THE ENCYCLOPEDIA

of the

REPUBLICAN PARTY

Volume One

THE ENCYCLOPEDIA

of the

REPUBLICAN PARTY

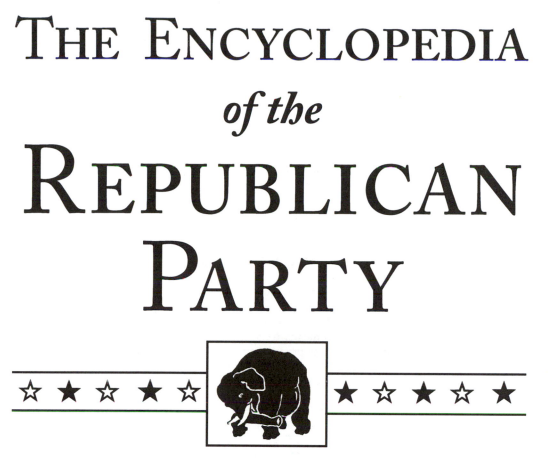

★ ★ ★ ★ ★ ★ ★ ★ ★ ★

Volume One

Edited by

GEORGE THOMAS KURIAN

JEFFREY D. SCHULTZ
Associate Editor

Sharpe Reference

An imprint of M.E. Sharpe, INC.

1997 Library Reference Edition published by Sharpe Reference
Sharpe Reference is an imprint of M.E. Sharpe INC.

M.E. Sharpe INC.
80 Business Park Drive
Armonk, NY 10504

Library of Congress Cataloging-in-Publication Data

Kurian, George Thomas.
[Encyclopedia of the Republican Party]
The encyclopedia of the Republican Party ; The encyclopedia of the Democratic Party /
George Thomas Kurian.
p.   cm.
Includes bibliographical references (p.   ) and index.
Contents: v. 1–2. The encyclopedia of the Republican Party — v. 3–4. The encyclopedia of the Democratic Party.
ISBN 1-56324-729-1 (set)
1. Republican Party (U.S. : 1854–)—Encyclopedias.
2. Democratic Party (U.S.)—Encyclopedias.
I. Kurian, George Thomas. Encyclopedia of the Democratic Party.
II. Title.
JK2352.K87   1996
324.2734'03—dc20
96-12187
CIP

Printed and bound in the United States of America

The paper used in this publication meets the minimum requirements of
American National Standard for Information Sciences—Permanence of
Paper for Printed Library Materials,
ANSI Z 39.48-1984.

∞

EB (c)   10   9   8   7   6   5   4   3   2   1

CONTENTS

Volume 1

Volume 2

Editor

George Thomas Kurian

Contributors

Bruce E. Altschuler
Department of Political Science,
State University of New York,
Oswego, New York

Monica Bauer
Iona College,
New Rochelle, New York

Stephen D. Van Beek
Department of Political Science,
San Jose State University,
San Jose, California

Patricia A. Behlar
Department of Social Sciences,
Pittsburg State University,
Pittsburg, Kansas

William C. Binning
Political Science Department,
Youngstown State University,
Youngstown, Ohio

Arthur Blaser
Political Science Department,
Chapman University,
Orange, California

Steve D. Boilard
Department of Government,
Western Kentucky University,
Bowling Green, Kentucky

Robert J. Bookmiller
Millersville University,
Millersville, Pennsylvania

Joan Axelrod-Contrada

Robert E. Dewhirst
Department of Government and
Economics, Northwestern Missouri
State University, Maryville,
Missouri

William E. Dugan
Border Research Institute,
Las Cruces, New Mexico

James W. Endersby
Department of Political Science,
University of Missouri,
Columbia, Missouri

J. David Gillespie
Department of Political Science,
Presbyterian College,
Clinton, South Carolina

Christian Goergen
College of DuPage,
Glen Ellyn, Illinois

Gary L. Gregg II
Clarion University,
Clarion, Pennsylvania

Douglas Harris
Department of Political Science,
The John Hopkins University,
Baltimore, Maryland

David Hatchett

Steve Hoenisch

Rogan Kersh
Department of Political Science,
Yale University,
New Haven, Connecticut

Quentin Kidd
Department of Political Science,
Texas Tech University,
Lubbock, Texas

Lisa Langenbach
Department of Political Science,
Middle Tennessee State University,
Murfreesboro, Tennessee

Tom Lansford
Old Dominion University,
Norfolk, Virginia

Cynthia J. Levy

W. Adam Mandelbaum

Janet B. Manspeaker
Department of Political Science,
Cheyney State University,
Cheyney, Pennsylvania

Jack J. Miller

Kimberly J. Pace

William D. Pederson
Department of History,
Louisiana State University,
Baton Rouge, Louisiana

Russell L. Riley
Political Science Department,
University of Pennsylvania,
Philadelphia, Pennsylvania

John S. Robey
Social Sciences Department,
University of Texas,
Brownsville, Texas

Joseph C. Santora

Frauke Schnell
Department of Political Science,
West Chester University,
West Chester, Pennsylvania

Diane L. Schultz

Jeffrey D. Schultz
Colorado College,
Colorado Springs, Colorado

Larry M. Schwab
Political Science Department,
John Carroll University,
Cleveland Heights, Ohio

Edward W. Siskel

Daniel Stanhagen

B. Kim Taylor

Susan L. Thomas
Department of Political Science,
Hollins College,
Roanoke, Virginia

Michael J. Towle
Department of Government,
Mount St. Mary's College,
Emmitsburg, Maryland

Gil Troy

Jessamyn West

John K. White
Department of Politics,
Providence College,
Providence, Rhode Island

Frank J. Williams
Associate Justice,
Superior Court of Rhode Island,
Providence, Rhode Island

John F. Yarbrough

PREFACE

There can be but two great political parties in this country.
—Stephen A. Douglas, 1858

Exactly 200 years ago, in 1796, Thomas Jefferson became a candidate for the presidency of the United States on the Jeffersonian Republican (later Democratic-Republican) ticket, and this event marks the beginning of party politics in the United States. *The Encyclopedia of the Republican Party* and *The Encyclopedia of the Democratic Party* are designed to mark the bicentennial of parties and party politics in the United States.

Although the definitions of Republican and Democrat have changed over the years, the United States is one of the few countries in the world where a strict two-party system has flourished. It was not always so. The history of political parties is filled with paradoxes. Parties are not mentioned at all in the Constitution, and the framers did not consider them essential, or even desirable. George Washington himself often spoke of "the baneful effect of parties" and condemned the Democratic-Republican groups as "self-created societies."

Yet, parties have become the primary mechanism outside the Constitution for transforming the perceived popular will into legislative acts and executive policies and programs. During the early years, parties coalesced around issues rather than personalities, and their labels and names changed as these issues lost urgency. Party labels were always fluid and sometimes misleading. It is interesting that Democratic and Republican are among the blandest political labels in the world. In one sense, they are perfectly interchangeable and neutral. Party symbols are even more meaningless: one is a jackass, the other an elephant.

There are at least two reasons why these two parties have flourished whereas more conventional political parties have not. The first is structural. The United States is not a fertile ground for extremism of any kind. Americans are not essentially apolitical, but they are uncomfortable with ideology-driven political activism. Barry Goldwater was dead wrong when he said that "extremism in the defense of liberty is no

vice," and his statement reveals a common but pernicious confusion between ends and means. Extremism is not justifiable in defense of anything. The last time Americans espoused extremism in the defense of liberty was in the Civil War, an avoidable conflagration that cost tens of thousands of lives. As a corollary, Americans have not encouraged ideological purity in their parties or leaders. George McGovern was one of the most logical and ideologically consistent political personalities in recent times. Adlai Stevenson II was one of the most articulate and eloquent champions of a rational and just society in the twentieth century. Yet, both of them, like many others of their ilk, have ended on the wrong side of the ledger of American history. Another corollary is that whenever members of an extremist faction or peripheral group try to take over a party, they lead it into political wilderness. This happened when the limousine liberals took over the Democratic Party in the 1960s and converted it into their playground. It happened again when certain extremist factions tried to take over the Republican Party in the 1980s and early 1990s. It has been said that the middle of the road is only for armadillos and road kills. But the strength of both the Democratic and Republican parties is in the middle, and it is when they return to the middle that they are able to renew their vision and communicate with the American people on the right wavelength.

The second reason for the durability of the Democratic and Republican parties is historical. The early political leaders followed the Westminster model of binary politics, in which there are only two camps: Conservative (Tory) and Liberal (Whig). William Gilbert (the better-known half of Gilbert and Sullivan) wrote:

> I often think it's comical
> How Nature does always contrive
> That every boy and every gal
> That's born into the world alive
> is either a little Liberal
> or else a little Conservative.

The success of the Democratic and Republican parties and the relative failure of third parties to strike deep roots illustrate Gilbert's insight into the biology of politics. This is in contrast to the Continental model of multiple parties. In Italy at one time there were 46 political parties, each a fiefdom for some unemployed or disgruntled politician. The election ballot papers would run into many pages. Multiple parties would require runoffs after the first elections, something that is constitutionally impossible in the United States.

The Encyclopedia of the Republican Party and *The Encyclopedia of the Democratic Party* is not only high history but high drama. It tries to capture the sweep of electoral and convention history. The quadrennial political paroxysm that begins with the primaries and ends on election night is more Barnum and Bailey than strict Constitution. Even before the advent of television, American politics was part spectacle and part carnival. The encyclopedia also presents the varied tableau of ideas, rivalries, issues, conflicts, identities, and movements that the campaign rhetoric often hides. While many issues have changed, may others have endured. For most of the twentieth century, the driving themes in the party platforms of both parties have been the linkages between politics, on the one hand, and, on the other, economy, religion, foreign policy, immigration, society, law, environment, finance, crime, race, women's rights, civil rights, education, and social values. That these issues should recur every four years is a tacit admission that they have no easy solutions.

In many cases party positions on these issues undergo subtle shifts. Sometimes parties completely reverse themselves and adopt contradictory positions, trusting in the public's short memory to overlook these somersaults and U-turns. One of the most ironic is how the Democratic Party evolved over the years from a viciously racist party willing to shed blood rather than give civil rights to black slaves into a doughty champion of African Americans. The changes in the Republican positions have been less dramatic but nonetheless striking. After waging a Civil War to enforce federal authority over the states, Republicans have become strong defenders of states' rights.

In his *Cycles of American History*, Arthur Schlesinger has provided a broadbrush framework for aligning the fortunes of the two major political parties with social, economic, and political cycles. Since 1860, the Republicans have been in the White House for 84 years and the Democrats for 52 years. The Democrats have controlled the House for 80 years and the Republicans for 56 years. The Democrats have controlled the Senate for 62 years and the Republicans for 72 years. (They were equally divided in the Senate of the 47th Congress.) All the four major wars of this century (World Wars I and II, the Korean War, and the Vietnam War) have been under the Democrats; the Great Depression, under the Republicans.

In trying to weave history, issues, biography, and party platforms together, this encyclopedia tries to give perspective and depth to the political moment. Writing about politics cannot be separated from interpretation. In the Issues and Ideology section there is a wide range of significant interpretations. Reference books are expected to provide accurate and definitive information consistent with the highest standards of scholarship. This encyclopedia attempts to meet this expectation. But it goes beyond that to offer vibrant, cutting-edge analysis and to convey the vitality and excitement that drive party politics.

THE ENCYCLOPEDIA OF THE REPUBLICAN PARTY

The Encyclopedia of the Republican Party chronicles the evolution of the Republican Party, the younger of the two major parties. The meteoric rise of the Republican Party (also known for some time as the Union Party, or the party for keeping the union of states) is unparalleled in the annals of politics. Within four years of its founding and its first convention, the party captured the White House, and then went on to win a bloody Civil War and to govern the United States for all but 16 of the next 72 years. It managed to do this without any charismatic leadership. With the exception of Lincoln (and possibly Theodore Roosevelt, who was a progressive rather than a conservative), the party has produced only leaders of modest capabilities and attainments. The strength of the Republican Party is to be sought, instead, in its ability to project the values and aspirations of Main Street America, whose citizens want nothing more than to lead quiet lives without any interference, official or otherwise. No party has so successfully converted the absence of an overarching national vision into a positive asset at the polling booth. The closest the Republican Party has come to ideology is its espousal of a strong anticommunist plank during the Cold War. Otherwise, the Republican ideal was to keep the ship of state on an even keel, sheltered from all storms. Even though religious and social values have figured prominently in recent party platforms, they were peripheral concerns during the party's first 100 years. Early campaign slogans, such as "A Chicken in Every Pot" and "A Full Dinner Pail," reveal that the strength of the party was its direct appeal to pocketbook issues. In a real sense, the Republican Party is a party of normalcy, the infelicitous word that Warren Harding coined to express the goal of his administration. "What is normal is Republican" is a belief that continues to infuse Republican leaders such as Newt Gingrich, who described his opponents as not being "normal Americans."

Although the Republican Party appears as a monolithic organization, it has two distinct personalities, joined at birth. There is a humanitarian party, the party of Lincoln and also Theodore Roosevelt, and there is a radical conservative party, of which the classic expression was Goldwaterism. Other contradictions abound within the party, such as the coexistence of internationalism and isolationism. Such contradictions, however, have rarely hurt the party's chances at the polls. Republicans have an enormous capacity, much admired by outside observers, to forget their internal differences and present a united front just before elections. It is perhaps one of its strengths that these contradictions are sublimated rather than allowed to become divisive issues. In groups, the coexistence of contradictions may be a healthy sign. As Walt Whitman wrote:

> Do I contradict myself
> Very well, then I contradict myself
> I am large, I contain multitudes.

Even though crippled by the New Deal for nearly half a century, the Republican Party remains the dominant American party of the twentieth century. During the first 96 years, its 11 presidents together have held the White House for 52 years. Despite its apparent periodic somnolence, it has reserves of surging energy, as the 1994 elections proved. It is entering the twenty-first century much stronger than it was in 1900, when the party was in power under the archetypal Republican, William McKinley.

My list of acknowledgments begins with Evelyn Fazio, vice president and publisher at M.E. Sharpe. Her perseverance, enthusiasm, and commitment to the creation of solid reference books were strong assets for the project and sustained it during its gestation. The production department, headed by Carmen Chetti, did a superb job in record time. Eileen Gaffney, who handled production, was a model of efficiency and tact. Also at M.E. Sharpe, Aud Thiessen helped the project to move along smoothly. The encyclopedia also benefited immeasurably from the efforts of associate editor Jeffrey D. Schultz, who handled many of the major entries and provided important leads.

Above all, I must thank my wife, Annie Kurian, who has been, as always, a wellspring of encouragement and support.

George Thomas Kurian

Ulysses S. Grant's Inauguration, 1873. *Source:* Library of Congress.

HISTORY

When General Colin Powell declined to run for president in the fall of 1995, he called on the "party of Lincoln" to "move, once again, close to the spirit of Lincoln." At the time, few Americans remembered that the Republican Party sprang from the radical antislavery movement in the 1850s and that for decades the Democratic Party was the conservative party in the United States. The Republican Party has thrived for over a century and a half by accommodating mainstream beliefs instead of maintaining ideological consistency. The character of the two-party system, the Civil War, the rise of big business, and the challenge of governing while questioning government all helped steer the Republican Party away from its radical origins.

THE TWO-PARTY SYSTEM

Americans in the 1850s took their party identities very seriously. "There are few stronger feelings in the American heart than that of party fealty," the *Cincinnati Gazette* noted in 1854. Americans expressed their party loyalty year-round, in the home, at school, in taverns, as well as on the streets and at the voting booths during election time.

America's founders never expected to see such loyalty. They hoped the Constitution would prevent parties from forming. By the 1790s, a rudimentary "first-party system" of Federalists and Democratic-Republicans had developed. The peculiarities of America's winner-take-all electoral setup favored a two-party system with both parties appealing to the center. Candidates needed broad-based coalitions to achieve the 50% + 1 of the vote that gave them power. Splinter parties, such as the Free Soil Party of the 1840s and 1850s, could not sustain themselves without the power-sharing arrangement of a proportional representation system.

The Federalist Party eventually disintegrated, and the Democratic-Republicans became known as the Democrats by the 1830s. At the time, assorted opponents of Andrew Jackson united in the Whig Party against his more populist Democratic Party. Under this Jacksonian or "second-party system," both the Whigs and the Democrats were as parochial and as diffuse as the nation itself. These coalitions of autonomous state parties assembled every four years in national conventions to select a nominee and a party platform. Since 1848, the Democrats had used a national committee to raise money, organize correspondence, and allocate resources in critical swing states. But these parties specialized in mobilizing the masses on the local level. The center of gravity remained in the local committees. From its inception, the Whig Party was more fragile and less organized than the Democratic Party. As the nation debated slavery expansion, neither party would be able to keep its warring northern and southern factions united—but the Whigs would fail first.

DEMISE OF THE WHIG PARTY

During the 1850s, the growing tensions over the expansion of slavery, the onset of an economic recession, and the nativist backlash against immigration destroyed the Whig Party. An influx of German and Irish immigrants during the 1830s and 1840s had triggered a backlash. Protestant "natives" attacked the mostly Catholic newcomers by seeking to limit immigration, establish free public schools, and prohibit liquor. In the 1840s, secret societies of nativists formed, consisting of people who were supposed to say they "know nothing" about their organization. With 90% of Catholics belonging to the Democratic Party, the Whigs had always appealed to moralistic Protestants. As the Whig Party deteriorated in the 1850s, many party members naturally turned to the Know-Nothing, or American, Party. It would prove to be a way station for many members going from Whiggery to Republicanism.

In 1852, the Whig Party convention endured 53 ballots before nominating a war hero, General Winfield Scott. Scott lost to the Democrats' compromise candidate, Franklin Pierce. When southern Whigs helped Democrats pass the Kansas–Nebraska Act of 1854, both parties suffered. The bill repealed parts of the Missouri Compromise, leaving the decision about slavery in the hands of the settlers in the two new territories. So many northern "conscience" Whigs abandoned their party that the Whigs soon ceased to exist, while enough "anti-Nebraska" northern Democrats left their party to shift the balance of power toward southern Democrats. As the Democrats solidified their standing in the South, enraged abolitionists pushed for a new party to unite the growing anti-Democratic majority in the North.

THE ORIGINS OF THE REPUBLICAN PARTY

The new party was founded haphazardly. Dissidents convened throughout the North during the Kansas–Nebraska crisis. One of the earliest mass meetings took place in Ripon, Wisconsin, on March 20, 1854, making this the ostensible birth date of the new party. One participant, Alvin E. Bovay, recalled, "We went into the little meeting held in a schoolhouse Whigs, Free Soilers, and Democrats. We came out of it Republicans," thus resurrecting the name of Thomas Jefferson's political party. Two months later, 30 anti-Nebraska Whig, Democratic, and Free Soil congressmen met but failed to establish any kind of institutional mechanism or issue any formal appeal.

"The dispersion of the old parties was one thing," one of the founders of the party, George Julian, would later recall, "but the organization of their fragments into a new one on a just basis was quite a different thing." The new party of Whigs, Free Soilers, anti-Nebraska Democrats, and Know-Nothings strained to establish common ground. Abolitionists opposed to the "peculiar institution" squabbled with moderates who tolerated slavery in the South but resisted its expansion out West; free-trading western farmers fought protectionist eastern manufacturers; patrician reformers detested machine politicians, just as nativists detested Germans and other immigrants. That fall, fusion proved most successful in the West. In fact, during the 1854 midterm elections, the nativists siphoned more Democratic votes in many eastern and border states than the Republicans did. Two-thirds of the electorate in Massachusetts voted for the Know-Nothings.

In calling their antislavery party *Republican,* the founders championed the Constitution's limited government devoted to liberty and equality. The American revolutionaries considered themselves *republicans,* an ideology spawned in ancient Rome that flourished in seventeenth- and eighteenth-century England. Republicanism feared power as corrupting. Only virtuous leaders stemming from a modest and virtuous citizenry could avoid the dual temptations of monarchy, on the one hand, and demagoguery, on the other. Such virtue would thrive amid a citizenry of free, equal, independent property owners, republicans agreed. The Whigs, having taken their name from the English antimonarchist party, emphasized their opposition to Andrew Jackson's grab for executive power, which he achieved democratically. In naming themselves after Jefferson's party, Republicans embraced a broad and positive vision that still emphasized the limits they sought to impose on their "democratic" rivals. Ironically, the only way this Republican Party would be able to achieve its paramount goal of ending slavery would be through an unprecedented assertion of national power.

THE 1856 CAMPAIGN

During the next two years, the Republican movement continued to grow. In the 34th Congress, convening in 1855, a small majority of the House of Representatives, 118 members, were identified as anti-Nebraska, but not all were Republican. When Republicans elected a former Democrat, Nathaniel P. Banks Jr., as Speaker of the House, they celebrated their "first and most important triumph." "The Republican Party is now Inaugurated," the former Whig boss, Thurlow Weed of New York, rejoiced.

More than half of the party's 1856 platform addressed the question of "Bleeding Kansas"—the violence that had broken out in the new territory. The rest of the platform developed the Republican Party ideology beyond antislavery. The platform advocated a transcontinental railroad and internal improvements financed by Congress. Appealing to abolitionists and businessmen, the platform advanced a vision of a prosperous country filled with equal citizens whose government deferred to individual prerogatives while doing what was necessary for "the accommodation and security of our existing commerce."

For its first presidential nominee in 1856, the two-year-old party chose the dashing John C. Frémont rather than an abolitionist zealot. "That must be a very dark and squat log cabin into which the fame of Colonel Frémont has not penetrated ere this," Horace Greeley of the *New York Tribune* observed, stressing Frémont's essential qualification: popularity. As

Thomas Nast's Republican Elephant as the New King of the Forest. *Source:* Library of Congress.

Greeley freely admitted, when it came to politics, the 43-year-old explorer "don't know the ABC's."

The Republican campaign for "Free Labor, free speech, free men, free Kansas and Frémont" galvanized state forces throughout the North. As usual, the canvass triggered a series of freewheeling, entertaining street festivals. "It is difficult to sit still with such excitement in the air," wrote Henry Wadsworth Longfellow. Republicans trusted their enthusiastic crusade against slavery to compensate for their rudimentary organization. "It was a struggle between two civilizations," the abolitionist George W. Julian recalled. Paramilitary Wide-Awake companies drilled in the streets, garbed in black oilcloth capes and caps. At night bonfires and torches illuminated the parades. People serenaded the "Pathfinder" and his popular wife, Jesse Benton Frémont. To the tune of "Pop Goes the Weasel," they sang: "What's the noise that goes about? What's the great commotion? Here and there and everywhere, The people are in motion. Ho my friends I tell you true, Here's the agitation. 'Tis for FREEmont and Jessie, too, Glory to the nation!"

A newcomer to the United States, E.L. Godkin, was repelled by the "little arts" used to woo the "uneducated," yet impressed by the serious "themes . . . under popular discussion." When they were not marching, millions of Americans were reading—in 1850 the white illiteracy rate was as low as 10 or 15%. Thousands of circulars clogged the mails. Circulation of crucial journals such as Greeley's *New York Tribune* soared.

Although he lost to the Democrat James Buchanan, Frémont won majorities in 11 of the 16 northern states, attracting almost as many popular votes as Scott had for the Whigs in 1852, and 72 more electoral votes. State legislatures sent 20 Republicans to the Senate—senators would not be directly elected until 1913—and voters sent 92 Republicans to the House. The fledgling party emerged as the principal minority party in the United States.

THE PARTY OF LINCOLN

By 1860, slavery had also divided the Democratic Party. The political system splintered, with four major candidates vying for the presidency. John Bell, a former Whig leader from Tennessee, ran as the standard-bearer of the Constitution Union Party, whose only platform was the Constitution. Southern Democrats nominated Vice President John C. Breckinridge of Kentucky, while northern Democrats turned to the architect of the divisive Kansas–Nebraska Act, Senator Stephen A. Douglas of Illinois. Meeting at the great wigwam in Chicago, the second Republican National Convention nominated Douglas's rival, Abraham Lincoln of Illinois.

This one-time Whig congressman had kept a low profile to secure the nomination against more prominent opponents, such as the former Whig William Henry Seward and the former Free Soil Democrat Salmon P. Chase. "Our policy," Lincoln explained, "is to give no offence to others—leave them in a mood to come to us, if they shall be compelled to give up their first love." Once again, expediency ruled. A tamer antislavery candidate improved Republicans' chances of winning. Once nominated, Lincoln continued to avoid giving offense. He made his acceptance letter "sufficiently brief to do no harm." He reached out to his defeated rivals, sending word through his ally David Davis that he "neither is nor will be . . . committed to any man, clique, or faction; and that . . . it will be his pleasure . . . to deal fairly with all." In keeping with political custom, Lincoln minimized his correspondence and his public appearances. He asked one question of each contemplated move: "Will it help or hurt?"

Naturally, Lincoln embraced the Republican platform, which now offered a fuller and more positive program championing the rights of Free Labor. Republicans centered their abolitionism in a broad movement praising capitalism and advocating middle-class prosperity for the laboring masses. Aiming at what one Republican called "men of moderate means . . . men of enterprise," the platform affirmed that "the development of the industrial interests of the whole country secures to the workingmen liberal wages, to agriculture remunerative prices, to mechanics and manufacturers adequate regard for their skill, Labor and enterprise, and to the nation commercial prosperity and independence." Respect for immigrants who had been naturalized as citizens, support for the homesteading movement, federal money for internal improvements, and opposition to slavery came naturally to this party of Free Labor.

The Republicans won the election, capturing the White House and both houses of Congress with 31 of 50 senators and 105 of 178 representatives. Still, Lincoln secured barely 40% of the popular vote. In ten of the slave states Lincoln failed to get a single vote. This new party's triumph triggered a wave of secessions from southern states. The party of Lincoln became the party of Civil War.

Lincoln as the Confederate Cartoonists Saw Him.
Source: Library of Congress.

Before defeating the South, Lincoln had to conquer his own party. He invited key rivals to join his government, explaining with characteristic self-deprecation to Thurlow Weed that "their long experience in public affairs and their eminent fitness" gave them "higher claims than his own for the place he was to occupy." With William Henry Seward of New York as secretary of state and Salmon P. Chase of Ohio as secretary of the treasury, Lincoln assembled a fractious cabinet. The powerful egos would tax the president's abilities. The new party remained a loose coalition of rival factions.

While supervising the bloody Civil War, the savvy Lincoln forged a formidable party organization. Republicans adapted the contemporary party structure based on local and state committees building up to a national convention. But, characteristically, they made their party more centralized and better funded than its predecessors. The party bought the loyalty of businessmen throughout the North by carefully distributing millions of dollars in war-generated government contracts and thousands of new patronage jobs. In return, the party assessed officeholders 5% of their salaries and expected those with government contracts to contribute generously. "They would remove any man who is not openly with us and of our party organization," one disillusioned cabinet member, Gideon Welles, muttered. Democrats "have to contend against the greatest patronage and the greatest money power ever wielded in a presidential election," the *New York World* complained in 1864.

Of course, most Republicans defended their tactics as necessary in the fight against the "plantation and bank paper aristocracy." The Republicans linked their future with the country's future. The Gettysburg Address symbolized Lincoln's emergence as the great bard of American nationalism. In 1864, his Republican Party convened in a "National Union" convention, renominating him and giving him a southern Democratic former slaveholder, Andrew Johnson, as a running mate. The Democrats nominated one of Lincoln's former generals, George B. McClellan.

The president claimed that he had neither the time nor the inclination to campaign. Lincoln's message was summarized in the aphorism he bequeathed to American politics: "Don't swap horses while crossing the stream." But as he struck the pose of statesmanlike disinterest, he worked behind the scenes. "The President is too busy looking after the election to think of anything else," Secretary of the Treasury William Pitt Fessenden grumbled. "All has been done that *can* be done here," Thurlow Weed reported to the president from New York City on the eve of the election. "Every ward—here and in Brooklyn—and every Election District, is abundantly supplied with material aid."

Lincoln's campaign, however, ultimately relied on neither party nor personality, but the battlefield. "I am a beaten man," Lincoln said, "unless we can have some great victory." During the bitter 1862 elections, the Democrats had gained 33 seats in the House and had recaptured the state legislatures of Illinois, Indiana, and Pennsylvania. Anticipating another defeat, Lincoln even drew up plans for the period between the election and his successor's inauguration. On September 1, General William T. Sherman conquered Atlanta. Two months later, Lincoln won 2,206,938 popular votes to McClellan's 1,803,787, but won 212 electoral votes to McClellan's 21. His Union Party increased its majorities in both the Senate and the House.

Lincoln's assassination shortly after his second inauguration gave the nation and the party a martyr. "Father Abraham" became the great saint who had sacrificed his life so that the party could rule and the nation could survive. The party of Lincoln became the party of American nationalism, prosperity, and equality.

THE RADICAL REPUBLICANS

Lincoln's death left Republicans with a former southern Democrat in the White House. Lincoln himself had struggled with the Radical Republicans in Congress, who chided him for being indecisive during wartime and too lenient in designing the peace. These Radicals had celebrated the Democratic gains in 1862 for rebuking the president and his "incompetent pro-slavery generals." Radicals such as Charles Sumner of Massachusetts, Thaddeus Stevens of Pennsylvania, and Benjamin Wade of Ohio had no patience with the pragmatic compromises characteristic of American politics. They were revolutionaries seeking to purify their nation.

Victory on the battlefield and in the voting booths energized congressional Republicans, who in 1865 enjoyed majorities of 42 to 10 in the Senate and 149 to 42 in the House. The more sure they were of their power, the more radical they became. They had not fought a war, sustaining 360,000 casualties, simply to return to the status quo.

Pragmatic political considerations strengthened various policy positions. All Republicans agreed with the Radical Thaddeus Stevens "that upon the continued ascendancy" of the Republican Party "depends the safety of this great nation." Radicals realized that the Republican Party needed a base in the South, which stood to gain as many as nine congressional seats in the next reapportionment from the freed slaves who now counted as full citizens. Radicals wanted to woo blacks, while moderates wanted to appease white Southerners.

Andrew Johnson lacked Lincoln's political skill and national standing. The new president alienated the Radicals with his boorish manners, his headstrong ways, and his laxness toward his fellow Southerners. Beginning in December 1865, congressional Radicals seized the initiative from the president by creating a Special Joint Committee on Reconstruction, to govern the readmittance and reorganization of southern states. Stevens led the Radicals in asserting congressional power over the southern states, which he considered to be vanquished territories whose very borders were now undefined.

Blacks Celebrate the Abolition of Slavery in Washington, April 19, 1866. *Source:* Library of Congress.

Andrew Johnson's Impeachment. *Source:* Library of Congress.

These congressional Republicans precipitated a constitutional crisis. Advocating harsher plans for the defeated South than the moderate president did, the Radicals curtailed presidential power. They limited the president's appointive and military authority. During the 1866 elections, Johnson campaigned against them in a controversial "swing around the circle." The Radicals responded with withering assaults aided by their own fund-raising campaign committee. The Radical state legislatures that emerged throughout the North forced the retirement of several moderates from the Senate. When Republicans returned with two-thirds of the seats in both houses of Congress, they sought revenge. "The present incumbent is a nullity and will be treated as such," Senator Charles Sumner declared. In March 1868 the Radicals impeached the president, although they failed to secure a conviction in the Senate by one vote.

At the same time, the Radicals engineered the passage and ratification of the 13th, 14th, and 15th amendments to the Constitution. These amendments abolished slavery, made black men citizens, and allowed them to vote. In the process, these amendments helped define the nature of American citizenship and established the basis of a constitutional revolution that expanded individual rights and federal government power over the next century.

The Republicans' first eight years in power transformed "these United States" into "the United States." While Democrats tended to champion states' rights, Republicans tended to trust the centralized government. Spurred by its free labor ideology and wartime exigencies, the Republican regime expanded federal prerogatives in transportation, finance, even agriculture. The Homestead Act of 1862 offered any citizen 160 acres of public domain after five years of residence; the Morrill Act of 1862 endowed land-grant colleges with substantial tracts of land; the Pacific Railway Act, also in 1862, allocated tracts of land to encourage railroad construction. By 1863, northerners who had not paid federal excise taxes for decades were paying national taxes in a national currency, with local banks and currencies taxed into extinction by the ever more powerful federal government. Assessing the changes since Lincoln's inauguration, the historian George Ticknor wrote in 1869 that "it does not seem to me as if I were living in the country in which I was born."

RECONSTRUCTION IN THE SOUTH

Southerners were certainly struck by how much their region had changed. The Radical Congress's 1st Reconstruction Act of 1867, passed over Johnson's veto, had divided the South into five military districts. By 1870, all of the former Confederate states had met the Radicals' conditions and reentered the Union. Most states were controlled by a Republican coalition of blacks, northern carpetbaggers, and southern "scalawags"—mostly white nonslaveholding small farmers. During this period, 16 blacks served in Congress, 600 served in state legislatures, and hundreds more held local offices. The reconstructed states outlawed discrimination, established the first state-funded public school systems in the South, and weakened plantation owners' grip on the region's economy. These dramatic changes triggered a backlash. Once white Southerners were "redeemed" and returned to power, the South would remain solidly Democratic for decades.

PRESIDENT GRANT

In 1868 the Republicans nominated the Civil War hero Ulysses S. Grant to succeed Andrew Johnson. Both parties had tried to draft the popular general. Republican Senator Benjamin Wade admitted: "We desire to bring him forward as our candidate for the Presidency; yet we do not exactly know where he stands." Grant's election solidified the party's electoral strategy over the next three decades. It would dominate national politics by "waving the bloody shirt"— evoking the patriots who died saving the Union. It would prefer presidents who deferred to Congress. And it would try to maintain the profitable alliance that Lincoln himself had forged between the party and big business.

A formidable coalition of Civil War veterans— known as the Grand Army of the Republic—along with eastern manufacturers, northern Protestants, and midwestern farmers, supported the party. Under the able leadership of William Chandler, secretary of the Republican National Committee, the party raised enough money to buy out many Democratic newspapers, to distribute as many as 150,000 documents a day, and to bribe Washington correspondents for as much as $3,500 a month. The Congressional Campaign Committee collected officeholders' assessments, while the Republican National Committee raised money from businessmen. The election solidified Republican control over New England and the Mississippi Valley for a generation. New York, New Jersey, and Indiana would be among the few two-party northern states remaining, becoming critical "swing" states. Republicans dominated the Senate throughout Grant's two terms in office, while splitting control over the House.

THE PARTY MACHINE

The Republican Party was no longer a crusading movement but an increasingly corrupt political organization. Patronage, bribery, and nepotism proliferated during Ulysses S. Grant's administration. The president was rumored to have 42 relatives on the government payroll. Grantism was not the only manifestation of corruption. Like a premature adolescent, whose body grows faster than his emotional and intellectual abilities, American society and politics were changing so fast that procedures and mores could not keep up. Corruption became an essential lubricant as government and corporations acted on a hitherto unprecedented scale. The Democrats in 1871 suffered from the Boss Tweed scandal, wherein New York's Tammany Hall bilked the city of millions by billing outrageous sums such as $179,729.60 for 40 old chairs and three tables. The Republicans in 1872 suffered from the Crédit Mobilier scandal, wherein the Union Pacific's construction company bought congressional cooperation by offering stock to prominent politicians, including rising stars such as James G. Blaine and James A. Garfield.

Politicians were not apologetic; their job was to keep the system moving, to distribute services to the needy, and to build parks, roads, buildings, for all to enjoy. They were the pragmatists, the doers. They boasted about their scientific efficiency. Republican Senator Roscoe Conkling would declare in an 1876 campaign speech: "We are told the Republican Party is a machine. Yes. A government is a machine, the common-school system of the state of New York is a machine; every organization which binds men together for a common cause is a machine."

In the big cities, elaborate local machines, mostly Democratic but some Republican, emerged. Resting on a solid foundation of immigrant votes, fueled by patronage and graft, the machines bored into the expanding municipal bureaucracies. The men running these machines concentrated on the power and the spoils extracted from their own locales.

Republicans throughout the North also established powerful state machines fueled by federal patronage. State leaders plunged into national politics to monitor the flow of jobs and contracts. Senators such as Roscoe Conkling of New York, Simon Cameron of Pennsylvania, John A. Logan of Illinois, and Oliver P. Morton of Indiana were uniquely positioned to work the state legislatures and the national government. Despite their avowals of party loyalty, they did not support a candidate unless they were assured of receiving their patronage rewards. If the characteristic Democratic

Grant as an Acrobat. *Source:* Library of Congress.

scandal was New York's Tweed Ring, the characteristic Republican scandal was the Whiskey Ring, a conspiracy between Internal Revenue agents and western distillers to avoid federal excise duties. The ring, exposed in 1875, pumped money throughout the state Republican machines up to the president's private secretary, Orville E. Babcock, and, some charged, U.S. Grant himself.

These corrupt political machines rested on a remarkably democratic system. Many party members participated in the local affairs of their precinct ward. The wards then selected representatives who met at township or county conventions. These mass conventions nominated candidates for local office, appointed campaign committees, and chose delegates to attend state conventions, which in turn selected delegates to the national conventions. As many as 18,000 people attended the Republican National Convention in 1880. Rarely have political parties been so responsive to their constituents or so brazen in their excesses.

THE LIBERAL REPUBLICAN REVOLT

Genteel Republicans mourned their party's moral and ideological decline. These political reformers could not believe that their republic or their party had come to this. They attacked the vengeful Radicals, the vulgar masses, the nouveau riche robber barons, the decline of a proper sensibility. Fears of losing power and money to their social inferiors intensified the criticism. The "best men" looked back to the 1850s as the glory days when good Americans united in a noble cause. Henry Adams would later label Grant's administration "the dividing line between what we hoped, and what we have got."

After four years of Grant, the reformers rebelled. A founder of the Republican Party, George W. Julian, recalled: "I could not aid in the reelection of Grant without sinning against decency and my own self-respect." The reformers launched the Liberal Republican Party at Cincinnati in May 1872. Angling for popular support, the convention nominated the publisher of the *New York Tribune*, one-time founder of the Republican Party, and well-known eccentric Horace Greeley.

Greeley was a bad choice. He opposed many of the reformers' proposals, including civil service reform and tariff reduction. Most disturbing of all, he had spent years attacking the Democrats, whom the reformers needed to defeat Grant. "Why, the honest, thinking mass of Democrats could no more vote [for Horace Greeley] than a Jew be persuaded to eat pork!" the *New York World* sputtered. When the Democrats nominated Greeley, the election became "a choice of two evils" for many, one Republican said. "Has the country no choice for ruler," the *World* asked in May, "between a scheming, sordid despot and a good-natured, hare-brained dreamer?"

Republican regulars dismissed the reformers as elitists, as dreamers, as throwbacks. "The whole movement had the questionable aspect of proceeding downward from the leaders, instead of upward from the masses," one observer wrote, embracing the democratic ethos furthered by the Civil War. Such reformers, one senator would sneer, were "effeminate without being either masculine or feminine; unable to beget or to bear; possessing neither fecundity nor virility; endowed with the contempt of men and the derision of women, and doomed to sterility, isolation and extinction." Liberal Republicans, Julian recalled, were branded as "apostates" to antislavery, "but slavery had perished forever"; called "Rebels," but "the war had been over seven years and a half." The reformers insisted that they had not changed sides, "the sides themselves had been changed by events."

Ultimately, party loyalty prevailed. As one disillusioned Republican regular, Henry Lee, explained, "We shall 'return to our vomit' and not try the new purge." New York and New Jersey went Republican as the party once again captured the White House and two-thirds of the House and the Senate. Frustrated that the crusade had been lost in the talk about Greeley's trademark white coat and Grant's military heroics, one reformer, Carl Schurz, mourned, "We designed it to be a campaign of ideas, and it became a campaign of personalities."

Underlying this clash between the upper-class reformers and the hard-headed businessmen and politicians was a deeper struggle over the future of the Republic. The Republican Party had become the dominant party. From 1854 to 1873, Walter Dean Burnham would show, Republicans won 70% of the electoral college, 58.4% of the available House seats, 60.7% of the Senate seats, and 69.2% of the state gubernatorial races. Such control, along with Grant's reelection in 1872, marked the triumph of party pragmatism over ideology, of the businessman over the visionary. The party of Lincoln had become a machine.

THE ELECTORAL DEADLOCK OF 1876

The Republicans demonstrated just how efficient a machine they had created in 1876. The Republican governor of Ohio, Rutherford B. Hayes, ran a desultory campaign against the shrewd Democratic governor of New York, Samuel Tilden. The Democrats were regrouping. The Panic of 1873, and the ensuing backlash against the Republicans' probusiness tight-money policy, had caused 85 seats to change hands in 1874, giving the Democrats a majority in the House, 169 to 109. Several key state legislatures in the Midwest had also gone Democratic, or been taken over by some of the independent political movements agitating for change. Hayes realized that even though more than a decade had passed since the end of the war, "Our strong ground is a dread of a solid South, rebel rule, etc. It leads people away from hard times, which is our deadliest foe."

Campaign contributions dried up, fortunes created by the war disappeared in the peacetime panic. The patrician Hayes benefited from the Republican organization, even as he distanced himself from some tactics. When informed that an estimated $100,000 was needed for "money and speakers" in Indiana, he wrote in his diary: "The use of money I have little faith in, and I am confident no such large sums can be raised." When he heard that federal employees were being assessed, he warned Republican officials that such assessments are "a plain departure from correct principles and ought not to be allowed. I trust the Committee will have nothing to do with it." Hayes's scruples enraged the Republican National Committee chairman, Zachariah Chandler. While Chandler had sometimes resented the extra burdens caused by Grant's disinterest in party affairs, the party chairman jealously guarded his power. Such power struggles between nominees and party committee members were typical of the period, as party regulars such as Chandler refused to surrender control of the party machinery to the fly-by-night and often self-righteous nominees.

In this age of party organization, party chairmen were less likely to be wealthy individuals bankrolling the limited national effort; they were party regulars like Chandler coordinating the cross-country canvass. Party members were beginning to take a candidate's preference for chairman into account, along with such questions as seniority, party unity, and fund-raising ability. As the presidency would grow in importance over the next century, the chairman and party organization would gradually become subservient to the nominees.

For all his posturing, Hayes did not complain when Republican Party officials schemed to thwart Samuel Tilden's victory. On election night, Tilden enjoyed a 250,000-vote lead in the popular vote and was just shy of a victory in electoral votes. Chandler sent telegrams to three critical southern states, hinting, "Hayes elected if we have carried S.C., Fla., and La. Can you hold your state? Answer immediately." The three states remained under military rule, and the Republicans' sway. By the next afternoon, Republicans in those states were claiming victory. Democrats protested, convinced that Tilden was being robbed.

Once again the Republic was deadlocked. Talk of civil war filled the air. Once again Congress assembled to try to solve a national crisis. This time, rather than clash ideologically, the politicians negotiated pragmatically. A special electoral commission consisting of five members of the House, five senators, and five associate justices of the Supreme Court convened. The 15 broke down to 8 Republicans and 7 Democrats, which is the way they voted on every issue. As a result, Hayes won with 185 electoral votes to Tilden's 184.

The Compromise of 1877 also called for Hayes to withdraw the remaining federal troops from the South and countenance the overthrow of the Republican regimes in South Carolina and Louisiana. The Republicans kept the presidency and ended Reconstruction.

Democrats consoled themselves with control of the Post Office. When Hayes appointed a Democrat, David M. Key, as postmaster general, he gave up a crucial source of patronage. At the time, the thousands of postal appointments to be made represented a considerable percentage of federal patronage jobs, which would double in number from 51,000 in 1871 to more than 100,000 in 1880. Postmasters were also strategically placed to control the flow of political information. The postmaster of Madison, Wisconsin, for 21 years, Elisha Keyes, affirmed that "Post Offices should be filled by men who are competent to run the Party machine in their vicinity."

PARTY EQUILIBRIUM, 1876–1896

The close race between Tilden and Hayes reflected the rough balance between Democrats and Republicans on a national level. The Congress was also closely divided, with a Republican majority of 39 to 36 in the Senate and a Democratic majority of 153 to 140 in the House. Over the next four presidential elections, the difference in the popular vote would be as little as 7,018 out of nearly 9 million cast in 1880 and only as much as 62,683 out of nearly 10 million cast in 1884. In 1888 Benjamin Harrison would beat Grover Cleveland 233 to 168 in the electoral college, while losing by 4,287 popular votes. Overall, from 1874 to 1892, Republicans would win 48.3% of the electoral college, 41.7% of the House, 51% of the Senate, and 49.5% of the governorships. During this time of political paralysis, the cartoonist Thomas Nast would identify the Democrats with a donkey and the Republicans with an elephant.

The country was polarized. Republicans dominated the North and the West, while Democrats dominated the South. The Democrats often controlled the House of Representatives, but the Republicans usually controlled the Senate, the White House—except during Grover Cleveland's two nonconsecutive terms—and most northern gubernatorial mansions. From the Civil War to 1890, Illinois, Iowa, Minnesota, Nebraska, and Vermont always had Republican governors; in Pennsylvania, Michigan, Wisconsin, Kansas, and Rhode Island, Republicans lost the gubernatorial race only once.

The end of Reconstruction made it difficult for Republicans to compete in the South and, as a result,

President Hayes's Inauguration Ceremonies, March 1877. Photograph by Matthew Brady. *Source:* Hayes Library.

to sustain majorities in the House of Representatives. Once southern states were "redeemed," whites kept blacks and Republicans out of power. Poll taxes, literacy tests, and threats inhibited black voting. By 1888, Republicans carried only 89 of 293 predominantly black counties throughout the South. Senator William E. Chandler of New Hampshire thundered: "A Republican can believe in tariff reduction or even free trade and yet properly adhere to the party. But he cannot fail to advocate the Fifteenth Amendment and all proper laws to supplement it and to enforce it and yet be a Republican." The push for racial justice—or at least for a continued flow of black votes—became a matter of party survival in the fight against "the Negro-baiting, Republican-killing democracy."

During this era of party power, presidents were political eunuchs. They were to keep quiet, get elected, and dispense the patronage to the allies of the political bosses and congressional fat cats who wielded the real power. Looking back on this period, the novelist Thomas Wolfe would ask about these mediocre incumbents, "Which had the whiskers, which the burnsides: which was which?"

Still, elections generated great interest and high voter turnout. With party identities strong and stable, electoral efforts emphasized mobilizing party loyalists and convincing a relatively small number of voters with extraordinary influence. The rural North was often as instinctively Republican as the South was Democratic. One man, recalling his childhood in Ohio, said that "the Republican Party was not a faction, was not a group, not a wing, it was an institution like those Emerson speaks of in his essay on politics, rooted like oak trees in the center around which men group themselves as best they can. . . . It was inconceivable that any self-respecting man should be a Democrat." Republican Boss Thomas Platt admitted that throughout his long political career, the "main consideration with me" in all matters was "the welfare of the Republican Party, which I have never discriminated from the welfare of the State and the nation." His explanation for why he became a Republican was simple: "I could not be a Democrat."

Religious and ethnic loyalties as well as a continuing sense of patriotism reinforced many northerners' identities. The Republican Party was the party of pietistic Protestantism, the party of moral reform. Most northern Methodists, northern Baptists, Norwegian Lutherans, Swedish Lutherans, Congregationalists, Episcopalians, Presbyterians, and Quakers were Republican. Patriotism, party pride, ethnic solidarity, and religious devotion dictated opposition to public funding of Catholic schools and support for temperance, prayer in schools and Sunday blue laws. Politicians encouraged this kind of ethnocultural identification, while dreading the battles they unleashed. "Questions based upon temperance, religion, morality, in all their multiplied forms, ought not to be the basis of politics," John Sherman complained in 1873. Such questions made it difficult to forge the kinds of compromises necessary to maintaining broad coalitions.

Republican moral crusaders did not object to their party's alliance with big business. Most wanted their government to encourage prosperity and equated support for business with support for free enterprise and the American dream. Occasional populist outbursts against the growing concentration of economic power could not compete with the enduring commitment to private property and the pursuit of wealth. The few tensions that did emerge between "Main Street" and "Wall Street" Republicans were eclipsed by overheated rhetoric about the Civil War and the various crusades needed to restore America's soul.

LAISSEZ-FAIRE CONSERVATISM

Yet while the *petit bourgeois* continued to trust the government to foster growth, businessmen began reevaluating the role of government in American economic life. The interventionist Free Labor ideology promised to help laborers and their bosses by harnessing government power to serve the business community. But more and more businessmen—many of whose fortunes originated from working with the government—began fearing that the same impulse that led the government to encourage development could lead to regulation. Embracing the traditional liberal belief in limited government expressed in the Constitution and consecrated by Thomas Jefferson, many conservative Americans began demanding a smaller, more restrained government. Herbert Spencer, William Graham Sumner, and other theorists who applied Charles Darwin's theories of evolution to society concluded that biology demanded government restraint. Social Darwinists condemned government regulations of business, of sanita-

tion, of housing, as an unnatural intrusion. "Fostering the good-for-nothing at the expense of the good is an extreme cruelty," Spencer preached. The political scientist Clinton Rossiter would call the emergence of this *laissez-faire* conservatism the great train robbery of American intellectual history.

Of course, as long as businessmen could influence the federal government through the Republican Party, they curbed their Jeffersonian instincts. The Liberal Republican revolt had failed to save the party from the influence peddlers. Parties needed the money, and corporations needed the access. An 1880 cartoon, "The Two Rival Political Huckster Shops," dismissed all politicians as greedy. Said the "Spirit of Washington" to the "Spirit of Jefferson" as they surveyed an election scene in which both Republicans and Democrats had "Nominations for Sale": "Behold the result of our sacrifices and labors!"

"STALWARTS," "HALF-BREEDS," AND THE FIGHT OVER CIVIL SERVICE REFORM

Meanwhile, fights over the spoils paralyzed the Republican Party. One faction of "Stalwarts" opposed civil service reform. Bosses such as Simon Cameron of Pennsylvania, Zachariah Chandler of Michigan, and Roscoe Conkling of New York had forged their political identities in the fight over Reconstruction. Self-styled members of the "Old Guard," they continued fighting the Civil War as a way of bringing victory—and patronage—to their "Grand Old Party," which was all of 25 years old in 1880. Their primary opponents, known as "Half-Breeds," were younger and wanted to end their party's obsession with the past. James Blaine of Maine and John Sherman of Ohio were willing to accept some civil service reform, or at least pay homage to it as necessary. Cameron, Lincoln's first secretary of war, dismissed this "new school of politicians who indulge in modish sentimentalism and cowardice calling them statesmanship, and go about sneering at obsolete courage and political conviction, calling them 'radicalism.' "

The two sides clashed during the 1880 convention in Chicago. Hoping to repeat their winning formula, Conkling's Stalwarts supported U.S. Grant for a third term. Joseph B. McCullagh, the editor of the *St. Louis Globe-Democrat*, described the Grant "boom" and introduced a new term to American politics, as he compared the effort to what a Mississippi riverboat pilot shouts when a river overflows: "By Jove, but she's booming." The Half-Breeds blocked Grant's nomination, but were themselves divided. Sherman refused to release enough votes to allow Blaine's nomination. After 34 frustrating ballots, the Wisconsin delegates switched 16 votes to a dark-horse, James Garfield, an Ohio Half-Breed acceptable to both Sherman and Blaine. On the 36th ballot, Garfield was nominated by a vote of 309 to 306.

To appease the Stalwarts, the convention nominated the former abolitionist Chester A. Arthur to be vice president. President Grant had appointed Arthur to be collector at the lucrative port of New York, while President Hayes had fired Arthur for meddling in politics despite an executive order barring federal officials from political involvement. This nomination thus disavowed President Hayes's attempts at civil service reform.

Garfield often had to choose between allowing his enemies to undermine his efforts or alienating them further. The Stalwarts were trying to centralize the Republican National Committee and control fund raising and strategy from New York. Individual state organizations resisted these attempts and competed with the national party for funds. The assistant secre-

tary of the committee eventually agreed to affirm that "we place no speakers upon the stump except upon the demands of the committees of the States."

The Stalwarts also tried to impose a national chairman on the candidate. Garfield's ally William E. Chandler thwarted this effort. As a result, the nominee had unprecedented input in selecting a new chairman, Marshall Jewell. But now Stalwarts had more reasons to oppose Garfield. Conkling was furious.

In August, Garfield left his front porch in Ohio and traveled to New York to meet with Conkling at the urging of party leaders. Conkling boycotted this "treaty of Fifth Avenue." Garfield, who had resisted the visit because he expected that the Stalwarts would eventually fall "into line," refused to chase after the pompous New York senator. "If the Presidency is to turn on that, I do not want the office badly enough." Eventually, Conkling and Garfield met in Garfield's home state. After speaking in Warren, Ohio, and barely acknowledging Garfield's candidacy, Conkling papered over his differences with Garfield in the "Treaty of Mentor."

The Greatest Presidential Puzzle. Cartoon Showing Senator Conkling Playing the "15 Puzzle," Which Was the Rage of the Day, with Blocks Representing Presidential Hopefuls, March 17, 1880. *Source:* Library of Congress.

REPUBLICAN PROTECTIONISM

Despite such division, the Republican fund-raising apparatus could still flood critical areas with campaign pamphlets and cash. Republicans distributed as many as 12 million documents in 1880. Manufacturers kept the party of protection well financed. The Civil War had reversed the trend toward lower tariffs seen in the Democratic tariffs of 1846 and 1857. Revenues were needed and manufacturers had to be coddled. Thus, the tariffs of 1862 and 1865 were rather steep. Democrats became more clearly defined by their commitment to free trade, just as Republicans came to be defined by their belief in protection. Free trade unified a Jeffersonian Democratic Party that feared a centralized government, just as protectionism appealed to the Republican Party, which was trying to harness government in the service of Free Labor and American industry.

The two camps became polarized. Trade policy was no longer simply a distinguishing mark between Republicans and Democrats but between good and evil. In 1880 the Democratic candidate, Winfield Scott Hancock, tried to finesse the tariff problem. Republicans had gained in manufacturing states by claiming that American industry was threatened by the Democrats' embrace of "free trade," which in the hands of Republican orators could appear as unsavory as free love. Hancock responded in an interview with the Paterson, New Jersey, *Daily Guardian*. He explained that even though the platform supported a "tariff for revenue only," Democratic tariff rates would still protect industry. Anyway, he added, "the tariff is a local question."

Hancock's explanation was economically sound but politically disastrous. In fact, attitudes toward the tariff were often determined by regional economic needs. Still, and especially in a presidential campaign, the broader symbol obscured minor variations and such incidental concerns as the truth. "That," the Republican Edwin Cowles chuckled, "is one interview too many." Republicans charged that Hancock would violate traditional American tariff policy at the cost of millions of jobs. Shocked Republicans doubted "whether any ten-year-old boy could be found" in Pennsylvania who was so "ignoran[t] of his ignorance." Democrats blamed Hancock's interview for his and their subsequent defeat. The Republicans regained the majority in both the House and the Senate, while Garfield narrowly won. One observer chided William Chandler, saying, "I honestly think you fellows elected Garfield by the use of money, systematically and methodically

FARMER GARFIELD
Cutting a Swath to the White House.

Cartoon of Garfield. *Source:* ICS/USIA.

employed. I think you bought Indiana as you would buy so much beef. . . . Where this side of h——l are we going to stop?"

The fight between the Half-Breeds and the Stalwarts had tragic consequences. When Garfield appointed Blaine as secretary of state and then tried to impose his own appointee as collector of the port of New York, Conkling resigned from the Senate in protest. Conkling assumed that the New York State legislature would reelect him, but he miscalculated. The Half-Breeds were triumphant, the Stalwarts in eclipse.

Six weeks after Conkling's resignation, one of his admirers, Charles Guiteau, shot President Garfield. "I am a Stalwart and now Arthur is President," the frustrated office seeker shouted. From his jail cell, the assassin preached that "the President's tragic death was a sad necessity but it will unite the Republican Party and save the Republic." The assassination reflected the Republicans' degeneration in 20 years from grand ideological concerns to petty party squabbles. This president was a victim of factionalism, not a martyr to liberty and union.

PUCK.

A HARMLESS EXPLOSION.

Roscoe Conkling Resigns from U.S. Senate. Cartoon by
Joseph Keppler. *Source:* Library of Congress.

The new president now became a most unlikely
champion of civil service reform. The former dispenser
of customs patronage had no choice but to sign the
Pendleton Civil Service Act of 1883. Under Chester A.
Arthur the United States finally had a law mandating
at least some merit-based federal appointments and
barring the levying of political campaign assessments
on federal officeholders.

THE MUGWUMP REVOLT, 1884

Still, the Pendleton Act failed to cleanse the
Republican Party or American politics. Disappointed
liberal Republicans continued trying to save their
party. When the Half-Breed leader James Blaine secured the Republican nomination in 1884, these reformers abandoned their party once again. A charming
man with piercing black eyes and a General Grant
beard, Blaine was a popular politician with one minor
flaw. Despite a yearly salary rarely exceeding $5,000,
he had become a millionaire. *The Nation's* editor, E.L.
Godkin, called Blaine's candidacy a "conspiracy of
jobbers to seize the Treasury, under the lead of a most
unprincipled adventurer." As in 1872, reformers were
forced to focus on personalities rather than the broader
issues. *Harper's* editor, George Curtis, mourned the triumph of expedience over idealism, saying, "I was at
the birth of the Republican Party, and I fear I am to witness its death."

Once again party regulars dismissed the rebels as ef-
fete and unrealistic. Regulars called reformers
Mugwumps, an Algonquin Indian word meaning
"Chief." Some redefined the term as an indecisive bird
sitting on a fence with his mug on one side and his
wump on the other. Others defined it as "a person educated beyond his intellect." This division helped
cause the first Democratic presidential victory since
the Civil War.

The attacks on Blaine's integrity and his considerable abilities as a speaker emboldened him. Violating
the nineteenth-century tradition of candidate passivity, he took to the stump. After a triumphant tour
through Ohio, Blaine met with Republican clergymen
in New York on October 29. The Reverend Samuel D.
Burchard greeted Blaine by denouncing the Democrats
as "the party whose antecedents have been Rum,
Romanism and Rebellion." Burchard's alliteration testified to the intersection of moralism, religion, and patriotism that made political identities so firm and political clashes so explosive during this era. Blaine,
whose sister was a nun and who had long dodged accusations that he was a Catholic, ignored the offending
remark; the alert chairman of the Democratic National
Committee did not. Senator Arthur Pue Gorman had
assigned men to shadow Blaine and transcribe all public remarks made at Republican functions. By the next
morning, thousands of Irish Catholic votes and, many
believe, the election itself, had been lost.

On Election Day, Cleveland received 4,879,507 popular votes, 219 electoral votes. Blaine received
4,850,293 popular votes, 182 electoral. The Democrats
retained the House; the Republicans, the Senate. The
Democrats won New York's 36 electoral votes by a
margin of 1,149 out of 1,125,000 votes cast. Historians
have long debated the effects of Blaine's being "bur-
chardized." In the 1960s, Lee Benson argued that

Harrison with Blaine as the Raven. Cartoon by Joseph Keppler. *Source:* Library of Congress.

Blaine reversed the Republican decline in six states and that, given the long-term voting trends, personalities were insignificant. Blaine's papers, however, are filled with estimates of the thousands driven away by the Burchard remarks. Blaine said he would have "carried New York by 10,000 if the weather had been clear on election day and Dr. Burchard had been doing missionary work in Asia Minor."

THE TARIFF FIGHT OF 1887–1888

The Democrats' return to the White House for the first time in a quarter of a century did not break the electoral stalemate. Cleveland alienated many Democratic Party regulars and in 1887 handed the Republicans a great issue for the election campaign: protectionism. Cleveland turned his entire annual message in December into a plea for a lower protective tariff. Shrewdly, Cleveland and the Democrats treated the tariff as an unjust tax that was gouging the American worker. Cleveland blamed high tariffs for "crippling our national energies, suspending our country's development, preventing involvement in productive enterprise, threatening financial disturbance, and inviting schemes of public plunder." The 1888 Democratic platform was equally hysterical, spelling out just how central this debate over trade was: "upon this great issue of tariff reform, so closely concerning every phase of our national life, and upon every question involved in the problem of good government, the Democratic Party submits its principles and professions to the intelligent suffrage of the people."

Democratic protectionists deserted the president as Republicans pounced. Pro-Republican high-tariff associations such as the American Iron and Steel Association poured thousands of dollars into the campaign. William McKinley of Ohio demonstrated how Republicans could wrap any issue in Old Glory when he praised the tariff as a friend of the workingman, not the businessman. McKinley and other Republicans urged voters to "stand by American industries, stand by that policy which believes in American work for American workmen, that believes in American wages for American laborers, that believes in American homes for American citizens." The 1888 Republican platform declared: Democratic free traders "serve the interests of Europe; we will support the interests of America. . . . The protective system must be maintained. Its abandonment has always been followed by general disaster to all interests, except those of the usurer and the sheriff." "The issue cannot now be obscured," the Republican nominee, Benjamin Harrison, thundered. "It is not a contest between schedules, but between wide-apart principles."

Looking back, one Nebraska Democrat would mourn his president's bad timing. "Had Cleveland's tariff reform message been dated December 1886, instead of 1887, we should win victory everywhere," J. Sterling Morton claimed. "The people would have become educated before this time, but the term of school has been too short for teaching economics to 60,000,000 people."

The black-and-white tariff issue became a vehicle for expressing frustration with America's new industrializing order and for articulating different visions of the

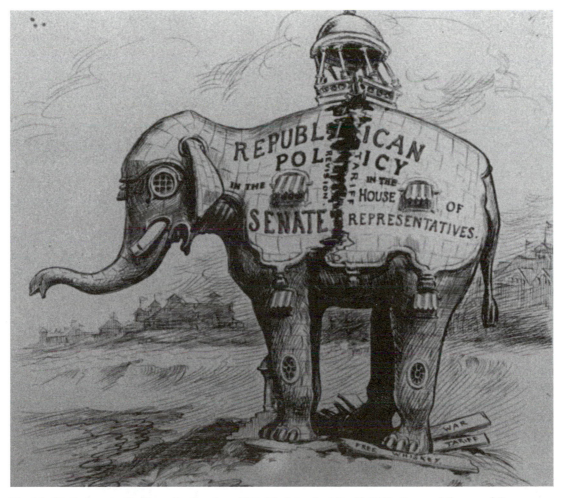

Doubly Unfortunate: Built on the Sand and Divided Against Itself, 1888. *Source:* Library of Congress.

future. Free trade became a rallying cry for Americans anxious to limit government power and corporate influence, just as protectionism became the identifying mark for sophisticated Americans who appreciated the realities of a new industrial order. The historian Morton Keller explains: "It was through the tariff and currency issues that the political system began to grapple with the economic problems of an industrial society. Their very familiarity as political issues, and the strong emotional content that inhered in protection and free trade, free silver and hard money, added to their political saliency."

Chastened by the 1884 defeat, inspired by the tariff battle, Republicans united behind Benjamin Harrison of Indiana. "Some men," a Republican newspaper admitted, "are born great, some achieve greatness, some have greatness thrust upon them, and others live in pivotal states." Matthew S. Quay, the Pennsylvania boss considered to be "the greatest po-

litical general of the century" by his peers, managed the campaign. Quay recognized that the electoral college made the presidential campaign a series of state elections. He upset locals by directing the efforts in key states, rather than simply coordinate fund raising, speech making, and printing at the national headquarters.

Republican fund raising was aggressive. James P. Foster, the president of the Republican League of the United States, a high-tariff association, advised: "I would put the manufacturers of Penn. under the fire and fry all the fat out of them." This "boodle" campaign raised as much as $3.3 million for the national Republican effort. Republicans made more than 20,000 speeches. They distributed more than a million propaganda tracts, including 300,000 lithographs of the candidate. "Money was used in this election with a profusion never before known on Am[erican] soil," one Mugwump complained.

The battle was particularly intense in Harrison's home state. The Republican National Committee treasurer, W.W. Dudley, tried to buy swing voters, or "floaters" as they were known, wholesale. He told his minions to "divide the floaters into blocks of 5 and put a trusted man w[ith] the necessary funds in charge of these 5 and make him responsible that none get away and that all vote our ticket." When these embarrassing instructions were publicized, "Blocks of Five Dudley" became a symbol for the Republicans' underhanded campaign efforts in 1888—and throughout the period.

For all the campaign efforts, there were very few "floaters" available. The voting patterns proved remarkably stable. On Election Day, President Cleveland increased his share of the popular vote by 0.1% while Harrison ran 0.3% behind Blaine's effort in 1884. Still, Republicans won the White House and both houses of Congress. Only two states changed hands. Harrison carried his home state of Indiana by 0.4% while Cleveland, without Reverend Burchard's help, lost his home state of New York by 1.1%.

Harrison somewhat presumptuously thanked a higher authority. "Providence has given us the victory," he exclaimed. Matt Quay, aware of "how close a number of men were compelled to approach the gates of the penitentiary" to ensure victory, snapped: "Providence hadn't a damned thing to do with it."

"CZAR" THOMAS REED

Republicans elected Thomas B. Reed of Maine, the Speaker of the House, to preside over the 51st Congress. This crafty parliamentarian developed "Reed Rules" to modernize congressional procedure. In so doing, he expanded the Speaker's discretionary power. With Reed's prodding, Republicans indulged their traditional zeal for internal improvements, Civil War pensions, and other expensive schemes. Democrats exploited the fears of Americans who expected more modest federal programs by complaining about this "billion dollar Congress." The Speaker, dubbed "Czar" Reed, would refuse to apologize for his activist approach to government. He believed that the United States was a "billion dollar country" and deserved a bold and effective Congress and party. "The democracy has one great advantage," he would explain. "The republican party does things; the democratic party finds fault. It follows . . . that the republican party must take positive ground on some known spot of the earth. The democrats are free then to skirmish through all creation. Of course that gives them

during the early part of the conflict the appearance of occupying the earth."

BACKLASH AGAINST THE "BILLION DOLLAR CONGRESS"

Like Cleveland, Harrison refused to acknowledge his debt to the party regulars. The new president resented the party demands for patronage payoffs. "Those who did most to place Harrison . . . in the Presidency, found him a marble statue when they asked for recognition of their services," Boss Thomas Platt of New York complained. For his part, Harrison grumbled that "the Senators and Representatives appear to think that the President of the United States has nothing else to do but fill the offices."

These party squabbles distracted Republicans at a time when their grip on the electorate was slipping. The McKinley Tariff of 1890 raised duties on manufactured goods to an average of about 49.5%—enraging

Harrison Rooster and Campaign Egg. *Source:* J. Doyle Dewitt Collection.

farmers and laborers, who blamed the Republicans' tariff for higher prices. Republicans were also alienating Catholics, immigrants, and other key constituents with their moralistic crusades against alcohol and against public funding for state-supported schools. In the decade preceding the critical midterm elections of 1890, 16 of the 21 states outside the South considered prohibiting the sale of alcohol by referendum. Only six voted for Prohibition—and Rhode Island reversed its decision three years later. Democrats complained about Republican "paternalism," cleverly rolling the Republicans' economic activism and cultural crusading into an assault on "personal liberty."

As a result, Republicans were repudiated during the midterm elections. The Democrats gained 76 seats in 1890. In the reconstituted House of Representatives, Democrats outnumbered the Republicans 3-to-1, with a total of 235 out of a possible 332 seats.

The party bosses tried to dump the weakened president at the 1892 convention. "I don't want this . . . ," he said, "but a Harrison never runs from a fight." Unable to find an alternative candidate, the Republican Convention reluctantly renominated Harrison. Harrison retaliated by nominating a reformer, Whitelaw Reid, as vice president and installing his own puppet as Republican national chairman. The "'leaders of the party' . . . are tremendously unfriendly to me," he explained. "[I]f I am to be elected I must elect myself."

THE POPULIST REBELLION

Republicans in 1892 fought the same fight about the distribution of spoils and the purity of their aims that had occupied them since the days of Reconstruction. Once again they focused on the tariff in their attempt to secure Harrison's reelection. "We reaffirm the American doctrine of protection," the platform declared. "We maintain that the prosperous condition of our country is largely due to the wise revenue legislation of the Republican Congress." But new challenges were emerging as well. Americans were grumbling about corrupt parties, concentrated wealth and industrial displacement. Especially in the West and the South, the Populist movement became a vehicle for expressing many of these complaints, while in the East and in the cities, Progressivism offered citizens a modern way of analyzing and changing their flawed society and polity.

Since the 1870s, farmers had felt squeezed by modern industrializing America. One Nebraska farm editor complained: "We have three crops: corn, freight rates and interest. The farmers farm the land, and the businessmen farm the farmers." More and more southern and western farmers looked to politics to solve their economic problems and end their sense of cultural displacement. They defined their agricultural way of life as the American way. Dozens of alliances and parties sprouted throughout the United States from the 1870s through the 1890s. In the cities, frustrated workers dreamed of a Farmer–Labor alliance to free America from the grip of Wall Street.

Gradually, this movement that began with dejected individuals who banded together in local groups, then regional groups, then interregional groups, decided to go national. By the 1890s, American farmers were in crisis. The problems of exorbitant shipping charges, greedy middlemen, and extortionate mortgage rates many had been complaining about for decades were compounded by a series of crop failures. Land prices and farm income plummeted.

These disparate efforts culminated on July 4, 1892, in Omaha, when 800 delegates from 22 farm, labor, and reform organizations founded the People's Party of America to mobilize "the power of government" in favor of farmers and laborers and against the money power's "vast conspiracy against mankind." The Omaha platform articulated the growing frustration of millions: "The people are demoralized; most of the States have been compelled to isolate the voters at the polling places to prevent universal intimidation and bribery. The newspapers are largely subsidized or muzzled, public opinion silenced, business prostrated, homes covered with mortgages, Labor impoverished, and the land concentrated in the hands of the capitalists." The People's presidential candidate, James Weaver, would siphon off over a million votes and 22 electoral votes from the two major-party candidates in 1892, 8.5% of the popular vote total. The People's Party would send a dozen congressmen to Washington while seizing the governor's chairs in Kansas, North Dakota, and Colorado.

Still, 1892 was the Democrats' year. For the first time since 1856, they secured majorities in the House and the Senate while winning the White House. Democrats even won in Lincoln's home state of Illinois. Cleveland interpreted this triumph over the Republicans and the Populists as a mandate for governmental restraint. "The lessons of paternalism ought to be unlearned and the better lesson taught that while the people should patriotically and cheerfully support the government, its functions do not include support of the people," he declared in his inaugural address.

Cleveland's stolidity would prove disastrous for his party when the Panic of 1893 devastated the American economy. During the 1894 midterm elections, the Republicans returned to congressional power, picking up 117 seats in the House and 5 seats in the Senate. The Republicans recaptured the rebellious states in the Great Plains and the Rocky Mountains except for Nevada, and solidified their hold on the Northeast. "Czar" Reed returned to rule the House until 1899. Such lurches from one party to the next suggested that the period of electoral stalemate was over. A major realignment was occurring in American politics.

The Depression of 1893 convinced many Populists that farmers and laborers needed to unite. But fighting both political parties seemed futile—better to try conquering one. Just as abolitionists had talked about fusion as the Whig Party shattered, Populists began searching for fusion with the Democrats on a free-silver platform. Silver had become a crucial symbolic issue for farmers and westerners, a way to woo mining interests and loosen credit for all. Grover Cleveland firmly believed in the gold standard. He considered all talk of "bimetallism" un-American.

THE 1896 REALIGNMENT

The Democrats were so badly divided at their 1896 convention that the platform committee could not agree on most issues. It took a 36-year-old, two-term congressman from Omaha, Nebraska, William Jennings Bryan, to break the impasse. Addressing the currency question directly, he roared, "Having behind us the producing masses of this nation and the world, supported by the commercial interests, the laboring interests and the toilers everywhere, we will answer their demand for a gold standard by saying to them: You shall not press down upon the brow of Labor this crown of thorns, you shall not crucify mankind upon a cross of gold." As a result of Bryan's oratory, the Democrats endorsed a Populist platform recognizing that "the money question is paramount to all others at this time." It called for "the free and unlimited coinage of both silver and gold," while attacking "the absorption of wealth by the few" in all facets of American life. Bryan was nominated to lead this crusade.

In noting how many of the Populists' initially radical reforms eventually became adopted by both parties, the historian Richard Hofstadter would deem third parties the bumblebees of American politics, stinging the major parties, then dying after their venom entered the system. In 1896 the Democrats proved more allergic to this toxin than the Republicans. Fusion enervated the Populists

Song Sheet, 1896 Republican Campaign. *Source:* New York Public Library.

and the Democrats. It demoralized southern Populists who had been rebelling against the Democratic Party's alliance with southern landowners, and radical Populists who found the Democratic platform too moderate. It also alienated Grover Cleveland's gold-standard Democrats. "I am a Democrat still," said David B. Hill, the New York Democratic boss, "very still."

The ensuing "battle of the standards" reduced the myriad and sometimes overlapping disagreements between Democrats and Republicans to one explosive issue: whether American currency should continue to be anchored in gold or expanded and cheapened by being redeemed for silver as well. "The whole country has been set to talking about coinage—a matter utterly unfit for public discussion," Lincoln's former secretary John Hay moaned. The polarized debate, coming on the heels of a devastating depression, terrified Americans. Two irreconcilable systems clashed. Republicans such as Henry Cabot Lodge were "fighting to save the country from a disaster which would be second only to 1861." Similarly, Democrats such as E.C. Wall of Wisconsin believed the "fight today is . . .

whether there shall be a republic or not. Whether a few men of wealth shall govern this land or the people."

The Republican nominee, William McKinley, offered a safe, traditional, dignified, solidly midwestern contrast to the fire-breathing Bryan. McKinley had built his career on the protective tariff crusade. At the beginning of this great battle over currency, "Czar" Reed observed, "McKinley isn't a silver-bug, McKinley isn't a gold-bug, McKinley is a straddle-bug." Theodore Roosevelt of New York discovered that at national headquarters "there is no demand whatever for literature on the tariff, but . . . they have to send out tons of mail matter on finance and that they only wish they had more documents." A "great politician," according to Senator Charles Dick, McKinley embraced the gold standard.

McKinley's political skills often were underestimated because of his reliance on Mark Hanna and because of his aspirations to statesmanship. Hanna was a wealthy Ohio industrialist who retired to direct McKinley's presidential effort. Hanna became Republican national chairman and organized one of the greatest Republican campaigns in American history. Building on the innovations of the previous few years, he helped reshape party politics.

Hanna combined old-fashioned partisan methods with modern tactics tailored to the new industrializing polity that was emerging. Many Americans no longer were as rooted in their communities and in their parties as their parents had been. The traditional bottom-up organization, building from local wards up toward the state, then the national, effort, had to be supplemented with a top-down approach that educated the masses and organized them by interest group rather than geographic locale. Hanna established different bureaus to appeal to different constituencies—Germans, blacks, traveling salesmen, wheelmen, even women. These categories heralded an America where people defined themselves by their professions, their hobbies, and their ethnic groups, rather than their neighborhoods.

As Matt Quay had in 1888, Mark Hanna viewed the national committee as a nerve center, not a clearinghouse. Hanna organized the campaign systematically—raising money, deploying 1,400 speakers, and distributing pamphlets as efficiently as Standard Oil produced and marketed its product. The campaign was honest and businesslike. Crude but extensive polls identified decisive areas. Well aware of Hanna's passion for efficiency, his subordinates carefully monitored their output. They distributed 200 to 300 million copies of 275 different items in a dozen different languages, weighing 2,000 tons. The committee spent $469,079.84 on printing; $42,693.84 in sending out 1.5 million mail packages from Chicago. Some estimated that the number of documents Republicans distributed in 1896 exceeded by 50% the total number of documents the Republican National Committee had issued since its founding.

More Americans were experiencing elections by reading at home than marching in the streets. Hanna fed partisan newspapers' growing demand for stories with boilerplate items. In all, nearly 5 million families every week read newspapers with copy from the Republican Bureau of Publication and Printing.

All these efforts required enormous sums—no party would spend as much money again until 1920. Hanna created a formidable fund-raising apparatus. He recognized that corporations controlled vast funds and that officeholders were no longer legal sources of money. His efforts benefited from the fact that the few Democrats who served as directors of railroads and banks abandoned Bryan and supported McKinley. Without critics to object, corporations donated "directly from their corporate treasuries . . . for the first time," according to Zachariah Chandler. "It was a very dangerous practice to inaugurate," the former Republican national chairman recognized. One Philadelphia bank president said that in his ten years at the helm, he had "never before contributed a cent to politics, but the present crisis we believe to be as important as war." He donated $25,000. According to Chauncey Depew, corporate executives compared their contributions to "taking out an insurance policy" to protect their "general interests."

The campaign solidified the bond between the Republican Party and the nation's businessmen. For the next century, the Republican Party would usually raise more money than the Democrats. The party became addicted to its corporate constituents and their policy demands. The Populist crusade had awakened the incipient Jeffersonianism of the nation's businessmen. *Laissez-faire* conservatism gave their desire to limit government intellectual respectability and would make the Republican Party the home to those who remained skeptical of government attempts to manage the economy and society.

Amid all these innovations, Republicans continued to wrap their campaign and their candidate in the American flag. They were so successful in appropriating national symbols as party props that their celebration of Flag Day on June 14 became an American tradition. A traveling Patriotic Heroes Battalion of war veterans reminded Americans that the Republicans were the party of union and the Democrats, the party of disunion.

Hanna's impressive organizational efforts were somewhat extraneous. Republicans emerged as the true fusion party in 1896. They terrified and inspired the northern masses—a trend clearly forecast in the midterm elections of 1894. After years of Democratic depression, factory workers were more tempted by McKinley's "full dinner pail" than Bryan's free silver. City dwellers, be they rich or poor, resented Bryan's agrarianism and hostility to industrialism. When Bryan called the Northeast "the enemy's country" and dreamed of a dry, Jeffersonian Protestant providence, immigrants and workers forgave the Republicans their anti-Catholicism, their bias toward big business, and their moralism. William McKinley became the first president since Ulysses S. Grant to win more than 50% of the popular vote. The electoral stalemate was broken.

The Republicans emerged from the 1896 election as the new majority party of the United States, having assembled a formidable coalition of farmers, laborers, middle-class workers, gold-standard Democrats, and industrialists throughout the North, the Midwest, and the Far West. The national campaign benefited from local efforts like those undertaken by Boss Thomas Platt in New York to expand the party's base in the cities. The "electoral realignment" of 1896 was sectional. Throughout the North and the West, the Democratic Party collapsed. Michigan, Pennsylvania, and other states became as solidly Republican as the South was Democratic. The Democrats' populist coalition of the dispossessed became a strained alliance between white southerners and western agrarians. Except for 1912, 84.5% of the total electoral vote for Democratic presidential candidates between 1896 and 1928 would be from the South. Republican gubernatorial candidates would win 83.1% of their races in the Northeast, 67.2% in the Midwest and West, 38.9% in the border states, and 2.6% in the 11 former Confederate states.

THE PARTY OF PROSPERITY

Thanks to Hanna, this reconstituted Republican Party suited the new American polity. This well-organized, well-managed, and well-financed party embraced the urban-industrial values—and realities—of modern America. While Bryan and the Democrats looked to an agrarian past, the Republicans united factory workers and owners with a vision of a prosperous future. This commitment to prosperity papered over growing divisions between capital and labor. The Free Soil ideology—promising dignity for all through prosper-

ity—no longer applied to a world of huge cities, multimillion-dollar corporations, and industrial plants.

The rejuvenated Republican Party flourished. An economic boom further cast the Republicans as the party of prosperity and the Democrats as the party of depression. The Spanish-American War of 1898 further cast the Republicans as the party of patriotism and the Democrats as the party of the doubters. Bryan would declare imperialism the "paramount issue" of his 1900 rematch against McKinley—and lose. "The Spanish War finished us off," the fiery Southern populist Tom Watson mourned. "The blare of the bugle drowned the voice of the reformer."

McKinley's passivity during the 1900 campaign accentuated his image as a dignified chief executive guiding the nation. The country was prosperous; the dinner pail was full. "There is only one issue in this campaign," Mark Hanna said, "and that is, let well enough alone." One farmer scoffed at Bryan's tirades against McKinley's imperialism: "What the hell do we care about the downtrodden Filipino as long as beef cattle are ten cents a pound?"

The 1900 contest solidified the new Republican majority. McKinley benefited from the rebound in farm prices and won in South Dakota, Kansas, Wyoming, Utah, Washington, and Bryan's own home state of Nebraska. Republicans enjoyed solid majorities in both houses of Congress as well.

McKinley's assassination in 1901 by an anarchist was a critical turning point for the Republican Party. Major McKinley was the last of the Civil War soldiers to serve in the White House. He and his peers had engineered the Republican Party's transition from an antislavery insurgency to the establishment party. They had created a formidable political organization. They had mastered a politics that buried conflict in rhetoric about prosperity and patriotism, intensified by the occasional wave of the "bloody shirt." They were the last of the ward politicians turned statesmen, the proud veterans of a popular politics of street parades and enduring party loyalties, a politics suited to the small-town and rural encampments of nineteenth-century America.

"We are too old to heal of such a wound," the 64-year-old John Hay wrote to Whitelaw Reid ten months after the assassination. To accentuate this sense of generational change, the new president, Theodore Roosevelt, was the youngest president in American history. At 43, his most vivid Civil War era memory was watching Lincoln's casket marched down Broadway. To Roosevelt and his generation, the Republican Party was not a welcome and evolving creation but an enduring and often impassive institution.

THE REPUBLICAN ROOSEVELT

Theodore Roosevelt embodied the contradictions of the Republican Party at the turn of the century. Overwhelmingly popular, he was a creature of both the East and the West, acceptable to Main Street and Wall Street, popular among reformers and pragmatists. Roosevelt mastered the modern arts of publicity and modern forms of communication to publicize his commitment to old-fashioned virtues. He conjured up the martial spirit of the Civil War by exaggerating his exploits during the "splendid little war" against Spain. And while he fancied himself a Progressive, he remained indebted to big business.

Progressivism vexed Republicans just as Populism had vexed Democrats. The temptation to embrace Progressivism was balanced by the fear that the movement would destroy the party, not just reform it. The Progressive movement was actually a series of movements that emerged between the 1890s and World War I in response to the challenges posed by the new industrial polity, particularly the growth of big business and big government. Characterized by simultaneous efforts of reformers on local, state, and national levels,

Roosevelt Campaigning. *Source:* Smithsonian Institution.

Progressivism incorporated a variety of goals: political reforms to destroy the urban machines and make government at all levels more democratic and more effective; economic reforms to curtail corporate power; and social reforms to help the victims of industrialization, especially the urban poor and the immigrants. To achieve these diverse goals, Progressives advocated a bewildering array of reforms including the ballot initiative, issue referendums, executive recall, regulation of public utilities and other corporations, antitrust legislation, tariff reform, city-manager plans, zoning regulations, education to Americanize the immigrant, immigration restriction, regulation of child and female labor, and even Prohibition.

Theodore Roosevelt was enough of an eastern patrician to want to purify politics and enough of a western cowboy to make the compromises necessary for political success. Roosevelt was a conservative, committed to achieving order in an industrial society. But, he explained, "The only true conservative is the man who resolutely sets his face toward the future." Roosevelt hoped for gradual changes within established institutions. He offered a "Square Deal" to all in this "era of federation and combination," trusting the federal government to referee among business, labor, and consumers. Behavior, not size, was the problem, he explained. "Those who would seek to restore the days of unlimited and uncontrolled competition," he would say, "are attempting not only the impossible, but what, if possible, would be undesirable."

Roosevelt's more immediate problem when he took office in 1901 was to consolidate power without violating McKinley's memory. Mark Hanna, now a senator, was unwilling to relinquish his hold on the Republican Party. One of Roosevelt's allies, Boss Matt Quay of Pennsylvania, anticipated trouble, because "we have two Executive Mansions," the White House and Hanna's headquarters at the Arlington Hotel. Roosevelt's ascension helped Quay and other eastern bosses wrest power away from Hanna and the other midwestern bosses who had advanced McKinley's candidacy. Through careful exercise of patronage in key states, Roosevelt created his own network of party loyalists.

THE "OLD GUARD"

Roosevelt had to tread carefully when dealing with Congress as well. Republicans held commanding leads in both houses, meaning that most of Roosevelt's headaches came from other Republicans, rather than Democrats. From 1903 to 1911, the Speaker of the House, Joseph G. Cannon of Illinois, ruled. "Uncle

Joe" exploited his ability to recognize speakers from the floor and the power of the Rules Committee to squelch his opponents and strangle legislation he disliked. In the Senate, power usually rested with the chairmen of the Finance and Appropriation Committees. The chairman of the Finance Committee, Nelson W. Aldrich of Rhode Island, would serve in the Senate for 30 years, from 1881 to 1911. During that time, he, along with William B. Allison of Iowa and John C. Spooner of Wisconsin, dominated the institution, dictating committee assignments and exploiting the newly developed party caucus system. In many ways, Aldrich and his cronies gave the notoriously individualistic upper chamber its first taste of effective leadership, building power through seniority instead of simply serving one term and moving on.

Cannon, Aldrich, and other members of the "Old Guard" wanted to "stand pat"—a poker-playing phrase—at a time of great change. The "standpatters" were committed to a high tariff and to supporting business. They feared that many of Roosevelt's regulatory schemes would swell the government and threaten the economy. For decades, the Republican Party had been able to serve business interests without becoming the party of *laissez-faire* conservatism. The Progressive demands to fix the fallout from industrialism would upset this balance.

THE "BULLY PULPIT"

The conservative opposition in Congress, as well as his own instinct for publicity and power, led Roosevelt to refashion the American presidency. He used the "bully pulpit" of the White House to speak to the "plain people." This Jacksonian vision of the presidency unsettled Republicans in Congress, who expected deferential presidents. The Old Guard recognized that such presidential power would eclipse congressional power while expanding the federal government's role in daily life. These tensions between Roosevelt and the Old Guard would eventually divide the party.

Roosevelt's popular presidency suited a modern political system where Americans no longer lived in what one historian calls "island communities." They were aware of new, complex national and international problems. The "plain people" needed a national focal point; Roosevelt offered his presidency. They worried about the perplexing new challenges; he offered cures. In this world, public opinion was more volatile and more powerful than party loyalty, interest groups had to be mollified, and politicians communicated through the press, not the party.

Newspapers were now independent institutions willing to "muckrake" and expose sensational scandals. President Roosevelt treated reporters as the most influential people in the country. He "corrupt[ed] the press," Oswald G. Villard of *The Nation* complained. "He warped and twisted, consciously or unconsciously, by his fascinating personality, the judgments of the best of the reporters." Theodore Roosevelt knew what reporters wanted, and he gave it to them—colorful news. They reciprocated with adoring press coverage.

In Roosevelt's presidency can be seen hints of the growing voter independence and party decline that would characterize modern American politics. These changes were occurring on the state level as well. In New York, such reformers as Charles Evans Hughes were beginning to address the economic and social challenges of industrialization and economic concentration. A politics of issues, rather than allegiances, of autonomous voters, rather than party loyalists, of independent candidates, rather than party bosses, developed.

The 1904 presidential campaign was a referendum on Roosevelt. "Your personality has been the Administration," Secretary of War Elihu Root told the president. Roosevelt continued his takeover of the Republican Party by choosing the officers of the Republican convention and dictating the platform. He installed his secretary, George B. Cortelyou, as Republican national chairman. The president "threw pretense aside," the journalist William Allen White gleefully recalled. "He assumed full responsibility."

While conquering the party, and playing to the people, Roosevelt also wooed Wall Street. Roosevelt's "trust-busting" rhetoric and Progressive pretensions unsettled the traditional donors. Corporations hesitated to bankroll their self-proclaimed nemesis. Roosevelt and Cortelyou strove to reconquer the corporate hearts. While Cortelyou solicited corporations, Roosevelt wooed the Wall Street moguls. He lobbied the railroad baron E.H. Harriman for $250,000. For the rest of his life, people whispered about Roosevelt's surrender to the money men.

His Democratic opponent, Judge Alton B. Parker, assailed Roosevelt's "shameless . . . willingness to make compromise with decency." Thus began a decades-long Democratic assault on the Republicans' selling of the presidency.

Roosevelt never doubted he would win, but the size of his landslide "stunned" him. Never before had a candidate secured 56.4% of the popular vote. Never before had a candidate won 336 electoral votes, or more than 300 electoral votes for that matter. Never before had the majority party secured 250 seats in the House of Representatives. To his wife, Roosevelt crowed: "My

Roosevelt as His Opponents Saw Him. *Source:* Library of Congress.

dear, I am no longer an accident!" At the height of his power, Roosevelt announced that he would respect George Washington's two-term precedent and retire in 1909. Roosevelt wanted to distinguish between using power vigorously and usurping it.

During his second term, Roosevelt often clashed with members of the Old Guard. They curbed his reformist zeal, while he forced them to pass precedent-setting if not path-breaking legislation. In his annual message to Congress in 1905, Roosevelt explained his approach. In advocating railroad regulation, he said he preferred management "by private individuals than by the government" as long as "justice is done the public. . . . What we need to do is to develop an orderly system, and such a system can only come through the gradually increased exercise of the right of

efficient government control." Roosevelt's zest for order, and his faith that government control could achieve both justice and efficiency, defined him as a Progressive. His continued flirtations with money men and the Old Guard, who preferred "private" managers over government bureaucrats, defined him as a pragmatist. "My business was to take hold of the conservative party and turn it into what it had been under Lincoln, that is, a party of *progressive* conservatism, or conservative radicalism," he said in 1908.

THE PRESIDENCY OF WILLIAM HOWARD TAFT

Roosevelt's hand-picked successor, Secretary of War William Howard Taft, lacked his predecessor's political finesse or stomach for conflict. It "is awful to be made afraid of one's shadow," as most campaigners are, Taft thought. The lumbering lawyer would have preferred serving on the Supreme Court to running the country and heading a political party.

Taft offered a tempting target to the Democrats and their nominee, William Jennings Bryan. The Democratic platform blasted Roosevelt's attempt to coronate a successor: "A forced succession to the Presidency is scarcely less repugnant to public sentiment than is life in that office." Bryan defined the "over-shadowing" question of the campaign as "Shall the People Rule?"

Republican Candidates for President and Vice President 1908: Taft and Sherman. "Grand Old Party Standard Bearers, 1856–1908." *Source:* National Archives.

He would charge that Taft was supported by office-holders, big businessmen, newspapers, "and an enormous campaign fund so tainted that he dare not let the people know where it comes from until they have voted."

Bryan refused donations from corporations and publicized all the contributions his campaign received. Half of the Democratic funds came from contributions under $100, and only eight contributors gave more than $1,000. As usual, the $1,658,000 the Republicans raised more than doubled the $630,000 the Democrats collected. Taft refused to publicize campaign contributions before the election, but he promised to publicize them afterward. He explained to Roosevelt that "I would like to have an ample fund to spread the light of Republicanism, but I am willing to undergo the disadvantage to make certain that in the future we shall reduce the power of money politics for unworthy purposes." Taft also turned down money from people connected to trusts, to U.S. Steel, to railroads. The Republican National Committee treasurer, George R. Sheldon, asked, "Where I am going to get the money?" Taft scoffed. "It is very difficult to get it out of Sheldon's head that the place to get money is confined to a narrow strip of street in New York."

Republican regulars still followed Mark Hanna's strategies. The Republican National Committee invited a prominent American Jew, Oscar Straus, to stump for Taft. Straus refused to speak "at any meeting gotten up on sectarian or hyphenated political lines." He condemned the practice of appealing to the "former national sympathies" of the "foreign born." This method was "un-American and inimical to the solidarity of our Americanism." Straus claimed that the chairman of the speaker's bureau agreed to end the practice, "and through that campaign at least put an end to advertising and meetings based on race or creed appeal." But, like corporate fund raising, appealing to ethnic groups in their own language proved too effective a tactic in this new polity to discontinue.

Taft's 51.6% share of the popular vote was closer to McKinley's shares in 1896 and 1900 than to Roosevelt's record-breaking 56.4% in 1904. The similarity between the Taft and McKinley vote totals suggests that Republicans could now consistently rely on a majority of the popular vote and that Roosevelt's personal popularity increased his constituency by approximately 10%. In another indication of party strength, Republicans retained control of two-thirds of the Senate seats and 56% of the House of Representatives.

As president, Taft pursued trust busting and some Progressive policies more zealously than Roosevelt had. Taft stressed "economy in expenditures" and called for a Commission on Efficiency and Economy, which recommended establishing a national budget. He also advocated a "Publicity Act" requiring representatives to detail their campaign contributions. But publicly he accommodated the Old Guard more than the fiery Roosevelt had.

REPUBLICAN INSURGENTS: THE "REVOLT AGAINST CANNONISM"

Republican Progressives began to rebel against the president and the congressional leadership. They renounced their party's traditional commitment to protectionism and its historic ties to big business. Senator Robert M. La Follette of Wisconsin led the fight over the Payne–Aldrich Tariff of 1909 against Senator Aldrich, who championed high rates and opposed an inheritance tax. La Follette and his self-styled "insurgents" turned their ire on the president when he endorsed the bill as "the best tariff bill that the Republican Party has ever passed."

On the House side, 40 Republican insurgents joined the Democratic minority to attack "Uncle Joe" Cannon's autocracy. Led by George Norris of Nebraska, the March 1910 "Revolt against Cannonism" was an assault on his precious Rules Committee. The rebels expanded the membership from 5 to 15, demanded that members be elected by the House and not appointed by the Speaker, and excluded the Speaker from the committee.

During the midterm elections of 1910, the insurgents battled the "regulars" aligned with the president. Ohio Senator Joseph B. Foraker, a standpatter, noted that, in Washington, "all the fighting talked about was among Republicans. I did not hear of any Republican, from the President down, talking or planning about any fighting with the Democrats." Democrats gained 56 House seats, establishing a firm majority for the first time since the 1896 "realignment." They also won 26 governorships, including New York and New Jersey, for the first time in decades, and reduced the Republican majority in the Senate from 29 to 10. The 1910 elections repudiated the "standpatters," not the insurgents. Many of the eastern regulars lost, while only 3 of 98 insurgent congressmen fell.

THEODORE ROOSEVELT VERSUS WILLIAM HOWARD TAFT

Roosevelt was frustrated that he had walked away from the presidency. He was too young to play the elder statesman. He lashed out, saying Taft had sold out

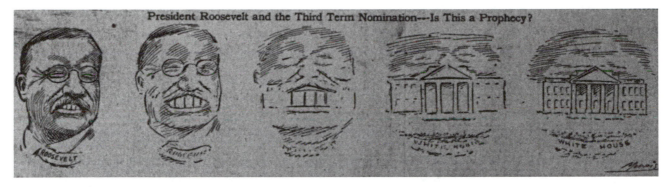

President Roosevelt and the Third Term Nomination. "Is This a Prophecy?" William Morris, 1907. *Source:* National Archives.

to the Republican Old Guard. The Republican Party had to decide, Roosevelt believed, whether to be "the party of the plain people" or "the party of privilege and of special interest." He embraced Progressive reforms expanding popular power, including the direct primary to nominate presidential candidates.

The direct-primary crusade resulted from the same feelings of frustration that impelled the Populist and Progressive movements. Many people were fed up with the manipulation of nominations by the party bosses. "Go back to the first principles of democracy; go back to the people," Senator La Follette declared in 1897. By 1912, a dozen states allowed voters to choose delegates to the national convention directly. For the first time in American history, a popular preconvention campaign was possible.

The direct primaries offered Roosevelt his one chance at seizing the Republican Party from his protégé. Otherwise, Taft's ties with the Old Guard made him unbeatable. Unconsciously echoing his nemesis, William Jennings Bryan, Roosevelt proclaimed that the major issue is "the right of the people to rule." In February 1912, borrowing a phrase cowboys used when they were ready to fight, Roosevelt announced: "My hat is in the ring." *Harper's Weekly* sneered that Roosevelt's "Hate, not hat, is in the ring."

The headstrong Roosevelt ripped into Taft and the Old Guard. He advanced a series of proposals, called the "New Nationalism," advocating a strong, Hamiltonian government to balance out big business. He called for more regulation of corporations, a graduated income tax, a reformed banking system, labor legislation, a direct primary, and a corrupt practices act—much as the Omaha platform had done. Roosevelt was no longer mollifying big business. He now felt free to advocate an activist government and to let loose rhetorically. Roosevelt portrayed Taft as standing "against the cause of justice for the helpless and the wronged, and on the side of . . . privilege and injustice." His fury inspired the Republican rank and file but split the party. The attacks launched a reluctant Taft into the campaign and virtually guaranteed that the still-powerful regulars would block Roosevelt's nomination. "Theodore Roosevelt has parted company with his better self!" one long-time Roosevelt ally exclaimed.

Taft/Roosevelt Split, 1912. *Source:* Culver Pictures.

Throughout the spring, the two former friends battled in the Republican primaries. Bitter, they fought like schoolboys. "Puzzlewit," "fathead," "egotist," "demagogue," they called each other. Arbiters of taste in the nation were appalled. "Are party wreckers more desirable than party leaders—bosses?" the *Washington Post* asked.

ROBERT M. LA FOLLETTE'S "WISCONSIN IDEA"

The Wisconsin Progressive Robert M. La Follette also joined the fray. Progressivism proved more influential in Wisconsin and other states than it was on the federal level. A representative of the western agrarian strain of radicalism that often allied with eastern Progressivism, La Follette had opposed the Republican machine in Wisconsin since 1880, when he had run for district attorney in Dane County. Since then, he had served in Congress from 1885 to 1891, as governor from 1901 to 1906, and would serve in the Senate from 1906 until 1925. La Follette's "Wisconsin idea" became a model of Progressivism, as government was made more responsive and more efficient. In 1903 Wisconsin enacted a primary law to circumvent boss rule. Legislation in 1905 established a railroad commission to circumvent the market and bring experts into the transportation industry.

Eventually, Roosevelt won Republican hearts, but Taft won the Republican nomination. The former president won 51% of the primary vote, securing 236 delegates in six state primaries while also carrying four state conventions. Taft won only a third of the popular vote and 34 delegates in the primaries. La Follette received 15.4% of the vote. But the primaries chose less than a quarter of the Republican delegates. At the Republican National Convention in Chicago, the party "steamroller" of bosses and officeholders renominated Taft.

THE 1912 DEBACLE

Roosevelt stormed out of the convention hall—and out of the Republican Party. At the Progressive Party convention, Roosevelt declared himself as "strong as a bull moose."

In accepting the nomination of what came to be known as the "Bull Moose Party," Roosevelt declared war on the two-party system. "Our fight is a fundamental fight against both of the old party machines, for both are under the dominion of the plunder league of the professional politicians who are controlled and

sustained by the great beneficiaries of privilege and reaction," he fumed. Displaying an evangelical fervor, Roosevelt affirmed: "We stand at Armageddon and we battle for the Lord!"

His triumphant Progressive Party nomination exhilarated Roosevelt. But he soon discovered that the freedom he enjoyed from political constraints reflected his weakness, not his strength. Relying on a makeshift organization, deprived of the Republicans' formidable network, shorn of his powers, cut off from corporate funds, Roosevelt could only peddle his charisma. And while public opinion was increasingly important, parties still ruled American politics. During a rally before the New Jersey primary in June, Roosevelt had knowingly said, "If you only vote as you shout, the thing is done." Throughout the fall of 1912, it became clear that Roosevelt had the crowds, but the Democrat Woodrow Wilson would get the votes.

"Good old Teddy," Wilson said, "what a help he is." The Republican split gave the Democrats their only shot at the White House in a generation. Taft even had trouble raising money. Many who contributed during the primaries were unwilling to do so again. Besides, Taft told his brother Charles, "the agitation about contributions makes everybody who is willing to give sensitive . . . lest his name may be dragged out in a public way." For the only time in the twentieth century, Republicans raised less than $1 million.

Thanks to Theodore Roosevelt, Republicans lost the White House and the Senate in 1912—the House stayed Democratic. Still, Roosevelt proved to be the most successful third-party candidate in history. His 4 million popular votes and 88 electoral votes made Taft the only major-party nominee since the founding of the Republican Party to come in third place. Together, Roosevelt and Taft received more than 7 million votes to Wilson's 6 million—a mark of the chance for a Republican victory squandered in the internecine fight.

OPPOSITION TO WILSONIANISM

Woodrow Wilson interpreted the Democratic sweep as a mandate to enact his "New Freedom," a Progressive attempt to keep business and government small. Wilson's first term was extraordinarily productive, lowering the tariff, passing antitrust legislation, and revolutionizing the nation's banking system with the Federal Reserve Act of 1913. Two constitutional amendments initiated during the Taft administration that were finally adopted during Wilson's first year also furthered this Progressive revolution. The 16th Amendment gave the federal government the right to levy income tax, and the 17th Amendment provided for the popular election of senators.

Wilson ignored the warnings about government "paternalism" of his Democratic predecessor, Grover Cleveland. The Wilson revolution defined the Democrats as the party of activist government. Yet this activism was not necessarily what future generations called "liberal." Wilson did little to advance women's suffrage and revealed his party's reliance on the "Solid South" when he supported segregation in federal departments in Washington, D.C.

The spread of segregation in Washington during the Wilson administration kept many blacks in the Republican Party for at least another generation. Both Roosevelt and Taft had disappointed blacks. Roosevelt had hosted Booker T. Washington at the White House, distributed some federal patronage to blacks, and condemned lynching. But when some black soldiers rioted in Brownsville, Texas, Roosevelt discharged three companies of black infantrymen. Taft proved even more disappointing, ignoring black concerns and depriving them of patronage in the South. Overall, however, blacks stuck with the party of Lincoln because, as one South Carolinian noted in 1928, "what little that has been done for us the Republicans gave to us."

The Republican attack against Wilson's "New Freedom" anticipated both parties' future positions on the question of big government. The Republican platform of 1916 would pay homage to the Progressive impulse to regulate "the great corporations of the country," then blast Wilson's program as expensive, inefficient, and intrusive. Playing to the *laissez-faire* conservatism of their corporate supporters, Republicans charged that "business success, no matter how honestly attained, is apparently regarded by the Democratic party as in itself a crime. Such doctrines and beliefs choke enterprise and stifle prosperity." The platform declared that "the Republican party believes in encouraging American business."

A PARTY IN DISARRAY

The Republican Party in 1916 was in disarray. Democrats had lost 61 seats in the House during the midterm election, and Wilson looked vulnerable. But a bewildering array of often irreconcilable factions identified with the party. On domestic issues, Progressives and members of the Old Guard were still bickering about the 1912 catastrophe. Regarding foreign affairs, Rooseveltian interventionists, midwestern isolationists, and German-American ethnics debated America's role in Europe's Great War. In the end, Republicans

settled on a call for "a strict and honest neutrality between the belligerents in the great war in Europe," and they nominated someone who had avoided partisan squabbles since 1910, Supreme Court Justice Charles Evans Hughes.

A Progressive Republican governor from 1906 to 1910, Hughes had watched the 1912 showdown from the safety of his Supreme Court seat. Now, after six years away from the tumult of American politics, Hughes had to get up to date without alienating any of his divided party's constituents. Every Hughes pronouncement, every meeting, every endorsement, was risky. Hughes could not criticize Wilson's Progressive programs without alienating some group that had benefited from them or appearing hypocritical himself. Also, Hughes nobly hesitated to say anything that would result in bad policy were he to win.

Hughes began by slighting the Republican National Committee. He filled his own 17-member steering committee with a mix of standpatters, Bull Moosers, and Progressives. By mid-September, the cracks appeared in the Republican facade. The rift between the Progressives and the Old Guard crippled organizational efforts throughout the country. State bosses often seemed more interested in defeating their intraparty rivals than in electing the standard-bearer. In New York, the doormat of Republican headquarters said "Welcome Progressives," while the reelection campaign of Governor Charles S. Whitman cried, "Quick death to the Progressives."

Hughes himself suffered in California when the Old Guard Republicans arranged a visit that at no time enabled Hughes to pay respects to the popular Progressive Republican Hiram Johnson, who was running for the Senate. At one point, an unknowing Hughes was even in the same hotel as Johnson: an oversight became a snub. When Hughes lost California, and thus the presidency, by under 4,000 votes, this "forgotten handshake" and the divisions underlying it appeared to have robbed Republicans of victory.

Hughes often failed to help the situation. With his party failing to support him, he needed to appeal to the public via the press. Yet his insistence on speaking extemporaneously, and his tendency to repeat the same speech at each stop, hindered newspaper coverage of his tour. All too often, reporters had nothing new to report. Advisers warned him, in vain, that in this new political world, it was foolish to deliver speeches "to the audiences that have heard them and not to the whole hundred millions of the American people."

The Republican campaign received its biggest boost in early September when the Adamson Act imposed an eight-hour day and time-and-a-half for overtime on the interstate railroads. Businessmen flocked to Republican headquarters with big checks to defeat the hated Wilson. The Republicans raised almost $2.5 million, nearly $1 million more than the Democrats did.

Although the Democrats lost 14 more seats in the House of Representatives, Wilson eked out a victory. The election was so close that on election night, both Hughes and Wilson went to sleep convinced that the president had lost. Only after the West Coast returns were in did Wilson's slim margin emerge. Wilson had polled 9.1 million popular votes to Hughes's 8.5 million. Wilson thus won 277 electoral votes, only 23 more than Hughes, with California's 13 electoral votes going to the president by only 3,773 popular votes.

In voting for Wilson, thousands of Republicans thought they were voting for peace. Ironically, within weeks of Wilson's second inauguration, the United States declared war on Germany. America's entry onto the world stage unsettled the Republican Party. Just as Theodore Roosevelt epitomized a tradition of vigorous involvement in international affairs to advance the nation's interests, Robert La Follette epitomized an older tradition of isolationism to preserve America's idealism against European chicanery.

In leading the nation into war, Woodrow Wilson caused both major parties to reverse their foreign policy stands. Since the outbreak of the Spanish-American War, the Republicans had championed American involvement overseas, while William Jennings Bryan had defined the Democrats as anti-imperialist. At the start of the war, Theodore Roosevelt and other interventionist Republicans had chided Wilson for not being sufficiently aggressive. But as Wilson led his party and the nation toward war, Republicans began to voice caution. Much of the party's rank and file, most of those outside the Northeast, and many of the Progressives were isolationists.

By the end of the war, the northeastern Teddy Roosevelt, traditionally interventionist wing of the Republican Party would provide the critical leadership in the fight against Wilson's League of Nations, an extraordinary reversal in a few short years. Both factions of the party could unite to oppose Wilson's League of Nations, with Roosevelt's heirs arguing that the United States should not cede its national prerogatives to a foreign body and isolationists demanding noninvolvement. But over the ensuing decades, the Republican Party would rarely find it so easy to paper over this rift.

The cooperation between business and government during World War I and the huge scale of distribution and production made Wilson's New Freedom look like Roosevelt's New Nationalism. The war exhausted Progressivism's crusading spirit even as the government institutionalized so many Progressive reforms. In 1918 Americans abandoned Wilsonian Progressivism in droves. The Democrats lost not only both Houses of Congress, the 240 Republican representatives constituted the largest party delegation since the Roosevelt landslide, and the third-largest Republican delegation in history. Looking back on the period, Calvin Coolidge of New England would note how quickly "the radicalism which had tinged our whole political life from soon after 1900 to the World War period . . . passed. There were still echoes of it and some of its votaries remained, but its power was gone."

THE ELECTION OF WARREN G. HARDING

Americans' simple, agrarian Arcadia had become an urbanized, industrialized, bureaucratized world power. "Fifty years ago the United States was mostly a country of villages and small towns," the *New York Times* would marvel—and overstate. "Now everybody, pretty nearly, is essentially urban and sophisticated."

The bureaucratization and centralization brought about by America's involvement in the European conflict helped transform the Republican Party. In 1918, Will Hays of Indiana established the first permanent national party headquarters of any party in Washington, D.C. The Republican National Committee would no longer be an ad hoc organization established every four years but a constant fixture on the Washington scene. An Advisory Committee on Policies and Platforms would help ensure ideological continuity as well as bureaucratic consistency. Hays also established a National Council of Republican Women, in anticipation of the 19th Amendment, which would grant women the right to vote in 1920.

Hays spent two years working to eliminate the amateurishness and divisiveness that helped elect Woodrow Wilson. Hays wanted a modern, sophisticated advertising effort set up to peddle the candidate. Long before the convention would meet in 1920 to look for a nominee, Hays and his advertising experts knew that their candidate would possess the 18 "vital qualities of mind and heart" their circulars would list. Whomever they chose would be distinguished by "his poise of mind his soundness of judgment his hold on fundamentals his appreciation of the needs of today and of tomorrow [and] his love of the people." During the campaign, such generic qualities would be trumpeted by advertising men such as Robert G. Tucker of Chicago, who wanted a "candidate" to come across as "a 'flesh and blood man' " on the newsreels. . . . After all the Americans are sentimental. They like to think of their leaders in a sentimental way." The generic qualities, the emotional appeal, the analysis of "the candidate" as an interchangeable product, and of "the Americans" as one massive market, characterized advertising's approach. Parties and campaigns were being reconceptualized and retooled to suit modern American consumer culture.

Anticipating such a "salesmanship campaign," dispirited by the squabbles generated by charismatic figures like Hughes and Roosevelt, suspicious of heroic politicians like Wilson who could not resist expanding the government and meddling in corporate life, Republicans in 1920 searched for a mediocre candidate. "Warren Harding is the best of the second-raters," Senator Frank Brandegee admitted. Harding had earned a well-deserved reputation for party regularity and personal geniality. He emerged as the compromise candidate in the soon-to-be-legendary "smoke-filled room" of Will Hays. A cabal of Old Guard senators who wanted a deferential nominee met at night to discuss alternatives when the convention deadlocked over the militant General Leonard Wood of New Hampshire and the wealthy Governor Frank Lowden of Illinois.

Harding repudiated Roosevelt's and Wilson's approaches. "I am appealing to Americans to put the Republican Party back in power because of the things to which that party is committed," Harding said. "My personality is of mere secondary importance." Most Republicans agreed that the party shaped the nominee's policies and not the other way around. Tired of "dictatorship," they argued that an average American was a more fitting president than an overachieving activist like Wilson. A Republican victory, they asserted, would mark a return to traditional, constitutional government in which the Congress and the president worked together as equals.

The Republican campaign, one observer noted, was run with "the smooth power of a high class business organization." Hays and his men perfected techniques using new communication technologies, encouraging telephone conferences as well as moving picture and phonograph appeals. The advertising whiz Albert Lasker and the chewing-gum magnate William Wrigley Jr. promised "the biggest advertising drive ever launched in a political campaign." They boasted that "no newspaper reader will be able to escape

1920 Republican Convention. Harding Medal.
Source: Harding Memorial Library.

breakfast without being confronted by the slogan which will meet his eye again on billboards on his way to work." Despite an immense campaign fund—as much as $8 million, some estimated—Wrigley was shocked at the limited budget. "The only thing that worries me is that we don't happen to have any money to advertise this wonderful man to the voters," he said in August. "We received about as much so far as I spend every week advertising a penny stick of Chewing Gum."

With Hays coordinating publicity, fund raising, and organization, Warren Harding's men in Marion, Ohio, managed the candidate. Trying to avoid controversy, they kept Harding on his front porch until late

September. They entertained the candidate and his press entourage with a host of special days tailored to the new forms of identity Americans were assuming. Judson Welliver and others carefully edited Harding's speeches for Governor's Day, First Voter's Day, Women's Day, Foreign Voter's Day—an appeal to disaffected hyphenates—and Travelling Salesmen's Day—an attempt to exploit derogatory remarks made by the newspaper owned by James Cox, the Democratic candidate. These efforts, combined with the collapse of Wilson's health, his foreign policy, and his political support, gave Harding a resounding victory. The Republicans gained 10 seats in the Senate for a margin of 59 to 37 and gained 63 seats in the House for an overwhelming margin of 303 to 131. As the first presidential candidate to win more than 60% of the vote, Harding promised to fulfill his mandate and return Americans "to normalcy."

HARDING'S CABINET

Warren G. Harding assembled a cabinet reflecting the diversity of the Republican coalition that now dominated the nation. Secretary of State Charles Evans Hughes and Secretary of Commerce Herbert Hoover represented the Progressive commitment to an efficient and just government that harked back to Lincoln's day and whose patron saint was Theodore Roosevelt. Secretary of the Treasury Andrew W. Mellon and the tax-reduction efforts he made throughout the decade embodied the enduring bond with big business and wealthy Americans the party had forged during the Civil War and maintained for so long. Attorney General Harry M. Daughtery of Ohio underscored the power of individual state organizations and the president's loyal cadre. And Secretary of the Interior Albert Fall, the former senator from New Mexico, illustrated the kind of local politicians who amassed power under the federal system.

Hughes, Hoover, and Mellon would serve with distinction. Mellon served all three presidents in the 1920s, Hoover ended up as president, and Hughes ended up as chief justice of the United States. Both Fall and Daughtery, however, would be disgraced. Fall would become the first cabinet officer in history sent to jail, the result of the Teapot Dome Scandal. A Senate committee discovered that Fall and others had been bribed to lease various U.S. Navy oil reserves, one of which was at Teapot Dome, Wyoming. Daugherty would resign amid accusations that he and his "Ohio Gang" peddled influence with an abandon not seen since the days of the Grant administration.

THE COOLIDGE PRESIDENCY

By the time Daughtery and Fall were exposed, Harding had died of an embolism. Harding's successor, Calvin M. Coolidge of Vermont, was so honest that most voters resented what the *New York Times* called the "assassins of character," rather than the corrupt politicians. This backlash reflected the waning of Progressive zeal throughout the country and saved the Republican Party from the kind of bloodletting the Watergate scandal caused half a century later.

Calvin Coolidge symbolized traditional virtues and steady leadership at a time of great change. "Mr. Coolidge's genius for inactivity is developed to a very high point," the columnist Walter Lippmann would note. "It is far from being an indolent inactivity. It is a grim, determined, alert inactivity which keeps Mr. Coolidge occupied constantly." Coolidge advocated a small central government and economic growth. "I am for economy," he said. "After that, I am for more economy. At this time and under present conditions, that is my conception of serving all the people."

Behind Coolidge's *laissez-faire* rhetoric was what one historian calls a "Hamiltonian approach." Rather than keep government out of business affairs, Coolidge allowed the government to aid businessmen and the booming corporations. "Never before, here or anywhere else, has a government been so completely fused with business," the *Wall Street Journal* exulted. Coolidge's famous aphorism that "the business of America is business" revealed that this symbol of old-fashioned virtues was in fact quite a modern thinker.

While Herbert Hoover and other cabinet members worked with businessmen to bring about a "new era" in governing, Coolidge refused to help out farmers who were already mired in a deep depression. "Well, farmers have never made money," he said. "I don't believe we can do much about it." Coolidge's refusal to help farmers deepened the fissure in the Republican Party between western farmers and eastern business-

Sticker from 1924 Campaign. *Source:* J. Doyle Dewitt Collection.

men. Westerners organized a bipartisan farm bloc in Congress that advanced their sectional economic interests and harassed the easterners. Agrarian Progressives from the West attacked the "lackeys of Wall Street," who responded by calling Senators Hiram Johnson of California, George Norris of Nebraska, Robert M. La Follette of Wisconsin, and other western Republicans "sons of the wild jackass" who blocked high tariffs and other probusiness measures.

The fight over the McNary–Haugen Farm Relief Bill symbolized this deep split. The bill called for federal price supports of basic farm commodities. Coolidge and his northeastern allies rejected such blatant market intervention. The bill was introduced in Congress five times and vetoed by President Coolidge twice. The presidential landslides of 1924 and 1928 papered over this division in the Republican Party but made it easier for farmers to desert the party in 1932.

In approaching the 1924 campaign, the honest New Englander revealed his preferences for businessmen like his old college classmate Frank Stearns over machine politicians. The journalist William Allen White said that Coolidge "remade the Republican Party." He took it away from the old guardsmen and gave it "frankly, openly, proudly" to businessmen. The Republican National Convention appeared to White as "an outing of chambers of commerce and bankers and Rotarians."

The chairman of the Republican National Committee, William M. Butler, ran the committee like a business. Accountants monitored fund raising and spending, limited expenditures to revenues, and issued public reports. Over 90% of the Republican funds came from corporations, who applauded the probusiness climate Coolidge encouraged. "The nation now knows that the predatory interests have, by supplying Republican campaign funds, systematically purchased legislative favors and administrative immunity," the Democratic platform of 1924 would charge. "The practices must stop; our nation must return to honesty and decency in politics."

Coolidge had two major opponents. A divided Democratic Party endured 102 ballots before nominating a Wall Street lawyer from West Virginia, John W. Davis, and a new Progressive Party led by Robert M. La Follette sought to resurrect the reforming spirit in America. After 18 years as a Progressive gadfly in the Senate, La Follette did succeed in attracting nearly 5 million votes, demonstrating that over 15% of the voters still yearned for an alternative to the two parties.

The Coolidge campaign continued to use the tools Mark Hanna had introduced and Will Hays had perfected. The advertising executive Bruce Barton urged the president to speak to the masses via radio in non-partisan venues, emphasizing patriotism rather than party loyalty. In the same vein, the public relations executive Edward Bernays worked on the Non-Partisan League for Coolidge. Bernays arranged a delegation of stage people, who "symbolized warmth, extroversion and Bohemian camaraderie" to dramatize the deadpan president's "warm, sympathetic, personality." The *New York Times* estimated that fully 40% of the $4.3 million the Republicans raised was spent on publicity, 20% was spent on speakers, and 25% was spent on establishing headquarters in key cities. These mass-oriented publicity campaigns broadened the party's appeal while diluting the intensity of the canvass.

THE "VANISHING VOTER"

During this period, the search for what some observers called the "Vanishing Voter" began. Since the electoral realignment of 1896, the percentage of eligible voters turning out to vote had plummeted from 79% to 49%. The end of the electoral stalemate and the shift from partisan organizing to mass appeals made politics less compelling. Progressive assaults had weakened parties, whose multifaceted operations were less useful in an age of specialization. Mass newspapers replaced partisan screeds, professional associations and unions fostered different kinds of allegiances, government now delivered services impartially, and mass entertainments such as sports, the theater, moving pictures, and radio proved more diverting. For more and more Americans, politics was no longer a way of life, party loyalty was no longer central to their identities.

The ratification of the 19th Amendment in August 1920, providing for woman suffrage, had further depressed the rate of electoral turnout. Although millions of women exercised their new right to vote, millions of others continued the habit of nonvoting that had been ingrained in them since youth. The number of voters jumped from over 18 million in 1916 to over 26 million in 1920 and over 29 million in 1924, but the participation rate dropped from 63% to 49%. The entry of women into the system did not usher in the new day for American politics suffragettes promised. Most of the women who chose to vote, voted as their husbands did. To some, this proved that women were still passive; to others, this proved that long before they had received the right to vote, women had influenced their husbands' ballots.

Coolidge won with 54.1% of the popular vote and 382 electoral votes. This landslide was not quite as resounding as Harding's, but it was great news for the Republican Party. The Democratic percentage of the popular vote dropped from 34.6% to 28.8%—which was even lower than the 29.4% of the vote Stephen Douglas received when the Democratic Party shattered in 1860. In Congress, the 56-to-39 split in the Senate and the 247-to-183 split in the House continued the Republican lock on both Houses and broke the spirit of the Progressives in Congress who had checked many of Harding's and Coolidge's legislative initiatives. Finally, in 1926, Andrew Mellon would be able to set the tax rate he wanted. The Revenue Act of 1926 eliminated the gift tax, halved estate taxes, and lowered the maximum income tax rate to 20%.

During this Republican decade, the party struggled with its new role as the party of isolationism. Midwestern Progressives continued to agitate for distance from Europe. The end of World War I evoked widespread disillusionment. This backlash would culminate in 1934 with Republican Senator Gerald Nye's Senate inquiry blaming America's involvement in World War I on a conspiracy of greedy munitions manufacturers. Harding found it easy to declare the League of Nations as "dead as slavery" and to continue to push for high tariffs. His secretary of state, Charles Evans Hughes, united idealists and isolationists by championing disarmament at the Washington Conference in 1921. But the United States had become a great world power. It was difficult to insulate the country—and the party—from the challenges of an increasingly interconnected world.

THE NEW ERA

Despite his continuing popularity, Coolidge tersely announced in August 1927: "I do not choose to run for president in nineteen twenty-eight." Even his wife expressed surprise at the announcement. Coolidge's heir apparent was Herbert Hoover, the secretary of commerce, and as one chagrined rival put it, "Under-Secretary of all other departments." Serving under both Harding and Coolidge, Hoover had steered a middle path between the supposedly *laissez-faire* business boosterism of Old Guard Republicans, on the one hand, and the crusading but critical spirit of Progressive Republicans, on the other. Hoover's Progressivism was a process-oriented, expert-filled, cautious plan to achieve efficiency through cooperation. Hoover's "associational corporatism" envisioned the government as umpire, keeping the economy flowing while facilitating cooperation among big business, labor, and consumers. Hoover foresaw the "mutualization of the postwar economy" and viewed the Department of Commerce as the central "transforming

station" of the new "associative state" he hoped to build. Coolidge found Hoover's ambitious plans to rationalize the entire American government exasperating. "That man has offered me unsolicited advice for six years, all of it bad," the President muttered in May 1928, months before Hoover was nominated to fill Coolidge's shoes.

Coolidge was one of the few Americans Hoover had failed to charm. Despite the public fascination with gangsters, movie stars, and baseball players during the Roaring Twenties, the dour Hoover enjoyed tremendous popularity. His reputation was, according to Walter Lippmann, "a work of art." Viewing public relations as an "exact science," Hoover had publicity men informing the press and public of his accomplishments. His presidential campaign of 1928, one observer later noted, was to be his "last successful public relations drive."

In 1928 Hoover won 58.2% of the popular vote and strong majorities in both houses of Congress with a dignified canvass. "There will not be any relaxing of resolute endeavor to keep our elections clean, honest and free from taint of any kind," the Republican platform declared, as it promised monthly accountings "of all contributions, the names of the contributors, the

Republican Campaign Cards, 1928. *Source:* National Archives.

Republican Campaign 1928. "The Bandwagon Rush." Drawing by C.K. Berryman, 1928. *Source:* National Archives.

Hoover from 1928 Campaign Poster. *Source:* J. Doyle Dewitt Collection.

amounts expended, and for what purposes." Party publicists distributed copper coins labeled "The Hoover Lucky Pocket Piece—Good for 4 Years of Prosperity" and promised Americans "two chickens in every pot and a car in every garage."

Hoover ran a high-minded effort, trusting disaffected Democrats to attack their own party's candidate. The Democrats' nomination of Alfred E. Smith, the Catholic governor of New York, outraged evangelical Protestants concentrated in the South and the Midwest, most of whom were Democrats. The preacher Billy Sunday attacked Smith's male supporters as "damnable whiskey politicians, bootleggers, crooks, pimps and businessmen who deal with him," and Smith's female supporters as "streetwalkers." Hoover wisely distanced himself from the anti-Catholic campaign. "The lower rank and file of party workers on both sides did not show the elevation of spirit one could desire," he later admitted in his memoirs, comparing some slurs against his pro-British sympathies with the ugly assault on Smith's religion. The victory of the Iowa orphan turned statesman over the tough-talking graduate of "F.F.M."— Fulton Fish Market—reassured traditionalists. The *St. Paul Pioneer Press* exulted that "America is not yet dominated by its great cities. Control of its destiny still remains in the smaller communities and rural regions, with their traditional conservatism and solid virtues. . . . Main Street is still the principal thoroughfare of the nation."

Despite the party's solid marriage with Wall Street, Republicans continued to control Main Street as well. For nearly 70 years, Republicans had dominated national politics. The economic boom seemed to ratify their extraordinary record as the party of peace and prosperity, of national strength and capitalist expansion. In retrospect, signs of slippage would become apparent, especially in agricultural areas that did not benefit from the boom and in eastern cities where immigrants resented Prohibition. The 1928 election would herald a new Democratic coalition based in the cities uniting blacks, ethnics, immigrants, and workers in an uncomfortable alliance with southern Democrats. At the time, however, the Republican lock on the White House, the House of Representatives, the Senate, and 30 governorships seemed unassailable.

THE GREAT DEPRESSION

As president, Herbert Hoover was doubly victimized: by the unrealistic expectations his election engendered and then by the devastating depression that began under his watch. Hoover's chicken in every pot became an unemployed man on every street corner—or so it seemed. The Great Humanitarian, the Boy Engineer, the Champion Progressive, had built his career managing American prosperity. He was unprepared for an economic downturn. Furthermore, as one who had risen so far in politics despite his disdain for politicking, he was unprepared to calm American fears and lead the people. By the time the stock market crashed in 1929, his public relations men had become yes men. Hoover would learn that popularity based on an individual's publicity was more volatile and more fleeting than that based on party loyalty.

The true tragedy of Herbert Hoover is that Americans would remember him as doing nothing to fight the depression, when he did all he could. Hoover himself was responsible for this impression. He tried to talk his way out of the depression, trying to convince businessmen to continue producing; trying to convince labor leaders to forego demands for better wages or fewer hours; trying to convince the public that "the fundamental business of this country, that is, production and distribution of commodities, is on a sound and prosperous basis." When a delegation of businessmen arrived in the White House in June 1930

to discuss further government assistance, he pronounced, "Gentlemen, you have come sixty days too late. The Depression is over." To demonstrate his calm, he continued to hold formal dinners every night in the White House, offering the inappropriate picture of the president feasting in white tie and tails as Americans picked through garbage looking for food.

This was the public Hoover, and the image that burdened him—and his party—for decades. But at the same time, Hoover tried to fight while remaining within the ideological limits of the time. Democrats and Republicans, liberals and conservatives, agreed that the federal government's budget should be balanced. Still, Hoover tried to "prime the pump" with

"Believe It or Not—It Happens Every Four Years." *Source: St. Louis Post-Dispatch.* Reprinted in the *Kansas City Star,* November 21, 1929.

government money. He proposed an increase of $423 million in federal public works programs. He pushed for state and local governments to build public works. He believed that each dollar the government spent would generate more money as workers consumed, producers purchased, invested, and gradually regained confidence.

By the spring of 1931, Hoover's position had deteriorated. Voters repudiated Republicans in the midterm elections of 1930. A 17-seat majority in the Senate dwindled to 1 seat; a 100-seat majority in the House became a 6-seat deficit. Hoover's name soon became synonymous with economic distress. Shantytowns outside cities were known as "Hoovervilles." Old newspapers were "Hoover blankets." Empty pockets were "Hoover flags." And yet, Hoover still acted cautiously.

By December 1931, conditions were so desperate that Hoover moved more boldly. As many as 25% of all American workers were now unemployed. Hoover and Congress established structures to support mortgages to keep banks afloat. He encouraged New York financiers to float a $500 million fund for troubled banks. In January 1932 he signed legislation establishing the Reconstruction Finance Corporation (RFC), issuing tax-exempt bonds and extending credit to banks, life insurance companies, agricultural credit corporations, and railroads. Eventually the RFC would be authorized to provide funds to local governments for public works projects and relief.

Gradually, the ground was shifting. More and more Americans were expecting the federal government to save them. The Democrats were on their way to becoming the party of the welfare state. The Republicans were going to be stuck championing the *laissez-faire* conservatism they had often preached and rarely practiced precisely when Americans lost faith in the philosophy. Big businessmen, however, were about to discover just how much they could dislike big government.

Even as they approved Hoover's unprecedented attempts to expand federal power, Democrats attacked. Congressional leaders painted the RFC as a break for business, and Hoover's proposed sales tax to pay for these expenditures as proof of his contempt for the common man. "With hundreds of millions the President would come to the rescue of the bondholders of the land banks, to the succor of the commercial banks, to the support of the railroads, and to the aid of industry of one kind and another," an Alabama Democrat railed. "To these interests he would open the Treasury, but to starving men, women and children he would not give a red cent."

The 1932 presidential campaign became a referendum on Hoover and the Republicans. "General Depression" would defeat "General Prosperity" and the president. The Republican National Convention was a dispirited affair. Hoover was nominated in the same hall in Chicago where the Democratic candidate Franklin D. Roosevelt was nominated, but the hall was one-third empty. The band played "California Here I Come," which is precisely where Hoover went to retire. "I'll tell you what our trouble is," the president would say. "We are opposed by 6,000,000 unemployed, 10,000 bonus marchers, and ten-cent corn. Is it any wonder that the prospects are dark?"

During the campaign, the president was abused. He was mobbed, booed, and pelted with rotten eggs. He received one telegram suggesting, "Vote for Roosevelt and make it unanimous." One Secret Service man who had been traveling with presidents since Theodore Roosevelt told *Time* magazine that "never before have I seen one actually booed, with men running out into the streets to thumb their noses at him. It's not a pretty sight."

The campaign depressed the president. One Hoover aide told former President Coolidge "that whereas the publicity director in past campaigns would bring out each day some new testimonial, some new expression of support and confidence, there is not today one Republican leader in banking or industry whose support would not bring jeers of derision. In 1924, Henry Ford's support meant a great deal. Today it would lose Mr. Hoover thousands of votes in Detroit, and so on down the line." Hoover resented the "systematic and unprecedented" assault on "me personally" rather than "on my policies and even on the Republican Party." He insisted that "the whole Democratic performance was far below the level of any previous campaign in modern times. . . . My defeat would no doubt have taken place anyway. But it might have taken place without such defilement of American life."

The Democratic contender, Franklin Roosevelt, kept the focus on Hoover. Beyond calling for a balanced budget and the repeal of Prohibition, he avoided details. When Roosevelt made his few campaign addresses, his talk of a "new deal" for the "forgotten man" and his attacks on Hoover sufficed. While some Democrats had to admit that their candidate was "disappointingly vague," even many Republicans found the contrast between Roosevelt's "bright, gay manner" and Hoover's "sour" mien "startling."

Roosevelt's call for Americans to "rendezvous with destiny" by rallying around his New Deal—not merely his party—"made men and women who are for the New Deal feel that they are engaged in a holy war," one Wilsonian Democrat gushed. On the other hand, *The Nation* complained that "neither of the two great parties, in the midst of the worst depression in our history, has had the intelligence or courage to propose a single fundamental measure that might conceivably put us on the road to recovery."

This time, both parties avoided extravagance. Huey Long of Louisiana, complaining that the Democrats "have all the votes and no money," had jokingly suggested selling "President Hoover a million votes for half what he is going to pay to try to get them. We can spare the votes and we could use the money." In this campaign, however, the Republicans' $2.9 million campaign fund was not much more than the Democrats' $2.25 million. For the first time in 20 years there was no congressional oversight committee to monitor financial abuses; there was no need.

Purchasing radio time was the largest single item of expenditure for both parties. The Republicans spent over 20% of their budget purchasing 70 hours of network time. The reliance on radio increased the campaigns' reliance on public relations specialists and nonpartisan appeals. Addressing millions throughout America simultaneously, politicians on the radio were more entertaining, more vague, less partisan, and less shrill.

Hoover's reelection effort reversed the effects of Harding's landslide. Sixty Democrats were in the Senate, as opposed to the 59 Republicans in 1921, 310 Democrats were in the House, as opposed to the 303 Republicans in 1921, and Roosevelt received 57.3% of the popular vote to Harding's 61%. "A few years ago you had to use the whole house for your caucus—now you can hold it in a phone booth," one Democratic congressman kidded a Republican rival. As only the third Democratic president since the Civil War, Franklin D. Roosevelt would enjoy extraordinary power in forging a new electoral coalition that would dominate the nation for much of the next half century.

Republicans from 1896 through 1932 had not completely repudiated their Free Labor roots or their role as defender of the blacks. Yet the Republican Party ended its reign tagged as the party of big business and *laissez faire*. For the next 20 years, Herbert Hoover would be the Democrats' favorite whipping boy, the symbol of Republican subservience to fat cats and monopolies. This stereotype overlooked the strong Progressive tradition within the party and Hoover's impressive Progressive record as secretary of commerce and president. Progressivism had been too ubiquitous for the majority party to ignore. Republicans had remained the party of big business while forging a role for the central government. The divided legacy of the Republican era, and the continued search for the political center, would confuse Republicans during their years as the opposition party. As much as Republicans' corporate supporters would want to undo the New Deal, the rank and file would become dependent on the expanded federal government.

THE NEW DEAL

Franklin D. Roosevelt's New Deal redefined liberalism and redrew the electoral landscape. Liberalism no longer entailed a Jeffersonian belief in limited government but a Rooseveltian commitment to use government to protect "the forgotten man." Roosevelt mobilized the disaffected to support his policies. A Gallup poll in 1936 would show that only 42% of people with higher incomes supported Roosevelt; 60% of middle-income people supported him, and 76% of lower-income people supported the president. Carefully, he kept southerners within the Democratic Party while reaching out to urban ethnics, union members, and blacks.

The Roosevelt realignment was based more on class cleavages than on sectional divisions. As a powerful president expanding government power in an age of urbanization and industrialization, he made the Democratic Party viable throughout the nation. With the South and border states still solidly Democratic, the Northeast, Midwest, and West experienced vigorous two-party competition. From 1932 to 1966, Republicans would win 56.7% of the gubernatorial races in the Northeast, 53.7% of the races in the Midwest and West.

The Democratic Party's image and constituency changed, seemingly overnight. The most dramatic transformation took place among African Americans. Smith's 1928 campaign had made some inroads in the black community—as it had with immigrants and laborers—attracting 27% of the vote in the black precincts in Cleveland, 28% of the vote in Harlem. But even in 1932, blacks who registered as Democrats were condemned as traitors. Hoover's share of the black vote actually increased that year. Over the next four years, blacks would abandon the party of Lincoln, joining Italians, Germans, Poles, and Jews in supporting the party of Roosevelt.

Roosevelt made it easier for Republicans to support him by exploiting the increasingly nonpartisan nature of American politics. Over the radio he invited "my friends" to "rendezvous with destiny." He attacked Hoover and his business supporters, rather than the Republican Party. At the same time, he used the surviving partisan machinery to reward his friends. The expansion of government under his New Deal gave Roosevelt and his successors unprecedented amounts of federal "pork" to distribute.

The triumph of Roosevelt's New Deal flummoxed the Republican Party. Republicans were unsure where to position themselves in the changing political universe and what ideology to embrace. Some Progressive Republicans abandoned their party, just as some conservative Democrats abandoned theirs. Herbert Hoover and the conservatives sought to rally their party around a defense of its traditional ideals—and of his administration. Hoover warned that the "penetration of Socialist methods even to a partial degree will demoralize the economic system, the legislative bodies, and in fact the whole system of ordered Liberty." Hoover's rhetorical attacks were similar to those made by the American Liberty League, a group of Democratic and Republican businessmen financed by the du Pont family and other millionaires. But Hoover was too much the Progressive to ally with this ultraconservative "smear brigade." I have "no more confidence in the Wall Street model of human liberty, which this group so well represents, than I have in the Pennsylvania Avenue model upon which the country now rides," he sneered.

At the same time, other Republicans accepted some New Deal measures but claimed that Roosevelt was moving too far too fast. These pragmatic Republicans earned Hoover's and the Liberty Leaguers' contempt but could not ally with the powerful critics of the New Deal, such as Father Charles Coughlin, Dr. Francis E. Townsend, and Senator Huey Long, who demanded more radical approaches. Exploiting their opponents' confusion, Democrats in 1934 bolstered their majorities in both houses of Congress. This rare victory in midterm elections demonstrated voters' broad approval for the bold leadership Franklin D. Roosevelt had demonstrated since his path-breaking "First Hundred Days."

The impotence of the Republican opposition and the growing popularity of the demagogues' attacks pushed Roosevelt to the left after 1934. His Second New Deal advocated higher taxes and passed the Social Security Act of 1935. This measure attempted to satisfy some of Townsend's and Long's criticisms and became the cornerstone of the welfare state. This extraordinarily popular piece of legislation repudiated the traditional American commitment to a decentralized federal government.

THE 1936 CAMPAIGN

During the 1936 campaign, the Republican Party failed to offer a clear alternative to the New Deal. The party's nominee, Governor Alfred M. Landon of Kansas, was an affable former Bull Mooser from the party's pragmatic wing. In Kansas, Governor Landon had copied some New Deal initiatives and would not mount the fire-breathing campaign Hoover and his allies demanded. Yet Landon ran on a platform largely dictated by the Old Guard. "For three long years the New Deal Administration has dishonored American traditions and flagrantly betrayed the pledges on which the Democratic Party sought and received public support," the platform charged. After detailing all of the Roosevelt administration's abuses, Republicans affirmed that "to a free people, these actions are insufferable. This campaign cannot be waged on the traditional differences between the Republican and Democratic parties. The responsibility of this election transcends all previous political divisions. We invite all Americans, irrespective of party, to join us in defense of American institutions."

Fortunately for the Republicans, their ideological confusion was belied by organizational mastery. John D.M. Hamilton, the first full-time, salaried national chairman of a major American political party, established a formidable party bureaucracy. When he first became chairman, party headquarters did not have a list of all the county chairmen—and he soon discovered that many counties did not even have chairmen. Hamilton built up the local organizations, worked with advertising executives to market Landon, and tried to ensure that the party organization survived even as its candidate suffered a devastating defeat.

Landon lost every state but Maine and Vermont. Republicans still enjoyed support in the farm belt and in the suburbs, but Roosevelt solidified his ruling coalition in the 1936 landslide. For the first time, a majority of blacks voted for the Democratic Party. In abandoning the party of Lincoln for a Democratic president with a mediocre record on civil rights, blacks voted with their pocketbooks, along with millions of others. Roosevelt won over 60% of the black vote in Cleveland, over 80% of the black vote in New York. As blacks flocked to the Democratic Party, many Republicans would become less concerned with civil rights, although liberal Republicans would provide critical support for civil rights well into the 1990s.

THE RISE OF THE CONSERVATIVE COALITION

Flush with victory, President Roosevelt miscalculated. Two weeks after his second inauguration, he tried to reorganize the Supreme Court, which had invalidated some of his first-term initiatives. This "Court-packing plan" united Old Guard and Progressive Republicans for the first time in decades. They succeeded in blocking the Judiciary Reorganization Bill by allying with conservative southern Democrats. The conservative coalition formed in 1937 would curb liberal initiatives over the next 20 years. Republicans would periodically unite with southern Democrats to dilute or defeat approximately one-fifth of the bills introduced in the ensuing ten Congresses—and many of the boldest ones.

The leading Republican congressman, Joseph P. Martin, explained that "it was simply a matter of finding issues on which we saw alike . . . when an issue of spending or new powers for the President came along, I would go to Representative Howard Smith of Virginia, for example, and say, 'Howard, see if you can't get me a few Democratic voters here.' " After he retired, Smith admitted that the whole arrangement "was very informal," but effective. Even as the national Democratic Party became more liberal, the local party in the South would remain conservative.

The Court-packing fight, along with the "Roosevelt recession" of 1937, weakened the Democrats. In the 1938 midterm elections, Republicans scored significant gains for the first time in a decade. They added 11 governorships to the 5 they already held while gaining 7 Senate seats and 75 House seats. They did not regain a majority in either house, but actually won a majority of the votes cast outside the Solid South. The all-important midwestern farmers and northeastern city dwellers were returning to their party.

In Ohio, President Taft's son, Robert A. Taft, unseated the Democratic Senate incumbent with an aggressive campaign assailing the New Deal. In New York, the crusading district attorney Thomas E. Dewey almost unseated the popular governor Herbert Lehman with a more moderate appeal. For the next decade and a half, these two young intelligent rivals would struggle for control of the party, representing the contest between Main Street isolationism and Wall Street internationalism, conservative purity and liberal pragmatism.

THE WENDELL WILLKIE BOOM

The tensions in Europe threatened the Republicans' comeback plans. The traditional split in domestic issues between the conservative eastern business interests and the Progressive western faction, with the midwestern farmers usually allying with the easterners, was complicated by the isolationism of the midwesterners and the western farmers. Northeastern business interests were too tied to Europe to accept such a position. In the fight for the presidential nomination,

Robert Taft of Ohio and Arthur Vandenberg of Michigan split the isolationist vote, while the boy wonder of New York, Thomas E. Dewey, championed the interests of what became known as the "eastern establishment."

These party regulars were swept away in the popular boom for Wendell Willkie. In a few short months, he had gone from a little-known but well-respected utilities magnate to the Republican standard-bearer. Modern public relations techniques helped draft the tousle-haired ex-Democrat. Willkie seemed to combine the small-town virtues of Elwood, Indiana, and the big-city smarts of Wall Street, the businessman's pragmatism and the politician's charisma. He inspired intense devotion. "For the first time in my life I have a leader I can yell for and mean it," a young Willkieite would write to his father after spending a month's salary on the drive. Willkie Clubs sprouted throughout the nation. Within months, 500,000 people had joined 4,000 clubs. These devotees overwhelmed the Republican Convention in Philadelphia. Willkie was nominated. Willkie, the *New York Times* declared, was "the biggest smash since Mickey Mouse."

Willkie believed that the "American people do not give their votes to policies. They give their votes to men." This personal campaign would challenge Franklin D. Roosevelt on his own terms and further undermine the party grip on American politics. The Associated Willkie Clubs of America tried to woo independents and Democrats, distancing the candidate from his party. Willkie had secured the nomination by campaigning against the party establishment. "I've entered into no deals or understanding with any political leaders or anybody else," he boasted. "If I accidentally am nominated and elected President of the United States, I shall go in completely free of any obligations of any kind." Such independent candidacies would become increasingly frequent with the spread of primaries in the coming decades.

Republican National Chairman Joseph P. Martin acknowledged that "the Willkie clubs were a tonic that the Republican organization needed. They brought enthusiasm, aggressiveness and color into the campaign—and they raised a great deal of money." At the same time, they perpetuated a great deal of confusion. Willkie and his publicity men alienated the regulars, dumping Hamilton as party chairman and ignoring the national committee. "Two-thirds of my time was devoted to making peace among quarreling factions," Martin later recalled. "There were days I was so exasperated that I told my associates I would give $10,000 to get out of the job." The columnist Raymond Clapper reported that "seldom has there been more chaos in a

Republican National Convention 1940. Presidential
Nominee Willkie. "The Performer Who Stole the Show."
Source: Kansas City Star.

Presidential campaign. Congressional cloakrooms
echo with stories of confusion, hurt feelings, unan-
swered telegrams and letters, crossed wires and general disorganization . . . the Willkie train . . . seems to
operate with all the confusion of an amateur road
show."

Willkie further demoralized party regulars by supporting the president's foreign policy. When Roosevelt, just before the convention, had enlisted former
Republicans Henry Stimson and Frank Knox as secretary of war and secretary of the navy to enhance national unity, Hamilton had read the two out of the
Republican Party. One reporter had advised Willkie
that the only way to win the election was to oppose the
draft. Willkie said he "would rather not win the election than do that." Willkie's interventionist stance deprived the party of a major issue and exacerbated tensions between isolationists and interventionists. At the
same time, it fostered the bipartisan foreign policy that

would prove critical during World War II and the Cold
War.

Both parties were further weakened during the 1940
campaign by the implementation of the Hatch Act,
which limited campaign contributions and prohibited
participation by federal workers in presidential campaigns. The Hatch Act harked back to the Gilded Age
debates about the civil service while trying to fix the
perennial problem of money in politics. The $3 million
spending limit imposed on each party and the limit of
$500,000 dollars on contributions were easily circum-
vented. Money ordinarily funneled through the party
was now spent independently, as Republicans spent
nearly $15 million and Democrats spent $6 million.

Roosevelt shrewdly ignored the charismatic Willkie
and his nonpartisan appeals. On the stump, Roosevelt
attacked Herbert Hoover and his Old Guard allies in
Congress, including Joseph P. Martin, the adman
turned silk-stocking congressman Bruce Barton, and
the isolationist Hamilton Fish. The effectiveness of
Roosevelt's attack on the party of "Martin, Barton and
Fish" revealed that the Republicans had not yet recovered from the debacle of 1932.

Although Roosevelt won an unprecedented third
term, his share of the popular vote declined. Roosevelt's 27,743,466 votes represented a drop of half a million in four years, while Willkie won nearly 6 million
more votes than Landon had, ending up with
22,304,755 popular votes. Democrats picked up only
seven new seats in the House and lost another three in
the Senate. Many Americans objected to a third term,
even for Roosevelt. They were tired of the New Deal.
After the election, Roosevelt confessed to Willkie's
manager, Russell Davenport: "You and your friend
Wendell Willkie waged a much more effective campaign than I expected. I had to abandon my policy of
keeping quiet and go out and make a series of
speeches. If I hadn't you might have won."

REPUBLICANS DURING WORLD WAR II

After the Japanese attack on Pearl Harbor, the two
Republican "traitors" in Roosevelt's cabinet, Henry
Stimson and Frank Knox, helped Republicans prove
their loyalty. With the nation rallying around the flag,
even isolationist Republicans muted their attacks on
the president. Still, less than a year after Pearl Harbor,
the incumbent Democrats suffered a stinging defeat
during the congressional elections. Republicans had
shrewdly and cautiously criticized Roosevelt's domestic policy without seeming to undermine his conduct

of the war. The federal bureaucracy had expanded enormously. The Office of Price Administration (OPA) rationed essential goods and regulated wages and prices. Subsequently considered "the most intrusive federal bureaucracy ever created in America," the OPA became a popular target for conservatives fearful of centralized government. "It was, in effect, a jarring reversal of the New Deal of the 1930s," historian Alan Brinkley has written: "government acting now not to distribute largesse but to restrict access to goods and services." Its outspoken director, Leon Henderson, became a symbol of the arrogant, statist, uncontrollable New Deal.

Republicans also benefited from the many young Democrats who were in uniform or had moved and were ineligible to vote in their new communities. Turnout among Democrats dropped considerably, but held steady among Republican voters. The result was a 44-seat gain for the Republicans in the House, 7 new Senate seats, and some critical gubernatorial chairs. Republicans recaptured the belt running from Ohio to Colorado. "The victorious candidates," *Fortune* magazine wrote, "rode an anti-Roosevelt and anti-Washington wave. They were almost entirely normalcy men, quiet, churchgoing, family men, not quite prohibitionists, men whose outlook was limited to their states and their regions. They may be relied upon to investigate Washington thoroughly. Many of them think they have a mandate to repeal all New Deal reforms." A month after the election, the conservatives' favorite target, Leon Henderson, resigned.

A DRIFT TO THE RIGHT

The Old Guard's impassioned attacks against the New Deal were finally resonating. The battles of the 1930s had polarized the two parties' positions in domestic politics. Just as the Democrats had become the party of the welfare state, the Republicans had become the party of free enterprise. "The social experimentation and reckless extravagance of the New Deal are on the way out because the common sense of the people is reasserting itself," the Indiana conservative Charles Halleck had cried, plaintively, in 1936. Six years later, it was becoming more true. The 1942 results invigorated the conservative coalition of Southern Democrats and Republicans. "The balance of [Roosevelt's] term is going to be an obstacle race," one journalist predicted.

The middle-aged Republican conservatives who joined the Congress in 1943 were no longer apologetic. After ten years of the New Deal, they were ready to at-

tack. Many congressmen were more conservative than the rest of the country, but they were buoyed by the growing backlash against the New Deal. The American people were tired of the high taxes, the growing deficit, the smothering bureaucracies they now identified with the New Deal. Liberalism, Leon Henderson complained, "is in temporary eclipse." Liberal leaders "abdicated" as the conservatives tried to dismantle the New Deal, program by program, eliminating the Civilian Conservation Corps, the Works Progress Administration, the National Youth Administration. Even the president recognized that "he has probably gone as far as he can on domestic questions," the New Dealer Thomas Corcoran reported, "that someone else would have to mop up after him." At the end of 1943, a weary president admitted that "Dr. Win the War" had replaced "Dr. New Deal."

Republican conservatives further justified their attacks by using German fascism and Russian communism to illustrate the dangers of untrammelled bureaucracy, of statist planning. As G.I. Joes defended freedom abroad, Republicans cast themselves as the defenders of liberty at home. Beginning their hunt for "un-American activities," conservative congressmen railed against the New Deal's "gigantic bureaucracy" and the many communists and fellow travelers who had wormed their way into key offices in Washington.

The party's drift to the right dismayed its titular head, Wendell Willkie. He ran against "the ultra-nationalists, the economically selfish . . . the religious and racial bigots" whom he feared were overtaking the party. His book, *One World,* advocated global awareness and interventionism. Willkie was repudiated by his own party in the Wisconsin primary and died before the election was held.

Still, Republican regulars realized that they needed to unite their party and moderate their positions enough to capture the political center in 1944. In September 1943 they gathered at the Grand Hotel in Mackinac Island—without Willkie—to forge a common approach on international affairs. The party leaders approved a resolution calling for "responsible participation by the United States in a postwar cooperative organization among sovereign nations to prevent military aggression and to attain permanent peace with organized justice." Internationalists such as Thomas Dewey were pleased with the promise of participation; isolationists Taft and Vanderberg took solace in the commitment to retaining each nation's sovereignty.

Domestic affairs were equally tricky. While opposing the New Deal, Republicans had to be constructive. They—and their pollsters—noticed that most of the public accepted much of the New Deal. The platform of 1944 would reflect these tensions. It called for a "restoration of harmony in government, for a balance of legislative and executive responsibility, for efficiency and economy . . . for an entirely new spirit in our Federal government." At the same time it supported extending "the existing old-age insurance and unemployment insurance systems to all employees not already covered," the "stimulation by Federal aid of State plans to make medical and hospital service available to those in need," and other aspects of the New Deal's social welfare state. Roosevelt's secretary of labor, Frances Perkins, rejoiced that the 1944 Republican platform showed "that the New Deal has won forever."

GOVERNOR THOMAS E. DEWEY

The 42-year-old governor of New York, Thomas E. Dewey, was well suited to champion this platform. A cautious internationalist, he was a moderately Progressive governor who increased social services and tried to prove that government could provide for the needy in a more efficient and less heavy-handed way than the New Deal did. Dewey would build on Theodore Roosevelt's and Wendell Willkie's examples, giving the Republicans' eastern establishment a Progressive tinge to ally with westerners against midwestern regulars. Trim, mustachioed, and energetic, Dewey still enjoyed considerable fame from his days as a gang-busting prosecutor. Though somewhat stiff and self-righteous in manner, he demonstrated impressive popular appeal both in the presidential primaries and in the New York gubernatorial races. Republicans wanted him to lead a campaign of youth against the "tired old men" of the New Deal.

As the first major party nominee born in the twentieth century, Dewey relied on modern methods such as polling, radio speeches, and advertising. Often, when campaigning, Dewey played to the radio audience, to the dismay of the partisan crowd he faced. In fact, Dewey avoided crowds whenever he could and would have been more comfortable broadcasting radio speeches from an empty studio.

Republican Candidate for President Dewey Campaigning, Mattoon, Illinois. *Source:* Office of War Information, August 8, 1944.

Together, the two parties would buy almost $2.5 million in airtime. With such a big investment, it was inevitable that radio advertising techniques would begin to overwhelm the political efforts. Campaign managers began referring to their own work as "a straight selling job" and their candidates as "the product." The election campaign itself was becoming, one reporter wrote, simply "a test of opposing radio sales methods."

With almost twice as much money as their competitors, Republicans could afford full 30-minute spots. But what most excited Republican strategists, and was most significant for the party's future, was the growing importance of the advertising men in molding the candidate's public and nonpartisan identity. Governor Dewey's Off the Record Advisory Committee on Publicity and Public Relations Problems linked prominent ad men with the candidate. Bruce Barton and his committee helped staff the campaign with advertising people and offered advice on "selling the candidate." "Personal appearances" in crucial states were essential. So, too, Barton insisted, was a "continuing theme" that allowed the candidates' day-to-day activities to "add up," leaving "one definite thought in the voters' minds such as we try to put into the buyers' minds in respect to an advertised product."

But Barton and his men could not agree just what this overall theme should be. They, along with Dewey and his managers, were not sure how much the campaign should be anti-Roosevelt, and how much pro-Dewey. If Dewey were too vicious he would be called disrespectful and even disloyal; if too kind, there would be no reason to abandon Roosevelt.

Described even by his admirers as "cold—cold as a February icicle," Dewey was an aggressive campaigner. He considered most New Dealers "greedy" and "power-hungry" and hoped to "restore the Government to the people of the United States." He attacked the New Deal's incompetence, its ties to party bosses and labor leaders, its economic program and its military strategy. When all else failed, Dewey waved the Red flag, charging that "the Communists are seizing control of the New Deal."

As their standard-bearer indicted the president on multiple charges, Republican partisans traded stories and pictures illustrating Roosevelt's failing health. Even with this assault, Dewey stopped short of calling for a return to the age of Hoover. In fact, the Republican platform made it difficult for Dewey to attack many of the New Deal's actual programs.

With its careful preparation and concern for target audiences, Dewey's approach revealed advertising's impact on the Republican campaign. His reliance on the experts frustrated regulars. "The whole headquar-

ters is run by New Yorkers and Tom Dewey takes no advice from anyone," Robert Taft muttered. This insularity did not help him with the Middle Americans who remained suspicious of an eastern internationalist, even though his running mate was Ohio's conservative governor, John Bricker. Republican ideologues ended up with another pragmatic nominee who was too moderate and too centrist.

Once again Republicans whittled away at Roosevelt's margin of victory without unseating the president. Dewey received 44.5% of the popular votes, Roosevelt 52.8%. Democrats lost 2 seats in the Senate but gained 24 seats in the House. The gains offset some of the losses of 1942 but did not return the Democrats to the dominant congressional position they enjoyed in the 1930s. The New Deal coalition was vulnerable but still strong.

"MR. REPUBLICAN"

Roosevelt died in April 1945, shortly after his fourth inauguration. His successor, Harry Truman, inherited an increasingly dispirited Democratic Party facing increasingly defiant Republicans. Truman's "Fair Deal" would attempt to summon the unity and commitment Roosevelt's New Deal had evoked, while Republicans rallied to assault Roosevelt's welfare state. Republicans mounted their 1946 congressional campaign united by the slogan "Had enough? Vote Republican!" Robert Taft charged that Truman wanted a Congress "dominated by a policy of appeasing the Russians abroad and of fostering Communism at home." This aggressive campaign restored control of Congress to the Republicans, winning a margin of 51 to 45 in the Senate and 246 to 188 in the House. Republicans looked confidently toward 1948.

In the Republican-dominated 80th Congress, Republicans muted their attacks on Truman's foreign policy while lambasting his domestic policy. In January 1945 Senator Arthur H. Vandenberg had repudiated isolationism and become the leading advocate of bipartisanship in foreign policy. Even the isolationist Taft endorsed the new United Nations. In domestic affairs, Taft criticized the Democrats harshly and eloquently. His Taft–Hartley bill of 1947 banned the closed shop. Republicans boasted about their independence of New Deal pressure groups as Democrats denounced their rivals' greedy subservience to big business.

Taft, who would emerge as "Mr. Republican" during these years of exile from the White House, was a brilliant legislative tactician but a ham-handed public relations man. The irrepressible Alice Roosevelt

Longworth, who liked the dour senator, had speculated earlier in the decade that having Taft replace Franklin Roosevelt in the White House would be like having a glass of milk after a slug of Benzedrine. Taft wanted to cut taxes and expenditures regardless of the political consequences. Asked what Americans buffeted by the postwar inflation should do about high food prices, he suggested they "eat less." In the long run, he would accept the precedents the New Deal established and support Social Security and federal housing subsidies. Still, his stiff demeanor would cast him as the naysayer to Democrats and moderate Republicans eager to distribute federal goodies.

"PRESIDENT" DEWEY

While Democrats suffered with a candidate who seemed neither to look like a president nor act like one, Republicans celebrated their embarrassment of riches. Senator Taft, Governor Dewey, and Governor Harold Stassen of Minnesota were among the Republican contenders for the nomination in 1948. As the 1944 standard-bearer, Dewey considered himself the presumptive nominee. He positioned himself as the centrist, pragmatic, generous alternative to Taft.

As Dewey awaited his coronation at the Republican convention, Taft and Stassen foraged for delegates. Taft lined up delegates by flexing his political muscles in the Senate; Stassen opted for the more popular route, barnstorming wherever state primaries were held. Bolstered by the Gallup polls that declared him the popular favorite, and disdainful of primaries that reflected voter preference but did not bind delegates, Dewey remained in New York's executive mansion, above the fray. Stassen surprised everyone with upset victories in the Wisconsin and Nebraska primaries in the spring of 1948. Stassen even had the temerity to challenge Taft in the senator's home state of Ohio, a violation of the gentlemen's rule that candidates were never contested in their home states. Slipping in the polls, and worried about Stassen's momentum, Dewey all of a sudden found time in his schedule to campaign in Oregon. Dewey's victory seemingly proved his popularity.

Although Dewey entered the Republican Convention in Philadelphia with a commanding lead, he still lacked a majority of delegates. On the first ballot, Dewey had 434 votes, Taft had 224, Stassen had 157, with the remaining 279 distributed among various favorite sons, including Governor Earl Warren of California. In the new Republican Party, delegates from the Far West held the balance of power between Taft's provincial midwesterners and Dewey's cos-

Dewey–Warren Campaign Button, 1948. *Source:* Library of Congress.

mopolitan easterners. On the third ballot, Warren threw his support to Dewey—and ended up as the vice presidential nominee.

Dewey attributed his defeat in 1944 to his shrill attacks on the New Deal. This time he would be more presidential. Besides, all the polls assured him that he would win. He ran the campaign with an eye toward ensuring a smooth transition to his administration. "We will build in this country," Dewey promised, "a sense of fair play and of unity and give and take which can increase our productivity, increase the internal peace within the country with a government which believes in our people and which has absolute faith in them and in the freedom by which this country was built."

Harry Truman, however, refused to cooperate. He believed that he could keep the Roosevelt coalition intact. In the wake of the New Deal, politicians like Truman conceived the electorate as a serious of "pressure groups"—farmers, laborers, "liberals," blacks, Jews, Catholics, Italians, "aliens"—who received benefits from the government and not the party boss. Each constituency had to be wooed with particular governmental programs and with specially tailored symbolic appeals.

Truman's acceptance speech listed all the benefits the Democrats had bestowed on the different constituencies in American society, then challenged the Republican Congress's defense of "special privilege." To cast the Republicans as the Herbert Hoovers of the 1940s, Truman called "the good-for-nothing, do nothing, Taft–Hartley 80th Congress" back for a special session, on what was known in his native Missouri as Turnip Day, to enact his housing, health, civil rights, Social Security, and power legislation. Now, Truman said, the nation could judge the Republicans' commitment, articulated in their platform, to fair housing and lower prices.

As expected, Taft and the Republicans did nothing. Truman ran hard against Taft and the "worst Congress" ever. This bravura combination of folksiness and calculation epitomized the Truman campaign. Truman would play Santa Claus to the Republicans' Scrooge. Against Dewey, he would play the farm boy to the city-slicker; the rugged midwesterner to the effeminate easterner; the defender of tradition to the slave of modernity.

Toward the end of the campaign, Dewey noticed the growing intensity of the crowds greeting Truman's vigorous whistle-stop campaign. As he continued with his bloodless homages to unity—"The next thing we know he'll be endorsing matrimony, the metal zipper and the dial telephone," the actress Tallulah Bankhead sneered—he sensed his campaign drifting. He and his campaign manager, Herbert Brownell Jr., considered raising the rhetorical temperature. But Dewey was imprisoned by his own pretensions. Brownell canvassed between 125 and 150 state and national Republican leaders. All but one said, "Don't rock the boat." Dewey respected the consensus, lost, and, inevitably, had to shoulder the blame alone.

Mainstream Republicans attacked the smug "Albany group" that ran the campaign. They ignored the fact that Republicans lost in Congress as well. Dewey's two losses, on the heels of Willkie's loss, vindicated the regulars and convinced many to trust to the party professionals, to run more aggressive campaigns. More broadly, Americans hailed the campaign as the defeat of the slick, manipulative, "Young & Rubicam and Hollywood" success-oriented, "efficiency-expert[ed]," advertising-intensive modern campaign. Americans had voted for "free, informed, intelligent discussion," wrote Eliot V. Cohen, the editor of *Commentary.*

THE RISE OF REPUBLICAN ANTICOMMUNISM

Despite these optimistic assessments, the political climate soon turned ugly. Within weeks of the election,

Dewey Wins GOP Nomination, 1948. *Source:* Library of Congress.

Congressman Richard Nixon was charging the administration with a cover-up in the case of Alger Hiss, a State Department official accused of spying for the communists. Nixon, a navy veteran from California, discovered with many of his colleagues that anticommunism was an effective weapon against the Democrats. The "pinkish" hue of the Roosevelt administration, along with the widespread shock that America was now engaged in a Cold War with its World War II ally, gave credence to theories that a communist conspiracy was afoot. The presence of communist moles in government helped explain the New Deal's hostility to free enterprise and, Senator Taft insisted, "the fact that this administration has lost the peace after the American people won the war."

The anticommunist crusade would place the Democrats on the defensive and help the Republicans recruit blocs of new voters. Many Catholics, appalled by communist atheism and by the Soviet domination of heavily Catholic Eastern Europe, flocked to the Republican Party. Catholics found it easier to abandon the Democratic machine as prosperity brought them from the cities to the suburbs. The anticommunist crusade also allowed Republicans to wipe away the taint of pre–Pearl Harbor isolationism and demonstrate their patriotism.

The outbreak of the Korean War in June 1950 traumatized the nation. Months later, Republicans gained modestly in the midterm elections by chiding the administration for being "soft on communism." The country was reeling from the war, the fall of China, Senator Joseph McCarthy's anticommunist demagoguery, raging inflation, a wave of labor strikes, and the continuing struggles with the Soviet Union. Truman and the Democrats appeared demoralized, ineffectual, spent.

Once again, Republicans looked confidently toward elections, sure that this time they could remove the Democrats from the White House. Once again, they would have to choose whether to nominate a pragmatic Republican who would appeal to Democrats or an ideological Republican who would keep the faith— and satisfy the faithful. Senator Taft assumed that he would receive the nomination. "Mr. Republican" enjoyed the support of party leaders and had solid con-

servative credentials that Dewey, Willkie and Landon had lacked. Yet Taft lacked the charisma and popular appeal necessary to compete in modern politics. Some searched for a more popular alternative, while northeastern businessmen suspicious of Taft's isolationism searched for a more internationalist candidate.

EISENHOWER REPUBLICANS

For these disaffected Republicans, Dwight D. Eisenhower was the obvious choice. The hero of World War II, supreme commander of the Allied powers in Europe since 1951, Eisenhower was the most popular man in America. He had no domestic record, but Republican businessmen knew he would help the United States fulfill its global responsibilities. In the winter of 1952, an independent committee determined to draft him. By the spring, Eisenhower clearly was the people's choice, but Senator Taft remained the Republican leaders' favorite. For half a decade, Eisenhower had been saying that he would run only if called, that the people had to seek him out. But if he wanted the nomination in 1952, Eisenhower would

Eisenhower Speaks from His Campaign Train, Jefferson City, Missouri. *Source:* International News, September 22, 1952.

have to work for it. In June, Eisenhower returned to America from NATO headquarters in Paris, resigned his commission, and began to campaign.

The battle between Taft and Eisenhower was not resolved until the Republican National Convention met at Chicago in July. Eisenhower's primary victories were offset by Taft's strength among party officeholders and in the National Committee itself. Before the convention, the committee sided with Taft in procedural disputes between Eisenhower rebels and party regulars in Georgia, Louisiana, Mississippi, and Texas. Eisenhower's forces brought the question to the convention floor. The general's men won the first round when they passed the "Fair Play Amendment" forbidding disputed delegates from voting on contested seats until their own status had been clarified. That victory, and a switch of Minnesota's delegation from the perennial candidate Harold Stassen to the general, gave Eisenhower a victory on the first ballot. Eisenhower mollified Taft supporters by accepting Senator Richard Nixon as the vice presidential nominee and supporting a platform advocating conservative measures such as a balanced budget, "progressive tax relief," and ardent anticommunism.

Eisenhower knew that he was his "own best salesman." He had learned from the primaries and from Dewey's sorry experience not to take his popularity for granted. Eisenhower also realized that in the event of a defeat, he, like Dewey, would become the scapegoat. He was therefore determined that "no lack of personal effort on my part" would be blamed. He felt the Republican campaign plan drawn up by the national chairman Arthur Summerfield gave "too much weight to nationwide familiarity with my name" and not enough to principle. Still, he recognized the value of the strategy. The people wanted to see and honor their hero.

When he did address issues during his vigorous whistle-stop tour, Eisenhower echoed his party's three-pronged indictment against the entrenched Democrats, symbolized by the formula K_1C_2—Korea, communism, and corruption. On all three issues, the Democrats were vulnerable. But as one of the architects of American foreign policy since the 1940s, Eisenhower had to tread carefully. As the campaign progressed, Eisenhower's attacks on the Democrats intensified. He refused to condemn Joe McCarthy's shrill anticommunism. And toward the end of the campaign, he promised, if elected, to go to Korea. This ploy exploited Eisenhower's image as a military man of peace. It made what had been a bipartisan policy the sole province of the Democrats. The crassness of the move "shocked and disappointed" Harry Truman.

THE "CHECKERS" SPEECH

In mid-September, Democrats thought they had an opportunity to throw the corruption issue back at the Republicans. The *New York Post* discovered that Nixon supporters had created an $18,000 fund to cover some of the California senator's expenses. Headlines blazed about the "Secret Nixon Fund!" Many urged Eisenhower to drop Nixon from the ticket. Eisenhower hesitated. "I am taking my time on this," he told reporters on his campaign train who, by a vote of 40-to-2, suggested dumping Nixon. For three days Nixon waited, Republicans agonized, and Democrats pelted Nixon with pennies when he spoke.

Thomas Dewey interceded, suggesting that Nixon refute the charges in a nationally televised address. On September 23, 1952, following the "Milton Berle Show," Nixon delivered what came to be known as the "Checkers Speech" to an estimated audience of 58 million. Nixon's maudlin defense of his honesty, his wife's "Republican cloth coat" and the dog he received as a gift inspired a flood of telegrams defending the beleaguered senator and prevented Eisenhower from dumping Nixon.

Eisenhower–Nixon. *Source:* United Press International.

Eisenhower soundly defeated the Democratic nominee, Adlai Stevenson, winning 55.2% of the popular vote and 442 electoral votes. The general even made inroads on the Solid South, carrying Tennessee, Virginia, Florida, and Texas, as well as the North and the West. The Republican Congress that swept into office on the general's coattails had a slim majority of one in the Senate and nine in the House. Republicans would not win a majority in the Senate again until 1980 and would have to wait until 1994 before recapturing the House of Representatives.

As the first Republican president since Hoover, enjoying majorities in both the House and the Senate, Eisenhower could have dismantled the Democrats' welfare state. Instead, he legitimized and expanded it. Under Eisenhower, Congress passed a public works project that dwarfed any of Franklin Roosevelt's schemes. The Highway Act of 1956 allocated $32 billion over the next 13 years to construct a 41,000-mile interstate system for highways and to complete construction of the federal aid system of highways. The federal government promised 90% of construction costs for the interstate and 50% for the federal aid system. The funding came from higher gasoline taxes and other duties, which went into a Highway Trust Fund. This project represented a giant step forward in the spread of federal power and the homogenization of American life. The ability to withhold highway funds from particular states would give Congress and the president unprecedented influence over local decisions, while the Federal Highway System's ubiquitous green signs with white borders and white lettering would impose a standard look on the country from coast to coast.

Similarly, Eisenhower stayed the course on foreign policy. The United States continued maneuvering in its Cold War against the Soviet Union, although Eisenhower's secretary of state, John Foster Dulles, preferred to talk about the "liberation" of communist-controlled areas, rather than their "containment." Isolationism was not considered an option, especially after Taft died in 1953. The bipartisan foreign policy consensus first forged under Truman and identified with Senator Arthur Vanderberg would continue with a Republican president enjoying the support of key Democratic senators like Lyndon Johnson. Most Republicans stood by their president as Eisenhower continued 20-years' worth of Democratic policy.

Just as congressional Democrats' cooperation pleasantly surprised Eisenhower, he was often frustrated by congressional Republicans. Taft's death made it difficult to contain the conservatives, many of whom felt betrayed by Eisenhower. Senators H. Styles Bridges of New Hampshire, William F. Knowland of California, and Eugene Millikin of Colorado tried to show themselves worthy of succeeding Taft by hindering the president. Senator McCarthy continued attacking the government, ignoring the fact that his party was now in control. Eventually, after the dramatic Army–McCarthy hearings of 1954 broadcast McCarthy's antics, the Senate censured the Wisconsin senator.

Eisenhower's cabinet looked very similar to Harding's, with idealists like Dulles balanced out by big businessmen like Secretary of the Treasury George M. Humphrey and Secretary of Defense Charles E. Wilson and party regulars like Postmaster General Arthur E. Summerfield and Attorney General Herbert Brownell Jr. Wilson was credited with coining the phrase "What's good for General Motors is good for the country," an attitude that captured Eisenhower's probusiness orientation.

Eisenhower's corporate supporters tried to modernize the Republican Party and run it on business principles. The new chairman, Leonard Wood Hall, eventually hired a permanent staff of 100 at party headquarters, which ballooned to 300 in an election year. The party mounted its first direct-mail fund-raising campaign, hoping to raise money from the masses rather than the corporate bigwigs.

Hall wanted to modernize campaigning methods as well. He believed that "politics is show business." His disdain for whistle-stopping as silly and archaic stemmed from his experience managing the Eisenhower campaign "special." "When the President is on television he goes into everyone's living room and you get the same impact as if he were there in person. And he certainly can meet more people that way than he can by any other method," Hall believed. Managing such "productions" gave the party a new role in this television age as a permanent public relations organization. To celebrate one of the president's birthdays, Hall mounted an elaborate "Salute to Eisenhower." The closed-circuit television special, complete with "pretty lady singers" and a short but moving speech by the president, raised over $5 million. "They got all the impact as though the President were there in person," Hall said of the 63,000 people at 53 different dinners. "The emotion was there, the tears were there."

The growing importance of the National Committee stemmed from the decline of the local party machines. With the New Deal, the federal government usurped the machines' traditional social welfare role. The proliferation of primaries and the rise of interest groups made independent candidates more viable, and more important. The spread of civil service reform in the cities also deprived machines of patronage. Finally, voters themselves were more independent and more oriented toward the national leaders they saw on television and read about in news magazines.

Despite Eisenhower's continuing popularity, less than 30% of Americans surveyed called themselves Republicans. "The Republican Party is not strong enough to elect a President," Richard Nixon explained. "We have to have a presidential candidate strong enough to get the Republican Party elected."

Eisenhower himself was more comfortable playing the role of national leader than party boss. In the waning days of his reelection rematch against Adlai Stevenson in 1956, when Soviet tanks rolled in Hungary and war broke out along the Suez Canal, Eisenhower addressed the nation as "the President of all Americans rather than the candidate of one party." Americans rallied around their president. Eisenhower had won World War II and ended the Korean War; he would help America out of this crisis too. Eisenhower's already strong lead was increased by an estimated five percentage points in the popular vote. Americans trusted "Ike" to "best handle the international crisis, keep us out of war, and deal with Russia." His defeated opponent, Adlai Stevenson, laughed that millions took "refuge *with* Eisenhower *from* Eisenhower's disastrous" foreign policy.

Even with this dramatic final flourish, Eisenhower failed to bring in a Republican Congress. For the first time since 1848, voters chose the president from one party while a majority in both houses went to another party. Despite Eisenhower's impressive 57.4% share of the popular vote, Democrats returned to Washington

Eisenhower Campaign Button. *Source:* J. Doyle Dewitt Collection.

with a margin of 49 to 47 in the Senate and 232 House seats as opposed to 199 for the Republicans. An estimated 4 of 10 voters split their ticket. This blaze of ticket splitting revealed the weakening of party ties and the continuing failure of the Republican Party to recover the majority it lost during the Hoover administration.

Eisenhower missed an opportunity to redefine his party's vision. His instinct for consensus and his aversion to rhetoric kept liberal northeasterners and stalwart midwesterners in the party fold. His cooperation with the Democratic majority leader, Lyndon B. Johnson, illustrated his preference for accommodation over confrontation.

When Republicans suffered heavy losses during the 1958 midterm elections, one of the few bright spots was in New York State, where the liberal Republican Nelson Rockefeller captured the governorship. Rockefeller and his fellow liberals were committed to civil rights, supported federal and state initiatives to aid the poor, and, unlike their Democratic rivals, supported big business and free enterprise enthusiastically. Another bright spot was in Arizona, where the conservative Senator Barry Goldwater won a resounding reelection victory. Goldwater and Rockefeller would vie for the soul of the party in the 1960s as intensely as Taft and Dewey had competed in the 1940s.

During his second term, with his health failing,

Eisenhower Campaigning in Minneapolis. *Source:* International News, October 16, 1956.

Eisenhower often found himself reacting to events instead of shaping them. The Soviets' launching of *Sputnik* into space, the fall of Cuba to the communists, the civil rights crisis in Little Rock, Arkansas, made it seem that the world had shifted, that Ike's midwestern conservatism could not meet the new challenges. An aging, frail president now came to epitomize a country whose greatest triumphs might be in the past. The public reaction surprised and depressed Eisenhower. "Alleged interservice rivalry, guided missiles, Sputnik II, Little Rock, Syria, and a variety of other problems seem to clog my memory these days," he sighed.

RICHARD NIXON

By contrast, Eisenhower's vice president, Richard Nixon, seemed young, dynamic, and ready to take charge. A World War II veteran, a freshman in Congress with John F. Kennedy in 1947, the son of a grocer peddling his own version of the American dream, Nixon had been the most prominent man of his generation dating back to his nomination as vice president in 1952. For eight years, he had played the role of Eisenhower's aggressive lieutenant. In the process, Nixon had strengthened the vice presidency, hauling the job out of its traditional obscurity. But along the way, Nixon had collected some bruises, many associated with his campaigning style. His initial runs for Congress in 1946 and for the Senate in 1950 became legendary for their Red-baiting slurs against Jerry Voorhis and Helen Gahagan Douglas. In 1952, Nixon slithered along the low road against Adlai Stevenson and his "Ph.D. degree from [Secretary of State Dean] Acheson's College of Cowardly Communist Containment." By 1956, Nixon had adopted a statesman-like tone, as Eisenhower encouraged: "Give 'em heaven." That year, Republicans considered him "the best campaigner we've got, bar none." In preparing for his presidential run in 1960, Nixon presented himself as an experienced statesman, a more mature version of the anticommunist hatchet man of the late 1940s and early 1950s.

Rockefeller and other liberals, however, did not trust the vice president. Although he could not match Nixon's popularity with the public or with party regulars, the New York governor had enough political clout and family money to force Nixon to negotiate with him. On the eve of the Republican Convention, Nixon felt compelled to visit his rival. In the "Compact of Fifth Avenue" Rockefeller imposed a 14-point program on Nixon that liberalized the Republican platform, particularly in the area of civil rights, and insulted Eisenhower by demanding a more aggressive defense policy.

The Republican Platform Committee consisted of two delegates from each state. Most of them were party regulars chosen by the state bosses. Watching the committee members in Chicago struggle to design a platform broad enough to unite their party, one Republican sneered that "in this party you have to run as hard as possible to stay in the same place; getting them to approve what Eisenhower has already done is an achievement in itself." The summit agreement negated all these efforts. As Theodore White noted, "Never had the quadrennial liberal swoop on the regulars been more nakedly dramatized. . . . Whatever honor they might have been able to carry from their services on the Platform Committee had been wiped out. A single night's meeting of two men in a millionaire's triplex apartment in Babylon-by-the-Hudson 830 miles away, was about to overrule them; they were exposed as clowns for all the world to see." Conservatives such as Barry Goldwater denounced the "Munich of the Republican Party," but the deal with Rockefeller gave Nixon the nomination he had earned after eight years of indentured servitude to Eisenhower.

While his Democratic opponent, John F. Kennedy, could range widely in the campaign, Nixon had to tread carefully. The vice president had to champion the administration without being too defensive. He had to inject passion into the campaign without being unstatesmanlike. And he had to project confidence without becoming another Thomas E. Dewey.

Nixon achieved these goals in his acceptance speech. He wanted to "break the stolid and unimaginative stereotype" of the Eisenhower administration that the Democrats advanced and "challenge people with the rather daring idea that a Republican campaign could be exciting and even inspiring." Nixon promised to lead America to a "victory of freedom over tyranny, of plenty over hungry, of health over disease," in every country of the world.

Nixon insisted that the man was more important than his party. He asked Americans to "decide on the basis of what" the candidates "say" and "believe." For the nominee of the minority party, this declaration was shrewd. It also recognized the decline of the party. Neither Nixon nor Kennedy was a slave to the party bosses; in fact, both men were independent, a worrying sign to those concerned with the party's future. The four televised debates between Kennedy and Nixon also emphasized the man, not the party. Press attacks on the vice president's appearance and performance in the first debate revealed the new standards for political success. As television became more important to the campaign, candidates would become more independent, parties more irrelevant.

Nixon wanted to win the campaign on his own in 1960, without Eisenhower and without the Republican National Committee. He was his own favorite adviser. "He reduced us all to clerks," one Republican Party official complained.

The election was extraordinarily close. Kennedy received 49.7% of the popular vote, Nixon 49.6%. Republicans gained 24 seats in Congress. The hard-fought campaign raised the voter turnout to 64.3%, the highest since 1908. Had 32,500 votes out of a record 69 million switched—or, as some speculated, if fewer corpses had voted in Chicago and Dallas—Nixon would have become the 36th president of the United States.

THE GOLDWATER CRUSADE

In the 1960s, the Republican Party was becoming increasingly polarized. Rockefeller, along with other liberal Republicans such as Senators Jacob Javits of New York and Clifford Case of New Jersey, wanted the party of Lincoln to fulfill its historic mission by helping the blacks. They hoped to replicate Theodore Roosevelt's coalition of "the plain people" and big businessmen. But Republican conservatives began rallying around different ideals and envisioning a different kind of coalition. Over a quarter of a century of government expansion and foreign struggles spawned a libertarian and nationalist conservatism that called for government restraint in domestic affairs but took pride in a strong military that could demonstrate American power around the world.

The Democrats were vulnerable. Southerners were disgusted by their national party's commitment to civil rights. Second-generation ethnics and children of union members were moving out to the suburbs and fearful of being overtaxed as they sought to fulfill the American dream. Westerners enamored of individualism were suspicious of a distant and powerful central government. Together, conservatives believed, these groups could redefine the Republican Party and reorient American government.

The 1964 primary face-off between Nelson Rockefeller and Barry Goldwater pitted these two visions of the Republican future against each other. Goldwater relied on a well-organized drive orchestrated by a New Yorker, F. Clifton White, of the National Federation of Young Republicans. At the same time, Rockefeller suffered from the scandal caused by his recent divorce after 31 years of marriage and his hasty remarriage to another divorcee. Goldwater's narrow victory over

Rockefeller in the California primary forced Rockefeller's withdrawal but did not clinch the nomination. Other governors, such as William Scranton of Pennsylvania, grasped at the nomination, while Richard Nixon waited for a deadlocked convention to turn to him. One poll on the eve of the convention showed Scranton more popular among Republican voters than Goldwater by 60% to 34%. Still, Goldwater's well-organized forces at the Cow Palace in San Francisco engineered a victory for the Arizona senator.

Barry Goldwater offered his conservative ideology as a response to the upheavals America was experiencing. The challenges of the 1960s, so praised in the previous campaign, appeared daunting by 1964. Questions about racism, crime, the Vietnam War, and urban decay confounded Americans. Promising a return to a simpler America, Goldwater's acceptance speech rejected compromise in the defense of liberty. "We must and we shall return to proven ways—not because they are old, but because they are true," he declared, promising that his America would not "stagnate in the swampland of collectivism" or "cringe before the bullying of communism." After hearing the speech, one reporter gasped: "My God, he's going to run as Barry Goldwater." For the campaign, the Republicans' slogan was "In your heart you know he's right." "Yes," cynics responded, "far right."

Goldwater resisted any suggestions that he modify his tactics or his ideas. He saw himself as a man of integrity. He believed that whenever he attempted to tailor his message to one particular group or another, he stumbled. As a result, he dismissed many good suggestions by complaining, "They're trying to change me."

Like all challengers, Goldwater wondered how far he could go in opposing the president. He referred to Johnson as the "interim President" or simply "Lyndon." He enjoyed criticizing Johnson's "giveaway" programs at the politically riskiest spots, denouncing Medicare in Florida, the poverty program in Appalachia, and the Tennessee Valley Authority in Tennessee. "I guess Barry just had to prove that he isn't chicken," one frustrated supporter noted. But Goldwater cancelled a 30-minute campaign film attacking the "immorality issue." The film featured incendiary footage of "stripteasing babes, wild Twisters, Negro riots" and a "black Lincoln Continental limousine careening madly along country roads, with beer cans being tossed out of the driver's window," as Johnson was alleged to have done. "This," Goldwater snapped, "is a racist film," even as it anticipated the battlelines of future Republican campaigns.

Goldwater and his aides identified the Midwest and the South as his areas of greatest vote-getting potential. His tour of the "lily white" South revealed how hard it would be to take the high road. The subtext of almost every meeting was racist, as "great numbers of unapologetic white supremacists" turned Goldwater rallies into "great carnivals of white supremacy," Richard Rovere observed. And as the campaign progressed, and his frustration mounted, Goldwater began chanting that all Johnson did was "lie and lie and lie." This descent muddied Goldwater's message and disappointed many who, as Goldwater had claimed to at the outset, respected the office, if not the man.

The Democratic landslide gave Lyndon Johnson the liberal mandate Franklin D. Roosevelt did not have after 1938 and that neither Truman nor Kennedy had ever enjoyed. With 61.1% of the popular vote—more than Roosevelt ever received—and more than two-thirds of both the House and the Senate, Johnson had enough votes to break the conservative coalition that had frustrated liberals for decades. With an ambitious program to build a "Great Society," Johnson and the Democrats expected to dominate Washington for another three decades.

The Republican Party seemed to be in a shambles. One poll estimated that 53% of those surveyed identified themselves as Democrats and only 25% identified themselves as Republicans. Almost 73% said that issues had motivated their vote, a devastating repudiation of Goldwater conservatism, it seemed. Yet, in retrospect, there were signs of optimism. Barry Goldwater continued the Republican assault on the Solid South. His impressive inroads heralded a revolution. In Mississippi, Goldwater received 87% of the vote; in Alabama he received 70%. Sixteen new Republican congressmen from the South joined the overwhelmingly Democratic 89th Congress. Having ceded the black vote to the Democrats, Republicans needed southern whites and could afford to play to their prejudices. With the population and power of the Northeast declining, and the South and West booming, Goldwater's loss pointed the way to a Republican future that was far brighter than anyone in 1964 would have dared to predict.

NIXON RETURNS

The leadership of the Republican Party was up for grabs. In the House of Representatives, a group of young moderate congressmen deposed the old stalwart Charles Halleck as minority leader and replaced him with the affable Gerald Ford. Out West, Ronald Reagan, a Hollywood actor and former New Deal Democrat whose nationwide speech electrified the

Goldwater campaign, agreed to run for governor of California. And in New York, exiled to a Fifth Avenue apartment and a lucrative Wall Street law practice, Richard Nixon planned his return.

Nixon realized that the 1964 campaign had crippled his two biggest rivals for the 1968 race, Goldwater and Rockefeller. After losing the 1962 gubernatorial race in California and bitterly declaring that the gentlemen of the press would no longer have him "to kick around," Nixon had tried to play party peacemaker in 1964. Two years later, Nixon and his new Wall Street friends spearheaded an effort to elect a Republican Congress. He traveled 30,000 miles and visited 82 congressional districts, raising tens of thousands of dollars for the cause—and collecting dozens of political debts.

"Congress '66" also reawakened hopes of a Nixon presidency. "It wasn't a Nixon-for-President group in the beginning," his aide Peter Flanigan insisted. "I suppose we all would have said at the beginning 'it'd be nice—but he can't be elected.' And then ... the night of the election in '66, with the telephone calls coming in from all over the country—we knew we were in business." Republicans had gained 47 seats in the House and 4 seats in the Senate. The Great Society was proving to be expensive and chaotic.

By January 1967, Nixon gathered his aides and said: "I'm not going to be coy with my oldest friends. . . . I want you to proceed with plans for winning the Republican presidential nomination next year." Nixon concluded that he was the one to unite Wall Street and Main Street, to cash in his party debts and exploit his fame. As Nixon undertook a world tour for *Reader's Digest* to stay in the public eye but out of trouble, he ordered his aides "to work your tails off getting the job done."

The "New Nixon" triumphed in 1968 by appealing to what he called "the silent center, the millions of people in the middle of the American political spectrum who do not demonstrate, who do not picket or protest loudly." Nixon realized that the "vocal minority" that dominated the evening news did not reflect the American mainstream. While Democrats sought to mollify the radicals, Nixon led the Republican Party toward what he later called the "silent majority," the "quiet Americans" who "have become committed to answers to social problems that preserve personal freedom."

As he had been doing since the 1940s, Nixon attracted critical elements of the New Deal coalition toward the Republican Party by labeling the Democrats as radicals. Nixon exploited the divisions among the Democrats. Southerners led by Governor George Wallace of Alabama were in revolt. Middle-class ethnics and blue-collar workers resented the "college kids," the welfare cheats, the crime in the streets, and the growing tax burdens at home. Even liberals had lost faith in the Johnson–Humphrey administration because of Vietnam. Nixon's narrow victory by less than half a million votes over Vice President Hubert Humphrey proved that "the movement" during the 1960s was only a small if loud insurgency that did more to undermine liberalism and strengthen conservatism than is generally appreciated.

Nixon entered office vowing to dismantle the New Deal. In August 1969 he declared that "after a third of a century of power flowing from the people and the States to Washington it is time for a New Federalism in which power, funds and responsibility will flow from Washington to the States and to the people." He developed creative ideas for welfare reform, revenue sharing, and tax reduction. He would blame his failure to implement these changes on the hostile Democratic Congress. But Nixon, like all the Republican presidents of this era, was a New Dealer at heart. Even as he undermined Americans' faith in government by questioning its efficacy, he and his administration championed programs to advance civil rights, improve the environment, deliver health care to all, and eliminate poverty. Richard Nixon, not some liberal Democrat, took the United States off the gold standard and instituted wage and price controls. Nixon's administration also implemented affirmative action and school busing. For all their rhetorical conservatism, Republicans throughout the 1960s, 1970s, and 1980s would find it politically impossible to resist using the federal government's power to seduce various constituencies with particular programs.

This phenomenon was particularly evident with what came to be known as middle-class entitlements. Social Security, which Goldwater dared to challenge, had become not only an accepted part of American government but sacrosanct. In 1972 Congress indexed Social Security benefits to inflation. As a result, with a growing percentage of the budget protected from debate, the federal budget, and the deficit, mushroomed.

The federal deficit problem was exacerbated by the expensive and bloody war Americans were fighting in Southeast Asia. The debate over Vietnam once again blurred party lines. Conservative Republicans repudiated their isolationist past and criticized the military for not prosecuting the war aggressively enough, just as liberal Democrats revived isolationism and denounced American imperialism. Nixon himself did not want to appear weak on the issue and refused to be the first president to lose a war. At the same time, he had been elected on a dovish-sounding promise to end the war. His policy of "Vietnamization"—training and equipping South Vietnamese forces to replace American soldiers—tried to appease both wings of his party and both extremes in American society.

Nixon's continued prosecution of the war made him the target of the same intense protests that helped encourage Lyndon Johnson to retire. Nixon blamed the "liberal media" for stirring up the protests. For the next three decades, Republicans would score political points by accusing the television networks, the leading newspapers, and the news weeklies of political bias. Polls of reporters consistently demonstrated their liberal leanings. The president and his men considered "ninety-five percent of the members of the Washington press corps . . . unalterably opposed to us because of their intellectual and philosophical background. Some of them will smirk and pander to us for the purpose of getting a story but we must remember that they are just waiting for the chance to stick the knife in deep and to twist it." With most of the press "out to get us," Nixon and his men had to be just "as tough, ruthless and unfeeling as they are."

In picking a fight with the press, Nixon had chosen his target wisely. Reporters were no longer the anonymous and cowed scribblers of a previous era. While fewer and fewer publishers were known and feared as Joseph Pulitzer and William Randolph Hearst had been in their day, reporters, especially those on television, had become independent and quite celebrated agents. More and more, it became apparent that reporters did not merely mirror what happened; they shaped the news. Journalists had a particular agenda and particular conventions for reporting. At the same time, the power of the press became more concentrated as newspaper chains gobbled up independent papers, and the "prestige papers," such as the *New York Times* and the *Washington Post*, worked with each other and the three major television networks to protect the ever-widening prerogatives of the press. The publication of the secret "Pentagon Papers," exposing the government's doubts about the Vietnam War, signified the new journalism's adversarial and arrogant approach. More and more people began to talk about the power of the "media"—a word invented by advertising agencies that encompassed the television networks, daily newspapers, and magazines.

For Nixon's men the term neatly encapsulated the increasingly arrogant institution that was the voice of the "liberal elite" they disdained. "This hasn't been our town," Nixon's speechwriter Pat Buchanan said of Washington, but he could have included vast parts of Boston and New York as well. "They live in Georgetown with their parties; they never invited us, they ignored us." Convinced that these parochials were out of touch with America's "silent majority," Nixon's men were determined to master the media's conventions and transcend the bias. By controlling access to the White House and staging events that the networks had no choice but to cover, Nixon's men hogtied their enemies.

WATERGATE

This same bunker mentality led Nixon's men to make their own rules, to fancy themselves above the law. They justified any action to advance their cause, no matter how irregular, by pointing to the hostile forces surrounding them and saying that the Democrats had done it too. Wary of most institutions, including their own party's establishment, they organized an independent election effort, called the Committee to Reelect the President. Its acronym proved irresistible and suggestive: CREEP. In his memoirs Nixon would proudly quote Theodore White's conclusion that the committee was "one of the most spectacularly efficient exercises in political technology of the entire postwar era." This combination of paranoia and zeal began a series of petty crimes and abuses that snowballed into the Watergate scandal.

Throughout the 1972 campaign, even after evidence linked the June break-in and bugging attempt at Democratic headquarters with CREEP, the Watergate issue failed to stir the American people. While some dismissed it as typical election-year hijinks, others found it hard to believe that anyone would even bother eavesdropping on the Democratic National Committee. "Anyone who knew anything about politics would know that a national committee headquarters was a useless place to go for information on a presidential campaign," Nixon himself would later write.

In 1972 the Democratic opposition to Nixon did not seem to warrant such crimes. Senator George McGovern snared the Democratic nomination by exploiting the new, open primary rules his McGovern–Fraser Commission had implemented. McGovern became the symbol of Democratic extremism to his opponents, proof that the party was occupied by the forces of "Acid, Abortion and Amnesty," in Republican Senate Minority Leader Hugh Scott's devastating phrase. McGovern's candidacy damaged the Democratic Party more than Goldwater's candidacy had damaged the Republicans. In November, Nixon won over 47 million votes, an unprecedented 60.7% of the popular vote. Subsequently, Democrats would have difficulty distancing themselves from the radical positions attributed to McGovern. Over 20 years later, cultural conservatives would still find it convenient to condemn permissive opponents as "McGovernik."

THE END OF PARTY?

The democratized nominating process that the McGovern–Fraser Commission and other reformers championed transformed the parties. Candidates now mobilized their own forces and forged their own identities, while using the parties for tactical support. For nearly a decade observers had been saying what David Broder of the *Washington Post* said in his 1971 book, *The Party's Over*. Independent candidates and the mass media diluted party loyalties. The massive ticket splitting of the Eisenhower years continued over the ensuing decades, as most Republican presidents ended up with heavily Democratic Congresses. Polls in the 1970s showed barely a quarter of the population strongly identifying with particular parties and as many as 38% identifying themselves as Independents. Especially on the presidential level, more and more Americans were willing to vote for the "best man," rather than their party's leader. Many believed that there was no substantial difference between the two parties, that they were simply packaging labels like Colgate and Crest. Sensing that these new, hollowed-out parties suited modern American culture, one political consultant blamed the new politics on "the telephone, television and the Model T."

Ironically, even though Watergate resulted from the declining power of the national party, the scandal devastated the Republican Party. The effects of Nixon's 48-state electoral sweep over George McGovern dissipated rapidly. When Richard Nixon finally resigned in August 1974, barely a fifth of Americans were willing to call themselves Republicans. The elections that fall would send only 144 Republicans to the House of Representatives, placing the party back where it had been ten years before.

Nixon's resignation, coming on the heels of the turbulent 1960s, made whatever inbred cynicism Americans had about politicians and the political system appear inadequate. One poll found that in 1976 only 35% of Americans surveyed trusted the "government in Washington to do what is right" always or most of the time, down from 54% in 1972 and 75% in 1958. At the same time, the scandal triggered an orgy of campaign reform. Now, optimists hoped, politics would be "fixed."

Many attributed the Watergate scandals to the mushrooming cost of campaigning. The professionalization of campaigning, with its consultants and elaborate "ad-buys," added to the cost, as did the fact that in an age of declining party loyalty, candidates had to spend more money to build organizations and a public image. Party committees that had spent $20 million combined to elect candidates in 1960 spent $100 million in 1972; the estimated $200 million spent to elect candidates at all levels in the United States in 1964 more than doubled to $425 million in 1972. The Watergate-inspired finance reforms limited individual contributions to $1,000 per candidate and established a taxpayer-supported federal election fund for the presidential campaign.

The age of the fat cat was over. But reformers had unwittingly ushered in the age of the PAC. Political action committees, first established by labor unions, were formed by corporations eager to pump money into campaigns while staying within the limits of the new law. As one campaign finance expert soon noted, "the large contributor, in effect, has been replaced by the large solicitor"—PAC managers, corporate executives, entertainment moguls, and direct-mail consultants. The finance reform further splintered American politics by shifting power away from the parties and rewarding individual candidates who forged lucrative relationships with particular PACs.

GERALD FORD, MIDWESTERN CONSERVATIVE

Nixon's successor, Gerald R. Ford, was the first president not to face the electorate at large, having succeeded Vice President Spiro Agnew, who resigned in an unrelated scandal. Ford was a midwestern Republican whose career reflected the changes the party had undergone since World War II. A Grand Rapids, Michigan, native, Ford had unseated an older, isolationist, machine-supported Republican congressman in 1948. As a war veteran, Ford was an interventionist who supported American involvement in Vietnam. He was a consensus politician known more for his constituent services than his bombast, more for his compromises than his strong stands, more for his ability to secure pork for his district than for his commitment to reducing the federal budget. Growing up in Robert Taft's neighborhood, Ford considered himself a conservative, but it was an affable conservatism blunted by prosperity and years of accommodation. In Congress, Ford was always more successful in limiting programs instead of eliminating them. As president, he, too, would have aides compiling lists of all the

Ford and Elephant, 1976. *Source:* USICA.

government programs his administration initiated, all the goodies he was distributing across America.

Ford made two political blunders early in his term. His pardon of Nixon within weeks of taking office alienated Democrats and the all-important news media whose beneficence he badly needed. And his selection of Nelson Rockefeller as vice president alienated right-wing Republicans still mourning Nixon's downfall and suspicious of the accommodating midwesterner now living in the White House.

Nixon's towering reputation as one of the great conservative anticommunists of his generation had dulled conservative attacks against his activist domestic policy and his détente with the Soviet Union and the People's Republic of China. In his absence, attacks mounted against the architect of détente, Henry Kissinger, and the "liberalism" of the Nixon–Ford domestic program. After two successful terms as governor of California, the most popular conservative in the party, Ronald Reagan, decided to violate the "Eleventh Commandment"—thou shalt not attack a fellow Republican—and challenge Ford for the nomination in 1976.

Reagan and his followers argued that antigovernment rhetoric was not enough. Republicans had to begin dismantling the ever-burgeoning federal bureaucracy with its oppressive regulations, its burdensome taxes, its runaway deficit. In soothing, well-delivered homilies, Reagan conjured up an older, simpler America of small-town brotherhood, individual initiative, free enterprise, and limited government. Reagan's push for the nomination took advantage of the growing number of states that used popular primaries, rather than caucuses or conventions, to select delegates to the national convention. In 1976, 28 state primaries would select 67.9% of the delegates, nearly doubling the numbers from 1968, when 16 state primaries selected 34.3% of the delegates. The number of Americans participating in the process nearly tripled, from 11 million in 1968 to 30 million in 1976. Circumventing the Republican establishment, Reagan appealed to the masses and split the party.

Ford's narrow victory over Reagan crippled the party going into the fall campaign. Polls estimated that the Democratic nominee Jimmy Carter enjoyed a lead of 27 to 34 points over his Republican rival. "In order to win, we must persuade over 15 percent (or about 10 million people) to change their opinions," Ford's strategist Stuart Spencer estimated. Spencer then listed all the factors that made the task appear even more daunting: Democrats enjoyed a registration advantage of almost 2-to-1; the post-Watergate reforms limited campaign spending; and voters were not about to be bought off by major government giveaways in the wake of what Spencer delicately called "the broken promises of 1972." To top it off, Ford was not effective on the stump.

In the end, Ford's most effective campaign tactic was a major television time-buying spree in late October. With the slickness associated with more mechanical Fords, the Republican advertising men bathed the president in a pool of American patriotism. "I'm feeling good about America, I'm feeling good about me," Ford's commercials sang. The commercials praised Ford's "sensitivity," his "trustworthiness," his role as a "family man." Ford closed the huge popularity gap with Carter, but still fell short. Miraculously, the easy victory Democrats expected was decided by only 1.7 million popular votes and 57 electoral votes.

The attempts that Ford and Carter made to woo the center contributed to the feeling that party labels were meaningless. "Issues did not dominate this campaign," Ford's chief of staff, Richard Cheney, admitted. "Now, people can blame television for that, but we're no more virtuous than they are in that sense. We played it that way."

THE REAGAN REVOLUTION

Throughout the Carter presidency, Ronald Reagan marshaled his forces. Reagan's Goldwater-conservatism-with-a-smile united disparate constituencies: Protestant evangelicals, blue-collar Catholics, southerners, neoconservative intellectuals alienated by the legacy of the 1960s, corporate leaders, homeowners, and residents of the Sunbelt fed up with high taxes and burdensome regulations. Carter's dour style, his warnings of American decline, the corrosive effects of double-digit inflation, and his impotence during the Iranian hostage crisis made it easier to peddle Reagan's upbeat and muscular message promising a stronger, prouder, freer, and richer America.

Reagan's successful push for the nomination shocked many liberal Republicans, who assumed that Goldwater conservatism was a dead letter. Reagan did not have the long-standing ties to Wall Street that often moderated right-wingers. Even Richard Nixon had moved toward the center before he became president. Liberal Republicans found an unlikely champion in a midwestern evangelical conservative, John Anderson. A ten-term but little-known congressman from Illinois, Anderson wooed liberals, the eastern establishment, and the media by addressing issues forthrightly and positioning himself to Reagan's left. While his Republican rivals pandered to the gun lobby in New Hampshire, Anderson declared for gun control. While all the other candidates flipped pancakes, drove tractor trailers, and kissed babies, Anderson spoke about issues. By April, discouraged by Reagan's lock on the Republican Party yet encouraged by his enthusiastic followers, Anderson abandoned his party. He established the National Unity Campaign, eventually releasing a 350-page platform and attracting as many as 15% of the respondents in public opinion polls. By Election Day, most voters returned to the conventional two-party choices. Anderson received less than 7% of the vote and no electoral votes. In New York, an obscure county executive from suburban Nassau County, Alphonse D'Amato, beat Jacob Javits, one of the greatest liberal Republican senators of the postwar era. D'Amato's victory sounded the death knell for liberal Republicanism in its stronghold.

Reagan's campaign against Carter benefited from the groundwork of the Republican National Committee chairman, Bill Brock. Much like Will Hays had done in 1918, Brock, in 1977, modernized the party to avoid another defeat. He instituted a direct-mail program that raised over $42 million on the eve of the campaign. He spent that money producing commercials critical of Carter and Democratic House Speaker "Tip" O'Neill, and building the party up on the local level. More than 10,000 Republicans attended seminars sponsored by the local elections division. Brock proved that political parties had an important function in the age of independent candidates. In fact, national party structures proved more elaborate than ever before in an age of supposedly waning influence. Parties offered an institutional apparatus that could support the nominee, even as he came in with his own campaign staff and his own political identity. The contrast between Reagan's and Anderson's general election campaigns demonstrated that parties were now the prizes a nominee won. They were essential in establishing credibility and reaching millions of voters in a few months.

Brock also tried to trigger some intellectual ferment. Despite the obvious cultural and ideological differences between most Republicans and Democrats, critics pointed to their broad-based natures and their pragmatic approaches as proof that they stood for nothing. Brock sponsored a quarterly journal, *Commonsense*, to facilitate internal party debate, and a less reflective, hard-hitting, monthly tabloid, *First Monday*, to differentiate the Republicans from the Democrats.

The tumult of the 1960s and 1970s made many voters more passionate about certain issues, and most candidates responded. Republicans and Democrats disagreed about the role of government in the economy, solutions to social issues, the management of the Cold War. They released reams of position papers on issues ranging from abortion and air pollution to Zimbabwe and Zaire. With the explosion of national news coverage, reporters generated more stories about issues, even if the overall percentage of substantive coverage decreased. And while three-quarters of Americans surveyed believed that candidates "mostly just say . . . what they need to say in order to get elected," studies showed that twentieth-century presidents stuck to approximately three-fourths of the issue positions they took while campaigning.

On election eve 1980, as the nation's secular high priest, Walter Cronkite, recited the president-elect's résumé, many were struck by how unlikely it was that a former sportscaster, Las Vegas pitchman, and "B" movie star would fill George Washington's chair. Yet Reagan had campaigned longer and harder than had most candidates in the modern era. He was no Jimmy Carter rising from the ashes of Watergate, or even a Gerald Ford emerging from congressional obscurity. Reagan the politician had been in the public eye for almost two decades. He left a substantial paper trail of speeches, radio talks, and policy decisions. Moreover, he was the most ideological Republican nominee since Barry Goldwater. He had sharp positions on every major issue facing the American people—defense, abortion, the economy. One could accuse him of being simplistic; one could not accuse him of being vague or uncontroversial.

At the same time, Reagan was aided by a corps of professional campaigners such as Stuart Spencer and Roger Ailes, who had been involved in Republican presidential campaigns since 1960. They, along with Michael Deaver and other Reagan aides, provided a professional veneer to the campaign and insulated the candidate as much as possible. Reagan himself was "telegenic" and used to taking direction. The result was an image that belied the conservative warhorse he was. Reagan's paradox was the paradox of modern politics. He was, at the same time, the most ideological and the most evanescent candidate of the modern era. Without the conservative grounding, he would have floated away. Without the image making, he would have sunk under the weight of his rhetoric. Reagan and his men would exploit this paradox over the next eight years.

The electoral coalition that swept Reagan into office seemed to herald another realignment. Fewer people would claim in the 1980s and 1990s that there was no difference between Republicans and Democrats, arresting the "dealignment" experts had predicted. For the first time since 1954, Republicans had a majority in at least one house of Congress, the Senate. White mainline and white evangelical Protestants voted 2 to 1 in favor of Reagan over Carter. Catholics went 5 to 4 for Reagan; while blacks, Jews, and Hispanics remained with the Democratic Party. Although in the 1960s one campaign aide had noticed a "hormone gap," whereby many women swooned and were more likely than men to support the handsome Hollywood actor, by 1980 Ronald Reagan worried about a "gender gap," whereby many women disliked his policies on national defense, abortion, and feminism and thus were less likely to support him. On Election Day, 54% of all male voters chose Reagan, but only 46% of women chose him, the largest difference between the sexes since Gallup had begun collecting such data in 1952. Geographically, the West and South were solidly Republican. "Reagan Democrats," Catholic and working-class members of the New Deal coalition who soured on the high taxes and big government of the Great Society, gave Republicans a strength in the Midwest and Northeast they had lacked for decades.

In Congress, Reagan resurrected the "conservative coalition" of Republicans and southern Democrats to pass his first-term program. Some of these "boll-weevil" Democrats eventually joined the Republican Party, including Phil Gramm of Texas, whose Gramm–Rudman–Hollings Act of 1985 demonstrated congressional support for the idea of a balanced budget. Ronald Reagan's successful first term revolution-

Reagan in a Lighter Moment. *Source:* United Press International.

ized Americans' rhetoric about government. Reagan saw government as the problem, rather than view it as the obvious solution to social problems. He inspired new generations of Republican voters and politicians with his odes to small government and traditional American values. But, like Eisenhower, Nixon, and Ford, Ronald Reagan could not resist distributing government largesse. The trillion-dollar budget deficit that emerged under the Reagan administration was not only because of his military buildup and his support for middle-class entitlements. Every year, administration aides assembled a document called the "Reagan Record" that listed the new programs the Reaganites had created, including a National Commission on Excellence in Education in the first term, and a new Superfund program in the second term authorizing $8.5 billion over five years "for the cleanup of abandoned hazardous waste sites." At best, the Reagan administration could boast about curbing the "average annual rate of growth" in domestic spending from an average of 6.6% per year from 1960 to 1980, to "slightly more than 2 percent" from 1981 to 1986.

Even on social issues Reagan's record did not quite match his rhetoric. Reagan was the hero of the Religious Right. These evangelical Protestants and an-

tiabortion Catholics decried the "secular humanism" of society in general and blasted the Supreme Court's approval of abortion and disapproval of school prayer. Recognizing that these right-wingers would never abandon him for the Democratic Party, President Reagan refused to expend much political capital fighting abortion. His administration also made sure to boast about its civil rights gains and its women appointees—most notably Sandra Day O'Connor to the Supreme Court. But the terms of debate about these social issues changed. Social conservatives flocked to the Republican Party, demonstrating disproportionate influence in the party primaries and local elections. And even though Reagan enraged conservatives by failing to place Robert Bork on the Supreme Court, in the long run, his three Supreme Court appointees and dozens of lower court appointees changed the direction of American jurisprudence.

While delivering the goods to businessmen, farmers, and middle-class Americans, Reagan played Franklin D. Roosevelt to Carter's Hoover, arguing, in a sense, that there was no cause for malaise but malaise itself. Buoyed by an economic upturn, Reagan brought "pride back to America." In the White House, he and his aides applied many of the techniques they had honed on the campaign trail. News was managed, massaged, and in the *au courant* phrase, "spun." Every morning, at 8:15 A.M., Reagan's deputy chief of staff, Michael Deaver, and about ten others would meet in the office of Chief of Staff James A. Baker III to plan out the day's news coverage. They wanted one major story a day, dramatically illustrated. Deaver and his men understood what television producers needed for a good story. The "visual is as critical as what we're saying," Deaver preached, acknowledging that "100 million people across this country get all of their news from network television."

In the deft hands of the Reagan handlers, the invasion of the tiny island of Grenada became a national triumph, even a national vindication. Reagan's "Teflon," his image as the president of military might, fiscal restraint, and law and order, no matter what happened under his watch, stemmed from his and his party's fortunate positioning on the political spectrum. The Republicans in the Reagan era outflanked the Democrats. Even if crime soared while Reagan was president, Republicans took a tougher stance on crime than did Democrats. Even if the budget mushroomed while Reagan was president, Republicans always suggested budget cuts, which Democrats instinctively opposed. Even if the United States suffered humiliations in the Middle East with the bombing of Marine headquarters in Lebanon and the Iran–contra hostage farce, Republicans always sounded more militant and more patriotic than Democrats. The rhetoric appealed to the American mainstream, even as the gap between the Reagan reality and Republican rhetoric increased Americans' cynicism.

REAGAN'S REELECTION CAMPAIGN

Reagan's 1984 campaign against Walter Mondale illustrated the president's political genius—and good fortune. As with Carter and Reagan in 1980, and with McGovern and Nixon in 1972, Mondale and Reagan offered the American people a stark choice. Mondale was still very much a New Deal Democrat, trusting the federal government as an instrument of justice. He favored arms control, abortion, and higher taxes to reduce the gargantuan federal deficit. Reagan, in contrast, was a Goldwater Republican, committed to a smaller government, a large defense buildup, curbs on abortion, and spending cuts rather than tax increases. The two candidates' political strategies reflected their differing philosophies. Mondale took his campaign of issues to the New Deal coalition in what was now called the "Rust Belt"; Reagan relied on television and

carefully crafted appearances to fashion his new coalition anchored in the Sunbelt stretching from California to Florida.

"Hawks" in the Reagan camp wanted a "bold campaign," emphasizing these differences and pushing for a Republican Congress to revitalize the right-wing agenda on social issues, economic reform, and a strong defense. This stance would allow Reagan to continue being Ronald Reagan, conservative, and could result in a mandate to complete the Reagan "revolution." It would also prepare the American people for some hard choices they might have to make.

Yet Reagan preferred playing to the American mainstream. He listened to the "patriots" who suggested the campaign remain, as the White House special assistant Richard Darman put it, "relatively nonspecific programmatically, . . . more abstract." This approach stressed patriotism not conservatism, themes not policies. In an interview with *Newsweek*, Reagan endorsed this approach by recalling his push for welfare reform during his second term as governor of California. "I never mentioned them in the campaign for reelection," he said, explaining that he "didn't want to politicize it. And immediately after the reelection we went to work on them and we achieved them." Reagan would, therefore, ignore "what's-his-name," try to avoid the press, and wrap himself in the flag. Such phrases as "the opportunity society," "a positive vision of our citizens and our country," and "freedom's next step" abounded. This red-white-and-blue strategy comported with the pollster Robert Teeter's "one-sentence strategy that if there was a good economic recovery under way and no American troops anywhere and we were at peace, Ronald Reagan would be reelected."

As a result, Reagan's right-wing rhetoric was absent from his campaign commercials. Some ads featured stirring scenes of the president with World War II veterans at Normandy, the president greeting foreign dignitaries, the president being feted abroad. Others interspersed stirring patriotic music and breathtaking views of the American landscape with tributes to Reagan from ordinary Joes—and Janes. To rebut Mondale's claim that the president would attack Social Security, the Republicans featured pictures of happy grandmothers and grandfathers; to disprove the charges of racism and sexism, blacks, Asians, and women were featured in the testimonials. The commercials, which had Mondale workers in tears when they previewed them, had the texture of advertisements for all-American companies like Coca-Cola or McDonald's, rather than for a president. This approach, however, once again proved to conservatives like Office of Management and Budget Director David

Stockman that Reagan "was a consensus politician not an ideologue."

The 1984 election landslide marked an impressive personal victory for Ronald Reagan. He had entered the White House with barely half of the popular vote and the highest negative ratings recorded by pollsters since they had begun asking such questions three decades before. Four years later, he received a higher percentage of the popular vote than Dwight Eisenhower had, nearly 59%, and more electoral votes, 525, than anyone ever had. Even though he would lose the Republican Senate in 1986 and failed to wrest the House of Representatives from the Democrats, he revitalized the Republican Party. Republicans now had a vigorous party apparatus, and a positive message, something they had been seeking ever since Franklin D. Roosevelt's New Deal.

GEORGE BUSH AND THE REPUBLICAN IDENTITY CRISIS

Ronald Reagan was an ideologue parading as a pragmatist. By wooing the American center, he made the Reagan revolution more rhetorical than real. He ended up charting a course that he could not follow. Reagan's successor, George Bush, was a pragmatist parading as an ideologue. Representatives of different aspects of Reagan Republicanism had vied to succeed the president in 1988. The evangelical broadcaster Pat Robertson represented the Religious Right, whose crusades helped transform the courts from liberal path-breakers to conservative bastions. A former quarterback and congressman, Jack Kemp, represented the conservative intellectuals, whose commitment to "supply-side" economics trumped four decades of "Keynesian" deficit spending. Kansas Senator Bob Dole represented the farmers and small-town citizens of the Midwest, whose dislike for government did not extend to defense spending, agricultural subsidies, Social Security, or Medicare. The eventual winner, Vice President Bush, represented the eastern businessmen who mastered the ways of Washington and the western rebels who distrusted denizens of the nation's capital.

Bush's career, which took him from Andover and Yale to the Texas oil fields, reflected the awkward marriage within the Republican Party between Wall Street and Main Street, between the business establishment and Middle America. Bush's jerky body language and his goofy syntax, his professed penchant for pork rinds while using "summer" as a verb, illustrated that, like his party, he was unsettled at the core of his being. Bush had risen through the ranks by serving patrons

like Richard Nixon and Ronald Reagan. He seized Reagan's mantle by parroting the hard line on abortion, taxes, and national defense. His servility to Reagan revealed how thoroughly the president had conquered all elements of his party.

Bush lacked the president's popularity and his charisma. Facing a 17-point deficit going into his 1988 campaign against Michael Dukakis, Bush lashed out. He declared Dukakis and the liberals "out of the mainstream," exploiting the continuing anxiety about the revolution in morals triggered by the 1960s. George Bush embraced what he called "the Norman Rockwell vision of America—the vision of kids and dogs and apple pie and flags on parade."

WILLIE HORTON AND THE SOLID SOUTH

The Republicans devastated the Democrats by attacking Dukakis's support for a prison furlough program that enabled a convicted murderer, Willie Horton, to rape a woman and terrorize her fiancee. Beginning in June, Bush began mentioning Horton in his speeches. In September, the National Security Political Action Committee broadcast an advertisement juxtaposing photos of a swarthy Dukakis with Willie Horton's mug shot and attacking the furlough program. The commercial was replayed on news shows, giving the Republicans free airtime. Barbara Bush would complain that even though it was "a pro-George independent committee—not our campaign" that "used the image of a sinister-looking Willie Horton, who was black . . . we got blamed for dirty politics and racism." The independent ad was so effective that when the Republicans broadcast an ad attacking Dukakis's "revolving door" approach to crime, they did not need to mention Willie Horton's name.

Democrats charged that "Willie Horton" was simply the latest in a series of racist code words the GOP had used to court southerners and encourage the white backlash against civil rights. "It's a wonderful mix of liberalism and a big black rapist," one Republican would confess. Nixon's cry for "law and order," Reagan's attack on "welfare queens," Democrats claimed, lured white southerners into the party of Lincoln and made it clear that blacks did not belong. The reversal was stunning: 86% of blacks now voted for the once-reviled Democratic Party. The South was as solidly Republican as it once had been Democratic. Two-thirds of white southerners now voted for the Republicans. Bush would win all the southern states, as Nixon had in 1972 and Reagan had in 1980 and

1984. Some Republicans acknowledged that their party had benefited from the switch, although most Republicans resented the charge of racism and pointed to the bipartisan support for school busing, affirmative action, and other civil rights measures through the 1990s.

In defining their party as the opponent of big government, Republicans diverged from what had become the civil rights agenda. Before the 1960s, when governments in the South oppressed blacks and the national government ignored their plight, the Republican desire to attract black votes coincided with the Republicans' hostility toward the southern regimes. But as the civil rights movement came to define the fight against racism as a responsibility of the federal government, and Democrats took the lead in the fight, African Americans and Republicans were bound to part ways. After signing the Civil Rights Act of 1964, Lyndon Johnson sighed, "I think we just delivered the South to the Republican Party for a long time to come."

Democrats also attacked the Willie Horton ad as proof that the Republicans preferred mudslinging to debating, images to issues. The Republicans usually had more money than Democrats, and with closer ties to the business community, Republicans had taken the lead in injecting innovative marketing techniques into politics. But the Democrats' lament lacked sincerity, as they struggled to catch up and outdo the Republicans. Only the most committed of partisans really believed that one party was more virtuous or less willing to pander than the other.

Bush defeated Dukakis with a smaller cushion than Reagan enjoyed of 53.4% of the popular vote. He did, however, win 426 electoral votes, benefiting from the Republicans' virtual lock on the South and the West. Bush recognized attacks on the "Willie Horton" campaign as assaults on his mandate. He defended his legitimacy by casting the discussions as attacks on the American people and the democratic process. The president trusted the "ability of the American people to judge candidates on the issues and not, as many cynics claim, on the basis of imagery." Eager to emphasize that he, not his handlers, won the election, he insisted that campaigns "are ultimately about ideas and leadership. . . . No consultant can make up for a candidate who is deficient in these vital areas."

Asserting himself after eight years as Reagan's vice president, Bush emerged as a pragmatist. Within months, his masquerade as a Reaganaut would appear as unconvincing as his masquerade as a Texan. The new president seemed most concerned with injecting old-fashioned values of congeniality, honesty, modesty, stability, loyalty, and dignity into modern government. Bush appointees, disappointed Reaganauts muttered, "don't have agendas. They have mortgages. They want jobs."

Bush soon discovered that distancing himself from Reagan pleased the press but alienated conservative supporters. Like an overambitious son blindly seizing the reins of a family business, George Bush did away with some of the most successful elements of Reaganism simply to make his mark. Gone were the rhetorical appeals, the broad vision, the fundamental principles. Lacking a clear policy agenda, anxious for public approval and positive press stories, Bush would spend much of his presidency buffeted between conservative ideologues on his right and media critics on his left. Trying to please both without Ronald Reagan's resolute bottom line, George Bush zigzagged, conveying the impression of an aimless leader. The result was chaos within the White House and a blurred image outside.

The president was resolute, however, in foreign policy. George Bush thrived during the Persian Gulf crisis of 1990–1991. During these difficult months, Bush forded the gap between the Yale campus and the Texas oil fields, blending Wall Street's needs for a steady oil flow with Main Street's patriotism. Bush viewed the Gulf War as America's opportunity to exorcise the "Vietnam syndrome" and defined the Republican Party as the party of aggressive interventionism, not isolationism.

During the 1992 New Hampshire primary, Reagan's former communications director Patrick Buchanan reprised his old boss's role as crusading conservative against Gerald Ford in 1976. Buchanan criticized the president for betraying the Reagan revolution. Buchanan's Reaganism-with-a-scowl was not broadly based enough to stop Bush's renomination, but it damaged the president and affirmed the power of the party's right wing. The party's 1992 convention in Houston became a pep rally for the spirit of Ronald Reagan, with a venom Reagan always knew to avoid. Pat Buchanan and others declared a "cultural . . . war" on the Democrats, warning that their nominee, Bill Clinton, lacked "moral authority" and would ruin "a nation we still call God's country."

The convention highlighted George Bush's failure to contain the nastier side of the right wing, as his mentor had done. It also raised the question of how inclusive the party should be, especially on the explosive issue of abortion. Pragmatists argued that their party was a "big tent" able to contain pro-choice and pro-life activists. They contrasted the Republican Party's tolerance with the Democrats' refusal to allow a pro-life speaker at their convention. But right-wingers fed up with Bush's dithering insisted that the party had to stand for particular principles, even if that included some "litmus tests."

Despite this clash, the 1992 Republican National Convention was pallid compared to many of its predecessors. In the age of primaries, nominations were usually decided months before the convention. Nominees created some artificial suspense by refusing to announce their running mate, although the president insisted that he would stick with his controversial vice president, Dan Quayle. Conventions functioned more as coronations, staged for the benefit of millions watching at home on television. But the three major networks had begun cutting back coverage of both major party conventions. Sitcom reruns and made-for-TV movies drew higher ratings.

Buchanan's campaign also resurrected the debate about foreign policy in the party. Buchanan was a nationalist "American Firster" who embraced isolationism as a way of placing his country's interests first. He was opposed by business-oriented free traders who yearned for open markets throughout the world, as well as more militant nationalists who took pride in America's role as the world policeman protecting national interests and democracy throughout the world.

Bush's failure to enact Reagan's mandate also triggered one of the most successful third-party crusades in the twentieth century. Billionaire Ross Perot exploited Americans' growing frustration with the two established parties and the still-untamed federal budget deficit. He set himself up as the straight-talking outsider who would apply business principles to government administration.

Democrats tried to define Bill Clinton's defeat of George Bush as a repudiation of Reaganism. But that assessment overlooked the fact that Clinton received only marginally more votes than Michael Dukakis had in 1988. Clinton won 43% of the popular vote and 370 electoral votes, while Bush won 37.5% of the popular votes, 168 electoral votes. Ross Perot, with over 19 million votes, had 18.8% of the popular vote. Bush lost because of the economic downturn, his own disinterest in domestic affairs, an incompetent campaign, and Perot's clever campaign that appealed to the "Reagan Democrats."

THE NEW REPUBLICAN CONGRESSIONAL MAJORITY

Conservative Republicans viewed Bush's defeat as a punishment for lacking principles in politics. They

vowed not to let Perot or anyone else coopt their attacks on Washington. Bush's identity crisis helped the Republican Party clarify its own identity. Saddled with a Democratic administration for the first time in 12 years, Republicans set their sights on winning a Republican Congress in 1994.

Even shortly before the midterm elections of 1994, the goal of a Republican Congress seemed quixotic. Democrats had controlled the lower house since 1955, and the upper chamber for all but six years since that time. It was easier to speculate about why Americans preferred Republican presidents and Democratic legislators than to overthrow the existing order.

In 1994 a group of young Republican congressmen rejected their defeatist leadership in the House and mounted a brilliant campaign against the entrenched Democratic Congress. They complained that the system was rigged against them, that when Republican candidates won 47% of the total vote, they won only 40% of the seats because of gerrymandered districts, and ended up with only 35% of the committee seats and 17% of the committee staff. Led by a bold, reckless, former history professor from the Atlanta suburbs, Newt Gingrich, these insurgents exploited the backlash against Congress and against President Clinton's own weakness. They nationalized the campaign, recruiting congressional candidates throughout the country to sign a ten-point Contract with America. The manifesto promised to reform Congress and to fulfill the promises Ronald Reagan had made in the 1980s of a balanced budget and a limited federal government. Gingrich respected Reagan's rhetoric more than his record, calling him "the brilliant articulator of a vision that will take a generation to sort out."

While forging a nationwide message, Gingrich and his colleagues also pumped money and expertise into state and local races. GOPAC, created in 1979, had been part of Bill Brock's attempt to modernize the Republican Party after Watergate. Gingrich used GOPAC to train a new generation of Republican politicians who could master politics in the age of the sound byte. In 1994, the efforts paid off. Republicans gained 500 seats in state legislatures, approaching a majority of seats for the first time since 1957. For the first time since 1970, Republicans won a majority of gubernatorial races, capturing the gubernatorial mansions of the states with a combined total of 70% of the population. The 52 new Republican congressmen and 8 new senators who helped conquer both houses of Congress for the first time in 40 years ignored the polls suggesting that most voters did not agree with the contract and were simply punishing the Democratic incumbents. The new congressmen—and the

Speaker—had given themselves a mandate, which they would try to fulfill.

Within weeks, Gingrich and his fabled corps of Republican freshmen had changed the terms of debate in the nation's capital. Both parties now agreed that the budget had to be tamed, that the bureaucracy had to be cut; they simply quibbled about how much and how quickly. "In modern America, compassion equals bureaucracy," Gingrich complained, repudiating the legacies of the New Deal and the Great Society. In fashioning a budget, Gingrich and his forces had to decide whether to compromise and win mainstream approval or stick to their principles and transform the country.

The budget negotiations of 1995, more than the Reagan revolution, marked the end of the New Deal era. A new Republican coalition of the South, the West, the Midwest, and parts of the Northeast seemed quite firm. Republicans appealed most to whites, males, married people, college but not postcollege graduates, Catholics, Protestants, Fundamentalists, and high-income earners, especially professionals, managers, and white-collar workers. The Democrats enjoyed more support among blacks, Hispanics, women, singles, high school graduates and high school dropouts, Jews, union members, and those making under $25,000 a year.

The Republican Party was no longer the post–New Deal opposition party hospitable to big business but unsure of its ideology. Nor was it the nineteenth-century party of big business and activist government. An instinctive distrust in government supplanted a traditional faith in government. A commitment to foster economic growth for all supplanted the modern commitment to mobilizing federal forces to help the poor. The alliance with business interests remained strong. The faith in *laisser faire* revived.

The party was positioning itself as the conservative party of traditionally liberal ideas of individualism, limited government, and free enterprise, repudiating the big-government tradition that stemmed from Abraham Lincoln and the Republican Roosevelt as well as from Lyndon Johnson and the Democratic Roosevelt. While Gingrich and his zealous freshmen demanded ideological purity in the tradition of Robert Taft, moderate successors to Thomas Dewey, such as Indiana Senator Richard Lugar, warned: "The Republican Party is in danger of marginalizing its message by resorting to extremist rhetoric." Lugar wanted the party to "unify . . . Americans for common purpose." Once again, Republicans would have to decide whether to follow Lincoln's example and appeal to the center or follow his radical critics' example and follow their consciences. In the long run, it was most

likely that the great American party tradition of pragmatism would domesticate the zealots' ideology.

Gil Troy

SEE ALSO Abraham Lincoln, Andrew Johnson, Ulysses S. Grant, Rutherford B. Hayes, James A. Garfield, Chester A. Arthur, Benjamin Harrison, William McKinley, Theodore Roosevelt, William Howard Taft, Warren G. Harding, Calvin Coolidge, Herbert Hoover, Dwight D. Eisenhower, Richard M. Nixon, Gerald R. Ford, Ronald Reagan, George Bush

BIBLIOGRAPHY

Baker, Jean H. *Affairs of Party: The Political Culture of Northern Democrats in the Mid-Nineteenth Century.* Ithaca: Cornell University Press, 1983.

————. "The Ceremonies of Politics: Nineteenth-Century Rituals of National Affirmation." In *A Master's Due: Essays in Honor of David Herbert Donald*, ed. William J. Cooper Jr., Michael F. Holt, and John McCardell, 161–178. Baton Rouge: Louisiana State University Press, 1985.

Beck, Paul Allen, and Frank J. Sorauf. *Party Politics in America.* 7th ed. New York: HarperCollins, 1982.

Benson, Lee. "Research Problems in American Political Historiography." In *Common Frontiers of the Social Sciences*, ed. Mirra Komarovsky, 113–183. Glencoe, IL: Free Press, 1957.

Black, Earl, and Merle Black. *The Vital South: How Presidents Are Elected.* Cambridge: Harvard University Press, 1992.

Blum, John Morton. *The Republican Roosevelt.* Cambridge: Harvard University Press, 1954.

————. *V Was for Victory: Politics and American Culture during World War II.* New York: Harcourt Brace Jovanovich, 1976.

Blumenthal, Sidney. *Pledging Allegiance: The Last Campaign of the Cold War.* New York: HarperCollins, 1990.

Bone, Hugh A. *Party Committees and National Politics.* Seattle: University of Washington Press, 1958.

Brinkley, Alan. *The End of Reform: New Deal Liberalism in Recession and War.* New York: Knopf, 1995.

Burnham, Walter Dean. "The Changing Shape of the American Political Universe." *American Political Science Review* 59 (March 1965): 7–28.

Chambers, William Nisbet, and Walter Dean Burnham, eds. *The American Party System: Stages of Political Development.* New York: Oxford University Press, 1967.

Chatham, Marie. "The Role of the National Party Chairman: From Hanna to Farley." Ph.D. dissertation, University of Maryland, 1953.

Cotter, Cornelius P., and Bernard C. Hennessy. *Politics without Power: The National Party Committees.* New York: Atherton Press, 1964.

Donald, David Herbert. *Lincoln.* New York: Simon and Schuster, 1995.

————. *The Politics of Reconstruction, 1863–1867.* Rev. 2d ed. Cambridge: Harvard University Press, 1965, 1984.

Downey, Matthew T. "Horace Greeley and the Politicians in the Liberal Republican Convention in 1872." *Journal of American History* 53 (March 1967): 727–750.

Foner, Eric. *Free Soil, Free Labor, Free Men: The Ideology of the Republican Party Before the Civil War.* New York: Oxford University Press, 1970.

Gienapp, William E. *The Origins of the Republican Party, 1852–1856.* New York: Oxford University Press, 1987.

Glad, Paul W. "McKinley, Bryan, and the People." In *Critical Periods of History*, ed. Robert D. Cross. Philadelphia: Lippincott, 1964.

Hertsgaard, Mark. *On Bended Knee: The Press and the Reagan Presidency.* Rev. ed. New York: Schocken Books, 1988, 1989.

Hofstadter, Richard. *The Age of Reform.* New York: Random House, 1955.

———. *The American Political Tradition and the Men Who Made It.* New York: Random House, 1948, 1973.

Jensen, Richard. "Armies, Admen and Crusaders, Types of Presidential Campaigns." *History Teacher* 2 (January 1969): 33–50.

———. *The Winning of the Midwest, Social and Political Conflict, 1888–1896.* Chicago: University of Chicago Press, 1971.

Julian, George W. *Political Recollections, 1840 to 1872.* Chicago: Jansen, McClurg, 1884.

Keller, Morton. *Affairs of State: Public Life in Late Nineteenth Century America.* Cambridge: Harvard University Press, 1977.

Kleppner, Paul. *The Cross of Culture: A Social Analysis of Midwestern Politics, 1850–1900.* New York: Free Press, 1970.

Leuchtenburg, William E. *The Perils of Prosperity, 1914–1932.* Chicago: University of Chicago Press, 1958.

"Man of the Year: Newt Gingrich." *Time*, December 25, 1995–January 1, 1996, pp. 48–83.

Mayer, George H. *The Republican Party, 1854–1964.* New York: Oxford University Press, 1964.

McCormick, Richard L. *From Realignment to Reform: Political Change in New York State, 1893–1910.* Ithaca: Cornell University Press, 1981.

———. *The Party Period and Public Policy: American Politics from the Age of Jackson to the Progressive Era.* New York: Oxford University Press, 1986.

McGerr, Michael E. *The Decline of Popular Politics: The American North, 1865–1928.* New York: Oxford University Press, 1986.

Morgan, H. Wayne. *From Hayes to McKinley: National Party Politics, 1877–1896.* Syracuse, NY: Syracuse University Press, 1969.

Nevins, Allan. *Ordeal of the Union*, vol. 2, *A House Dividing, 1852–1857.* New York: Scribner's, 1947.

Nie, Norman H., Sidney Verba, and John R. Petrocik. *The Changing American Voter.* Enlarged ed. Cambridge: Harvard University Press, 1979.

Polakoff, Keith Ian. *Political Parties in American History.* New York: Knopf, 1981.

Polsby, Nelson W., and Aaron Wildavsky. *Presidential Elections: Contemporary Strategies of American Electoral Politics.* 8th ed. New York: Free Press, 1992.

Porter, Kirk H., and Donald Bruce Johnson, eds. *National Party Platforms, 1840–1968.* 4th ed. Urbana: University of Illinois Press, 1970.

Reichley, A. James. *The Life of the Parties: A History of American Political Parties.* New York: Free Press, 1992.

Rossiter, Clinton. *Conservatism in America.* 2nd ed. Cambridge: Harvard University Press, 1982.

Safire, William. *Safire's Political Dictionary: An Enlarged Up-to-Date Edition of the New Language of Politics.* Rev. ed. New York: Ballantine Books, 1978.

Schlesinger, Arthur M., Jr., ed. *History of U.S. Political Parties.* 4 vols. New York: Chelsea House, 1973.

Smith, Richard Norton. *Thomas E. Dewey and His Times.* New York: Simon and Schuster, 1982.

Sorauf, Frank J. *Party Politics in America.* 4th ed. Boston: Little, Brown, 1980.

Sproat, John G. *The Best Men: Liberal Reformers in the Gilded Age.* New York: Oxford University Press, 1968.

Troy, Gil. *See How They Ran: The Changing Role of the Presidential Candidate.* Rev. ed. Cambridge: Harvard University Press, 1996.

Wattenberg, Ben J. *Values Matter Most.* New York: Free Press, 1995.

Wattenberg, Martin. *The Decline of American Political Parties, 1952–1980.* Cambridge: Harvard University Press, 1984.

Weiss, Nancy. *Farewell to the Party of Lincoln: Black Politics in the Age of FDR.* Princeton: Princeton University Press, 1983.

Westbrook, Robert. "Politics as Consumption: Managing the Modern American Election." In *The Culture of Consumption: Critical Essays in American History*, ed. Richard Wightman Fox and T.J. Jackson Lears, chap 5. New York: Pantheon Books, 1983.

White, Theodore. *The Making of the President, 1960.* New York: Atheneum, 1961.

Wiebe, Robert H. "The Search for Order, 1877–1920." In *The Making of America*, ed. David Herbert Donald. American Century Series. New York: Hill and Wang, 1967.

Wilson, Joan Hoff. *Herbert Hoover: Forgotten Progressive.* Boston: Little, Brown, 1975.

Republican National Convention, Chicago, 1952. *Source:* IPS/Mottar.

ISSUES AND IDEOLOGY

Abortion

Abortion is arguably the most divisive issue in modern American politics. Since the Supreme Court decided the *Roe* v. *Wade* case in 1973, some of the strongest, least compromising political forces in American history have been unleashed. The abortion issue arouses a level of intensity among activists that is seldom seen in American politics. Over the past 30 years, few other political issues have inspired widespread marches, civil disobedience, and violence. Pro-life activists block entrance to clinics performing abortions, harass women attempting to get legal abortions, and even occasionally murder doctors who perform abortions. Pro-choice activists are equally vocal if somewhat less disruptive and violent—largely because, for now, they are on the winning side. The effects of this highly visible, divisive, and inflammatory issue on the Republican Party have been noticeable, though electorally sometimes unimportant.

For over 20 years, the Republican Party has been identified with the pro-life cause, largely because of Republican support of evangelical Christians who seek to impose a particular morality, family tradition, and way of life on Americans through the political process. The abortion issue is not simply about a particular "right to privacy" as defined by the Supreme Court, although that is one of the primary arenas in which the battle has been fought. Abortion involves, at least partially, a debate about proper sexual behavior, as abortion has been regarded by some as a means by which women could avoid the consequences of sex outside marriage. Abortion is part of a larger cluster of values about sexual morality, the appropriate roles of women, and the centrality of childrearing and family life to society. The Republican Party has been consistently committed to this cluster of values—though President Reagan certainly intensified that commitment—and has therefore opposed abortion for many years.

Initially, however, the abortion issue did not fall out over strict partisan lines. The *Roe* Court was dominated by an unlikely mix of Republican-appointed, left-leaning justices whose tendencies had been to extend the sphere of protected liberties, often by direct judicial intervention. In this sense, the *Roe* decision (made by a 7-to-2 margin) was consistent with the Court's earlier decisions on other issues—abortion was found to be a matter of "privacy," a right that the Court had ruled was implied by the "penumbra" of protections found in the First, Third, Fourth, Fifth, and Ninth amendments. The Court found that despite the fact that the Constitution makes no explicit mention of a right to privacy and certainly no mention of a right to abortion, such rights are implicitly contained in the Bill of Rights. Previous precedents, also handed down by liberal and judicially active Courts, held that the Bill of Rights applied to the states as well as the federal government—a legal position that allowed the Supreme Court to strike down the Texas law at issue in *Roe*.

For over a decade after *Roe*, the Supreme Court consistently struck down attempts by the states to restrict access to legal abortions, overturning measures requiring parental consent for the abortions of minors and allowing the prospective father a veto over a woman's abortion decision. The Court also struck down a variety of state laws designed to discourage women from having abortions: exposure to mandatory, detailed descriptions of fetal development; descriptions of the risks and possible psychological traumas; and reminders about the availability of support from the father or from social service agencies. The only important exception to this slew of rulings that protected nearly unlimited access to abortions came in *Maher* v. *Roe* and *Harris* v. *McRae*, in which Congress was allowed to restrict Medicaid funding for abortions.

By 1989, the abortion issue was very much a partisan issue. Over the 16 years during which the original abortion cases were heard, the liberal majority on the Court was declining as the original justices from *Roe* retired and were replaced by antiabortion appointees. By 1989, the two dissenters in *Roe*, Rehnquist and White, were reinforced by three Reagan appointees, two of whom were avowedly antiabortion and the third of whom, Justice O'Connor, leaned toward the pro-life position. With the makeup of the Court thus, the string of rulings in support of abortion was interrupted in 1989 in the case of *Webster* v. *Reproductive Health Services*, where the Court ruled, by a 5-to-4 margin, that some state-imposed restrictions on abortion are constitutionally permissible. The issue in *Webster* was a preamble to a Missouri law that declared that human life begins at the moment of conception. *Webster* did not overturn *Roe*—though Republican-appointed Justice Antonin Scalia urged the Court to do so—but it did invite state legislatures to write restrictive abortion laws that might pass constitutional muster.

By the time of the *Webster* ruling, the two sides of the abortion issue were almost wholly identifiable by party affiliation. While the Court itself had only two Democratic appointees—one of whom, Justice White, not only voted with the majority in *Webster* but had been an opponent of the "right to abortion" since *Roe*—support for and against the "right to abortion" in the Congress and the presidency had increasingly fallen out over party lines, and by 1989, this identification was almost absolute. Of the 23 senators who signed the antiabortion *amici* briefs sent to the Supreme Court, only one was a Democrat, and of the 25 senators who signed a pro-choice brief sent in 1989, only three were Republican.

Presidential politics, however, had much earlier diverged along the lines drawn by the abortion issue. Though Nixon campaigned for reelection in 1972 as an antiabortion candidate, the issue had not yet achieved national attention, despite the efforts of pro-choice groups and liberal women's organizations. The pro-life plank in the Republican platform of those years was a relatively unimportant one, and Nixon's major stance on the abortion issue came before *Roe*, when he reversed a federal regulation making abortions more available in hospitals on military bases. His order that the policy on abortions in these hospitals should conform to the laws of the states where they are located did little more than avoid controversy by leaving the battle where it already was—in the state legislatures. When the battle over abortion was made a national political issue in 1973 with the *Roe* ruling, Nixon was unable to assert any leadership, for he was in the middle of the political troubles with Watergate that would eventually drive him from the White House.

Gerald Ford, Nixon's successor, was plagued with other political problems, particularly as he faced the 1976 election without a previous electoral mandate and with the stain of his unconditional pardon of Nixon, and he did not directly face the abortion issue despite the opposition that had been sparked by the *Roe* decision. When he had the opportunity to appoint a justice to the Supreme Court, he chose the moderate John Paul Stevens, who would later side with the pro-choice justices, instead of either a woman or a hardline conservative like Robert Bork. Ford cautiously opposed *Roe*, saying that the Court had "gone too far," declaring that the states should have the power to decide, but he opposed any constitutional amendment that would limit or overturn *Roe*. Ford was criticized by both sides of the abortion debate for his fence-straddling (his wife, Betty, however, publicly supported the right to abortion).

Ronald Reagan was the major figure in the effort to get the Republican Party to adopt a strong antiabortion position. The 1980 Republican platform supported a constitutional amendment and other congressional legislation aimed at overturning *Roe*. More important, Reagan's Department of Justice scrutinized potential appointees to the federal bench, screening out those deemed potentially supportive of pro-choice positions. The 1984 Republican platform applauded "President Reagan's fine record of judicial appointments" and reaffirmed "support for the appointment of judges at all levels of the judiciary who respect traditional family values and the sanctity of innocent human life." Reagan also sought to curtail abortion through restrictive regulations that would only be able to be challenged in federal courts packed with Reagan judges. He also made executive branch appointments in line with his antiabortion policy. Surgeon General C. Everett Koop made public attacks not only against abortion but also against the use of contraceptives. When he left office in 1989, he announced that he was withholding from publication a long-awaited medical report that had concluded that there was little evidence that abortion causes women significant physical or psychological harm. Reagan's secretary of health and human services was also an outspoken supporter of the antiabortion movement, lobbying Congress to ban funding for abortions and counseling on abortion and at the same time pushing for funding of religious organizations.

Reagan unabashedly erased the distinction between public and private morality, giving presidential legitimacy to the antiabortion movement's moral views and pressing for the legal enforcement of these views. Further, he infused the abortion debate with the inflammatory rhetoric of "traditional family values," "parents' obligation and right to guide their minor children," and the "fundamental right of the unborn child." He also succeeded in changing the ideological nature of the Supreme Court in the direction that led to *Webster*. Reagan, more than any other single figure, was responsible for the polarization of the abortion issue in the 1980s.

Reagan's successor, George Bush, underwent a political transformation during his eight years in the Reagan administration. In addition to converting to what he had earlier called "voodoo economics," Bush also changed his stance on abortion. When running against Reagan for the Republican presidential nomination in 1980, Bush had opposed a constitutional amendment banning abortion, but running in 1988, he called for the "criminalization of abortion," which would provide penalties for doctors performing abortions, as in the days before *Roe*. Bush also continued to give presidential support, legitimacy, and prestige to the antiabortion movement. Speaking to the March for Life rally in 1989, Bush called for the overturning of *Roe* by constitutional amendment and promised that "the president hears you now and stands with you in a cause that must be won." In 1990 Bush vetoed appropriations bills for funding abortions for poor women in the District of Columbia who had been made pregnant by rape or incest. Bush also retained Reagan's solicitor general, Charles Fried, who successfully presented the administration's position on abortion in *Webster*.

In 1992, three groups of Republican officials—the National Republican Coalition for Choice, Pro-Choice America, and Republicans for Choice—were organized to combat the party's antiabortion stance. Some Republican governors urged the party to ease its antiabortion line, and the Young Republican National Federation voted to ask the party to remove the antiabortion plank from the 1992 platform. The pro-choice elements in the party were strong enough that Massachusetts Governor William Weld was allowed to address the convention in support of women's right to choose abortion. And, in a television interview, the first lady, Barbara Bush, expressed her disapproval of her party's strong antiabortion position; abortion, she said, was a private matter that had no place in the platform. Although the efforts of these Republican groups failed to alter the party's position on abortion, they drew attention to the fact that one could be a Republican without being against abortion, and that one's position on the abortion debate did not necessarily line up with one's party affiliation.

Since 1973, the Republican Party has come to hold a more and more uncompromising antiabortion stance. Since 1984, the Republican platform has affirmed that

unborn children have a "fundamental right to life," and the presidential campaigns of Reagan and Bush emphasized an unbending commitment to the antiabortion position. Despite the fact that for nearly 20 years the Republican Party has been identified with the pro-life cause, voters for Republican presidential candidates are not overwhelmingly pro-life, and many Republican congressmen, governors, and state legislators have won office with pro-choice positions. And recently, even with the apparent turnaround in the Supreme Court, the Republican Party has become concerned about the effect of its strong antiabortion position on electoral success.

The 1994 election that put the Republicans back in power on Capitol Hill also brought big gains for the antiabortion movement—at least 35 seats in the House and 5 in the Senate. They can now claim a majority in each house on many abortion-related questions. And at least five of the most ardent of the newly elected abortion foes are women, blurring the battle lines of gender for the first time. But the antiabortion forces are picking their shots carefully, and rather than try to overturn *Roe* entirely, they are focusing on more narrow questions, such as federal funding of clinics that offer abortion counseling, the legality of abortion in military hospitals, and various restrictions on particular abortion procedures. The Republican Congress, aware of past abortion battles both on Capitol Hill and in the nation, is taking a cautious approach to change. Ralph Reed, executive director of the Christian Coalition, whose Contract with the American Family is the blueprint for much of the legislation, said, "We don't want to overplay our hand with a pro-life Congress the way the pro-abortion people overplayed their hand."

The Republican Congress also faces other difficulties with the abortion issue. The party's budget cutting has been coming into conflict with the antiabortion stance. In 1995, Republicans were split over the proposal to deny welfare mothers benefits for any additional children born after benefits had begun; some pro-life Republicans opposed this measure because they said it would encourage abortions among welfare mothers. This conflict is central to the new Republican coalition between traditional business-sector supporters who are interested in cutting the budget and the Christian Right, which has been an increasingly important element in Republican electoral success and which opposes legal abortion.

Despite these problems, turnarounds, and oppositions, Reagan's legacy in the abortion issue will continue to be strongly felt as the Rehnquist Court follows its decision in *Webster* and reviews, in a manner increasingly hostile to *Roe*, the state laws that are being passed in the wake of *Webster*'s partial reversal of the Court's rulings on abortion. Republican control of the Senate can also make it difficult for Democratic presidents' judicial appointments. The Reagan revolution, in combination with Rehnquist's control of the Supreme Court and Republican control of Congress, is succeeding in its attempt to roll back the gains for abortion rights that have been made since 1973.

Jessamyn West

SEE ALSO Women

BIBLIOGRAPHY

Cook, Elizabeth Adell, Ted G. Jelen, and Clyde Wilcox. *Between Two Absolutes: Public Opinion and the Politics of Abortion.* Boulder, CO: Westview Press, 1992.

Craig, Barbara Hinkson, and David M. O'Brien. *Abortion and American Politics.* Chatham, NJ: Chatham House, 1993.

Tribe, Laurence H. *Abortion: The Clash of Absolutes.* New York: Norton, 1990.

Affirmative Action

Affirmative action programs were developed by federal agencies given the authority to make rules and regulations under the Civil Rights Act of 1964 for desegregating activities receiving federal funding. President Lyndon Johnson issued an executive order in 1965 that promoted affirmative action for employment and promotion in the federal government, and for businesses contracting to do work for the federal government. In 1972 the U.S. Office of Education issued guidelines that contained "goals" for university admission and hiring policies for both African Americans and women.

Progress in affirmative action is generally measured in terms of the number of minorities or women admitted to a university or employed or promoted at a company. In order to retain federal funding many companies and universities have felt pressured to show "progress." This pressure can lead to preferential treatment and challenges to the traditional methodologies that have been used for school admissions (e.g., the scholastic aptitude test, or SAT). Some minority groups have argued that these tests are not good predictors of academic success. For example, women score lower on the SAT than men, but have higher graduation rates. In addition, it is alleged that the SAT is culturally biased in favor of middle-class Anglos.

The main constitutional issue posed by affirmative action is whether these programs discriminate against whites and violate the Equal Protection Clause of the 14th Amendment. This has led to a string of decisions but unfortunately not a clear-cut answer.

In *Regents of the University of California* v. *Bakke* (1978) the Court struck down a special admissions program at a state medical school on the basis that it excluded a white applicant on the basis of his race. Bakke had applied to the University of California–Davis medical school twice and had been rejected both times. African American applicants with significantly lower grade-point averages and medical aptitude text scores had been admitted through a special admissions program that reserved 16 places in the class of 100 for minority applicants. The University of California argued that its use of race was "benign." That is, it was designed to help minorities, not hurt them. The special admissions program was designed to counter the effects of past discrimination and increase the number of underrepresented minorities in the medical school. In addition, the university argued that it would obtain those benefits that are derived from having an ethnically diverse student body.

The Supreme Court held that the objectives of the university were legitimate but that maintaining a *separate* admissions program with a quota of openings that were not available to white applicants violated the Equal Protection Clause. The mandate to provide equal protection could not mean one thing to one individual and something else when applied to another individual. As a consequence, the Court ordered that Bakke be admitted to the medical school and that the special admissions program be eliminated. It also recommended that the university examine the Harvard program that considers an applicant's ethnicity a "plus" but does not have a numerical quota that excludes persons from competing for all positions.

This line of thinking was the guiding force in determining a more recent case in U.S. 4th Circuit Court of Appeals. The court held in *Podberesky* v. *Kirvin* (1994) that the University of Maryland may *not* fund a scholarship program that awards aid only to African American students. The decision is binding only on the states in the 4th District (i.e., Maryland, North and South Carolina, Virginia, and West Virginia), and it is probable that the case will be appealed to the Supreme Court. Nevertheless, it may be indicative that the courts continue to look with disfavor on programs that entirely exclude a racial group or create a quota.

Some cases have upheld the practice of affirmative action. In *United Steelworkers of America* v. *Weber* (1979) the Supreme Court approved of a plan developed by the Kaiser Aluminum Corporation and a union that reserved 50% of higher-paying jobs for minorities. Only 2 percent of skilled technical jobs were held by African Americans, but they comprised 39% of the workforce. Weber was excluded from a training program that would have led to a higher-paying job, but African American employees with less seniority and fewer qualifications were accepted. Weber could not claim that his rights to equal protection under the 14th Amendment had been abridged because the 14th Amendment applies only to the "state." Instead, he argued that the affirmative action program violated provisions of the 1964 Civil Rights Law that forbade discrimination on the basis of race.

The Supreme Court ruled that the 1964 Civil Rights Act did not prohibit affirmative action plans and that it would be "ironic" if private efforts to deal with the vestiges of past discrimination were to be found impermissible based on a piece of legislation passed with the goal of assisting the minority groups that had experienced the past discrimination.

The Supreme Court has continued to express concern about whites who are adversely affected by affirmative action programs. In *Firefighters Local Union* v. *Stotts* (1984) the Court held that a city could not lay off white firefighters in favor of African American firefighters with less seniority. And in *Richmond* v. *Crosen* (1989) the Supreme Court held that a minority set-aside program that allotted 30% of all city construction contracts to minorities violated the Equal Protection Clause.

In a 1995 decision the Supreme Court cast doubt on the constitutionality of affirmative action programs that award federal contracts even for "benign" purposes. In *Adarand* v. *Pena* the Court examined a law that mandated that at least 10% of federal money spent on highway projects go to businesses owned by "disadvantaged individuals." A job in the San Juan National Forest in southern Colorado was awarded to Mountain Gravel and Construction, a firm owned by an alleged disadvantaged individual. Adarand Contractors, owned by a white man, submitted a bid for the work that was $1,700 less than the bid of Mountain Gravel, but Adarand was still not awarded the contract. The company sued, challenging the constitutionality of the set-aside program.

Justice Sandra Day O'Connor, writing for the majority, found that federal programs that classify people by race, even for ostensibly a benign purpose such as increasing opportunities for minorities, are unconstitutional unless they are subject to the most searching judicial inquiry, are "narrowly tailored," and accomplish a "compelling governmental interest." The Court stopped short of voiding federal affirmative action entirely, but it did establish a formidable obstacle with the "compelling governmental interest" standard.

Justices Scalia and Thomas would have gone further and wrote in their concurring opinions that affirmative action programs can *never* be justified. The ruling cast doubt on the validity of *Fullilove* v. *Klutznick* (1980), which had upheld a 10% federal set-aside program for minority contractors. Justice Thomas, the Court's only African American, wrote that he found "benign discrimination" every bit as noxious as "malicious prejudice."

The change in attitude of the Court is dramatic when comparing the Adarand decision with that of *Metro Broadcasting* v. *Federal Communications Commission* (FCC) just four years earlier. In the *Metro* case the Court ruled that the federal government may use "benign racial classifications" to give a preference to African Americans in awarding radio and television licenses. Because fewer than 1% of the nation's radio and television stations were owned by minorities in 1978, the FCC said that it would consider it a "plus factor" in awarding future licenses if the application was submitted from a minority.

Metro Broadcasting, a predominately white Florida firm, lost a bid for a new television station license in Orlando to a company owned by a Hispanic, and Metro sued. The Court upheld the FCC's use of "benign racial classifications" not just to remedy past discrimination but also to give African Americans and other minorities a greater share of federal benefits.

By the mid-1990s the makeup and thinking of the Court, and perhaps much of the nation, regarding affirmative action had changed. Congress had amended Title VI of the Civil Rights Act to make it clear that employers were not required to meet statistical quotas reflecting the available workforce. In addition, several Republican leaders (e.g., Phil Gramm, Bob Dole, Lamar Alexander, and Pat Buchanan) believe that affirmative action should be curtailed.

Governor Pete Wilson of California announced that California's state universities were abandoning affirmative action as a tool to guarantee the diversity of the student body and employees. Governor Wilson made his opposition to affirmative action the cornerstone in his short-lived presidential campaign. But he did highlight the issue in the minds of the electorate.

In October 1995 President Clinton announced in a major address on racial harmony at the University of Texas that he did not like affirmative action but that it was still necessary in order to remedy the lingering effects of past discrimination. The same day the president spoke at the University of Texas Louis Farrakhan lead a "million man march" in which he called for African American men to take greater control of their lives and responsibility for their families. He presented a vision of the future where civil rights organizations would free themselves from reliance on white funding sources, bureaucratic decisions, and legal opinions (e.g., those that deal with promoting the welfare of African Americans through affirmative action programs). His view was that the system has been built on the wrong idea (i.e., white supremacy) and that there is really no way that African Americans could integrate into white society, be it through affirmative action or other programs, and maintain their self-respect.

On the other hand, President Clinton presented a defense of affirmative action and governmental assistance that should be linked to greater personal responsibility among African Americans. How can the decisions and opinions of divergent views found in the courts, among African American leaders and politicians regarding affirmative action be reconciled? Perhaps they cannot. Rather than look for consistency in the law or among politicians, we may need to resign ourselves to some uncertainty about how far affirmative action programs can go. At some point they do indeed become "reverse discrimination," but that point may vary from program to program, and each program may have to be judged separately.

If the courts want to announce a clear-cut national policy, they will shortly have the opportunity. A case that is being appealed to the U.S. Supreme Court involves an affirmative action program at the University of Texas Law School. In 1992 the law school admitted 41 African Americans and 55 Mexican Americans using a separate committee to evaluate the credentials of Anglo applicants and another committee to evaluate the qualifications of minority applicants. Use of the "Texas Index" resulted in a white applicant having a 1% chance of being admitted to the law school and a Mexican American applicant a 90% chance.

Four white students who were denied admission but who had better Law School Admission Test scores than most of the minority applicants that were admitted sued. The university responded that if they had not used the "Texas Index," the number of African Americans admitted would have dropped from 41 to 9 and the number of Mexican American students in the law school would have declined from 55 to only 18. The "Texas Index" called for the use of separate admission committees and the use of a formula based on standardized test scores and grade-point averages. White and minority applicants had separate cutoff points.

The lower court ruled that Texas's use of separate admission committees and separate cutoff scores was not permissible but that the goal of achieving student population diversity and the need to rectify the lingering effects of past discrimination did warrant considering race as a factor in admissions decisions.

This decision may be threatening to similar programs at other universities. For example, the University of Wisconsin's law school admits all minority applicants thought to be able to succeed in the law school program. If there are additional seats, then Anglo applicants may compete for them. The Texas decision is being appealed, and if the Supreme Court grants it a hearing, the Court will have an opportunity to reconcile many of the ambiguities that currently surround affirmative action programs.

John S. Robey

SEE ALSO African Americans, Other Minorities

BIBLIOGRAPHY

Glazer, Nathan. *Affirmative Discrimination.* Cambridge: Harvard University Press, 1987.

Hacker, Andrew. *Two Nations.* New York: Charles Scribner, 1992.

Hero, Rodney E. *Latinos and the U.S. Political System.* Philadelphia: Temple University Press, 1992.

Sigelman, Lee, and Susan Welch. *Black Americans' View of Racial Inequality.* Cambridge, MA: Cambridge University Press, 1991.

African Americans

Perhaps no U.S. institution has been as influenced by the destiny of African Americans as the Republican Party. It started out midway through the nineteenth century as the party of racial tolerance and justice. Yet it would win three presidential elections in the 1980s with coalitions fundamentally pivoted on fear and resentment of African Americans. The ebb and flow between these two polar extremes is one of the most profound stories in U.S. political history.

The GOP was organized in 1854 to thwart what historian A.J. Reichley calls the "imperial ambitions of the southern planter class" and its chief political vehicle, the Democratic Party. The Republicans were the party of free labor, capital accumulation, and an emerging industrial capitalism. Southern slaveowners who wanted a low tariff and insisted on holding a portion of the labor force in bondage represented the very antithesis of these goals.

The new party got Abraham Lincoln elected to the presidency in 1860, followed shortly thereafter by the departure of most of the southern states from the Union and the beginning of the Civil War. Though deeply divided on whether African Americans should be should be granted full citizenship rights, the party managed to hold together well enough to win the war.

Lincoln was assassinated just before the war's conclusion. And his vice president, Andrew Johnson, took over the presidency. He was a man of intense dislikes.

He hated the planter class of his home state of Kentucky, but he despised African Americans even more.

The new president declared that African Americans had less "capacity for government than any other people" soon after he took office. Former rebel sympathizers and officials of the breakaway government were quickly restored to power in the southern states. They then passed discriminatory laws—known as the Black Codes—which left African Americans in the South free in name only.

Northern public opinion was outraged. The Republican Party went into an uproar. Even Republicans who were lukewarm toward equality between the races were outraged. It seemed as if the war had been fought in vain. Uniting behind its radical wing, which favored total equality between the races, the GOP used its control of both houses of Congress to wrestle control of the postwar South away from the president.

African American citizenship rights were codified into law by the passage of a Civil Rights Bill in the summer of 1866. This was followed by the 14th Amendment, forbidding the states from "depriving any person of life, liberty or property without due process of law," and the 15th Amendment, outlawing racial discrimination.

Led by Pennsylvania's Thaddeus Stevens in the House and Charles Sumner of Massachusetts in the Senate, and prodded by African American leaders such as Frederick Douglass outside Congress, the Republican government sent troops to the South to protect the rights of the newly freed blacks. This set the stage for what has been historically known as Reconstruction and the greatest period of African American upward mobility in the nation's history.

The newly freed African Americans provided immediate dividends for the Republicans. Republican war hero Ulysses S. Grant won the presidential election of 1868 over Democrat Horatio Seymour by 310,000 votes—3,012,833 to 2,703,249. Nearly half a million of his votes came from newly enfranchised African Americans.

Enthusiastic African Americans elected representatives to office in numbers that are still unmatched. Between 1865 and 1900, 16 African Americans were elected to Congress, and 800 served in state legislatures. Such men as Governor P.B.S. Pinchback in Louisiana, Mississippi speaker of the lower house J.R. Lynch, and Representative J.M. Langston in Virginia changed southern society. They established the first public school systems in the region. They ended the use of the whipping post, the branding iron, and other medieval forms of punishing criminals.

But the tide soon changed. With the rebellious South firmly underfoot by the early 1870s, an increasingly large number of people began to call for political reconciliation with the region. White newspapers began to hammer away at alleged corruption in the Reconstruction governments. Cries of "reverse discrimination" against whites became part of public discourse. And business owners began to argue that the incessant political conflict in the region was undermining economic development. The Radical Republicans, a minority even in their own party, were increasingly isolated by the mid-1870s.

Southern Democrats wasted little time responding to the changed circumstances. They had voting booths placed in swamps and other remote places to depress the African American turnout on Election Day. When these efforts failed, they organized vigilante groups to bar African Americans forcibly from the ballot box. Pitched battles were fought between these groups, and black militias were organized to counter them. Untold numbers of people were killed or injured. The fighting was intense. But the Democrats had greater resources and access to cannons and other heavy weapons, and they gradually prevailed.

The decisive moment came after the presidential election of 1876. National electoral machinery was brought to a halt by disputed electoral votes in South Carolina, Florida, and Louisiana. The GOP was able to get the Ohio governor, Rutherford B. Hayes, elected to the White House only by agreeing to withdraw federal troops from the South.

This tipped the balance of power in the region decisively in favor of the Democrats, who gradually restored the descendants of the pre–Civil War planter class to hegemony. By the 1890s, the black militias had been disarmed and most southern states had rewritten their constitutions, denying African Americans the right to vote and reducing them to a state of economic and social peonage. North Carolina's George White, the last Reconstruction-era African American congressman, left the House of Representatives in 1901. And the Republicans were all but shut out of the South for nearly 100 years.

Republican leaders turned first one way and then the other as they tried to respond to the Democratic transgressions in the South. The GOP won the White House again in 1880 when James A. Garfield bested Civil War hero General Winfield Scott Hancock, the Democratic standard-bearer. During his inauguration speech, Garfield announced that "under our institutions there is no middle ground for the Negro race between slavery and equal citizenship. There can be no permanent disfranchised peasantry in the United

States." But the Ohioan also tossed a bone to the white southerners working to disenfranchise African Americans by calling their arguments that blacks should be denied the right to vote because they were largely uneducated a matter of "supreme importance."

Benjamin Harrison, another Republican, won the presidency in 1888 only by accumulating more electoral votes than his Democrat opponent. He decided to remedy his devastating losses in the South by reviving Republican support for African American voting rights in the region. A bill was introduced in the House of Representatives by Henry Cabot Lodge of Massachusetts that would have allowed the federal government to overrule southern local electoral practices that denied African Americans the right to vote. The bill passed the House but got sidetracked in the Democratic-controlled Senate.

The first years of the twentieth century found African Americans beginning the first wave of a massive 60-year migration from the South to the urban areas of the North and West. But the Republican ambivalence toward their plight continued. After Republican President William McKinley was assassinated in September 1901, Theodore Roosevelt, his vice president, took over the presidency. Roosevelt is best remembered for outraging white southerners by allowing Booker T. Washington to spend a night at the White House. But, in fact, Roosevelt tried to move the GOP away from close identification with African Americans. He supported efforts to replace "blacks and tans" with an all-white southern GOP. He also took a hard line toward African American troops who had fought a bloody brawl with white civilians in Brownsville, Texas.

The Republicans won the White House in 1920 behind Warren G. Harding, who also tried to straddle the fence on the "Negro question." He told the semicentennial celebration in Birmingham, Alabama, in 1921 that he would oppose "social equality" for African Americans, but they should have equal access to the ballot box.

The large numbers of African Americans settling in the North and Midwest began to elect representatives to office under the Republican banner by the 1920s. In 1928, Chicago's Oscar De Priest became the first African American elected to Congress since George White left the body in 1901.

But African American–GOP relations took a plunge when Herbert Hoover was elected president in 1928. Hoover had campaigned among African American Republicans in the South in his efforts to win the Republican presidential nomination. Once in office, however, he purged them from important party positions in the South. "This is my golden opportunity to clean up the Republican Party in the South," he said.

But the former secretary of commerce's inability to end the Great Depression struck the fatal blow. African Americans suffered more than any other group from the economic downturn. As a result, Democratic presidential nominee Franklin Delano Roosevlt received 25% of the African American vote in northern cities in the 1932 presidential elections.

Once in office, Roosevelt's New Deal social welfare programs provided token jobs and access to public housing and welfare for African Americans struggling to make ends meet. And with this, the party of the segregationist South and the pre–Civil War planter class won most of the African American vote in the presidential elections of 1936, 1940, and 1944. Roosevelt also won most of the southern white vote.

Following in the wake of the voters, African American political leaders began to change parties. Chicago's Arthur Mitchell became the first African American elected to Congress as a Democrat in 1934.

The New Deal coalition held together until African Americans and their supporters began to push the Democrats to take stronger stands on civil rights in the late 1940s. Once rabidly pro-Democratic southern political leaders began to hedge their bets. Many of them encouraged their constituents to vote Democratic in local and statewide elections and Republican in national contests. This cost the Democrats Florida, Virginia, and a number of other southern states in the 1952 and 1956 presidential elections and opened the way for two successive terms in the White House by Republican war hero Dwight Eisenhower.

The 1960 presidential election featured Massachusetts Senator John F. Kennedy against Richard Nixon, Eisenhower's vice president. Both had undistinguished civil rights records, but Kennedy actively solicited the African American vote. The result was a drop in the Republican vote total in the African American community from 40% in 1956 to 32% and a razor-thin Kennedy win in 1960.

But as a whole, the GOP remained committed to racial equality. Even under Nixon, the party had adopted a strong civil rights platform at its national convention in 1960. When in one opinion survey pollsters asked people which party treated African Americans more fairly on job and housing issues, 22% of the respondents said the Democrats and 21% said the Republicans. But forces were already in motion to change that.

Thirty-two businessmen, lawyers, small-town newspaper publishers, oilmen, and bankers met in 1961 to work toward ridding the GOP of liberal influences. Their efforts culminated in Arizona's Senator Barry Goldwater winning the Republican nomination for president in 1964.

Goldwater was a conservative ideologue of the first rank. He was against farm subsidies, Social Security, and the Tennessee Valley Authority. And in line with this, he was deeply opposed to federal efforts to end segregation.

Goldwater lost 44 states to Kennedy's vice president, Lyndon Johnson. But Goldwater's conservative stance on civil rights struck a totally unexpected cord with white southerners. Five of the six states he won were in the Deep South: Mississippi, Alabama, South Carolina, Georgia, and Louisiana. And for the first time since Reconstruction, the GOP seemed to have found a way to compete in the region.

By 1968, the GOP had also made gains among working-class whites in other parts of the country. Many of them were fearful of the African American rebellions sweeping the nation's large urban areas in the mid-1960s. They also resented the Democratic-led antipoverty and affirmative action programs, which were seen as aiding minorities at whites' expense.

Into this breach stepped Richard Nixon as the Republican nominee for president in 1968. Preaching law and order and the maintenance of the status quo, he slipped by the Democrats' Hubert Humphrey in a close election. But Nixon's percentage of the African American vote fell from 32% in 1960 to 12% in 1964. And the party of Lincoln, which once depended on African Americans for control of national politics, now needed the fear and resentment of them to hold together a reverse coalition.

Once in office, Nixon carried out his agenda with unparalleled ferocity. Time and again in 1971 and 1972 he attacked "forced busing" and "forced integration." He scaled back spending on social programs for minorities and the poor and sanctioned a widespread campaign of electronic surveillance of African American activists and civil rights leaders.

Nixon won another term in office in 1972 when he crushed George McGovern, a liberal Democrat, by 18 million votes. But his assault on African Americans and liberals was cut short by the Watergate scandal and his resignation from office on August 9, 1974. The fallout from the scandal temporarily stalled the conservative onslaught. The Democrats were able to recapture the White House as Georgia Governor Jimmy Carter defeated Nixon's vice president, Gerald Ford, in the 1976 presidential election.

The mood of the country continued to darken as inflation eroded earnings and African Americans and whites sparred over affirmative action and federal spending on social programs. Into this mix stepped Ronald Reagan, a former film star, as the Republican nominee for president in 1980. He reunited Nixon's old coalition of frustrated lower-middle-class and working-class whites from northern urban areas with white southerners and Protestant evangelicals.

The Republican candidate sharpened the edge of white resentments by peppering his campaign speeches with anecdotes about "welfare cheats" and other abusers of government social programs. The fact that most people would see these unnamed individuals as African Americans was cleverly left unstated, in the best Goldwater–Nixon tradition.

Reagan beat Carter in 45 states and began a revolution against "big government." From 1984 to 1988, Reagan cut $100 billion from federal social programs. In 1980 alone, $1.7 billion was taken out of child nutrition programs, and 400,000 families were removed from the welfare rolls. The cuts so disproportionately affected African Americans that the African American median income fell 5.2% that year.

Reagan opposed the establishment of Dr. Martin Luther King Jr.'s birthday as a national holiday. He supported tax-exempt status for a number of colleges and universities that refused to admit African Americans and opposed the extension of the Voting Rights Act.

In 1984 Reagan was given another four years to carry out his policies after he blasted Walter Mondale, Carter's vice president, by 17 million votes. For the second straight election, the Republicans won less than 10% of the African American vote.

But Reagan was more than just a Beltway-based talking head. He was an outgrowth of a national conservative movement, many of whose core supporters were opposed to civil rights laws and government spending on social programs that were thought to aid African Americans.

Conservative Republican businessmen Howard Jarvis and Paul Gann put together Proposition 13, a grassroots movement in California in the late 1970s that resulted in a cap on property tax increases. Revenues from these levies were widely perceived as being used to aid African Americans and Hispanics. More than 17 states had passed similar measures by 1986.

David Duke's election to the Louisiana legislature in 1989 as a Republican brought national attention to the fact that the Republican Party had also become home to many white supremacists. A former member of a Ku Klux Klan chapter, Duke was the head of the National Association for the Advancement of White People. He advocated sterilizing welfare mothers and wrote about forcing Jews, Latinos, African Americans, and other minorities into segregated "ethnic homelands."

Duke was denounced by mainstream Republican leaders, but he was only narrowly defeated in a 1990 bid to unseat GOP Senator Bennett Johnson. Klan and other right-wing extremist groups have played a part in the election of a number of other Republican elected officials around the country.

George Bush, Reagan's vice president, won 40 states and defeated Democratic nominee Michael Dukakis during the 1988 presidential election. But Bush shocked African Americans by putting pictures of convicted murderer Willie Horton on his campaign literature. Horton is African American, and his victims were white. This was widely seen as being a none-too-subtle effort to pander to white fears about African American crime. Bush also initially vetoed the 1990 Civil Rights Act, which sought to protect workers against job discrimination.

Bush was defeated in the 1992 presidential election by Democratic nominee Bill Clinton, the governor of Arkansas. But two years into the new administration, the Republicans seized the national stage again when they won control of both houses of Congress in the November 1994 congressional elections.

Led by Republican House Speaker Newt Gingrich, the new GOP congressional majorities renewed the assault on government and social programs where Reagan and Bush had left off. High on their agenda was a dramatic trimming of the welfare rolls and the elimination of affirmative action.

The Congressional Black Caucus (CBC) was another target of Gingrich and his supporters. Claiming they were trying to shrink the size of the federal bureaucracy, the Republicans eliminated three House committees. But two of them—the Post Office and Civil Service and the District of Columbia committees— were dominated by CBC members. The Republicans also eliminated hundreds of committee staff jobs, many of them held by recently hired African Americans.

A 1992 study found that fewer than 1% of African American elected officials categorized themselves as Republicans. And Bush won just 11% of the African American vote in that year. But many whites see the GOP as the last bulwark against "reverse discrimination." This makes African Americans as much a part of the Republican political equation as they were in the days when they propelled Republican presidents into the White House—and they will be for the foreseeable future.

David Hatchett

SEE ALSO Affirmative Action

BIBLIOGRAPHY

Bennett, Lerone, Jr. *Before the* Mayflower: *A History of Black America*. New York: Penguin Books, 1984.

Boller, Paul F., Jr. *Presidential Campaigns*. New York: Oxford University Press, 1984.

Edsall, Thomas Byrne, with Mary D. Edsall. "Race." *Atlantic Monthly*, May 1991, pp. 53–86.

———. *Chain Reaction: The Impact of Race, Rights and Taxes on American Politics*. New York: Norton, 1992.

Hagerstrom, Jerry. *Beyond Reagan: The New Landscape of American Politics*. New York: Penguin Books, 1988.

Henry, Charles P. "Jesse Jackson and the Decline of Liberalism in Presidential Elections." *Black Scholar*, January–February 1989, pp. 2–12.

Kazin, Michael. *The Populist Persuasion: An American History*. New York: Basic Books, 1995.

Lusane, Clarence. *African Americans at the Crossroads: The Restructuring of Black Leadership and the 1992 Presidential Elections*. Boston: South End Press, 1994.

Marable, Manning. *Race, Reform and Rebellion: The Second Reconstruction in Black America, 1945–1982*. Jackson: University of Mississippi Press, 1984.

———. *Black American Politics: From the Washington Marches to Jesse Jackson*. London: Verso, 1985.

Polsby, Nelson W., and Aaron Wildavsky. *Presidential Elections: Strategies and Structures of American Politics*. Chatham, NJ: Chatham House, 1992.

Reichley, James A. *The Life of the Parties: A History of American Politics*. New York: Free Press, 1992.

Ridgeway, James. "The Posse Goes to Washington: How the Militias and Far Right Got a Foothold on Capital Hill." *Village Voice*, May 23, 1995, pp. 17–18.

———. "Divided We Stand: How Government Is Redrawing the Racial Map of America." *Village Voice*, October 24, 1995, pp. 26–27.

Tryman, Mfanya D. "Blacks and the Democrats: Dissolution of an Irreconcilable Marriage." *Black Scholar*, November–December 1986, pp. 28–33.

Arms Control

The Republican position on arms control is rooted in the experiences of war. The lessons of the period before World War II weigh heavy on many Republicans' minds. To them, the spiral model failed the critical test when Western policies of appeasement exploded after the Munich conference of 1938. Chamberlain's pronouncement "that there would be peace in our time" proved disastrous (Jervis 1976, 59). The Republican attitudes toward arms control evolve from the early years of the Cold War. Their early position can easily be summarized by the popular conservative statement: "He who wants peace, must prepare for war."

The conservative consensus on arms control for the first 20 years of the Cold War can be illustrated by the provocative yet accurate adage "better dead, than Red." Early conservatives were convinced that a strong, sophisticated military, equipped with nuclear weapons, was essential to arresting communist forces in assaults on the free world (Levine 1990, 3). Arms control was generally undesirable because the Soviets could not be trusted to honor their agreements.

Although the "better dead, than Red" language had all but disappeared by the early 1970s, rhetorically the Republican position was largely unchanged. Even in the early 1980s President Reagan would consistently refer to the Soviet Union as the "evil empire." On the other hand, substantively the Republican position had completely evolved. Thoughtful conservatives were convinced that meaningful arms-control agreements could be negotiated, but only from a "position of strength." It is ironic that the most important arms-control agreements (SALT I and START) between the Soviet Union and the United States were negotiated by Republican presidents with impeccable conservative credentials.

If the existence of the "Red menace" explains the impetus for the Republican doctrine of "peace through strength," then the Republicans' enmity for the doctrine of MAD (Mutually Assured Destruction) provides the other essential key to understanding their current arms-control policy initiatives. Republicans generally reject that the central deterrent capability of the U.S. strategic arsenal rests in its ability to annihilate enemy civilian population centers. Reagan's Defense Secretary Caspar Weinberger clearly illustrates this point: "True believers in the disproven MAD concept hold that the prime, if not only, objective of strategic nuclear forces of both the US and the Soviet Union is the ability to destroy each others cities" (Levine 1990, 145). Republicans assert that the policy of holding civilian populations hostage constitutes nuclear terrorism and is morally bankrupt.

Opposition to MAD produced the Republican drive for the Strategic Defense Initiative (SDI) and the subsequent attempt to reinterpret the 1972 anti-ballistic missile treaty to support the research, funding, and deployment of SDI. At the core of the SDI movement was the feeling that President Nixon and Secretary Kissinger had sold out by negotiating SALT I and the anti-ballistic missile (ABM) treaty. These treaties reinforced the theory of assured destruction and brought the Soviets "dangerously" close to nuclear parity with the United States.

At the time of Ronald Reagan's presidential inauguration in January 1981, Mutually Assured Destruction was a reality. The Soviet Union and the United States had equally sufficient strategic assets to guarantee the destruction of all of each other's major population centers in the event of a nuclear conflict. The United States had adopted a policy of "massive retaliation." The acceptance of MAD was simply unacceptable to conservatives. The SDI was only the theoretical option to counter the morally bankrupt concept of MAD.

Ronald Reagan promised the American people that he would build a ballistic missile defense system that would render nuclear weapons "impotent and obsolete" (Sheehan 1988, 159). Although the scientific feasibility of such a system is highly questionable, by advocating SDI, conservatives were able to undermine the consensus in favor of nuclear deterrence (Sheehan 1988, 159). Critics argued that pursuing SDI would invalidate the ABM treaty, escalate the spiral of tension with the USSR, and waste enormous resources on a fantasy they dubbed "Star Wars."

The debate over the ABM treaty and development of SDI forms the nucleus of the differences between the Republican and Democratic positions on arms control. Republicans favor a liberal interpretation of Agreed Statement D of the ABM treatment. Agreed Statement D prevents the development of "exotic weapons" for use in missile defense systems (Levine 1990, 178). Republicans, in an obvious attempt to subvert the treaty, claim that high-technology weapons, such as laser and rail guns, are not exotic. Democrats, on the other hand, contend that most of the systems funded under SDI constitute a breakout from the ABM treaty.

Although SDI is an extremely tenuous idea, the Republicans' desire to move away from the theory of assured destruction provided the foundation for wide political consensus behind the desire for negotiating substantial reductions in strategic arms. Democrats supported the START talks because they believed that arms reduction lowers the spiral of nuclear tension, and Republicans saw START as an opportunity to diffuse MAD as well as increase the effectiveness of SDI by reducing the number of warheads an ABM system would have to counter. Furthermore, conservatives believed that President Reagan, the consummate conservative, would never sell them out.

Despite differences in philosophy, the last decade has seen a broad consensus on a wide range of arms-control issues, including the Non-Proliferation Treaty, the Chemical Weapons Convention, as well as START. START II, which reduces U.S. and Soviet strategic arsenals to between 3,500 and 3,000 warheads each, was recently ratified by the U.S. Senate. The largest difference on arms control remains the deployment of ABM systems.

Although funding for SDI has been substantially reduced over the past decade, and the emphasis has been shifted from national to theater ballistic missile defense, the issue remains highly contested. The House Republicans continue to promote legislation that would require the deployment of a multiple-site national missile defense system by the year 2003 (information available on the Internet).

Although deep-seated differences over deterrence and MAD remain, the end of the Cold War has resulted in a rhetorical shift. Republicans no longer illustrate SDI as an umbrella that will protect the United States from a massive nuclear assault but as a required system that will protect American cities from the missile attack of a Third World dictator. Democrats no longer emphasize the destabilizing effects of SDI but oppose the unnecessary and exorbitant costs of the system.

The end of the Cold War leaves U.S. policymakers void of a clear strategic vision. The move from bilateral to multilateral arms agreements dramatically increases the complexity of negotiations. The domestic political situation will ultimately define the direction of new arms-control agreements. Understanding the inherent differences in the philosophies of the competing political parties is important to explaining specific congressional policy initiatives. The debates over "better dead, than Red" and "mutually assured destruction" define the essence of the modern Republican position on arms control and SDI.

Cynthia J. Levy

SEE ALSO Defense

BIBLIOGRAPHY

Jervis, Robert. *Perceptions and Misperceptions in International Politics.* Princeton: Princeton University Press, 1976.
Levine, Robert A. *Still the Arms Debate.* Brookfield, VT: Dartmouth, 1990.
Sheehan, Michael. *Arms Control.* New York: Basil Blackwell, 1988.

Big Government

Ruminating on the "declining American dream" in 1995, a Michigan Republican congressman, Peter Hoekstra, declared that "the bottom line is this: government has grown too big for too long and attempts to do too much." Slashing the swollen federal government, he concluded, alone could "return America to its historic greatness" (Hoekstra 1995).

Today's American voter routinely associates the Republican Party with such a position, influenced most notably by Ronald Reagan. In fact, Republican animus toward big government has waxed and waned over the century and a half since the party's founding. Frequently the story has been one of rhetorical opposition, although through such GOP-led periods as Reconstruction, Theodore Roosevelt's turn-of-the-century reign, the Eisenhower 1950s, and Nixon's presidency, the Leviathan state steadily grew. Long-standing American suspicion of centralized power has regularly won rhetorical champions in Congress and the White House, but the cause has not always been led by Republicans nor have Republicans in power always promoted limits on the size of the U.S. national government.

Nonetheless, among present-day Republicans, especially in the House led by Speaker Newt Gingrich, a staunchly anti-big-government position is fundamental. This party sentiment likely will be aired in platforms, and judged by voters, into the coming millennium.

Questions surrounding big government invoke a variety of related topics: federalism and public administration, most notably. Given this literally encyclopedic forum, discussion here focuses specifically on Republican Party approaches to the size and growth of the U.S. federal government, particularly with respect to national efforts at taxing, spending, and regulating.

HISTORICAL ROOTS

Ironically, in the light of contemporary Republicans' identification with devolutionary assaults on big government, the party's formative years marked a particularly significant period of federal growth—the Civil War and its aftermath in Reconstruction. Republicans controlled the presidency, both houses of Congress, and the Supreme Court throughout this period, a time when total federal employment grew sharply (up almost 40%, from 36,000 to 51,000 workers, between 1861 and 1871) and when the national government wielded unprecedented power. Though massive wartime mobilization of personnel and materiel was swiftly reversed after 1865, other sources of activist federal government remained—in the South, fulfilling wide-ranging Reconstruction policies legislated by a Republican Congress; and in the growing system of pensions for Civil War veterans.

All these postwar efforts at national expansion were initiated by, and widely identified with, the Republican Party. Democrats' support for the nascent pension system was tempered by concern about fraud and waste, while "Republicans waxed ever more eloquent in their advocacy of generosity to the Union veterans" (Skocpol 1992, 125). As the preservers of the federal Union, Republicans acted with alacrity to requisite national programs—economic, pension, patronage reform—in its service.

The Gilded Age's *laissez-faire* ethos eventually drew Republicans back to the language of "smaller is better," at least in government. Bigness in business was far more acceptable, and indeed GOP opposition to 1890s–1900s reform efforts at the federal level helped smooth the rise of corporate giantism. Yet it was the Republican "Billion-Dollar" Congress of 1889–91 that achieved the most expansive (and extravagant, hence the title) legislative record of this period, extending federal activity in areas ranging from military pensions to antitrust laws. And in another ostensible historical irony, it was a Republican who epitomized the growth of federal regulation and the American administrative state—big government, on turn-of-the-century terms.

TR AND THE ADMINISTRATIVE STATE

Progressive reformers initially concentrated their efforts at state and local levels, but issues such as railroad regulation and environmental conservation required a national response. And in Theodore Roosevelt, acceding to the presidency on McKinley's assassination in 1901, Progressives found their champion. Foremost among President Roosevelt's basic aims was "to make [the federal] government the most important single influence in national affairs" (Wiebe 1967, 190), and his success in this area, especially given enduring public suspicion of federal activity, was considerable. Thus the titular and, arguably, spiritual head of early twentieth-century Republicans served as the "intellectual father and driving force" (Chandler 1987, 4) of the American administrative state. Roosevelt's "new Nationalism" inspired, among other efforts, construction of the Panama Canal, at the time the largest engineering project ever undertaken.

Despite a severe depression in 1907, Roosevelt's Republican heirs in Congress and the White House continued this big-government reform and regulation legacy. Taft's presidency saw passage of a major railroad regulation act and the 16th Amendment to the Constitution, establishing the first U.S. federal income tax.

Out of power in both branches after 1912, Republicans adopted an oppositional posture centered on fiscal austerity. Never again would the party's leaders be so strongly identified with expansionist policies as un-

der Roosevelt and Taft, though federal growth would occur during later Republican presidencies. Still, limited-government proposals by GOP leaders before the New Deal were minor, mostly involving administrative tinkering and budgetary restraint.

Herbert Hoover stands as an early example of this tension between *laissez-faire* principle and reformist practice. While echoing period GOP denunciation of government largess, he was among the most able administrative reformers ever to attain the White House. Hoover's efforts along these lines continued well past his humbling 1932 electoral defeat. In the late 1940s he headed a commission on reorganization of federal activities that remains a high-water mark for ambition and achievement: nearly 70% of the Hoover Commission's hundreds of proposals were enacted.

GOP RESPONSES TO THE NEW DEAL—AND AFTER

Republican opposition to big government solidified with the Great Depression's ushering in of Franklin Roosevelt's New Deal. GOP response to the dramatic expansion of federal activity was unwavering critical during Roosevelt's 12-year tenure. The 1936 national party platform declared that Americans' "political liberty, individual opportunity, and character as free citizens . . . today for the first time are threatened by Government itself." Four years later, Republicans convened to affirm that New Dealers had "failed America . . . by seducing our people to become continuously dependent on government, thus . . . quenching the traditional American spirit." Antigovernment sentiment lodged deeply in the Republican mind, in short, largely in response to Franklin Roosevelt's string of expansive lawmaking, and would remain rhetorically prominent thereafter, although political reality would frequently prove a poor fit.

When Dwight Eisenhower ended two decades of Democratic executive (and, briefly, legislative) branch dominance in 1952, the stage seemed set for wholesale dismantling of the national apparatus erected in civilian and military spheres alike. Yet most major New Deal programs remained in effect—Social Security, for example, which GOP national and state-level candidates had run against for years. Although a small decline was registered in overall civilian government employment, the federal budget steadily increased throughout Eisenhower's tenure. Among Eisenhower's earliest programmatic efforts was creation of the first U.S. domestic policy "superdepartment," Health, Education, and Welfare; and a major achievement of his presidency was the federally funded creation of the interstate highway system. Efficiency through centralization was the rationale behind many period Republican programs; a ratchet or two upward in big federal government was the result.

With reasserted Democratic control of both branches, by the 1960s Republican denunciations of the bloated public sector were approaching the purple. The 1964 party platform, an arrow aimed at the heart of Johnson's nascent Great Society, began: "Humanity is tormented once again by an age-old issue . . . are men in government to serve, or are they to master, their fellow men?" Much on the need to strangle the federal Leviathan followed. Barry Goldwater, as party standard-bearer, had embodied antiwelfare statism since his *Conscience of a Conservative*, published four years earlier. Gallup and other surveys from this period indicate that Republican voters reflected (or inspired) this view: not until the mid-1990s would the partisan split over attitudes toward big government again be so dramatic.

All the more extraordinary, then, that the 1968 torch-passing from LBJ's liberal Democratic "Great Society" to Richard Nixon's avowedly limited government "New Federalism" made virtually no difference in the drumbeat of expanding government services and regulatory activities. Nixon presided over an immense expansion of the welfare state: new social and environmental programs ranged from a host of urban aid programs, including the first publicly financed jobs for unemployed Americans since the New Deal, to sweeping clean water and clean air acts. To be sure, Nixon did not necessarily originate or promote all these policies, but rarely did he noticeably oppose them. Nor did fellow Republicans in Congress: the water pollution act passed the Senate 86–0, for example.

As for regulatory activity, more new federal agencies and statutes regulating business and state/local government activity were established under Nixon than in the Truman, Kennedy, Johnson, and Carter administrations combined (Mayhew 1991, 83).

Political historians puzzling over this record reach for various explanations, from fluctuating economic fortunes to congressional Democrats' dominance of the policy agenda to shifting "public moods." Whatever the causes, the apparently anomalous fact is that a mere generation or two ago, a conservative Republican president did little to halt, and much to further, a profound expansion in federal services and administrative regulation. A consensus about the benefits of big government prevailed from the New Deal into the early 1970s, in sum, essentially regardless of the party in power.

REAGAN REPUBLICANS AND BIG GOVERNMENT

National attitudes seemed considerably different a decade later, when Ronald Reagan swept into office declaring, in his first inaugural address, that "government is not the solution to our problem; government is the problem." Indeed, as the 1980s began there was palpable international agreement on this score, at least among industrialized nations: from Japan to Northern and Western Europe to the United States, leaders were "groping with aspects of . . . the 'government is too big' issue" (Campbell 1985, 471). As in the past, Republican Party attitudes were at least partly shaped by larger forces. Simultaneously, Reagan's portrayal of a swollen Leviathan undeniably influenced Americans' outlook toward big government—for a time.

Three factors are worthy of note in assessing Reagan Republicans' effect on government services and regulation, and on national attitudes thereof.

First, antigovernment policy proposals during the 1980s were more extensive than those of preceding twentieth-century administrations, Republican or Democratic. Traditional tinkering, on the order of procedural reform and incremental change, was brushed aside; instead, broad cuts in federal activity were promoted, if rarely enacted in full. Though blunted by extensive increases in defense spending, initial Reagan proposals for slashing federal government represented the first real attempt at retrenchment in several decades. And at the outset, results were achieved, from major cuts in personal and corporate income taxes to elimination of some 75 categorical federal programs.

Second, Reagan-era policies differed in kind as well as degree from previous Republican devolutionary plans, at least since the New Deal. Reagan's approach to Leviathan was foremost economic: the government would be reined in through such measures as balancing the budget, privatization, tax cuts, and devolution of fiscal responsibilities to the state and local levels. Such policies had been floated before, by leaders of both parties, but never as a systematic package of controls targeting the federal sector.

With the emergence, early in Reagan's presidency, of the federal budget deficit as a sustained concern, these economic policies took on added salience and urgency. Republicans' disdain for federal spending was coupled with real fiscal limitations, apparently fueling further Reagan administration government-cutting fervor.

Yet—and here is the third general point about Reagan-era animus toward big government—federal activity did *not* shrink during Reagan's tenure.

Civilian government employment rose steadily, especially at the federal level; more familiarly, the federal budget grew apace, topping the trillion-dollar level for the first time ever in 1985. Reagan Republicans' inability to affect this growth was perhaps symbolized most in attempts to eliminate two cabinet departments (Education and Energy). Not only did these remain, but among Reagan's last presidential acts was creation of a new cabinet department, Veterans Affairs. While public sentiment supported general cuts in federal services, especially when advertised as eliminating waste and fraud, most particular programs proved stoutly resistant to elimination or meaningful reduction.

Thus it is less surprising to learn that Americans' attitudes toward the public sector altered positively during the 1980s. Opinion polls display a significant shift toward a preference for bigger government by the end of Reagan's rule (Bennett and Bennett 1990, 141). Part of this shift likely owed to a backlash against Republican efforts to cut highly popular programs, particularly Social Security. But also at play was a more subtle development. Chroniclers of the "imperial presidency" note that presidents at least since Franklin Roosevelt come for many Americans to personify the national government. Reagan, as an immensely well-liked leader, symbolized a friendlier, grandfatherly federal government—one he tried and mostly failed to reduce.

Republicans' apparent inability to shift permanently the terms of debate over big government received confirmation in the campaigns and presidency of George Bush, Reagan's vice president and successor as 41st president. Whether owing to his lifetime of public service or to shrewd reading of public opinion, Bush mainly eschewed the antigovernment rhetoric and policies of his predecessor. Republicans grumbled, especially when a 1990 budget agreement violated the president's famous "Read my lips: no new taxes" pledge. Halfway through Bush's presidency, political scientists were concluding that "we may well have seen the last campaign centered on the theme of vastly curtailing big government" (Bennett and Bennett 1990, 145).

REPUBLICAN REVOLUTION II

On the presidential level, this may yet prove true; but the 1994 congressional elections heralded a signal, if perhaps temporary, renewal of Republican opposition to big government. The Contract with America, the House GOP campaign platform, principally featured policies aimed at reducing federal regulations and services. All four of the ideological planks of Reagan's antigovernment message—devolution of national ac-

tivities to the states, balanced federal budget, tax cuts, and privatization of public responsibilities—appear prominently in the Contract and in accompanying Republican arguments. In policy areas from environment to welfare, health care to immigration, Republicans (especially in the House of Representatives, led by Speaker Newt Gingrich) promised "revolutionary" reductions in national government.

How revolutionary are these changes? In historical perspective, the term seems germane, if premature. A half century of federal growth, slowed very little by Reagan Republicans' frontal attacks, was by 1995–1996 supplemented with extensive attention to state-level policy initiatives and renewed praise for "states' rights." Republicans from House freshmen to presidential candidate Bob Dole constantly invoked the Tenth Amendment (reserving policies not explicitly assigned to Congress to the states). "In itself, this represents considerable movement off the old nation-centered perspective," concluded two scholarly observers early in the 104th Congress (Pagano and Bowman 1995).

Moreover, in keeping with a tradition of mutual partisan adaptation to apparent public mood shifts on big government, many Democratic leaders adopted a more openly antifederal stance. President Clinton, whose "reinventing government" policies were a centerpiece of his 1992 campaign and extensively promoted during his administration, declared repeatedly after the 1994 Republican election victories that "the era of big government is over." A combination of general public sentiment, Republican rhetoric and ideology, Democratic accommodation, and overstretched federal accounts seemed by the mid-1990s to have effected a change in national mood similar in depth, if opposite in character, to that of the New Deal–Great Society years.

Revolutionary ambition rarely translates into enduring change in the American system of separated powers, however. Republicans' legislative program for transforming the federal government bogged down within months of GOP resumption of majority party control of House and Senate, slowed by presidential vetoes and Senate caution. The script seems reminiscent of the Reagan years, when Americans' attachment to particular federal benefits ultimately outweighed a predisposition to reducing the national government.

Rogan Kersh

BIBLIOGRAPHY

Bennett, Linda L.M., and Stephen Earl Bennett. *Living with Leviathan: Americans Coming to Terms with Big Government.* Lawrence: University Press of Kansas, 1990.

Campbell, John C. "Research Roundtable: Governmental Responses to Budget Scarcity." *Policy Studies Journal* 13 (1985).

Chandler, Ralph Clark, ed. *A Centennial History of the American Administrative State.* New York: Free Press, 1987.

Hoekstra, Peter. "Renewing the American Dream." *Public Manager* 18 (1995).

Mayhew, David R. *Divided We Govern: Party Control, Lawmaking, and Investigations, 1946–1990.* New Haven: Yale University Press, 1991.

Pagano, Michael A., and Ann O'M. Bowman. "The State of American Federalism, 1994–95." *Publius: The Journal of Federalism* 25 (1995).

Skocpol, Theda. *Protecting Soldiers and Mothers: The Origins of American Social Policy, 1870–1920.* Cambridge: Harvard University Press, 1992.

Wiebe, Robert H. *The Search for Order: 1877–1920.* New York: Hill and Wang, 1967.

Campaign Finance and Campaign Finance Reform

Running for office has always meant spending money. Even before the American Revolution, there are records of candidates spending money to gain elected office. There is an account of George Washington's race for the Virginia House of Burgesses in 1757, which required that he offer "the customary means of winning votes," which included rum punch, wine, beer, and other libations (Thayer 1973).

Almost immediately, campaign money and where it came from became a hot issue in American politics. As early as 1832, President Andrew Jackson spoke to Congress on the topic, stating that "it is to be regretted that the rich and powerful too often bend the acts of government to their selfish purposes . . . the humble members of society . . . who have neither the time nor the means of securing like favors to themselves, have the right to complain of the injustices of their government" (Bauer 1994).

Machine politics in the urban areas of the nation honed political fund raising to a fine art in the nineteenth century. Such organizations as Tammany Hall in New York, the Pendergasts in Kansas City, Frank Hague in Jersey City, "Big Bill" Thompson of Chicago, and Mayor James Curley of Boston were known for their corruption scandals, often revolving around campaign money. Campaigns could be funded from kickbacks due from patronage employees into the party's coffers or from those who, desiring to build, buy, or sell to the state or local government, were obliged to contribute to the party in power in order to stay in business.

SCANDAL LEADS TO REFORMS

After the Civil War, with the federal government now in the position to help or hinder numerous business interests, money from persons interested in legislation poured into federal and presidential campaigns. An example was the fund raising done by Marcus Alonzo "Dollar Marc" Hanna, an Ohio businessman who raised money for William McKinley for president in 1896. Because of the Teapot Dome scandal that flowed from Hanna's fund-raising practices, Congress passed a law prohibiting corporate donations to political campaigns in 1907 (the Tillman Act) and followed that up in 1910 with a law mandating disclosure of the sources of federal campaign funds (Beck and Sorauf 1992).

The 1925 Corrupt Practices Act banned corporate contributions to political candidates and limited expenditures for House races to $5,000 and Senate races to $25,000. Under the 1925 act, all expenditures directly under the control of the candidate must be reported to the clerk of the U.S. House, but any amount spent by committees without the express knowledge of the candidate need not be reported. The act contained no provisions for enforcement: no mechanism to compel the filing of reports or to scrutinize them for their accuracy. It was the first of many campaign finance reforms containing loopholes and omissions.

In 1943 the Tillman Act ban on contributions from corporations was extended to labor unions. In response to the ban, the Congress of Industrial Organizations developed the first political action committee. This PAC allowed union members to pool their voluntary donations into a fund that could be used to disburse funds to political candidates, thus circumventing the letter of the 1943 reform. Eventually business and other organized interest groups adopted the same practice.

Before 1950, most campaigns were a matter of radio and newspaper advertisements, followed by grassroots volunteer efforts to get out the vote. After the advent of television, first used in a 1948 Connecticut Senate race, campaign costs began to soar, and the costs of running for president tripled between 1960 and 1968 (see Tables 1 and 2).

By the 1950s, a majority of states also had laws limiting campaign expenditures on the books, but these laws also applied only to spending done by the candidate, exempting committees spending on his behalf. Also exempted from these statutes were expenditures for such key campaign tools as printing, stationery, and postage (Clapp 1963). In a study on the attitudes of congressmen conducted by the Brookings Institution in 1959, a congressman pointed out the inadequacies of the prevailing campaign finance laws: "I don't believe you can be

Table 1

Total Political Costs for All Offices in the United States During Presidential Years

| Year | Total expenditures in millions | | Percentage change since past election | |
	Actual	Adjusted	Actual	Adjusted
1952	$ 140	$140	—	—
1956	155	151	+10.7	+7.9
1960	175	157	+12.9	+4.0
1964	200	171	+14.3	+8.9
1968	300	229	+50.0	+33.9
1972	425	270	+41.7	+17.9
1976	540	252	+27.1	−6.7
1980	1,200	388	+122.8	+54.0
1984	1,800	470	+53.3	+18.9
1988	2,700	666	+48.3	+41.7

Note: The largest increase occurs between the 1964 and 1968 elections, and again between the 1976 and 1980 elections. The largest increase in the safety margin for House incumbents also took place during this period of time, with the number of competitive House seats dwindling. The logical explanation for this is that by the 1968 campaign, the use of expensive television advertising was becoming the norm even in congressional races. Because of television ads, new, and expensive, consultants were added to campaigns in order to create tailored spots to best fit the circumstances of each campaign.

There is a dip in expenditures in 1976, which was the first election held under the new Federal Election Campaign Act rules. Campaigns were struggling to understand and comply with new rules, and the number of political action committees had not yet exploded to take advantage of the new legal routes of obtaining large amounts of campaign money. There were only 608 PACs operating in federal elections. Since this was also the first post-Watergate election, campaign managers were extremely cautious in their fund raising and were careful to stay within the confines of the law. If there was a doubt as to the meaning of the Federal Elections Campaign Act, the campaigns were more likely to err on the side of caution in 1976.

By the 1980 election, the number of PACs had increased, a new profession of campaign law had sprung up, and campaigns were more confident of their abilities to raise money while remaining technically within the boundaries of the Federal Elections Campaign Act.

How are such vast sums of money spent? A look at the 1988 contest, where there were no major independent candidates for the presidency, shows what a typical two-party contest costs and for what services the money is spent (see Table 2).

Sources: Alexander and Bauer 1988; Beck and Sorauf 1992.

---

elected in some of these districts, mine included, within the spirit of the law. You can do it within the technicalities. What we had to do was technically legal: we created a whole slew of committees, each of whom would take over a portion of the campaign" (Clapp 1963).

THE MODERN REFORM ERA

In 1971, Common Cause sued the Republican and Democratic national committees under the 1925 Corrupt Practices Act. It had long been common knowledge that the parties received large amounts of money from contributors who could remain behind the scenes, while the voters were unable to discover whose money was financing American politics. Under pressure of this suit, the Federal Elections Campaign Act of 1971 was born. As both Democrats and Republicans scrambled to finish their fund raising for the 1972 elections before the new law took effect, Common Cause struck again, this time suing the Committee to Re-Elect the President (Nixon's reelection campaign) under the

1925 law still in effect. This lawsuit led to the discovery of slush funds and money laundering of huge campaign contributions made by big business, all illegal under the 1925 act.

The last unregulated presidential campaign in American history seemed to the reform lobby proof that campaign finance was in desperate need of regulation. The Republicans raised the largest campaign treasury in American history for the 1972 reelection campaign of Richard Nixon. Over $60 million was raised, most of it before the April 7, 1972, deadline when the new election law took effect. One of Nixon's chief fund raisers that year, Maurice Stans, was subsequently convicted for his role in funneling cash to pay for the illegal actions in the Watergate scandal.

THE 1971 FEDERAL ELECTION CAMPAIGN ACT

The Federal Election Campaign Act was the first major reform of campaign finance since 1925. It mandated re-

Table 2

Costs of Nominating and Electing a President, 1988 (in millions)

Prenomination		
Spending by candidates for major party nomination	$199.6	
Compliance costs	12.4	
Independent expenditures	4.1	
Communication costs	0.2	
Labor spending	15.0	
Spending by minor party candidates	2.1	
Delegate candidate expenditures	0.1	$233.511
Conventions		
Republicans' expenditures	$18.0	
Democrats' expenditures	22.4	$40.4
General Election		
Spending by major party candidates	$92.2	
Spending by minor party candidates	3.0	
Compliance costs	6.1	
Party committee spending	61.6	
Republican National Committee media	5.8	
Expenditures by labor, corporations, and associations	27.5	
Independent expenditures	10.1	
Communication costs	2.0	$208.3
Miscellaneous expenses	17.8	$500.0

Note: The term *communication costs* indicates the monies spent by organizations such as labor unions and corporations to urge their members or employees to vote for a particular candidate. Compliance costs are monies spent to hire accountants and attorneys to prepare and file the campaign finance disclosure forms required by the Federal Election Commission on a quarterly basis for all federal campaigns. In addition to the federal requirement, many states have their own campaign finance laws, which also require compliance.
Source: Alexander and Bauer 1991.

forms in four categories. The first category of reforms concerned the actions of candidates, the second concerned the actions of individual donors, the third regulated donations by multicandidate committees, and the fourth applied to donations given by groups other than multicandidate committees. Every candidate for federal office since 1972 has filed reports according to its provisions. It was the single most important campaign finance reform of the twentieth century.

Federal Candidates

1. Candidates for federal office must disclose the names, addresses, employers, and occupations of any donor giving a cumulative total of over $200 to the campaign, in reports submitted to the Federal

Election Commission at specified intervals in and between election cycles.
2. Party and PAC contributions, no matter what the amount, must be reported.
3. Reports of all campaign receipts and expenditures must be submitted in reports to the Federal Election Commission at specified intervals; these reports must also be filed locally, normally with the state election commissioner.
4. Campaign contributions from businesses, corporations, and labor unions are not allowed.

Individuals

1. Individuals wishing to influence elections are limited to donating $1,000 to any candidate or candidate committee per election in any given year (so an individual could double their contribution by contributing $1,000 in the primary and $1,000 in the general election).
2. Individuals are allowed to donate no more than $20,000 to any national party committee in any calendar year.
3. Individuals are allowed to give up to $5,000 per year to a PAC or political committee.
4. Individuals may contribute no more than $25,000 in total to these sources in any calendar year.

Political Action Committees

1. All political action committees must submit detailed reports quarterly to the Federal Election Commission that disclose contributions and their sources and disbursement to candidates or groups.
2. Committees that support fewer than five candidates and have fewer than 50 contributors may contribute $1,000 per election (primary and general elections counting as separate elections) to any particular candidate; they are limited to donating $20,000 to any national party committee and $5,000 to any other political committee. There is no limit on what the committee may contribute in a calendar year or election cycle.
3. Multicandidate committees (defined as any group that gives to more than five different candidates, has more than 50 contributors, and has been registered as a group for at least six months) may donate $5,000 per election (primary and general counting as separate elections) to individual campaigns. They may contribute up to $15,000 to the national party and $5,000 to any other political committee. There is no limit on what the multicandidate committee may contribute in a calendar year or election cycle.

This last provision in the law led to an explosion in the number of political action committees (PACs) from 600 in 1974 to more than 4,000 in 1996. Since the FECA severely limited individual contributions, the PAC became a handy mechanism for raising the large sums of money needed in modern congressional campaigns, but it has been widely criticized for contributing to incumbents over challengers. Nine out of every ten PAC dollars go to a congressional incumbent. Some political scientists believe this has led to higher reelection rates and safer seats for House incumbents in particular (Bauer and Hibbing 1989).

THE FEDERAL ELECTION COMMISSION

To correct a major flaw in the 1925 Corrupt Practices Act, the 1974 legislation created the Federal Election Commission. The FEC is made up of six members appointed by the president, with equal representation from the two major parties to keep the commission from becoming a tool for partisan advantage. Commissioners serve six-year staggered terms.

The commission has been frequently criticized for timidity in the enforcement of campaign laws. With each party represented by three members, it is easy to see how controversial actions that would put either party in a bad light could be blocked by a tie vote. As a result, most of the penalties meted out in the first 20 years of its existence have been relatively minor, most often calling for the payment of fines long after the campaigns are over.

Along with an enforcement function, the commission plays an important role in collecting and disseminating information to the public. Statistical reports are published before and after each round of federal elections, allowing the media to report on the ways campaigns are raising and spending their money. Individuals may request copies of the disclosure forms for any federal candidate, allowing anyone willing to pay a modest fee the chance to see exactly where individual candidates got their funds and how these funds were spent. This has allowed ordinary citizens to track campaign funds in a way not possible before 1974, while opening up new areas of inquiry in fields such as political science, history, and journalism. These reports may be accessed by contacting the Public Records Office of the Federal Election Commission, 999 E. Street Northwest, Washington, DC 20463.

Disclosure forms for any candidate for federal office may also be viewed by computer at terminals in many state election commission offices at no charge, or on-line at a home personal computer for a fee of $20 per hour. In addition to individual disclosure forms, FEC bulletins may also be downloaded to personal computers, allowing anyone with the right equipment the chance to become thoroughly educated on all aspects of campaign finance.

THE 1974 FECA AMENDMENTS

In response to the Watergate scandal, the FECA was amended to create a system of public funding of presidential campaigns, through a voluntary $1 check-off on the income tax form. By 1992, the federal treasury was supplying over $55 million each to the Republican and Democratic nominees for president. Only 19% of taxpayers in 1995 were contributing to the public financing of presidential campaigns, and by 1996 the fund was having trouble paying matching funds to candidates in the Republican primaries in a timely manner (Dye and Zeigler 1996).

This reform was designed to take special-interest money out of presidential elections, by fully funding the general election campaigns of both major party candidates with an equal amount. Here is how it works. In the contest for the nomination, campaign contributions of $250 or less given by individuals would be matched, dollar for dollar, by federal money, according to the following rules:

1. The presidential candidate must raise at least $5,000 in 20 states, from small donations.
2. After qualifying, the candidate would continue to receive matching funds until they received less than 10% of the vote in two primaries in a row.

The amendments included a set amount to be given equally to fund the Republican and Democratic National Conventions.

THE SUPREME COURT AND CAMPAIGN FINANCE

The FECA had to be amended again in 1976, when certain provisions of the law were ruled unconstitutional by the Supreme Court in the case of *Buckley* v. *Valeo*. In the Buckley ruling, the Court said that spending on campaigns was a form of free speech. Therefore the law could not simply limit spending; this would be limiting speech. It would be legal to grant a benefit, such as public financing, only to those who abided by the spending limits, thus ensuring that most candidates would spend within the limits of the law. If a candidate wanted to spend over the limit, however, there was no constitutional way to prohibit it.

The first presidential candidate to spend over the legal limit was a multimillionaire businessman who did not need federal funds to mount his campaign. Texan H. Ross Perot spent $59 million of his own money and garnered 19% of the vote in 1992. In the 1996 Republican presidential primary contest, multimillionaire publisher Steve Forbes ignored spending limits to fund his campaign from his own pocketbook.

In the same ruling, the Court also declared unconstitutional any limitations placed on independent groups wishing to spend money in behalf of a candidate. The 1976 FECA amendments allowed such "independent expenditure" committees to raise and spend unlimited funds in behalf of candidates. By the 1988 election, such groups had become a factor in American politics, raising and spending money in behalf of both major party candidates.

SOFT MONEY

In 1979, the FECA was amended once again, this time to create a category of campaign money that would not be limited or recorded. "Hard" money must be reported to the FEC by amount and donor. Unregulated funds are considered "soft money" and were allowed as a tool for political parties to engage in "party-building activities," activities meant to help the entire party instead of a single candidate. The amendments were adopted at the urging of leaders of both political parties, who argued that the political parties had been marginalized by the strict funding limits of the 1974 act. Although soft money may be subject to state laws, it is currently unregulated at the federal level.

The 1979 amendments allowed the following monies to be raised in unlimited amounts, without public disclosure of donors: funds for printing, preparation, and distribution of lists of endorsed candidates, including distribution through the mail; campaign materials such as yard signs, bumper stickers, and brochures, paid for by local party committees; and voter registration and get-out-the-vote activities to benefit their party's nominees for president and vice president, including funds for telephone banks designed by professionals but utilized by volunteers.

Soft-money contributions allowed individuals, corporations, and labor unions to give large sums of money to political parties, often in contributions of $100,000 or more. Corporations, which had been prohibited from direct contributions to campaigns since 1907, were once more able to give direct contributions.

Table 3

Soft Money Expenditures (in millions)

Year	Republicans	Democrats
1980	$15.1	$4.0
1984	$15.6	$6.0
1988	$22.0	$23.0
1992	$49.6	$35.3

Source: Citizen's Research Foundation and the Center for Responsive Politics.

Managers of presidential campaigns contend that without soft money, they would be unable to mount adequate campaigns. For example, the amount given to the campaigns of George Bush and Bill Clinton in 1992 by the federal check-off program provided only about 36% of the amount actually spent in the election (Greenberg and Page 1996).

Soft money could come from groups and individuals simply interested in improving government as a function of their being good citizens. Or it could come from individuals and groups with a strong motivation to influence government policy for their own benefit. It is this second category that alarms some political analysts. The major donors of soft money seem to fall almost exclusively into the second category, giving large contributions, often to both parties, while seeking benefits from the federal government for their companies.

RECENT ATTEMPTS AT REFORM

In 1990 two important attempts were made at campaign finance reform, and both attempts failed to produce tangible results. The leader of the Republican and Democratic parties in the Senate appointed a bipartisan Campaign Finance Reform Panel made up of experts, academics, and party activists. They proposed the following reforms: reduced broadcast and postal rates for candidates, free broadcast time for parties to allocate to candidates, and exemptions from the spending limits for a percentage of funds raised in the candidate's home state (Beck and Sorauf 1992).

The second attempt was made through the political process, when campaign finance reform bills were passed in the House and Senate. This attempt failed, in large part, because the House and Senate bills disagreed on fundamental issues and were impossible to reconcile. Even if the bills had been reconciled in Conference Committee, the bill faced a probable presidential veto from President George Bush. The debate

Table 4

Receipts of the Major Parties (in millions)

	1978	1980	1982	1984	1986	1988	1990	1992	1994
Democrat	$26.4	$37.2	$39.3	$98.5	$64.8	$127.9	$85.7	$177.7	$139.1
Republican	$84.5	$169.5	$215	$279.9	$255	$263.3	$206.3	$267.3	$245.6
Total	$110.9	$206.7	$254.3	$396.4	$320	$391.2	$292	$445	$384.7

Source: Federal Election Commission.

on these proposals showed clear partisan positions on campaign finance reform, with Republicans objecting to spending caps and Democrats objecting to the elimination of PAC money. The 1990 debate showed the partisan interests on display, and led to a legislative deadlock (Beck and Sorauf 1992).

When President Bill Clinton was elected in 1992, his campaign speeches promised campaign finance reform. But bills passed separately in the House and Senate were never reconciled, and the Clinton administration was unable to pass campaign finance reform legislation while the Democratic Party held both the White House and both houses of Congress.

By 1995, the Republicans were in control of both the House and the Senate, and campaign finance reform did no better in the atmosphere of a divided government. During a joint speaking engagement in the summer of 1995, Speaker of the House Newt Gingrich shook hands with President Bill Clinton, pledging to appoint yet another joint commission to study campaign finance reform. As this volume goes to press, months after the historic handshake, no commission members have been appointed, and the only campaign reform legislation to be signed into law was a bill that mandated that all lobbyists register as such, which limited the ability of lobbyists to pay for gifts and meals for legislators.

By 1996, the group that formed around Ross Perot's surprisingly effective third-party presidential candidacy in 1992, United We Stand America, had placed campaign finance reform at the center of their efforts. At a campaign forum held in Concord, New Hampshire, on January 20, 1996, the executive director of United We Stand America, Russell Varney, described the current campaign finance system as "organized graft" (Randolph T. Holhut, "Getting Big Money Out of Politics," from an Internet posting February 1996, The Written Word, mdle@primenet.com Michael Lewis).

One of the obstacles to an overhaul of campaign finance has been the lack of consensus among groups lobbying for changes in the system. Three nonpartisan public-interest lobbies have focused on campaign fi-

nance reform: Common Cause, the group that began reform by suing the political parties in 1971; Public Citizen, a Ralph Nader–sponsored group of public-interest lobbyists; and the Center for Responsive Politics, the youngest reform organization, founded in the late 1980s to research and report on campaign finance. Only the Center for Responsive Politics calls for full public financing of all federal campaigns, while the older groups take more moderate positions.

Monica Bauer

SEE ALSO Monetary Policy

BIBLIOGRAPHY

Alexander, Herbert, and Monica Bauer. *Financing the 1988 Election.* Boulder, CO: Westview Press, 1991.

Bauer, Monica. "Money and Politics: In Pursuit of an Ideal." In *Presidential Campaigns and American Self Images*, ed. Arthur H. Miller and Bruce E. Gronbeck. Boulder, CO: Westview Press, 1994.

Beck, Paul Allen, and Frank J. Sorauf. *Party Politics in America.* 7th ed. New York: HarperCollins, 1992.

Clapp, Charles L. *The Congressman: His Work as He Sees It.* Washington, DC: Brookings Institution, 1963.

Dye, Thomas R., and Harmon Zeigler. *The Irony of Democracy.* 10th ed. Belmont, CA: Wadsworth, 1996.

Greenberg, Edward S., and Benjamin I. Page. *The Struggle for Democracy.* New York: HarperCollins, 1996.

Thayer, George. *Who Shakes the Money Tree.* New York: Simon and Schuster, 1973.

Campaign Materials

SYMBOLS

In November 1874, just before the midterm elections, *Harper's Weekly* cartoonist Thomas Nast introduced the elephant to represent the "Republican vote." The Democrats in that election secured a majority in the House of Representatives for the first time since before the Civil War. Indeed, with the Democrats shut out of the presidency since 1861, the capture of the House was the party's first national triumph in almost two decades. Nast, an avid Republican, chose a marauding elephant to depict the vote, which the illustrator believed had become aimless and confused. Subsequent Nast cartoons shifted the animal from merely representing the vote to depicting the party itself. The symbol quickly caught on, and soon Republicans had embraced the pachyderm as their own. While Democrats experimented with a number of animal images, starting with the rooster and ultimately settling on the donkey, the Republican Party by the late nineteenth century had clearly established the elephant as its trademark. Nast also receives the credit for linking the Democratic Party with the donkey. In a December 1879 illustration, he utilized both animals for the first time in the same cartoon.

The elephant has historically evoked both praise and derision. In the early 1900s New York State Senator N.A. Elsberg stated that "among the elephant's known characteristics are cleverness and unwieldiness. He is an animal easy to control until he is aroused; but when frightened or stirred up, he becomes absolutely unmanageable. Here we have all the characteristics of the Republican vote...." Two-time Democratic standard-bearer Adlai Stevenson offered a slightly different observation about the animal: "The elephant has a thick skin, a head full of ivory, and as everyone who has seen a circus parade knows, proceeds best by grasping the tail of its predecessor."

SLOGANS

Slogans were as diverse as Republican presidential candidates, and technological innovations allowed for interesting vehicles to make catch phrases popular. The famous western explorer John C. Frémont was the first Republican presidential nominee in 1856. Frémont's likeness and his nickname, "Pathfinder," adorned many political artifacts ranging from cloth ribbons to medal tokens to glassware and ceramics. "The Rocky Mountains Echo Back Frémont," declared one item. Others coupled the Frémont battle cry with the divisive issue of slavery that was gripping the nation. Indeed, Republicans launched their new party to protest its further expansion. "Free Speech/Free Press/Free Soil/Free Men/Frémont and Victory" proclaimed one artifact, while another trumpeted "Free Soil! Free Speech! Freedom for Kansas!" Frémont's campaign materials paired him with his wife, Jessie, and was one of the first instances where a candidate's spouse was named on political items. Mrs. Frémont was the daughter of antislavery Democratic Senator Thomas Hart Benton, and this lineage was probably factored into touting Frémont as "Jessie's Choice." While the association with Benton was designed to attract dissatisfied Democrats to the Frémont ticket, it failed. Democratic nominee James Buchanan won the presidency.

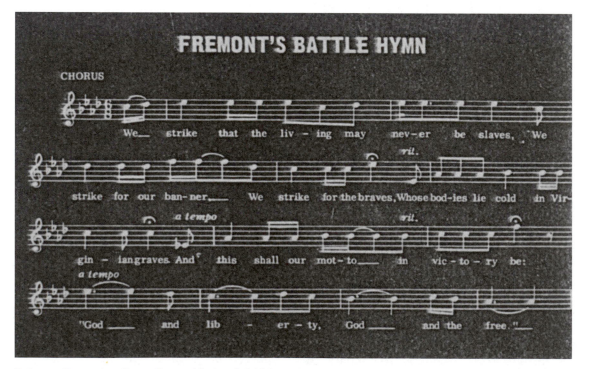

Frémont Campaign Song. *Source:* National Archives.

Lincoln Ribbon, 1860. *Source:* Smithsonian Institution.

As the Republican Party's debut largely coincided with breakthroughs in photography, candidates' likenesses were also produced for partisan articles. In the 1860s, ferrotype lapel pins containing a photograph surrounded by a metal frame added to the luster of campaigning. Abraham Lincoln's pictorial image in the 1860 contest was that of an ordinary American. In addition to using his likeness, much political capital was gained through slogans accenting Lincoln's rail-splitting days and stories of his honesty. He was the "Rail Splitter" and "Honest Abe" or "Old Abe, Prince of Rails." Medalets portrayed Lincoln as "the Rail Splitter of the West" coupled on the reverse with the call for "No More Slave Territory." Others suggested "Let Liberty Be National and Slavery Sectional." In 1864 the president sought reelection on the platform of "Peace/Amnesty and Emancipation." A series of union battlefield victories late in the 1864 campaign provided the means for an impressive win for Lincoln over his challenger, General George McClellan.

Ulysses S. Grant's past as general of the Union armies during the Civil War was a major selling point for the candidate in 1868 and 1872. One ribbon declared "He Saved the Union in the Field—Let Us Preserve It at the Ballot Box," while another designated him the "Hero of Appomattox/Freedom's Defender." Yet, after two undistinguished terms, the Republican Party thwarted Grant's bid for a third term in 1876 by nominating Rutherford B. Hayes. Hayes's campaign tried to undermine the Democrats by linking them with Tammany Hall corruption in New York City; this regardless of the fact that nominee Samuel Tilden had prosecuted Tammany Boss William Tweed. "Hurrah! For Hayes & Honest Ways" was one popular catch phrase. Despite vows of honesty, Hayes assumed the presidency after a much-disputed election in which Tilden had won more popular votes. In a compromise designed to end Reconstruction in the South, Democrats in the electoral vote count traded the election in return for federal troop withdrawals from the former Confederate states. This bargain prompted Hayes's detractors to refer to him as RutherFRAUD Hayes.

Relatively few unique campaign materials were present in either James Garfield's successful White House run in 1880 or James Blaine's failed bid in 1884. This was not the case in 1888. Benjamin Harrison heavily relied on nostalgic references in this race. As the grandson of President William Henry Harrison, the candidate rejuvenated his grandfather's symbols of the log cabin and cider barrel. He also invoked the elder Harrison's nickname, "Tippecanoe," which was first utilized in 1840. The 1888 contest depicted Benjamin as "A Chip Off the Old Block," while he and his running mate, Levi Morton, were known as "Tippecanoe and Morton Too." Other themes were prevalent as well. One campaign banner contained a biblical reference by calling on the public to vote for "The Tribes of Benjamin and Levi." In a completely different vein, Harrison, a strict protectionist, branded the incumbent Grover Cleveland's trade policies as favorable to Great Britain. The candidate therefore championed, "The Protection of American Industries/The Keystone of National Prosperity." During the 1892 rematch between Harrison and Cleveland, Republicans resurrected the theme again, painting their opponent as a chump of Great Britain for promoting free trade. Harrison was for protective tariffs: "Harrison & Protection" and "Protection/Reciprocity/Honest Money." In the rematch, however Cleveland bested Harrison. It should be noted that the first Harrison–Cleveland matchup was also significant for the revival of textiles as a political artifact. Red bandanas picturing both Republican and Democratic candidates were a frequent sight.

With the 1896 race came new advancements in technology, which in many ways revolutionized campaigning strategies. The use of a thin layer of celluloid over a candidate's photograph allowed for creative and colorful items and at the same time provided for a less expensive means of producing political buttons. More than 1,000 varieties of these objects were released during this contest. The introduction of celluloid buttons began the "Golden Age," which lasted until 1916. Colors and designs that were impossible under previous methods now could be found in abundance.

McKinley Poster. *Source:* Library of Congress.

McKinley Campaign Song. *Source:* National Archives.

In 1896 and 1900, the presidential contenders from both parties remained the same: William McKinley for the Republicans and William Jennings Bryan for the Democrats. The 1896 race in particular concentrated on currency issues and whether the dollar would be pegged to gold or to silver. Called the "Battle of the Standards," each campaign promoted the metal of choice. The GOP, for example, was as "Good as Gold" and Republicans pronounced "I Am a Gold Bug. But No Humbug." This election again revisited the tariff issue. McKinley was an ardent supporter of protective tariffs, having championed this cause in Congress. "Sound Money, Protection and Prosperity" were what separated the Republicans from Bryan. In addition, McKinley coopted the Democrat's antibusiness trust philosophy with "In McKinley We Trust, In Bryan We Bust." McKinley sought also to portray himself as untainted by political machine influence with the battle cry "The People against the Bosses."

McKinley and Roosevelt Campaign Lantern in the Shape of a "Full Dinner Pail." *Source:* Library of Congress.

Roosevelt for President, 1904. *Source:* National Archives.

In the 1900 race, after McKinley's successful prosecution of the Spanish-American War, foreign policy issues became an important factor in a presidential election for the first time in decades. Deflecting Bryan's criticism of U.S. imperialism, key campaign material was pulled from a McKinley speech, "The American Flag Has Not Been Planted in Foreign Soil to Acquire More Territory, but for Humanity's Sake." The phrase was accompanied by images of Cuban liberty. Given the popularity of the war and the selection of Teddy Roosevelt as the vice presidential candidate, a number of items featured Roosevelt alone; a historical rarity at this point for a running mate. Much was made of his wartime "Rough Rider" exploits, and many items featured a uniformed Roosevelt against backdrops of the charge up San Juan Hill in Puerto Rico or standing next to big-game animals such as lions. Republicans also emphasized sound fiscal policy and domestic prosperity along with attempts to capitalize on the wave of patriotism engendered by the war. GOP campaign trinkets trumpeted: "Prosperity at Home/Prestige Abroad" and "Protection/Expansion/Prosperity." A more focused attack included "A Full Dinner Pail," as the ticket

Trying to Kick It Over. GOP Protection. Full Dinner Pail. Free Trade Democracy, 1904. *Source:* Library of Congress.

tried to appeal to blue-collar workers with the promise of full employment.

In 1904, the Spanish-American War theme reappeared as Roosevelt took advantage of his "Rough Rider" image for his own presidential quest. Rebus puzzle items that mix images and words to produce slogans pictured a rose and the word "velt" (Rose + velt) and were popular pro-Roosevelt artifacts. Playing off of the candidate's well-known toothy smile and sense of humor, grinning caricatures of Teddy adorned campaign materials along with references to his own domestic prosperity package, known as the "Square Deal." Other buttons employed historical motifs, marking the 50th anniversary of the Republican Party in 1904 and featuring portraits of Roosevelt with Lincoln.

In 1908, a bandana issued for William Howard Taft's candidacy made the most of his size with "A Big Man for a Big Office and a Big Party to Elect Him." Taft was equated with the popular Roosevelt, who had hand-picked him as his successor. Less clear, however, is the significance of Taft's equation with an opossum.

Numerous artifacts, especially postcards, affectionately offer a caricature of Taft as "Billy Possum." The campaign also poked fun at the Democrats for nominating Bryan for a third White House run with "Three Strikes and Out" and "Vote for Taft This Time—You Can Vote for Bryan Any Time." Taft faced a tougher battle in 1912 when in addition to facing the Democrat Woodrow Wilson, his former mentor Teddy Roosevelt mounted a third-party challenge under the Progressive/ Bull Moose label. Taft lamely tried to counter the Roosevelt bid with "Good Republicans Don't Bolt a Party Ticket." Charles Evans Hughes in 1916 attempted to mend the party fences by appealing to the dissident Progressive "Bull Moosers" who had supported Roosevelt in 1912. Many items jointly pictured an elephant and a moose with the slogan "Republicans/ Bull Moosers/Get Together."

World War I and the subsequent push for isolationism in foreign affairs heavily flavored GOP strategies in 1920. "Back to Normalcy," touted one slogan, and "America First" was another frequent Warren Harding refrain. Blaming the Democrats for bringing America into World War I, one poster depicted Harding in front of a U.S. flag and the Democratic candidate James Cox raising the banner of the League of Nations. "Under Which Flag?" the poster queried. Isolationism was not the only hot-button issue of the day. Harding actively courted the women's vote after the passage of the 19th Amendment. One GOP ad warned "Women! For Your Own Good Vote the Republican Ticket." It stated further:

> From the beginning of time woman has been the enemy of War. From the beginning of time, she has been its most unhappy victim. In proportion as woman's influence molds the politics of nations wars will diminish. For woman is for peace. . . . Your interest as a woman, your interest as a mother, your interest as a citizen, your interest as the financial manager of the home combine to require the return to Republican principles.

In 1924 automobile license-plate attachments made their debut and advertised Calvin Coolidge's run for the presidency. The popular "Keep Cool with Coolidge" and "Deeds—Not Words," a reference to Coolidge's "Silent Cal" image, decorated many Republican items. Herbert Hoover's candidacy in 1928 coincided with the introduction of matchbook

Hoover Bumper Sticker. *Source:* National Archives.

covers with political messages. A variety of Hoover materials contained images of owls with inscriptions such as "Hoo Hoo Hoover for President" and "Hoo But Hoover." As secretary of commerce under Harding and Coolidge, the Hoover camp emphasized the good economics with "Four More Years of Prosperity! Why Change?" A number of negative items from 1928 alluded to the Democrats' selection of Al Smith as the first Catholic to be nominated by a major party. Hoover was portrayed as "A Christian in the White House" and "100% American." Hoover's reelection bid in 1932 played up Franklin Roosevelt's radical image, "Vote for Hoover and Be Safe." Economic themes were emphasized and despite the devastating effects of the Great Depression, banners heralded President Hoover's and Vice President Charles Curtis's quest by encouraging voters to "Keep Them on the Job" because "We Want to Turn the Corner to Prosperity."

In 1936, Kansan Alfred Landon utilized his home state's flower, the sunflower, on many items. Another

Coolidge Campaign Song. *Source:* National Archives.

Landon–Knox Decal Sticker. *Source:* Smithsonian Institution.

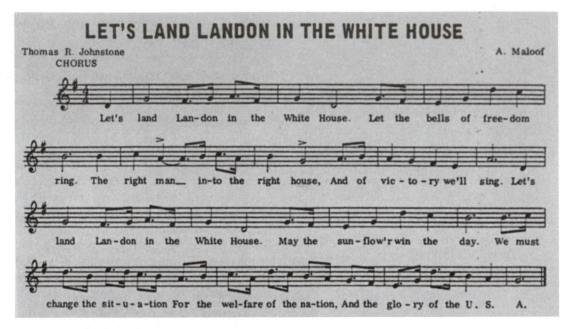

Landon Campaign Song. *Source:* National Archives.

approach was the numerous plays on his last name: "Land on Roosevelt" and "Landon on the New Deal," picturing an elephant flattening a donkey. His running mate's name, Frank Knox, was also used in the clever slogan "Landon Knox Out Roosevelt." "Landon, Deeds Not Deficits" addressed the Republican concern over the enormous cost of FDR's New Deal domestic policies.

Wendell Willkie's campaign in 1940 produced a variety of rebus puzzle items picturing a key ("Will" + key). He was the "Key to Prosperity," and voters were

Willkie Campaign Song. *Source:* National Archives.

Willkie Poster. *Source:* Franklin Delano Roosevelt Library.

encouraged to "Let Willkie Unlock Opportunity." Additional catch phrases touted "Life Begins in '40" and "We Want Willkie." Roosevelt's unprecedented third-term run unleashed an equally unparalleled number of negative campaign objects from the Republicans. Among the anti-Roosevelt offerings in 1940 were "Washington Wouldn't/Grant Couldn't/Roosevelt Shouldn't"; "No Dictator"; "No Third Termites"; "Third International/Third Reich/Third Term"; "Two Times Is Enough for Any Man"; "Two Good Terms Deserve a Rest"; and "Dr. Jekyll of Hyde Park"; the last a reference to the Roosevelt family home. They targeted the first lady as well with "We Don't Want Eleanor Either" and "No Royal Family." The war in Europe played a minor role in the 1940 campaign with "Draft Roosevelt and He'll Draft You," and "Wallace And Roosevelt"—a button that featured Roosevelt's and his running mate, Henry Wallace's, last names with larger first letters to spell WAR. A companion piece simply stated "Guard Our Peace," with the larger first letters also indicating GOP. Willkie levied criticism too at the administration's domestic agenda. The New Deal was renamed the "Raw Deal" or the "Misdeal," and FDR's policies were compared with those envisioned under the Republicans: "Roosevelt and Relief/Willkie and Work." Election Day, November 5, was billed by Republicans as "Dethronement Day," but voters thought otherwise and elected Roosevelt to a third term.

New York Governor Thomas Dewey opposed Roosevelt in 1944. "Peace & Jobs Quicker with Dewey & [John] Bricker" and other buttons critical of FDR's war leadership had Dewey–Bricker surrounded by the words "Mothers, Sisters, Sweethearts, Wives." Change was a constant theme of the Republican camp: "Dewey/We Are Due for a Change," and voters were encouraged to "Go Forth (4th) With Dewey." In 1948, Dewey returned as the GOP nominee and hence the phrase "Dewey's Due in '48." His 1948 opponent, Harry Truman, was fodder for a number of slogans. One button was embossed with a "4-H Club: Help Hurry Harry Home," while a second declared "I want a True-man/Not Harry." Another, alluding to the refurbishing of the White House, intoned "Truman Was Screwy to Build a Porch for Dewey." In the end, Truman kept the presidency and the porch.

Flasher buttons and bumper stickers were inaugurated during the 1952 race. These were put to good use with arguably the most effective campaign slogan ever—Dwight Eisenhower's "I Like Ike" (and in 1956, "I Like Ike Even Better"). Voters were also urged to "Let's Clean House with Ike and Dick." In a reference to the famous photograph of opponent Adlai Stevenson with a hole in his shoe, the Eisenhower campaign issued a button with the shoe, "Don't Let This Happen to You—Vote for Ike." Mamie Eisenhower and Pat Nixon were promoted heavily in 1952 to portray their husbands as family men. In a veiled allusion to Stevenson's divorced status, one button in 1956 pleaded "Mothers for Mamie/Keep a Mother in

Eisenhower Campaign Song. *Source:* National Archives.

the White House." In 1952 there was an accent on peace and security given Eisenhower's military background and the increasingly unpopular war in Korea. One Ike brochure in 1956 intoned, "He stopped the War in Korea/He proved he could keep the peace/Under his administration we have jobs with peace. . . . Let's keep it that way."

In 1960, Vice President Richard Nixon underscored his experience ("Experience Counts") and his expertise in foreign affairs. Running mate Henry Cabot Lodge and

Campaign Buttons For and Against Eisenhower. *Source:* National Archives.

his tenure as U.S. ambassador to the United Nations were also touted. With numerous allusions to the famous 1959 "kitchen debate" between Nixon and Soviet leader Nikita Khrushchev, buttons stressed that Nixon was "The One Man to Deal with Khrushchev." A different button addressed Democrat John F. Kennedy's wealth. It pictured a sign in front of the White House proclaiming, "Not for Sale, Elect Nixon." Similar to his vice presidential bids, the 1960 campaign also heavily promoted Pat Nixon as an asset with "We Want Pat."

Barry Goldwater was "A Choice Not an Echo" in 1964. Clever pro-Goldwater items utilized his trademark horn-rimmed glasses, while others contained the chemical formulas for gold and water, AU H_2O, or pictured a glass containing a gold-colored liquid engraved "H_2O." Novelty items such as a golden-hued canned soda were lauded as "The Right Drink for the Conservative Taste" (LBJ countered with a less inspired "Johnson Juice"). Perhaps the best known of the Goldwater slogans was an attempt to deflect his radical image: "In Your Heart, You Know He's Right." Buttons also featured a quote from Goldwater's acceptance speech, "Extremism in the Defense of Liberty Is No Vice; Moderation in the Pursuit of Justice Is No Virtue."

In 1968, Nixon returned as the Republican standard-bearer, prompting phrases such as "This Time, Nixon" and "Nixon's the One." An interesting Nixon artifact from this campaign was a doorhanger patterned after a "Peanuts" cartoon character, "Even the Great Pumpkin is Voting Nixon–[Spiro] Agnew." Running for reelection in 1972, Nixon attempted a more formal campaign. There were few items in this election that referred to him by his nickname, "Dick," although the need for Nixon was "Now More Than Ever." Instead, voters were simply asked to "Reelect the President in 1972." A series of ethnically oriented trinkets heralding various communities' support for the president appeared too in 1972. In the wake of Watergate, "Cubans for Nixon" assumed a whole new meaning.

Gerald Ford's 1976 run highlighted the restoration of hope and dignity he had brought in Watergate's aftermath: "He's Making Us Proud Again." The campaign promoted slogans such as "Prosperity/Peace/Public Trust." First Lady Betty Ford was also featured prominently as voters were reminded, "Betty's Husband for President in 1976." Another GOP tactic was to underscore the "Jimmy Who?" feelings about relatively unknown challenger Jimmy Carter by noting "You Can Be Sure with Ford." Carter's peanut farmer background was an additional source of ire as Americans were presented with the choice of "Peanuts on Your Table/or a Ford in Every Garage." They were also warned with "Don't Settle for Peanuts—Elect Ford," which pictured an elephant crushing a peanut (wearing Carter's toothy grin) in its trunk.

In the fallout of the Iran hostage crisis and other issues that caused the Carter administration to appear weak in 1980, Ronald Reagan campaigned on the slogans "Let's Make America Great Again" and "The Time Is Now." More humorous ones suggested "Carter to the Peanut Patch; Reagan to the White House." In 1984 the Reagan campaign went all out to close the so-called gender gap and to counter the novelty of a woman, Geraldine Ferraro, running for vice president on the Democratic ticket. Numerous "Women for Reagan" items were launched in 1984. The Republicans also heralded that Reagan–Bush were "Bringing America Back" and that it was "Morning in America." The GOP invoked patriotism as well, and citizens were encouraged to "Help Keep America Great/Re-elect Reagan." George Bush made history in 1988 by becoming the first sitting vice president since Martin Van Buren to win the presidency. One pro-Bush flasher button interchanged Democrat Michael Dukakis's image with Carter, along with the alternating words "Here We Go Again/Tax and Spend." Another, in the shape of a beer can, intoned "This Bush Is for You." In Bush's 1992 reelection bid, the overriding national issue might have been change, but Bush was still fighting old Democratic Party adversaries with "Clinton Is a Repackaged McGovern/Carter Copy/Recycled Mondale/Dixie Dukakis . . . Bush in '92. The *Real* Change." Others unsuccessfully invoked Bush's Gulf War win by promoting the candidate on a button shaped like a medal and the logo "Victory in '92."

Robert J. Bookmiller

BIBLIOGRAPHY

Fischer, Roger A. *Tippecanoe and Trinkets Too: The Material Culture of American Presidential Campaigns, 1828–1984.* Urbana: University of Illinois Press, 1988.

Frank, Beryl. *The Pictorial History of the Republican Party.* Secaucus, NJ: Castle Books, 1980.

Keller, Morton. *The Art and Politics of Thomas Nast.* New York: Oxford University Press, 1968.

Schlesinger, Arthur M., Jr., Fred L. Israel, and David J. Frent, eds. *Running for President: The Candidates and Their Images.* New York: Simon and Schuster, 1994.

Sullivan, Edmund B. *Collecting Political Americana.* New York: Crown, 1980.

Campaigns and Elections

Electioneering practices have always been essential to the Republican Party and its predecessors (the Federalist and Whig parties) because the major purpose of a political party is to gain power through contesting and winning elections. Nomination processes, campaign regulations, and voting procedures directly influence electioneering practices. The general trend in U.S. elections has been from party-centered nominations and campaigns to candidate-centered campaigns. Electoral modifications and the commercialization of campaigns have severely limited the power of party elites to select and control the campaigns of their party's candidates since the beginning of the twentieth century. Nonetheless, the Republican party, with its well-financed, highly organized, technologically advanced national party committees, and its common ideology, has a significant impact on elections.

In the early 1790s nomination practices varied from state to state. In some states, committees of correspondence nominated and campaigned for candidates. In many states, nominations were solicited at outdoor mass meetings. Consequently, many candidates competed for each elected office. Gradually, patriotic societies and fraternal organizations began to nominate and campaign for candidates. Before 1800, suffrage was extremely limited, and most voting was done by the viva-voce method. Election officials required voters to announce their selection publicly at the voting place. This method was very time consuming and open to intimidation. In addition, different governments held their elections on different dates.

Partisan electioneering methods conformed to the nomination and voting procedures. One of the first electioneering activities of the nascent political parties was to acquire auxiliaries among the press. In 1792, Alexander Hamilton used U.S. Treasury Department funds to subsidize a friendly Philadelphia paper, *Gazette of the United States*, published by John Fenno, to advocate the Washington administration's policies. Democratic-Republicans quickly responded with the *National Gazette*.

The presidential election of 1800 was the first party-centered U.S. election. While the Democratic-Republicans were better organized, the Federalist Party used federal government patronage to mobilize its supporters. The party also received the endorsement of clergy from established churches who urged their parishioners to save the country from the heretical Thomas Jefferson. Like its opponents, Federalist activists urged members to cast a straight party vote for state and local elections.

By 1824, most white males could vote, and electoral processes were modified to accommodate the increased number of voters. States reduced the sizes of electoral districts and started to use paper ballots that were printed and distributed by the parties. The

Democratic-Republican Party became very organized at local and state levels and campaigned systematically. School-district and township committees in rural areas and ward and county committees in the cities met frequently, sponsored local candidates, and produced political information. State party committees performed a wide range of functions including distributing literature, collecting funds, printing ballots, preparing lists of eligible voters, measuring voter preferences, and organizing political rallies.

During the second administration of Andrew Jackson, the Whig Party developed as a reaction to the president's war on the National Bank. The Whigs had remarkable success in a relatively short time by using effective campaign techniques. Like the Federalists, Whigs relied on the support of established churches and portrayed their campaigns in moral terms as struggles between virtue and vice, natives and immigrants, Protestants and Catholics. Leaders such as Thurlow Weed systematically solicited contributions from businessmen to support Whig campaigns. Whig politicians held mass rallies complete with parades, picnics, speeches, and political memorabilia. Candidates for congressional, state, and local offices also conducted individual or joint canvasses with their opponents, usually consisting of long speeches and debates. In the mid-1800s, Whig Party activists responded to fraudulent Democratic electioneering practices with their own illegal tactics. For example, Whig operatives hired "repeaters," got them drunk, and transported them to different polling places to cast many votes. The party-centered nature of electioneering practices was reflected in presidential campaigns. Party managers conducted the national campaign with the assistance of state and local leaders, while the presidential candidate stayed at home and appeared unconcerned by the election.

In the 1840 election, the Whig Party bypassed prominent party leaders and chose a popular military hero, General William Henry Harrison, to lead the presidential ticket. When Democrats satirized Harrison as an "Old Granny" who would be content to "spend the rest of his days in a log cabin with a barrel of cider," Whig campaigners launched a counterattack centered on an alliterative slogan, "Tippecanoe and Tyler too." Whig contributors raised a massive campaign war chest to pay an army of canvassers to get out the vote for "Old Tip." Whig papers used the slogan "Van, Van, . . . used up man" to attack President Van Buren, and monster rallies featuring a log cabin and a barrel of cider were held in major cities. The Whig electioneering strategy was so successful that the party won control of the federal government in

1840. Unfortunately, the party began to disintegrate over the slavery issue. Before it collapsed, however, Whigs captured the presidency in 1848 by choosing another celebrated military general, Zachary Taylor, leaving a legacy of nominating military heros to its successor.

The Republican Party used its predecessor's electioneering practices. During the 1860 election, "Wide Awakes" marching clubs paraded through northern cities marshaling support for Republican candidates. In the Republican era, party bosses used political patronage to a far greater extent than their predecessors. As an illustration, throughout the Civil War, President Lincoln went beyond any previous president in using federal government resources to strengthen his party. For example, when Republican governors in Pennsylvania, Connecticut, and Ohio faced reelection difficulties, federal government employees from those respective states were assessed 1% of their salaries to fund the governors' campaign expenses and given free railroad passes to go home and vote. As Lincoln campaigned for reelection, the Republican National Committee used government offices and systematically assessed contributions from all federal government employees.

From the late 1860s to the end of the 1890s, the Gilded Age, parties had their greatest influence on election outcomes. Elections were conducted with torchlight parades, gigantic rallies, and presidential "front porch" campaigns. Republicans dominated the national government and most northern states in the early 1870s, and created strong political machines. Republican activists established interlocking relationships with corporate leaders and raised huge war chests. Candidates waved "the bloody shirt," characterizing their opponents as traitors and copperheads, and urged men "to vote the way they shot." Illegal electioneering practices also flourished. Republican machine operatives hired repeaters, printed their ballots on distinctive colored paper, sometimes paid or intimidated voters at polling places, and stuffed ballot boxes.

While Republican congressional, state, and local candidates canvassed voters, party leaders still conducted presidential campaigns. For example, President Grant refused to make any statements during his campaigns. In 1880, Republican presidential campaign tactics began to change when James Garfield's home was only eight miles from a main line railroad station. Garfield gave carefully worded front-porch speeches to crowds who journeyed to his farm. After James Blaine unsuccessfully broke with tradition by touring the country in 1884, Benjamin Harrison deliberately built his pres-

idential campaign in 1888 around voter pilgrimages to his Indianapolis home. Campaign managers organized the crowds into delegations, scheduled their visits, and gave them prepared questions.

In 1883 the Pendleton Act ended assessments of federal appointees. Republican bosses turned to state employees and corporate contributions to replace lost revenues. Mark Hanna, a millionaire businessman, waged an unprecedented nationwide campaign to elect William McKinley in 1896. Hanna established Republican headquarters in New York and Chicago and divided campaign activities among national, state, and interest-group committees. Party officials installed a complete bookkeeping and auditing system to regulate the flows of campaign monies. Republican operatives distributed more than 200 million pieces of literature during the election season and levied fixed assessments on corporations and banks. Hanna's committees raised a Republican campaign war chest of between $10 million and $16 million, while businessmen encouraged their employees, clients and customers to vote for Republicans. While the Democratic presidential candidate, William Jennings Bryan, toured the country, McKinley stayed home in Canton, Ohio, and successfully campaigned from his front porch.

Electoral reforms initiated by Progressive Republicans such as voter registration, the Australian ballot, voting machines, and primary elections were widely adopted by the end of the nineteenth century. In the early 1900s, campaign contributions for federal elections were strictly regulated. As these reforms gradually took effect, candidate-centered electioneering practices began to replace party-centered methods. In 1912 mass advertising techniques, movies, and recordings were used in the presidential campaigns. Regional tours became common for state and national candidates, and presidential aspirants also began to canvass voters. But party officials continued to solicit candidates and dominate presidential nominations at party conventions.

During the interwar period, candidates began to rely on professional expertise and technology. Radio campaign advertisements were used in the 1920s and private public relations firms and opinion polls became features of major campaigns in the early 1930s. Since the 1950s, electioneering activities have become increasingly capital intensive, commercialized, and candidate centered. In 1952 Dwight Eisenhower used regional television ads in his campaign, and in 1960 televised candidate debates were initiated. The commercialization of campaigns spread rapidly to state and local elections in the 1960s. Television, commercial polls, and computerized voter and contributor lists made it possible for candidates to bypass party officials and activists. Though the cost of campaigns soared, the new-style campaign methods freed candidates from labor-intensive party campaigns. For the past 45 years, candidates have developed their own campaign organizations to conduct electioneering activities. For example, in 1968 and 1972, Richard Nixon's personal organization conducted both the nomination and election campaigns, excluding the Republican National Committee.

Party power over nominations also has eroded in the past 25 years. Reforms initiated after the 1968 Democratic National Convention resulted in the increase of primaries, dramatically decreasing the power of state and city party leaders. Despite its loss of power, Republican Party leaders continue to be key players in electioneering activities. County parties in conjunction with candidate campaign efforts distribute literature, post signs, place newspaper advertisements, and issue press releases. Local parties are also very effective in conducting voter registration drives and get-out-the-vote campaigns, and state parties provide research and polling data as well as campaign literature and seminars to candidates.

Under a loophole in the 1979 campaign finance law amendment, contributions to political parties are virtually unlimited ("soft money"). These donations are for party-building activities such as gathering voter and contributor lists, polling, conducting campaign schools for candidates, advertising promoting the party as a whole, and contributing to state and local parties. In the late 1970s, the Republican National Committee under the direction of William Brock dramatically increased its resources by extensive direct-mail programs. Brock used the money to expand the RNC's electioneering activities and to serve state parties. In 1980 the committee ran very effective national television ads targeting the Democratic leadership and urging viewers to "vote Republican, for a change." The RNC also started a new division to revive state and local parties, recruit and train local candidates, and influence primary elections. For example, between 1977 and 1980, more than 10,000 Republicans attended campaign seminars and the RNC financially supported more than 4,000 state legislative candidates.

Throughout the past 15 years, Republican candidates have harnessed the power of television. For example, during his campaigns Reagan skillfully used television ads and manipulated media coverage to appeal to voters on an ideological level. He and his successor, George Bush, used images, sound bytes, and negative ads to sell themes, such as "a Kinder, Gentler Nation," and weaken their opponents. During the 1994 election, Republican candidates for the House of Representatives successfully coordinated their campaigns on an ideological level with the Contract with America and recaptured control of Congress. Consequently, though electioneering activities are increasingly candidate centered, Republicans may be returning to traditional party campaigns in the sense that their candidates are campaigning with a partisan ideology. Moreover, the RNC and Republican congressional committees continue to have a significant impact on U.S. elections in terms of finance, technology, and support for local and state parties.

Janet B. Manspeaker

SEE ALSO Presidential Nominations and Elections, The Presidential Nomination Process

BIBLIOGRAPHY

Mayer, George. *The Republican Party: 1854–1964.* New York: Oxford University Press, 1964.

Merrill, Horace Samuel, and Marion Galbraith Merrill. *The Republican Command: 1897–1913.* Lexington: University Press of Kentucky, 1971.

Reichley, A. James. *The Life of the Parties.* New York: Free Press, 1992.

The Cold War

Many in the Republican Party were very hesitant about the United States' getting involved in a Cold War when it began around 1947, but just over four decades later, Republican presidents could claim credit for bringing it to a successful end. After overcoming an initially strong isolationist tendency, the Republican Party, led by Dwight D. Eisenhower, accepted America's global responsibility and became the party of the strong president and the party of the active foreign policy agenda. As the Cold War progressed, the Republican Party's 1940s isolationism, as represented by Senator Robert Taft of Ohio, became the 1980s internationalism, as represented by President Ronald Reagan.

When President Harry Truman went to a Republican-controlled Congress in 1947 to outline his plans for America's role in a Cold War with the Soviet Union, one of the biggest hurdles he had to overcome was the Republican isolationism that had been especially prevalent since the end of World War I. The Republican Party was split between a more liberal internationalist wing and a more conservative isolationist wing, and Congress was where the isolationist wing was most powerful. Truman succeeded in winning over many Republican conservatives by raising the specter of global communism and arguing that the

United States was the only nation that could stop the expansion-minded Soviet Union.

Part of Truman's success at convincing both the Congress and the American people of the necessity of containing Soviet communism was the advice he received from Republican Senator Arthur Vandenberg of Michigan, who was himself more of an internationalist than an isolationist. Vandenberg advised Truman that the only way to get an economy-minded Republican Congress to accept the commitments implied in Truman's containment doctrine was to scare them into accepting an international role in a moral struggle against the evils of communism.

By the time that Eisenhower became president, the internationalist wing of the Republican Party was clearly winning the internal debate over the direction that America's Cold War policy should take. In his 1953 inaugural address, Eisenhower defined the range of American interests in broad terms and soundly rejected the "fortress America" mentality propagated by isolationists such as Senator Taft. Eisenhower ran for president as much to keep Taft and the isolationist wing of the Republican Party out of power as for any other reason. Eisenhower's administration continued to follow the principles of containment, but given the extraordinary commitments it required in both monetary and manpower terms, adjustments were deemed necessary. His "new look" approach to containment involved a shift in strategy that relied more on nuclear weapons and the threat of nuclear retaliation to deter the Soviet Union and relied less on American ground forces and equipment. As a result of implementing this new strategy, Eisenhower was able to appease conservatives in his own party by limiting the use of America's conventional military resources but still maintain an internationalist posture by relying on new and advanced nuclear technology to keep the "pressure" on the Soviet Union.

By the 1950s, the Cold War had also helped bring to an end the congressional bipartisanship on foreign policy that had existed for several decades. Americans were becoming increasingly anxious about communism, and while differences between the two parties over policy were certainly evident, many Republicans felt that the Roosevelt and Truman administrations had fostered an environment where communism could flourish in America. After Alger Hiss, a State Department employee in the Roosevelt administration, was convicted of perjury in 1950, Senator Joseph McCarthy of Wisconsin charged that the case helped explain the foreign policy failures of the Roosevelt and Truman administrations. As examples, McCarthy cited America's failure to protect Eastern Europe from the

Soviet Union and the "loss" of China. While many in the Republican Party were uncomfortable with McCarthy's extreme rhetoric, others were more than happy to use the situation for political gain.

In the 1952 presidential campaign, Eisenhower pledged that he would "go to Korea," and within a few months of his taking office he brought the war there to an end. The remainder of the 1950s was consumed with Cold War diplomacy that was largely driven by Eisenhower's conviction that resources were finite and sooner or later the differences between the United States and the Soviet Union would have to be brought to a conclusion. Eisenhower's eagerness to come to an understanding with the Soviet Union was not always appreciated by his own foreign policy advisers. For instance, John Foster Dulles, Eisenhower's secretary of state, often stressed the risks more than the advantages of negotiating with the Soviet Union and frequently pushed for a much tougher line against communism than Eisenhower liked. Given this struggle, perhaps it is not so hard to understand why the Eisenhower years are difficult to categorize. Eisenhower, the victorious war general, was also Eisenhower, the man of peace. He was also the prophet who warned of the emerging military-industrial complex very early in the Cold War. Yet Eisenhower also advocated a defensive posture that spotlighted nuclear weapons and left the Kennedy administration to deal with ongoing covert operations in such troubled spots as Cuba and Vietnam.

The 1960s were relatively quiet for the Republican Party because, while the nation was being turned upside down over the Vietnam War, Republicans controlled neither the executive nor legislative branches of government for any length of time during that decade. In any event, most Republicans were in general agreement with the Johnson adminsitration's escalation of the Vietnam War, and both Kennedy and Johnson knew that they could count on at least tacit Republican backing for U.S. involvement in Vietnam. In reality, Republican support for the war effort lasted only as long as public support lasted. In 1964, Republican presidential candidate Barry Goldwater advocated a "let's win" strategy of total military victory in Vietnam while his Democratic opponent, Lyndon Johnson, pledged that he would not commit American fighting forces in Southeast Asia. Johnson broke that pledge only months after his inauguration. By 1968, when public opinion toward the war had turned sour, Republican candidate Richard Nixon promised to get America out of the war and Johnson decided not to seek reelection.

The Nixon administration found it just as hard to deal with Vietnam as did the Johnson administration. While Nixon and his chief foreign policy adviser,

Henry Kissinger, were busy working on an exit strategy from Vietnam that combined "peace with honor," a Democratic Congress was slowly pulling the rug out from under them. The Nixon strategy for exiting Vietnam was to force the Viet Cong and North Vietnamese to give up and at the same time withdraw U.S. troops. By the end of Nixon's first term, American forces had dropped more tons of bombs in Indochina than during the four years that the Johnson administration had carried on the war, sent troops into Cambodia, and carpet-bombed suburbs of Hanoi. While Nixon's strategy of escalating the war to force an end may have eventually succeeded, neither the American public nor the Congress had the stomach for it. Congress began passing extremely restrictive antiwar measures and in 1973 passed the War Powers Resolution, which was designed to limit the president's ability unilaterally to deploy U.S. troops abroad.

Yet, despite the mess that Nixon inherited in Vietnam, his administration also made considerable progress toward easing Cold War tensions with China and the Soviet Union. In 1972 Nixon ignored his own staunch anticommunist attitude and traveled to China seeking and eventually achieving improved Sino-American relations. Simultaneously, he sought to improve relations with the Soviet Union through the strategy of détente, which included assurances to the Soviets that the United States had no immediate military or political aims on Moscow and included negotiations aimed at reducing the size and scope of both Soviet and American strategic nuclear weapons systems. The Cold War thaw initiated by the Nixon administration's détente strategy lasted until 1979, when the Soviet Union invaded Afghanistan, and President Jimmy Carter imposed economic sanctions in response.

In 1981 Ronald Reagan swept into power with a reenergized vision of America's role in the world. By listening to the confrontational and aggressive rhetoric of the Reagan administration it would have been hard to predict the vast improvements in Soviet–American relations that were to come within the decade. In just a few years, President Reagan went from condemning Russia as an "evil empire" to calling Mikhail Gorbachev his "friend." Reagan came into office with the conviction that détente was nothing more than the United States' surrendering itself to the Soviet Union and that the Soviet threat was global and absolute. He saw the world in a very simple and straightforward way. The root of all evil was the Soviet Union, and the only way to overcome that evil was to reenergize America's economic and military strength.

Reagan was, on one hand, a hardliner who surrounded himself with people who advocated an assertive and expensive foreign policy that would force the Soviet Union into a corner. In his first budget, Reagan called for dramatic increases in military spending with renewed emphasis on research and development, not simply to maintain the status of containment, but to regain the initiative in the Cold War. The new and improved American military would be one that included B-1 bombers, theater nuclear forces in Europe, a Strategic Defense Initiative to protect America from missile attacks, and a 600-ship navy. The Soviet economy, Reagan contended, could not keep up with such rapid and expensive increases, and thus it would force the communists to make some tough decisions about war and peace. On the other hand, Reagan was also a pragmatist who saw the wisdom of negotiating with the Soviet Union from a position of strength. In a new period of détente, the Reagan administration concluded the Intermediate Nuclear Forces Treaty (INF) and opened talks on the Strategic Arms Reduction Treaty (START).

In 1985 Gorbachev assumed power in the Soviet Union, and within a short while it became obvious that he was not a "typical" Soviet leader. Gorbachev was a very outgoing and personable man, and he and Reagan got along well. Together the two leaders set the stage for the end of the Cold War.

Between 1989 and 1991, President George Bush presided over the fall of the Iron Curtain across Eastern Europe and the collapse of the Soviet Union. Bush strongly supported Russia's first democratically elected president, Boris Yeltsin, even as some advised him not to get too close, and by 1993, Democratic President Bill Clinton was offering Yeltsin increased U.S. aid to help Russia through the transition phase to democracy.

With the Cold War over, isolationism crept back into American politics in the 1990s, and Republicans in Congress best represented the new isolationist mood. With the collapse of the Soviet Union and the end of the Cold War, many Americans began to question the necessity of continuing the internationalism that had characterized U.S. foreign policy for the past four decades. A couple of factors added strength to the traditional isolationist tendencies of Americans. For one, there no longer appeared to be a threat. From Truman's presidency forward, communism was the enemy, and Americans believed that they could not afford to turn their backs on the world. President Clinton's was the first administration in nearly four decades not to have a single Cold War issue from which to define itself. Second, economic factors had made it such that Americans felt as though a "peace dividend" was well overdue. With high budget deficits and public anxiety about the fundamental health of the nation's economy, Americans appeared ready to get their own house in order. Perhaps nothing exemplified the new isolationism better than the difficulty that foreign aid bills had making it through Congress or the difficulty that President Clinton had convincing a Republican Congress to support his committment of 20,000 American troops to the Bosnian peace mission in late 1995.

Quentin Kidd

SEE ALSO Foreign Policy

BIBLIOGRAPHY

Crockatt, Richard. *The Fifty Years War.* London: Routledge, 1995.

Gaddis, John Lewis. *Strategies of Containment.* Oxford: Oxford University Press, 1982.

———. *The United States and the End of the Cold War.* Oxford: Oxford University Press, 1993.

Hersh, Seymour M. *The Price of Power: Kissinger in the Nixon White House.* New York: Summit Books, 1983.

LaFeber, Walter. *America, Russia, and the Cold War 1945–1984.* New York: Knopf, 1985.

Levering, Ralph B. *The Cold War, 1945–1972.* Arlington Heights, IL: Harlan Davidson, 1982.

McCormick, Thomas J. *America's Half-Century, United States Foreign Policy in the Cold War and After.* Baltimore: Johns Hopkins University Press, 1995.

Talbott, Strobe. *Deadly Gambits.* New York: Vintage Books, 1985.

Congressional Elections

The Republican Party dominated Congress throughout the Civil War and Reconstruction. During this period, the GOP won landslide victories in most of the House and Senate elections. The party's dominance ended in the 1870s. From that point on, until the mid-1890s the two parties competed almost evenly in congressional elections. The Republicans won most of the Senate elections, and the Democrats won the majority of the House elections.

Another Republican era in congressional elections began in the 1890s and lasted until 1932. During these years, Republicans won the majority of House and Senate seats in all but four elections (1910–1916). To offset the Democrats' dominance in the South, the Republicans piled up huge majorities in the Northeast, Midwest, and West.

This electoral pattern, however, ended abruptly in the 1930s. Congressional Republicans fell victim to the Democratic realignment that swept through the entire political system. An incredible shift occurred in con-

gressional voting patterns. From 1928 to 1936, the number of Republican representatives dropped from 267 to 89, and the number of Republican senators declined from 56 to 17. The Democrats kept their southern base and expanded to dominate in other regions as well. Only the most Republican districts and states elected Republicans. There were questions whether the Republican Party could survive as a viable party in congressional elections.

But the Republicans' fortunes started to improve in the late 1930s. In the 1938 election, they gained 80 House seats and 6 Senate seats. These results followed the typical pattern of the party of the president's (or both the president and the majority in Congress) losing seats in a midterm election. The Republicans continued to gain ground in the 1940s. By 1944, they had pushed their seat totals to 190 in the House and 38 in the Senate.

In another election following the midterm pattern, the Republicans in 1946 picked up 56 House seats and 13 Senate seats to win back the majority in both chambers. So the Republicans controlled Congress in 1947 for the first time since 1932. They won by winning back many of the districts and states outside the South that they had lost in the 1930s.

Their success was short lived, however. In an enormous turnaround in 1949, the Democrats returned as the majority party in both houses as the Republicans lost 75 House seats and 9 Senate seats. An important part of the campaign was the debate over the record of the Republican Congress. Congressional Republicans defended their record against attacks from President Truman and congressional Democrats.

The 1950s began with promising developments for congressional Republicans but ended in disaster. After cutting the Democrats' House and Senate majorities in the 1950 election, the Republicans won a big victory in 1952. For the first time since 1928, they won the presidency and the majority in both houses of Congress. With this victory, a new Republican era appeared to be at hand. As it turned out, this was not to be. In fact, the 1954 election began the worst period ever for Republicans in congressional elections. They did not win both the House and Senate again in the same election until the 1990s. They lost the remaining congressional elections of the 1950s. The 1958 defeat was especially significant. Not only did they lose by a landslide, but the Democrats cut into their midwestern and northeastern bases. This did not bode well for the future. The Republicans needed to do well in northern states to make up for their weakness in the South.

The Republicans' misfortunes continued through the 1960s as they lost all the congressional elections during the decade. The worst defeat was in 1964 when they dropped to only 140 representatives and 38 senators. These low numbers made it difficult for the Republicans to stop the Democrats from passing the Great Society programs and the other parts of the Democratic agenda. There were, however, two favorable developments during the 1960s for the congressional Republicans. First, the Republican Party finally started making some inroads in southern House and Senate elections. Second, the Republicans rebounded in the 1966 and 1968 elections to reduce the Democrats' lead in the House and Senate.

The Republicans' recovery from the 1964 disaster gave them hope for the 1970s. But problems developed, and their losing streak in congressional elections continued through the decade. The Democrats won another landslide victory in 1974. This election followed the revelations associated with the Nixon administration and the Watergate scandal. The Republicans lost by a wide margin again in 1976, but they picked up a few seats in 1978. One bright spot for the Republicans in the 1970s was their continued improvement in the South. They had advanced to the point of winning a substantial minority of the southern congressional seats. The Republicans kept losing the House and Senate elections, however, because the Democrats had gained enough new seats in northern areas to offset their southern losses.

The Republicans' losing string in congressional elections finally ended, at least in the Senate, in 1980. They gained 12 Senate seats to win the majority for the first time since the 1952 election. They picked up 33 House seats, but fell short of a majority in the House. The Republicans benefited from the decline in the popularity of President Carter and congressional Democrats that resulted from various economic and foreign policy problems. With their increased strength in the House and Senate, the Republicans were able to pass some of the major parts of the Reagan administration's agenda in 1981 and 1982.

Another big turnaround occurred in the 1982 House election as the Democrats added 26 seats to their majority. The Republicans were hurt by the recession of the early 1980s and the opposition of some voters to the Republicans' domestic policies. With their reduced numbers, the House Republicans were in a much weaker position to defend the policies of the Reagan administration. Even though the Democrats won the majority of the national vote in the 1982 Senate election, the Republicans retained the majority of Senate seats. Split-party majorities continued in 1984 as the Democrats won the House election, and the Repub-

licans won in the Senate. The presidential coattail effect was weak in the election as President Reagan won reelection by a landslide, but the Republicans picked up just a few seats in the House and lost two in the Senate.

The Republicans lost control of the Senate in 1986 as the Democrats gained 8 seats. The Republicans also lost a few seats in the House as the results followed the typical midterm election pattern. So the Republicans were back to being the minority party again in the House and Senate.

The 1988 election produced another divided government as George Bush won the presidential race and the Democrats retained control of the House and Senate. This pattern continued through 1992 as the Democrats won yet another congressional election in 1990. The split-party control ended with the 1992 election as Bill Clinton won the presidency and the Democrats kept their congressional majorities.

During the many years of Republican losses in congressional elections, political observers offered a variety of reasons for the party's difficulties. One of the Republicans' claims was that their weakness in House elections was caused, at least in part, by the Democrats' control of the redistricting process in many states. Democrats, of course, disagreed and argued that they won because they had better candidates and more popular policies. Many analysts thought that the Democrats were aided by the high reelection rate of incumbents that developed in the 1960s. As the majority party, the Democrats benefited more from this because they entered each congressional election with more incumbents. In addition, the Democrats were helped by their lead in party identification. During most of this period, more Americans considered themselves Democrats than Republicans.

Finally, in the 1994 election, the Republicans won control of both the House and Senate for the first time in 40 years. They had lost 20 consecutive House elections and 17 of the previous 20 Senate races. The Republicans' victory was based on a large shift in partisan voting patterns. The Republican House candidates received the majority of the total House vote for the first time since 1946. Newt Gingrich and the other Republican House leaders organized a national House Republican campaign based on the Contract with America, their policy platform. The Republicans' success in the South was one of the major factors that produced the voting changes. After many years of steady growth in the South, the Republicans finally won the majority of southern seats.

Larry M. Schwab

BIBLIOGRAPHY

Abramson, Paul R., John H. Aldrich, and David W. Rohde. *Change and Continuity in the 1992 Elections.* Rev. ed. Washington, DC: CQ Press, 1995.

Ross, Baker K. "The Congressional Elections." In *The Election of 1988*, ed. Gerald M. Pomper. Chatham, NJ: Chatham House, 1989.

Duncan, Philip D., and Christine C. Lawrence. *Politics in America 1996.* Washington, DC: CQ Press, 1995.

Erikson, Robert S. "The Puzzle of Midterm Loss." *Journal of Politics* 50 (1988): 1011–1029.

Hinkley, Barbara. *Congressional Elections.* Washington, DC: CQ Press, 1981.

Jacob, Charles E. "The Congressional Elections and the Outlook." In *The Election of 1976*, ed. Gerald M. Pomper. New York: McKay, 1977.

———. "The Congressional Elections." In *The Election of 1980*, ed. Gerald M. Pomper. Chatham NJ: Chatham House, 1981.

Jacobson, Gary C. "Congress: Politics After a Landslide without Coattails." In *The Elections of 1984*, ed. Michael Nelson. Washington, DC: CQ Press, 1985.

———. *The Politics of Congressional Elections.* 3rd ed. New York: HarperCollins, 1992.

Jones, Charles O. *Every Second Year.* Washington, DC: Brookings Institution, 1967.

Maisel, Louis Sandy, and Joseph Cooper, eds. *Congressional Elections.* Beverly Hills, CA: Sage, 1981.

Mann, Thomas E., and Norman J. Ornstein. *The American Elections of 1982.* Washington, DC: American Enterprise Institute, 1983.

Mayhew, David R. "Congressional Elections: The Case of the Vanishing Marginals." *Polity* 6 (1974): 295–317.

McAdams, John C., and John R. Johannes. "The 1980 House Elections: Reexamining Some Theories in a Republican Year." *Journal of Politics* 45 (1983): 143–162.

Wilcox, Clyde. *The Latest American Revolution? The 1994 Elections and Their Implications for Governance.* New York: St. Martin's Press, 1995.

Congressional Party Leadership

Along with committees, political parties are the central organizing institutions in the Congress. Although political parties are traditionally more important in the House of Representatives, they are important in the Senate as well. In the House, it is along party lines that the Speaker is selected and House rules are adopted. In both the House and the Senate, parties organize competition, aid in building coalitions, and provide formal leadership.

PARTIES IN CONGRESS: PROCEDURAL AND SUBSTANTIVE COALITIONS

Political parties are central to the organization of the Congress. Two-party politics in the United States usually allows for a clear majority and minority within both houses of Congress. Charles O. Jones has identified two kinds of majorities in congressional parties: procedural and substantive majorities. Although substantive majorities—those "necessary to pass legislation"—vary greatly from issue to issue (and thus are not necessarily congruent with partisan majorities), "normally, membership of procedural majorities and minorities coincides with that of the two political parties" (Jones 1992, 233). Elsewhere, Jones makes this organizational role of parties more explicit: "the party willingly assumes the responsibility for organizing the process—providing personnel (including leadership), making rules, establishing committees" (Jones 1964, 5). Through procedural organization, political parties gain control of the House Speakership, the administration of Congress, as well as the schedules and committee systems in both chambers.

In 1835 (the 24th Congress), the Whigs (the precursor to the Republican Party) became the oppositional minority in both the House and the Senate. By the 25th Congress, the Whigs had only one less House member than the Jacksonian Democrats who controlled the chamber. Two Congresses later, the Whigs became the majority party in both the House and the Senate for the first time. From 1841 to 1855, the Whigs would trade control of the House with the Democrats, having lost control of the Senate for good in 1844.

In 1855, the Republican Party became the majority party in the House and the primary opposition in the Senate. During the Civil War era and until the 1874 elections, Republicans controlled both the House and the Senate. Although controlling the Senate for all but two Congresses (the 46th and the 53rd) from the 1870s until 1912, Republicans were relegated to minority status in the House from 1875 to 1894 with the exception of two Congresses (the 47th and the 51st).

In the twentieth century, Republicans have, for the most part, played the role of the minority in both the House and the Senate. Of the 48 Congresses from 1901 to 1996, Republicans have controlled the Senate in 18 Congresses and the House in only 14 Congresses. Since 1931, Republicans have controlled the House in only 3 of 33 Congresses (the 80th, the 83rd, and the 104th), gaining a House majority on the coattails of Dwight Eisenhower in 1952, and during the midterm elections of the administrations of Democratic Presidents Truman and Clinton.

Aside from this procedural role, parties also help to organize both the House and Senate as floor voting coalitions. Although substantive majorities do vary, Melissa Collie and David W. Brady (1985) claim that from "a historical perspective the congressional parties have proved the broadest and most stable basis of coalition formation in the Congress" (p. 284). Perhaps more important than party in building coalitions, however, are personal ideology, constituency, and the numerous other factors that cause one to be either a Republican or a Democrat. Cooper, Brady, and Hurley (1977) found that, from 1887 to 1969, electoral factors were "a highly influential determinant of party voting" in Congress (p. 159). Indeed, electoral factors in addition to a changing issue agenda can have an impact on the extent to which party is important in creating and maintaining substantive majorities; at times in U.S. history, party voting in Congress has been relatively high, while at other times factors such as region have predominated (Sinclair 1978).

For most of the twentieth century, party has been a less important consideration in congressional floor voting. Examining data from 1887 to 1969, Cooper, Brady, and Hurley (1977) found that over "the course of this century there has been a clear and substantial decline in the strength of party as a determinant of voting" (p. 137). Extending this analysis through the 1970s, Collie and Brady (1985) found that "the salience of the partisan cleavage declined in the 1950s and again in the 1970s" (p. 282), although there has been "a striking resurgence of partisanship" in the 1980s. Pointing to extremely high unity among House Democrats in 1987 and 1988, David W. Rohde says: "To find a Congress in which Democratic unity was higher than that, one has to go back to the Sixty-first Congress (1909–1911), when 'Boss' Cannon was Speaker. Republican unity also increased, albeit not so sharply, from 71 percent in 1969 to 80 percent in 1988" (Rohde 1991, 14).

LEADERSHIP POSITIONS AND ACTIVITIES: AGENCY AND CONTENT

Any examination of leadership in Congress must examine the methods and norms that govern parties' selection of leaders. Robert L. Peabody (1976) found that Republican succession in the House is marked by "open competition and even revolt against established leadership" (p. 291). In the Senate, Republican succession has involved much less conflict and much more stability than in the House. Examining seven case studies of leadership change, Peabody finds external variables to have the least impact on leadership selec-

tion. He says, "Leadership selection is primarily, although not exclusively, determined by individual competition played out within positional and institutional restraints" (p. 469).

Congressional party leaders are selected by the majority of their party in the House and Senate, respectively. Thus the congressional party caucus represents each leader's constituency. One valuable way of studying congressional party leadership views leaders as "agents of the members who select them and charge them with advancing members' goals" (Sinclair 1995, 9). In attempting to further members' collective goals, party leaders throughout history have had to accomplish different tasks while enjoying varying levels of resources. Joseph Cooper and David W. Brady (1981) offer a contextualist view of party leadership that helps explain the variability of leadership activity; they suggest that "the impact of institutional context on leadership power and style is determined primarily by party strength" (p. 424). By comparing the leadership styles of Speakers Cannon and Rayburn, Cooper and Brady find that "institutional context rather than personal skill is the primary determinant of leadership power" (p. 423), as well as leadership style. Thus it is within varying contexts and as agents of their fellow partisans in Congress that party leaders can best be understood.

House Leaders

In the House, the core party leadership posts are the Speaker, the floor leaders, and the whips within each party. The House Speaker serves the dual role of leader and spokesperson for both the House as an institution and his or her (historically the former) party within the House. Mary Parker Follett suggests that American Speakers have unique parliamentary powers beyond those powers typically afforded speakers in legislative assemblies. Speakers have the political powers of appointment and control of the Rules Committee, the political power of attempting to influence party followers, and the rights commonly afforded any member of the House (Follett 1896, 299–301). As Barbara Sinclair suggests, the Speaker's parliamentary and political powers are used in tandem, one reinforcing the power of the other: "The Speaker wears two hats; he is an officer of the House and the leader of his party in the chamber. The two roles are neither clearly separable nor of equal importance. The Speakership is predominantly a partisan position; within the limits of fairness, he is expected to use the resources provided by the first role to help him perform the second" (Sinclair 1983, 34).

Second in command in the majority party and first

in the minority party are the House floor leaders. The majority leader's position is defined by the leader's relationship to the Speaker and thus varies depending on the desires of the Speaker and the implicit or explicit negotiation of that role by the Speaker and the majority leader. Traditionally, majority leaders are "responsible for scheduling legislation for floor consideration" as well as acting as the party's leader on the floor, and taking "the lead on issues that are important to the party but that are politically too risky for the Speaker" (Sinclair 1983, 42). The minority floor leader is the leader of his party in the House. "Minority leaders promote unity among party colleagues, monitor the progress of bills through committees and subcommittees, and forge coalitions with like-minded members of the opposition party" (Davidson and Oleszek 1994, 175).

Parties in the House also employ party whips and rather elaborate whip systems, which aid Speakers and floor leaders by providing a conduit of information from leaders to followers, and vice versa. Whips also attempt to persuade colleagues, encourage and facilitate attendance for floor votes, and count votes that often provide leaders with the knowledge of the outcome before a vote even takes place.

Senate Leaders

The Senate—described as "an institution rife with rampant individualism" (Davidson and Oleszek 1994, 177)—has considerably weaker party leadership than does the House. In the Senate, the floor leaders are the heads of both parties. Formal party floor leadership did not exist in the Senate until the early twentieth century. In the Senate as in the House, majority and minority whips assist floor leaders in carrying out leadership tasks. As in the House, Senate whips' chief functions are relaying information and counting votes.

THE HOUSE REPUBLICANS: DOMINANCE, RESIGNATION, AND RESURGENCE

In the late nineteenth and early twentieth centuries, House Republican leaders exercised substantial control over the legislative process. From 1889 to 1891 and from 1895 to 1899, Representative Thomas Brackett "Czar" Reed served as the Speaker of the House. Holding a thin majority in the House, Speaker Reed's Republicans were at the mercy of the minority House Democrats, who used parliamentary techniques to impede the work of the House Republican majority. The

most famous technique is known as the *disappearing quorum*. In order for a House vote to count, a quorum (i.e., half the House membership) must be present. Democrats who were present refused to vote so as to prevent the presence of a quorum. Using the power of the Speaker's chair, "Czar" Reed counted as present Democrats who refused to vote. Claiming that the "object of a parliamentary body is action," Reed exerted the right of the majority in the House to accomplish its goals.

Building on the powers established by Reed, Republican Speaker Joseph Cannon led the House from 1903 to 1911. Cannon used the power to assign members to committees, refer bills to committee, control the House Committee on Rules, and the Speaker's chair during floor debate to control the House. Having extended his powers beyond their limits, however, Cannon agitated Democrats and Progressive Republicans, who would join forces to strip Cannon of many of his powers (Jones 1992).

Republicans controlled the House from 1919 until 1931, but divisions within the party caused Republicans to decentralize power in the House rather than strengthen party leaders. Democrats took control of the House in 1931 and, with the exceptions of the 80th and the 83rd Congresses, continued to control the House until the 104th Congress. The Republicans' experience in the minority from 1955 to 1995 was more than twice the time any party in American history had languished in the minority.

In the 1980s and 1990s, divisions within the House Republican Party over the minority's role in policymaking sharpened. Republican leader Robert Michel of Illinois led, for the most part, as an accommodationist, pragmatically working with Democratic leaders to change policy where possible. Representative Newt Gingrich represented a different style, however. "Gingrich and other junior Republicans formed the Conservative Opportunity Society (COS), a group devoted to sharpening partisan distinctions on the House floor" (Connelly and Pitney 1994, 27). These more vocal Republicans sought actively to criticize the Democrats controlling Congress in an attempt to build a Republican majority in the House.

Working from the backbench of the House Republican Party, Gingrich used the media and his confrontational style to build support among fellow Republicans. In 1989, Gingrich was selected Republican whip by a narrow margin. And when Michel announced his retirement in 1994, Gingrich fended off challenges to become Republican leader. As Gingrich solidified his position as leader, House Republicans were building a House majority that would make Gingrich the first

Republican Speaker since Speaker Joseph Martin Jr. in the 83rd Congress.

SENATE REPUBLICAN LEADERSHIP: PARTICIPATION AND ACCOMMODATION

Senate party leaders on both sides of the aisle were strong in the 1950s. Republican leaders William Knowland and Everett Dirksen "helped to centralize what was a much 'flatter' hierarchy compared with that of the House" (Ornstein, Peabody, and Rohde 1993, 25). Nevertheless, Donald Matthews's assertion that, compared to Senate Democrats, Republican Senate leadership is "more formalized, institutionalized, and decentralized" has proved, with occasional exceptions, to be true from the 1970s to well into the 1990s (Ornstein, Peabody, and Rohde 1993, 23). Since the 1950s, however, Senate leadership in both parties has been more collegial, with the party sharing power with rank-and-file senators.

Republican senators' frustration with being the minority party has not equaled that of their colleagues in the House. For one reason, Republican senators did not languish in the minority as long as did House Republicans. Although Democrats took over the Senate in 1933, Senate Republicans, like their House counterparts, would capture the majority of seats in the 80th and 83rd Congresses and would control the Senate from 1981 to 1987. Second, even while in the minority, Senate Republicans have considerable influence on policymaking. According to Bader and Jones (1993), "Even as minority leader, [Senate Republican Robert] Dole could affect scheduling to allow room for compromise. Filling a variety of policy roles, Dole . . . and other Republicans made important contributions" (p. 300). As a result of this share in policymaking, Senate Republicans have not punished their leaders as House Republicans traditionally have.

NEW STYLES OF CONGRESSIONAL LEADERSHIP

Students of congressional party leadership focus on the internal tools party leaders have at their disposal. Indeed, these scholars have explained a great deal of leadership activity by focusing on party leaders' use of the whip system, power over committee appointments (both standing committees and conference committees), power over the Rules Committee, power to refer bills, and many other significant internal tools. But scholars have paid little attention to the external leadership strategies party leaders employ. Perhaps the most significant new strategy is the use of the media to build coalitions within the House. On the Republican side, this new strategy is most associated with Speaker Newt Gingrich, who, as a backbencher, used C-SPAN to focus attention on possible ethics violations by then Speaker Jim Wright. As Speaker, Gingrich used the media to set the agenda of the House, build winning coalitions, and challenge President Clinton. Gingrich is not the only party leader to use the media, however. Increasingly, members of Congress "have come to expect their party leaders to function as outward-oriented public leaders" (Sinclair 1995, 260). Progressively, party leaders have met these increasing expectations to shape the public debate through the mass media.

Douglas Harris

BIBLIOGRAPHY

Bader, John B., and Charles O. Jones. "The Republican Parties in Congress: Bicameral Differences." In *Congress Reconsidered*, 5th ed., ed. Lawrence C. Dodd and Bruce I. Oppenheimer, 291–314. Washington, DC: CQ Press, 1993.

Collie, Melissa P., and David W. Brady. "The Decline of Partisan Voting Coalitions in the House of Representatives." In *Congress Reconsidered*, 3rd ed., ed. Lawrence C. Dodd and Bruce I. Oppenheimer, 272–287. Washington, DC: CQ Press, 1985.

Connelly, William F., Jr., and John J. Pitney Jr. *Congress' Permanent Minority?* Lanham, MD: Rowman and Littlefield, 1994.

Cooper, Joseph, and David W. Brady. "Institutional Context and Leadership Style: The House from Cannon to Rayburn." *American Political Science Review* 75 (1981): 411–425.

Cooper, Joseph, David W. Brady, and Patricia A. Hurley. "The Electoral Basis of Party Voting: Patterns and Trends in the U.S. House of Representatives, 1887–1969." In *The Impact of the Electoral Process*, ed. Louis Maisel and Joseph Cooper, 133–165. Beverly Hills: Sage.

Davidson, Roger H., and Walter J. Oleszek. *Congress and Its Members*. 4th ed. Washington, DC: CQ Press, 1994.

Follett, Mary Parker. *The Speaker of the House of Representatives*. New York: Longmans, Green, 1896.

Jones, Charles O. *Party and Policy-Making: The House Republican Policy Committee*. New Brunswick, NJ: Rutgers University Press, 1964.

Jones, Charles O., Joseph G. Cannon, and Howard W. Smith. "The Limits of Leadership in the House of Representatives." In *New Perspectives on the House of Representatives*, 4th ed., ed. Robert L. Peabody and Nelson W. Polsby, 233–259. Baltimore: Johns Hopkins University Press, 1992.

Ornstein, Norman J., Robert L. Peabody, and David W. Rohde. "The U.S. Senate in an Era of Change." In *Congress Reconsidered*, 5th ed., ed. Lawrence C. Dodd and Bruce I. Oppenheimer, 13–40. Washington, DC: CQ Press, 1993.

Peabody, Robert L. *Leadership in Congress: Stability, Succession and Change*. Boston: Little, Brown, 1976.

Rohde, David W. *Parties and Leaders in the Postreform House*. Chicago: University of Chicago Press, 1991.

Sinclair, Barbara. "From Party Voting to Regional Fragmentation, 1933–1956." *American Politics Quarterly* 6 (1978): 125–146.

———. *Majority Leadership in the U.S. House*. Baltimore: Johns Hopkins University Press, 1983.

———. *Legislators, Leaders and Lawmaking*. Baltimore: Johns Hopkins University Press, 1995.

Contract with America

The Contract with America was a written pledge by Republican incumbents and candidates for the House of Representatives in 1994 that promised that a majority Republican House of Representatives would hold floor votes on ten separate provisions as well as change the manner in which the House of Representatives conducts itself. On September 27, 1994, Representative Newt Gingrich of Georgia presided over a ceremony at which more than 330 Republican members of Congress and candidates for the House signed the Republican Contract. The Contract had been written and presented by Republicans on the advice and counsel of political consultants who had constructed the broad themes of the document after conducting opinion polls and focus groups (Burger 1994).

The Contract with America promised that if Republicans became the majority party in the House as a result of the November 8 elections, the House Republican majority would reform House rules as well as hold floor votes on ten legislative provisions. The prologue of the Contract dealt specifically with changing rules and procedures of the House of Representatives. First, Republicans promised to remove congressional exemptions from laws that apply to the rest of the country. In addition, Republicans promised to hire an independent auditing firm to investigate "waste, fraud, or abuse" in Congress. Republicans would also alter the House committee system by reducing the overall number of committees, placing term limits on committee chairpersons, banning proxy voting in committee, and reducing the size of committee staffs by one-third. Further reforms promised by Republicans included the requirement of a three-fifths majority to pass a tax increase and the reform of federal budget accounting procedures.

Republicans also promised a "more open" House of Representatives through a reform of the practices under which bills can be debated and amended on the floor of the House. In contrast to the practices of the Democratic House of the 1980s, Republicans hoped to bring bills to the House floor under less restrictive rules, thus allowing for more amending flexibility at the floor stage of the legislative process. Republicans found, however, that there are procedural advantages for the majority in using restrictive rules, and they used them more frequently throughout the 104th Congress. Democrats attempted to score political points early in the 104th Congress by complaining that the Republican package that would change the House rules was brought to the House floor under a rule that prohibited floor amendments.

The main text of the Contract with America included ten proposals for legislation that were to be brought to the House floor for a vote. The Republican Contract did not promise passage of legislation, but rather floor votes on each of the provisions of the Contract during the first 100 days of the 104th Congress. The ten provisions called for (1) a constitutional amendment requiring a balanced federal budget allowing the president a line-item veto; (2) an anti-crime bill that would limit habeas corpus appeals, mandate minimum sentences for certain crimes, and provide federal block grants for local law-enforcement agencies; (3) a bill that would limit federal Aid to Families with Dependent Children (AFDC); (4) a bill designed to give tax credits to adoptive parents and those caring for elderly dependents; (5) a bill designed to give tax credits for families with children and a reduction in taxes for some married couples; (6) a bill to restrict U.S. participation in UN activities; (7) a bill to expand Social Security benefits for some senior citizens; (8) a measure to cut the capital gains tax; (9) a bill to require losers of civil lawsuits to pay the legal expenses of the winner; and (10) a constitutional amendment limiting terms of senators and representatives to 12 years.

With such Contract plank titles as the "Taking Back Our Streets Act," the "Personal Responsibility Act," the "American Dream Restoration Act," and the "Common Sense Legal Reform Act," the Contract had a public relations objective in addition to its policy objective. Republicans spoke of the Republican "revolution" of 1994, which they hoped would have an impact not only on public policy but also on the political process. Moreover, the Republicans hoped to show that they could get something accomplished, that they could end Washington "gridlock."

The Contract with America sought to nationalize the 1994 midterm congressional elections. Congressional elections are often fought over issues of local rather than national importance. And when midterm congressional elections are nationalized, it is usually in the form of a referendum on the performance of the president. The 1994 midterm congressional elections, which saw the Republican Party recapture the U.S. Senate and take control of the House of Representatives for the first time in 40 years, were, argued Republicans, decided on the public's reaction to the Contract with America. There is, however, no consensus regarding the extent to which the Contract was a factor in the GOP's 1994 electoral victory. The 1994 elections may, in fact, have been a referendum on Democratic performance from 1993 to 1994, but by adopting a midterm platform, Republicans attempted to nationalize the elections on ideological, issue-oriented grounds. As Republican leader Newt Gingrich claimed, the Contract was an attempt to set forth a "positive governing agenda" (Burger 1994).

The significance of the Contract rests primarily in its position as a focal point for the new Republican majority in the 104th Congress. In the first 100 days of the Republican Congress, GOP leaders fulfilled their contract by having a House floor vote on each of the ten provisions. The Contract established an agenda and a goal for House Republicans and thus produced a remarkably productive House of Representatives. By March 31, 1995, the Congressional Research Service reported that the House had been in session nearly four times as many hours, on average, as it had in the same period of time over the previous 20 years. Similarly, the CRS reported that the 104th Congress passed 111 bills by March of 1995, compared with an average production of 86 for that amount of time in the previous 20 years. Republicans were quite successful in securing House passage for their Contract as well. Nine of the ten provisions were passed. Only the Contract provision calling for a constitutional amendment limiting congressional terms to 12 years failed to pass the House as a coalition of senior Republicans and Democrats voted against the provision. Despite this high level of activity, however, it is important to note that overall production in Congress is down: "Through April 7, five public laws had been enacted. By the same date in 1993, 13 had been enacted. In 1991, the number was 25 under President George Bush" (Cassata 1995, 990).

Some claim that this productivity is a result of stronger, more activist Republican Party leadership in Congress. Certainly Speaker Gingrich and House Majority Leader Dick Armey of Texas were as active as congressional leaders have been in the House in recent years. But in many ways their tasks were more easily achieved than those of previous congressional leaders. First, the Republican majority was more ideologically homogeneous than recent Democratic majorities had been. Second, the Contract with America purposefully

avoided including controversial provisions that would be difficult to pass (Katz 1995).

Political scientist David W. Rohde suggests that congressional leadership can be described as "conditional party government," wherein party leaders use their powers only when the majority of their party supports a particular bill (Rohde 1991). In the case of the Contract with America, Republican leaders specifically sought to include provisions that were popular with Republican members of Congress, Republican congressional candidates, and the public. Controversial issues were left out of the Contract. Thus, each provision met the requirements of conditional party government. When one views the Contract and the 104th Congress in the light of Rohde's conclusions, the leadership's success seems less extraordinary.

The Republican Contract with America helped nationalize the 1994 midterm congressional elections and lent credence to the Republican "revolution." For these reasons, the Contract is an important document. But distilled to its bare minimum, the Contract seems to be a somewhat less significant document. It established easily met requirements. It promised no passage of legislation but simply a floor vote on its provisions. What is voted on the floor of the House is determined by the House Committee on Rules, usually an arm of the majority party leadership. Each of the issues included in the Contract was supported by the majority of Republicans, thus the Contract represented only a prearrangement of what would have otherwise been the Republican congressional agenda. The Contract was, in fact, only a promise by Republicans to act like a majority party in Congress if they won a majority of the congressional seats.

The shift in the policy agenda resulting from the Republican takeover of the House is certainly significant. Furthermore, the Contract served as a centralizing document that produced an extremely active first session of the 104th Congress. In terms of the Republican "revolution," however, it was the fact that Republicans had won a majority that was revolutionary, rather than the circumstances under which they won that majority. The Republican agenda, with or without the Contract, would have been the same.

Douglas Harris

SEE ALSO Newt Gingrich

BIBLIOGRAPHY

Burger, Timothy. "Democrats Break Silence on GOP 'Contract.'" *Roll Call*, September 26, 1994, 1.

Cassata, Donna. "Republicans Bask in Success of Rousing Performance." *Congressional Quarterly Weekly Report*, April 8, 1995, 986–990.

Katz, Jeffrey L. "GOP Faces Unknown Terrain Without 'Contract' Map." *Congressional Quarterly Weekly Report,* April 8, 1995, 979–981.

Rohde, David W. *Parties and Leaders in the Postreform House.* Chicago: University of Chicago Press, 1991.

Crime

Until the dawn of the twentieth century and the social problems that accompanied urbanization and industrialization, crime policy was often viewed as properly belonging to state and local authorities. The U.S. Constitution, combined with a tradition of federalism, reserved police powers for the states, and both the federal and state governments were satisfied to keep it that way.

Before the 1900s, most of the federal government's forays into crime policy involved regulating interstate commerce and the railroads, protecting the mails, combating counterfeiting, and conducting such moral purity crusades as those against pornography and lotteries. With the Sherman Antitrust Act in the late 1800s, Congress struck out against monopolies.

The 1920s, however, first propelled crime to an issue of national political status. The 1930s followed with a dramatic war on crime, prompted by a series of brazen kidnappings and bank robberies. Since then, crime policy has emerged episodically as a national political issue, often in response to a rising crime rate, inner-city strife, or other social situations, such as the civil rights and antiwar demonstrations of the 1960s. Crime became an important political issue of the 1960s, taking the public spotlight in, for instance, the election of 1964. Before the 1960s, little federal money was allocated for crime control. Yet the 1960s were not the first years in U.S. history during which crime arose as a major political issue. The 1920s saw crime rise to the fore, as did the 1980s and 1990s. The issue continues to be one of importance, with Republican candidates for public office often attempting to outdo one another with law-and-order rhetoric.

Since the rise of the federal government's involvement in crime, the typical Republican position has been to advocate a strong law-and-order response to social and criminal unrest, focusing on repressing it through such policies as bolstering law enforcement and lengthening prison sentences.

In 1908 Republican President Theodore Roosevelt helped increase the federal government's anticrime role by proposing the creation of a Bureau of Investigation within the Department of Justice. But recalling allegations that Roosevelt had misused the Secret Service for his political ends and wary of the president's motives, Congress rejected his proposal. The president reacted by establishing the bureau by executive order. Meantime, the Republican Party platform of 1908 lauded President Theodore Roosevelt for his "brave and impartial enforcement of the law."

In 1910 Congress passed a piece of landmark legislation, the Mann Act, officially the White Slave-Trade Act, prohibiting the transportation of women across state lines for prostitution. A few years later, Congress passed the Webb–Kenyon Act over Republican William H. Taft's veto. The act forbade the use of interstate commerce for the movement of liquor into dry states.

And in 1914 the seeds of the drug war of the 1980s were planted as Congress passed the landmark Harrison Narcotics Act, which regulated professionals dealing with narcotic drugs. Enforcement of the legislation increasingly criminalized drug trafficking and the use of narcotics, which in turn prompted still more legislation.

As the century moved on, crime increasingly moved into the spotlight as a political issue, and the Prohibition period brought yet more attention to it. In 1928 the Republican Party's platform reaffirmed its loyalty to the enforcement of the Constitution's laws and the 18th Amendment, which prohibited the sale, transportation, and manufacture of alcohol. During the presidential election that year, Prohibition was a major point of contention between Democratic candidate Alfred E. Smith and the Republican nominee, Herbert Hoover, who went on to win the election. The Republican platform of 1932 commended President Hoover's "intensive and effective drive" against criminals and stated that the party favors the enactment of rigid penal laws to help stamp out "gangsters." Yet Hoover lost that year to Democrat Franklin D. Roosevelt, who as part of his New Deal went on to expand Hoover's drive against criminals into a war on crime.

Although organized crime had certainly existed in America before World War I, federal legislators had generally considered the problem to be the province of state and local authorities. But as organized crime increasingly pervaded the national consciousness, Congress began to react—first with anti-racketeering statutes enacted in 1934 and 1946 and later with the proceedings of the Senate Special Committee to Investigate Organized Crime in Interstate Commerce, otherwise known as the Kefauver Crime Committee, after its chairman, Estes Kefauver, a Tennessee Democrat. The committee, formed in 1950, included Republicans Charles W. Tobey of New Hampshire and Alexander Wiley of Wisconsin.

During the second half of the twentieth century, growing concern over organized crime, drug abuse, and violent crime, as well as the advent of the civil rights movement, brought a massive increase in federal involvement in law-and-order issues. And in the mid-1960s, a dramatic shift in national attitude took place: crime began to be viewed as a national problem warranting a national solution. In fact, it was largely the 1964 presidential campaign battle among Republican Senator Barry Goldwater, Independent candidate George Wallace, and Democrat Lyndon B. Johnson that returned crime to the national spotlight as a policy issue. In reaction to civil rights demonstrations and a rising crime rate, both Goldwater and Wallace included a strong law-and-order plank in their campaigns. Goldwater, in particular, often referred to "crime in the streets" and the need for "law and order." Both Goldwater and Wallace accused Johnson of fostering a leniency that abetted crime. Holding to conservative tradition, Goldwater and Wallace promised to repress crime with a stricter enforcement of the criminal code. Johnson responded not so much with a war on crime as a War on Poverty, hoping to reduce the crime rate by ameliorating what such Democratic liberals as Johnson saw as its root cause.

In 1967, as the next presidential election was approaching, the crime issue remained alive, kept to the fore of public and political consciousness by a high crime rate and continuing racial tensions. In February, President Johnson presented a detailed message to Congress on crime that included a proposal for the enactment of the Safe Streets and Crime Control Act of 1967. The act established within the Justice Department a large-scale categorical grant program to aid states and localities in their battle against crime.

The president's bill encountered formidable opposition in Congress, particularly from Republicans but also from southern Democrats, both of which groups were becoming increasingly disenchanted with Johnson's Great Society program, which, they believed, had made big promises but had fulfilled few of them. The objection to the president's bill, though, was not over the need for it, but over how the funds should be allocated. Johnson's bill would distribute money to the cities; Republicans wanted the grants delivered to the states. Amid rioting in Newark and Detroit, a subcommittee of the House Judiciary Committee held hearings on the bill.

Meantime, as the debate over Johnson's proposal continued into spring 1968, law and order again rose as a central issue in the presidential election. Richard M. Nixon, seeking the presidency for the Republican Party, employed the issue in his campaign, as did George Wallace, who was running for the presidency as an Independent candidate. Both Nixon and Wallace argued that decisive action needed to be taken against crime—and that action meant enforcing the criminal laws more forcefully. The voting public, having its attention further focused on crime by the campaign messages of Nixon and Wallace, waited to see what Congress would do with Johnson's proposal.

Despite the lack of enthusiasm among Republicans and conservative southern Democrats for the administration's bill, the House Judiciary Committee reported out a bill that, in accordance with the president's proposal, provided direct grants to local authorities. Yet 12 of the 15 Republicans on the Judiciary Committee lobbied strongly against the bill when it was introduced to the floor. Republican Representatives William Cahill of New Jersey, Thomas Railsback of Illinois, and Edward Beister of Pennsylvania, along with support from House Minority Leader Gerald R. Ford, galvanized not only their fellow Republicans but also conservative southern Democrats to oppose the bill in its present form. They argued that the bill would usurp states' rights and allow the central government to dictate the law enforcement policies of local authorities.

The Republicans counterattacked with an alternative named the Cahill Amendment, after its sponsor. It proposed distributing block grants to state agencies rather than grants-in-aid to local authorities. Besides House Republicans and many southern Democrats, 47 of 50 governors, many of whom were members of the Republican Party, supported the Cahill Amendment. In contrast, big-city majors, a group that also included some Republicans, backed the administration's bill. Thus, division arose within the Republican Party over the Safe Streets and Crime Control Act.

But the small fracture between the Republican mayors and Republican governors did not keep Republicans in the House of Representatives from rejecting the administration's bill in favor of a bill sanctioning a stronger state role, which was what the Republican governors had wanted.

Next, the Senate Judiciary Committee began considering the administration's bill. The committee's chairman, Democrat John McClellan of Arkansas, frowned on Johnson's proposal. Backed by three other southern Democrats on the Judiciary Committee, Democrat McClellan joined committee Republicans to rewrite the administration's bill to emphasize a strong state role in fighting crime. Republican Senator Roman Hruska of Nebraska, a conservative, became a chief sponsor of the version that was finally adopted. But some of the more liberal Senate Democrats, arguing that the revised bill was anti-city, obtained a compromise stipulating that states had to funnel percentages of the grants to local government units. In the end, as in the House, Republicans joined forces with conservative southern Democrats to rout the administration's bill and substitute a state-oriented version for it. President Johnson reluctantly signed the Omnibus Crime Control and Safe Streets Act of 1968 into law, saying that it contained "more good than bad." The act, which included the establishment of the Law Enforcement Assistance Administration, was a victory for critics of the Great Society, including the Republican Party. The enforcement administration survived into the 1980s, when battles over the federal budget phased it out.

In the late 1960s and early 1970s, the administration of Republican President Richard Nixon continued the attack against crime begun by Johnson, but with an emphasis on law and order. Nixon's policy, however, came under attack, largely from liberals, who saw Nixon's law-and-order campaign as attempts to put down civil rights activists and antiwar demonstrators. President Nixon, in contrast, used the rising public sentiment that city streets were unsafe to assail members of the Democrat Party as being "soft on crime."

President Nixon helped several pieces of anticrime legislation become law, including the landmark Organized Crime Control Act of 1970. Sponsored by Senator McClellan, the conservative southern Democrat from Arkansas, and Senator Samuel J. Ervin, a conservative Democrat from North Carolina, the act included Title IX, the Racketeer Influenced and Corrupt Organizations statute, which launched a concerted drive against organized crime. The statute established severe criminal and civil penalties for using racketeering money or procedures in authentic businesses. But it also led to numerous civil lawsuits, which in turn prompted Congress to review the statute.

In 1970 President Nixon also helped encourage passage of the Comprehensive Drug Abuse and Control Act, which reinforced narcotics penalties. Yet the act did not stop the issue of drug abuse from reappearing in nearly every election year thereafter; the issue eventually culminated during the 1980s in conservative Ronald Reagan's War on Drugs and, later, passage of the 1988 Anti-Drug Abuse Act, which further increased penalties for both users and dealers, established a cabinet-level drug czar, and set aside additional federal funds to fight drugs.

But Nixon's criticism of the Democrats and his anticrime crusade soon ebbed, as he found himself accused of perpetuating criminal acts as part of the Watergate affair. Several of his high-ranking administration officials, including Attorney General John N. Mitchell, were convicted of violating the law.

The 1980 campaign of conservative Republican presidential candidate Ronald Reagan revived the Republican Party's law-and-order theme and reinvigorated crime as a national political issue after it had flagged slightly during the latter half of the 1970s. After being elected president, Reagan's anticrime policies focused on repressing, rather than preventing, crime. During Reagan's tenure, fighting crime translated into combating drug trafficking and abuse. He expanded the federal government's drug interdiction effort, while Nancy Reagan, the first lady, led a "Just Say No" campaign that equated drug use with immorality. In 1986 Congress passed the Anti–Drug Abuse Act, which greatly expanded Reagan's war against trafficking and abuse.

As Reagan's drug war heated up, a three-way division emerged among prominent Republicans in administration over how to carry out the drug war. Attorney General Edwin Meese, a conservative Republican, advocated getting tough with drug users. He said drug testing should be required of all workers, arguing that it reduces accidents and boosts productivity while keeping people from disobeying the law. Another faction, led by Otis Bowen, Reagan's secretary of health and human services, stressed education and rehabilitation, an approach often advocated by Democrats. William J. Bennett, a conservative who served as Reagan's secretary of education, argued for greater military involvement in stemming the influx of drugs. He also urged Reagan to appoint a drug czar, but the president opposed it on grounds that it would mean more "big government."

Despite the Reagan administration's efforts to eradicate drugs, many political analysts saw the issue as a political defeat for Reagan, largely because the war against drugs had not been won. And many thought it could not be won.

But that view did not stop Republican President George Bush from continuing Reagan's antidrug drive among his crime-fighting efforts. After passage of the Anti–Drug Abuse Act of 1988, which created a cabinet-level drug czar, Bush appointed Bennett to the post after Republican Senator Dennis DeConcini of Arizona turned it down. Bennett focused on combating street sales of drugs and on financing antidrug efforts in the countries from which the drugs were originating.

In the 1990s, crime has remained a dominant political issue. Following the bombing of the World Trade Center in New York and the attack on the Federal Building in Oklahoma City, President Bill Clinton, a moderate Democrat, fought for a crime bill aimed at combating terrorism.

In late 1994, conservative Republicans, led by Newt

Gingrich, the Speaker of the House from Georgia, tendered a plan to reduce crime prevention spending by $5 billion, starting a conflict that polarized the Republican Party along conservative–moderate lines. Conservatives maintained that such spending is wasteful, while the moderates in the party favored crime-prevention spending, arguing that it is cheaper than building prisons. Conservative Gingrich, in particular, has called crime prevention proposals "pork." The proposals include such programs as the establishment of "drug courts" that obtain treatment for addicts and midnight basketball leagues that give teenagers an alternative to hanging out on city streets.

Moderate Republicans—including not only some of those in Congress but also those at the state and local levels—insisted that Congress allow local authorities flexibility in how to combat crime.

Besides cutting federal money for crime prevention, conservatives in Congress, especially the authors of the Contract with America, have sought to alter President Clinton's "community policing" drive to emphasize hiring more police officers and buying more crime-fighting hardware. Newt Gingrich has said that people who dial 911 want "a policeman, not a social worker."

Other Republicans in Congress disagreed with Gingrich and his allies. Utah Senator Orrin Hatch, chairman of the Judiciary Committee, argued that federal crime policy should be aimed at empowering local citizens against crime by allowing them to spend federal anticrime money without detailed restrictions. Representative Henry Hyde of Illinois, an independent-minded Republican who is chairman of the House Judiciary Committee, has also voiced disagreements with Gingrich's approach.

Despite opposition from some of his fellow conservative Republicans, Gingrich has held firm. In fact, he has hardened his repression-over-prevention approach further. Speaking to the Republican National Committee in July 1995, Gingrich called for the death penalty for anyone caught shipping narcotics into the country.

Meanwhile, the Clinton administration has resisted attacks on its crime policies by the conservative Contract with America Republicans. Attorney General Janet Reno, appointed by President Clinton, has argued forcibly for the effectiveness of community policing, adding that it has the overwhelming support of the public. Clinton also set up a National Commission on Crime Control and Prevention and charged it with developing a strategy for controlling and preventing crime and violence.

Other major points of contention over crime policy during the mid-1990s have included search-and-seizure rights and, especially, federal aid. Expanding police powers of search and seizure has been high on the GOP anticrime agenda. In particular, Republicans have been seeking to alter the "exclusionary rule" to permit illegally obtained evidence to be used in court as long as the police officer involved believed that he was acting in good faith at the time of seizure.

Reports in 1995 showed the overall level of crime declining slightly for the third year in a row, and such Republicans as Representative Bill McCollum of Florida attributed some of the dip to making convicts serve longer prison sentences, another policy Republicans have advocated during the 1990s. In fact, the Grand Old Party's anticrime proposal of 1995 included a provision that would require violent criminals to serve 85% of their prison terms. Such hardline policies as determinate sentencing, advocated by conservative Republicans, have not been without their costs, however, resulting in a U.S. prison population proportionately larger than that of any other country.

During the 1996 Republican presidential primaries, gambling became an issue. Ultraconservative candidate Pat Buchanan said the gambling industry in such states as Louisiana "corrupts communities, beginning with politicians." Senator Richard Lugar, at one time a Republican 1996 presidential candidate, called for a national study of gambling's effects on crime.

As the presidential election of 1996 approaches, the issue of crime, whether it focuses on drug control, gambling, prison sentences, or prevention, promises to remain a prominent issue that will continue to divide not only Republicans from Democrats but also moderate Republicans from conservatives.

Steve Hoenisch

SEE ALSO Gun Control

BIBLIOGRAPHY

Bacon, Donald C., Roger H. Davidson, and Morton Keller, eds. *The Encyclopedia of the United States Congress.* New York: Simon and Schuster, 1995.

Barnes, Fred. "Dopey." *New Republic,* May 23, 1988.

Feeley, Malcolm M., and Austin D. Sarat. *The Policy Dilemma: Federal Crime Policy and the Law Enforcement Assistance Administration.* Minneapolis: University of Minnesota Press, 1980.

Gest, Ted. "Congress and Cops." *U.S. News & World Report,* December 26, 1994.

Harris, Richard. *Justice: The Crisis of Law, Order, and Freedom in America.* New York: Dutton, 1970.

Porter, Kirk H., and Donald Bruce Johnson. *National Party Platforms: 1840–1964.* Urbana: University of Illinois Press, 1966.

Tromanhauser, Edward D. *The Shaping of Crime Policy.* Chicago: Union Institute, 1990.

Defense

In his autobiography, former President Ronald Reagan, the vicar of Republican conservative values, explains that the impetus behind the massive military buildup of the early 1980s was to "assure that we would regain and sustain military *superiority* over the Soviet Union" (Reagan 1994, 294). In general, Republicans believe that the best means of securing peace is maintaining the world's most formidable military force (information available on the Internet). Military *superiority* deters any potential aggressor and enables the United States to negotiate arms-control agreements from the essential position of strength required to reach meaningful agreements with its adversaries (Reagan 1994, 294).

During the first 20 years of the Cold War, there was widespread political consensus for maintaining a strong military. Rising out of the Vietnam quagmire, the peace movement radically changed the political environment. While many Jacksonian Democrats supported robust military spending, the election of the "propeace" Democrats in the early 1970s caused a split in the party. An increasing number of congressional Democrats began to believe that the "tendency of the United States to seek overwhelming military superiority serves only to foster a threatening global environment that is detrimental to international stability" (information available on the Internet). This influential faction of Congress was successful at substantially reducing military expenditures during the 1970s. These military reductions combined with the Iranian hostage crisis and the Soviet invasion of Afghanistan gave rise to the image of the United States as a "hollow giant." Capitalizing on the public dissatisfaction with America's diminished world stature, President Reagan set out to renew America's military might.

During his two terms as president, Reagan clearly reestablished the American armed forces as the best in the world. The collapse of the Soviet Union, the negotiation of START I and II, and the overwhelming victory of U.S. forces in the Gulf War reinforced the Republican belief in *peace through strength*. The Reagan disciples elected to a majority in both houses of Congress in 1994 continue to advocate military *superiority*, to the dismay of their colleagues across the aisle.

Former Senate Majority Leader Robert Dole, in a 1995 speech to American war veterans, emphasized the Republican position: "For the demands of freedom require us to modernize our forces, to maintain our technological edge, and to ensure that America remains the world's one and only superpower. Our goal is not just to be strong enough to turn back a threat.

We must be so strong no one ever again is even tempted to threaten us, at all." The Republicans' desire to maintain a superior military directly opposes the Democratic impulse to invest the "peace dividend" in social programs. These conflicting priorities, combined with immense pressure to balance the federal budget, set the stage for the battle over the defense expenditures.

The Republicans' Contract with America accused congressional Democrats and the Clinton administration of cutting defense forces "so deeply that we risk a return to the 'hollow military' of the late 1970s" (Gingrich et al. 1994). Arguing that the proliferation of nuclear, biological, and chemical weapons of mass destruction, the emergence of genocidal nationalism, and the existence of regional threats such as China, North Korea, and Iran, makes for an extremely dangerous international environment, the newly elected Congress acted quickly to bolster defense spending. Over the objection of the Democratic minority, they were able to stop the decline in defense spending, fund the canceled B-2 bomber and Seawolf submarine, and add $7 billion to the budget for national missile defense.

Obtaining the reluctant cooperation of the Clinton administration, the Republicans easily passed most of their defense agenda. In a minor setback, the Republicans found themselves in a contentious fight over missile defense. Convinced that the Republican attempt to revitalize the Strategic Defense Initiative (SDI) would violate the 1972 anti-ballistic missile (ABM) treaty, the Democratic minority persuaded the president to veto the defense authorization bill.

Representative Floyd Spence, Chairman of the House National Security committee, defended the need for the missile system: "The American people want to restore and revitalize our national security. They are outraged when they find out that we have no defense against ballistic missiles, which could do irreparable harm to them and their loved ones in our country. They cannot understand why we do not have national missile defense" (information available on the Internet). The Democrats argued that abrogating the ABM treaty would hamper America's ability to negotiate further reductions in the world's nuclear arsenals. In a compromise measure, the Republicans altered the language, calling for deployment of the national missile defense, and agreed to place military readiness ahead of SDI. A shallow victory for the Democrats, the final budget still retained a substantial amount of funding for missile defense.

In his 1983 speech on the "evil empire" President Reagan urged Americans "to speak out against those who would place the United States in a position of military inferiority" (Reagan 1995, 570). Today Republicans are speaking our against those who would redirect defense dollars to "wasteful" social programs. According to Republicans, the first and foremost priority of the federal government is national defense (Gingrich et al. 1994). The demanding post–Cold War international environment mandates the necessary defense investment to ensure that the United States remains the "world's most formidable military power" (information available on the Internet).

The philosophy of *peace through strength* has dominated the American strategic culture since the end of World War II. Except for a brief lapse in the late 1970s, the United States has consistently sought military superiority over its adversaries. Despite Democratic congressional critics, the United States continues to invest four times more on defense than its closest competitor. The collapse of the Soviet Union matches the United States against more elusive, yet equally deadly, threats. Facing the uncertain security challenges of the next century, the key to understanding Republican defense policy resides in the cult of superiority. The compelling question for Republicans is, superior to whom or what?

Cynthia J. Levy

SEE ALSO Arms Control

BIBLIOGRAPHY

Gingrich, Newt, Dick Armey, and House Republicans. *Contract with America.* New York: Random House, 1994.
Reagan, Ronald. *An American Life.* New York: Simon and Schuster, 1990.

Drug Policy

Members of the Republican Party have played a leading role in the often bipartisan issue of drug control. The party has generally stood unified on the need for drug control; splits within the party usually have taken place over the priorities, funding levels, or strategies for controlling drugs.

Although the drug issue has persisted in U.S. political history since Congress moved in 1887 to restrict the importation of opium into the United States and later enacted the landmark Harrison Narcotics Act to regulate professionals dealing with narcotic drugs in 1914, it was conservative Republican President Ronald Reagan who elevated the issue to the national spotlight with his War on Drugs early in the 1980s. Since then, the issue has remained of significant public and political importance, with members of the Republican Party trying during elections to outdo one another

with antidrug promises and elected officials of the party quarreling over the best way to interdict drugs and squelch abuse.

In the 1980s, President Reagan expanded the federal government's drug interdiction effort, while Nancy Reagan, the first lady, led a "Just Say No" campaign that equated drug use with immorality. During the Reagan administration, Congress passed the Anti–Drug Abuse Act of 1986, which greatly expanded the war against trafficking and abuse. A three-way division soon emerged among prominent Republicans in the Reagan administration over how to carry out the drug war. Attorney General Edwin Meese advocated getting tough with drug users. He said drug testing should be required of all workers, arguing that it reduces accidents and boosts productivity while keeping people from disobeying the law. Another faction, led by Otis Bowen, Reagan's secretary of health and human services, stressed education and rehabilitation, an approach often taken by Democrats. William J. Bennett, a conservative who served as Reagan's secretary of education, argued for greater military involvement in stemming the influx of drugs. He also urged Reagan to appoint a drug czar, but the president opposed it on grounds that it would mean more "big government."

Despite the Reagan administration's efforts to eradicate drugs, many political analysts saw the issue as a political defeat for Reagan, largely because the war against drugs had not been won. And many thought it could not be won.

That view did not stop Republican President George Bush from continuing Reagan's antidrug efforts. After passage of the Anti–Drug Abuse Act of 1988, which created a cabinet-level drug czar, Bush appointed Bennett to the post after Republican Senator Dennis DeConcini of Arizona turned it down. Bennett focused on combating street sales of drugs and on financing antidrug efforts in the countries from which the drugs were originating.

Other Republicans have also played a significant role in fighting drug use. In 1970 Republican President Richard Nixon helped encourage passage of the Comprehensive Drug Abuse and Control Act, which reinforced narcotics penalties. In the mid-1990s, Republicans, led by conservative Newt Gingrich of Georgia, the Speaker of the House, pressured the administration of Democratic President Bill Clinton to rethink its emphasis on providing drug addicts with treatment while limiting support for overseas antidrug campaigns. The Clinton approach, Republicans argue, fails to diminish effectively the supply of illicit drugs, thereby stimulating drug use.

Gingrich, in particular, has been among the most

outspoken conservatives against drug traffickers during the mid-1990s. He said that anyone responsible for shipping drugs into the country should be put to death.

In view of such antidrug campaigns as those of Gingrich, Bennett, and Reagan, it has been conservatives who have usually led the antidrug charge among Republicans, but they have often been backed by their more moderate colleagues.

Steve Hoenisch

BIBLIOGRAPHY

Bacon, Donald C., Roger H. Davidson, and Morton Keller, eds. *The Encyclopedia of the United States Congress*. New York: Simon and Schuster, 1995.

Barnes, Fred. "Dopey." *New Republic*, May 23, 1988.

Feeley, Malcolm M., and Austin D. Sarat. *The Policy Dilemma: Federal Crime Policy and the Law Enforcement Assistance Administration*. Minneapolis: University of Minnesota Press, 1980.

Gest, Ted. "Congress and Cops." *U.S. News & World Report*, December 26, 1994.

Education

Throughout most of its history, the Republican Party has alternated between outright opposition to federal involvement in education and limited support for it. Yet the party in its early years backed federal educational assistance; in fact, Republicans were among the first U.S. politicians to propose significant federal aid for education. By the twentieth century, however, the party had shifted its position to a general skepticism that at times gave way to limited support. Even when backing limited aid, though, the party retained its stipulation that in administering the aid, the federal government must in no way interfere with state and local control of schools. There have also been occasional periods of strong Republican support for federal educational assistance, particularly during the 1960s, often in response to social crises or threats to national security.

Within the party, conservative Republicans have in general taken a stronger stance against federal involvement in education, while moderate Republicans have most often leaned toward supporting it. Oregon Senator Wayne Morse, for instance, began his political career as a moderate Republican who increasingly worked to pass legislation supporting education. Eventually, Morse switched to the Democratic Party and became an even stronger voice for educational legislation.

In the party's early years, many Republicans not only backed education but also proposed laws to assist education. Among the first attempts to render such aid was made by a Republican representative, Justin Morrill of Vermont. The Morrill Act, introduced in 1857, sought to donate land to states and territories for colleges. Morrill's measure was vetoed in 1857 by Democratic President James Buchanan, who maintained that the act unconstitutionally interfered with states' rights, an objection that would later be adopted by the Republican Party and used against proposals offered by the Democrats.

While the objection that federal involvement in education interferes with states' rights has often been used by the Republican Party, the constitutionality of federal aid for public schooling is considered by many to have been settled by precedent. Nevertheless, some in the Republican Party still consider it a legitimate objection. Legally, the argument seems to hold little validity. Indeed, even in the early years of the battle over aid for education, the constitutionality argument failed to persuade Congress. A resubmitted Morrill Act was passed in 1862 and signed into law by President Abraham Lincoln, himself a Republican.

Constitutionality aside, the proper role of the federal government in public education was increasingly to become a point of contention between Democrats and Republicans. The two parties would put forth various arguments for and against such aid. The more prominent arguments were over the need for federal aid for education, the appropriate extent of federal involvement in education, whether the federal government can and should try to help equalize education, and whether the federal government could afford to offer its help. But before these arguments became fully articulated, the education issue, long at the margins of political debate and legislation, had to evolve into one of greater prominence.

After the Civil War, President Andrew Johnson, a so-called War Democrat nominated by the Union Party, the name adopted by the Republican National Convention of 1864, approved a federal Department of Education in March 1867. The department was soon demoted and renamed the Office of Education; from 1870 to 1939, it was subsumed under the Federal Security Agency, later the Department of Health, Education, and Welfare. Congress reestablished the Department of Education on May 4, 1980.

In 1870 Republican President Ulysses S. Grant urged Congress to support primary education with grants, making him the first president actively to back federal aid for education. Grant further implored Congress to use all its power to encourage education. During the year of Grant's request, the congressional struggle over the issue began when George F. Hoar, a Republican representative from Massachusetts, introduced a bill to provide general aid to public schools. Although Hoar's bill never came to a vote, it served to focus attention on the issue.

Two years later, in 1872, the Republican Party began using federal aid for education in its campaign literature, which exhibited the party's support for federal educational assistance, a stance that would be reversed by the 1920 presidential election. In 1876—the first year in which federal involvement in education was mentioned in a major party platform—the Republican Convention vowed to support a constitutional amendment forbidding the use of public funds for sectarian education. In 1879 Republican President Rutherford B. Hayes continued Grant's policies, urging Congress to formulate measures that would supplement local funds with federal aid. In 1880 James A. Garfield, also a Republican, captured the presidency with a campaign platform that included national backing for education. The Republican who took the helm after Garfield's death, Chester Arthur, backed federal educational aid in the speeches he made to Congress, as did Republican Benjamin Harrison after being elected president in 1888.

In 1876 the Democratic Party took a view that the party and its candidates would repudiate after having remained nearly silent on the issue for several election years: the platform declared that the establishment and support of the public schools belonged exclusively to the states. Then, as the Republican platforms of 1880 and 1884 and the Republican presidents of 1880 and 1888 endorsed national support for education, the Democrats kept quiet. From 1880 to 1920, the Democratic Party platforms made little mention of the subject. After the 1888 presidential election, the Republicans also dropped the issue, which did not resurface significantly until the party platform of 1920 expounded a different view: it endorsed support for vocational and agricultural training. The Democrats, in contrast, now favored federal aid to education. The parties' respective positions had begun their reversal.

During the early 1920s, Republican President Warren G. Harding opposed a cabinet-level Department of Education, validating the Republican Party's shift on the issue. But in 1924 another slight alteration occurred. The Republican Party's platform exhorted the establishment of a cabinet department of education and relief. As president, Republican Calvin Coolidge paid little attention to the issue, which was taking place largely in Congress at the time. In 1928 the Republican platform merely cited the enrollment increases at colleges and technical schools as signs of the Coolidge administration's success.

Meanwhile, the twentieth century brought social crises that manifested themselves in bills, occasionally proposed by Republicans, for new legislation to assist education. The rate of Selective Service rejections, for instance, prompted demands for aid in 1918, just as the rejections during the World War II draft rekindled the debate over federal aid. World War II also brought legislation to supplement education in communities affected by the war effort. And World War II prompted an extensive program that gave millions of returning veterans the money to attend college: the GI Bill, passed in 1944 under the official name of the Service Man's Readjustment Act. After World War II, a teacher shortage inspired the aid proposals of the late 1940s. The Great Depression of the 1930s led to emergency aid to education. And the baby boom of the 1950s spawned school construction bills. The Cold War and the Soviet Union's launching of *Sputnik* in 1957 helped spur the National Defense Education Act. The civil rights demonstrations of the 1960s encouraged legislation to equalize educational opportunity. Yet, to a degree beyond that established by any one of these social crises, initiatives, including some from Republicans, emerged for general federal assistance for education, though they were not to arise in earnest until the 1930s.

Republican President Herbert Hoover, however, in a remark encouraging to those in favor of federal aid to education, said in his inaugural address: "Although education is primarily a responsibility of the states and local communities and rightly so, yet the nation as a whole is vitally concerned in its development everywhere to the highest standards and to complete universality." Hoover's secretary of the interior, Ray Lyman Wilbur, soon disillusioned those previously encouraged by the president's inaugural remark by rejecting both federal aid and the establishment of a Department of Education. President Hoover, responding to the controversy over the federal government's proper role in education, appointed a committee, the National Advisory Committee on Education, to study the matter.

In October 1931 the committee unveiled its report, the first comprehensive survey of federal educational activities. The panel's recommendations included creating a Department of Education, having the Office of Education conduct further studies to determine whether federal aid was needed, and eliminating educational grants for vocational education. The committee concluded that if vocational education was to be subsidized, it should be done through general federal grants exercised at the discretion of the states. Hoover chose to heed only the suggestion to end the vocational program, but his proposal was quashed by Congress.

During the election years of 1936 and 1940, a hush fell over the issue of education, with Republican platforms denouncing the New Deal administration in general as usurping states' rights and "failing America." The 1944 platform, again blasting the New Deal in general, mentioned that the federal government should avoid involvement in education to keep schools "free."

The postwar era ushered in a period of federal involvement in education that expanded the government's role to proportions previously unseen. Party platforms in the years after the war reveal that the Republican Party generally opposed educational assistance, though it supported limited aid in 1956 and 1960. Meantime, the Democrats consistently favored federal aid to education.

Yet after the war, certain elected Republicans campaigned in favor of limited assistance, and some of these Republicans possessed such power that other party members in Congress followed. For example, between 1943 and 1947, Republican Senator Robert A. Taft of Ohio, a member of the Committee on Labor and Public Welfare, began to lean toward the cause of education. Senator Taft's inclinations were highly influential. Many committee senators, as well as many in the rest of the Senate, were willing to listen to Senator Taft, who was considered an expert on education policy. Known as "Mr. Republican" for his conservative views, Senator Taft was the chairman of the committee from 1947 to 1949. But Senator Taft's backing of education was not without its intraparty conflicts. For instance, he often clashed with Republican Representative Fred Hartley of New Jersey, who led the House Labor and Education Committee from 1947 to 1949. As Taft and Hartley battled it out, the Republican Party's plank, as contained in the platform of 1948, vaguely favored "equality of educational opportunity for all and the promotion of education and educational facilities."

By the election of 1952, the issue had moved further into the spotlight, and the Democratic and Republican parties took sharply contrasting positions. The Democratic Party refined its position of the previous elections by calling for aid for school construction, teachers' salaries, and school repair. The Republican Party countered with the following platform statement: "The responsibility for sustaining this system of popular education has always rested with local communities and the states. We subscribe fully to this principle."

Following five terms and 20 continuous years of Democrats in the White House, newly elected Republican President Dwight D. Eisenhower, holding firm to his party's platform, strongly opposed federal support for education. The Eisenhower administration asked Congress to postpone action on the issue until after the White House Conference on Education, scheduled for 1954. A majority of the conference participants endorsed federal education aid, and a large majority recommended construction aid to meet a shortage of classrooms. The conference's recommendations helped shift the Eisenhower administration's position. In 1955, 1956, and 1957 President Eisenhower endorsed, with tempered enthusiasm, federal measures of limited magnitude to facilitate school construction. The president was willing to back school construction because it strictly limited the amount of money to be allocated and because it reduced the likelihood of federal control over schools.

Meantime, by 1956 the Republican Party itself turned toward supporting education, lessening in the process some of its differences with the Democrats, who continued promoting an array of educational programs. In its platform, the Republican Party cited the action by their elected officials that created the Department of Health, Education, and Welfare. And at the convention, the Grand Old Party praised the Eisenhower administration's school construction initiative and vowed to renew party efforts to ensure its approval.

In 1958, however, the Eisenhower administration revoked its backing of school construction, instead urging Congress to approve the National Defense Education Act. With the Republican president advocating the measure and Congress sanctioning it with bipartisan support, its passage signaled an expanded role for the federal government in education. The expansion was prompted in part by concerns over the country's national defense and rate of scientific advancement. These concerns had arisen after the Soviets launched *Sputnik* the previous year and in response to the Cold War in general. The act supported science, math, and foreign language programs in public schools.

With the next presidential election, partisan controversy over education gathered renewed vigor. Although the platforms of both parties supported federal aid in principle in 1960, the kind of support they had in mind was different. The Republicans maintained that the primary responsibility for education should remain with local communities and the state, but endorsed selective federal assistance for school construction. The party platform also voiced support for efforts to equalize educational opportunities and to strengthen vocational schooling. But the party stopped short of endorsing the wide-ranging assistance program advocated by the Democrats. In arguing against such a program, the Republican platform restated what had by now become one of its standard objections: "Any large plan of federal aid to education, such as direct contributions to or grants for teachers' salaries, can only lead ultimately to federal domination and control of our schools." The Democrats called for generous financial support for, among other educational programs, teachers' salaries and construction of classrooms and other facilities. The contrast between the two parties' policies blossomed into a major domestic issue of the presidential campaign—a campaign that also compelled the two parties in Congress to solidify their positions.

Senator John F. Kennedy, the Democratic presidential candidate in 1960, seized on federal support for schools and attempted to make it a major issue in the election. He blasted President Eisenhower for giving only limited support to the issue and attacked the Republican candidate for president, Vice President Richard M. Nixon, for backing only a limited construction program and for referring to federal aid for education as "too extreme." After the election, which the Republican presidential ticket lost, the Kennedy–Johnson administration's vigorous advocacy for education and a sympathetic Congress resulted in several major measures that provided schools with federal aid.

The rift between the parties only grew during the 1964 presidential campaign, which was characterized by vast differences in ideological positions among the candidates and their parties. Presidential candidate Senator Barry Goldwater, Republican from Arizona, maintained that support for education was a step toward subordinating state and local governments to administrative divisions of the central government in Washington. He also held that there was no educational problem requiring federal aid. Senator Goldwater has been one of the most prominent and unrelenting voices against federal intervention in education on constitutional grounds. The 1964 platform of the Republican Party did allow tax credits for those burdened by the costs of higher education.

In contrast, Democratic President Lyndon B. Johnson was a strong advocate of the strengthened role of the federal government and the strongest supporter of federal aid for education yet to occupy the White House. Johnson's platform promised additional and expanded aid to supplement those programs enacted by what had been dubbed the "Education Congress of 1963."

By the election of 1968, the Republican Party again shifted to a more moderate position, citing inadequate education in urban areas and pledging to bring about high-quality education for all. The platform backed grants, loans, and work–study programs for students as well as continuing to favor tax credits to help offset the cost of college for needy students. The platform advocated expanded programs for preschool children and suggested the establishment of a commission to study educational quality.

In 1968, Republican Richard M. Nixon was elected president. Among the actions he took on education was telling Congress in 1970 to establish a National Institute of Education. A bill creating the institute became law in 1972. President Nixon also sent Congress a proposal to halt court-ordered busing. Instead, Nixon proposed to allocate $2.5 billion to improve school quality while preserving neighborhood schools.

In 1972 the Republican Party, in agreement with its president, opposed busing for racial balance. The party's platform statement also lauded the 60% increase in the amount spent on elementary and secondary education by the Office of Education during the past four years of Republican rule. Such spending—and Republican Party backing of it—was to fall during the Republican administrations of Presidents Ronald Reagan and George Bush that began in 1980, the next year in which a Republican sat in the White House after the Nixon–Ford administration.

During the administration of Democrat Jimmy Carter, the tuition tax credit emerged as an issue. Introduced in January 1977 by Republican Senator William Roth of Delaware and backed by many other Republican senators, the tax-credit bill was originally intended to set up a credit for tuition paid for postsecondary schooling. The bill was expanded to cover tuition spent on private elementary and secondary schooling by Senator Robert Packwood, an Oregon Republican. In 1978 a bill to furnish students with financial aid was offered in response to the tuition tax credit and became law. The measure, however, did not end but only postponed additional Republican calls for a tuition tax credit.

Taking office in 1980, President Ronald Reagan, a conservative Republican, redefined the education policy of the federal government, in effect ending 30 years of liberal educational spending that often received at least limited bipartisan backing. President Reagan successfully directed the focus of federal education policy away from funding programs and toward using moral suasion to hasten change. He significantly reduced the government's role in education and decentralized many programs. He failed, however, to fulfill his campaign promises of abolishing the Department of Education, passing a school prayer amendment, and instituting a tuition tax credit.

In 1985, after Reagan's first secretary of education, Terrel Bell, resigned, conservative William J. Bennett took his place. Bennett announced that he would use the post as a "bully pulpit" to push conservative policies and values. Bennett argued for a Western Civilization–based core curriculum and against multicultural and other liberal programs.

Republican George Bush, formerly Reagan's vice president, was elected president in 1988, partly on the plank of being "the education president." In general, President Bush, though slightly less conservative than Reagan, continued Reagan's policy of devolution in education. The first Bush budget, however, did contain some new initiatives. For instance, it earmarked money for the Drug Free Schools and Communities Act and for magnet schools. Republican calls for educational reform during the era advocated institutional competition among schools and adequate training for entering the job market. President Bush also renewed the call for a tuition tax credit.

In the elections of 1994, Republicans gained control of Congress and quickly set out to slash funds from various education programs, arguing that the government's deficit necessitated cutbacks. Republican Representative Newt Gingrich's Contract with America further targeted education and job training for budget reductions as Congress and the Democratic Clinton administration clashed over balancing the budget.

In the Republican primaries of 1996, the issue surfaced over whether parents should be given school vouchers to send their children to private, public, or religious schools. Bob Dole, Phil Gramm, and Dick Lugar came out in support of vouchers, arguing that they would allow parents greater freedom in deciding how their children should be educated. Pat Buchanan said he would favor vouchers only if there were no "government strings" attached. Lamar Alexander supported scholarships that students can use at public, private, or religious schools.

The positions of the presidential candidates of 1996 illustrate how Republican positions toward education have changed with the political and social climates of the times. The party's general position has moved from its early proposals of support to giving the issue little attention during the earlier part of the twentieth century. After World War II, the party's position alternated between limited backing and disavowal of all support. The 1960s brought a time of expanded federal involvement in education, and many elected Republicans played a part in sanctioning the programs. The conservative presidencies of Reagan and Bush brought a renewed and intensified conservative Republican attack on federal education programs, leading to sub-

stantial cutbacks in many of the programs established during the 1950s, 1960s, and 1970s. The Republican Party of the 1990s continues its call for less government on ideological grounds and less aid to education because of fiscal restraints. Continuing a long-running Republican demand of the twentieth century, the chorus of current Republicans stipulates that if the federal government does provide aid for education, it must do so without interfering with local control of schools and, increasingly, the freedom of parents to do what they think is right for their children.

Steve Hoenisch

BIBLIOGRAPHY

Johnson, Donald Bruce. *National Party Platforms: Volume II, 1960–1976.* Urbana: University of Illinois Press, 1978.

Meranto, Philip. *The Politics of Federal Aid to Education in 1965: A Study in Political Innovation.* Syracuse: Syracuse University Press, 1967.

Mitchell, Douglas E., and Margaret E. Goertz, eds. *Education Politics for the New Century.* Bristol, PA: Falmer Press, Taylor and Francis, Inc., 1990.

Munger, Frank J., and Richard F. Fenno Jr. *National Politics and Federal Aid to Education.* Syracuse: Syracuse University Press, 1962.

Porter, Kirk H., and Donald Bruce Johnson. *National Party Platforms: 1840–1964.* Urbana: University of Illinois Press, 1966.

Spring, Joel. *Conflicts of Interest: The Politics of American Education.* White Plains, NY: Longman, 1988.

Tiedt, Sidney W. *The Role of the Federal Government in Education.* New York: Oxford University Press, 1966.

Foreign Policy

A thread of consistency exists in Republican foreign policy that corresponds to the party's conservative tradition. Republicans traditionally have followed the principles of Realpolitik and national self-interest, which they align with ordered liberty. Democrats, in contrast, have been more idealistic, which corresponds to that party's focus on liberalism and equalitarianism. While this characterization is not a perfect means of differentiating the parties, it is useful in describing Republican foreign policy. Despite the party's underlying focus on national self-interest, Republicans have been divided about whether to adopt an interventionist or isolationist foreign policy.

The Republican Party also has had a great interest in developing a coherent foreign policy, particularly during the twentieth century. As the dominant party, Democrats campaigned on their domestic and foreign policy records. Conversely, Republicans often used foreign policy issues to show how their party could more effectively manage the country's international position. Unfortunately, Republican leaders often disagreed over the proper role of the United States in world politics, which weakened the party's electoral success.

Republican foreign policy is rooted in Federalist and Whig foreign policy, since most Federalists joined the Whig Party after their party's demise in the 1820s, and four out of five original Republicans came from the Whig party. Republican foreign policy can be categorized into five historical periods, Federalist and Whig foreign policy (1793–1850s), Republican expansionism (1860–1912), Republican isolationists versus interventionists (1913–1941), the struggle between moderate Republicans and militant anticommunist Republicans (1945–1988), and contemporary Republican foreign policy (1988 to 1996).

FEDERALIST AND WHIG FOREIGN POLICY

The division between Republican and Democratic foreign policy goes back to the early days of the U.S. political system when the nascent parties had competing interpretations of the French Revolution and the proper response of the United States to the subsequent European war. Typically, Federalists supported President Washington's Proclamation of Neutrality. High Federalists pushed for the establishment of a provisional army to repel an invasion, suppress domestic opponents, and conquer Florida and Louisiana. But President John Adams supported only the maintenance of a small defensive army and the expansion of the U.S. Navy.

During the War of 1812, many Federalists believed that the Republicans had engineered the war. They resisted tax measures, contested national calls on state militias, traded with Canada, and gave supplies to the British fleet. Voters accused Federalists of being disloyal, and the party became one casualty of the War of 1812.

In the mid-1800s, the Whig Party's support for economic progress did not translate into approval of Democratic expansionism. Whigs feared the acquisition of Texas and other territories would cause rapid and destabilizing economic growth and increase the political power of the slaveholders. Consequently, most Whigs resisted territorial expansion and opposed the Mexican-American War. The Whig Party successfully won the presidency by nominating military heros, William Henry Harrison in 1840 and Zachary Taylor in 1848, and by avoiding clear foreign policy

positions. The Whig administrations were interludes from Democratic expansionism, though President Tyler approved the annexation of Texas.

REPUBLICAN EXPANSIONISM

Republicans were concerned with preventing European intervention on the side of the Confederacy during the Civil War. Consequently, Republicans were unable to prevent Spanish and French interventions in the Western Hemisphere and the installation of a satellite French government in Mexico until 1866 when President Andrew Johnson sent troops to the border and demanded the withdrawal of French forces.

After the Civil War, the Republican Party focused on domestic problems and the pacification of the West. The major foreign policy accomplishment of the Johnson administration was the purchase of Alaska in 1867 for $7.2 million by Secretary of State William Seward, a vigorous expansionist. But congressional Republicans rejected Seward's request for the purchase of several Caribbean islands and the annexation of Hawaii.

In the late nineteenth century Republican foreign policy became expansionist as a result of European imperialism, the influence of Alfred T. Mahan, a revival of the ideology of Manifest Destiny, and Social Darwinism. According to Mahan, the United States needed to counteract the Europeans with a program of mercantile imperialism. America could keep pace with its rivals only if it built up foreign markets, expanded its merchant marine fleet, constructed a navy to protect shipping lanes, and acquired overseas bases. Social Darwinists also legitimated U.S. imperialism and asserted that superior races were justified in their territorial conquests because of the survival of the fittest. The ideology of Manifest Destiny further supported U.S. expansionism, since an imperialism of righteousness would extend the blessings of Christianity and civilization to heathens. The United States had to assume the white man's burden to protect its interests and fulfill its noble destiny.

Republican expansionism increased under James G. Blaine, secretary of state in the Garfield and Benjamin Harrison administrations. "Jingo Jim" hosted the First International American Conference in 1889 to promote Pan-Americanism, and advocated the annexation of Hawaii and the creation of a U.S. isthmian canal. Republican jingoism continued to gather steam during the Cleveland administrations, which led to foreign policy confrontations over Hawaii and Cuba. From 1897 to 1911, when the Republicans controlled the executive and legislative branches, the party used an activist internationalist foreign policy starting with the annexation of Hawaii and seizure of Spanish holdings in 1898. Yet small numbers of anti-imperialist Republicans stridently opposed U.S. expansionism.

After the sinking of the *Maine* in Havana harbor and sensational press stories regarding Spanish atrocities in Cuba, President McKinley bowed to demands and asked for a declaration of war in April 1898. While the Spanish-American War satisfied Republican imperialists eager for conquest and military glory, the Teller Amendment initiated by anti-imperialist Republicans prohibited the annexation of Cuba. Spain ceded control of Cuba, Guam, Puerto Rico, and the Philippine Islands to the United States in December 1898.

The congressional debate over the Spanish treaty was one of the most heated foreign policy discussions of the Republican Party. Anti-imperialists broke with President McKinley and opposed the treaty for national interest and philosophical reasons. They argued that forcibly annexing people violated the principle of popular sovereignty and the Monroe Doctrine. Conversely, imperialists argued that only those people capable of self-government should have self-government, and it was America's duty to extend an uplifting hand to less civilized people. Opponents of the treaty failed by two votes to block its ratification when key Democrats supported the McKinley administration.

The leadership of Theodore Roosevelt had a lasting impact on Republican foreign policy. Roosevelt believed that global progress created situations of potential instability, and it was the duty of the civilized countries to reduce chaos. Consequently, the United States had an obligation to be prepared to exert its power in international politics. This activist foreign policy was exemplified by the Roosevelt corollary to the Monroe Doctrine in 1904, which stated that the United States would not interfere with Latin American nations as long as they conducted their affairs with decency. But any "brutal wrongdoing" might require intervention by a civilized power, such as the United States.

Roosevelt's personal motto, "Speak Softly and Carry a Big Stick," applied to Republican foreign policy during his administration. Republicans modernized and strengthened American armed forces, particularly the navy. The United States intervened in Cuba, made the Caribbean an area of U.S. influence, and began the Panama Canal. President Roosevelt mediated the Russo-Japanese War in 1905 and dispatched the U.S. battle fleet on a voyage around the world in 1907 to demonstrate U.S. capabilities.

President Taft continued Republican expansionism by using dollar diplomacy rather than direct military force. Taft stated that the U.S. government should encourage and support American industrialists and bankers in securing profit overseas. Unlike Roosevelt and his followers, who believed in power politics, Taft was confident that courts of law could resolve international problems. Administration officials negotiated trade agreements with other great powers in 1911. But Roosevelt supporters attached so many unacceptable amendments to the treaties that President Taft removed them from consideration. The division between Taft's and Roosevelt's domestic and foreign policy positions split the party in 1913.

ISOLATIONISTS VERSUS INTERNATIONALISTS

Before World War I, Republicans were deeply divided over foreign policy after the sinking of the *Lusitania* in 1915. Roosevelt and his supporters wanted a hardline response against German aggression, while Progressive Republicans asserted that the United States should stay out of European conflicts that would weaken the impulse for domestic reforms and could draw the country into collaboration with imperialist regimes. Other Republicans, though isolationists, agreed with the necessity of a U.S. presence in World War I for security interests. Finally, many prominent Republicans favored the establishment of a new international order ruled by English-speaking people.

The left wing of the Progressive Republican movement vigorously opposed the U.S. declaration of war in 1917. During World War I, Republicans criticized the conduct of the war and reacted negatively to Wilson's 14 Points speech. Republican isolationists were horrified with the prospect of U.S. involvement in redrawing European boundaries, while the Roosevelt and Lodge wing of the party regarded the 14 Points as propaganda.

Republicans interpreted their winning of congressional majorities in both houses in 1918 and the presidency in 1920 as a foreign policy mandate for a return to normalcy. Republican rejection of the League of Nations was a key element of the party's noninternationalist foreign policy in the interwar period. While most Republican senators initially supported the treaty, they added conditions about a U.S. role in the League of Nations that corresponded to Roosevelt's foreign policy goals, rather than isolationism. The rejection of the treaty and the League enabled America to turn its back on Europe after World War I, which strengthened the isolationist wing of the party.

Republican foreign policy during the Harding, Coolidge, and Hoover administrations focused on disarmament, the payment of European war debts, aloofness from the League of Nations, and the renunciation of U.S. imperialism in Latin America. The major foreign policy accomplishment of the Harding presidency was the 1921 Four-Power and Nine-Power disarmament treaties in which the world's great powers agreed to limit the size of their navies. In 1928, 15 nations signed the Peace of Paris, which outlawed war and demanded the settlement of all disputes by "pacific means." Though some Roosevelt supporters and isolationists sneered at the symbolic treaty, most Republicans hailed it as a means to cut expenditures, disarm, and collect war debts. In 1930 President Hoover formally repudiated the Roosevelt corollary to the Monroe Doctrine and abandoned dollar diplomacy. At the end of his term, Hoover supported the isolationist wing of the party when he refused to coordinate U.S. reactions to the Japanese invasion of Manchuria with European nations.

The division between Republican isolationists and interventionists weakened the party before World War II. Congressional Republican isolationists supported strict economic and military neutrality laws, resisted President Franklin Roosevelt's request to reach commercial agreements with foreign nations, and almost defeated an extension of the draft. But Wendell Willkie tried quiet isolationism during his campaign for the presidency in 1940 and called for increased aid to England. Other Republicans supported an isolationist policy toward Europe while urging a stronger stand against Japanese encroachments in Asia. The Japanese attack on Pearl Harbor in 1941 ended the interventionist-isolationist debate within both parties.

MODERATE AND MILITANT ANTICOMMUNIST REPUBLICANS

The Republican Party was divided over President Truman's containment policy and the Korean War after World War II. Tensions between moderate Republicans and militant anticommunists replaced partisan divisions between isolationists and internationalists. The communist issue translated into Republican majorities in 1950; however, Republican leaders were divided over the Korean War. Some Republicans demanded that the United States withdraw from "Mr. Truman's war" while others demanded that America widen the scope of the war and invade China. Senator Joseph McCarthy's accusations about communist infiltration of America also affected

Republican foreign policy. From his perspective, communist subversion and treason were the reasons that America was not able to save Eastern Europe and China from communism. Republican leaders used McCarthy as a rallying point in the 1952 presidential election. Senator Taft, the leading contender, called for a reexamination of U.S. foreign policy and argued that the United States could not sustain its containment policy. Taft and his supporters asserted that the only way to avoid costly international entanglements was a defense policy based on air and naval superiority, as well as propaganda and clandestine support for democratic movements in communist countries. Many Republicans recognized the paradoxical nature of their foreign policy proposal because it relied on the same methods used by the enemy. Nonetheless, they believed that using subversion and propaganda was necessary if a limited foreign policy and military posture was to succeed.

The internationalist wing of the party sponsored the candidacy of General Eisenhower. During the campaign, Eisenhower asserted that containment was "negative, futile, and immoral" and called for a total victory in Korea. Ironically, his administration accepted the premises of the Cold War and institutionalized containment while using Taft's foreign policy prescriptions. According to the Republican leadership, defense policy should provide for maximum deterrent at a bearable cost. A strategy of massive nuclear deterrence was initiated to defend Europe and check Soviet aggression, while containment was expanded with military alliances. President Eisenhower threatened to use nuclear weapons in China and initiated massive air strikes in North Korea to force a quick resolution to the Korean War.

In the 1950s and 1960s, Republicans (and Democrats) interpreted Third World nationalist movements from a containment perspective and used economic and military assistance as well as the CIA as routine counterrevolutionary instruments of American intervention. For example, the Eisenhower administration believed the armed conflict in Vietnam began with a Chinese intervention to spread communism. They supported French military force to suppress the rebellion and sent U.S. advisers into the country in 1955.

While Eisenhower moderates enjoyed bipartisan foreign policy support, they had to contain the militant anticommunist wing of the party. The struggle between moderate and militant Republicans became more open when Senator Barry Goldwater and Governor Nelson Rockefeller competed for the 1964 presidential nomination. Rockefeller, representing establishment and moderate Republicans, supported

Eisenhower's foreign policy. Goldwater and his militant conservative supporters considered communism to be the mortal foe of everything the United States represented. These Republicans, though fiscally conservative, were foreign policy interventionists who supported military modernization. While Goldwater's defeat was interpreted as a victory for a moderate Republican foreign policy, the militant anticommunist wing of the Republican party gained power.

Republican foreign policy during the Nixon and Ford administrations returned to its national interest roots. President Nixon faced a dual problem: how to honor his campaign commitments to withdraw U.S. troops from Vietnam with honor while continuing the containment policy. He used massive bombings of North Vietnam, invaded Cambodia in 1971, and initiated the Vietnamization policy to pressure North and South Vietnamese leaders to agree to "peace with honor" in 1973.

President Nixon and his foreign policy adviser, Henry Kissinger, also modified the containment policy with the Nixon Doctrine. While the United States would continue its global responsibilities and commitments, direct U.S. interventions would be based strictly on American national interests. The Nixon administration opened direct negotiations with the Soviet Union to bring order to the Soviet and American strategic balance of power. President Nixon offered to recognize the Soviet Union as a great power and increase trade relations, if the Soviet Union would relax its support of Third World insurgencies. The Strategic Arms Limitation Talks (SALT) began seriously in 1969, and the first agreement was completed in 1972 before the right wing of the Republican Party created a stalemate on SALT II at the end of the Ford administration. Under the Republican foreign policy of détente, American relations with the Soviets were still very competitive, but Republican leaders did not view communism as a monolithic bloc directed by the Soviet Union or China or both.

During the Reagan administration, the militant anticommunist wing of the party dominated Republican foreign policy, which became more like traditional Democratic foreign policy based on U.S. exceptionalism. According to Republican leaders, the chief threat to the United States was Soviet expansion driven by communist ideology and totalitarianism. Foreign policy in the early 1980s reverted to confrontations with the "evil empire" and increased defense spending based on the assumption the Soviets had gained strategic superiority during détente. In 1983 President Reagan added a new element to Republican foreign policy, the vision of a space-based antimissile defensive system designed to replace deterrence, the

Strategic Defensive Initiative (SDI). Reagan's morality was so intense that he practiced linkage politics and refused to negotiate with the Soviet leadership until the end of his administration.

Republicans considered insurgency movements in Latin American and other Third World countries the result of Soviet expansionism. For example, conservative Republicans were convinced that the war in Nicaragua was part of the superpower rivalry and the Sandinistas were a Soviet beachhead in the Western Hemisphere. The National Security Council became a shadow CIA, and key covert operations were privatized to circumvent Democratic congressional restrictions regarding assistance to Nicaraguan contras.

Republican foreign policy faced new challenges in the Bush administration with the collapse of the Soviet Union, the removal of Soviet control over Eastern Europe, and Iraq's seizure of Kuwait. President Bush forged a cooperative relationship with the Soviets during his tenure, thereby ending the Cold War. He became extremely popular when he organized an international coalition to oppose Iraq and militarily forced the Iraqis to withdraw from Kuwait. Unfortunately, President Bush was unable to translate the success of Republican foreign policy to the 1992 election.

After Bill Clinton took office in 1992, Republicans lost their enthusiasm for the use of military force. Many leaders believe that military power should be used to protect vital U.S. strategic or economic interests, not for idealistic goals. Consequently, congressional Republicans resisted sending U.S. troops to Somalia and Haiti and insisted on fixed withdrawal dates. Republicans also criticized the Clinton administration's handling of the Bosnian civil war and objected to the Dayton Peace Agreement, which pledged the use of U.S. peacekeeping troops. As a legacy of the Vietnam War, Republicans have been careful to differentiate their criticism of Democratic foreign policy from their unqualified support of U.S. armed forces. Consequently, congressional leaders advocated continued funding for President Clinton's foreign policy actions. Unlike contemporary Democratic foreign policy, however, Republican foreign policy seems to be based on national interest.

Janet B. Manspeaker

SEE ALSO The Cold War

BIBLIOGRAPHY

Mayer, George. *The Republican Party: 1854–1964.* New York: Oxford University Press, 1964.

Merrill, Horace Samuel, and Marion Galbraith Merrill. *The Republican Command: 1897–1913.* Lexington: University Press of Kentucky, 1971.

Nathan, James, and James Oliver. *United States Foreign Policy and World Order*. 3rd ed. Boston: Little, Brown, 1985.

Reichley, A. James. *The Life of the Parties*. New York: Free Press, 1992.

Spanier, John, and Eric Uslaner. *American Foreign Policy Making and the Democratic Dilemmas*. 6th ed. New York: Macmillan, 1994.

Freedom of Speech

It is another irony of American politics that in the early days of the Republican Party the Jeffersonian Republicans included freedom of speech in their campaign platform—and won, in part, on the plank. Now, conservative Republicans are the group most likely to oppose wide-scale freedom of speech, usually on moral grounds. Moderate Republicans, in contrast, have been less likely to appeal to morality as a justification for legislation limiting free speech.

The history of free speech battles in the United States begins with the Alien and Sedition Acts of 1798, which included sections that made it illegal to utter or publish any "false, scandalous, and malicious writing" against the U.S. government or writing that defamed or brought disrepute to Congress or the president. At the time, the act fueled partisan politics, with the Republicans using it to defeat the Federalists in 1800. Thomas Jefferson made the principle that the First Amendment denies government the right to control speech a cornerstone of his platform, winning the presidency. His fellow Republicans also used the plank to gain control of Congress. As they promised during the election campaign, the Republicans allowed the acts of 1798 to expire in 1801.

By 1872, the Republican platform had become decidedly more conservative, foreshadowing the antiliberty policies advocated during the first half of the next century. Congress and Republican President Ulysses S. Grant were praised for suppressing "treasonable organizations."

The World War I era was marked by government repression, witch hunts, and violations of personal liberties. The policies of Republicans contributed to these violations. The Congress of 1919–1920 introduced more than 70 measures aimed at restricting, among other activities, peacetime sedition, the display of the Red flag, and the sending of seditious material in the mail. Among the most flagrant attempts to restrict speech was the Sedition Act of 1918, an amendment to the wartime espionage act. Introduced into the Senate by Republican Knute Nelson of Minnesota at the urging of U.S. Attorney General A.

Mitchell Palmer, the bill defined as punishable sedition any activity aimed at changing the government or the laws of the United States. Endorsed by President Wilson, the act became law. In 1920, Attorney General Palmer used the act to carry out the so-called Palmer raids. More than 4,000 people labeled as communists or associated with communist labor parties were arrested. Palmer said they were plagued with a "disease of evil thinking."

The prosecution of those who publicly advocated communism continued during the 1930s, when Representative Hamilton Fish of New York, a reactionary Republican, called for a House investigation of communists' activities and urged formation of a committee to hear testimony.

Communication technology that emerged during the twentieth century often stimulated restrictive legislation—and partisan conflict. In particular, interparty confrontation arose following the Radio Act of 1927, which established the Radio Commission. Passed at the suggestion of Republican Secretary of Commerce Herbert Hoover, who had been appointed by Republican President Warren G. Harding, the measure required broadcasters to act in the "public interests"—a phrase that allowed a Republican-appointed commission to evaluate program content when considering the renewal of stations' licenses. In 1931 the committee rejected the Chicago Federation of Labor's renewal application based on the station's programming content, triggering a battle between Republicans and Democrats that culminated in the Communications Act in 1934, which New Deal Democrats used to rewrite the Radio Act and establish the Federal Communications Commission (FCC). After seeing how newspapers had in general supported Republicans, the New Deal Democrats wanted to ensure that radio and television would be nonpartisan. The act strengthened the provisions of the law applying equal time for candidates and ballot measures. But it was not until 1949 that the FCC promulgated the Fairness Doctrine, which required the presentation of contrasting viewpoints on controversial issues of public consequence.

By 1940, however, the Republican Party had moderated its position; its platform stood behind licensing without censorship or arbitrary controls. And in 1944, the party's platform urged a clarification of the FCC's role. Yet, partisan conflict over the act did not end in the 1940s. Five decades later, the FCC repealed the Fairness Doctrine under pressure from conservative Republican President Ronald Reagan.

The split within the Republican Party of greatest historical significance came during the now infamous communist hysteria caused by Republican Joseph McCarthy, elected by Wisconsin to the U.S. Senate in 1946. McCarthy believed the federal government to be threatened by communist infiltration—a contention that appealed mostly to conservative Republicans, who saw McCarthy and his anticommunist hysterics as a partisan political asset. In fact, during the congressional elections of 1950, McCarthy was the "most frequently invited speaker by senators seeking reelection." Thus it was no surprise that McCarthy's anticommunist fever was catching. The Republican Party platform of 1952 included a vehement attack on communists.

On February 9, 1950, Senator McCarthy alleged that there were 205 communists in the State Department, igniting a national debate on the issue and prompting Democratic Senate Majority Leader Scott Lucas of Illinois to ask the Foreign Relations Committee to investigate the allegations. The investigating committee found McCarthy's allegations to be "a fraud and a hoax perpetuated on the Senate of the United States and the American people." Meantime, President Dwight D. Eisenhower, himself a Republican, spoke out against McCarthy, but failed to reel him in. Eisenhower has been criticized for not keeping Republican leaders, especially conservatives, from treating McCarthy as an asset.

On December 2, 1954, the Senate censured McCarthy in a 67–22 vote, with all Democrats and 22 Republicans voting against him.

Amid the anticommunist sentiment of 1948, the House Un-American Activities Committee, chaired by Republican Richard Nixon, held hearings that led to compromising Alger Hiss, a top State Department official, as being part of a communist cell.

More recently, freedom of speech has become an issue in funding for the arts through the National Endowment for the Arts. Republican Senator Jesse Helms of North Carolina introduced legislation to prohibit the National Endowment for the Arts from funding, among other restrictions, any "indecent" and "obscene" art. Although Congress rejected Helms's proposal, it did adopt, for the first time in the NEA's history, a restriction that barred funding for material determined by the NEA to be obscene.

The advent of wide-ranging public access to the Internet has also prompted calls for restrictive legislation. The Exon–Coats Amendment would outlaw making "indecent communication" available to Internet users younger than 18 years of age. It was drafted by Senators Jim Exon, a Nebraska Democrat, and Daniel R. Coats, an Indiana Republican.

Steve Hoenisch

BIBLIOGRAPHY

Bacon, Donald C., Roger H. Davidson, and Morton Keller, eds. *The Encyclopedia of the United States Congress*. New York: Simon and Schuster, 1995.

Hentoff, Nat. *The First Freedom: The Tumultuous History of Free Speech in America*. New York: Delacorte Press, 1980.

Maisel, L. Sandy, ed. *Political Parties and Elections in the United States: An Encyclopedia*. New York: Garland, 1991.

Murphy, Paul L. *The Meaning of Freedom of Speech: First Amendment Freedoms from Wilson to FDR*. Westport, CT: Greenwood Press, 1972.

Porter, Kirk H., and Donald Bruce Johnson. *National Party Platforms: 1840–1964*. Urbana: University of Illinois Press, 1966.

Smith, Craig R. *Freedom of Expression and Partisan Politics*. Columbia: University of South Carolina Press, 1989.

Gun Control

Gun control is a highly salient topic within the Republican Party. Both as a litmus test of ideological orthodoxy and as a political hot button for rallying popular support, gun control is an issue on which the Republican Party is seldom silent.

Gun control did not become a sustained national issue until increasing violence and a wave of assassinations prompted a political response that resulted in the Gun Control Act of 1968. From that time forward, gun control has been a highly emotional and partisan issue. The debate revolves around two primary questions. First, how intrusive should the government be in the regulation of private possession of handguns? Answers run the gamut from disallowing any governmental restrictions to prohibiting private ownership altogether. Possible answers between those two extremes include mandatory handgun registration, mandatory waiting periods for purchase, and prohibitions on gun ownership by certain people (such as convicted felons). The other dimension of the gun-control issue centers on the distinction between types of guns. Rifles are typically presumed less concealable than handguns, and thus less potentially dangerous. Automatic weapons are considered more destructive and less justifiable as weapons for sport or self-defense. Although governmental policy has established some basic principles on both these dimensions of the gun-control issue, a vociferous debate continues at the boundaries of that limited consensus.

Republicans vigorously oppose efforts to tighten or extend gun-control laws. In part this is a logical extension of the party's general opposition to excessive regulation and its ideological commitment to creating a smaller, less intrusive government. The Republicans often justify their opposition to gun control on constitutional grounds; the Second Amendment guarantees "the right of the people to keep and bear arms," and extensive regulation of arms is viewed as tantamount to violating that right. Gun-control advocates of course challenge this interpretation of the Second Amendment. Yet, aside from a case in 1939 (*United States* v. *Miller*), which upheld a federal ban on transporting sawed-off shotguns, the Supreme Court has not ruled on gun control's constitutionality. For the Republicans, opposition to gun control is at once a reflection of individualism and patriotism.

The Republican Party's virtual ownership of law and order as a campaign issue complicates its opposition to gun control. After all, gun control is continuously justified as a necessary response to extraordinarily high numbers of armed robberies, murders, and other crimes that plague America. While accepting the premise that the government needs to respond to the level of crime in the country, Republicans generally make the opposite conclusion about gun control, namely, that the best way to combat armed criminals is with armed law-abiding citizens. The government should fight crime with tougher penalties and stricter enforcement of existing laws. Finally, Republicans object to the alleged unworkability of gun-control laws. By definition, criminals exist outside the law, and thus presumably will find a way to circumvent legal restrictions on the possession of weapons.

As the gun-control battle has worn on in Washington and in state legislatures, gun-control opponents have largely held the line against further restrictions. Politically supported and financially backed by the National Rifle Association (NRA), gun-control opponents have emerged as a force to be reckoned with. The Republican Party has courted this group, and vice versa. Politically, it would be very difficult for a Republican officeholder or candidate to appear as a gun-control advocate.

Nevertheless, a small number of high-profile conservatives have supported gun control, including Robert Bork, President George Bush's nominee to the Supreme Court. And in recent years there has been a sense among some party members that the NRA has pushed its position too far and that gun control has not been allowed to go far enough. The assassination attempt on President Ronald Reagan in 1981 provided the first serious opportunity for Republican moderates to allow some slight tightening of existing laws. The president's press secretary, James Brady, was severely wounded in that attack, and since that time he and his wife, Sarah, have lobbied tirelessly for a gun-control package that imposed a national waiting period and background check for handgun purchases.

Even then, Reagan did not endorse the idea until after he had left office, and President Bush threatened to veto the "Brady Bill," as it came to be known. It was not until 1993, with a Democratic president as well as a Democratic-controlled Congress, that the Brady Bill was passed and signed. Later, when the NRA began to escalate its antigovernment rhetoric to provocatively incendiary levels, former President Bush gave the NRA a public upbraiding by resigning his lifetime membership. This action by a former Republican president symbolized the moderates' frustration with their party's allegiance to the NRA. Some perceived the NRA's storied political clout to be waning.

The 1994 congressional elections bolstered the ranks of conservative Republicans in the House of Representatives, and it appeared unlikely that the party would shift its ideological stance on regulation to the left. Following up on campaign pledges, Republican congressional leaders initially promised to overturn an assault weapons ban that the Democratic-controlled Congress had passed in 1994. Republican Speaker Newt Gingrich of Georgia proclaimed in a letter to the NRA in 1995 that "no gun control legislation is going to move in committee or on the floor of the House" while he was Speaker. State legislatures moved toward loosening gun-control laws, in particular making it easier to carry a concealed weapon.

Yet without any noticeable reduction in crime and, more to the point, murders, the political debate over gun control showed no signs of abating. The Republican Party continued to seek a balance between its insistence that the government should act more harshly toward criminals and its ideological aversion to greater regulation.

Steve D. Boilard

BIBLIOGRAPHY

Idelson, Holly. "Gun Rights and Restructuring: The Territory Reconfigured." *Congressional Quarterly* 51 (April 24, 1993): 21–26.

Nisbet, Lee, ed. *The Gun Control Debate: You Decide.* Buffalo, NY: Prometheus Books, 1990.

"Party Positions on National Issues." *Congressional Digest*, October 1992, pp. 234–255.

Robin, Gerald D. *Violent Crime and Gun Control.* Cincinnati: Anderson, 1991.

Health Care

Although federal health care began after the prompting of a Republican senator, the Grand Old Party, increasingly weary of enlarging the central government, soon became opposed to most health legislation. Conservative Republicans of the twentieth century have stood almost without exception against federal involvement in health initiatives beyond research, arguing that such programs usurp states' rights and can lead only to socialized medicine. The positions of moderate Republicans have varied by elected politician, with some occasionally proposing or supporting legislation to expand federal health services. Among the Republicans who have significantly battled to thwart health care legislation stands President Dwight D. Eisenhower, who quelled for nearly a decade the gaining momentum of Democrats in Congress fighting for a national insurance act. Republican Senator Reed Smoot of Utah proved himself to be a formidable early opponent of federal health care. In contrast, a few moderate Republicans, notably Senator Jacob K. Javits and Representative James S. Parker, both of New York, became legislative forces behind an expansion of federal health services.

Federal health care began in 1798 with an Act for Relief of Sick and Disabled Seamen, which created the Marine Hospital Service, the progenitor of the Public Health Service, the name that the agency took following passage of the Public Health and Marine Service Act of 1902. The bill was enacted after Republican Senator John C. Spooner of Wisconsin asked for changes in the public health service.

But by 1908, the Republican Party's attitude began to show signs of opposition to the public health bureaucracy. The party's platform commended efforts to secure greater efficiency in health agencies and favored legislation toward that end.

Then in 1922 and 1925, Republican Senator Smoot tried unsuccessfully to combine the Public Health Service with the Veterans Bureau and to curtail its authority. Smoot's early attempt at consolidation and devolution, which would be followed by additional and at times more successful Republican attempts at reductions, was thwarted by Surgeon General Hugh Cumming.

But during the 1920s, not all members of the Republican Party sought to curtail federal health care. In 1926, Republican Representative James S. Parker of New York, urged by Surgeon General Cumming, introduced a bill to expand the authority and services of the Public Health Service. In 1928 the Parker bill passed both houses only to be vetoed by Republican President Calvin Coolidge.

Also in 1926, Democratic Senator Joseph E. Ransdell of Louisiana, chairman of the Public Health Committee, introduced a bill to create a national institute of health. The proposal, however, languished in Congress for four years, encountering indifference from many members and facing determined opposition from Republican President Calvin Coolidge's Bureau of the Budget. During 1928, Republican Senator Smoot prevented the Ransdell bill's passage.

Yet in 1930, despite the early opposition, both the Parker and Ransdell acts became law, determining the direction of the Public Health Service for the next 40 years. The Parker Act, officially known as the Public Health Service Amendments of 1930, enhanced the authority and operations of the service. The Ransdell Act was officially known as the National Institute of Health Act. Acting contrary to what would become a general opposition of most elected members of the Republican Party to federal health care, Republican President Herbert Hoover was supportive of the bills, helping to cultivate their chances of passage. Congressional interest in cancer research and crises of influenza and psittacosis also helped propel the bills' passage.

The next big battle over health care came in 1946 when Democratic Senators Lester Hill of Alabama and Harold H. Burton of Ohio introduced a bill to help defray the costs of hospital construction. But the influential Senator Robert A. Taft, an Ohio Republican, frowned upon the bill because, he believed, it allowed for too much federal control. In order to gain his backing, Senator Taft wanted the measure to contain assurances of states' rights and local control, money set aside according to state assessments of need, and matching funds for local hospital boards.

Hill's measure appealed to many southern Republican conservatives in Congress because it promised to funnel aid to their states. Even Senator Taft was eventually persuaded to back the bill by a funding formula that awarded the largest sums to the poorest states.

Democratic President Harry S. Truman announced in his State of the Union speech in 1948 that his goal was "to enact a comprehensive insurance system which would remove the money barrier between illness and therapy." For Truman, national health insurance was an issue of equality, and his speech triggered the Democratic-backed drive for a national insurance program. Republicans, however, disagreed with both the need for and the philosophy behind such a program.

In early 1949, President Truman urged Congress to act on medical insurance. Soon thereafter, Democrats presented a proposal to Congress, but it met with strong opposition from Republicans who had formed a coalition with anti-Truman conservative southern Democrats. They combined forces to block the insurance proposal; it was never reported out of committee.

In 1950, 1951, and 1952, President Truman continued to push for compulsory health insurance. But the prospects for such a bill's passage appeared bleak after 1949, especially when the elections of 1950 increased the Republicans' presence in the House by more than 25 members and nearly allowed them to take control of the Senate.

Despite their crusade against Truman's insurance proposal, many Republicans in Congress were committed to funding the medical research of the federal government. One Republican in particular, H. Styles Bridges of New Hampshire, teamed up with several Democrats to gain passage of the National Heart Institute Act in 1948 and the Omnibus Medical Research Act of 1950, which established new institutes for health research.

Through the 1950s and especially after 1955, Congress maintained strong bipartisan support for medical research, resulting in increased funding for the National Institutes of Health in 1957 and 1958.

The 1952 election that installed Republican Dwight D. Eisenhower as president shattered all possibility of a Democratic-supported compulsory insurance bill. In fact, under President Eisenhower, no substantial medical bill had a chance of passage. Even after the Democratic Party regained control of Congress in 1954, they still lacked enough votes to ensure a favorable majority.

The year 1958 rekindled the debate over a national health insurance program. During that year, a member of the House Ways and Means Committee, where at least one earlier proposal for national health insurance had died a quiet death, Aime J. Forand, a Rhode Island Democrat, reintroduced an insurance bill. During the 1950s, statistics began to show that the aged had substantial health and financial problems. But despite the statistics, the Forand bill soon drew opposition from conservative members of Congress, including many Republicans, who argued that it was regressive and limited. They said it would not offer substantial assistance to those who needed it most while covering those who did not need it. Opponents further argued that Americans are not poor enough to warrant compulsory government health insurance. They added that the bill would encroach on states' rights, a refrain often repeated by Republicans. Although Forand's bill was rejected by the House Ways and Means Committee in 1959 by a 17–8 vote, it did serve to revive the battle over federal health care.

The dawn of the 1960s and the presidential election of Democrat John F. Kennedy, who campaigned on a strong social welfare platform, again put the Republicans on the defensive against federal involvement in health services.

In February 1961, true to his party's campaign promises, President Kennedy called for an extension of Social Security benefits to cover hospital and nursing home costs but not surgical expenses for those over age 65. Senator Clinton P. Anderson, a New Mexico Democrat who was a high-ranking member of the Finance Committee, and Representative Cecil R. King, a California Democrat who sat on the Ways and Means Committee, introduced the president's proposal as the King–Anderson bill.

The bill, however, did not have bipartisan backing, and Representative Mills, though a Democrat, was determined to consider in the crucial Ways and Means Committee only a proposal that had bipartisan support.

Besides Mills, there were other significant barriers to passage of the King–Anderson bill. One was the determined opposition of Republicans on the House Ways and Means Committee who had formed a coalition with several conservative southern Democrats. Together, they formed a strong enough bloc to override the favorable votes of the committee's urban, prolabor Democrats. In the House, though, the Medicare bill did have the backing of several liberal Republicans.

Yet the aggregation of negative factors—opposition from the Ways and Means Committee's Republicans and southern Democrats, especially Chairman Mills, and President Kennedy's focus on other priorities—effectively killed the Medicare bill without even a formal committee vote. But the battle for a national program of health insurance was not over yet; it was only postponed.

Following the assassination of President Kennedy, the ascendancy of Democrat Lyndon B. Johnson to the presidency brought to the White House a liberal administration committed to social reforms as part of a War on Poverty. The election of Johnson over Senator Barry Goldwater, a conservative Republican from Arizona, was a turning point for the loss that the Republicans were to suffer on Medicare. Goldwater, a long-time critic of the expanding role of the federal government, had maintained in his campaign that any federal health care programs were a usurpation of states' rights and a step toward socialized medicine, an objection often articulated by conservative Republicans.

Following the 1964 election, the composition of committees was changed to reflect the strength of the parties in the House as a whole. Thus, in 1965, the Ways and Means Committee shifted from 15 Democrats and 10 Republicans to 17 Democrats and 8 Republicans, further ensuring a bloc favorable to Medicare. The fate of the reintroduced King–Anderson bill had changed from being a possibility to a certainty. The bill continued to include coverage of the aged, limited hospitalization and nursing home insurance benefits, and Social Security financing.

Republicans reacted to the reintroduction of the King–Anderson measure by starting to talk about alternative programs that they saw as more positive. They put forth the following arguments as grounds for opposing the King–Anderson bill in favor of an alternative: it contained inadequate benefits, with too many exclusions and limits; it was too costly; and it did not distinguish between the poor and wealthy among the aged. To address these concerns, Representative John W. Byrnes of Wisconsin, the ranking Republican on the Ways and Means Committee, proposed a bill for a voluntary insurance system. Byrnes's bill was also driven by the desire of Republicans on the Ways and Means Committee to prevent the Democrats from taking exclusive credit for the health insurance legislation that now seemed to be a certainty.

Representative Mills, foreseeing that passage of the King–Anderson bill was now inevitable, sought to build bipartisan consensus for it. In a brilliant legislative move that at once strengthened the proposal and brought Republican backing to it, Mills moved to draft legislation combining the King–Anderson hospital insurance bill with Byrnes's voluntary plan and an expanded state-administered Kerr–Mills program for all medically needy people. Thus Mills succeeded in winning bipartisan support for his combination bill because it appealed to the Republicans, many of whom wanted, at most, a voluntary plan.

In 1965, the Social Security Amendments of 1965 passed both houses and were signed into law by President Johnson, establishing Medicare and Medicaid and ending in defeat for the Republican Party a long, bitter fight against national health insurance that began with the Roosevelt administration and spanned the administrations of Presidents Truman and Kennedy and part of Johnson's. Perhaps the most far-reaching health care legislation passed in U.S. history, the amendments included a hospital insurance program for Social Security recipients over age 65, funded from payroll taxes, and voluntary medical service insurance for the same group, funded by small premiums and general revenues. It also expanded the Kerr–Mills program for all medically needy people.

The battle of a federal health insurance program, however, did not end with the passage of Medicare and Medicaid. The battle merely shifted—to what the appropriate level of funding for such programs should be. The origins of Medicare during the 1960s also shaped the dispute over national health insurance in the 1970s, an era during which health policy continued to have strong appeal among Democrats and a few Republicans in Congress.

Among the Republicans, Senator Jacob K. Javits of New York emerged as a strong voice advocating health care legislation. His leadership in Congress, however, was counterbalanced by Republican President Richard M. Nixon's mild antagonism toward federal health programs, an antagonism that manifested itself by calling attention to what he saw as an overburdened health budget. President Nixon tried to regulate federal health programs better and to terminate some of them. In particular, the Nixon administration attacked the Public Health Service as being too independent and too powerful.

In 1971 President Nixon suggested a plan to cut health care costs and spur development of health maintenance organizations (HMOs) for providing care for Medicare and Medicaid recipients. Although the plan eventually lost favor with the White House, it was embraced by several influential congressional Republicans, notably Senator Javits and Representative William R. Roy of Kansas. Working with several key Democrats, they adopted Nixon's plan. After three years of legislative effort, the Health Maintenance Organization Act of 1973 created an experimental program to underwrite HMO development and became a forerunner to the debate over stimulating HMO use during the 1990s.

President Nixon announced in 1972 that he intended to end federal backing for the Hill–Burton Act and several other programs and to cut funding for other programs. He also said he would revoke funds already appropriated to certain health care programs. Congress reacted with anger, securing appropriations for the programs. Congress eventually secured the grant programs at least temporarily in the Special Health Revenue Sharing Act of 1975, passed over Republican President Ford's veto. Many members of Congress, resenting Ford's tactics, backed the health care leaders.

Also in 1972, Senator Wallace F. Bennett, a Utah Republican, introduced the Public Health Service Amendments, which mandated that hospitals receiving federal funds conduct reviews of need.

The late 1970s saw the election of Democrat Jimmy Carter to the presidency and a subsequent respite from the health care debate. During the 1970s, however, many in Congress, particularly Republicans, became increasingly concerned over the rising costs of health care and voiced those concerns during hearings on continuing the programs.

Conservative Republican President Ronald Reagan, soon after his election in 1981, launched an assault on the federal health care system, announcing plans to consolidate all 26 health services programs into two block grants, one for health services, the other for preventive health. He also announced plans to slash spending on health by 25%. The president's announcement set off a battle in Congress, with conservatives in both parties taking up Reagan's charge. In the Senate, Orrin Hatch, a conservative Republican from Utah, and Phil Gramm, a Texas Republican, led the president's battle to disassemble the federal health care programs. In the House, Republican Representatives Edward R. Madigan of Illinois, James T. Broyhill of North Carolina, and William E. Dannemeyer of California played key leadership roles for the Reagan agenda.

With a few concessions to Democrats, conservative Republicans, backed by many conservative Democrats and moderate Republicans, passed the Omnibus Budget Reconciliation Act of 1981. It reduced funding for all health services programs, collapsed funding for many categorical grant programs into block grants to states, and increased local and state governance over remaining programs. The concessions to congressional Democrats came only after last-minute lobbying by a group of Republican governors.

During the tenure of the Republican Reagan administration, Congress also passed the Tax Equity and Fiscal Responsibility Act of 1982, which tightened regulations on Medicare and Medicaid and established their reimbursement rates.

Also in the early 1980s, President Reagan tried to relax federal rules for nursing homes, but his effort met with bipartisan outcry and eventually led to the passing of a detailed law protecting the rights and stipulating the care of nursing home patients.

Republican President George Bush, elected in 1988, continued the Reagan administration's forceful opposition to health programs, often with the backing of many conservative members of Congress.

Running against the general Republican antihealth trend of the 1980s and early 1990s, one Republican congresswoman joined forces with two Democrats to pass the Women's Health and Equity Act. Olympia Snowe, a Republican of Maine, worked with Senator Barbara Mikulski, a Maryland Democrat, and Representative Patricia Schroeder, an influential Colorado Democrat, to secure passage of the bill, which created an office for research on women's health at the National Institutes of Health.

The election of Democratic President Bill Clinton returned health care to the fore of national politics in 1992. Clinton campaigned on a plank of reforming the nation's health care system. True to his promise, he unveiled his proposal in a speech to Congress and the nation on September 22, 1993, saying that Hillary Rodham Clinton had consulted with government leaders of both parties. He proposed a concept first conveyed by Republican President Richard M. Nixon—that every employer and every individual would be asked to contribute to national health care.

But some conservative Republicans in the House objected to any mandate requiring employers to pay for health insurance. And, in general, Republicans argued that the Clinton plan contained excessive controls and would put an undue burden on small businesses to pay for workers' insurance.

Even though Clinton's initiative did reflect several ideas that some Republicans found appealing—including an attempt to control health care not so much by government directive as by limiting insurance premiums—the proposal was not alluring enough to survive challenges from the strong Republican minority, led by Republican Bob Dole, the powerful Senate minority leader.

In late 1995 and early 1996, Republicans, now in control of Congress, pushed legislation to transform Medicare into a market-driven program in order to help balance the federal budget. Such a program, Republicans argued, would open up the Medicare market to hundreds of private health insurers, giving elderly people a wider variety of plans. Conservative Republican Newt Gingrich of Georgia, the Speaker of the House, played a key role in the highly partisan battle to cut Medicare spending. He won the support of the American Medical Association, a powerful special-interest lobbying group, by making concessions to their concerns that the plan would reduce Medicare payments to doctors. President Clinton has threatened to veto Congress's Medicare and Medicaid reform plan, arguing that it would devastate the quality of care for the elderly, especially those in nursing homes.

Republicans in Congress have also promoted proposals to repeal tough federal standards for the quality of nursing home care as part of their general effort to shift power and responsibility from the central government to the states.

Meanwhile, on the local level, elected Republicans have attempted to reform medical care through privatization, with such cities as Los Angeles and New York spinning off city health services. In particular, New York Mayor Rudolph Giuliani, a Republican, has said he wants New York to get out of the hospital business. Arguments for privatization say that the current system is inefficient, delivers poor care, and is unprepared to compete in a managed-care marketplace.

Thus the push and pull over the future of health care policy continues. The nature of the government's involvement in providing health services remains contested ground, as it has since the beginning of the twentieth century. And, much as they have throughout the century, the battle lines remain drawn along ideological lines, with a strong coalition of conservative Republicans fighting vigorously against a federal role and a less cohesive group of moderate Republicans taking a more lenient position.

Steve Hoenisch

BIBLIOGRAPHY

Bacon, Donald C., Roger H. Davidson, and Morton Keller, eds. *The Encyclopedia of the United States Congress*. New York: Simon and Schuster, 1995.

Eckholm, Erik, ed. *Solving America's Health-Care Crisis: A Guide to Understanding the Greatest Threat to Your Family's Economic Security*. New York: Times Books, 1993.

"Health Care: Clinton's Plan and the Alternatives." *New York Times*, October 17, 1993, p. 22.

Johnson, Donald Bruce. *National Party Platforms: Volume II, 1960–1976*. Urbana: University of Illinois Press, 1978.

Maisel, L. Sandy, ed. *Political Parties and Elections in the United States: An Encyclopedia*. New York: Garland, 1991.

Marmor, Theodore R. *The Politics of Medicare*. Chicago: Aldine, 1973.

Porter, Kirk H., and Donald Bruce Johnson. *National Party Platforms: 1840–1964*. Urbana: University of Illinois Press, 1966.

Stevens, Robert, and Rosemary Stevens. *Welfare Medicine in America: A Case Study in Medicaid*. New York: Macmillan, 1974.

Immigration

WHAT IS IMMIGRATION?

Throughout American history immigration has encompassed a vast array of people and experiences. There is no single motive that all immigrants share. Nor is there a common path that all immigrants follow. Immigrants do not necessarily wish to become citizens or to remain in America indefinitely. Many maintain citizenship in their native country and live in the United States as resident aliens. Still others enter the country illegally or move back and forth following seasonal work.

Debate over immigration in the United States has historically addressed three distinct categories of immigrants: legal immigrants, refugees, and illegal immigrants. At various moments in American history these categories were given different meanings or referred to different groups of people. For example, the term *refugee* has been used in different eras to describe

people fleeing genocide, ideological conflict, or even economic crisis. In each era, however, immigration policy has prioritized offering asylum to refugees.

Arguments for and against immigration are made on economic, political, and moral grounds. People opposed to immigration or favoring a more restrictive immigration policy argue that immigrants take away much-needed jobs from Americans and become dependent on the generous welfare system of the United States. Immigrants are portrayed as a drain on the U.S. economy because they send their earnings to relatives in their native countries. At times, immigrants have been depicted as agents of foreign powers, who vote according to whatever foreign policy is best for their families back home. Furthermore, immigrants are accused of diluting American culture and of a moral depravity that threatens the values essential to American life. Republican politicians have incorporated many of these arguments to rationalize a restrictionist immigration platform.

Politicians who favor a more liberal immigration policy argue that, historically, immigrant labor has contributed greatly to U.S. expansion and industrialization. Today, they add, immigrants play a necessary role in the division of labor by taking jobs American workers will not accept. Proponents of immigration point out that immigrants contribute tax dollars and Social Security payments in amounts that far outnumber the social services they consume. Immigration, they point out, is a net gain for the U.S. economy.

Moreover, they explain that immigrants have made invaluable contributions to the political and cultural development of the country. Those individuals who emigrate to the United States are often fleeing repressive regimes or extreme poverty, and they tend to be not only ambitious but also ardent supporters of American democracy.

Whereas the Republican Party is often associated with restrictive policies and the Democratic Party with a liberal immigration platform, their respective party positions have changed over time in response to shifts in the economic and political climate of the United States. The result is an extremely diverse set of policies that, over the course of U.S. immigration history, have failed to articulate a consistent position.

THREE PHASES OF U.S. IMMIGRATION POLICY

The history of U.S. immigration policy can be divided into three phases, each with very different objectives and each resulting in new patterns of immigration. The first, leading up to the 1880s, was a time of relatively few restrictions on immigration. The country was expanding rapidly, and it was generally understood that a growing population was necessary to push the frontier forward. From 1880 to 1965, the United States developed ever more restrictive policies on the number of immigrants that could enter in any given year. This period is marked by the creation of a national origins quota system. It was a time of intense anti-immigrant sentiment, but also rapid advancements in the standard of living for newly arrived immigrants. With the 1965 amendments to U.S. immigration law, an era of liberal policy began and the national-origin system was altered so as to create equity between groups seeking to emigrate.

Pre-1880s

From its inception, the United States has truly been a nation of immigrants. The colonies were founded by refugees fleeing religious and ideological persecution. The early U.S. economy was fueled by the forced immigration of slave labor and the contract labor of indentured servants.

Despite a deeply ingrained ideology of openness and freedom, forged as each new wave of immigrants was integrated into American society, there was a great deal of nativism in the political rhetoric of the time. In particular, during the early development of the two-party system, immigration policy played an important role in articulating the opposing national party platform.

In the 1850s after the dissolution of the Whig Party and during the early formation of the Republican Party, immigration played an important role in Republicans' attempts to define a party platform that would represent a viable opposition to the Democrats on a national level. The primary issue in their anti-Democratic platform was the slavery question. The Republican Party, from the beginning, was the antislavery party.

The break-up of the Whigs, however, left several factions, including the Know-Nothing Party, many of which established regional control based on an anti-immigrant platform. It was the difficult task of early Republican politicians to incorporate the constituencies of these various factions and at the same time navigate between the Democratic Party and nativism. In the end, the nativist agenda was relegated to the fringe of the Republican Party platform because most party members feared issues such as immigration and the temperance movement would obscure the most important issue for the national Republican agenda, namely the antislavery platform (Foner 1970).

1880–1965

Until the 1880s, U.S. policy remained relatively open and, in the case of contract laborers, often encouraged immigration. In 1882, this era of openness came to an end. Economic instability brought on by rapid industrialization combined with social instability resulting from rapid urbanization caused increased unrest among many Americans. This unrest resulted in several important pieces of anti-immigrant legislation. While Democratic politicians attempted to protect the country's open immigration policy, there was overwhelming support for restrictive measures. The Chinese Exclusion Act of 1882, for example, resulted in the elimination of almost all Chinese immigration to the United States. The act, which was initially opposed but eventually signed by Republican President Chester Arthur, was the first of several measures restricting Asian immigration; the National Origins Act completely blocked Japanese immigration for the next 40 years (Mink 1986).

It was the Immigration Act of 1924, or National Origins Act, that created an entirely new system for controlling the flow of immigrants into the country. Under the new law, visas were allocated based on national origin and determined as 2% of the U.S. population originating from that same nation according to 1890 census data. The 1924 measure effectively limited immigration to around 300,000 and controlled the composition of that immigration so that a majority of the newcomers were European (Daniels 1990).

While most immigration during this period was severely restricted, one category flourished. At the end of World War II, Europe was ravaged, and a large refugee population had been created. Victory in Europe left many Americans with renewed faith in democracy and a sense of moral responsibility for the rest of the world. As a result, there was a great deal of public support for resettling refugees in the United States. A bipartisan coalition in Congress passed the Displaced Persons Act of 1948, which admitted 205,000 refugees. The act was an extremely popular piece of legislation, so when Republicans claimed sole responsibility for the bill during that year's presidential campaign, the Democrats called for even more refugees to be admitted (Cafferty 1983).

During the Cold War, refugees from political repression were also admitted in large numbers. This group of immigrants was met with ambivalence, though, as suspicions about Soviet infiltration increased. The Immigration and Nationality Act of 1952, also referred to as the McCarran–Walter Act, essentially continued the national-origin quota system, but added a provision excluding communists. President Harry Truman vetoed the bill, arguing that the national-origin aspect "discriminates, deliberately and intentionally, against many of the peoples of the world" (Daniels 1990). A Republican-dominated Congress passed the McCarran–Walter Act over Truman's veto, however, and it was another 13 years before a policy was enacted that did not discriminate on the basis of national origin.

1965–Present

The liberal politics of the 1960s and the resulting advances made during the civil rights movement led to a corresponding change in Americans' attitudes toward immigrants. Increased awareness of race and a growing national dialogue about institutional racism resulted in calls for a more enlightened immigration policy. By 1964 President Lyndon Johnson, in his State of the Union speech, was urging reform of federal immigration laws (Cafferty 1983).

The next year, a series of amendments to the Immigration and Nationality Act drastically changed U.S. immigration policy by doing away with the national-origin quota system. The 1965 amendments, which ended years of strict limits on Asian immigration, caused a dramatic shift in immigration patterns and the racial makeup of America's immigrant population (Cafferty 1983). The new policy also allowed immediate relatives of U.S. citizens to enter the country with very few restrictions. Current patterns of immigration to the United Sates are a direct result of the 1965 amendments.

One consequence of this more liberal immigration policy was that all attention became focused on the issue of illegal immigrants. In November 1986 a Democratic Congress and Republican President Ronald Reagan enacted the Immigration Reform and Control Act (IRCA). Introduced by Senator Alan Simpson (R-Wyoming) and Representative Romano Mazzoli (D-Kentucky), the bill was a bipartisan effort to strengthen enforcement of existing immigration law. The most important aspect of the legislation, however, was that it combined sanctions for companies that employed illegal aliens with amnesty for illegal immigrants residing in the United States since 1981. Through IRCA, over 3 million illegal immigrants were accepted into the amnesty program and began the naturalization process (Daniels 1990).

Current debate on immigration policy centers on the issue of illegal immigrants. Nevertheless, campaign rhetoric in both parties has responded to growing public sentiment that restrictions even on legal immigration might be necessary. Measures such as the 1994 California state referendum Proposition 187 represent the first time that anti-immigrant sentiment has turned into the legislated denial of social services such as health care and education to the children of illegal immigrants. Proposition 187 was supported by most of California's Republican politicians including Governor Pete Wilson, who for a short time entered the 1996 presidential race on a primarily anti-immigration platform.

During the 1994 Republican revolution in Congress and the 1996 presidential primaries, immigration occupied an important place in candidates' rhetoric. Republicans continue to call for lower levels of immigration and stronger measures against illegal immigration, such as eliminating protections for the rights of illegal immigrants and their children.

Edward W. Siskel

BIBLIOGRAPHY

Abrams, F. "American Immigration Policy: How Strait the Gate?" In *U.S. Immigration Policy*, ed. Richard Hofstetter. Durham: Duke University Press, 1984.

Cafferty, P., B. Chiswick, A. Greeley, and T. Sullivan. *The Dilemma of American Immigration: Beyond the Golden Door*. New Brunswick, NJ: Transaction Books, 1983.

Daniels, Roger. *Coming to America: A History of Immigration and Ethnicity in American Life*. New York: HarperCollins, 1990.

Foner, E. *Free Soil, Free Labor, Free Men: The Ideology of the Republican Party Before the Civil War*. New York: Oxford University Press, 1970.

Gienapp, W. *The Origins of the Republican Party: 1852–1856*. New York: Oxford University Press, 1987.

Higham, J. *Strangers in the Land*. New York: Oxford University Press, 1977.

Mink, G. *Old Labor and New Immigrants in American Political Development: Union, Party, and State, 1875–1920*. Ithaca: Cornell University Press, 1986.

Seller, M. "Historical Perspectives on American Immigration Policy: Case Studies and Current Implications." In *U.S. Immigration Policy*, ed. Richard Hofstetter. Durham: Duke University Press, 1984.

Jews

While traditionally identified as a major Democratic voting block and a liberally oriented citizenry, growing numbers of Jews are Republican oriented and conservatively directed, as America heads toward the close of the century.

Traditional values, of work, community, and religious involvement, are shared not only by Protestants, who are traditionally Republican, but also by growing numbers of conservative Jews.

Newt Gingrich, outspoken House Speaker, have been well received by American conservative Jewry, with his recent promises of moving the American Embassy in Israel from Tel Aviv to Jerusalem, and his seeking to reorient American education toward a traditionally disciplined learning institution.

In New England, conservative Jewry, which have been noted to be more fiscally than socially conservative, are paying more and more attention to the Republican Party candidates, although no clear favorite has yet emerged.

In New Jersey, the National Jewish Coalition has helped create a Jewish influence in the Republican Party. The executive director of this organization, Matt Brooks, was campaign manager in Massachusetts for the 1988 presidential nomination try of Republican Jack Kemp.

Brooks views New Jersey as a "critical swing state in the '96 Presidential election," in a recent interview with *MetroWest Jewish News* and feels New Jersey will "get lots of attention from presidential candidates."

The National Jewish Coalition is seeking to play a key role in the interface between a Republican-controlled Congress and the Jewish community. "Under age 30, Jews are much more conservative in their voting," say key members of the coalition.

Following up on the growing tendency toward conservativism among younger Jewish voters, the *Young Jewish Leadership PAC*, a group of Jewish conservatives aged 20 to 35, seeks to "fund conservative candidates in close races" who are highly supportive of Israel, and Jews have historically contributed to the campaigns of candidates who are pro-Israel, ignoring party affiliation.

In New York, almost 50% of the Jewish vote went to outspoken Republican Senator Alphonse D'Amato, thus showing a growing tendency in the highly Jewish concentrated East toward a new view of Republican politics.

In former presidential elections, 80% of the Jews voted Democratic in 1992, and the same percentage was evident in 1994 regional elections. But it is viewed by some that the polls of Jewish voters exaggerate the loyalty of Jewish voters to the Democrats.

The Democrats have used the specter of the Christian Right to attempt to retain the Jewish vote, but there is evidence that the Jewish voter is not necessarily "buying in" to this scare tactic.

Robert Leiter, in his article relating to the Jews and the Religious Right, in the *Jewish Exponent*, quotes Marshall Breger, associated with the conservative Heritage Foundation in Washington, as saying, "Instead of reaching out to the Republican majority, Jews have made themselves irrelevant in the debate (with the Christian Right)." In Breger's opinion, "Jews must make political alliances with the religious conservatives."

The stronger military orientation of the Republican Party is another attraction for Jews concerned about the security of Israel, and while Colin Powell was considering the presidential race, he was viewed as a most attractive Republican candidate to American conservative Jewry.

Major players in national Republican politics, such as Gingrich and Dole, in meeting with Jewish conservative representatives after the 1994 elections, assured Jews of their commitment to Israel as a strategic ally of the United States. Dole is courting the Jewish vote among conservatives even though they are a minority, because they play important roles in presidential fund-raising efforts.

Despite a public relations position to the contrary, however, Jews view Dole as hostile to the interests of Israel, based on his voting record. In 1990, Dole, while approving hundreds of millions of dollars in loan guarantees to Iraq, opposed a $400 million loan guarantee to help Israel house incoming Soviet Jews.

While nobody is predicting that the majority of Jews are going to become a strong Republican voting block, the decline of economic stability in America, the serious depreciation in American education (with education being a strong traditional Jewish cultural value), and growing challenges to the security of the state of Israel are the winds of political change that are blowing younger and more conservative Jews into the fields of the Republican candidates and political leaders.

W. Adam Mandelbaum

SEE ALSO Other Minorities

BIBLIOGRAPHY
Bloomfield, Douglas M. "On the GOP Train in New Hampshire." *MetroWest Jewish News*, November 2, 1995.
Leiter, Robert. "Jews Missing the Boat on Ties with Religious Right." *Jewish Exponent*, July 14, 1995.
Jolkovsky, Binyamin. "They're Young, They're Jewish, They're Republican." *Forward*, October 13, 1995.

McCarthyism

In the early 1950s, Republican Senator Joseph R. McCarthy of Wisconsin rose to national attention by making a series of unsubstantiated claims about the growth of communism within the United States. With the communist takeover of China, the beginning of the Korean War, and the espionage cases of Alger Hiss and Ethel and Julius Rosenberg, many Americans became unduly anxious over the potential threat of communism to the nation. McCarthy capitalized on this "Red scare" in an attempt to further his political career. His name became so associated with this period that the term *McCarthyism* became synonymous with the Red scare of the 1950s.

In the midst of his 1950 reelection campaign, McCarthy made a speech in Wheeling, West Virginia, in which he forecast an American loss of the Cold War due to a communist conspiracy within the State Department. He claimed to have a list of some 205 subversives within the Truman State Department—though the number of subversives rose as he repeated his allegations. McCarthy's wild accusations were quickly shown to be inaccurate at best, but the senator had already gained the attention of the American media. Over the next four years, McCarthy inflamed the American public through increasingly extreme accusations over the presence of communist infiltrators in the American government and American society in general.

McCarthy's brand of rabid anticommunism quickly took center stage in American politics as politicians from both the Republican and Democratic parties rushed to join the anticommunist bandwagon. In actions that often showed little regard for the basic civil liberties of Americans, numerous investigations were launched into a diffuse panorama of the society. The House Un-American Activities Committee (HUAC) examined the influence of communism in Hollywood. As a result, a number of prominent Hollywood figures found themselves blacklisted and thus unable to work in American entertainment. Meanwhile, the Senate Internal Security Subcommittee investigated the United Nations as a vehicle for subversion. Even President Truman felt compelled to demonstrate his anticommunist credentials. Truman issued executive orders that introduced new standards for investigating supposed subversives in the government and his administration. He also signed the McCarran–Walter Immigration Act, which gave the president broad powers to deny immigration to suspected communists.

In the end, McCarthy was responsible for his own downfall. With the 1952 election of Republican Dwight D. Eisenhower, McCarthy found it much more difficult to assert his allegations. Eisenhower's administration offered far fewer targets for McCarthy than had Truman's, which forced the senator to broaden his search for subversives. When McCarthy attempted to charge the U.S. Army with being soft on communism, his political fortunes unraveled. During televised coverage of the Army–McCarthy Hearings in 1954, the American public was able to see firsthand the viciousness of McCarthy's tactics.

Public sentiment turned against McCarthy after the hearings. The Senate voted to censure McCarthy for "unbecoming conduct," and most political figures distanced themselves from the senator. McCarthyism quickly faded from American politics. McCarthy lost political clout and died in disgrace three years later, in 1957.

Tom Lansford

BIBLIOGRAPHY

Landis, Mark. *Joseph McCarthy: The Politics of Chaos.* London: Associated University Press, 1987.
Reeves, Thomas C. *The Life and Times of Joe McCarthy: A Biography.* New York: Stein and Day, 1982.
Rogin, Michael P. *The Intellectuals and McCarthy: The Radical Specter.* Cambridge: MIT Press, 1967.

Media

Like the Democratic Party, the Republican Party has had a changing relationship with the media—sometimes feeling that its leaders could manipulate the media and that Republicans were well represented in the media, especially among publishers and owners; at other times fearing that the media were a hostile outside enemy out to destroy the Republican Party and its leaders. The changes are attributable in part to changes in the Republican Party, and in part to changes in the media.

Among the issues that led to the Republican Party's concern with the media were perceived incompatibility between national security and media independence, regulation of pornographic and indecent material, attempts to ensure fairness in the political process, and regulation of new forms of technology.

Restrictions on the media in the name of "national security" were pronounced by a relatively new Republican Party during the Civil War. Legislators of the Republican Party, which believed in the Union fighting a civil war against southern secessionists, generally supported the restrictions. Papers were closed, editors were jailed, and presses were confiscated. Typical of congressional votes was a May 1864 motion to suspend the House Rules, allowing consideration of a resolution condemning the seizure of two New York newspapers' offices. The motion failed, but every Democrat voted for it. During Reconstruction, government controls on southern newspapers continued, lest their editors try to foment a new rebellion.

Republicans in the leadership were joined by Democrats in supporting the Spanish-American War, dubbed by Secretary of State John Hay as "a splendid little war." Indeed, the vote on appropriations to support that war was unanimous. Future leaders, including a future president, Theodore Roosevelt, distinguished themselves by service in and support of this war.

Critics held the "yellow press," and especially the influential Republican William Randolph Hearst, responsible. The claim that the media could incite violence has been echoed by pacifists who claim that the media stir up passions for war, then sound caution during a later phase. A minority of Democrats agreed with Senator George Hoar of Massachussetts, explicitly opposed to imperialism, in which they contended the media played a large role.

During most of the major U.S. wars of the twentieth century, by contrast, Democratic presidents were in office. During the World War I, most Republicans joined Democrats who supported the Wilson administration in setting up a federal censorship board.

The Republican candidate opposing Wilson in the 1916 election was Justice Charles Evans Hughes, who later complained: "We have seen the war powers . . . exercised broadly after the military exigency has passed . . . and we may well wonder whether constitutional government . . . could survive another great war." This was a typical Republican attitude—not endorsing unrestrained coverage by the media—but claiming that government controls had gone too far.

During World War II a voluntary press code limited the reporting of war and economic information. Most Republicans joined the Democrats in searching for enemies of American interests, wherever they might be found, including the media.

Republican legislators joined with Democrats to override President Truman's veto of the McCarran Act, an attempt to root out alleged subversives in the media and elsewhere, in the aftermath of World War II. And Republicans as well as Democrats condoned or encouraged "little HUACs" (state copies of the federal House Un-American Activities Committee, which often investigated subversive influences on and in the media).

And during the wars in Korea and Indochina most Republicans joined Democrats who supported censorship, infiltration, or disinformation to stop what they viewed as unfair criticism of war efforts.

The 1968 election found friends and enemies in both major political parties. The Democratic convention was held in Chicago, where the mayor, Richard Daley, accused the media of giving comfort to the enemy. Cynics saw so little difference between Hubert Humphrey, the Democratic nominee, and Richard Nixon, the Republican nominee, that they thought an appropriate response to the Republican campaign slogan "Nixon's the One" was "Hubert's the Other."

Nixon won the election, and his mutual animosity with the media continued. It reached its height when the administration sought unsuccessfully to stop publication of the "Pentagon Papers" in the *New York Times*; the attempt failed in part because key Republicans including Senators Mark Hatfield and Lowell Weicker did not share their president's hostility toward the media. The Supreme Court did not argue that prior restraint of the newspapers was unconstitutional; instead they just argued that the Nixon administration had not met its heavy burden of proof. At the Senate impeachment hearings, several Republicans joined Democratic Senator Sam Ervin, who emerged as a champion of constitutional rights, including press freedom.

Nixon's first vice president, Spiro Agnew, was renowned for his criticism of the press, which he called "nattering nabobs of negativism." The Republican Party, however, included defenders as well as critics of press freedom. One of the most ardent defenders was Paul ("Pete") McCloskey, who served in the House and was an unsuccessful presidential candidate.

With Republican leadership of the last stages of the war in Indochina, and of the interventions in Grenada, Panama, and the Persian Gulf, most Democrats became critics of controls on the media, and of many covert operations, to which media access was impossible. In 1982 many Republicans successfully endorsed the passage of legislation making it a federal crime to publish anything they had reason to know would disclose the identity of U.S. intelligence agents.

When the Reagan administration invaded Grenada in 1983, it ordered an unprecedented 48-hour news blackout. Criticism of the blackout from Democrats and others led to the appointment of a panel recommending that press pools accompany future U.S. interventions and that news not be blacked out. When Panama was invaded in 1979, under the George Bush administration, a press pool was used, but during the first hours of the invasion, the pool was in a windowless room in Fort Smith, Arkansas.

During the Gulf War, press pools were used with general support but some criticism from Democratic leaders. Similarly, press pools were used when the Democrat-led Clinton administration intervened in Somalia, Haiti, and Bosnia.

From their start, foreign broadcast services, such as Radio Free Europe, Radio Liberty, and Radio Marti, were a contentious issue. Most Republicans, including Ronald Reagan and George Bush, supported funding the services, as valuable antidotes to closed societies, during and after the Cold War. Other Republicans opposed funding the services as an unnecessary waste of money.

In the years following the party's founding, Republican politicians endorsed the Comstock Laws (named for Anthony Comstock, who served for 43 years as secretary of the New York Society for the Suppression of Vice, and served in the unpaid federal position of special agent for the U.S. Postal Service), defined through the English *Hicklin* case of 1868 whereby material was obscene if isolated passages could produce prurient or lustful thoughts in a particularly susceptible person. Even at common law, the category of "obscene libel" reflected a general agreement that liberty of the press did not include license to publish materials that might be thought immoral.

Indecent or pornographic material was a local matter, unless interstate commerce was involved, as it was when the mails were used or material was broadcast on radio or television. Attitudes toward indecent material and pornography became a litmus test for Supreme Court justices, with Democratic senators more likely to allow the media to disseminate questionable materials. Indecent material may not be obscene. The key is that it is "patently offensive" and either sexual or excretory.

Recent Republican administrations have given access to antipornography forces. For the Eisenhower administration, this meant access for New York's Francis Cardinal Spellman. Eisenhower and Spellman were disappointed when Justice William Brennan, a Catholic and lifelong Democrat, helped render decisions that were not viewed favorably by antipornography forces.

During the Johnson administration pornography was one of many issues in battles over the appointment of Abe Fortas to the Supreme Court. Initially, Everett Dirksen, the minority leader in the Senate, had been supportive of Fortas. An antipornography group, Citizens for Decent Literature, helped Dirksen to change his mind.

The election of Richard Nixon partly represented public endorsement of his pledge to appoint federal judges including Supreme Court justices, who, in marked contrast to Democratic appointees, would allow less latitude for pornographers. In 1970, however, a Commission on Obscenity and Pornography (the Lockhart Commission) revealed its studies. That commission discounted claims that pornography was linked to sex crimes or to violence. President Nixon rejected the findings of the commission, saying, "I have evaluated that report and reject its morally bankrupt conclusions." All but one of the commission's members had been picked by Nixon's predecessor, Lyndon Johnson. The one was Charles Keating, founder of Citizens for Decent Literature. Justice Warren Burger (a Nixon appointee) cited the minority report of dissenting members, which said that pornography might be related to harmful behavior.

A 1972 surgeon general's Study of Television and Social Behavior was more to President Nixon's liking. It reached a tentative conclusion that violence on television was related to violence in society. That finding echoed a 1969 National Commission on the Causes and Prevention of Violence and would later be echoed by Republican Surgeon General C. Everett Koop.

Democratic legislators were more likely than Republicans to object to attacks on the media by Nixon and his first vice president, Spiro Agnew, and to object to child pornography legislation and the report issued by a commission headed by Edwin Meese and begun by President Ronald Reagan's first attorney general, William French Smith, linking pornography to crime. That commission had called for the adoption of new obscenity statutes and the enforcement of existing ones, along with a broadened conception of what might be considered "obscene."

It was, however, during a Democratic administration (Carter's) that the Protection of Children Against Sexual Exploitation Act of 1977 was adopted, and other new regulations on the exposure of children to indecent materials were introduced.

Republicans have also voiced opposition to government involvement in and control of the media at the international level. President Reagan's ambassador to the United Nations, Jeane Kirkpatrick (herself a Democrat turned Republican) objected to proposals for a New World Information and Communications Order and endorsed the U.S. withdrawal from the UN Educational, Scientific, and Cultural Organization (UNESCO).

Republicans, led by Senator Jesse Helms of North Carolina and Congressman Dana Rohrabacher of California, attacked the National Endowment of the Arts for funding projects that they viewed as "obscene." President George Bush was more content to threaten the endowment and to appoint a new director than to end its funding altogether. Critics were more successful in reducing the amount of funding and encouraging self-censorship than in regulating content.

Media portrayals were one theme of Republican Senator Robert Dole's presidential campaign in 1996. Dole argued that Hollywood's glorification of sex and violence undermined traditional American values. Another candidate, Pat Buchanan, who had been press secretary to President Nixon, wrote in 1989 that there should be "a cultural revolution in the 90's," by which he meant less permissiveness in the media.

Current concerns include the dissemination of "cyberporn" over the Internet, to which minors have access, and pornography on television and in the movies. Republicans have varied in the degree to which they would regulate "cyberporn," however. Indeed, Republican Representative Rick White of Washington tried unsuccessfully to engineer a compromise proposal when most of his fellow Republicans supported restrictions proposed by a Democrat, Senator James Exon of Nebraska.

Democrats and Republicans have tended to endorse media efforts to find a "safe haven"—hours during which children are usually not in the audience—hence when more explicit materials can be disseminated.

Attempts to make the political process more fair included the Fairness Doctrine of the 1950s, codified by Congress in 1959 amendments to the Communications Act, the Equal Opportunity Doctrine, the Zapple Doctrine, and right-of-reply laws. At the national level the desire for political fairness was embodied in the 1934 Communications Act (although that act makes explicit reference instead to national defense, and safety of life and property in requiring that broadcasters operate in the "public interest") adopted during a Democratic administration, that of Franklin Roosevelt, but also supported by many Republicans. The issue was not so much whether to regulate the new media as how to do so.

The act superseded the Radio Act of 1927 and established the Federal Communications Commission, which in theory, although not in practice, is immune to partisan pressure. As mentioned earlier, at the point the statute was adopted, the issue was not whether communication should be regulated, but how, since the number and strength of radio stations were proliferating rapidly.

The Fairness Doctrine referred to the obligation of broadcasters to "provide reasonable opportunity for the discussion of conflicting views." There were two parts to the obligation: (1) to spend a reasonable amount of time discussing controversial issues and (2) to do so fairly, that is, to give some coverage to every side of the controversy. It assumed that there was a scarcity of radio frequencies and that there could be a limited number of television stations. Because advances in cable television technology created new possibilities for many more stations, it was repealed in 1987 by the Federal Communications Commission, and vetoed by President Reagan when the then majority Democratic Congress sought to reinstate it. Despite the repeal, licenses were still obligated to serve the "public interest."

Similarly, equal rates are to be charged political candidates for advertising, and if one candidate is allowed to use the airwaves, her or his opponents can demand equal time. Republicans have tended to argue for a narrow definition of "use"; some successfully argued when Ronald Reagan was a candidate that each showing of one of his movies was not a "use."

In 1971, with Republican support and despite Democratic opposition, the requirements that candidates be allowed to advertise at the lowest unit cost were loosened so that the rules applied only to a short period before elections. In general, Republican candidates are better financed than their Democratic opponents and will resist attempts to "level the playing field."

Food and drug advertising through the media is regulated by the Federal Trade Commission. In general, Democrats have been less willing than Republicans to apply free speech arguments to commercial speech and more willing to regulate advertising, particularly advertising directed toward children.

Democrats as well as Republicans could object to what they perceived to be unfair media attacks. During the 1990s, Democratic President Bill Clinton objected to attacks from conservative talk radio and talk television hosts including the Republican Rush Limbaugh. Republican Congressman Robert Dornan, sometimes a substitute for Limbaugh, also demonstrated an ability to use the airwaves.

Some Republicans, as well as Democrats, saw public broadcasting as a guarantor of fairness, although most did not. Spokespeople for controversial causes were often critical of Republicans and claimed that they had difficulty competing in the marketplace and gaining access to the media. Many Republican members of Congress therefore would consistently vote against continuing or increasing government funding of broadcasting. For instance, Republican leaders, including Speaker of the House Newt Gingrich, argued that with new technology people had access to many sources of information, and controversial viewpoints had many outlets in the media. The original rationale for public broadcasting was therefore no longer valid.

A concern with "leaks" to the media was held by both major parties when they were in power, but has probably recently been more pronounced during Republican administrations. A reflection of this was a threat (not carried out) by Richard Thornburgh, George Bush's attorney general, to require reporters to turn over their telephone records.

The concern about the impact of the media on the political process (indeed, the saying that the four branches of the American government are ABC, NBC, CBS, and CNN is probably incorrect only in that it excludes Fox) reflects the importance of new technology. The telegraph brought with it the ability to report information or misinformation instantly from the battlefield. Radio brought with it a need to regulate the number of stations and how they would be used. Motion pictures brought concerns about where and how explicit sexual material would be shown.

In general, the advent of new media contributed to a decline in the influence of both parties. Parties tended to adapt to the media, rather than the other way around. Gone were the days when the media were supposed to represent partisan opinion.

Leaders were expected to hold regular press conferences, to be on the Internet, and to deliver major speeches when the television audience was large. A candidate who hid things (for instance, drug experimentation, finances, or a war record) was thought to have something to hide. Most media could be expected to "follow the flag" and to give support in the initial stages of any intervention, regardless of the party in power. As the conflict continued, however, the media would be increasingly critical.

The media have changed, but some elements have remained the same. Allegations of a one-party press are made, but usually tend only to apply to some people in some media. In general, those at the bottom of the media hierarchy are likely to be Democrats; those at the top are likely to be Republicans. We can generally expect that most reporters and correspondents will be Democrats, although only a minority of publishers and owners will be. In this respect, the media are similar to American society in general.

Arthur Blaser

BIBLIOGRAPHY

Blumberg, N.B. *One-Party Press?* Lincoln: University of Nebraska Press, 1954.

Carter, T. Barton, Juliet Lushbough Dee, Martin J. Gaynes, and Harvey L. Zuckman. *Mass Communication Law in a Nutshell.* 4th ed. St. Paul, MN: West, 1994.

Emerson, Thomas. *The System of Free Expression.* New York: Vintage, 1970.

Levy, Leonard W. *Emergence of a Free Press.* New York: Simon and Schuster, 1985.

Linfield, Michael. *Freedom under Fire: U.S. Civil Liberties in Times of War.* Boston: South End Press, 1990.

McCloskey, Paul, Jr. *Truth and Untruth: Political Deceit in America.* New York: Simon and Schuster, 1972.

The Minimum Wage

In 1968, the official platform of the Republican Party said it planned to take a "flexible approach to minimum wage laws." That statement has characterized much of the party's position since Congress passed the Fair Labor Standards Act in 1938, establishing a minimum wage. Since then, Congress has significantly revised and broadened its terms.

But even though minimum-wage proposals have often drawn bipartisan support, members of the Republican Party have at times found themselves at odds on the issue. The most common fracture has been along conservative–moderate lines. Many conservatives favor a policy of letting the free market establish wages, and some maintain there should be no minimum wage at all. Senator Orrin Hatch, a conservative Republican from Utah and the senior Republican on the Committee on Labor and Human Resources, and Representative Steve Bartlett, a Texas Republican on the House Committee on Education and Labor, have fought against recent attempts to raise the minimum wage, arguing that a higher wage will increase unemployment and inflate prices, actually hurting the people that proponents say would be helped. House Majority Leader Richard Armey, Republican of Texas, vowed to fight Democratic President Bill Clinton's proposed increase in the minimum wage with "every fiber" of his body.

Moderate Republicans, in contrast, have not been so adamant. Although some of them reject an increase in the minimum wage as unnecessary, others have tended to argue that workers in entry-level positions deserve pay adequate enough to live on and that raising the minimum wage does not necessarily increase unemployment or inflation.

Additional debate among party members has focused not so much on whether there should be a minimum wage, but what it should be.

Throughout his eight years in the White House, conservative Republican President Ronald Reagan was content to keep the minimum wage the same, but that did not stop Republican George Bush, Reagan's vice president, from pledging to raise the wage during his 1988 campaign for president. The most controversial part of Bush's plan turned out to be the so-called training wage, a condition of his campaign pledge. The proposal drew opposition from Democrats.

Other Republicans have sought to address the minimum-wage issue by proposing alternative methods of helping the working poor. For example, Representative Thomas Petri, a Republican from Wisconsin, has introduced legislation to expand the earned-income tax credit, the subsidy paid to low-income working parents. Petri's proposal, however, which pegs the tax credit to the number of children in a family, also drove a wedge into party unity. Ultraconservative Republicans condemn it as social engineering.

Before becoming Bush's Republican vice president, Dan Quayle of Indiana, at the time senior Republican on the Senate's subcommittee on labor, supported an increase in the earned-income tax credit along with a gradual increase in the minimum wage.

Steve Hoenisch

BIBLIOGRAPHY

"An Honest Day's Pay?" *The Economist*, September 3, 1988.

Du Pont, Pete. "Pay Hazard." *National Review*, May 1, 1995.

McClenahen, John S. "Take a Hike: A Rise in the Minimum Wage Is Unlikely in 1995." *Industry Week*, March 6, 1995.

Mencimer, Stephanie. "Take a Hike: The Minimum Wage and Welfare Reform." *New Republic*, May 23, 1994.

"Wages of Politics." *The Economist*, March 18, 1989.

Modern Republicanism

Modern Republicanism is that certain brand of Republicanism that marked the campaigns, elections, and administrations of President Dwight Eisenhower. Also known as "Eisenhower Republicanism," "progressive moderation," and "dynamic conservatism," this mid-century Republican philosophy must be understood in its historical context, the ways in which it grew out of early twentieth-century Republicanism, and the ways in which it affected the Republican Party that arose in its wake.

The political forces within the Republican Party that would come to support Dwight Eisenhower for the Republican presidential nomination in 1952 had been resurrected from the Progressive era and nurtured and solidified in the 1940s by presidential candidates Wendell Willkie and Thomas E. Dewey. Progressive Willkie–Dewey Republicans were considerably more liberal than Republicans typically had been in the first half of the twentieth century. These precursors of "modern Republicans" were also internationalist in regard to American foreign policy. Considering that traditional Republicanism of the time was associated with the conservative, isolationist "stand-pat Republicanism" of Senator Robert A. Taft of Ohio, the Willkie–Dewey forces, if successful, could substantially have altered twentieth-century Republicanism.

In 1952 Dwight Eisenhower became the standard-bearer for this particular brand of progressive Republicanism. Prior to his candidacy, few people knew whether Eisenhower was a Republican or a Democrat. Eisenhower had been considered a potential presidential candidate by forces in both parties, insisting all the while that he was not seeking the presidency but would accept the position only out of a sense of duty. In one sense, the uncertainty about Eisenhower's political affiliation and his broad personal appeal made it clear that Eisenhower's political strength could be tapped by following an ideologically moderate course. Second, in juxtaposition to his chief rival for the Republican nomination, Senator Taft, Eisenhower appeared to be a somewhat more moderate Republican alternative. According to political scientist V.O. Key Jr., "Mr. Taft had come to personify standpat Republicanism. Precisely what sort of Republican General Eisenhower was, nobody knew, but he was presumably different from Taft, an impression enormously helpful in the presentation of the General as a new Republican" (Key 1964, 193).

Eisenhower's moderate stance was a product of several factors. Aside from the political positioning vis-à-vis Taft, Eisenhower sought to present a moderate Republican image in order to counter the considerable advantage Democrats enjoyed in presidential electoral politics. The Democrats and their New Deal were still quite popular, while traditional Republicans were still incurring the political costs of the Great Depression. In order to win the White House, Republicans would need to reach out to Independent voters and disenchanted Democrats. Coupled with Eisenhower's personal popularity, the moderation of traditional Republicanism attracted these crucial non-Republican votes. Sinclair Weeks said, "With General Eisenhower as our presidential candidate, Republicans and many joining with us for the first time will . . . bring about a victory" (PDE 1989, 1260). In his 1952 Republican convention speech nominating Eisenhower, Maryland Governor Theodore R. McKeldin proclaimed, "Among independent and new voters, [Eisenhower] leads the next Republican candidate almost three to one. Among disillusioned Democrats—and they are legion—he is far in front. And we shall need the help of these independents and liberated Democrats."

Perceiving the need to reach out to non-Republican voters, Eisenhower took steps to lessen the perceived difference between the parties on social welfare issues that had previously benefited Democrats. On many issues, Eisenhower accepted, and in some instances extended, New Deal policies. In the areas of public housing, Social Security, and unemployment, Eisenhower conceded to Democrats the importance of federal government involvement. This strategy of concession on many domestic issues served Eisenhower well in the elections of 1952 and 1956. The authors of *The American Voter* credit the "willingness of the Eisenhower administration to embrace . . . the New Deal" with lessening "an important difference the public had perceived between the parties" (Campbell, Converse, Miller, and

Stokes 1960, 46). Lessening the perceived partisan difference on these issues subsequently reduced the salience of the issues; thus modern Republicans could focus voter attention on different dimensions of opinion: "Corruption, Korea, and Communism" (Campbell, Converse, Miller, and Stokes 1960, 551).

Although he is credited with extending the New Deal, Eisenhower feared many of the trends he perceived to be put in motion by New Deal policies. Having referred in private to New Deal programs as "creeping socialism," Eisenhower's personal antipathy for the New Deal is evident. The seeds of this modern Republicanism were in the electoral/political motivations of Eisenhower rather than in his personal political philosophy. When his brother, Edgar, complained that President Eisenhower was being too liberal in his support of New Deal programs, Eisenhower replied, "Should any political party attempt to abolish social security and eliminate labor laws and farm programs, you would not hear of that party again in our political history" (Leuchtenberg 1985, 49). It was the temper of the times that Eisenhower cited in defending his moderate positions to vice presidential nominee Richard Nixon: "I have labored hard and earnestly to eliminate divisions in the Republican party and to state and to re-state a firm middle of the road policy at home, and an intelligent, forward-looking program in the foreign field. *In these times*, I do not see how an honest man can do much more. We are faced with facts—we must meet them as they exist, not as we would like them to be" (PDE 1989, 1369).

In an attempt to disassociate himself with the Republican past, Eisenhower proffered modern Republicanism, which involved changes in both domestic and foreign policies. In the area of domestic policy, Eisenhower hoped to convince voters that he would react more quickly and vigorously than did Herbert Hoover should another economic depression occur. Eisenhower stressed his support of New Deal safeguards such as Social Security and public relief and public works. Where Republicans in the 1930s and 1940s had opposed some aspects of Social Security, modern Republicans in 1952 favored amending the system to provide coverage for those citizens who were still excluded from the system. And where Republicans of the 1930s and 1940s called for an end to many of the relief agencies established by the New Deal, modern Republicans conceded that the federal government has a legitimate role in such endeavors. The 1952 Republican platform stated that "the Federal Government and state and local governments should continuously plan programs of economically justifiable public works." This represents a subtle word change from

previous Republican platforms, but the lack of direct repudiation of federal involvement in relief and public works betrays a softening of Republican philosophy against federal involvement in the economy.

In the area of foreign policy, Eisenhower had a substantial impact on Republican philosophy. Modern Republicanism meant more international activity for the United States and more presidential authority in foreign policy (Reichard 1975). In fact, even those who doubt that Eisenhower had a significant impact on domestic Republicanism concede that he changed the way many Republicans viewed America's role in the world. One close Eisenhower associate claims that during "Eisenhower's first two years in office, rhetoric and the very real shift of the Republican party toward internationalism combined to create an aura of change and revitalization about the GOP" (Larson 1956, 237).

THE MODERN REPUBLICAN LEGACY

Political scientist Stephen Skowronek places presidents into a typology in which both the strength of the existing political regime (established by a previous president) and the affiliation of the president with, or the opposition of the president to, the existing regime are considered. Skowronek suggests that the relationship of these two factors produces patterns of presidential politics. As a Republican entering the White House during the Democratic New Deal era, Eisenhower could represent one of two types of presidential politics described by Skowronek: the politics of reconstruction or the politics of preemption. Reconstructive presidents are those presidents who have the most enduring impact on American politics. These presidents, who are opposed to vulnerable existing regimes, have an opportunity to change political discourse and fundamentally alter political coalitions in American politics. If, however, the president is in opposition to a regime that is still strong, that president can only hope to preempt the regime. Perhaps the preemptive president has an opportunity to curtail the legacy of the existing regime, but he is in no position to reconstruct the political system.

Where, then, do Dwight Eisenhower and his modern Republican philosophy fit? In fact, most agree that Eisenhower did not reconstruct American politics. He had a great deal of impact on foreign policy within the Republican Party, but in terms of domestic policy, Eisenhower's chief contribution was making the New Deal permanent. Because of Eisenhower's victory in 1952, the New Deal was partially accepted in both parties. Although the Republican Party "could chip away at New Deal measures . . . , it could not re-open settled questions" (Key 1964, 224). Although he reconstructed the Republican Party in some ways, Eisenhower did not reconstruct American politics. He accepted that the public welcomed the New Deal, and thus he could not get rid of it altogether. Nevertheless, Eisenhower sought, where politically feasible, to curtail the trends he believed so ominous.

Douglas Harris

BIBLIOGRAPHY

Campbell, Angus, Philip E. Converse, Warren E. Miller, and Donald E. Stokes. *The American Voter.* Chicago: University of Chicago Press, 1960.

Key, V.O., Jr. *Politics, Parties, and Pressure Groups.* 5th ed. New York: Thomas Y. Crowell, 1964.

Larson, Arthur. *A Republican Looks at His Party.* New York: Harper, 1956.

Leuchtenberg, William E. *In the Shadow of FDR.* Ithaca: Cornell University Press, 1985.

The Papers of Dwight Eisenhower (PDE), ed. Louis Galambos. Baltimore: Johns Hopkins University Press, 1989.

Reichard, Gary W. *The Reaffirmation of Republicanism.* Knoxville: University of Tennessee Press, 1975.

Skowronek, Stephen. *The Politics That Presidents Make.* Cambridge: Harvard University Press, 1993.

Monetary Policy

Before the development of the modern banking and currency system of the United States, monetary policy consisted of either supporting the gold standard or the unlimited coinage of silver. Historically, Republicans had supported the gold standard that controlled and limited the supply of money in circulation and therefore had a deflationary impact.

Today, the goals of monetary policy are full employment, price stabilization, economic growth, and balance-of-payments equilibrium. Full employment does not mean that 100% of the people have jobs. Economists recognize that there will always be some frictional unemployment of 3% or 4%. Price stabilization does not mean no growth in the Consumer Price Index, but rather controlled slow growth of 2% or less. Concerns over economic growth focus on how fast the economy can grow while avoiding inflation. Finally, balance-of-payments equilibrium has to do with how much deficit can be incurred without adversely affecting the economy or the strength of the dollar. While there is little dispute that these goals are desirable, there is considerable difference of opinion as to how to achieve them, how to measure them, and what numbers are acceptable.

While monetary policy is the responsibility of the independent Federal Reserve Board, whose members are appointed by the president and confirmed by the Senate, the impact of "the Fed's" decisions have made it an extremely political issue. The Fed accomplishes its task by buying and selling government bonds in open market operations or by changing reserve requirements—the amount of money banks must hold in reserve to secure deposits—or by changing the conditions under which banks can borrow reserves at the discount window, that is, raise or lower the discount rate it charges banks to borrow funds. Decisions of the Federal Reserve can have a strong influence on interest rates, the money supply, and, in the end, employment and inflation.

Republicans are generally monetarists in their approach to the economy. This means that they believe that by controlling the rate of growth of the money supply, they can control economic activity. This view was dominant during the Reagan administration and continued through the Bush administration. Republicans sought the support of the Fed in establishing a constant rate of growth in the money supply in order to maintain steady growth. In addition, they believed that steady monetary growth would result in greater price stability. But Republicans have been unable to institutionalize this economic view in any significant way. During the Reagan administration, both the administration and the Federal Reserve, under the leadership of Paul Volcker, chairman of the Fed, pursued monetarist policies, but there is no legislation that forces the Fed or the administration to do so.

Many do not believe that monetarist policies are the appropriate way to achieve the economic goals outlined above. In fact, until the late 1970s, the Fed generally focused its policies on the control of interest rates as a way to control the economy. Even during the Reagan years, the Fed often pursued its more traditional object of interest-rate control, rather than money supply.

In the end, Republicans tend to see inflation as resulting from excess demand caused by an excessive supply of money. Under this model, budget deficits are not seen as stimulating economic growth. Furthermore, under this model it makes a difference whether deficits are reduced by raising taxes or cutting spending. Republican monetarists argue that higher taxes and increased government spending are inherently anti-growth, while lower spending and taxes result in the stimulation of the economy. Therefore, while monetary policy is not an area under direct political control, it has a dramatic impact on how elected officials choose to encourage the growth of the economy.

Jeffrey D. Schultz
Diane L. Schultz

BIBLIOGRAPHY

Alesina, Alberto, and Geoffrey Carliner. *Politics and Economics in the Eighties*. Chicago: University of Chicago Press, 1991.

Bartlett, Bruce. "Inflation and Democrats." *National Review* 45 (April 26, 1993), 34.

Mayer, Thomas. *Monetary Policy in the United States*. New York: Random House, 1967.

Nominating Conventions

William Marcy Tweed, boss of New York City's Tammany machine in the late nineteenth century, once said, "I don't care who does the electing just so I can do the nominating" (Davis 1983, 4). This statement is a testament to the importance of party nominations of candidates to electoral politics. As the presidency is the highest elected office in the U.S. government, the study of presidential nominating politics is of particular importance. The national convention—the institution by which political parties in America nominate presidential candidates—has remained remarkably stable for most of American history.

In the early days of the republic, congressional caucuses—meetings of a party's members of Congress—were the predominant means by which nominees for the presidency and vice presidency were selected. Many found this process undemocratic, however. Furthermore, some parties wishing to field presidential candidates did not have sufficient numbers of partisans in Congress to sustain a caucus. Thus an alternative had to be developed. In 1831, as part of the democratizing spirit of the Jacksonian era, the first national party convention was held by the Antimasonic Party. Although this party was relatively unimportant in the history of party politics in America, it did devise an important institution that solved the unique problem of nominating national candidates in the federal system of the United States. Political scientist V.O. Key Jr. once said, "The national convention represents the solution by American parties of the problem of uniting scattered points of political leadership in support of candidates for the Presidency and Vice Presidency. Thus, it is the basic element of national party apparatus" (Key 1964, 396).

Partially in response to the successful use of conventions by the Jacksonian Democratic-Republicans, the Whig Party (a precursor to the Republican Party) held its first convention in December 1839. Although Senator Henry Clay of Kentucky was favored to win the party's nomination, several of the rules adopted by the Whigs for their first convention worked to erode Clay's support. And although Clay led on the first bal-

lot, General William Henry Harrison of Ohio became the Whig's first national presidential candidate.

In 1854, as the Whig Party declined in importance and the salience of the slavery issue heightened, the Republican Party was born. The Republican Party was founded in large part on the sectionalism that typified the era immediately preceding the Civil War. According to Paul T. David and his colleagues, "the organizing impetus came from radical northern and middlewestern groups that were strongly opposed to the extension of slavery into the territories" (David, Goldman, and Bain 1960, 24). In their first convention in 1856, Republicans nominated John C. Frémont of California for president and selected opposition to slavery in the territories as their main issue.

As with the Democrats, Republican conventions would gain legitimacy through usage. In some ways the legitimacy of convention nominations was secured more quickly for the Whigs and Republicans than for Democrats. According to Byron Shafer, "The convention . . . quickly acquired authority over party endorsement. A Whig convention actually deposed a sitting president, John Tyler, in 1844 and then another, Millard Fillmore, in 1852" (Shafer 1988, 12). And in 1876, the Republican convention sought its own nominee instead of the three candidates who came to the convention as "serious contenders." At the convention, Rutherford B. Hayes, a "favorite son" candidate, secured the presidential nomination on the seventh ballot (Shafer 1988, 16). Since this legitimating period, conventions have remained the authoritative, if not always determinative, forum for presidential nominations.

CONVENTION FUNCTIONS, RULES, AND PROCESSES

Typically, national nominating conventions are held in the summer prior to the election. Nelson Polsby observes two chief patterns of convention timing: "One is that the 'out' party will normally hold its convention before the 'in' party, on the theory that its candidate will need more of a publicity boost earlier. . . . Also, if there is an incumbent president, he will schedule the convention to fit his timetable" (Polsby 1983, 117). Conventions are usually four-day events. The first day of the convention is used to welcome delegates, who then "approve the installation of temporary officers and the formal appointment of committees" (Davis 1983, 85). The opening day ends with the convention's keynote address. The second day is allotted for the reports of the committees on rules, credentials, and the platform. Day three of a typical convention is when the names of presidential candidates are put in for the party's nomination. Once the nominating speeches are complete, balloting begins to determine the party's presidential nominee. The final day of the convention is devoted to the selection of the vice presidential nominee and the acceptance speeches of the presidential and vice presidential candidates (Davis 1983, 85).

According to James W. Davis, national party conventions serve the following manifest functions: (1) to nominate presidential and vice presidential candidates; (2) to provide "the impetus and encouragement to divergent elements of the party to close ranks behind the newly anointed nominee"; (3) to shape the choice of the vice presidential candidate; (4) to write the party's platform; (5) to provide a "rally mechanism" for the general election campaign; and (6) to serve as the "supreme governing-body of the national party" (Davis 1983, 5–8). In addition to these more concrete functions, national conventions also serve the latent functions of (1) legitimating nonconsensus nominees; (2) building consensus within the party more generally; (3) providing "party ritual that reinforces the democratic nature" of the proceedings; (4) providing a forum for intraparty debate; and (5) democratizing the choice of the president by essentially nullifying the electoral college (Davis 1983, 8–10).

The themes that run through these functions are consensus and democracy. Consensus is sought and cultivated around the party's nominees and its programmatic platform. The democratic nature of conventions lies in the participatory nature of the nomination, the ratification of the platform, and the increasing public control over delegate selection. The functions of conventions have been remarkably stable throughout convention history, although their relative importance has varied over time. One cause of the change in importance of convention functions is the changes in convention rules and processes. There have been important changes in the rules governing the institution in the Republican Party, including the use of the unit rule and the formula for delegate apportionment.

The "unit rule," which was employed in Democratic conventions consistently from 1831 to 1968, allows a state delegation to cast all its votes for the candidate supported by the majority of the delegation. The unit rule was one of the procedures used by the first Whig convention that helped destroy Henry Clay's chances at the presidential nomination, because Clay had substantial strength in many state delegations in which he did not have a majority (Congressional Quarterly 1983, 23). But in ensuing Whig conventions, the rules of which were used as precedent for Republican conventions, the unit rule was not employed. In

Republican conventions between 1860 and 1880, a number of states and supporters of specific presidential candidates saw a potential advantage in using the unit rule and thus attempted to institute some form of unit voting. After one such attempt in 1880, the Republican Party redrafted convention rules "again rejecting the unit rule and in addition clarifying the right of any delegate to have his delegation polled" (David, Goldman, and Bain 1960, 203).

The fight over the unit rule has been described as a fight between forces that value minority voice and more localized control of delegates and those who value states' rights and the strength of state parties in nominating politics. The power of individual states in the nominating process has also been the subject of the battle over apportionment: how many convention delegates each state would be apportioned. James W. Davis claims that "almost from its birth, the Republican party has been plagued with controversy over delegate apportionment rules" (Davis 1983, 56). Traditionally, both Republicans and Democrats had apportioned delegates to states "in accordance with their strength in the electoral college." But because this rule of apportionment "presupposed a more or less even spread of party strength over the entire country," and because Republican strength was not evenly distributed, this traditional apportionment rule "led to party disaster for the Republicans and eventually to its modification by them" (Key 1964, 405).

In the post-Reconstruction South, the Republican Party was so weak that the apportionment rule gave Republicans in southern states far more delegates than their numbers warranted. In 1908, some Republicans proposed a new system of apportionment that would have redressed the imbalance of southern strength at Republican conventions. Had this new system been adopted, the 1912 convention probably would have nominated Theodore Roosevelt rather than President William Howard Taft (Davis 1983, 57). At the 1912 Republican convention, Taft's support among the "rotten borough" delegates from southern states allowed him a great deal of control over the convention. Taft secured the nomination, but significant numbers of Republicans preferred Roosevelt. Roosevelt's third-party candidacy and the resulting split among Republicans helped Democrat Woodrow Wilson win the general election.

In 1913, Republicans approved a rule for the 1916 convention that decreased the representation of Republicans in the South by 76 votes. According to Key, this "new rule left the weak [southern] Republican areas still overrepresented in relation to their Republican voting strength," and a "series of subsequent modifications, either by or under the authority of the national conventions of 1920, 1940, and 1952, made further adjustments designed to penalize those areas with relatively few Republican votes and to increase the relative strength of those states with heavier Republican popular strength" (Key 1964, 406).

Republicans also have addressed the apportionment problem by awarding bonus votes to states that the Republican candidate for president had carried in the previous election. Since the reapportionment for the 1916 convention, the Republican Party has had some type of victory bonus, but again apportionment questions have proven problematic for Republicans. In 1971 the Ripon Society, a group of moderate Republicans, sued the Republican Party over the convention bonus system, maintaining that "a uniform bonus rule ran afoul of the Fourteenth Amendment, violative of the one-person, one-vote standard." But in the end, a federal appeals court "upheld the paramount authority of the Republican National Convention to determine delegate apportionment" (Davis 1983, 55).

NOMINATION BATTLES

Despite the fact that the Republican Party has not used the two-thirds rule, which has forced Democrats into so many tumultuous nomination battles, Republicans have nonetheless had significant contests for their presidential nomination. In 1880, only four years after the Republicans selected Rutherford B. Hayes as a favorite son, "dark-horse" candidate, James A. Garfield became the Republican's second "dark-horse" candidate. At the beginning, the 1880 convention was divided into two factions: one supporting the nomination of Ulysses Grant for a third term and the other a coalition of groups opposed to Grant. On the 34th ballot of the stalemated convention, Garfield received 16 votes. Above his protestations that he was not a candidate for president, Garfield received a majority of the convention's votes and the Republican nomination on the 36th ballot.

Another significant battle for the Republican nomination occurred in 1912 when former President Theodore Roosevelt challenged President William Howard Taft. This was very much a battle between popularity and party control. Although Roosevelt had defeated Taft in most of the presidential primaries, Taft's organizational strength, particularly among southern delegations, ensured that Taft, rather than Roosevelt, would receive the party's presidential nomination. Although Roosevelt's name would not be placed in nomination at the 1912 Republican conven-

tion, his supporters met the following day to plan their own national convention later that summer.

THE REFORM ERA

Since 1968, the Democratic Party has regularly established commissions to evaluate and alter the rules governing its nominating conventions. The Republican Party, however,

> remains unreformed: its apportionment formula for delegates to national conventions is still weighted toward the electoral college; the 1976 recommendations of its Rule 29 Committee to provide for monitoring of state delegation selection processes were rejected by the Republican National Committee and the 1976 Convention; the Republicans have no enforceable demographic quotas or affirmative action standards; convention committees reflect state equality in apportionment of members; and the confederate legal structure of the party has been retained. (Polsby 1983, 53–54)

Although the Republican Party has not engaged in a series of its own reforms, it has not escaped the impact of Democratic reforms. Byron Shafer claims that "reform begat reform—and primaries begat primaries—until the Republican party had actually outpaced the Democrats in some institutional regards" (Shafer 1988, 48). Where state legislatures codified Democratic convention reform, some laws were written to extend to Republicans as well. In addition, reform had an impact on the Republican Party in part because "many of the forces which were pushing Democratic leaders" toward reform were influencing Republicans as well: "They too were sensitive to demands and arguments for 'democratization' of the process; they too possessed a large—probably larger—segment of white-collar independents, for whom such reforms were especially attractive" (Shafer 1988, 47).

CONTEMPORARY CONVENTIONS

For most of American history, party conventions were deliberative and authoritative institutions in presidential nominating politics. It was the Republican Convention of 1860 that gave the United States its President Lincoln. In fact, prior to the convention, Senator William H. Seward of New York was the Republican front-runner in 1860. Lincoln did not secure his party's nomination until the third ballot. Modern conventions no longer have this power over the nomination. With the expansion of presidential primaries, the presidential nominating system has been democratized. By the time of the convention, the party's nominee is already known. Nelson Polsby writes that conventions have "been transformed. Instead of a body of delegates from the state parties meeting to ratify the results of a complex series of negotiations conducted by party leaders at the convention, the convention is now a body dominated by candidate enthusiasts and interest group delegates who meet to ratify a choice made prior to the convention" (Polsby 1983, 75–76).

Nominating conventions may no longer have the power to nominate candidates. This does not mean that conventions are unimportant. They still represent a forum in which party disputes can be resolved, and perhaps more important, they represent a highly publicized campaign commercial for the party's nominee. Norman Ornstein claims that "in the television age, the convention has also become an easy way for voters who normally tune out politics to judge the nominees and assess their mettle and the state of their organization." Ornstein argues that one can predict general election outcomes by monitoring conventions: "since 1964, the party with the smoothest-running convention has prevailed" in the general election (Ornstein 1995).

As the real organizational strength of parties in the United States rests in state parties, it is often difficult to assess the state of the national party. Conventions represent the essence of the national party. And decisions made at conventions regarding the party platform represent the issue orientation of the party. This is not to say that party platforms in the United States are binding, as they are in many European parties, but they do represent the collective, negotiated positions of the collected partisans, officials, and state party organizations. Thus, conventions and platforms are indicators of the positions and power of American political parties.

Douglas Harris

SEE ALSO The Presidential Nomination Process, Primary Elections

BIBLIOGRAPHY

Congressional Quarterly. *National Party Conventions, 1831–1980*. Washington, DC: CQ Press, 1983.

David, Paul T., Ralph M. Goldman, and Richard C. Bain. *The Politics of National Party Conventions*. Washington, DC: Brookings Institution, 1960.

Davis, James W. *National Conventions in an Age of Party Reform*. Westport, CT: Greenwood Press, 1983.

Key, V.O., Jr. *Politics, Parties and Pressure Groups*. 5th ed. New York: Crowell, 1964.

Ornstein, Norman. "Who Will Win the White House?" *Fortune*, October 30, 1995.

Polsby, Nelson W. *Consequences of Party Reform*. Oxford: Oxford University Press, 1983.

Shafer, Byron E. *Bifurcated Politics: Evolution and Reform in the National Party Convention*. Cambridge: Harvard University Press, 1988.

Other Minorities

While the Republican Party actively recruits "ethnic" minorities such as Hispanics, Asian Americans, and immigrants, it simultaneously stresses traditional values such as strong family bonds, patriotism, respect for law and order, and the work ethic. Consequently, Republicans attract upper- and middle-class members of minority groups who share their ideology. The party also has been restricted in its ability to attract members of minority groups because of its conservatism and nativistic history.

Throughout the nineteenth and most of the twentieth centuries, Republican values and conservatism served the party well as one of the more salient features of U.S. politics. While Democrats were more likely to attract ethnic-religious minority groups and immigrants, their support was transitory. As religious or ethnic minority groups acculturated and gained acceptance, they joined the core American culture advocated by the Republican Party (or the Whig Party) and switched party affiliations. Often minority group defections to the Republican or Whig parties were accelerated when the Democratic Party welcomed new ethnic groups. (Only African Americans have been the exception, moving from the Republican to the Democratic Party.)

Based on its historical success, the Republican Party continues to recruit minority voters by stressing core U.S. values. While this strategy has been effective with certain elements of contemporary ethnic minority groups such as Cuban Americans, recent Southeast Asian immigrants, and neoconservative Asian Americans, most members of ethnic minority groups view Republican efforts with suspicion. Nevertheless, many analysts believe that Hispanics, Asian Americans, and other ethnic-religious minority groups are relatively conservative and not strongly committed to the Democratic Party. Therefore, if racial barriers are dismantled, Hispanic and Asian Americans could follow the historical pattern and defect to the Republican Party. Given the rapid growth of the Hispanic and Asian American populations, several key Republican leaders, such as Jack Kemp, are convinced that the party must develop new strategies to recruit actively these potentially powerful minorities.

HISTORICAL OVERVIEW

The first precursor to the Republican Party, the Federalists, represented the conservative elements and dominant religious groups of U.S. society. For example, the state-sponsored Congregationalist churches in New England supported the party, as well as Old Line Presbyterians, Episcopalians, and Quakers in the election of 1800.

The Federalist Party's successor, the Whig Party, was the first truly national conservative party, since it added cultural and moral appeals to its economic policy. Whigs believed they represented social virtue, while their opponents represented the dregs of society. Unlike Democrats, who argued that all white men were equal by virtue of their birth, Whigs generally maintained that there were graded hierarchies of citizenship and humanity. They asserted that the poor, immigrant, and minority groups of society should become full citizens only after they improved themselves and moved up the hierarchy.

In the mid-1800s, a surge of immigrants came to the United States from predominately Catholic regions in Ireland and Germany. Concurrently, the Second Great Awakening revitalized U.S. Protestantism, which resulted in a wave of nativism (opposition to immigration, the foreign born, and their respective cultures) and anti-Catholicism in the northern states. Third parties such as the Know-Nothings, the American Republican Party, and the Anti-Masons attained regional power by maligning Catholics and immigrants. Whig labor groups also resented economic competition from immigrants and pushed party leaders toward nativism. During the 1840s and 1850s, while the Whig Party did not officially advocate nativism, leaders avoided any unnecessary attacks on nativist emotions. Whigs also tried to benefit from nativistic fears by supporting anti-immigrant and anti-Catholic reforms such as the prohibition of liquor and "blue laws" governing recreation, dress, and sexual relations. Whigs joined Protestant reformers' proposals for free public schools so that immigrant children would be forced to learn English. The Whigs' strategy was effective as many evangelical Protestants left the Democratic Party in the mid-1800s. This realignment inaugurated the long-term trend in U.S. politics of minority groups leaving the Democratic Party when they became part of mainstream America. The Protestant migration to the Republican Party also initiated an ethnoreligious split between the U.S. political parties lasting for approximately 100 years.

Most northern Whigs joined the Republican Party after their party collapsed. Abraham Lincoln and other Republican leaders actively recruited German Americans by opposing legislation restricting political rights for immigrants and naturalized citizens. Consequently, many Protestant German Americans joined the Republican Party in 1860. But most northeastern Republican candidates adopted the Whig strategy and supported Protestant reform proposals and state immigration restriction efforts along with the abolition of slavery.

During the Gilded Age, another wave of immigrants came to the United States, primarily from southern and eastern Europe. In some cities, such as Philadelphia, Pittsburgh, Cincinnati, and San Francisco, local Republican Party organizers recruited immigrants. Nonetheless, most immigrants joined the Democratic Party.

In the late 1800s many descendants of earlier settlers regarded the new immigrants as racially inferior and un-American. Republicans also believed that government at all levels should carry out moral reforms. Consequently, a powerful Republican-inspired crusade to purify U.S. society of its sins and foreign contagions was begun in the 1870s. Progressive Republicans instituted a series of electoral reforms, such as the Australian ballot, registration laws, and naturalization requirements, designed to restrict the suffrage of immigrants and reduce vote fraud. Republicans supported the prohibition of the use of any language except English in public schools and immigration restrictions, though always exempting English immigrants. In the 1890s, the second great crossing over of white ethnic minority groups occurred as large numbers of traditionally Democratic urban voters switched to the Republican Party.

During the late 1960s and throughout the 1970s and 1980s, more ethnoreligious white minority groups moved to the Republican Party as a result of their economic success and the inclusion of "new" nonwhite minority groups in the Democratic Party. As an illustration, in the 1950s many Catholics grew dissatisfied with containment and the Democrats' relatively moderate views on communism and joined the Republican Party. Whereas only 36% of Catholic voters supported the Republican presidential candidate in 1948, by 1956, 47% of Catholics voted for Dwight Eisenhower. Catholics voted as a religious bloc in 1960 and 1964 in favor of John F. Kennedy and his successor. In 1968, 39% of the Catholic voters supported Richard Nixon, who became the first Republican presidential candidate to receive a majority of the Catholic votes four years later, 52%. Throughout the 1970s and into the 1980s, as Republican candidates supported religious issues such as school prayer and antiabortion positions, more Catholic voters left the Democratic Party. In 1984, Ronald Reagan received 59% of Catholic votes, and 53% and 56% of Catholic voters supported George Bush in 1988 and 1992.

HISPANICS AND
THE REPUBLICAN PARTY

Hispanics are the second-largest, youngest, and one of the fastest-growing ethnic minority groups in the United States, consisting of approximately 24 million people and representing 9.5% of the U.S. population. Hispanic Americans are a very diverse minority, including three main subgroups, Mexican Americans (approximately 64% of the total Hispanic population), Puerto Ricans (approximately 11%) and Cuban Americans (approximately 5%), as well as clusters of groups from the Caribbean and Central and Latin America. Today, 75% of Hispanic Americans are concentrated in the metropolitan areas of California, Texas, New York, and Florida, with the remaining 25% residing primarily in Illinois, New Mexico, New Jersey, Arizona, Colorado, and Michigan. Hispanics constitute more than 25% of the population of California, New Mexico, and Texas, and from 1980 to 1992 the number of Hispanics in ten midwestern states increased from 1.2 million to 1.8 million. The socioeconomic status of Hispanics, except for Cuban Americans, is considerably below that of Anglo Americans. In 1993, 30% of Mexican Americans and 36% of Puerto Ricans were living below the poverty level, compared with 18% of Cuban Americans and 11.6% of Anglo Americans.

Despite the rapid increase in the Hispanic population, many observers have called the Hispanic vote the "sleeping giant," since this ethnic group has lower registration and voting rates than other minorities. The main reason for reduced electoral participation is that about one-third of all Hispanics are resident aliens. Hispanic citizens also have been reluctant to register and vote. For example, from 1980 to 1992, Hispanic registration figures were relatively low, averaging 36.7% for presidential election years and 31.5% for congressional election years, while Hispanic voter turnout averaged 30% and 23%, respectively. Nevertheless, generalizations about Hispanic voting behavior must be tempered, since Mexican Americans and Puerto Ricans have much lower registration and voting rates than do Cuban Americans.

The partisan loyalty of Hispanic voter patterns is difficult to ascertain because Cuban American vote totals are usually combined with those of Mexican Americans and Puerto Ricans. But Hispanics are not a cohesive political bloc; Cuban Americans are predominately Republicans for foreign policy and socioeconomic reasons, while most Mexican Americans and Puerto Ricans are Democrats. Moreover, many analysts believe that Mexican Americans and Puerto Ricans are more conservative and only moderately attached to the Democratic Party. Affluent and highly educated Hispanics also are leaning toward the Republican Party. Conversely, younger Cuban Americans may be leaning toward the Democratic Party.

Before the 1960s, voting and racial barriers instituted by both political parties were able to limit severely the electoral power of Hispanic Americans to New Mexico. In the 1960s the Chicano movement also increased the politicalization of Hispanics because leaders applied their organizational skills, developed during a series of grape and lettuce boycotts, to voter registration drives and political campaigns. Hispanics were predominately Democrats with only 10% to 15% voting for Republican presidential candidates in the 1960s.

The Voting Rights Acts increased the potential political power of Hispanics in the 1970s. Between 1970 and 1980, the Hispanic population increased from 9 million to 14.6 million people, and population projections predicted that Hispanic Americans would outnumber African Americans in the early 2000s. Consequently, the Republican Party became increasingly aware of the potential impact of Hispanic voters. Republican leaders developed the "southwest strategy" for the 1972 election, believing that Hispanics were dissatisfied with the paternalistic behavior of the Democratic Party. They created the Republican National Hispanics Assembly and state organizations such as the Mexican American Republicans of Texas, whose aims were to recruit Hispanic voters and candidates for the Republican Party. Republicans targeted the small but prospering Hispanic middle class and stressed traditional Republican values. Richard Nixon received approximately 30% of the Hispanic vote and did well in middle-class Hispanic communities. Cuban Americans also began to exert their political power in Florida.

President Nixon was the first U.S. president to recognize the importance of appointing Hispanics to positions in his administration for symbolic reasons. He appointed Ramona Banuelos to serve as U.S. treasurer and Hillary Sanchez as director of the Small Business Administration. Republicans continued to receive almost one-third of Hispanic votes in presidential elections throughout the 1970s.

During the 1980s, the Hispanic population increased

by another 47%, to 21.4 million. The number of Hispanic elected officials increased dramatically during the 1980s with the most notable gains occurring in Arizona, California, Florida, New Mexico, New York, and Texas. The Republican Party began actively to promote Cuban Americans to key positions in the party and the government. The Cuban American National Foundation, a strong conservative lobby group, was formed in 1980 with strong ties to the Republican Party. Critics charged that the Republicans used Cuban Americans to build the image that they had general Hispanic support. Nevertheless, more Hispanics voted for Republican presidential candidates; 45% percent of Hispanics voted for Ronald Reagan in 1980 and 1984. Ironically, the visibility of Hispanics declined markedly in the Reagan administration as there were very few Hispanic appointees and no Hispanic cabinet officials, though President Reagan appointed a Hispanic U.S. treasurer and selected Katherine Ortega to be a keynote speaker at the Republican National Convention in 1984. Interestingly, despite the visibility of his Hispanic daughter-in-law and grandchildren, Hispanic support for George Bush dropped slightly to 38% in 1988 and 31% in 1992.

In the past 30 years, Republican Party leaders formed unique alliances with Hispanic political leaders in many states as legislatures developed new district apportionment plans in compliance with the Voting Rights Acts. Hispanics actively participated in the 1971, 1981, and 1991 redistricting process and often had to seek relief in the courts against Democratic-controlled state legislatures. They charged that Democratic leaders split Hispanic communities into several districts to ensure the election of more Democratic representatives. Republican leaders, on the other hand, supported the establishment of Hispanic and African American districts. In fact, Democrats accused Republicans of attempting to "pack" Hispanics into one or two districts to increase partisan competition in the remaining predominately Anglo districts. Hispanic and Republican reapportionment efforts were relatively successful. After the 1990 census, six new congressional districts were created for Hispanics. In 1992, 19 Hispanics were elected to Congress, compared to 10 before the 1992 election.

In conclusion, the Republican Party has actively recruited Hispanic members with limited success. Upper- and middle-class Hispanics, most notably in the Cuban American community, have responded to traditional Republican values. It will be interesting to see if the Republican Party develops new strategies to broaden its appeal to include working-class Hispanics.

ASIAN AMERICANS AND THE REPUBLICAN PARTY

Asian Americans are the third-largest minority group in the United States with a population of 8.4 million people representing 3.3% of the total population. Despite low fertility rates, Asian Americans are the fastest-growing minority group in the United States due to immigration. The Asian American population is projected to increase to 7% of the total population by 2020. Like Hispanics, Asian Americans are a diverse minority group with different ethnic subdivisions. Currently, there are 1.6 million Chinese Americans, 1.4 million Filipinos, and 847,000 Japanese Americans living in the United States. Other significant Asian/Pacific Islander minority groups include Indian Asians, Korean Americans, and Vietnamese citizens.

Asian Americans also tend to reside in concentrated areas. California has the most Asians and Pacific Islanders with 2.84 million, followed by New York and Hawaii with approximately 694,000 and 685,000 Asian/Pacific Islanders, respectively. Texas, Illinois, New Jersey, and Washington also have relatively large Asian/Pacific American populations. The Asian American vote could have a have a significant impact in these states, particularly in California, where Asian Americans constitute almost 10% of the population. Ironically, though Asian Americans disproportionately contribute to political campaigns, particularly for Asian American candidates, they have a low registration and voter turnout rate. For example, only about 30% to 35% of eligible Japanese, Chinese, and Filipino Americans registered to vote in 1980. The registration rates for other groups of Asian/Pacific Islander Americans were lower, ranging from 4% for Vietnamese Americans to 28% for Samoan Americans. Consequently, while Asian Americans are a major source of money, they are a minor source of votes, which limits their political power.

Most Asian Americans support the Democratic Party, which worked harder than the Republican Party to win their votes. Nevertheless, Asian Americans are not a solid bloc of Democratic voters because they have weak party loyalties and engage in crossover voting. Many Asian Americans also are more conservative than other minorities. Newer immigrants and Southeast Asian refugees are considered the "Cubans" of the Asian community. These Asian Americans have gravitated toward the Republican Party due their strident anticommunist and conservative political beliefs. A small number of Asian American neo-conservatives also are joining the Republican Party.

Most Asian Americans were politically apathetic

during the post–World War II era, except for a Hawaii majority, part of the Democratic political party. During the 1960s, some politicalization occurred in the Asian American community. In 1968 the Republican Party organized the Heritage Group to recognize small minority groups, including the Chinese American National Federation. But it was the Democratic Party that reached out to Asian Americans in the 1970s, particularly in 1976 when the Asian/Pacific American unit was established to help Jimmy Carter's candidacy. The role of Democratic Asian Americans became more visible in 1983 when the Asian Pacific Caucus was established. Republican Asian Americans petitioned for an analogous Republican caucus at the Republican National Convention in 1984. Their petition was rejected because Republican Party leaders asserted that special caucuses were not necessary. At the time, Republicans assured Asian Americans that the African American, Hispanic, and Jewish Republican caucuses would eventually be disbanded.

In the 1980s and early 1990s more Asian Americans entered the political arena. Nonetheless, Asian Americans' political power remains limited. Less than 1% of locally elected officials (60 to 70 people) were Asian Americans in 1992. Nationally, Asian Americans have had more influence. For example, in 1986 the bipartisan Interim Coordinating Committee for Chinese Americans (ICCCA) persuaded all the presidential candidates to commit themselves to appointing at least three Chinese Americans to policymaking positions in their administrations. This strategy was effective, since President Bush appointed 30 Chinese Americans after the 1988 election.

Several Republican leaders argue that a basic affinity exists between Asian American and Republican beliefs that has yet to be exploited. For example, many Asian Americans oppose communism, have strong family values, and believe in capitalism and the work ethic. Ties between Asian Americans and the Republican Party could increase if party leaders develop new strategies to recruit Asian American candidates.

Janet B. Manspeaker

SEE ALSO African Americans, Jews

BIBILOGRAPHY

de la Garza, Rodolfo, et al. *Latino Voices: Mexican, Puerto Rican, and Cuban Perspectives on American Politics.* San Franciso: Westview Press, 1992.

Garcia, F. Chris, ed. *Latinos and the Political System.* Notre Dame: Notre Dame Press, 1988.

Kitano, Harry, and Roger Daniels. *Asian Americans: Emerging Minorities.* 2nd ed. Englewood Cliffs, NJ: Prentice Hall, 1995.

Vigil, Maurilio. *Hispanics in American Politics: The Search for Political Power.* New York: New York University Press, 1987.

Wei, William. *The Asian American Movement.* Philadelphia: Temple University Press, 1993.

Party Discipline

Party discipline, according to one student of British political behavior, "refers both to the existence of a high degree of cohesion, and to the methods of maintaining this cohesion in a political party." Thus, there are two elements to the definition. One relates to the extent of internal solidarity within the party (usually implying a coherence across a broad range of domestic and foreign policies), the other to the availability of political rewards and punishments to maintain solidarity in the face of possible dissent.

American parties in general, and the Republican Party in particular, have *not* commonly been characterized by a high level of cohesion (see the companion essay in *The Encyclopedia of the Democratic Party*). Indeed, the internal histories of both American parties are more notable for their divisions than for their discipline.

In his classic work *The Making of the President 1960*, Theodore H. White explored what he termed "that spectacular Republican schizophrenia which for a century has baffled all observers." "The Republican Party," White continued, "is twins and has been twins from the moment of its birth—but the twins who inhabit its name and shelter are Jacob and Esau: fratricidal, not fraternal, twins." The party originally emerged from an uneasy union of New England abolitionists and seasoned Whig politicians, the latter more interested in power than moral issues. In the early part of the twentieth century, a mix of cleavages within the Republican Party—some derived from issue differences, some personality politics—festered and eventually led to an open split, with progressive elements following former President Theodore Roosevelt (New York) away from "standpatter" conservative Republicans into the Bull Moose Party. Although that formal division did not last, for decades thereafter Republican Party politics was characterized by internal tension between party "regulars"—those relatively conservative Republicans such as Senator Robert Taft of Ohio—and more liberal Republicans, in the Roosevelt tradition—such as Governor Thomas E. Dewey of New York. By the 1980s one of those "twins"—the liberal Republicans (then commonly associated with New York Governor Nelson Rockefeller)—had died, based largely on the vast success of Ronald Reagan. Although a more ideologically pure conservative party did result, new cleavages arose in the party in the 1980s, with some Republicans stressing economic conservatism as the core of the party's agenda, others advancing conservatism on social issues. These long-standing divisions within the party—which have showed up in both congressional and presidential politics—severely complicate efforts to exercise discipline.

The shortage of discipline among the nation's Republicans (and Democrats) has been a persistent concern of those who study American politics because political parties are almost alone in their potential for giving unity of purpose to a government designed by the framers to be divided against itself. Parties thus hold promise of binding together in common purpose that which the Constitution separates—if the parties themselves are cohesive.

Indeed, many American observers see in the rigorously disciplined behavior of some parties—especially those of the English Parliament—a model for behavior in the United States. Prominent political scientists have long argued that the inherent inefficiencies of government in the United States can be remedied only through the emergence of strong, disciplined governing parties—in the British mold—which experts call "party government."

A comparison of the dynamics of Britain's parties with their American counterparts will illuminate why the discipline of the former has not been a customary feature of the latter. Such a comparison gives context for understanding how the notion of party discipline relates to Republican Party behavior in the United States.

British political parties are highly centralized, highly organized, highly routinized entities that spring from a political culture that places great value on adherence to party standards. They are hierarchically oriented, with relatively stable channels for member advancement through the party ranks into leadership positions. Both the internal politics of British parties and the broader political environment that shapes them tend to reward conformist behavior. "I would remind you," a British party leader once wrote a wavering member, that "you were elected not because you were [an individual with a very good record] but simply because you were a Labour candidate. I cannot speak for your constituents but I am certain that they expect you, as mine expect me, to vote for the Labour government and to ensure its continuance in office."

Voters for members of the British Parliament have commonly been more party centered than candidate centered in their voting decisions. Thus, those who go to the House of Commons usually do so with the understanding that they are there to advance the broad program of the party.

The contrasts with the American political system are striking, with almost every difference magnifying the problems American parties confront in approaching the disciplined behavior of their British equals.

The most fundamental difference is the decentralized character of American politics. As a matter of history, American parties at the national level have been essentially federalist in nature, an aggregation of state and local parties that, whatever they might have shared in the way of commitments to broad governing principles or allegiance to an agreed-on presidential candidate, had to respect the diversity of their membership. Accordingly, American parties have usually left a wide range of discretion to their members in staking out positions on even the most consequential of public issues.

Underlying this enormous freedom of choice within American parties is a political culture that places a very high value on localism and independence, rather than centralization and conformity. "A local spirit will infallibly prevail" among those selected to serve in Congress, wrote James Madison in *The Federalist Papers*, No. 46. In other words, American lawmakers are expected by their constituents not to pledge primary allegiance to a party program (as do their British counterparts), but to look after the needs and concerns of their districts first and foremost. That is the most powerful source of influence operating on most members of Congress most of the time. Those partisan demands that are so influential as a centripetal force on members of Parliament, then, confront an almost irresistible counterforce on American soil. The American political culture rewards a kind of political behavior that is not conducive to the spirit of party discipline prevalent in Britain.

A second major obstacle to party discipline in the United States—added to the decentralized nature of American politics—appears precisely in that area where disciplined parties are expected to serve their most useful function: the environment of separated institutions sharing powers. The prospects for, and influence of, disciplined parties in Britain is vastly magnified by the nature of their governing arrangements. For all practical purposes, governance there is a function of the prerogatives of the Lower House. The majority party of the Commons establishes the executive branch of the government, while the House of Lords brings relatively minimal powers to the lawmaking process. Thus, there is a fairly simple calculus of governance there: a parliamentary party campaigns on a well-defined program, effectively is issued a mandate by the voters on Election Day to bring that program into being, and then organizes the government to enact the program, with little in the way of internal obstacles to frustrate their designs.

Those simplicities do not exist in the United States. The American framers constitutionalized a system such that even if a single party nominally commands the elected government—that is, if the Republicans control both houses of Congress and the White House—there are obstacles to unified, disciplined action on policy. For example, each institution represents a different constituency in time and space. Those partisans who staff the Senate, the House, and the presidency are the products of staggered elections, different popular impulses registered at different times in the life of the nation, when the mix of relevant issues and concerns may not be the same. Accordingly, the partisan product of one election may be vastly different from the partisan product of another. For example, the House Republican class elected in 1994, in the Republican "revolution" that resulted in their reclaiming control of the lower chamber for the first time in four decades, was far more aggressive in its antigovernment activism than Republicans elected even two or four years before.

The effect of these differing impulses is amplified by the presence of competing claims by each institution for a key role in the nation's lawmaking processes. In *The Federalist* No. 51 Madison claimed that the founders had successfully given "to those who administer each department [of the government] the necessary constitutional means and personal motives to resist encroachments of the others." In practice, this has meant that partisans in each branch of the government have jealously guarded their institutional prerogatives, to the point of being wary of giving up authority even to those with whom they share a common party allegiance. Richard Nixon, for example, could not automatically count on Republican members of Congress to support his claims of executive privilege in the Watergate affair. The enduring nature of these institutional rivalries, sustained by those who believe that a part of their constitutional obligation is to maintain the equally independent political institutions they inherited, serves to complicate the work of partisans who seek to make the entire government an agency of a disciplined governing party.

Despite the fact that the Republican Party does not routinely act in the disciplined fashion of its British counterparts, some elements of party discipline can be recognized here. Within the confines of American practice, the Republicans are commonly thought to be a more disciplined lot than the Democratic Party, at least in modern times. There are two reasons for this greater cohesiveness. First, the Republicans have been, since perhaps the 1930s, a more sociologically homogeneous party than the Democrats. African Americans have overwhelmingly moved into the Democratic Party, as have activists promoting greater sexual equality, creating internal party tensions along racial and gender lines to a degree largely absent among the Republicans. Second, because the Republicans have long been considered the "probusiness" party—President Calvin Coolidge famously declared in 1925 that "the chief business of America is business"—Republicans have been disposed to treat politics in a businesslike fashion. The recruitment of candidates and financial support from business communities has thus disposed the Republicans to mimic private-sector organizational arrangements in the public sector, bringing "sound business principles" such as hierarchical organizational structures to the government.

The best place to look for the exercise of party discipline among the Republicans is within the legislative party. Extensive studies of Congress demonstrate that the party label is the single most important factor for explaining roll-call voting in both the House and the Senate. For example, one index—called a "party unity score," which measures the percentage of members who vote with the majority of their party on those roll-call votes on which a majority of the two parties divide—shows that congressional Republicans voted together nearly 80% of the time from 1954 to 1986. Such statistics, however, developed from roll-call voting patterns, tend to overstate the extent to which congressional policymaking is subjected to the influence of disciplined party decisions. Party unity at the final stage of the legislative process (i.e., on floor votes) in the American Congress is commonly the product of well-balanced compromises, representing what members of Congress can agree on, not what any one partisan prefers. Such unity is of a different character than that produced by a disciplined party system, in which unity proceeds from partisan attachments alone, allowing party leaders to pass legislation without compromising on their conceptions of what the most coherent policy should be. The "best" policy attainable under a system of divided powers—and thus the one most likely to gain the broadest support—is likely to be a mix of policy compromises that departs substantially from what a single rational agent (such as a disciplined political party) would prescribe for dealing with a particular public problem. Thus, while a high level of cohesion in Congress may signify some measure of discipline by party members, it may not be a signal of the kind of *coherent* policymaking usually associated with parliamentary parties.

Congressional parties also are the best place to see the tools of party discipline in practice in the United States, to the extent that they exist. The most prominent party power for congressional parties is the power to organize. Those leading the congressional party have access to the appointment power for keeping their partisans in line, either by granting or denying committee or subcommittee appointments based on performance in relation to the party's standards. In recent history, however, the use of the appointment power by congressional party leadership for specific disciplinary purposes has been rare. For example, at least in the awarding of chairs, the seniority rule has predominated, whereby those majority party members with the longest service on the committee assume its headship position, irrespective of their individual agendas. Nonetheless, a reserve power does exist for use in unseating those who clearly cannot serve the majority's interest. This power was exercised in 1995 when reform-oriented Republicans in the House generally rewarded with party chairs only those members they felt were committed to enacting their governing program, the Contract with America.

Congressional party leaders may use other tools to keep their forces unified on policy, including control of rules and floor action; support for a cooperative member's pet projects; and selective channeling of information to the party membership, keeping favored partisans up-to-date on the status of private negotiations and the likely scheduling of important votes. Party leaders can also be useful sources of campaign money. In recent times this support has commonly been channeled through official instruments—the Republican Senatorial and the Republican Congressional Campaign Committees—although the long-time practice of helping cooperative junior members make connections with sympathetic private funding sources remains an important mechanism for channeling party favors. Moreover, the support of high-profile party leadership may be denied those who do not adhere to the leadership's standards of behavior. During the 104th Congress, Speaker of the House Newt Gingrich of Georgia selectively canceled personal appearances at a series of fund-raising rallies for Republicans who refused to vote for a budget compromise endorsed by the leadership.

Yet missing from the arsenal of weapons available to party leaders in Washington is a power crucial to the maintenance of party discipline in London: an effective power of expulsion. Denial of the party name usually wrecks a dissenter's political career in Britain be-

cause local party organizations there are adjuncts of the national party structure. The local electorate's commitment to the national party is commonly so strong that expulsion is taken as a confirmed sign of bad faith.

The national party's inability to influence directly local nominations and elections in the United States renders expulsion a useless weapon for party leaders here. Again, in the United States, a legislator's primary commitment is commonly to his or her constituency, which may or may not be well served, in specific instances, by the party's position on a host of complicated issues. Under this construction, a legislator's rejection of the party's position on specific issues may be easily defended to his or her constituency as a necessary service to them. In this environment, the ability of a party to discipline its members effectively is severely circumscribed.

A useful example of the limited extent to which the Republican Party leadership may use the tools of party discipline arose, ironically, in the House of Representatives in 1995, during a period when the House Republicans were usually working as a model governing party. In October, the Republican chairman of the House Appropriations Committee removed from service on a military appropriations subcommittee a freshman member who had voted against final floor passage of a defense money bill that had gained committee support. The leadership intended to maintain party discipline by punishing a junior member disloyal to the party's position on that measure.

But that effort to discipline a rebellious member encountered immediate, significant resistance. Other conservative members of the Republican class elected in the 1994 Republican "revolution" rallied to support their colleague. When they threatened to withold their unified support for other elements of the leadership agenda unless the Neumann incident was rectified, Speaker Gingrich acquiesced, rewarding the maverick member with a coveted slot on the House Budget Committee.

Both the organizational culture of the House of Representatives and the nation's political culture reinforced that member's claim to act as he did, and consequently undermined the Republican leadership's ability to punish him for it. He was supported by a significant faction of the party that was willing to defy the party's formal leadership. More fundamentally, however, the recalcitrant member won that confrontation because he could make a powerful case that the two most important claims on his vote as a legislator were the interests of his constituency—as he, not the Republican leadership, understood them—and the dictates of his own conscience. Against those demands, the call of party discipline in the United States does not fare well.

Russell L. Riley

BIBLIOGRAPHY

Bradshaw, Kenneth, and David Pring. *Parliament and Congress*. Austin: University of Texas Press, 1972.

Epstein, Leon. *Political Parties in the American Mold*. Madison: University of Wisconsin Press, 1986.

Jackson, Robert J. *Rebels and Whips: An Analysis of Dissension, Discipline and Cohesion in British Political Parties*. New York: Macmillan, 1968.

Ripley, Randall. *Congress: Process and Policy*. 4th ed. New York: Norton, 1988.

Stokes, Michael. "When Freedoms Conflict: Party Discipline and the First Amendment." *Journal of Law and Politics* 11 (1995).

Party Organization in Congress

Over the past 60 years, the Republicans have been the minority party in Congress for all but a few years. So the Republicans were organized as the minority party for most of this period. The Republicans have similar, but not identical, organizational structures in the House and Senate. These organizations include four main parts: the leadership, caucus, whip system, and party committees.

In the House, most Speakers in the early 1900s were Republicans because of the numerous Republican victories in House elections during this period. Since 1933, however, most Speakers have been Democrats. Thus, during this Democratic era in Congress, the Republican House leader has usually been the minority leader.

In the 40 consecutive years of Democratic control of the House (1955–1994), the minority leaders were Joseph Martin, Charles Halleck, Gerald Ford, John Rhodes, and Robert Michel. They attempted to develop alternative policies to the Democrats' programs and publicize these policies. They also tried to defeat the legislation of the Democratic leadership by promoting unity within their party and seeking votes from Democrats. Their favorite target for Democratic votes was conservative southerners. By forming a conservative coalition with several southern Democrats, the Republicans were able to defeat some of the legislation sponsored by moderate and liberal Democrats. Social issues such as civil rights were one of the main policy areas in which the coalition developed.

In addition, when there were Republican presidents, the minority leaders promoted the administration's programs in Congress. The success of Republican minority leaders in these situations varied widely. Robert Michel, for instance, successfully worked with the Reagan administration in 1981 and 1982 to pass several important parts of the Republican program. But during the remainder of the Reagan administration and all of the Bush administration, Michel and the House Republicans had much less success in the battle against the House Democratic majority.

The House Republican leaders faced many problems during the 40 straight years of being in the minority. The biggest problems were the shortage of votes and the Democrats' control of the top leadership positions (i.e., Speaker, majority leader, committee chairs, and subcommittee chairs). Another difficulty was the diversity and independence of the House Republicans. The House Republican leaders, just as their Democratic counterparts, had few effective rewards and sanctions to deal adequately with the ideological and constituency differences and force their party colleagues to follow the party line.

Moreover, as the minority status continued, Republican minority leaders had to contend with a growing sense of frustration. Many House Republicans became angry and frustrated from being in the minority year after year. They focused much of their anger and frustration on the House Democrats and the Democratic leaders. They claimed that the Democrats misused their power and treated the Republicans unfairly. But a number of frustrated House Republicans also became upset with the performance of their own leaders. In the 1980s, for example, Robert Michel came under attack from a group of young conservatives led by Newt Gingrich of Georgia. This group proposed that the House Republicans take a more aggressive and partisan stance against the Democrats.

Finally in 1994, after 20 consecutive losses, the Republicans won the majority of House seats. This meant, among other things, that the Republican House leader after 40 years would be the Speaker, rather than the minority leader. Unfortunately for Robert Michel, his dream of being Speaker was never realized because he retired in 1994. But, even if he had not retired, he probably would have been unable to retain his position as Republican leader. Instead of Michel, Newt Gingrich became the first Republican Speaker since 1955.

The Speaker is the leader of the House and of the majority party. Gingrich used the powers from both positions to become one of the most powerful Speakers of the century. The usual pattern since the early 1900s, when several major powers were taken from the Speaker, was for the Speaker to allow much of the legislative program of the party to develop in the standing committees and then to coordinate the efforts to pass the legislation on the floor. Also, Speakers had limited control over the standing committees and the committee chairs because the chairs were selected through the seniority system. Speaker Gingrich, on the other hand, set most of the House's policy agenda and selected the committee chairs. He told the chairmen which major bills their committees should consider. The agenda in 1995 was based on the House Republican platform (i.e., the Contract with America) for the 1994 election. The Speaker and the other House Republican leaders were able to persuade most of their Republican colleagues to rally around the leadership's agenda.

By the end of 1995, Gingrich had achieved a number of successes but had suffered several setbacks. The House had passed most of the legislation from the Republican platform and approved a budget based on the priorities of the Republican leadership. But much of this legislation and their budget had failed to make it all the way through the system. Several key bills were either defeated in the Senate or vetoed by President Clinton. Also, public opinion polls indicated that the popularity of Speaker Gingrich and the House Republicans had declined significantly. And the polls showed that more Americans blamed the congressional Republicans than President Clinton for the gridlock in Washington.

The second-highest position in the majority party of the House is the majority leader. The primary job of the majority leader is to aid the Speaker in his role as leader of the majority party. Majority leaders are usually involved in the day-to-day activities associated with leading the majority party, especially scheduling and coalition building for floor votes. In 1995 Dick Armey became the first Republican majority leader in 40 years. Armey worked closely with Speaker Gingrich in the leadership's efforts to pass their budget and the Contract with America legislation.

The House majority whip is the third-highest position in the majority party, and the minority whip is the second-highest position in the minority party. The whip coordinates a communications network between the leadership and rank-and-file members. Key aspects of this communication are attempts to persuade the party members to support the leadership's positions on floor votes. The whip position often serves as a steppingstone for higher offices in the House Republican leadership. Robert Michel, for example, was minority whip before he became minority leader,

and Newt Gingrich held the position before he became Speaker.

The next position in the House Republican hierarchy is the caucus (conference) chairman. As the head of the organization representing all House Republicans, the conference chairman usually is an important member of the leadership team. He or she is often included in leadership meetings to plan strategy on upcoming floor votes.

The conference selects the House Republican leader, who will become either the Speaker or minority leader, the majority leader (if the party is in the majority), the whip, and the conference chairman. Also, the House Republicans will at times develop policy proposals through the conference. And it often serves as a forum for the House Republicans to discuss policy issues and party matters. In 1995 and 1996 Gingrich and Armey, for instance, spoke at conference meetings several times to encourage their colleagues to support the leadership's position on key policy decisions.

The whip organization consists of the whip, the chief deputy whip, and several deputy and assistant whips. The members of the whip organization assist in the effort to communicate with all the House Republicans. They inform the rank and file about legislation and schedules and lobby them for their support of bills coming up on the floor. And they continually poll all the House Republicans to provide the leadership with estimates of the support for bills.

Finally, several important party functions are carried out by the party committees. The Steering Committee (formerly known as the Committee on Committees) makes the standing committee assignments for House Republicans. The Policy Committee considers proposals on policy issues. And the National Republican Congressional Committee provides campaign funds for House Republican candidates.

When the Republicans are in the majority in the Senate, their top leadership positions are the majority leader and majority whip (assistant majority leader). If they are in the minority, these positions are the minority leader and minority whip (assistant minority leader). The conference chairman is the third-ranking position in both situations.

By winning three elections during the 1980s, the Senate Republicans had a little more experience with majority leadership during recent decades than House Republicans. While Democratic Speakers and majority leaders led the House through the 1980s, Republicans Howard Baker (1981–1984) and Robert Dole (1985–1986) held the office of majority leader for six years. In 1995 Republican leaders took control of both chambers as Dole returned to his former position as majority leader and teamed up with Gingrich as the congressional leaders.

Like the Speaker, the majority leader is the overall leader of the chamber and the leader of the majority party. So Senator Dole, for instance, had the responsibility to schedule legislation on the floor, oversee the floor debate, maintain the Senate Republican organization, and lead his party colleagues to victory on floor votes. The majority leader uses his or her powers as Senate leader, such as the control over scheduling, to enhance the role of party leader. Dole, for instance, scheduled floor votes at times when he believed there was majority support for the Republican leadership's position and delayed votes on bills that appeared to lack support.

Besides leadership within the Senate, the majority leader must represent the Senate with the public and other key players in the national political system. Senator Dole, as majority leader, met with the media almost daily to explain what was happening in the Senate and defend his policy positions. In addition, he met with the Speakers O'Neill and Gingrich and with Presidents Reagan and Clinton. Of course, the meetings with fellow Republicans usually revolved around how best to promote the Republican agenda, while meetings with Democratic leaders generally involved attempts to resolve differences. There were, however, exceptions to these patterns. For example, several meetings with Reagan and later with Gingrich as Speaker involved negotiations to resolve significant differences on budget policies. And on a few occasions, such as in the debate over the NAFTA trade agreement, Dole and Clinton met to plan strategy on how to seek support for major legislation they both approved.

The majority leader faces many difficulties in leading the Senate. The power and independence of individual senators create a decentralized power structure in the chamber. Also, this significant influence of an individual senator, along with the filibuster, allows the minority party to have a bigger impact on legislation in the Senate than in the House. This could be seen in the mid-1990s when the Senate Democrats had much more success in their battle against the Republican program than their Democratic colleagues did in the House.

During the many years since the 1920s when the Republicans were in the minority, the Senate minority leaders had to deal with many of the same problems and frustrations as the House minority leaders. They had to struggle year after year with a shortage of votes and often with little hope of major legislative victories. But they were able at times to use the opportunities available to the minority party in the Senate.

Senate minority leaders employed similar strategies as their House counterparts. They attempted to build majorities on floor votes through the conservative coalition, negotiated with Democratic presidents and congressional leaders, and promoted the programs of Republican presidents.

The whip heads the whip organization and assists the majority/minority leader with party leadership responsibilities. Senator Trent Lott became majority whip in 1995 (and majority leader in June 1996, after Dole's resignation). He developed a good working relationship with Senator Dole. He communicated with the other Senate Republicans on party matters and promoted the policy positions of the leadership.

The Senate Republicans also call their caucus a conference. This organization elects the Senate Republican leaders and makes some policy statements. Unlike the Democrats, the Senate Republicans elect a senator other than their leader as conference chairman.

Their whip system is a small organization. It consists of just the whip, the chief deputy whip, three deputy whips, and five regional whips. Because of the smaller size of the Senate, there is much less need for party members to communicate through a whip system.

Finally, the Senate Republicans operate with three party committees. The Policy Committee makes recommendations on party activities and policy issues. The Steering Committee determines the Republican standing committee assignments. And the National Republican Senatorial Committee provides campaign support for Senate Republican candidates.

Larry M. Schwab

BIBLIOGRAPHY

Bader, John B., and Charles O. Jones. "The Republican Parties in Congress: Bicameral Differences." In *Congress Reconsidered*, ed. Lawrence C. Dodd and Bruce I. Oppenheimer, 5th ed. Washington, DC: CQ Press, 1993.

Burton, Larry. "Leadership Roles in the Senate: Functions and Change." In *Congress and Public Policy*, ed. David C. Kozak and John D. Macartney, 2nd ed. Chicago: Dorsey Press, 1987.

Congressional Quarterly. *How Congress Works*. 2nd ed. Washington, DC: CQ Press, 1991.

———. *Players, Politics and Turf of the 104th Congress*. Washington, DC: CQ Press, 1995.

Duncan, Philip D., and Christine C. Lawrence. *Politics in America 1996*. Washington, DC: CQ Press, 1995.

Jones, Charles O. *The Minority Party in Congress*. Boston: Little, Brown, 1970.

Matthews, Donald R. *U.S. Senators and Their World*. New York: Random House, 1960.

Oleszek, Walter T. *Majority and Minority Whips in the Senate: The History and Development of the Party Whip System in the U.S. Senate*. Washington, DC: Government Printing Office, 1979.

Peabody, Robert. *Leadership in Congress*. Boston: Little, Brown, 1976.

Smith, Steven S. "Forces of Change in Senate Party Leadership and Organization." In *Congress Reconsidered*, ed. Lawrence C. Dodd and Bruce I. Oppenheimer, 5th ed. Washington, DC: CQ Press, 1993.

The Presidential Nomination Process

The national nominating convention, one of the means by which a party selects a presidential candidate, was an established political norm by the time of the Republican Party's founding in the mid-1850s. Adopting this method from their Whig predecessors, the Republican Party established a process whereby the delegates to the national convention fixed the rules and procedures of the convention and selected the presidential nominee. In this system, each of the states was generally granted a specified number of delegates based on the size of the state's congressional delegation. Delegate selection at the state level was determined by the state party organization, usually through some combination of local and state conventions or caucuses. Throughout the nineteenth cenury, the party leadership, particulary at the state level, acted as political brokers. Serving state and regional interests (in addition to fulfilling individual political agendas), this leadership generally conducted the most important business of the convention behind closed doors. While this system enhanced the power of individual state party leaders, the party rank-and-file membership played a limited role in the process.

The presidential primary evolved from the public demand for wider popular partication in government, the expression of which resulted in numerous legal reforms during the 1880–1920 period. In the first decade of the new century numerous states enacted legislation providing for the direct election of party candidates for statewide office. The election of state party delegates to the national presidential nominating convention was a logical extension of the primary idea. Presidential primaries appeared shortly after the turn of the century, and by 1916 the number of states holding Republican primaries grew to 20. While a majority of the delegates to the party convention were selected through this process in 1916, many were not bound to vote for specific candidates at the convention. These uncommitted delegates were, in large part, subsequently coopted into dominant coalitions by party leadership. Thus the primary vote did not determine the outcome of the convention, and state party leaders

were able to maintain their influence in the nomination of the party's presidential candidates. Nevertheless, the primary election posed a threat to the power of the leadership. Contending that these elections were expensive and turnout was generally low, the Republican leadership was successful in reducing the impact of the primary in the selection of the party's presidential nominee. In subsequent years, the number of primaries declined as some states reverted to previous methods of selecting delegates to the national convention (i.e., caucuses or state conventions or combinations of these two formats). In many states that continued to hold primaries, these were viewed as an advisory, rather than mandatory, means for selecting delegates. Through the election of 1968, the primary was not considered the principal vehicle by which a candidate obtained the party's presidential nomination.

The divisive Democratic National Convention of 1968 marked the demise of the leadership-controlled nomination process for both parties. Beginning in 1969, the Democratic national organization adopted a series of reforms designed to make the process more representative of the party membership and the American public. While the reform movement was initiated by the Democrats, the Republican Party was compelled to make changes as well. The programs adopted by the Democratic national organization were frequently at odds with existing state statutes. Therefore, at the state level, Democratic-controlled legislatures enacted laws that were compatible with the party's new rules. These new state laws subsequently affected the procedures of the Republican Party. While the Republican national organization did not follow the Democrats' lead in establishing rules pertaining to the demographic composition of state delegations, the party supported the inclusion of women and minorities in the nomination process. By 1984, approximately half of the delegates to the national convention were women. This was accomplished largely through the appeals of the national leadership to the state party organizations. Minority representation among the delegates remains much more limited.

The current system of nominating Republican presidential candidates is characterized, most notably, by importance of the primary election. The direct primary has become the principle means by which delegates are selected for the national convention. Since 1968, an increasing number of states have established the primary election as a means of selecting delegates. In 1968, 16 states held Republican presidential primaries in which approximately 34% of the delegates were selected. In contrast, 28 states staged primaries in 1976, selecting 67% of the delegates in this fashion. This trend, in general, has continued through the most recent election, with 39 states holding Republican primaries in 1992.

The states that continue to hold conventions or caucuses or both have also been affected by the reform movement. In general, delegates are selected in the calendar year of the national convention (there are exceptions); state parties are required to publicize the time, place, and rules of meetings; and information concerning the presidential preferences of would-be delegates must be made public by the state party organization. These changes are designed to eliminate the backroom politics characteristic of earlier times and dilute the influence of state party chairmen in the selection of delegates.

A second prominent feature of the current nomination system is the multifaceted nature of the process and the division of power between the national party organization, the state parties, and the state legislatures. While primaries have become increasingly important in the selection of delegates, these elections can take a number of forms. The form that primary elections (as well as conventions and caucuses) take is largely determined by the state party organizations. While the national party organization has some influence over the procedure, the state party organizations (in concert with state legislatures) determine the process by which delegates are chosen, that is, primary, convention, caucus (or some combination of these), the allocation of delegates (by congressional district or statewide), and the dates of caucuses and conventions. The state parties, however, do not operate in a vacuum and therefore cannot directly change their method of selecting delegates to the national convention. The state legislatures enact the laws governing the selection process and determine the dates of primary elections. In recent years, state legislation has generally provided the parties with the option of selecting the process by which delegates are chosen. (This serves to explain why, in some states, one party selects delegates by a primary election while the other party employs the caucus or convention system. Given the flexibility afforded state party organizations in determining the procedure, it is conceivable that there could be 50 different variations of this process, for each party.)

Given this division of power, however, state legislatures are sometimes at odds with the national party organization. In recent elections, a front-loaded schedule, that is, an increasing number of early primaries, has become the norm. In response, the New Hampshire legislature has threatened to pass legislation mandating that its state primary (for both parties) be held one week before any other state's primary. New Hampshire has traditionally held the first primary, and the legislature does not want the state to lose the

political and economic benefits associated with this position. Unlike the Democrats, however, the Republican Party has chosen not to establish national party rules regulating the time frame for the selection of delegates. Nevertheless, the threat of legislative action has allowed New Hampshire to maintain its distinction as the first primary state.

The conflict between party organizations and the states has not always been so easily resovled. In several instances this discord has resulted in legal battles decided by the courts. In a recent ruling, *Tashjian* v. *Republication Party of Connecticut* (107 S. Ct. 544, 1986), the Supreme Court upheld the party's right of freedom of association. In this case, the Court overturned a state law that had prohibited open primaries. Unable to change the law in the Democrat-controlled state legislature, the Republican state party initiated legal action, claiming that this legislation violated the rights of freedom of association (specifically, the rights of independents to vote in the primary of their choice). Basing its decision on previous rulings, the Supreme Court sided with the party. Such decisions have bolstered the parties' authority to enforce their own rules, thus granting greater control over the method of delegate selection.

Also characteristic of the post-1968 nomination process is the trend of shifting primary dates. The early contests tend to have a greater impact on the selection process than those held in June. Candidates who do well in the early primaries establish their position as front-runners for the nomination. This status enhances their name recognition as well as the ability to raise funds for succeeding contests. In addition, the citizens of New Hampshire and the early March primary states generally have a broader slate of candidates to select from than do voters in the late primary states. For example, six Republican candidates were entered in the 1988 New Hampshire primary. By the time California, Montana, New Jersey, and New Mexico held their primaries in early June, George Bush had secured the party's nomination. This pattern was reenacted in 1996, with Bob Dole securing the party nomination (in a nine-candidate field) by the end of March.

In an effort to temper the importance of the Iowa caucus and the New Hampshire primary, the Democrats proposed an early regional primary, Super Tuesday, in which a number of southern states would hold elections on the same date. The Republican Party also embraced this regional approach. In 1988, 14 states across the southern tier of the nation held Republican primaries on the second Tuesday in March. In the next presidential election year, the Republicans held eight primaries on Super Tuesday. Reflecting their own set of regional concerns, in 1992 several western states moved their primary or caucus date to the week before Super Tuesday. The trend to a front-loaded primary schedule continued in 1996 when the California state legislature switched that state's primary from June to March. With the largest state delegation at the Republican National Convention, this move may further reduce the influence of the early, small-state contests as well as that of the southern regional primary

Just as the debate pertaining to the role of political parties and the representative nature of the system shaped the transformation of the nomination process in the 1820s and early 1900s, the current system is marked by these same concerns. The platform of the Republican Party and the degree to which the process represents the party membership and the American public is central to the changing rules and norms associated with the selection of presidential candidates.

William E. Dugan

SEE ALSO Nominating Conventions, Primary Elections

BIBLIOGRAPHY

Asher, Herbert B. *Presidential Elections and American Politics: Voters, Candidates, and Campaigns Since 1952.* 5th ed. Pacific Grove, CA: Brooks/Cole, 1992.

Chase, James S. *Emergence of the Presidential Nominating Convention, 1789–1832.* Urbana: University of Illinois Press, 1973.

Polsby, Nelson W. *Consequences of Party Reform.* New York: Oxford University Press, 1983.

Stanley, Harold W., and Richard G. Niemi. *Vital Statistics on American Politics.* 2nd ed. Washington, DC: CQ Press, 1990.

Wayne, Stephen J. *The Road to the White House: The Politics of Presidential Elections.* 5th ed. New York: St. Martin's Press, 1995.

Presidential Nominations and Elections

During the past 30 years, the Republican Party has transformed itself into a clearly conservative party. This change has been particularly notable on the presidential level. When the New Deal realignment in the 1930s changed the Democrats from the minority to the majority party, the Republicans reacted by nominating a series of moderate presidential candidates. Neither Wendell Willkie in 1940 nor Thomas Dewey in 1944 was able to defeat Franklin Roosevelt. After Roosevelt died, however, Dewey was favored to defeat incumbent Harry Truman, but the latter surprised the pundits by winning the 1948 election.

Nevertheless, the Republicans stuck with moderation in 1952, nominating war hero Dwight Eisenhower

rather than the favorite of the conservatives, Senator Robert Taft. This time, the party was rewarded as Eisenhower not only won that year but was easily reelected in 1956. Because the adoption of the 22nd Amendment to the Constitution prevented Eisenhower from running for a third term, the party turned to Vice President Richard Nixon. In an election marked by the first-ever televised debates between two candidates, Nixon lost to John Kennedy by a popular-vote margin of only 50.1% to 49.9%.

The Republican move to the right began dramatically in 1964 with the nomination of Arizona Senator Barry Goldwater. Nixon's defeat in the 1962 California gubernatorial election had left the party without a clear front-runner for the presidential nomination. At first, Nelson Rockefeller seemed a likely possibility. The New York governor had easily won reelection the same day that Nixon had been beaten. Possessed of charm, intelligence, and great wealth, Rockefeller took an early lead in trial heat polls but, having been divorced in 1961, his remarriage to a recently divorced woman coincided with the beginning of a decline in his national popularity. Furthermore, Rockefeller's liberalism made him more appealing to Democrats and Independents than to those Republicans who would select the nominee. This meant that his only hope was to put together a string of primary victories, but by the time he declared his candidacy late in 1963, his ratings in the Gallup poll trial heats against other Republican contenders had dropped to about 12%.

Almost by default, Senator Goldwater had moved near the head of the pack despite press commentary suggesting that he was too conservative to have a chance of winning the election. Furthermore, Lyndon Johnson, who had succeeded to the presidency after Kennedy's assassination, came from the Southwest, thereby negating Goldwater's strongest geographical appeal. Goldwater countered with claims that the polls had missed a hidden conservative majority within the country.

The New Hampshire primary struck a strong blow against Goldwater. Although Henry Cabot Lodge was neither on the ballot nor able to campaign because he was in Saigon as ambassador to South Vietnam, a write-in campaign on his behalf garnered 35% of the vote, well ahead of Goldwater and Rockefeller. Despite the momentum generated by this victory, Lodge's presence in Vietnam prevented him from even announcing his candidacy, let alone campaigning. While a series of inconclusive primaries followed, Goldwater's supporters were piling up commitments from delegates in the nonprimary states. Since these states provided a majority of the delegate total, the last chance to prevent Goldwater's nomination would be the California primary. When only Rockefeller opposed him in that state, Goldwater was able to clinch the nomination with a narrow victory. Goldwater interpreted his nomination as a mandate to move the Republican Party in a more conservative direction, declaring to cheers at the nominating convention that "extremism in the defense of liberty is no vice."

Such statements allowed President Johnson to portray Goldwater as a dangerous extremist, resulting in an overwhelming Democratic win in the 1964 election. When the more moderate Richard Nixon launched a political comeback that won him not only the 1968 Republican nomination for president but also a narrow general election over Vice President Hubert Humphrey, most experts claimed that centrism had permanently triumphed over conservatism within the Republican Party. What they overlooked was that the Goldwater candidacy had established a grassroots base for the party's conservatives, although Goldwater had carried only six states, five in the Deep South (the sixth being his home state of Arizona). Many conservative whites whose votes had automatically gone to the Democrats were so alienated by the national party's civil rights initiatives that they voted Republican in protest. Where there had been virtually no Republican organizations in many southern states, the Goldwater campaign established them. Eventually they were to become a foundation block for a transformed Republican Party.

The second change was financial. Lacking the large contributors who had often bankrolled presidential candidates, the Goldwater campaign turned to direct mail. Although the election failed to show the hoped-for hidden conservative vote, the direct-mail effort proved wildly successful, raising nearly $6 million from more than 400,000 contributors. Thus it was clear that an identifiably conservative candidate could count on a large number of small contributors for a financial base.

With President Nixon again a candidate in 1972, this seemed of little consequence. The president easily turned back challenges to his renomination from two members of Congress, the liberal Paul McCloskey and the conservative John Ashbrook. His 62% majority against liberal Senator George McGovern seemed to many to cement the triumph of the center over the extremes. But the Watergate break-in, which had seemed merely a minor annoyance that McGovern had been unable to turn into a serious campaign issue, was to prove the president's undoing. First, Vice President Spiro Agnew resigned after being charged with corruption in his previous offices in Maryland. Nixon's nomination of House Minority Leader Gerald Ford

was quickly confirmed by Congress. When the Watergate allegations became so serious that Congress was on the verge of impeaching the president, Nixon resigned, elevating Ford to the presidency.

Having never been elected by a constituency larger than his Michigan congressional district, Ford was a unique incumbent. At first, the public found his down-to-earth behavior and honesty refreshing enough to give him an approval rating of 71% in an August 1974 Gallup poll. Soon his unconditional pardon of former President Nixon caused that rating to plummet, dropping below 50% later that year, then to 37% at the start of 1975. As a result, Ford nearly became the first president to be denied renomination since Chester Arthur in 1884. Although Ford himself was generally regarded as a conservative, his challenger was the clearly more conservative former governor of California, Ronald Reagan. Reagan had first come to national attention as a result of his rousing speech in support of Goldwater at the 1964 convention. A tentative challenge to Richard Nixon at the 1968 convention came too late to affect the result but helped make Reagan the leading spokesman for the party's conservative wing.

Ford's weakness made a challenge by a campaigner as effective as Reagan possible in a nomination contest that now stressed primaries instead of giving party leaders the predominant voice. Ford narrowly won the first primaries in New Hampshire and Florida; then he more easily won several more. Just as many began to write Reagan off, he rallied, winning a series of southern states as well as Indiana. Then it was Ford's turn with victories in Michigan and Maryland. In the final week, Ford was able to counter Reagan's home state win in California with his own triumphs in Ohio and New Jersey. Nevertheless, the president's delegate edge at the convention remained narrow enough to be in jeopardy until he was officially nominated. To preserve that advantage, the Ford forces conceded several major platform planks to the conservatives, including opposition to abortion and indirect criticism of Ford's own policy of détente with the Soviet Union. They had already dropped Rockefeller from the ticket and now replaced him with a considerably more conservative senator, Robert Dole. Although Ford kept his modest lead, winning the nomination with 52.5% of the delegate vote, the conservative wing had clearly captured the Republican presidential party.

Although Ford started the campaign well behind in the polls, he staged a spirited rally, despite a few gaffes such as his debate statement that Eastern Europe was not dominated by the Soviet Union. Ultimately, Democrat Jimmy Carter won a close election by a popular vote margin of 51%–49%.

The Carter administration, however, was plagued by economic troubles from energy shortages to large increases in inflation and interest rates at a time of little economic growth. With Carter facing his own challenge from Edward Kennedy, the Republican Party had a serious opportunity to oust an incumbent president. Front-runner Reagan faced several challengers, most notably George Bush. When the relatively moderate Bush won the Iowa caucuses, some saw the party as moving away from its more conservative faction, but Reagan, who had previously run a noncommittal front-runner campaign, quickly switched to a more aggressive stance, resulting in a primary victory in New Hampshire that was the first of a series of wins. By the end of May, Reagan had locked up a clear convention majority. Although the choice of Bush as vice presidential nominee was a gesture to the party's moderates, the platform itself was clearly conservative, going so far as to reverse the party's 40-year commitment to the Equal Rights Amendment to the Constitution.

In the general election campaign, President Carter, as Johnson had done in 1964, sought to portray his opponent as an extremist too unreliable to trust with America's nuclear arsenal. Reagan's amiable nature reduced the effectiveness of such tactics, while Carter's vigorous attacks caused many to see him as mean-spirited. For his part, Reagan emphasized the weak economy, asking voters at the end of his debate with Carter, "Are you better off now than you were four years ago?" In the end, voter concern about the economy, whether or not they accepted Reagan's conservative proposals of tax cuts, increased defense spending, and cuts in social programs, won out as the public gave Reagan a victory margin of nearly 10%.

By 1984 the economy recovered and Reagan faced no opposition for the nomination and little challenge in the general election from Democrat Walter Mondale. His second term achieved far less than the first, however, culminating in the Iran–contra scandal. Nevertheless, Reagan supported Vice President Bush as his successor. During his eight years in office, Bush had accepted most of Reagan's policy positions while courting conservative leaders. Although he faced half a dozen challengers, Bush's early primary defeats of Robert Dole, who had won the Iowa caucuses, in New Hampshire and the predominantly southern Super Tuesday contests quickly ended all doubt about the nominee. Bush continued wooing conservatives with a platform virtually unchanged from 1980 and 1984, as well as a conservative running mate in Dan Quayle. When postconvention polls showed him trailing Democrat Michael Dukakis, he began to attack his opponent vigorously, stressing issues such as crime and national security. With Dukakis unable to counter, Bush was elected.

After successfully invading Panama and regaining Kuwait quickly in the Gulf War, Bush's popularity ratings soared to unprecedented heights. With the best-known Democrats deciding not to run, reelection seemed assured. But a declining economy caused those ratings to plunge. Although a primary challenge from conservative Pat Buchanan had little chance of success, it indicated that conservatives had still not accepted Bush as one of them. Bush sought to mollify conservatives by allowing many to speak at the convention, but their strident rhetoric turned many voters off. With both Democrat Bill Clinton and billionaire Independent Ross Perot stressing economic issues, Bush was put on the defensive. An attempt to resurrect the success of his 1988 attack strategy by going after Clinton's character proved inadequate, and Clinton was elected president.

As the 1996 election approaches, the triumph of conservatism in the Republican Party seems complete. All the major contenders for the nomination are clearly conservative. Party platforms for the past 20 years have espoused the conservative philosophy. With a campaign based on the conservative Contract with America triumphing in the 1994 elections, there seems little reason for the conservatives who now lead the party to expect a sudden change of direction.

Bruce E. Altschuler

BIBLIOGRAPHY

Mayer, William G., ed. *In Pursuit of the White House: How We Choose Our Presidential Nominees.* Chatham, NJ: Chatham House, 1996.

Pika, Joseph A., and Richard A. Watson. *The Presidential Contest.* 5th ed. Washington, DC: CQ Press, 1996.

Pomper, Gerald M., et al. *The Election of 1992.* Chatham NJ: Chatham House, 1993.

Wayne, Stephen J. *The Road to the White House 1996.* New York: St. Martin's Press, 1996.

Primary Elections

The primary election, also referred to as the *direct primary*, is the process whereby voters choose a political party's candidates for public office. This process is contrasted with the party caucus or convention, where candidates are chosen by party leaders and activists. At present, all states employ the primary process, sometimes in conjunction with caucuses or conventions or both, to nominate candidates for a variety of public posts.

The adoption of the primary election as the principal means of nominating party candidates for public office grew out of the reforms of the Progressive era. During the last two decades of the nineteenth century, the party convention and caucus (indirect methods of nomination) came under increasing attack from party membership. Combined with public demand for wider popular participation in government, the direct election of candidates became a central element in the crusade for responsible party government.

While the first state legislation pertaining to primary elections was enacted in California in 1866, the reform of the nomination process was sporadic and incomplete until after the turn of the century. Through 1889, state laws regulating the conduct of party primaries were generally limited in scope (addressing certain kinds of fraudulent activity) or optional (with the party deciding whether to invoke the legal protections and abide by statutory provisions). Several states enacted mandatory laws, but these applied only to major metropolitan areas. For the most part, primary elections were conducted by the political parties beyond the effective regulation of the state.

This situation began to change during the 1890s as states enacted more complete and effective statutes. Following the turn of the century, support for primary elections gained widespread acceptance across the country. State primary laws passed during the first two decades of the twentieth century were characterized by the statewide application of mandatory regulations. In other words, the political parties (in most states) no longer had the option of orchestrating the manner in which these elections were conducted. The statutes governing general elections were also enforced with respect to primary elections. Furthermore, an increasing number of states embraced the direct primary as a means of nominating party candidates for a wide range of public offices. For example, in 1904 only Wisconsin and Oregon held mandatory, legally regulated direct primaries covering nominations for state offices; by 1917, 32 of the 48 states held such elections.

The expansion of the primary election in the old "Solid South" was largely a product of changes in state Democratic Party rules rather than legislative activity. As the dominant party, the Democrats controlled nearly every elective position (local and statewide) throughout the region. The Democratic primary thus became more significant in determining who would hold elective office than the general election, in which the Democratic nominee frequently ran uncontested or was pitted against a weak Republican candidate. The Republican Party's noncompetitive position in the southern states was reflected by the absence of primaries. As an example, prior to 1960, only 4 of the 11 southern states nominated candidates for the U.S. Senate in Republican primaries.

At present, primary elections take one of several forms, depending on state law. A majority of states hold closed primaries, where participation is limited to those voters who are registered with or declare a preference for one of the major parties. For example, only registered Republicans can vote in the Republican primary in this system. One criticism of the closed primary is that it restricts participation of those voters who identify themselves as Independents. Some states employ the open primary, a system in which registered voters may vote in either party's primary regardless of registration status. While the open primary provides the voter increased flexibility, in both the open and closed primary, the voter is restricted to voting for only one party's slate of candidates for a variety of public offices. A variation of the open primary known as the blanket or wide-open primary allows voters to cast a ballot for each office in either party's primary. In this system a voter may vote for a gubernatorial candidate from one party's slate while choosing among candidates for the state legislature from the other party. The blanket primary has been employed in Alaska, Louisiana, and Washington. Party leaders and activists are generally opposed to the blanket and open primary, arguing that Independents and members of one party may vote for weaker candidates of the other party.

A number of states also have provisions for runoff primaries. A runoff election is held when several candidates (three or more) for a given elective office run in the party primary and none receives a majority of the vote. The runoff election pits the two highest vote-getters in the primary against each other for the party nomination. The runoff primary was particularly important in the southern states prior to the time when the Republican Party began effectively to compete for public office.

The presidential primary, that is, the direct election of state party delegates to the national presidential nominating convention, was a logical extension of the primary idea sweeping the country in the early years of the twentieth century. Florida was the first state to provide political parties with this option (1904). A year later, Wisconsin passed legislation providing for a presidential primary and was followed in succession by Pennsylvania (1906), South Dakota (1909), and Oregon (1910). By 1916, 20 states held Republican presidential primaries.

In part, the intent of the presidential primary was to reduce the influence of the state party bosses by removing the delegate selection process from their control. While a majority of the delegates to the 1916 Republican National Convention were selected in primaries, many of these delegates were not bound to vote for specific candidates. These uncommitted delegates were, in large part, coopted into dominant coalitions by the party leadership. While the primary vote did not determine the outcome of the 1916 convention, this method of delegate selection posed a threat to the party leadership. Contending that these elections were expensive and turnout was generally low, the leaders of both parties were successful in reducing the impact of the primary in the selection of presidential nominees. The number of Republican primaries declined as some states reverted to previous methods of selecting delegates (i.e., caucuses and state conventions). In many states that continued to hold primaries, these were viewed as an advisory, rather than mandatory, means for selecting delegates. The party leadership continued to wield considerable influence in the nomination process through the 1968 elections. During this period, the presidential primary was not considered the principal means by which a candidate obtained the party's nomination. Instead, support of the party leadership remained the most decisive element in this process.

Since the contentious Democratic Convention of 1968, the presidential nomination process has undergone extensive reform. The Democrats, reacting to charges that the process did not represent the interests of the rank-and-file party membership, initiated a series of rule changes. Most notable were guidelines requiring increased representation of women and minorities on state delegations. The new rules subsequently made the presidential primary the preferred method of delegate selection in that this process satisfied the criteria of openness and equal representation. Unlike the Democrats, the Republican Party has not established a sweeping set of national rules governing the presidential nomination process. Instead, the party has prescribed that delegate selection procedures conform to the laws of the states. With a growing number of states providing for a presidential primary, the Republican state organizations have opted to employ this method of delegate selection. In 1968, 16 states held Republican presidential primaries. This increased to 28 and 39, respectively, in 1976 and 1992.

These numbers reflect the increasing impact of presidential primaries on the nomination process over the course of the past 20 years. The process, however, is by no means uniform; these elections can take a number of forms. For example, one type of primary may involve the election of delegates that are pledged to a particular candidate, while a second type may provide an expression of nominee preference with no delegates elected. Other forms include the election of unpledged delegates, with no presidential candidates on the ballot, and an election that reflects presidential preference followed by a separate election for delegates. Furthermore, primary rules in the various states allow delegates to be allocated by two separate methods: at the substate level (usually apportioned by congressional district) and at large (statewide).

While the presidential primary has become a crucial element in the nomination of candidates, there are objections to this process as well. One criticism of the system pertains to increasing campaign expenditures. In order to compete in a large number of front-loaded and regional primaries, a candidate must spend large sums of money for televised campaign messages. This requires effective fund-raising activities. Critics contend that the $1,000-a-plate dinners and special-interest contributions buy political influence. Another objection is that direct primaries reduce the power of party officials in the nomination process. While this was the original intent of the primary process, critics argue that candidates are no longer accountable to the party. The consequences of this development include decreasing levels of party discipline, which results in less coherent legislation and ineffective leadership. Another criticism of this system is that presidential primaries have become media events that detract from the serious discussion of issues. Instead, media coverage focuses on candidate personalities and treats the process much like a horserace. Finally, many observers note that the low turnout in primary elections has not expanded the scope of political participation in the nomination process. Despite these objections, primaries are likely to remain an important feature in the nomination of presidential candidates.

William E. Dugan

SEE ALSO Nominating Conventions, The Presidential Nomination Process

BIBLIOGRAPHY

Aldrich, John H. *Before the Convention*. Chicago: University of Chicago Press, 1980.

Overacker, Louise. *The Presidential Primary*. New York: Macmillan, 1926.

Polsby, Nelson W. *Consequences of Party Reform*. New York: Oxford University Press, 1983.

Stanley, Harold W., and Richard G. Niemi. *Vital Statistics on American Politics*. 2nd ed. Washington, DC: CQ Press, 1990.

Wayne, Stephen J. *The Road to the White House: The Politics of Presidential Elections*. 5th ed. New York: St. Martin's Press, 1995.

Public Perception of Parties and Candidates

In his ground-breaking work on public opinion, Walter Lippmann (1922) pointed out that people's behavior is usually in response to a pseudo environment, based on perceptions of reality. Especially for abstract, intangible objects, such as political parties, these "pictures in our heads" are often simplified models of a very complex reality. Today, politicians and scholars agree that public perceptions of candidates, parties, and policies are crucial determinants of political success.

Public opinion research has uncovered several rules and limitations related to public perceptions of parties and candidates. First, one has to keep in mind that public perceptions are in constant flux. Since candidates change frequently, their role is quite volatile in regard to public opinion. Accordingly, studies have found that candidate evaluation is an important source of short-run change in election outcomes, with candidates either assets or liabilities for parties (Converse, Clausen, and Miller 1965). While party images are more resistant to change, they are not carved in stone. During Dwight Eisenhower's administration, the Democratic Party lost most of the advantage it had enjoyed, being perceived as the party of prosperity. Moreover, during the past 30 years, Democrats and Republicans have exchanged their public image in regard to which party is better able to keep the country out of war. For the future, it might even be possible that the Republicans will replace the Democrats as the party of the South, a label the Democrats held for more than 100 years.

Secondly, to talk of a (*single*) public perception is misleading, since different parts of the public have quite different views of the parties and candidates. The main reason for those differences is the fact that perceptual signals cannot by themselves serve as a basis for understanding. People first have to give those signals meaning by putting them into the appropriate categories of their *conceptual framework*. The pioneer work on how people conceptualize political signals was done in the late 1950s by the Center for Political Studies (CPS) of the University of Michigan. A series of questions about what people liked or disliked about parties and candidates revealed four main levels of conceptualization (Campbell et al. 1960). On the lowest level (about 22% of respondents), people seemed to have little to no understanding of political issues or events and either had no evaluation, or could not defend their evaluation, of candidates or parties. About 24% of respondents were found to refer to the *nature of*

times ("times are good, so why change?") when evaluating parties and candidates. The biggest group (42%) referred to *group benefits*. Respondents on this level liked or disliked parties and candidates because they thought they were good or bad for a group they identified with (farmers, working people, middle class). Finally, only about 10% of all answers indicated a deeper, more structured understanding of the political world. People in this category used ideological labels to describe their political preferences. The levels of conceptualization/sophistication have led to an intensive debate over the limits of public understanding and knowledge (Converse 1964; Nie, Verba, and Petrocik 1979), but it seems fair to say that a large proportion of the public has only a rudimentary understanding of political issues and processes.

On top of the cognitive limitations of public perceptions, people's beliefs and attitudes about politics are strongly "colored" by their membership in groups and social categories and their identification with a party. V.O. Key (1966) claimed that public perceptions echo the alternatives and outlooks presented to them. This might be justified insofar as historical reality cannot be changed, but political issues or events are often subject to perceptual distortion (Campbell et al. 1960). Thus we find that people's perceptions are strongly influenced by membership in primary groups (family, colleagues, friends) and, to a lesser degree, social categories such as race, class, or religion (Conover 1984). Party identification, the sense of attachment a person feels to a party, has been identified as the main point of reference for making sense of political events, issues, or personalities. The relationship between those different factors has been studied intensively and is one of interdependence. But it seems that the intensity of one's party identification can explain the direction of many other political perceptions (Niemi and Weisberg 1984). Thus, what a white male executive, living in a suburb and identifying strongly with the Republicans, will perceive when he looks at the Democratic Party or candidate will likely be very different from a poor, inner-city black, female's view.

Keeping the above limitations in mind, one can try to identify the pattern of perceptions voters seem to hold about the Republican Party and its candidates. Historically, very little empirical evidence exists about public perceptions before the onset of public opinion research. After its foundation in 1854, the Republican Party was the antislavery party. It also became very quickly the party of the North and was associated with industrial and business interests. The Civil War discredited the Democrats and started a 70-year period of political dominance for Republicans. They were seen as the party of Reconstruction and led the United States to become one of the foremost industrial powers. The modern image of the Republicans as the party favoring business was fixed in the 1920 and early 1930s by a series of presidents—Harding, Coolidge, and Hoover—who favored *laissez-faire* economic policies. The Great Depression and 1932 triggered a large-scale political realignment that resulted in a massive decline in support for the Republican Party.

Since Franklin D. Roosevelt and his New Deal policies helped the poor, aged, unemployed, and labor unions, the Democratic Party was more and more perceived as the party of "the common man" and economic prosperity. Republicans were slow to reshape their image, and it took them until 1952 to recapture the presidency by nominating a popular war hero. Dwight Eisenhower helped the Republicans overcome the label of the party of depression. The GOP also acquired the image of the party of peace and was seen as better equipped to handle foreign affairs.

Perceptions of the Republican Party changed again dramatically during the late 1960s as a result of the combined effect of the Vietnam War and the civil rights movement. A majority of the public thought that racial integration was pushed too fast and too far and wanted the government to stay out of issues such as school integration. By 1967–1968, most people were tired of the Vietnam War and 63% disapproved of President Lyndon B. Johnson's handling of the war (Page 1978, 33). After the crucial election of 1968, the Democrats were more and more seen as the party of minority interests, and African Americans became loyal Democrats, which alienated much of the white southern Democrats and led to a slow but steady increase in support for Republican candidates in the South. Increasingly, the Republicans were seen as tougher on issues of law and order and less willing to accept a variety of lifestyles. Until 1968, Republicans profited from an increasingly negative image of the Democratic Party, which changed more rapidly than that of the opposition. This confirms that the actions of the incumbent party are more likely to be known and evaluated than the words of the opposition. Thus, incumbents will usually have a sharper image.

Despite discernible differences in some areas, Page's (1978) analysis of Republican and Democratic party identifiers finds few sharp differences in 1968. On about half of the 63 issues he analyzed, he did not find any appreciable difference between party positions. On most others, the differences were very moderate. This finding supports the familiar claim that the two major parties are often indistinguishable, mainly because they try to be all things to all people. While party conflict was strongest and most obvious before and during the Civil War, and again during the New Deal, Democrats and Republicans stood for much of the same things even during the late 1960s, when the American society seemed quite polarized.

These similarities are reflected in public perceptions of parties and candidates. Between 1952 and 1976, around 45% of the public could not see any important differences between the two major parties. This proportion declined about 10% during the 1980s, probably as a result of the Reagan presidency. Several other measures, however, show a long-term decline in the relevance of parties, especially when it comes to evaluations (Wattenberg 1990) and problem-solving capacity. While in 1964 almost 70% of a national sample named one of the two major parties as "likely to do a better job in dealing with this [the most important] problem," this proportion had declined to 44% by 1988. Wattenberg (1991) shows that citizens are more and more likely to conceptualize issues in terms of candidates and less in terms of parties. This also means that the perceptual link between parties and candidates has deteriorated. Bill Clinton ran in 1992 as a "different kind of Democrat" mainly to avoid the "liberal Democrat" label.

With the increasing use of the mass media and political action committees, candidates have come to assume a more prominent role in the public mind. While earlier studies (Goldberg 1966) found that party identification influenced candidate choice directly and indirectly via its impact on issue evaluations, more recent analyses affirm the crucial role of candidates in the dynamics of electoral choice (Markus and Converse 1984). Starting with Eisenhower, the perception of presidential candidates' personality, experience, skills, and "attractiveness" has been crucial for electoral outcomes. It is also well known, however, that the perception of candidates' stands on issues varies from voter to voter. One of the best-known systematic distortions is caused by "projection" effects. Voters may project their own issue position onto candidates they like for other reasons. The reverse effect occurs when people perceive issue stands of candidates they do not like as opposed to their own. It speaks for the increasing importance of candidates that Eisenhower, Nixon, and Reagan were all elected by a public in which Democrats clearly outnumbered Republicans. They also changed the image of their party. Eisenhower helped the Republicans overcome the negative economic association, Nixon damaged his party with Watergate, and Reagan helped give the Republicans a big advantage in the area of defense politics.

While the media have helped candidates to gain direct access to the electorate, they also seem to have lowered the quality of public discourse. Television, especially, often prefers images over issues, and tends to emphasize the negative, sensational, or theatrical. This has added to increasing public frustration and negativity about politics in general (Patterson 1994; Graber 1993).

Public confidence in the parties has declined, but the Republicans retain a core image that shows more than marginal differences from the Democratic Party. When asked which political party would do a better job, Democrats in 1992 held a more than 30% advantage over Republicans on the issues of economic conditions, unemployment, health care, environmental protection, race relations, education, and abortion. The public also thought that Democrats would be more likely to keep the United States out of World War III. But on issues such as foreign affairs, national defense, public order, moral decay, and a balanced budget, the Republicans are perceived as the party doing a better job (*Gallup Poll Monthly*, April and July 1992). While these assessments might change in the future, they are much more likely to be persistent than are public evaluations of candidates. The fact that President Bush's level of public approval fell from an unprecedented 91% in January 1991 to less than 50% one year later is proof of the volatile nature of public support for candidates.

Christian Georgen

BIBLIOGRAPHY

Campbell, Angus, Philip Converse, Warren Miller, and Donald Stokes. *The American Voter*. New York: Wiley, 1960.

Conover, Pamela J. "The Influence of Group Identification on Political Perception and Evaluation." *Journal of Politics* 46 (1984): 761–785.

Converse, Philip E. "The Nature of Belief Systems in Mass Publics." In *Ideology and Discontent*, ed. David E. Apter. New York: Free Press, 1964.

Converse, Philip E., Aage R. Clausen, and Warren Miller. "Electoral Myth and Reality: The 1964 Election." *American Political Science Review* 59 (1965): 321–343.

Converse, Philip E., and Gregory B. Markus. "Plus ça change . . . : The New CPS Election Study Panel." In *Controversies in Voting Behavior*, 2nd ed. Washington, DC: CQ Press, 1984.

Goldberg, Arthur S. "Discerning a Causal Pattern among Data on Voting Behavior." *American Political Science Review* 60 (1966): 913–922.

Graber, Doris. *Mass Media and American Politics*. 4th ed. Washington, DC: CQ Press, 1993.

Nie, Norman H., S. Verba, and J. Petrocik. *The Changing American Voter*. Cambridge: Harvard University Press, 1979.

Niemi, Richard G., and Herbert F. Weisberg, eds. *Controversies in Voting Behavior*. 2nd ed. Washington, DC: CQ Press, 1984.

Key, V.O., Jr. *The Responsible Electorate*. Cambridge: Harvard University Press, 1966.

Lippmann, Walter. *Public Opinion*. New York: Macmillan, 1922.

Page, Benjamin I. *Choices and Echoes in Presidential Elections: Rational Man and Electoral Democracy*. Chicago: University of Chicago Press, 1978.

Patterson, Thomas E. *Out of Order*. New York: Random House, 1994.

Sundquist, James. *Dynamics of the Party System: Alignments and Realignments of Political Parties in the United States*. Washington, DC: Brookings Institution, 1980.

Wattenberg, Martin P. *The Decline of American Political Parties, 1952–1988*. Cambridge: Harvard University Press, 1990.

———. *The Rise of Candidate-Centered Politics*. Cambridge: Harvard University Press, 1991.

Reaganomics

Reaganomics was one of the most controversial attempts to change the course of U.S. economic policy fundamentally in the past 40 years. Even Reagan's vice president, George Bush, while an opponent of Reagan in the 1980 Republican primaries, called the proposals "voodoo economics." In a kinder and gentler world, Reaganomics have become known as *supply-side economics*. The term *supply-side* is used to distinguish it from its older Keynesian cousin, *demand-side economics*.

When President Ronald Reagan took office in January 1980, the economy was in a severe recession. Economic growth was negative. The consumer inflation rate was 12%. Unemployment had reached more than 7%. The real value of corporate equities (stocks) had declined more than 40% in less than 20 years. Federal spending had increased to more than 22% of the gross national product. These serious economic realities helped shape the program known as Reaganomics.

At the heart of his proposals were the four core elements Reagan outlined in a speech on February 18, 1981: (1) budget reform that would cut the rate of growth in federal spending, (2) reduction in personal income tax rates by 10% a year over three years and an acceleration in the depreciation for business investment in plant and equipment, (3) regulatory relief, and (4) a new monetary policy that would restore a stable currency and healthy financial markets. At the heart of these proposals was Reagan's belief that the greatest cause of economic problems was the government.

In order for the new economic program to work, the rate of growth in spending had to be controlled. While candidate Reagan had specifically promised to reduce "waste, fraud, extravagance, and abuse," all concerned knew that if the plan was to work, reductions in spending on entitlements was necessary to bring the spending in line. Even deeper cuts would be necessary in order to finance the defense spending that Reagan had considered integral to the United States as a world leader. Perhaps it was in this area that Reaganomics failed the most. Reagan was unable to curb spending effectively. This failure was caused in large part by Democratic control of Congress. Congressional Democrats saw no reason to follow the course laid out by the president. They had seen their electoral victories tied to a government that spent huge sums of federal money in entitlements and on programs that reached their districts. Despite attempts by Reagan to change the way in which spending decisions were made, he was ultimately unsuccessful. The result was the ballooning of federal deficits.

While some critics blame the substantial tax cuts of the Reagan years for the dramatic increase in the deficit, the revenues generated do not support that position. During the Reagan years, revenues increased sharply despite the tax cut. Reagan and many conservative economists believed that by cutting taxes, the economy would grow. They believed that the growth in the economy would more than make up for the lost revenues by generating new revenues. Reagan hoped that a simpler and fairer tax system would offer relief to an economy that had unlimited potential. Congress approved much of the Reagan plan on taxes in 1982. The tax reform of 1986 continued to follow the plan with top rates on individual income tax half of what they were in 1980. Reagan was successful in structuring a simpler, fairer, and lower rate tax structure. He had been correct in his assessment that lower taxes would result in economic expansion and more revenues.

In the two decades that preceded Reagan's inauguration, more than 20 new regulatory agencies had been established. Most of these agencies were responsible for the regulation of health, safety, environment, and energy. Several studies argued that the growth of regulation led to a one-tenth decline in American productivity. Other studies stated that over 1.5 billion hours of labor were expended yearly filling out federal forms. Reagan believed, as did Office of Management and Budget Director David Stockman, that what was needed was not regulatory reform but relief. In a December 1980 memo known as "the economic Dunkirk," Stockman called for "a dramatic, substantial recision of the regulatory burden." The argument was that such relief would do much "to boost business." By executive order, Reagan ordered federal agencies to use a net benefit method for determining regulations. Large numbers of pending regulations were suspended for 60 days so that they could be reviewed. During Reagan's first term, few areas of the federal bureaucracy escaped regulatory changes. A special commission established to assess the success of the changes estimated that tens of billions of dollars were saved by the changes. But the antiregulatory movement of the Reagan administration stalled at the end of his first term, for several reasons. First, Reagan was unsuccessful in making necessary changes at the legislative level. Second, the administration had little in the way of specifics to offer at the legislative level. At best, Reagan was able to slow the growth of new regulations.

Monetary policy under Reaganomics used the control of the money supply as the primary means of reducing inflation and stabilizing growth. The administration first sought to control the supply of money in order to curb high inflation. As inflation came down in 1982, the administration changed courses, encouraging a dramatic increase in the money supply. The result was the most rapid sustained peacetime growth rate. Fundamental to Reaganomics is the belief that the Federal Reserve should stabilize the money supply, rather than toy with interest rates. The result of this substantial shift in how to handle monetary policy was a decade of low inflation, low interest rates, and steady economic growth. In many ways, monetary policy was the biggest success of Reaganomics. The major flaw with the approach was the failure of either the administration or the Federal Reserve to institutionalize their approach to monetary policy.

Reaganomics did not produce a revolutionary change in the government's economic policies. While many economists and elected officials have adopted the theoretical underpinnings of Reagan's economic policy, it has not been adopted wholeheartedly by the majority of elected officials. Nevertheless, there is a growing adherence to the primary tenets of Reaganomics even by those formerly opposed to it for political reasons. President Bill Clinton, no friend of Ronald Reagan's or his stated economic policies, has adopted many of the specifics of Reaganomics, such as a cut in the rate of growth of federal spending, deregulation, and tax cuts to spur economic growth. The experiments under Reagan have shown an alternative path. As this path becomes more mainstream, more of it will be adopted and institutionalized. The revolution of Reaganomics is not over yet.

Jeffrey D. Schultz
Diane L. Schultz

BIBLIOGRAPHY

Niskanen, William A. *Reaganomics: An Insider's Account of the Policies and the People.* New York: Oxford University Press, 1988.

Roberts, Paul Craig. *The Supply-Side Revolution*. Cambridge: Harvard University Press, 1984.

Stone, Charles F., and Isabell V. Sawhill. *Economic Policy in the Reagan Years*. Washington, DC: Urban Institute Press, 1984.

Realignment and Dealignment

While the term *realignment* describes an enduring change in the relative strength of parties, *dealignment* refers to a decline in political party loyalty and a rise in political independence. The increasing number of voters who do not identify with any of the parties, increased split-ticket voting, and the shift from party politics toward candidate-centered politics are all signs of a party dealignment in contemporary American politics. A realignment, in contrast, would be indicated by a complete change in the identity of the major parties (as when the Republicans replaced the Whigs in the 1850s) or a significant change in the party balance (as when the Democrats became the majority party in the 1930s).

Central to an understanding of both realignment and dealignment is the concept of *party identification*, which has been set firmly in the minds of political scientists ever since the publication of *The American Voter* (Campbell et al. 1960). *The American Voter* defines party identification as a long-term stable influence on voters' decision-making processes. Further, it is a psychological attachment to one of the two major parties that is the result of a childhood socialization process. While party identification is a relatively strong and stable influence on voters' decisions, political scientists and historians have noted that there appear to be periodic shifts in party identification that change the political environment for decades at a time.

The first work to note these shifts was V.O. Key's "A Theory of Critical Elections" (1955). Key argued that critical elections were the signal that a realignment was occurring within the electorate that was "both sharp and durable" (1955, 11) and altered the preexisting cleavages within the electorate. Key identified the elections of 1896 and 1932 as examples of two such critical elections. Historians have also identified the 1860 victory of the first Republican candidate, Abraham Lincoln, as a landmark in American politics. The 1896 election of William McKinley heralded the dominance of the Republican Party in American politics that persisted until 1932 brought the Roosevelt revolution. The pro-Republican realignment in 1896 solidified Republican dominance and was mainly caused by the conversion of northern, mostly urban, Democrats. The

probusiness Republicans continued to control national government until 1932, holding a majority in one or both houses of Congress except for the period from 1913 to 1928.

The major realigning electoral period that, according to some scholars (e.g., Sundquist 1983), continues to influence the current cycle of electoral politics occurred during the 1932, 1934, and 1936 elections. The Great Depression and the failure of the Republican Hoover administration to take decisive efforts to alleviate the economic crisis brought massive switches in party identification in almost all classes of voters.

Lasting rearrangements of party support are driven by policy, in other words by ideals about what the government should and should not do. Thus, realignments are issue centered. The issues causing realignment have been moral (slavery in the 1850s) or economic as in the 1890s and 1930s.

For the past 30 years, election analysts have debated the question of a new realignment. For instance, Carmines, Renten, and Stimson (1984) argue that racial issues caused a realignment during the 1960s. According to Carmines et al., Republican identification increased among southern whites. Black voters, in contrast, became more firmly Democratic. Although these changes did not affect total party identification figures, the coalitional makeup of the parties was altered. Yet, there is much scholarly disagreement on the question of whether or not a realignment occurred in 1964. Sundquist (1983) argues strongly against such a realignment. He sees the South belatedly conforming to class-based patterns of party identification adopted by the rest of the nation during the New Deal realignment (see also Silbey 1991).

The possibility of a new realignment favorable to the Republican Party was raised again by the victories of Republican Presidents Ronald Reagan and George Bush in 1980, 1984, and 1988. Similar to Roosevelt's success in 1932, Reagan's election was the result of widespread dissatisfaction with incumbent President Carter. Reagan's economic and social policies constituted a significant departure from previous policies, and Bush's electoral victory constituted the first time in four decades that the incumbent party has won the White House for two consecutive elections. Yet the realignment process seems to be incomplete because Republicans were unable to capture both houses of Congress. Although Republicans continued to dominate in presidential elections, they actually lost House seats in 1988. Bush won the presidency with a solid margin of 54% to 46%, yet Democrats were able to increase the number of seats they held in the House and the Senate. Further, there has been little discernible movement in state and local politics toward the kind of ideological division needed for party realignment (Huckshorn 1984).

It is possible that a new realignment favorable to the Republicans is in the making. The impressive gains of conservatives in the 1994 midterm election could signal the beginning of a new period of realignment caused by the emergence of a new coalition of conservative voters. The 1994 election gave Republicans a solid majority in the House and the Senate. All Republican incumbents who sought reelection to the House, Senate, or a governorship won in 1994. Yet it remains to be seen if the conservative gains from 1994 will be followed up in the 1996 presidential election. In sum, scholarly work on realignment rejects the idea that the Republican victories in the 1980s and 1990s should be interpreted as signs of a major period of nationwide realignment. Yet much of the speculation on realignment has focused on the South, which is now characterized by Republican dominance among southern white voters. Throughout the 1980s and 1990s, southern whites continued to endorse Republican presidential candidates. In 1994, Republicans were able to capture a majority of House and Senate seats from southern states.

An alternative to the realignment thesis is dealignment, and many scholars argue that the question of whether or not a realignment has occurred in the past 30 years is moot because the political system has been experiencing dealignment during that period. The dealignment argument contends that instead of people changing from one party to another or new voters joining one party in large numbers, the American political system is characterized by voters' rejection of parties and a move toward independent status. Where once the great majority of Americans closely identified with a political party, strong attachments to the parties and support for the party system generally have fallen to all-time historical lows. Survey data collected by the Center for Political Studies at the University of Michigan document the erosion of support for the parties.

Throughout the 1950s, only about 21% of the electorate considered themselves to be Independents. From 1964 on, however, the situation changed dramatically. Independent voters increased in the 1960s to 25.8%, and in the 1970s to 34.8%. In recent years, anywhere from one-third to 40% report Independent status. This trend toward independence has been less pronounced for the Republicans than for the Democrats. Weak identification with the Republican Party remained relatively stable over the past 40 years; however, the party has lost support among individuals who strongly identify with the Republicans. For in-

stance, in 1956 15% of the public identified strongly with the Republican Party; in 1976 only 9% considered themselves to be strong Republicans. The number of independent Republicans has increased over time.

What have been the consequences of this process of dealignment? Throughout the 1950s, party identification was the key predictor of an individual's vote. For instance, 83% of American voters who identified with a party voted consistently with that identification in the 1956 election (Nie, Verba, and Petrocik 1984). Yet in 1972, about half of the voters were not guided by their party identification. Although strong identification with Republicans is lower than with Democrats, strong Republicans are less likely to defect than strong Democrats (Crotty 1984). In the 1988 election, 91% of Republicans voted for Bush; only 82% of Democrats voted for Dukakis. Not only have there been marked increases in partisan defection in voting but also concomitant increases in ticket splitting. Ticket splitting occurs when a voter casts his or her ballot for candidates of two or more parties for different offices in the same election. As recently as 1960, almost two-thirds of the electorate reported voting a straight party ballot in presidential elections. By 1972, however, these percentages nearly reversed as 62% of the electorate reported voting a split ticket.

What is behind the steady and dramatic decline in partisanship since 1964? Norpoth and Rusk's analysis (1982) indicates that the decline was caused by the entrance of new voters who came with a discernible lower partisanship level than those voters who entered the electorate between 1952 and 1964, as well as the desertion of parties by those already in the electorate. Thus, dealignment has occurred in all age groups since 1964. But the generations that entered the electorate after 1964 are much less likely to have ties to one of the political parties. These generational differences in the strength of party attachment point toward an incomplete transmission of partisanship from parents to children. In other words, parental partisanship was either less salient or was rejected in the generations entering the electorate after 1964.

Additional causes of party dealignment can be found by investigating citizens' attitudes toward the parties, as well as structural changes in the parties that have taken place during the past 30 years. More than ever before, voters distrust parties. Confidence in the parties is particularly low among the young. In 1984, 56% of those under age 35 felt better represented by interest groups, while only 25% chose parties. Clyde Wilcox (1995) reports a postelection poll indicating that the majority of Americans were pleased with the Republican victory, yet they were also cynical that the

Republicans would behave differently than the Democrats.

As far as structural changes in the parties are concerned, scholars point toward the decline of the urban political machine, the parties' diminished role in the recruitment and nomination of candidates, as well as the emergence of new campaign technologies as sources of party dealignment. Although changes in the presidential nomination process (i.e., the introduction of open primaries) were initially introduced by the Democratic Party, the 1968 and 1972 Republican National Conventions adopted a number of rules requiring the party to end discrimination and broaden participation. GOP reforms were not as dramatic as those implemented by the Democrats in 1972; however, Republican nominations have also been affected by the reform spirit, in part by GOP-initiated reforms and because of changes in state laws made in conformity with the new Democratic rules.

The introduction of new campaign technologies contributed to a further shift in the balance of power away from the parties and to the candidates. Campaign assets once received from the party organization (i.e., skills, manpower, information, and campaign funds) are now often provided by pollsters, fund raisers, the media, and public relations experts (Sorauf 1976). Consequently, a candidate's success depends on his or her ability to attract financial support from organized interests and create a favorable media image. The modern candidate is relatively independent from the party, and candidates are forced to proclaim allegiance to their party only when it seems politically expedient to do so (Bennett 1996).

Regardless of its causes or extent, the weakening of the parties and the growing alienation of the electorate from the major U.S. parties has produced significant changes in political behavior and the political system. For the past 30 years, American politics has been characterized by an increase in political independence among both citizens and politicians that manifests itself in personality-oriented politics and a decreased reliance on party cues.

Frauke Schnell

SEE ALSO Voting Behavior

BIBLIOGRAPHY

Andersen, Kristi. *The Creation of a Democratic Majority, 1928–1936*. Chicago: University of Chicago Press, 1979.

Bennett, Lance B. *The Governing Crisis: Media, Money, and Marketing in American Elections*. New York: St. Martin's Press, 1996.

Burnham, Walter D. *Critical Elections and the Mainsprings of American Politics*. New York: Norton, 1970.

Campbell, Angus, Philip E. Converse, Warren E. Miller, and Donald E. Stokes. *The American Voter*. New York: Wiley, 1960.

Carmines, Edward G., Steven H. Renten, and James A. Stimson. "Events and Alignments: The Party Image Link." In *Controversies in Voting Behavior*, ed. Richard G. Niemi and Herbert F. Weisberg. Washington, DC: CQ Press, 1984.

Converse, Philip E. *The Dynamics of Party Support*. Beverly Hills: Sage, 1976.

Crotty William. *American Parties in Decline*. Glenview, IL: Scott, Foresman, 1984.

Erikson, Robert S., and Kent L. Tedin. "The 1928–1936 Partisan Realignment: The Case for the Conversion Hypothesis." *American Political Science Review* 75 (1981): 951–962.

Huckshorn, Robert J. *Political Parties in America*. Monterey, CA: Brooks/Cole, 1984.

Key, V.O. "A Theory of Critical Elections." *Journal of Politics* 17 (1955): 3–18.

Nie, Norman, Sidney Verba, and John R. Petrocik. *The Changing American Voter*. Cambridge: Harvard University Press, 1979.

Norpoth, Helmut, and Jerold Rusk. "Partisan Dealignment in the American Electorate." *American Political Science Review* 76 (1982): 522–537.

Silbey, Joel H. "Beyond Realignment and Realignment Theory: American Political Eras, 1789–1989." In *The End of Realignment? Interpreting American Electoral Eras*, ed. Byron E. Shafer. Madison: University of Wisconsin Press, 1991.

Sorauf, Frank J. *Party Politics in America*. Boston: Little, Brown, 1976.

Sundquist, James L. *Dynamics of the Party System*. Washington, DC: Brookings Institution, 1983.

Wilcox, Clyde. *The Latest American Revolution? The 1994 Elections and Their Implications for Governance*. New York: St. Martin's Press, 1995.

Religion

The U.S. Constitution contains two passages strictly divorcing religion from the government. Article VI maintains that "no religious Test shall ever be required as a Qualification to any Office or public Trust under the United States," and the First Amendment begins "Congress shall make no law respecting an establishment of religion, or prohibiting the free exercise thereof." These provisions do not, however, remove religion from the arena of politics, and they cannot force citizens and voters to forget their religious affiliations and biases. In practice, American politics are often intricately interwoven with religious concerns, though the largely Protestant makeup of the United States often conceals the blatantly religious elements of public life that have been given official sanction: presidents traditionally take the oath of office with their hand resting on a Bible; since the 1860s, U.S. currency has borne the motto "In God We Trust," which was made the national motto in 1956; the Pledge of Allegiance, given federal sanction for recitation in public schools, has included the phrase "one nation, under God" since 1954; Christmas, but no other major religious holiday of any creed, is both a federal holiday and a state holiday in all 50 states.

The United States is undoubtedly a Christian nation, as these facts attest, yet significant, and often influential, elements of society do not adhere to one of the sects of the dominant form of Christianity in America: Protestantism. Struggles over the inclusion of certain moral precepts in legislation, the imposition of certain religious rites in public functions and institutions, and the issues of religious tolerance, religious separation, and religious privilege have made religion a central feature of electoral and partisan politics. Without artificially drawing lines, the two major parties can be readily identified with certain attitudes about religion: since World War II, both Roman Catholics and Jews have consistently voted Democratic, while white Protestants have consistently voted Republican. These voting patterns have deep historical roots and have been reinforced by the recent movement of the Religious Right into the mainstream of the Republican Party and the corresponding reaction of the Democratic Party against moralistic legislation and judgments in Republican-dominated courts.

The Republican Party was born as the party of evangelical Protestantism, basing its early electoral successes on antislavery and Prohibition positions; it has maintained that character through its nearly century-and-a-half of existence. The Republican Party has not only courted but sometimes overlapped with temperance groups like the Anti-Saloon League and evangelical groups like the Moral Majority. It has also consistently stood for the introduction of religion into American public life and successfully campaigned for legislation achieving a kind of modified "civic religion." White Protestants, particularly the affluent, have consistently voted Republican and generally support the attempts of Republican officeholders to legislate for the rest of the nation their morality.

These voting patterns have deep historical roots and have been reinforced by the recent movement of the Religious Right into the mainstream of the Republican Party. Established in 1854, the party was initially organized to provide a unified antislavery front in the North, where evangelical Protestants were agitating for abolition and calling for direct government intervention to solve the slavery issue. When Abraham Lincoln, who had campaigned (unsuccessfully) for a Prohibi-

tion amendment to the Illinois constitution, took over the party leadership in 1860, Republicans added an additional morality plank into the party's platform by adopting a prohibitionist stance, a position largely favored by white Anglo-Saxon Protestants and generally opposed by other religious and ethnic groups, particularly immigrant Catholics. Since then, the Republican Party has consistently striven to pass morally charged and religiously oriented legislation, from mandatory prayer in school to restrictions on abortion and the consumption of alcohol and certain drugs.

Republican reformers and officeholders have been successful in passing a number of other religiously inspired laws, including an amendment to the U.S. Constitution (the 18th); however, Democratic control of Congress and the Supreme Court in the 1930s and 1940s, and throughout the 1960s and 1970s, unraveled these successes by repealing Prohibition, Sunday closing laws, and mandatory prayer in school; by removing Nativity scenes from government property; and by legalizing abortion. The 1980s witnessed a resurgence of religious involvement in American politics, and the Republican Party received the necessary support from its traditional ally, evangelical Protestantism, in the form of groups like the Moral Majority, to elect Ronald Reagan, a president firmly committed to "family values," prayer in school, opposition to abortion, and the reinvigoration of "traditional" (i.e., Protestant) morality in America. The Religious Right was also largely responsible for rallying "grassroots" support of Republican congressional candidates in the 1994 elections that brought a Republican majority to the House of Representatives. Current Republican control of the Supreme Court and Congress promises to reintroduce at least some of the religious legislation repealed or overruled by the Democrats.

The Republican Party has consistently fought for the introduction of religion into public life. An early Republican-backed measure to bring God back into American public life was undertaken by the first Republican administration of Abraham Lincoln. In 1861, the Reverend M.R. Walkinson of Ridleyville, Pennsylvania, wrote a letter to Secretary of the Treasury Salmon P. Chase. In his letter the clergyman called for the phrase "God, Liberty and Law" to be added to U.S. coins. He expressed a view still heard today, that many of the nation's problems stemmed from what he called "our national shame in disowning God." Chase directed the Mint to begin producing coins with the motto "In God We Trust," which by 1864 was on every U.S. coin. It was not until 1954, however, that another Republican administration, backed by a Republican Congress, passed a law directing that from then on, all U.S. currency must include the motto "In

God We Trust." Shortly thereafter, the same Congress and president passed a law including the phrase "one nation, under God" in the Pledge of Allegiance.

Republicans have also given strong support to religion in public schools, and even after the Supreme Court ruled that mandatory prayer in school violated the First Amendment's Establishment Clause, the 1972 Republican platform called for voluntary school prayer: "We reaffirm our view that voluntary prayer should be freely permitted in public places—particularly, by school children while attending public schools." Various states, under Republican leadership, attempted to introduce various forms of secular or nonsectarian prayer, including the "silent moment." With a Republican majority in the Supreme Court since Reagan appointed Sandra Day O'Connor in 1981, various rulings have rolled back the strict separation of church and state mandated by the Democratically controlled Court, giving states greater leeway to pass formerly prohibited legislation that introduces certain religious elements into official public life.

Chief Justice Rehnquist, originally appointed to the Court by President Nixon and elevated to Chief Justice by President Reagan, has been consistently arguing that the Court's rulings in Establishment Clause cases that block states from providing aid to religious schools are flawed and must be reversed. With control of the Court and a Republican majority, Rehnquist has succeeded in getting certain religious statutes past constitutional scrutiny; in 1983, the Court upheld a town's Christmas crèche display and Nebraska's legislative prayer, and even while invalidating Alabama's moment-of-silence law, several justices noted that more carefully drawn legislation would not be struck down. Rehnquist's Court has at least partially succeeded in promoting the Republican attitude about the strong relationship between religion and American public life. The Court has indicated that the First Amendment does not bar the government from recognizing America's religious heritage, which in their hands is dominated by the concerns of evangelical Protestantism.

Jack J. Miller

SEE ALSO School Prayer

BIBLIOGRAPHY

Maisel, L. Sandy, ed. *Political Parties and Elections in the United States.* New York: Garland, 1991.

Noll, Mark A., ed. *Religion and American Politics: From the Colonial Period to the 1980s.* New York: Oxford University Press, 1990.

Wald, Kenneth D. *Religion and Politics in the United States.* Washington, DC: CQ Press, 1992.

Republican National Committee

The Republican National Committee (RNC) was established following the first Republican National Convention held in Philadelphia in June 1856. Initially, the RNC acted as a committee of correspondence for state party leaders during those times when campaigns were not being conducted. In presidential election years, it distributed campaign literature and coordinated the speeches of surrogate speakers. The RNC functioned only sporadically until the chairmanship of Will Hays (1918–1921), who transformed it into a year-round operation replete with a paid staff. (The Democratic National Committee followed suit after Alfred E. Smith's defeat in 1928.) Despite Hays's efforts, however, the RNC remained an embryonic organization until the early 1960s. In 1964, political scientists Cornelius P. Cotter and Bernard C. Hennessy described it as engaging in a "politics without power." As an example, one Midwest state party chair refused to make an anticipated $25,000 annual dues payment. RNC members excoriated the recalcitrant state chair but were powerless to do more.

INSTITUTIONAL GROWTH OF THE REPUBLICAN NATIONAL COMMITTEE

Historically, the institutional growth of the RNC has been sporadic—with the greatest advances occurring after landslide losses in presidential elections. For example, after Franklin D. Roosevelt routed Alfred M. Landon in 1936, RNC chair John Hamilton authorized construction of a permanent headquarters. But the national committee languished until Barry M. Goldwater's overwhelming loss in 1964. Newly installed RNC chair Ray C. Bliss, a self-styled "nuts and bolts" man, began rebuilding the largely decimated Republican state and local parties, especially those in the large industrial cities. Bliss's extraordinary tenure ran from 1965 until 1969, when Richard M. Nixon was elected president.

The next major evolution of the RNC occurred during the chairmanship of William E. Brock (1977–1981). Brock, a former Republican U.S. senator from Tennessee, won the post in a five-way contest following Gerald R. Ford's narrow loss in 1976. Like Bliss, Brock focused on rebuilding state and local Republican organizations—this time using money and computerized technology to obtain the desired results. State parties were encouraged to hire full-time political directors, and regional directors were chosen to report to the RNC chair. Brock also named regional finance directors to assist state parties with fund raising. Enamored of the new computer technology, Brock made it available to the state parties to help in their accounting practices, fund raising, and analysis of survey research. Finally, he created a Local Elections Division that would recruit prospective candidates, sponsor campaign-management seminars, and furnish office-seekers with on-site technical assistance. In short, Brock appropriated to the RNC functions that heretofore had been largely left to the state parties.

But Brock's greatest innovation was in developing a direct-mail system that would underwrite the many new duties he had undertaken. Until the 1960s, the RNC was supported by assessments of state parties based on a given state's population, percentage of Republican votes, and personal income. But payments were sporadic, and the system collapsed following Goldwater's nomination, which alienated many wealthy GOP moderates. Brock instituted a multimillion-dollar direct-mail campaign backed by the new computerized technology that would raise funds from individual donors. By 1978, the RNC had a donor base of 511,638 contributors, 58% of whom paid $25 or less. Ten years later, the base grew to 1.2 million contributors, each making an average payment of $61.25. In 1992, the RNC raised $85.4 million for Republican candidates and "party-building" efforts at the state and local level. With the increased funding has come an explosion of full-time staff: in 1972, the RNC employed 30 people; by 1990, that figure had increased to 400. Today few would argue that the RNC is engaged in a form of "politics without power." As one midwestern state Republican chair noted: "I figure that I should go along with the National Committee as much as possible because I want as much of their money as I can get."

REPUBLICAN NATIONAL CHAIR

The Republican national chair has changed from that of a part-time, unsalaried position in the first half of the twentieth century to a full-time administrative officer and partisan spokesperson in the latter half. Selection of the chair largely depends on control of the presidency. A Republican president will routinely name the chair, and the choice is usually ratified without dissent. In 1971, for example, President Nixon selected Senator Robert J. Dole of Kansas to be RNC

chair. Similarly, President Bush (who served as RNC chair from 1973 to 1974) chose campaign operatives Lee Atwater (1989–1990), Clayton Yeutter (1991–1992), and Rich Bond respectively (1992–1993), without a hint of opposition. But in these circumstances, the national chair is often droned out by the presidential megaphone and plagued by White House interference. Richard Richards, who was chosen by President Reagan to head the RNC in 1981, said, "It is a tough, tough job to be National Chairman when you have the White House . . . every clerk and secretary in the White House thinks they can do your job better than you can, and they don't even know what you do." When the Democrats occupy the White House, the RNC chair is a more visible and powerful public figure, as the tenures of Ray Bliss and Bill Brock attest. In these situations, the contest is often a spirited one. For example, in 1993, following George Bush's loss to Bill Clinton, Republicans chose Haley Barbour in a hotly contested race. Barbour had prior experience as a White House political director during the Reagan administration, and thanks to the ties he established with local and state party leaders he was catapulted to the national chairmanship. Barbour has been an outspoken public figure, making frequent television appearances, and is credited with much of the Republican success at the polls in 1994.

The Rules of the Republican Party state that the national committee is responsible for the "general management of the Republican party subject to direction from the national convention." In reality, day-to-day management of the RNC falls to the chair, who acts as chief executive officer. Over the years, the RNC assumed the characteristics of a large corporation with myriad tasks, including the following:

1. *Fund Raising*. The Finance Division is responsible for raising and spending monies contributed to the Republican National Committee and development of the direct-mail campaign.
2. *Voter List Development*. This includes the creation of a computer-generated list of 100 million names to assist the RNC in its get-out-the-vote drives during presidential election years.
3. *Voter Contact Programs*. This involves direct solicitation of voters by mail coordinated by the RNC and state and local parties. In 1988 the RNC instituted Victory '88, which generated 30 million pieces of mail and an equal number of telephone calls to potential Republican supporters.
4. *Technical Services*. This includes candidate seminars, hiring professional poll takers to measure voter re-

sponse to targeted Republican candidates and issues, providing legal help in complying with state
and federal election laws (especially campaign finance statutes), preparation of print and electronic
media advertising, as well as redistricting and other
computer-based electioneering programs.

5. *Generic Advertising.* In 1988, the RNC spent $11.5
million on "generic" television advertising to promote the Republican Party.

6. *Communications.* This includes "opposition research" on Democratic opponents and issuing "line-
of-the-day" messages to Republican candidates so
that the party can present a coordinated message on
national and local media outlets—especially on
television and radio talk programs.

7. *Speaker's Bureau.* More than 500 speakers are made
available by the RNC to raise money for and speak
on behalf of state and local Republican office seekers.

8. *State and Local Party Development.* The RNC provides regional directors to assist state parties in developing stronger organizations and awards financial grants to them.

9. *Managing the National Convention.* The RNC is responsible for selecting the site of and managing the party's
quadrennial presidential nominating convention.

SIZE OF THE
REPUBLICAN NATIONAL COMMITTEE

In addition to the chair and the permanent staff, the
RNC is overseen by a board of directors. Until the
1960s, national committee membership consisted of
two persons from each state (one male, one female). In
1968 the committee was expanded to include state
chairs (a bow to the Republican Party's newfound
southern strength). Under rules adopted in 1988, the
national committee totals 165—including 1 national
committeeman and committeewoman from each state,
the District of Columbia, Guam, Puerto Rico, American Samoa, and the Virgin Islands (110) and the 50
state chairs plus representatives from the District of
Columbia and the U.S. territories (55). Four selection
methods are used: (1) partisan primary election, (2) state
party convention, (3) state party central committee, or
(4) the state party's delegation to the national convention. National committeemen and women serve for
four years; state party chairs serve for the length of
their tenure. A study of committee members conducted in the 1960s found that most were college educated, more than 45 years old, Protestant, and white-
collar professionals (with a high percentage being
lawyers or business owners).

The composition of the RNC reflects its "confederate" nature, as deference is usually given to the mores
of individual state parties. Unlike the Democratic
National Committee, the RNC has refrained from in-
truding into the presidential nominating procedures of
the individual states. To date, the greatest effort to control the presidential nominating contest was made by
the Delegates and Organization Committee (the "DO
Committee"), which was established by the RNC in
1968. Among the DO Committee's recommendations
were (1) open meetings should be held throughout the
delegate selection process in order to assure that all
qualified Republicans could participate in the nominating process; (2) no fees should be assessed against
prospective convention delegates; (3) no proxy voting
should be permitted; (4) "automatic delegates"—that
is, those who became delegates by virtue of holding a
particular party or elective office—should not be
seated; (5) each convention committee should be expanded to include one delegate from each state who is
under 25 years of age and one delegate from a designated minority group; (6) each state should be encouraged to seek equal representation between men and
women in its national convention delegation; (7) states
should be required to seek delegate representation by
persons less than 25 years of age in proportion to their
voting strength in the general population; and (8) the
RNC should assist states in their efforts to inform citizens on the delegate selection process. The 1972
Republican National Convention adopted all of the
DO Committee's recommendations with the exception
of that calling for proportional representation of
young people. But the RNC has refrained from further
intrusion into state delegate selection procedures.
With so many states scheduling their presidential primaries in the first few months of 1996, however, Haley
Barbour has proposed another RNC-sponsored commission to examine delegate selection procedures with
an eye toward greater national party control.

John K. White

BIBLIOGRAPHY

Bibby, John F. "Party Renewal in the National Republican
Party." In *Party Renewal in America: Theory and Practice*, ed.
Gerald M. Pomper. New York: Praeger, 1981.

Bibby, John F., and Robert J. Huckshorn. "Out-Party Strategy:
Republican National Committee Rebuilding Politics,
1964–1966." In *Republican Politics: The 1964 Campaign and Its
Aftermath for the Party*, ed. Bernard Cosman and Robert J.
Huckshorn. New York: Praeger, 1968.

Bone, Hugh A. *Party Committees and National Politics.* Seattle:
University of Washington Press, 1958.

Committee for Party Renewal. *Party Line.* February 1983.

Cotter, Cornelius P., and John F. Bibby. "Institutional

Development of Parties and the Thesis of Party Decline."
Political Science Quarterly 95 (Spring 1980): 1–27.

Cotter, Cornelius P., and Bernard C. Hennessy. *Politics without Power: The National Party Committees.* New York: Atherton Press, 1964.

Freeman, Jo. "The Political Culture of the Democrats and Republicans." *Political Science Quarterly* 101 (1986): 327–356.

Goldman, Ralph M. *The National Party Chairmen and Committees.* Armonk, NY: M.E. Sharpe, 1990.

Herrnson, Paul S. *Party Campaigning in the 1980s.* Cambridge: Harvard University Press, 1988.

Kayden, Xandra, and Eddie Mahe Jr. *The Party Goes On: The Persistence of the Two-Party System in the United States.* New York: Basic Books, 1985.

Klinkner, Philip A. *The Losing Parties: Out-Party National Committees, 1956–1993.* New Haven: Yale University Press, 1994.

Reichley, A. James. *The Life of the Parties.* New York: Free Press, 1992.

School Prayer

Although members of the Republican Party as a whole have been more inclined to support a school prayer amendment than have their Democratic brethren, the party has by no means stood unified on the issue.

School prayer has split Republicans in Congress largely along conservative–moderate lines, but that is not to say that all conservatives support it while all moderates do not. On an issue as deeply personal as religion, elected Republicans—including both those in Congress and those in past administrations—have often been impelled by personal reasons, ideologies, or beliefs to either support or denounce freedom of prayer in public schools. Their positions have also been swayed by historical or legal arguments.

The issue, long at the margins of U.S. political history, took center stage after the 1982 election of conservative Republican President Ronald Reagan, who proposed an amendment to remove the legal barrier to prayer in public schools, making him the first chief executive to turn the country's attention to the issue. The Supreme Court banned prayer from public schools in the 1960s.

After Reagan's proposal, some of the most intensive lobbying of the 1980s took place as right-wing Christian fundamentalists rallied behind the amendment. But fierce opposition from liberal, Protestant, and Jewish organizations kept proponents from amassing the required votes to secure passage.

Reagan's proposal quickly divided the Republican Party as the Senate debated the president's proposal in 1984. Ultraconservative Republican Senators Jesse Helms of North Carolina, a long-time supporter of school prayer, and Orrin G. Hatch of Utah played forceful roles in the drive to pass the legislation. They were backed by conservatives Alan Simpson of Wyoming and William V. Roth of Delaware.

Among the conservatives who opposed the school prayer plan was Arlen Specter of Pennsylvania.

Many moderate Republicans fought against Reagan's amendment. Both of Oregon's moderate senators, Bob Packwood and Mark O. Hatfield, argued against it, as did John C. Danforth of Missouri and William S. Cohen of Maine. Lowell P. Weicker, a moderate-to-liberal Republican who later served as the Independent governor of Connecticut, strongly contested the amendment throughout the debate. Slade Gorton of Washington also resisted it.

Moderate conservatives argued that the amendment would render prayer insignificant by diluting it to serve the diverse religions represented in America's schools or would be used as religious indoctrination by the dominant majority. Some also maintained that it would violate the country's tradition of separation between church and state. Besides, they said, it would for all practical purposes be impossible to implement such legislation.

Conservatives cited the omnipresence of God in the classroom and the right of students to pray to Him. And they rebutted the moderates by maintaining that local communities could be entrusted to resolve the problem of implementing the amendment and the possibility of trivializing prayer. They contended that the federal government should not place limits of expression on local communities.

Although Congress rejected the school prayer amendment, it passed the Equal Access Act of 1984, which prohibits school districts from discriminating against high school religious clubs. Religious Right lobbyists and ultraconservative Republicans viewed the act as a partial victory.

In the mid-1990s, the Christian Coalition revived the issue of school prayer, pushing a Religious Equality Amendment to the Constitution that would allow expression of religion in such public forums as schools. The amendment has received the blessing of ultraconservative Representative Newt Gingrich of Georgia, the Speaker of the House, and his more moderate Republican colleague Robert Dole of Kansas, the Senate majority leader until June 1996 and a 1996 presidential candidate.

Steve Hoenisch

SEE ALSO Religion

BIBLIOGRAPHY

Bacon, Donald C., Roger H. Davidson, and Morton Keller, eds. *The Encyclopedia of the United States Congress.* New York: Simon and Schuster, 1995.

Fenwick, Lynda Beck. *Should the Children Pray: A Historical, Judicial, and Political Examination of Public School Prayer.* Waco, TX: Baylor University Press, 1989.

Social Security

The Republican Party takes credit for emphasizing the fiscal integrity of Social Security as a program of the U.S. government and for efforts to strengthen state, local, and voluntary efforts to promote social welfare policies. Indeed, before the enactment of Social Security as a government program, and sometimes since, most Republicans argued that providing social welfare was a responsibility of the private sector. Social welfare programs are still a patchwork of national efforts, state efforts, and private efforts. Leaders of the Republican Party have tried to ensure that increases in Social Security taxes have kept pace with increases in benefits.

The founders of the Republican Party saw social welfare more as something to be provided by individuals free of government interference than as something to be provided by government.

Indeed, the notion that ours was a nation of joiners, many of whom came to America because individual initiative was valued and government interference was not, was important in American culture. But during the Great Depression many people saw the limits to individual initiative and voluntary organization. People who thought of themselves as great successes realized just how vulnerable they were to the whims of the marketplace.

Most increases in spending on social programs came during periods of social unrest, the Progressive era at the beginning of the twentieth century, the New Deal period of the 1930s, and during the Great Society of the 1960s. Thus the Republican Party tended not to attack all efforts to promote social welfare programs but to argue that there were more practical means than those proposed by the Democrats.

One program, however, that Republicans were more likely to support than were Democrats was the old-age and disability pensions given to veterans of the Civil War. As the veterans died, so too did the programs. Republicans were likely to oppose most other schemes for having the government aid unemployed people of the 1800s as "wild-eyed" and "impractical." These included an Independent Party proposal in 1876 that workers without jobs settle western lands and be employed on government improvement projects; an 1878 Greenback–Labor Party proposal that the unemployed be aided through loans, public works programs, and

settlement in the West; and various ideas of the influential American socialist Edward Bellamy.

During World War I, Britain, perhaps America's staunchest ally, extended unemployment insurance to cover munitions workers and others involved in support of the war effort. Eventually, benefits were extended to cover all British workers, who came to see them as an entitlement, rather than a privilege.

The advancement of industrialism and capitalism was accompanied by the declining influence of families, churches, and even civic mindedness, so many Democrats were skeptical about the ability of the nongovernmental "social safety net" to provide for the social welfare of all Americans. Certain risks and obligations would not be borne by private insurance companies or by other institutions; in the face of this vacuum, government was a last and necessary resort.

Social welfare was guaranteed or proposed for limited groups of Americans by several laws enacted or introduced prior to the Social Security Act of 1935. In 1917, the Robinson–Keating bill proposed federal grants-in-aid and a cooperative federal–state–local administration. In 1933, the Wagner–Peyser Act created the U.S. Employment Service, which would later be transferred to the Social Security Board, within the Department of Labor.

The congressional election of 1934 saw a decisive Republican loss. Third parties to the far left of the Republicans and even to the left of the Democrats now held ten seats in the House of Representatives and two in the Senate. The question was no longer whether the government should be involved in promoting social welfare, but how. The election was in part a mandate for the New Deal policies of Franklin Delano Roosevelt and a sign that there was not much public opposition to a government rule in providing social welfare, but also in part a sign that there was public sentiment for more decisive change.

The Social Security Act was passed in 1935 and was signed into law by President Franklin Roosevelt. Originally it meant a 1% tax on payrolls, which has since increased to many times that amount. When passed, it was even viewed by some of its staunchest advocates as a temporary relief measure and a response to a crisis, rather than as a permanent entitlement.

Instead of withering away, in the later years of the twentieth century, demands for public assistance became greater, and leaders of the Republican Party were more likely to oppose the size of the changes, rather than the changes themselves. Indeed, instead of limiting the program, Roosevelt and Truman's successor, Republican President Dwight D. Eisenhower, accepted it.

A major issue has always been what percentage of

Social Security revenues should come from the worker, and what percentage from the government. This helps determine the degree to which income is redistributed or the program functions like a bank account, with those with higher incomes putting in more and taking out more. Among the two major parties, Republicans have leaned toward the latter view, Democrats the former.

For example, when Republican President Gerald Ford proposed in his 1976 State of the Union address that Social Security taxes be increased, Democratic Congressman Al Ullman of Oregon countered that there should instead be a new tax on commercial transactions.

Particularly influential in the act's adoption was President Roosevelt, who faced little outright Republican opposition when he observed in his 1933 inaugural, "I see a third of a nation ill-fed, ill-clad, and ill-housed." Roosevelt's "Four Freedoms" speech also indicated that "freedom from want" was a major reason for fighting World War II. He felt that enactment of the Social Security Act had been a significant step toward providing that freedom at home.

Partly because a federal government guarantee was new in the United States, some Republicans branded Democratic supporters as communists, or at least as dupes helping to establish an important step on the agenda of Karl Marx. Indeed, some in the administration did see the act as an important step forward in establishing a Bill of Economic Rights, to accompany the civil and political guarantees of the Bill of Rights.

Members of the Republican Party have not been united in their responses to the Social Security Act. Some became reluctant supporters, while others became critical opponents. Still others argued that social welfare could be guaranteed in a better way, such as through the states.

Changes at the national level were followed by programs in the states, many of them opposed by some Republicans. In general the states were slow to act (Wisconsin was the only state with an unemployment insurance program) and, as with the federal Social Security statute, did very little to redistribute wealth.

Republican leaders tended to accept several amendments to the Social Security Act to broaden coverage, which, in many cases, were successful. These include the 1956 introduction of disability insurance (blindness was covered in the original legislation) and Medicare for senior citizens. Earlier amendments, made in 1939, were also designed to ensure that benefits were not strictly proportioned to contributions.

In 1972, many Republicans were unsuccessful in opposing efforts to index Social Security benefits to infla-

tion. In fact, because benefits were to rise 1% faster than the Consumer Price Index, it was charged that they, too, were a source of inflation.

Key constituencies of the Republican Party are skeptical of government efforts to provide social welfare. Many businesses found their obligations to be onerous, while some taxpayers' groups resented the ever-higher taxes. Also, some interest groups resented the intrusion of government into functions previously performed by religious groups and other charities.

When the Social Security Act was adopted, important pressure groups argued that the Democrats should have gone further. These included the American Association for Old Age Security, later the American Association for Social Security (AASS). The AASS wanted a more comprehensive system, one like the British one. Earlier the AASS had complained: "Our present American doles are degrading and niggardly; British insurance payments are self-respecting and three times as adequate." For its part, the *London Times* welcomed the act's passage, saying that if it had been in force before the depression, the effects would not have been as swift or severe.

When the act was adopted, there was serious question whether it, and similar statutes introduced in various states, would be consistent with state and federal constitutions. But just as other federal institutions became more accepting of the increased governmental role, so too did the judiciary. Many federal judges were appointed by the Roosevelt administration but opposed by many Republicans, and tended to find provisions of the act constitutional.

State judges appointed by Democratic governors, and even those appointed by Republican governors, had every incentive to find the act consistent with their state constitutions, since if they did not, it would only mean that other states, and not theirs, would receive federal funds.

Particularly significant were two cases, *Steward Machine Company* v. *Davis* and *Helvering* v. *Davis*, for both of which Justice Cardozo wrote the majority (5–4) opinions. In the latter case, Justice Cardozo disagreed with many Republicans, but agreed with Democrats who argued that there were lessons to be learned from 1929 and that one of these was that the federal Congress must be able to legislate for the general welfare.

A later legal question concerned the applicability of the Due Process Clause of the Constitution to Social Security benefits. For example, was there a constitutional right to property in money paid into the Social Security fund, and was there a constitutional right to an evidentiary hearing prior to the termination of Social Security benefits? The answer of the Supreme

Court, expressed in *Flemming* v. *Nestor* and *Mathews* v. *Eldridge*, was no. Speaking for a majority of the Court in the latter case, Justice Powell differentiated between welfare benefits and Social Security benefits, contending that "the disabled worker's need is likely to be less than that of a welfare recipient." Significantly, the two dissenters in the *Mathews* case, Justices Brennan and Marshall, argued that in many cases, Social Security benefits can be very significant, and an evidentiary hearing should be available prior to their termination. Most Republicans would disagree with them.

In comparison to other industrialized countries, the Social Security Act in the United States is rather meager. Indeed, many Republicans expressed fears of additional protections that might be granted and of efforts to have existing protections widened. They would dislike a system more like New Zealand's, for instance, in which medical care is guaranteed, and that has the effect of redistributing income downward. In the United States, by contrast, most medical care is privately paid for and provided, and some individuals go without, choosing to use their limited income for other things.

Cross-national comparisons lend support to the idea that the Republican Party would be supportive of government social welfare guarantees. Labor and Social Democratic parties and governments tend to be more supportive of government programs than are parties and governments representing business or propertied classes.

Programs have very seldom given rights to the powerless. Indeed it is precisely because many recipients of Social Security benefits demand that the benefits be retained or broadened that many Republican officeholders will adapt their policies to get reelected. Especially those representing an aging constituency have their political futures determined by how they vote on Social Security issues. And because most voters hope to be recipients of Social Security benefits, many Republican politicians will have self-interested motivations, rather than charitable ones, for voting that appropriations be continued or increased.

Some of the differences are no doubt cultural, but others have to do with the political structure. In the United States, power is divided so that even if key constituencies placing a priority on comprehensive social welfare are able to obtain positions of leadership within the Republican Party, their opponents are able to block change. Indeed, Republican opponents of reform measures have consistently been able to block major changes.

One important difference between countries is in competing notions of civil rights and human rights.

The French Declaration of the Rights of Man of 1789 describes public assistance as a "sacred debt."

By contrast, the American Declaration of Independence proclaimed individuals' inalienable rights to "life, liberty, and the pursuit of happiness," and the Bill of Rights emphasizes freedom from government. Even when Democratic President Jimmy Carter urged (unsuccessfully) that the United States join most other industrial nations by ratifying the United Nations Covenant on Economic, Social and Cultural Rights, he proposed reservations indicating that in the United States many social services were to be provided by individuals or by agencies other than the federal government. This was in response to the urging of Republican leaders, who would block efforts at major change.

In the 1990s, many Republicans joined Democrats in their concern over the budget deficit. A bipartisan commission, co-chaired by Bob Kerrey, an influential Democratic senator from Nebraska, and Missouri Republican Senator John Danforth, proposed, among other things, that the minimum age for receiving old-age Social Security benefits from the government be raised from 65 to 67. This change, the commission indicated, would save billions of dollars a year. The commission's proposed changes were induced largely by demographic factors: more people were considered to be of "old age" than ever before, thanks to advances in health care; they were likely to live longer; and there were not enough people of "working age" to support them.

Another major change was the popularity of work requirements, more popular among Republicans than among Democrats. In the United States, unlike in most other industrialized countries, the Social Security Administration deals with those labeled as "beyond working age" and people with disabilities. People without disabilities who are considered of working age are handled mainly by welfare systems administered by the states, many of which have work requirements for eligibility.

Just as Republican politicians at the national level were likely to argue that government programs of social services should be more fiscally responsible, so too were Republican politicians at state and local levels. In the rhetoric of the political battlefield, this meant that they were critical of "bleeding hearts" but in turn were accused by their opponents of being "heartless." They were likely to cite the unfairness or atypicality of examples of individuals who ate dog food or died of heat exhaustion because they could not afford other groceries or purchase a fan on their meager Social Security earnings. They were likely to argue that more should be spent on the military, which would mean that less could be spent for domestic purposes such as social security. They would criticize people like Democratic President Lyndon Johnson and his followers, who would argue that we could have both "guns and butter."

Certain prominent politicians came to be identified in the public mind as "friends" or "enemies" of Social Security. Republican President Ronald Reagan, before and during his presidency, was identified with remarks he had made early in his political career suggesting that Social Security should be made voluntary. In other words, an individual could choose not to participate, not to have contributions deducted from his or her paycheck, and not to have them matched by the employer. In contrast, many prominent opponents of the Republican Party sought to be identified as "friends" of the Social Security program. One who succeeded was New York Senator Daniel Patrick Moynihan, who engaged in many legislative efforts to keep the program viable. On the other hand, Moynihan took the unpopular position, shared by many Republicans, that the Social Security Administration be taken "off the budget," in other words, the program must not be allowed to operate at a deficit, to be made up for elsewhere.

In fact, Social Security benefits tended to rise at a rate greater than the rate of inflation. Between 1970 and 1975, for example, the Consumer Price Index increased 40%, while Social Security benefits increased 58%.

Many prominent Republican politicians, though, were frightened by calls for new initiatives with government involvement in areas considered as "social security" elsewhere, but not in the United States. With staunch Republican opposition, Democratic President Bill Clinton and Senator Edward Kennedy sought unsuccessfully to increase massively the federal government's involvement in health care. Many Republicans also fought the efforts of others, concerned about the great disparity in state programs of workers' compensation and unemployment, who sought to have them moved to the federal level.

A big question was how Social Security programs could best be administered, especially as they got bigger. With the creation of a separate Department of Education, the Department of Health, Education, and Welfare became the Department of Health and Human Services. Eventually, in the 1990s, the Social Security Administration became an independent agency. Although there was bipartisan support for the changes, leadership came from members of the Democratic Party. Coordination of the monumental tasks of social welfare had long been recognized as a problem. Soon

after the Social Security Act became law, President Franklin Roosevelt formed a special interdepartmental coordinating committee, including administrators from the Public Health Service, and the Departments of the Interior, Agriculture, and Labor.

As voters toward the end of the twentieth century were likely to complain that their taxes were too high, leading Republican politicians sought to ensure that Social Security would not be rolled back or frozen. Importantly, though, the debate was no longer over whether government had a role in guaranteeing social welfare; it was instead over how great that role should be.

The battle between Social Security as an assistance program, redistributing wealth, and as an insurance program, serving essentially as a bank account, was a divisive one, within and between the major parties. Since the program's enactment, members of the Democratic Party were more likely to be protective of the assistance features of the program, members of the Republican Party of the insurance features. For instance, when Republican President Gerald Ford proposed a small increase in payroll taxes in 1976, Democratic legislative leaders balked because an increase in the payroll tax, while it might make for a sounder insurance program, would not redistribute wealth. Similarly, Ford once proposed a ceiling on increases in benefits, which was rejected by Democratic leaders in the Senate because the proposed increase was less than the rate of inflation. Because Social Security was a popular program, Ford reversed himself.

During the administration of Republican President Ronald Reagan, members of the executive and legislative branches again became alarmed that increases in Social Security expenditures exceeded increases in revenues. A commission headed by Robert Dole of Kansas reccommended that payroll taxes be increased, a strategy that has generally been preferred by Republicans to funding from general revenues.

Some Republicans chose to attack Social Security by arguing from anecdote. Congressman Newt Gingrich, for example, referred to 40 Denver alcoholics who had their disability checks mailed to a liquor store.

Most voters made a distinction between social programs, which they did like, and welfare programs, which they did not. In both cases, Republicans would often oppose changes, taking into account the rising cost of living, and would be likely to be portrayed in their attempts to cut benefits as "mean." They disagreed with Democrats who argued that it was unrealistic to expect churches and voluntary agencies to do everything that government did not. At the close of the twentieth century they tended to find limiting government expenditures for all purposes, including

Social Security, to be one of their most effective campaign issues.

Arthur Blaser

SEE ALSO Welfare

BIBLIOGRAPHY

Epstein, Abraham. *Insecurity: A Challenge to America; a Study of Social Insurance in the U.S. and Abroad.* New York: H. Smith and R. Hoar, 1933.

Lampmann, Robert J., ed. *Social Security Perspectives: Essays in Honor of Edwin E. Witte.* Madison: University of Wisconsin, 1962.

Lubove, Roy. *The Struggle for Social Security, 1900–1935.* Cambridge: Harvard University Press, 1968.

Richards, Raymond. *Closing the Door to Destitution: The Shaping of the Social Security Acts of the United States and New Zealand.* University Park: Pennsylvania State University Press, 1994.

States' Rights

While Republicans and their predecessors have always considered federalism a valid feature of the U.S. political system, throughout most of the party's history, they have favored the expansion of federal or national governmental power to promote traditional Republican goals, ordered liberty and economic growth. Federalists, National Republicans, Whigs, and early Republicans believed that a strong central government was necessary to provide the proper climate for economic prosperity. As the Democrats began to dominate the national government after the Great Depression, however, Republicans began to view states' rights as a way to reduce the size of federal governmental spending and eliminate harmful regulations. Republicans also advocated the return of power to the states to reduce federal governmental interference with liberty. Therefore, while early Republicans favored the development of an active national government to support economic goals, modern Republicans have attempted to reduce the size and power of the federal government. Traditional Republican values have remained constant, however. Paradoxically, as Republicans embraced states' rights, Democrats abandoned their traditional support for the doctrine and converted to a positive theory of national government. Like early Republicans, modern Democrats support the development of an active national government, but for different reasons. Whereas early Republicans sought to promote economic prosperity and growth, Democrats have attempted to use the federal government to achieve social and political equality. To paraphrase Abraham Lincoln, when it comes to states' rights, the two modern political parties are indeed wearing each other's clothes (means) but have stayed in their original bodies (ends).

Early Republicans adopted the northern Whig position on states' rights and the proper role of the national government that originated with the National Republican theory of government predicated on the beliefs of the Federalist Party. Consequently, an overview of Federalist, National Republican, and Whig interpretations of states' rights and the proper role of the national government are presented here before the Republican position is discussed.

Alexander Hamilton is the architect of traditional Republican views on states' rights and the role of the national government. During President Washington's administration, Hamilton, in his position as secretary of the treasury, proposed an ambitious economic plan centered on the federal government. Hamilton argued that if the United States was going to prosper, its credit would have to be sound to encourage investments. Therefore, the national government should assume all previous foreign, national, and state debts. Hamilton admitted that by having the national government pay state government obligations, the federal government would become more powerful at the expense of the state governments. Hamilton proposed a federal tariff to protect and subsidize manufacturers. Consequently, manufacturing interests would be loyal to the central government rather than state governments. While Hamilton won the support of President Washington, Thomas Jefferson and James Madison vigorously attacked his plans, asserting that Hamilton was attempting to sabotage the principles of a representative government, infringe on liberty, and restore a monarchy.

The congressional debate over Hamilton's plans in 1790 and 1791 revealed a deep division among the nation's representatives. Hamilton and his supporters believed that a strong central government was essential to protect the nation and to provide the requisites for economic growth. The Federalists also argued that the national government should be biased toward the interests of commerce and manufacturing and be guided by the wealthy and educated members of society who were better equipped to govern ("the wise, and the good, and the rich"). Conversely, Jefferson and his supporters advocated protection of states' rights and a minimal role for the federal government based on a strict interpretation of the U.S. Constitution. The Federalists were able to pass key elements of Hamilton's plans over mounting Democratic-Republican opposition. The federal government paid its debts and imposed tariffs on some imported goods. Congress also established the First National Bank of the United States to serve as the country's central financial institution.

The Federalist philosophy regarding the need for a strong central government was adopted by leading officials in the Adams administration, who continued to take their orders from Hamilton. After the XYZ Affair in 1797, the Federalists established a provisional army paid for by federal taxes and used the power of the national government to repress its critics under the Sedition Act of 1798. Ironically, after the Democratic-Republicans became the dominant party in 1800, they accepted major aspects of their opponents' positions including the provisional army and tariffs.

The Federalists also left one other important legacy, Chief Justice John Marshall, who continued to espouse Federalist principles long after the party had dissolved. Throughout his tenure on the U.S. Supreme Court (1801 to 1835) Marshall promoted the establishment and expansion of federal power and limited the power of state courts and governments by broadly interpreting the national supremacy and implied powers clauses of the Constitution. Consequently, the Federalist position on states' rights and the proper role of the national government provided a strong foundation for the Republican Party.

During the Era of Good Feelings, sectional differences regarding states' rights divided the Democratic-Republican party. Key officials in the Monroe administration including Henry Clay and John C. Calhoun advocated the American system, which called for federal power to nurture U.S. industry and promote commerce. Elements of the system included federally financed internal improvements, another national bank, and a protective tariff. The expansion of federal power angered western and southern Democratic-Republicans, who favored states' rights and a limited role for the national government. During the Monroe and John Quincy Adams administrations, northern National Republicans were able to charter the Second Bank of the United States in 1816 and pass high protective tariffs designed to protect U.S. manufacturers over the objections of southern legislators in 1824, 1828, and 1832, respectively.

When Jackson and his Democratic Party gained control of Congress in 1826 and the presidency in 1828, they declared war on the Second Bank, which they considered a tool of commercial interests in the northeastern states. Nevertheless, Jackson supported the constitutionality of the tariff and condemned South Carolina's nullification ordinance of 1832. The Whig Party developed as a reaction to Jackson's dismantling

of the bank in 1832 and his stand against nullification. Consequently, the Whig Party was divided over states' rights and slavery at its inception. Southern Whigs favored states' rights and slavery, while northern Whigs supported the American system, an expansion of federal power, and opposed slavery. In the 1840s and 1850s partisan and sectional differences concerning states' rights centered on slavery rather than economic issues. The Whig Party, despite its remarkable electoral success, failed to develop a unified position regarding slavery and states' rights and disintegrated.

The Republican Party, which formed as a response to slavery, also endorsed the northern Whig economic program of higher tariffs and federally financed internal improvements. During the Civil War, Lincoln maintained that the Union and the power of the national government must be preserved with military force and limitation of states' rights. Republicans also instituted the American system with an unprecedented body of legislation including the National Banking, Agricultural College, and Homestead Acts and charters for five railroads.

Republican rule after the war resulted in unparalleled federal governmental favoritism toward business and corporations as Republican leaders developed a mutually beneficial interlocking relationship with corporate leaders. Fraud and graft were widespread as unscrupulous politicians and businessmen used federal and state governmental power to further their interests. In the 1870s a reform movement was initiated in the Republican Party to end corruption in the federal government, reform the Civil Service, reduce the tariff, and remove military occupation forces in the South.

At the turn of the century, party divisions concerning the proper role of the national government revolved around the necessity of a tariff, control of monopolies, and reforms. President Roosevelt led the Republican Party in a new direction when he initiated policies designed to secure more social justice and insisted that the federal government had the right to control important utilities. Roosevelt also expanded the role of the national government by creating the National Conservation Commission to expand forest reserves and national parks and passing the Meat Inspection and Pure Food and Drug Acts in 1906.

Progressive Republicans felt betrayed when following Republican administrations did not continue Roosevelt's program of federal expansion. In the 1920s, the Republican Party continued to protect U.S. businesses with high tariffs and assisted struggling railroads while the U.S. economy prospered. Despite emergency federal actions by the Hoover administration, however, the party was not able to deal with the stock market crash of 1929 and the Great Depression that followed. During the Roosevelt and Truman administrations, conservative and progressive Republicans resisted what they considered FDR's authoritarian tendencies and the creation of a strong centralized Democratic national government.

After the Republicans won control of the presidency in 1952, President Eisenhower did not attempt to repeal New Deal legislation; however, he tried to limit the role of the national government by reducing taxes and balancing the budget. Eisenhower also called for greater local control of governmental affairs. When the U.S. Supreme Court ordered states to end racial segregation in 1954, the southern states' rights movement gained new momentum. Despite his states' rights position, Eisenhower used federal troops to restore order in Little Rock, Arkansas, and protect the rights of black high school students in 1957.

At the beginning of the 1960s, moderates and conservatives in the Republican Party began to advocate the role of states in the U.S. political system. While moderate Republicans believed that the federal government had a role in meeting public needs, they asserted that it would be more efficient and equitable if state governments managed most service programs. Western conservative Republicans feared and resented the growing power of the national government, which they believed conflicted with liberty and impeded economic growth. Moreover, many western Republicans also disliked the federal government's ownership of huge tracts of land in their states. Southern Republicans resented federal actions to enforce school desegregation and civil rights legislation. Consequently, in the 1960s, the Republican Party began to focus on states' rights. In 1964 the Republican presidential candidate, Barry Goldwater, pledged to uphold states' rights and won many southern votes.

In 1968, many southern Republicans and Democrats, dissatisfied with their respective party's positions on civil rights, supported the third-party candidacy of George Wallace. Nonetheless, Richard Nixon employed a "southern strategy," pledging an increased role for state and local governments to win support. During his first term, Nixon sought to give power back to state and local governments under his New Federalism programs. He reduced federal welfare services, initiated the general revenue-sharing program, and appointed four "strict constructionist" justices to the U.S. Supreme Court.

In the late 1970s, a "sagebrush" rebellion against federal government environmental regulations in the western and southwestern states added to the Republican Party's support of states' rights. In 1980 Ronald Reagan launched an ambitious program to cut government spending and taxes, reduce the size of the federal government, and deregulate businesses and society. A key part of Reagan's New Federalism programs was to give state and local governments more freedom to spend a reduced amount of federal monies. Reagan also terminated the general revenue-sharing program, created a new block grant program, and proposed a "turn back" of programs from the federal to the state governments. President Bush continued the New Federalist programs. For example, in education and transportation, state and local governments assumed more responsibility. Bush also proposed a variety of turnover of federal programs to the states, including Medicaid, AFDC, and Community Development block grants.

New Federalism continues to be an important feature of Republican proposals. For example, in 1994 many Republican candidates for Congress and governorships promised to limit the role of the national government and give greater power to state and local governments. Consequently, modern Republicans have abandoned the party's traditional emphasis on the national government to support economic growth and have adopted a states' rights position to achieve economic progress and liberty.

Janet B. Manspeaker

BIBLIOGRAPHY

Mayer, George. *The Republican Party: 1854–1964*. New York: Oxford University Press, 1964.

Merrill, Horace Samuel, and Marion Galbraith Merrill. *The Republican Command: 1897–1913*. Lexington: University Press of Kentucky, 1971.

Reichley, A. James. *The Life of the Parties*. New York: Free Press, 1992.

Term Limits

Since the movement began to limit the number of terms legislators may serve, members of the Republican Party—activists, officeholders, and voters—have provided the leadership, financial support, and votes for the national movement. The first official statement made by Republicans for legislative term limits was contained in their 1988 national platform adopted in New Orleans prior to that year's general election. Early support from activists such as Republican Eddie Mahe Jr., who founded the political organization Americans to Limit Congressional Terms, provided key resources to launch and continue the effort.

Initially, national Republicans focused on the U.S. Congress, where they noted that more than 90% of members seeking reelection were routinely successful despite well-documented public dissatisfaction with the institution. Congress was a tough target, however, since Democrats could not be expected to vote to limit their own terms, thereby increasing Republican prospects. Some congressional Republicans, such as Mitch McConnell of Kentucky, also were critical. He said that "people should not be denied the right to vote for someone simply because of an arbitrary limit" (McConnell 1995). The early efforts, therefore, began in states where proponents did not have to rely on incumbents limiting themselves.

In December 1990, San Jose, California was the gathering point for term-limit activists from around the nation (for an excellent description, see Rothenberg 1992). During the meeting, they analyzed term-limit efforts and developed future strategies. Provided to advocates was information about how to get a constitutional amendment on the ballot in states with the initiative process (allowing voters to circulate a petition and vote directly on a constitutional amendment); how to raise money for the effort; and how to coordinate and direct the campaigns. The experiences of Colorado, Oklahoma, and California furnished successful case studies for discussion because voters in each of those states passed limitations on their state legislators just a month before the meeting. Colorado voters also agreed to limit the service of a member of Congress, placing six two-year limitations on House members and two six-year limitations on senators. Opponents to this latter provision immediately prepared legal challenges, claiming that the restrictions violated the U.S. Constitution's clause that specifies the legal qualifications for members of Congress.

Term-limit proposals generated such excitement in Republican and conservative activist circles because they simultaneously addressed several issues. First, term limits would help thwart the advantages incumbent officeholders had in defending their seats at elections. Because of government-funded constituency mailings and legislative staff, fund-raising advantages, and public visibility, many thought incumbents faced little prospect of defeat. As Paul Jacob, of U.S. Term Limits (an advocacy group), noted, "The only way an incumbent gets in trouble these days is if he gets his hand caught in the till" (Galvin 1992). Second, term limits were a direct attack on the Democratic Party, since it controlled the majority of state legislative chambers and both houses of Congress. Limits would create "open seats," providing Republican challengers with a better chance of taking the seats and eventually gaining control in the legislatures. And third, term limits just might break up what many thought was an entrenched alliance of lobbyists, career bureaucrats, and self-interested legislators who were a barrier to sound decision making.

A key strategic decision for term-limit advocates was to solicit progressive and Democratic support. In so doing they broadened their base of appeal and deflected charges that the effort was simply a Republican power grab. Among the recruits were Cleta Mitchell, a former Oklahoma Democratic legislator who joined Mahe's group; Ralph Nader, founder and leader of Public Citizen, who gave his group's support; and Jerry Brown, 1992 Democratic presidential aspirant, who made term limits part of his campaign platform.

Following their early successes, term-limit advocates set their sights on other states. They also began to target members of Congress in Washington, where Republicans tried, without success, to limit the service of incumbent legislators retroactively. The initiative would have permitted only one more election for those who had served the maximum number of terms. Democratic Speaker of the House of Representatives Thomas Foley led a successful counterattack by opponents to the proposal, and it was narrowly defeated. Even with that setback, proponents regrouped in Washington, as well as in 13 other states, to pass nonretroactive limits on state and national legislators in 1992. By the turn of the century, this will result in the complete turnover of legislators in about 20 states.

Despite the loss of term-limit advocate and President George Bush to opponent Bill Clinton in 1992, Republican prospects brightened again in 1994 when voters in seven more states passed limits. During that campaign, Republican strategists and candidates targeted congressional Democrats who had come out against term limits, foremost of whom was Tom Foley, who had filed a lawsuit to block implementation of I-573, Washington's 1992 initiative limiting congressional terms. Republican efforts were successful beyond their greatest expectations. Foley was defeated by the unknown George Nethercutt and, nationwide, Republicans picked up 52 House seats and 8 Senate seats, giving them control of Congress.

Republican congressional candidates had placed in their Contract with America a promise to bring a constitutional amendment to a vote if they gained control of the House. In March 1995 they brought up the issue in several different forms. None received the 290 votes necessary to propose the amendment, which, together with two-thirds of senators supporting the measure, would send the amendment to state legislatures for ratification (where it would need the support of 38 states). The amendment offered by Representative Bill McCollum of Florida would have allowed six two-year terms for House members and two six-year terms for senators. It received 227 votes, 63 short of passage. Highlighting their continuing support, Republicans voted for the amendment 189 to 40, Democrats opposed it by 162 to 38. Perhaps because of their new-found power, Republicans favored a 12-year proposal over a 6-year version and a retroactive proposal.

In May 1995 the U.S. Supreme Court made clear that a constitutional amendment was necessary for congressional term limitations when it ruled unconstitutional Washington's, and every other state's, imposed term limit on members of Congress.

Stephen D. Van Beek

BIBLIOGRAPHY

Benjamin, Gerald, and Michael J. Malbin. *Limited Legislative Terms*. Washington, DC: CQ Press, 1992.

Galvin, Thomas. "Limits Score a Perfect 14-for-14, but Court Challenges Loom." *Congressional Quarterly Weekly Report*, November 7, 1992, pp. 3593, 3994.

McConnell, Mitch. "Representation without Limitation." *Washington Post Weekly Edition*, March 27, 1995.

Rogers, David. "Term Limit Campaign Gets Financing Mainly from Wealthy Conservatives." *Wall Street Journal*, November 4, 1992.

Rothenberg, Stuart. "Transplanting Term Limits." In *Limiting Legislative Terms*, ed. Gerald Benjamin and Michael Malbin. Washington, DC: CQ Press, 1992.

U.S. Term Limits, Inc. v. Thornton (115 S.Ct. 1842), 1995.

Will, George. "Presidency Is Not the Top Election." *San Jose Mercury News*, October 1, 1992.

Third Parties

Some historians and many third-party advocates contend that the Republican Party was born in 1854 as a *third* party but then soon intruded itself into the ranks of the national major parties, replacing the Whigs as the principal challengers of the Democrats. If so, the story is unique; no other U.S. third party ever has gone on to achieve national major-party status. It is clear that by the time of Republican birth, the Whig Party, hopelessly divided on slavery and sectionalism, was in a downward spiral toward oblivion. Congressional and presidential election returns from 1856 suggest that the GOP was a major party virtually from the moment of its creation. The Republicans made it, whereas Liberty and Free Soil, two earlier antislavery parties, had not. That too suggests that early-day Republicans benefited mightily from a rising partisan vacuum needing to be filled.

Of the major parties today, the Republicans may be somewhat more idea centered than the Democrats. Some prominent GOP voices seek to make conservative ideology or positions on abortion or some other issue the litmus test for receiving the party's embrace. Even so, it was Republican strategist Lee Atwater who created the "big tent" metaphor for the major parties. Atwater strongly averred that his own party should be an open big tent. The Republican Party is, like the Democratic Party, a coalition of diverse interests. Both major parties exist in service of primarily electoral objectives.

Third parties, in contrast, often expend more of their energies on articulating ideas, even exposing visions of a nation transformed. Some of America's noblest policy innovations first were ideas either conceived by third parties or taken up and pushed by third parties years before Republicans or Democrats grasped their political profitability.

Women were among those who created the Prohibition Party, this nation's oldest still-living third party, in 1869, and women took seats at Prohibition's first national convention. Republicans and Democrats finally placed suffrage planks into their 1916 platforms. Their tardy act had been preceded by the more timely suffrage activism of a half dozen or more third parties.

People who build, lead, and take part in third parties sometimes are motivated by hopes of altering the character of U.S. party politics or of surmounting the barriers that peripheralize them. Desires notwithstanding, third parties have been relegated to the margins, sometimes influencing but rarely if ever entering the political mainstream.

Unloved though they may be, the two relatively nonideological undifferentiated major parties are ingenious in coopting the ideological space occupied by a large majority of the U.S. electorate. Direct primaries and other procedures for open participation encourage dissidents to enter into major parties rather than pursue "quixotic" third-party strategies. It has been suggested too that Americans have tended toward neat division on policy issues (business vs. labor, segregation vs. civil rights, pro-choice vs. pro-life), a bifurcation rationalizing a system of just two major parties.

Structural barriers also disadvantage third parties. Multiparty competition would be encouraged by proportional representation (PR) election systems; it is deterred instead by single-member district, winner-take-all elections, the norm in America. The 1992 electoral college produced no electoral votes for H. Ross Perot, despite the 19% the voters gave him. The Federal Election Campaign Act and other campaign finance laws discriminate substantially against third-party participants. State-imposed barriers to ballot access may be the most formidable structural obstacles in the way of third-party access to the mainstream. Finance and ballot-access legislation is, after all, the creation of Republican and Democratic lawmakers.

Third parties themselves may be characterized by reference to relative distance from the main thrust of political life. *Continuing doctrinal parties* (sometimes designated "minor" parties) exist for decades far removed, their longevity undergirded by commitment to, and the radicalism of, party doctrine. Communists, Libertarians, and other doctrinal parties sometimes *have* claimed loyalty among important sectors of the body politic. Issues raised by doctrinal parties are occasionally appropriated by one or both major parties, thus influencing the policy process. But doctrinal party voter strength has determined electoral outcomes only rarely. Never has the presidential tally of a doctrinal party candidate exceeded the 6% taken in 1912 by Socialist Eugene V. Debs.

There also are the *non-national parties*. This is the type of third party that may become significant, even a *major* party, in the politics of a community or an entire state, but that either does not seek or does not attain a significant presence in national politics (except perhaps in the U.S. congressional delegation from the particular state). Historic examples abound: the Minnesota Farmer–Labor Party, the Progressive Party of Wisconsin, the American Labor Party in New York. The Farmer–Labor Party, founded at the close of World War I, managed in the 1920s to supplant the Democrats as Minnesota's major opposition to the ruling state GOP. For several of the 1930s depression years Farmer–Labor enjoyed the status of ruling party in Minnesota. In 1944, the Minnesota Democratic and Farmer–Labor parties formally merged. To this day, Democrats run against Republicans in Minnesota on the DFL ballot line.

The electoral strength and influence of the Progressive Coalition of Burlington, Vermont, produced in that city the only true three-party system existing in the United States in the 1980s and 1990s. Burlington's Republicans and Democrats, known to some as Republicrats, sometimes coalesce, offering a single nominee in opposition to the Progressives.

The significance of partisan New York Liberals, Conservatives, and Right-to-Lifers late in the twentieth century has been largely the result of an extraordinary New York state cross-endorsement provision allowing a candidate's name to appear on the ballot as the nominee of more than one party. Frequently Conservatives and Right-to-Lifers endorse or nominate Republican nominees. Sometimes one of those

natural allies of the Republicans runs a separate campaign. Some prominent national and New York Republicans gave tacit support to the successful 1970 U.S. Senate campaign of Conservative James L. Buckley, even though Buckley's opponents included an incumbent Republican.

The most formidable partisan challenge to Republican and Democratic domination of mainstream politics comes from the nationally organized *transient* or *short-lived parties*. These parties' rise is meteoric, often indicating dysfunction or failure in major-party ranks. The Know-Nothings of the 1850s and the Populists four decades later almost achieved national major-party status.

Some transient parties originate as protest movements. Others secede from one or the other major party. The participation of the Southern Democrats, a secessionist splinter from the national Democratic Party, in the presidential election of 1860 helped secure the defeat of national Democrat Stephen A. Douglas by Republican Abraham Lincoln. The secession of Theodore Roosevelt's Bull Moose Progressives from the GOP sealed the 1912 victory of Democrat Woodrow Wilson; Bull Moose was the only third party ever to beat a major party for second place in a presidential vote.

The short lives of these parties, their defining characteristic, indicates vulnerability but also their clout. Voter appeal by a transient party often poses the threat that it will determine election outcome. Neutralizing the threat means appropriating what appeals. Major parties thus gobble up transient parties' popular policy demands. The Republican Party adopted its southern strategy and began to redefine itself as compatible with that strategy primarily to neutralize the 1968 threat from George Wallace's American Independent Party. AIP thus affected major-party relationships and the relative popularity and influence of Republicans and Democrats for all the years since.

In the nineteenth century, before state-printed secret ballots made it impossible to do so, a major and a transient party sometimes fused in a unified presidential campaign. The Liberal Republican Party of the early 1870s was the first party originating as a movement in secession from the GOP. Democrats in 1872 nominated Liberal Republican nominee Horace Greeley and adopted the Liberal Republican platform verbatim. Populists in 1896 nominated the Democratic nominee William Jennings Bryan, who went down to defeat against Republican William McKinley. In joining with the Bryan Democrats, Populists charted their own third-party's course to extinction. The classic case of big-fish-swallows-small, the Democratic-Populist story also bears testimony to third-party clout and potential. Bryan-era Democrats devoured the Populists by incorporating almost every important element of the Populist platform. No other third party ever has matched Populist success in affecting the nation's public policy.

As the nation approached the twenty-first century, the window of third-party opportunity was more widely open than at any time since the 1930s. Opinion polls in the 1990s showed a breakdown in belief in public institutions, especially in the legitimacy of the major parties. Most Americans said they longed for a third *major* party in competition with Republicans and Democrats.

Connecticut and Maine elected third-party governors, both renegade former Republicans, in 1990. An Independent took the 1994 gubernatorial race in Maine. Ross Perot, who took the third-highest percentage ever for a non-major-party presidential candidate in 1992 (the highest for any such candidate not running as an ex-president), regrouped his forces and organized the Reform Party in 1996. Libertarians, Greens, Progressives, and Independents held elective offices in places scattered nationwide.

In the 1990s there was serious third-party talk by, or centered on, prominent people: Colin Powell, Bill Bradley, Paul Tsongas, Lowell Weicker, Pat Buchanan, Jesse Jackson, and others. Many of these people had come to politics through the Republican or the Democratic Party. Some were well-known liberals or conservatives. But many of the most persistent advocates of third-party creation in the 1990s wanted a centrist party. Now, they said, the Republicans and Democrats had become *too* polarized, *too* partisan. Success seemed most likely to reach the grasp of some new party that would, in articulating its vision, combine fiscal conservatism with a liberal outlook on choice and lifestyle issues.

J. David Gillespie

BIBLIOGRAPHY

Black, Gordon S., and Benjamin D. Black. *The Politics of American Discontent: How a New Party Can Make Democracy Work Again.* New York: Wiley, 1994.

Gillespie, J. David. *Politics at the Periphery: Third Parties in Two-Party America.* Columbia: University of South Carolina Press, 1993.

Hesseltine, William B. *Third-Party Movements in the United States.* Princeton: Princeton University Press, 1962.

Mazmanian, William A. *Third Parties in Presidential Elections.* Washington, DC: Brookings Institution, 1973.

Rosenstone, Steven J., Roy L. Behr, and Edward H. Lazarus. *Third Parties in America: Citizen Response to Major Party Failure.* Princeton: Princeton University Press, 1984.

Tort Reform

The current tort system encompasses two general and previously separate categories of injuries. The first occurs when the injured and injurer have no prior relationship. The best example from this category is a car accident. The second category is when the injured and injurer have some previous relationship, such as doctor–patient, employer–employee, and manufacturer–consumer.

Until fairly recently, these two categories of injury cases had been handled differently. The former was under tort law—an area of the common law—while the latter was an aspect of contract law. Since the 1960s, however, in two state injury cases, *Henningsen* v. *Bloomfield Motors* in New Jersey and *Greenman* v. *Yuba Power Products Co.* in California, the contract aspect has given way to the tort law. In these cases, privity (a contractual term limiting damages payments to direct purchasers of a product) was removed and replaced with strict liability for product-related injuries, even if the parties specified another standard for liability.

As a result of these changes, the state and federal courts in recent years have witnessed an unprecedented growth in personal injury lawsuits. The flood of litigation involves medical malpractice, unsafe products, and environmental hazards. Jury awards and out-of-court settlements have led to an increase in premiums for liability insurance or the withdrawal of coverage completely.

For more than a decade, Republicans have attempted to reform the tort system of the United States. They have argued that the costs of litigation have driven up the cost of insurance and consumer goods. It is estimated that 2.5% of the cost of the average product is built into the price to offset potential liability claims. With certain items—stepladders and vaccines—the percentage is as high as 95% of the consumer price. In addition, both innovation and jobs have been lost to the growing litigiousness of Americans spurred on by large damage awards. The Senate Commerce Committee reported that two of the three companies that produced the diphtheria-tetanus-pertussis (DTP) vaccine stopped production because of liability costs.

Many groups, including engineers, doctors, municipal governments, small businesses, storeowners, and car rental companies, sought relief from a system that they claimed unfairly exposed them to risk. In his study of American productivity and economic prospects for the future, Vice President Dan Quayle specifically cited tort reform as an important change necessary to increase American business opportunities. According to a 1994 Business Roundtable survey of 20 major U.S. corporations, liability is a major hindrance to productivity. Currently, litigation-related costs account for 4.5% of the gross domestic product.

Several attempts at reform were tried in the 1980s. Republican Senator Robert Kasten of Wisconsin in the 97th Congress attempted to create a federal standard of negligence rather than strict liability. Under this proposed system, manufacturers would have escaped liability if their products met all relevant federal safety standards. The proposal, however, never got out of the Senate Commerce Committee. More recently, Republican Senator John Danforth of Indiana sponsored the Product Liability Reform Bill of 1986, which was voted out of committee but never had a full Senate vote. Similar measures were introduced in the U.S. House of Representatives, where they met with similar fates.

The largest stumbling block for the Republican agenda of tort reform had been Democratic control of Congress. With the ascension of the Republican Party in the 1994 elections, prospects for reform looked good. As part of the Contract with America, Republicans sought to limit punitive damages, force courtroom losers to pay winners' legal fees, and protect defendants from having to pay all the damages in cases where they were only partly responsible for injuries. After passage of a sweeping reform bill in the House of Representatives, however, the legislation was bogged down in the Senate when a coalition of Republicans and Democrats, including bill co-sponsors Republican Senator Slade Gordon of Washington and Democratic Senator John D. "Jay" Rockefeller IV of West Virginia, could not muster the 60 votes necessary to end a Democratic-led filibuster. In the end, a watered-down version of tort reform passed the Senate.

Opposition to tort reform was led by the Association of Trial Lawyers of America (ATLA) and consumer groups, notably Public Citizen, a group founded by consumer activist Ralph Nader. The ATLA used its extensive lobbying power to convince enough senators, mostly Democrats, not to support the measure. The ATLA's influence is considerable among Democrats because it is one of the largest contributors to Democratic campaign coffers. While it does not have a political action committee, ATLA contributed over $56 million to Democratic candidates in 1990 alone. President Bill Clinton considered vetoing any tort reform measure. While the ATLA and President Clinton argued that the Republican bill would have hurt consumers and protected wrongdoers, it is hard to ignore the fact that 30% to 40% of Clinton's 1992 campaign funds came from trial lawyers.

In addition to the force of ATLA and consumer groups, Democratic senators threatened to add an amendment forcing tobacco companies to pay for Medicare costs attributed to smoking. This threat helped to scare off enough senators, preventing the passage of the more sweeping House version.

Critics of the Republican plan for tort reform attacked the GOP's attempt to impose a single federal standard on tort law. These critics cite the fact that central to the Contract with America is returning power to the states. They argue that tort law has been a fundamental area of state regulation and that to change this situation is at a minimum inconsistent with the Republicans' stated philosophy. In fact, according to opponents, many states have enacted legislation that would limit punitive damages and frivolous lawsuits.

Republicans respond to this charge of inconsistency by citing the fact that tort law often involves interstate commerce, which is the sole domain of the national government. Republicans argue that interstate commerce is stifled because of the state-based liability rulings. In fact, they want the tort system to reflect the market in that liability insurance rates are currently set at a national level by insurance companies. Therefore, to set tort standards at the national level follows the dictates of market forces. Additionally, they argue that loss of jobs through company relocations to other countries must be dealt with at the national level. Republicans cite cases such as Johnson Controls, which moved its battery manufacturing facilities to Mexico because of increased risk of being sued by American employees.

In the end, the traditional Republican argument of devolution and federalism gives way to a compelling interstate commerce issue that cannot be resolved on a state-by-state basis.

Jeffrey D. Schultz
Diane L. Schultz

BIBLIOGRAPHY

Abraham, Spencer. "The Federal Case for National Tort Reform." *Policy Review*, no. 73 (Summer 1995).

Bogus, Carl T. "The Contract and the Consumer." *American Prospect*, no. 21 (Spring 1995): 53–57.

Reske, Henry. "A Classic Battle of Loyalists." *ABA Journal* 81 (June 1, 1995): 22.

Rubin, Paul H. *Tort Reform by Contract*. Washington, DC: AEI Press, 1993.

Trade Policy

Major partisan and sectional disagreements over trade policy, particularly over the level of tariffs, have been an interesting feature of U.S. politics. While both parties recognized the necessity of tariffs after the War of

1812, Republicans and their predecessors generally advocated high tariffs to stimulate industrialization, and Democrats favored low tariffs to avoid corruption and reduce prices. After the Great Depression, Republicans abandoned protectionism and supported the philosophy of free trade as U.S. exports grew rapidly. During the past 25 years, internal and external partisan differences undermined the U.S. trade policy consensus. Currently, most Republicans support free-trade initiatives. But Republicans from "rustbelt" states advocate a return to protectionist measures to improve the current trade imbalance. Consequently, the Republican Party does not have a uniform trade policy.

Until the 1930s, the Republican Party, and its predecessors, generally advocated high tariffs to support manufacturing and economic development. Alexander Hamilton, in his position as secretary of the treasury, laid the framework for Republican protectionism in 1791. In his *Report on Manufactures,* Hamilton argued that industrial independence was a prerequisite for political independence and that tariffs should be implemented to raise revenues and "encourage" U.S. industries. With the support of President Washington, Congress levied a tariff on some imported goods. During the French Revolution and the resulting European war, the United States based its foreign trade policy on the rights of neutrals to trade with all European nations and their colonies. Though President John Adams sympathized with England, he realized that depending on the goodwill of the British navy was harmful to U.S. commerce. Therefore, in 1798 he persuaded Congress to establish a Department of the Navy and finance the construction of three squadrons of U.S. warships. Consequently, the Federalists set the foundation for Republican trade policy by establishing a protective tariff, asserting trade rights for neutrals, and strengthening the navy to protect U.S. commerce.

Many elements of Federalist trade policy were scaled back by the Democratic-Republicans when they came to office in 1800–but not tariffs. Before he left office, however, President Madison adopted a Hamiltonian/Federalist trade policy as the Northeast became a great manufacturing center. Congressional leaders such as Henry Clay and his Nationalist Republicans advocated the American system during the Era of Good Feelings. A key element of the system was a protective tariff to stimulate U.S. manufacturing, create domestic markets for agricultural commodities, and finance internal improvements. In 1816 Congress increased the tariff duties to an average of 20%. Madison and his successor, James Monroe, refused to implement the entire American system program for fear of unconstitutionally expanding the power of the national government.

By the end of the Monroe administration, three sections of the United States began to develop different economic structures that affected U.S. trade policy. The northeastern states advocated protectionism to support their growing manufacturing sector, while the southern states, which were dependent on British markets for their cotton exports, pressed for a low tariff policy. The western states wanted federally financed internal improvements and security but viewed tariffs as an instrument to protect the wealthy. After John Quincy Adams became president in 1824, Congress raised the tariff to 36% and even higher in 1828. Southerners militantly opposed the new tariff measures, which they considered "peculiar" taxes on their region.

After Andrew Jackson was elected in 1828, southern and western Democrats expected him to revise the tariff. But Jackson declared that Congress was within its rights to levy the protective tariff. In 1832 Congress passed another highly protective tariff, which South Carolina nullified. Jackson threatened military action to collect tariff duties but also pressured Congress to pass a tariff reduction measure, gradually returning the tariff to its 1816 levels. A series of panics hit President Van Buren's administration in the late 1830s, which brought the Whig Party to power in 1840.

The Whig Party accomplished major trade policy goals during the Tyler, Taylor, and Fillmore administrations. Northern Whigs argued that protective tariffs would create an increasing and diversified industrial sector and more jobs for the poor by closing out foreign goods. Despite his low tariff position, President Tyler approved the Tariff of 1842, which reestablished the level of duties imposed in 1832. By the mid-1840s, American merchants prospered as new markets opened in Europe. From 1840 to 1860, the combined value of U.S. exports and imports increased from approximately $220 billion to $690 billion. Though only 5% of American trade was with Asia, U.S. merchants wanted to increase their access to the Far East and pressured the U.S. government to intervene in China. President Tyler successfully concluded the Treaty of Wanghia in 1844, which granted U.S. traders the same rights as those given to Europeans. In 1852 President Fillmore responded to merchants' demands and sent Commodore Perry to open trade relations with Japan.

During the Civil War, Republicans used a high tariff to pay for the war and protect industries, raising tariff rates to an average level of 47% by 1864. After the war, most Republican leaders continued to view a high tariff as an essential barrier to promote U.S. industrialization. They argued that cheaper prices for goods inevitably resulted in a meaner and poorer society, pointing to the plight of the working classes in Europe and Asia as evidence to support their argument. Minor tariff reductions were made in 1780 and 1872 when a dissident group of Liberal Republicans led a movement to lower prices. In 1873 the country plunged into a recession, and Republicans quickly restored high tariff duties. During the panic, many dissatisfied groups blamed the protective tariff as one source of economic problems. But congressional Republicans blocked modest tariff reform proposals.

At the end of Grover Cleveland's first term, the tariff became the leading partisan issue when the president attempted to pass modest tariff reductions. During the presidential campaign of 1888, Republicans charged that Cleveland was a British agent who wanted to crush American industry by removing all barriers to lower-priced English goods. Republicans portrayed themselves as nationalists and promised even higher tariffs to protect jobs. Republicans fulfilled their campaign pledges after the election and passed the McKinley tariff bill, which increased the tariff by another 4%. But the Republicans also acknowledged that tariff rates affected U.S. exports. Consequently, the tariff bill contained a "reciprocity clause" threatening to raise U.S. tariffs even higher if other countries did not lower their tariffs. Public reaction to the tariff temporarily swept the Republicans from congressional power in 1890 and the presidency in 1892.

The financial panic of 1893 helped return the Republicans to power in 1896. For the next 40 years (except the eight years under President Wilson), the Republican Party dominated the political system and trade policy. U.S. trade policy centered on protectionism and reciprocal trade agreements, especially with Caribbean and Central American countries. Congress passed the Dingley Act of 1897, raising duties to an average of 52%, and strengthened the navy to protect U.S. commerce. In the late 1890s, as U.S. exports increased, other countries began to consider protecting their markets against U.S. goods. The eminent dissolution of China by imperialist European countries also threatened American opportunities in the Far East. With his Open Door notes in 1899, Secretary of State John Hay established the principle of nondiscrimination as the future basis of Republican and U.S. trade policy.

In the first ten years of the twentieth century, Progressive Republicans pressed for tariff reductions to limit the concentration of business and promote exports. In 1909 the next Republican tariff bill, the Payne–Aldrich Act, reflected the party's commitment to nondiscrimination. Though Congress reduced tariff duties only slightly, the bill established a system of minimum and maximum tariff rates and allowed the president to impose additional penalties against any country discriminating against U.S. exports. Advocates for the bill argued that the United States should treat all competitors and producers alike. Nevertheless, most Republicans wanted to keep tariffs firmly in place.

President Wilson dramatically lowered tariffs in 1913, but subsequent Republican administrations returned to the principle of reciprocity after World War I and passed modest tariff increases under the 1922 Fordney–McCumber Act. The act also contained elements of the Open Door policy because it allowed the president to punish discriminatory countries. Nonetheless, in 1922 the Harding administration also began to move to a more liberal trade policy as it adopted the unconditional form of the most-favored-nation (MFN) principle. During the interwar years, Republicans and Democrats recognized that U.S. exports depended on revitalized European markets and tried to assist the European recovery effort with loans. After the stock market crash, however, Republicans resorted to high tariffs and passed the party's last major protectionist legislation, the Smoot–Hawley Act of 1930.

Republican-dominated trade policy ended when the Roosevelt administration passed the Reciprocal Trade Agreements Act in 1934. After the mid-1930s, the major goal of American trade policy was to reduce trade barriers through bilateral and multilateral negotiations. The United States and other industrialized nations formed the General Agreement on Tariffs and Trade (GATT) in 1947 to coordinate trading policy and liberalize the world market. From the 1930s to the late 1960s, both parties supported trade liberalization because U.S. exports dominated the world market. Major partisan trade policy disagreements did not resurface until 1968 when GATT and the Bretton Woods system seemed to be collapsing and the United States was nearing an import deficit caused by trade imbalances.

Since 1968, disagreements over American trade policy have occurred between and within both political parties. Democrats with some notable exceptions switched to protectionism, while Republicans were divided along regional lines. Many Republicans supported free trade to open export markets and stimulate economic growth. But Republicans from states or districts adversely affected by rising imports joined the Democrats. Moreover, while Presidents Nixon, Reagan, and Bush were ardent free-trade supporters, they occasionally backed strong protectionist measures during their respective tenures.

From 1969 to 1992, partisan trade conflicts were often between Republican presidents and Democratic-controlled Congresses. In 1969 President Nixon failed to obtain congressional authority to participate in GATT negotiations. Congress tried to enact a protectionist trade bill in 1986 with support from the Democratic-controlled House of Representatives and the Republican-controlled Senate. President Reagan vetoed the measure, which resurfaced in 1987 with the support of 40% of Republican legislators and unanimous Democratic approval. After the stock market crash in October, however, Congress enacted a less protectionist measure that became law over President Reagan's veto. President Reagan also imposed restrictions on the number of Japanese cars imported into the United States and placed tariffs of up to 100% on electronic components in 1987. President Bush agreed to congressional retaliatory measures that contradicted free-trade principles in 1988: "Super 301" and the Structural Impediments Initiative. He also threatened to close American markets if Japan did not liberalize its trading policy. Nonetheless, Bush negotiated a free-trade agreement with Canada that was ratified in 1988 and the North American Free Trade Agreement (NAFTA) in 1992, which was ratified in 1993. Bush also supported the creation of a free trade zone in the Western Hemisphere, which led to the 1994 Free Trade Area of the Americas summit.

As a result of the budget deficit and continuing trade imbalance, differences within the Republican Party over trade policy have continued in the 1990s. During the 1992 presidential campaign season, Republican presidential hopefuls including Pat Buchanan and the independent candidate Ross Perot challenged Bush's free trade position with effective results. Congressional Republicans for the most part voted for NAFTA and the 1994 GATT agreement, which substantially reduces trade barriers. Nonetheless, trade policy continues to be an important element in the 1996 presidential race as Republican candidates debate the wisdom of free trade versus protectionism. Consequently, despite the Republican-sponsored free-trade initiatives of the 1980s, the party does not have a uniform trade policy.

Janet B. Manspeaker

BIBLIOGRAPHY

Blum, John M., et al. *The National Experience*. 4th ed. New York: Harcourt Brace, 1977.

Frieden, Jeffry, and David A. Lake, eds. *International Political Economy*. New York: St. Martin's Press, 1991.

Spanier, John W., and Eric M. Uslaner. *American Foreign Policy Making and Democratic Dilemmas*. 6th ed. New York: Macmillan, 1994.

Voting Behavior

The study of voting behavior seeks to explain the determinants of the individual vote choice, voting patterns, and trends. Voting is the most common act of political participation and for some citizens the only form of political participation in which they engage. Elections are the primary instrument of self-government in a democracy, and, once elected, the concern about reelection imposes a significant restraint on the elected leaders. Public officials who want to be reelected are likely to be responsive to broad segments of the citizenry. In addition, elections link public attitudes to public policy and confer legitimacy and authority on the government. Although elections usually do not determine the exact policy outcome, voting for one party is usually associated with distinct policy goals. Generally, voting Republican usually means favoring conservative or business views.

Systematic research on voting behavior emerged from the development of statistical sampling theory, which slowly led to the methodological refinement of political polling. The 1920s and 1930s saw the first reports of political polls in the media and political science research. For instance, in 1936 *Literary Digest*, a popular weekly magazine, sent out 10 million questionnaires asking respondents if they would vote for Democratic candidate Franklin D. Roosevelt or for the Republican Alfred M. Landon. The sample utilized by the magazine was a nonrandom or haphazard sample. Because of the lack of comprehensive lists of voters, questionnaires were sent to car owners, as well as citizens listed in the telephone directories. The base of Roosevelt's support, the unemployed, underemployed, and poor, were excluded from the magazine's sample. Only 2 million questionnaires were returned. Not surprisingly, the *Literary Digest* predicted a landslide victory for Republican Landon (55%). Actual election results, however, gave his Democratic opponent, Roosevelt, an overwhelming margin of support (61%). Commercial researchers such as George Gallup and Elmo Roper used systematic sampling procedures and predicted the right winner of the 1936 election.

In contrast to commercial polling, scientific studies of voting behavior that began to emerge in the early 1940s are less concerned about correct predictions of electoral outcomes, but focus on in-depth analyses of the determinants of the individual vote. The first major study of voting behavior was conducted by Columbia University's Bureau of Applied Statistics with a random sample of respondents from Erie County. *The People's Choice*, the seminal work by Paul Lazarsfeld, Bernard Berelson, and Hazel Gaudet

(1944), relied on a sociological model to analyze voting behavior in the 1940 election. Lazarsfeld et al. argued that a person's vote decision was mainly determined by sociodemographic background variables, most importantly religious affiliation, socioeconomic status, and place of residence. For example, Protestants from rural areas and with high socioeconomic status were most likely to vote for the Republican candidate Thomas E. Dewey. The authors of *The People's Choice* concluded that "a person thinks politically, as he is, socially" (1944, 27).

The basic findings of the sociological Columbia model were confirmed in a second major study conducted in 1948 (Berelson, Lazarsfeld, and McPhee 1954). Similar to the first study, the authors of *Voting* concluded that social-group factors accounted for most of the differences in voting behavior. The most serious criticisms directed toward the Colombia model of voting behavior point toward the social determinism of the model and the lack of attention paid to the political aspects of an election. Further, the Columbia model is not useful in explaining political change across elections. Different parties are elected in different years even if social-group characteristics do not change much.

The book that gives the most comprehensive analysis of electoral behavior and stands at the fore of academic research in the field is *The American Voter* by University of Michigan researchers Angus Campbell, Philip E. Converse, Warren E. Miller, and Donald E. Stokes. In contrast to the purely sociological Columbia model, Campbell et al.'s analysis of the 1952 and 1956 presidential elections emphasizes three psychological aspects of an individual's vote choice: the person's attachment to a party, orientation toward the major issues, and evaluation of the candidates. Central to an understanding of voting behavior is the concept of party identification, which acts as a long-term and stable influence on voters' decision-making processes. Party identification is a psychological attachment to one of the two major parties, which is the result of a childhood socialization process. Party identification predisposes individuals to vote for their own party's candidate. For instance, in the 1952 election, 99% of strong Republicans voted for a Republican candidate, Dwight Eisenhower. Although the influence of party identification has declined over the past 40 years, its impact on individual vote choices continues to be significant.

While party identification is a long-term influence affecting the vote, issues, candidate characteristics, and party images represent short-term factors specific to the election. As a result of these short-term influences, an individual's vote may "deviate" from his or her party identification and be cast for the opposition party's candidate. Despite the marked differences between the Columbia and Michigan models, both theories rest on the assumption that the electorate is apathetic and irrational. Issues do not have much impact on the vote because voters' interest in the campaign is low, and their understanding of issue positions is shallow and superficial.

Yet, *The American Voter* study relied on data from the 1950s, a period in which few political events agitated the electorate. Issue or policy voting became somewhat more important in the post-1960 elections, which centered on a new set of foreign policy and social issues, the Vietnam War, civil rights, and desegregation. According to Carmines and Stimson (1980), issue voting was especially prevalent during the 1972 electoral contest between incumbent Republican Richard Nixon and Democratic challenger George McGovern (see also Nie, Verba, and Petrocik 1976). In order for issues to matter, however, issues have to be salient, and parties and candidates have to stake out distinguishable positions on this issue. Carmines and Stimson (1980) argue that desegregation fell into this category of "easy" issues. The Vietnam War issue, in contrast, did not induce issue voting because the candidates did not stake out sufficiently distinct positions on U.S. involvement in the war.

This implies that the lack of issue awareness cannot be solely attributed to an unsophisticated electorate. Carmines and Stimson show that voters choose candidates according to issues, provided the parties' different positions are discernible. Voting on the basis of issues continued to be important in the 1980s and 1990s. Citizens' dissatisfaction with the performance of the economy, the federal deficit, and the national debt were important issues in the 1992 election, and voters who were unsatisfied with Republican Bush's economic record were significantly more likely to endorse the Democratic challenger Bill Clinton. Although voters were not able to exactly compare Clinton's and Bush's economic platform, vote choices were made on the retrospective evaluation of the incumbent president's ability to handle the nation's economy. In a similar vein, Republican Ronald Reagan won the 1980 election because retrospective evaluations of Jimmy Carter's handling of foreign policy and economic matters were unfavorable.

The influence of party identification, the most important determinant of the vote choice in the 1950s, declined throughout the 1960s and 1970s, which were characterized by a decrease in political party loyalty and a rise in political independence. This decrease, however, affected the Republican Party less than the Democrats. The role of partisanship as a determinant of individual vote choices increased again in the 1988 and 1992 elections. Exit polls indicated that 85% of strong and weak Republicans cast their vote in favor of Republican incumbent George Bush. Bush was endorsed by 91% of Republicans in 1988.

An entirely different approach to the study of voting behavior was taken by rational choice theorists (Downs 1957). According to the economic theory of voting, the decision to cast a ballot and the decision for which candidate to vote are determined by an economic cost–benefit analysis. Voters will vote for the candidate closest to them on important issues and will cast a ballot only if the perceived benefits of voting outweigh the costs associated with voting.

This economic model of voting behavior is especially useful in explaining low electoral turnout in the United States. In 1960, turnout in presidential elections peaked at 63%, but it has since declined to about 50%, although it increased slightly in the 1992 presidential election to about 53%. Electoral turnout in off-year congressional elections, primaries, and local elections is substantially lower. These numbers are even more dramatic if one considers that the education of the electorate increased steadily since the 1960s and that educated citizens are more likely to vote than those with less education (Wolfinger and Rosenstone 1980). Thus, turnout should have increased and not decreased.

Downs's model of voting behavior explains electoral turnout by pointing toward the costs and benefits associated with casting a ballot. Registration, the act of voting itself, and the search for information needed to make an informed choice involves costs. These costs will induce the citizen to stay home unless he or she can see that the returns offered by becoming informed and voting are greater than the costs. Applying the cost–benefit model to the decline in electoral participation implies that many citizens perceive little benefit in voting. Costs associated with voting have actually declined since the 1960s. Registration is less an institutional obstacle course than 30 years ago. In particular, the "Motor Voter Law," which came into effect in 1995 and allows for voter registration when citizens apply for or renew their licenses, has made registration significantly easier. Yet it remains to be seen if this law will result in an increase in electoral participation.

This decline in the costs associated with voting, however, has not been accompanied by increases in the perceived benefits of citizen participation. Instead, the electorate's trust in the government decreased steadily since the early 1960s, reaching a low point in 1988 and staying at about this level throughout the early 1990s. In 1988, 58% of Americans indicated that government can never or only some of the times be trusted. Only 32.7% of the citizenry indicated that government is run for the benefit of all. Almost 70% believe that government is run by big interests. Obviously, citizens who feel alienated from the government are less likely to vote than those who place trust in the governing institutions. In a similar vein, citizens' likelihood of detecting differences between the parties, policy platforms has decreased. It must make a difference to the voter which candidate wins the election. The larger the party differential, that is, the ideological- or performance-based difference between the parties the greater the benefit derived from voting.

In comparison to research on voting conducted in the 1940s and 1950s, recent studies of electoral behavior rely on increasingly sophisticated methodologies and high-quality data. Yet a commonly accepted theory of voting behavior has still to evolve. The theoretical framework developed by *The American Voter* (Campbell et al. 1960) continues to influence current investigations of voting patterns. Nevertheless, the major emphasis on the role of party identification as the main determinant of the individual vote choice has been replaced by more dynamic models of the electoral decision process (e.g., Page and Jones 1979). These models are trying to account for the fact that candidate, party, and issue factors interact. For instance, party loyalties do not function merely as a fixed determinant of the vote but are themselves influenced by issue and candidate factors.

The more complicated models developed throughout the 1970s, 1980s, and 1990s did not necessarily provide definite conclusions. There has been a great deal of electoral volatility during the postwar years. None of the discussed models can entirely account for change and stability in American electoral behavior. Yet their combined conclusions give a fairly comprehensive picture of the determinants of electoral choices.

Frauke Schnell

SEE ALSO Realignment and Dealignment

BIBLIOGRAPHY

Asher, Herbert B. *Presidential Elections and American Politics.* 5th ed. Chicago: University of Chicago Press, 1992.

Berelson, Bernard R., Paul F. Lazarsfeld, and William N. McPhee. *Voting.* Chicago: University of Chicago Press, 1954.

Campbell, Angus, Philip E. Converse, Warren E. Miller, and Donald E. Stokes. *The American Voter.* New York: Wiley, 1960.

Carmines, Edward G., and James A. Stimson. "The Two Faces of Issue Voting." *American Political Science Review* 74 (1980): 78–91.

Downs, Anthony. *An Economic Theory of Democracy.* New York: Harper and Row, 1957.

Key, V.O. (with Milton C. Cummings). *The Responsible Electorate: Rationality in Presidential Voting, 1936–1960*. New York: Vintage Books, 1966.

Lazarsfeld, Paul F., Bernard R. Berelson, and Helen Gaudet. *The People's Choice*. New York: Columbia University Press, 1948.

Miller, Warren E. "The Puzzle Transformed: Explaining Declining Turnout." *Political Behavior* 14 (1882): 1–40.

Nie, Norman H., Sidney Verba, and John R. Petrocik. *The Changing American Voter*. Cambridge: Harvard University Press, 1979.

Niemi, Richard G., and Herbert F. Weisberg. *Controversies in Voting Behavior*. Washington, DC: Congressional Quarterly, 1984.

Page, Benjamin I. *Choices and Echoes in Presidential Elections*. Chicago: University of Chicago Press, 1978.

Page, Benjamin I., and Calvin Jones. "Reciprocal Effects of Policy Preferences, Party Loyalties and the Vote." *American Political Science Review* 73 (1979): 1071–1089.

Piven, Frances E., and Richard A. Cloward. *Why Americans Don't Vote*. New York: Pantheon Books, 1988.

Pomper, Gerald M., ed. *The Election of 1988: Reports and Interpretations*. Chatham, NJ: Chatham House, 1993.

Teixeira, Ruy A. *The Disappearing American Voter*. Washington, DC: Brookings Institution, 1992.

Wolfinger, Raymond E., and Steven J. Rosenstone. *Who Votes?* New Haven: Yale University Press, 1980.

Welfare

WHAT IS WELFARE?

The term *welfare* is used broadly to refer to direct or indirect financial subsidies to individuals. People receive direct subsidies individually from the government by means of a check or other financial benefit. Social Security payments and subsidized student loans are direct subsidies. Indirect subsidies are not paid individually to beneficiaries. Instead, the government provides goods and services that are used collectively; for example, government supports education. Students receive a government service at only a fraction of its real cost because taxpayers in the school district, state, and nation pay. A third kind of subsidy is one provided through tax benefits. A tax-break subsidy permits some people and corporations to pay less in taxes than others of the same income. Most tax subsidies go directly to middle- and upper-income people through corporate tax breaks. Since shareholders of corporations are usually upper-income people, they profit the most from these tax subsidies.

The American welfare system is usually dated from the Social Security Act of 1935. After defeating the Republican president, Herbert Hoover, who opposed a federal response to the depression, the Democratic president, Franklin D. Roosevelt, enacted several temporary emergency relief programs for poor people and unemployed workers. Only with the passage of the 1935 Social Security Act did the United States begin to develop a nonemergency, permanent welfare act. That act established a "safety net" to catch those falling into poverty. It did so through a system of entitlements for the elderly, the unemployed, and poor fatherless children and created a program for maternal and child health care. Health insurance, originally part of the package, was removed to deflect strong opposition from business, the medical profession, and the insurance industry. In 1937, the Supreme Court upheld the constitutionality of the act, which made the federal government's responsibility for social welfare permanent. The fourth program created by the Social Security Act is actually a series of programs, now known as Supplemental Security Income (SSI) (Katz 1995).

The centerpiece of the Social Security Act was the establishment of a national pension program for retired workers—Old Age Insurance (OAI), popularly known as Social Security. The payments were available to many, but not all, workers who retired at age 62 or later. Agricultural workers, domestic workers, unpaid female homemakers, those employed by nonprofit religious, scientific, literary, or educational institutions, as well as employers covered by the Railroad Retirement Act, were excluded from coverage (Abramovitz 1988). The 1939 amendments to the act extended coverage to include a retired or deceased worker's dependents. In subsequent years the act was modified by a series of amendments and court cases stretching from 1939 through the 1970s to include the most needy groups, for example, people of color, the very poor, unmarried mothers, and other workers not protected under the original act.

Social Security is financed through a payroll tax on employees and employers paid to a trust fund. In 1995, the tax was slightly over 7.6% of the first $61,200 of an employee's wages. Individuals who qualify collect their Social Security benefits upon reaching retirement age. Partial benefits can be collected before age 65, full benefits after. Recent changes in law mean that younger workers have to wait longer to collect full benefits. Individuals who receive Social Security do not believe they are collecting welfare because they are only getting back what they paid into the program through payroll deductions. This is not wholly accurate, however, because recipients receive back their contributions, with interest, in 6 years, while they typically receive Social Security for 14 years (Peters 1986).

The Social Security Act also included unemployment insurance to protect some workers against the loss of income due to temporary or involuntary joblessness. States determine their own eligibility requirements, rules of coverage, benefit levels, waiting periods, and financing systems, within broad guidelines. Most states' regulations limit unemployment insurance benefits to persons who are actively seeking a job and who can establish that their unemployment is for a "good cause," that is, involuntary. Most state unemployment programs disqualify workers who quit a job voluntarily without good cause; are fired for work-related misconduct; refuse a suitable job; are directly involved in a strike; or make fraudulent claims.

Another program created by the Social Security Act was a public assistance program, Aid to Families with Dependent Children (AFDC). Commonly referred to as "welfare," this is the major welfare program that provides cash assistance for families below the official poverty line. It is a program for children deprived of parental care and support due to parental death, continued absence from the home, incapacity, or unemployment. Until recently, two-parent families were ineligible for benefits in most states. The caseload consists mainly of women and their children (Zopf 1989). Since the recipients are poor, they have been means tested; that is, individual recipients must periodically demonstrate eligibility by showing they are poor. In between times, any change, for example, births, deaths, or change or address, must be reported to the welfare bureaucracy. Almost every aspect of a welfare recipient's life is subject to scrutiny by welfare officials. Federal AFDC grants match state welfare and local general assistance expenditures up to specified amounts for individuals not already covered by old-age or Social Security insurance. This results in widely varying welfare grants in different states, ranging from a high of $924 a month for a family of three in Alaska to a low of $120 a month in Mississippi.

In the 1990s there has been a significant return of state authority over social and moral behavior of welfare recipients (Kleniewski 1995). Although under the federal grant-in-aid law, states retain a great deal of discretion over AFDC, states cannot generally impose additional eligibility requirements (such as denying aid for a child conceived while the mother was receiving AFDC) or withhold money for behavioral matters (such as failure to attend school). The Department of Health and Human Services (HSS) has been granting the states waivers to institute these policies (Savner and Greenberg 1995). This waiver practice has been going on since 1962, but it became increasingly popular during the Reagan and Bush administrations and increased during the Clinton administration. Now, even more state control over AFDC under block grants, with or without federal restrictions, is a central feature of the debate over welfare reform in the new Republican-controlled Congress.

REPUBLICAN PARTY APPROACH TO WELFARE

Republican Party philosophy generally opposes welfare programs and increases in benefits for poor people. One reason is the Republican belief that welfare measures undermine economic efficiency. Because the welfare state modifies the forces of the market, Republicans believe that it upsets incentive structures that are essential if the market is to operate efficiently. Welfare programs are believed to introduce disincentives to work, save, and invest. The effect, according to Republican Party philosophy, is the diminution of the welfare of society as a whole, and of poor people most particularly (Kaus 1986). Another Republican objection to welfare is moralistic. Republicans believe that welfare state transfers take money from the deserving and give it to the undeserving. In a less extreme form, Republicans accuse the welfare state of ignoring the differential moral deserts among claimants to welfare benefits. Some people have misbehaved badly and have come to their plight through their own misconduct. Others (widows, orphans) have fallen into poverty through no fault of their own. Universal welfare programs treat all alike. Republicans prefer the "deserving" poor to be treated one way, the "undeserving" another (Goodin 1988; Rector 1993). Finally, Republicans criticize welfare programs for having created more dependency than they have cured. The government, Republicans maintain, should therefore decrease its role in promoting social welfare and leave many, if not most, of the social problems it currently tackles to be resolved by the individuals most directly concerned (Mead 1991; Murray 1994).

Republicans believe that caring for poor people should not be a federal government responsibility; welfare should be instead a state, local, and private responsibility. Friends and neighbors should provide assistance to the deserving poor. Republicans seek to reform welfare to return to the custom of localism that guided the provision of assistance to poor people in the United States from colonial times. Republican President Herbert Hoover, faithful to the tradition of localism, was loath to see the federal government take a role in providing welfare to poor people; private charity and local efforts could, he believed, assist burgeoning numbers of destitute people during the Great Depression.

As a consequence, Republicans seek to reduce the size and scope of social welfare programs and reduce welfare benefits for poor people. At the federal level, Republican President Ronald Reagan signed into law the Family Support Act of 1988, which ties the obligation to participate in job search, job training, or work experience to the receipt of AFDC benefits. The principal changes enacted by the Republicans during the 1980s were to restrict welfare eligibility, cut back sharply on work incentives, and encourage states to experiment with various work programs by reducing federal funding (Katz 1989).

At the state level, Republican welfare reforms reflect a consensus that poverty is primarily behavioral rather than economic or environmental, the fault of the individual. The two most popular of the Republican state reforms are Learnfare, in which benefits are reduced if a child fails to attend school, misses too many school days, or fails to maintain certain grades; many states have also adopted the Family Cap, in which additional welfare benefits are denied to children born to women already eligible and enrolled on AFDC, children whose paternity has not been established, or children who are born outside marriage to a minor mother unless the mother married the father or someone adopts the child (Thomas 1994a, 1994b).

In 1994, with the Republican takeover of Congress, welfare reform suddenly reappeared on the national agenda. The Republicans decided that, after a decade of minor tinkering with the welfare system, it was time for a major overhaul. One of the most comprehensive welfare reform proposals was made during the 104th Congress, under the initiative of Speaker Newt Gingrich and the Republicans in Congress. The plan was designed to end a bedrock principle of the Democratic Party for the past 60 years: that the federal government will guarantee some support to the country's poorest families, no matter what.

The Republican plan would repeal the 30-year-old law under which certain categories of people are automatically entitled to health care and health insurance and would abolish the individual right, or entitlement, to public assistance (AFDC) for any poor family that meets the eligibility requirements. The plan would give the states new authority to run welfare programs with minimum federal regulation. Specifically, the Republican plan would set a time limit on welfare, would tighten eligibility criteria for poor people seeking assistance, would impose an array of new work requirements on welfare recipients, and would give states broad new authority to design their own sys-

tems. Most significantly, the plan would replace an array of federal antipoverty programs with block grants, limited lump-sum payments to the states, a provision that would give state officials broad authority to run their own welfare programs, no strings attached. Finally, the Republican plan encourages localities to contract out to religious groups for welfare services by providing a tax deduction for charitable activity assisting poor people, and would prohibit states from spending federal money on additional benefits for children born to women already enrolled on welfare; on direct cash benefits to a minor who has a child outside marriage; or on benefits to a woman who cannot establish the paternity of her child (Backer 1995).

President Clinton vetoed the Republican welfare reform bill in January 1996. The president argued that the Republican blueprint for changing the welfare system would be too tough on children in many ways, including cutting funds for disabled children and not providing enough money to care for children whose parents take jobs (Shogren 1996).

Susan L. Thomas

SEE ALSO Social Security

BIBLIOGRAPHY

Abramovitz, M. *Regulating the Lives of Women: Social Welfare Policy from Colonial Times to the Present.* Boston: South End Press, 1988.

Backer, L.C. "Welfare Reform at the Limit: The Futility of 'Ending Welfare as We Know It.'" *Harvard Civil Rights–Civil Liberties Law Review* 30 (1995): 339–405.

Goodin, R.E. *Reasons for Welfare: The Political Theory of the Welfare State.* Princeton: Princeton University Press, 1988.

Katz, M.B. *The Undeserving Poor: From the War on Poverty to the War on Welfare.* New York: Pantheon Books, 1989.

———. *Improving Poor People: The Welfare State, The "Underclass," and Urban Schools as History.* Princeton: Princeton University Press, 1995.

Kaus, M. "The Work Ethic State." *New Republic,* July 7, 1986, pp. 22–33.

Kleniewski, N. "The War Against Welfare Moves to the States." *Research in Politics and Society* 5 (1995): 193–215.

Mead, L.M. "The New Politics of the New Poverty." *The Public Interest* 103 (1991): 3–19.

Peters, C. "Tilting at Windmills." *Washington Monthly,* June 1986, p. 10.

Rector, R. "Fighting Behavioral Poverty." *Georgetown Journal on Fighting Poverty* 1 (1993): 69–73.

Savner, S., and M. Greenberg. *The CLASP Guide to Welfare Waivers: 1992–1995.* Washington, DC: Center for Law and Social Policy, May 1995.

Shogran, E. "Clinton Vetoes GOP's Welfare Overhaul Plan." *Los Angeles Times,* January 16, 1996.

Thomas, S.L. *Gender and Poverty.* New York: Garland, 1994a.

———. "From the Culture of Poverty to the Culture of Single

Motherhood: The New Poverty Paradigm." *Women & Politics* 14 (1994b): 65–97.

Zopf, P.E. *American Women in Poverty.* New York: Greenwood Press, 1989.

Women

Certain political issues have been identified as *women's issues*, namely, those particular battles fought to correct certain inequalities between women and men, such as women's right to vote and workplace equality (in terms of status, pay, and opportunity). Other women's issues are related to uniquely female biological functions, such as reproductive rights (abortion, contraception, family-planning counseling) and workplace problems such as sexual harassment, while some are related to concerns traditionally associated with females, such as maternity leave, day care, and child support. Mainstream women's movements have fought for these causes on three major fronts: the suffrage movement, the Equal Rights Amendment, and the abortion issue.

It would be a mistake to assume that all women have been proponents of these causes and most men have been opponents or that one of the mainstream, male-dominated political parties has consistently supported or opposed these movements. The Republican Party was the first major party to advocate women's suffrage, and Republican-controlled state legislatures were active in promoting women's rights in the late nineteenth and early twentieth centuries. Recently, however, the Republican Party has adopted notably antifeminist positions on abortion and the Equal Rights Amendment, and although the Reagan administration put women in top administrative positions for the first time, the emphasis on "traditional family values," which includes the nonworking housewife and compliant mother, marks the Republican Party as the party antithetical to the progressive interests of women.

WOMEN'S SUFFRAGE

The women's suffrage movement had its origins in the mid-nineteenth century among crusaders for social justice and proponents of freeing the slaves, but the movement achieved its most notable successes during the Progressive era, when many reforms were adopted. To many Progressive-era women's activists, such as Jane Addams and Florence Kelley, women's rights were merely a part of the larger cluster of rights to be fought for, particularly workers' rights, such as working conditions and pay. To other women reformers of the Progressive era, women's rights were the central issue. There was, however, great diversity among these reform groups. There were a few militant champions of sexual liberation, among whom was Emma Goldman, an immigrant later deported for her radical anarchist activities. Goldman advocated birth control and free love, saying that "women must no longer keep their mouths shut and their wombs open."

A less radical advocate of birth control was Margaret Sanger. Sanger's followers, largely middle class, did not favor free love or critique the nuclear family; some were conservatives who feared that Anglo-Saxon Protestants were committing "race suicide" through the immigration policies of the United States. They believed that birth control could reduce the population growth of immigrant masses. Others in the movement were not such xenophobes but merely wanted to give women a way out of the tyranny of unwanted pregnancy—a theme that would later be picked up by abortion rights advocates. By 1918, Sanger succeeded in getting the courts to permit doctors to distribute birth-control information; states, however, continued to prohibit the sale of contraceptives.

Other feminists opposed the traditional role of women not out of a desire for sexual freedom or in order to destroy marriage but to allow women to be liberated from the burdens of housework and motherhood and provide them with the opportunities afforded to men to pursue freedom and satisfaction through meaningful work and creative effort. Charlotte Perkins Gilman was a leading advocate of this position, and in her book *Women and Economics* (1898), which prefigured much of what the National Organization for Women (NOW) would say 70 years later, she called for a form of communalism featuring large housing units, day nurseries, central kitchens, and maid service to relieve women of domestic chores. Gilman's ideas were once again aimed at middle-class Anglo-Saxon Protestant women and as such had little widespread appeal, particularly among the large population of women already working not out of the desire to find fulfillment but because of economic necessity.

The suffrage movement did not suffer from the limited appeal of other women's movements of the time, though its leaders were largely middle-class women. Although women were not granted the vote by the United States until 1920, when the 19th Amendment was passed, the suffrage movement had been active in the United States since the demand for the enfranchisement of American women was first seriously formulated at the Seneca Falls Convention (1848). The Seneca Falls Convention, the first women's rights assembly in the United States, was organized by Lucretia

Women's Suffrage Association at the Republican National Convention, 1856. *Source:* National Archives.

Coffin Mott and Elizabeth Cady Stanton and met at Seneca Falls, New York, on July 19–20, 1848. The 68 women and 32 men present passed a Declaration of Sentiments, which paralleled the language of the Declaration of Independence and listed 16 forms of discrimination against women, including denial of suffrage and of control of their wages, their own persons, and their children. Twelve resolutions calling for various rights were passed. Eleven received unanimous approval, whereas one, advocating the vote for women, was adopted over Mott's opposition. The convention was moved to Rochester, New York, two weeks later to win broader support for its goals.

After the Civil War, agitation by women for the ballot became increasingly vociferous. In 1869, however, a rift developed among feminists over the proposed 15th Amendment, which gave the vote to black men. Susan B. Anthony, Elizabeth Cady Stanton, and others refused to endorse the amendment because it did not give women the ballot. Other suffragists, however, including Lucy Stone and Julia Ward Howe, argued that once the black man was enfranchised, women would achieve their goal. As a result of the conflict, two organizations emerged. Stone created the American Woman Suffrage Association, which aimed to secure the ballot through state legislation. Stanton and

Anthony formed the National Woman Suffrage Association to work for suffrage on the federal level and to press for more extensive institutional changes, such as the granting of property rights to married women.

In 1872, Anthony went to the polls and asked to be registered. The two Republican members of the board were convinced by her claim that the 14th Amendment's privileges and immunities clause granted women the right to vote (a claim later rejected by the Supreme Court, which declared that voting is not a privilege of citizenship) and agreed to receive her name, against the advice of their Democratic colleague and a U.S. supervisor. Anthony and 13 other women were arrested when they voted, but Republican president Ulysses S. Grant unconditionally pardoned them in 1872. In 1878, Anthony wrote and submitted to Congress a proposed right-to-vote amendment that later became the 19th Amendment to the U.S. Constitution.

In 1890 the two groups united under the name National American Woman Suffrage Association (NAWSA). In the same year, Wyoming entered the Union, becoming the first state with general women's suffrage (which it had adopted as a territory in 1869). In 1896, the Republican Party became the first major party to favor women's suffrage officially, and that same year a Republican senator, A.A. Sargent of California, introduced a proposal in the Senate to give women the right to vote. The proposal was defeated four times in the Democratic-controlled Senate.

In the 1910s, the suffrage movement made major gains. The membership of NAWSA was 75,000 in 1910, a major increase from 17,000 in 1905. In that year, Washington, whose legislature was Republican controlled, became the fifth state to approve women's suffrage. By the time the federal amendment was passed, 12 states, all Republican, had given women full suffrage. In 1917, Jeannette Rankin, a Montana Republican, became the first woman to serve in the House. By the end of 1917, NAWSA claimed 2 million members and the support of former Republican president Theodore Roosevelt. When the Republican Party regained control of Congress, the Equal Suffrage Amendment, with the original language as drafted by Anthony, finally passed (304–88)—only 16 of the 88 opposing votes were cast by Republicans. When the amendment was submitted to the states, 26 of the 36 states that ratified it had Republican-controlled legislatures. Of the nine states that voted against ratification, eight were controlled by Democrats.

Following the success of the suffrage movement, the League of Women Voters, an offshoot of the National American Woman Suffrage Association, was organized in 1920. The league's aim was to educate the female electorate in the use of their right to vote. Despite the fervor surrounding the passage of the 19th Amendment, women did not turn out in great numbers during the 1920s, and when they voted, they tended to vote overwhelmingly Republican, lending force to the Republican domination of both the presidency and Congress throughout that decade.

THE EQUAL RIGHTS AMENDMENT

The next major step in the women's movement was the introduction of the Equal Rights Amendment (ERA). Dissatisfied with continued gender-based discrimination, despite women's right to vote, the National Woman's Party, headed by Alice Paul, drafted a proposed amendment to the Constitution stating that "equality of rights under the law shall not be denied or abridged by the United States nor by any State on account of sex." The ERA was originally introduced in Congress in 1923, but it was not acted on until 1970, when the National Organization for Women (NOW) greatly heightened awareness of women's issues and forced politicians to take notice of the ERA.

The ERA was approved by the House of Representatives in 1971 and by the Senate in 1972. The deadline for ratification was originally March 1979, but in 1978 it was extended three years. Despite being endorsed by two Republican presidents, Nixon and Ford, the controversial ERA was strongly opposed by conservative Republican majorities in various state legislatures. Between 1979 and 1982, ERA supporters employed economic boycotts against states that did not ratify the amendment, but when Republican nominee Ronald Reagan opposed the ERA in 1980 and forced the Republican Party to drop support for the ERA from its platform, the ERA seemed doomed. Although national polls indicated that a majority of Americans favored passage of the ERA, with the aid of the newly elected president, the anti-ERA movement, spearheaded by STOP ERA, an organization founded by Phyllis Schlafly in 1972, managed to quash what support remained for the ERA. On June 30, 1982, ratification of the ERA fell three states short of the 38 needed. Efforts to regain congressional approval of the proposal, however, were defeated in the House on November 15, 1983.

ABORTION

Besides fighting for equal political rights and official sanction of gender-based discrimination, the women's movement also concentrated on reproductive rights as fundamental to women's control of their lives. Margaret Sanger's birth-control movement had been an attempt to get women out from under the domination of the male-imposed "biologically determined" social roles. The right to abortion was a further step in women's liberation from the often confining position of wife and mother. Outlawed by most states since the mid-nineteenth century, abortion was made legal in one broad sweep in 1973, when the Supreme Court struck down a Texas abortion law in *Roe* v. *Wade*. The *Roe* Court was dominated by the unlikely mix of Republican-appointed, left-leaning justices whose tendency had been to extend the sphere of protected liberties, often by direct judicial intervention. The *Roe* decision (made by a 7-to-2 margin, with five of the justices in the majority belonging to the Republican Party) found abortion to be a matter of "privacy," which early Republican-dominated Courts had ruled was implied by the "penumbra" of protections found in the First, Third, Fourth, Fifth, and Ninth amendments. The Court found that despite the fact that the Constitution makes no explicit mention of a right to privacy, and certainly no mention of a right to abortion, such rights are implicitly contained in the Bill of Rights.

For over a decade after *Roe*, the Supreme Court consistently struck down attempts by the states to restrict access to legal abortions. Though personally opposed to abortion, Republican presidents Nixon and Ford were hesitant to directly attack *Roe*. Ronald Reagan was the major figure in the effort to get the Republican Party to adopt a strong antiabortion position. The 1980 Republican platform supported a constitutional amendment and other congressional legislation aimed at overturning *Roe*. More important, Reagan's Department of Justice scrutinized potential appointees to the federal bench, screening out those deemed potentially supportive of pro-choice positions. The 1984 Republican platform applauded "President Reagan's fine record of judicial appointments" and reaffirmed "support for the appointment of judges at all levels of the judiciary who respect traditional family values and the sanctity of innocent human life." Reagan also sought to curtail abortion through restrictive regulations that would only be able to be challenged in the federal courts, which were packed with Reagan judges. He also made executive branch appointments in line with his antiabortion policy. Surgeon General C. Everett Koop made public attacks not only against abortion but also against the use of contraceptives. When he left office in 1989, he announced that he was withholding from publication a long-awaited medical report that had concluded that there was little evidence that abortion causes women significant physical or psychological harm. Reagan's secretary of health and human services was also an outspoken supporter of the antiabortion movement, lobbying Congress to ban funding for abortions and counseling on abortion and at the same time pushing for funding of religious organizations.

By 1989, the liberal majority on the Court had declined significantly as the original justices from *Roe* retired and were replaced by antiabortion appointees. By 1989 the two dissenters in *Roe*, Rehnquist and White, were reinforced by three Reagan appointees—two of whom were avowedly antiabortion and the third of whom, Justice O'Connor, leaned toward the pro-life position. With the makeup of the Court thus, the string of rulings in support of abortion was interrupted in 1989 in the case of *Webster* v. *Reproductive Health Services*, where the Court ruled, by a 5-to-4 margin, that some state-imposed restrictions on abortion are constitutionally permissible. As the 1988 Republican nominee, George Bush, who opposed a constitutional amendment banning abortion when running against Reagan in 1980, called for the "criminalization of abortion," which would provide penalties for doctors performing abortions, as in the days before *Roe*. Bush also nominated for the Supreme Court Clarence Thomas, who was not a strong supporter of women's rights. When sexual harassment allegations were brought against Thomas by Anita Hill, the Bush administration once again came under fire for its poor record on women's issues.

Although the Republican Party initially supported women's rights more vigorously than other major parties, this position was reversed during the Reagan and Bush administrations. In the 1980s, the Republican Party did take measures to further the position of women in important government positions. Reagan's first term included several notable appointments, including Sandra Day O'Connor as the first female Supreme Court justice, Elizabeth Dole as the first female secretary of transportation, and Jeane Kirkpatrick as the first female U.S. representative to the United Nations. With Dole, Kirkpatrick, and Margaret Heckler as the secretary of health and human services, it was also the first time in history three women served concurrently in a president's cabinet. Republican opposition to the Equal Rights Amendment and abortion rights, however, led many women to view the Republican Party as antifeminist and reactionary in terms of women's rights. Indeed, the vociferous opposition of the Reagan and Bush administrations to *Roe*, and Reagan's outspoken advocacy of "traditional family values," belie the tokenism in Reagan's appointments.

The Republican Party continues to press for traditional family values against the rights and interests of women. The Republican Congress's Contract with America not only comes out against abortion but aims at cuts in welfare spending for single working mothers. The Republican economic agenda is premised on the very nuclear family that has often been the target of women's movements.

Jessamyn West

SEE ALSO Abortion

BIBLIOGRAPHY

Hecker, Eugene A. *A Short History of Women's Rights*. Westport, CT: Greenwood Press, 1971.

Langley, Winston E., and Vivian C. Fox, eds. *Women's Rights in the United States: A Documentary History*. Westport, CT: Greenwood Press, 1994.

Le Veness, Frank P., and Jane P. Sweeney, eds. *Women Leaders in Contemporary U.S. Politics*. New York: Lynne Rienner, 1987.

Front Page of the *Washington Post*, November 9, 1904. *Source: Washington Post.*

BIOGRAPHIES

Presidents

CHESTER A. ARTHUR

The 21st president of the United States, Chester Alan "Chet" Arthur, was born in Fairfield, Vermont, on October 5, 1829. He died in New York shortly after leaving the presidency, on November 18, 1886. In 1880 Arthur was selected as the vice presidential candidate to balance the Republican ticket of nominee James A. Garfield. Soon after his election, Garfield was assassinated, and Arthur became president. Despite his long tenure as a spoilsman in the Republican political machine in New York, President Arthur led the fight for modern civil service reform.

Prior to his entry into politics, Chet Arthur was a schoolteacher in Vermont and New York. His parents, William and Malvina Stone Arthur, had moved the family from town to town because of his father's occupation as a Baptist preacher. Arthur attended Union College in Schenectady and studied law while teaching. He embarked on a successful legal career in New York City. In the *Lemmon Slave Case*, Arthur argued that blacks transported through New York State were no longer slaves but free. In another case, he defended the rights of a black passenger riding on a New York trolley, which led to desegregation of that city's public transportation system.

Arthur was attracted to the abolitionist views of the new Republican Party and joined soon after the formation of the party. Thereafter, he actively campaigned for Republican candidates. He served in the New York State militia from 1858 to 1862, rising to the rank of quartermaster general during the Civil War. Following the war, Arthur held several prominent positions in the Republican Party organization in New York.

His active support for the candidacy of Ulysses S. Grant resulted in a presidential appointment as collector of the port of New York in 1871. The collector was responsible for collecting fees and tariffs on imports from ships arriving in New York and New Jersey. At this time, up to three-quarters of all federal duties on ships were collected through this port authority. Arthur used the office to obtain compulsory party contributions from workers at the customhouse and to serve the interests of New York senator and party boss Roscoe Conkling. Arthur served as a delegate to the 1876 convention in Cincinnati. He initially supported the presidential aspirations of Conkling, but he voted for Rutherford B. Hayes on the final ballots as it became clear that Conkling could not win the nomination.

As collector, "Elegant Arthur" was the most highly paid federal bureaucrat in the nation, and he began to amass some degree of wealth. During his tenure, Arthur ignored rules to hire employees based on merit and filled the customhouse with party supporters. Since the administration of Andrew Jackson (1829–1837), federal employees were chosen through a national system of patronage. Key supporters of the president's political party, or often a faction within the party, were rewarded with government jobs following the election. This spoils system led to wholesale replacement of government employees after a new president was elected. As government grew bigger, this amateur bureaucracy became more inefficient and corrupt. The Grant administration (1869–1877) has been considered particularly inept by most scholars.

Many politicians, including Republican Rutherford B. Hayes, called for reform and an end to the spoils system. After his election as president in 1876, Hayes's suggestions for voluntary reforms were ignored by most of the members of his cabinet, and Hayes encountered significant congressional opposition to reform. In 1877, however, the Jay Commission investigated charges of corruption and mismanagement in the New York customhouse. The commission found blatant rule violations. Following the recommendations of the commission, Chester Arthur, as collector, was ultimately removed from office by President Hayes.

Chester A. Arthur. *Source:* Library of Congress.

Arthur returned to his law practice but was selected as a delegate to the 1880 Republican National Convention in Chicago. Hayes declined to run for reelection. Delegates at the convention divided into two camps. The "Stalwarts" were those Republicans who supported the nomination of Grant for an unprecedented third term. Arthur was a member of this faction, which was led by Senator Roscoe Conkling. Those opposing Grant constituted a majority but did not initially unify around any single candidate. This wing, which later became known as the "Half Breeds," supported civil service and other liberal reforms. The 1880 convention was the most divisive of all Republican conventions. Ohio reformer James A. Garfield was finally chosen the party's nominee on the 36th ballot.

To placate the Stalwarts, as well as to balance the ticket geographically, the convention nominated Chester Alan Arthur as vice president on the first ballot. Arthur accepted the nomination over the objections of Roscoe Conkling. Arthur had not been a candidate for any elective office before his vice presidential nomination. Elections during this era were decided primarily by party loyalty. Presidential elections, therefore, were more a function of mobilization than persuasion. Nationally, the Republican Party maintained a slight majority of voters in post–Civil War elections, and the compromise ticket of Garfield and Arthur satisfied most factions within the party. James A. Garfield was elected president in November by a slim margin over Democratic nominee General Winfield Hancock. Arthur became vice president.

Arthur enjoyed his job as vice president; this is unusual because the position carries so little formal power. The U.S. Senate, however, was evenly divided between Democrats and Republicans after the election. Vice President Arthur, as presiding officer of the Senate, cast votes breaking ties that gave the Republicans majority status in the chamber, enabling them to fill committees and leadership positions.

Garfield did not shower convention delegates or other party supporters with the spoils of presidential appointments, although he was inundated with requests for patronage. Garfield's appointment of a liberal (or Half Breed) Republican, William H. Robertson, as collector of the port of New York, however, produced a fiercely negative reaction from the Conkling machine. In the ensuing controversy, Chester Arthur allied with the Stalwarts rather than the president. Eventually, Roscoe Conkling and fellow New York Senator Thomas Platt resigned their seats in protest, temporarily giving the Democrats a Senate majority.

President Garfield would not back down to demands for patronage and continued to press for reform of the federal civil service. Only four months into his term, Garfield encountered a frustrated, insane office seeker who yelled, "I am a Stalwart and Arthur is President now!" as he shot Garfield twice. One bullet lodged in Garfield's spine, and his physical condition worsened over the next few days. Arthur rejected suggestions that he serve as acting president. Garfield died several weeks later, and on September 20, 1881, Chester Arthur ascended to the presidency.

As president, the former machine politician began to modify his views regarding reform. Responding to public opinion as well as to false rumors that the Stalwarts were responsible for the assassination, Arthur pressed for civil service reform. He proposed a new civil service modeled on business, with uninterrupted employment assigned on the basis of merit rather than party service. He pushed for investigations of abuse and misconduct in government. Democrats won a majority of seats in the House in the 1882 election, and the Republicans responded to pressure for new legislation before power changed hands.

President Arthur signed the Pendleton Act, which was passed by Congress in January 1883. It reestablished the Civil Service Commission and a merit system with competitive examinations for certain classified positions. A similar agency had been briefly created during the Grant administration, but it was soon abolished. Arthur had originally opposed merit tests for employment but compromised on the issue. Only about 10% of federal positions were covered by this legislation in 1883, but presidents were later given discretion to increase the number of positions covered by the act. Over subsequent administrations, especially during the Progressive era, the number and percentage of merit system employees grew.

Arthur continued to support racial equality, though he seemed unconcerned with the economic advancement of African Americans and other minorities. He did veto legislation with the intent to prohibit Chinese immigration and to deny citizenship to Chinese in the United States, but he later compromised for a bill limiting immigration. Arthur lobbied for clearer rules of presidential succession, yet the circumstances of his own succession provided the stimulus for reform. American foreign policy was a mixture of inconsistencies and setbacks. The Arthur administration sought a fairer policy on tariffs but continued a protectionist policy for American industry. The administration did improve the American navy and merchant marine: building new ships, establishing the Naval War College, reducing the number of officers, and creating a merit system. Republican policy emphasized a free market within the domestic economy with protection of international trade.

President Chester Arthur sought renomination at the 1884 convention in Chicago. James G. Blaine, former House Speaker, senator, and secretary of state under Garfield, had been a reformist presidential candidate in the previous conventions of 1876 and 1880 and opposed Arthur. Blaine quickly emerged as the front-runner, though Blaine lost several procedural votes at the convention. Arthur's coalition, for instance, won an early battle to name a black Mississippi delegate, John Lynch, as temporary chair of the convention. The Stalwarts, however, distrusted Arthur because of civil service reforms, and Arthur could not convince the liberal Republican wing to accept his recent transformation. Arthur finished a strong second on the first three convention ballots, but support for Blaine grew. On the

fourth ballot, Blaine was selected as the Republican presidential nominee. Blaine's nomination and Arthur's defeat signaled the end of the national power of the Stalwart faction.

Arthur suffered from kidney disease during his administration, and his health declined sharply following his term of office. Throughout his term, Arthur sought personal privacy, and his illness was successfully hidden from most observers. Arthur married Ellen "Nell" Lewis Herndon of Virginia in 1859. She died of pneumonia in January 1880, and Arthur's sister acted as first lady during his presidency.

The Chester Arthur administration can be characterized as competent and efficient. Arthur as president was far better than Arthur the machine politician. His term in office, however, emphasized the symbolic and the ceremonial over the substantive and the progressive. He was largely passive, in part due to illness, but as President Chester Arthur, he did expand executive authority by seeking foreign markets for U.S. products, improving and modernizing the navy, and vetoing pork-barrel legislation. Arthur's term was an important turning point for civil service reform and the establishment of a probusiness ideology within the Republican Party. His administration marked the end of the Stalwarts and a movement toward a new brand of Republicanism.

James W. Endersby

SEE ALSO History

BIBLIOGRAPHY

Doenecke, Justus D. *The Presidency of James A. Garfield and Chester A. Arthur.* Lawrence: Regents Press of Kansas, 1981.

Hoogenboom, Ari Arthur. *Outlawing the Spoils: A History of the Civil Service Reform Movement, 1865–1883.* Urbana: University of Illinois Press, 1961.

Howe, George F. *Chester A. Arthur: A Quarter-Century of Machine Politics.* New York: Dodd, Mead, 1934.

Peskin, Allan. "Who Were the Stalwarts? Who Were Their Rivals? Republican Factions in the Gilded Age." *Political Science Quarterly* 99 (1984): 703–716.

Pletcher, David M. *The Awkward years: American Foreign Relations under Garfield and Arthur.* Columbia: University of Missouri Press, 1962.

Reeves, Thomas C. "Chester A. Arthur and the Campaign of 1880." *Political Science Quarterly* 84 (1969): 628–637.

———. *Gentleman Boss: The Life of Chester Alan Arthur.* New York: Knopf, 1975.

GEORGE BUSH

George Herbert Walker Bush (b. June 12, 1924, Milton, Massachusetts) can be remembered as ambassador to

George Bush. *Source:* Library of Congress.

the United Nations (1970), chair of the Republican National Committee (1972), ambassador to China (1974–1975), a member of Congress from Texas, director of the Central Intelligence Agency (1976–1977), or Ronald Reagan's vice president (1981–1989). Referring to his many opportunities in and out of politics, someone from Texas said of Bush that he was born on third base but always thought that he had hit a triple. But he is most often remembered as the 41st president of the United States, serving from 1989 to 1993. He was a graduate of Yale University and helped found an oil company in Texas in 1953.

In 1964 Bush lost a bid for a Senate seat from Texas but was elected to the House of Representatives in 1966 and reelected in 1968. Bush's backers cited his lengthy résumé as evidence of his suitability for the presidency.

When Bush was elected president in 1988, he promised to work toward a "kinder, gentler America," to promote environmental quality, and to be "the edu-

cation president." At the beginning of his administration, he held an "education summit" at the White House to symbolize the high priority that would be given to education. Teachers and environmental activists were among those who opposed Bush's reelection in 1992. But when Bush took office in 1989, it appeared that his administration would be more moderate than the Reagan administration that preceded it. He made a memorable promise, "Read my lips. No new taxes"—a promise that was popular but one that he did not keep. Whether he could have kept the promise was a topic of much debate.

To get elected, Bush defeated Michael Dukakis, a former governor of Massachusetts. An influential advertisement that was not actually placed by the Bush campaign told the story of Willie Horton, who committed murder after having been paroled in Massachusetts. The ad implied that Dukakis was unduly "soft" on crime but that a Bush administration would not be. It also represented an implied appeal to racism because Horton was African American.

Bush picked as his running mate Senator J. Danforth Quayle, who had won his Senate seat by a large majority, but as vice president, Quayle was never popular with the American people. Polling data indicated that the Democratic nominee for the vice presidential slot, Senator Lloyd Bentsen of Texas, was more popular and judged to be the winner in a debate with Quayle. Quayle nevertheless had some attributes that Bush lacked and so provided the ticket with balance. Quayle was much younger than Bush and more conservative. His nomination was designed to reassure some conservative Republicans, such as members of the Religious Right.

In foreign policy Bush promised a "new world order," which would mean a greater reliance on multilateralism involving the United Nations and regional institutions. With an end to the Cold War and eventually the demise of the Soviet Union, Bush felt that times were ripe for American leadership. His style was termed "Rolodex diplomacy" because he used the phone so often.

It was said that one of Bush's big concerns was not to appear to be a "wimp," a "ghost," or an "empty suit," as critics referred to him. To many critics, his "finest hour" was the Persian Gulf War, in which the United States resoundingly defeated Iraq. Bush stopped short, though, of deposing Iraqi leader Saddam Hussein. Nevertheless, during the campaign, Bush laid claim to the title "foreign policy president" and declared that such missions as Desert Storm (the U.S. response to the Iraqi invasion of Kuwait), Operation Just Cause (the U.S. invasion of Panama) and two operations called Restore Hope (one an airlift of food to starving Kurds in Iraq, the other the provision of food to people in the Confederation of Independent States) had been great successes.

He depicted the Gulf War as a struggle between good and evil, saying, "I might have said to hell with them [the United Nations, which authorized the intervention]—it's right and wrong, it's good and evil, he's evil and our cause is right." Bush was backed, even prodded, in his decisions by key allies, most notably the prime minister of Great Britain, Margaret Thatcher. The conflict with Iraqi leader Saddam Hussein persisted even after the Bush presidency: Hussein tried to engineer the assassination of Bush during a 1994 trip the former president took to Kuwait to accept an honorary doctorate from the University of Kuwait.

When American troops were sent to the Persian Gulf, it was labeled a response to Iraq's invasion of Kuwait. But one reason cited by many of the war's proponents was American dependence on Gulf oil. Bush did not discourage this view when he said that the American way of life was threatened.

Changes begun during the Reagan administration in the Soviet Union and Eastern Europe, generally reflecting liberalization, continued. In April 1989, the old communist government fell in Czechoslovakia. Also in that year, Germany was unified. In 1989, Solidarity, the trade union movement in Poland, regained its legal status, and in May 1990, Poland held its first free election in 68 years. Also in 1990, the Baltic states (Estonia, Latvia, and Lithuania) declared their independence from the Soviet Union and took steps to ensure it.

Bush endorsed the sending of Peace Corps volunteers to Eastern Europe and agreed with Soviet Prime Minister Mikhail Gorbachev at a summit held in Washington, D.C., in June 1990 to increase trade, reduce chemical weapons stockpiles, and establish student exchanges. In the face of a declining Soviet threat, though, Bush continued to fight for the Strategic Defense Initiative ("Star Wars"), the MX missile, and the Stealth bomber. Bush continued policies of détente with the Soviet Union and Eastern Europe.

With respect to China, Bush was viewed by his critics as too concerned about close relations with the government and not concerned enough about human rights. During his administration, demonstrators in Tiananmen Square in Beijing were attacked by government troops, and about 5,000 died. After initially suspending weapons shipments to China in protest, the Bush administration resumed them. Many influential members of Congress wished to grant visas to Chinese students in the United States, a move Bush opposed. He viewed his policy as one of power politics and realism as opposed to idealism and human rights.

In the Philippines, the United States backed the government of Corazon Aquino. There were, however, repeated coup attempts and a guerrilla insurgency led by the New People's Army. Through Clark Air Base, near Manila, the United States responded to a coup attempt in December 1989. Because of intense anti-Americanism, Peace Corps volunteers were withdrawn.

During the Bush administration, in February 1990, the incumbent Sandinista government lost an election in Nicaragua, and the candidate whom Bush preferred, Violeta Barrios de Chamorro, won the presidency. The United States had openly supported and subsidized the United Nicaraguan Opposition, and with its victory came an end to a bloody civil war in which the United States had, with Bush's enthusiastic support, backed and funded the rebels, known as *contras.* Although problems in Haiti would extend beyond Bush's term in office, it was during the Bush administration, in 1991, that a coup culminating in the rule of Colonel Raul Cedras overthrew the democratically elected government of President Jean-Bertrand Aristide. In strong contrast to the United Nations, which viewed the coup as "an internal matter," Bush led multilateral efforts to impose sanctions and to assure Aristide's safety.

President Bush backed the broadcasting efforts of Radio Free Europe and Radio Marti. He argued that their programming represented democracy in a world in which closed societies still posed a danger, and not, as critics charged, the antithesis of democracy, as state-operated media, rendered unnecessary by the ending of the Cold War.

Bush generally did not place Africa high on his foreign policy agenda. With respect to South Africa, he was more inclined to favor the relaxation of sanctions against the apartheid government and was generally viewed as an enemy (favoring "constructive engagement" with the rulers), rather than a friend, of majority rule. Bush did, however, support the sanctions during the early years of his administration, and lifting them was to be a reward for reforms. In Liberia, Bush did not change the view that America's intimate involvement in that country had been divisive. In 1990, when the regime of Samuel Doe was toppled and a bloody civil war began, Bush approved the use of U.S. troops to evacuate American citizens.

So-called high-politics issues of war and security took priority over low-politics issues of the economy, education, and the environment. Bush was a very reluctant participant in the United Nations Conference on the Environment and Development, held in Rio de Janeiro, Brazil, in 1992. Bush did not indicate support for either of the two treaties to come out of the conference—the Convention on Biological Diversity and the United Nations Framework Convention on Climate Change. Nor did the Bush administration fully agree with most of the representatives to the conference as to the Agenda 21, adopted at the conference in 1992, or the Rio Declaration on Environment and Development, which stated that development was a right and that priority should be given to "the special situation and needs of developing countries." It was clear that most of the conference's delegates supported a different kind of new world order than did George Bush.

Environmental activists complained that, during the Bush years, businesses could undo or circumvent regulations they did not like. Businesses would appeal to the Competitiveness Council at the White House, and the economy would take precedence over the environment. Bush's defenders, though, argued that his environmental record was good. Although it did not satisfy most of the delegates at Rio, who wanted a freeze, he did promise to limit U.S. production of chlorofluorocarbons (CFCs). He endorsed a new Clean Air Act, which was enacted into law during his administration.

In the economic area, Bush was an unabashed free trader, often, his opponents feared, at the cost of environmental degradation. He was a supporter of the North American Free Trade Agreement (NAFTA) and of the strengthening of the General Agreement on Tariffs and Trade (GATT). His term was marked by a period of recession; he therefore pledged that the economy would improve if he were reelected.

During the Bush administration, the rich–poor gap increased both intranationally and internationally. Even President Bush felt that inflation was unacceptably high. The economy as a whole was sluggish, and Bush was generally unsuccessful in solving trade problems with Japan. In 1992, during a bout with intestinal flu, he made matters worse by throwing up in the lap of Japanese Prime Minister Kiichi Miyazawa.

Bush was very concerned about the charge that he was insensitive to the plight of poor people. In his 1992 State of the Union address, for instance, he proposed tax relief, which he said would benefit everyone.

A big legislative achievement was the enactment of the Americans with Disabilities Act of 1990, compared by Bush to "the freeing of the slaves." This was a civil rights statute, endorsed by the Chamber of Commerce and the National Association of Manufacturers and passed with large majorities on both sides of the aisle.

Bush made one appointment to the Supreme Court, Clarence Thomas, who, it was alleged, had sexually harassed a woman he supervised while head of the Equal Employment Opportunities Commission, Anita Hill, now a law professor. Thomas was narrowly confirmed by the Senate and became perhaps the most conservative member of the Court.

There was a gender gap with respect to feelings about Bush, with men tending to view him more favorably than women. One reason was that Bush several times vetoed legislation that would have liberalized abortion laws. In addition, Bush tended to be a "hawk" on military issues while women tended to be more "dovish" than men.

There were notable improvements on the crime front, although some administration critics argued that this had more to do with the population's getting older than with the "get-tough" attitude of the public and of many officials. Bush appointed tougher judges, fought against gun registration, and favored capital punishment.

Part of Bush's campaign to control crime was the 1989 invasion of Panama in the name of the "war on drugs." Bush felt that Panama's president, Manuel Noriega, was engaged in drug trafficking and money laundering. The invasion had four declared objectives: (1) to keep the Panama Canal open, (2) to restore democracy to Panama, (3) to protect U.S. citizens' lives, and (4) to arrest Noriega and charge him with drug trafficking. As a result of the invasion, Noriega was forcibly brought to the United States to stand trial.

Bush felt, though, that education and crime control were primarily state and local, not federal, responsibilities. In this, he was supported by many Republican federal, state, and local officials. Indeed, he felt that many efforts should not be undertaken by government at all; they should instead be undertaken by voluntary agencies. This was the essence of his "thousand points of light" initiative extolling the virtue of ordinary Americans, the one thing he asked President Bill Clinton to continue. With this in mind, at the unveiling of the official portraits of the Bushes in 1995, Clinton praised Bush for his "compassion, civility, responsibility and optimism" as well as for his "integrity and decency."

In running against Clinton in 1992, Bush tried to emphasize his war record and contrast it with the background of Clinton, who had been an opponent of the Vietnam War rather than a participant. Bush argued that his own service during World War II (he had been a fighter pilot in the navy) had been meritorious and demonstrated his ability to withstand the pressures of the presidency. But the persistent lesson best expressed by Democratic strategist James Carville—"It's the economy, stupid"—carried sway because many voters' expectations were not matched by their achievements.

Bush tried unsuccessfully to run against a Congress that he viewed as an obstacle, as Democratic President

Harry Truman had done successfully in 1948. Bush tried to blame the persistence of many of the problems the country faced on the "do-nothing, good for nothing 80th Congress." The vast majority of the members of that Congress were returned to office, but Bush was not. A complicating factor was the role of independent candidate Ross Perot, who persuaded a substantial number of voters that Bush, as well as the Congress, was responsible for an oversized government. So when Bush parodied the Democratic promise to "put people first" by referring to the "government-first crowd," there were those who felt that Bush, too, was part of that crowd.

Another issue that Bush attempted unsuccessfully to use was "family values." Some opponents tried to portray him as an old man who was out of touch with the voters and pointed to this issue as evidence. Clinton's wife, Hillary, had an established career, which Barbara Bush did not, and the Clintons were seen as role models by a substantial number of voters. Often the attacks were made by innuendo, as in a statement by Marilyn Quayle, wife of Bush's vice president, that in the sixties, "not everyone demonstrated, dropped out, took drugs, joined in the sexual revolution or dodged the draft" or believed "that the family was so oppressive that women could only thrive apart from it."

Bush was also criticized for his party's opposition to homosexual rights and for not doing enough about AIDS (acquired immune deficiency syndrome). In an effort to combat the latter perception, on a night devoted to "family values," the Republican National Convention was addressed by Mary Fisher, an artist with AIDS, who insisted, "We do the President's cause no good if we praise the American family, but ignore a virus that destroys it." Nevertheless, throughout the campaign, Bush was heckled by demonstrators asking, "What about AIDS?"

After his presidency, Bush remained active in politics. One of his sons, George Bush Jr., was elected as governor of Texas, while another, Jeb Bush, came close to being elected as governor of Florida in 1994. George Bush's wife, Barbara, was very popular with the American people. Some were even interested in the welfare of the Bushs' pet dog, Millie. The delivery of Millie's first litter in 1989 reportedly brought tears to the president's eyes.

Before, during, and after Bush's presidency, he was tainted by the Iran–contra scandal. Many people insisted that he knew too much, even if he had done little. At the end of his presidency, in 1993, Bush pardoned former Secretary of Defense Caspar Weinberger and five others, saying that the pardons were motivated by "honesty, decency, and fairness."

In contrast to popular feelings about Bush's predecessor, Ronald Reagan, very few people felt either an intense love for George Bush or an intense hatred of him. Most remember his presidency as one of foreign policy success but domestic failure. Bush hated the "vision thing," something he would be criticized for lacking.

One observer, scholar Richard J. Barnet, was moved to comment that the president left "the impression that he didn't know quite what to do, but was determined to do it prudently." Bush's defenders as well as his critics feel that his presidency was characterized by moderation. They only disagree as to whether this quality was an asset or a liability.

Arthur Blaser

SEE ALSO History

BIBLIOGRAPHY

Bernhart, Larry. *American Hero*. New York: Pantheon, 1993.

Campbell, Colin, and Bert A. Rockman. *The Bush Presidency: First Appraisals*. Chatham, NJ: Chatham House, 1991.

Duffy, Michael, and Dan Goodgame. *Marching in Place: The Status Quo Presidency of George Bush*. New York: Simon and Schuster, 1992.

Podhoretz, John. *Hell of a Ride: Backstage at the Whitehouse Follies, 1989–1993*. New York: Simon and Schuster, 1994.

Tiefer, Charles. *The Semi-Sovereign Presidency: The Bush Administration's Strategy for Governing without Congress*. Boulder, CO: Westview Press, 1995.

CALVIN COOLIDGE

(John) Calvin Coolidge—born on July 4, 1872, in the town of Plymouth Notch, Vermont—was the 30th president of the United States. Coolidge presided over an era of governmental frugality and probusiness policies that were popular at the time but later regarded as misconceived. Coolidge, nicknamed "Silent Cal," was noted for his cautious reserve, public taciturnity, and pronounced frugality, but he was also a competent administrator, a skillful manipulator of the media, and a man devoted to career and family. Throughout his tenure, Coolidge remained a remarkably popular president, but the Great Depression brought his *laissez-faire* policies into disrepute, and most historians now regard him as having been overly complacent and inactive, lacking in vision, and ill equipped to deal with the period's emerging problems.

Early Life

Coolidge was raised in a rural farming community of 1,200 people where his family had lived since 1781. His father, a former merchant, held many public of-

Calvin Coolidge. *Source:* Library of Congress.

fices, ranging from superintendent of schools to state senator. His mother died of tuberculosis when he was 12. Coolidge was educated in a one-room schoolhouse next door to his home and, though very quiet, did well in his studies. At the age of 14, he was sent to Black River Academy in the nearby town of Ludlow in order to attain further education. He became secretary of his class and delivered a commencement speech praising the role of oratory in molding public opinion. At the urging of his principal and his father, he decided to sit for entrance exams at Amherst College. After failing the first round of exams due to a bad cold caught on the train, he did postgraduate study at St. Johnsbury

Academy, which granted him a college entrance certificate to Amherst College in 1891. Coolidge, the first member of his family to attend college, graduated from Amherst in 1895 and went into law practice in Northampton, Massachusetts, in 1897.

Early Political Career

Coolidge became a member of the Republican Party and served as city councillor and solicitor from 1899 to 1902. He was elected to the state legislature in 1907. His work there attracted little notice, but after being elected mayor of Northampton in 1909 and 1910, Coolidge left his law practice and devoted himself fully to his political career. In 1911 he went to the state Senate, where his thorough work earned him leadership positions, and by 1913 he was president of the Senate. Coolidge was a consistent opponent of big government. In his inaugural address as president of the Senate, he said, "Don't expect to build up the weak by pulling down the strong."

Coolidge cultivated friendship with Republican Party leaders, who admired his ability to voice the needs of business interests in Massachusetts. In 1915 Coolidge was elected lieutenant governor, and his popularity in the party brought him the governorship in 1918. It was in his role as governor that Coolidge stepped into the national spotlight.

As governor, Coolidge had to deal only with minor matters until the dramatic Boston police strike of 1919. This strike developed out of the inflation that followed World War I, as police officers saw their wages hold steady while the cost of living and the incomes of other groups rose. Although it was illegal for the police to form a labor union, they did so anyway. When Boston authorities threatened disciplinary action against the union leaders, the officers countered with a strike, during which criminal elements roamed the city, and there was rioting, violence, and property damage. On the second day of the strike, Governor Coolidge called out the state militia to restore order. In a public exchange of letters with Samuel Gompers, president of the American Federation of Labor, Coolidge made the statement, "There is no right to strike against the public safety by anybody, anywhere, anytime."

His use of the state militia to end the Boston police strike in 1919 won Coolidge a somewhat undeserved reputation for decisive action and brought him to the attention of the leadership of the Republican Party. Some forces within the party promoted him as a candidate for the presidential nomination in 1920. That year the Republicans were badly divided, and many strong candidates came forward to vie for the party nomination, which would almost surely lead to the presidency, since the Democrats were even more hopelessly torn and were irreparably associated with the by then unpopular Woodrow Wilson.

On the initial ballot, General Leonard Wood had more delegates than anyone else—but considerably fewer than enough to win the nomination. Coolidge ranked well down on the list, with only 34 votes. As the League of Nations debate caused the front-runners to knock each other off on successive ballots, Coolidge gradually lost delegates, and Warren G. Harding was finally adopted as the compromise candidate on the tenth ballot. Party leaders had selected Senator Irving Lenroot of Wisconsin for the vice presidential nomination, but when the Oregon delegation offered Coolidge as their candidate by way of complimenting Coolidge's admirers, the delegates chose Coolidge instead. In addition to settling for two compromise candidates, the Republicans did not offer a party platform.

The Republican ticket campaigned with slogans such as the vacuous "Let's Have Done with Wiggle and Wobble" and "Back to Normalcy" that played on the isolationist sentiment popular in the United States at the time. In the first presidential election that included female voters, the Harding–Coolidge ticket overwhelmingly defeated the Democrats, winning by more than 7 million votes out of fewer than 30 million cast, with an electoral count of 404 to 127. As Harding's vice president, Coolidge did little, remaining in the background of the scandal-plagued Harding administration.

Presidency

While Harding was on a trip to Alaska attempting to escape the pressures of the various scandals raging in Washington, Coolidge was visiting his family home in Vermont. Harding died in San Francisco on August 2, 1923, and the next day, Coolidge took the oath of office in the same farmhouse where he was born. The oath was given by his father, a notary public and justice of the peace, who read it by the light of a kerosene lamp. After being sworn in, the new president—along with his wife, father, and a few others—went across the street to Miss Cilley's Store, where they toasted the austere occasion with Moxie. Moxie was Coolidge's favorite soft drink, and he did not scruple to publicly support the beverage even as the nation's most visible public figure; there were several newspaper accounts of Coolidge and Moxie during his tenure as president.

Coolidge was also the first president to make radio broadcasts from the White House. His address on George Washington's birthday, transmitted from his study on February 22, 1924, was heard on 42 stations from coast to coast.

Following Harding's death, Coolidge moved quickly to neutralize the effects of the scandals that had been plaguing the late president's administration. Largely because of his inactivity, Coolidge was able to distance himself from the disreputable practices of his predecessor. His careful and skillful handling of the Washington scandals managed to save the Republican Party from public blame for widespread corruption and helped him secure the 1924 presidential nomination.

He campaigned with the slogan "Keep Cool with Coolidge," and to attract women voters, he distributed the Coolidge thimble—a device that failed in its purpose of encouraging women, recently granted suffrage, to vote. Despite the scandal associated with the Harding administration, the country was generally content with the Republican policies of limited government and withdrawal from international affairs following World War I. Coolidge easily won the election in November, receiving 54 percent of the popular vote. The electoral vote count was 382 for Coolidge, 136 for Democrat John W. Davis and 13 for Progressive Robert M. La Follette.

Coolidge's victory seemed to confirm both the appeal of his public image and the popularity of the conservative policies that he claimed were responsible for a growing national prosperity. Adopting his own saying that "The business of America is business," Coolidge felt the nation needed to attend to local affairs rather than worrying about big new public programs. In his 1925 inaugural address as president, Coolidge said, "Economy is idealism in its most practical form." Later that year, in an address to the New York Chamber of Commerce, he said, "Government and business should remain independent and separate; one directed from Washington, the other from New York." This style of governing, combined with a booming economy, made Coolidge very popular.

During Coolidge's administration, the economy prospered and the stock market flourished, but the prosperity did not benefit all sections of the nation equally. Industries such as coal mining remained depressed, and some cities had unemployment rates surpassing 10%. The cuts in federal taxes and expenditures that the president secured tended to favor business, as did his reorganization of regulatory policy. His maintenance of a high protective tariff adversely affected certain sectors of the economy, particularly agriculture.

After commercial farmers had lobbied in Congress for relief from depressed conditions, Coolidge vetoed the resulting McNary–Haugen Bill. When the farmers argued that manufacturers received substantial federal help from the high protective tariff and that the government ought to do something for agriculture, the president replied that the farmers were also aided by the tariff. His vetoes prevailed over the farm bloc in Congress.

Coolidge tended to remain distant from foreign affairs, leaving the formation of policy to his secretaries of state, Charles Evans Hughes and Frank B. Kellogg, who continued the search for improved international relations through mechanisms operating outside the League of Nations, which the U.S. Senate had failed to ratify. Among his administration's diplomatic achievements were the Dawes Plan, for scaling down German reparations; the Stimson accords, for pacifying Nicaragua; and the Kellogg–Briand Pact; outlawing war.

The Coolidge presidency was famous for its practical nonexistence. Coolidge was reluctant to appear in public or make policy statements, which he explained by saying, "If you don't say anything you can't be called on to repeat it." Coolidge's probusiness stance was aided by his silence and inactivity. In part because of metabolic need, Coolidge had to have a nap every afternoon as well as ten hours of sleep a night; he averaged four hours of work per day. Dorothy Parker, informed that Coolidge had died, responded, "How could they tell?" and H.L. Mencken complained that "Nero fiddled but Coolidge only snored."

Postpresidency

In 1927, when his teenage son died of blood poisoning, Coolidge announced that he would not be a candidate for president again, declaring simply, "I do not choose to run." He was not active in the successful 1928 campaign of fellow Republican Herbert Hoover, and in March 1929, when Hoover was inaugurated, Coolidge returned to Northampton. He engaged in the composition of his autobiography, published as *The Autobiography of Calvin Coolidge* in 1929, and wrote a daily newspaper column entitled "Thinking Things Over with Calvin Coolidge." He died in Northampton on January 5, 1933, and was buried in the family plot in Plymouth Notch, Vermont.

Jessamyn West

SEE ALSO History

BIBLIOGRAPHY

McCoy, Donald R. *Calvin Coolidge: The Quiet President*. New York: Macmillan, 1967.
White, William Allen. *Calvin Coolidge: The Man Who Is President*. New York: Macmillan, 1925.
Woods, Robert A. *The Preparation of Calvin Coolidge*. Boston: Houghton Mifflin, 1924.

DWIGHT D. EISENHOWER

Dwight David Eisenhower, the 34th president of the United States, began his life of public service as a career officer in the United States Army. Although he entered politics late in life, Eisenhower, known to the country as "Ike," became one of the most popular and successful postwar presidents. Eisenhower's calm, grandfatherly presence in the White House offered a measure of reassurance to a nation beset with a host of both foreign and domestic troubles.

Born to a large but poor family in Denison, Texas, in 1890, Eisenhower grew up in Abilene, Kansas, where he absorbed the hardworking midwestern values that would later characterize him. Attracted by the possibility of a free college education and the opportunity to play football, Eisenhower entered the U.S. Military Academy at West Point in 1911. He proved to be an average student and, in fact, received numerous demerits for minor infractions such as smoking. He graduated 61st out of a class of 164. One year after graduating from West Point and being commissioned a second lieutenant in the army, Eisenhower met and subsequently married Marie "Mamie" Geneva Doud. The couple eventually had one son who lived to maturity, John Sheldon Doud Eisenhower.

Dwight D. Eisenhower. *Source:* Library of Congress.

The early years of Eisenhower's military career were unexceptional. He served in a variety of positions until 1932, when he was posted to the staff of General Douglas MacArthur. He followed MacArthur to the Philippines and served there from 1935 to 1939. With the beginning of World War II, Eisenhower attracted the attention of Army Chief of Staff George C. Marshall, who considered him one of the most able officers in the army. Eisenhower would go on to command three major Allied invasions, including the invasion of Normandy, and would be appointed supreme Allied commander in Europe by the end of World War II.

After the war, Eisenhower became army chief of staff and then temporarily retired from the military to serve as president of Columbia University. He was recalled by President Harry S. Truman to serve as NATO's first supreme commander in 1951. Eager to seek the presidency but wary of actively campaigning for it, Eisenhower nonetheless showed tremendous strength in the early Republican presidential primaries of 1951 as a write-in candidate. This led to a popular movement to "draft" him to run. At the 1952 convention, Eisenhower easily defeated the more conservative Senator Robert Taft of Ohio on the first ballot, with 845 votes to Taft's 280. Eisenhower picked Senator Richard M. Nixon of California, who had made a name for himself as a staunch anticommunist through the Alger Hiss spy case, as his running mate.

At a time when communist expansion, the Korean War and McCarthyism all seemed to point to an overall American decline, Eisenhower seemed to many Americans like the solution to the nation's woes. The Republican campaign slogan "I Like Ike" seemed to testify to Eisenhower's personal appeal. Eisenhower pledged to end the Korean War, while Nixon hammered away at the Democrats for being soft on communism. The Democratic candidate, Adlai Stevenson, appeared to many Americans to be too intellectual and too removed from the average person. Stevenson's formality was especially damaging when compared to Eisenhower's grandfatherly presence on the new medium of television.

Eisenhower won the election with 55% of the popular vote to Stevenson's 44%. The Republican ticket swept 39 states and 442 electoral votes to the Democrat's 9 states and 89 electoral votes. Eisenhower also broke the Solid South—by carrying four states in the region. In addition, the Republicans gained narrow majorities in both the House of Representatives and the Senate.

During his first term, Eisenhower clearly demonstrated that he was a moderate and, hence, would not bow to the more conservative elements of the Republican Party. Many conservatives expected Eisenhower, the first Republican president since 1932, to dismantle many of the New Deal and Fair Deal programs. Instead of slashing government programs and spending, Eisenhower actually increased them. He broadened the Social Security system, increased farm subsidies, and created the Department of Health, Education and Welfare. Furthermore, during his tenure, Eisenhower greatly expanded the White House staff. He created new positions such as the office of chief of staff and increased the number of personnel on various other staffs.

Eisenhower also showed a willingness to expand the federal government's role in the national economy. He increased the minimum wage from 75¢ to $1.00 an hour and supported revisions to the union-restricting Taft–Hartley Act. In 1954 he signed the St. Lawrence Seaway Act, which called for a joint construction project with Canada to allow oceangoing ships to travel the Great Lakes. Two years later the president signed the Interstate Highway Act, which authorized the construction of a 42,000-mile system of highways to span the nation.

In spite of these spending increases, Eisenhower did carry out a number of conservative reforms during his first term. These actions were aimed mainly at the American business community. He reduced the income tax on the wealthy, cut out many price controls and decreased business regulations. For instance, he supported the Atomic Energy Act of 1954, which allowed private companies to produce nuclear energy. While many criticized Eisenhower for being too probusiness, his policies helped spur an economic boom that began in 1954 and lasted well into 1958.

Eisenhower's moderate nature was also reflected in his actions toward the Red scare of the 1950s known as McCarthyism. While campaigning, Eisenhower deliberately refrained from using the harsh rhetoric and tactics espoused by Senator Joseph McCarthy of Wisconsin. Instead, Eisenhower allowed Nixon to attack the Truman administration for being soft on communism. After the election, Eisenhower continued to try to distance himself from McCarthy and his supporters. He spoke out against McCarthy-inspired book burnings and worked behind the scenes to undermine support for the senator. When McCarthy lost public favor by attacking the U.S. Army in the infamous Army–McCarthy Hearings of 1954, Eisenhower supported the Senate's resolution to censure the Wisconsin senator. This censure effectively ended the McCarthy era.

The modern civil rights movement came fully into existence during Eisenhower's first term. In 1954 the

Supreme Court, led by Eisenhower appointee Earl Warren, issued the *Brown* v. *Board of Education* decision, which declared that segregation in the public school system was unconstitutional. Eisenhower would eventually have to use federal troops to enforce that ruling.

Eisenhower actually began implementing his foreign policy before he even took the oath of office. He traveled to Korea in 1952 and helped institute a truce agreement that was formalized in July 1953. This fulfilled Eisenhower's campaign promise to restart negotiations and effectively ended the Korean War.

The death of Joseph Stalin in 1953 seemed to offer the United States an opportunity to improve relations with the Soviet Union. Eisenhower attempted to further reduce tensions between the two superpowers through actions such as his atoms-for-peace proposal to the United Nations in 1953 and his open-skies proposal at the Geneva Conference of 1955. Nonetheless, competition between the two nations intensified during Eisenhower's presidency as both states attempted to increase their influence in the Third World through trade and both military and economic aid. Eisenhower dramatically increased the role of the CIA in conducting American foreign policy. With his approval, the CIA carried out coups in both Iran and Guatemala to replace leftward-leaning governments with staunch anticommunist leaders.

The French withdrawal from Indochina brought about an increased American presence in the region, exemplified by the creation of the Southeast Asia Treaty Organization (SEATO), which was supposed to mirror its European counterpart, the North Atlantic Treaty Organization (NATO), as a defensive alliance to contain communist expansion. In 1955 tensions flared in Asia when Communist China threatened to invade Taiwan. Eisenhower reacted vigorously by obtaining congressional authority to use American troops if necessary to protect Taiwan. This action deterred the Chinese, who withdrew their troops.

In the Middle East, Eisenhower refused to support an Anglo-French intervention over the Suez Canal in 1956. This action soured relations with France but forced Great Britain closer to the United States because it demonstrated the necessity for securing American support before undertaking significant foreign policy initiatives.

Eisenhower suffered a heart attack on September 24, 1956. He was hospitalized for seven weeks but recovered quickly enough to run for a second term. As in the previous election, the Democrats nominated Adlai Stevenson to run against Eisenhower. Also, as in the previous election, Eisenhower easily defeated Stevenson, receiving 35,582,236 popular votes and 457 elec-

toral votes to Stevenson's 26,031,322 popular votes and 73 electoral votes. Despite Eisenhower's impressive margin of victory, however, the Republicans failed to capture either house of Congress. Eisenhower's victory was clearly a personal one.

Early in his second term, Eisenhower faced a number of both domestic and foreign crises. In September 1957 the president was forced to send troops to Little Rock, Arkansas, after rioting broke out in response to Arkansas Governor Orval Faubus's refusal to integrate the city's public school system. In October of the same year, the American public was shocked when the Soviet Union launched the world's first satellite, *Sputnik*, and thus started the space race. Only after a year of some notable failures was the United States able to respond to the Soviet Union's space lead with the launching of *Explorer I.*

Eisenhower's domestic problems were complicated by the beginnings of a recession that lingered for most of his second term. Partially in response to the recession and to the start of the space race, Eisenhower submitted the largest peacetime budget yet proposed in 1957. At a record $71.8 billion, this deficit-financed budget alienated most conservative Republicans. The budget included vast increases in defense spending, the space program and various social programs.

The expanded military spending came as Eisenhower exercised an increasingly hard line against the Soviet Union. He undertook an immense buildup of the nation's nuclear arsenal as part of America's new strategic doctrine of "massive retaliation" as a deterrent against the Soviet Union. Also, in 1957 Congress approved a new foreign policy tenet known as the "Eisenhower Doctrine," which gave the president authority to use military force to aid nations that faced communist aggression. Eisenhower invoked this doctrine in 1958 to send troops to Lebanon and to send ships to protect Taiwan in response to Chinese attacks on Taiwanese islands.

Relations between the Soviet Union and the United States briefly thawed with Premier Nikita Khrushchev's visit to the United States in 1959 and a planned summit between the two leaders in Paris a year later. The thaw abruptly ended when the Soviets shot down an American U-2 "spy plane" prior to the Paris summit. Khrushchev demanded that Eisenhower apologize for such flights and end the U-2 project. Eisenhower refused, and most of the earlier goodwill rapidly dissipated. Eisenhower suffered a further foreign policy setback late in his second term when Fidel Castro toppled the dictatorship of Fulgencio Batista in Cuba. Relations between Cuba and the United States quickly deteriorated when Castro began enacting socialist reforms on the island that included nationalizing land owned by American companies. Castro gradually positioned Cuba closer to the Soviet Union, which prompted Eisenhower to break off diplomatic relations with the island in January 1961. This action, in turn, prompted Castro to move firmly into the Soviet orbit.

Prevented from running for a third term by the 22nd Amendment to the Constitution, Eisenhower endorsed Vice President Nixon in the 1960 presidential election. Despite his ambivalence toward Nixon, Eisenhower was genuinely shocked when Nixon lost the election. Eisenhower had little confidence in the ability of John F. Kennedy to effectively govern the nation and, in his farewell speech, warned America about the dangers of a growing military-industrial complex—a complex that his policies had helped facilitate.

After leaving office, Eisenhower retired to private life in Gettysburg, Pennsylvania. There he wrote his memoirs and continued to engage in his favorite sport, golf. In his last major political act, he again endorsed Nixon for the presidential race in 1968. He suffered a series of heart attacks in 1969 that eventually weakened him to the point that he contracted pneumonia. He died of the disease on March 28, 1969, and was given a full military burial in his hometown of Abilene, Kansas.

Tom Lansford

SEE ALSO History

BIBLIOGRAPHY

Ambrose, Stephen E. *Eisenhower: Soldier and President.* New York: Simon and Schuster, 1990.

Burk, Robert F. *Dwight D. Eisenhower: Hero and Politician.* Boston: Twayne Publishing, 1986.

Lee, R. Alton. *Dwight D. Eisenhower: Soldier and Statesman.* Chicago: Nelson–Hall, 1981.

Saulnier, Raymond. *Constructive Years: The U.S. Economy under Eisenhower.* Lanham, MD: University Press of America, 1991.

GERALD R. FORD

For more than a quarter century, Gerald Rudolph Ford reigned as a major force in the Republican Party. He represented the party's moderate wing after World War II and eventually served as Republican minority leader in the U.S. House of Representatives during the 1960s and early 1970s. An Eisenhower internationalist who had his worldview changed as a result of his military service during World War II, Ford's ultimate goal was to lead the Republicans to a congressional victory so that he could become Speaker of the House. His reliable "workhorse" style and open, congenial personality won

Gerald R. Ford. *Source:* Library of Congress.

him friends among both Republicans and Democrats. Denied a House majority, Ford planned to retire in 1976. But fate intervened in late 1973 when Spiro T. Agnew resigned and Ford assumed the vice presidency. Less than a year later, fate again interjected itself into Ford's career when Richard M. Nixon, Ford's 1948 congressional classmate, resigned, catapulting Ford into the presidency. Gerald R. Ford became the first unelected president of the United States on August 9, 1974.

Although Ford shared many of Nixon's domestic and foreign policy views, their personalities were very different. Ford's political philosophy and personality were products of his midwestern roots. Born on July 14, 1913, in Omaha, Nebraska, as Leslie Lynch King Jr. to a father he met for the first time sixteen years later, Ford was adopted in 1917 by his mother's second husband and assumed his stepfather's name. He had his name legally changed in 1935 after he had graduated from college. In many ways, Ford's ambition derived from an apparent need for public acceptance. His work ethic, honesty, and openness derived from an affectionate and stable childhood. Ford's trusting and optimistic outlook was reinforced through his dedicated participation in scouting, which was demonstrated by his achievement of Eagle Scout rank at age 14.

His stepfather encouraged his interest in school and in athletics. After Ford's high school football team won the Michigan championship, Ford was named all-state center and captain of the all-state team. Athletics offered Ford a vehicle to acquire his undergraduate and graduate college degrees during the Great Depression. He played football while he worked his way through the University of Michigan (1931–1935) and earned a bachelor's degree in economics. His collegiate athletic prowess gained him offers from two professional football teams, but he turned them down to pursue a law degree. During his White House years, Ford was maligned by the media as uncoordinated, but he was America's most natural athlete in the presidency.

Though much later in his career he would disparagingly refer to himself as "a Ford and not a Lincoln," Gerald Ford and Abraham Lincoln shared such traits as congeniality, a moderate philosophy, and a similar career path. Ford's initial interest in a political career grew out of winning a local high school popularity contest in Grand Rapids, Michigan. He visited Congress and would later use the legal profession as his route into politics. He demonstrated an early interest in law by taking two courses at the University of Michigan Law School before financial restraints forced him to accept a position as an assistant coach at Yale University, which later admitted him on a trial basis as a part-time law student in the spring of 1938. While still a law student in 1939, Ford registered as a Republican. The next year, he served in the Wendell Willkie campaign and in Philadelphia attended his first Republican National Campaign. Ford, already dabbling in national party politics, went on to graduate in the top third of the Yale Law class of 1941.

The new graduate, entertaining political aspirations, rejected offers from major law firms in the East and opted to return to his midwestern roots to open a law office with Philip Buchen, one of the top law graduates from the University of Michigan.

From the start of this partnership, it was clear that Ford was more interested in politics than the practice of law. Soon he was elected president of a Grand Rapids citizens' organization formed to overthrow Frank McKay, the corrupt state Republican Party political boss. Ford's political plans were put on hold by World War II. His four-year enlistment as a naval officer serving in the Pacific theater resulted in a transformation of Ford's midwestern isolationist philosophy into a broader worldview. When he returned home, he found himself at odds with the traditional isolationist establishment in his party.

Ford immediately joined the prestigious law firm of Butterfield, Keeny and Amberg, where Philip Buchen, his first law partner, was already a member. He soon built a political base by joining a host of local civic or-

ganizations, and within a year decided to run for Congress. In a bold assertion of his new political views, he challenged five-term incumbent Bartel J. Jonkman, a Republican hand-picked and supported over the years by Frank McKay. Jonkman was an old-school isolationist opposed to the new internationalism being championed by Michigan's then-senior senator Arthur Vandenberg, who supported the Marshall Plan and the United Nations. Although the Dutch made up 60% of the district and western Michigan traditionally had espoused an America First outlook, Ford shrewdly appealed to members of the Dutch Reformed Church, rather than the Dutch Christian Reformed Church to which Jonkman belonged. Through an energetic campaign, Ford defeated the veteran Republican in the September 14, 1948, primary by a 26,632 to 14,341 vote. Although Harry Truman pulled off an even more surprising victory in the November general election that year, Ford was elected with 60.5% of the vote in Michigan's Fifth Congressional District. His 1948 House classmates included John F. Kennedy and Richard M. Nixon.

Ford's first alliance in Congress was as a founder of the Chowder and Marching Society, a group of 15 Republicans, primarily World War II veterans, including Nixon. This informal organization would eventually produce many of the Republican Party's leaders during the next three decades. Ford shared Nixon's political philosophy as well as a mutual interest in sports. The society's monthly meetings included members' wives and brought the Fords and Nixons even closer together. By 1950, the Fords lived near the Nixons in Alexandria, Virginia.

In Congress, Ford's skills and his diligence soon earned him his "workhorse" reputation. In 1950 he was selected for an opening on the powerful Appropriations Committee. After five losing presidential campaigns, in the 1952 election Ford backed Eisenhower over Robert Taft. Republican control of the House and Senate in 1952 led to Ford's appointment as chairman of the Army Subcommittee on Appropriations. In 1956 he was selected for membership on the five-member Intelligence Subcommittee of Appropriations with oversight of the CIA budget. Ford made Nixon's short list for consideration as his 1960 running mate. In 1961, the American Political Science Association recognized Ford's political accomplishments as a legislative force and a moderate conservative.

By 1962, Ford had earned a "godfather" role in his party in recognition of his career contributions. He was selected by a group of fellow young Republicans (Melvin Laird, Robert Griffin, Charles Goodell, and Donald Rumsfeld) to challenge the leadership of

Charles Hoeven from Iowa for chairmanship of the House Republican Conference, the third-ranking leadership position among House Republicans. The Old Guard was defeated 86 to 78.

Though the contest was already decided, as a symbol for his state's moderate Republican philosophy, Ford nominated Michigan Governor George Romney for president at the 1964 Republican National Convention in San Francisco. During that fall's election, Ford campaigned for Barry Goldwater, hoping that more Republicans might be elected to Congress. After the disastrous November election left the House Republicans reduced to their lowest number since 1936, the same group of Republican "Young Turks" in 1962 persuaded Ford to challenge Charles Halleck, the 64-year-old House Republican leader. Ford won by a 73-to-67 vote and was reelected to the position during his remaining years in the House. Ford's "brain trust," which worked to develop policy alternatives to the Democrats, included Laird, Goodell, and John Rhodes.

Unrelenting strain on his family, particularly his concern for the health of his wife, Betty, exacerbated by his extended absences from home for political reasons, coupled with his mounting frustration with the Nixon White House, led Ford to plan his retirement from Congress in 1976, even though he had never realized his ambition to become Speaker of the House. Ironically, it was not the Speaker of the House—or Spiro Agnew, the man who had been elected vice president in 1972—who ultimately succeeded Nixon when he resigned on August 9, 1974. Instead, it was Ford, a politician whose personality was the polar opposite of his two disgraced predecessors, who was appointed vice president and later took the oath as the 38th president of the United States.

Ford brought to the executive office the same leadership approach that served him so well in the legislative branch of government. His foreign policy was dominated by Henry Kissinger, who had developed ties with Ford early in Ford's congressional career. Ford's open staff dispelled the paranoia that had enveloped the White House under Nixon. Unfortunately, his decision to pardon Nixon as a means to heal the nation and move beyond the Watergate scandal was misunderstood by the public, which disapproved of judicial short-circuits. Nonetheless, the pardon was characteristic of America's greatest presidents. The clemency record shows that Ford had the most generous pardoning rate of presidents since World War II. Moreover, despite his hawkish view on Vietnam, Ford also supported an amnesty for Vietnam War resisters.

The conservative wing of the Republican Party challenged Ford's leadership during the 1976 primaries. He was able to defeat the strong challenge from Ronald Reagan by winning 16 of 26 primaries, but the final Republican nominee was not decided until the Republican Convention, when Ford won on the first ballot with 1,187 to 1,070 votes. Ford selected as his running mate Senator Robert Dole of Kansas. Ultimately the "workhorse" Ford nearly defeated Jimmy Carter in a close election (49% to 51% of the popular vote and an electoral college margin of 240 to 297), this despite his accidental presidency, his primary struggle, and his pardon of Nixon.

William D. Pederson

SEE ALSO History

BIBLIOGRAPHY

Cannon, James. *Time and Chance. Gerald Ford's Appointment with History*. New York: HarperCollins, 1994.

Firestone, Bernard J., and Alexej Ugrinsky, eds. *Gerald R. Ford and the Politics of Post-Watergate America*. Westport, CT: Greenwood Press, 1992.

Ford, Gerald R. *A Time to Heal*. New York: Harper and Row, 1979.

Greene, John R. *Gerald R. Ford. A Bibliography*. Westport, CT: Greenwood Press, 1994.

———. *The Presidency of Gerald R. Ford*. Lawrence: University of Kansas Press, 1995.

Peabody, Robert L. *The Ford–Halleck Minority Leadership Contest*. New York: McGraw-Hill, 1966.

Pederson, William D., ed. *The "Barberian" Presidency*. New York: Peter Lang, 1989.

JAMES A. GARFIELD

The relatively short life of James Abram Garfield (b. November 19, 1831; d. September 19, 1881) is in many ways a chronicle of a tumultuous period in American history. Born in a log cabin to a struggling pioneer family in a region of Ohio called the Western Reserve, Garfield graduated from college, became a teacher, principal, part-time preacher, officer in the Union army, legislator at both the state and national levels, respected statesman and politician, and for a short period, president of the United States.

The decade of Garfield's life spanning his late teens to late twenties was spent first at Geauga Academy, a private religiously oriented secondary school, then at Western Reserve Eclectic Institute at Hiram, Ohio, and then later at Williams College in Massachusetts, from which he graduated. After graduation, he returned to Hiram to teach full-time and preach on weekends in the recently formed Disciples of Christ denomination, of which he was at that time a devout member. His early twenties were additionally marked by frequent

James A. Garfield. *Source:* Library of Congress.

public-speaking engagements on philosophical and religious themes, which while he seemed totally uninterested in politics at the time, caused him to address moral issues such as slavery that were soon to become significant political issues. In a theme that was to follow him for the rest of his life, he was appointed president of the college at Hiram over older and more experienced teachers. Somehow, James A. Garfield always managed to have the right friends in the right places at the right moments in history and, as such, won for himself many notable appointments and offices, starting with the presidency of what was soon to be known as Hiram College.

In an era in which the office sought the candidate, Garfield's friend Harmon Austin, influential in the

newly formed Republican Party, nominated the 27-year-old Garfield for the Ohio state senate. Since the district in which he was nominated was heavily Republican in sentiment, Garfield won the position easily and in January 1860 was sworn in. His two years in the state senate were marked by growing friendships with many up-and-coming influentials in the Republican Party of Ohio. By 1861, he spent a good deal of time speaking out loudly and strongly against slavery and for the preservation of the Union—by war if necessary. While loyal to the new Republican President Abraham Lincoln, he was frustrated by Lincoln's perceived inaction regarding slavery and the southern resistance and was highly critical of him.

In August 1861, totally inexperienced as a soldier or commander, he was appointed to a post as colonel of a new regiment. He commanded a battle in Kentucky in January 1862 and saw battle at Shiloh (April 1862). While he showed a distaste for professional military men and their seeming preoccupation with battle strategy over the larger moral issues of vanquishing slavery, he spent a good deal of 1862 and 1863 in command positions in the Union army.

While Garfield was serving in the army in 1862, friends got him nominated to the United States Congress on the Republican Party ticket. Again, he was easily elected in the fall of 1862 with little or no campaigning, for a term of Congress that was to begin in December 1863. The interim he spent as chief of staff for General William S. Rosecrans in their encounters in middle Tennessee. Following the loss of an important battle at Chickamauga, Garfield directed hostile allegations at Rosecrans regarding his actions in the battle, and Rosecrans was removed from command, ending what had become a good friendship.

Garfield began what were to be 18 years in the House of Representatives when the congressional term opened in December 1863. During his tenure, he became both a significant leader of his party, despite policy and personal disagreements that frequently arose, and a respected leader in Congress.

While Lincoln was popular with the people, he was not so popular with Congress. The Democrats thought the war should be ended by negotiation even if that meant recognizing the Confederate States as a new nation. The Republicans in Congress were of two factions—those who supported the president and those Radical Republicans who saw Lincoln as weak. These Republicans, among them Garfield, criticized the president for postponement of emancipation, his doubts regarding African American suffrage, and his desire to keep Reconstruction in his hands and return the various states to self-government as soon as possible.

Garfield and other Radical Republicans in Congress vehemently opposed Lincoln's desires for political privileges and property for pardoned rebels in 1863. Garfield urged harsh treatment of rebels and confiscation of their property, opposing the president on most points. Yet when Lincoln was assassinated, Garfield was among the many mourners, deeply feeling the loss.

Lincoln's successor, Andrew Johnson, began a Reconstruction modeled after Lincoln's plan. In 1864, three states—Arkansas, Louisiana and Tennessee—had been recognized. Johnson prepared to recognize the eight remaining states of the Confederacy on the same formula and offered a broad amnesty as Lincoln had wanted. But the Radical Republicans insisted that the newly admitted states abolish slavery, with no mention of suffrage for ex-slaves. Garfield, however, went on record as supporting not only immediate abolition of slavery but suffrage as well.

Calls in Congress for Johnson's impeachment accelerated in 1865 when he vetoed a Radical Republican–pushed bill that would have provided for indefinite military occupation of the South. While Garfield was largely in the Radicals' camp, he vacillated but eventually supported impeachment.

Throughout the 1870s, Garfield gained in stature in Congress, holding posts on the Ways and Means Committee and serving as chair of the Appropriations Committee. These positions allowed him to develop some expertise in fiscal matters. On the issues of the day, Garfield took anti-inflationary, high-tariff, protectionist positions that would shelter Ohio's emerging steel industry. In general, he was a believer in sound currency, a pragmatic fiscal conservative.

Republican Ulysses S. Grant was elected to the first of two terms as president in 1868. During the ensuing eight years, Garfield was a respected leader in Congress and within his party, but he was highly critical of the president and his policies. By 1871, a large rift appeared in the Republican Party. The Republicans opposed to Grant nominated Horace Greeley for president, while the other Republicans nominated Grant for a second term. Even though Garfield was greatly displeased with Grant, he supported his candidacy as a choice of the lesser of two evils. This began Garfield's period of more intense party loyalty.

In the early 1870s, Garfield was caught up in several scandals and controversies surrounding some members of Congress regarding the purchase of railroad stock, a perceived salary grab by Congress, and other events that students of government 100 years later would see as conflicts of interest. At the time, however, such ethical qualms were not so well developed, and many government officials regularly engaged in such behavior. Garfield was associated with these controversies, but none apparently did him permanent political damage.

In 1876, the Republican Party nominated Rutherford B. Hayes for president, and the Democrats nominated Samuel Tilden. This was a very closely contested race, with Tilden winning the popular vote but Hayes winning a one-vote majority in the electoral college. Because of the closeness of the outcome, the election was contested in four states—Florida, Louisiana, South Carolina, and Oregon. Because of Garfield's stature in the House of Representatives and within his party, he was appointed to a group charged with examining contested states' returns. In Louisiana, the Democrats had won with a mere 6,000 votes; Garfield charged that voter intimidation had prevented a Republican victory and thus gave that state to the Republicans. There were many allegations of election fraud, pursued by both sides, and Garfield found himself right in the middle of the dispute. The result was that the three disputed states in the South each sent two sets of election returns to be counted in Washington, one showing Republican victory, the other Democratic.

Since this problem had not occurred before and the Constitution is not clear on the issue, the dilemma was who should count the votes (and thus, which sets of returns would they accept). Garfield played a very large role in quiet negotiations with both sides, attempting to exact the Democrats' price for having the votes counted by the Senate—a move that would assure Hayes of victory. The result was that an agreement was made that an Electoral Commission would be created, composed of five senators, three of whom would be Republicans; five members of the House, three of whom would be Democrats; and five members of the Supreme Court, two of each party and the fifth to be chosen jointly by the initial 14 members of the commission. The commission's decision would be final.

Garfield was elected to serve as one of the Republicans from the House. The fifth justice was Joseph P. Bradley, a nominal Republican who was respected by both sides and who most believed would be an impartial judge of the returns. After the commission reviewed all contested states, the vote was along party lines, with Bradley voting for the Republican Hayes to be president.

Hayes's four years passed with Garfield as minority leader in the House. When Hayes decided not to seek reelection, Garfield's name was suggested by some as a possibility. But there were lots of hats in the ring in the 1880 election, and Garfield decided not to seek the nomination actively, but not to refuse it if it were offered him. The major contenders for the nomination were James G. Blaine, Ulysses S. Grant, and John Sherman, for whom Garfield was serving as manager. Thirty-four ballots could not produce a nominee at the horribly deadlocked convention. Garfield's name was offered as a compromise candidate, and on the 36th ballot, he won the majority of votes and became his party's nominee for president, with Chester A. Arthur as the vice presidential nominee.

The general election of 1880 saw Garfield pitted against the Democrats' General Winfield Scott Hancock. It proved to be another close election. Only 10,000 votes separated the two candidates, although Garfield won 214 electoral votes to Hancock's 155.

The months between the election and his inauguration were filled with office seekers and people wanting favors from the president-elect. Once Garfield assumed the office of president on March 4, 1881, the endless stream of office seekers did not die away but merely intensified as hundreds begged for government jobs and cabinet appointments. In an attempt to please both factions of the Republican Party, Garfield filled large numbers of appointments both with people from the Grant or Stalwart camp and with people who had supported Blaine. Instead of appeasing his critics, this attempt to mollify them merely infuriated them. One of the many individuals to whom Garfield denied a federal post was Charles Jules Guiteau.

On July 2, 1881, while waiting at the Washington, D.C., train station, en route to a family vacation, Garfield was shot twice by Guiteau. One shot grazed his arm, but the other lodged somewhere in his back, placing the president in grave danger. Because antibiotics and X-rays had not yet been invented, the gunshot wound would eventually take his life. For two days, Garfield's life hung by a thread, then he seemed to get somewhat better.

It was clear that Garfield was unable to execute his duties and responsibilities as president, yet there was no consensus as to whether Vice President Arthur should take the oath of office immediately or merely serve as acting president, so he did neither. Since Congress was not in session that summer and no pressing problems were before the nation, Garfield lingered on as president in a deteriorating condition until his death on September 19. Guiteau, who upon shooting Garfield had yelled, "I am a Stalwart," was arrested, tried, and executed.

Lisa Langenbach

SEE ALSO History

BIBLIOGRAPHY

Clancy, Herbert J. *The Presidential Election of 1880.* Chicago: Loyola University Press, 1988.

Doenecke, Justus D. *The Presidencies of James A. Garfield and Chester A. Arthur.* Lawrence: University Press of Kansas, 1981.

Peskin, Allan. *Garfield.* Kent, OH: Kent State University Press, 1978.

ULYSSES S. GRANT

Ulysses Simpson Grant, Civil War general and 18th president of the United States, was born Hiram Ulysses Grant on April 27, 1822, in Point Pleasant, Ohio, near Cincinnati. U.S. Grant had a varied career as businessman, farmer, military officer, and politician. In all these pursuits, Grant experienced the range from glorious success to the depths of despair, and he became one of the most recognized and beloved figures of American political history. He died on July 23, 1885, in Mount McGregor, New York.

Grant's father arranged for his appointment to West Point in 1838, and his academic performance there was mixed. His name was erroneously changed to Ulysses Simpson Grant during his enrollment. He preferred this name and kept it. Grant did not particularly like the army but served in the infantry from 1843 to 1854, including campaigns in the Mexican War, an action he

Ulysses S. Grant. *Source:* Library of Congress.

privately opposed. Later, he moved to St. Louis and through an unsuccessful series of careers as farmer, partner in a real estate firm, and customhouse employee. When the Civil War began, Grant worked in his father's leather goods store in Galena, Illinois.

Grant requested to be recommissioned in the Union army but was not. In 1861 he received a gubernatorial appointment to raise and command a regiment of Galena volunteers. Later that year, he was promoted to brigadier general of volunteer troops in southeastern Missouri. In 1862 he captured Fort Donelson in Tennessee, an important Union victory that attracted attention and a promotion. Subsequent victories in the western campaigns attracted President Lincoln's favor, and Grant was promoted to commander of all Union armies in 1864. Grant fought the forces of Robert E. Lee until the Confederate general's surrender at Appomattox, Virginia, in 1865, effectively ending the war. Throughout his military career, Grant understood the linkages between military and political success.

In 1868 there was deep dissatisfaction with the administration of Andrew Johnson, who became president after Lincoln's assassination. Reconstruction policy under Johnson had moved toward a restoration of power of the antebellum aristocracy. Both Democrats and Republicans sought the candidacy of war hero Ulysses Grant. Grant was essentially nonpartisan, and it was his dissatisfaction with Johnson and the weak attempts at Reconstruction that led him into the Republican camp. Partisan squabbling, Grant believed, worked against national unity. He served briefly as secretary of war after President Johnson's removal of Edwin Stanton produced a backlash from Radical Republicans who sought the president's impeachment. Grant cooperated with congressional Republicans and joined the party of Lincoln.

Grant viewed politics as an obligation and an indication of his acceptance and popularity. He had never been politically involved, voting for president only twice prior to his nomination. Grant wanted to strengthen the policy of Reconstruction in the South, to promote racial justice, and to encourage economic progress. Yet, Grant, like most of the Republicans at the time, preferred a caretaker president with an active Congress. The legislative branch set national policy, and the executive, Grant thought, should merely enforce it.

At the Chicago convention of the "National Union Republican Party" in May, delegates unanimously selected Ulysses Grant as their presidential nominee. The convention ultimately chose House Speaker Schuyler Colfax of Indiana as the vice presidential nominee and approved a platform denouncing Andrew Johnson's

presidency, lauding the Reconstruction policy of the Radical Republicans, proposing a hard-currency approach to economic crises, and supporting guarantees of suffrage and civil rights of blacks in the South, immigrants, and naturalized citizens.

This was an age when presidential candidates were expected to be quiet and passive, making few speeches and fewer policy pronouncements. Grant was the ideal candidate for this age, in part, quite frankly, because Grant had nothing to say. In his letter accepting the nomination, however, Grant set the campaign theme: "Let us have peace." Grant's view of a passive presidency ignored issues of the day because he expected to be merely an administrative officer. His strengths were his popularity and character.

The Republican electoral strategy was to "wave the bloody shirt," that is, to make defense of the Union in the Civil War the primary issue in the campaign. The Democratic Party was fractured and weakened by the war and the Johnson administration. Grant's nomination symbolized union and victory. The Democrats nominated Horatio Seymour, an effective orator but a weak presidential candidate. The Democratic vice presidential nominee, Francis Blair of Missouri, gave prosouthern speeches that played into the hands of Republican attempts to label the Democrats as the party of secession. Grant won convincingly in the November election, with 52.7% of the popular vote and 214 electoral votes (to Seymour's 80).

Grant distrusted politicians and, with Lincoln gone, had few political allies. His initial presidential appointments were mostly composed of friends and colleagues, including his wartime advisers. The Grant administration was rocked by scandals. The first, Black Friday, involved gold speculators Jay Gould and James Fisk, who attempted to corner the gold market, using their influence with Grant and the White House. Grant eventually realized this and ordered the Treasury Department to flood the gold market. But that ruined many investors, and charges of greed and corruption implicated the administration from that point on.

Poor choices for appointments continued to plague Grant. He appointed two new justices to the Supreme Court, shortly after its decision to declare part of a congressional statute to authorize wartime paper currency as legal tender as unconstitutional and void. The two justices joined the dissenting faction, reversing the decision and upholding the act. The sudden reversal implied that Grant tried to pack the Court. The Crédit Mobilier scandal further damaged the administration's reputation. Stock in this holding company was discounted to administration officials, including Vice

President Colfax, in order to avoid federal investigation of schemes to skim profits from construction of the Union Pacific railway.

In June 1872, Grant easily won renomination at the Republican convention in Philadelphia, and Massachusetts Senator Henry Wilson was nominated for vice president. The Republican platform was one of rights (for women and blacks), reform, and Reconstruction. Grant's campaign strategy mirrored that of 1868. He withdrew from visible activity and ran what would later become known as a "front-porch campaign." The Democrats' advantage was "Grantism," the corruption inherent to the administration. Many liberal Republicans repulsed by the scandals of the Grant administration temporarily allied with the Democrats.

A coalition of liberal Republicans and Democrats had emerged victorious in the 1870 Missouri legislative elections. The Liberal Republican Party held its convention in Cincinnati in January 1872. Delegates eventually chose *New York Tribune* editor Horace Greeley and Missouri Governor B. Gratz Brown as their presidential and vice presidential nominees. The Democrats held a convention in Baltimore in July lasting only a few hours. They endorsed the Liberal Republican ticket and platform, in spite of some obvious inconsistencies on issues. Greeley, like Horatio Seymour before him, traveled the countryside making speeches, but tended to alienate many potential voters. The Democrats and Liberal Republicans in 1872 had no unifying cause other than simple opposition to Grant's reelection. The disorganized opposition created an environment that would make the election difficult for Grant to lose, despite the scandals and incompetence of his administration. In the final tally, Grant received 55.6% of the popular votes and 286 electoral votes. Greeley died shortly after the general election, so his 66 electoral votes were shared by other Democrats.

Scandal, however, remained characteristic of the second Grant administration. Orville Babcock, Grant's secretary, was involved in a conspiracy known as the Whiskey Ring, a fraudulent diversion of millions of dollars of liquor tax revenues. Secretary of the Treasury William Richardson resigned following a scheme that allowed collectors of delinquent tax to keep 50% of all revenues. Secretary of War W.W. Belknap resigned following revelations that he accepted bribes from traders at Indian posts.

Grant's second term was also a period of economic upheaval. The Panic of 1873 produced a depression and brought in a new era of financial instability. Thousands of businesses failed, and millions of workers were unemployed. Republican efforts to acquire gold reserves to back all legal tender stabilized the currency and strengthened public confidence. But the depression that originated in the panic lasted for several more years and became the worst episode of economic dislocation in American history until the Great Depression. The panic emphasized the nationalization and internationalization of the American economy and the need for the national government to intervene to preserve financial stability. It would also lead to public dissatisfaction with the politics of the time.

Throughout both terms, the public policy goals of the administration were frequently conflicting. For instance, Grant sought two aims regarding rehabilitation of the South. He wanted racial justice and equality for the former slaves. His second term oversaw passage of the Civil Rights Acts of 1875. But he also wanted to supervise the transition of power back to the southern states. In his first term, Grant used the southern occupation by federal troops to enforce laws and stop the terrorist activities of the Ku Klux Klan. As time passed, he became more reluctant to resort to military power to enforce federal law. The public in the North was losing interest in Reconstruction and intervention in the South.

Grant's foreign policy was successful when shepherded by his able secretary of state, Hamilton Fish. A treaty in 1871 avoided conflict through an international arbitration of wartime damage claims between Great Britain and the United States. But there were failures too. Grant sought to annex Santo Domingo (the Dominican Republic) as a potential homeland for blacks, but the proposal was simplistic and never received the support of Congress.

George Washington had established a precedent that presidents should serve only two terms in office, though this pattern was a tradition and not a rule. Stalwart Republicans, however, were unhappy with the reformists' notions of Grant's successor, President Rutherford B. Hayes. Hayes opted not to run for reelection, and the Stalwarts rallied to nominate Ulysses Grant for an unprecedented third term at the 1880 convention in Chicago. The Stalwarts, however, would ultimately lose as the reformists would ultimately lose in the most divisive Republican convention ever. Grant supporters could not persuade other delegates to cast ballots for his nomination. The Stalwart faction voted for Grant on every roll through the 36th when dark-horse candidate James Garfield won the nomination.

Ulysses Grant embarked on a world tour after his second term and later moved to New York. There he invested all his income, and a substantial sum of borrowed money, into his son's brokerage partnership.

The firm went bankrupt, as did the former president. Grant was diagnosed with cancer of the mouth and throat, probably due to his long tradition of smoking cigars. Grant worked diligently to finish his *Personal Memoirs of U.S. Grant* during his illness. His hope that the book would help pay for personal debts came true; the volume is a classic autobiography. Ulysses Grant died shortly after completing the work in 1885.

Grant recognized the errors of his scandal-ridden administration, resulting from poor selection of staff and aides. The president operated above these failures and was never directly involved in any scandal. The era from Grant's first election onward has become known as the Gilded Age. It is characterized by political corruption, the rise of big business, and machine politics. This was an age of strong partisanship with Republican domination in the North and white Democratic domination in the South, but national politics was evenly split. The Republican Party moved from a third party with a limited range of attractive issue positions to a well-organized, national party characterized by a high degree of voter loyalty. The attention of Republicans, and the nation, moved from civil rights and Reconstruction to economic prosperity and political reform. Disinterested in politics and administration, Ulysses Grant nevertheless oversaw the growth and development of the Republican Party into a permanent and strong institution.

James W. Endersby

SEE ALSO History

BIBLIOGRAPHY

Catton, Bruce. *U.S. Grant and the American Military Tradition; Grant Moves South; Grant Takes Command.* Boston: Little, Brown, 1954, 1960, 1979.

Gillette, William. *Retreat from Reconstruction, 1869–1879.* Baton Rouge: Louisiana State University Press, 1979.

Goldhurst, Richard. *Many Are the Hearts: The Agony and the Triumph of Ulysses S. Grant.* New York: Reader's Digest Press, 1975.

Grant, Ulysses S. *Memoirs and Selected Letters: Personal Memoirs of U.S. Grant, Selected Letters 1839–1865.* New York: Library of America, 1990.

Hesseltine, William B. *Ulysses S. Grant: Politician.* New York: Dodd, Mead, 1935.

Mantell, Martin E. *Johnson, Grant, and the Politics of Reconstruction.* New York: Columbia University Press, 1973.

McFeely, William S. *Grant: A Biography.* New York: Norton, 1981.

Simpson, Brooks D. *Let Us Have Peace: Ulysses S. Grant and the Politics of War and Reconstruction, 1861–1868.* Chapel Hill: University of North Carolina Press, 1991.

WARREN G. HARDING

Warren Gamaliel Harding, 29th president of the United States (1921–1923), was born on November 2, 1865, in the Ohio village of Corsica (now Blooming Grove). After a successful career as an Ohio newspaperman, he launched his political career in the Ohio Republican Party, where he achieved success on the principle of attaining harmony among conflicting groups of politicians and citizens. His presidency was marked by efforts to readjust to the normal conditions of peacetime following the disruptions of World War I. A conservative Republican of the progressive era mold, Harding achieved some moderate reforms in civil rights and agriculture and succeeded in greatly helping business, which his successor, Calvin Coolidge, valorized with his famous dictum: "The chief business of America is business." His administration was marred by scandal, and since his death, Harding has largely been considered an unimaginative, unimportant president.

Early Political Career

Harding graduated from Ohio Central College in 1882, and in 1884, with the aid of his father, he and two as-

Warren G. Harding. *Source:* Library of Congress.

sociates purchased a failing newspaper, the *Marion Daily Star*. As editor and publisher, and an aspiring businessman with an eye on profit, Harding was careful to keep his Republican sympathies out of the *Daily Star*. He wrote in 1888 that "most newspapers are run for money, 'tis true, and this is one of them." The *Daily Star* made no editorial comment on either issues or candidates in the 1885 and 1887 Ohio gubernatorial elections nor in the 1884 presidential election. Though Harding personally supported Blaine against Cleveland in 1884, he wrote just prior to Cleveland's inauguration, "Only one month until we live and breathe under a Democratic administration. The sun will shine just the same and the great political change will be scarcely noted except by office-holders."

Under Harding's carefully neutral management, the newspaper prospered where before it had foundered, and as his business holdings were secure, Harding began to become more political in his editorial comments. In the early 1890s, Harding challenged the elders in the Republican Party with the idea that the time had come for a youth movement in the party's leadership. Harding claimed that the Civil War heroes and founders of the party had had their day, and in 1891 he supported the campaign of ex-governor Joseph B. Foraker against Senator John Sherman in his attempt to win a sixth term. Though Sherman won the election, Harding had successfully introduced his "antiboss" theme into the pages of the *Daily Star*, and his continued efforts on the part of the younger generation of Ohio Republicans allowed him to move into the center of Republican Party politics. He continued to politicize his editorials throughout the 1890s, though he adopted the careful compromising strategy that would endear him to all segments of the party and result in his election to the Ohio Senate in 1898 with both "boss" and "antiboss" elements of the party supporting him. Ohio Republican politics of the time were deeply riven with factionalism, but Harding earned a reputation for being able to harmonize conflict, and he rose to a position of leadership in the Ohio Senate.

After his term in the Senate, Harding served briefly as lieutenant governor (1904–1905), then, although he returned to his newspaper full-time, he continued to be active in the Republican Party, working to mediate intraparty disputes. In 1910 Harding was chosen as the Republican nominee for governor, but the Democratic Party, under the leadership of Governor Judson Harmon, succeeded in revealing the corruption of the Republican Party, and Harding was defeated by 100,000 votes, the worst defeat ever suffered by the Ohio Republican Party. Harding, however, largely escaped blame for the devastating defeat, and his ability

to harmonize, compromise, and mediate kept his political career afloat until he ran for the U.S. Senate in 1914. With the 17th Amendment having recently taken effect, making senators popularly elected instead of chosen by the state legislature, Harding had to run against Senator Foraker in the state's first primary election. His popular appeal as a pleaser of all factions brought him victory there as well as in the November general election, when he became Ohio's first popularly elected senator.

Harding was a relatively unspectacular senator; he introduced no bills of national importance and attempted to cast his votes so as to avoid alienating any important group of Ohio constituents. The only noticeable stance he took was at the end of World War I, when Harding, then a member of the Senate Foreign Relations Committee, staunchly opposed the League of Nations.

In 1920 Harding ran for president, initially to solidify his position in the Ohio Republican Party, but the Republicans nationally were once again badly divided. Many strong candidates came forward for the party nomination, which would almost surely lead to the presidency, as the Democrats were even more hopelessly torn and were irreparably associated with the by then unpopular Woodrow Wilson. The League of Nations debate, which had been raging for almost a year, caused the front-runners to knock each other off, and a deadlock developed at the convention. After nine ballots, a group of Republican senators, meeting in the historic "smoke-filled" room 404 of the Hotel Blackstone, decided on the amorphous and malleable Harding, who was finally adopted as the compromise candidate, winning on the tenth ballot. The Republicans also decided not to offer a party platform.

During the ensuing campaign, which was rather listless because of the lack of subtantive issues or solid candidates, the party was careful to keep Harding off the campaign trail because, as one Republican boss noted, "If he goes out on tour somebody's sure to ask him questions and Warren's just the sort of damned fool who will try to answer them." Instead, Harding and the Republicans campaigned with slogans such as the vacuous "Let's Have Done with Wiggle and Wobble" and "Back to Normalcy" that appeared on a Harding coinage and strong isolationist sentiment left over from before World War I that was heightened by the disillusionment brought on by that atrocious conflict. In the first presidential election to include women voters, Harding overwhelmingly defeated the Democratic nominee, James M. Cox, by more than 7 million votes out of fewer than 30 million cast, with an electoral count of 404 to 127. However, the election showed that there were signs of discontent with the two parties and their uninspiring candidates, evidenced both by low turnout and by a relatively strong showing by Eugene V. Debs, who garnered almost a million votes, the largest socialist tally in American history, despite his having conducted his campaign from the federal penitentiary in Atlanta.

Presidency

Having built his early newspaper and political careers on avoiding alienating readers and voters, preventing conflict among various groups, and generally taking the middle road, Harding, as president, continued to pursue harmony, but he also initiated many extremely conservative policies that would mark the Republican-dominated twenties. His administration was active in promoting the implementaton of these policies, and though the decade of the twenties is often seen as a period of government retrenchment and as a break with the "progressive" past, the effect of Harding's presidency was generally to broaden, not shrink, the importance of the public sector in American life.

In foreign policy, Harding followed the general trend of withdrawal from world affairs that was so strong at the time. The United States, vehemently isolationist until its reluctant entry into World War I, attempted to return to its prewar status as a nation free of foreign entanglements. Harding called for a return to "normalcy," and his foreign policy reflected the desire to continue the retreat from world politics that began when the Senate rejected U.S. participation in the League of Nations in 1920. Harding encouraged the rapid demobilization that had begun as soon as the war had ended, and he took further steps toward disarmament in the Washington Conference of 1921–1922, which led to international agreements to reduce naval forces. He also fought for and won a high protective tariff, the Fordney–McCumber Act of 1922, which attempted to seal America off from the world economy. The renewed strength of isolationist rhetoric and policy did not, however, prevent the United States from extending its sphere of influence inside the Western Hemisphere, where American investments, both capital and political, skyrocketed; by 1924 the United States was directing the finances of ten Latin American nations.

In domestic affairs, Harding was generally flexible and agreeable, and he favored policies intended to reduce conflict. He was popular with Congress and encouraged rationalization of the operation of the federal government with the development of the Bureau of the Budget, which adopted a federal budget in place of the previous "system" that had left federal spending to the discretion of congressional committees. In many ways a typical progressive-era conservative, Harding supported programs to keep America in touch with changing times: he called for a Department of Public Welfare, intervened to end the 12-hour day in steel mills, and approved legislation assisting farm cooperatives and liberalizing farm credit. He also advocated a federal antilynching law and not only let Eugene Debs out of jail but received him at the White House. In typical Harding fashion, he attempted to avoid alienating either side of the era's most divisive issue, Prohibition, by supporting the 18th Amendment while at the same time failing to take steps to effectively enforce the Volstead Act, which had banned the manufacture and sale (but not the private consumption) of liquor.

Harding was, however, a conservative first and foremost, and correspondingly a supporter of big business. He believed that businessmen were the natural leaders of society and that the talented few who built the new factories, produced the new inventions, and made the nation's industry and commerce hum with increasing efficiency should enter politics and keep it from being spoiled by lazy Democratic demagogues and Republican Party machine bosses. Agencies like Herbert Hoover's Commerce Department and the Agriculture Department provided businessmen with data and advice and developed close ties with the large concerns that were coming to be known as "agribusiness." Harding's executive agencies also promoted infrastructure improvements that would enhance commercial activity, and though they overrode efforts to develop the Tennessee Valley region, they approved plans for the Boulder Dam, the first federally sponsored large-scale, multipurpose river basin development project.

Harding's economic policies were notably, even outstandingly, probusiness, as his choice of multimillionaire industrialist Andrew Mellon for the post of secretary of the treasury attested. Like J.P. Morgan, Mellon was certain that the same principles that drove big business to profit could curb wasteful competition and lead to the capitalist utopia. These ideas resulted in policies based on the idea that government intervention was necessary to assist holders of capital, and Harding initiated the Republican policy of cutting taxes on the rich and on corporations.

Harding's political nature and his ties with some of the shadier aspects of the Republican Party eventually got him in trouble. Despite having appointed several highly respected individuals to his cabinet, Harding also had a tendency to associate with the kind of party hacks and hustlers who had helped him rise from a moderate midwestern newspaper publisher to the presidency of the United States. As a result, Harding's administration is often best known for scandals, the most famous of which was the Teapot Dome affair. Secretary of the Interior Albert B. Fall was accused of turning over valuable federally owned mineral reserves to private developers in exchange for bribes. Attorney General Harry Daugherty, a longtime Harding confidant and known Republican Party toady, was also implicated in graft, and other corruption came to light in the Veterans Bureau and the Office of the Alien Property Custodian. The president was never directly implicated in these scandals, but concern over their effect on his administration and his friends weakened his health, which was already affected by a heart condition, and he died of a heart attack on August 2, 1923, while returning from a trip to Alaska.

Jack J. Miller

SEE ALSO History

BIBLIOGRAPHY

Downes, Randolph C. *The Rise of Warren Gamaliel Harding: 1865–1920*. Columbus: Ohio State University Press, 1970.

Mee, Charles L. *The Ohio Gang: The World of Warren G. Harding*. New York: M. Evans, 1981.

Murray, Robert K. *The Harding Era: Warren G. Harding and His Administration*. Minneapolis: University of Minnesota Press, 1969.

BENJAMIN HARRISON

Benjamin Harrison, the 23rd president of the United States (1889–1893), was the only grandson of a former president ever to serve in that high office. His grandfather was William Henry Harrison, the ninth president (1841), who died of pneumonia just one month after delivering a long inaugural address on March 4, 1841, in Washington's abysmal weather. Born on August 20, 1833, in North Bend, Ohio, Benjamin Harrison was named after his great-grandfather, who was a signer of the Declaration of Independence. The Harrisons were as formidable a political dynasty as America has ever seen.

Harrison graduated from Miami University in Oxford, Ohio, in 1852 and, after a year of studying law in Cincinnati, married Caroline Scott, the daughter of a faculty member at Miami. The Harrisons settled in Indianapolis, Indiana, where he established a law practice and began his political career. Harrison became an early organizer of the Republican Party and won several local political positions, including that of reporter for the Indiana Supreme Court in 1860.

Benjamin Harrison. *Source:* Library of Congress.

In 1862 Indiana's governor, Oliver P. Morton, asked Harrison to recruit and command a regiment of Indiana volunteers for service in the Civil War. Harrison organized the 70th Indiana Regiment and served under the command of General William Tecumseh Sherman. Harrison was a respected officer who earned a reputation for courage and gallantry during the campaign in Georgia in 1864 and was promoted to brigadier general the following year. Just 32 years old in 1865, Harrison returned to Indiana a genuine war hero.

Harrison rose steadily in the legal community in Indiana and in the state Republican Party. In 1876 scandal befell the party's gubernatorial candidate, and Harrison was pressed to run in his place. He lost the election by several thousand votes, but the contest only enhanced his stature within the party itself. With the death of former Governor and U.S. Senator Morton, Harrison emerged as the most prominent party leader in the state after 1877. In 1879 President Rutherford B. Hayes gave Harrison his first national exposure when he considered him for several positions and eventually appointed him to the Mississippi River Commission.

Harrison led the Indiana delegation to what would be a deadlocked Republican National Convention in

1880. Harrison was pledged to the candidacy of the influential Senator James G. Blaine against former President Ulysses S. Grant, who sought a third term as president. After 35 ballots, Harrison and the convention agreed on the compromise candidacy of James Garfield, who would go on to win the presidency in the general election. The Indiana legislature then sent Harrison to the Senate, where he would hone his influence and build his political strength over the next six years.

Supporters had been working for some time to position Harrison to win the Republican nomination for president in 1888, but the first ballot at the convention found him in fifth place. Blaine provided a great boost to Harrison's candidacy when the longtime candidate refused to run and instead seemed to express confidence in Harrison's electability. By the eighth ballot, the Indianan had become the party's nominee. The convention chose New York's Levi P. Morton to be Harrison's running mate.

The Harrison candidacy was largely limited to speeches delivered from the candidate's front porch in Indianapolis. In the election, the South gave incumbent Democrat Grover Cleveland a 95,000-vote edge in the popular vote, but the Harrison–Morton ticket was able to win swing states like New York and Indiana and amass an electoral college victory of 233–168. Harrison's victory in 1888 marked the last time a candidate who lost the popular vote won in the electoral college. Republicans also gained majorities in the Senate and the House in the election, which gave them full control over the elected branches of government for the first time in more than a decade.

Indebted to the colorful and charismatic Blaine for his rise in the Republican Party, Harrison appointed him secretary of state, a post he had previously held in the James A. Garfield administration. Harrison micromanaged the appointment process but proved particularly inept at building his base within his party through the patronage system. Except for Blaine, the president passed over nearly all other powerful figures in the Republican Party as he formed his cabinet. Party leaders were alienated by this seeming lack of appreciation, which helped lead to serious opposition within the party to Harrison's renomination in 1892.

As president, Harrison has not been treated enthusiastically by historians. He has often been portrayed as being aloof or indifferent as president, and his single term in the Senate certainly provided only scant preparation for high office. Part of the problem for Harrison is that he has become associated with two particular scandals involving his appointments. James S. Clarkson, the first assistant postmaster general,

doled out thousands of postmaster positions to loyal members of the Republican Party, and James R. Tanner, commissioner of pensions for just six months, did his best to promulgate or increase pensions to as many Civil War veterans as he could.

Scholars have also been critical of what they take to be Harrison's unwillingness to assert a leadership role in domestic affairs and to build or protect presidential power. Though there had been some attempts at a resurgent presidency in the mid–nineteenth century, Harrison's tenure was unquestionably one of congressional dominance. A former senator who had clashed with President Grover Cleveland on questions of presidential power, Harrison had no problems endorsing the congressionally centered view of American government, and his term in office was very much based on such a Whiggish understanding.

Both houses of Congress would undergo major changes during Harrison's tenure—some of which would further strengthen the hand of the legislative branch in the national government. Six new states were added to the Union during Harrison's term (Idaho, Montana, North Dakota, South Dakota, Washington, and Wyoming), and each of them would send two new and aggressive Republicans to the Senate. These new western Republicans asserted their prerogatives from the start and caused some considerable problems for the established Republican Party in the Northeast and Midwest, though they eventually found ground for compromise to advance their agenda. In the Senate, several powerful leaders were able to impose procedural and party discipline to a degree seldom before seen in the upper house.

Even more dramatically than in the Senate, Speaker of the House Thomas B. Reed was able to assert his power and the power of the majority party over the lower house. Reed swiftly removed the minority party's techniques for delaying or stopping the agenda of the leadership, and what remained was a considerably streamlined legislative process. In particular, Reed refused the Democrats their use of the "disappearing quorum," in which they would sit silently, refusing to answer the quorum call so as to deny the Speaker the quorum he needed to conduct business. Reed would simply count the silent Democrats as being present and move on with the business of the House. This and other "Reed rules" helped pave the way for an even more influential Congress than had previously been the case. Whereas Congress had initially been organized as a deliberative body, it had been reorganized into a disciplined governing body.

Harrison's tenure of office saw several important pieces of legislation signed into law. The protectionist

McKinley Tariff Act was passed, as was the Sherman Silver Purchase Act. The administration is probably best known, however, for the passage of the Sherman Antitrust Act of 1890, which formed the government's basic antimonopoly law.

In foreign policy, Harrison sometimes took an active leadership role, especially during Secretary of State Blaine's at times incapacitating illness. Often depicted as aggressive or militant in his foreign policy, Harrison supplied an impetus for what would become America's empire. He helped convince Congress to begin deployment of a two-ocean navy, with the construction of three battleships being authorized in 1890. He entered into a protectorate agreement over the Samoan Islands with Germany and Great Britain. And in January 1892 Harrison mobilized the fleet against Chile, which had refused to apologize and pay reparations for the October 1891 murder of two American sailors on shore leave there. Chile backed down in the face of such pressure, thereby avoiding war with the United States. In February 1893 Harrison attempted to annex the recently created Republic of Hawaii by negotiating and signing an annexation treaty with the new republican government. By that time a lame duck with a lame duck Senate, Harrison eventually withdrew the treaty from Senate consideration when it became obvious it had no chance of winning approval.

Harrison was challenged for the Republican nomination in 1892 by his secretary of state, Blaine, and future president William McKinley, then governor of Ohio, but Harrison survived the challenge. The Democrats nominated former President Grover Cleveland, and for the first time in American history, both parties' candidates had been president of the United States. Harrison did not offer the Republicans much leadership, and the party seemed simply to be drifting through the election of 1892. Tragedy befell the White House on October 25, when Mrs. Harrison died of tuberculosis, and the president seemed eager simply to see an end to the closing days of the campaign. In the final analysis, the outcome was predictable. Cleveland won with 277 electoral votes to Harrison's 145. The upstart Populist Party garnered 22 votes of its own.

Harrison spent the remainder of his life in private practice in Indianapolis, lecturing at Stanford University, and serving as counsel for Venezuela in its boundary dispute with British Guiana. In 1896 he married Mary Lord Dimmick, a relative of his late wife. Harrison's remarriage resulted in the birth of a daughter in 1897 but also led to his estrangement from his other children. Harrison died on March 13, 1901.

Gary L. Gregg II

SEE ALSO History

BIBLIOGRAPHY

Sievers, Harry Joseph. *Benjamin Harrison.* 3 vols. Chicago: Regnery, 1968.

Socolofsky, Homer E., and Allan B. Spetter. *The Presidency of Benjamin Harrison.* Lawrence: University Press of Kansas, 1987.

RUTHERFORD B. HAYES

The presidency of Rutherford Birchard Hayes, 19th president of the United States, brought an end to Reconstruction and put the government on the path toward civil service reform. Although accused at first of having "stolen" the highly contested election of 1876 by only one electoral vote, Hayes eventually earned praise for his sincerity and honesty. He and his wife Lucy, a temperance advocate popularly known as Lemonade Lucy, adopted a policy of not serving liquor in the White House. Amid the partisan politics of the Gilded Age, Hayes stood out as the conciliator known

Rutherford B. Hayes. *Source:* Library of Congress.

for the memorable phrase "He serves his party best who serves his country best."

Born on October 4, 1822, in Delaware, Ohio, Rutherford B. Hayes was the son of Sophia Birchard Hayes and the late Rutherford Hayes Jr., a business-man who died suddenly of a fever a couple of months before the future president was born. Sophia Hayes was a strict Presbyterian who taught her son the value of working hard and observing the Sabbath. In ele-mentary school, Rutherford was a champion speller. He attended private secondary schools and graduated from Kenyon College in Gambier, Ohio, at the top of his class in 1842. Then Hayes headed east to Harvard Law School, where he developed the scholarly in-stincts that would influence his style in political office. After law school, Hayes moved back to Ohio to prac-tice law, first in Lower Sandusky (later Fremont), then Cincinnati. He joined the recently formed Cincinnati Literary Club and made a name for himself as a de-fense attorney in three high-profile murder trials.

On December 30, 1852, Hayes married Lucy Ware Webb, a recent graduate of Wesleyan Female College with strong temperance and abolitionist beliefs who was destined to become the first American first lady to be a college graduate. In 1858 the Cincinnati City Council elected Hayes city solicitor by a single vote on the 13th ballot. This marked the start of his famed good luck in winning close elections. When the Civil War broke out, Hayes became an officer with the 23d Ohio Volunteer Infantry, rising from major to brevet general by war's end. Hayes was wounded four times but emerged from the struggle with modest fame and a seat in the U.S. House of Representatives.

As a congressman from 1865 until 1867, Hayes sup-ported the 14th and 15th Amendments and oversaw improvements to the Library of Congress. The re-served and scholarly Hayes disliked the partisan dis-cord of Congress, however. In July 1867 he resigned his seat to run for governor of Ohio against a promi-nent Democrat, Judge Allen G. Thurman. Hayes, who supported an unpopular black suffrage amendment to the state constitution, was expected to lose. Never-theless, he won by a narrow margin of less than 3,000 votes out of nearly half a million cast. After two terms as governor, Hayes took a three-year hiatus from poli-tics, during which time he lived quietly with Lucy and their five children in Fremont, Ohio, studying the his-tory of the region and managing his real estate hold-ings. In 1875 Hayes ran for a third term as governor and won yet another close race, defeating incumbent Governor William Allen by 297,817 to 292,273.

Meanwhile the scandal-riddled second term of President Ulysses S. Grant was drawing to a close against a backdrop of economic depression and politi-cal factionalism. On one end of the Republican Party were the party regulars, or Stalwarts, led by Senator Roscoe Conkling of New York. On the other was a mi-nority of reform-minded liberals.

To win the election of 1876, the Republican Party sought a candidate attractive to party regulars but un-tainted by scandal. Rutherford B. Hayes emerged as the party's choice, partially by default. At the Republican National Convention in June 1876, Hayes picked up enough strength as a second-choice candi-date to win the race away from the front-runners by five votes on the seventh ballot.

In his formal acceptance of the Republican Party's nomination, Hayes advocated political reform and promised not to seek a second term. Two weeks later, the Democrats, declaring themselves the party of re-form, nominated New York Governor Samuel J. Tilden, famous for helping to prosecute and expose the notorious Tweed ring.

When the polls closed on the evening of election day, November 7, 1876, Tilden looked like the obvious winner in the popular vote by about 250,000 votes. The next day however, Republican Party chieftains real-ized that if Hayes won certain key states in the elec-toral college, he'd win the election. Four states— Louisiana, South Carolina, Florida and Oregon—had sent in two sets of returns: one from Democrats, the other from Republicans. Both claimed victory. If Hayes kept all 20 Republican votes, he'd win the election by 185 to 184 in the electoral college.

Faced with the conflicting returns, Congress, on January 24, 1877, called for the formation of an electoral commission comprised of 15 members—five from the Senate, five from the House and the remaining five from the Supreme Court. The decision of the electoral commission would be final unless voted down by both houses of Congress. Although Democrats argued that the partisan election boards of the South had de-frauded Tilden of votes, the commission, with seven Democrats and eight Republicans, voted along strict party lines to award the election to Hayes. In exchange for accepting the commission's decision, congressional Democrats got Republicans to agree to the withdrawal of federal troops from the South. At 4:10 A.M. on March 2, 1877, Rutherford B. Hayes was declared the duly elected president of the United States.

House Democrats protested the next day with a reso-lution saying that Tilden had been "elected." Rumors circulated about the possibility of an attempted coup by Democrats. To prevent an inter-regnum between the Constitutional date of the president's takeover, which fell on Sunday, March 4, 1877, and the formal inauguration the next day, Hayes was sworn in at a private ceremony on Saturday night. Because of the long and bitter election dispute, no inaugural ball or parade was held.

On Monday, March 5, 1877, Hayes was sworn in at a formal ceremony boycotted by Democratic members of Congress. In his inaugural address, Hayes discussed several issues that would figure prominently in his presidency: the southern question, currency, civil service reform, and the contested election. Hayes rejoiced that the election dispute had been settled peacefully. Newspaper headlines, however, referred to him as "His Fraudulency" and "Rutherfraud B. Hayes."

Hayes got to work assembling an independent cabinet based on merit rather than favoritism. Among his choices: David M. Key, a former Confederate colonel, as postmaster general to foster unity between North and South and Frederick Douglass, the celebrated abolitionist, a U.S. marshal of the District of Columbia.

Although Hayes had supported radical Reconstruction in his early days as a congressman, he had come to regard bayonet rule of the South as a failed experiment and so adopted a policy of reconciliation. The troops that remained in the South were essentially performing political duty in Louisiana and South Carolina, where contested elections had given rise to two separate state governments, each with its own governor. White southerners wanted the federal troops attached to the Republican statehouses withdrawn so Democrats could be installed. Fear of violence, however, led Hayes to proceed with caution.

Hayes invited the rival governors of South Carolina to a conference at the White House, where Republican Governor Daniel Chamberlain surrendered power to Democratic Governor Wade Hampton, who, in turn, promised in writing to protect the Constitutional rights of blacks. A commission dispatched by Hayes to Louisiana worked out a similar agreement. On April 10 and April 24, 1877, federal troops left the statehouses. In June the poet Oliver Wendell Holmes honored Hayes in a poem as a "Healer of Strife!"

The president's hopes of drawing white southerners into the Republican Party, however, were soon dashed by the congressional elections of 1878. With white southerners firmly in the grip of the Democratic Party, fraud, intimidation and mob violence prevented blacks throughout the South from exercising their Constitutional right to vote. In a political clash between whites and blacks in Louisiana, between 30 and 40 people were killed. In South Carolina, federal marshals arrested 22 whites for intimidating blacks, but legal maneuverings by the all-white juries prevented convictions. The governors of Louisiana and South Carolina had failed to keep their promises.

Workers throughout the country, meanwhile, were suffering from the effects of the economic depression. In the summer of 1877, the Great Strike—the first strike of national-emergency proportions in the history of the nation—broke out along the railway lines after a number of railroads cut employee wages by 10% rather than reduce management salaries or stock dividends.

The strike spread from the East through the Midwest across the Mississippi River and into Missouri and Iowa before ending a few weeks later. After careful deliberation, Hayes dispatched federal troops to four states—West Virginia, Maryland, Pennsylvania and Illinois. In each case, the disturbance was quelled without the loss of life, thus establishing a precedent for federal intervention in labor disputes.

To address the economic depression behind the disturbance, Hayes favored a "sound money" policy based on the gold standard. Proponents of "cheap money," on the other hand, pushed for the expansion of low-cost silver and paper currency to help farmers and businessmen pay off their debts. In 1878 Congress passed the Bland–Allison Act calling for the U.S. Treasury to resume its minting of silver dollars. Hayes vetoed the bill, but Congress overrode his veto, and Bland–Allison became law. The president, however, muted its impact by coining only the $2 million monthly minimum of silver.

On the issue of paper money, Hayes won congressional support to resume redeeming with gold the "greenbacks" printed to finance the Civil War. On January 2, 1879, the U.S. Treasury redeemed the greenbacks, and American currency became equivalent to that of the commercial world. Foreign trade picked up; crop prices improved; and the five-year depression ended in 1879.

To win congressional support for resumption, however, Hayes had to compromise on civil service reform. Although he succeeded in reorganizing the New York Customhouse, he failed to interest Congress in introducing civil service exams and other reforms throughout the system. Ironically, Chester A. Arthur, one of the customhouse spoilsmen ousted by Hayes, went on to become the president credited with civil service reform.

In Hayes's cabinet, Secretary of the Interior Carl Schurz came the closest to carrying out the spirit of civil service reform. As overseer of the Office of Indian Affairs, he curtailed the widespread cheating of Native Americans and blocked an effort to move Indian Affairs back to the War Department.

Ten days after Hayes was nominated for president, the Sioux defeated General George A. Custer, but the president left office with the last of the major Indian wars fought. In response to pleas by the Ponca tribe, Hayes, on February 1, 1881, outlined a four-point Indian policy calling for education, land rights, fair compensation for Indian lands, and citizenship, thus laying the groundwork for the Dawes Severalty Act of 1887.

In other matters, a congressional committee under Representative Clarkson N. Potter of New York reopened the question of fraud in the election of 1876 but unwittingly embarrassed the Democrats instead of the Republicans. In foreign policy, the Hayes administration recognized the Mexican government of Porfirio Díaz and negotiated an agreement with China to limit immigration. Hayes toured the American West Coast in 1880, becoming the first president to cross the country while in office. In an era of bearded presidents, he wore the longest beard.

As promised, Hayes refused to seek reelection. He retired to his country estate in Fremont, Ohio, and involved himself in philanthropic pursuits, including an educational foundation for southern blacks whose recipients included W.E.B. Du Bois. While waiting to board a train in Cleveland on January 14, 1893, Hayes was striken by a pain in his chest. He died at home three days later.

Joan Axelrod-Contrada

SEE ALSO History

BIBLIOGRAPHY

Barnard, Harry. *Rutherford B. Hayes and His America.* Indianapolis and New York: Bobbs-Merrill, 1954.

Davison, Kenneth E. *The Presidency of Rutherford B. Hayes.* Westport, CT: Greenwood Press, 1972.

Hoogenboom, Ari. *The Presidency of Rutherford B. Hayes.* Lawrence: University Press of Kansas, 1988.

Severn, Bill. *The Long and Short of It: Five Thousand Years of Fun and Fury over Hair.* New York: David McKay, 1971.

Williams, T. Harry, ed. *Hayes: The Diary of a President, 1875–1881.* New York: David McKay, 1964.

HERBERT HOOVER

Herbert Clark Hoover, 31st president of the United States (1929–1933), was born on August 10, 1874, the son of a blacksmith in the Iowa village of West Branch. Hoover had a brilliant early career as a mining engineer, voluntary war relief administrator, and secretary of commerce. Hoover attempted to lead a public life in accordance with his principles, encouraging voluntary social cooperation by his example and assisting others through his work with various relief and commerce agencies. Hoover earned a well-deserved reputation

as a "great humanitarian" through these efforts, but this view of him was shattered during his first year as president, when the Wall Street crash of 1929 occurred, and his inaction was seen as the cause of the ensuing collapse of the economy. After losing his bid for reelection to Franklin Delano Roosevelt, Hoover remained active in public life, as a volunteer once again, warning that the New Deal would be the end of American initiative, drive, efficiency, and greatness and attempting, through his work with two Hoover Commissions, to make the executive branch more efficient. He died in New York City on October 20, 1964, at the age of 90.

Early Career

Hoover was orphaned at the age of eight and sent to live with an uncle in Oregon. The uncle became mod-

Herbert Hoover. *Source:* Library of Congress.

erately wealthy, and young Herbert was able to study mining engineering at the newly opened Stanford University. He was in the first Stanford graduating class (1895) and, upon graduating, worked in California mines as an ordinary laborer. Hoover soon obtained a position in Australia directing a new gold-mining venture, and during the next two decades, he traveled through much of Asia, Africa, and Europe as a mining entrepreneur, becoming a millionaire by the age of 40.

At the outbreak of World War I in August 1914, Hoover was in London, and he volunteered to direct the exodus of American tourists from Europe. Afterward, he headed the Commission for Relief in Belgium from 1915 to 1919. This position earned him the reputation as a "great humanitarian"—a well-earned title, as his commission fed 10 million people during the war and left funds for Belgian postwar reconstruction. When the United States entered the war in April 1917, Hoover returned to Washington to serve as food administrator for the Woodrow Wilson administration. This was a special wartime office, created to encourage American agricultural production and food conservation and to coordinate the rational distribution of food. When the war ended in November 1918, Hoover attended the Versailles Conference as an adviser to President Wilson, who afterward appointed him head of the American Relief Administration, an agency intended to relieve the suffering in Europe caused by the war's destruction.

Hoover was renowned internationally as a result of his high-profile activities in these offices, and though he had never held elected office, his public reputation in the United States was enormous. He was considered a potential presidential candidate as early as 1920. Franklin Roosevelt remarked at the time, "Hoover is certainly a wonder, and I wish we could make him President of the United States." At the time Hoover had no party affiliation, and his political stance was unclear. He had supported Republican Theodore Roosevelt in 1912, but he had also worked closely with the Democratic Wilson administration during the war years. His self-made fortune and sense of rugged individualism made him an ideal Republican, and he was too prominent and able to be ignored. Hoover declared himself a member of the Republican Party while at the same time refusing to seek the presidency.

In 1921 President Warren G. Harding appointed Hoover secretary of commerce, a post he held for the next eight years, during the entirety of both the Harding and Calvin Coolidge administrations. As secretary of commerce, Hoover was concerned with applying rational principles in order to end the escalating conflict between newly organizing labor and increasingly big business, and he was instrumental in bringing about the eight-hour workday and legislation against child labor. He also worked toward bringing the benefits of cooperative action to business owners and farmers without destroying individual initiative. To this end his department encouraged firms to join together in voluntary trade associations and thereby develop and share vital information about costs of production and distribution and about available markets. Hoover expanded the Commerce Department's activities with great success, and by 1928, when President Coolidge announced that he would not seek reelection, Hoover was the obvious choice for the Republican presidential nomination, receiving that honor on the first ballot at the convention.

The Republicans were viewed at that time as largely responsible for the continuing prosperity of the postwar America of the twenties, and in his acceptance speech at the Kansas City Republican National Convention, Hoover proclaimed, "The poorhouse is vanishing from among us." Republican campaigners declared that Hoover would provide "A Chicken in Every Pot, a Car in Every Garage." Hoover was pitted against Al Smith, the first Catholic to receive a major party presidential nomination, and religious smears sometimes marred the campaign. Hoover won a landslide victory, sweeping a huge Republican majority into Congress on his coattails.

Presidency

As secretary of commerce, Hoover had initiated policies designed to encourage voluntary cooperation among businesses and among farmers, and his department had assisted this undertaking by providing vital data and advice. As president, Hoover wished to continue these efforts, which he felt were along scientific lines, and he quickly established the Research Committee on Social Trends. The committee made use of the best minds in American social science and brought together members of earlier-established voluntary organizations like the National Institute of Public Administration and the Social Science Research Council. Hoover expressed the belief that the committee could find ways to abolish poverty and provide for a future of peace and ever-increasing economic prosperity. The committee's 1,600-page report, *Recent Social Trends in the United States*, was not ready until 1933, when Hoover was already on his way out of office; ironically, many of the report's methods and recommendations—which included a leveling of income, unemployment payments to be financed from workers' earnings, and price fixing on thousands of commodities—were adopted by the New Deal, which Hoover sharply criticized throughout his later life.

Early in Hoover's term the most noticeable economic problem America faced was the agricultural depression that had been chronic for nearly a decade. The Agricultural Marketing Act, passed by Congress in 1929, established a new Agricultural Marketing Administration (AMA), which, following Hoover's policies as secretary of commerce, promoted the idea of marketing cooperatives among farmers to increase their efficiency while the government purchased surplus commodities until individual cooperative action could maintain farm prosperity without government intervention. The AMA, however, did not try to control overproduction, which was the main cause of depressed prices, and soon Hoover and the country had more serious economic difficulties to face, when the Wall Street crash of October 1929 occurred.

The onset of the Great Depression crippled Hoover's ability to promote his scientific policies, and despite the demonstrated success of central planning, he refused to mobilize the resources of the federal government to save the collapsing economy, fearing that government intervention would destroy the integrity and initiative of the individual. Hoover, like many others, assumed that the crash was a temporary dip in the natural business cycle, but when conditions deteriorated, he was forced to take some action, however minimal. The actions that he did take, however, were either futile or detrimental. The tax cut of $160 million that he asked for in 1930 had little effect, for few Americans at that time paid federal taxes anyway. The Hawley–Smoot Tariff of 1930, which established record-high rates, had little impact on domestic prices, but it provoked retaliation by other countries, and America's exports were cut in half between 1930 and 1932, deepening the economic difficulties. The Reconstruction Finance Corporation (RFC), established in late 1931, was authorized to lend nearly $500 million to financial institutions, which were supposed to direct the "trickling down" of money to the public. This move made Hoover the target of criticisms that he was willing to offer help to businesses but denied aid to the unemployed; in 1932 Hoover reluctantly agreed to let the RFC lend $300 million to states for unemployment relief.

Hoover's inability to end the economic depression quickly overshadowed his reputation as the "great humanitarian," and his staunch resistance of congressional appropriations for direct relief of the unemployed contributed greatly to the misery of the millions of Americans who had lost their jobs, some of whom were actually starving by the winter of 1932–

1933. Hoover's most vicious and foolish move was his action against the "bonus army" of 1932, a ragged collection of around 20,000 unemployed citizens claiming to be veterans of World War I. The group descended on Washington to lobby for the immediate payment of bonuses due to them in 1945 for their military service. Hoover ordered the police to clear the veterans from near the White House, and he commanded the army to chase the veterans out of their encampment across the Potomac in Anacostia Flats. Two veterans were killed by gunfire, 1,000 people were gassed, and 63 were injured as the army, under the leadership of General Douglas MacArthur, charged the crowd with fixed bayonets and burned the pathetic shacks of the "army."

By the election of 1932, Hoover's defeat was certain, as he had made no progress in alleviating the sufferings brought on by the depression and was seen as a major contributor to the nation's deep economic problems. Franklin D. Roosevelt easily won the election by promising Americans the kind of government action that many felt would be needed to end the country's woes.

Postpresidency

Hoover, whose first elected office had been the presidency, never ran for office again, though he remained active in public life much as he had before entering partisan politics in 1921. He criticized the policies of the New Deal, saying that they made Americans dependent on the government, and he continued to attempt to set a positive example of voluntarism, dedicating much of his time to the Hoover Institution, which established a huge manuscript library at Stanford, the Boy and Girl Scouts, the Boys' Clubs, and Mills College. He returned to mining, but his public activities occupied so much of his attention that his business ventures suffered, and only sinecures such as his appointment to the board of New York Life Insurance Company kept him prosperous.

After World War II, Hoover once again came to the aid of war-torn Europe, as he had so brilliantly in the previous world war, serving as coordinator of the European Food Program from 1946 to 1947. He remained an active critic of government policy, opposing the dropping of atomic bombs on Japan and the military intervention in Korea and favoring the withdrawal of American forces from Europe. In 1950 he refused President Harry S. Truman's invitation to serve as chairman of a bipartisan committee to investigate communists in government. He told Truman, "I doubt if there are any consequential card-carrying communists in government."

Hoover's final contribution in public service began in 1947, when he was appointed to the newly formed Commission on Organization of the Executive Branch of the Government (called thereafter the Hoover Commission). Hoover consulted expert advisers in an attempt to make the government more efficient and the executive branch more accountable to the Congress and the public, but the commission actually increased the strength of the presidency and diminished the role of Congress. A second Hoover Commission, appointed under the Dwight D. Eisenhower administration, was charged with contemplating changes in social and economic policy. Eisenhower was unhappy with the right-wing character of some of the recommendations and delayed transmitting the commission's proposals to Congress until many were out of date; Congress subsequently rejected most of the commission's recommendations.

Jack J. Miller

SEE ALSO History

BIBLIOGRAPHY

Burner, David. *Herbert Hoover, a Public Life.* New York: Knopf, 1979.

Nash, George H. *The Life of Herbert Hoover.* New York: Norton, 1983.

Patterson, James T. *America in the Twentieth Century.* New York: Harcourt, Brace, Jovanovich, 1983.

Robinson, Edgar Eugene. *Herbert Hoover, President of the United States.* Stanford: Stanford University Press, 1975.

ANDREW JOHNSON

Andrew Johnson, 17th president of the United States, occupied the White House during one of the most turbulent times in U.S. history. Although a lifelong Democrat, he was the Republican choice for vice president during Abraham Lincoln's second term and thus is considered to have been a Republican president. Nonetheless, his relationship with the Republican Party in Congress proved so stormy that Andrew Johnson remains the only president to have been impeached by the House of Representatives and tried by the Senate. His presidency was spared, however, when the Senate failed by one vote to muster the constitutionally required two-thirds vote for removal.

Johnson was born in Raleigh, North Carolina, in 1808. At the age of ten, lacking any formal education, Johnson was apprenticed to a tailor with whom he stayed for six years. During those years, Johnson learned to read and developed an interest in politics. In 1826 he settled in the eastern Tennessee city of Greeneville, where he met and married Eliza McCardle, who

Andrew Johnson. *Source:* Library of Congress.

continued his education by teaching him arithmetic and writing.

Johnson worked as a tailor in Greeneville, and his shop became a local gathering place. From this vantage he was elected first a city alderman in 1828, then mayor in 1830, and then to the state legislature in 1835, and to the U.S. House of Representatives in 1843. In 1852 the Whig Party gerrymandered his district to eliminate Democratic support; Johnson responded by successfully running for governor, a post he held from 1853 to 1857. In 1857 the state legislature elected him to the United States Senate.

It was from the Senate that Johnson gained national prominence. In 1860, at the start of the U.S. Civil War, Johnson became famous by being the only southern senator to oppose secession. When Tennessee held a referendum on the issue, Johnson returned home to urge his fellow citizens to stay with the Union. But the referendum passed, placing Tennessee in the Confederacy. Johnson fled for his life and became the only senator from a Confederate state to maintain his seat. When General Ulysses S. Grant occupied Tennessee in 1862, Lincoln appointed Johnson as military governor.

In 1864 the Republican Party chose Johnson to run as Lincoln's vice president, and the two men successfully campaigned on what they called the "Union Party" ticket. In March 1865 Johnson's vice presidential inauguration proved to be an embarrassing moment for him that would cloud his reputation. Johnson became inebriated that morning, claiming that he needed whiskey to maintain his strength after a recent bout of typhoid fever. He was clearly drunk during his inaugural address. Although it is questionable whether this behavior was typical for him, the incident would prove quite costly, as Johnson's opponents would later portray him as a drunkard.

On April 15, just six days after the Civil War was ended by the surrender of Confederate General Robert E. Lee at Appomattox, Abraham Lincoln was killed. This left Johnson with Lincoln's most difficult remaining political question—how to deal with the South after the war. Lincoln favored a relatively lenient Reconstruction policy that would quickly bring the southern states back into the Union. Others in the Republican Party, commonly called the "Radical Republicans," sought to impose more stringent conditions on the Confederate states.

At first, the Radicals believed that they had an ally in the White House. But it soon became apparent that Johnson opposed placing harsh conditions on the rebel states. Johnson issued a series of proclamations between May and July 1865 that pardoned most former participants in the rebellion and allowed them to participate in the establishment of new state governments upon taking an oath of loyalty to the Union. It did not, however, establish any requirements concerning the voting rights of southern blacks. This fact concerned the so-called moderate Republicans and angered many of the Radicals, because the southern state legislatures had begun instituting "black codes," which violated the civil rights of southern blacks.

In February 1866 Congress sent the president a bill to continue the existence of the Freedmen's Bureau, which had been created in 1865 to protect blacks throughout the South. The 1866 bill greatly expanded the scope and authority of the Freedmen's Bureau, including the use of military tribunals. It was a partisan bill with unanimous Republican support and Democratic opposition, and Johnson's veto decision clearly put him at odds with his own party. To make matters worse, a few days later Johnson gave a speech to a crowd gathered at the White House in which he denounced as "traitors" those who were seeking to centralize power in the federal government, specifically naming two northern Republican senators.

In late March, Johnson vetoed the Civil Rights Act, which granted citizenship to blacks and protected their rights. Johnson argued that the bill unconstitutionally violated states' rights and would "operate in favor of the colored and against the white race." This action unified the moderate wing of the Republican Party

with the Radicals. In early April, Congress overrode Johnson's veto. This was followed in June by congressional passage of the 14th Amendment, which, among other things, would constitutionally guarantee the protections of the Civil Rights Act of 1866. Although it was now up to the states to ratify the amendment, Johnson again angered Republicans by declaring that he was opposed to it because the ex-Confederate states were not yet represented in Congress.

As president, Johnson never formally left the Republican Party. But he came close in the summer of 1866, when he helped create the National Union Club, which consisted of Republican and Democratic supporters of the administration. The club held a national convention in August, which urged voters to choose candidates who were supportive of Johnson and favored rapid southern readmission to the Union; in essence, it called for the defeat of most Republican members of Congress. In late August, Johnson went on a whistle-stop speaking tour through the North and Midwest, hoping that he could defeat the Radicals in the fall congressional elections. Instead, Johnson's occasionally inflammatory rhetoric against his opposition served only to infuriate Republicans.

In the fall elections of 1866, the voters gave the Republicans a sufficiently large margin in Congress to allow them to control Reconstruction. In February 1867 Congress passed the first in a series of Military Reconstruction Acts, which established military rule in the South and gave blacks the right to vote. Johnson vetoed the measure, and Congress overrode the veto, thus making clear its domination over the executive branch.

But it was the Tenure of Office Act that proved to be Johnson's greatest problem. Passed over Johnson's veto in March 1867, the act required the president to seek Senate approval before removing any official whose appointment had previously received Senate approval. The congressional Republicans were attempting to prevent Johnson from removing Republicans from appointed positions, particularly Secretary of War Edwin Stanton. (The act, which would not be repealed until 1885, was of questionable constitutionality. Indeed, in 1926, the Supreme Court would declare that removal powers were primarily executive powers and that the president had sweeping authority to remove executive officials.)

In August, while Congress was out of session, Johnson suspended Secretary Stanton according to the provisions of the Tenure of Office Act and appointed General Ulysses S. Grant as acting secretary. In January 1868 Grant resigned the post, and the Senate reinstated Stanton. In February, Johnson fired Stanton outright, in violation of the Tenure of Office Act. This infuriated congressional Republicans. Three days later, the House of Representatives voted to impeach Johnson, with all Republicans supporting impeachment and all Democrats opposing it.

According to the Constitution, an impeachment by the House of Representatives is followed by a trial in the Senate to determine whether the president should be removed from office. The House transmitted to the Senate 11 articles of impeachment, most of which involved Johnson's violation of the Tenure of Office Act, but two of which involved Johnson's rhetorical attacks against Congress. The impeachment trial went on through the month of May. In the end, Johnson was saved by one vote. Seven Republicans had voted against removal, partly because they believed that removal would establish a bad precedent, partly because they could not find an impeachable offense in Johnson's actions, and partly because they disliked the man who would be Johnson's successor, Senate President Pro Tempore Benjamin Wade.

Soon after his acquittal, Johnson sought the nomination of the Democratic Party for president in 1868. The Democrats, however, had decided that northern delegates would choose the nominee, thus taking away Johnson's southern support. Johnson was in second place after the first ballot at the convention but gained no further support in subsequent balloting.

Other events of note during the Johnson presidency include the U.S. purchase of Alaska from Russia and the first official visit of a Chinese delegation to the United States.

After his presidency, Johnson returned to Tennessee. In January 1875, the Tennessee State legislature again elected Johnson to the United States Senate, making him the only former president elected to the Senate. He served briefly; in July he died suddenly from a stroke in his daughter's Tennessee home.

Michael J. Towle

SEE ALSO History

BIBLIOGRAPHY

Bowers, Claude G. *The Tragic Era: The Revolution after Lincoln.* Cambridge, MA: Riverside Press, Houghton Mifflin, 1929.

Castel, Albert. *The Presidency of Andrew Johnson.* Lawrence: Regents Press of Kansas, 1979.

Dewitt, David Miller. *The Impeachment and Trial of Andrew Johnson.* New York: Russell and Russell, 1903; reissued 1967.

Foner, Eric. *A Short History of Reconstruction: 1863–1877.* New York: Harper and Row, 1984.

McKitrick, Eric L. *Andrew Johnson and Reconstruction.* Chicago: University of Chicago Press, 1960.

Milkus, Sidney M., and Michael Nelson. *The American Presidency: Origins and Development, 1776–1990.* Washington, DC: CQ Press, 1990.

Milton, George Fort. *The Age of Hate: Andrew Johnson and the Radicals.* New York: Coward–McCann, 1930.

Nash, Howard P., Jr. *Andrew Johnson: Congress and Reconstruction.* Cranbury NJ: Associated University Presses, 1972.

Sefton, James E. *Andrew Johnson and the Uses of Constitutional Power.* Boston: Little, Brown, 1980.

Smith, Gene. *High Crimes and Misdemeanors: The Impeachment and Trial of Andrew Johnson.* New York: William Morrow, 1977.

Stryker, Lloyd Paul. *Andrew Johnson: A Study in Courage.* New York: Macmillan, 1936.

ABRAHAM LINCOLN

Elected in 1860 to become the Republican Party's first successful presidential candidate, and only its second candidate to make a presidential bid, Abraham Lincoln (1809–1865) endures as the most important political figure in Republican Party history. His significance is magnified by a presidency (1861–1864) that scholars rank as the most important in American history. The magnanimity of Lincoln's behavior so transcended partisanship that he has come to exemplify the American creed for both major political parties, and through his presidential legacy Lincoln today symbolizes democratic leadership for the rest of the world.

Lincoln's origins represent a classic study of the self-made person. Born on February 12, 1809, he was the second child and first son of Thomas and Nancy Hanks Lincoln, who lived near Hodgenville, Kentucky, on the

Abraham Lincoln. *Source:* Baker and Goodwin, 1860.

edge of the frontier, later institutionalized in school history lessons as his log-cabin birth. The young farm family moved to southern Indiana in December 1816. Two years later, Nancy Lincoln died of "milk sickness." In 1819 his father married Sarah Bush Johnston from Elizabethtown, Kentucky, who became Lincoln's beloved stepmother. As a boy, Lincoln had less than one year of formal schooling, and his self-taught education came "by littles." Having more education than his parents (his stepmother was illiterate), and from experience, Lincoln recognized yeoman farming on the frontier as hard. He could not wait to leave it for something better—a desire that would lead to his political belief that all people had "a right to rise" through their own labor. This cultural belief is demonstrated in the Lincoln family's relocation in 1830 for a second and final time as Thomas Lincoln continued to try to improve his family's life.

As soon as he came of age, Lincoln left home to seek his own career. His rapid succession of jobs reinforced his belief in the dignity of work while allowing him to find his identity as an individual. Almost immediately after establishing his independence, Lincoln began seeking political office. He declared for the Illinois House of Representatives in March 1832 on a platform of "internal improvements" and education, keys to his own advancement. Reflecting his understanding of the founding fathers (at this time primarily in the life of George Washington), his campaign ad in the *Sangamon Journal* stated: "Every man is said to have his own peculiar ambition," and he had "no other so great as that of being truly esteemed of my fellow men."

In addition to campaigning for political office as a Whig while he served as a storekeeper in New Salem, Illinois, Lincoln enlisted in the 31st Regiment of the Illinois Militia in April 1832, during the Black Hawk War, a decision that modeled George Washington's example. The militia company elected Lincoln captain, "to his own surprise." Much later in his life, Lincoln remembered it as "a success which gave me more pleasure than any I have had since," reflecting the needs of a healthy political personality. In the short run, his military service worked against his first attempt at elected office because it left him too little time to campaign. He carried New Salem in that election, but ran eighth among 13 candidates. Of more lasting significance than the outcome of the election, however, was the fact that he had found his life's calling and had made political contacts and friends who would encourage him to pursue a law practice as a vehicle into further politics.

In a rapid second bid for public office, Lincoln was elected on August 4, 1834, to serve in the Illinois House of Representatives from Sangamon County. The election brought Lincoln into contact again with his future lawyer partner, John Todd Stuart, a Whig leader who also had served in the Black Hawk War. Stuart encouraged Lincoln to study law.

Lincoln reinforced his primary calling in life—politics—by serving four terms in the Illinois legislature. He became a master at party organization and discipline, reaching out for voters at the precinct level. In a remarkably short interval, Lincoln emerged from obscurity to a major Whig leadership role in the statehouse. His legislative work reflected a lifelong commitment to economic development and industrialization based on his belief that government had a role to play in economic development by assisting people when they were unable to help themselves. Lincoln led the Sangamon delegation in relocation of the state capital from Vandalia to Springfield, and he supported large borrowing to finance railroads, roads, and river improvements. He was against governmental policies that diminished people's potential. Although not an abolitionist, Lincoln was one of only five legislators who voted against a resolution condemning abolitionism. With one other Whig, Lincoln introduced a resolution that "the institution of slavery is founded on both injustice and bad policy."

Lincoln began practicing law in 1836 and became certified as an attorney on March 1, 1837. He would ultimately have three law partners, a number that ironically parallels the number of romantic relationships in which he was involved. In each relationship, Lincoln ascended to greater equality with his successive partners. His first law partnership was with John Todd Stuart (1837–1841), the second with Stephen T. Logan (1841–1844), and the third and final with William H. Herndon beginning in 1844. His first two partners brought him greater experience, but denied him equal recognition as a junior partner. His partnership with Herndon was based strictly on an equal splitting of fees, as well as a recognition that the younger Herndon was more in tune with the progressive ideals of the age.

Meanwhile, in his personal life, Lincoln experienced brief, early relationships with Ann Rutledge and Mary Owens before becoming engaged to Mary Todd. The engagement was broken, but they reconciled and wed in 1842. Lincoln's spouse came from a higher socioeconomic background than his. Mary Todd was from a distinguished Kentucky family, a former neighbor and admirer of Henry Clay, the national Whig leader with whom Lincoln shared common political philosophies. She worked incessantly to refine Lincoln, and she served as a continued source of encouragement for his political ambition. Despite her temperamental episodes, the marriage endured; Lincoln's own moodiness moderated as he learned to deal with his wife's moods. They had four sons.

Within four years of their marriage, on August 3, 1846, Lincoln was elected overwhelmingly to the U.S. House of Representatives for his first and only term, having agreed to serve only one term so that a fellow Whig could run for the office in 1848. The only Whig from Illinois, he opposed Democratic President James K. Polk's war against Mexico. Always politically practical, Lincoln did not object to the United States' acquiring some territory seized from Mexico as long as it was not "so far south, as to enlarge and agrivate [sic], the distracting question of slavery." Voting several times for the Wilmot Proviso, which would have excluded slavery from territory acquired by the war, Lincoln also drafted a bill to abolish slavery, with compensation to slaveowners, in the District of Columbia.

In June 1848, Lincoln attended the Whig convention in Philadelphia to support General Zachary Taylor, who was nominated. Despite his hard campaigning for the successful nominee, Lincoln was denied appointment as commissioner of the General Land Office and refused the secretaryship and governorship of Oregon Territory.

Lincoln returned to his law practice in earnest and seemed to lose interest in politics. But his active participation in politics was renewed by the passage of the Kansas–Nebraska Act in 1854 under the leadership of Illinois Senator Stephen A. Douglas. Its passage outraged Lincoln. The act shifted the precarious slavery balance that had existed for a generation by repealing the Missouri Compromise of 1820 that prohibited slavery above 36°30', where Nebraska Territory existed. Douglas's "popular sovereignty" concept allowed citizens of a territory to decide the fate of slavery.

On November 7, 1854, Lincoln was elected to a fifth term in the Illinois House, but he resigned to become a candidate for the U.S. Senate. On February 8, 1855, in order to break a deadlock and to prevent the election of Democrat Joel A. Matteson, Lincoln threw his votes for the Senate seat to Lyman Trumbull.

Lincoln was a key player in the formation of the Illinois Republican Party. On February 22, 1856, at a meeting of anti-Nebraska editors in Decatur, he urged adoption of a statement of principles. He had previously refused to join the Republican Party because he thought it was dominated by abolitionists. Lincoln knew that the new Republican Party could not beat the Democrats without alliance with the anti-Catholic and anti-immigrant Know-Nothings, whose principles he detested. He accepted them as Republicans, however, for they included many of his "old political and personal friends." In 1857 Lincoln opposed the "erroneous" *Dred Scott* decision that ruled that blacks were excluded from the equality espoused in the Declaration of Independence. To Lincoln, the Declaration was an essential part of America's political creed.

Nominated yet again for the U.S. Senate, on June 16, 1858, Lincoln delivered the famous biblical admonition that "a house divided against itself cannot stand," evidence of his belief that the United States could no longer endure as half slave, half free. By this time he was part of the Radical wing of the Republican Party, in contrast to his earlier inclination to leave slavery alone where it already existed, placing it on the road to "ultimate extinction." That summer Lincoln debated his opponent, Senator Douglas, attacking Douglas's popular sovereignty as nothing more than "the perpetuity and nationalization of slavery." While Republicans received a majority of 5,000 popular votes, holdover state Democratic senators ensured Douglas's reelection.

In 1859 Lincoln campaigned in Ohio for Republican candidates as a national Republican political insider and minor hopeful for the 1860 Republican presidential nomination.

By 1859 he had already dabbled in national politics, having received 110 votes in an informal ballot for vice president at the first Republican convention in 1856. He spoke at Cooper Institution in New York City on February 27, 1860, and made several other speeches in New England cities, his introduction to easterners and part of his strategy for the 1860 nomination.

For the 1860 election, Republicans needed to keep the states they carried in 1856 and to win Pennsylvania along with either Illinois or Indiana. Lincoln was attractive to Midwest party leaders and voters, and his stand on increasing tariffs would satisfy Pennsylvania. His lack of political reputation meant that he was not as well known as his Republican rivals William H. Seward, Salmon P. Chase, Edward Bates, or Simon Cameron, but it also meant that he had fewer political enemies.

The Republicans met on May 19, 1860, in Chicago. Lincoln remained in Springfield, while his campaign manager, Judge David Davis, led Lincoln's charge at the convention. Other delegates switched to Lincoln when their first choice failed. Lincoln won on the third ballot. With a split in the Democratic Party, Lincoln and his vice presidential running mate, ex-Democrat Hannibal Hamlin of Maine, were assured victory. Following the practice of the day, Lincoln did not campaign. On November 6, 1860, Lincoln received 39% of the vote, defeating northern Democrat Stephen A. Douglas, southern Democrat John C. Breckinridge, and Constitutional Unionist John Bell.

In his inaugural address on March 4, 1861, Lincoln promoted the Republican Party platform that prohibited the extension of slavery. He beseeched his countrymen that "we are not enemies but friends. . . . Though passion may have strained, it must not break our bonds of affection. . . ."

Faced with *de facto* secession, Lincoln, in a strategy to force the Confederacy's hand and garner northern support, attempted to supply Fort Sumter, causing the ensuing bombardment on April 12, 1861, and subsequent evacuation on April 14. Congress was not in session, and Lincoln exercised war powers normally reserved by the Constitution to the legislative branch. He called for 75,000 troops, suspended the writ of habeas corpus, and established a blockade of southern ports and an increase in the regular army and navy. Congress had little choice but to ratify these acts when it convened on July 4, 1861. In his message to Congress, Lincoln referred to the struggle facing the nation as "a People's Contest."

Despite his lack of executive experience, Lincoln had the self-confidence to appoint political rivals, thought by most to be superior to Lincoln, to his cabinet. The three outstanding cabinet members were Secretary of State William H. Seward, Secretary of the Treasury Salmon P. Chase, and Secretary of War Edwin M. Stanton. Yet Lincoln led his cabinet.

As the leader of the Republican Party, he remained on good terms with party members and did not forget the importance of patronage. He outmaneuvered Chase, who coveted the presidential nomination in 1864, as well as the Radicals in Congress who thought Lincoln too slow in defining and implementing war aims. He refused to allow them to dictate policy, especially on emancipation and Reconstruction. To the consternation of ideologues, he argued that his policy was to have no policy, allowing himself maximum flexibility to achieve his goals. For this, he took a political beating but remained unintimidated. Few Radicals joined the movement to replace him on the ticket in 1864, and he was easily nominated for reelection.

While initially insisting that saving the Union was his "paramount object," it became apparent to the president, ever flexible on tactical matters, that Union war policy required emancipation. On July 22, 1862, he read the preliminary Emancipation Proclamation to his cabinet, but Seward suggested postponement until a military victory. Lincoln waited until September 22, five days after General George B. McClellan forced General Robert E. Lee to retreat after Antietam. The proclamation would take effect on January 1, 1863. Moral virtues and the change in his previous policy notwithstanding, the ever-practical Lincoln also wanted to tap the unused resource of the black man to fill the depleted ranks of the Union Army.

Although the pressures of the wartime presidency were immense, Lincoln retained his focused mind and performed his duties as chief executive as well as commander in chief. He followed the Whig Party tradition of rarely submitting legislation to Congress. He allowed Congress to introduce and pass important bills such as the Homestead Act, the Land Grant College Act, and the protective tariff. At Chase's urging, Lincoln lobbied Congress for the National Banking Act of 1863. Only on the issue of slavery did Lincoln take an active role in legislative matters. After his reelection, he pressed for passage of the proposed 13th Amendment to abolish slavery, furiously lobbying for the few remaining votes needed in the House for approval.

Lincoln's interest in foreign affairs was limited primarily to blocking foreign support for the Confederates. Because Lincoln could delegate matters to competent cabinet members, Secretary of State Seward handled the details of diplomacy involved for the president. Lincoln's military experience when he assumed the presidency was limited to the Black Hawk War, but he became very active in military affairs after Union army disasters at the beginning of the war, for he realized that ultimately the responsibility would rest upon him as commander in chief. Preferring initially to rely on "professional" soldiers, in typical manner the self-taught Lincoln gained self-confidence as a military leader, recognizing that his instincts were as good as or superior to the West Point–trained generals.

Even though he feared defeat for a second term in the 1864 election, Lincoln insisted that a constitutional amendment ending slavery be part of the Republican platform. With military victories at Atlanta and Mobile Bay, Lincoln ran with Andrew Johnson on the National Union Party ticket. They easily defeated Democrat McClellan with 55% of all votes cast. The Republican Party of Lincoln was firmly entrenched.

The legacy of Abraham Lincoln to the Republican Party is immense. His presidency is the activist model for the party, although with the exception of Theodore Roosevelt no Republican would enjoy Lincoln's long-term success. Nonetheless, his stature as a Republican would assure that the party remained a competitive force in American politics.

Beyond a heroic partisan legacy, Lincoln's leadership in promoting human rights and maintaining respect for the election process and political opponents even during a civil war is an enduring model of the democratic ideal in practice. Never an ideologue, he seemed intuitively to appreciate the necessary role of political opposition as he skillfully maneuvered to achieve America's ultimate goal of reconciling the values of the Declaration of Independence with the U.S.

Constitution. Lincoln's political leadership remains a timeless democratic legacy in self-government.

Frank J. Williams

SEE ALSO History

BIBLIOGRAPHY

Donald, David H. *Lincoln*. New York: Simon and Schuster, 1995.

Gienapp, William E. *The Origins of the Republican Party*. New York: Oxford University Press, 1987.

Neely, Mark E., Jr. *Abraham Lincoln and the Promise of America. The Last Best Hope of Earth*. Cambridge: Harvard University Press, 1993.

Oates, Stephen B. *With Malice toward None. The Life of Abraham Lincoln*. New York: Harper and Row, 1977.

Paludau, Philip S. *The Presidency of Abraham Lincoln*. Lawrence: University of Kansas Press, 1994.

Williams, Frank J., and William D. Pederson, eds. *Abraham Lincoln Contemporary: An American Legacy*. Campbell, CA: Savas Woodbury, 1995.

Williams, Frank J., William D. Pederson, and Vincent J. Marsala, eds. *Abraham Lincoln: Sources and Style of Leadership*. Westport, CT: Greenwood Press, 1994.

WILLIAM McKINLEY

William McKinley, 25th president of the United States, was a career politician who epitomized the conservative wing of the Republican Party at the end of the nineteenth century with his staunch support of big business and high tariffs. As president, McKinley's policies reflected his probusiness stance and his willingness to assert American power around the world. The United States became both an imperialist power and a major rival to the great European states during McKinley's tenure. His career was cut short by an assassin's bullet.

The seventh of eight children of William and Nancy McKinley, the future president was born on January 29, 1843, in Niles, Ohio. When McKinley was nine, his family moved to the small town of Poland, Ohio, where he spent the rest of his formative years. McKinley developed a gift for oratory at a young age and refined this skill during his early education through his school's debate society. After graduating from high school, he enrolled at Allegheny College in Meadville, Pennsylvania, but illness forced him to drop out after less than a year. Financial pressures prevented McKinley from returning to school, so he worked for a period before volunteering for the army at the outbreak of the Civil War in 1861. He rose from the rank of private to brevet major by the war's end.

After the Civil War, McKinley studied law and was

William McKinley. *Source:* Library of Congress.

admitted to the Ohio bar in 1867. He established a practice in Canton, Ohio, where he soon became active in the local Republican Party. In 1869 he was elected county prosecutor, and in 1876 he was elected to the U.S. House of Representatives, where he served from 1877 to 1883 and again from 1885 to 1891. While in the House, McKinley gained national attention as the leading proponent of protectionism. In 1890 he drafted the McKinley Tariff, which brought about a sharp rise in consumer prices. Angry Ohio voters turned McKinley out of office that same year, but he rebounded and was elected governor of Ohio two years later, serving as governor for two terms.

McKinley married Ida Saxton on January 25, 1871. The couple had two daughters, both of whom died in infancy. The stress of the infants' deaths caused Mrs. McKinley to suffer a nervous breakdown. Her condition was further complicated when she developed epilepsy. McKinley remained completely devoted to his wife, despite her health problems. His deep affection for his fragile wife struck a chord with many Americans and clearly added to his popularity both as governor of Ohio and later as president.

An ally of Republican boss Mark Hanna, McKinley quickly became the front-runner for the 1896 Republican presidential nomination. Hanna conducted a masterful campaign, which culminated in McKinley's nomination at the Republican National Convention in St. Louis. The Republicans adopted a platform that included maintenance of the gold standard, protective tariffs, and the acquisition of Hawaii. McKinley chose as his running mate Garret Hobart of New Jersey, who, although little known outside his home state, proved quite a welcome addition to the Republican ticket when New Jersey went Republican for the first time since 1872.

As their candidate, the Democrats chose William Jennings Bryan on the momentum generated by his famous "Cross of Gold" speech, and developed a platform that advocated free silver, tariff reduction and the establishment of an income tax. These measures formed the core of the populist movement, and by including them in their platform, the Democrats virtually co-opted the Populist Party. On the other hand, the inclusion of these measures caused conservative Democrats to break ranks and support McKinley, who won the election with 7,035,638 votes (51% of the popular vote) to Bryan's 6,467,946 (47%). McKinley was also aided by the generous support of industrialists who helped him raise $3 million for his bid—five times as much as Bryan raised. This money helped McKinley carry the larger, vote-rich, industrial states of the Northeast (New York, New Jersey, Pennsylvania, and so forth) while Bryan's support came mainly from the traditionally Democratic states of the South and the prosilver states of the West.

The Republicans had a substantial majority in both houses of Congress, which allowed McKinley to pursue his agenda with little effective opposition from the Democrats. In 1897 Congress passed the Dingley Tariff, which set protective tariffs at an average of 46% of the value of the goods. The Gold Standard Act of 1900 officially placed the United States on the gold standard. In response to a joint resolution of Congress in 1898, McKinley's administration also carried out its pledge to formally annex Hawaii.

The Spanish-American War of 1898 added more territory to the growing colonial possessions of the United States and confirmed America as a world power. The war began when sympathy for Cuban insurgents, fighting for independence from Spain, was dramatically increased through the questionable actions of "yellow journalism," which exaggerated and even fabricated accounts of Spanish atrocities on the island. Tensions between the United States and Spain rapidly deteriorated with the publication of the de Lôme letter, in which the Spanish ambassador to the United States characterized McKinley as weak and spineless. One week after the publication of the de Lôme letter, the American battleship *Maine* exploded and sank in Havana harbor with the loss of the majority of its crew. This incident aroused a war fever in the United States that McKinley found unstoppable. The president actually wanted to avoid war because he feared the effect such a conflict might have on business and trade. Nonetheless, bowing to public pressure, he rejected concessions from the Spanish government and asked Congress for a declaration of war on April 11, 1898.

The war went very well for the United States (prompting Secretary of State John Hay to describe it as "a splendid little war"). With the battle cry "Remember the *Maine*," American forces easily captured Cuba, Puerto Rico, Guam and the Philippines. Disease proved to be more deadly than the Spanish, as only 500 of the 5,000 American casualties died from battle wounds. The rest fell to a variety of tropical diseases such as malaria and yellow fever. The Treaty of Paris ended the war; granted Cuba independence; and gave Guam, the Philippines and Puerto Rico to the United States. The United States paid Spain $20 million in compensation for the Philippines. While Cuba was granted nominal independence, the American Congress in 1901 passed the Platt Amendment, which gave the United States the right to intervene in Cuba in order to maintain stability. The amendment also gave America two naval bases on Cuban soil. Under an agreement with Germany that split the island territory, McKinley added Samoa to the list of American colonies in 1899.

The retention of the Philippines as a colony of the United States sparked a rebellion on the island chain. Led by Emilio Aguinaldo, the Filipinos engaged American forces in a costly guerrilla war. It took the Americans two years to capture Aguinaldo and end the rebellion. Anti-imperialist factions in the United States used the rebellion to highlight the similarities between the United States and other colonial powers, and the episode became one of the major issues in the election of 1900.

With the acquisition of the various territories in the Pacific, American businesses became increasingly interested in trade with China. However, American interests were at a disadvantage since the Europeans and the Japanese had already begun to carve China into various spheres of influence. Concerned that American businesses would be shut out of the lucrative China trade, McKinley responded with the "open-door" policy. He directed Secretary of State John Hay to work out an understanding with the major powers that would maintain open trade in the region. With the support of Great Britain, Hay managed to reach an agreementwith all the major European powers and Japan under the terms of which these nations pledged to open their spheres of influence to free and unrestricted trade with the other major powers in China. As a result, most tariffs and other restrictions were dropped for foreign businesses trading in the region.

America soon intensified its involvement in Asia. In June 1900 a Chinese nationalist group known as the Boxers rose up against the foreign powers in China. The Boxers massacred some 300 foreign businessmen, missionaries, and diplomats and laid siege to the foreign missions in Beijing. The United States became the main force behind organizing a relief expedition for Beijing. A multinational coalition of troops defeated the Boxers and rescued the foreign nationals besieged in Beijing. China was forced to pay an indemnity of some $333 million to the foreign powers. The American share of this compensation was $25 million—an amount that far exceeded American losses during the incident. McKinley directed that $17 million of the payment be returned to the Chinese government, which subsequently used the funds to send Chinese students to American colleges.

The election of 1900 once again pitted McKinley against Bryan. The currency issue faded into the background as new discoveries of gold in Alaska and South Africa allowed McKinley to lock the United States into the gold standard at a favorable rate through the Gold Standard Act of 1900. In addition, the American economy was booming under McKinley's administration. Events such as the Alaska gold rush, the Spanish-American War, and the subsequent acquisition of various colonies and the new open-door policy all combined to stimulate the economy to such a level as to overcome high consumer prices caused by protectionist tariffs. McKinley's campaign slogan during the election was "Four More Years of the Full Dinner Pail."

The main issue in the campaign became imperialism. For Bryan and the Democrats, the insurrection in the Philippines and the Boxer Rebellion in China clearly demonstrated that the United States was no longer the champion of freedom and independence but that, under McKinley's administration, it had instead become a traditional imperial power bent on acquiring territory around the globe. Bryan called for the immediate independence of the Philippines and other territory acquired during the Spanish-American War. McKinley and the Republicans countered that the United States had a moral duty to bring American ideals and values to the so-called backward people of the world and that American imperialism differed from and was more "uplifting" than European imperialism because of these values.

Bryan also called for such progressive reforms as the direct election of senators, tariff reductions, and statehood for the western territories such as New Mexico. Besides an increased American presence in the world, McKinley emphasized the need for continuity in administrations in order to preserve the relative prosperity of the period and called for measures such as restrictions on immigration, an increase in the age limit for child labor, and the construction of a canal across Central America. While Bryan crisscrossed the nation in campaign appearance after campaign appearance, McKinley remained aloof at the White House, leaving the overwhelming majority of campaigning to his new running mate, Theodore Roosevelt.

McKinley's first vice president, Garret Hobart, died in office in 1899, and McKinley allowed the 1900 Republican National Convention to decide his replacement. The clear choice of the delegates was the tremendously popular governor of New York, Theodore Roosevelt. Roosevelt, who came to fame through his actions during the Spanish-American War, was known as a progressive. The inclusion of Roosevelt helped balance the Republican ticket by giving a nod toward the reform-minded elements of the country. Roosevelt's vigorous campaigning and the economic prosperity of the day easily propelled McKinley to victory again. He won with 7,219,530 (52%) of the popular vote to Bryan's 6,358,071 (46%) and carried 28 states to Bryan's 17.

On September 6, 1901, in Buffalo, New York, an avowed anarchist, Leon Czolgosz, fired two bullets at the president. The first was deflected by a button, but the second struck McKinley in the abdomen and lodged in his pancreas. Initially doctors were optimistic about the president's chances for recovery. However, gangrene set in along the track of the bullet, and McKinley succumbed to his wound early on the morning of September 14. His last words were reported to be, "It is God's will. His will, not ours, be done."

Tom Lansford

SEE ALSO History

BIBLIOGRAPHY

Damini, Brian P. *Advocates of Empire: William McKinley, the Senate and American Expansion, 1889–1899.* New York: Garland, 1987.

Dobson, John. *Reticent Expansion: The Foreign Policy of William McKinley*. Pittsburgh: Duquesne University Press, 1988.

Morgan, H. Wayne. *William McKinley and His America*. Syracuse, NY: Syracuse University Press, 1963.

RICHARD M. NIXON

Richard Milhous Nixon, 37th president of the United States (1969–1974), was born on January 9, 1913, in Yorba Linda, California. Nixon was one of the most controversial politicians of the twentieth century. He built his political career on the communist scare of the late forties and early fifties, but as president he achieved détente with the Soviet Union and opened relations with the People's Republic of China. His administration occurred during the domestic upheavals brought on by the civil rights movement and the Vietnam War. He was reelected in 1972 by an overwhelming margin, but less than two years later he was forced to become the first man to resign the presidency, amid the scandal and shame of Watergate. He had staged a difficult political comeback in 1968, after

Richard M. Nixon as Congressman, 1948. *Source:* Library of Congress.

purportedly retiring from politics, and by the end of his life, he had shed some of the scourge of Watergate and was once again a respected elder statesman, largely because of his record on foreign policy. He died on February 22, 1994. His writings include three autobiographical works: *Six Crises* (1962), *RN: The Memoirs of Richard Nixon* (1978), and *In the Arena* (1990).

Early Political Career

Nixon came from a southern California Quaker family, where hard work and integrity were deeply rooted and heavily emphasized. Always a good student, he was invited by Harvard and Yale to apply for scholarships, but his older brother's illness and the depression made it necessary for him to remain close to home, and he attended nearby Whittier College, where he graduated second in his class in 1934. He went on to law school at Duke University, where his seriousness and determination won him the nickname "Gloomy Gus." He graduated third in his class and applied for jobs with both large northeastern law firms and the FBI. His applications were all rejected, however, and he was forced to go home to southern California, where his mother helped get him a job at a friend's local law firm.

At the outbreak of World War II, Nixon went to work briefly for the tire-rationing section of the Office of Price Administration in Washington, D.C., and eight months later, he joined the navy and was sent to the Pacific as a supply officer. He was popular with his men and such an accomplished poker player that he was able to send enough of his comrades in arms' money back home to help fund his first political campaign. Shortly after returning from the war, Nixon entered politics, answering a Republican Party call in the newspaper for someone to run against five-term Democratic Congressman Jerry Voorhis. Nixon seemed the perfect man for the job, and he was welcomed generously by the California Republican Party, which considered him "salable merchandise."

The style of Nixon's first campaign set the tone for the early part of his political career, in which he achieved national renown as a fierce anticommunist. He accused Congressman Voorhis of being a communist and even went so far as to have campaign workers make anonymous calls to voters stating that as a fact and advising that a vote for Nixon was therefore the best move. This sort of straightforward communist baiting was new at the time, and fear of the Soviet Union, which appeared to be spreading its influence throughout Asia (China fell to Mao Zedong's communist forces in 1949), made it a particularly persuasive tactic. "Of course I knew Jerry Voorhis wasn't a communist," Nixon later said, "but I had to win."

Nixon defeated Voorhis with 60% of the vote, and upon taking his seat in Congress, he became the junior member of the infamous House Committee on Un-American Activities. Nixon's dogged pursuit of Alger Hiss, a former adviser to Franklin Roosevelt and one of the organizers of the United Nations, brought him national exposure. Hiss had been accused of being a communist and of transmitting secret State Department documents to the Soviets, and though many believed him innocent, Nixon fiercely pushed the case forward, eventually getting Hiss convicted of perjury and jailed. At the age of 35, Nixon was a national figure, and he rode this fame to an easy victory in his Senate race against three-term Congresswoman Helen Gahagan Douglas in 1950, once again adopting a communist-baiting campaign strategy. He accused Ms. Douglas, who opposed the efforts of the House Un-American Activities Committee, of being "pink right down to her underwear." In return, Douglas dubbed Nixon "Tricky Dick," which became his long-standing nickname.

Nixon was only in the U.S. Senate for a year and a half when, in 1952, the Republican National Convention selected him to be General Dwight D. Eisenhower's running mate. Much of Nixon's success and notoriety up to that point had been built on the political and personal ruination of his honest Democratic foes, and Nixon was expected to do much of the dirty work of campaigning, leaving Eisenhower to take the "high road," remaining pure and untarnished by messy politicking. Nixon performed his task admirably, casting doubt on the abilities and patriotism of his and Eisenhower's Democratic opponent, Adlai Stevenson.

Nixon himself had to face close scrutiny during the campaign, and when the *New York Post* announced that he had received secret campaign contributions from wealthy sources, he was nearly pushed off the ticket. Instead of giving up, Nixon went on national, prime-time television and appealed directly to the voters. He delivered what has come to be known as the "Checkers Speech," fully exposing his financial situation and revealing that he was not a wealthy man. The speech was an unprecedented success, and the Republican National Committee received thousands of telegrams of support. Nixon remained on the ticket and became vice president when Eisenhower overwhelmingly defeated Stevenson.

When Eisenhower decided to run again in 1956, Nixon's presence on the ticket was not assured; however, Nixon pressured the president into making a de-

cision, and refused Eisenhower's offer of a cabinet position, and the Republican ticket once again contained Richard Milhous Nixon as the vice presidential candidate. In the second campaign, Nixon moved away from his muckraking, communist-baiting techniques, and the press began speaking of a "new Nixon." Because of Eisenhower's apparent support, Nixon was considered by many the Republican heir apparent, and he became more active in his second term. Eisenhower sent him on tours of South America, where his motorcade was spat upon and attacked, and the Soviet Union, where Nixon challenged Nikita Khrushchev to an impromptu debate, known as the "Kitchen Debate."

Nixon was unanimously nominated at the Republican National Convention in 1960, and only 14 years after first running for office, he was one election away from the presidency. Many were confident of Nixon's ability to win the election easily, being a prominent, national figure running against the young, inexperienced John F. Kennedy, who was little known nationally and had a reputation as a playboy inside Washington circles. Kennedy, however, took advantage of modern campaigning techniques, which employed television more than personal contact, and he was given a big push by the first-ever televised presidential debates. The healthy, attractive, charming Kennedy came off as strong, confident, and in control, while Nixon, who refused to wear makeup, looked haggard, almost ghostlike. The election was one of the closest in history, with Kennedy winning by only 100,000 votes nationwide. Some of the most crucial votes came from Cook County, Illinois, which was controlled by party boss Richard Daley, and many suspected election fraud, but Nixon refused to demand a recount, stating that it would be political suicide if he lost.

Nixon ran for governor of California in 1962, but he had never been a locally active politician, and his years in Washington had put him out of touch with the situation in California. He lost soundly to incumbent Pat Brown. In a press conference shortly after the results were announced, Nixon berated the media for giving him a hard time since the Hiss case, urged greater fairness in political coverage, and claimed that this would be his last press conference. "You don't have Nixon to kick around anymore," he said. He took a job as a Wall Street lawyer but soon tired of private life and took to the campaign trail in 1966, stumping successfully for Republican congressional candidates and bringing himself once again into the heart of Republican Party affairs.

After a grueling four-continent tour during which he familiarized himself with foreign affairs, the dogged Nixon was back in the electoral arena again, running for president a second time in 1968. Nixon avoided the tricky issue of the Vietnam War, stating only that he would find an "honorable end" to the conflict. He let the Democrats, badly split over the war, tear themselves asunder, further setting himself apart by running a "law-and-order" campaign that blamed America's most visible, divisive problems on the liberal Democrats. Nixon's appeal to the "forgotten Americans," who felt themselves ignored in the upheavals of the sixties, brought him a close victory over Hubert Humphrey.

Presidency

Upon his election, Nixon pledged that he would bring America together, but his margin of victory had been slim and based primarily on white, middle-class, hawkish, and patriotic voters. As president, he concentrated primarily on foreign affairs, hoping to bring about a generation of peace and a new world order. Chief of Staff H.R. Haldeman and John Erhlichman, a top campaign official and one of Nixon's closest advisers, handled much of domestic policy and shielded Nixon from many of the irksome daily details of the administration, leaving the president free to concentrate on foreign policy. Nixon often bypassed the Defense and State Departments, instead working closely with National Security Adviser Henry Kissinger, a former Harvard professor and newcomer to official foreign policy circles.

The Vietnam War, which had destroyed Nixon's predecessor, was the major obstacle to the new president's designs. Even before his inauguration, Nixon had Kissinger engage in secret peace talks with North Vietnam, hoping to speed American withdrawal from Vietnam. Early in his term, Nixon announced a gradual replacement of American fighting forces with South Vietnamese, planning to have all American troops out of Vietnam by the end of 1970. However, Nixon did not want to be the first president to lose a war, and he could not be satisfied with a simple withdrawal from Vietnam, being convinced, as were many Americans, that abandoning South Vietnam to the communists would invite further communist aggression in the region. Nixon had to face a vigorous antiwar movement, and he appealed to the "silent majority," another version of his "forgotten Americans," who he felt supported his foreign policy. He pledged not to back down and in early 1970 escalated the war, authorizing bombings of North Vietnam and attacks on Cambodia. After his reelection, Nixon once again ordered an escalation in the bombings, which Alexander Haig, Kissinger's deputy, described as "brutalizing" the north. Two weeks after the bombings began,

Nixon announced that peace negotiations were soon to resume, and by January 28, 1973, a cease-fire was established that allowed the United States to remove its reamaining 23,700 troops and end its 12-year military involvement in Vietnam.

Domestically, Nixon adhered to a standard Republican spending-cut program, cutting back and opposing federal welfare services and proposing antibusing legislation. He also implemented the "new economic policy," which called for a 10% tax on many imports; repeal of certain excise taxes; tax breaks for industries undertaking new investment; and a 90-day freeze on wages, prices, and dividends designed to halt inflation. These policies were initially successful, causing American exports to become cheaper and improving the balance of trade, but when the wage and price commissions began to give in to pressures from both labor and business interests, inflation accelerated again, inaugurating a decade-long rise in the cost of living that negatively impacted many segments of American society.

But Nixon is best remembered for his foreign policy achievements, despite his failure to bring a speedy, or even an "honorable," end to the Vietnam War, and Kissinger's inability to end the Middle East tensions that were brought on by Israel's victory over Arab countries in the Six-Day War of 1967. Perhaps this notoriety is based on the fact that Nixon was one of the few presidents in American history who practiced foreign policy by design, setting certain goals and moving steadily, if sometimes secretly and ruthlessly, toward them, instead of merely reacting to the conditions of world affairs as had many previous chief executives. He repudiated his anticommunist past and became the first U.S. president to visit the Soviet Union when he traveled to Moscow in May 1972. He sought peace with the opposing superpower and initiated negotiations with the Soviet Union to limit nuclear weapons, which resulted in the Strategic Arms Limitation Treaty (SALT). At the same time, he was making secret contact with the other great communist nation, the People's Republic of China, which he visited publicly in February 1972, thus opening official diplomatic relations with China for the first time since the communist takeover in 1949.

Despite the finally peaceful outcome of the Vietnam situation and his diplomatic accomplishments, Nixon's vicious, unrelenting policies and his blatant scoffing at the antiwar movement had ignited serious domestic upheavals, including the shooting of 12 students at a Kent State University antiwar demonstration. The visible public dissatisfaction with the president, which could be seen outside the White House from 1970 on, exacerbated Nixon's famous insecurity and brought out what some of his aides called Nixon's "dark side." The paranoia that resulted led Nixon to form the Special Investigations Unit, known as the "plumbers," an outfit illegally equipped by the CIA and sent on missions to embarrass and discredit potential Democratic opponents. He also formed the Committee to Re-elect the President (CREEP), which collected $60 million, much of it in violation of existing campaign laws, and disbursed funds for "dirty tricks," which included tapping the phone of the chair of the Democratic National Committee.

Nixon needed little of this help to secure reelection in 1972, as he faced a badly divided Democratic Party headed by a self-righteous and indecisive George McGovern. Nixon won the election with 60.7% of the vote, but a host of revelations in 1973 undermined Nixon's presidency and finally brought about his resignation. The involvement of the CIA, supposedly under Nixon's direction, in a military coup that overthrew Chile's Salvador Allende, the Western Hemisphere's first popularly elected Marxist, was exposed, and Vice President Spiro Agnew was forced to resign when it was revealed that he had cheated on his income taxes and had taken more than $100,000 in payoffs from contractors between 1966 and 1972. The IRS also disclosed that Nixon himself owed more than $400,000 in back taxes and penalties, and critics pointed out that the Nixon administration had raised subsidies to milk producers, which then donated more than half a million dollars to the Republican Party.

The final blow came when Nixon's involvement in the plumbers' Watergate burglary was revealed by investigative reporters. Nixon's involvement was documented on audiotapes of White House conversations, which Nixon refused to turn over to investigators. Nixon cited "executive privilege" and national security as reasons for keeping the tapes, but the Supreme Court rejected his appeal. A few days later, the House Judiciary Committee voted to impeach the president on three counts. Nixon finally released the incriminating tapes, and over the next few days, both Republican and Democratic senators, enough to get a conviction, indicated that they would vote against the president if articles of impeachment were passed by the House. On August 9, 1974, before the House could vote to impeach him, Nixon resigned the presidency, the first incumbent ever to do so.

Postpresidency

Nixon was succeeded by Gerald Ford, the man he had appointed to replace Spiro Agnew as vice president.

Soon after taking office, Ford granted Nixon a pardon for any crimes he might have committed as president. Unlike some of his aides, Nixon never went to jail. After resigning the presidency, Nixon sought to portray himself as an elder statesman. He published five books on U.S. foreign policy: *The Real War* (1980), *Real Peace* (1983), *No More Vietnams* (1985), *1999: Victory without War* (1988), *Seize the Moment* (1992), and *Beyond Peace* (1994). By the 1990s, much of the scandal had been forgotten, and Nixon was once again hailed as a genius of foreign policy and jokingly considered a possible Republican presidential candidate. T-shirts and bumper stickers appeared bearing the motto "He's tan, he's rested, and he's ready: Nixon in '92."

Jack J. Miller

SEE ALSO History

BIBLIOGRAPHY

Aitken, Jonathan. *Nixon: A Life*. Chicago: Regnery, 1993.
Ambrose, Stephen E. *Nixon: The Education of a Politician, 1913–1962*. New York: Simon and Schuster, 1988.
Genovese, Michael A. *The Nixon Presidency: Power and Politics in Turbulent Times*. Westport, CT: Greenwood Press, 1990.
Hoff-Wilson, Joan. *Nixon Reconsidered*. New York: Basic Books, 1994.
WGBH Boston. *Nixon*. PBS Video, 1990, videorecording.

RONALD REAGAN

Ronald Wilson Reagan, 40th president of the United States, came to politics relatively late in life after a career in both radio and film. The skills that he developed as a radio announcer and actor served him well in politics—earning him the nickname "the Great Communicator." One of the most conservative presidents of the twentieth century, Reagan used his considerable ability to communicate with the American people to become one of the most popular twentieth-century presidents as well, through his ability to rise above the problems that confronted his administration.

Born on February 6, 1911, Reagan grew up in a lower-middle-class home in Illinois. Although an average student, Reagan was a popular and athletic youth who was elected president of the student body and played on the football, basketball and track teams in high school and went on to attend Eureka College in Illinois from 1928 to 1932, on a partial football scholarship. Finding that he had a gift for oratory, Reagan chose to enter the field of radio broadcasting after his graduation from Eureka College in June 1932.

Reagan was a sports broadcaster from 1932 until 1935, when a friend suggested that he try film acting. After a screen test in 1937, he went on to act in some 50

Ronald Reagan. *Source:* Library of Congress.

ernment and fiscal responsibility. He served two terms as governor, compiling an impressive record as a conservative by limiting the size and growth of the state government, balancing the state budget and reforming California's welfare system.

Reagan ran for the Republican presidential nomination in 1968, placing third behind Richard M. Nixon and Nelson Rockefeller. Reagan again ran for president in 1976 and came just 60 votes short of denying Gerald Ford the nomination at the Republican National Convention in Kansas City. By this time, Reagan had established himself as the leader of the conservative wing of the Republican Party.

Reagan was successful in his third run for the presidency in 1980. Rising above other conservatives, he dominated the early primaries and easily won the Republican nomination on the first ballot at the July 1980 convention in Detroit. When former President Gerald Ford declined an invitation to be the vice presidential candidate, Reagan chose his former opponent George Bush. The Republicans adopted a platform that incorporated Reagan's main campaign themes: a balanced budget, tax cuts, restrictions on the growth of government, and increases in defense spending.

Beset by a host of problems that ranged from runaway inflation and gasoline shortages to the lingering hostage crisis in Iran, Reagan's opponent, President Jimmy Carter, was unable to overcome the public's perception of him as a weak president. Carter campaigned on traditional Democratic themes, which included increased government spending for social programs and national health insurance. John Anderson, a moderate Republican, ran as an independent and offered himself as a compromise choice between Reagan's conservatism and Carter's liberalism.

Reagan won the 1980 election by a landslide. He received 43,899,248 popular votes (51%) and 489 electoral votes and carried 44 states. Carter received 35,481,435 popular votes (41%) and 49 electoral votes and carried 6 states. Anderson received 5,719,437 popular votes (7%) but failed to win any electoral votes or carry any states. On Reagan's coattails, the Republicans gained control of the Senate. Reagan's election confirmed a shift in southern politics that had begun with Nixon's presidency as conservative Democrats, often called "Reagan Democrats," found themselves increasingly pulled toward the Republican Party and away from the Democratic Party, which many viewed as being controlled by the liberal wing of the party and thus out of touch with much of middle America.

Reagan survived an assassination attempt soon after taking office. On March 30, 1981, John Hinckley Jr. fired six shots from a .22-caliber revolver at President Rea-

movies, including such classics as *Knute Rockne—All-American* (1940) and *King's Row* (1941). While working for Warner Brothers Film Studios, Reagan met and eventually married actress Jane Wyman in 1941. The couple had one daughter, Maureen, and adopted a son, Michael, in 1945. In part because of Reagan's increasing political activism, the two divorced in 1949. Reagan was the first president to have been divorced. He was remarried to actress Nancy Davis in March 1952. The couple had two children, Patti (Reagan) Davis and Ronald Prescott Reagan.

As his film career declined in the late 1940s, Reagan was drawn to politics. Twice elected president of the Screen Actors Guild, Reagan testified before the House Un-American Activities Committee as a "friendly witness" in 1947, though he privately criticized the tactics of Congress during the McCarthy period. Despite his previous allegiance to the Democratic Party, Reagan supported Dwight D. Eisenhower in both of his presidential bids and actively campaigned for Richard M. Nixon in 1960. Two years later, he officially switched parties and became a Republican. He attracted nation-al political attention in 1964 with a televised speech on behalf of Barry Goldwater's presidential candidacy. This episode served as a springboard for Reagan's own political career.

Reagan successfully ran for governor of California in 1966 by campaigning on a platform of limited gov-

gan as he left the Washington, D.C., Hilton. Hinckley's shots wounded Reagan, Press Secretary James Brady, and two others (the round that hit Reagan penetrated one of his lungs and lodged one inch from his heart). Despite the severity of his wounds, Reagan made a quick and full recovery and was back at the White House in 12 days. The assassination attempt generated immense popular support for Reagan and helped him win passage of his initial agenda.

Reagan implemented elements of his "New Federalism" immediately after taking office. He imposed a hiring freeze on federal employees and secured passage of a package of tax cuts and large reductions in federal spending. Reagan went on to initiate an economic program based on supply-side economics. By cutting taxes on the wealthy and on businesses, Reagan reasoned that large amounts of capital would be freed for investment and thus spur economic growth and cause a "trickle down" of benefits to the middle and lower classes as new businesses and jobs were created. Reagan's fiscal policies, aided by high interest rates and a drop in world oil prices, drove inflation down from more than 13% to less than 3% within two years of his taking office. Unfortunately, those same high interest rates also helped drive the economy into a recession. Unemployment rose from 7% to almost 11%, while bank, business and farm failures reached levels not seen since the Great Depression. As a result of the recession and tax cuts, federal receipts fell sharply, forcing dramatic increases in the federal deficit. At the same time, the trade deficit between the United States and other nations also ballooned as Americans bought record amounts of relatively inexpensive foreign goods. The United States was transformed from the world's largest creditor nation to the world's largest debtor nation.

By late 1982, the recession had ended, and the economy began to expand. Unemployment fell steadily as the United States embarked upon the longest economic recovery since World War II. This expansion was partially fueled by dramatic increases in defense spending. Reagan called for these increases in an effort to give the United States the power needed to reassert itself as leader of the "free world" and thus counter the relative Soviet gains of the 1970s. Reagan also intended to engage the Soviet Union in an arms race in which he felt confident that the Soviets could not keep up with the Americans.

With a more assertive foreign policy posture and the economic recovery of the early 1980s, Reagan went into the 1984 election buoyed by immense popularity. He ran unopposed for the Republican nomination and dominated the polls against his Democratic challenger,

former Vice President Walter F. Mondale. Reagan campaigned on a platform that contained pledges not to raise taxes, to promote global free trade and to work toward a balanced budget amendment. Mondale chose the first woman, Geraldine Ferraro, to run as a vice presidential candidate for a major party and campaigned on a platform that called for tax increases on businesses and the wealthy and vainly attacked Reagan's record. On election day, Reagan received the largest electoral total in American history, with 525 electoral votes and 54,281,858 popular votes (59%), and carried 49 states. Mondale received 13 electoral votes and 37,457,215 popular votes (41%) and won only his home state of Minnesota and the District of Columbia.

Like his first term, Reagan's second was marked by continuing record deficits. Nonetheless, Reagan continued to emphasize tax reform. The 1986 Tax Reform Act was the most sweeping change in the federal tax code since World War II. The act simplified the tax code and lowered the tax rates for most individuals. Reagan felt that this reform was one of the most important of his second term.

Despite record losses on Wall Street in October 1987, when the Dow Jones Industrial Average lost 36% of its value, the American economy continued to grow during Reagan's second term. Unemployment dropped below 6% in 1987 and 1988 as a record 117 million Americans were employed. At the same time, though, the dollar rose dramatically against other currencies. This continued to fuel America's large trade deficit as American consumers stocked up on relatively cheap imports of cars, clothes and electronic goods.

In both his terms as president, Reagan's foreign policy was characterized by an increased American assertiveness around the globe. Through programs such as the Strategic Defense Initiative (SDI) and the massive naval buildup, Reagan's policies would eventually spur the reform efforts of Mikhail Gorbachev, which, in turn, led to the demise of the Soviet Union and the end of the Cold War. Ronald Reagan the Cold Warrior became Ronald Reagan the Peacemaker as he and Gorbachev met in a series of summits that eventually culminated in the Strategic Arms Limitation Treaty (SALT) of December 1987, which cut the nuclear stockpiles of the two superpowers by some 2,500 warheads.

Reagan also showed a willingness to break the "Vietnam syndrome" and engage American troops in combat operations to further or protect U.S. interests around the globe. Actions such as the invasion of Grenada in 1983, the American bombing of Libya and related air skirmishes, and the reflagging of Kuwaiti tankers in 1987 all demonstrated a reassertion of

American power in the world. At the same time, however, Reagan's two terms were plagued by both terrorist attacks and the kidnapping of American hostages. From the bombing of the marine barracks in Lebanon in 1983, which killed 241 American marines, to the downing of a Pan Am passenger flight over Lockerbie, Scotland, in 1988, which killed 259 passengers, the United States seemed impotent against international terrorism.

The administration's attempts to recover American hostages held by Islamic extremist groups led to the biggest scandal of Reagan's presidency. In 1985 Reagan agreed to sell weapons to Iran covertly in exchange for the release of American hostages. While some hostages were released, still others were taken, and more important, the proceeds from the Iranian arms sales were illegally diverted to aid the anticommunist contras in Nicaragua. Although Reagan was cleared of any direct involvement in the illegal flow of funds to the contras, the Iran–contra scandal dramatically reduced his influence during his last two years in office—a fact exacerbated by the Republican loss of the Senate in 1986.

After appointing Sandra Day O'Connor as the first female justice on the Supreme Court, Reagan generally tilted the Court to the right through the nominations of William Rehnquist as chief justice and Antonin Scalia as associate justice. In 1987, however, two of Reagan's Supreme Court nominations were blocked by the Senate after lengthy, televised hearings. These hearings signaled a new era in Senate confirmations as presidential appointees came under increasing scrutiny over their views on contentious issues such as abortion.

In 1988, in one of his last major acts as president, Reagan signed the U.S.–Canada Free Trade Pact, which began dismantling trade barriers between the two nations and laid the groundwork for the later North American Free Trade Agreement (NAFTA). Reagan endorsed Vice President Bush as his successor in 1988 and actively campaigned for him. After Bush's victory, Reagan retired to Bel Air, California, from whence he remained active in Republican politics. Reagan also retained his personal popularity in retirement, remaining one of the best-liked, though controversial, American political leaders of his time.

Tom Lansford

SEE ALSO History

BIBLIOGRAPHY

Berman, Larry, ed. *Looking Back on the Reagan Presidency.* Baltimore: Johns Hopkins University Press, 1990.

Boaz, David, ed. *Assessing the Reagan Years.* Washington, DC: Cato Institute, 1988.

Boyarsky, Bill. *Ronald Reagan: His Life and Rise to the Presidency.* New York: Random House, 1981.

Reagan, Ronald. *An American Life.* New York: Simon and Schuster, 1990.

Thompson, Kenneth W. *Leadership in the Reagan Presidency.* New York: Madison Books, 1992.

THEODORE ROOSEVELT

Courageous outdoorsman, savvy politician, Theodore Roosevelt made the journey from Oyster Bay Cove, Long Island, New York, to Washington, D.C., to become the nation's youngest president, taking office in 1901, just before his 43rd birthday. While it was the assassination of then President William McKinley that ushered Roosevelt into office, it was a popular vote that confirmed the decision of the fates, in 1904.

Born in 1858, Roosevelt transformed himself from a sickly youth to a strapping hunter, soldier, explorer and statesman. Letting neither his defective eyesight nor his asthma stand in his way, as a youth, Roosevelt

Theodore Roosevelt. *Source:* Library of Congress.

exercised in a gym built by his father and later took up the manly art of boxing, becoming a member of the Harvard University boxing team. It was a boxing accident that left him blind in one eye.

The rugged physique he developed via persistent effort imbued in Roosevelt a lifelong advocacy of the benefits of physical exertion and mental endeavor. His competitive nature, nurtured through pugilistic contests, served him equally well in the political "ring."

While in the White House, Roosevelt would appear on horseback, play tennis, or hike, often with companions who were to become known as the "Tennis cabinet."

Roosevelt obtained his early education from private tutors, never attending public school. Showing a strong inclination toward natural history while a small boy, he started with two of his cousins the "Roosevelt Museum of Natural History," collecting bones, stones, and animal carcasses housed in a dresser drawer.

Roosevelt made an early first trip to Europe with his family. During a later trip to Europe, in 1872, the family journeyed throughout Egypt, sailing up the Nile, and Roosevelt, dedicated to his "museum," collected many exhibits, which led him to become skilled in both hunting and taxidermy.

Continuing with his tendency to be a "founder," Roosevelt, while living in Dresden, Germany, along with two other cousins, formed the "Dresden Literary American Club," via which they shared their creative writings.

Returning from the second European trip at the age of 15, Roosevelt was prepared by his tutors for his entry into Harvard University, which he attended from 1876 to 1880.

Roosevelt took up other interests besides the offerings of academia and, in his senior year, fell in love with the woman who became his wife, Alice Lee. They married and moved to New York City, where for a time Roosevelt attended Columbia Law School but never finished.

When only 23 years old, Roosevelt was elected to the New York State legislature, gaining the respect of his older colleagues and becoming well known as an opponent of the widespread corruption of New York politics of the time.

Three years after his entry into the legislature, he was made chair of the New York State delegation to the Republican National Convention.

But all was not incessant progress and triumph. In the year Roosevelt became chair, his wife, Alice Lee, died, leaving him with a two-day-old daughter, also named Alice. Adding to this tragic loss was the death of his mother on the same night in the same house.

After completing his term in the legislature, Roosevelt moved to his ranches in North Dakota, leaving his daughter in the care of his sister, Anna.

Roosevelt spent two years in the rough and wild of North Dakota—hunting, cowboying, and serving as a deputy sheriff—before his second marriage, to his childhood friend Edith Carrow.

They settled in Long Island, in Oyster Bay Cove, at Sagamore Hill, which today is still preserved as a national historic site. Never idle, they produced five children, who were later referred to as the "Roosevelt Gang."

At Sagamore Hill, Roosevelt's passion for physical exercise was visited upon the children, who swam in Long Island Sound, often in their clothes, and went on hikes.

Roosevelt was interrupted from writing the *History of the West* when President Benjamin Harrison selected him as civil service commissioner in 1889, in which capacity Roosevelt served for six years, gaining a reputation as a reformer.

Back from Washington, in 1895 Roosevelt took the post of police commissioner of New York City, becoming the enemy of graft and corruption in the police force. Strongly opposed by politicians and journalists alike, he was somewhat less than entirely successful.

After two years of fighting corruption in the New York City Police Department, Roosevelt became assistant secretary of the navy, at the invitation of President McKinley. The president sometimes referred to Roosevelt as a "bull in a china shop."

As a war with Spain approached, Roosevelt undertook preparations on his own initiative, raising a volunteer cavalry regiment with his associate, then Colonel Leonard Wood. The cowboy backgrounds of many of the members earned them the name "Rough Riders."

In action in Cuba, Roosevelt's "ranch hand" background served him well, forewarning him just before an ambush. While looking at some barbed wire, he noticed it was freshly cut, alerting him to the presence of Spanish soldiers, who quickly confirmed his deduction via repeated volleys of Mauser bullets.

Roosevelt, of course, is well remembered as a hero for leading the charge on Kettle Hill, which has been mistakenly called San Juan Hill. Roosevelt was later made a colonel, on his way to becoming governor of New York in 1898.

An unconventional politician and a publicity hound, Roosevelt did not produce significant legislative changes as governor of New York. However, his less than heroic performance as governor did not hinder him in the least from becoming vice president under the reelected McKinley in 1900.

McKinley's assassination in Buffalo, New York, by an anarchist ushered in the young Roosevelt as president of the United States in 1901.

In 1904 the people chose him as the commander in chief, and as elected president, Roosevelt inaugurated a program he referred to as the "Square Deal." This program of social legislation added new federal regulation of big business, control over interstate railroads, and an environmental program.

This program was not met with universal welcome. In 1902 the United Mine Workers Union struck in Pennsylvania, seeking less work and more money, together with recognition of their union. Naturally, the owners of the mine resisted their efforts.

Roosevelt threatened to use troops to operate the mines and forced the owners to negotiate with the union. From these efforts the miners got a shorter workday and more wages, but the union was not given legitimacy. At the time, this was accepted.

Further federal regulation under Roosevelt was evidenced by passage of the Pure Food and Drugs Act of 1906, creating the FDA.

Big business was often a target of the Roosevelt administration. Targeting the huge industrial monopolies of the time, then known as "trusts," Roosevelt urged and obtained the creation of the Department of Commerce and Labor and what was then called a Bureau of Corporations.

Investigations were conducted into big business monopolies, and warnings were issued. Suits were brought under the Sherman Anti-Trust Act of 1890, causing the dissolution of the railroad monopoly of the Northern Securities Company and resulting in more than two dozen indictments of monopolists.

Interstate transportation rates were fixed by the newly created Interstate Commerce Commission, which, of course, still functions today to regulate the interstate transport of goods.

In his environmental programs, Roosevelt was chiefly concerned with preserving the Old West, timberland, and wildlife. In his 1908 conference on conservation issues, Roosevelt was able to bring about the creation of conservation commissions in 41 states and the birth of the National Conservation Commission.

Under the National Reclamation Act, dams were built and arid lands were reclaimed via irrigation. Roosevelt had shown himself to be one of the early politicians oriented toward fighting graft but promoting "green" in the environment.

One of the most famous issues confronting the Roosevelt presidency was the Colombian threat to the Panama Canal Zone. Roosevelt ordered naval vessels to protect the integrity of the region and recognized the new nation of Panama, which several days later gave the United States control over a narrow strip of the Isthmus of Panama. This served to protect the interests of the French Panama Canal Company, which would have lost many millions of dollars if it could not sell its rights to the United States.

In other areas of world politics, Roosevelt was instrumental in bringing about the end of the Russo-Japanese War in 1905, temporarily keeping the lid on hostilities between France and Germany over Morocco, and settling the rights of American fishermen in Canada.

The Roosevelt administration was marked by a considerable military buildup and a show of American military might.

Having entered the presidency at a young age, Roosevelt also retired from it at a young age, stepping down at 50 from his White House duties.

From the political jungle of Washington, he journeyed to Africa to hunt, later touring throughout Europe to much acclaim, pomp, and circumstance.

However, politics called Roosevelt to the forefront once more, and he again ran for president on what became known as the "Bull Moose" ticket. He was shot at, slightly wounded, and narrowly lost the election to Woodrow Wilson.

Back to the jungles, this time in Brazil, in 1913–1914, Roosevelt explored unknown regions, caught malaria, and injured his leg. After this exploration, in 1917 Roosevelt explored how he might be of service to Washington when World War I brought the United States into conflict with Germany. His efforts were rebuffed by reelected President Wilson, although the sons of the former Rough Rider served in the war.

Never quiet during his active political life, Roosevelt died quietly in his sleep on January 6, 1919, leaving a legacy equaled by few subsequent presidents.

W. Adam Mandelbaum

SEE ALSO History

BIBLIOGRAPHY

Blum, John Morton. *The Republican Roosevelt*. Cambridge: Harvard University Press, 1977.

Busch, Noel Fairchild. *T.R.: The Story of Theodore Roosevelt and His Influence on Our Times*. New York: Reynal, 1963.

Gould, Lewis L. *The Presidency of Theodore Roosevelt*. Lawrence: University Press of Kansas, 1991.

Harbaugh, William H. *The Life and Times of Theodore Roosevelt*. New York: Oxford University Press, 1975.

Morris, Edmund. *The Rise of Theodore Roosevelt*. New York: Ballantine, 1986.

Mowry, George E. *Era of Theodore Roosevelt, 1900–1912*. New York: HarperCollins, 1991.

Pringle, Henry F. *Theodore Roosevelt: A Biography*. New York: Harcourt Brace, 1956.

WILLIAM HOWARD TAFT

William Howard Taft, 27th president of the United States and tenth chief justice of the United States, was born September 15, 1857, into a politically active family that had adopted Ohio as its home some 19 years before his birth. His father, Alfonso Taft, was an active member of the Republican Party who held two cabinet positions in the Ulysses S. Grant administration and earlier had attended the Republican National Convention of 1860, which nominated Abraham Lincoln. Clearly the future president was exposed to politics from his earliest years. Elective politics, however, held no great attraction for the younger Taft.

After attending Yale and graduating second in his class in 1878, Will Taft decided to follow his father's footsteps into the legal profession. He returned home to Cincinnati and studied law at the Cincinnati Law School. After being admitted to the bar, he worked as a newspaper reporter before beginning to practice his new profession. He then held a series of appointed positions, beginning with an appointment to fill a vacancy on the Superior Court in Cincinnati in 1886, to

William Howard Taft. *Source:* Library of Congress.

which he was elected to a full term in 1888. It was a time of labor unrest, strikes, and violence. Taft thought of organized labor as seriously threatening the nation.

By 1889 Taft was aspiring to sit on the United States Supreme Court. The governor of Ohio recommended him to President Benjamin Harrison to fill a vacancy on the Court; however, he was young and relatively inexperienced and did not receive the appointment. Harrison did appoint him solicitor general of the United States, a position he held from 1890 to 1892. As solicitor general, Taft represented the United States before the Supreme Court and won most of his cases. In 1892 he returned to Cincinnati to take a seat on the federal Court of Appeals for the Sixth Circuit. While on the Court of Appeals, Taft privately expressed his hostility toward strikers and toward boycotts instituted by labor organizations. But he was also opposed to anti-competitive business conspiracies. In a case involving a pipe company, he carefully distinguished the case from a contrary Supreme Court decision and found the company's practices to be a restraint on interstate commerce. The Supreme Court affirmed the decision.

Taft had ties to President William McKinley, a fellow Ohioan, which he hoped would get him his coveted Supreme Court appointment. At this time, he was friendly with Theodore Roosevelt, who was beginning to look beyond New York politics toward the national political arena. Roosevelt had supported McKinley, and Taft personally spoke to the president on his behalf. McKinley appointed Roosevelt assistant secretary of the navy, but Taft did not get a Supreme Court appointment, even though there was a vacancy in 1898.

In 1900 McKinley asked Taft to accept a position that would take him outside the United States. During the Spanish-American War, the United States had acquired control of the Philippine Islands, and the president wanted Taft to serve on, or possibly head, a commission to help prepare the Filipinos for self-government. Taft was reluctant to accept the appointment because it would have meant giving up his judicial position. McKinley, however, promised him a Supreme Court appointment if another vacancy occurred. Moreover, Mrs. Taft welcomed the opportunity to travel and had urged her husband to accept. Taft conditioned his acceptance on being appointed to head the commission, and the president acquiesced. In 1901 Taft became civil governor. Although he had anticipated being in the Philippines for only a short time, he spent four years there. After Theodore Roosevelt became president, Taft was twice offered his long-desired Supreme Court appointment, which he declined rather than desert the Filipino people, with whom he had developed a very warm relationship. As Taft and Roosevelt communicated concerning the Supreme Court, their friendship grew.

Roosevelt brought Taft back from the Philippines to be his secretary of war, but he really intended for him to be an adviser on a broad range of matters. Roosevelt believed Taft's presence would strengthen his administration and would be helpful in the 1904 election. Indeed, Taft did support him and campaigned actively for him even though campaigning was not something he enjoyed doing.

Roosevelt won the presidency in his own right in 1904, and when another Supreme Court vacancy occurred, he offered it to Taft. Again Taft declined. His family had developed presidential ambitions for him, which initially he had not shared, but in time they won him over. It was the third time he had declined a Supreme Court nomination, although he probably would have accepted had the position been chief justice.

As early as 1905, Taft said that he had no organization to secure the Republican presidential nomination but that he would accept the nomination if the party selected him. By 1907 he did have an organization. Its function was to win for Taft the support of party leaders who would be selecting delegates to the Republican National Convention. Roosevelt lent his support by directing federal patronage to Taft supporters, making it clear that Taft was his chosen successor.

There was, however, opposition to Taft's nomination. Conservatives in the party considered Roosevelt a radical and were convinced that Taft would be like him. William Jennings Bryan, while seeking the Democratic nomination, advocated public ownership of the railroads. Taft, while out campaigning, would talk about how much public money Bryan would spend on the railroads if elected. In the process, conservative Republicans began to feel more comfortable with the Taft candidacy, and the convention gave him the nomination. The congenial, rotund Ohioan went on to win the electoral college vote by a margin of 321 to Bryan's 162.

William Howard Taft entered his presidency without an abundance of self-confidence. He did nevertheless make his own cabinet selections, retaining two members from Roosevelt's cabinet, and later encountered incorrect allegations that he broke a promise to keep Roosevelt's entire cabinet. He had made no such promise.

As his presidency unfolded, Taft's restrained interpretation of his office prevented him from exercising leadership in his relations with conservative Republicans who held power in Congress. When Taft sought a downward revision of the tariff in the belief that its purpose should be revenue rather than protec-

tion, he was unable to achieve his objective. The kind of tariff he wanted would have resulted in lower prices for American consumers, but the Payne–Aldrich Tariff that Congress sent him was very protectionist in nature. He would not veto it, however, because he did not wish to alienate the congressional leadership, whose support he expected to need later, on other legislation. Instead, he alienated the progressive wing of the party. By the end of his term, they did not want four more years of Taft.

Although Taft had hoped to bring greater unity to his party, the split between the Old Guard and the progressive Republicans grew ever wider during his presidency. When Richard Fallinger, his secretary of the interior, and Gifford Pinchot, the chief forester, who had originally been appointed by Roosevelt, became embroiled in a dispute over coal leases on public lands, Taft tried to make peace between them. Failing in that, he sided with Ballinger and dismissed Pinchot, who was a favorite of the progressives.

It seemed that nothing Taft did pleased the progressives. Although his administration brought more antitrust suits in four years than Roosevelt's had in seven, the progressive Republicans did not approve of Taft's prosecutions of what they considered to be "good" corporations, even if they might be guilty of violations. Taft did not believe that he could rightly refuse to bring Sherman Act prosecutions against violators.

Taft's foreign policy toward Latin America, known as dollar diplomacy, reflected the belief that the United States government had an obligation to protect American investments in Latin American countries. There was also the Panama Canal to be protected. Other nations of the hemisphere were as resentful of Taft's foreign policy as of Roosevelt's before him.

In 1912 Taft sought a second term. To the delight of progressive Republicans, Theodore Roosevelt challenged him for the nomination. When the Republican National Convention met in Chicago, the incumbent president's supporters were in firm control of the party machinery. Disputes, such as those over delegates' credentials, were generally decided in Taft's favor. Although he was denied the Republican nomination, former President Roosevelt became the candidate of a third party, the Progressive Party, whose members believed that both major parties were dominated by special interests. The Democratic Party, however, had nominated a progressive Democrat, Woodrow Wilson. Because of the split in Republican ranks, Wilson was elected, and Taft became a one-term president.

After his presidency, Taft joined the faculty of Yale Law School and remained there for eight years. He and Roosevelt reconciled during the years of the Wilson presidency. In 1918 Wilson appointed Taft one of two joint chairs of the National War Labor Board, a position that taught him much about the lives of working people.

In 1920 the Republican Party reclaimed the presidency with the election of Warren G. Harding, thus permitting Taft to culminate his public career on the Supreme Court in the chair of the chief justice. Following the death of Chief Justice Edward Douglass White, whom Taft had himself appointed, Harding nominated Taft, and the Senate confirmed him. Taft thus became the only former president to serve on the Supreme Court. His first major opinion on the Court involved labor law and seemed to be a throwback to his antilabor days as a judge in Ohio and on the Sixth Circuit Court of Appeals. In *Truax* v. *Corrigan*, Taft wrote for a divided Supreme Court that an Arizona law that greatly limited the authority of state courts to issue injunctions in labor disputes violated the due process clause of the 14th Amendment. There were times when he wrote like a conservative justice and other times when he wrote like a progressive Republican. In 1922 both sides of the chief justice were displayed. In *Stafford* v. *Wallace*, he wrote an opinion upholding the power of the federal government to regulate stockyards under the commerce power, but in *Bailey* v. *Drexel*, he wrote that Congress could not use its tax power to regulate child labor, which he considered to be within the reserved powers of the states. The following year, in 1923, the Supreme Court struck down congressional legislation requiring the payment of a minimum wage to women working in the District of Columbia on the grounds that it violated freedom of contract. In his dissent in *Adkins* v. *Children's Hospital*, the chief justice wrote that freedom of contract was meaningless to some people, that their economic conditions were such that they had to take what they were offered. But the opinion that Taft considered his most important was *Myers* v. *United States*, decided in 1926, which strengthened the power of the president to remove executive officials from office.

Taft's greatest contributions to the Supreme Court came not from his opinions but from his efforts to bring administrative reforms to the federal courts and from his efforts on behalf of the construction of a Supreme Court building. Never in its history had the Court had its own building. Taft lived long enough to know that the construction would take place, when President Herbert Hoover signed the bill appropriating the necessary funds in December 1929. William Howard Taft died March 8, 1930.

Patricia A. Behlar

SEE ALSO History

BIBLIOGRAPHY

Coletta, Paolo E. *The Presidency of William Howard Taft.* Lawrence: University Press of Kansas, 1973.

Kelly, Frank K. *The Fight for the White House: The Story of 1912.* New York: Crowell, 1961.

Mason, Alpheus Thomas. *William Howard Taft, Chief Justice.* Lanham, MD: University Press of America, 1983.

Pringle, Henry F. *The Life and Times of William Howard Taft.* 2 vols. New York: Farrar and Rinehart, 1939.

Ross, Ishbel. *An American Family: The Tafts, 1678–1964.* Cleveland: World Publishing, 1964.

Vice Presidents

SPIRO AGNEW

Spiro Theodore "Ted" Agnew was born in Baltimore, Maryland, on November 9, 1918. His father, Theodore Spiro Agnew, was a Greek immigrant, who came to the United States in 1899. The elder Agnew settled in Boston but eventually moved the family to Baltimore, where he became an active member of the Greek community and a local leader of the Democratic Party. The younger Agnew wrote his father's political speeches.

Agnew attended Baltimore's Johns Hopkins University for three years as a chemistry major before transferring to night classes at the University of Baltimore's law school. His studies were temporarily interrupted by World War II. Agnew served in the army during the war; he entered as a second lieutenant and was later promoted to captain. Immediately following the conclusion of the war, he returned to finish law school. He graduated in 1947 and settled in the town of Towson, Maryland. Agnew was a registered Democrat, emulating his father, but business acquaintances persuaded him that the Republican philosophy was closer to his own, so he switched parties.

Agnew's foray into public life began with the PTA (Parent-Teacher Association) of his children's schools. He became president of the PTA. In 1960 he decided to try his hand in the political arena. He ran for a 15-year term as an associate circuit judge and lost. Winning a resounding victory over the overwhelming Democratic opposition, he became Baltimore county executive in 1962.

Agnew's political agenda was a progressive one. His accomplishments included the first civil rights program south of the Mason–Dixon Line and the addition of a public kindergarten to local schools. His major issue was urban development. Agnew was elected governor of Maryland in 1966. In just two short years, Richard Nixon tapped him to become his running mate in the 1968 election. Essentially, Agnew had only eight years of governmental experience to bring to the job. It was his work in urban development and renewal that tipped the scales in his favor.

On November 4, 1968, Agnew became the 39th vice president of the United States. He assumed a very active role in the Nixon administration, serving on the National Aeronautics and Space Council, the National Council on Marine Resources and Engineering Development, the President's Council on Youth Opportunity, the Peace Corps National Advisory Council, the National Security Council, the Council on Urban Affairs, and the Environmental Quality Council. In addition, he was very active in foreign policy, particularly in Southeast Asia.

Nixon and Agnew were reelected in 1972. In the midst of the Watergate scandal Agnew resigned as vice president of the United States on October 10, 1973. On the same day, he pleaded no contest to the allegation of income tax evasion for the year 1967. Agnew was only the second person in the history of the United States to quit while serving as vice president (John C. Calhoun was the first, in 1832) and the only one who resigned under duress.

Kimberly J. Pace

SEE ALSO Richard M. Nixon

BIBLIOGRAPHY

Agnew, Spiro T. *Go Quietly . . . Or Else*. New York: Morrow, 1980.

Cohen, Richard M., and Jules Witcover. *A Heartbeat Away: The Investigation and Resignation of Vice President Spiro T. Agnew*. New York: Viking Press, 1974.

Lucas, Jim G. *Agnew: Profile in Conflict*. New York: Scribner's, 1970.

SCHUYLER COLFAX

Schuyler Colfax (b. March 23, 1823, New York City; d. January 13, 1885, Mankato, Minnesota) was Ulysses S. Grant's vice president (1869–1873) and a former member of Congress from Indiana (1854–1869). His party affiliation changed from Whig to Know-Nothing to Republican. Colfax was selected as a vice presidential candidate because he was suitably ambitious, a good orator, and more radical (meaning more willing to place restrictions on the southern states that had seceded from the Union) than Grant, although less radical than his principal rival for the nomination, Senator Ben Wade.

Schuyler Colfax's paternal grandfather, William Colfax, was the commander of General George Washington's bodyguard during the Revolutionary War. Schuyler Colfax was appointed deputy auditor of Saint Joseph County, Indiana, by his stepfather, who was then the auditor. (Colfax's birth father died before he was born; he was raised by his mother and his stepfather, who was only 14 years his senior.) He studied law but was never admitted to the state bar. He worked for or owned newspapers in Indianapolis (the *Indiana State Journal*) and South Bend (the South Bend *Free Press,* a weekly that Colfax made an organ of Whig opinion, changing its name to the *St. Joseph Valley Register*). He served the various newspapers as correspondent, publisher, and editor.

As have numerous politicians, Colfax appealed to many positions in order to get elected. While an editor in South Bend, he preached Whig philosophies. Although, as a Radical Republican, he preached racial equality, he appealed to anti-Masonic prejudices in order to get elected. Colfax initially ran with the support of the Know-Nothings and was bitterly critical of the foreigners, immigrants, and Catholics whose support he would seek when running for vice president. He was a delegate to a Know-Nothing convention but denied the association.

In 1844 Colfax made presidential campaign speeches backing John C. Calhoun, a Democrat. In 1848 he was a delegate to the Whig National Convention; two years later he was a delegate to Indiana's Constitutional Convention; and in 1851 he was an unsuccessful candidate for Congress on the Whig ticket. But when the Republican Party was formed, he became an earnest advocate for it.

While serving in Congress, Colfax made a notorious stagecoach ride to what, at the time, were the western territories. He delivered orations during a journey that took weeks (the journey, not the orations). Colfax was initially leery of what he viewed as strange doctrines being preached in the West, at one time asking, "Will Brigham Young fight?"

Also, during Colfax's service in the House, he delivered one of his famous orations, opposing the use of the army in Kansas until the territory's laws were approved by Congress. More than a million copies of that speech were circulated, which heightened his reputation as an orator, although his legislative record was minimal.

Colfax's service as chair of the Committee on Post Offices and Post Roads was widely said to be meritorious. He was credited with the advent of overland mail service to California. In large part because of that, President Abraham Lincoln considered him as a nominee for postmaster general but opted for another instead, stating that Colfax's relative youth was a factor mitigating against him.

Although Colfax served three terms as Speaker of the House, he was not as well known as many of his contemporaries. Colfax had been elected Speaker on December 8, 1863, receiving 101 votes to 42 for Sunset Cox of Ohio, with 39 votes split among the six other candidates. The fact that he did not have a well-defined national reputation (beyond being a relatively Radical Republican, although not as radical as Thaddeus Stevens, for instance) was as much an asset as a liability in the 1868 race for the White House.

Colfax was associated with the antislavery amendments to the Constitution that were enacted during his time as Speaker. During Reconstruction he was known as a polished speaker on, and an advocate of, civil rights. He also voted "Yes" on the question of President Andrew Johnson's impeachment, an extremely popular position at the time.

As Speaker, Colfax was expected to preside, and very seldom to make speeches or introduce major legislation, and he did not disappoint. Although Colfax expressed some strong beliefs and to some is remembered as an uncompromising and sometimes Radical Republican, as Speaker he did not engage in any parliamentary maneuvers that would be perceived as "unfair."

For instance, he rejected a suggestion that he engage in "quorum counting," a practice in which Thomas Brackett Reed later engaged as Speaker. Under this practice, legislators could be counted as "present" even though they did not respond to roll calls. Business might therefore be conducted when members of the minority party (under Colfax's speakership, the Democrats) wishing to filibuster were not present.

Colfax resigned from the speakership on March 3, 1869, one day before his inauguration as vice president. He was replaced by another Republican, Theodore M. Pomeroy, notorious for serving in the post only one day.

At the 1868 Republican National Convention, in Chicago, Colfax was far from a consensus choice. Senator Ben Wade of Ohio received a plurality on the early ballots. (Had Andrew Johnson been impeached, Wade, under the rules of the time, would have assumed the presidency.) The fifth ballot was the first time any candidate received a majority, and the nod went to Colfax, with the convention later making his nomination unanimous.

Colfax served on the ticket more for electability than for what he could do. Indeed, he accomplished little during his years as vice president. Nor was the Ulysses S. Grant administration in which he served particularly distinguished. As historian Samuel Eliot Morison said, "It would have been better for the coun-

try had that elderly lawyer and politician of the Jackson–Van Buren line [Grant's opponent, Horatio Seymour] been President for the next eight years, instead of General Grant."

Indeed, Colfax had been considered as a nominee for the presidency prior to the Republican National Convention of 1868. He was Indiana's "favorite son" during a period in which there were several other favorite sons: Hannibal Hamlin, Thomas Ewing, Galusha Grow, and James G. Blaine; Senators William Howard of Michigan, Henry Wilson of Massachusetts, Richard Williams of Oregon, and Benjamin Wade of Ohio; and ex-Governors William Buckingham of Connecticut, Reuben Fenton of New York, and William Newell of New Jersey. The platform adopted at that convention condemned the corruption of the preceding Andrew Johnson administration and promised encouragement to immigration. Only Ulysses S. Grant's name was placed in nomination for the presidency, and he was nominated unanimously and enthusiastically.

There was no such unanimity regarding who should be the vice presidential nominee. Of the ten leading candidates, Wade, Colfax, and Fenton were the most popular. As mentioned, Wade received a plurality on the first four ballots, with Colfax coming in second. On the fifth ballot, the deadlock was broken, and Colfax was nominated. Generally, Colfax was regarded not as a strong person but as a friendly person. His nickname, "Smiley," bore this out.

Colfax was associated with Radical Republicans in the House of Representatives who were not anxious for reconciliation with what they regarded as the conquered provinces of the South. As Colfax said in his letter accepting the Republican Party's nomination, "Certainly no one ought to have claimed that they should be readmitted under such rule that . . . they could ever again . . . defy the national authority or destroy the national unity." In comparison to Colfax, Grant, the war hero, appeared moderate.

In the wake of the Civil War, the Republican Party was much stronger than the Democratic Party. Some observers have noted that Grant lacked a program, but the public did not seem to care. Grant clubs and Republican clubs were popular, and eventually the Grant–Colfax ticket was elected by a large majority.

During his time in office, Colfax did not accomplish much. As president of the Senate, Colfax was implored by the popular Democratic senator from Massachussetts Charles Sumner to stop his boss from proceeding with what Sumner believed was the imminent annexation of the Dominican Republic. Sumner urged that the administration not follow the policies of Andrew Jackson, James Buchanan, and Franklin

Pierce. Grant did not annex the Dominican Republic, but not because of anything Sumner or Colfax said. A far greater factor was the opposition and restraining influence of a member of Grant's cabinet, Hamilton Fish.

In 1871, while still serving as vice president, Colfax would be offered Fish's job as secretary of state. He declined it, preferring to remain vice president. Colfax's interests were always primarily domestic, not international. Besides, the vice presidency was a better springboard for the presidency, to which Colfax still aspired.

Colfax shared the interventionist fervor of the Grant administration. The southern states were beneficiaries of Union ideas. So, too, could be Cuba and the Dominican Republic. In many ways, this line of thinking foreshadowed that of Senator Albert Beveridge and other self-proclaimed imperialists of the late nineteenth century.

Colfax was dropped from the ticket in Grant's race for a second term in 1872 because he was regarded as more of a liability than an asset. Colfax was a candidate for the position, but the Philadelphia convention preferred Henry Wilson, with a first-ballot vote of $364\frac{1}{2}$ for Wilson to $321\frac{1}{2}$ for Colfax. Colfax was associated with scandal at a time when the federal government was rife with scandal and still reeling from the scandals of the Andrew Johnson administration.

Some observers suggest that largely to distract attention from the scandals, Colfax became allied in the antipornography crusade with Anthony Comstock, a special agent of the U.S. Postal Service and for 34 years secretary of New York's Society for the Suppression of Vice. Comstock's "chamber of horrors" (a collection of sex literature and aphrodisiacs) was located in Colfax's vice presidential office.

As vice president, Colfax was regularly upstaged by cabinet members, who received more attention both from the press and from President Grant. Of them, the first among equals was probably Hamilton Fish, the secretary of state.

By the 1872 campaign, Colfax was much better known, and not renominated, although President Grant was and was elected to a second term. Three things were held against Colfax. First and foremost, in what was known as the Crédit Mobilier scandal, a construction company made large donations to several politicians. They had made large donations to Colfax while he was a congressman, but those donations were only made public after Colfax was serving as vice president. The company had made huge profits and declared huge dividends due to westward expansion and the building of the Union Pacific Railroad. Colfax escaped formal censure by the House, but the veracity of his absolute denials was challenged. Tarnished by this scandal and others, Colfax lived his last 12 years in infamy, although he remained a popular speaker and commentator on national affairs.

Second, $4,000 in contributions from a government contractor to the 1868 campaign were exposed. (Specifically, the contractor provided envelopes for the government.) Colfax had chaired the House Committee on Post Offices and Post Roads, and the contributions were thought to have influenced policy.

Third, Colfax certainly did not discourage a group of Radical Republicans who eventually failed in their attempt to create a Liberal Republican Party. That party's ideology would have been more in tune with the Radical Republicans, and it would have been less willing to seek compromises with the southern states. The fact that Colfax failed to discourage those who wanted him to be that party's nominee in 1872 did not endear him to President Grant. Nor did he discourage those who wanted him to be the Republican Party's nominee instead of Grant.

The legacy of Colfax's vice presidency is not a good one, although he did enjoy a career as a public speaker after his term of office. Colfax was also offered the editorship of the *New York Tribune*, an offer he declined (a friend and supporter of Colfax's, Horace Greeley, had edited the *Tribune* for years), and was an active member of the Odd Fellows. He did very little in an administration that did very little. What Colfax's contribution lacked in quantity it did not make up for in quality; indeed, his period of service is remembered more for his involvement in scandal than for anything else.

Arthur Blaser

SEE ALSO Ulysses S. Grant

BIBLIOGRAPHY

Briskin, James S. *The Campaign Lives of Ulysses S. Grant and Schuyler Colfax.* Cincinnati: C.F. Vent and Company, 1868.

Hollister, Ovando James. *Life of Schuyler Colfax.* New York: Funk and Wagnalls, 1885.

House of Representatives, 70th Congress, First Session on H. J. Res. 27 and H. R. 160, a Joint Resolution, *Memorials to Casimir Pulaski and Schuyler Colfax.* Washington, DC: Government Printing Office, 1928.

Smith, Willard H. *Schuyler Colfax: The Changing Fortunes of a Political Idol.* Indianapolis: Indiana Historical Bureau, 1952.

CHARLES CURTIS

A Kansas congressman, U.S. senator, and Herbert Hoover's vice president from 1929 to 1933, Charles Curtis was born in North Topeka, Kansas, on January 25, 1860. His mother, who was part Kaw Indian, died when he was young, and his father, a cavalry officer, left his son with his two grandmothers, who took turns raising him. Graduating from high school in 1879, he clerked for a Topeka lawyer and was admitted to the bar in 1881. In 1892 he was elected to Congress, where he remained for seven consecutive terms until 1907. In 1914 he was elected to the U.S. Senate in the first election in which senators were chosen by popular vote under the new 17th Amendment. Although his critics labeled him "the apotheosis of mediocrity," he was elected majority leader in 1924. In the Senate he supported Prohibition, voting rights for women, and bills helping farmers and Indians. He also gained a reputation as one of the best poker players on the Hill. Despite being a poor speaker and totally lacking in imaginative ideas, Curtis built up good relations with his constituents and excelled as a mediator.

After Calvin Coolidge rejected his bid for the vice presidency in 1924, Curtis set his sights higher and contended as a favorite son for the presidential nomination in 1928. When his effort failed, he accepted the second spot on the ticket with Hoover. Both candidates on the Hoover–Curtis ticket were from west of the Mississippi, but they won handily. Curtis's tenure as vice president was undistinguished. He was renominated as Hoover's running mate in 1932 but lost in the Republican debacle of that year. Curtis died four years later, on February 8, 1936.

SEE ALSO Herbert Hoover

BIBLIOGRAPHY

Ewy, Marvin. *Charles Curtis of Kansas, Vice President of the United States.* Emporia: Kansas State Teachers College, 1961.

Seitz, Don C. *From Kaw Teepee to Capitol: The Life Story of Charles Curtis.* New York: Frederick A. Stokes, 1928.

CHARLES G. DAWES

Charles Gates Dawes (b. August 27, 1865, Marietta, Ohio; d. April 23, 1951, Evanston, Illinois) is probably best known as a federal civil servant, as a negotiator of the Dawes Plan (rescheduling German reparations after World War I), and as Calvin Coolidge's vice president. He also had major accomplishments as a businessman, lawyer, and musician.

Dawes's father had been a general in the Civil War and had served a term in Congress. One of his grandfathers accompanied Paul Revere on the famous ride immortalized by Longfellow and, indeed, was probably more instrumental than Revere in warning of the arrival of the British.

Dawes, who was born in Marietta, Ohio, attended Marietta College and the University of Cincinnati Law School, leaving Ohio to practice law in Lincoln, Nebraska. Two years after moving to Lincoln, Dawes married Carol Blymer, by whom he had a son and a daughter; they adopted two more children. Among the causes that Dawes advanced in Lincoln was his criticism of the railroads for what was perceived to be discrimination against farmers. His support of farm interests would later bring him into conflict with President Coolidge.

Dawes moved to Illinois to pursue his career as a utilities official and banker. His move was prompted by the fact that he was $20,000 in debt, not unusual for the Panic of 1893. Dawes invested borrowed money in gas and electric companies in La Crosse, Wisconsin.

Although he was not Coolidge's first choice as his running mate, Dawes's selection increased Coolidge's bipartisan appeal. Many people perceived Dawes to be "above politics"; although he had been a Republican candidate for the Senate in Illinois, he had never held elective office.

Dawes's first job with the federal government was as comptroller of the currency with the McKinley administration, a partial reward for Dawes's help in the election against Dawes's friend William Jennings Bryan. Dawes was allied with the powerful machine of Mark Hanna, as was McKinley. In his position, Dawes helped to reorganize several banks that had collapsed in earlier years.

After leaving that office, Dawes made what would be his only try for an elective position. He failed to get the 1901 Republican nomination as a candidate for U.S. senator from Illinois.

Once Dawes was defeated, he entered banking by founding the Central Trust Company of Illinois, a career in which he would be very successful.

During World War I, Dawes served with the American Expeditionary Force in France as general purchasing agent. He worked closely with General Pershing, a longtime friend from Lincoln, Nebraska. Dawes was commissioned as a major in 1917 and was promoted to brigadier general in 1918. He readily admitted that his service was much different from that of the "boys in the trenches."

Dawes did not succumb to the isolationist fervor that swept the country following the war. He supported America's involvement in the League of Nations and argued that America had no choice about whether to be involved in Europe. The war had demonstrated that the fates of America and Europe were connected.

After World War I, Dawes and many of his fellow Republicans sought to reduce the federal budget, which by 1919 had reached $25.5 billion (up from a mere $1.2 billion in 1914), and the federal deficit. After Warren G. Harding was elected president in 1920, Dawes turned down an offer to be secretary of the treasury but accepted an offer to be the first director of the Bureau of the Budget, created under the 1921 Budget and Accounting Act. In the one year he held the post, Dawes had a decisive impact.

Indeed, one reporter said that in his first days on the job, Dawes "swept sweltering Washington as with a cyclonic electric fan." In that post, Dawes was able to continue efforts he made on the Liquidation Board at post–World War I downsizing. When Dawes finished work on a $3.5-billion budget for fiscal year 1922, he had done what he had been appointed to do, and so he resigned and left Washington.

Soon after his appointment, Dawes testified before a congressional commission to refute the widely held belief that huge and fraudulent profits had been made by America's World War I suppliers. It was then that he uttered the saying with which he is often associated and that became his nickname, "Hell and Maria," in response to a member of the commission who had asked him about the price paid for French mules.

Dawes is often associated with the Dawes Plan, which set a revised schedule for German reparations after World War I. Germany had been unable to pay the 20 billion marks required under the Treaty of Versailles. The plan was adopted with America's World War I allies (Belgium, Britain, France, Italy, and the United States had two seats each on the Allied Reparations Commission), which saw Dawes and the American government he represented as having great credibility.

In 1925, Dawes shared the Nobel Peace Prize with Sir Austen Chamberlain, Britain's foreign secretary. In Dawes's case, the prize honored his work on the German reparations. The Dawes Plan, admittedly a stopgap measure, was replaced by the Young Plan in 1929. Dawes's share of the prize money was used to help fund an endowed Chair in International Affairs at the Page School of Johns Hopkins University.

Largely on the strength of his reputation as the "savior of Europe," Dawes was eventually catapulted to the vice presidency. As mentioned previously, Dawes was not Calvin Coolidge's first choice for his running mate but was eventually selected. Coolidge's first choice had been Senator Borah, but as was customary at the time, he deferred to the wishes of the majority of Republicans in Congress.

In addition to Borah, Senator Jim Watson of Indiana, Governor Frank Lowden of Illinois, former senator and now Judge William Kenyon, Senator Charles Curtis of Kansas, and Herbert Hoover were potential nominees. Lowden was nominated before indicating that he did not wish the honor. Eventually, at the Republican National Convention in Cleveland, Dawes defeated Herbert Hoover (preferred by Coolidge, though Dawes was acceptable) for the second spot on the Coolidge ticket, by a vote of $682\frac{1}{2}$ to $234\frac{1}{2}$. Indeed, there were no strong feelings against Dawes's selection. The entire 1924 Republican National Convention was so uneventful that humorist Will Rogers commented that the delegates could have stayed at home and held the convention by postcard.

Coolidge had assumed the presidency when his predecessor, Warren G. Harding, died in office. The strategy his campaign advisers had devised for him required that he be efficient but not visible, which meant that his running mate, Dawes, did much of the public campaigning. This was modeled after William McKinley's having had his vice presidential nominee, Theodore Roosevelt, do the bulk of the ticket's campaigning.

The Democratic Party was badly split, with John Davis the eventual nominee. Davis was a New York lawyer to wealthy clients, which was part of the reason why the Progressive Robert La Follette mounted a third-party challenge to represent the unrepresented and underrepresented. Some important Democrats, including Senator Burton K. Wheeler, who eventually became La Follette's vice presidential candidate, defected to the Progressives, which helped the Coolidge–Dawes ticket.

Davis's running mate, Governor Charles Bryan of Nebraska, brother of William Jennings Bryan, was as far to the left of the Democratic Party as Davis was to the right. Dawes had the job of portraying Bryan and La Follette as dangerous threats to capitalism.

Just as Davis and Bryan represented different ideas, so did Coolidge and Dawes, with Dawes being much more internationalist and sympathetic to agriculture. As a vice presidential candidate and eventually as vice president, Dawes had to conform to the wishes of the Coolidge administration.

This meant that Dawes had to oppose U.S. participation in the League of Nations, a position he had previously favored. Dawes emphasized that the administration would follow League mandates and adhere to the commissions of the League but would not join the League itself. He explained that the American people had made their opposition clear and the complexities of participation were prohibitive.

In contrast, the Democratic platform of 1924 called for a public referendum on American participation in the League, which had first been proposed by the previous Democratic president, Woodrow Wilson. In contrast to the League, the World Court was deserving of U.S. participation, according to Coolidge and Dawes, since it involved no entangling alliances.

A big issue during and after the campaign was the Ku Klux Klan. Klan members had been present at the 1924 convention but were not welcomed by Dawes or the other delegates. A big issue of the time was how public and active a stance the major parties took in opposing the Klan, and the Republican Party's strategy was largely one of hoping that the Klan would go away.

In conducting the campaign, Dawes discovered that he had to tone down his rhetoric. The expression "Hell and Maria" with which he was associated was changed to a more acceptable "I wonder," to the surprise of the media. Dawes was found to have an appealing way of using radio, which was a fairly new technology, so he often tended to speak for the campaign, with the moderation that the new medium required.

Dawes would continue to use the radio during and after the vice presidency, arguing that a radio audience could give a more detached and thoughtful response than a live audience, which might react hastily and emotionally.

The 1924 election was a huge victory for the Republicans and for the Coolidge–Dawes ticket. The ticket received 382 electoral votes, with Davis–Bryan receiving 136 and the La Follette ticket 13. The Senate (over which Dawes was to preside) had 55 Republicans, 40 Democrats, and 1 Farmer–Laborite. The House had 264 Republicans, 148 Democrats, and 1 Socialist.

As vice president, Dawes's greatest efforts were devoted to the reform of the Senate rules, including the filibuster, which Dawes viewed as a major impediment to action. Several important senators opposed the changes, including one of the most influential Republicans, William Borah of Idaho. President Coolidge therefore had the difficult choice of whether to support his vice president, Dawes, or leading members of his own party in the Senate. Coolidge decided in favor of the latter, dooming Dawes's efforts.

Dawes had not endeared himself to Coolidge because his speech at the inaugural was livelier and better received by the public than was the president's. The Senate, though, was not pleased and would rather have heard the usual passive, status quo–oriented speech than one challenging its cherished traditions.

Soon after assuming the job of vice president, Dawes was caught up in the confirmation battle over Coolidge's nominee for attorney general, lawyer Charles B. Warren, accused by opponents of ties to the "sugar trust." The first vote was 40 to 40, but Dawes, who could have cast the tie-breaking vote, was at home taking a nap, much to President Coolidge's con-

sternation. The Senate eventually chose not to confirm the nomination, by a 46–39 vote.

Dawes and Coolidge differed over an important farm relief bill and over the issue of allowing branch banking. Dawes was reported to be organizing a senatorial coalition in support of the changes, which drew a presidential veto.

Dawes was a very popular vice president, arguably even more popular than President Coolidge. In 1928, Coolidge decided not to run for a second term. There were therefore many people who wanted Dawes to run for president that year, and Dawes encouraged them. Others subsequently proved to be more popular, and Dawes supported the eventual Republican nominee and president, Herbert Hoover.

As vice president, Dawes is more often associated with a notable failure than with success. Dawes, who as vice president was chair of the Senate (he always enjoyed a Republican majority in the Senate, 55–43 following the election of 1924), attempted to reform the rules of that body, including the practice of the filibuster.

Dawes was also a flutist and pianist, a composer of some note, an ambassador to Great Britain, head of the Reconstruction Finance Corporation in Herbert Hoover's administration, and the author of several published works on his experiences in government (including his diaries while vice president) and business. He was also interested in archeology and ancient history.

How, then, were Dawes's selection and service as vice president significant in American history and politics? First, the country was in a mood for efficient management, not for boisterous politics. Second, the Republicans were now clearly the party of business and finance rather than an arbiter between interests.

Arthur Blaser

SEE ALSO Calvin Coolidge

BIBLIOGRAPHY

Dawes, Charles. *Notes as Vice-President, 1928–1929*. New York: Putnam, 1935.

Gilbert, Clinton W. *You Takes Your Choice*. New York: G.P. Putnam's Sons, 1924.

Leach, Paul R. *That Man Dawes*. Chicago: Reilly and Lee, 1930.

Timmons, Bascom. *Portrait of an American: Charles Gates Dawes*. New York: Holt, 1953.

White, William Allen. *Politics and People: The Ordeal of Self-Government in America*. New York: Macmillan, 1924.

CHARLES FAIRBANKS

A U.S. senator and Theodore Roosevelt's vice president from 1905 to 1909, Charles Warren Fairbanks was born on May 11, 1852, in a one-room farmhouse in Unionville, Ohio. After graduating from Ohio Wesleyan University, he was admitted to the bar in 1874. He moved to Indianapolis and became a wealthy attorney specializing in railroad litigation. A powerful speaker and a leader in the Indiana Republican Party, he delivered the keynote address at the 1896 Republican Convention. The next year, he was elected to the U.S. Senate, where he was one of McKinley's staunchest supporters. Although he was considered for the vice presidential nomination in 1900, Theodore Roosevelt was nominated instead. Representing the conservative wing of the party, he accepted the second place on the winning Republican ticket in 1904 as Roosevelt's running mate. The liberal Roosevelt and the conservative Fairbanks were a classic mismatch. Fairbanks was excluded from an active role in the Roosevelt administration and was publicly ridiculed by the president. His presidential ambitions were again thwarted when Roosevelt endorsed William Howard Taft for the 1908 presidential race. Fairbanks never held public office after 1909 but remained a powerful figure in Republican politics. In 1912, as chairman of the Republican National Convention, he supported Taft against Roosevelt. In 1916 he was Charles Evans Hughes's running mate on the losing Republican ticket. He died two years later, on June 14, 1918.

SEE ALSO Theodore Roosevelt

HANNIBAL HAMLIN

A Jacksonian Democrat who switched to the Republican Party because of Democratic tolerance of slavery, Hannibal Hamlin served as vice president during President Abraham Lincoln's first term (1861–1865), brought on the ticket by the younger Lincoln because of Hamlin's New England background, extensive legislative experience and opposition to slavery. As vice president, Hamlin was not given significant duties by Lincoln but today is remembered for his outspoken opposition to slavery and support of radical emancipation of blacks.

Born in 1809 in Paris Hill, Maine, Hamlin served at virtually every level of government during a lifetime in public service, including three separate tenures in the U.S. Senate, his final Senate term coming after his term as vice president. After first taking charge of the family farm in Maine and working as a surveyor and schoolteacher, Hamlin studied law and practiced in Hampden, Maine, while serving in the Maine legislature from 1836 to 1841 and again in 1847, including three years as speaker. He was elected to the U.S. Congress in 1842

and served during the 28th and 29th Congresses (1843–1847) before unsuccessfully running for the U.S. Senate in 1846. But he won a Senate seat in 1848, backed by the antislavery wing of the DemocraticParty, in a special election to fill the vacancy caused by the death of the incumbent, John Fairfield.

It was during his first Senate tenure that Hamlin broke with the Democratic Party. Having taken an antislavery position on sectional issues, he left the party in 1856 because of its endorsement of the Kansas–Nebraska Act, which extended slavery into the territories, and was elected governor of Maine the same year as a Republican. After serving one month, he returned to the Senate as a Republican in 1857. Nominated for vice president on the second ballot by the Republican National Convention in 1860, Hamlin wrote to his wife Ellen that he "neither expected or desired" the nomination but that, as a faithful member of his new party, he felt an obligation to accept it.

In 1864 Lincoln, seeking to appease moderate southerners, replaced Hamlin with Andrew Johnson on the Republican ticket. After leaving the vice presidency, Hamlin served as collector of the Port of Baltimore but resigned in 1866 because of his growing opposition to President Andrew Johnson's policies toward the South and became president of a small railroad running from Bangor to Dover. Upon his election to the Senate for the third time, from 1869 to 1881, Hamlin worked to uphold radical Reconstruction and chaired the Foreign Relations Committee. He later was appointed U.S. minister to Spain by President James A. Garfield and served in that post from 1881 to 1882.

Hamlin spent the last years of his life in Bangor, tending a farm and enjoying retirement. In 1891, he died on July 4.

John F. Yarbrough

SEE ALSO Abraham Lincoln

GARRET A. HOBART

Garret Augustus Hobart—24th vice president of the United States (1897–1899), politician, and businessman—was born on June 3, 1844, in Long Branch, New Jersey, the son of Addison W. Hobart, a teacher, and Sophia Vanderveer.

Upon his graduation from Rutgers College (New Jersey) in 1883 at the age of 19 with an A.B. degree, Hobart taught school in Marlboro, New Jersey. After a few years, he abandoned teaching as a profession to pursue the study of law in Paterson, New Jersey, under Socrates Tuttle, an attorney and close friend of his father's. He was admitted to the bar at 22, became a

Garret A. Hobart. *Source:* Library of Congress.

counselor at law in 1869, and served a six-year apprenticeship under Tuttle, whose daughter, Jennie, became his wife on July 21, 1869. The couple had two children, a son and a daughter.

Hobart had a varied political career over two decades. In 1871 he was chosen counsel of Paterson. One year later, he was elected counsel to the Board of Freeholders and a Republican member of the state assembly. His involvement in state politics bolstered his political career. He was reelected to the state legislature (1873), served as speaker of the New Jersey House (1874), served in the state Senate (1876), and won reelection (1879). Hobart held the position of president pro tempore of the New Jersey Senate for two years (1881–1882) and gained a reputation as a skillful parliamentarian.

In 1884 Hobart was nominated as New Jersey's representative to the United States Senate, but his strong desire to remain in New Jersey to tend to his considerable array of business interests caused him to decline nomination to that federal office five times. Hobart's business and public-sector appointments included directorships in some 60 companies and governmental agencies.

From 1880 to 1890, he served as the chair of the State Republican Committee, concurrent with being a member and vice chair of the Republican National Committee. Hobart also worked vigorously in the presidential campaigns of two Republican candidates: James G. Blaine, who lost the election of 1884, and Benjamin Harrison, who was elected the 23rd president of the United States (1889–1893). In 1896 Hobart was nominated to run as vice president on the Republican ticket with William McKinley. Following their election victory, McKinley and he were inaugurated on March 4, 1897.

McKinley and Hobart enjoyed one of the best personal and working relationships ever between an American president and his vice president. McKinley heeded Hobart's counsel in both personal and political matters. Hobart played a pivotal role in McKinley's administration as liaison to Congress. In 1899 he cast the tie-breaking vote against the treaty with Spain that provided for the future independence of the Philippines. His diplomacy and tact were widely known in political circles. Such traits made him highly successful in helping McKinley secure the July 19, 1899, resignation of Secretary of War General Russell A. Alger, a troublesome cabinet member. McKinley's reliance on Hobart expanded the role of the vice president considerably and restored credibility and stature to the position.

Hobart served as vice president of the United States for two years and eight months before his untimely death in Paterson, New Jersey, in 1899, at the age of 55, after a long illness.

Theodore Roosevelt replaced Hobart as the 1900 vice presidential candidate on the Republican ticket with McKinley. When McKinley was assassinated in 1901, Roosevelt became president.

Joseph C. Santora

SEE ALSO William McKinley

LEVI P. MORTON

Levi Parsons Morton, vice president of the United States and governor of New York, was primarily a prominent New York banker who remained exceedingly successful in financial affairs even through the panic of 1907. A descendant of old New England stock, Morton was born on May 16, 1824, in Shoreham, Vermont. He gained early experience in business working as a storekeeper in Hanover, New Hampshire. Forgoing a college education, Morton threw himself into the business of banking.

It was in New York on January 1, 1855, that he began his banking career as head of Morton, Grinnell & Company. Southern secession would destroy this company in 1861, but Morton saw in the Civil War great opportunity. He emerged from the war as one of the nation's most prominent businessmen. By the 1870s his firm—Morton, Bliss and Company—had become so successful that it had expanded into England and was trusted to help fund the national debt during the resumption of specie payment.

Morton's first foray into politics and diplomacy was with the Joint High Commission of 1871. President Ulysses S. Grant and Secretary of State Hamilton Fish were in constant touch with the proceedings in Geneva, during which Morton and his fellow commissioners secured $15.5 million in payment from Great Britain for damages incurred during the Civil War. With this achievement, Morton ran for a seat in the House of Representatives as a Republican in 1876 and, though he was unsuccessful, ran well in a typically Democratic district.

Morton was elected to the House in 1878 and 1880, though he did not serve his second term after he was

Levi P. Morton. *Source:* Library of Congress.

made U.S. minister to France. Morton chose the position in France over James Garfield's 1880 offer of the vice presidency, a position for which New York's political boss, the powerful Roscoe Conkling, discouraged Morton from running. Morton heeded Conkling's advice, and the vice presidency fell to Chester A. Arthur, a fellow New Yorker who chose to ignore Conkling's pressure and would later ascend to the presidency upon Garfield's death.

After his service in France, Morton made two unsuccessful runs for the U.S. Senate in 1885 and 1887. When Benjamin Harrison offered him the spot of running mate, Morton accepted and served as vice president from 1889 to 1893. Morton's experience in France prepared him well for the ever-growing ceremonial function of the vice presidency, but he took his role of presiding officer of the Senate seriously. As presiding officer, he gained a reputation for fairness and integrity. Morton often irritated Republican bosses for his refusal to accede to their demands, perhaps remembering that Conkling's advice had cost him the presidency.

His independence as Senate leader kept the Republicans from renominating Morton for Harrison's second bid for the presidency. Morton made a foray into state politics with his election to the governorship of New York in 1895, but his one term would end his political career at the age of 75. Morton would continue in his successful business until his retirement in 1909. He died in Rhinebeck, New York, on May 16, 1920, at the age of 96.

Daniel Stanhagen

SEE ALSO Benjamin Harrison

DAN QUAYLE

Having served just two terms in the House of Representatives (1977–1980) and eight years in the Senate (1981–1989), J. Danforth "Dan" Quayle (b. 1947) was little known outside his home state of Indiana when George Bush selected him as his running mate in 1988. A conservative, Quayle provided some ideological balance to Bush's more moderate reputation.

Quayle immediately was beset by controversy and media scrutiny surrounding his service in the Indiana National Guard during the Vietnam War and what some took to be inadequate qualifications for high office. Intense media scrutiny would follow him throughout his tenure as vice president.

As vice president, Quayle chaired the Bush administration's Council on Competitiveness and the White House Space Council. His role as chair of the Council on Competitiveness was especially controversial as the council was responsibile for the oversight of the nation's regulatory policy and was designed as a check on government regulations of business that were found to inhibit competitiveness in the world market.

Quayle became best known for a much-derided May 1992 address in which he spoke of the importance of two-parent families and attacked the entertainment industry for setting bad examples for America's youth. For particular criticism he singled out the television character "Murphy Brown" and her decision to be a single mother. The media firestorm that followed the speech propelled Quayle's issues into the national spotlight. In subsequent years other politicians and writers would take up the "family values" issues with which Quayle was concerned.

Well known to harbor presidential ambitions of his own, Quayle passed up the 1996 race for the Republican nomination, citing a desire to spend more time with his family.

Gary L. Gregg II

SEE ALSO George Bush

NELSON ROCKEFELLER

Nelson Aldrich Rockefeller was governor of New York from 1958 to 1973 and Gerald Ford's vice president from 1974 to 1977.

Born July 8, 1908, in Bar Harbor, Maine, to one of America's wealthiest families, Nelson Rockefeller was named after his maternal grandfather, Nelson Aldrich, the powerful U.S. senator and champion of big business at the turn of the century. After graduating from Dartmouth College in 1930, Nelson Rockefeller turned early to public service, serving the Franklin Roosevelt administration as assistant secretary of state for Latin American affairs and the Eisenhower administration as the first undersecretary in the new Department of Health, Education, and Welfare. After gaining his spurs in Washington, Rockefeller turned his attention to elective office. In 1958 he successfully challenged Averill Harriman, the incumbent Democratic governor. The contest between the two, called the "battle of the millionaires," was notable for the way in which Rockefeller established his image as a social liberal and a fiscal conservative. Winning by more than half a million votes against an older and formidable opponent, Rockefeller went on to capture the governor's mansion three more times. By the time he resigned in 1973 he had served as governor longer than anyone else since the early 1800s and had gained a reputation as one of the ablest governors in modern times. He also changed the skyline of Albany, the state capital, by initiating a monumental building program. But he was

Nelson Rockefeller. *Source:* Library of Congress.

criticized for financing a host of social programs through higher tax burdens and budgetary deficits. Beginning in 1960, Rockefeller tried to use the governor's mansion and his record in Albany as a springboard to the White House. But thrice he lost his bid. In 1960, Vice President Nixon was able to preempt him; in 1964, he was hurt by a messy divorce from his first wife and remarriage to a much younger woman; in 1968, the Republican nomination again eluded him as the more conservative and religious elements within the party became dominant. In fact, Rockefeller was unable to escape the stigma of being an eastern establishment liberal for the rest of his career. In 1973 Rockefeller resigned his office as governor to concentrate on the Commission on Critical Choices for America. But the drama of Watergate unfolding in Washington at that time and the resignation of Vice President Spiro Agnew set in motion a chain of events that led to Gerald Ford's becoming the president with Rockefeller as vice president. The appointment was ironic because Rockefeller had gone on record as saying that he never wanted to be "vice president of anything." His short tenure in office was marred by opposition from conservative Republicans. Perceived as a liability to Ford's reelection chances, Rockefeller withdrew from consideration as Ford's running mate in 1976. He never again held any public office and died in somewhat mysterious circumstances on January 26, 1979.

SEE ALSO Gerald R. Ford

BIBLIOGRAPHY

Benjamin, Gerald, and T. Norman Hurd. *Rockefeller in Retrospect*. Albany: Rockefeller Institute of Government, 1984.

Connery, Robert, and Gerald Benjamin. *Rockefeller of New York*. New York: Oxford University Press, 1974.

Kramer, Michael, and Sam Roberts. *I Never Wanted to be Vice President of Anything*. New York: Basic Books, 1976.

Pepsico, Joseph. *The Imperial Rockefeller*. New York: Simon and Schuster, 1983.

Underwood, James, and William L. Daniels. *Governor Rockefeller in New York: The Apex of Pragmatic Liberalism in the U.S.* Westport, CT: Greenwood Press, 1982.

JAMES SCHOOLCRAFT SHERMAN

Against the advice of his father, James Schoolcraft Sherman (b. 1855) entered political life as a Republican when he was elected mayor of Utica, New York, in 1884. In 1886 he was elected to the United States House of Representatives, where he served from 1887 to 1891 and from 1893 to 1909.

While in the House, Sherman was a party regular, supporting the policies of Thomas Brackett Reed and Joseph Cannon. He was a gifted parliamentarian, playing a considerable role in the formation of the Rules Committee. Sherman also served as chair of the Committee of the Whole during important debates out of respect for his parliamentary knowledge. He unsuccessfully sought the post of Speaker of the House upon Reed's retirement.

Sherman was nominated as the Republican Party's vice presidential candidate on the ticket headed by William H. Taft in 1908. Renominated for the post in 1912, Sherman died before the election in November.

Jeffrey D. Schultz

SEE ALSO William Howard Taft

WILLIAM ALMON WHEELER

William Almon Wheeler, vice president of the United States, was born on June 30, 1819, in Malone, New York. Wheeler attended the University of Vermont for two years but left in 1840 due to financial troubles. He returned to Malone and studied law under Asa Hascell, passing the bar exam in 1845. The next year he was appointed district attorney for Franklin County, a

James Schoolcraft Sherman. *Source:* Library of Congress.

job he held until 1849. After his term as district attorney, he practiced law successfully for three years before leaving law to manage a local bank.

Although successful as a banker, Wheeler decided to enter politics and in 1850 was elected to the New York State legislature. He left the Assembly in 1851, when he received an appointment as trustee for the mortgage holders of the Northern Railway, a position he held until 1866. Wheeler did not let his political career suffer and was elected to the state Senate in 1858 and to the United States House of Representatives in 1860. He left the House in 1863 because he had an agreement with two other politicians that the counties of the district would rotate the office. He continued to be involved in politics by presiding over the Republican State Conventions in 1867 and 1868.

In 1868 Wheeler again ran for the House of Representatives and was swept to victory in the Republican landslide that carried Ulysses S. Grant to the White House. Wheeler served in the House until 1877 and developed a reputation for honesty and integrity. In 1874 the state elections in Louisiana were

William Almon Wheeler. *Source:* Library of Congress.

challenged by 12 Democrats running for the lower house. The "Wheeler Compromise" left the Republicans in control of the state Senate but seated the 12 Democrats over their Republican opponents, thereby giving the Democrats a majority in the lower house. Wheeler also refused gifts from railways and returned congressional pay increases to the government. In 1876 he was nominated to run with Rutherford B. Hayes as a candidate for the vice presidency. Wheeler was selected because of his reputation for honesty and his popularity in the South due to the Wheeler Compromise on the disputed Louisiana election returns.

Wheeler did not support Hayes's Reconstruction policy for the South. Wheeler's position on these issues temporarily alienated him from the administration, until the midterm elections repudiated the president's policies. Wheeler left office in 1881, after the Republican National Convention did not renominate him or Hayes in 1880 for a second term. Wheeler ran for the Senate in 1880 but was defeated easily and so retired to private life. He died of a stroke on June 4, 1887, in Malone at the age of 68.

Daniel Stanhagen

SEE ALSO Rutherford B. Hayes

HENRY WILSON

Henry Wilson, United States senator and vice president of the United States, was born Jeremiah Jones Colbath in Farmington, New Hampshire, on February 16, 1812. Wilson's family was so impoverished that on his 11th birthday he was indentured to a neighboring farmer. Wilson worked hard for ten years and left his servitude at the age of 21 with only several farm animals to his name. He changed his name, with the permission of his parents, and walked to Natick, Massachusetts, to begin a new life.

He learned the trade of shoemaking and opened his own shop while continuing to educate himself through reading and debating. In 1836 Wilson traveled to Virginia and Washington, D.C., to recover his health, nearly broken after 15 years of hard labor. In Washing-

Henry Wilson. *Source:* Library of Congress.

ton he attended numerous debates about the merits and evils of slavery and left determined "to see the emancipation of the United States."

When he returned to Natick, Wilson studied at several schools and debated regularly. In 1841 he was elected to the Massachusetts House of Representatives and served two one-year terms. In the next ten years, he served four terms in the state legislature and was a delegate to the Whig National Convention. However, he left the Whig Party because of its soft position on the abolition of slavery. He helped start the Free Soil Party and headed its first convention in Buffalo, New York. Not satisfied with the slavery platform of the Free Soil Party, he left and for a short time embraced the Know-Nothings.

Wilson was appointed to the United States Senate in 1854, after the resignation of Edward Everett, and won reelection in 1859, 1865, and 1871. From the beginning, he fought hard and spoke eloquently for the emancipation of the slaves and for the repeal of the fugitive slave law. With the outbreak of the Civil War, he had a heavy responsibility because of his position in the Massachusetts Militia, as a brigadier general, and his assignment to the Committee on Military Affairs in the Senate. He was instrumental in shaping the organization and recruitment of the vast army that fought the war to a successful conclusion. Wilson urged President Abraham Lincoln to free the slaves, and in 1865 he sponsored the bill for the establishment of the Freedmen's Bureau. He was a bitter opponent of President Andrew Johnson's Reconstruction policy.

In 1872 Wilson was nominated to run as Ulysses S. Grant's vice president. As vice president, Wilson sought to improve education and working conditions, but to little avail. Wilson died in his third year as vice president, on March 4, 1875. He authored several books, including *History of the Anti-Slave Measures of the Thirty-seventh and Thirty-eighth United States Congress* and *History of the Rise and Fall of Slave Power in America.*
Daniel Stanhagen

SEE ALSO Ulysses S. Grant

Losing Presidential Candidates

JAMES G. BLAINE

James Gillespie Blaine was U.S. secretary of state in 1881 and again in 1889–1892; he was a member of the House of Representatives and Speaker of the House from 1869

to 1875. He was a U.S. senator from 1876 to 1881 and the Republican presidential candidate in 1884.

Blaine was born January 31, 1830, in West Brownsville, Pennsylvania, and was educated at Washington College. After studying law, he moved to Maine, where his wife's relatives helped him to become editor and publisher of the *Kennebec Journal* in 1884. One of the founders of the Republican Party in Maine, he was a delegate to the first Republican National Convention in 1856, and from 1859 to 1881 was chairman of the Maine Republican Party while serving in the Maine lower house as speaker. His national career was launched in 1862 when he was elected to the U.S. Congress. A strong supporter of civil rights, he was an eloquent orator whose "bloody shirt" speeches roused and inspired thousands of veterans. In 1869 he was elected Speaker of the House. In 1876 he was appointed to an unexpired Senate term and later elected to a full term. He relinquished his seat in the Senate in 1881 to become the secretary of state under the newly elected President James A. Garfield. Blaine was walking with Garfield through a Washington, D.C., railroad station when the president was shot by an assassin. Blaine resigned from the cabinet shortly thereafter.

Blaine attempted to secure the Republican presidential nomination in both 1876 and 1880. His first try was aborted when the "Mulligan Letters" implicated him

James G. Blaine. *Source:* Library of Congress.

in a railroad scandal. He was accused of giving favors to a railroad company in return for money and of profiting from railroad stocks. The convention chose Rutherford B. Hayes instead. In 1880 Blaine was the acknowledged leader of the Half Breeds, a faction of the Republican Party opposed to President Ulysses S. Grant's attempt to seek an unprecedented third term. The convention, however, chose a dark horse, James A. Garfield. Blaine's political fortunes rose after his brief service as Garfield's secretary of state, particularly after the publication of his *Twenty Years in Congress.* His influence as the "Plumed Knight" of the Republican Party grew, and his support of civil rights, sound currency, and tariff reduction made him immensely popular with the moderates in the party and in the western states. He gained the presidential nomination on the first ballot in 1884. But earlier charges of corruption, the factionalism engendered in his struggle with the Stalwarts, the revolt of the Mugwumps, the independent Republicans, and the loss of Catholic support following the "Rum, Romanism and Rebellion" speech by an associate on the eve of the election led to Blaine's defeat at the hands of Grover Cleveland, the first loss by a Republican candidate in over a quarter of a century. Blaine declined to be a candidate in 1888; instead, he supported Benjamin Harrison. After Harrison's victory, Blaine was named secretary of state for the second time in a decade. His greatest successes during the next four years were in reshaping the bases of U.S. foreign policy, particularly toward Latin America. He presided over the first Pan-American Conference in 1890 and abjured notions of hegemony in favor of trade and friendship in dealing with nations of the hemisphere. He also was responsible for the annexation of the Hawaiian Islands. Blaine resigned in 1892 to make a final bid for the White House, but was beaten by Harrison on the first ballot. He died within a year, on January 27, 1893. Tall and dignified in appearance and an eloquent orator, Blaine dominated Republican politics for over 30 years.

BIBLIOGRAPHY

Muzzy, David S. *James G. Blaine: A Political Idol of Other Days.* New York: Dodd, Mead, 1934.

THOMAS E. DEWEY

Thomas E. Dewey was born in Owosso, Michigan, on March 24, 1902, and it was there that he spent his childhood. He attended Michigan State University in Ann Arbor for his undergraduate studies. He completed his legal studies at Columbia Law School in

Thomas E. Dewey. *Source:* Library of Congress.

New York City. His move to New York was in part prompted by an intense love of singing, and he felt he could receive better vocal training in New York. His love of music and singing would remain one of his passions throughout his life.

Following graduation from law school in 1925, Dewey worked in a number of New York City law firms before becoming U.S. attorney in 1932. At the age of 31, he was the youngest person ever to hold that title. Although Dewey achieved remarkable success, he was replaced by President Roosevelt with someone more in line with the New Deal philosophy, and Dewey returned to private practice two years after his appointment.

In 1935, Dewey was appointed as a special prosecutor, specifically to investigate organized crime. Within a short time his effectiveness in this task won him national acclaim. In the late 1930s, Dewey achieved mass exposure by going after and convicting many of New York City's most famous gangsters, including "Lucky" Luciano, Louis Lepke, "Dutch" Schultz, "Waxy" Gordon, and dozens of others. Dewey became New York City's district attorney in 1937, and from that office he continued his assault on organized crime.

Making the logical leap into politics, Dewey became

the Republican governor of New York State in 1942. He was reelected in 1946 with 58.6% of the vote—the largest majority in the history of gubernatorial elections in New York.

In 1948 Governor Dewey was the Republican party's presidential nominee. Advance polls predicted the Republican candidate would handily defeat President Truman. In a race Dewey seemed destined to win, the unthinkable happened. He lost. Newspapers were so confident of his winning the presidency they prematurely printed papers with the headline *Dewey Defeats Truman*. Governor Dewey returned to New York and was elected for a third term in 1950.

During his tenure as governor, Dewey could count among his accomplishments a state-funded university, a thruway, and the first civil rights legislation enacted in the United States. As governor, he never submitted an unbalanced budget, and when he left office in 1955, state taxes were 10% lower than they had been when he was first elected.

Although Dewey ultimately lost his presidential bid, he did emerge as the titular head of the Republican Party. He has been called the father of the modern-day Republican Party. In his newfound role he was instrumental in the elections of both Eisenhower and Nixon.

In his lifetime Dewey managed to beat tuberculosis and cancer. He suffered a massive heart attack on March 16, 1971, and died shortly thereafter.

Kimberly J. Pace

BIBLIOGRAPHY

Dewey, Thomas E. *Twenty Against the Underworld*. Garden City, NY: Doubleday, 1974.

Smith, Richard Norton. *Thomas E. Dewey and His Times*. New York: Simon and Schuster, 1982.

JOHN C. FRÉMONT

Born January 21, 1813, in Savannah, Georgia, John Charles Frémont grew up in Charleston, South Carolina. His father died when he was five, and his early education was sponsored by relatives and friends. After attending Charleston College, he joined the navy in 1831. He resigned from the navy in 1835 to become a second lieutenant in the U.S. Topographical Corps in 1838. Handsome, bright, and dashing, Frémont was an explorer at heart, and his lively account of a journey with frontiersman Kit Carson as his guide in 1842 to chart the best route to Oregon brought him fame and fortune.

A year earlier he had married Jessie Benton, daughter of a powerful U.S. senator, Thomas Hart Benton of Missouri, and Frémont owed his later successes not a little to the encouragement and patronage of his father-in-law. Jessie helped her husband write his reports and memoirs, and later, during hard times, supported him through her own literary activities.

In 1843 he was commissioned to survey Oregon, and during the course of the next year, he explored the entire Northwest, including northern California. He returned to St. Louis in August 1844 as a national hero, and his reports and maps became important travel guides to the West for many decades. Now at the acme of his career as explorer, he earned the title of the "Pathfinder of the West."

In 1845, while Frémont was on another exploratory mission in northern California, war broke out between the United States and Mexico. Frémont journeyed to Sonoma and encouraged U.S. settlers to revolt successfully against Mexico and establish the Bear Flag Republic, the nickname of the newly independent Republic of California. He commanded U.S. forces in California until the arrival of Commodore Robert F. Stockton as governor. But, a conflict of instructions from Washington over the formation of civil government and the refusal of Frémont to take orders from General Stephen W. Kearney led to Frémont's arrest and court-martial. The incident, which was a cause célèbre at the time, resulted in Frémont's conviction for disobedience and mutiny. He was subsequently sentenced to dismissal from the army, but President Polk canceled the punishment as a favor to an old friend. Nevertheless, Frémont resigned his commission in protest.

After his resignation, Frémont continued to lead private expeditions, the first to prove that the Sangre de Cristo and San Juan mountains were passable for railroad traffic in the winter and the second to find a southern railroad route to the Pacific. Meanwhile, gold found on Frémont-owned land in the Sierra foothills, along with shrewd real estate investments in San Francisco, made him wealthy.

He retired to his huge ranch at Mariposa, but emerged from retirement to be elected as one of the first U.S. senators from California in 1850. He was one of the founding fathers of the Republican Party, which chose him as its standard-bearer in 1856. The fledgeling party hoped to ride on Frémont's national visibility and fame, and the campaign slogan was "Free Soil, Free Speech and Frémont." Frémont was the darling of the northern antislavery intelligentsia, including Ralph Waldo Emerson, William Cullen Bryant, and Henry Wadsworth Longfellow. But the Republican Party's lack of organization and the hostility of the South led to his rout at the hands of James Buchanan, the Democratic candidate. Frémont returned to California to develop his mining interests.

Soon after the outbreak of the Civil War, Lincoln appointed Frémont commander of the Department of the West. He was soon relieved of this command and transferred to western Virginia following his decision to impose martial law in Missouri and free ths slaves of the Confederate owners under his jurisdiction without the approval of the president. It was feared that this impetuous act would prompt many more slave-holding border states to secede from the Union. Frémont also was charged with corruption and mismanagement. He thereupon resigned from the army.

In 1864 a group of radical anti-Lincoln Republicans nominated him as their candidate, but he withdrew from the race when no prominent party leader came forward to back him. Frémont's later years were marked by financial ruin. He lost his entire Mariposa estate, and the gold also ran out. He lost the remainder of his fortune through bad railroad investments. To save him from destitution, Rutherford B. Hayes named him territorial governor of Arizona in 1878, and Congress voted him a pension just before his death on July 13, 1890.

BIBLIOGRAPHY

Nevins, Allan. *Frémont: The West's Greatest Adventurer*. New York: Harper, 1928.
————. *Frémont, Pathfinder of the West*. New York: Longman, 1955.

BARRY GOLDWATER

A Phoenix, Arizona, businessman who spent World War II flying noncombat missions in the U.S. Army Air Force, Barry Goldwater (b. 1909) was first elected to the United States Senate in 1952 and served into the mid-1980s. As a senator and a Republican presidential candidate in 1964, Goldwater was known to many as "Mr. Conservative."

In 1960 *The Conscience of a Conservative* was published under Goldwater's name. This slim volume put forward in simple, practical terms the conservative vision for the nation. Goldwater criticized big government and the welfare state, spoke in defense of states' rights, and argued for lower taxes and a hard line against what he termed "the Soviet menace." Above all, Goldwater purported to speak in defense of individual freedom against what he took to be its enemies both at home and abroad. The book instantly became a political classic. It would go through eight printings in its first ten months alone and would eventually sell more than 4 million copies.

The success of *The Conscience of a Conservative* garnered Goldwater considerable media coverage and

Barry Goldwater. *Source:* Library of Congress.

speculation as to his being a prospective future Republican presidential nominee. Without his support, in 1961 a group of influential conservatives secretly formed the Draft-Goldwater Committee in hopes of paving the way for his becoming the Republican nominee in 1964 and for conservatives to take control of the Republican Party itself. In 1963 the group went public, eventually with the support of the senator himself.

Although Goldwater lost the New Hampshire primary to Henry Cabot Lodge and would later lose in places like Oregon to the moderate Republicans' favorite candidate, Nelson Rockefeller, he eventually gathered enough delegates to the 1964 Republican National Convention in San Francisco to be nominated on the first ballot as the party's presidential candidate.

In the general election of 1964, Goldwater was portrayed by his opponents as a trigger-happy warrior who couldn't be trusted in the age of nuclear weapons. He was defeated handily by the incumbent Democratic president, Lyndon Johnson. Goldwater won just six states and 39% of the popular vote to Johnson's landslide of 44 states and 61%.

Goldwater's personal defeat, however, masks the much more important meaning of the 1964 race. Goldwater's nomination by the Republican Party marked the ascendance of the conservative wing of the party and the decline of the established liberal wing most often associated with Nelson Rockefeller. The Goldwater campaign was also responsible for training and giving a start in politics to a vast array of individuals who would come to form the leadership of the conservative movement and the Republican Party. Two decades later these trends would culminate in the election as president of Ronald Reagan, who was himself one of those individuals who got their political start working for the Goldwater candidacy in 1964.

Long recognized as a principal figure in conservative politics, Goldwater became problematic for many fellow conservatives in the 1990s, when he began to express support for abortion rights and gay rights, both of which had become anathema to most in the movement he had helped found.

Gary L. Gregg II

BIBLIOGRAPHY

Goldwater, Barry. *The Conscience of a Conservative.* Shephardsville, KY: Victor, 1960.

CHARLES EVANS HUGHES

Born April 11, 1862, in Glens Falls, New York, the son of a Baptist minister, Charles Evans Hughes chose a career in the law rather than in the church. He entered politics in 1905 and made a name for himself in the role of counsel to legislative committees investigating utility companies and the insurance industry in New York. In 1906 he successfully sought the office of governor of New York, defeating William Randolph Hearst. Hughes, who disliked campaigning, appeared aloof but was nevertheless the only Republican candidate to win statewide office that year.

His first brush with presidential politics was as a New York favorite son at the 1908 Republican National Convention. William Howard Taft won the nomination and offered him the vice presidential nomination, but Hughes declined. After being elected to a second term as governor, he was largely unsuccessful in achieving reforms that he sought and considered leaving politics. In 1910 President Taft appointed him an associate justice of the Supreme Court.

Hughes won the Republican presidential nomina-

tion in 1916. His opponent was incumbent President Woodrow Wilson, who ran as a peace candidate who had kept the nation out of war in Europe. In the election, Hughes faced problems that he could not overcome. One was his own personality; many people continued to perceive him as aloof. Another problem was that his party was not unified. He was unable to heal the split between the progressive wing and the Old Guard. Wilson won the election.

After his loss, Hughes saw the nation enter World War I, saw Wilson broken in its aftermath, and believed that the same thing would have happened to him had he won. Without regret, he returned to the practice of law and did not again seek the presidency. After the Republican Party regained the White House, Hughes served as secretary of state in the Warren G. Harding administration from 1921 to 1925. From 1928 to 1930, he served on the Permanent Court of International Justice in the Netherlands.

In late 1929 William Howard Taft, who had become chief justice of the United States, was in failing health and wanted Hughes to be his successor. President

Charles Evans Hughes. *Source:* Library of Congress.

Herbert Hoover appointed Hughes chief justice in 1930. On the Court, Hughes became one of the two "swing" voters whose votes determined whether the liberal bloc or the conservative bloc prevailed. Because the Court held key New Deal legislation unconstitutional, President Franklin D. Roosevelt attempted to "pack" the Court with supporters of his policies. This threat to the Court led the two swing voters to vote with the liberal bloc to uphold New Deal legislation. Primarily because of his leadership qualities and his devotion to the Court, Hughes is generally included among the great chief justices to serve on the Supreme Court.

Hughes retired from the Court in 1941 at the age of 74. When he retired, he withdrew from public life. He died August 27, 1948.

Patricia A. Behlar

ALFRED M. LANDON

A Kansas governor, oil businessman and politician who became identified with Kansas progressivism, Alfred Mossman Landon ran unsuccessfully as a Republican candidate for president against Franklin Delano Roosevelt in 1936, in an election that seemed close throughout but ended with Landon's winning only the electoral votes of Vermont and Maine. But "Alf" Landon is remembered today not simply for the 1936 defeat but for a half-century of influence in politics.

Elected governor of Kansas in 1932 and reelected in 1934, the only Republican gubernatorial incumbent to win that year in a victory that led to his presidential candidacy, Landon had a reputation for reducing taxes and balancing the budget. His interest in politics began early, with his support of Theodore Roosevelt's Progressive Party in 1912, and he worked diligently in Kansas Republican politics all his life, from serving as a secretary to Kansas Governor Henry Allen to being Republican state chairman. He sought to make the Republican Party a moderate force rather than a conservative one, from regulating the excesses of capitalism to supporting essential welfare needs.

Few Republicans of national stature were left following the 1934 elections; Hoover was too closely connected to the grief of the depression; and there was a desire to nominate a candidate from west of the Alleghenies. Hence, Landon seemed the right candidate—a midwestern governor who blended Republican ideals with a moderate reputation for liberalism. As an oil man who had championed the Progressive Party and had even been a Rough Rider in the Spanish-American War, his supporters felt that Landon would appeal to a wide spectrum of voters.

Alfred M. Landon. *Source:* Library of Congress.

Born in West Middlesex, Pennsylvania, on September 9, 1887, the son of a successful businessman and a minister's daughter, Landon moved to Kansas with his parents in 1904, received a law degree from the University of Kansas in 1908 and entered the oil business in 1912 after first entertaining a career in banking. He attended the Bull Moose Convention of the Progressive Party in 1912 and campaigned for Theodore Roosevelt in Kansas. In World War I, he served in the U.S. Army in the chemical warfare division.

After his defeat in the presidential campaign, Landon did not seek elective office again but remained active in Republican politics and in the petroleum business. Having reached the age of 100 a month earlier, Landon died in Topeka, Kansas, on October 12, 1987. His daughter, Nancy Landon Kassebaum, was elected to the U.S. Senate from Kansas in 1978 and has served three terms, announcing her retirement in 1995.

John F. Yarbrough

WENDELL WILLKIE

Born in Elwood, Indiana, in 1892, Willkie was a lawyer who eventually became an industrialist. He rose to national prominence as president of a mammoth utility holding company called the Commonwealth and Southern Corporation. In his younger years, he was a pioneer in the quest to reduce utility rates and for Americans to use more electrical products; he also battled the competition of the Tennessee Valley Authority (TVA).

As an Ohio delegate to the Madison Square Garden convention of 1924, Willkie voted for Al Smith. Willkie removed his support from the Democratic Party to the Republican Party in 1938. Known for his disarming charm, Willkie had little trouble inspiring people to create a network of pro-Willkie clubs that would raise

Wendell Willkie. *Source:* Museum of Modern Art.

a considerable campaign fund, slate him for personal appearances at important events, write press releases, and book him on popular radio shows. Willkie rose in the Gallup poll rankings with amazing rapidity.

Willkie was nominated as a presidential candidate by the Republicans in 1940 and was narrowly defeated. He was generally considered an unlikely candidate at the time because he was a political "outsider." Nevertheless, his credentials as a proven administrator and outspoken internationalist garnered enthusiasm in Republican circles at that time, since France had just fallen to Germany, and Roosevelt was underscoring the importance of foreign policy. Willkie found himself in a strange Republican position when he publicly supported the basic goals of the New Deal, hoping to make inroads into Roosevelt's impressive 1936 majority. He was also in an anomalous position when he endorsed Roosevelt's destroyers-for-bases deal with England and Selective Service.

Willkie reduced Roosevelt's Gallup poll lead by chipping away at the third-term issue and by trying to portray the president as a warmonger. Part of Willkie's campaign oratory included this observation: "If [President Roosevelt's] promise to keep our boys out of foreign wars is no better than his promise to balance the budget, they're almost on the transports!"

In the election, the voting pattern was similar to that of four years earlier. Willkie carried more than twice as many counties as Landon and halved Roosevelt's popular plurality, but Roosevelt won 54.8% of the vote to Willkie's 44.8%.

Once freed of the pressure to deliver campaign speeches, Willkie criticized the administration's aid to Britain at the time as inadequate—and proved to be more of an interventionist than the president. In 1941 and 1942 Willkie traveled the world, representing the president. He was a staunch opponent of isolationism and was the leader of the left-wing element within the Republican Party.

When it appeared that Roosevelt, tough as ever to beat, might seek a fourth term, Willkie, then the Republican Party's titular head, loudly proclaimed his support for Wilsonian internationalism. This dismayed many of his supporters, in addition to Republicans in general. The fact that Willkie seemed to enjoy insulting politicians who disagreed with him also contributed to his faltering stature. He entered the primary in isolationist Wisconsin, and despite two weeks of hard campaigning there, his delegates were crushed by a slate pledged to Governor Thomas E. Dewey, who had not even declared his candidacy. Willkie died suddenly in October 1944.

B. Kim Taylor

Speakers

NATHANIEL P. BANKS

Rather than pursue a career in the law when he was admitted to the bar in 1839, Nathaniel Prentiss Banks (1816–1894) served as an inspector in the Boston customshouse. Although he was unsuccessful in his first seven attempts as a candidate for the lower branch of the Massachusetts legislature, Banks was elected to that body in 1849. In 1851 he was elected as the speaker of the house. Two years later, he served as president of the Massachusetts constitutional convention. Later, in 1853, Banks entered the U.S. House of Representatives as a Democrat. To the subsequent Congress, he was elected as the candidate of the Know-Nothing or American Party. In a hard-fought election for the position of Speaker of the House in which he declared that he would not allow the repeal of the Missouri Compromise to aid the spread of slavery, Banks was elected on the 133rd ballot. Many observers and historians marked his election as Speaker as the first defeat of slavery. Banks was considered one of the ablest and most efficient Speakers. He was even known to give some of his most strident opponents chairmanship of committees. He declined the 1856 nomination for president by the North American Party, a splinter antislavery faction of the American Party that had nominated former President Milliard Fillmore. Instead, in 1957, Banks accepted the Republican nomination for governor of Massachusetts. In an innovative move, Banks stumped the state and defeated his incumbent opponent by a wide margin. He held the post of governor from 1858 to 1860. At the end of his third term in 1861, Banks moved to Chicago, succeeding George B. McClellan as president of the Illinois Central Railroad. On May 16 of that year, he was commissioned by President Abraham Lincoln as a major general. After serving with distinction, Banks left the army in August 1865. On his return to Boston, he was reelected as a Republican to the U.S. House of Representatives to fill a vacancy. He was defeated for reelection in 1872, in large part because he supported the candidacy of Horace Greeley over President Ulysses S. Grant. In 1874 he was elected to the Massachusetts Senate, serving only one term. In 1875 he returned to the U.S. House of Representatives, this time as a Democrat. In 1877, he was reelected as a Republican. Banks was then appointed by President Rutherford B. Hayes as U.S. Marshal for Massachusetts, a post he held from 1879 to 1888. In 1888 he was once again elected to the House of Representatives as a Republican. Health concerns prevented him from running for reelection in 1890, however. He died in 1894.

Jeffrey D. Schultz

JOSEPH G. CANNON

A partisan Republican Speaker of the House whose authoritarian rule prompted the word *Cannonism* and ultimately led to a rebellion against his control, Joseph Gurney Cannon held the speakership at a time when the powers of the office were broad, and he used that power to defeat legislation he opposed. In succeeding years he has been viewed more favorably by House Speakers from Sam Rayburn to Newt Gingrich, whose powers over House business in the years since have been diminished.

Running the House with an iron hand, often refusing to recognize members on the floor, "Uncle Joe" Cannon of Illinois rose to the chairmanship of the House Appropriations Committee and then to Speaker of the House, where he held power from 1903 to 1911, and was a consistently conservative member who at that time in House history held great power through his ability to appoint all committees of the House and

Joseph G. Cannon. *Source:* Library of Congress.

their chairs. He was distrustful of President Woodrow Wilson's domestic programs; critical of the administration's foreign policy, particularly regarding the League of Nations; and adamantly opposed to a downward revision to the tariff.

Combined with his chairmanship of the House Rules Committee, controlling legislative procedure, Cannon's power came under fire from both Republicans and Democrats for his using it to defeat progressive legislation. In March 1910 insurgent Republicans and Democrats, led by George W. Norris of Nebraska and others from the Midwest, curbed Cannon's powers by enlarging the Rules Committee, providing for its election by the House, and excluding the Speaker from membership. After losing the speakership when the Democrats won a majority in the 61st Congress and then losing reelection in 1912, Cannon regained his congressional seat in 1914 and remained in Congress as a respected elder legislator until his retirement.

Born to Quaker parents in New Garden, North Carolina, on May 7, 1836, Cannon moved with his family to Indiana in 1840 and went on to study law at Cincinnati Law School before moving to Illinois and practicing, ultimately settling in Danville. After a failed run for the U.S. Congress in 1870, he was elected as a Republican in 1872 and served until 1891, when he lost his reelection bid, then won again in 1892 and served in the next ten Congresses. He rose rapidly in the House under the wing of Speaker Thomas B. Reed and was emblematic of the small-town politician who rose to prominence through seniority and popularity within the party.

Cannon decided not to run for reelection in 1922 and retired to Illinois. He died in Danville on November 12, 1926.

John F. Yarbrough

FREDERICK H. GILLETT

Frederick Huntington Gillett, a reserved and scholarly Republican from western Massachusetts, was elected Speaker of the House of Representatives in 1919. He served as Speaker for three consecutive terms before deciding not to seek reelection in 1924 so that he could become the Republican Party's candidate for the United States Senate from Massachusetts. He was elected to the Senate in 1924 and served one term before retiring from public life in 1931.

Born in Westfield, Massachusetts, in 1851, Gillett attended Amherst College and Harvard Law School, and was first elected to Congress in 1893 after having served as the assistant attorney general of Massachusetts and as a representative to the Massachusetts

State House for two years. In the United States House, Gillett served on several important committees, including the Appropriations, Judiciary, and Foreign Affairs Committees. He also chaired the Committee on Civil Service Reform for 12 years and in that time became known as the stepfather of the merit system. Gillett's tenure as Speaker of the House was not marked by any significant events.

Gillett ran for the Senate in 1924, having been persuaded to become the Republican Party's nominee after the original nominee decided to become the manager of Calvin Coolidge's presidential campaign. In the Senate, Gillett worked for the establishment of the Department of Education and Public Welfare and strongly supported the 18th Amendment and the Volstead Act. He also supported the creation of the World Court even though he had opposed the League of Nations while in the House. Gillett was a personal friend of President Coolidge and was regarded as one of the president's closest advisers and confidants.

Upon his retirement in 1931, Gillett returned to Massachusetts to pursue his scholarly interests and wrote a biography of George Frisbie Hoar, which was published in 1934. He died from leukemia in Springfield, Massachusetts, on July 31, 1935.

Quentin Kidd

NEWT GINGRICH

Newton "Newt" Gingrich became the central figure in the Republican Party in 1994, when the Republicans gained a majority in Congress for the first time in 40 years. Gingrich was elected Speaker and took control of the House of Representatives in a way that previous Speakers had been unable to do. He controlled the Republican conference and determined major committee assignments, dramatically altering the manner in which the House of Representatives conducted its business.

Newt Gingrich was born June 17, 1943, as Newton McPherson Jr. in Harrisburg, Pennsylvania. His mother divorced Newton McPherson and married Robert Gingrich, an army artillery officer, who adopted Newton. Newt had three sisters. Robert Gingrich was a professional soldier, and Newt spent his formative years living on or near various military bases. In 1960 the family moved to Columbus, Georgia, where Robert Gingrich was assigned to serve at Fort Benning. When his family moved again, Newt stayed in Georgia and attended Emory University in Atlanta, from which he earned his bachelor's degree in history in 1965.

Gingrich, an avid reader, went to graduate school at

Tulane University in New Orleans to work on his doctoral degree. He was becoming an adopted son of the South, from where the newly energized Republican Party would eventually emerge, influenced greatly by Gingrich. He wrote his doctoral thesis on Belgian education in the Congo.

Gingrich took a teaching position in 1970 at West Georgia College in Carrollton, Georgia, located in the Sixth Congressional District. Although Gingrich was a very popular professor, his real interest was in politics. He ran for Congress in 1974 against longtime incumbent Democrat Jack Flynt. In this campaign, Gingrich ran as a moderate Republican and lost. Not discouraged, he ran against Jack Flynt again in 1976. This time the election was influenced by the presidential candidacy of Georgia's son Jimmy Carter, and Gingrich lost a second time, but by a mere 2%.

In 1978 Gingrich once again sought the Sixth Congressional District seat in Georgia. The incumbent, Jack Flynt, had decided not to run; Gingrich's opponent was Virginia Shapard. Gingrich raised $219,000, took more conservative positions, and won. In Congress Gingrich sought and received an appointment to the House Administration Committee, where he would be a close student of the rules and business matters of the House of Representatives. This would serve him well in his climb to the top.

Gingrich ran well-financed reelection campaigns for his House seat and won easily, except in 1990, when he faced stiff resistance and won by a mere 974 votes. His district, after the 1990 census, became more Republican. Gingrich concentrated his energies on positioning the Republican Party in the House to take control once the Republicans were in the majority. In Gingrich's view, the established Republican leadership was too accommodating to the Democratic majority. In the 1982 election, the House Republicans were defeated, and Gingrich argued for a more aggressive posture for the party. He organized the Conservative Opportunity Society, a group of young conservative House members, to change the party's direction. These Republicans discovered that the newly created C-Span would be a useful outlet to deliver their message.

In 1987 Gingrich started criticizing Speaker Jim Wright's ethical abuses, and Wright resigned from office in June 1989, earning Gingrich the respect of the Republicans and the enmity of the Democrats. In 1989 House Whip Dick Cheney was nominated to be President George Bush's secretary of defense. Although President Bush and minority leader Robert Michel favored Illinois House member Edward Madigan to fill the important Republican leadership position of House whip, Gingrich challenged Madigan

and won by two votes. In 1990 Gingrich, as Republican whip, refused to support the Bush budget deal with Congress that raised taxes and brought attention to Bush's famous "Read my lips" pledge.

The 1992 election of Democrat William Jefferson "Bill" Clinton as president gave Gingrich an opportunity that suited his style. He could define his philosophy of government as an alternative to that of the party in power. He also demonstrated that he could work in a bipartisan manner by producing the votes Clinton needed to pass the North American Free Trade Agreement (NAFTA).

The 1994 congressional elections brought Gingrich to the forefront of American politics. He worked tirelessly to recruit Republican candidates and help elect them to Congress. He was the leader of the Republicans when they attained majority status in the House of Representatives for the first time in 40 years. Gingrich and his allies nationalized the congressional elections by putting out the "Contract with America" pledge, which included ten pieces of proposed legislation: a balanced budget amendment, a term-limit amendment, a tax cut, a line-item veto for the president, and other goals that promised Americans less government.

William C. Binning

GALUSHA A. GROW

A member of the House of Representatives and Speaker of the House from 1861 to 1863, Galusha Aaron Grow was born in Ashford (now Eastford), Connecticut, on August 21, 1823. His family moved to Glenwood, Pennsylvania, where he attended school. He graduated from Amherst College in Massachusetts in 1844. Returning to Pennsylvania, he studied law and was admitted to the bar. He was elected to Congress as a Democrat in 1850. A strong opponent of slavery, he joined the Republican Party as a founding member in 1854 and served as a Republican in Congress until 1863. His opposition to slavery was so strong that in 1859 he was involved in a fistfight on the floor of the House with a southern Democrat. He was elected Speaker of the 37th Congress. As Speaker, his principal accomplishment was the passage of the Homestead Act, and he is remembered as the Father of the Homestead Law. The absence of southern legislators during the Civil War helped Grow secure the passage in 1862 of the Homestead Act, granting 160 acres of federal domain to settlers. In 1863 Grow was gerrymandered out of his district and returned to the practice of law and his extensive business interests in railroads, lumber, soft coal, and oil. But he remained active in Pennsylvania Republican politics and managed to come back to Congress in 1894, where he served until 1903. He died on March 31, 1907.

BIBLIOGRAPHY

Duboid, James T., and Gertrude S. Matthews. *Galusha A. Grow: Father of the Homestead Law.* Boston: Houghton Mifflin, 1917.

Ilsevich, Robert D. *Galusha A. Grow: The People's Candidate.* Pittsburgh: University of Pittsburgh Press, 1988.

DAVID B. HENDERSON

A member of the House of Representatives and Speaker of the House from 1899 to 1902, David Bremner Henderson was born March 14, 1840, in Old Deer, Scotland, and immigrated with his parents to Illinois in 1846. Henderson enlisted in the Union army in 1861 after attending Upper Iowa University. He was wounded twice, and his leg was partially amputated. After the war, he studied law and established a legal practice in Dubuque, Iowa. He was elected on the Republican ticket to the 48th Congress and to the nine succeeding Congresses. As a standpat Republican, Henderson supported Civil War veterans' pensions, the gold standard, and protective tariffs, and he was instrumental in the passage of the first major bankruptcy bill. He was elected Speaker of the House in 1899, serving in that capacity between two important Speakers, Thomas B. Reed and Joseph Cannon. Henderson's own failing health kept him from becoming a strong Speaker, and he declined reelection in 1902.

BIBLIOGRAPHY

Smith, William Henry. *Speakers of the House of Representatives of the United States.* New York: AMS Press, 1971.

JOSEPH WARREN KEIFER

After valiant service in the Union army during the Civil War, Joseph Warren Keifer (b. January 30, 1836; d. April 22, 1932) was elected to the Ohio State Senate, serving from 1868 to 1869. He also served as a delegate to the Republican National Conventions in 1876 and 1908.

In 1876 he was elected to the United States House of Representatives, where he was a leading member of the Stalwart Republicans. In 1881 he was elected Speaker of the House, in large part because of his length of service and commitment to Republican ideas. He was not an effective Speaker and was defeated for reelection in 1884.

From June 9, 1898, until May 12, 1899, he served as a major general during the Spanish-American War. Keifer was reelected to Congress in 1905 and served until 1911, having been defeated for reelection in 1910. During his second tenure in the House, he advocated reducing southern representation in proportion to the number of citizens disenfranchised by southern legislatures.

Keifer was an active member of the Interparliamentary Union, which called for the third Hague Conference in 1915. While in private life, he wrote extensively on the Civil War and his life. He died in 1932, at the age of 96.

Jeffrey D. Schultz

NICHOLAS LONGWORTH

An expert on parliamentary procedures and son-in-law of President Theodore Roosevelt, Nicholas Longworth presided as Speaker of the House during the 1920s with firmness, tact and a genial temperament that brought him respect from both Republicans and Democrats in the House.

After working his way up in Ohio politics and joining the U.S. Congress in 1903, Longworth was promoted to majority leader in 1923 and then to Speaker in 1925. Despite his loyalty to the Republican Party, he opposed President Calvin Coolidge's naval program and also passed a bonus-loan bill for soldiers over President Herbert Hoover's veto. His marriage to Alice Lee Roosevelt, daughter of Theodore Roosevelt, was not always a blessing, for when his famous father-in-law ran on a third-party ticket in 1912, Longworth supported President William Howard Taft without offending Roosevelt, but he lost reelection that year in the House.

Born in Cincinnati, Ohio, on November 5, 1869, Longworth came from a prominent Cincinnati family. His grandfather had started one of the nation's first wineries and was a friend of Abraham Lincoln. After graduating from Harvard University and Cincinnati Law School, Longworth practiced in Cincinnati and began his political career serving on the Cincinnati Board of Education and by serving the Republican Party in Cincinnati, which was headed by George B. Cox. He was elected to the Ohio House of Representatives in 1899 and served until 1900 before moving to the state Senate from 1901 to 1903. Longworth was elected to the U.S. Congress as a Republican in 1903 and served in the next four Congresses. He lost reelection in 1912 but won his congressional seat again in the 64th Congress and served from 1915 until his death while on a visit to Aiken, South Carolina, on April 9, 1931.

John F. Yarbrough

JOSEPH W. MARTIN JR.

A prominent conservative Republican member of the United States House of Representatives from Massachusetts for 42 years, Joseph Martin (b. November 3, 1884; d. March 6, 1968) had a Capitol Hill career that included a pair of 2-year terms as Speaker (1947–1948 and 1953–1954) plus 16 years as the minority leader (1939–1946, 1949–1952, and 1955–1959). Martin was the only Republican to be elected Speaker during the 1931–1994 period. He came to the House in 1925 following 5 years in the Massachusetts legislature.

During the early years of his House career, Martin served first on the Foreign Affairs Committee, where he supported protectionist policies, before earning a place on the powerful Rules Committee. His career progressed to the point at which, in 1933, Martin won election as assistant floor leader, a position he held for 5 years. The numerous party positions Martin held at some point in his career included national convention chair, presidential elector, convention delegate, and chair of the Congressional Campaign Committee.

During this time Martin used his new position to work toward attaining two goals. First, he was an outspoken opponent of parts of the New Deal. Second, Martin helped form what has become known as the "conservative coalition" of Republicans and conservative Democrats to fight domestic legislation sought by presidents Franklin Roosevelt and Harry Truman. His opposition to Roosevelt inspired Martin to help win passage of the 22nd Amendment, limiting presidents to two terms. In addition, his struggles with Truman led Martin in 1951 to read publicly a letter from General Douglas MacArthur criticizing the president, an act that ignited the general's firing for insubordination.

Ironically, by 1959 his good working relationship with the Democratic Speaker, Sam Rayburn, helped spark a successful rebellion among younger Republicans to oust Martin as minority leader in favor of a more confrontational and ideological delegation spokesman. Martin retired after losing a primary renomination bid in 1966.

Robert E. Dewhirst

WILLIAM PENNINGTON

William Pennington, Speaker of the House of Representatives and governor of New Jersey, was born in Newark, New Jersey, on May 4, 1796. His father, William Sandford Pennington, was at one time governor of New Jersey. Pennington attended the College of New Jersey (now Princeton University) and graduated

in 1813 with a degree in law. His first job was with Theodore Frelinghuysen, Henry Clay's future running mate. Pennington worked for the courts until 1826, when he decided to take advantage of his father's influence and enter politics. He was elected to the New Jersey State Assembly in 1827 as a Democrat but became a Whig after his election. He served in the Assembly uneventfully for ten years before being elected governor and chancellor of New Jersey.

The most significant political event during Pennington's five 1-year terms as governor was the "Broad Seal War" of 1837–1838. Five of New Jersey's congressional seats were contested that year, and despite allegations of corruption, Pennington certified the results with the "Seal of New Jersey." The issue was brought to Congress, and after ten days of debate, the Democrats were seated over Pennington's Whigs. In 1843 he left the office of governor and returned to practicing law. For 15 years he tried to obtain an appointment as a minister to Europe or as the chancellor of New Jersey, no longer an elected position. He refused President Millard Fillmore's offer to serve as governor of the Minnesota Territory and in 1850 refused an opportunity to act as a claims judge under the recent treaty with Mexico.

In 1858 Pennington was elected to the House of Representatives as a Republican. When the House convened in January 1859 to elect a Speaker, the Democrats were fractured by the bloody events in Kansas, and the Republicans lacked the votes to elect John Sherman to the speakership. After eight weeks of battle and compromise, the unknown and uninspiring freshman congressman Pennington was elevated to the post of Speaker of the House of Representatives. He was elected with an exact majority of the votes, 177, and became the second freshman, Henry Clay being the first, elected Speaker.

Pennington's performance as Speaker was so dismal that he even failed to win reelection in 1860. Although Pennington was not qualified to be Speaker, it should be taken into account that the fractured House, and nation, cast onto Pennington's shoulders the weight of issues they could not resolve themselves. Pennington died in 1862 in Newark.

Daniel Stanhagen

THEODORE M. POMEROY

Theodore Medad Pomeroy, Speaker of the House of Representatives, was born in Cayuga, New York, on December 31, 1824. He attended public school and the Munro Collegiate in Elbridge, New York, graduated from Hamilton College in 1842, then clerked for four years before being admitted to the bar. He began practicing law in Auburn, New York, in 1846. Pomeroy was district attorney of Cayuga County from 1850 to 1856, when he was elected to the State Assembly. In 1860, he was a delegate to the New York Republican Convention and later that year was elected to the 37th Congress. In four terms in the House, he served as chairman of the Committee on Expenditures in the Post Office Department and on the Committee on Banking and Currency. In November 1868, he decided not to seek reelection. As an administrative motion, he was elected Speaker of the House for March 3, 1869.

After leaving office, he became the first vice president of the American Express Company and in 1875 was elected mayor of Auburn, New York. In 1876, he served as temporary chairman of the Republican National Convention. His last political position was one term in the New York State Senate, after which he retired from public life. He died in Auburn on March 23, 1905.

Daniel Stanhagen

THOMAS B. REED

Thomas Brackett Reed (b. 1839) served Maine's First Congressional District in the House of Representatives from 1876 until 1898. He was elected Speaker of the House in 1889 and served as either Speaker or minority leader of the Republican Party until he retired in protest over the United States' annexation of the Philippines. Reed strongly disagreed with the application of the colonial theory to the Constitution and had opposed the earlier annexation of Hawaii, arguing that such actions violated the principles of self-government.

While serving as Speaker, from 1889 to 1891 and from 1895 to 1899, Reed pushed through the so-called Reed rules, which greatly increased the powers of the Speaker. He introduced the practice of counting all members of Congress who were recognized in the chamber whether they answered their names when called or not. This change greatly increased the flow of legislation through the House and forced representatives to publicly announce their positions. The result was an increase in the chances of securing the passage of popular Republican legislation. Reed also arbitrarily used his powers not to recognize opposing representatives who wished to be heard. For this reason he came to be known as Czar Reed, and opposition to him mounted even as his dominance grew.

Among the great issues facing the country during Reed's tenure in Congress, perhaps the most important was the issue of free coinage of silver. In 1890 Congress passed the Sherman Silver-Purchase Bill, which Reed had strongly opposed and then had worked to

Thomas B. Reed Portrayed as a Tyrant. *Source:* Library of Congress.

have watered down when passage became inevitable. The bill required the federal government to purchase 4.5 million ounces of silver each month on the open market and issue treasury notes redeemable in gold in return. The thinking behind the plan was that the value of silver would go up and thus reduce the gap that existed between the intrinsic value of silver and gold dollars.

Reed strongly opposed subsidizing the price of silver, and by 1893 it had become obvious that the intentions of the original bill were not being realized. Rather than going up, the price of silver had actually gone down, and many people feared that the government would not be able to maintain gold payments. Reed joined forces with President Grover Cleveland, amid strong opposition from Democrats, and had the Silver-Purchase Bill repealed.

After retiring from Congress, Reed practiced law in New York City and traveled abroad. In 1902, while in Washington to conduct business before the Supreme Court, Reed fell ill and died a few days later of chronic Bright's disease.

Quentin Kidd

Other Notable Republicans

Nelson W. Aldrich (1841–1915)   Nelson Wilmarth Aldrich entered politics as an independent Republican on the Providence Common Council in 1869. In 1875 he was elected to the first of two terms in the state legislature. He declined the chance to run for governor in 1877 offered by the leading faction of the deeply divided Rhode Island Republican Party. The following year he was sent to the 46th Congress and served there until the death of Senator Ambrose E. Burnside in 1881, when he chose to run for the vacated seat. In the Senate, he established himself as a man of extraordinary range and grasp of subjects. He was a strident protectionist and a great parliamentarian. When the Democrats made large gains in the election of 1890, they targeted Aldrich's seat. Despite the battalion of stump speakers sent to unseat him, he survived the election. Along with William B. Allison of Iowa, Orville H. Platt of Connecticut, and John C. Spooner of Wisconsin, Aldrich formed the Big Four, who were the core of the Republican Senate from 1897 to 1905. The Big Four were at the height of their power with the re-election of William McKinley as president in 1900. When Teddy Roosevelt assumed the presidency, they rallied around his policies, including his position regarding Panama. After going abroad to study modern banking practices, Aldrich was instrumental in drafting and passing the Aldrich–Vreeland Act, which curbed the panic of 1907. The election of 1908 would turn on the issue of the tariff, and the Payne–Aldrich Tariff helped to settle that issue in a manner acceptable to the western states and their leader, Robert M. La Follette of Wisconsin, thereby preventing its replacement with an income tax. While actively supporting Taft for president in 1908, Aldrich chose not to seek re-election.

William B. Allison (1829–1908)   From the Democratic stronghold of Dubuque, Iowa, William Boyd Allison worked to unite the state's Republicans. Through his efforts, the party was successful in electing Samuel J. Kirkwood as governor in 1859. At the Republican National Convention in Chicago in 1860, Allison switched his support from Salmon P. Chase to Abraham Lincoln. In 1862 he was elected to Congress and served four terms. Allison was a strong supporter of the Lincoln administration and garnered a reputation as a thought-ful moderate. After unsuccessful senatorial bids in 1869 and 1870, he was elected to the Senate in 1872 on a wave of anti-Harlanism, a liberal Republican movement in Iowa to defeat conservative incumbent James Harlan. While he was in the Senate, Allison's political power grew immensely because of his membership in the powerful Republican Senate inner circle known as the Big Four (which also included Nelson W. Aldrich of Rhode Island, Orville H. Platt of Connecticut, and John C. Spooner of Wisconsin). From 1881 until 1908, Allison was chair of the Senate Finance Committee. In 1897 he served a turn as chair of the Republican caucus. At the time of his death in 1908, he was the most senior senator.

Henry B. Anthony (1815–1884)   As editor of the *Providence Journal*, Henry Bowen Anthony rose in the political ranks because of his reporting on Dorr's Rebellion, an 1841–1842 uprising that led to the adoption of a new Rhode Island State constitution in 1843. The conservative elements of Rhode Island elected him governor in 1849 and reelected him in 1850. He refused to run for a third term and returned to the newspaper as editor. In 1858 he reentered public life as a U.S. senator. His colleagues selected him as president pro tempore in 1869, 1870, 1871 and again in 1884. Throughout his senatorial tenure, he worked to have the *Congressional Record* become a faithful transcript of the proceedings of Congress.

Howard H. Baker (1902–1964)   Howard Henry Baker entered public life when he was elected to the Tennessee House in 1929 and again in 1930. In 1931 he ran a successful campaign for the Scott County Board of Education, where he served two one-year terms. While serving as the attorney general for the 19th circuit of Tennessee, Baker ran unsuccessful campaigns for governor in 1938 and for the United States Senate in 1940. In the latter year, Baker was a delegate to the Republican National Committee, a role he played in the next four presidential nominating conventions. In 1950, he was elected to the United States House of Representatives, where he served until his death in 1964. While in the House, Baker was an influential member of the Ways and Means Committee.

Howard H. Baker Jr. (1925–)　Howard Henry Baker Jr., the son of Congressman Howard H. Baker, was the first Republican senator to be directly elected by the people of Tennessee in 1966. A moderate Republican, Baker was twice reelected to the Senate, in 1972 and 1978. In 1973 he served as the ranking Republican on the Senate Watergate Committee. He served as minority leader from 1977 to 1981 and as majority leader from 1981 to 1985. He sought the Republican nomination for president in 1980, but withdrew from the race, hoping instead for the number-two spot on a ticket headed by Ronald Reagan. However, Baker's moderate pragmatism had little support among the more conservative forces in the Reagan camp. Ironically, President Reagan convinced Baker to serve as chief of staff beginning in 1987, when the White House was embroiled in the Iran–contra affair. After the end of Reagan's second term, Baker returned to his law practice in Tennessee.

Haley Barbour (1947–)　Haley Barbour was elected chair of the Republican National Committee on January 29, 1993, on the heels of the defeat of the Republican ticket in the 1992 election. For the preceding 12 years, the Republican Party had been controlled by the Republican president in the White House, who selected the national chair. The last chair chosen by President George Bush was Rich Bond, who followed the popular and skillful Lee Atwater.

Haley Barbour, who was 45 when elected, is a native of Yazoo City, Mississippi. He started working for the Republican Party as the executive director of the Mississippi Republican Party after graduating from the University of Mississippi Law School. Barbour worked on the Ford campaign in 1976. He was the Republican nominee for the U.S. Senate in 1982 but lost to Democratic incumbent Senator John C. Stennis.

In his campaign for national chair, Barbour was criticized for his recent work as a Washington lobbyist. He overcame that with strong support from southern members of the Republican National Committee. He was elected chair on the third ballot, with 90 of the 165

committee votes, defeating Spencer Abraham of Michigan.

As chair, Haley Barbour has the role of spokesperson for the Republicans. His task was to rebuild the party, and he and the Republican Party enjoyed great success in the 1994 midterm election, capturing both houses of Congress and a majority of the nation's governorships. Haley Barbour will preside over the Republican National Convention in San Diego in August 1996. It is customary for the national party to maintain a neutral stance until the convention.

William C. Binning

Albert J. Beveridge (1862–1927)　Albert Jeremiah Beveridge was elected to the Senate as a compromise candidate of the Illinois legislature in 1899. In many ways, his rise to prominence was a Horatio Alger story of a poor midwestern farmer being appointed to public office. He served in the Senate until 1911, distinguishing himself as one of the most powerful and popular orators of his time. He soon became one of the leaders of the progressive wing of the Republican Party. He was a strong supporter of President Theodore Roosevelt's Square Deal policies. He was also the chief sponsor of reforms in the meat-packing industry, child labor laws, and antitrust legislation. He broke with the party in 1912, choosing to support Roosevelt's third-party run for the presidency. However, in 1916 he returned to the party after failed attempts to win election as governor and senator. He was nominated for the Senate by the Republicans in 1922 but was defeated by Harry S. New. After this defeat, he retired from politics and became one of the country's great historians. His masterpiece is a four-volume work, *The Life of John Marshall*.

William E. Borah (1865–1940)　The Lion of Idaho, William Edgar Borah, first ran for public office as a Silver Republican in 1896. Although unsuccessful in that campaign, he gained national recognition for his prosecution of labor radicals in Idaho. In his 33-year tenure in the Senate, which began in 1907 and ended with his death in 1940, he was fiercely independent, often being referred to as "The Great Opposer." As a member of the "Irreconcilables," he was a leading opponent of President Woodrow Wilson's policies regarding the Treaty of Versailles and U.S. entry into the League of Nations. Although he initially supported President Herbert Hoover, Borah came to believe the president was not doing enough to end the depression. His Senate colleagues appointed him chair of the Senate Committee on Education and Labor. Much to their dismay, rather than attack organized labor, Borah was instrumental in creating the Department of Labor and the Children's Bureau. In addition, he led the fight for an eight-hour workday for federal employees. Fundamentally a Jeffersonian Democrat in his political philosophy, Borah disliked federal centralization, believing the states better able to respond to the needs of their citizens.

Frank B. Brandegee (1864–1924)   In 1888, the same year he entered into a law practice, Frank Bosworth Brandegee was chosen as a delegate to the Republican National Convention in Chicago, a post he held again in 1892, 1900 and 1904. The following year he was elected to the Connecticut House of Representatives. He was reelected in 1898 and served as speaker of the Connecticut House in 1899. In 1902 he was chosen to fill a vacant seat in the U.S. House of Representatives. Reelected twice to the House, Brandegee resigned in 1905 upon his election to the U.S. Senate, replacing Orville H. Platt. His senatorial career was one of obstructionist tactics. Brandegee used parliamentary procedure and his vote to limit inquiries into the elections of William Lorimer and Truman H. Newberry. He actively opposed U.S. entry into the League of Nations. Found dead in his Washington, D.C., home on October 14, 1924, Brandegee had committed suicide by inhaling gas because of growing financial difficulties.

Charles R. Brayton (1840–1910)   Charles Ray Brayton, the son of a congressman, was the Republican boss of Rhode Island. He left Brown University in 1859 to organize a Civil War militia company, the Third Rhode Island Volunteers, rising to the rank of brigadier general on May 13, 1863, "for faithful and meritorious services." After the war, Brayton held various political patronage posts in his home state. He worked tirelessly to control the state legislature and was willing to give or take bribes to achieve his ends. He allied himself with the powerful U.S. Senator Nelson W. Aldrich. In 1900 Brayton was struck blind but continued to serve as a party leader. However, with the election of a Democratic governor in 1906, he was pressured to retire.

John W. Bricker (1893–1986)   John William Bricker rose through the Republican political ranks to become Ohio's attorney general in 1933, a post he held until 1937. In 1938 he ran a successful campaign for governor and was reelected in 1942. In 1944 he was the vice presidential nominee on the Republican ticket headed by Thomas E. Dewey. Elected to the United States Senate in 1946, Bricker was reelected in 1952. As chair of the Committee on Interstate and Foreign Affairs, Bricker sought to limit the power of the federal government to infringe on traditional areas of states' rights. He sponsored the famous Bricker Amendment,

which sought to limit the scope of the president's treaty-making power. The amendment's chief goal was to limit the president's power to send troops overseas under the authority of the United Nations. Bricker was defeated for reelection in 1958.

H. Styles Bridges (1898–1961)   Henry Styles Bridges entered public life when he was appointed to the New Hampshire Public Service Commission in 1930. In 1934, at the age of 36, he became the Granite State's youngest governor. His two-year tenure was marked by a balanced budget and state-sponsored unemployment compensation. In 1936, Bridges won election to the United States Senate, defeating former Senator George H. Moses in a hard-fought primary. He remained in the Senate until his death in 1961. From 1952 to 1953 he was the Republican floor leader, and from 1953 to 1955 he served as president pro tempore. In the Senate he was an outspoken opponent of President Franklin D. Roosevelt's New Deal policies. An ardent anticommunist, Bridges opposed the lend–lease deal with Russia and attacked Secretary of State Dean Acheson's defense of Alger Hiss. He defended General Douglas MacArthur in congressional hearings after President Harry S. Truman fired MacArthur. He also tried to protect Senator Joseph McCarthy of Wisconsin from censure. Bridges, a fiscal conservative, chaired the Appropriations Committee, where he pushed for cuts in foreign aid, which he considered wasteful.

Patrick J. Buchanan (1938–)   Patrick Joseph Buchanan, one of nine children, was born on November 2, 1938, in Washington, D.C. He received his A.B. degree from Georgetown University and a master's degree from Columbia University. He started his journalism career as an editorial writer for the *St. Louis Globe Democrat* in 1962 and went on to become a speechwriter for Richard Nixon. Buchanan later served as a syndicated columnist, television talk show host, and commentator, cohosting CNN's *Crossfire*, and was a regular panelist on *The McLaughlin Group*. Buchanan also served as President Ronald Reagan's communications director from 1985 to 1987 and became well known for his conservative views.

Patrick Buchanan ran for president against incumbent George Bush in 1992 and is a Republican presidential candidate in 1996. In the 1992 election he ran a strong race in New Hampshire, garnering 37% of the vote. Many Bush supporters blamed Buchanan's candidacy for President Bush's loss to Bill Clinton in November 1992. Buchanan gave a major address at the 1992 Republican National Convention and stated that America was in a "culture war." He emphasized social issues in his 1992 campaign and continued those themes in his 1996 campaign. Buchanan, who adheres to a very strong antiabortion position, is an isolationist and protectionist in his foreign policy positions. Like Senator Phil Gramm and others, he failed to make much headway after the first few primaries.

Theodore E. Burton (1851–1929)   Theodore Elijah Burton was elected to public office in Cleveland, Ohio, where he served on the City Council from 1886 to 1888. In 1888 he was elected to the U.S. House of Representatives. Although defeated for reelection in 1890, he was reelected in 1894 and served until 1909, when he was appointed to the Senate. Fearing that he would not win under the new direct-election rule, Burton retired from office in 1913. His Republican replacement, Warren G. Harding, used the seat as a springboard to the White House. Burton returned to politics in 1920, being elected to the House of Representatives. In 1928 he was elected to the Senate, though he died within the year. In addition to his duties as a legislator, Burton was an active scholar of financial history. His works *Financial Crises and Periods of Industrial and Commercial Depression* and *John Sherman* increased his legislative influence in the financial arenas. Regarded as an independent Republican, Burton often embarrassed his Republican colleagues with his voting record.

Nicholas Murray Butler (1862–1947)   Nicholas Murray Butler began his political career as a delegate to the Republican National Convention in 1888, a position he held again from 1904 to 1932. Although he turned down opportunities to run for mayor of New York City and governor of New York State, he served on several commissions on administrative reorganization and as an informal adviser to the state Constitutional Conventions of 1894 and 1915. Butler was a trusted adviser to Presidents Theodore Roosevelt and William H. Taft. He first broke with Roosevelt when the president announced his plans to further regulate the economy and then helped Taft ward off the Roosevelt forces at the 1912 Republican National Convention. Regarding himself as a Hamiltonian, Butler sought to preserve limited government and government by the trained. He opposed most progressive reforms, such as the direct election of senators and the initiative, recall and referendum. He sought the party's nomination for president in 1920 but failed to gain any real support. President Warren G. Harding used Butler as an influential, informal adviser. Butler grew increasingly dissatisfied with the Republican Party over the issues of Prohibition and the protective tariff. He ran for the Republican nomination in 1928, hoping to remove the Prohibition plank

from the platform. He was instrumental in the drafting and adoption of the Kellogg–Briand Pact, which was a bilateral renunciation of war between the United States and France. Through the huge endowment of the Carnegie Corporation, Butler worked on many international issues. He received the Nobel Peace Prize in 1931.

Simon Cameron (1799–1889)   Simon Cameron began his political career when he moved to Washington, D.C., in 1822 to work for the company that printed the congressional debates. In his spare time, he observed Congress and made influential friends. After two years, Cameron returned to Harrisburg, Pennsylvania, and bought a newspaper, *The Republican*. In 1830 he headed the state's movement to reelect Andrew Jackson, having had Martin Van Buren nominated vice president instead of John C. Calhoun. He earned the nickname "The Great Winnebago Chief" because of his work settling Indian claims, often with notes drawn on his own bank. Cameron was appointed to the U.S. Senate in 1845, when James Buchanan resigned to enter President James K. Polk's cabinet. The following year, however, he failed to achieve reelection by the coalition of Whigs, Nativists, and Protectionist Democrats. After a time in private life, Cameron ran for the U.S. Senate in 1855 as the candidate of the Know-Nothing Party. In 1856 he switched to the Republican Party and won appointment to the Senate, helping to build the state's machine. In the Senate, Cameron was an ardent foe of Buchanan. At the 1860 convention his presidential electors were traded to Lincoln for a cabinet position, secretary of war. During Cameron's tenure as secretary, corruption became rampant in the administration of governmental contracts. In addition Cameron actively endorsed the plan of arming freed slaves. Lincoln, in order to save face, appointed Cameron as minister to Russia. Displeased with his new appointment, Cameron ran unsuccessfully in 1863 and 1867 for the Senate. In 1873, however, he was once again sent to the Senate. Exercising his extensive political influence, he secured for his son, James Donald Cameron, an appointment as secretary of war in the Ulysses S. Grant administration. When President Rutherford B. Hayes removed Cameron's son from the post, Cameron resigned his Senate seat on the promise that the Pennsylvania State legislature would appoint his son to replace him.

Arthur Capper (1865–1951)   Arthur Capper, a successful journalist and publisher, rejected the populism of his home state of Kansas and built a strong publishing empire, which he used as a forum for more conservative Republican ideas. In 1912 Capper lost his race for governor by 29 votes. However, in 1914 he became the first native-born Kansan to be elected governor. Capper served two terms as governor before being elected in 1918 to the United States Senate, where he served until his retirement in 1949. While in the Senate, he was a leader of the farm bloc. He sponsored several important farm bills that bear his name, including the Capper–Ketchum Act, which funded 4-H clubs, and the Capper–Volstead Act, which aided cooperatives. Although a staunch isolationist, Capper voted for U.S. entry into the League of Nations. In addition, he was often criticized by his fellow Republicans in the 1930s for his support of some New Deal legislation.

Daniel Clark (1809–1891)   Daniel Clark was an active organizer of the Republican Party in New Hampshire. In 1857 he was nominated to serve the remainder of Senator James Bell's term. Regarded as a brilliant orator and an uncompromising foe of slavery, Clark was reelected in 1860, though not in 1866 because of New Hampshire's belief in rotation of office. President Andrew Johnson, however, appointed him the district judge in Manchester, New Hamsphire, in 1866.

Roscoe Conkling (1828–1888)   Roscoe Conkling was elected mayor of Utica, New York, in 1858, resigning later in the year upon his election to the U.S. House of Representatives. He served in the House from 1858 to 1867, except for 1863–1865. Although a staunch Republican, he married the daughter of the Democratic governor of New York. Conkling was often ridiculed as "the finest torso in public life" because of his almost fanatical concern with his health. When William Seward, the leader of the New York Republicans, decided to support President Andrew Johnson in his Reconstruction plan, Conkling and the more radical Republicans were energized. He was elected to the Senate in 1867 and reelected twice (in 1873 and 1879). In 1873 he was offered the post of chief justice of the United States but declined because he preferred the wrangle of partisan politics. He opposed Rutherford B. Hayes's nomination for president, seeing it as the end of the Ulysses S. Grant dynasty. In 1880 he led the renominate-Grant movement, which split the party and produced a James A. Garfield–Chester A. Arthur ticket. In 1881 he resigned from the Senate because he opposed appointments made by Garfield in his home state. Conkling mistakenly believed that the legislature in Albany would reelect him as a sign of support.

John Jordan Crittenden (1786–1863)   John Jordan Crittenden believed that political service was most meaningful at the state level. In 1811 he was elected to

the Kentucky State House, where he served until 1817, when he was elected to the U.S. Senate. In 1823 he did not stand for reelection because he preferred to return to his home state. In 1825 he ran unsuccessfully for the state House, but the assassination of his opponent necessitated a special election, which he won. He was reelected in 1829 and served as speaker of the House. Crittenden was appointed by President John Quincy Adams as district attorney but was later removed by President Andrew Jackson. Appointed to the Senate in 1835, Crittenden opposed Jackson's bank policies. Reelected in 1840, he resigned to serve as attorney general in President Benjamin Harrison's administration. He resigned this post on September 11, 1841, with several other cabinet members because of disarray in the John Tyler administration. Elected to the Senate in 1842 to fill Henry Clay's seat, Crittenden was subsequently reelected in 1843. He supported Clay as the party's standard-bearer in 1844 as he had done in 1824. However, in 1848 he supported Zachary Taylor because he did not believe Clay could win. Crittenden's support of Taylor led to a break with Clay that ended with a reunion at Clay's deathbed. Out of respect for Clay, he refused any appointments in the Taylor administration. Crittenden resigned from the Senate in 1848 to return to Kentucky and serve as governor. After Taylor's death, he accepted the post of attorney general under President Millard Fillmore. In 1854 he was once again elected to the Senate, where he introduced the "Crittenden Propositions," which were designed to be a more moderate solution to the problem of slavery. In 1860, Crittenden advocated the election of the John Bell–Edward Everett ticket over the party's official candidate, Abraham Lincoln. Returning to Kentucky, Crittenden urged the state to remain in the Union. Elected to the special session of Congress in 1861, he worked to limit the scope and effects of the Civil War.

Shelby M. Cullom (1829–1914)   Shelby Moore Cullom is best known for his authorship of the Interstate Commerce Act, which created the Interstate Commerce Commission. He strongly believed that states were the primary source of regulation. However, he recognized the limitations of this position and the need for federal action. Cullom first entered politics as an active supporter of Abraham Lincoln for the Senate in 1858 and for the presidency in 1860. He served as speaker of the Illinois State legislature, as a member of the U.S. House of Representatives (1865–1871), and as governor of Illinois (1876–1883) before being elected to the U.S. Senate in 1883. Cullom served in the Senate until 1913, having lost his 1912 reelection bid.

Albert B. Cummins (1850–1926)   An unsuccessful candidate for the Senate in 1894 and 1899, Albert Baird Cummins announced his candidacy for governor of Iowa in 1901 with the hope of reducing machine politics. His candidacy split the Republican Party, but he was still elected on the first ballot to represent the party as its nominee in the general election. His progressive movement captured a second term in 1903 and a third in 1906. In 1908 Cummins made another attempt to gain a seat in the Senate. Once again controversy grew between his progressive wing and the conservative wing of the party. Under a new primary law, however, he was selected as the party's nominee. Cummins won the general election and served in the Senate until 1925, the last six years of his tenure as the president pro tempore.

Bronson M. Cutting (1888–1935)   Bronson Murray Cutting was active in the foundation of the New Mexico Progressive Republican Party, serving as its treasurer and chair. In 1916 he attended the Progressive National Convention in Chicago. During World War I he served in military intelligence and later as military attaché at the American Embassy in London. After the war, Cutting was unsuccessful in his early attempts to enter political office because his progressive leanings were not in favor among the Republican leadership. However, in 1928 he was appointed by the governor to fill a vacancy in the Senate. Later that year, Cutting won the seat in his own right. An ardent liberal, he was a critic of the Herbert Hoover administration. He was supportive of Franklin D. Roosevelt's New Deal, voting for many of its legislative planks. In a bitter 1934 reelection contest, Cutting's opponent, Democrat Dennis Chaves, alleged voter fraud. After Cutting was sworn in, he returned to New Mexico to investigate the charges himself. It was on the return trip to Washington, with papers he believed exonerated him, that Cutting died in an airplane crash—becoming the first sitting senator to die in a plane accident. Ironically, Chaves was appointed to fill Cutting's seat and held it for nearly 30 years.

Henry Winter Davis (1817–1865)   Henry Winter Davis was a strong supporter of Whig General Winfield Scott's failed 1852 bid for the presidency. In 1855 he was elected as a member of Congress from Maryland and soon became a prominent leader of the Know-Nothings. Supporting Millard Fillmore in 1856, Davis continued his stance of neutrality on slavery. In January 1860 Davis cast the tie-breaking vote for William Pennington that gave control of the House of Representatives to the Republicans. During the Civil War, he was an outspoken Unionist in his home state

and throughout the country. He was returned to the House in a hotly contested race in 1863. Davis, who opposed the Louisiana Plan because it usurped legislative authority, was the chief author of an alternative plan that President Abraham Lincoln pocket vetoed. In response, he coauthored the Wade–Davis Manifesto, which attacked Lincoln's Reconstruction plan. After his defeat for reelection in 1864, Davis became an outspoken opponent of presidential Reconstruction.

Everett McKinley Dirksen (1896–1969)   Although he lost a close Republican primary for the House of Representatives in 1930, Everett McKinley Dirksen of Illinois defeated the Republican incumbent, William Hull, in 1932 in the Republican primary and then won the general election. Dirksen supported many of the domestic policies of the Franklin D. Roosevelt administration while taking an ardent isolationist, antiadministration stance in foreign policy. In 1938 he became the chair of the Republican National Committee, a post he held until 1946. A moderate Republican, Dirksen attempted unsuccessfully to secure the party's nomination for president in 1944 and for vice president in 1952 and 1960. He retired from the House in 1948 for medical reasons. However, by 1950 Dirksen had recovered and waged a successful bid for the Senate, where he stayed until his death in 1969. In the 1950 election he defeated the Democratic majority leader, Scott Lucas, with the help of the conservative wing of the Republican Party. While Dirksen was initially a supporter of conservative Senators Robert A. Taft and Joseph R. McCarthy, his 1956 reelection brought him into the camp of President Dwight D. Eisenhower. After his reelection, he was chosen party whip and then party leader in 1959. Dirksen's strengths were his ability to bargain hard and to compromise when prudent. He was an effective leader who was able to supply key votes for Democratic legislation. As a result, his opponents considered Dirksen a great statesman. He was an extremely visible politician, holding weekly televised press conferences. Nicknamed "The Wizard of Ooze" for his rhetorical style, Dirksen cut an album, *Gallant Man*, a collection of patriotic readings that sold 500,000 copies.

Joseph M. Dixon (1867–1934)   In 1990 Joseph Moore Dixon was elected to the Montana State House after serving in various appointed legal posts in the state. After only a single term in the state House, he was elected to the United States House of Representatives in 1902, serving until 1907. While in the House, he chaired the Committee on the Conservation of Natural Resources. In the election of 1906 Dixon succeeded in obtaining a seat in the Senate. However, he was not reelected in 1912. In a break with the more conservative forces in the Republican Party, Dixon chaired the 1912 National Progressive Convention, which nominated Theodore Roosevelt. In 1920 he was elected as a progressive governor of Montana, serving one term. In 1924 his reelection bid was unsuccessful. After a failed run for the Senate in 1928, Dixon was appointed the first assistant secretary of the interior, a post he held from 1929 to 1933.

Robert Dole (1923–)   Robert Joseph Dole was born in Russell, Kansas, on July 22, 1923, to Doran and Bina Dole. He was an outstanding athlete as a young man in Kansas. He attended the University of Kansas from 1941 to 1943 where he was involved in college athletics. Dole was severely wounded in April 1945 in Italy in the closing days of World War II. He spent three years in Veterans Administration hospitals recovering from his wounds and lost the use of his right arm. He continues to hold a pen in that hand, which he cannot use even to button his shirt.

He attended Washburn University on the GI Bill and graduated with both an A.B. degree and a law degree in 1952. Dole's family had been Roosevelt Democrats; Dole ran as a Republican for the Kansas state legislature and won in 1951. He was elected county attorney in 1953 and served until 1961. He was elected to the U.S. House of Representatives in 1960. He served four terms in the House, where he concentrated on agricultural issues. He was elected to the U.S. Senate from Kansas in 1968 with 60% of the vote. He was reelected four times by large margins, except in 1974, when he won with a slim 51% of the vote.

Bob Dole is one of postwar America's most successful politicians. He is known for his sharp wit. He has been a consensus builder and an effective parliamentarian. These skills have served him well. In the early 1980s Dole became chairman of the powerful Senate Finance Committee and in 1984 he became the majority leader of the Republicans in the Senate, where he served Presidents Bush and Reagan effectively and loyally.

Dole served as chairman of the Republican National Committee from 1971 to 1973 as President Richard Nixon's choice. He was replaced by George Bush. Dole was the vice presidential nominee of Gerald Ford in 1976 and was blamed for the ticket's loss that year. Dole sought the Republican nomination for president in 1980 and 1988 and failed in those bids.

Dole, who was divorced from his first wife, Phyllis, in 1972, married Mary Elizabeth Hanford Dole in 1975. Elizabeth Dole served in the Nixon administration, as

secretary of transportation under Reagan, and as secretary of labor under President Bush. The Doles have one daughter.

Robert Dole has long reflected midwestern Republican values. He is pragmatic. He was not an advocate of supply-side economics; he preferred a traditional conservative balanced budget. After the 1994 Republican takeover of the House, Dole was eclipsed by Speaker Newt Gingrich as the spokesman of the Republicans. Bob Dole ran for the Republican presidential nomination in 1996. He resigned his position as Senate majority leader and also from the Senate in May 1996.

William C. Binning

Thomas C. du Pont (1863–1930)   Thomas Coleman du Pont, a prominent Wilmington, Delaware, businessman, was appointed to the Republican National Committee in 1908. Using his immense personal wealth, he built a $5 million highway from one end of Delaware to the other and gave it to the people of the state. Though du Pont ran for president in 1916, he had little support at the convention. In 1921, the governor appointed him to fill an unexpired term in the Senate. He lost his 1922 bid for election to the seat in his own right. However, in 1924 du Pont ran for the Senate again and was successful. He resigned from office in 1928 because of failing health.

George F. Edmunds (1828–1919)   The strongly independent George Franklin Edmunds began his public service as a Vermont State Representative (1854–1859), serving the last three years as speaker of the state House. In 1861–1862 he was elected to the state Senate and served there until appointed special counsel in 1864 in the extradition of the St. Albans raiders. Edmunds held strong antislavery views that shaped much of his service in the U.S. Senate, which began in 1866. A supporter of radical policies in Reconstruction, he supplied the needed vote to override President Andrew Johnson's veto of the Civil Rights Bill and opposed the admission of Colorado as a state because of its white suffrage provision. Edmunds is considered to have been one of the greatest constitutional lawyers to serve in the Senate. He chaired the Judiciary Committee from 1872 until his death in 1891. The only piece of legislation to bear his name is an antipolygamy statute. Following the death of President James A. Garfield, Edmunds was elected president pro tempore. He received modest support for president in 1880. However, in 1884 Edmunds was strongly backed by reform elements of the party. He was not a popular member of the Senate because he used his sarcasm against all whom he thought deserving.

Stephen B. Elkins (1841–1911)   Stephen Benton Elkins began his life of public duty by enlisting in the Union army against the wishes of his father and brother, who had enlisted as Confederate soldiers. In 1864 he moved to New Mexico and was elected to the territorial legislature the following year. After his service as territorial attorney general from 1866 to 1872, Elkins was elected as a delegate to the 43rd Congress, serving in that capacity until 1877. Around 1890 he moved to Elkins, West Virginia, a town he had founded. During the presidential campaign of 1884, he was a senior adviser to James G. Blaine. Elkins was an important member of the Republican National Committee for three successive elections. In 1891 he was appointed secretary of war. Elected in 1895 to the U.S. Senate from West Virginia, Elkins served there until his death in 1911.

Rebecca Latimer Felton (1835–1930)   Rebecca Latimer Felton was the first woman senator. In recognition of her work to reform politics, Governor Thomas W. Hardwick of Georgia appointed her to serve in 1922 following the death of one senator but before the winner of the seat could be sworn in. Felton gained a political reputation because of her work with her husband, who was active in Georgia politics. Together, they sought to advance liberal ideas against the more conservative elements in the state. Felton was an ardent advocate of equal rights for women, temperance, and penal reform. Her service in the Senate lasted only one day, as she was sworn in on November 21 and her successor was sworn in the following day.

Simeon D. Fess (1861–1936)   An ardent Republican, Simeon Davidson Fess began his career in public life in 1912 by serving as a member and then as president of Ohio's Constitutional Convention. Later that year, he was elected to the House of Representatives, a position he held until 1922, when he was elevated to the Senate. Regarded as the leader of the Old Guard, Fess was a prominent critic of President Woodrow Wilson. He served as chair of the Republican Congressional Campaign Committee in 1918. In the 1920 presidential campaign, Fess supported Warren G. Harding. In 1922 he defeated incumbent Senator Atlee Pomerene. In the Senate, Fess continued his solid party support. He was a staunch prohibitionist, demanding strict enforcement of the Volstead Act. At the 1928 Republican Presidential Nominating Convention, Fess was the keynote speaker. Upon his reelection to the Senate that year, he became the party whip. In 1930 he was elected to the Republican National Committee. However, in 1932 Fess was forced from the committee by more progressive elements. He was defeated for reelection in 1934 and retired from politics.

William Pitt Fessenden (1806–1869)   Despite his close personal ties to Daniel Webster (his godfather), William Pitt Fessenden of Maine opposed Webster's campaign for president in 1852. He was first elected to the state legislature in 1831 on an anti-Jackson ticket, serving a second term beginning in 1839. In 1840 Fessenden was elected to a single term in the U.S. House of Representatives. He returned to the state legislature for several more single terms in 1845 and 1853. The antislavery majority in the Maine legislature appointed Fessenden to the U.S. Senate in 1854. In his first official speech, he rose in opposition to the Kansas–Nebraska Act. During the Civil War, he chaired the important Finance Committee. In 1864 Fessenden resigned from the Senate upon his appointment as secretary of the treasury. He soon resigned from that post, however, after putting the nation's financial affairs in order. In 1865 he resumed his tenure in the Senate. On December 21, 1865, Fessenden became chair of the Joint Committee on Reconstruction. He believed that the South had few rights as it had been defeated. He also believed that Reconstruction was a legislative, not a presidential, matter. Despite the overwhelming sentiment of the people of Maine, Fessenden voted not guilty in the impeachment trial of President Andrew Johnson. He died before he could face reelection.

William P. Frye (1830–1911)   William Pierce Frye, who as a law student studied under William Pitt Fessenden, served in the Maine legislature in 1861, 1862 and 1867. In 1867 he was elected as the state attorney general. He was first elected to the U.S. House of Representatives in 1871 and served there until chosen as the replacement for Senator James G. Blaine, who resigned to enter President James A. Garfield's cabinet. Serving in the Senate until 1911, Frye earned a reputation as a strict Republican. With the elevation of Teddy Roosevelt to the presidency, Frye became the Senate's permanent presiding officer for five years.

Walter Q. Gresham (1832–1895)   Walter Quitin Gresham's early political life was tied to the issue of slavery. In his youth, he believed that the passage of time would bring a peaceful end to slavery. He spent a short time in the Know-Nothing Party but quickly joined the Republican Party. In 1856, Gresham stumped for the party's standard-bearer, John C. Frémont. In 1860 he was elected to the Indiana legislature. However, with the outbreak of war, Gresham sought a military commission from the governor. When he was refused, he formed a volunteer company and was elected its captain. After fighting at Shiloh and Vicksburg, Gresham was appointed brigadier general in 1863. In 1865 he was promoted to major general for his gallantry at Atlanta. Running for Congress as a Unionist in 1866, he lost. In 1868 Gresham was a state delegate to the Republican National Convention in Chicago. Though offered a number of political patronage positions, he refused most of them. At the 1888 Republican National Convention, Gresham was second on the first ballot. However, the nomination went to the compromise candidate, Benjamin Harrison, on the eighth ballot. By 1892 his growing break with the party would lead Gresham to vote for the Democratic presidential candidate, Grover Cleveland. After Cleveland won, Gresham was offered the post of secretary of state. Gresham declined and instead served as an unofficial adviser to the president on foreign policy issues.

Robert P. Griffin (1923–)   After a successful law practice specializing in labor issues, Robert Paul Griffin defeated the incumbent Ruth Thompson, a staunch conservative and Michigan's first female representative, in the 1956 Republican primary and then won the general election. In the House, Griffin was much more moderate than his predecessor. He served on the House Education and Labor Committee, continuing to work on issues of labor throughout his political career. Reelected in 1958, he served continuously in the House until his appointment to fill a vacancy in the Senate in 1966. Griffin won the seat in his own right later in 1966 and was reelected in 1972. From 1969 until 1977 he served as party whip. Griffin was defeated for reelection in 1978 and retired from public life.

Herbert S. Hadley (1872–1927)   Herbert Spenser Hadley served as attorney general of Missouri from 1905 to 1909. In 1909 he was elected the first Republican governor of the state since Reconstruction. Hadley held that post until 1913, having been defeated for reelection. A progressive Republican, he served as the floor leader of the Theodore Roosevelt forces at the 1912 Presidential Nominating Convention. When William H. Taft secured the nomination, Hadley refused either to bolt the convention or to support the party's standard-bearer.

Charles A. Halleck (1900–1986)   Charles Abraham Halleck of Indiana often referred to himself as Mr. Republican. He was first elected to the House in 1934 to fill the vacancy created by the death of a candidate-elect. He retained that seat until his retirement. In the House, Halleck served as both majority leader (1947, 1953, and 1959) and minority leader (1962–1968). While serving as minority leader, Halleck was instrumental in securing Republican support for the Civil Rights Act of 1964. In the 1960s, along with Senator

Everett M. Dirksen, he attacked Democrats and their policies in press conferences dubbed "The Ev and Charlie Show." Halleck served as the permanent chair of the Republican National Convention in 1960. Often considered a prime candidate for the party's vice presidential nomination, he retired from politics in 1969.

Marcus A. Hanna (1837–1904)   Marcus "Mark" Alonzo Hanna was one of the first politicians to recognize the natural links between business and politics when in 1880 he organized the Cleveland, Ohio, businessmen to support James A. Garfield for president. In 1888 he championed favorite son John Chairman, an Ohio senator, for president. Hanna's contributions to campaigns in Ohio in 1891 helped secure the election of William McKinley as governor. In 1896, due in large part to Hanna's behind-the-scenes efforts, McKinley was nominated as the Republican candidate for president on the first ballot. When selected as chair of the Republican National Committee, Hanna brought professionalism to the organization with paid campaigners and unprecedented national expenditures. Offered the position of postmaster general in McKinley's cabinet, he declined. Instead, Hanna sought and received an appointment as a senator when John Chairman was appointed secretary of state. Hanna's early years in the Senate were not active ones. However, as the issues facing the Senate turned from foreign affairs to business, he became more active. Though a proponent of big business, Hanna was also a firm believer in organized labor. Many of the eastern business interests wanted Hanna to be the standard-bearer in 1904. He declined to pursue the presidency, preferring to play the role of kingmaker.

Mark O. Hatfield (1922–)   Mark Odom Hatfield began his political career as an Oregon State legislator from 1950 to 1954. In 1954 he was elected to the state Senate, where he served until 1956. After serving two years as secretary of state, Hatfield ran for governor in the heavily Democratic state. Despite landslide victories for Democrats nationwide, he was successful in his bid and was reelected in 1962. At the Republican National Convention in 1960, Hatfield was chosen to place Richard M. Nixon's name in nomination. In 1964 he delivered the keynote address at the convention. In 1966 he narrowly won a seat in the United States Senate by stressing both his opposition to President Lyndon B. Johnson's Vietnam policies and the economic problems of his state. Hatfield still holds that seat today. His continued opposition to the war in Vietnam after Nixon replaced Johnson made him a foe of the White House. A liberal Republican, Hatfield often votes with his Democratic colleagues. When he assumed the chair of the Senate Appropriations Committee in 1981, he initially supported President Ronald Reagan's tax and budget cuts. However, along with Democratic Senator William Proxmire, Hatfield organized the Senate to override the president's veto of an appropriations bill in 1982. When the Republicans took control of the Senate after the 1994 midterm elections, Hatfield was once again elevated to chair of the Appropriations Committee. As before, he continued to show his independence by voting against the balanced budget amendment, a cornerstone of the new Republican majority's fiscal plans. Hatfield announced his retirement, to be effective when his current term expires in 1997.

Jesse A. Helms (1921–) Jesse Alexander Helms served two United States senators before returning to North Carolina and being elected to the Raleigh City Council, a post he held from 1957 to 1961. Helms served as an executive in radio from 1960 until 1972. He used his position to air editorials on academic freedom, which he thought had gone too far; busing, which he opposed; the dangers of communism; and government waste. In 1970 the archconservative switched from the Democratic Party to the Republican Party. He defeated a heavily favored Democrat to join the United States Senate in 1972. At the Republican National Convention in 1976, he supported Ronald Reagan but was approached about forming a conservative third party. He won reelection to the Senate in 1978, 1984, and 1990. A strong supporter of the American military and a quasi isolationist, he chairs the powerful Senate Foreign Relations Committee.

George F. Hoar (1826–1904) George Frisbie Hoar was an active player in the formation of the Republican Party in Massachusetts. He served a single term in the state House in 1852 and one in the state Senate in 1857. In 1869, while in England, Hoar was elected to Congress, where he served until his election as a senator in 1877. He was regarded by his colleagues as a man of high morals. While twice offered the post of minister to England, modest financial resources prevented him from accepting. Serving numerous times as a delegate to state and national conventions, Hoar chaired the 1888 Republican National Convention, which nominated James A. Garfield.

Hiram W. Johnson (1886–1945) Hiram Warren Johnson's first taste of politics was as the successful manager of his father's campaign for Congress in 1894. However, Johnson was more attuned with the progressive elements of politics than with the more conservative ones of his father. In 1901, upon the election of a reform candidate whom Johnson had supported for mayor of Sacramento, Johnson was appointed city attorney. As an assistant district attorney, he prosecuted graft in San Francisco. Johnson's success in convicting Abraham Ruef led to his being nominated for governor by the Lincoln–Roosevelt League, a progressive faction within the Republican Party. While easily defeating the other Republican candidates in the primary, Johnson narrowly won the general election of 1910. The reform ticket that he had headed also won control of the legislature. As governor, he proposed many reforms, including the popular reversal of judicial decisions. Johnson did not leave many areas untouched as he reformed primary laws and created a civil service system and conservation commission. His most important piece of legislation was the Public Utilities Act, which increased the power of the railroad commission at the expense of the Southern Pacific Railroad, a company Johnson had targeted as a candidate. At the national level, Johnson was a charter member of the National Progressive Republican League, which supported former President Theodore Roosevelt's bid for the party nomination. He led the California delegates out of the 1912 Republican National Convention when it renominated William H. Taft. He chaired the newly formed third party's convention and was the vice presidential nominee. The Lincoln–Roosevelt League's political influence started to wane after the election of President Woodrow Wilson. However, Johnson continued his political success, being reelected to the governorship in 1914. In 1916 Johnson did not actively campaign for the Republican presidential nominee, Charles Evans Hughes. While Johnson was overwhelmingly elected to the Senate that year, Hughes lost California by a narrow margin and thus the White House. Johnson was charged with party treason for his lackluster support of Hughes. He reluctantly supported President Wilson's call for war but remained a vocal critic of the administration. He became the leader of the "Irreconcilables" in Congress over Wilson's policies regarding the Treaty of Versailles and U.S. entry into the League of Nations. In the 1920 Republican Presidential Nominating Convention, Johnson ran third on the first four ballots. When the nomination finally went to Warren G. Harding, he refused the nomination for vice president. Despite Republican control of Congress and the White House, Johnson often differed with his party in his legislative votes. Domestically he supported the twice-vetoed McNary–Haugen Bill and other western progressive pieces of legislation. In the realm of foreign policy, he led the opposition to joining the World Court and opposed the London Naval Pact. Rather than oppose the renomination of President Herbert Hoover in 1932,

Johnson urged progressives to support the Democratic nominee, Franklin D. Roosevelt. While he was an early supporter of Roosevelt, by 1936 Johnson began to criticize the president's agenda, especially the Court-packing plan. In foreign policy, Johnson attacked the administration's program by voting against nearly every proposal. While opposed to a third term for Roosevelt, he was unhappy with the Republican nomination of Wendell Willkie in 1940. During World War II, Johnson supported the acts necessary to prosecute the war successfully. However, in 1945 his was the lone vote against sending the United Nations Charter to the Senate floor. Because of illness, Johnson was unable to lead the opposition to the adoption of the charter. He died later that year at Bethesda Naval Hospital.

Nancy Kassebaum (1932–)   Nancy Landon Kassebaum was born July 29, 1932, in Topeka, Kansas, the daughter of Alfred M. Landon, the Republican presidential candidate in 1936. She graduated from the University of Kansas, and two years later married Philip Kassebaum, executive of Kassebaum Communications, owner of radio stations in Kansas. From 1975 to 1976 she worked in the Washington office of Senator James B. Pearson. When Pearson decided not to run in 1978, Kassebaum announced her candidacy and easily won the Republican primary and the general election, capitalizing on her father's standing in Kansas politics. She was reelected in 1984 and 1990. In the Senate, Kassebaum generally voted along conservative party lines, except for her limited support of federal funding for abortions. Her record on feminist issues is mixed, and she opposed an extension of time for the ratification of the Equal Rights Amendment. Her field of expertise is foreign affairs and national security, and since 1980 she has been on the prestigious Senate Foreign Relations Committee. Kassebaum announced her intention to resign from the Senate in 1997.

Preston King (1806–1865)   Preston King was elected to the New York Assembly in 1834 and served there until several of his friends were arrested for their participation in the Canadian Rebellion of 1837–1838. The event led to King's breakdown and a short, voluntary stay in an asylum in Hartford, Connecticut. He returned to politics in 1843, being elected to the U.S. House of Representatives. King broke with the Whig Party over the issue of slavery, joining the Free Soil Party at its Buffalo convention of 1848. Though not a candidate, King was elected to Congress on the Free Soil Party ticket in 1848 and reelected in 1850. He supported Franklin Pierce in 1852 but later opposed the Pierce administration and the Kansas–Nebraska Act.

While considered for the vice presidency on the John C. Frémont ticket in 1856, King was instead elected to the Senate. He supported Abraham Lincoln in 1860, serving as chair of the Republican National Committee from 1860 to 1864. At the 1864 Republican National Convention in Baltimore, he urged the nomination of Andrew Johnson as vice president. King retired from the Senate at the end of his 1856 term.

William F. Knowland (1908–1974)   When William Fife Knowland was 12 years old, he made speeches for Warren G. Harding's presidential campaign. At 16 he was the treasurer of his local Coolidge–Dawes Club. Despite a Democratic landslide in the election of 1932, Knowland—at the age of 24—was elected to the California State Assembly. Two years later he was elected to the state Senate. Prior to his service in the army during World War II, Knowland was appointed to the Republican National Committee in 1938, becoming its chair in 1941. While serving in France in 1945, he was appointed to the U.S. Senate to fill the vacated seat of Senator Hiram W. Johnson. A year later Knowland defeated Democratic candidate Will Rogers Jr. for the seat. In 1952 both the Republicans and the Democrats placed his name on the ballot as their candidate for the Senate. Knowland, a moderate Republican, became an active member of the "Young Turks" who challenged the leadership of conservative Senator Robert A. Taft. Although Knowland was nominated for the party leadership in the Senate, the conservative Taft forces defeated him. Taft tried to woo the California senator to support him at the 1952 Presidential Nominating Convention. However, Knowland and the delegates were committed to California Governor Earl Warren. In the end, Knowland was outmaneuvered by Richard M. Nixon, the junior senator from California, who secured the vice presidential nomination. Knowland served as majority leader from 1953 to 1955, when he became minority leader, a post he held until 1958 when he left the Senate to run unsuccessfully for governor of California.

Thomas H. Kuchel (1910–1994)   Thomas Henry Kuchel was elected to the California legislature from Orange County in 1936, at the age of 26. He served there until he won election to the state Senate in 1940, being selected as the chair of the Republican State Central Committee. While serving as a lieutenant in the navy during World War II, Kuchel maintained his seat in the Senate. In 1946 Governor Earl Warren appointed him state controller. He served in that capacity until 1953, when Warren appointed him to replace Senator Richard M. Nixon, who had resigned to accept the post of vice president. Kuchel was reelected to his

Senate seat in 1956 and again in 1962, holding the post of party whip from 1959 to 1969. A moderate Republican, he worked closely with the senior senator from California, William F. Knowland, rather than with fellow Californian Vice President Nixon.

Melvin R. Laird (1922–)   Melvin Robert Laird successfully waged a campaign to fill the Wisconsin State Senate seat vacated by his father's death in 1946. After attending the Republican National Convention in 1948, he stood for reelection unopposed the same year for a full four-year term as a state senator. He chaired the Committee on Taxation, which issued the Laird Report, a standard on the Wisconsin tax system. Again in 1952 Laird was a delegate to the Republican National Convention, where he supported the unsuccessful bid of Senator Robert A. Taft of Ohio. Later that same year he was elected to the United States House of Representatives, where he served until 1969. Laird chaired the Platform Committee at the 1964 Republican National Convention. While he publicly supported the party's nominee, conservative Senator Barry Goldwater, Laird preferred a more moderate candidate who could stress what all Republicans shared. A moderate himself, he left the House in 1969 to assume the heavy responsibility of secretary of defense under President Richard M. Nixon. Serving in that position for Nixon's first term, Laird had the difficult task of constructing an effective Vietnam policy. Although Laird resigned from the cabinet, President Nixon asked to be his chief domestic adviser. Laird was instrumental in the selection of House Minority Leader Gerald R. Ford to replace Spiro T. Agnew following Agnew's resignation of the vice presidency. As the president's role in Watergate became clearer, Laird resigned from his post, believing that Nixon should be impeached.

Henry Cabot Lodge (1850–1924)   Among the many distinctions that Henry Cabot Lodge could claim was that he held the first Ph.D. in political science from Harvard University. In 1882 he ran an unsuccessful campaign for Congress. At the 1884 Republican Presidential Nominating Convention, he worked with Theodore Roosevelt in a failed attempt to prevent the nomination of James G. Blaine of Maine. A party loyalist, however, he actively campaigned for the Blaine ticket. Elected to the House of Representatives in 1886, he was regarded as one of its finest orators. He left the House in 1893 to assume a seat in the Senate, where he served until 1924. Lodge was an odd mix of progressive (in the areas of antitrust legislation and the reform of food and drug production) and conservative (in his opposition to free silver and support for American ex-

pansion in Panama and the Philippines). As a senator, he voted against the direct election of senators, woman suffrage, and the 18th Amendment. As chair of the Foreign Relations Committee, he led the fight against the Treaty of Versailles, opposing the coupling of peace with U.S. entry into the League of Nations.

Henry Cabot Lodge Jr. (1902–1985)   Henry Cabot Lodge Jr., the grandson of Henry Cabot Lodge, began his political career as a committed isolationist. In 1936 he was elected to the United States Senate from Massachusetts. He was reelected in 1942 but resigned when the War Department prohibited short-term service in World War II by legislators between sessions. Having repudiated his isolationist stance, Lodge served as a combat officer in the United States Army. After the war he was reelected to the Senate in 1946. However, he failed in his 1952 reelection bid against John F. Kennedy. President Dwight D. Eisenhower appointed Lodge United States ambassador to the United Nations, where he served from 1953 to 1960. He was the Republican Party's nominee for the vice presidency on the unsuccessful 1960 ticket headed by Vice President Richard M. Nixon. Lodge was regarded as one of the great statesmen of his time. President Kennedy appointed Lodge to serve as ambassador to South Vietnam, a post he held from 1963 to 1967. After Lodge served as ambassador to Germany from 1968 to 1969, President Nixon sent him to the Vietnam peace talks in Paris as one of the chief negotiators. In 1970 Lodge was appointed as special envoy to the Vatican. In 1977 he retired from public life and returned to the Bay State.

William Lorimer (1861–1933)   On July 13, 1912, the U.S. Senate invalidated the 1909 election of William Lorimer from Illinois. His was the last election invalidated under the old system of state legislatures' choosing senators. Known as the Blond Boss because of his powerful machine—which was responsible for the election of three Chicago mayors, two governors, and one senator—Lorimer was elected to the Senate on the 94th ballot by a split Republican Party in the state legislature. His opponents petitioned to have Lorimer's election invalidated because of his bribery of state legislators. The Senate initially exonerated Lorimer in 1910. However, a more progressive Republican Senate voted 55–28 to remove him in 1912.

Joseph R. McCarthy (1908–1957)   Joseph Raymond McCarthy began his political career as a Democrat running unsuccessfully for district attorney of Shawano County, Wisconsin. Later he served as an elected judge of the tenth circuit. While in the marine corps in the Pacific during World War II, McCarthy unsuccessfully sought the Republican nomination for the Senate in 1944. In 1946, with the aid of the conservative Republican Voluntary Committee, he defeated incumbent Republican Senator Robert M. La Follette Jr. in the primary. He easily won the general election that November and remained in the Senate until his death in 1957. McCarthy gained national attention and notoriety for his charge that communists were developing the United States foreign policy in the State Department. When he became chair of the Committee on Government Operations in 1953, McCarthy started an investigation to prove his claims. His hearings, which became vitriolic and petty as time went on, led to a resolution to censure the senator. After lengthy debate and hearings, the Senate voted 67–22 on December 2, 1954, to censure McCarthy for behavior that was "contemptuous, contumacious, and denunciatory." McCarthy spent the remainder of his term as a man without a party.

James McMillan (1838–1902)   James McMillan successfully managed the 1878 congressional campaign of his business partner, John S. Newberry. As chair of the Michigan Republican Committee, he reorganized the party in 1886. McMillan initially refused a nomination for the Senate in 1886 but was unanimously elected by the Republican legislature, serving in the Senate until his death in 1902. While a senator, McMillan was an active member of the Republican circle facetiously called the SOPC (School of Philosophy Club). The group, which included many of the most important party members in the Senate and the administration, met to play cards, shoot billiards, and discuss Republican policies. His most lasting service in the Senate was on the District of Columbia Committee, which developed the future growth and development plans for the city.

Charles L. McNary (1874–1944)   Charles Linza McNary served in a variety of county and state posts, including a stint on the Oregon State Supreme Court, until he was appointed to the United States Senate in 1917, where he remained until his death in February 1944. Considering himself to be a progressive Republican, during World War I McNary supported many of the initiatives of the Woodrow Wilson administration, including the Treaty of Versailles. He was aligned with other western progressives such as Robert M. La Follette of Wisconsin and Hiram W. Johnson of California. However, McNary was also loyal to the party, often serving as the link between the western progressives and the eastern conservatives. During the Great Depression, he supported many of the New Deal programs of Franklin D. Roosevelt, especially the

Tennessee Valley Authority. In 1944 he was the Republican Party's vice presidential nominee on a ticket headed by Wendell Willkie.

Robert H. Michel (1923–)   After serving as a well-decorated World War II combat infantryman and receiving his bachelor's degree from Bradley University, Robert Henry Michel went to Washington, D.C., to serve as administrative assistant to Representative Harold Velde of Illinois from 1949 to 1956. Velde was chair of the House Un-American Activities Committee when he announced in 1956 that he would not seek reelection. Michel defeated the local Republican for the party's nomination and won the general election. He served in the House of Representatives from 1957 until his retirement in 1995. A committed conservative in his early days as a congressman, Michel voted with the conservative coalition of southern Democrats and Republicans. In 1964 he campaigned vigorously for conservative Senator Barry Goldwater against the eastern liberal wing's candidate, Nelson A. Rockefeller. He was a delegate to the Republican National Conventions from 1964 through 1992. In 1966 he was given the post of assistant minority whip for the Midwest. After being warned by Melvin Laird, Michel declined an offer to join Richard M. Nixon's administration as White House congressional liaison. Serving as chair of the National Republican Congressional Campaign Committee from 1973 to 1974, Michel tried to increase the meager Republican numbers in the wake of Watergate. After the disastrous 1974 election, he was chosen minority whip, a post he held until 1981. When John Rhodes did not seek reelection to the post of House minority leader, Michel was selected because, although he was a conservative, he was on good working terms with party moderates. In addition, he was seen as a good parliamentarian and able to arrive at compromises. When Republicans gained control of the White House and Senate in the 1980 election, Michel was able to build a coalition between Republicans and conservative Democrats in order to secure passage of much of President Ronald Reagan's legislative agenda during his first term.

Edwin D. Morgan (1811–1883)   Edwin Denison Morgan began his political career in 1849, when he was elected to the New York City Board of Aldermen. In 1851 he was elected to the state Senate, serving two terms. Morgan was instrumental in the founding of the Republican Party in New York State, serving as the vice president of the conference planning the first convention. He was the chair of the Republican National Committee from 1856 until 1864. In 1858 he was a surprise winner of the governorship, and was reelected in

1860. Three years later, he was chosen to succeed Senator Preston King in the United States Senate. He declined an appointment as secretary of the treasury in 1865. In a bitter contest with Reuben E. Fenton, Morgan was defeated for reelection to the Senate. He again headed the Republican National Committee from 1872 to 1876. In that year, he decided to run for governor. However, the powerful political machine of Senator Roscoe Conkling did not support Morgan, and as a result, he lost. President Chester Arthur nominated Morgan as secretary of the treasury, and although he was confirmed, Morgan declined the appointment and retired from public life.

Oliver H.P.T. Morton (1823–1877)   Oliver Hazard Perry Throck Morton began his career as a Democrat. However, he openly broke with the party because of the Kansas–Nebraska Act and was instrumental in the formation of the Republican Party in Indiana. In 1856 Morton was the party's unsuccessful gubernatorial candidate. In 1860 he was offered the post of lieutenant governor on the ticket headed by Henry S. Lane. He accepted the post because he was promised that if the Republicans were victorious, the legislature would send Lane to the Senate and Morton would be governor. As governor, he believed that the Civil War was necessary and inevitable and actively pursued Unionist policies. He ardently used his office to prosecute the war and prevent any Copperhead gains in Indiana. When the Democrats and pacifists gained control of the state legislature in 1862, he borrowed funds from private citizens and Washington to bypass the legislature. Despite a stroke in the summer of 1865 that left him disabled, Morton refused to retire from politics. In 1867 he was elected to the Senate and served there until his death. He became a strong supporter of thorough Reconstruction of the South rather than the more lenient policies of Presidents Abraham Lincoln and Andrew Johnson. He was a contender for the Republican presidential nomination in 1876 despite his physical condition. However, his inability to raise money and his partisan ways prevented his nomination. In 1877 Morton suffered another stroke and died.

Thruston B. Morton (1907–1982)   Thruston Ballard Morton was first elected to the United States House of Representatives from Kentucky in 1946, and was reelected three times. From 1953 until 1956 he served as assistant secretary of state for congressional relations in the Dwight D. Eisenhower administration. Morton was elected to the United States Senate in 1956, serving until 1969. In the Senate he was the leader of the moderate wing of the Republican Party. He was an early opponent of United States involvement in Vietnam as well as a strong supporter of civil rights legislation. From 1959 to 1961 he served as chair of the Republican National Committee. Declining to run for reelection in 1968, he returned to his home state of Kentucky.

Truman H. Newberry (1864–1945)   Truman Handy Newberry, a wealthy automobile executive, defeated another automobile executive, Henry Ford, in the 1918 campaign for the United States Senate from Michigan. Newberry's campaign, however, spent $176,000 on advertising and publicity even though the Federal Corrupt Practices Act limited spending to $3,750. Ford asked the Senate to investigate Newberry's campaign for violations. While the Senate was holding hearings, Newberry and 134 members of his campaign staff were indicted on a charge of criminal conspiracy. In March 1920 Newberry and 16 codefendants were found guilty. He received a two-year prison sentence and a fine of $10,000. However, the United States Supreme Court voted five to four to overturn the conviction because of an error in the jury instructions. In January 1922 the Senate voted 47–41 to seat Newberry, though it expressed grave concerns about his expenditures. When the controversy continued into the fall, Newberry resigned from the Senate.

George W. Norris (1861–1944)   George William Norris was elected as a Republican to the House of Representatives in 1903 from a heavily populist Nebraska district in a close race in which he defeated the Democratic incumbent. Although elected with the help of the conservative powers of the Republican Party, Norris joined other more liberal Republicans in an attempt to limit the power of House Speaker Joseph Cannon. This failed attempt led to Norris's running his 1908 reelection campaign without the help of either the state or the national party. With the election of William H. Taft to the White House, there was growing tension between the liberal and conservative camps in the Republican Party. In 1910 Norris successfully curbed Cannon's power by having the Rules Committee chosen by election rather than by appointment. He was easily reelected to his fifth term in 1910. Norris was chosen as first vice president of the National Progressive Republican Party, backing Robert M. La Follette for the presidential nomination in 1912. After defeating the incumbent Republican senator, Norris was elected to the Senate in a year in which Nebraska went Democratic. He remained in the Senate for 30 years, until he lost his reelection bid in 1942. In the Senate, Norris continued his independent voting ways. He was critical of the Woodrow Wilson administration but supported World War I once it started. He did not like the strong ties between

Republican administrations and big business and often voted against the confirmation of individuals he thought too connected in both worlds. After the death of Robert M. La Follette, Norris became the leading spokesperson for farm interests and for the public ownership of hydroelectric power. In 1928 he broke with his party and endorsed the candidacy of the Democratic nominee, Alfred E. Smith. In 1932 he endorsed Franklin D. Roosevelt, becoming one of the Senate's strongest supporters for much of the New Deal legislation. Norris authored the Tennessee Valley Authority Act and the Rural Electrification Act. In 1936 he ran as an independent, endorsed by President Roosevelt and the Democratic Party, for reelection to the Senate. In 1942 he was defeated while running again as an independent because of Nebraskans' growing dissatisfaction with the Roosevelt administration.

Thomas C. Platt (1833–1910)   Thomas Collier Platt, a close ally of Roscoe Conkling, was an influential New York political boss. In 1871, along with Conkling, he overthrew Reuben E. Fenton to take control of the party machine. Platt traded political favors in order to win a seat in the House of Representatives in 1873, where he remained until his appointment to the Senate in 1881. As a senator, he did not make a significant mark, although he continued to control the New York machine with Conkling. In 1880 Platt supported the draft–Ulysses S. Grant campaign over the selection of James Garfield of Ohio. When Garfield appointed a political enemy of Conkling's and Platt's to the post of collector for the Port of New York, both senators resigned on May 16, 1881. They believed that the state legislature would reappoint them as a sign of support. However, the legislature in Albany chose others to send to Washington. In 1884 Platt supported James G. Blaine of Maine over incumbent President Chester Arthur when Arthur refused to undo Garfield's appointments. Still in control of the New York machine, Platt traded the votes of the New York delegation in 1888 to Benjamin Harrison in return for the post of secretary of the treasury. Harrison, however, did not keep his bargain and instead appointed Platt as ambassador to Spain. Feeling slighted, Platt did not campaign for the Harrison ticket in 1892, helping Grover Cleveland take New York. At the 1896 Presidential Nominating Convention, Platt worked to have Theodore Roosevelt placed on the ticket as vice president in order to get the progressive governor out of New York. However, Roosevelt's successor, William Odell, became an active progressive after assuming the governorship. Platt returned to the Senate in 1897 and was reelected in 1902, though his power in Washington was limited.

Matthew S. Quay (1833–1904)   Matthew Stanley Quay first gained attention when he secured enough delegates to elect Andrew G. Curtin as governor of Pennsylvania in 1860. During the Civil War, he served as the assistant commissary general and private secretary to the governor. In 1865 he was elected to the state House, where he chaired the Ways and Means Committee. From 1872 until his appointment to the Senate in 1887, Quay held a number of important state positions. He served in the Senate until his death on May 28, 1904. In addition to his tenure in the Senate, Quay served on the Republican National Committee, managing Benjamin Harrison's 1888 campaign.

Jeanette Rankin (1880–1973)   Jeanette Rankin was the first woman ever elected to the U.S. House of Representatives. She was elected in 1916, four years before the 16th Amendment gave women the right to vote. Her home state, Montana, was one of several western states in which women were allowed to vote. A strident pacifist, she voted against U.S. entry into World War I. Rankin was also the first woman to run for the United States Senate. In 1918, after losing a primary contest in the Republican Party, she ran as the candidate of the National Party, a coalition of progressives, farmers, and prohibitionists. Despite her loss in 1918, she was reelected to the House of Representatives in 1940 and was the only member of Congress to vote against entry into World War II. After serving two terms, she retired and spent the rest of her life dedicated to working for peace.

Hiram R. Revels (1827–1901)   On February 25, 1870, the U.S. Senate voted 48–8 to seat Hiram Rhoades Revels of Mississippi—the first black ever elected to that body. Several southern senators objected to the seating of a black man. They charged that the Reconstruction government of Mississippi was illegitimate and that the 14th Amendment was not a valid part of the Constitution. During the Civil War, Revels organized two Negro regiments in Maryland. Prior to coming to the Senate, he was a state senator, elected in 1868. He retired after one term in the Senate in order to assume the presidency of Alcorn University, a post he held for three years. Fundamentally a conservative, Revels worked actively for the Democrats in 1875 to remove the carpetbaggers.

John J. Rhodes (1916–)   John Jacob Rhodes, along with Phoenix City Councilman Barry Goldwater, began a long political friendship when they masterminded the 1950 gubernatorial campaign of Howard Pyle. Rhodes stood for election to the post of attorney general that year; however, he lost. Riding the coattails of President Dwight D. Eisenhower, he was successful in unseating eight-term Democratic Congressman John R. Murdock in 1952. In winning the election, Rhodes became the first Republican congressman from the state of Arizona. Despite many challenges, he remained in the House of Representatives until 1983, having chosen not to stand for reelection in 1982. Rhodes was a conservative, whose voting record shows his strong support for defense and limited federal expenditures on social programs. He worked his way up through the ranks of the House structure. In 1965, in a clash with the new minority leader, Gerald R. Ford, Rhodes was unanimously elected as chair of the Policy Committee, making him the number-four Republican in the House. He opposed almost all of the Great Society legislation of the Lyndon B. Johnson administration. He was one of only 34 Republicans to vote against the Civil Rights Act of 1964. Rhodes supported the Tonkin Gulf Resolution, a vote he later regretted. In 1964 he served as the floor manager for the Goldwater forces at the Republican National Convention. In 1972 he chaired the Platform Committee. When Ford was elevated to the vice presidency in 1973, Rhodes announced his interest in becoming minority leader. He served in that post until his retirement in 1983. While initially believing President Richard M. Nixon to be innocent in regard to Watergate, Rhodes urged the Democratically controlled House Judiciary Committee to conduct an impeachment inquiry. When it became clear that Nixon was deeply involved, Rhodes announced that he would vote for impeachment. Rhodes wrote *The Futile System*, a highly critical examination of Congress in which he argued that an effective minority was as crucial as an effective majority. Rhodes would know because he was in the majority for only the first of the 15 terms he spent in Congress.

George W. Romney (1907–1995)   George Wilcken Romney served as an aide to Democratic Senator David I. Walsh from 1929 to 1930. He remained in Washington, D.C., as a lobbyist for the aluminum industry until 1939. While serving as president of American Motors, Romney became active in Michigan politics. He formed the nonpartisan Citizens for Michigan committee, which sought to write a new state constitution. He served as a delegate to and vice president of the 1961–1962 constitutional convention. He decided to run for governor as a Republican in 1962. Romney succeeded in defeating the incumbent Democratic governor, John B. Swainson. Despite the United Auto Workers' opposition to the new constitution, citizens adopted the charter, which, among its other provisions, lengthened the term of the governor

from two to four years. The rising star was encouraged to run for the Republican presidential nomination in 1964 by former President Dwight D. Eisenhower and former Vice President Richard M. Nixon. Eisenhower and Nixon saw Romney as a moderate alternative to conservative Senator Barry Goldwater and liberal Governor Nelson A. Rockefeller. Romney declined to run. He was, however, reelected in 1964 to the governor's mansion. In 1968 he actively sought the party's presidential nomination but withdrew before the first primary. During President Nixon's first term, Romney served as secretary of housing and urban development.

Dwight M. Sabin (1843–1902)   Dwight May Sabin served as a Minnesota State senator from 1872 to 1875. He was elected to the United States House of Representatives in 1878 for one term and again in 1881 for a single term. In 1882 he was elected to the United States Senate, where he chaired the Committee on Railroads. After being a member of the Republican National Committee from 1878 through 1884, he served as the national chair from 1883 to 1884. He was unsuccessful in his reelection bid in 1888, returning to Minnesota and his railroad and timber interests.

Everett Sanders (1882–1950)   Everett Sanders was elected to the U.S. House of Representatives from Indiana in 1916, serving until 1924. He declined the opportunity to run again for the House in 1924. Instead, he became the director of the speakers' bureau for the Republican National Committee. A personal friend of President Calvin Coolidge, Sanders served as his secretary from 1925 to 1929. In 1932 he began a two-year stint as chair of the Republican National Committee before retiring in Washington, D.C. In his retirement years, he authored a book on President Coolidge, *Coolidge Character*.

Hugh D. Scott Jr. (1900–1994)   Hugh Doggett Scott Jr. was elected to the House of Representatives from Pennsylvania in 1940, serving until 1945, when his reelection bid was unsuccessful. From 1945 until his reelection to the House in 1946, he served on active duty as a lieutenant in the United States Navy. Scott served in the House until 1959, having been elected to the United States Senate in 1958. He was the leader of the liberal wing of the Republican Party in the state of Pennsylvania. In 1960 he considered a run for governor of the state but decided against it when former President Dwight D. Eisenhower convinced Representative William Scranton to run. Staying in the Senate, Scott served there until his retirement from politics in 1977. From 1948 to 1949 he chaired the Republican National Committee, a post he gained for his efforts on behalf of Thomas E. Dewey. He was elected minority leader of the Senate in 1969. During Watergate, Scott defended President Richard M. Nixon until almost the very end. Scott, House Minority Leader John Rhodes, and Senator Barry Goldwater met with Nixon the day before Nixon's resignation to inform the president that he could not be protected from impeachment.

William W. Scranton (1917–)   William Warren Scranton came from a very political family: his mother was a Republican National Committee member from 1928 to 1951. After engaging in several successful business ventures, Scranton entered politics as the special assistant in charge of briefing the press on State Department policy for Secretary of State John Foster Dulles. After Dulles's retirement, Scranton remained in that post for the new secretary of state, former Massachusetts Governor Christian Herter. In addition to this duty, Scranton represented the United States in conferences of the North Atlantic Treaty Organization. Scranton was convinced by the local Republican Committee to run against the incumbent Democratic Congressman Stanley A. Prokop in the heavily Democratic district that included Scranton, Pennsylvania—a town founded by his ancestors. Victorious in the election, Scranton served in Congress only one term. During that term, however, he showed himself to be independent of the party, often siding with the John F. Kennedy administration. As a moderate, he was persuaded by former President Dwight D. Eisenhower to run for governor of Pennsylvania in order to avoid a split of the party between its conservative and liberal wings. In 1964 he stood for the party's presidential nomination as the representative of its moderate-liberal wing. His candidacy was unsuccessful as the conservative forces selected Senator Barry Goldwater on the first ballot. While Scranton did not stand for elected office again, he served as a delegate to the Pennsylvania Constitutional Convention of 1967–1968, on several presidential advisory boards during the Richard M. Nixon and Gerald R. Ford administrations, and as ambassador to the United Nations from 1976 to 1977.

William H. Seward (1801–1872)   Drawn to the anti-Masonic movement in western New York, William Henry Seward was elected to the state's Senate in 1830 at the age of 29. Although he played a prominent leadership role, Seward was defeated for reelection in 1833. Chosen unanimously as the Whig Party's candidate for governor in 1834, he was unsuccessful in his bid. In 1838 Seward again stood as the Whig candidate for governor after a closely fought bid for nomination. He was successful in this second at-

tempt and was reelected in 1840. Seward worked hard for internal improvements even during a recession, which caused the discounting of the bonds issued to finance the projects. He advocated native-language education, a position from which he later backed away. He gained a reputation as an opponent of slavery when he refused to extradite three sailors who had encouraged a fugitive slave to run to New York from Virginia. Seward's growing antislavery sentiment led to his election to the U.S. Senate in 1848. He stood against any compromise on slavery, urging its limitation, and advocated the repeal of the Fugitive Slave Law. Seward supported the presidential candidacies of Zachary Taylor in 1848 and General Winfield Scott in 1852. While the election of 1852 resulted in large Whig loses, the ill-fated Kansas–Nebraska Act reinvigorated the antislavery movement and its leaders, including Seward. At the Republican National Convention of 1860, Seward was a leading candidate for president, but his radical views on slavery deprived him of the nomination. He campaigned vigorously for Abraham Lincoln. After several states had seceded, Seward gave an impassioned speech for Union and called for a constitutional convention of all states to resolve the issue. He accepted the post of secretary of state in the Lincoln cabinet on December 28, 1860. In his famous memorandum "Thoughts for the President's Consideration," Seward advocated waging war on France and Spain as a means of solidifying the Union. Despite this imprudent memo, his conduct as secretary during the war was outstanding. Seward was artful in his dealings with European leaders, including the famed seizure of Mason and Slidell on the *Trent*. Seward encouraged expansion of the Union by purchasing Alaska, negotiating to buy the Danish West Indies (an acquisition that was never ratified), and favoring the annexation of Hawaii. During the Andrew Johnson administration, Seward advocated a conciliatory policy toward the South. Seward drafted many of the president's veto messages and made speeches in support of Johnson. He retired at the end of Johnson's term in 1868. By that time he was almost completely disabled, having been in a carriage accident in 1865 and having been severely beaten in his house on the night of Lincoln's assassination.

John Sherman (1823–1900)   John Sherman was one of many Whig politicians who joined the Republican Party after the collapse of the Whig Party over the issue of slavery. He was first elected to the House of Representatives from Ohio in 1854. He served there until his election as a United States senator in 1861. He was recognized by his colleagues for his knowledge in the area of finance. In the House he had chaired the Ways and Means Committee and in the Senate the Finance Committee. Though he favored a moderate approach to Reconstruction, he voted for most of the radical measures. In 1877 President Rutherford B. Hayes appointed Sherman as secretary of the treasury. In that post he fought against the free coinage of silver and for a protective tariff. Sherman unsuccessfully sought the party's nomination for president in 1880, 1884, and 1888. In 1881 he returned to the Senate, where he remained until his appointment as secretary of state in 1897. He resigned from the William McKinley administration in 1898, when the cabinet voted in favor of war with Spain.

Margaret Chase Smith (1897–1995)   Margaret Chase Smith of Maine was elected to the United States House of Representatives in 1940 to fill the vacancy created by the death of her husband, Clyde Harold Smith. Her first vote in the House was in favor of the Selective Service Act, much to the chagrin of her Republican colleagues. She won reelection to the House for three additional terms. In 1948 she made a successful bid for the United States Senate, serving there until 1973. In both the House and Senate, she had a reputation as a highly independent liberal Republican. She was considered for several prominent posts in the Franklin D. Roosevelt and Harry S. Truman administrations. Smith was an outspoken critic of Senator Joseph McCarthy. From the floor of the Senate in 1950, she gave an impressive speech known as "The Declaration of Conscience" condemning McCarthyism. She also condemned the John F. Kennedy administration's unwillingness to use nuclear weapons if necessary. Soviet Premier Nikita Khrushchev once referred to Smith as "the devil in a disguise of a woman." Smith holds the record for the most roll-call votes without missing one (2,941). Her record would have been even more impressive except that she missed a vote in 1955 when she had been assured that there would be no votes. She was unsuccessful in her 1972 reelection bid and returned to Maine.

Thaddeus Stevens (1792–1868)   Thaddeus Stevens began his political career as part of the anti-Masonic movement. In 1831 he attended the Anti-Masonic Convention in Baltimore, where he gave a rousing speech condemning secret orders. He was a successful candidate for the Pennsylvania House in 1833 on the Anti-Masonic Party ticket, serving until 1841. While in the state legislature, he worked to extend public education and pass a protective tariff. He was elected to the United States House of Representatives as a Whig in 1848. Stevens left Congress in 1853 because he be-

lieved the Whigs to be too moderate on the issue of the extension of slavery into the territories. He returned to Pennsylvania to help found the Republican Party. In 1858 he was reelected to the House as a Republican who denounced slavery and supported a protective tariff. During the Civil War, he chaired the powerful Ways and Means Committee. By 1864 Stevens was committed to the total defeat of the South. Considering the Wade–Davis Bill inadequate, he was interested in reducing the South to territorial status. After President Abraham Lincoln's assassination, Stevens chaired the Joint Committee on Reconstruction and was responsible for the passage of the legislation creating the Freedmen's Bureau and the Civil Rights Act over President Andrew Johnson's vetoes. With the landslide Republican victories of 1866, Stevens used the majority to impose a military Reconstruction and secure the passage of the 15th Amendment. He introduced the impeachment resolution against President Johnson for violating the Tenure of Office Act by removing Secretary of War Edwin M. Stanton in 1868 without seeking congressional approval. Shortly after Johnson's acquittal in 1868, Stevens died.

Charles Sumner (1811–1874)   After practicing law in Boston, Charles Sumner was instrumental in founding the Free Soil Party, which was dedicated to keeping slavery out of the territories. In that same year, 1848, he ran unsuccessfully for Congress. However, in 1851 Sumner was elected to the United States Senate by a coalition of Free Soilers and Democrats. In 1854 he worked to found the Republican Party in opposition to the conservative Whig Party. The following year, after delivering a powerful speech condemning the Kansas–Nebraska Act and the many defenders of slavery, Sumner was severely beaten by Representative Preston Brooks of South Carolina because of his views on slavery and unflattering comments about the representative's relative Senator Andrew Butler. The beating was so severe that Sumner was absent from the Senate for more than three years recovering. In the meantime the legislature in Boston reelected him in 1856. Returning on the eve of the Civil War, Sumner worked to persuade President Abraham Lincoln to emancipate the slaves. Early in the war, he led the legislative effort to secure civil rights for the freedmen. In 1861 he was appointed chair of the Senate Foreign Relations Committee, a post he held until 1871, when he was removed for his opposition to President Ulysses S. Grant's annexation of the Dominican Republic. Sumner joined Thaddeus Stevens in calling for the rigorous Reconstruction of the South. He believed that formulating the plan for Reconstruction was the responsibility of Congress and not the president. During the impeachment trial of President Andrew Johnson, Sumner used his formidable oratorical skills to condemn the president as one of the greatest enemies of the United States. Sumner served in the Senate until March 11, 1874, when he died of a heart attack.

Robert A. Taft (1889–1953)   Robert Alphonso Taft, the son of President and Chief Justice William Howard Taft, began his political career as a legal adviser to Herbert Hoover at both the Food Administration and the American Relief Administration. Many of his ideas about the nature and extent of government were shaped by Hoover. Like Hoover, he opposed big government because of its inefficiency and threats to liberty. He shared Hoover's view of international law and a world court as a solution to political problems. In 1920, after forming a new law firm with his brother, Taft ran successfully for the Ohio legislature. He served there until 1926, the last two years as majority leader and speaker. Taft was elected to one term as a state senator before being defeated in a statewide Democratic landslide in 1932. Upon his election to the United States Senate in 1938, he became one of the leading opponents of the Franklin D. Roosevelt administration in both domestic and foreign policy. During 1939 Taft voted against all the administration's efforts to aid the Allied war effort in Europe. At the 1940 Republican National Convention, internationalist Wendell Willkie defeated isolationist Taft on the sixth ballot. After winning a close reelection campaign in 1944, Taft became the leader of a conservative block of legislators that dominated Capitol Hill for nearly a decade. He used his power to advance his fiscally conservative and isolationist positions. He opposed most of the Harry S. Truman administration's expenditures in foreign affairs, including military aid to Greece and Turkey and the North Atlantic Treaty Organization. In 1948 Taft again failed to secure the Republican nomination, which went to Thomas E. Dewey. In 1950 he became more partisan in his bid for reelection. He supported the investigations by Senator Joseph McCarthy of communists in the government, endorsed U.S. participation in the Korean War, and blamed Truman for China's fall to the communists. In 1952 Taft thought that he would easily secure the Republican nomination for president. He had written a short book, *A Foreign Policy for Americans,* which outlined his views. However, Thomas Dewey and Senator Henry Cabot Lodge Jr. of Massachusetts encouraged Dwight D. Eisenhower to run for the nomination because they disapproved of Taft's isolationist stance. Eisenhower won the nomination but had to cut a deal with Taft in order to gain the senator's support. Eisenhower agreed to much of Taft's domestic policy of fiscal conservatism. Taft and Eisenhower worked closely until Taft's death in the summer of 1953.

Robert A. Taft Jr. (1917–1993)   Robert Alphonso Taft Jr., the grandson of President William Howard Taft and son of Senator Robert A. Taft, began his political career when elected to the Ohio legislature in 1955. He served there from 1956 to 1962, holding the post of majority leader from 1961 to 1962. In 1962 he ran a successful campaign for the House of Representatives. Forgoing reelection to the House, he was unsuccessful in his bid for the United States Senate in 1964. He was reelected to the House of Representatives in 1966 and again in 1968. In 1970 he won a seat in the Senate but failed to win reelection in 1976. Like his father, Taft was a fiscal conservative, urging that the federal government trim its ever-growing expenditures. After losing his reelection bid, he returned to Ohio to practice law.

William H. Thompson (1867–1944)   Persuaded by a wealthy friend, William Hale "Big Bill" Thompson ran a successful campaign for the Chicago Board of Aldermen in 1899. Although he ran as a reformer, Thompson did not participate actively in the affairs of the board and declined to run again in 1901. However, with the help of the powerful William Lorimer, Thompson was elected to the Cook County Board of Commissioners in 1902. He left politics in 1904 to pursue his real love, athletics—founding the Illinois Athletic Club. After Thompson garnered much publicity for his yatching victories, the new boss of Republican politics, Fred Lundin, had Thompson elected mayor of Chicago in 1915. This first term as mayor was one in which Thompson paid little attention to the reforms he had promised. Instead, many critics believed that Lundin was in charge, giving big payoffs on government contracts. After an unsuccessful bid for the United States Senate in 1918, Thompson won reelection as mayor in 1919. In this second term, he began an active program of internal improvements to the city's infrastructure. However, Thompson was also criticized for his handling of a race riot, and the Illinois courts overturned his firing of the school superintendent. Planning a third term as mayor, Thompson was forced to withdraw from the race when a grand jury indicted Lundin and 22 other members of his campaign staff for fraud. In a closely contested race for mayor in 1927, Thompson was reelected with the help of Al Capone. Using strong-arm tactics to replace enemies on the school board, Thompson became the focus of national criticism. He was defeated in his reelection bid in 1931. His 1936 run for governor on the Union Party ticket and his 1939 run for the Republican mayoral nomination both failed.

Strom Thurmond (1902–)   Strom Thurmond began his political career as a populist Democratic governor of South Carolina (1947–1951), where he championed, among other things, an end to the poll tax. Opposed to President Harry S. Truman's desegregation of the United States Army and attempts to secure passage of federal legislation to end racial discrimination, he ran for president on the States' Rights ticket in 1948. Thurmond was elected to the United States Senate in 1954, a seat he holds to this day, as a result of a vigorous write-in campaign when the party passed him over because of his 1948 presidential run. Thurmond is the only United States senator to have been elected as a write-in candidate. As promised, he resigned in 1956 and ran for the full six-year term. In response to the Supreme Court's decision in *Brown* v. *Board of Education* (of Topeka), Thurmond penned a "Declaration of Constitutional Principles," popularly known as "The Southern Manifesto," in which he argued that the Court's decision should be nullified. In 1960 he supported Lyndon B. Johnson for the party's nomination. When the nomination went to John F. Kennedy, he refused to support the ticket. He switched his party affiliation in 1964. Thurmond gained a reputation as an opponent of federal civil rights legislation and holds the record for the longest filibuster in the Senate's history. He became a powerful force in Republican politics at the presidential level. After the failed 1964 run by conservative Senator Barry Goldwater, Thurmond was instrumental in the nomination of Richard M. Nixon in 1968. However, he criticized the administration's deficit spending and ballooning welfare expenditures. In 1976 he supported former Governor Ronald Reagan over the moderate incumbent Gerald Ford. However, he supported John Connally of Texas in 1980 instead of Reagan. At the end of his current term (1997), Thurmond will break another Senate record by being, at the age of 94, the oldest person ever to serve.

Arthur H. Vandenberg (1884–1951)   Arthur Hendrick Vandenberg, the editor of the *Grand Rapids Herald,* was appointed to the Senate in 1928 upon the death of Senator Woodbridge N. Ferris. In the Senate, he was instrumental in the passage of the bill that requires the redistricting of Congress after every census. An early supporter of President Herbert Hoover, he later became a critic as he believed Hoover was not doing enough to end the depression. As a result, Vandenberg voted in favor of most of the early New Deal legislation proposed by President Franklin D. Roosevelt. Winning reelection in 1934, Vandenberg was one of only 25 Republicans in the Senate. Elected minority leader, he was an ardent opponent of the later elements of Roosevelt's plan. He declined the 1936 Republican nomination for vice president. Working with conservative Democrats in the Senate, Vandenberg was successful in defeating New Deal legislation, including the Court-packing plan. An ardent isolationist prior to World War II, he moderated his views while working closely with the Roosevelt administration and others in Congress. He helped the administration get the Senate's approval to participate in the United Nations. President Harry S. Truman appointed him to be a delegate to the first and second United Nations General Assemblies. With little campaigning, Vandenberg was easily reelected in 1946 to the Senate, where he served until his death in 1951. With the Republican takeover in 1946, he was made president pro tempore of the Senate and chair of the Senate Foreign Relations Committee. Again convincing the 1940 Republican presidential candidate, Wendell Willkie, to leave foreign policy out of the election, Vandenberg continued his bipartisan efforts in the area of foreign policy. Those efforts often put him at odds with his fellow Republicans, especially conservatives like Robert A. Taft. Vandenberg supported Truman's decision to send troops to Korea under U.N. guidelines and to station troops in Europe as part of the North Atlantic Treaty Organization, despite his deep concerns about those decisions.

Benjamin F. Wade (1800–1878)   Benjamin Franklin Wade was elected to the United States Senate by the Whig majority in the Ohio legislature in 1851 after serving for four years as president–judge of the Third State Judicial Circuit. He remained in the Senate until 1869. During his tenure, he was a forceful member of the radical Republicans, who believed that the Civil War was being poorly executed by the Abraham Lincoln administration. An early critic of General George B. McClellan, Wade was selected to chair the uncompromising Committee on the Conduct of the War. After Lincoln vetoed the Wade–Davis Bill, Wade, with Senator Henry W. Davis, issued the Wade–Davis Manifesto, which claimed supremacy for the legislature, not the president. Although he supported replacing Lincoln with Salmon P. Chase, Wade campaigned for Lincoln in 1864. When President Andrew Johnson proved to be as reluctant as Lincoln to engage in harsh Reconstruction tactics, Wade began to attack the president. Chosen president pro tempore of the Senate in 1867, Wade worked for the impeachment of Johnson, which would have meant his own elevation to the presidency. In 1868 he lost his bid for reelection and retired to practice law in Ohio.

James E. Watson (1863–1948)   James Eli Watson, who at the age of 12 accompanied his father to the 1876 Presidential Nominating Convention, first gained public office in 1894, when he defeated incumbent Democrat William S. Holman for a seat from Indiana in the House of Representatives. Although defeated for reelection in 1896, Watson was returned to the House in 1898 and served five consecutive terms. Aligned with the Old Guard Republicans, Watson was elevated to party whip by House Speaker Joseph G. Cannon. In 1908 he ran unsuccessfully for governor of Indiana. At the 1912 Presidential Nominating Convention, he was the effective floor leader of the William Howard Taft forces. Watson was elected to the Senate in 1918 to fill the unexpired term of Benjamin F. Shively. He was reelected to full terms in 1920 and 1926. Throughout his years in the Senate, Watson was a consistent member of the conservative wing of the Republican Party, believing in high tariffs and isolationism, although he did support the passage of the 19th Amendment and the McNary–Haugen Bill to raise farm price supports. Watson retired from politics in 1932 after having served as majority leader since 1928, during which time he had considerable differences of opinion with President Herbert Hoover, whom he had opposed for the 1928 presidential nomination.

Wallace H. White Jr. (1877–1952)   Wallace Humphrey White Jr., the grandson of Senator William P. Frye of Maine, was elected to the United States House of Representatives from Maine in 1916. Early in his congressional career, he took an interest in the regulation of the radio industry, securing the passage of several pieces of legislation that bore his name. He stayed in the House until 1930, when he was elected to the United States Senate. In 1934 he wrote the Communications Act, which established the Federal Communications Commission. He continued to sponsor legislation to reorganize the commission and to better regulate the radio industry. From 1944 to 1947 he served as minority leader in the Senate. He became majority leader in 1947, serving until his retirement from office in 1949.

Leonard Wood (1860–1927)   Leonard Wood, a military surgeon, became the personal physician to President William McKinley in 1895 after having served in several campaigns in the West. Later Wood joined Theodore Roosevelt's Rough Riders and led the first assault at Las Guásimas, Cuba. After the end of the Spanish-American War, he became the military governor of Santiago. Under his leadership the city was restored to its prewar charm. In December 1899, he was appointed the military governor of Cuba. For three years he worked to improve the conditions of the island's educational system, police operations and infrastructure. In 1903 he was made governor of the Moro Province of the Philippines, serving there until 1906. In 1910 he returned to Washington, D.C., to assume the post of army chief of staff and to oversee the reorganization of the War Department. When he was passed over for command during World War I, Wood sought the 1920 Republican presidential nomination in Chicago. Despite considerable delegate support, he failed to capture the nomination. After a brief stint on a special mission to the Philippines, Wood was appointed governor-general of the territory, a post he held until his death in 1927.

Members of Congress

AANDAHL, Fred George (N.Dak.) April 9, 1897–April 7, 1966; House 1951–53; Gov. Jan. 4, 1945–Jan. 3, 1951.

ABBOT, Joel (Ga.) March 17, 1776–Nov. 19, 1826; House 1817–25.

ABBOTT, Joseph Carter (N.C.) July 15, 1825–Oct. 8, 1881; Senate July 14, 1868–71.

ABBOTT, Nehemiah (Maine) March 29, 1804–July 26, 1877; House 1857–59.

ABDNOR, James (S.Dak.) Feb. 13, 1923–; House 1973–81; Senate 1981–87.

ABEL, Hazel Hempell (Nebr.) July 10, 1888–July 30, 1966; Senate, Nov. 8–Dec 31, 1954.

ABELE, Homer E. (Ohio) Nov. 21, 1916–; House 1963–65.

ABRAHAM, Spencer (Mich.) Senate, 1995–.

ACHESON, Ernest Francis (Pa.) Sept. 19, 1855–May 16, 1917; House 1895–1909.

ACKERMAN, Ernest Robinson (N.J.) June 17, 1863–Oct. 18, 1931; House 1919–Oct. 18, 1931.

ADAIR, Edwin Ross (Ind.) Dec. 14, 1907–May 5, 1983; House 1951–71.

ADAMS, Charles Francis (son of John Quincy Adams, grandson of President John Adams) (Mass.) Aug. 18, 1807–Nov. 21, 1886; House 1859–May 1, 1861.

ADAMS, Charles Henry (N.Y.) April 10, 1824–Dec. 15, 1902; House 1875–77.

ADAMS, George Everett (Ill.) June 18, 1840–Oct. 5, 1917; House 1883–91.

ADAMS, Henry Cullen (Wis.) Nov. 28, 1850–July 9, 1906; House 1903–July 9, 1906.

ADAMS, Robert Jr. (Pa.) Feb. 26, 1849–June 1, 1906; House Dec. 19, 1893–June 1, 1906.

ADAMS, Sherman (N.H.) Jan. 8, 1899–Oct. 27, 1986; House 1945–47; Gov. Jan. 6, 1949–Jan. 1, 1953.

ADAMS, Silas (Ky.) Feb. 9, 1839–May 5, 1896; House 1893–95.

ADGATE, Asa (N.Y.) Nov. 17, 1767–Feb. 15, 1832; House June 7, 1815–17.

ADKINS, Charles (Ill.) Feb. 7, 1863–March 31, 1941; House 1925–33.

AIKEN, George David (Vt.) Aug. 20, 1892–Nov. 19, 1984; Senate Jan. 10, 1941–75; Chrmn. Senate Expenditures in the Executive Departments 1947–49; Chrmn. Senate Agriculture and Forestry 1953–55; Gov. Jan. 7, 1937–Jan. 9, 1941.

AINEY, William David Blakeslee (Pa.) April 8, 1864–Sept. 4, 1932; House Nov. 7, 1911–15.

AITKEN, David Demerest (Mich.) Sept. 5, 1853–May 26, 1930; House 1893–97.

ALBAUGH, Walter Hugh (Ohio) January 2, 1890–Jan. 2, 1942; House Nov. 8, 1938–39.

ALBERT, William Julian (Md.) Aug. 4, 1816–March 29, 1879; House 1873–75.

ALBRIGHT, Charles Jefferson (Ohio) May 9, 1816–Oct. 21, 1883; House 1855–57.

ALCORN, James Lusk (Miss.) Nov. 4, 1816–Dec. 19, 1894; Senate Dec. 1, 1871–77; Gov. March 10, 1870–Nov. 30, 1871.

ALDRICH, Cyrus (Minn.) June l8, 1808–Oct. 5, 1871; House 1859–63.

ALDRICH, James Franklin (son of William Aldrich) (Ill.) April 6, 1853–March 8, 1933; House 1893–97.

ALDRICH, Nelson Wilmarth (father of Richard Steere Aldrich, cousin of William Aldrich, great-grandfather of John Davison "Jay" Rockefeller IV, grandfather of Vice Pres. Nelson Aldrich Rockefeller and Gov. Winthrop Rockefeller of Ark.) (R.I.) Nov. 6, 1841–April 16, 1915; House 1879–Oct. 1, 1881; Senate Oct. 5, 1881–1911.

ALDRICH, Richard Steere (son of Nelson Wilmarth Aldrich, great-uncle of John Davison "Jay" Rockefeller IV, uncle of Vice Pres. Nelson Aldrich Rockefeller of Ark.) (R.I.) Feb. 29, 1884–Dec. 25, 1941; House 1923–33.

ALDRICH, Truman Heminway (brother of William Farrington Aldrich) (Ala.) Oct. 17, 1848–April 28, 1932; House June 9, 1896–97.

ALDRICH, William (father of James Franklin Aldrich, cousin of Nelson Wilmarth Aldrich) (Ill.) Jan. 19, 1820–Dec. 3, 1885; House 1877–83.

ALDRICH, William Farrington (brother of Truman Heminway Aldrich) (Ala.) March 11, 1853–Oct. 30, 1925; House March 13, 1896–97, Feb. 9, 1898–99, March 8, 1900–01.

ALEXANDER, De Alva Stanwood (N.Y.) July 17, 1846–Jan. 30, 1925; House 1897–1911.

ALEXANDER, Evan Shelby (cousin of Nathaniel Alexander) (N.C.) about 1767–Oct. 28, 1809; House Feb. 24, 1806–09.

ALEXANDER, John (Ohio) April 16, 1777–June 28, 1848; House 1813–17.

ALEXANDER, John Grant (Minn.) July 16, 1893–Dec. 8, 1971; House 1939–41.

ALEXANDER, Nathaniel (cousin of Evan Shelby Alexander) (N.C.) March 5, 1756–March 7, 1808; House 1803–Nov. 1805; Gov. Dec. 10, 1805–Dec. 1, 1807 (Democratic Republican).

ALGER, Bruce Reynolds (Tex.) June 12, 1918–; House 1955–65.

ALGER, Russell Alexander (Mich.) Feb. 27, 1836–Jan. 24, 1907; Senate Sept. 27, 1902–Jan. 24, 1907; Gov. Jan. 1, 1885–Jan. 1, 1887; Secy. of War March 5, 1897–Aug. 1, 1899.

ALLARD, Wayne (Colo.) Dec. 2, 1943–; House 1991–.

ALLEE, James Frank (Del.) Dec. 2, 1857–Oct. 12, 1938; Senate March 2, 1903–07.

ALLEN, Amos Lawrence (Maine) March 17, 1837–Feb. 20, 1911; House Nov. 6, 1899–Feb. 20, 1911.

ALLEN, Clarence Emir (Utah) Sept. 8, 1852–July 9, 1932; House Jan. 4, 1896–97.

ALLEN, Edward Payson (Mich.) Oct. 28, 1839–Nov. 25, 1909; House 1887–91.

ALLEN, George Felix (Va.) March 8, 1952–; House Nov. 12, 1991–93; Gov. Jan. 15, 1994–.

ALLEN, Heman (Vt.) Feb. 23, 1779–April 7, 1852; House 1817–April 20, 1818.

ALLEN, Henry Crosby (N.J.) May 13, 1872–March 7, 1942; House 1905–07.

ALLEN, Henry Justin (Kans.) Sept. 11, 1868–Jan. 17, 1950; Senate April 1, 1929–Nov. 30, 1930; Gov. Jan. 13, 1919–Jan. 8, 1923.

ALLEN, John Beard (Wash.) May 18, 1845–Jan. 28, 1903; House (Terr. Del.) March 4–Nov. 11, 1889; Senate Nov. 20, 1889–93.

ALLEN, John Clayton (Ill.) Feb. 14, 1860–Jan. 12, 1939; House 1925–33.

ALLEN, John Joseph Jr. (Calif.) Nov. 27, 1899–; House 1947–59.

ALLEN, Leo Elwood (Ill.) Oct. 5, 1898–Jan. 19, 1973; House 1933–61; Chrmn. House Rules 1947–49, 1953–55.

ALLEY, John Bassett (Mass.) Jan. 7, 1817–Jan. 19, 1896; House 1859–67.

ALLISON, William Boyd (Iowa) March 2, 1829–Aug. 4, 1908; House 1863–71; Senate 1873–Aug. 4, 1908.

ALLOTT, Gordon Llewellyn (Colo.) Jan. 2, 1907–Jan. 17, 1989; Senate 1955–73.

ALSTON, Lemuel James (S.C.) 1760–1836; House 1807–11.

AMBLER, Jacob A. (Ohio) Feb. 18, 1829–Sept. 22, 1906; House 1869–73.

AMES, Adelbert (father of Butler Ames, son-in-law of Benjamin Franklin Butler) (Miss.) Oct. 31, 1835–April 12, 1933; Senate Feb. 23, 1870–Jan. 10, 1874; Gov. June 15, 1868–March 10, 1870 (Military), Jan. 4, 1874–March 20, 1876.

AMES, Butler (son of Adelbert Ames, grandson of Benjamin Franklin Butler) (Mass.) Aug. 22, 1871–Nov. 6, 1954; House 1903–13.

AMES, Oakes (Mass.) Jan. 10, 1804–May 8, 1873; House 1863–73.

ANDERSEN, Herman Carl (Minn.) Jan. 27, 1897–July 26, 1978; House 1939–63.

ANDERSON, George Washington (Mo.) May 22, 1832–Feb. 26, 1902; House 1865–69.

ANDERSON, Isaac (Pa.) Nov. 23, 760–Oct. 27,1838; House 1803–07.

ANDERSON, John Alexander (Kans.) June 26, 1834–May 18, 1892; House 1879–91 (1879–87 Republican, 1887–89 Independent Republican).

ANDERSON, John Bayard (Ill.) Feb. 15, 1922–; House 1961–81.

ANDERSON, John Zuinglius (Calif.) March 22, 1904–Feb. 9, 1981; House 1939–63.

ANDERSON, Richard Clough Jr. (Ky.) Aug. 4, 1788–July 24, 1826; House 1817–21.

ANDERSON, Sydney (Minn.) Sept. 18, 1881–Oct. 8, 1948; House 1911–25.

ANDERSON, William (Pa.) 1762–Dec. 16, 1821; House 1809–15, 1817–19.

ANDERSON, William Coleman (Tenn.) July 10, 1853–Sept. 8, 1902; House 1895–97.

ANDRESEN, August Herman (Minn.) Oct. 11, 1890–Jan. 14, 1958; House 1925–33, 1935–Jan. 14, 1958.

ANDREW, Abram Piatt Jr. (Mass.) Feb. 12, 1873–June 3, 1936; House Sept. 27, 1921–June 3, 1936.

ANDREWS, Arthur Glenn (Ala.) Jan. 15, 1909–; House 1965–67.

ANDREWS, Mark (N.Dak.) May 19, 1926–; House Oct. 22, 1963–81; Senate 1981–87.

ANDREWS, Samuel George (N.Y.) Oct. 16, 1796–June 11, 1863; House 1857–59.

ANDREWS, Walter Gresham (N.Y.) July 16, 1889–March 5, 1949; House 1931–49; Chrmn. House Armed Services 1947–49.

ANDREWS, William Ezekiel (Nebr.) Dec. 17, 1854–Jan. 19, 1942; House 1895–97, 1919–23.

ANDREWS, William Henry (N.Mex.) Jan. 14, 1846–Jan. 16, 1919; House (Terr. Del.) 1905–Jan. 7, 1912.

ANDREWS, William Noble (Md.) Nov. 13, 1876–Dec. 27, 1937; House 1919–21.

ANDRUS, John Emory (N.Y.) Feb. 16, 1841–Dec. 26, 1934; House 1905–13.

ANGELL, Homer Daniel (Oreg.) Jan. 12, 1875–March 31, 1968; House 1939–55.

ANKENY, Levi (Wash.) Aug. 1, 1844–March 29, 1921; Senate 1903–09.

ANSORGE, Martin Charles (N.Y.) Jan. 1, 1882–Feb. 4, 1967; House 1921–23.

ANTHONY, Daniel Read Jr. (Kans.) Aug. 22, 1870–Aug. 4, 1931; House May 23, 1907–29.

ANTHONY, Henry Bowen (R.I.) April 1, 1815–Sept. 2, 1884; Senate 1859–Sept.–2, 1884; elected Pres. pro tempore March 23, 1869, April 9, 1869, May 28, 1870, July 1, 1870, July 14, 1870, March 10, 1871, April 17, 1871, May 23, 1871, Dec. 21, 1871, Feb. 23, 1872, June 8, 1872, Dec. 4, 1872, Dec. 13, 1872, Dec. 20, 1872, Jan. 24, 1873, Jan. 23, 1875, Feb. 15, 1875; Gov. May 1, 1849–May 6, 1851 (Whig).

APLIN, Henry Harrison (Mich.) April 15, 1841–July 23, 1910; House Oct. 20, 1901–03.

APPLEBY, Stewart Hoffman (son of Theodore Frank Appleby) (N.J.) May 17, 1890–Jan. 12, 1964; House Nov. 3, 1925–27.

APPLEBY, Theodore Frank (father of Stewart Hoffman Appleby) (N.J.) Oct. 10, 1864–Dec. 15, 1924; House 1921–23.

APSLEY, Lewis Dewart (Mass.) Sept. 29, 1852–April 11, 1925; House 1893–97.

ARCHER, John (father of Stevenson Archer, grandfather of Stevenson Archer born in 1827) (Md.) May 5, 1741–Sept. 28, 1810; House 1801–07.

ARCHER, Stevenson (son of John Archer) (Md.) Oct. 11, 1786–June 26, 1848; House Oct. 26, 1811–17, 1819–21.

ARCHER, William Reynolds Jr. (Tex.) March 22, 1928–; House 1971–Chrmn. House Ways and Measures Committee, 1995–.

ARENDS, Leslie Cornelius (Ill.) Sept. 27, 1895–July 17, 1895; House 1935–Dec. 31, 1974.

ARENTZ, Samuel Shaw "Ulysses" (Nev.) Jan. 8, 1879–June 17, 1934; House 1921–23, 1925–33.

ARMEY, Richard Keith (Tex.) July 7, 1940–; House 1985–; Majority leader 1995–.

ARMSTRONG, Orland Kay (Mo.) Oct. 2, 1893–April 15, 1987; House 1951–53.

ARMSTRONG, William Hepburn (Pa.) Sept. 7, 1824–May 14, 1919; House 1869–71.

ARMSTRONG, William Lester (Colo.) March 16, 1937–; House 1973–79; Senate 1979–91.

ARNELL, Samuel Mayes (Tenn.) May 3, 1833–July 20, 1903; House July 24, 1866–71 (July 24, 1866–67 Unconditional Unionist).

ARNOLD, Isaac Newton (Ill.) Nov. 30, 1815–April 24, 1884; House 1861–65.

ARNOLD, Samuel Greene (great-uncle of Theodore Francis Green) (R.I.) April 12, 1821–Feb. 14, 1880; Senate Dec. 1, 1862–63.

ARNOLD, Samuel Washington (Mo.) Sept. 21, 1879–Dec. 18, 1961; House 1943–49.

ARNOLD, Warren Otis (R.I.) June 3, 1839–April 1, 1910; House 1887–91, 1895–97.

ARNOLD, William Carlile (Pa.) July 15, 1851–March 20, 1906; House 1895–99.

ASHBROOK, Jean Spencer (widow of John Milan Ashbrook, daughter-in-law of William Albert Ashbrook) (Ohio) Sept. 21, 1934–; House July 12, 1982–83.

ASHBROOK, John Milan (husband of Jean Spencer Ashbrook, son of William Albert Ashbrook) (Ohio) Sept. 21, 1928–April 24, 1982; House 1961–April 24, 1982.

ASHCROFT, John (Mo.) May 9, 1942–; Senate, 1995–.

ASHLEY, Delos Rodeyn (Nev.) Feb. 19, 1828–July 18, 1873; House 1865–69.

ASHLEY, James Mitchell (great-grandfather of Thomas William Ludlow Ashley) (Ohio) Nov. 14, 1824–Sept. 16, 1896; House 1859–69; Gov. (Mont. Terr.) 1869–70.

ASPER, Joel Funk (Mo.) April 20, 1822–Oct. 1, 1872; House 1869–71.

ATKESON, William Oscar (Mo.) Aug. 24, 1854–Oct. 16, 1931; House 1921–23.

ATKINSON, Eugene Vincent (Pa.) April 5, 1927–; House 1979–83 (1979–Oct. 14, 1981 Democrat).

ATKINSON, George Wesley (W.Va.) June 29, 1845–April 4, 1925; House Feb. 26, 1890–91; Gov. March 4, 1897–March 4, 1901.

ATKINSON, Louis Evans (Pa.) April 16, 1841–Feb. 5, 1910; House 1883–93.

ATWOOD, David (Wis.) Dec. 15, 1815–Dec. 11, 1889; House Feb. 23, 1870–71.

ATWOOD, Harrison Henry (Mass.) Aug. 26, 1863–Oct. 22, 1954; House 1895–97.

AUCHINCLOSS, James Coats (N.J.) Jan. 19, 1885–Oct. 2, 1976; House 1943–65.

AUSTIN, Albert Elmer (stepfather of Clare Boothe Luce) (Conn.) Nov. 15, 1877–Jan. 26, 1942; House 1939–41.

AUSTIN, Archibald (Va.) Aug. 11, 1772–Oct. 16,1837; House 1817–19.

AUSTIN, Richard Wilson (Tenn.) Aug. 26, 1857–April 20, 1919; House 1909–19.

AUSTIN, Warren Robinson (Vt.) Nov. 12, 1877–Dec. 25, 1962; Senate April 1, 1931–Aug. 2, 1946.

AVERILL, John Thomas (Minn.) March 1, 1825–Oct. 3, 1889; House 1871–75.

AVERY, Daniel (N.Y.) Sept. 18, 1766–Jan. 30, 1842; House 1811–15, Sept. 30, 1816–17.

AVERY, John (Mich.) Feb. 29, 1824–Jan. 21, 1914; House 1893–97.

AVERY, William Henry (Kans.) Aug. 11, 1911–; House 1955–65; Gov. Jan. 11, 1965–Jan. 9, 1967.

AVIS, Samuel Brashear (W.Va.) Feb. 19, 1872–June 8, 1924; House 1913–15.

AYER, Richard Small (Va.) Oct. 9,1829–Dec. 14, 1896; House Jan. 31, 1870–71.

AYRES, William Hanes (Ohio) Feb. 5, 1916–; House 1951–71.

BABBITT, Elijah (Pa.) July 29, 1795–Jan. 9, 1887; House 1859–63.

BABCOCK, Joseph Weeks (grandson of Joseph Weeks) (Wis.) March 6, 1850–April 27, 1909; House 1893–1907.

BACHARACH, Isaac (N.J.) Jan. 5, 1870–Sept. 5, 1956; House 1915–37.

BACHMANN, Carl George (W.Va.) May 14, 1890–Jan. 22, 1980; House 1925–33.

BACHUS, Spencer (Ala.) Dec. 28, 1947–; House 1993–.

BACON, Ezekiel (son of John Bacon, father of William Johnson Bacon) (Mass.) Sept. 1, 1776–Oct. 18, 1870; House Sept. 16, 1807–13.

BACON, John (father of Ezekiel Bacon, grandfather of William Johnson Bacon) (Mass.) April 5, 1738–Oct. 25, 1820; House 1801–03.

BACON, Mark Reeves (Mich.) Feb. 29, 1852–Aug. 20, 1941; House March 4–Dec. 13, 1917.

BACON, Robert Low (N.Y.) July 23, 1884–Sept. 12, 1938; House 1923–Sept. 12, 1938.

BACON, William Johnson (son of Ezekiel Bacon, grandson of John Bacon) (N.Y.) Feb. 18, 1803–July 3, 1889; House 1877–79.

BADHAM, Robert Edward (Calif.) June 9, 1929–; House 1977–89.

BAER, John Miller (N.Dak.) March 29, 1886–Feb. 18, 1970; House July 10, 1917–21.

BAFALIS, Louis Arthur (Fla.) Sept. 28, 1929–; House 1973–83.

BAGLEY, George Augustus (N.Y.) July 22, 1826–May 12, 1915; House 1875–79.

BAILEY, Alexander Hamilton (N.Y.) Aug.14, 1817–April 20, 1874; House Nov. 30, 1867–71.

BAILEY, Goldsmith Fox (Mass.) July 17, 1823–May 8, 1862; House 1861–May 8, 1862.

BAILEY, John Mosher (N.Y.) Aug. 24, 1838–Feb. 21, 1916; House Nov. 5, 1878–81.

BAILEY, Ralph Emerson (Mo.) July 14, 1878–April 8, 1948; House 1925–27.

BAILEY, Wendell (Mo.) July 30, 1940–; House 1981–83.

BAILEY, Willis Joshua (Kans.) Oct. 12, 1854–May 19, 1932; House 1899–1901; Gov. Jan. 12, 1903–Jan. 9, 1905.

BAIRD, David (father of David Baird Jr.) (N.J.) April 7, 1839–Feb. 25, 1927; Senate Feb. 23, 1918–19.

BAIRD, David Jr. (son of David Baird) (N.J.) Oct. 10, 1881–Feb. 28, 1955; Senate Nov. 30, 1929–Dec. 2, 1930.

BAIRD, Joseph Edward (Ohio) Nov. 12, 1865–June 14, 1942; House 1929–31.

BAKER, Charles Simeon (N.Y.) Feb. 18, 1839–April 21, 1902; House 1885–91.

BAKER, Edward Dickinson (Oreg.) Feb. 24, 1811–Oct. 21, 1861; House 1845–Jan. 15, 1847 (Whig Ill.), 1849–51 (Whig Ill.); Senate Oct. 2, 1860–Oct. 21, 1861.

BAKER, Ezra (N.J.) ?–?; House 1815–17.

BAKER, Henry Moore (N.H.) Jan. 11, 1841–May 30, 1912; House 1893–97.

BAKER, Howard Henry (husband of Irene Bailey Baker, father of Howard Henry Baker Jr.) (Tenn.) Jan. 12, 1902–Jan. 7, 1964; House 1951–Jan. 7, 1964.

BAKER, Howard Henry Jr. (son of Howard Henry Baker, stepson of Irene Bailey Baker, son-in-law of Everett McKinley Dirksen) (Tenn.) Nov. 15, 1925–; Senate 1967–85; Senate minority leader 1977–81; Senate majority leader 1981–85.

BAKER, Irene Bailey (widow of Howard Henry Baker, stepmother of Howard Henry Baker Jr.) (Tenn.) Nov. 17, 1901–; House March 10, 1964–65.

BAKER, John Harris (brother of Lucien Baker) (Ind.) Feb. 28, 1832–Oct. 21, 1915; House 1875–81.

BAKER, LaMar (Tenn.) Dec. 29, 1915–; House 1971–75.

BAKER, Lucien (brother of John Harris Baker) (Kans.) June 8, 1846–June 21, 1907; Senate 1895–1901.

BAKER, Richard Hugh (La.) May 22, 1948–; House 1987–.

BAKER, Stephen (N.Y.) Aug. 12, 1819–June 9, 1875; House 1861–63.

BAKER, William Benjamin (Md.) July 22, 1840–May 17, 1911; House 1895–1901.

BAKER, William Henry (N.Y.) Jan. 17, 1827–Nov. 25, 1911; House 1875–79.

BAKER, William Pond (Calif.) June 14, 1940–; House 1993–.

BAKEWELL, Charles Montague (Conn.) April 24, 1867–Sept. 19, 1957; House 1933–35.

BAKEWELL, Claude Ignatius (Mo.) Aug. 9, 1912–March 18, 1987; House 1947–49, March 9, 1951–53.

BALDRIDGE, Howard Malcolm (Nebr.) June 23, 1894–Jan. 19, 1985; House 1931–33.

BALDWIN, Henry Alexander (Hawaii) Jan. 12, 1871–Oct. 8, 1946; House (Terr. Del.) March 25, 1922–23.

BALDWIN, Henry Porter (Mich.) Feb. 22, 1814–Dec. 31, 1892; Senate Nov. 17, 1879–81; Gov. Jan. 6, 1869–Jan. 1, 1873.

BALDWIN, John Denison (Mass.) Sept. 28, 1809–July 8, 1883; House 1863–69.

BALDWIN, John Finley Jr. (Calif.) June 28, 1915–March 9, 1966; House 1956–March 9, 1966.

BALDWIN, Joseph Clark (N.Y.) Jan. 11, 1897–Oct. 27, 1957; House March 11, 1941–47.

BALDWIN, Raymond Earl (Conn.) Aug. 31, 1893–Oct. 4, 1986; Senate Dec. 27, 1946–Dec. 16, 1949; Gov. Jan. 4, 1939–Jan. 8, 1941, Jan. 6, 1943–Dec. 27.

BALL, Joseph Hurst (Minn.) Nov. 3, 1905–Dec. 18, 1993; Senate Oct. 14, 1940–Nov. 17, 1942, 1943–49.

BALL, Lewis Heisler (Del.) Sept. 21, 1861–Oct. 18, 1932; House 1901–03; Senate March 3, 1903–05, 1919–25.

BALL, Thomas Raymond (Conn.) Feb. 12, 1896–June 16, 1943; House 1939–41.

BALL, William Lee (Va.) Jan. 2, 1781–Feb. 28, 1824; House 1817–Feb. 28, 1824.

BALLENGER, Cass (great-great-grandson of Lewis Cass) (N.C.) Dec. 6, 1926–; House 1987–.

BALLOU, Latimer Whipple (R.I.) March 1, 1812–May 9, 1900; House 1875–81.

BANKS, Nathaniel Prentice (Mass.) Jan. 30, 1816–Sept. 1, 1894; House 1853–Dec. 24, 1857, Dec. 4, 1865–73, 1875–79, 1889–91 (1853–55 Democrat, 1855–57 American Party, March 4–Dec. 24, 1857 Republican, Dec. 4, 1865–67 Union Republican, 1867–73 Republican, 1875–77 Independent); Speaker Feb. 2, 1856–57; Gov. Jan. 6, 1858–Jan. 2, 1861.

BANNON, Henry Towne (Ohio) June 5, 1867–Sept. 6, 1950; House 1905–09.

BANTA, Parke Monroe (Mo.) Nov. 21, 1891–May 12, 1970; House 1947–49.

BARBER, Hiram Jr. (Ill.) March 24, 1835–Aug. 5, 1924; House 1879–81.

BARBER, Isaac Ambrose (Md.) Jan. 26, 1852–March 1, 1909; House 1897–99.

BARBER, Joel Allen (Wis.) Jan. 17, 1809–June 17, 1881; House 1871–75.

BARBER, Levi (Ohio) Oct. 16, 1777–April 23, 1833; House 1817–19, 1821–23.

BARBOUR, Henry Ellsworth (Calif.) March 8, 1877–March 21, 1945; House 1916–33.

BARBOUR, Lucien (Ind.) March 4, 1811–July 19, 1880; House 1855–57.

BARBOUR, William Warren (N.J.) July 31, 1888–Nov. 22, 1943; Senate Dec. 1, 1931–37, Nov. 9, 1938–Nov. 22, 1943.

BARCHFELD, Andrew Jackson (Pa.) May 18,1863–Jan. 28, 1922; House 1905–17.

BARCLAY, Charles Frederick (Pa.) May 9, 1844–March 9, 1914; House 1907–11.

BARD, David (Pa.) 1744–March 12, 1815; House 1795–99, 1803–March 12, 1815.

BARD, Thomas Robert (Calif.) Dec. 8, 1841–March 5, 1915; Senate Feb. 7, 1900–05.

BARHAM, John All (Calif.) July 17, 1843–Jan. 22, 1926; House 1895–1901.

BARKER, Joseph (Mass.) Oct. 19, 1751–July 5, 1815; House 1805–09.

BARNARD, William Oscar (Ind.) Oct. 25, 1852–April 8, 1939; House 1909–11.

BARNETT, William (Ga.) March 4, 1761–April 1832; House Oct. 5, 1812–15.

BARNEY, Samuel Stebbins (Wis.) Jan. 31, 1846–Dec. 31, 1919; House 1895–1903.

BARR, Bob (Ga.) House, 1995–.

BARR, Samuel Fleming (Pa.) June 15, 1829–May 29, 1919; House 1881–85.

BARRERE, Granville (nephew of Nelson Barrere) (Ill.) July 11, 1829–Jan. 13, 1889; House 1873–75.

BARRETT, Frank Aloysius (Wyo.) Nov. 10, 1892–May 30, 1962; House 1943–Dec. 31, 1950; Senate 1953–69; Gov. Jan. 1, 1951–Jan. 3, 1953.

BARRETT, William Emerson (Mass.) Dec. 29, 1858–Feb. 12, 1906; House 1895–99.

BARROWS, Samuel June (Mass.) May 26, 1845–April 21, 1909; House 1897–99.

BARRY, Alexander Grant (Oreg.) Aug. 23, 1892–Dec. 28, 1952; Senate Nov. 9, 1938–39.

BARRY, Henry W. (Miss.) April 1840–June 7, 1875; House Feb. 23, 1870–75.

BARRY, Robert Raymond (N.Y.) May 15, 1915–June 14, 1988; House 1959–65.

BARRY, William Taylor (Ky.) Feb. 5, 1784–Aug. 30, 1835; House Aug. 8, 1810–11; Senate Dec. 16, 1814–May 1, 1816; Postmaster Gen. April 6, 1829–April 30, 1835.

BARTHOLDT, Richard (Mo.) Nov. 2, 1855–March 19, 1932; House 1893–1915.

BARTINE, Horace Franklin (Nev.) March 21, 1848–Aug. 27, 1918; House 1889–93.

BARTLETT, Dewey Follett (Okla.) March 28, 1919–March 1, 1979; Senate 1973–79; Gov. Jan. 9, 1967–Jan. 11, 1971.

BARTLETT, Harry Stephen "Steve" (Tex.) Sept. 19, 1947–; House 1983–March 11, 1991.

BARTLETT, Josiah Jr. (son of Gov. Josiah Bartlett of N.H.) (N.H.) Aug. 29, 1768–April 16, 1838; House 1811–13.

BARTLETT, Roscoe Gardner (Md.) June 3, 1926–; House 1993–.

BARTON, Bruce (N.Y.) Aug. 5, 1886–July 5, 1967; House Nov. 2, 1937–41.

BARTON, Joe Linus (Tex.) Sept. 15, 1949–; House 1985–.

BARTON, Silas Reynolds (Nebr.) May 21, 1872–Nov. 7, 1916; House 1913–15.

BASS, Charles (N.H.) House, 1995–.

BASS, Lyman Kidder (N.Y.) Nov. 13, 1836–May 11, 1889; House 1873–77.

BASS, Perkins (N.H.) Oct. 6, 1912–; House 1955–63.

BASSETT, Burwell (Va.) March 18, 1764–Feb. 26, 1841; House 1805–13, 1815–19, 1821–29.

BATEMAN, Herbert Harvell (Va.) Aug. 7, 1928–; House 1983–.

BATES, Arthur Laban (nephew of John Milton Thayer) (Pa.) June 6, 1859–Aug. 26, 1934; House 1901–13.

BATES, George Joseph (father of William Henry Bates) (Mass.) Feb. 25, 1891–Nov. 1, 1949; House 1937–Nov. 1, 1949.

BATES, William Henry (son of George Joseph Bates) (Mass.) April 26, 1917–June 22, 1969; House Feb. 14, 1950–June 22, 1969.

BATTIN, James Franklin (Mont.) Feb. 13, 1925–; House 1961–Feb. 27, 1969.

BAUMAN, Robert Edmund (Md.) April 4, 1937–; House Aug. 21, 1973–81.

BAUMHART, Albert David Jr. (Ohio) June 15, 1908–; House 1941–Sept. 2, 1942, 1955–61.

BAXTER, Portus (Vt.) Dec. 4, 1806–March 4, 1868; House 1861–67.

BAYNE, Thomas McKee (Pa.) June 14, 1836–June 16, 1894; House 1877–91.

BEACH, Clifton Bailey (Ohio) Sept. 16, 1845–Nov. 15, 1902; House 1895–99.

BEALE, Charles Lewis (N.Y.) March 5, 1824–Jan. 29, 1900; House 1859–61.

BEALE, Joseph Grant (Pa.) March 26, 1839–May 21, 1915; House 1907–09.

BEALES, Cyrus William (Pa.) Dec. 16, 1877–Nov. 14, 1927; House 1915–17.

BEALL, James Glenn (father of John Glenn Beall Jr.) (Md.) June 5, 1894–Jan. 14, 1971; House 1943–53; Senate 1953–65.

BEALL, John Glenn Jr. (son of James Glenn Beall) (Md.) June 19, 1927–; House 1969–71; Senate 1971–77.

BEALL, Reasin (Ohio) Dec. 3, 1769–Feb. 20, 1843; House April 20, 1813–June 7, 1814.

BEAMAN, Fernando Cortez (Mich.) June 28, 1814–Sept. 27, 1882; House 1861–71.

BEAMER, John Valentine (Ind.) Nov. 17, 1896–Sept. 8, 1964; House 1951–59.

BEAN, Curtis Coe (Ariz.) Jan. 4, 1828–Feb. 1, 1904; House (Terr. Del.) 1885–87.

BEARD, Robin Leo Jr. (Tenn.) Aug. 21, 1939–; House 1973–83.

BEATTY, John (Ohio) Dec. 16, 1828–Dec. 21, 1914; House Feb. 5, 1868–73.

BECK, James Montgomery (Pa.) July 9, 1861–April 12, 1936; House Nov. 8, 1927–Sept. 30, 1934.

BECK, Joseph David (Wis.) March 14, 1866–Nov. 8, 1936; House 1921–29.

BECKER, Frank John (N.Y.) Aug. 27, 1899–Sept. 4, 1981; House 1953–65.

BECKWITH, Charles Dyer (N.J.) Oct. 22, 1838–March 27, 1921; House 1889–91.

BEDE, James Adam (Minn.) Jan. 13, 1856–April 11, 1942; House 1903–09.

BEDINGER, George Michael (uncle of Henry Bedinger) (Ky.) Dec. 10, 1756–Dec. 7, 1843; House 1803–07.

BEEDY, Carroll Lynwood (Maine) Aug. 3, 1880–Aug. 30, 1947; House 1921–35.

BEERMANN, Ralph Frederick (Nebr.) Aug. 13, 1912–Feb. 17, 1977; House 1961–65.

BEERS, Edward McMath (Pa.) May 27, 1877–April 21, 1932; House 1923–April 21, 1932.

BEESON, Henry White (Pa.) Sept. 14, 1791–Oct. 28, 1863; House May 31, 1841–43.

BEGG, James Thomas (Ohio) Feb. 16, 1877–March 26, 1963; House 1919–29.

BEGOLE, Josiah Williams (Mich.) Jan. 20, 1815–June 5, 1896; House 1873–75; Gov. Jan. 1, 1883–Jan. 1, 1885.

BEIDLER, Jacob Atlee (Ohio) Nov. 2, 1862–Sept. 13, 1912; House 1901–07.

BELCHER, Page Henry (Okla.) April 21, 1899–Aug. 2, 1980; House 1951–73.

BELDEN, James Jerome (N.Y.) Sept. 30, 1825–Jan. 1, 1904; House Nov. 8, 1887–95, 1897–99.

BELFORD, James Burns (cousin of Joseph McCrum Belford) (Colo.) Sept. 28, 1837–Jan. 10, 1910; House Oct. 3, 1876–Dec. 13, 1877, 1879–85.

BELFORD, Joseph McCrum (cousin of James Burns Belford) (N.Y.) Aug. 5, 1852–May 3, 1917; House 1897–99.

BELKNAP, Charles Eugene (Mich.) Oct. 17, 1846–Jan. 16, 1929; House 1889–91, Nov. 3, 1891–93.

BELKNAP, Hugh Reid (Ill.) Sept. 1, 1860–Nov. 12, 1901; House Dec. 27, 1895–99.

BELL, Alphonzo (Calif.) Sept. 19, 1914–; House 1961–77.

BELL, Charles Henry (nephew of Samuel Bell, cousin of James Bell) (N.H.) Nov. 18, 1823–Nov. 11, 1893; Senate March 13–June 18, 1879; Gov. June 2, 1881–June 7, 1883.

BELL, James (son of Samuel Bell, uncle of Samuel Newell Bell, cousin of Charles Henry Bell) (N.H.) Nov. 13, 1804–May 26, 1857; Senate July 30, 1855–May 26, 1857.

BELLINGER, Joseph (S.C.) 1773–Jan. 10, 1830; House 1817–19.

BELLMON, Henry Louis (Okla.) Sept. 3, 1921–; Senate 1969–81; Gov. Jan. 14, 1963–Jan. 9, 1967, Jan. 12, 1987–.

BENDER, George Harrison (Ohio) Sept. 29, 1896–June 18, 1961; House 1939–49, 1951–Dec. 15, 1954; Senate Dec. 16, 1954–57.

BENEDICT, Cleveland Keith (W.Va.) March 21, 1935–; House 1981–83.

BENEDICT, Henry Stanley (Calif.) Feb. 20, 1878–July 10, 1930; House Nov. 7, 1916–17.

BENHAM, John Samuel (Ind.) Oct. 24, 1863–Dec. 11, 1935; House 1919–23.

BENJAMIN, John Forbes (Mo.) Jan. 23, 1817–March 8, 1877; House 1865–71.

BENNET, Augustus Witschief (son of William Stiles Bennet) (N.Y.) Oct. 7, 1897–June 5, 1983; House 1945–47.

BENNET, Benjamin (N.J.) Oct. 31, 1764–Oct. 8, 1840; House 1815–19.

BENNET, William Stiles (father of Augustus Witschief Bennet) (N.Y.) Nov. 9, 1870–Dec. 1, 1962; House 1905–11, Nov. 2, 1915–17.

BENNETT, Charles Goodwin (N.Y.) Dec. 11, 1863–May 25, 1914; House 1895–99.

BENNETT, David Smith (N.Y.) May 3, 1811–Nov. 6, 1894; House 1869–71.

BENNETT, Granville Gaylord (Dakota) Oct. 9, 1833–June 28, 1910; House (Terr. Del.) 1879–81.

BENNETT, Henry (N.Y.) Sept. 29, 1808–May 10, 1868; House 1849–59 (1849–57 Whig).

BENNETT, John Bonifas (Mich.) Jan. 10, 1904–Aug. 9, 1964; House 1943–45, 1947–Aug. 9, 1964.

BENNETT, Joseph Bentley (Ky.) April 21, 1859–Nov. 7, 1923; House 1905–11.

BENNETT, Marion Tinsley (son of Philip Allen Bennett) (Mo.) June 6, 1914–; House Jan. 12, 1943–49.

BENNETT, Philip Allen (father of Marion Tinsley Bennett) (Mo.) March 5, 1881–Dec. 7, 1942; House 1941–Dec. 7, 1942.

BENNETT, Robert Foster (son of Wallace Foster Bennett) (Utah) Sept. 18, 1933–; Senate 1993–.

BENNETT, Wallace Foster (father of Robert Foster Bennett) (Utah) Nov. 13, 1898–Dec. 19, 1993; Senate 1951–Dec. 20, 1974.

BENSON, Alfred Washburn (Kans.) July 15, 1843–Jan. 1, 1916; Senate June 11, 1906–Jan. 23, 1907.

BENSON, Samuel Page (Maine) Nov. 28, 1804–Aug. 12, 1876; House 1853–57 (1853–55 Whig).

BENTLEY, Alvin Morell (Mich.) Aug. 30, 1918–April 10, 1969; House 1953–61.

BENTLEY, Helen Delich (Md.) Nov. 28, 1923–; House 1985–.

BENTON, Jacob (N.H.) Aug. 19, 1814–Sept. 29,1892; House 1867–71.

BENTON, Lemuel (great-grandfather of George William Dargan) (S.C.) 1754–May 18, 1818; House 1793–99 (1793–95 no party).

BEREUTER, Douglas Kent (Nebr.) Oct. 6, 1939–; House 1979–.

BERGEN, Christopher Augustus (N.J.) Aug. 2, 1841–Feb. 18, 1905; House 1889–93.

BERRY, Ellis Yarnal (S.Dak.) Oct. 6, 1902–; House 1951–71.

BETHUNE, Edwin Ruthvin Jr. (Ark.) Dec. 19, 1935–; House 1979–85.

BETHUNE, Marion (Ga.) April 8, 1816–Feb. 20, 1895; House Dec. 22, 1870–71.

BETTS, Jackson Edward (Ohio) May 26, 1904–Aug. 13, 1993; House 1951–73.

BETTS, Samuel Rossiter (N.Y.) June 8, 1787–Nov. 2, 1868; House 1815–17.

BEVERIDGE, Albert Jeremiah (Ind.) Oct. 6, 1862–April 27, 1927; Senate 1899–1911.

BEVERIDGE, John Lourie (Ill.) July 6, 1824–May 3, 1910; House Nov. 7, 1871–Jan. 4, 1873; Gov. Jan. 23, 1873–Jan. 8, 1877.

BIBB, William Wyatt (Calif.) Oct. 2, 1781–July 9, 1820; House Jan. 26, 18–Nov. 6, 1813; Senate Nov. 6, 1813–Nov. 9, 1816; Gov. Nov. 9, 1819–July 10, 1820 (Democratic Republican Ala.)

BIDDLE, Joseph Franklin (Pa.) Sept. 14, 1871–Dec. 3, 1936; House Nov. 8, 1932–33.

BIDWELL, Barnabas (Mass.) Aug. 23, 1763–July 27, 1833; House 1805–July 13, 1807.

BIDWELL, John (Calif.) Aug. 5, 1819–April 4, 1900; House 1865–67.

BIERY, James Soloman (Pa.) March 2, 1839–Dec. 3, 1904; House 1873–75.

BIESTER, Edward George Jr. (Pa.) Jan. 5, 1931–; House 1967–77.

BIGBY, John Summerfield (Ga.) Feb. 13, 1832–March 28, 1898; House 1871–73.

BILBRAY, Brian P. (Calif.) House 1995–.

BILIRAKIS, Michael (Fla.) July 16, 1930–; House 1983–.

BILLINGHURST, Charles (Wis.) July 27, 1818–Aug. 18, 1865; House 1855–59.

BINES, Thomas (N.J.) ?–April 9, 1826; House Nov. 2, 1814–15.

BINGHAM, Henry Harrison (Pa.) Dec. 4, 1841–March 22, 1912; House 1879–March 22, 1912.

BINGHAM, Hiram (father of Jonathan Brewster Bingham) (Conn.) Nov. 19, 1875–June 6, 1956; Senate Dec. 17, 1924–33; Gov. Jan. 7–Jan. 8, 1925.

BINGHAM, John Armor (Ohio) Jan. 21, 1815–March 19, 1900; House 1865–63, 1865–73.

BINGHAM, Kinsley Scott (Mich.) Dec. 16, 1808–Oct. 5, 1861; House 1847–51 (Democrat); Senate 1859–Oct. 5, 1861; Gov. Jan. 3, 1855–Jan. 5, 1859.

BIRCH, William Fred (N.J.) Aug. 30, 1870–Jan. 25, 1946; House Nov. 6, 1918–19.

BIRD, Richard Ely (Kans.) Nov. 4, 1878–Jan. 10, 1955; House 1921–23.

BIRDSALL, Benjamin Pixley (Iowa) Oct. 26, 1858–May 26, 1917; House 1903–09.

BIRDSALL, James (N.Y.) 1783–July 20, 1856; House 1815–17.

BISBEE, Horatio Jr. (Fla.) May 1, 1839–March 27, 1916; House 1877–Feb. 20, 1879, Jan. 22–March 3, 1881, June 1, 1882–85.

BISHOP, Cecil William "Runt" (Ill.) June 29, 1890–Sept. 21, 1971; House 1941–55.

BISHOP, Phanuel (Mass.) Sept. 3, 1739–Jan. 6, 1812; House 1799–1807.

BISHOP, Roswell Peter (Mich.) Jan. 6, 1843–March 4, 1920; House 1895–1907.

BIXLER, Harris Jacob (Pa.) Sept. 16, 1870–March 29, 1941; House 1921–27.

BLACK, Frank Swett (N.Y.) March 8, 1853–March 22, 1913; House 1895–Jan. 7, 1897; Gov. Jan. 1, 1897–Jan. 1, 1899.

BLACKBURN, Benjamin Bentley (Ga.) Feb. 14, 1927–; House 1967–75.

BLACKBURN, Edmond Spencer (N.C.) Sept. 22, 1868–March 10, 1912; House 1901–03, 1905–07.

BLACKBURN, Robert E. Lee (Ky.) April 9, 1870–Sept. 20, 1935; House 1929–31.

BLACKBURN, William Jasper (La.) July 24, 1820–Nov. 10, 1899; House July 18, 1868–69.

BLACKLEDGE, William (father of William Salter Blackledge) (N.C.) ?–Oct. 19, 1828; House 1803–09, 1811–13.

BLACKNEY, William Wallace (Mich.) Aug. 28, 1876–March 14, 1963; House 1935–37, 1939–53.

BLAINE, James Gillespie (Maine) Jan. 31, 1830–Jan. 27, 1893; House 1863–July 10, 1876; Speaker 1869–73, Dec. 1, 1873–75; Senate July 10, 1876–March 5, 1881; Secy. of State March 7–Dec. 19, 1881, March 7, 1889–June 4, 1892.

BLAINE, John James (Wis.) May 4, 1875–April 16, 1934; Senate 1927–33; Gov. Jan. 3, 1921–Jan. 3, 1927.

BLAIR, Austin (Mich.) Feb. 8, 1818–Aug. 6, 1894; House 1867–73; Gov. Jan. 2, 1861–Jan. 4, 1865.

BLAIR, Henry William (N.H.) Dec. 6, 1834–March 14, 1920; House 1875–79, 1893–95; Senate June 20, 1879–85, March 10, 1885–91.

BLAIR, Samuel Steel (Pa.) Dec. 5, 1821–Dec. 8, 1890; House 1859–63.

BLAKE, Harrison Gray Otis (Ohio) March 17, 1818–April 16, 1876; House Oct. 11, 1859–63.

BLAKE, John Jr. (N.Y.) Dec. 5, 1762–Jan. 13, 1826; House 1805–09.

BLAKE, John Lauris (N.J.) March 25, 1831–Oct. 10, 1899; House 1879–81.

BLAKENEY, Albert Alexander (Md.) Sept. 28, 1850–Oct. 15, 1924; House 1901–03, 1921–23.

BLANCHARD, George Washington (Wis.) Jan. 26, 1884–Oct. 2, 1964; House 1933–35.

BLAND, Oscar Edward (Ind.) Nov. 21, 1877–Aug. 3, 1951; House 1917–23.

BLAZ, Ben Garrido (Guam) Feb. 14, 1928–; House (Delegate) 1985–99.

BLEAKLEY, Orrin Dubbs (Pa.) May 15, 1854–Dec. 3, 1927; House March 4–April 3, 1917.

BLEDSOE, Jesse (uncle of Robert Emmett Bledsoe Baylor) (Ky.) April 6, 1776–June 25, 1836; Senate 1813–Dec. 24, 1814.

BLILEY, Thomas Jergme Jr. (Va.) Jan. 28, 1932–House 1981–; Chrmn. House Commerce Committee 1995–.

BLISS, Aaron Thomas (Mich.) May 22, 1837–Sept. 16, 1906; House 1889–91; Gov. Jan. 1, 1901–Jan. 1, 1905.

BLISS, Philemon (Ohio) July 28, 1813–Aug. 25, 1889; House 1855–59.

BLOOMFIELD, Joseph (N.J.) Oct. 18, 1763–Oct. 3, 1823; House 1817–21; Gov. Oct. 31, 1801–Oct. 28, 1802, Oct. 29, 1803–Oct. 29, 1812.

BLOUNT, Thomas (brother of William Blount, uncle of William Grainger Blount) (N.C.) May 10, 1759–Feb. 7, 1812; House 1793–99 (1793–95 no party), 1805–09, 1811–Feb. 7, 1812.

BLOUNT, William Grainger (son of William Blount, nephew of Thomas Blount) (Tenn.) 1784–May 21, 1827; House Dec. 8, 1815–19.

BLOW, Henry Taylor (Mo.) July 15, 1817–Sept. 11, 1875; House 1863–67 (1863–65 Unconditional Unionist).

BLUE, Richard Whiting (Kans.) Sept. 8, 1841 –Jan. 28, 1907; House 1895–97.

BLUTE, Peter Ignatius (Mass.) Jan. 28, 1956–; House 1993–.

BODEN, Andrew (Pa.) ?–Dec. 20, 1835; House 1817–21.

BOEHLERT, Sherwood Louis (N.Y.) June 28, 1936–; House 1983–.

BOEHNER, John Andrew (Ohio) Nov. 7, 1949–; House 1991–.

BOGGS, James Caleb (Del.) May 15, 1909–; House 1947–53; Senate 1961–73; Gov. Jan. 20, 1953–Dec. 30, 1960.

BOHN, Frank Probasco (Mich.) July 14, 1866–June 1, 1944; House 1927–33.

BOIES, William Dayton (Iowa) Jan. 3, 1857–May 31, 1932; House 1919–29.

BOLES, Thomas (Ark.) July 16, 1837–March 13, 1905; House June 22, 1868–71, Feb. 9, 1872–73.

BOLLES, Stephen (Wis.) June 25, 1866–July 8, 1941; House 1939–July 8, 1941.

BOLTON, Chester Castle (husband of Frances Payne Bolton, father of Oliver Payne Bolton) (Ohio) Sept. 5, 1882–Oct. 29, 1939; House 1929–37, Jan. 3–Oct. 29, 1939.

BOLTON, Frances Payne (widow of Chester Castle Bolton, granddaughter of Henry B. Payne, mother of Oliver Payne Bolton) (Ohio) March 29, 1885–March 9, 1977; House Feb. 27, 1940–69.

BOLTON, Oliver Payne (son of Chester Castle Bolton and Frances Payne Bolton, great-grandson of Henry B. Payne) (Ohio) Feb. 22, 1917–Dec. 13, 1972; House 1953–67, 1963–65.

BOND, Charles Grosvenor (nephew of Charles Henry Grosvenor) (N.Y.) May 29, 1877–Jan. 10, 1974; House 1921–23.

BOND, Christopher Samuel "Kit" (Mo.) March 6, 1939–; Senate 1987–; Gov. Jan. 8, 1973–Jan. 10, 1977, Jan. 12, 1981–Jan. 14, 1985. Chrmn. Senate Small Business Committee 1995–.

BONILLA, Henry (Tex.) Jan. 2, 1954–; House 1993–.

BONIN, Edward John (Pa.) Dec. 23, 1904–; House 1953–55.

BONO, Sonny (Calif.) House, 1995–.

BONYNGE, Robert William (Colo.) Sept. 8, 1863–Sept. 22, 1939; House Feb. 16, 1904–09.

BOOTHMAN, Melvin Morella (Ohio) Oct. 16, 1846–March 5, 1904; House 1887–91.

BOOZE, William Samuel (Md.) Jan. 9, 1862–Dec. 6, 1933; House 1897–99.

BORAH, William Edgar (Idaho) June 29, 1865–Jan. 1940; Senate 1907–Jan. 19, 1940.

BOREING, Vincent (Ky.) Nov. 24, 1839–Sept. 16, 1903; House 1899–Sept. 16, 1903.

BOREMAN, Arthur Inghram (W.Va.) July 24, 1823–April 19, 1896; Senate 1869–75; Gov. June 20, 1863–Feb. 26, 1869.

BOSCH, Albert Henry (N.Y.) Oct. 30, 1908–; House 1953–Dec. 31, 1960.

BOSCHWITZ, Rudolf Eli "Rudy" (Minn.) Nov. 7, 1930–; Senate Dec. 30, 1978–91.

BOTTUM, Joseph H. (S.Dak.) Aug. 7, 1903–July 4, 1984; Senate July 11, 1962–63.

BOULTER, Eldon Beau (Tex.) Feb. 23, 1942–; House 1985–89.

BOUND, Franklin (Pa.) April 9, 1829–Aug. 8, 1910; House 1885–89.

BOURNE, Jonathan Jr. (Oreg.) Feb. 23, 1855–Sept. 1, 1940; Senate 1907–13.

BOUTELL, Henry Sherman (Ill.) March 14, 1856–March 11, 1926; House Nov. 23, 1897–1911.

BOUTELLE, Charles Addison (Maine) Feb. 9, 1839–May 21, 1901; House 1883–1901.

BOUTWELL, George Sewel (Mass.) Jan. 28, 1818–Feb. 27, 1905; House 1863–March 12, 1869; Senate March 17, 1873–77; Gov. Jan. 11, 1851–Jan. 14, 1853 (Democrat); Secy. of the Treasury March 12, 1869–March 16, 1873.

BOW, Frank Townsend (Ohio) Feb. 20, 1901–Nov. 13, 1972; House 1951–Nov. 13, 1972.

BOWDEN, George Edwin (nephew of Lemuel Jackson Bowden) (Va.) July 6, 1852–Jan. 22, 1908; House 1887–91.

BOWDEN, Lemuel Jackson (uncle of George Edwin Bowden) (Va.) Jan. 16, 1815–Jan. 2, 1864; Senate 1863–Jan. 2, 1864.

BOWEN, Christopher Columbus (S.C.) Jan. 5, 1832–June 23, 1880; House July 20, 1868–71.

BOWEN, Henry (son of Rees Tate Bowen, nephew of John Warfield Johnston, cousin of William Bowen Campbell) (Va.) Dec. 26, 1841–April 29, 1915; House 1883–85 (Readjuster), 1887–89.

BOWEN, John Henry (Tenn.) Sept. 1780–Sept. 25, 1822; House 1813–15.

BOWEN, Thomas Mead (Colo.) Oct. 26, 1835–Dec. 30, 1906; Senate 1883–89; Gov. (Idaho Terr.) 1871.

BOWERS, George Meade (W.Va.) Sept. 13, 1863–Dec. 7, 1925; House May 9, 1916–23.

BOWERS, William Wallace (Calif.) Oct. 20, 1834–May 2, 1917; House 1891–97.

BOWERSOCK, Justin De Witt (Kans.) Sept. 19,1842–Oct. 27, 1922; House 1899–1907.

BOWIE, Walter (great–uncle of Thomas Fielder Bowie) (Md.) 1748–Nov. 9, 1810; House March 24, 1802–05.

BOWLES, Henry Leland (Mass.) Jan. 6, 1866–May 17, 1932; House Sept. 29, 1925–29.

BOWMAN, Charles Calvin (Pa.) Nov. 14, 1852–July 3, 1941; House 1911–Dec. 12, 1912.

BOWMAN, Frank Llewellyn (W.Va.) Jan. 21, 1879–Sept. 15, 1936; House 1925–33.

BOWMAN, Selwyn Zadock (Mass.) May 11, 1840–Sept. 30, 1928; House 1879–83.

BOWRING, Eva Kelly (Nebr.) Jan. 9, 1892–Jan. 8, 1985; Senate April 16–Nov. 7, 1954.

BOYD, Adam (N.J.) March 21, 1746–Aug. 15, 1835; House 1803–05, March 8, 1808–13.

BOYD, John Frank (Nebr.) Aug. 8, 1853–May 28, 1945; House (Terr. Del.) 1865–67, 1869–71.

BOYD, Sempronius Hamilton (Mo.) May 28, 1828–June 22,1894; House 1863–65 (Unconditional Unionist), 1869–71.

BOYD Thomas Alexander (Ill.) June 25, 1830–May 28, 1897; House 1877–81.

BOYLE, John (Ky.) Oct. 28, 1774–Feb. 28, 1835; House 1803–09.

BRADFORD, Allen Alexander (Colo.) July 23, 1815–March 12, 1888; House (Terr. Del.) 1865–67, 1869–71.

BRADLEY, Frederick Van Ness (Mich.) April 12, 1898–May 24, 1947; House 1939–May 24, 1947; Chrmn. House Merchant Marine and Fisheries 1947.

BRADLEY, Nathan Ball (Mich.) May 28, 1831–Nov. 8, 1906; House 1873–77.

BRADLEY, Thomas Wilson (N.Y.) April 6, 1844–May 30, 1920; House 1903–13.

BRADLEY, William O'Connell (Ky.) March 18, 1847–May 23, 1914; Senate 1909–May 23, 1914; Gov. Dec. 10, 1895–Dec. 12, 1899.

BRADLEY, Willis Winter (Calif.) June 28, 1884–Aug. 27, 1954; House 1947–49.

BRADY, James Dennis (Va.) April 3, 1843–Nov. 30, 1900; House 1885–87.

BRADY, James Henry (Idaho) June 12, 1862–Jan. 13, 1918; Senate Feb. 6, 1913–Jan. 13, 1918; Gov. Jan. 4, 1909–Jan. 2, 1911.

BRADY, Nicholas Frederick (N.J.) April 11, 1930–; Senate April 12–Dec. 20, 1982; Secy. of the Treasury Sept. 16, 1988–Jan. 19, 1993.

BRAINERD, Samuel Myron (Pa.) Nov. 13, 1842–Nov. 21, 1898; House 1883–85.

BRAMBLETT, Ernest King (Calif.) April 25, 1901–Dec. 27, 1966; House 1947–55.

BRAND, Charles (Ohio) Nov. 1, 1871–May 23, 1966; House 1923–33.

BRANDEGEE, Augustus (father of Frank Bosworth Brandegee) (Conn.) July 15, 1828–Nov. 10, 1904; House 1863–67.

BRANDEGEE, Frank Bosworth (son of Augustus Brandegee) (Conn.) July 8, 1864–Oct. 14, 1924; House Nov. 5, 1902–May 10, 1905; Senate May 10, 1905–Oct. 14, 1924.

BRAY, William Gilmer (Ind.) June 17, 1903–June 4, 1979; House 1951–75.

BRAYTON, William Daniel (R.I.) Nov. 6, 1815–June 30, 1887; House 1857–61.

BRECKINRIDGE, John (brother of James Breckinridge, grandfather of John Cabell Breckinridge and William Campbell Preston Breckinridge, great-grandfather of Clifton Bodes Breckinridge, great-great-grandfather of John Bayne Breckinridge, cousin of John Brown of Va. and Ky., James Brown, and Francis Preston) (Ky.) Dec. 2,

1760–Dec. 14, 1806; Senate 1801–Aug. 7, 1805; Atty. Gen. Aug. 7, 1805–Dec. 14, 1806.

BREHM, Walter Ellsworth (Ohio) May 25, 1892–Aug. 24, 1971; House 1943–53.

BREITUNG, Edward (Mich.) Nov. 10, 1831–March 3, 1887; House 1883–85.

BRENNAN, Vincent Morrison (Mich.) April 22, 1890–Feb. 4, 1959; House 1921–23.

BRENTANO, Lorenzo (Ill.) Nov. 4, 1813–Sept. 18, 1891; House 1877–79.

BRENTON, Samuel (Ind.) Nov. 22, 1810–March 29, 1857; House 1851–53 (Whig), 1855–March 29, 1857.

BRENTS, Thomas Hurley (Wash.) Dec. 24, 1840–Oct. 23, 1916; House (Terr. Del.) 1879–85.

BREWER, Francis Beattie (N.Y.) Oct. 8, 1820–July 29, 1892; House 1883–85.

BREWER, John Hart (N.J.) March 29, 1844–Dec. 21, 1900; House 1881–85.

BREWER, Mark Spencer (Mich.) Oct. 22, 1837–March 18, 1901; House 1877–81, 1887–91.

BREWSTER, Henry Colvin (N.Y.) Sept. 7, 1845–Jan. 29, 1928; House 1895–99.

BREWSTER, Ralph Owen (Maine) Feb. 22, 1888–Dec. 25, 1961; House 1935–41; Senate 1941–Dec. 31, 1952; Gov. Jan. 8, 1925–Jan. 2, 1929.

BRICK, Abraham Lincoln (Ind.) May 27, 1860–April 7, 1908; House 1899–April 7, 1908.

BRICKER, John William (Ohio) Sept. 6, 1893–March 22, 1986; Senate 1947–59; Chrmn. Senate Interstate and Foreign Commerce 1953–55; Gov. Jan. 9, 1939–Jan. 8, 1945.

BRIDGES, Henry Styles (N.H.) Sept. 9, 1898–Nov. 26, 1961; Senate 1937–Nov. 26, 1961; Chrmn. Senate Appropriations 1947–49, 1953–55; Senate minority leader Jan. 8, 1952–53; elected Pres. pro tempore Jan. 3, 1953; Gov. Jan. 3, 1935–Jan. 7, 1937.

BRIGGS, Frank Obadiah (son of James Frankland Briggs) (N.J.) Aug. 12, 1851–May 8, 1913; Senate 1907–13.

BRIGGS, George (N.Y.) May 6, 1805–June 1, 1869; House 1849–53 (Whig), 1859–61.

BRIGGS, James Frankland (father of Frank Obadiah Briggs) (N.H.) Oct. 23, 1827–Jan. 21, 1905; House 1877–83.

BRIGHAM, Elbert Sidney (Vt.) Oct. 19, 1877–July 5, 1962; House 1925–31.

BRIGHAM, Lewis Alexander (N.J.) Jan. 2, 1831–Feb. 19, 1885; House 1879–81.

BRISTOW, Henry (N.Y.) June 5, 1840–Oct. 11, 1906; House 1901–03.

BRISTOW, Joseph Little (Kans.) July 22, 1861–July 14, 1944; Senate 1909–15.

BRITT, James Jefferson (N.C.) March 4, 1861–Dec. 26, 1939; House 1915–17, March 1–3, 1919.

BRITTEN, Frederick Albert (Ill.) Nov. 18, 1871–May 4, 1946; House 1913–35.

BROCK, William Emerson III (grandson of William Emerson Brock) (Tenn.) Nov. 23, 1930–; House 1963–71; Senate 1971–77; Chrmn. Rep. Nat. Comm. Jan. 1977–Jan. 1981; Secy. of Labor April 29, 1985–Oct. 31, 1987.

BRODERICK, Case (cousin of David Colbreth Broderick and Andrew Kennedy) (Kans.) Sept. 23, 1839–April 1, 1920; House 1891–99.

BROGDEN, Curtis Hooks (N.C.) Nov. 6, 1816–Jan. 5, 1901; House 1877–79; Governor July 11, 1874–Jan. 1, 1877.

BROMWELL, Henry Pelham Holmes (Ill.) Aug. 26, 1823–Jan. 7, 1903; House 1865–69.

BROMWELL, Jacob Henry (Ohio) May 11, 1848–June 4, 1924; House Dec. 3, 1894–1903.

BROMWELL, James Edward (Iowa) March 26, 1920–; House 1961–65.

BROOKE, Edward William III (Mass.) Oct. 26, 1919–; Senate 1967–79.

BROOKHART, Smith Wildman (Iowa) Feb. 2, 1869–Nov. 15, 1944; Senate Nov. 7, 1922–April 12, 1926, 1927–33 (Nov. 7, 1922–25 Progressive Republican).

BROOKS, Charles Wayland (Ill.) March 8, 1897–Jan. 14, 1957; Senate Nov. 22, 1940–49; Chrmn. Senate Rules and Administration 1947–49.

BROOKS, Edward Schroeder (Pa.) June 14, 1867–July 12, 1957; House 1919–23.

BROOKS, Edwin Bruce (cousin of Edmund Howard Hinshaw) (Ill.) Sept. 20, 1868–Sept. 18, 1933; House 1919–23.

BROOKS, Franklin Eli (Colo.) Nov. 19, 1860–Feb. 7, 1916; House 1903–07.

BROOKS, George Merrick (Mass.) July 26, 1824–Sept. 22, 1893; House Nov. 2, 1869–May 13, 1872.

BROOKS, Micah (N.Y.) May 14, 1775–July 7, 1857; House 1815–17.

BROOMALL, John Martin (Pa.) Jan. 19, 1816–June 3, 1894; House 1863–69.

BROOMFIELD, William S. (Mich.) April 28, 1922–; House 1957–93.

BROPHY, John Charles (Wis.) Oct. 8, 1901–Dec. 26, 1976; House 1947–49.

BROSIUS, Marriott (Pa.) March 7, 1843–March 16, 1901; House 1889–March 16, 1901.

BROTZMAN, Donald Glenn (Colo.) June 28, 1922–; House 1963–65, 1967–75.

BROWER, John Morehead (N.C.) July 19, 1845–Aug. 5, 1913; House 1887–91.

BROWN, Arthur (Utah) March 8, 1843–Dec. 12, 1906; Senate Jan. 22, 1896–97.

BROWN, Charles Elwood (Ohio) July 4, 1834–May 22, 1904; House 1885–89.

BROWN, Clarence J. (father of Clarence J. Brown Jr. (Ohio) July 14, 1893–Aug. 23, 1965; House 1939–Aug. 23, 1965.

BROWN, Clarence J. Jr. (son of Clarence J. Brown) (Ohio) June 18, 1927–; House Nov. 2, 1965–83.

BROWN, Ernest S. (Nev.) Sept. 25, 1903–July 23, 1965; Senate Oct. 1–Dec. 1, 1954.

BROWN, Foster Vincent (father of Joseph Edgar Brown) (Tenn.) Dec. 24, 1852–March 26, 1937; House 1895–97.

BROWN, Garry Eldridge (Mich.) Aug. 12, 1923–; House 1967–79.

BROWN, George Hanks (Hank) (Colo.) Feb. 12, 1940–; House 1981–91; Senate 1991–.

BROWN, John (Md.) ?–Dec. 13, 1815; House 1809–10.

BROWN, John Robert (Va.) Jan. 14, 1842–Aug. 4, 1927; House 1887–89.

BROWN, Joseph Edgar (son of Foster Vincent Brown) (Tenn.) Feb. 11, 1880–June 13, 1939; House 1921–23.

BROWN, Norris (Nebr.) May 2, 1863–Jan. 5, 1960; Senate 1907–13.

BROWN, Robert (Pa.) Dec. 25, 1744–Feb. 26, 1823; House Dec. 4, 1798–1815.

BROWN, Seth W. (Ohio) Jan. 4, 1841–Feb. 24, 1923; House 1897–1901.

BROWN, Webster Everett (Wis.) July 16, 1851–Dec. 14, 1929; House 1901–07.

BROWN, William Ripley (Kans.) July 16, 1840–March 3, 1916; House 1883–87.

BROWN, William Wallace (Pa.) April 22, 1836–Nov. 4, 1926; House 1883–87.

BROWNBACK, Sam (Kans.) House, 1995–.

BROWNE, Edward Everts (Wis.) Feb. 16, 1868–Nov. 23, 1945; House 1913–31.

BROWNE, Thomas Henry Bayly (Va.) Feb. 8, 1844–Aug. 27, 1892; House 1887–91.

BROWNE, Thomas McLelland (Ind.) April 19, 1829–July 17, 1891; House 1877–91.

BROWNING, Orville Hickman (Ill.) Feb. 10, 1806–Aug. 10, 1881; Senate June 26, 1861–Jan. 12, 1863; Secy. of the Interior Sept. 1, 1866–March 4, 1869.

BROWNING, William John (N.J.) April 11, 1850–March 24, 1920; House Nov. 7, 1911–March 24, 1920.

BROWNLOW, Walter Preston (nephew of William Gannaway Brownlow) (Tenn.) March 27, 1851–July 8, 1910; House 1897–July 8, 1910.

BROWNLOW, William Gannaway (uncle of Walter Preston Brownlow) (Tenn.) Aug. 29, 1805–April 29, 1877; Senate 1869–75; Gov. April 5, 1865–Feb. 25, 1869.

BROWNSON, Charles Bruce (Ind.) Feb. 5, 1914–Aug. 4, 1988; House 1951–59.

BROYHILL, James Thomas (N.C.) Aug. 19, 1927–; House 1963–July 14, 1986; Senate July 14–Nov. 10, 1986.

BROYHILL, Joel Thomas (Va.) Nov. 4, 1919–; House 1953–Dec. 31, 1974.

BRUCE, Blanche Kelso (Miss.) March 1, 1841–March 17, 1898; Senate 1875–81.

BRUCE, Donald Cogley (Ind.) April 27, 1921–Aug. 31, 1969; House 1961–65.

BRUMAUGH, David Emmert (Pa.) Oct. 8, 1894–April 22, 1977; House Nov. 2, 1943–47.

BRUMM, Charles Napoleon (father of George Franklin Brumm) (Pa.) June 9, 1838–Jan. 11, 1917; House 1881–89 (1881–85 Greenbacker), 1895–99, Nov. 6, 1906–Jan. 4, 1909.

BRUMM, George Franklin (son of Charles Napoleon Brumm) (Pa.) Jan. 24, 1880–May 29, 1934; House 1923–27, 1929–May 29, 1934.

BRUNSDALE, Clarence Norman (N.Dak.) July 9, 1891–Jan. 27, 1978; Senate Nov. 19, 1959–Aug. 7, 1960; Gov. Jan. 3, 1951–Jan. 9, 1957.

BRYAN, Joseph (Ga.) Aug. 18, 1773–Sept. 12, 1812; House 1803–06.

BRYAN, Joseph Hunter (N.C.) ?–?; House 1815–19.

BRYAN, Nathan (N.C.) 1748–June 4, 1798; House 1795–June 4, 1798.

BRYANT, Ed (Tenn.) House, 1995–.

BUCHANAN, James (N.J.) June 17, 1839–Oct. 30, 1900; House 1885–93.

BUCHANAN, John Hall Jr. (Ala.) March 19, 1928–; House 1965–81.

BUCK, Alfred Eliab (Ala.) Feb. 7, 1832–Dec. 4, 1902; House 1869–71.

BUCK, Clayton Douglass (great-great-nephew of John Middleton Clayton) (Del.) March 21, 1890–Jan. 27, 1965; Senate 1943–49; Chrmn. Senate District of Columbia 1947–49; Gov. Jan. 15, 1929–Jan. 19, 1937.

BUCK, Ellsworth Brewer (N.Y.) July 3, 1892–Aug. 14, 1970; House June 6, 1944–49.

BUCK, John Ransom (Conn.) Dec. 6, 1835–Feb. 6, 1917; House 1881–83, 1885–87.

BUCKBEE, John Theodore (Ill.) Aug. 1, 1871–April 23, 1936; House 1927–April 23, 1936.

BUCKINGHAM, William Alfred (Conn.) May 28, 1804–Feb. 5, 1875; Senate 1869–Feb. 5, 1875; Gov. May 5, 1858–May 2, 1866.

BUCKLAND, Ralph Pomeroy (Ohio) Jan. 20, 1812–May 27, 1892; House 1865–61.

BUCKLEY, Charles Waldron (Ala.) Feb. 18, 1835–Dec. 4, 1906; House July 21, 1868–73.

BUCKMAN, Clarence Bennett (Minn.) April 1, 1851–March 1, 1917; House 1903–07.

BUDGE, Hamer Harold (Idaho) Nov. 21, 1910–; House 1951–61.

BUECHNER, John William "Jack" (Mo.) June 6, 1940–; House 1987–91.

BUFFETT, Howard Homan (Nebr.) Aug. 13, 1903–April 30, 1964; House 1943–49, 1951–53.

BUFFINGTON, James (Mass.) March 16, 1817–March 7, 1875; House 1855–63, 1869–March 7, 1875.

BULKELEY, Morgan Gardner (cousin of Edwin Denison Morgan) (Conn.) Dec. 26, 1837–Nov. 6, 1922; Senate 1905–11; Gov. Jan. 10, 1889–Jan. 4, 1893.

BULL, Melville (R.I.) Sept. 29, 1854–July 5, 1909; House 1895–1903.

BULLOCH, William Bellinger (Ga.) 1777–May 6, 1852; Senate April 8–Nov. 6, 1813.

BUNDY, Hezekiah Sanford (Ohio) Aug 15, 1817–Dec. 12, 1895; House 1865–67, 1873–75, Dec. 4, 1893–95.

BUNDY, Solomon (N.Y.) May 22, 1823–Jan. 13, 1889; House 1877–79.

BUNN, Jim (Oreg.) House, 1995–.

BUNNELL, Frank Charles (Pa.) March 19, 1842–Sept. 11, 1911; House Dec. 24, 1872–73 (no party), 1885–89.

BUNNING, James Paul David (Ky.) Oct. 23, 1931–; House 1987–.

BURCHARD, Horatio Chapin (Ill.) Sept. 22, 1825–May 14, 1908; House Dec. 6, 1869–79.

BURDET, Samuel Swinfin (Mo.) Feb. 21, 1836–Sept. 24, 1914; House 1869–73.

BURDICK, Clark (R.I.) Jan. 13, 1868–Aug. 27,1948; House 1919–33.

BURDICK, Theodore Weld (Iowa) Oct. 7, 1836–July 16, 1898; House 1877–79.

BURDICK, Usher Lloyd (father of Quentin Northrop Burdick, father-in-law of Jocelyn Birch Burdick, father-in-law of Robert Woodrow Levering) (N.Dak.) Feb. 21, 1879–Aug. 19, 1960; House 1935–45, 1949–59.

BURGENER, Clair Walter (Calif.) Dec. 5, 1921-; House 1973–83.

BURGES, Dempsey (N.C.) 1751–Jan. 13, 1800; House 1795–99.

BURK, Henry (Pa.) Sept. 26, 1850–Dec. 5, 1903; House 1901–Dec. 5, 1903.

BURKE, Charles Henry (S.Dak.) April 1, 1861–April 7, 1944; House 1899–1907, 1909–15.

BURKE, J. Herbert (Fla.) Jan. 14, 1913–June 16, 1993; House 1967–79.

BURKE, James Francis (Pa.) Oct. 21, 1867–Aug. 8, 1932; House 1905–15.

BURKE, Raymond Hugh (Ohio) Nov. 4, 1881–Aug. 18, 1954; House 1947–49.

BURKE, William Joseph (Pa.) Sept. 25, 1862–Nov. 7, 1925; House 1919–23.

BURKETT, Elmer Jacob (Nebr.) Dec. 1, 1867–May 23, 1935; House 1899–March 4, 1905; Senate 1905–11.

BURLEIGH, Edwin Chick (Maine) Nov. 27, 1843–June 16, 1916; House June 21, 1897–1911; Senate 1913–June 16, 1916; Gov. Jan. 2, 1889–Jan. 4, 1893.

BURLEIGH, Henry Gordon (N.Y.) June 2, 1832–Aug. 10, 1900; House 1883–87.

BURLEIGH, John Holmes (son of William Burleigh) (Maine) Oct. 9, 1822–Dec. 5, 1877; House 1873–77.

BURLEIGH, Walter Atwood (Dakota) Oct. 25, 1820–March 7, 1896; House (Terr. Del.) 1865–69.

BURLINGAME, Anson (Mass.) Nov. 14, 1820–Feb. 23, 1870; House 1855–61 (1855–57 American Party).

BURNHAM, Alfred Avery (Conn.) March 8, 1819–April 11, 1879; House 1859–63.

BURNHAM, George (Calif.) Dec. 28, 1868–June 28, 1939; House 1933–37.

BURNHAM, Henry Eben (N.H.) Nov. 8, 1844–Feb. 8, 1917; Senate 1901–13.

BURNS, Conrad (Mont.) Jan. 25, 1935–; Senate 1989–.

BURNSIDE, Ambrose Everett (R.I.) May 23, 1824–Sept. 13,1881; Senate 1875–Sept. 13, 1881; Gov. May 29, 1866–May 25, 1869.

BURNSIDE, Thomas (Pa.) July 28, 1782–March 25, 1851; House Oct. 10, 1815–April 1816.

BURR, Richard M. (N.C.) House, 1995–.

BURRELL, Orlando (Ill.) July 26, 1826–June 7, 1921; House 1895–97.

BURROUGHS, Sherman Everett (N.H.) Feb. 6,1870–Jan. 27, 1923; House June 7, 1917–Jan. 27, 1923.

BURROUGHS, Silas Mainville (N.Y.) July 16, 1810–June 3, 1860; House 1857–June 3, 1860.

BURROWS, Julius Caesar (Mich.) Jan. 9, 1837–Nov. 16, 1915; House 1873–75, 1879–83, 1885–Jan. 23, 1895; Senate Jan. 24, 1895–1911.

BURSUM, Holm Olaf (N.Mex.) Feb. 10, 1867–Aug. 7, 1953; Senate March 11, 1921–25.

BURTNESS, Olger Burton (N.Dak.) March 14, 1884–Jan. 20, 1960; House 1921–33.

BURTON, Charles Germman (Mo.) April 4, 1846–Feb. 25, 1926; House 1895–97.

BURTON, Danny Lee (Ind.) June 21, 1938–; House 1983–.

BURTON, Harold Hitz (Ohio) June 22, 1888–Oct. 28, 1964; Senate 1941–Sept. 30, 1945; Assoc. Justice Supreme Court Oct. 1, 1945–Oct. 13, 1958.

BURTON, Hiram Rodney (Del.) Nov. 13, 1841–June 17, 1927; House 1905–09.

BURTON, Joseph Ralph (Kans.) Nov. 16, 1850–Feb. 27, 1923; Senate 1901–June 4, 1906.

BURTON, Laurence Junior (Utah) Oct. 30, 1926–; House 1963–71.

BURTON, Theodore Elijah (Ohio) Dec. 20, 1851–Oct. 28, 1929; House 1889–91, 1895–1909, 1921–Dec. 15, 1928; Senate 1909–15, Dec. 15, 1928–Oct. 28, 1929.

BURWELL, William Armisted (Va.) March 15, 1780–Feb. 16, 1821; House Dec. 1, 1806–Feb. 16, 1821.

BUSBEY, Fred Ernst (Ill.) Feb. 8, 1895–Feb. 11, 1966; House 1943–45, 1947–49, 1951–55.

BUSH, George Herbert Walker (son of Prescott Sheldon Bush) (Tex.) June 12, 1924–; House 1967–71; Chrmn. Rep. Nat. Comm. Jan. 1973–Sept. 1974; Vice President 1981–89; President 1989–93.

BUSH, Prescott Sheldon (father of George Herbert Walker Bush) (Conn.) May 15, 1895–Oct. 8, 1972; Senate Nov. 4, 1952–Jan. 2, 1963.

BUSHFIELD, Harlan John (husband of Vera Cahalan Bushfield) (S.Dak.) Aug. 6, 1882–Sept. 27, 1948; Senate 1943–Sept. 27, 1948; Gov. Jan. 3, 1939–Jan. 5, 1943.

BUSHFIELD, Vera Cahalan (widow of Harlan John Bushfield) (S.Dak.) Aug. 9, 1889–April 16, 1976; Senate Oct. 6–Dec. 26, 1948.

BUSHONG, Robert Grey (grandson of Anthony Ellmaker Roberts) (Pa.) June 10, 1883–April 6, 1951; House 1927–29.

BUTLER, Benjamin Franklin (grandfather of Butler Ames, father-in-law of Adelbert Ames) (Mass.) Nov. 5, 1818–Jan. 11, 1893; House 1867–75, 1877–79; Gov. Jan. 4, 1883–Jan. 3, 1884 (Democrat/Greenback).

BUTLER, Ezra (Vt.) Sept. 24, 1763–July 12, 1838; House 1813–15; Gov. Oct. 13, 1826–Oct. 10, 1828 (Democratic Republican).

BUTLER, Hugh Alfred (Nebr.) Feb. 28, 1878–July 1, 1954; Senate 1941–July 1, 1954; Chrmn. Senate Public Lands 1947–48; Chrmn. Senate Interior and Insular Affairs 1948–49, 1953–54.

BUTLER, John Cornelius (N.Y.) July 2, 1887–Aug. 13, 1953; House April 22, 1941–49, 1951–53.

BUTLER, John Marshall (Md.) July 21, 1897–March 14, 1978; Senate 1951–63.

BUTLER, Josiah (N.H.) Dec. 4, 1779–Oct. 27, 1854; House 1817–23.

BUTLER, Manley Caldwell (Va.) June 2, 1925–; House Nov. 7, 1972–83.

BUTLER, Robert Reyburn (grandson of Roderick Randum Butler) (Oreg.) Sept. 24, 1881–Jan. 7, 1933; House Nov. 6, 1928–Jan. 7, 1933.

BUTLER, Roderick Randum (grandfather of Robert Reyburn Butler) (Tenn.) April 9, 1827–Aug. 18, 1902; House 1867–75, 1887–89.

BUTLER, Thomas (La.) April 14, 1785–Aug. 7, 1847; House Nov. 16, 1818–21.

BUTLER, Thomas Stalker (Pa.) Nov. 4, 1855–May 26, 1928; House 1897–May 26, 1928 (1897–99 Independent Republican).

BUTLER, William (father of Andrew Pickens Butler and William Butler, below, grandfather of Matthew Calbraith Butler) (S.C.) Dec. 17, 1759–Nov. 15, 1821; House 1801–13.

BUTLER, William Morgan (Mass.) Jan. 29, 1861–March 29, 1937; Senate Nov. 13, 1924–Dec. 6, 1926; Chrmn. Rep. Nat. Comm. 1924–28.

BUTTERFIELD, Martin (N.Y.) Dec. 8, 1790–Aug. 6, 1866; House 1859–61.

BUTTERWORTH, Benjamin (Ohio) Oct. 22, 1837–Jan. 16, 1898; House 1879–83, 1885–91.

BUTTON, Daniel Evan (N.Y.) Nov. 1, 1917–; House 1967–71.

BURTTZ, Charles Wilson (S.C.) Nov. 16, 1837–July 20, 1913; House Nov. 7, 1876–77.

BUYER, Stephen Earle (Ind.) Nov. 26, 1958–; House 1993–.

BYRNE, Emmet Francis (Ill.) Dec. 6, 1896–Sept. 25, 1974; House 1957–59.

BYRNES, John William (Wis.) June 12, 1913–Jan. 12, 1985; House 1945–73.

CABELL, Samuel Jordan (Va.) Dec. 15, 1756–Aug. 4, 1818; House 1795–1803.

CABLE, John Levi (great-grandson of Joseph Cable) (Ohio) April 15, 1884–Sept. 15, 1971; House 1921–25, 1929–33.

CAHILL, William Thomas (N.J.) June 25, 1912–; House 1959–Jan. 19, 1971; Gov. Jan. 20, 1970–Jan. 15, 1974.

CAIN, Harry Pulliam (Wash.) Jan. 10, 1906–March 3, 1979; Senate Dec. 26, 1946–53.

CAIN, Richard Harvey (S.C.) April 12, 1825–Jan. 18, 1887; House 1873–75, 1877–79.

CAKE, Henry Lutz (Pa.) Oct. 6, 1827–Aug. 26, 1899; House 1867–71.

CALDER, William Musgrave (N.Y.) March 3, 1869–March 3, 1945; House 1905–15; Senate 1917–23.

CALDERHEAD, William Alexander (Kans.) Sept. 26, 1844–Dec. 18, 1928; House 1895–97, 1899–1911.

CALDWELL, James (Ohio) Nov. 30, 1770–May 1838; House 1813–17.

CALDWELL, John Alexander (Ohio) April 21, 1852–May 24, 1927; House 1889–May 4, 1894.

CALHOUN, John Caldwell (cousin of John Ewing Colhoun and Joseph Calhoun) (S.C.) March 18, 1782–March 31, 1850; House 1811–Nov. 3, 1817; Senate Dec. 29, 1832–43, Nov. 26, 1845–March 31, 1850; Vice President 1825–Dec.

28, 1832 (Democratic Republican); Secy. of War Oct. 8, 1817–March 7, 1825; Secy. of State April 1, 1844–March 10, 1845.

CALHOUN, Joseph (cousin of John Caldwell Calhoun and John Ewing Colhoun) (S.C.) Oct. 22, 1750–April 14, 1817; House June 2, 1807–11.

CALKINS, William Henry (Ind.) Feb. 18, 1842–Jan. 29, 1894; House 1877–Oct. 20, 1884.

CALLAHAN, Herbert Leon "Sonny" (Ala.) Sept. 11, 1932–; House 1985–.

CALLAWAY, Howard Hollis "Bo" (Ga.) April 2, 1927–; House 1965–67.

CALLIS, John Benton (Ala.) Jan. 3, 1828–Sept. 24, 1898; House July 21, 1868–69.

CALVERT, Ken (Calif.) June 7, 1953–; House 1993–.

CAMERON, Angus (Wis.) July 4, 1826–March 30, 1897; Senate 1875–81, March 14, 1881–85.

CAMERON, James Donald (son of Simon Cameron) (Pa.) May 14, 1833–Aug. 30, 1918; Senate March 20, 1877–97; Secy. of War May 22, 1876–March 3, 1877; Chrmn. Rep. Nat. Comm. 1879–80.

CAMERON, Ralph Henry (Ariz.) Oct. 21, 1863–Feb. 12, 1953; House (Terr. Del.) 1909–Feb. 18, 1912; Senate 1921–27.

CAMERON, Simon (father of James Donald Cameron) (Pa.) March 8, 1799–June 26, 1889; Senate March 13, 1845–49 (no party), 1857–March 4, 1861, 1867–March 12, 1877; Secy. of War March 5, 1861–Jan. 14, 1862.

CAMP, David (Mich.) July 9,1953–; House 1991–.

CAMP, John Henry (N.Y.) April 4, 1840–Oct. 12, 1892; 1877–83.

CAMP, John Newbold Happy (Okla.) May 11, 1908–Sept. 27, 1987; House 1969–75.

CAMPBELL, Alexander (Ohio) 1779–Nov. 5, 1857; Senate Dec. 11, 1809–13.

CAMPBELL, Ben Nighthorse (Colo.) April 13, 1933–; House 1987–93 (Democrat); Senate 1993– (Republican from 1995).

CAMPBELL, Carroll Ashmore Jr. (S.C.) July 24, 1940–; House 1979–87; Gov. Jan. 14, 1987–.

CAMPBELL, Ed Hoyt (Iowa) March 6, 1882–April 26, 1969; House 1929–33.

CAMPBELL, George Washington (Tenn.) Feb 9, 1769–Feb. 17, 1848; House 1803–09; Senate Oct. 8, 1811–Feb. 11, 1814, Oct. 10, 1815–April 20, 1818; Secy. of the Treasury Feb. 9–Oct. 5, 1814.

CAMPBELL, Guy Edgar (Pa.) Oct. 9, 1871–Feb. 17, 1940; House 1917–33 (1917–23 Democrat).

CAMPBELL, Howard Edmond (Pa.) Jan. 4, 1890–Jan. 6, 1971; House 1945–47.

CAMPBELL, Jacob Miller (Pa.) Nov. 20, 1821–Sept. 27, 1888; House 1877–79, 1881–87.

CAMPBELL, John Wilson (Ohio) Feb. 23, 1782–Sept. 24, 1833; House 1817–27.

CAMPBELL, Philip Pitt (Kans.) April 25, 1862–May 26, 1941; House 1903–23.

CAMPBELL, Thomas J. (Calif.) Aug. 14, 1952–; House 1989–93.

CAMPBELL, William Wildman (Ohio) April 2, 1853–Aug. 13, 1927; House 1905–07.

CANADY, Charles Terrance (Fla.) June 22, 1954–; House 1993–.

CANDLER, John Wilson (Mass.) Feb. 10, 1828–March 16, 1903; House 1881–83, 1889–91.

CANFIELD, Gordon (N.J.) April 15, 1898–June 20, 1972; House 1941–61.

CANNON, George Quayle (father of Frank Jenne Cannon) (Utah) Jan. 11, 1827–April 12, 1901; House (Terr. Del.) 1873–81.

CANNON, Joseph Gurney (Ill.) May 7, 1836–Nov. 12, 1926; House 1873–91, 1893–1913, 1915–23; Speaker Nov. 9, 1903–05, Dec. 4, 1905–07, Dec. 2, 1907–09, March 15, 1909–11.

CANNON, Newton (Tenn.) May 22, 1781–Sept. 16, 1841; House Sept. 16, 1814–17, 1819–23; Gov. Oct. 12, 1835–Oct. 14, 1839 (Whig).

CAPEHART, Homer Earl (Ind.) June 6, 1897–Sept. 3, 1979; Senate 1945–63; Chrmn. Senate Banking and Currency 1953–55.

CAPPER, Arthur (Kans.) July 14, 1865–Dec. 19, 1951; Senate 1919–49; Chrmn. Senate Agriculture and Forestry 1947–49; Gov. Jan. 11, 1915–Jan. 13, 1919.

CAPRON, Adin Ballou (R.I.) Jan. 9, 1841–March 17, 1911; House 1897–1911.

CAPSTICK, John Henry (N.J.) Sept. 2, 1856–March 17, 1918; House 1915–March 17, 1918.

CAPUTO, Bruce Faulkner (N.Y.) Aug. 7, 1943–; House 1977–79.

CAREY, John (Ohio) April 5, 1792–March 17, 1875; House 1859–61.

CAREY, Joseph Maull (father of Robert Davis Carey) (Wyo.) Jan. 19, 1845–Feb. 5, 1924; House (Terr. Del.) 1885–July 10, 1890; Senate Nov. 15, 1890–95; Gov. Jan. 2, 1911–Jan. 4, 1915.

CAREY, Robert Davis (son of Joseph Maull Carey) (Wyo.) Aug. 12, 1878–Jan. 17, 1937; Senate Dec. 1, 1930–37; Gov. Jan. 6, 1919–Jan. 1, 1923.

CARLETON, Peter (N.H.) Sept. 19, 1755–April 29, 1828; House 1807–09.

CARLSON, Cliffard Dale (Ill.) Dec. 30, 1915–Aug. 28, 1977; House April 4, 1972–73.

CARLSON, Frank (Kans.) Jan. 23, 1893–May 30, 1987; House 1935–47; Senate Nov. 29, 1950–69; Chrmn. Senate Post

Office and Civil Service 1953–55; Gov. Jan. 13, 1947–Nov. 28, 1950.

CARMAN, Gregory Wright (N.Y.) Jan. 31, 1937–; House 1981–83.

CARNEY, William (N.Y.) July 1, 1942–; House 1979–87.

CARPENTER, Cyrus Clay (Iowa) Nov. 24, 1829–May 29, 1898; House 1879–83; Gov. Jan. 11, 1872–Jan. 13, 1876.

CARPENTER, Edmund Nelson (Pa.) June 27, 1865–Nov. 4, 1952; House 1925–27.

CARPENTER, Lewis Cass (S.C.) Feb. 20, 1836–March 6, 1908; House Nov. 3, 1874–75.

CARPENTER, Matthew Hale (Wis.) Dec. 22, 1824–Feb. 24, 1881; Senate 1869–75, 1879–Feb. 24, 1881; elected Pres. pro tempore March 12, 1873, March 26, 1873, Dec. 11, 1873, Dec. 23, 1874.

CARR, Francis (father of James Carr) (Mass.) Dec. 6, 1751–Oct. 6, 1821; House April 6, 1812–13.

CARRIER, Chester Otto (Ky.) May 5, 1897–Sept. 24, 1980; House Nov. 30, 1943–45.

CARRIGG, Joseph Leonard (Pa.) Feb. 23, 1901–; House Nov. 6, 1951–59.

CARSON, Henderson Haverfield (Ohio) Oct. 25, 1893–Oct. 6, 1971; House 1943–45, 1947–49.

CARTER, Albert Edward (Calif.) July 5, 1881 –Aug. 8, 1964; House 1925–45.

CARTER, Luther Cullen (N.Y.) Feb. 25, 1805–Jan. 3, 1875; House 1859–61.

CARTER, Thomas Henry (Mont.) Oct. 30, 1854–Sept. 17, 1911; House (Terr. Del.) March 4–Nov. 7, 1889, (Rep.) Nov. 8, 1889–91; Senate 1895–1901, 1905–11; Chrmn. Rep. Nat. Comm. 1892–96.

CARTER, Tim Lee (Ky.) Sept. 2, 1910–March 27, 1987; House 1965–81.

CARTER, Vincent Michael (Wyo.) Nov. 6, 1891–Dec. 30, 1972; House 1929–35.

CARTER, William Henry (Mass.) June l5, 1864–April 23, 1955; House 1915–19.

CARY, William Joseph (Wis.) March 22, 1865–Jan. 2, 1934; House 1907–19.

CASE, Charles (Ind.) Dec. 21, 1817–June 30, 1883; House Dec. 7, 1857–61.

CASE, Clifford Philip (N.J.) April 16, 1904–March 5, 1982; House 1945–Aug. 16, 1953; Senate 1955–79.

CASE, Francis Higbee (S.Dak.) Dec. 9, 1896–June 22, 1962; House 1937–51; Senate 1951–June 22, 1962; Chrmn. Senate District of Columbia 1953–55.

CASEY, Levi (S.C.) about 1752–Feb. 3, 1807; House 1803–Feb. 3, 1807.

CASEY, Lyman Rufus (N.Dak.) May 6, 1837–Jan. 26, 1914; Senate Nov. 25, 1889–93.

CASON, Thomas Jefferson (Ind.) Sept. 13, 1828–July 10, 1901; House 1873–77.

CASSEL, Henry Burd (Pa.) Oct. 19, 1855–April 28, 1926; House Nov. 5, 1901–09.

CASSIDY, James Henry (Ohio) Oct. 28, 1869–Aug. 23, 1926; House April 20, 1909–11.

CASTLE, Michael Newbold (Del.) July 2, 1939–; House 1993–; Gov. Jan. 15, 1985–Dec. 31, 1992.

CASTOR, George Albert (Pa.) Aug. 6, 1855–Feb. 19, 1906; House Feb. 16, 1904–Feb. 19, 1906.

CASWELL, Lucien Bonaparte (Wis.) Nov. 27, 1827–April 26, 1919; House 1875–83, 1885–91.

CATLIN, Theron Ephron (Mo.) May 16, 1878–March 19, 1960; House 1911–Aug. 12, 1912.

CATRON, Thomas Benton (N.Mex.) Oct. 6, 1840–May 15, 1921; House (Terr. Del.) 1895–97; Senate March 27, 1912–17.

CATTELL, Alexander Gilmore (N.J.) Feb. 12, 1816–April 8, 1894; Senate Sept. 19, 1866–71.

CAULFIELD, Henry Stewart (Mo.) Dec. 9, 1873–May 11, 1966; House 1907–09; Gov. Jan. 14, 1929–Jan. 9, 1933.

CAVICCHIA, Peter Angelo (N.J.) May 22 1879–Sept. 11, 1967; House 1931–37.

CEDERBERG, Elford Alfred (Mich.) March 6, 1918–; House 1953–Dec. 31, 1978.

CESSNA, John (Pa.) June 29, 1821–Dec. 13, 1893; House 1869–71, 1873–75.

CHABOT, Steve (Ohio) House, 1995–;

CHACE, Jonathan (R.I.) July 22, 1829–June 30, 1917; House 1881–Jan. 26, 1885; Senate Jan. 1885–April 9, 1889.

CHADWICK, E. Wallace (Pa.) Jan. 17, 1884–Aug. 18, 1969; House 1947–49.

CHAFEE, John Hubbard (R.I.) Oct. 22, 1922–; Senate Dec. 29, 1976–; Gov. Jan, 1, 1963–Jan 7, 1969; Chrmn. Senate Environment and Public Works Committee 1995–.

CHAFFEE, Jerome Bunty (Colo.) April 17, 1825–March 9, 1886; House (Terr. Del.) 1871–75; Senate Nov. 15, 1876–79.

CHALMERS, William Wallace (Ohio) Nov. 1, 1861–Oct. 1, 1944; House 1921–23, 1925–31.

CHAMBERLAIN, Charles Ernest (Mich.) July 22, 1917–; House 1957–Dec. 31, 1974.

CHAMBERLAIN, Jacob Payson (N.Y.) Aug. 1, 1802–Oct. 5, 1878; House 1861–63.

CHAMBLISS, Saxby (Ga.) House, 1995–.

CHANDLER, John (brother of Thomas Chandler, uncle of Zachariah Chandler) (Maine) Feb. 1, 1762–Sept. 25, 1841; House 1805–09 (Mass.); Senate June 14, 1820–29.

CHANDLER, Rod Dennis (great-great-great-nephew of Zachariah Chandler) (Wash.) July 13, 1942–; House 1983–93.

CHANDLER, Thomas Alberter (Okla.) July 26, 1871–June 22, 1953; House 1917–1919, 1921–23.

CHANDLER, Walter Marion (N.Y.) Dec. 8, 1867–March 16, 1936; House 1913–19 (1913–17 Progressive), 1921–23.

CHANDLER, William Eaton (N.H.) Dec. 28, 1835–Nov. 30, 1917; Senate June 14, 1887–89, June 18, 1889–1901; Secy. of the Navy April 16, 1882–March 6, 1885.

CHANDLER, Zachariah (nephew of John Chandler and Thomas Chandler, grandfather of Frederick Hale; great-great-great-uncle of Rod Dennis Chandler) (Mich.) Dec. 10, 1813–Nov. 1, 1879; Senate 1857–75, Feb. 22, 1879–Nov. 1, 1879; Secy. of the Interior Oct. 19, 1875–March 11, 1877; Chrmn. Rep. Nat. Comm. 1876–79.

CHANEY, John Crawford (Ind.) Feb. 1, 1853–April 26, 1940; House 1905–09.

CHAPMAN, Pleasant Thomas (Ill.) Oct. 8, 1854–Jan. 31, 1931; House 1905–11.

CHAPPELL, John Joel (S.C.) Jan. 19, 1782–May 23, 1871; House 1813–17.

CHAPPIE, Eugene A. (Calif.) March 28, 1920–May 31, 1992; House 1981–87.

CHARLES, William Barclay (N.Y.) April 3, 1861–Nov. 25, 1950; House 1915–17.

CHASE, Dudley (uncle of Salmon Portland Chase and Dudley Chase Denison) (Vt.) Dec. 20, 1771–Feb. 23, 1846; Senate 1813–Nov. 3, 1817 (Jefferson Democrat), 1825–31.

CHASE, Jackson Burton (Nebr.) Aug. 19, 1890–May 4, 1974; House 1955–57.

CHASE, James Mitchell (Pa.) Dec. 19, 1891–Jan. 1, 1945; House 1927–33.

CHASE, Ray P. (Minn.) March 12, 1880–Sept. 18, 1948; House 1933–35.

CHASE, Salmon Portland (nephew of Dudley Chase, cousin of Dudley Chase Denison) (Ohio) Jan. 13, 1808–May 7, 1873; Senate 1849–55 (Free-Soiler), March 4–6, 1861; Gov. Jan. 14, 1856–Jan. 9, 1860; Secy. of the Treasury March 7, 1861–June 30, 1864; Chief Justice U.S. Supreme Court Dec. 15, 1864–May 7, 1873.

CHAVES, Jose Francisco (N.Mex.) June 27, 1833–Nov. 26, 1904; House (Terr. Del.) 1865–67, Feb. 20, 1869–71.

CHEADLE, Joseph Bonaparte (Ind.) Aug. 14, 1842–May 28, 1904; House 1887–91.

CHEATHAM, Henry Plummer (N.C.) Dec. 27, 1857–Nov. 29, 1935; House 1889–93.

CHENEY, Person Colby (N.H.) Feb. 25, 1828–June 19, 1901; Senate Nov. 24, 1886–June 14, 1887; Gov. June 10, 1875–June 6, 1877.

CHENEY, Richard Bruce (Wyo.) Jan. 30, 1941–; House 1979–March 17, 1989; Secy. of Defense March 21, 1989–Jan. 20, 1993.

CHENOWETH, Helen (Idaho) House, 1995–.

CHENOWETH, John Edgar (Colo.) Aug. 17, 1897–Jan. 2, 1986; House 1941–49, 1951–65.

CHEVES, Langdon (S.C.) Sept. 17, 1776–June 26, 1857; House Dec. 31, 1810–15; Speaker Jan. 19, 1814–15.

CHICKERING, Charles Addison (N.Y.) Nov. 26, 1843–Feb. 13, 1900; House 1893–Feb. 13, 1900.

CHILCOTT, George Miles (Colo.) Jan. 2, 1828–March 6, 1891; House (Terr. Del.) 1867–69; Senate April 17, 1882–Jan. 27, 1883.

CHILDS, Robert Andrew (Ill.) March 22, 1845–Dec. 19, 1915; House 1893–95.

CHINDBLOM, Carl Richard (Ill.) Dec. 21, 1870–Sept. 12, 1956; House 1919–33.

CHIPERFIELD, Burnett Mitchell (father of Robert Bruce Chiperfield) (Ill.) June 14, 1870–June 24, 1940; House 1915–17, 1929–33.

CHIPERFIELD, Robert Bruce (son of Burnett Mitchell Chiperfield) (Ill.) Nov. 20, 1899–April 9, 1971; House 1939–69; Chrmn. House Foreign Affairs 1953–55.

CHIPMAN, Norton Parker (D.C.) March 7, 1836–Feb. 1, 1924; House (Del.) April 21, 1871–75.

CHITTENDEN, Simeon Baldwin (N.Y.) March 29, 1814–April 14, 1889; House Nov. 3, 1874–81 (Nov. 3, 1874–77 Independent Republican).

CHRISTGAU, Victor Laurence August (Minn.) Sept. 20, 1894–Oct. 10, 1991; House 1929–33.

CHRISTIANCY, Isaac Peckham (Mich.) March 12, 1812–Sept. 8, 1890; Senate 1875–Feb. 10, 1879.

CHRISTENSON, Jon (Nebr.) House, 1995–.

CHRISTIANSON, Theodore (Minn.) Sept. 12, 1883–Dec. 9, 1948; House 1933–37; Gov. Jan. 6, 1925–Jan. 6, 1931.

CHRISTIE, Gabriel (Md.) 1755–April 1, 1808; House 1793–97 (no party), 1799–1801.

CHRISTOPHERSON, Charles Andrew (S.Dak.) July 23, 1871–Nov. 2, 1951; House 1919–33.

CHRYSLER, Dick (Mich.) House, 1995–.

CHURCH, Marguerite Stitt (widow of Ralph Edwin Church) (Ill.) Sept. 13, 1892–May 26, 1990; House 1951–63.

CHURCH, Ralph Edwin (husband of Marguerite Stitt Church) (Ill.) May 5, 1883–March 21, 1950; House 1935–41, 1943–March 21, 1950.

CHURCHILL, George Bosworth (Mass.) Oct. 24, 1866–July 1, 1925; House March 4–July 1, 1925.

CHURCHILL, John Charles (N.Y.) Jan. 17, 1821–June 4, 1905; House 1867–71.

CLAFLIN, William (Mass.) March 6, 1818–Jan. 5, 1905; House 1877–81; Gov. Jan. 7, 1869–Jan. 4, 1872; Chrmn. Rep. Nat. Comm. 1868–72.

CLAGETT, Clifton (N.H.) Dec. 3, 1762–Jan. 25, 1829; House 1803–05 (Federalist), 1817–21.

CLAGETT, William Horace (uncle of Samuel Barrett Pettengill) (Mont.) Sept. 21, 1838–Aug. 3, 1901; House (Terr. Del.) 1871–73.

CLAGUE, Frank (Minn.) July 13, 1865–March 25, 1952; House 1921–33.

CLAIBORNE, John (son of Thomas Claiborne born in 1749, brother of Thomas Claiborne born in 1780) (Va.) 1777–Oct. 9, 1808; House 1805–Oct. 9, 1808.

CLAIBORNE, Thomas (father of John Claiborne and Thomas Claiborne born in 1780, uncle of Nathaniel Herbert Claiborne and William Charles Cole Claiborne, great-uncle of John Francis Hamtramck Claiborne, great-great-great-great-great-uncle of Corinne Claiborne Boggs) (Va.) Feb. 1, 1749–1812; House 1793–99, 1801–05.

CLAIBORNE, Thomas (son of Thomas Claiborne born in 1749, brother of John Claiborne) (Tenn.) May 17, 1780–Jan. 7, 1856; House 1817–19.

CLANCY, Donald Daniel (Ohio) July 24, 1921–; House 1961–77.

CLANCY, Robert Henry (Mich.) March 14, 1882–April 23, 1962; House 1923–25 (Democrat), 1927–33.

CLAPP, Moses Edwin (Minn.) May 21, 1851–March 6, 1929; Senate Jan. 23, 1901–17.

CLARDY, Kit Francis (Mich.) June 17, 1892–Sept. 5, 1961; House 1953–55.

CLARK, Ambrose Williams (N.Y.) Feb. 19, 1810–Oct. 13, 1887; House 1861–65.

CLARK, Amos Jr. (N.J.) Nov. 8, 1828–Oct. 31, 1912; House 1873–75.

CLARK, Charles Benjamin (Wis.) Aug. 24, 1844–Sept. 10, 1891; House 1887–91.

CLARK, Charles Nelson (Mo.) Aug. 21, 1827–Oct. 4, 1902; House 1895–97.

CLARK, Christopher Henderson (brother of James Clark, uncle of John Bullock Clark, great-uncle of John Bullock Clark Jr.) (Va.) 1767–Nov. 21, 1828; House Nov. 5, 1804–July 1, 1806.

CLARK, Clarence Don (Wyo.) April 16, 1851–Nov. 18, 1930; House Dec. 1, 1890–93; Senate Jan. 23, 1895–1917.

CLARK, Daniel (N.H.) Oct. 24, 1809–Jan. 2, 1891; Senate June 27, 1857–July 27, 1866; elected Pres. pro tempore April 26, 1864, Feb. 9, 1865.

CLARK, Ezra Jr. (Conn.) Sept. 12, 1813–Sept. 26, 1896; House 1855–59 (1855–57 American Party).

CLARK, Henry Alden (Pa.) Jan. 7, 1850–Feb. 15, 1944; House 1917–19.

CLARK, James (brother of Christopher Henderson Clark, uncle of John Bullock Clark, great-uncle of John Bullock Clark Jr.) (Ky.) Jan. 16, 1770–Sept. 27, 1839; House 1813–16, Aug. 1, 1825–31; Gov. June 1, 1836–Sept. 27, 1839 (Whig).

CLARK, James West (N.C.) Oct. 15, 1779–Dec. 20, 1843; House 1815–17.

CLARK, Linwood Leon (Md.) March 21, 1876–Nov. 18, 1965; House 1929–31.

CLARK, Rush (Iowa) Oct. 1, 1834–April 29, 1879; House 1877–April 29, 1879.

CLARK, Samuel Mercer (Iowa) Oct. 11, 1842–Aug. 11, 1900; House 1895–99.

CLARK, William Thomas (Tex.) June 29, 1831–Oct. 12, 1905; House March 3l, 1870–May 13, 1872.

CLARKE, Archibald Smith (brother of Staley Nichols Clarke) (N.Y.) 1788–Dec. 4, 1821; House Dec. 2, 1816–17.

CLARKE, Frank Gay (N.H.) Sept. 10, 1850–Jan. 9, 1901; House 1897–Jan. 9, 1901.

CLARKE, Freeman (N.Y.) March 22, 1809–June 24, 1887; House 1863–65, 1871–75.

CLARKE, John Davenport (husband of Marian Williams Clarke) (N.Y.) Jan. 15, 1873–Nov. 5, 1933; House 1921–25, 1927–Nov. 5, 1933.

CLARKE, Marian Williams (widow of John Davenport Clarke) (N.Y.) July 29, 1880–April 8, 1953; House Dec. 28, 1933–35.

CLARKE, Reader Wright (Ohio) May 18, 1812–May 23, 1872; House 1865–69.

CLARKE, Sidney (Kans.) Oct. 16, 1831–June 18, 1909; House 1865–71.

CLASON, Charles Russell (Mass.) Sept. 3, 1890–July 7, 1985; House 1937–49.

CLASSON, David Guy (Wis.) Sept. 27, 1870–Sept.6, 1930; House 1917–23.

CLAUSEN, Don Holst (Calif.) April 27, 1923–; House Jan. 22, 1963–83.

CLAWSON, Delwin Morgan (Calif.) Jan. 11, 1914–May 5, 1992; House June 11, 1963–Dec. 31, 1978.

CLAWSON, Isaiah Dunn (N.J.) March 30, 1822–Oct. 9, 1879; House 1855–59 (1855–57 Whig).

CLAY, Joseph (Pa.) July 24, 1769–Aug. 27, 1811; House 1803–08.

CLAY, Matthew (Va.) March 25, 1754–May 27, 1815; House 1797–1813, March 4–May 27, 1815.

CLAYTON, Charles (Calif.) Oct. 5, 1825–Oct. 4, 1885; House 1873–75.

CLAYTON, Powell (Ark.) Aug. 7, 1833–Aug. 25, 1914; Senate 1871–77; Gov. July 2, 1868–March 17, 1871.

CLEMENTS, Isaac (Ill.) March 31, 1837–May 31, 1909; House 1873–75.

CLENDENIN, David (Ohio) ?–?; House Oct. 11, 1814–17.

CLEVELAND, James Colgate (N.H.) June 13, 1920–; House 1963–81.

CLEVENGER, Cliff (Ohio) Aug. 20, 1885–Dec. 13, 1960; House 1939–59.

CLIFT, Joseph Wales (Ga.) Sept. 30, 1837–May 2, 1908; House July 25, 1868–69.

CLINGER, William Floyd Jr. (Pa.) April 4, 1929–; House 1979–. Chrmn. House Government Reform and Oversight Committee 1995–.

CLINTON, De Witt (half-brother of James Graham Clinton, cousin of George Clinton, nephew of Vice Pres. George Clinton) (N.Y.) March 2, 1769–Feb. 11, 1828; Senate Feb. 9, 1802–Nov. 4, 1803; Gov. July 1, 1817–Jan. 1, 1823, Jan. 1, 1825–Feb. 11, 1828.

CLINTON, George (cousin of De Witt Clinton and James Graham Clinton, son of Vice Pres. George Clinton) (N.Y.) June 5, 1771–Sept. 16, 1809; House Feb. 14, 1805–09.

CLIPPINGER, Roy (Ill.) Jan. 13, 1886–Dec. 24, 1962; House Nov. 6, 1945–49.

CLOPTON, John (Va.) Feb. 7, 1756–Sept. 11, 1816; House 1795–99, 1801–Sept. 11, 1816.

CLOUSE, Wynne F. (Tenn.) Aug. 29, 1883–Feb. 19, 1944; House 1921–23.

CLUETT, Ernest Harold (N.Y.) July 13, 1874–Feb. 4, 1954; House 1937–43.

COATS, Daniel Ray (Ind.) May 16, 1943–; House 1981–Jan. 1, 1989; Senate Jan. 3, 1989–.

COBB, Amasa (Wis.) Sept. 27, 1823–July 5, 1905; House 1863–71.

COBB, Clinton Levering (N.C.) Aug. 25, 1842–April 30, 1879; House 1869–75.

COBB, Howell (Ga.) Aug. 3, 1772–May 26, 1818; House 1807–12.

COBB, Stephen Alonzo (Kans.) June 17, 1833–Aug. 24, 1878; House 1873–75.

COBEY, William Wilfred Jr. (N.C.) May 13, 1939–; House 1985–87.

COBLE, Howard (N.C.) March 18, 1931–; House 1985–.

COBURN, John (Ind.) Oct. 27, 1825–Jan. 28, 1908; House 1867–75.

COBURN, Stephen (Maine) Nov. 11, 1817–July 4, 1882; House Jan. 2–March 3, 1861.

COBURN, Tom (Okla.) House, 1995–.

COCHRAN, James (grandfather of James Cochrane Dobbin) (N.C.) about 1767–April 7, 1813; House 1809–13.

COCHRAN, Thomas Cunningham (Pa.) Nov. 30, 1877–Dec. 10, 1957; House 1927–35.

COCHRAN, William Thad (Miss.) Dec. 7, 1937–; House 1973–Dec. 26, 1978; Senate Dec. 27, 1978–.

COCHRANE, Aaron Van Schaick (nephew of Isaac of Whitbeck Van Schaick) (N.Y.) March 14, 1858–Sept. 7, 1943; House 1897–1901.

COCHRANE, Clark Betton (uncle of George Cochrane Hazelton and Gerry Whiting Hazelton) (N.Y.) May 31, 1815–March 5, 1867; House 1857–61.

COCKE, William (father of John Cocke, grandfather of William Michael Cocke) (Tenn.) 1748–Aug. 22, 1828; Senate Aug. 2, 1796–March 3, 1797, April 22–Sept. 26, 1797, 1799–1805.

COCKS, William Willets (brother of Frederick Cocks Hicks) (N.Y.) July 24, 1861 –May 24, 1932; House 1905–11.

CODD, George Pierre (Mich.) Dec. 7, 1869–Feb. 16, 1927; House 1921–23.

CODDING, James Hodge (Pa.) July 8, 1849–Sept. 12, 1919; House Nov. 5, 1895–99.

COFFIN, Charles Edward (Md.) July 18, 1841–May 24, 1912; House Nov. 6, 1894–97.

COFFIN, Howard Aldridge (Mich.) June 11, 1877–Feb. 28, 1956; House 1947–49.

COGHLAN, John Maxwell (Calif.) Dec. 8, 1835–March 26, 1879; House 1871–73.

COGSWELL, William (Mass.) Aug. 23, 1838–May 22, 1895; House 1887–May 22, 1895.

COHEN, William Sebastian (Maine) Aug. 28, 1940; House 1973–79; Senate 1979–; Chrmn. Senate Special Aging Committee 1995–.

COLE, Albert McDonald (Kans.) Oct. 13, 1901–June 5, 1994; House 1945–53.

COLE, Cornelius (Calif.) Sept. 17, 1822–Nov. 3, 1924; House 1863–65 (Union Republican); Senate 1867–73.

COLE, Cyrenus (Iowa) Jan. 13, 1863–Nov. 14, 1939–; House July 19, 1921–33.

COLE, Nathan (Mo.) July 26, 1825–March 4, 1904; House 1877–79.

COLE, Ralph Dayton (brother of Raymond Clinton Cole) (Ohio) Nov. 30, 1873–Oct. 15, 1932; House 1905–11.

COLE, Raymond Clinton (brother of Ralph Dayton Cole) (Ohio) Aug. 21, 1870–Feb. 8, 1957; House 1919–25.

COLE, William Clay (Mo.) Aug. 29, 1897–Sept. 23, 1965; House 1943–49, 1953–55.

COLE, William Sterling (N.Y.) April 18, 1904–March 15, 1987; House 1935–Dec. 1, 1957.

COLEMAN, Earl Thomas (Mo.) May 29, 1943–; House Nov. 2, 1976–93.

COLEMAN, Hamilton Dudley (La.) May 12, 1845–March 16, 1926; House 1889–91.

COLEMAN, William Henry (Pa.) Dec. 28, 1871–June 3, 1943; House 1915–17.

COLES, Isaac (father of Walter Coles) (Va.) March 2, 1747–June 3, 1813; House 1789–91 (no party), 1793–97 (1793–95 no party).

COLFAX, Schuyler (Ind.) March 23, 1823–Jan. 13, 1885; House 1855–69; Speaker Dec. 7, 1863–65, Dec. 4, 1865–67, March 4, 1867–March 2, 1869; Vice President 1869–73.

COLHOUN, John Ewing (cousin of John Caldwell Calhoun and Joseph Calhoun) (S.C.) about 1749–Oct. 26, 1802; Senate 1801–Oct. 26, 1802.

COLLAMER, Jacob (Vt.) Jan. 8, 1791–Nov. 9, 1865; House 1843–49 (Whig); Senate 1855–Nov. 9, 1865; Postmaster Gen. March 8, 1849–July 22, 1850.

COLLIER, Harold Reginald (Ill.) Dec. 12, 1916–; House 1957–75.

COLLINS, James Mitchell (Tex.) April 29, 1916–July 21, 1989; House Aug. 24, 1968–83.

COLLINS, Mac (Ga.) Oct. 15, 1944–; House 1993–.

COLLINS, Samuel LaFort (Calif.) Aug. 6, 1895–June 26, 1965; House 1933–37.

COLSON, David Grant (Ky.) April 1, 1861–Sept. 27, 1904; House 1895–99.

COLT, LeBaron Bradford (R.I.) June 25, 1846–Aug. 18, 1924; Senate 1913–Aug. 18, 1924.

COLTON, Don Byron (Utah) Sept. 15, 1876–Aug. 1, 1952; House 1921–33.

COMBEST, Larry Ed (Tex.) March 20, 1945–; House 1985–, Chrmn. House Select Intelligence Committee 1995–.

COMINS, Linus Bacon (Mass.) Nov. 29, 1817–Oct. 14, 1892; House 1855–59 (1865–57 American Party).

COMPTON, C. H. Ranulf (Conn.) Sept. 16, 1878–Jan. 26, 1974; House 1943–45.

COMSTOCK, Daniel Webster (Ind.) Dec. 16, 1840–May 19, 1917; House March 4–May 19, 1917.

COMSTOCK, Oliver Cromwell (N.Y.) March 1, 1780–Jan. 11, 1860; House 1813–19.

COMSTOCK, Solomon Gilman (Minn.) May 9, 1842–June 3, 1933; House 1889–91.

CONABLE, Barber Benjamin Jr. (N.Y.) Nov. 2, 1922–; House 1965–85.

CONARD, John (Pa.) Nov. 1773–May 9, 1857; House 1813–15.

CONDICT, Lewis (N.J.) March 3, 1772–May 26, 1862; House 1811–17, 1821–33.

CONDIT, John (father of Silas Condit) (N.J.) July 8, 1755–May 4, 1834; House 1799–1803, March 4–Nov. 4, 1819; Senate Sept. 1, 1803–March 3, 1809, March 21, 1809–17.

CONGER, Edwin Hurd (Iowa) March 7, 1843–May 18, 1907; House 1885–Oct. 3, 1890.

CONGER, Omar Dwight (Mich.) April 1, 1818–July 11, 1898; House 1869–81; Senate 1881–87.

CONKLING, Alfred (father of Frederick Augustus Conkling and Roscoe Conkling) (N.Y.) Oct. 12, 1789–Feb. 5, 1874; House 1821–23.

CONKLING, Frederick Augustus (son of Alfred Conkling, brother of Roscoe Conkling) (N.Y.) Aug. 22, 1816–Sept. 18, 1891; House 1861–63.

CONKLING, Roscoe (son of Alfred Conkling, brother of Frederick Augustus Conkling) (N.Y.) Oct. 30, 1829–April 18, 1888; House 1859–63, 1865–March 4, 1867; Senate March 4, 1867–May 16, 1881.

CONLAN, John Bertrand (Ariz.) Sept. 17, 1930–; House 1973–77.

CONNELL, Charles Robert (son of William Connell) (Pa.) Sept. 22, 1864–Sept. 26, 1922; House 1921–Sept. 26, 1922.

CONNELL, William (father of Charles Robert Connell) (Pa.) Sept. 10, 1827–March 21, 1909; House 1897–1903, Feb. 10, 1904–05.

CONNELL, William James (Nebr.) July 6, 1846–Aug. 16, 1924; House 1889–91.

CONNER, James Perry (Iowa) Jan. 27, 1851–March 19, 1924; House Dec. 4, 1900–09.

CONNER, Samuel Shepard (Mass.) about 1783–Dec. 17, 1820; House 1815–17.

CONNOLLY, James Austin (Ill.) March 8, 1843–Dec. 15, 1914; House 1895–99.

CONNOLLY, James Joseph (Pa.) Sept. 24, 1881–Dec. 10, 1952; House 1921–35.

CONOVER, Simon Barclay (Fla.) Sept. 23, 1840–April 19, 1908; Senate 1873–79.

CONOVER, William Sheldrick II (Pa.) Aug. 27, 1928–; House April 25, 1972–73.

CONRAD, Frederick (Pa.) 1759–Aug. 3, 1827; House 1803–07.

CONTE, Silvio Otto (Mass.) Nov. 9, 1921–Feb. 8, 1991; House 1959–Feb. 8, 1991.

CONWAY, Martin Franklin (Kans.) Nov. 19, 1827–Feb. 15, 1882; House Jan. 29, 1861–63.

COOK, Burton Chauncey (Ill.) May 11, 1819–Aug. 18, 1894; House 1865–Aug. 26, 1871.

COOK, George Washington (Colo.) Nov. 10, 1851–Dec. 18, 1916; House 1907–09.

COOK, Joel (Pa.) March 20, 1842–Dec. 15, 1910; House Nov. 5, 1907–Dec. 15, 1910.

COOK, Marlow Webster (Ky.) July 27, 1926; Senate Dec. 17, 1968–Dec. 27, 1974.

COOK, Orchard (Mass.) March 24, 1763–Aug. 12, 1819; House 1805–11.

COOK, Samuel Andrew (Wis.) Jan. 28, 1849–April 4, 1918; House 1895–97.

COOK, Zadock (Ga.) Feb. 18, 1769–Aug. 3, 1863; House Dec. 2, 1816–19.

COOK, Edmund Francis (N.Y.) April 13, 1885–May 13, 1967; House 1929–33.

COOKE, Edward Dean (Ill.) Oct. 17, 1849–June 24, 1897; House 1895–June 24, 1897.

COOKE, Thomas Burrage (N.Y.) Nov. 21, 1778–Nov. 20, 1853; House 1811–13.

COOLEY, Wes (Oreg.) House, 1995–.

COOMBS, Frank Leslie (Calif.) Dec. 27, 1853–Oct. 5, 1934; House 1901–03.

COON, Samuel Harrison (Oreg.) April 15, 1903–May 8, 1980; House 1953–57.

COOPER, Allen Foster (Pa.) June 16, 1862–April 20, 1917; House 1903–11.

COOPER, Edward (W.Va.) Feb. 26, 1873–March 1, 1928; House 1915–19.

COOPER, Henry Allen (Wis.) Sept. 8, 1850–March 1, 1931; House 1893–1919, 1921–March 1, 1931.

COOPER, John Gordon (Ohio) April 27, 1872–Jan. 7, 1955; House 1915–37.

COOPER, John Sherman (Ky.) Aug. 23, 1901–Feb. 21, 1991; Senate Nov. 6, 1946–49, Nov. 5, 1952–55, Nov. 7, 1956–73.

COOPER, William Craig (Ohio) Dec. 18, 1832–Aug. 29, 1902; House 1885–91.

COPELAND, Oren Sturman (Nebr.) March 16, 1887–April 10, 1958; House 1941–43.

COPLEY, Ira Clifton (nephew of Richard Henry Whiting) (Ill.) Oct. 25, 1864–Nov. 1, 1947; House 1911–23 (1915–17 Progressive).

CORBETT, Robert James (Pa.) Aug. 25, 1905–April 25, 1971; House 1939–41, 1945–April 25, 1971.

CORCORAN, Thomas Joseph (Ill.) May 23, 1939–; House 1977–85.

CORDON, Guy (Oreg.) April 24, 1890–June 8, 1969; Senate March 4, 1944–55; Chrmn. Senate Interior and Insular Affairs 1954–55.

CORLETT, William Wellington (Wyo.) April 10, 1842–July 22, 1890; House (Terr. Del.) 1877–79.

CORLEY, Manuel Simeon (S.C.) Feb. 10, 1823–Nov. 20, 1902; House July 25, 1868–69.

CORLISS, John Blaisdell (Mich.) June 7, 1851–Dec. 24, 1929; House 1895–1903.

CORNELL, Thomas (N.Y.) Jan. 27, 1814–March 30, 1890; House 1867–69, 1881–83.

CORWIN, Franklin (nephew of Moses Bledso Corwin and Thomas Corwin) (Ill.) Jan. 12, 1818–June 15, 1879; House 1873–75.

CORWIN, Thomas (brother of Moses Bledso Corwin, uncle of Franklin Corwin) (Ohio) July 29, 1794–Dec. 18, 1865; House 1831–May 30, 1840 (Whig), 1859–March 12, 1861; Senate 1845–July 20, 1850 (Whig); Gov. Dec. 16, 1840–Dec. 14, 1841 (Whig); Secy. of the Treasury July 23, 1850–March 6, 1853.

COSTELLO, Peter Edward (Pa.) June 27, 1854–Oct. 23, 1935; House 1915–21.

COTTON, Aylett Rains (Iowa) Nov. 29, 1826–Oct. 30, 1912; House 1871–75.

COTTON, Norris H. (N.H.) May 11, 1900–Feb. 24, 1989; House 1947–Nov. 7, 1954; Senate Nov. 8, 1954–Dec. 31, 1974, Aug. 8–Sept. 18, 1975.

COUDERT, Frederick René Jr. (N.Y.) May 7, 1898–May 21, 1972; House 1947–59.

COUDREY, Harry Marcy (Mo.) Feb. 28, 1867–July 5, 1930; House June 23, 1906–11.

COUGHLIN, Clarence Dennis (uncle of Robert Lawrence Coughlin) (Pa.) July 27, 1883–Dec. 15, 1946; House 1921–23.

COUGHLIN, Robert Lawrence (nephew of Clarence Dennis Coughlin) (Pa.) April 11, 1929–; House 1969–93.

COURTER, James Andrew (N.J.) Oct. 14, 1941–; House 1979–91.

COUSINS, Robert Gordon (Iowa) Jan. 31, 1859–June 20, 1933; House 1893–1909.

COUZENS, James (Mich.) Aug. 26, 1872–Oct. 22, 1936; Senate Nov. 29, 1922–Oct. 22, 1936.

COVERDELL, Paul (Ga.) Jan. 20, 1939–; Senate 1993–.

COVINGTON, Leonard (Md.) Oct. 30, 1768–Nov. 14, 1813; House 1805–07.

COVODE, John (Pa.) March 17, 1808–Jan. 11, 1871; House 1855–63 (1855–57 Whig), 1867–69, Feb. 9, 1870–Jan. 11, 1871.

COWAN, Edgar (Pa.) Sept. 19, 1815–Aug. 31, 1885; Senate 1861–67.

COWGER, William Owen (Ky.) Jan. 1, 1922–Oct. 2, 1971; House 1967–71.

COWGILL, Calvin (Ind.) Jan. 7, 1819–Feb. 10, 1903; House 1879–81.

COWLES, Charles Holden (nephew of William Henry Harrison Cowles) (N.C.) July 16, 1875–Oct. 2, 1957; House 1909–11.

COWLES, George Washington (N.Y.) Dec. 6, 1823–Jan. 20, 1901; House 1869–71.

COX, Charles Christopher (Calif.) Oct. 16, 1952–; House 1989–.

COX, Jacob Dolson (Ohio) Oct. 27, 1828–Aug. 4, 1900; House 1877–79; Gov. Jan. 8, 1866–Jan. 13, 1868; Secy of the Interior March 5, 1869–Oct. 31, 1870.

COX, James (N.J.) June 14, 1753–Sept. 12, 1810; House 1809–Sept. 12, 1810.

COYLE, William Radford (Pa.) July 10, 1878–Jan. 30, 1962; House 1925–27, 1929–33.

COYNE, James Kitchenman III (Pa.) Nov. 17, 1946–; House.1981–83.

CRADDOCK, John Durrett (Ky.) Oct. 26, 1881–May 20, 1942; House 1929–31.

CRAGIN, Aaron Harrison (N.H.) Feb. 3, 1821–May 10, 1898; House 1855–59 (1855–57 American Party); Senate 1865–77.

CRAGO, Thomas Spencer (Pa.) Aug. 8, 1866–Sept. 12, 1925; House 1911–13, 1915–21, Sept. 20, 1921–23.

CRAIG, George Henry (Ala.) Dec. 25, 1845–Jan. 26, 1923; House Jan. 9–March 3, 1885.

CRAIG, Larry Edwin (Idaho) July 20, 1945–; House 1981–91; Senate 1991–.

CRAIG, Samuel Alfred (Pa.) Nov. 19, 1839–March 17, 1920; House 1889–91.

CRAIG, Joe (Calif) Dec. 25, 1877–March 2, 1938; House 1927–33.

CRAMER, William Cato (Fla.) Aug. 4, 1922–; House 1955–71.

CRAMTON, Louis Convers (Mich.) Dec. 2, 1875–June 23, 1966; House 1913–31.

CRANE, Daniel Bever (brother of Philip Miller Crane) (Ill.) Jan. 10, 1936–; House 1979–85.

CRANE, Philip Miller (brother of Daniel Bever Crane) (Ill.) Nov. 3, 1930–; House Nov. 25, 1969-.

CRANE, Winthrop Murray (Mass.) April 23, 1853–Oct. 2, 1920; Senate Oct. 12, 1904–13; Gov. Jan. 4, 1900–Jan. 8, 1903.

CRAPO, Michael Dean (Idaho) May 20, 1951–; House 1993–.

CRAPO, William Wallace (Mass.) May 16, 1830–Feb. 28, 1926; House Nov. 2, 1875–83.

CRAWFORD, Coe Isaac (S.Dak.) Jan. 14, 1858–April 25, 1944; Senate 1909–15; Gov. Jan. 8, 1907–Jan. 5, 1909.

CRAWFORD, Fred Lewis (Mich.) May 5, 1888–April 13, 1967; House 1935–53.

CRAWFORD, Joel (Ga.) June 15, 1783–April 5, 1858; House 1817–21.

CRAWFORD, William (Pa.) 1760–Oct. 23, 1823; House 1809–17.

CREAGER, Charles Edward (Okla.) April 28, 1873–Jan. 11, 1964; House 1909–11.

CREIGHTON, William Jr. (Ohio) Oct. 29, 1778–Oct. 1, 1851; House May 4, 1813–17, 1827–28, 1829–33.

CREMEANS, Frank A. (Ohio) House, 1995–.

CRESWELL, John Angel James (Md.) Nov. 18, 1828–Dec. 23, 1891; House 1863–65; Senate March 9, 1867; Postmaster Gen. March 6, 1869–July 6, 1874.

CRETELLA, Albert William (Conn.) April 22, 1897–May 24, 1979; House 1953–59.

CRIPPA, Edward David (Wyo.) April 8, 1899–Oct. 20, 1960; Senate June 24–Nov. 28, 1954.

CRIST, Henry (Ky.) Oct. 20, 1764–Aug. 11, 1844; House 1809–11.

CROCHERON, Henry (brother of Jacob Crocheron) (N.Y.) Dec. 26, 1772–Nov. 8, 1819; House 1815–17.

CROCKER, Alvah (Mass.) Oct. 14, 1801–Dec. 26, 1874; House Jan. 2, 1872–Dec. 26, 1874.

CROMER, George Washington (Ind.) May 13, 1856–1936; House 1899–1907.

CRONIN, Paul William (Mass.) March 14, 1938–; 1973–75.

CROOKE, Philip Schuyler (N.Y.) March 2, 1810–March 17, 1881; House 1873–75.

CROUCH, Edward (Pa.) Nov. 9, 1764–Feb. 2, 1827; House Oct. 12, 1813–15.

CROUNSE, Lorenzo (Nebr.) Jan. 27, 1834–May 13, 1909; House 1873–77; Gov. Jan. 13, 1893–Jan. 3, 1895.

CROUSE, George Washington (Ohio) Nov. 23, 1832–Jan. 5, 1912; House 1887–89.

CROW, Charles Augustus (Mo.) March 31, 1873–March 20, 1938; House 1909–11.

CROW, William Evans (father of William Josiah Crow) (Pa.) March 10, 1870–Aug. 2, 1922; Senate Oct. 24, 1921–Aug. 2, 1922.

CROW, William Josiah (son of William Evans Crow) (Pa.) Jan. 22, 1902–Oct. 13, 1974; House 1947–49.

CROWLEY, Richard (N.Y.) Dec. 14, 1836–July 22, 1908; House 1879–83.

CROWNINSHIELD, Jacob (brother of Benjamin Williams Crowninshield) (Mass.) March 31, 1770–April 15, 1808; House 1803–April 15, 1808.

CROWTHER, Frank (N.Y.) July 10, 1870–July 20, 1965; House 1919–43.

CROWTHER, George Calhoun (Mo.) Jan. 26, 1849–March 18, 1914; House 1895–97.

CROZIER, Robert (Kans.) Oct. 13, 1827–Oct. 2, 1895; Senate Nov. 24, 1873–Feb. 12, 1874.

CRUGER, Daniel (N.Y.) Dec. 22, 1780–July 12, 1843; House 1817–19.

CRUMP, Rousseau Owen (Mich.) May 20, 1843–May 1, 1901; House 1895–May 1, 1901.

CRUMPACKER, Edgar Dean (father of Maurice Edgar Crumpacker, cousin of Shepard J. Crumpacker Jr.) (Ind.) May 27, 1851–May 19, 1920; House 1897–1913.

CRUMPACKER, Maurice Edgar (son of Edgar Dean Crumpacker, cousin of Shepard J. Crumpacker Jr.) (Oreg.) Dec. 19, 1886–July 24, 1927; House 1926–July 24, 1927.

CRUMPACKER, Shepard J. Jr. (cousin of Edgar Dean Crumpacker and Maurice Edgar Crumpacker) (Ind.) Feb. 13, 1917–Oct. 14, 1986; House 1951–57.

CRUTCHFIELD, William (Tenn.) Nov. 16, 1824–Jan. 24, 1890; House 1873–75.

CUBIN, Barbara (Wash.) House, 1995–.

CULBERTSON, William Constantine (Pa.) Nov. 25, 1825–May 24, 1906; House 1889–91.

CULBERTSON, William Wirt (Ky.) Sept. 22, 1835–Oct. 31, 1911; House 1883–85.

CULBRETH, Thomas (Md.) April 13, 1786–April 16, 1843; House 1817–21.

CULKIN, Francis Dugan (N.Y.) Nov. 10, 1874–Aug. 4, 1943; House Nov. 6, 1928–Aug. 4, 1943.

CULLEN, William (Ill.) March 4, 1826–Jan. 17, 1914; House 1881–85.

CULLOM, Shelby Moore (nephew of Alvan Cullom and William Cullom) (Ill.) Nov. 22, 1829–Jan. 28, 1914; House 1865–71; Senate 1883–1913; Senate majority leader 1911–13; Gov. Jan. 8, 1877–Feb. 8, 1883.

CULVER, Charles Vernon (Pa.) Sept. 6, 1830–Jan. 10, 1909; House 1865–67.

CUMBACK, William (Ind.) March 24, 1829–July 31, 1905; House 1855–57.

CUMMINGS, Henry Johnson Brodhead (Iowa) May 21, 1831–April 16, 1909; House 1877–79.

CUMMINS, Albert Baird (Iowa) Feb. 15, 1850–July 30, 1926; Senate Nov. 24, 1908–July 30, 1926; elected Pres. pro tempore May 19, 1919, March 7, 1921; Gov. Jan. 16, 1902–Nov. 24, 1908.

CUNNINGHAM, Glenn Clarence (Nebr.) Sept. 10, 1912–; House 1957–71.

CUNNINGHAM, John Edward III (Wash.) March 27, 1931–; House May 17, 1977–79.

CUNNINGHAM, Paul Harvey (Iowa) June 15, 1890–July 16, 1961; House 1941–59.

CUNNINGHAM, Randy "Duke" (Calif.) Dec. 8, 1941–; House 1991–.

CURRIE, Gilbert Archibald (Mich.) Sept. 19, 1882–June 5, 1960; House 1917–21.

CURRIER, Frank Dunklee (N.H.) Oct. 30, 1853–Nov. 25, 1921; House 1901–13.

CURRY, Charles Forrest (father of Charles Forrest Curry Jr.) (Calif.) March 14, 1858–Oct. 10, 1930; House 1913–Oct. 10, 1930.

CURRY, Charles Forrest Jr. (son of Charles Forrest Curry) (Calif.) Aug. 13, 1893–Oct. 7, 1972; House 1931–33.

CURRY, George (N.Mex.) April 3, 1861–Nov. 27, 1947; House Jan. 8, 1912–13; Gov. (N.Mex. Terr.) 1907–11.

CURTIN, Willard Sevier (Pa.) Nov. 18, 1905–; House 1957–67.

CURTIS, Carl Thomas (Nebr.) March 15, 1905–; House 1939–Dec. 31, 1954; Senate Jan. 1, 1955–79.

CURTIS, Carlton Brandaga (Pa.) Dec. 17, 1811–March 17, 1883; House 1851–55 (Democrat), 1873–75.

CURTIS, Charles (Kans.) Jan. 25, 1860–Feb. 8, 1936; House 1893–Jan. 28, 1907; Senate Jan. 29, 1907–13, 1915–29; elected Pres. pro tempore Dec. 4, 1911 (to serve Dec.

4–Dec. 12, 1911); Senate majority leader Nov. 28, 1925–29; Vice President 1929–33.

CURTIS, George Martin (Iowa) April 1, 1844 –Feb. 9, 1921; House 1895–99.

CURTIS, Laurence (Mass.) Sept. 3, 1893–July 11, 1989; House 1953–63.

CURTIS, Newton Martin (N.Y.) May 21, 1835–Jan. 8, 1910; House Nov. 3, 1891–97.

CURTIS, Samuel Ryan (Iowa) Feb. 3, 1805–Dec. 25, 1866; House 1857–Aug. 4, 1861.

CURTIS, Thomas Bradford (Mo.) May 14, 1911–Jan. 10, 1993; House 1951–69.

CUSHMAN, Francis Wellington (Wash.) May 8, 1867–July 6, 1909; House 1899–July 6, 1909.

CUTCHEON, Byron M. (Mich.) May 11, 1836–April 12, 1908; House 1883–91.

CUTHBERT, Alfred (brother of John Alfred Cuthbert) (Ga.) Dec. 23, 1785–July 9, 1856; House Dec. 13, 1813–Nov. 9, 1816, 1821–27; Senate Jan. 12, 1835–43.

CUTLER, William Parker (Ohio) July 12, 1812–April 11, 1889; House 1861–63.

CUTTING, Bronson Murray (N.Mex.) June 23, 1888–May 6, 1935; Senate Dec. 29, 1927–Dec. 6, 1928, 1929–May 6, 1935.

CUTTING, John Tyler (Calif.) Sept. 7, 1844–Nov.24, 1911; House 1891–93.

CUTTS, Marsena Edgar (Iowa) May 22, 1833–Sept. 1, 1883; House 1881–Sept. 1, 1883.

CUTTS, Richard (Mass.) June 28, 1771–April 7,1845; House 1801–13.

DAGGETT, Rollin Mallory (Nev.) Feb. 22, 1831–Nov. 12, 1901; House 1879–81.

DAGUE, Paul Bertram (Pa.) May 19, 1898–Dec. 2, 1974; House 1947–67.

DAHLE, Herman Bjorn (Wis.) March 30, 1855–April 25, 1920; House 1899–1903.

DAILY, Samuel Gordon (Nebr.) 1823–Aug. 15, 1866; House (Terr. Del.) May 18, 1860–65.

DALE, Porter Hinman (Vt.) March 1, 1867–Oct. 6 1933; House 1915–Aug. 11, 1923; Senate Nov. 7, 1923–Oct. 6, 1933.

DALE, Thomas Henry (Pa.) June 12, 1846–Aug. 21, 1912; House 1905–07.

DALLINGER, Frederick William (Mass.) Oct. 2, 1871–Sept. 5, 1955; House 1915–25, Nov. 2, 1926–Oct. 1, 1932.

DALZELL, John (Pa.) April 19, 1845–Oct. 2, 1927; House 1887–1913.

D'AMATO, Alfonse Martello (N.Y.) Aug. 1, 1937–; Senate 1981–, Chrmn. Senate Banking, Housing and Urban Affairs Committee 1995–.

DAMRELL, William Shapleigh (Mass.) Nov. 29, 1809–May 17, 1860; House 1855–59 (1855–57 American Party).

DANA, Samuel (Mass.) June 26, 1767–Nov. 20, 1835; House Sept. 22, 1814–15.

DANAHER, John Anthony (Conn.) Jan. 9, 1899–Sept. 22, 1990; Senate 1939–45.

DANFORD, Lorenzo (Ohio) Oct. 18, 1829–June 19, 1899; House 1873–79, 1895–June 19, 1899.

DANFORTH, Henry Gold (N.Y.) June 14, 1854–April 8, 1918; House 1911–17.

DANFORTH, John Claggett (Mo.) Sept. 5, 1936–Senate Dec. 27, 1976–; Chrmn. Senate Commerce, Science, and Transportation 1985–87.

DANIEL, Robert Williams Jr. (Va.) March 17, 1936–; House 1973–83.

DANIELS, Charles (N.Y.) March 24, 1825–Dec. 20, 1897; House 1893–97.

DANIELS, Milton John (Calif.) April 18, 1838–Dec. 1, 1914; House 1903–05.

DANNEMEYER, William Edwin (Calif.) Sept. 22, 1929–; House 1979–93.

DARBY, Ezra (N.J.) June 7, 1768–Jan. 27, 1808–House 1805–Jan. 27, 1808.

DARBY, Harry (Kans.) Jan. 23, 1895–Jan. 17, 1987; Senate Dec. 2, 1949–Nov. 28, 1950.

DARLING, William Augustus (N.Y.) Dec. 27, 1817–May 26, 1895; House 1865–67.

DARLINGTON, Smedley (second cousin of Edward Darlington, Isaac Darlington, and William Darlington) (Pa.) Dec. 24, 1827–June 24, 1899; House 1887–91.

DARLINGTON, William (cousin of Edward Darlington and Isaac Darlington, second cousin of Smedley Darlington) (Pa.) April 28, 1782–April 23, 1863; House 1815–17, 1819–23.

DARRAGH, Archibald Bard (Mich.) Dec. 23, 1840–Feb. 21, 1927; House 1901–09.

DARRALL, Chester Bidwell (La.) June 24, 1842–Jan. 1, 1908; House 1869–Feb. 20, 1878, 1881–83.

DARROW, George Potter (Pa.) Feb. 4, 1859–June 7, 1943; House 1915–37, 1939–41.

DAUB, Harold John "Hal" Jr. (Nebr.) April 23, 1941–House 1981–89.

DAVENPORT, Frederick Morgan (N.Y.) Aug. 27, 1866–Dec. 26, 1956; House 1925–33.

DAVENPORT, Ira (N.Y.) June 28, 1841–Oct. 6, 1904; House 1885–89.

DAVENPORT, Samuel Arza (Pa.) Jan. 15, 1834–Aug. 1, 1911; House 1897–1901.

DAVIDSON, James Henry (Wis.) June 18, 1858–Aug. 6, 1918; House 1897–1913, 1917–Aug. 6, 1918.

DAVIS, Charles Russell (Minn.) Sept. 17, 1849–July 29, 1930; House 1903–25.

DAVIS, Cushman Kellogg (Minn.) June 16, 1838–Nov. 27, 1900; Senate 1887–Nov. 27, 1900; Gov. Jan. 7, 1874–Jan. 7, 1876.

DAVIS, George Royal (Ill.) Jan. 3, 1840–Nov. 25, 1899; House 1879–85.

DAVIS, Glenn Robert (Wis.) Oct. 28, 1914–Sept. 21, 1988; House April 22, 1947–57, 1965–Dec. 31, 1974.

DAVIS, Horace (Calif.) March 16, 1831–July 12, 1916; House 1877–81.

DAVIS, Jack (Ill.) Sept. 6, 1935–; House 1987–89.

DAVIS, James John (Pa.) Oct. 27, 1873–Nov. 22, 1947; Senate Dec. 2, 1930–45; Secy. of Labor March 5, 1921–Nov. 30, 1930.

DAVIS, Noah (N.Y.) Sept. 10, 1818–March 20, 1902; House 1869–July 15, 1870.

DAVIS, Robert Lee (Pa.) Oct. 29, 1893–; House Nov. 8, 1932–33.

DAVIS, Robert Thompson (Mass.) Aug. 28, 1823–Oct. 29, 1906; House 1883–89.

DAVIS, Robert William (Mich.) July 31, 1932–; House 1979–93.

DAVIS, Roger (Pa.) Oct. 2, 1762–Nov. 20, 1815; House 1811–15.

DAVIS, Thomas M. III (Va.) House, 1995–.

DAVIS, Thomas Terry (Ky.) ?–Nov. 15, 1807; House 1797–1803.

DAVIS, Thomas Treadwell (N.Y.) Aug. 22, 1810–May 2, 1872; House 1863–67 (1863–65 Unionist).

DAVIS, Timothy (Iowa) March 29, 1794–April 27, 1872; House 1857–59.

DAVIS, Timothy (Mass.) April 12, 1821–Oct. 23, 1888; House 1855–59 (1855–57 American Party).

DAVIS, William Morris (Pa.) Aug. 16, 1815–Aug. 5, 1891; House 1861–63.

DAVISON, George Mosby (Ky.) March 23, 1855–Dec. 18, 1912; House 1897–99.

DAVY, John Madison (N.Y.) June 29, 1835–April 21, 1909; House 1875–77.

DAWES, Beman Gates (son of Rufus Dawes, brother of Vice President Charles Gates Dawes) (Ohio) Jan. 14, 1870–May 15, 1953; House 1905–09.

DAWES, Henry Laurens (Mass.) Oct. 30, 1816–Feb. 5, 1903; House 1857–75 (no party); Senate 1875–93.

DAWES, Rufus (father of Vice President Charles Gates Dawes and Beman Gates Dawes) (Ohio) July 4, 1838–Aug. 2, 1899; House 1881–83.

DAWSON, Albert Foster (Iowa) Jan. 26, 1872–March 9, 1949; House 1905–11.

DAWSON, John (Va.) 1762–March 31, 1814; House 1797–March 31, 1814; Cont. Cong. 1788.

DAWSON, William Adams (Utah) Nov. 5, 1903–Nov. 7, 1981; House 1947–49, 1953–59.

DAY, Stephen Albion (Ill.) July 13, 1882–Jan. 5, 1950, House 1941–45.

DAY, Timothy Crane (Ohio) Jan. 8, 1819–April 15, 1869; House 1855–57.

DAYTON, Alston Gordon (W.Va.) Oct. 18, 1857–July 30, 1920; House 1895–March 16, 1905.

DEAN, Josiah (Mass.) March 6, 1748–Oct. 14, 1818; House 1807–09.

DEAN, Sidney (Conn.) Nov. 16, 1818–Oct. 29, 1901; House 1855–59 (1855–57 American Party).

DEBOE, William Joseph (Ky.) June 30, 1849–June 15, 1927; Senate 1897–1903.

DECKARD, Huey Joel (Ind.) March 7, 1942–; House 1979–83.

DEEMER, Elias (Pa.) Jan. 3, 1838–March 29, 1918–; House 1901–07.

DEERING, Nathaniel Cobb (Iowa) Sept. 2, 1827–Dec. 11, 1887; House 1877–83.

DE FOREST, Henry Schermerhorn (N.Y.) Feb. 16, 1847–Feb. 13, 1917; House 1911–13.

DEFREES, Joseph Hutton (Ind.) May 13, 1812–Dec. 21, 1885; House 1865–67.

DEGENER, Edward (Tex.) Oct. 20, 1809–Sept. 11, 1890; House March 31, 1870–71.

DEGETAU, Frederico (P.R.) Dec. 5, 1862–Jan. 20, 1914; House (Res. Comm.) 1901–05.

DE HAVEN, John Jefferson (Calif.) March 12, 1849–Jan. 26, 1913; House 1889–Oct. 1, 1890.

DELANO, Charles (Mass.) June 24, 1820–Jan. 23, 1883; House 1859–63.

DELANO, Columbus (Ohio) June 4, 1809–Oct. 23, 1896; House 1845–47 (Whig), 1865–67, June 3, 1868–69; Secy. of the Interior Nov. 1, 1870–Sept. 30, 1875.

DE LANO, Milton (N.Y.) Aug. 11, 1844–Jan. 2, 1922; House 1887–91.

DE LARGE, Robert Carlos (S.C.) March 15, 1842–Feb. 14, 1874; House 1871–Jan. 24, 1873.

DELAY, Thomas Dale (Tex.) April 8, 1947–; House 1985–.

DELLENBACK, John Richard (Oreg.) Nov. 6, 1918–House 1967–75.

DEMING, Henry Champion (Conn.) May 23, 1815–Oct. 8, 1872; House 1863–67.

DE MOTTE, Mark Lindsey (Ind.) Dec. 28, 1832–Sept. 23, 1908; House 1881–83.

DEMPSEY, Stephen Wallace (N.Y.) May 8, 1862–March 1, 1949; House 1915–91.

DeNARDIS, Lawrence Joseph (Conn.) March 18, 1938–; House 1981–83.

DENBY, Edwin (grandson of Graham Newell Fitch) (Mich.) Feb. 18, 1870–Feb. 8, 1929; House 1905–11; Secy. of the Navy March 6, 1921–March 10, 1924.

DENEEN, Charles Samuel (Ill.) May 1, 1863–Feb, 5, 1940; Senate Feb. 26, 1925–31; Gov. Jan. 9, 1905–Feb. 3, 1913.

DENISON, Dudley Chase (nephew of Dudley Chase, cousin of Salmon Portland Chase) (Vt.) Sept. 13, 1819–Feb. 10, 1905; House 1875–79 (1875–77 Independent Republican).

DENISON, Edward Everett (Ill.) Aug. 28, 1873–June 17, 1953; House 1915–31.

DENNEY, Robert Vernon (Nebr.) April 11, 1916–June 26, 1981; House 1967–71.

DENNIS, David Worth (Ind.) June 7, 1912–; House 1969–75.

DENNISON, David Short (Ohio) July 29, 1918–; House 1957–59.

DENNY, Arthur Armstrong (Wash.) June 20, 1822–Jan. 9, 1899; House (Terr. Del.) 1865–67.

DENNY, Harmar Denny Jr. (Pa.) July 2, 1886–Jan. 6, 1966; House 1951–53.

DENOYELLES, Peter (N.Y.) 1766–May 6, 1829; House 1813–15.

DENTON, Jeremiah Andrew Jr. (Ala.) July 15, 1924–; Senate Jan. 2, 1981–87.

DEPEW, Chauncey Mitchell (N.Y.) April 23, 1834–April 5, 1928; Senate 1899–1911.

DE PRIEST, Oscar (Ill.) March 9,1871–May 12,1951; House 1929–35.

DEROUNIAN, Steven Boghos (N.Y.) April 6, 1918–House 1953–65.

DERWINSKI, Edward Joseph (Ill.) Sept. 15, 1926–House 1959–83; Secy. of Veterans Affairs March 15, 1989–Sept. 26, 1992.

DESHA, Joseph (brother of Robert Desha) (Ky.) Dec. 9, 1768–Oct. 11, 1842; House 1807–19; Gov. June 1, 1824–June 1, 1828 (Democratic Republican).

DEVEREUX, James Patrick Sinnott (Md.) Feb. 20, 1903–Aug. 5, 1988; House 1951–59.

DEVINE, Samuel Leeper (Ohio) Dec. 21, 1915–; House 1959–81.

DEVITT, Edward James (Minn.) May 5, 1911–; House 1947–49.

D'EWART, Wesley Abner (Mont.) Oct. 1, 1889–Sept. 2, 1973; House June 5, 1945–55.

DEWEESE, John Thomas (N.C.) June 4, 1835–July 4, 1906; House July 6, 1868–Feb. 28, 1870.

DEWEY, Charles Schuveldt (Ill.) Nov. 10, 1880–Dec. 27, 1980; House 1941–45.

DEWINE Michael (Ohio) Jan. 5, 1947–; House 1983–91; Senate 1995–.

DE WITT, Francis Byron (Ohio) March 11, 1849–March 21, 1929; House 1895–97.

DE WOLF, James (R.I.) March 18, 1764–Dec. 21, 1837; Senate 1821–Oct. 31, 1825.

DEZENDORF, John Frederick (Va.) Aug. 10, 1834–June 22, 1894; House 1881–83.

DIAZ-BALART, Lincoln (Fla.) Aug. 13, 1954–; House 1993–.

DICK, Charles William Frederick (Ohio) Nov. 3, 1858–March 13, 1945; House Nov. 8, 1898–March 23, 1904; Senate March 23, 1904–11

DICK, John (father of Samuel Bernard Dick) (Pa.) June 17, 1794–May 29, 1872; House 1853–59 (1853–55 Whig).

DICK, Samuel Bernard (son of John Dick) (Pa.) Oct. 26, 1836–May 10, 1907; House 1879–81.

DICKENS, Samuel (N.C.) ?–1840; House Dec. 2, 1816–17.

DICKERSON, Mahlon (brother of Philemon Dickerson) (N.J.) April 17, 1770–Oct. 5, 1853; Senate 1817–Jan. 30, 1829; Gov. Oct. 26, 1815–Feb. 1, 1817; Secy. of the Navy July 1, 1834–June 30, 1838.

DICKEY, Jay (Ark.) Dec. 14, 1939–; House 1993–.

DICKEY, Oliver James (son of John Dickey) (Pa.) April 6, 1823–April 21, 1876; House Dec. 7, 1868–73.

DICKINSON, Lester Jesse (cousin of Fred Dickinson Letts) (Iowa) Oct. 29, 1873–June 4, 1968; House 1919–31; Senate 1931–37.

DICKINSON, William Louis (Ala.) June 5, 1925–; House, 1965–93.

DICKSON, Frank Stoddard (Ill.) Oct. 6, 1876–Feb. 24, 1953; House 1905–07.

DICKSON, William (Tenn.) May 5, 1770–Feb. 1816; House 1801–07.

DIEKEMA, Gerrit John (Mich.) March 27, 1859–Dec. 20, 1930; House March 17, 1908–11.

DIETRICH, Charles Henry (Nebr.) Nov. 26, l853–April 10, 1924; Senate March 28, 1901–05; Gov. Jan. 3–May 1, 1901.

DILLINGHAM, William Paul (son of Paul Dillingham Jr.) (Vt.) Dec. 12, 1843–July 12, 1923; Senate Oct. 18, 1900–July 12, 1923; Gov. Oct. 4, 1888–Oct. 2, 1890.

DILLON, Charles Hall (S.Dak.) Dec. 18, 1853–Sept. 15, 1929; House 1913–19.

DINGLEY, Nelson Jr. (Maine) Feb. 15, 1832–Jan. 13, 1899; House Sept. 12, 1881–Jan. 13, 1899; Gov. Jan. 7, 1874–Jan. 5, 1876.

DINSMOOR, Samuel (N.H.) July 1, 1766–March 16, 1835; House 1811–13; Gov. June 2, 1831–June 5, 1834 (Jacksonian).

DioGUARDI, Joseph J. (N.Y.)g Sept. 20, 1940–; House 1985–89.

DIRKSEN, Everett McKinley (father-in-law of Howard H. Baker Jr.) (Ill.) Jan. 4, 1896–Sept. 7, 1969; House 1933–49;

Chrmn. House District of Columbia 1947–49; Senate 1951–Sept. 7, 1969; Senate minority leader 1959–Sept. 7, 1969.

DITTER, John William (Pa.) Sept. 5, 1888–Nov. 21, 1943; House 1933–Nov. 21, 1943.

DIVEN, Alexander Samuel (N.Y.) Feb. 10, 1809–June 11, 1896; House 1861–63.

DIXON, Henry Aldous (Utah) June 29, 1890–Jan. 22, 1967; House 1955–61.

DIXON, James (Conn.) Aug. 5, 1814–March 27, 1873; House 1845–49 (Whig); Senate 1857–69.

DIXON, Joseph (N.C.) April 9, 1828–March 3, 1883; House Dec. 5, 1870–71.

DIXON, Joseph Moore (Mont.) July 31, 1867–May 22, 1934; House 1903–07; Senate 1907–13; Gov. Jan. 3, 1921–Jan. 4, 1925.

DIXON, Nathan Fellows (father of Nathan Fellows Dixon, below) (R.I.) May 1, 1812–April 11, 1881; House 1849–51 (Whig), 1863–71.

DIXON, Nathan Fellows (son of Nathan Fellows Dixon, above) (R.I.) Aug. 28, 1847–Nov. 8, 1897; House Feb. 12–March 3, 1885; Senate April 10, 1889–95.

DOAN, Robert Eachus (Ohio) July 23, 1831–Feb. 24, 1919; House 1891–93.

DOBBINS, Samuel Atkinson (N.J.) April 14, 1814–May 26, 1886; House 1873–77.

DOCKERY, Oliver Hart (son of Alfred Dockery) (N.C.) Aug. 12, 1830–March 21, 1906; House July 13, 1968–71.

DODD, Edward (N.Y.) Aug. 25, 1805–March 1, 1891; House 1855–59 (1855–57 Whig).

DODDS, Francis Henry (Mich.) June 9, 1858–Dec. 23, 1940; House 1909–13.

DODGE, Grenville Mellen (Iowa) April 12, 1831–Jan. 3, 1916; House 1867–69.

DODGE, William Earle (N.Y.) Sept. 4, 1805–Feb. 9, 1883; House April 7, 1866–67.

DOLE, Robert Joseph (Kans.) July 22, 1923–; House 1961–69; Senate 1969–; Chrmn. Senate Finance 1981–85; Senate majority leader 1985–87; Senate minority leader 1987–; Chrmn. Rep. Nat. Comm. Jan. 1971–Jan. 1973; Senate majority leader 1995–96.

DOLLIVER, James Isaac (nephew of Jonathan Prentiss Dolliver) (Iowa) Aug. 31, 1894–Dec. 10, 1978; House 1945–57.

DOLLIVER, Jonathan Prentiss (uncle of James Isaac Dolliver) (Iowa) Feb. 5, 1858–Oct. 15, 1910; House 1889–Aug. 22, 1900; Senate Aug. 22, 1900–Oct. 15, 1910.

DOLPH, Joseph Norton (uncle of Frederick William Mulkey) (Oreg.) Oct. 19, 1835–March 10, 1897; Senate 1883–95.

DOMENICI, Peter Vichi (N.Mex.) May 7, 1932–; Senate 1973–; Chrmn. Senate Budget 1981–87. Chrmn. Senate Budget Committee 1995–.

DOMINICK, Peter Hoyt (nephew of Howard Alexander Smith) (Colo.) July 7, 1915–March 18, 1981; House 1961–63; Senate 1963–75.

DONDERO, George Anthony (Mich.) Dec. 16, 1883–Jan. 29, 1968; House 1933–57; Chrmn. House Public Works 1947–49, 1953–55.

DONLEY, Joseph Benton (Pa.) Oct. 10, 1838–Jan. 23, 1917; House 1869–71.

DONNAN, William G. (Iowa) June 30, 1834–Dec. 4, 1908; House 1871–75.

DONNELL, Forrest C. (Mo.) Aug. 20, 1884–March 3, 1980; Senate 1945–51; Gov. Jan. 13, 1941–Jan. 8, 1945.

DONNELLY, Ignatius (Minn.) Nov. 3, 1831–Jan. 1, 1901; House 1863–69.

DOOLEY, Edwin Benedict (N.Y.) April 13, 1905–Jan. 25, 1982; House 1957–63.

DOOLITTLE, James Rood (Wis.) Jan. 3, 1815–July 23, 1897; Senate 1857–69.

DOOLITTLE, John Taylor (Calif.) Oct. 30, 1950–; House 1991–.

DOOLITTLE, William Hall (Wash.) Nov. 5, 1848–Feb. 25, 1914; House 1893–97.

DORN, Francis Edwin (N.Y.) April 18, 1911–Sept. 17, 1987; House 1953–61.

DORNAN, Robert Kenneth (Calif.) April 3, 1933–; House 1977–83, 1985–.

DORR, Charles Phillips (W.Va.) Aug. 12, 1852–Oct. 8, 1914; House 1897–99.

DORSEY, George Washington Emery (Nebr.) Jan. 25, 1842–June 12, 1911; House 1885–91.

DORSEY, Stephen Wallace (Ark.) Feb. 28, 1842–March 20, 1916; Senate 1873–79.

DOUGHERTY, Charles Francis (Pa.) June 26, 1937–House 1979–83.

DOUGLAS, Albert (Ohio) April 25, 1852–March 14, 1935; House 1907–11.

DOUGLAS, Chuck (N.H.) Dec. 2, 1942–; House 1989–91.

DOUGLAS, Fred James (N.Y.) Sept. 14, 1869–Jan. 1, 1949; House 1937–45.

DOUGLAS, William Harris (N.Y.) Dec. 5, 1853–Jan. 27, 1944; House 1901–05.

DOUTRICH, Isaac Hoffer (Pa.) Dec. 19, 1871–May 28, 1941; House 1927–37.

DOVENER, Blackburn Barrett (W.Va.) April 20, 1842–May 9, 1914; House 1895–1907.

DOWELL, Cassius Clay (Iowa) Feb. 29, 1864–Feb. 4, 1940; House 1915–35, 1937–Feb. 4, 1940.

DOWNEY, Stephen Wheeler (father of Sheridan Downey) (Wyo.) July 25, 1839–Aug. 3, 1902; House (Terr. Del.) 1879–81.

DOXEY, Charles Taylor (Ind.) July 13, 1841–April 30, 1898; House Jan. 17–March 3, 1883.

DRAKE, Charles Daniel (Mo.) April 11, 1811–April 1, 1892; Senate 1867–Dec. 19, 1870.

DRAKE, John Reuben (N.Y.) Nov. 28, 1782–March 21, 1857; House 1817–19.

DRAPER, William Franklin (Mass.) April 9, 1842–Jan. 28, 1910; House 1893–97.

DRAPER, William Henry (N.Y.) June 24, 1841 –Dec. 7, 1921; House 1901–13.

DREIER, David Timothy (Calif.) July 5, 1952–; House 1981–.

DRESSER, Solomon Robert (Pa.) Feb. 1, 1842–Jan. 21, 1911; House 1903–07.

DREW, Irving Webster (N.H.) Jan. 8, 1845–April 10, 1922; Senate Sept. 2–Nov. 5, 1918.

DRIGGS, John Fletcher (Mich.) March 8, 1813–Dec. 17, 1877; House 1863–69.

DRISCOLL, Michael Edward (N.Y.) Feb. 9, 1851–Jan. 19, 1929; House 1899–1913.

DRUKKER, Dow Henry (N.J.) Feb. 7, 1872–Jan. 11, 1963; House April 7, 1914–19.

DRYDEN, John Fairfield (N.J.) Aug. 7, 1839–Nov. 24, 1911; Senate Jan. 29, 1902–07.

DUELL, Rodolphus Holland (N.Y.) Dec. 20, 1824–Feb. 11, 1891; House 1859–63, 1871–75.

DUFF, James Henderson (Pa.) Jan. 21, 1883–Dec. 20, 1969; Senate Jan. 18, 1951–57; Gov. Jan. 21, 1947–Jan. 16, 1951.

DULLES, John Foster (N.Y.) Feb. 25, 1888–May 24, 1959; Senate July 7–Nov. 8, 1949; Secy. of State Jan. 21, 1963–April 22, 1969.

DUNBAR, James Whitson (Ind.) Oct. 17, 1860–May 19, 1943; House 1919–23, 1929–31.

DUNCAN, John James (father of John James "Jimmy" Duncan Jr.) (Tenn.) March 24, 1919–June 21, 1988; House 1965–June 21, 1988.

DUNCAN, John James "Jimmy" Jr. (son of John James Duncan) (Tenn.) July 21, 1947–; House Nov. 8, 1988–.

DUNHAM, Ransom Williams (Ill.) March 21, 1838–Aug. 19, 1896; House 1883–89.

DUNN, George Grundy (Ind.) Dec. 20, 1812–Sept. 4, 1857; House 1847–49 (Whig), 1855–57.

DUNN, James Whitney (Mich.) July 21, 1943–; House 1981–83.

DUNN, Jennifer (Wash.) July 29, 1941–; House 1993–.

DUNN, Thomas Byrne (N.Y.) March 16, 1853–July 2, 1924; House 1913–23.

DUNN, William McKee (Ind.) Dec. 12, 1814–July 24, 1887; House 1859–63.

DUNNELL, Mark Hill (Minn.) July 2, 1823–Aug. 9, 1904; House 1871–83, 1889–91.

DUNWELL, Charles Tappan (N.Y.) Feb. 13, 1852–June 12, 1908; House 1903–June 12, 1908.

du PONT, Henry Algernon (cousin of Thomas Coleman du Pont) (Del.) July 30, 1838–Dec. 31, 1926; Senate June 13, 1906–17.

du PONT, Pierre Samuel "Pete" IV (Del.) Jan. 22, 1935–; House 1971–77, Gov. Jan. 18, 1977–Jan. 15, 1985.

du PONT, Thomas Coleman (cousin of Henry Algernon du Pont) (Del.) Dec. 11, 1863–Nov. 11, 1930; Senate July 7, 1921–Nov. 7, 1922, 1925–Dec. 9, 1928.

DURELL, Daniel Meserve (N.H.) July 20, 1769–April 29, 1841; House 1807–09.

DURENBERGER, David Ferdinand (Minn.) Aug. 19, 1934–; Senate Nov. 8, 1978–; Chrmn. Senate Select Committee on Intelligence Activities 1985–87.

DUREY, Cyrus (N.Y.) May 16, 1864–Jan. 4, 1933; House 1907–11.

DURFEE, Nathaniel Briggs (R.I.) Sept. 29, 1812–Nov. 9, 1872; House 1865–59 (1855–57 American Party).

DURKEE, Charles (Wis.) Dec. 10, 1805–Jan. 14, 1870; House 1849–53 (Free-Soiler); Senate 1855–61; Gov. (Utah Terr.) 1865–69.

DURNO, Edwin Russell (Oreg.) Jan. 26, 1899–Nov. 20, 1976; House 1961–63.

DUVAL, Isaac Harding (W.Va.) Sept. 1, 1824–July 10, 1902; House 1869–71.

DUVAL, William Pope (Ky.) 1784–March 19, 1854; House 1813–15; Gov. (Fla. Terr.) 1822–34.

DUVALL, Gabriel (Md.) Dec. 6, 1752–March 6, 1844; House Nov. 11, 1794–March 28, 1796 (Nov. 11, 1794–95 no party); Assoc. Justice Supreme Court Nov. 23, 1811–Jan. 14, 1835.

DWIGHT, Jeremiah Wilbur (father of John Wilbur Dwight) (N.Y.) April 17, 1819–Nov. 26, 1885; House 1877–83.

DWIGHT, John Wilbur (son of Jeremiah Wilbur Dwight) (N.Y.) May 24, 1859–Jan. 19, 1928; House Nov. 2, 1902–13.

DWORSHAK, Henry Clarence (Idaho) Aug. 29, 1894–July 23, 1962; House 1939–Nov. 5, 1946; Senate Nov. 6, 1946–49, Oct. 14, 1949–July 23, 1962.

DWYER, Florence Price (N.J.) July 4, 1902–Feb. 29, 1976; House 1957–73.

DYER, David Patterson (uncle of Leonidas Carstarphen Dyer) (Mo.) Feb. 12, 1838–April 29, 1924; House 1869–71.

DYER, Leonidas Carstarphen (nephew of David Patterson Dyer) (Mo.) June 11, 1871–Dec. 15, 1957; House 1911–June 19, 1914.

EAGER, Samuel Watkins (N.Y.) April 8, 1789–Dec. 23, 1860; House Nov. 2, 1830–31.

EAMES, Benjamin Tucker (R.I.) June 4, 1818–Oct. 6, 1901; House 1871–79.

EARLE, Elias (uncle of Samuel Earle and John Baylis Earle, great-grandfather of John Laurens Manning Irby and Joseph Haynsworth Earle) (S.C.) June 19, 1762–May 19, 1823; House 1806–07, 1811–15, 1817–21.

EARLE, John Baylis (nephew of Elias Earle, cousin of Samuel Earle) (S.C.) Oct. 23, 1766–Feb. 3, 1863; House 1803–05.

EARLE, Samuel (nephew of Elias Earle, cousin of John Baylis Earle) (S.C.) Nov. 28, 1760–Nov. 24, 1833; House 1795–97.

EARLY, Peter (Ga.) June 20, 1773–Aug. 15, 1817; House Jan. 10, 1803–07; Gov. Nov. 5, 1813–Nov. 10, 1815 (Democratic Republican).

EAST, John Porter (N.C.)-May 5, 1931–June 29, 1986; Senate 1981–June 29, 1986.

EATON, Charles Aubrey (uncle of William Robb Eaton) (N.J.) March 29, 1868–Jan. 23, 1953; House 1925–53; Chrmn. House Foreign Affairs 1947–49.

EATON, John Henry (Tenn.) June 18, 1790–Nov. 17, 1856; Senate Sept. 5, 1818–21, Sept. 27, 1821–March 9, 1829; Secy. of War March 9, 1829–June 18, 1831; Gov. (Fla. Terr.) 1834–36.

EATON, Thomas Marion (Calif.) Aug. 3, 1896–Sept. 16, 1939; House Jan. 3–Sept. 16, 1939.

EATON, William Robb (nephew of Charles Aubrey Eaton) (Colo.) Dec. 17, 1877–Dec. 16, 1942; House 1929–33.

ECHOLS, Leonard Sidney (W.Va.) Oct. 30, 1871–May 9, 1946; House 1919–23.

ECKERT, Fred J. (N.Y.) May 6, 1941–; House 1985–87.

ECKLEY, Ephraim Ralph (Ohio) Dec. 9, 1811–March 27, 1908; House 1863–69.

ECTON, Zales Nelson (Mont.) April 1, 1898–March 3, 1961; Senate 1947–53.

EDDY, Frank Marion (Minn.) April 1, 1856–Jan. 13, 1929; House 1895–1903.

EDGE, Walter Evans (N.J.) Nov. 20, 1873–Oct. 29, 1956; Senate 1919–Nov. 21, 1929; Gov. Jan. 15, 1917–May 16, 1919, Jan. 18, 1944–Jan. 21, 1947.

EDGERTON, Alonzo Jay (Minn.) June 7, 1827–Aug. 9, 1896; Senate March 12–Oct. 30, 1881.

EDGERTON, Sidney (Ohio) Aug. 17, 1818–July 19 1900; House 1859–63; Gov. (Mont. Terr.) 1865, 1866.

EDMONDS, George Washington (Pa.) Feb. 22, 1864–Sept. 28, 1939; House 1913–25, 1933–35.

EDMUNDS, George Franklin (Vt.) Feb. 1, 1828–Feb. 27, 1919; Senate April 3, 1866–Nov. 1, 1891; elected Pres. pro tempore March 3, 1883, Jan. 14, 1884.

EDWARDS, Don Calvin (Ky.) July 13, 1861–Sept. 19, 1938; House 1905–11.

EDWARDS, Marvin Henry "Mickey" (Okla.) July 12, 1937–; House 1977–93.

EDWARDS, Ninian (Ill.) March 17, 1775–July 20, 1833; Senate Dec. 3, 1818–24; Gov. 1809–18 (Ill. Terr.), Dec. 6, 1826–Dec. 6, 1830.

EDWARDS, Thomas McKey (N.H.) Dec. 16, 1795–May 1, 1875; House 1859–63.

EDWARDS, Weldon Nathaniel (N.C.) Jan. 25, 1788–Dec. 18, 1873; House Feb. 7, 1816–27.

EDWARDS, William Jackson "Jack" (Ala.) Sept. 20, 1928–; House 1965–85.

EDWARDS, William Posey (Ga.) Nov 9, 1835–June 28, 1900; House July 25, 1868–69.

EGGLESTON, Benjamin (Ohio) Jan. 3, 1816–Feb. 9, 1888; House 1865–69.

EGGLESTON, Joseph (uncle of William Seger Archer) (Va.) Nov. 24, 1754–Feb. 13, 1811; House Dec. 3, 1798–1801.

EHRLICH, Robert L. Jr. (Md.) House, 1995–.

EINSTEIN, Edwin (N.Y.) Nov. 18, 1842–Jan. 24, 1905; House 1879–81.

EKWALL, William Alexander (Oreg.) June 14, 1887–Oct. 16, 1956; House 1935–37.

ELA, Jacob Hart (N.H.) July 18, 1820–Aug. 21, 1884; House 1867–71.

ELIOT, Thomas Dawes (Mass.) March 20, 1808–June 14, 1870; House April 17, 1854–1855 (Whig), 1859–69.

ELKINS, Davis (son of Stephen Benton Elkins, grandson of Henry Gassaway Davis) (W.Va.) Jan. 24, 1876–Jan. 5, 1959; Senate Jan. 9–Jan. 31, 1911, 1919–25.

ELKINS, Stephen Benton (father of Davis Elkins) (W.Va.) Sept. 26, 1841–Jan. 4, 1911; House (Terr. Del. N.Mex.) 1873–77; Senate 1895–Jan. 4, 1911; Secy. of War Dec. 17, 1891–March 5, 1893.

ELLERY, Christopher (R.I.) Nov. 1, 1768–Dec. 2, 1840; Senate May 6, 1801–05.

ELLICOTT, Benjamin (N.Y.) April 17, 1765–Dec. 10, 1827; House 1817–19.

ELLIOTT, Douglas Hemphill (Pa.) June 3, 1921–June 19, 1960; House April 26–June 19, 1960.

ELLIOTT, James Thomas (Ark.) April 22, 1823–July 28, 1876; House Jan. 13–March 3, 1869.

ELLIOTT, Richard Nash (Ind.) April 25, 1873–March 21, 1948; House June 26, 1917–31.

ELLIOTT, Robert Brown (S.C.) Aug. 11, 1842–Aug. 9, 1884; House 1871–Nov. 1, 1874.

ELLIS, Edgar Clarence (Mo.) Oct. 2, 1854–March 15, 1947; House 1905–09, 1921–23, 1925–27, 1929–31.

ELLIS, Hubert Summers (W.Va.) July 6, 1887–Dec. 3, 1959; House 1943–49.

ELLIS, William Russell (Oreg.) April 23, 1850–Jan. 18, 1915; House 1893–99, 1907–11.

ELLISON, Daniel (Md.) Feb. 14, 1886–Aug. 20, 1960; House 1943–45.

ELLSWORTH, Charles Clinton (Mich.) Jan. 29, 1824–June 25, 1899; House 1877–79.

ELLSWORTH, Franklin Fowler (Minn.) July 10, 1879–Dec. 23, 1942; House 1915–21.

ELLSWORTH, Matthew Harris (Oreg.) Sept. 17, 1899–Feb. 7, 1986; House 1943–57.

ELLWOOD, Reuben (Ill.) Feb. 21, 1821–July 1, 1885; House 1883–July 1, 1885.

ELMENDORF, Lucas Conrad (N.Y.) 1758–Aug. 17, 1843; House 1797–1803.

ELMER, Ebenezer (brother of Jonathan Elmer, father of Lucius Quintius Cincinnatus Elmer) (N.J.) Aug. 23, 1752–Oct. 18, 1843; House 1801–07.

ELMER, William Price (Mo.) March 2, 1871–May 11, 1956; House 1943–45.

ELSAESSER, Edward Julius (N.Y.) March 10, 1904–Jan. 7, 1983; House 1945–49.

ELSTON, Charles Henry (Ohio) Aug. 1, 1891–Sept. 25, 1980; House 1939–53.

ELSTON, John Arthur (Calif.) Feb. 10, 1874–Dec. 15, 1921; House 1915–Dec. 15, 1921 (1915–17 Progressive).

ELTSE, Ralph Roscoe (Calif.) Sept. 13, 1885–March 18, 1971; House 1933–35.

ELVINS, Politte (Mo.) March 16, 1878–Jan. 14, 1943; House 1909–11.

ELY, Alfred (N.Y.) Feb. 15, 1815–May 18, 1892; House 1859–63.

ELY, Frederick David (Mass.) Sept. 24, 1838–Aug. 5, 1921; House 1885–87.

EMERSON, Henry Ivory (Ohio) March 15, 1871–Oct. 28, 1953; House 1915–21.

EMERSON, Louis Woodard (N.Y.) July 25, 1857–June 10, 1924; House 1899–1903.

EMERSON, Norvell William (Mo.) Jan. 1, 1938–; House 1981–.

EMERY, David Farnham (Maine) Sept. 1, 1948–; House 1975–83.

EMRIE, Jonas Reece (Ohio) April 25, 1812–June 5, 1869; House 1855–57.

ENGEL, Albert Joseph (Mich.) Jan. 1, 1888–Dec. 2, 1959; House 1935–51.

ENGLAND, Edward Theodore (W. Va.) Sept. 29, 1869–Sept. 9, 1934; House 1927–29.

ENGLEBRIGHT, Harry Lane (son of William Fellows Englebright) (Calif.) Jan. 2, 1884–May 13, 1943; House Aug. 31, 1926–May 13, 1943.

ENGLEBRIGHT, William Fellows (father of Harry Lane Englebright) (Calif.) Nov. 23, 1855–Feb. 10, 1915; House Nov. 6, 1906–11.

ENGLISH, Phil (Pa.) House, 1995–.

ENOCHS, William Henry (Ohio) March 29, 1842–July 13, 1893; House 1891–July 13, 1893.

ENSIGN, John (Nev.) House, 1995–.

EPPES, John Wayles (Va.) April 7, 1773–Sept. 13, 1823; House 1803–11, 1813–15; Senate 1817–Dec. 4, 1819.

ERDAHL, Arlen Ingolf (Minn.) Feb. 27, 1931–; House 1979–83.

ERK, Edmund Frederick (Pa.) April 17, 1872–Dec. 14, 1953; House Nov. 4, 1930–33.

ERLENBORN, John Neal (Ill.) Feb. 8, 1927–; House 1965–85.

ERNST, Richard Pretlow (Ky.) Feb. 28, 1858–April 13, 1934; Senate 1921–27.

ERRETT, Russell (Pa.) Nov. 10, 1817–April 7, 1891; House 1877–83.

ERVIN, James (S.C.) Oct. 17, 1778–July 7, 1841; House 1817–21.

ESCH, John Jacob (Wis.) March 20, 1861–April 27, 1941; House 1899–1921.

ESCH, Marvin Lionel (Mich.) Aug. 4, 1927–; House 1967–77.

ESHLEMAN, Edwin Duing (Pa.) Dec. 4, 1920–Jan. 10, 1985; House 1967–77.

ESSEN, Frederick (Mo.) April 22, 1863–Aug. 18, 1946; House Nov. 5, 1918–19.

ESTEP, Harry Allison (Pa.) Feb. 1, 1884–Feb. 28, 1968; House 1927–33.

ESTERLY, Charles Joseph (Pa.) Feb. 8, 1888–Sept. 3, 1940; House 1925–27, 1929–31.

ESTY, Constantine Canaris (Mass.) Dec. 26, 1824–Dec. 27, 1912; House Dec. 2, 1872–73.

EUSTIS, William (Mass.) June 10, 1753 -Feb. 6, 1825; House 1801–05, Aug. 21, 1820–23; Secy. of War March 7, 1809–Jan. 13, 1813; Gov. May 31, 1823–Feb. 6, 1825.

EVANS, Alvin (Pa.) Oct. 4, 1845–June 19, 1906; House 1901–05.

EVANS, Daniel Jackson (Wash.) Oct. 16, 1925–; Senate Sept. 12, 1983–89; Gov. Jan. 11, 1965–Jan. 12, 1977.

EVANS, David Reid (S.C.) Feb. 20, 1769–March 8, 1843; House 1813–15.

EVANS, Henry Clay (Tenn.) June 18, 1843–Dec. 12, 1921; House 1889–91.

EVANS, Hiram Kinsman (Iowa) March 17, 1863–July 9, 1941; House June 4, 1923–25.

EVANS, Isaac Newton (Pa.) July 29, 1827–Dec. 3, 1901; House 1877–79, 1883–87.

EVANS, James La Fayette (Ind.) March 27, 1825–May 28, 1903; House 1875–79.

EVANS, Melvin Herbert (V.I.) Aug. 7, 1917–Nov.27, 1984; House (Terr. Del.) 1979–81.

EVANS, Robert Emory (Nebr.) July 15, 1856–July 8, 1925; House 1919–23.

EVANS, Thomas Beverley Jr. (Del.) Nov. 5, 1931–; House 1977–83.

EVANS, Thomas Cooper (Iowa) May 26, 1924–; House 1981–87.

EVANS, Walter (nephew of Burwell Clark Ritter) (Ky.) Sept. 18, 1842–Dec. 30, 1923; House 1895–99.

EVANS, William Elmer (Calif.) Dec. 14, 1877–Nov. 12, 1959; House 1927–35.

EVARTS, William Maxwell (grandson of Roger Sherman) (N.Y.) Feb. 6, 1818–Feb. 28, 1901; Senate 1885–91; Atty. Gen. July 15, 1868–March 3, 1869; Secy. of State March 12, 1877–March 7, 1881.

EVERETT, Terry (Ala.) Feb. 15, 1937–; House 1993–.

EVERHART, James Bowen (son of William Everhart) (Pa.) July 26, 1821–Aug. 23, 1888; House 1883–87.

EWART, Hamilton Glover (N.C.) Oct. 23, 1849–April 28, 1918; House 1889–91.

EWING, Thomas W. (Ill.) Sept. 19, 1935–; House July 10, 1991–.

FAIRBANKS, Charles Warren (Ind.) May 11, 1852–June 4, 1918; Senate 1897–1905; Vice President 1905–09.

FAIRCHILD, Benjamin Lewis (N.Y.) Jan. 5, 1863–Oct. 25, 1946; House 1895–97, 1917–19, 1921–23, Nov. 6, 1923–27.

FAIRCHILD, George Winthrop (N.Y.) May 6, 1854–Dec. 31, 1824; House 1907–19.

FAIRCLOTH, Lauch (N.C.) Jan. 14, 1928–; Senate 1993–.

FAIRFIELD, Louis William (Ind.) Oct. 15, 1858–Feb. 20, 1930; House 1917–25.

FALL, Albert Bacon (N.Mex.) Nov. 26, 1861–Nov. 30, 1944; Senate March 27, 1912–March 4, 1921; Secy. of the Interior March 5, 1921–March 4, 1923.

FANNIN, Paul Jones (Ariz.) Jan. 29, 1907–; Senate 1965–77; Gov. Jan. 5, 1959–Jan. 4, 1965.

FARIS, George Washington (Ind.) June 9, 1854–April 17, 1914; House 1895–1901.

FARNSWORTH, John Franklin (Ill.) March 27, 1820–July 14, 1897; House 1857–61, 1863–73.

FARQUHAR, John Hanson (Ind.) Dec. 20, 1818–Oct. 1, 1873; House 1865–67.

FARQUHAR, John McCreath (N.Y.) April 17, 1832–April 24, 1918; House 1885–91.

FARR, Evarts Worcester (N.H.) Oct. 10, 1840–Nov. 30, 1880; House 1879–Nov. 30, 1880.

FARR, John Richard (Pa.) July 18, 1857–Dec. 11, 1933; House 1911–19, Feb. 25–March 3, 1921.

FARRINGTON, Joseph Rider (husband of Mary Elizabeth Pruett Farrington) (Hawaii) Oct. 15, 1897–June 19, 1954; House (Terr. Del.) 1943–June 19, 1954.

FARRINGTON, Mary Elizabeth Pruett (widow of Joseph Rider Farrington) (Hawaii) May 30, 1898–July 21, 1984; House (Terr. Del.) July 31, 1954–57.

FARROW, Samuel (S.C.) 1759–Nov. 18, 1824; House 1813–15.

FARWELL, Charles Benjamin (Ill.) July 1, 1823–Sept. 23, 1903; House 1871–May 6, 1876, 1881–83; Senate Jan. 19, 1887–91.

FARWELL, Nathan Allen (cousin of Owen Lovejoy) (Maine) Feb. 24, 1812–Dec. 9, 1893; Senate Oct. 27, 1864–65.

FARWELL, Sewall Spaulding (Iowa) April 26, 1834–Sept. 21, 1909; House 1881–83.

FAUST, Charles Lee (Mo.) April 24, 1879–Dec. 17, 1928; House 1921–Dec. 17, 1928.

FAWELL, Harris Walter (Ill.) March 25, 1929–; House 1985–.

FELLOWS, Frank (Maine) Nov. 7, 1889–Aug. 27, 1951; House 1941–Aug. 27, 1951.

FELTON, Charles Norton (Calif.) Jan. 1, 1828–Sept. 13, 1914; House 1885–89; Senate March 19, 1891–93.

FENERTY, Clare Gerald (Pa.) July 25, 1895–July 1, 1952; House 1935–37.

FENN, Edward Hart (Conn.) Sept. 12, 1856–Feb. 23, 1939; House 1921–31.

FENNER, James (R.I.) Jan. 22, 1771–April 17, 1846; Senate 1805–Sept. 1807; Gov. May 6, 1807–May 1, 1811 (Demo–cratic Republican), May 5, 1824–May 4, 1831 (Democratic Republican), May 2, 1843–May 6, 1845 (Law & Order Whig).

FENTON, Ivor David (Pa.) Aug. 3, 1889– Oct. 23, 1986; House 1939–63.

FENTON, Lucien Jerome (Ohio) May 7, 1844–June 28, 1922; House 1895–99.

FENTON, Reuben Eaton (N.Y.) July 4, 1819–Aug. 25, 1885; House 1853–55 (Democrat), 1857–Dec. 20, 1864 (Democrat); Senate 1869–75; Gov. Jan. 1, 1865–Jan. 1, 1869 (Union Republican).

FENWICK, Millicent Hammond (N.J.) Feb. 25, 1910–Sept. 16, 1992; House 1975–83.

FERDON, John William (N.Y.) Dec. 13, 1826–Aug. 5, 1884; House 1879–81.

FERGUSON, Homer (Mich.) Feb. 25, 1889–Dec. 17, 1982; Senate 1943–55.

FERNALD, Bert Manfred (Maine) April 3, 1858–Aug. 23, 1926; Senate Sept. 12, 1916–Aug. 23, 1926; Gov. Jan. 6, 1909–Jan. 4, 1911.

FERRISS, Orange (N.Y.) Nov. 26, 1814–April 11, 1894; House 1867–71.

FERRY, Thomas White (Mich.) June 10, 1827–Oct. 13, 1896; House 1865–71; Senate 1871–83; elected Pres. pro tempore March 9, 1875, March 19, 1875, Dec. 20, 1875, March 5, 1877, Feb. 26, 1878, April 17, 1878, March 3, 1879.

FESS, Simeon Davison (Ohio) Dec. 11, 1861–Dec. 23, 1936; House 1913–23; Senate 1923–35; Chrmn. Rep. Nat. Comm. 1930–32.

FESSENDEN, Samuel Clement (brother of Thomas Amory Deblois Fessenden and William Pitt Fessenden) (Maine) March 7, 1815–April 18,1882; House 1861–63.

FESSENDEN, Thomas Amory Deblois (brother of Samuel Clement Fessenden and William Pitt Fessenden) (Maine) Jan. 23, 1826–Sept. 28, 1868; House Dec. 1, 1862–63.

FESSENDEN, William Pitt (brother of Samuel Clement Fessenden and Thomas Amory Deblois Fessenden) (Maine) Oct. 16, 1806–Sept. 8, 1869; House 1841–43 (Whig); Senate Feb. 10, 1854–July 1, 1864 (Feb. 10, 1854–59 Whig), 1865–Sept. 8, 1869; Secy. of the Treasury July 5, 1864–March 3, 1865.

FIEDLER, Roberta Frances "Bobbi" (neÈ Horowitz) (Calif.) April 22, 1937–; House 1981–87.

FIELD, Moses Whelock (Mich.) Feb. 10, 1828–March 14, 1889; House 1873–75.

FIELD, Richard Stockton (son of Richard Stockton) (N.J.) Dec. 31, 1803–May 25, 1870; Senate Nov. 21, 1862–Jan. 14, 1863.

FIELD, Walbridge Abner (Mass.) April 26, 1833–July 15, 1899; House 1877–March 28, 1878 (no party), 1879–81.

FIELDS, Jack Milton Jr. (Tex.) Feb. 3, 1952–; House 1981–.

FIELDS, William Craig (N.Y.) Feb. 13, 1804–Oct. 27, 1882; House 1867–69.

FINDLAY, William (brother of James Findlay and John Findlay) (Pa.) June 20, 1768–Nov. 12, 1846; Senate Dec. 10, 1821–27; Gov. Dec. 16, 1817–Dec. 19, 1820 (Democratic Republican).

FINDLEY, Paul (Ill.) June 23, 1921–; House 1961–83.

FINDLEY, William (Pa.) 1741 or 1742–April 4, 1821; House 1791–99 (1791–95 no party), 1803–17.

FINLEY, Charles (son of Hugh Franklin Finley) (Ky.) March 26, 1865–March 18, 1941; House Feb. 15, 1930–33.

FINLEY, Hugh Franklin (father of Charles Finley) (Ky.) Jan. 18, 1833–Oct. 16, 1909; House 1887–91.

FINNEY, Darwin Abel (Pa.) Aug. 11, 1814–Aug. 25, 1868; House 1867–Aug. 25, 1868.

FINO, Paul Albert (N.Y.) Dec. 15, 1913–; House 1953–Dec. 31, 1968.

FISCHER, Israel Frederick (N.Y.) Aug. 17, 1858–March 16, 1940; House 1895–99.

FISH, Hamilton (father of Hamilton Fish, below, grandfather of Hamilton Fish born in 1888, great-grandfather of Hamilton Fish Jr. born in 1926) (N.Y.) Aug. 3, 1808–Sept. 7, 1893; House 1843–45; Senate 1851–57; Gov. Jan. 1, 1849–Jan. 1, 1851; Secy. of State March 17, 1869–March 12, 1877.

FISH, Hamilton (son of Hamilton Fish, above, father of Hamilton Fish born in 1888, grandfather of Hamilton Fish Jr. born in 1926) (N.Y.) April 17, 1849–Jan. 15, 1936; House 1909–11.

FISH, Hamilton (son of Hamilton Fish born in 1849, father of Hamilton Fish Jr., below, grandson of Hamilton Fish born in 1808) (N.Y.) Dec. 7, 1888–Jan. 18, 1991; House Nov. 2, 1920–45.

FISH, Hamilton Jr. (son of Hamilton Fish Jr., above, grandson of Hamilton Fish born in 1849, great-grandson of Hamilton Fish born in 1808) (N.Y.) June 3, 1926–; House 1969–.

FISHER, Charles (N.C.) Oct. 20, 1789–May 7, 1849; House Feb. 11, 1819–21, 1839–41.

FISHER, Horatio Gates (Pa.) April 21, 1838–May 8, 1890; House 1879–83.

FISHER, John (N.Y.) March 13, 1806–March 28,1882; House 1869–71.

FISK, James (Vt.) Oct. 4, 1763–Nov. 17, 1844; House 1805–09, 1811–15; Senate Nov. 4, 1817–Jan. 8, 1818.

FISK, Jonathan (N.Y.) Sept. 26, 1778–July 13, 1832; House 1809–11, 1813–March 1815.

FITCH, Thomas (Nev.) Jan. 27, 1838–Nov. 12, 1923; House 1869–71.

FITZGERALD, Roy Gerald (Ohio) Aug. 25, 1875–Nov. 16, 1962; House 1921–31.

FITZGERALD, William Thomas (Ohio) Oct. 13, 1858–Jan. 12, 1939; House 1925–29.

FJARE, Orvin Benonie (Mont.) April 16, 1918–; House 1955–57.

FLACK, William Henry (N.Y.) March 22, 1861–Feb. 2, 1907; House 1903–Feb. 2, 1907.

FLAHERTY, Lawrence James (Calif.) July 4, 1878–June 13, 1926; House 1925–June 13, 1926.

FLANAGAN, James Winright (Tex.) Sept. 5, 1805–Sept. 28, 1887; Senate March 30, 1870–75.

FLANAGAN, Michael Patrick (Ill.) House, 1995–.

FLANDERS, Alvan (Wash.) Aug. 2, 1825–March 14, 1884; House (Terr. Del.) 1867–69; Gov. (Wash. Terr.) 1869–70.

FLANDERS, Ralph Edward (Vt.) Sept. 28, 1880–Feb. 19, 1970; Senate Nov. 1, 1946–59.

FLEEGER, George Washington (Pa.) March 13, 1839–June 25, 1894; House 1885–87.

FLEETWOOD, Frederick Gleed (Vt.) Sept. 27, 1868–Jan. 28, 1938; House 1923–25.

FLETCHER, Charles Kimball (Calif.) Dec. 15, 1902–Sept. 29, 1985; House 1947–49.

FLETCHER, Loren (Minn.) April 10, 1833–April 15, 1919; House 1893–1903, 1905–07.

FLETCHER, Thomas (Ky.) Oct. 21, 1779–?: House Dec. 2, 1816–17.

FLICK, James Patton (Iowa) Aug. 28, 1845–Feb. 25, 1929; House 1889–93.

FLINT, Frank Putnam (Calif.) July 15, 1862–Feb. 11, 1929; Senate 1905–11.

FLOOD, Thomas Schmeck (N.Y.) April 12, 1844–Oct. 28, 1908; House 1887–91.

FLOYD, John (Va.) April 24, 1783–Aug. 17, 1837; House 1817–29: Gov. March 4, 1830–March 31, 1834

FLYE, Edwin (Maine) March 4, 1817–July 12, 1886; House Dec. 4, 1876–77.

FLYNN, Dennis Thomas (Okla.) Feb. 13, 1861–June 19, 1939; House (Terr. Del.) 1893–97, 1899–1903.

FOCHT, Benjamin Kurtz (Pa.) March 12, 1863–March 27, 1937; House 1907–13, 1915–23, 1933–March 27, 1937.

FOELKER, Otto Godfrey (N.Y.) Dec. 29, 1875–Jan. 18, 1943; House Nov. 3, 1908–11.

FOERDERER, Robert Hermann (Pa.) May 16, 1860–July 26, 1903; House 1901–July 26, 1903.

FOGG, George Gilman (N.H.) May 26, 1813–Oct. 5, 1881; Senate Aug. 31, 1866–67.

FOLEY, Mark (Fla.) House, 1995–.

FOLGER, Walter Jr. (Mass.) June 12, 1765–Sept. 8, 1849; House 1817–21.

FONG, Hiram Leong (Hawaii) Oct. 1, 1907–; Senate Aug. 21, 1959–77.

FOOT, Solomon (Vt.) Nov. 19, 1802–March 28, 1866; House 1843–47 (Whig); Senate 1851–March 28, 1866 (1851–57 Whig); elected Pres. pro tempore Feb. 16, 1861, March 23, 1861, July 18, 1861, Jan. 15, 1862, March 31, 1862, June 19, 1862, Feb. 18, 1863, March 4, 1863, Dec. 18, 1863, Feb. 23, 1864, April 11, 1864.

FOOTE, Ellsworth Bishop (Conn.) Jan. 12, 1898–Jan. 18, 1977; House 1947–49.

FOOTE, Wallace Turner Jr. (N.Y.) April 7, 1864–Dec. 17, 1910; House 1895–99.

FORAKER, Joseph Benson (Ohio) July 5, 1846–May 10, 1917; Senate 1897–1909; Gov. Jan. 11, 1886–Jan. 13, 1890.

FORBES, Michael P. (N.Y.) House, 1995–.

FORD, Gerald Rudolph Jr. (Mich.) July 14, 1913–House 1949–Dec. 6, 1973; House minority leader 1965–Dec. 6, 1973; Vice President Dec. 6, 1973–Aug. 9, 1974; President Aug. 9, 1974–77.

FORD, Leland Merritt (Calif.) March 8, 1893–Nov. 27, 1965; House 1939–43.

FORDNEY, Joseph Warren (Mich.) Nov. 5, 1853–Jan. 8, 1932; House 1899–1923.

FOREMAN, Edgar Franklin (N.Mex.) Dec. 22, 1933–; House 1963–65 (Tex.), 1969–71.

FORNEY, Daniel Munroe (son of Peter Forney, uncle of William Henry Forney) (N.C.) May 1784–Oct. 15, 1847; House 1815–18.

FORNEY, Peter (father of Daniel Munroe Forney, grandfather of William Henry Forney) (N.C.) April 21, 1756–Feb. 1, 1834; House 1813–15.

FORSYTHE, Edwin Bell (N.J.) Jan. 17, 1916–March 29, 1984; House Nov. 3, 1970–March 29, 1984.

FORT, Franklin William (N.J.) March 30, 1880–June 20, 1937; House 1925–31.

FORT, Greenbury Lafayette (Ill.) Oct. 17, 1825–Jan. 13, 1883; House 1873–81.

FOSS, Frank Herbert (Mass.) Sept. 20, 1865–Feb. 15, 1947; House 1925–35.

FOSS, George Edmund (brother of Eugene Noble Foss) (Ill.) July 2, 1863–March 15, 1936; House 1895–1913, 1915–19.

FOSTER, Addison Gardner (Wash.) Jan. 28, 1837–Jan. 16, 1917; Senate 1899–1905.

FOSTER, Charles (Ohio) April 12, 1828–Jan. 9, 1904; House 1871–79; Gov. Jan. 12, 1880–Jan. 14, 1884; Secy. of the Treasury Feb. 25, 1891–March 6, 1893.

FOSTER, David Johnson (Vt.) June 27, 1857–March 21, 1912; House 1901–March 21, 1912.

FOSTER, Israel Moore (Ohio) Jan. 12, 1873–June 10, 1950; House 1919–25.

FOSTER, John Hopkins (Ind.) Jan. 31, 1862–Sept. 5, 1917; House May 16, 1905–09.

FOSTER, Lafayette Sabine (Conn.) Nov. 22, 1806–Sept. 19, 1880; Senate 1855–67; elected Pres. pro tempore March 7, 1865.

FOSTER, Stephen Clark (Maine) Dec. 24, 1799–Oct. 5, 1872; House 1857–61.

FOSTER, Wilder De Ayr (Mich.) Jan. 8, 1819–Sept. 20, 1873; House Dec. 4, 1871–Sept. 20, 1873.

FOULKROD, William Walker (Pa.) Nov. 22, 1846–Nov. 13, 1910; House 1907–Nov. 13, 1910.

FOWLER, Charles Newell (N.J.) Nov. 2, 1852–May 27, 1932; House 1895–1911.

FOWLER, John (Ky.) 1755–Aug. 22, 1840; House 1797–1807.

FOWLER, Tillie (Fla.) Dec. 23, 1942–; House 1993–.

FOX, John D. (Pa.) House, 1995–.

FRANCE, Joseph Irvin (Md.) Oct. 11, 1873–Jan. 26, 1939; Senate 1917–23.

FRANCHOT, Richard (N.Y.) June 2, 1816–Nov. 23, 1875; House 1861–63.

FRANCIS, George Blinn (N.Y.) Aug. 12, 1883–May 20, 1967; House 1917–19.

FRANK, Augustus (nephew of William Patterson of N.Y. and George Washington Patterson) (N.Y.) July 17, 1826–April 29, 1895; House 1859–65.

FRANK, Nathan (Mo.) Feb. 23, 1852–April 5, 1931; House 1889–91.

FRANKHAUSER, William Horace (Mich.) March 5, 1863–May 9, 1921; House March 4–May 9, 1921.

FRANKLIN, Jesse (brother of Meshack Franklin) (N.C.) March 24, 1760–Aug. 31, 1823; House 1795–97 (no party); Senate 1799–1805, 1807–13; elected Pres. pro tempore March 10, 1804; Gov. Dec. 7, 1820–Dec. 7, 1821 (Democratic Republican).

FRANKLIN, Meshack (brother of Jesse Franklin) (N.C.) 1772–Dec. 18, 1839; House 1807–15.

FRANKLIN, William Webster (Miss.) Dec. 13, 1941–; House 1983–87.

FRANKS, Gary (Conn.) Feb. 9, 1953–; House 1991–.

FRANKS, Robert Douglas (N.J.) Sept. 21, 1951–; House 1993–.

FRAZIER, Lynn Joseph (N.Dak.) Dec. 21, 1874–Jan. 11, 1947; Senate 1923–41; Gov. Jan. 3, 1917–Nov. 23, 1921.

FREAR, James Archibald (Wis.) Oct. 24, 1861–May 28, 1939; House 1913–35.

FREDERICKS, John Donnan (Calif.) Sept. 10, 1869–Aug. 26, 1945; House May 1, 1923–27.

FREE, Arthur Monroe (Calif.) Jan. 15, 1879–April 1, 1953; House 1921–33.

FREEMAN, Chapman (Pa.) Oct. 8, 1832–March 22, 1904; House 1875–79.

FREEMAN, James Crawford (Ga.) April, 1820–Sept. 3, 1885; House 1873–75.

FREEMAN, Nathaniel Jr. (nephew of Jonathan Freeman) (Mass.) May 1, 1766–Aug. 22, 1800; House 1795–99 (1795–97 Federalist).

FREEMAN, Richard Patrick (Conn.) April 24, 1869–July 8, 1944; House 1915–33.

FREER, Romeo Hoyt (W. Va.) Nov. 9, 1846–May 9, 1913; House 1899–1901.

FRELINGHUYSEN, Frederick Theodore (nephew and adopted son of Theodore Frelinghuysen, great-nephew of Frederick Frelinghuysen, uncle of Joseph Sherman Frelinghuysen, great-grandfather of Peter Hood Ballantine Frelinghuysen Jr.) (N.J.) Aug. 4, 1817–May 20, 1885; Senate Nov. 12, 1866–69, 1871–77; Secy. of State Dec. 19, 1881–March 6, 1885.

FRELINGHUYSEN, Joseph Sherman (nephew of Frederick Theodore Frelinghuysen, cousin of Peter Hood Ballantine Frelinghuysen Jr.) (N.J.) March 12, 1869–Feb. 8, 1948; Senate 1917–23.

FRELINGHUYSEN, Peter Hood Ballantine Jr. (cousin of Joseph Sherman Frelinghuysen, great-grandson of Frederick Theodore Frelinghuysen, great-great-nephew of Theodore Frelinghuysen, great-great-great-grandson of Frederick Frelinghuysen) (N.J.) Jan. 17, 1916–; House 1953–75.

FRELINGHUYSEN, Rodney (N.J.) House, 1995–.

FRENCH, Burton Lee (Idaho) Aug. 1, 1875–Sept. 12, 1954; House 1903–09, 1911–15, 1917–33.

FRENCH, Ezra Bartlett (Maine) Sept. 23, 1810–April 24, 1880; House 1859–61.

FRENCH, John Robert (N.C.) May 28, 1819–Oct. 2, 1890; House July 6, 1868–69.

FRENZEL, William Eldridge (Minn.) July 31, 1923–; House 1971–91.

FREY, Louis Jr. (Fla.) Jan. 11, 1934–; House 1969–79.

FRISA, Daniel (N.Y.) House, 1995–.

FRIST, Bill (Tenn.) Senate, 1995–.

FROEHLICH, Harold Vernon (Wis.) May 12, 1932–; House 1973–75.

FROMENTIN, Eligius (La.) ?–Oct. 6, 1822; Senate 1813–19.

FROST, Rufus Smith (Mass.) July 18, 1826–March 6, 1894; House 1875–July 28, 1876.

FROTHINGHAM, Louis Adams (Mass.) July 13, 1871–Aug. 23, 1928; House 1921–Aug. 23, 1928.

FRYE, William Pierce (grandfather of Wallace Humphrey White Jr.) (Maine) Sept. 2, 1830–Aug. 8, 1911; House 1871–March 17, 1881; Senate March 18, 1881–Aug. 8, 1911; elected Pres. pro tempore Feb. 7, 1896, March 7, 1901, Dec. 5, 1907.

FULKERSON, Frank Ballard (Mo.) March 5, 1866–Aug. 30, 1936; House 1905–07.

FULLER, Alvan Tufts (Mass.) Feb. 27, 1878–April 30, 1958; House 1917–Jan. 5, 1921 (1917–19 Independent Republican); Gov. Jan. 8, 1925–Jan. 3, 1929.

FULLER, Charles Eugene (Ill.) March 31, 1849–June 25, 1926; House 1903–13, 1915–June 25, 1926.

FULLER, Hawden Carlton (N.Y.) Aug. 28, 1895–Jan. 29, 1990; House Nov. 2, 1943–49.

FULLER, Timothy (Mass.) July 11, 1778–Oct. 1, 1835; House 1817–25.

FULLER, William Elijah (Iowa) March 30, 1846–April 23, 1918; House 1885–89.

FULTON, Charles William (brother of Elmer Lincoln Fulton) (Oreg.) Aug. 24, 1853–Jan. 27, 1918; Senate 1903–09.

FULTON, James Grove (Pa.) March 1, 1903–Oct. 6, 1971; House 1945–Oct. 6, 1971.

FUNDERBURK, David (N.C.) House, 1995–.

FUNK, Benjamin Franklin (father of Frank Hamilton Funk) (Ill.) Oct. 17, 1838–Feb. 14, 1909; House 1893–95.

FUNK, Frank Hamilton (son of Benjamin Franklin Funk) (Ill.) April 5, 1869–Nov. 24, 1940; House 1921–27.

FUNSTON, Edward Hogue (Kans.) Sept. 16, 1836–Sept. 10, 1911; House March 21, 1884–Aug. 2, 1894.

FURLOW, Allen John (Minn.) Nov. 9, 1890–Jan. 29, 1954; House 1925–29.

GAGE, Joshua (Mass.) Aug. 7, 1763–Jan. 24, 1831; House 1817–19.

GAHN, Henry Conrad (Ohio) April 26, 1880–Nov. 2, 1962; House 1921–23.

GAILLARD, John (uncle of Theodore Gaillard Hunt) (S.C.) Sept. 5, 1765–Feb. 26, 1826; Senate Dec. 6, 1804–Feb. 26, 1826; elected Pres. pro tempore Feb. 28, 1810, April 17, 1810, April 18, 1814, Nov. 25, 1814, March 6, 1817, March 31, 1818, Jan. 25, 1820, Feb. 1, 1822, Feb. 19, 1823, May 21, 1824, March 9, 1825.

GAINES, Joseph Holt (W.Va.) Sept. 3, 1864–April 12, 1951; House 1901–11.

GAINES, William Embre (Va.) Aug. 30, 1844–May 4, 1912; House 1887–89.

GALE, Richard Pillsbury (Minn.) Oct. 30, 1900–Dec. 4, 1973; House 1941–45.

GALLAGHER, James A. (Pa.) Jan. 16, 1869–Dec. 8, 1957; House 1943–45, 1947–49.

GALLEGLY, Elton William (Calif.) March 7, 1944–; House 1987–.

GALLINGER, Jacob Harold (N.H.) March 28, 1837–Aug. 17, 1918; House 1885–89; Senate 1891–Aug. 17, 1918; Senate minority leader 1913–Aug. 17, 1918; elected Pres. pro tempore Feb. 12, 1912 (to serve Feb. 12–Feb. 14, April 26–April 27, May 7, July 6–July 31, Aug. 12–Aug. 26, 1912; Dec. 16, 1912–Jan. 4, 1913; Jan. 19–Feb. 1, Feb. 16–March 3, 1913).

GALLO, Dean Anderson (N.J.) Nov. 23, 1935–; House 1985–.

GALLOWAY, Samuel (Ohio) March 20, 1811–April 5, 1872; House 1855–57.

GAMBLE, John Rankin (brother of Robert Jackson Gamble, uncle of Ralph Albernethy Gamble) (S.Dak.) Jan. 15, 1848–Aug. 14, 1891; House March 4–Aug. 14, 1891.

GAMBLE, Ralph Abernethy (son of Robert Jackson Gamble, nephew of John Rankin Gamble) (N.Y.) May 6, 1885–March 4, 1959; House Nov. 2, 1937–57.

GAMBLE, Robert Jackson (brother of John Rankin Gamble, father of Ralph Abernethy Gamble) (S.Dak.) Feb. 7, 1851–Sept. 22, 1924; House 1895–97, 1899–1901; Senate 1901–13.

GANNETT, Barzillai (Mass.) June 17, 1764–1832; House 1809–12.

GANSKE, Greg (Iowa) House, 1995–.

GARBER, Jacob Aaron (Va.) Jan. 25, 1879–Dec. 2, 1953; House 1929–31.

GARBER, Milton Cline (Okla.) Nov. 30, 1867–Sept. 12, 1948; House 1923–33.

GARDNER, Augustus Peabody (uncle of Henry Cabot Lodge Jr. and John Davis Lodge) (Mass.) Nov. 5, 1865–Jan. 14, 1918; House Nov. 3, 1903–May 15, 1917.

GARDNER, Francis (N.H.) Dec. 27, 1771–June 25, 1835; House 1807–09.

GARDNER, Gideon (Mass.) May 30, 1759–March 22, 1832; House 1809–11.

GARDNER, James Carson (N.C.) April 8, 1933–; House 1967–69.

GARDNER, John James (N.J.) Oct. 17, 1845–Feb. 7, 1921; House 1893–1913.

GARDNER, Mills (Ohio) Jan. 30, 1830–Feb. 20, 1910; House 1877–79.

GARDNER, Washington (Mich.) Feb. 16, 1845–March 31, 1928; House 1899–1911.

GARFIELD, James Abram (Ohio) Nov. 19, 1831–Sept. 19, 1881; House 1863–Nov. 8, 1880; President March 4–Sept. 19, 1881.

GARFIELDE, Selucius (Wash.) Dec. 8, 1822–April 13, 1881; House (Terr. Del.) 1869–73.

GARLAND, David Shepherd (Va.) Sept. 27, 1769–Oct. 7, 1841; House Jan. 17, 1810–11.

GARLAND, Mahlon Morris (Pa.) May 4, 1856–Nov. 19, 1920; House 1915–Nov. 19, 1920.

GARLAND, Peter Adams (Maine) June 16, 1923–; House 1961–63.

GARN, Edwin Jacob "Jake" (Utah) Oct. 12, 1932–; Senate Dec. 21, 1974–93; Chrmn. Senate Banking, Housing and Urban Affairs 1981–87.

GARNER, Alfred Buckwalter (Pa.) March 4, 1873–July 30, 1930; House 1909–11.

GARNETT, James Mercer (brother of Robert Selden Garnett, grandfather of Muscoe Russell Hunter Garnett, cousin of Charles Fenton Mercer) (Va.) June 8, 1770–April 23, 1843; House 1805–09.

GARNETT, Robert Selden (brother of James Mercer Garnett, cousin of Charles Fenton Mercer) (Va.) April 26, 1789–Aug. 15, 1840; House 1817–27.

GARTNER, Fred Christian (Pa.) March 14, 1896–Sept. 1, 1972; House 1939–41.

GAVIN, Leon Harry (Pa.) Feb. 25, 1893–Sept. 15, 1963; House 1943–Sept. 15, 1963.

GEAR, John Henry (Iowa) April 7, 1825–July 14, 1900; House 1887–91, 1893–95; Senate 1895–July 14, 1990; Gov. Jan. 17, 1878–Jan. 12, 1882.

GEARHART, Bertrand Wesley (Calif.) May 31, 1890–Oct. 11, 1955; House 1935–49.

GEKAS, George William (Pa.) April 14, 1930–; House 1983–.

GENSMAN, Lorraine Michael (Okla.) Aug. 26, 1878–May 27, 1954; House 1921–23.

GEORGE, Melvin Clark (Oreg.) May 13, 1849–Feb. 22, 1933; House 1881–85.

GEORGE, Myron Virgil (Kans.) Jan. 6, 1900–April 11, 1972; House Nov. 7, 1950–59.

GERLACH, Charles Lewis (Pa.) Sept. 14, 1895–May 5, 1947; House 1939–May 5, 1947.

GERMAN, Obadiah (N.Y.) April 22, 1766–Sept. 24, 1842; Senate 1809–15.

GERNERD, Fred Benjamin (Pa.) Nov. 22, 1879–Aug. 7, 1948; House 1921–23.

GEST, William Harrison (Ill.) Jan. 7, 1838–Aug. 9, 1912; House 1887–91.

GHOLSON, Thomas Jr. (Va.) ?–July 4, 1816; House Nov. 7, 1808–July 4, 1816.

GIBSON, Ernest Willard (father of Ernest William Gibson Jr.) (Vt.) Dec. 29, 1872–June 20, 1940; House Nov. 6, 1923–Oct. 19, 1933; Senate Nov. 21, 1933–June 20, 1940.

GIBSON, Ernest William Jr. (son of Ernest Willard Gibson) (Vt.) March 6, 1901–Nov. 4, 1969; Senate June 24, 1940–41; Gov. Jan. 9, 1947–Jan. 16, 1950.

GIBSON, Henry Richard (cousin of Charles Hopper Gibson) (Tenn.) Dec. 24, 1837–May 25, 1938; House 1895–1905.

GIDDINGS, Joshua Reed (Ohio) Oct. 6, 1795–May 27, 1864; House Dec. 3, 1838–March 22, 1842 (Whig.); Dec. 5, 1842–59 (Dec. 5, 1842–49 Whig. 1849–55 Free-Soiler).

GIFFORD, Charles Laceille (Mass.) March 15, 1871–Aug. 23, 1947; House Nov. 7, 1922–Aug. 23, 1947.

GIFFORD, Oscar Sherman (S.Dak.) Oct. 20, 1842–Jan. 16, 1913; House (Terr. Del. Dakota) 1885–89, (Rep.) Nov. 2, 1889–91.

GILBERT, Abijah (Fla.) June 18, 1806–Nov. 23, 1881; Senate 1869–75.

GILBERT, Newton Whiting (Ind.) May 24, 1862–July 5, 1939; House 1905–Nov. 6, 1906.

GILBERT, Sylvester (Conn.) Oct. 20, 1755–Jan. 2, 1846; House Nov. 16, 1818–19.

GILCHREST, Wayne Thomas (Md.) April 15, 1946–; House 1991–.

GILCHRIST, Fred Cramer (Iowa) June 2, 1868–March 10, 1950; House 1931–45.

GILES, William Branch (Va.) Aug. 12, 1762–Dec. 4, 1830; House Dec. 7, 1790–Oct. 2, 1798 (no party), 1801–03; Senate Aug. 11, 1804–15; Gov. March 4, 1827–March 4, 1830.

GILFILLAN, Calvin Willard (Pa.) Feb. 20, 1832–Dec. 2, 1901; House 1869–71.

GILFILLAN, John Bachop (Minn.) Feb. 11, 1835–Aug. 19, 1924; House 1885–87.

GILHAMS, Clarence Chauncey (Ind.) April 11, 1860–June 5, 1912; House Nov. 6, 1906–09.

GILL, Joseph John (Ohio) Sept. 21, 1846–May 22, 1920; House Dec. 4, 1899–Oct. 31, 1903.

GILLESPIE, Dean Milton (Colo.) May 3, 1884–Feb. 2, 1949; House March 7, 1944–47.

GILLESPIE, James (N.C.) ?–Jan. 11, 1805; House 1793–99 (1793–95 no party), 1803–Jan. 11, 1805.

GILLET, Charles William (N.Y.) Nov. 26, 1840–Dec. 31, 1908; House 1893–1905.

GILLETT, Frederick Huntington (Mass.) Oct. 16, 1851–July 31, 1935; House 1893–1925; Speaker May 19, 1919–21, April 11, 1921–23, Dec. 3, 1923–25; Senate 1925–31.

GILLETT, James Norris (Calif.) Sept. 20, 1860–April 20, 1937; House 1903–Nov. 5, 1906; Gov. Jan. 8, 1907–Jan. 3, 1911.

GILLETTE, Wilson Darwin (Pa.) July 1, 1880–Aug. 7, 1951; House Nov. 4, 1941–Aug. 7, 1951.

GILLIE, George W. (Ind.) Aug. 15, 1880–July 3, 1963; House 1939–49.

GILLMOR, Paul Edward (Ohio) Feb. 1, 1939–; House 1989–.

GILMAN, Benjamin Arthur (N.Y.) Dec. 6, 1922–; House 1973–, Charmn. House International Relations Committee 1995–.

GILMAN, Charles Jervis (great-nephew of John Taylor Gilman and Nicholas Gilman) (Maine) Feb. 26, 1824–Feb. 5, 1901; House 1857–59.

GILMAN, Nicholas (brother of John Taylor Gilman and great-uncle of Charles Jervis Gilman) (N.H.) Aug. 3, 1755–May 2, 1814; House 1789–97 (no party); Senate 1805–May 2, 1814; Cont. Cong. 1787–89.

GINGRICH, Newton Leroy (Ga.) June 17, 1943–; House 1979–.

GLASGOW, Hugh (Pa.) Sept. 8, 1769–Jan. 31, 1818; House 1813–17.

GLENN, Milton Willits (N.J.) June 18, 1903–Dec. 14, 1967; House Nov. 5, 1957–65.

GLENN, Otis Ferguson (Ill.) Aug. 27, 1879–March 11, 1959; Senate Dec. 3, 1928–33.

GLYNN, James Peter (Conn.) Nov. 12, 1867–March 6, 1930; House 1915–23, 1925–March 6, 1930.

GODSHALK, William (Pa.) Oct. 25, 1817–Feb. 6, 1891; House 1879–83.

GOEBEL, Herman Philip (Ohio) April 5, 1853–May 4, 1930; House 1903–11.

GOFF, Abe McGregor (Idaho) Dec. 21, 1899–Nov. 23, 1984; House 1947–49.

GOFF, Guy Despard (son of Nathan Goff, father of Louise Goff Reece, father-in-law of Brazilla Carroll Reece) (W.Va.) Sept. 13, 1866–Jan. 7, 1933; Senate 1925–31.

GOFF, Nathan (father of Guy Despard Goff, grandfather of Louise Goff Reece) (W.Va.) Feb. 9, 1843–April 24, 1920; House 1883–89; Senate April 1, 1913–19; Secy. of the Navy Jan. 7–March 6, 1881.

GOLDEN, James Stephen (Ky.) Sept. 10, 1891–Sept. 6, 1971; House 1949–55.

GOLDER, Benjamin Martin (Pa.) Dec. 23, 1891–Dec. 30, 1946; House 1925–33.

GOLDSBOROUGH, Phillips Lee (Md.) Aug. 6, 1865–Oct. 22, 1946; Senate 1929–35; Gov. Jan. 10, 1912–Jan. 12, 1916.

GOLDWATER, Barry Morris (father of Barry Morris Goldwater Jr.) (Ariz.) Jan. 1, 1909–; Senate 1953–65, 1969–87; Chrmn. Senate Select Committee on Intelligence Activities 1981–85; Chrmn. Senate Armed Services 1985–87.

GOLDWATER, Barry Morris Jr. (son of Barry Morris Goldwater) (Calif.) July 15, 1938–; House April 29, 1969–83.

GOOCH, Daniel Wheelwright (Mass.) Jan. 8, 1820–Nov. 11, 1891; House Jan. 31, 1858–Sept. 1, 1865, 1873–75.

GOOD, James William (Iowa) Sept. 25, 1866–Nov. 18, 1929; House 1909–June 15, 1921; Secy. of War March 6–Nov. 18, 1929.

GOODALL, Louis Bertrand (Maine) Sept. 23, 1851–June 26, 1935; House 1917–21.

GOODELL, Charles Ellsworth (N.Y.) March 16, 1926–Jan. 21, 1987; House May 26, 1959–Sept. 9, 1968; Senate Sept. 10, 1968–71.

GOODING, Frank Robert (Idaho) Sept. 16, 1859–June 24, 1928; Senate Jan. 15, 1921–June 24, 1928; Gov. Jan. 2, 1905–Jan. 4, 1908.

GOODLATTE, Robert William (Va.) Sept. 22, 1952–; House 1993–.

GOODLING, George Atlee (father of William Franklin Goodling) (Pa.) Sept. 26, 1896–Oct. 17, 1982; House 1961–65, 1967–75.

GOODLING, William Franklin (son of George Atlee Goodling) (Pa.) Dec. 5, 1927–; House 1975–; Chrmn, House Economic and Educational Opportunities Commitee, 1995–.

GOODRICH, Milo (N.Y.) Jan. 3, 1814–April 15, 1881; House 1871–73.

GOODWIN, Angier Louis (Mass.) Jan. 30, 1881–June 20, 1975; House 1943–55.

GOODWIN, Forrest (Maine) June 15, 1862–May 28, 1913; House March 4–May 28, 1913.

GOODWIN, Godfrey Gummer (Minn.) Jan. 11, 1873–Feb. 16, 1933; House 1925–Feb. 16, 1933.

GOODWIN, Henry Charles (N.Y.) June 25, 1824–Nov. 12, 1860; House Nov. 7, 1854–55 (Whig), 1857–59.

GOODWIN, John Noble (Ariz.) Oct. 18, 1824–April 29, 1887; House (Rep. Maine) 1861–63, (Terr. Del.) 1865–67; Gov. (Ariz. Terr.) 1863–65.

GOODWIN, Philip Arnold (N.Y.) Jan. 20, 1882–June 6, 1937; House 1933–June 6, 1937.

GOODWIN, Robert Kingman (Iowa) May 23, 1905–Feb. 21, 1983; House March 5, 1940–41.

GOODWYN, Peterson (Va.) 1745–Feb. 21, 1818; House 1803–Feb. 21, 1818.

GOODYKOONTZ, Wells (W.Va.) June 3, 1872–March 2, 1944; House 1919–23.

GORMAN, John Jerome (Ill.) June 2, 1883–Feb. 24, 1949; House 1921–23, 1925–27.

GORTON, Thomas Slade III (Wash.) Jan. 8, 1928–; Senate 1981–87, 1989–.

GOSS, Edward Wheeler (Conn.) April 27, 1893–Dec. 27, 1972; House Nov. 4, 1930–35.

GOSS, Porter (Fla.) Nov. 26, 1938–; House 1989–.

GOULD, Arthur Robinson (Maine) March 16, 1857–July 24, 1946; Senate Nov. 30, 1926–31.

GOULD, Norman Judd (grandson of Norman Buel Judd) (N.Y.) March 15, 1877–Aug. 20, 1964; House Nov. 2, 1915–23.

GOURDIN, Theodore (S.C.) March 20, 1764–Jan. 17, 1826; House 1813–15.

GOVE, Samuel Francis (Ga.) March 9, 1822–Dec. 3, 1900; House June 25, 1868–69.

GRADISON, Willis David Jr. (Ohio) Dec. 28, 1928–; House 1975–Jan. 31, 1993.

GRAFF, Joseph Verdi (Ill.) July 1, 1854–Nov. 10, 1921; House 1895–1911.

GRAHAM, George Scott (Pa.) Sept. 13, 1850–July 4, 1931; House 1913–July 4, 1931.

GRAHAM, James Harper (N.Y.) Sept. 18, 1812–June 23, 1881; House 1859–61.

GRAHAM, Lindsey (S.C.) House, 1995–.

GRAHAM, Louis Edward (Pa.) Aug. 4, 1880–Nov. 9, 1965; House 1939–55.

GRAHAM, William Harrison (Pa.) Aug. 3, 1844–March 2, 1923; House Nov. 29, 1898–1903, 1905–11.

GRAHAM, William Johnson (Ill.) Feb. 7, 1872–Nov. 10, 1937; House 1917–June 7, 1924.

GRAMM, William Philip "Phil" (Tex.) July 8, 1942–; House 1979–January 5, 1983 (Democrat), Feb. 22, 1983–85; Senate 1985–.

GRAMMER, Elijah Sherman (Wash.) April 3, 1868–Nov. 19, 1936; Senate Nov. 22, 1932–33.

GRAMS, Rodney (Minn.) Feb. 4, 1948–; House 1933–1995; Senate 1995–.

GRANATA, Peter Charles (Ill.) Oct. 28, 1898–Sept. 29, 1973; House 1931–April 5, 1932.

GRANDY, Frederick Lawrence (Iowa) June 29, 1948–; House 1987–.

GRANGER, Amos Phelps (cousin of Francis Granger) (N.Y.) June 3, 1789–Aug. 20, 1866; House 1855–59 (1855–57 Whig).

GRANGER, Bradley Francis (Mich.) March 12, 1825–Nov. 4, 1882; House 1861–63.

GRANT, James William (Fla.) Feb. 21, 1943–; House 1987–91 (1987–Feb. 21, 1989 Democrat).

GRANT, John Gaston (N.C.) Jan. 1, 1858–June 21, 1923; House 1909–11.

GRANT, Robert Allen (Ind.) July 31, 1905–; House 1939–49.

GRASSLEY, Charles Ernest (Iowa) Sept. 17, 1933–; House 1975–81; Senate 1981–.

GRAVELY, Joseph Jackson (Mo.) Sept. 25, 1828–April 28, 1872; House 1867–69.

GRAY, Edward Winthrop (N.J.) Aug. 18, 1870–June 10, 1942; House 1915–19.

GREEN, Isaiah Lewis (Mass.) Dec. 28, 1761–Dec. 5, 1841; House 1805–09, 1811–13.

GREEN, Sedgwick William "Bill" (N.Y.) Oct. 16, 1929–; House Feb. 21, 1978–93.

GREEN, William Raymond (Iowa) Nov. 7, 1856–June 11, 1947; House June 5, 1911–March 31, 1928.

GREENE, Frank Lester (Vt.) Feb. 10, 1870–Dec. 17, 1930; House July 30, 1912–23; Senate 1923–Dec. 17, 1930.

GREENE, William Stedman (Mass.) April 28, 1841–Sept. 22, 1924; House May 31, 1898–Sept. 22, 1924.

GREENHALGE, Frederic Thomas (Mass.) July 19, 1842–March 5, 1896; House 1889–91; Gov. Jan. 3, 1894–March 5, 1896.

GREENUP, Christopher (Ky.) 1750–April 27, 1818; House Nov. 9, 1792–97 (Nov. 9, 1792–95 no party); Gov. June 1, 1804–June 1, 1808.

GREENWOOD, James Charles (Pa.) May 4, 1951–; House 1993–.

GREGG, Andrew (grandfather of James Xavier McLanahan) (Pa.) June 10, 1755–May 20, 1835; House 1791–1807 (no party); Senate 1807–13; elected Pres. pro tempore June 26, 1809.

GREGG, Judd Alan (N.H.) Feb. 14, 1947–; House 1981–89; Gov. Jan. 4, 1889–Jan 7, 1993.

GRIEST, William Walton (Pa.) Sept. 22, 1858–Dec. 5, 1929; House 1909–Dec. 5, 1929.

GRIFFIN, Isaac (great-grandfather of Eugene McLanahan Wilson, great-great-grandfather of Charles Hudson Griffin) (Pa.) Feb. 27, 1756–Oct. 12, 1827; House May 24, 1813–17.

GRIFFIN, Michael (Wis.) Sept. 9, 1842–Dec. 29, 1899; House Nov. 5, 1894–99.

GRIFFIN, Robert Paul (Mich.) Nov. 6, 1923–; House 1957–May 10, 1966; Senate May 11, 1966–Jan. 2, 1979.

GRIFFITHS, Percy Wilfred (Ohio) March 30, 1893–June 12, 1983; House 1943–49.

GRIMES, James Wilson (Iowa) Oct. 20, 1816–Feb. 7, 1872; Senate 1859–Dec. 6, 1869; Gov. Dec. 9, 1854–Jan. 13, 1858 (Whig).

GRINNELL, Josiah Bushnell (Iowa) Dec. 22, 1821–March 31, 1891; House 1863–67.

GRISHAM, Wayne Richard (Calif.) Jan. 10, 1923–; House 1979–83.

GRISWOLD, Dwight Palmer (Nebr.) Nov. 27, 1893–April 12, 1954; Senate Nov. 5, 1952–April 12, 1954; Gov. Jan. 9, 1941–Jan. 9, 1947.

GRISWOLD, Harry Wilbur (Wis.) May 19, 1886–July 4, 1939; House Jan. 3–July 4, 1939.

GRISWOLD, John Augustus (N.Y.) Nov. 11, 1822–Oct. 31, 1872; House 1863–69 (1863–65 Democrat).

GRISWOLD, Matthew (grandson of Roger Griswold) (Pa.) June 6, 1833–May 19, 1919; House 1891–93, 1895–97.

GRONNA, Asle Jorgenson (N.Dak.) Dec. 10, 1858–May 4, 1922; House 1905–Feb. 2, 1911; Senate Feb. 2, 1911–21.

GROSS, Chester Heilman (Pa.) Oct. 13, 1888–Jan. 9, 1973; House 1939–41, 1943–49.

GROSS, Harold Royce (Iowa) June 30, 1899–Sept. 22, 1987; House 1949–75.

GROSVENOR, Charles Henry (uncle of Charles Grosvenor Bond) (Ohio) Sept. 20, 1833–Oct. 30, 1917; House 1885–91, 1893–1907.

GROTBERG, John E. (Ill.) March 23, 1925–Nov. 15, 1986; House 1985–Nov. 15, 1986.

GROUT, William Wallace (Vt.) May 25, 1836–Oct. 7, 1902; House 1881–83, 1885–1901.

GROVER, James Russell Jr. (N.Y.) March 5, 1919–; House 1963–75.

GROW, Galusha Aaron (Pa.) Aug. 31, 1823–March 31, 1907; House 1851–63 (1851–57 Democrat), Feb. 26, 1894–1903; Speaker July 4, 1861–63.

GRUNDY, Joseph Ridgway (Pa.) Jan. 13, 1863–March 3, 1961; Senate Dec. 11, 1929–Dec. 1, 1930.

GUBSER, Charles Samuel (Calif.) Feb. 1, 1916–; House 1953–Dec. 31, 1974.

GUDE, Gilbert (Md.) March 9, 1923–; House 1967–77.

GUENTHER, Richard William (Wis.) Nov. 30, 1845–April 5, 1913; House 1881–89.

GUERNSEY, Frank Edward (Maine) Oct. 15, 1866–Jan. 1, 1927; House Nov. 3, 1908–17.

GUGGENHEIM, Simon (Colo.) Dec. 30, 1867–Nov. 2, 1941; Senate 1907–13.

GUILL, Ben Hugh (Tex.) Sept. 8, 1909–; House May 6, 1950–51.

GUNCKEL, Lewis B. (Ohio) Oct. 15, 1826–Oct. 3, 1903; House 1873–75.

GUNDERSON, Steven Craig (Wis.) May 10, 1951–; House 1981–.

GURLEY, John Addison (Ohio) Dec. 9, 1813–Aug. 19, 1863; House 1859–63.

GURNEY, Edward John (Fla.) Jan. 12, 1914–; House 1963–69; Senate 1969–Dec. 31, 1974.

GURNEY, John Chandler "Chan" (S.Dak.) May 21, 1896–March 9, 1985; Senate 1939–51; Chrmn. Senate Armed Services 1947–49.

GUTKNECHT, Gil (Minn.) House, 1995–.

GUYER, Tennyson (Ohio) Nov. 29, 1913–April 12, 1981; House 1973–April 12, 1981.

GUYER, Ulysses Samuel (Kans.) Dec. 13, 1868–June 5, 1943; House Nov. 5, 1924–25, 1927–June 5, 1943.

GWINN, Ralph Waldo (N.Y.) March 29, 1884–Feb. 27, 1962; House 1945–59.

GWYNNE, John William (Iowa) Oct. 20, 1889–July 5, 1972; House 1935–49.

HADLEY, Lindley Hoag (Wash.) June 19, 1861–Nov. 1, 1948; House 1915–33.

HADLEY, William Flavius Lester (Ill.) June 15, 1847–April 25, 1901; House Dec. 2, 1895–97.

HAGANS, John Marshall (W.Va.) Aug. 13, 1838–June 17, 1900; House 1873–75.

HAGEDORN, Thomas Michael (Minn.) Nov. 27, 1943–; House 1975–83.

HAGEN, Harold Christian (Minn.) Nov. 10, 1901–March 19, 1957; House 1943–55 (1943–45 Farmer Laborite).

HAGER, Alva Lysander (Iowa) Oct. 29, 1850–Jan. 29, 1923; House 1893–99.

HAGGOTT, Warren Armstrong (Colo.) May 18, 1864–April 29, 1958; House 1907–09.

HAHN, John (Pa.) Oct. 30, 1776–Feb. 26, 1823; House 1815–17.

HAHN, Michael (La.) Nov. 24, 1830–March 15, 1886; House Dec. 3, 1862–63 (Unionist), 1885–March 15, 1886; Gov. March 4, 1864–March 3, 1865 (State Rights Free-Trader).

HAINER, Eugene Jerome (Nebr.) Aug. 16, 1851–March 17, 1929; House 1893–97.

HALE, Eugene (father of Frederick Hale) (Maine) June 9, 1836–Oct. 27, 1918; House 1869–79; Senate 1881–1911.

HALE, Fletcher (N.H.) Jan. 22, 1883–Oct. 22, 1931; House 1925–Oct. 22, 1931.

HALE, Frederick (son of Eugene Hale, grandson of Zachariah Chandler, cousin of Robert Hale) (Maine) Oct. 7, 1874–Sept. 28, 1963; Senate 1917–41.

HALE, James Tracy (Pa.) Oct. 1810–April 6, 1865; House 1859–65.

HALE, Nathan Wesley (Tenn.) Feb. 11, 1860–Sept. 16, 1941; House 1905–09.

HALE, Robert (cousin of Frederick Hale) (Maine) Nov. 29, 1889–Nov. 30, 1976; House 1943–59.

HALE, Robert Safford (N.Y.) Sept. 24, 1822–Dec. 14, 1881; House Dec. 3, 1866–67, 1873–75.

HALE, Salma (N.H.) March 7, 1787–Nov. 19, 1866; House 1809–11, 1813–17.

HALL, Albert Richardson (Ind.) Aug. 27, 1884–Nov. 29, 1969; House 1925–31.

HALL, Bolling (Ga.) Dec. 25, 1767–Feb. 25, 1836; House 1811–17.

HALL, Chapin (Pa.) July 12, 1816–Sept. 12, 1879; House 1859–61.

HALL, Darwin Scott (Minn.) Jan. 23, 1844–Feb. 23, 1919; House 1889–91.

HALL, Durward Gorham (Mo.) Sept. 14, 1910–; House 1961–73.

HALL, Edwin Arthur (great–grandson of John Allen Collier) (N.Y.) Feb. 11, 1909–; House Nov. 7, 1939–53.

HALL, Homer William (Ill.) July 22, 1870–Sept. 22, 1954; House 1927–33.

HALL, Joshua Gilman (N.H.) Nov. 5, 1828–Oct. 31, 1898; House 1879–83.

HALL, Leonard Wood (N.Y.) Oct. 2, 1900–June 2, 1979; House 1939–Dec. 31, 1952; Chrmn. Rep. Nat. Comm. April 1953–Feb. 1957.

HALL, Obed (N.H.) Dec. 23, 1757–April 1, 1828; House 1811–13.

HALL, Philo (S.Dak.) Dec. 31, 1865–Oct. 7, 1938; House 1907–09.

HALL, Robert Bernard (Mass.) Jan. 28, 1812–April 15, 1868; House 1855–59 (1855–57 American Party).

HALL, Thomas (N.Dak.) June 6, 1869–Dec. 4, 1958; House Nov. 4, 1924–33.

HALL, Willard (Del.) Dec. 24, 1780–May 10, 1875; House 1817–Jan. 22, 1821.

HALLECK, Charles Abraham (Ind.) Aug. 22, 1900–March 3, 1986; House Jan. 29, 1935–69; House majority leader 1947–49, 1953–55; House minority leader 1959–65.

HALPERN, Seymour (N.Y.) Nov. 19, 1913–; House 1959–73.

HALSEY, George Armstrong (N.J.) Dec. 7, 1827–April 1, 1894; House 1867–69, 1871–73.

HALSEY, Silas (father of Jehiel Howell Halsey and Nicoll Halsey) (N.Y.) Oct. 6, 1743–Nov. 19, 1832; House 1805–07.

HALSEY, Thomas Jefferson (Mo.) May 4, 1863–March 17, 1951; House 1929–31.

HALTERMAN, Frederick (Pa.) Oct. 22, 1831–March 22, 1907; House 1895–97.

HAMER, Thomas Ray (nephew of Thomas Lyon Hamer) (Idaho) May 4, 1864–Dec. 22, 1950; House 1909–11.

HAMILTON, Charles Mann (N.Y.) Jan. 23, 1874–Jan. 3, 1942; House 1913–19.

HAMILTON, Charles Memorial (Fla.) Nov. 1, 1840–Oct. 22, 1875; House July 1, 1868–71.

HAMILTON, Cornelius Springer (Ohio) Jan. 2, 1821–Dec. 22, 1867; House March 4–Dec. 22, 1867.

HAMILTON, Edward La Rue (Mich.) Dec. 9, 1857–Nov. 2, 1923; House 1897–1921.

HAMILTON, John (Pa.) Nov. 25, 1754–Aug. 22, 1837; House 1805–07.

HAMILTON, Morgan Calvin (brother of Andrew Jackson Hamilton) (Tex.) Feb. 25, 1809–Nov. 21, 1893; Senate March 31, 1870–77.

HAMLIN, Hannibal (Maine) Aug. 27, 1809–July 4, 1891; House 1843–47 (Democrat); Senate June 8, 1848–Jan. 7, 1857 (Democrat), 1857–Jan. 17, 1861; 1869–81; Gov. Jan. 8–Feb. 25, 1857; Vice President 1861–65.

HAMMERSCHMIDT, John Paul (Ark.) May 4, 1922–; House 1967–93.

HAMMOND, Jabez Delno (N.Y.) Aug. 2, 1778–Aug. 18, 1855; House 1815–17.

HAMMOND, John (N.Y.) Aug. 17, 1827–May 28, 1889; House 1879–83.

HAMMOND, Samuel (Ga.) Sept. 21, 1757–Sept. 11, 1842; House 1803–Feb. 2, 1805; Gov. (Upper Louisiana Terr.) 1805–24.

HAMPTON, Wade (S.C.) 1752–Feb. 4, 1835; House 1795–97, 1803–05.

HANBACK, Lewis (Kans.) March 27, 1839–Sept. 7, 1897; House 1883–87.

HANBURY, Harry Alfred (N.Y.) Jan. 1, 1863–Aug. 22, 1940; House 1901–03.

HANCHETT, Luther (Wis.) Oct. 25, 1825–Nov. 24, 1862; House 1861–Nov. 24, 1862.

HANCOCK, Clarence Eugene (N.Y.) Feb. 13, 1885–Jan. 3, 1948; House Nov. 8, 1927–47.

HANCOCK, Milton D. "Mel" (Mo.) Sept. 14, 1929–; House 1989–.

HAND, Thomas Millet (N.J.) July 7, 1902–Dec. 26, 1956; House 1945–Dec. 26, 1956.

HANLY, James Franklin (Ind.) April 4, 1863–Aug. 1, 1920; House 1895–97; Gov. Jan. 9, 1905–Jan. 11, 1909.

HANNA, John (Ind.) Sept. 3, 1827–Oct. 24, 1882; House 1877–79.

HANNA, John Andre (grandfather of Archibald McAllister) (Pa.) 1762–July 23, 1805; House 1797–July 23, 1805.

HANNA, Louis Benjamin (N.Dak.) Aug. 9, 1861–April 23, 1948; House 1909–Jan. 7, 1913; Gov. Jan. 8, 1913–Jan. 3, 1917.

HANNA, Marcus Alonzo (father of Ruth Hanna McCormick) (Ohio) Sept. 24, 1837–Feb. 15, 1904; Senate March 5, 1897–Feb. 15, 1904; Chrmn. Rep. Nat. Comm. 1896–1904.

HANRAHAN, Robert Paul (Ill.) Feb. 25, 1934–; House 1973–75.

HANSBROUGH, Henry Clay (N.Dak.) Jan. 30, 1848–Nov. 16, 1933; House Nov. 2, 1889–91; Senate 1891–1909.

HANSEN, Clifford Peter (Wyo.) Oct. 16, 1912–; Senate 1967–Dec. 31, 1978; Gov. Jan. 6, 1963–Jan. 2, 1967.

HANSEN, George Vernon (Idaho) Sept. 14, 1930–; House 1965–69, 1975–85.

HANSEN, James Vear (Utah) Aug. 14, 1932–; House 1981.

HANSEN, Orval Howard (Idaho) Aug. 3, 1926–; House 1969–75.

HARALSON, Jeremiah (Ala.) April 1, 1846–about 1916; House 1875–77.

HARDEN, Cecil Murray (Ind.) Nov. 21, 1894–Dec. 5, 1984; House 1949–59.

HARDING, Abner Clark (Ill.) Feb. 10, 1807–July 19, 1874; House 1865–69.

HARDING, John Eugene (Ohio) June 27, 1877–July 26, 1959; House 1907–09.

HARDING, Warren Gamaliel (Ohio) Nov. 2, 1865–Aug. 2, 1923; Senate 1915–Jan. 13, 1921; President 1921–Aug. 2, 1923.

HARDY, Alexander Merrill (Ind.) Dec. 16, 1847–Aug. 31, 1927; House 1895–97.

HARDY, Guy Urban (Colo.) April 4, 1872–Jan. 26, 1947; House 1919–33.

HARMER, Alfred Crout (Pa.) Aug. 8, 1825–March 6, 1900; House 1871–75, 1877–March 6, 1900.

HARNESS, Forest Arthur (Ind.) June 24, 1895–July 29, 1974; House 1939–49.

HARPER, John Adams (N.H.) Nov. 2, 1779–June 18, 1816; House 1811–13.

HARRELD, John William (Okla.) Jan. 24, 1872–Dec. 26, 1950; House Nov. 8, 1919–21; Senate 1921–27.

HARRIS, Benjamin Winslow (father of Robert Orr Harris) (Mass.) Nov. 10, 1823–Feb. 7, 1907; House 1873–83.

HARRIS, George Emrick (Miss.) Jan. 6, 1827–March 19, 1911; House Feb. 23, 1870–73.

HARRIS, Ira (grandfather of Henry Riggs Rathbone) (N.Y.) May 31, 1802–Dec. 2, 1875; Senate 1861–67.

HARRIS, John (cousin of Robert Harris) (N.Y.) Sept. 26, 1760–Nov. 1824; House 1807–09.

HARRIS, John Spafford (La.) Dec. 18, 1825–Jan. 25, 1906; Senate July 8, 1868–71.

HARRIS, Robert Orr (son of Benjamin Winslow Harris) (Mass.) Nov. 8, 1854–June 13, 1926; House 1911–13.

HARRIS, Stephen Ross (uncle of Ebenezer Byron Finley) (Ohio) May 22, 1824–Jan. 15, 1905; House 1895–97.

HARRIS, Thomas K. (Tenn.) ?–March 18, 1816; House 1813–15.

HARRISON, Benjamin (grandson of William Henry Harrison, son of John Scott Harrison, grandfather of William Henry Harrison born in 1896) (Ind.) Aug. 20, 1833–March 13, 1901; Senate 1881–87; President 1889–93.

HARRISON, Carter Bassett (brother of William Henry Harrison born in 1773) (Va.) ?–April 18, 1808; House 1793–99 (1793–95 no party).

HARRISON, Horace Harrison (Tenn.) Aug. 7, 1829–Dec. 20, 1885; House 1873–75.

HARRISON, John Scott (son of William Henry Harrison born in 1773, father of Benjamin Harrison) (Ohio) Oct. 4, 1804–May 25, 1878; House 1853–57 (1853–55 Whig).

HARRISON, William Henry (great-great-grandson of William Henry Harrison, grandson of Benjamin Harrison and Alvin Saunders) (Wyo.) Aug. 10, 1896–Oct. 8, 1990; House 1951–55, 1961–65, 1967–69.

HARSHA, William Howard (Ohio) Jan. 1, 1921–; House 1961–81.

HART, Alphonso (Ohio) July 4, 1830–Dec. 23, 1910; House 1883–85.

HART, Roswell (N.Y.) Aug. 4, 1824–April 20, 1883; House 1865–67.

HART, Thomas Charles (Conn.) June 12, 1877–July 4, 1971; Senate Feb. 15, 1945–Nov. 5, 1946.

HARTER, John Francis (N.Y.) Sept. 1, 1897–Dec. 20, 1947; House 1939–41.

HARTLEY, Fred Allan Jr. (N.J.) Feb. 22, 1902–May 11, 1969; House 1929–49; Chrmn. House Education and Labor 1947–49.

HARTMAN, Jesse Lee (Pa.) June 18, 1853–Feb. 17, 1930; House 1911–13.

HARTNETT, Thomas Forbes (S.C.) Aug. 7, 1941–; House 1981–87.

HARVEY, David Archibald (Okla.) March 20, 1845–May 25, 1916; House (Terr. Del.) Nov. 4, 1890–93.

HARVEY, James (Mich.) July 4, 1922–; House 1961–Jan. 31, 1974.

HARVEY, James Madison (Kans.) Sept. 21, 1833–April 15, 1894; Senate Feb. 2, 1874–77; Gov. Jan. 11, 1869–Jan. 13, 1873.

HARVEY, Ralph (Ind.) Aug. 9, 1901–; House Nov. 4, 1947–59, 1961–67.

HASBROUCK, Abraham Joseph (cousin of Abraham Bruyn Hasbrouck) (N.Y.) Oct. 16, 1773–Jan. 12, 1845; House 1813–15.

HASBROUCK, Josiah (N.Y.) March 5, 1755–March 19, 1821; House April 28, 1803–05, 1817–19.

HASKELL, Dudley Chase (grandfather of Otis Halbert Holmes (Kans.) March 23, 1842–Dec. 16, 1883; House 1877–Dec. 16, 1883.

HASKELL, Harry Garner Jr. (Del.) May 27, 1921–; House 1957–59.

HASKELL, Reuben Locke (N.Y.) Oct. 5, 1878–Oct. 2, 1971; House 1915–Dec. 31, 1919.

HASKINS, Kittredge (Vt.) April 8, 1836–Aug. 7, 1916; House 1901–09.

HASTERT, John Dennis (Ill.) Jan. 2, 1942–; House 1987–.

HASTINGS, Daniel Oren (Del.) March 5, 1874–May 9, 1966; Senate Dec. 10, 1928–Jan. 2, 1937.

HASTINGS, James Fred (N.Y.) April 10, 1926–; House 1969–Jan. 20, 1976.

HASTINGS, Richard "Doc" (Wash.) House, 1995–.

HATCH, Herschel Harrison (Mich.) Feb. 17, 1837–Nov. 30, 1920; House 1883–85.

HATCH, Jethro Ayres (Ind.) June 18, 1837–Aug. 3, 1912; House 1895–97.

HATCH, Orrin Grant (Utah) March 22, 1934–; Senate 1977–; Chrmn. Senate Labor and Human Resources 1981–87; Chrmn. Senate Judiciary Committee 1995–.

HATFIELD, Henry Drury (W.Va.) Sept. 15, 1875–Oct. 23, 1962; Senate 1929–35; Gov. March 4, 1913–March 4, 1917.

HATFIELD, Mark Odom (Oreg.) July 12, 1922–; Senate Jan. 10, 1967–; Chrmn. Senate Appropriations 1981–87; Gov. Jan. 12, 1959–Jan. 9, 1967; Chrmn. Senate Appropriations Committee 1995–.

HATHORN, Henry Harrison (N.Y.) Nov. 28, 1813–Feb. 20, 1887; House 1873–77.

HAUGEN, Gilbert Nelson (Iowa) April 21, 1859–July 18, 1933; House 1899–1933.

HAUGEN, Nils Pederson (Wis.) March 9, 1849–April 23, 1931; House 1887–95.

HAUGHEY, Thomas (Ala.) 1826–Aug. 5, 1869; House July 21, 1868–69.

HAVENS, Harrison Eugene (Mo.) Dec. 15, 1837–Aug. 16, 1916; House 1871–75.

HAVENS, Jonathan Nicoll (N.Y.) June 18, 1757–Oct. 25, 1799; House 1795–Oct. 25, 1799.

HAWES, Aylett (uncle of Richard Hawes, Albert Gallatin Hawes and Aylatt Hawes Bucker) (Va.) April 21, 1768–Aug. 31, 1833; House 1811–17.

HAWK, Robert Moffett Allison (Ill.) April 23, 1839–June 29, 1882; House 1879–June 29, 1882.

HAWKES, Albert Wahl (N.J.) Nov. 20, 1878–May 9, 1971; Senate 1943–49.

HAWKINS, Isaac Roberts (Tenn.) May 16, 1818–Aug. 12, 1880; House July 24, 1866–71 (July 24, 1866–67 Unionist).

HAWKINS, Joseph H. (Ky.) ?–1823; House March 29, 1814–15.

HAWKINS, Paula (Fla.) Jan. 24, 1927–; Senate Jan. 1, 1981–87.

HAWKS, Charles Jr. (Wis.) July 7, 1899–Jan. 6, 1960; House 1939–41.

HAWLEY, John Baldwin (Ill.) Feb. 9, 1831–May 24, 1895; House 1869–75.

HAWLEY, Joseph Roswell (Conn.) Oct. 31, 1826–March 17, 1905; House Dec. 2, 1872–75, 1879–81; Senate 1881–1905; Gov. May 2, 1866–May 1, 1867.

HAWLEY, Robert Bradley (Tex.) Oct. 25, 1849–Nov. 28, 1921; House 1897–1901.

HAWLEY, Willis Chatman (Oreg.) May 5, 1864–July 24, 1941; House 1903–33.

HAY, John Breese (Ill.) Jan. 8, 1834–June 16, 1916; House 1869–73.

HAYAKAWA, Samuel Ichiye (Calif.) July 18, 1906–Feb. 27, 1992; Senate 1977–83.

HAYDEN, Edward Daniel (Mass.) Dec. 27, 1833–Nov. 15, 1908; House 1885–89.

HAYES, Everis Anson (Calif.) March 10, 1855–June 3, 1942; House 1905–19.

HAYES, James Allison "Jimmy" (La.) Dec. 21, 1946–; House 1987– (Democrat until 1995).

HAYES, Philip Cornelius (Ill.) Feb. 3, 1833–July 13, 1916; House 1877–81.

HAYES, Rutherford Birchard (Ohio) Oct. 4, 1822–Jan. 17, 1893; House 1865–July 20, 1867; Gov. Jan. 13, 1868–Jan. 8, 1872, Jan. 10, 1876–March 2, 1877; President 1877–81.

HAYNES, Martin Alonzo (N.H.) July 30, 1842–Nov. 28, 1919; House 1883–87.

HAYS, Charles (Ala.) Feb. 2, 1834–June 24, 1879; House 1869–77.

HAYS, Edward Dixon (Mo.) April 28, 1872–July 25, 1941; House 1919–23.

HAYS, Edward Retilla (Iowa) May 26, 1847–Feb. 28, 1896; House Nov. 4, 1890–91.

HAYWARD, Monroe Leland (Nebr.) Dec. 22, 1840–Dec. 5, 1899; elected to the Senate March 8, 1988, to fill a vacancy but died before qualifying.

HAYWORTH, J.D. (Ariz.) House, 1995–.

HAZELTON, George Cochrane (brother of Gerry Whiting Hazelton, nephew of Clark Betton Cochrane) (Wis.) Jan. 3, 1832–Sept. 4, 1922; House 1877–83.

HAZELTON, Gerry Whiting (brother of George Cochrane Hazelton, nephew of Clark Belton Cochrane) (Wis.) Feb. 24, 1829–Sept. 29, 1920; House 1871–75.

HAZELTON, John Wright (N.J.) Dec. 10, 1814–Dec. 20, 1878; House 1871–75.

HAZLETT, James Miller (Pa.) Oct. 14, 1864–Nov. 8, 1941; House March 4–Oct. 20, 1927.

HEALD, William Henry (Del.) Aug. 27, 1864–June 3, 1939; House 1909–13.

HEATH, John (Va.) May 8, 1758–Oct. 13, 1810; House 1793–97.

HEATON, David (N.C.) March 10, 1823–June 25, 1870; House July 15, 1868–June 25, 1870.

HEATON, Robert Douglas (Pa.) July 1, 1873–June 11, 1933; House 1915–19.

HEATWOLE, Joel Prescott (Minn.) Aug. 22, 1856–April 4, 1910; House 1895–1903.

HERBERT, Felix (R.I.) Dec. 11, 1874–Dec. 14, 1969; Senate 1929–35.

HECHT, Jacob Chic (Nev.) Nov. 30, 1928–; Senate 1983–89.

HECKLER, Margaret Mary O'Shaughnessy (Mass.) June 21, 1931–; House 1967–83; Secy. Health and Human Services March 9, 1983–Dec. 13, 1985.

HEDGE, Thomas (Iowa) June 24, 1844–Nov. 28, 1920; House 1899–1907.

HEFLEY, Joel M. (Colo.) April 18, 1935–; House 1987–.

HEFLIN, Robert Stell (uncle of James Thomas Heflin) (Ala.) April 15, 1815–Jan. 24, 1901; House 1869–71.

HEIDINGER, James Vandaveer (Ill.) July 17, 1882–March 22, 1945; House 1941–March 22, 1945.

HEILMAN, William (great-grandfather of Charles Marion La Follette) (Ind.) Oct. 11, 1824–Sept. 22, 1890; House 1879–83.

HEINEMAN, Frederick Kenneth (N.C.) House 1995–.

HEINER, Daniel Brodhead (Pa.) Dec. 30, 1854–Feb. 14, 1944; House 1893–97.

HEINKE, George Henry (Nebr.) July 22, 1882–Jan. 2, 1940; House 1939–Jan. 2, 1940.

HEINTZ, Victor (Ohio) Nov. 20, 1876–Dec. 27, 1968; House 1917–19.

HEINZ, Henry John III (Pa.) Oct. 23, 1938–April 4, 1991; House Nov. 2, 1971–77; Senate 1977–April 4, 1991.

HELGESEN, Henry Thomas (N.Dak.) June 26, 1857–April 10, 1917; House 1911–April 10, 1917.

HELMICK, William (Ohio) Sept. 6, 1817–March 31, 1888; House 1859–61.

HELMS, Jesse Alexander (N.C.) Oct. 18, 1921–; Senate 1973–; Chrmn. Senate Agriculture, Nutrition and Forestry 1981–87; Chrmn. Senate Foreign Relations Committee 1995–.

HELMS, William (N.J.) ?–1813; House 1801–11.

HEMENWAY, James Alexander (Ind.) March 8, 1860–Feb. 10, 1923; House 1895–1905; Senate March 4, 1905–09.

HENDEE, George Whitman (Vt.) Nov. 30, 1832–Dec. 6, 1906; House 1873–79; Gov. Feb. 7–Oct. 6, 1870.

HENDERSON, Bennett H. (Tenn.) Sept. 5, 1784–?; House 1815–17.

HENDERSON, David Brenner (Iowa) March 14, 1840–Feb. 25, 1906; House 1883–1903; Speaker Dec. 4, 1899–1901, Dec. 2, 1901–03.

HENDERSON, John Earl (Ohio) Jan. 4, 1917–; House 1955–61.

HENDERSON, Thomas Jefferson (Ill.) Nov. 29, 1824–Feb. 6, 1911; House 1875–95.

HENDON, William Martin (N.C.) Nov. 9, 1944–; House 1981–83, 1985–87.

HENDRICKSON, Robert Clymer (N.J.) Aug. 12, 1893–Dec. 7, 1964; Senate 1949–55.

HENRY, Charles Lewis (Ind.) July 1, 1849–May 2, 1927; House 1895–99.

HENRY, Edward Stevens (Conn.) Feb. 10, 1836–Oct. 10, 1921; House 1895–1913.

HENRY, Lewis (N.Y.) June 8, 1885–July 23, 1941; House April 11, 1922–23.

HENRY, Paul Brentwood (Mich.) July 9, 1942–July 31, 1993; House 1985–July 31, 1993.

HENRY, Robert Kirkland (Wis.) Feb. 9, 1890–Nov. 20, 1946; House 1945–Nov. 20, 1946.

HEPBURN, William Peters (great-grandson of Matthew Lyon) (Iowa) Nov. 4, 1833–Feb. 7, 1916; House 1881–87, 1893–1909.

HERGER, Walter William "Wally" (Calif.) May 20, 1945–; House 1987–.

HERKIMER, John (N.Y.) 1773–June 8, 1848; House 1817–19, 1823–25.

HERMANN, Binger (Oreg.) Feb. 19, 1843–April 15, 1926; House 1885–97, June 1, 1903–07.

HERNANDEZ, Benigno Cardenas (N.Mex.) Feb. 13, 1862–Oct. 18, 1954; House 1915–17, 1919–21.

HERRICK, Manuel (Okla.) Sept. 20, 1876–Feb. 29, 1952; House 1921–23.

HERRICK, Samuel (Ohio) April 14, 1779–June 4, 1852; House 1817–21.

HERSEY, Ira Greenlief (Maine) March 31, 1858–May 6, 1943; House 1917–29.

HERSEY, Samuel Freeman (Maine) April 12, 1812–Feb. 3, 1875; House 1873–Feb. 3, 1875.

HERTER, Christian Archibald (Mass.) March 28, 1895–Dec. 30, 1966; House 1943–53; Gov. Jan. 8, 1953–Jan. 3, 1957; Secy. of State April 22, 1959–Jan. 20, 1961.

HESELTON, John Walter (Mass.) March 17, 1900–Aug. 19, 1962; House 1945–59.

HESS, William Emil (Ohio) Feb. 13, 1898–July 14, 1986; House 1929–37, 1939–49, 1951–61.

HEYBURN, Weldon Brinton (Idaho) May 23, 1852–Oct. 17, 1912; Senate 1903–Oct. 17, 1912.

HICKENLOOPER, Bourke Blakemore (Iowa) July 21, 1896–Sept. 4, 1971; Senate 1945–69; Gov. Jan. 14, 1943–Jan. 11, 1945.

HICKEY, Andrew James (Ind.) Aug. 27, 1872–Aug. 20, 1942; House 1919–31.

HICKMAN, John (Pa.) Sept. 11, 1810–March 23, 1875; House 1855–63 (1855–59 Democrat, 1959–61 Anti-Lecompton Democrat).

HICKS, Frederick Cocks (original name: Frederick Hicks Cocks, brother of William Willets Cocks) (N.Y.) March 6, 1872–Dec. 14, 1925; House 1915–23.

HICKS, Josiah Duane (Pa.) Aug. 1, 1844–May 9, 1923; House 1893–99.

HIESTAND, Edgar Willard (Calif.) Dec. 3, 1888–Aug. 19, 1970; House 1953–63.

HIESTAND, John Andrew (Pa.) Oct. 2, 1824–Dec. 13, 1890; House 1885–89.

HIESTER, Daniel (brother of John Hiester, cousin of Joseph Hiester, uncle of William Hiester and Daniel Hiester, below) (Md.) June 25, 1747–March 7, 1804; House 1789–July 1, 1796 (no party Pa.), 1801–March 7, 1804.

HIESTER, John (father of Daniel Hiester born in 1774, brother of Daniel Hiester born in 1747, cousin of John Hiester, uncle of William Hiester) (Pa.) April 9, 1745–Oct. 15, 1821; House 1807–09.

HIESTER, Joseph (cousin of John Hiester and Daniel Hiester born in 1747, grandfather of Henry Augustus Muhlenberg) (Pa.) Nov. 18, 1752–June 10, 1832; House Dec. 1, 1797–1805, 1815–Dec. 1820; Gov. Dec. 19, 1820–Dec. 16, 1823 (Democratic Republican).

HIGBY, William (Calif.) Aug. 18, 1813–Nov. 27, 1887; House 1863–69.

HIGGINS, Anthony (Del.) Oct. 1, 1840–June 26, 1912; Senate 1889–95.

HIGGINS, Edwin Werter (Conn.) July 2, 1874–Sept. 24, 1954; House Oct. 2, 1905–13.

HIGGINS, William Lincoln (Conn.) March 8, 1867–Nov. 19, 1951; House 1933–37.

HILBORN, Samuel Greeley (Calif.) Dec. 9, 1834–April 19, 1899; House Dec. 5, 1892–April 4, 1894, 1895–99.

HILDEBRANT, Charles Quinn (Ohio) Oct. 17, 1864–March 31, 1953; House 1901–05.

HILER, John Patrick (Ind.) April 24, 1953–; House 1981–91.

HILL, Charles Augustus (Ill.) Aug. 23, 1833–May 29, 1902; House 1889–91.

HILL, Ebenezer J. (Conn.) Aug. 4, 1845–Sept. 27, 1917; House 1895–1913, 1915–Sept. 27, 1917.

HILL, John (N.J.) June 10, 1821–July 24, 1884; House 1867–73, 1881–83.

HILL, John Boynton Philip Clayton (Md.) May 2, 1879–May 23, 1941; House 1921–27.

HILL, Joshua (Ga.) Jan. 10, 1812–March 6, 1891; House 1857–Jan. 23, 1861 (American Party); Senate Feb. 1, 1871–73.

HILL, Nathaniel Peter (Colo.) Feb. 18, 1832–May 22, 1900; Senate 1879–85.

HILL, Ralph (Ind.) Oct. 12, 1827–Aug. 20, 1899; House 1865–67.

HILL, William Henry (N.Y.) March 23, 1877–July 24, 1972; House 1919–21.

HILL, William Silas (Colo.) Jan. 20, 1866–Aug. 28, 1972; House 1941–59; Chrmn. House Select Committee on Small Business 1953–55.

HILLEARY, Van (Tenn.) House 1995–.

HILLELSON Jeffrey Paul (Mo.) March 9, 1919–; House 1953–55.

HILLINGS, Patrick Jerome (Calif.) Feb. 19, 1923–July 20, 1994; House 1951–59.

HILLIS, Elwood Haynes (Ind.) March 6, 1926–; House 1971–87.

HIMES, Joseph Hendrix (Ohio) Aug. 15, 1885–Sept. 9, 1960; House 1921–23.

HINDS, Asher Crosby (Maine) Feb. 6, 1863–May 1, 1919; House 1911–17.

HINDS, James (Ark.) Dec. 5, 1833–Oct. 22, 1868; House June 22–Oct. 22, 1868.

HINSHAW, Andrew Jackson (Calif.) Aug. 4, 1923–; House 1973–77.

HINSHAW, Edmund Howard (cousin of Edwin Bruce Brooks) (Nebr.) Dec. 8, 1860–June 15, 1932; House 1903–11.

HINSHAW, John Carl Williams (Calif.) July 28, 1894–Aug. 5, 1956; House 1939–Aug. 5, 1956.

HINSON, Jon Clifton (Miss.) March 16, 1942–; House 1979–April 13, 1981.

HIRES, George (N.J.) Jan. 26, 1835–Feb. 16, 1911; House 1885–89.

HISCOCK, Frank (N.Y.) Sept. 6, 1834–June 18, 1914; House 1877–87; Senate 1887–93.

HITCHOCK, Phineas Warrener (Nebr.) Nov. 30, 1831–July 10, 1881; House (Terr. Del.) 1865–March 1, 1867; Senate 1871–77.

HITT, Robert Roberts (Ill.) Jan. 16, 1834–Sept. 20, 1906; House Nov. 7, 1882–Sept. 20, 1906.

HOAR, Ebenezer Rockwood (son of Samuel Hoar, brother of George Frisbie Hoar, father of Sherman Hoar, uncle of Rockwood Hoar) (Mass.) Feb. 21, 1816–Jan. 31, 1895; House 1873–75; Atty. Gen. March 5, 1869–June 23, 1870.

HOAR, George Frisbie (son of Samuel Hoar, brother of Ebenezer Rockwood Hoar, father of Rockwood Hoar, uncle of Sherman Hoar) (Mass.) Aug. 29, 1826–Sept. 30, 1904; House 1869–77; Senate 1877–Sept. 30, 1904.

HOAR, Rockwood (son of George Frisbie Hoar, nephew of Ebenezer Rockwood Hoar, cousin of Sherman Hoar, grandson of Samuel Hoar) (Mass.) Aug. 24, 1855–Nov. 1, 1906; House March 1, 1905–Nov. 1, 1906.

HOARD, Charles Brooks (N.Y.) June 5, 1805–Nov. 20, 1886; House 1857–61.

HOBLITZELL, John Dempsey Jr. (W.Va.) Dec. 30, 1912–Jan. 6, 1962; Senate Jan. 25–Nov. 4, 1958.

HOBSON, David Lee (Ohio) Oct. 17, 1936–; House 1991–.

HOCH, Homer (Kans.) July 4, 1879–Jan. 30, 1949; House 1919–33.

HODGES, Asa (Ark.) Jan. 22, 1822–June 6, 1900; House 1873–75.

HODGES, George Tisdale (Vt.) July 4, 1789–Aug. 9, 1860; House Dec. 1, 1856–57.

HOEKSTRA, Peter (Mich.) Oct. 30, 1953–; House 1993–.

HOEVEN, Charles Bernard (Iowa) March 30, 1895–Nov. 9, 1980; House 1943–65.

HOFFECKER, John Henry (father of Walter Oakley Hoffecker) (Del.) Sept. 12, 1827–June 16, 1900; House 1899–June 16, 1900.

HOFFECKER, Walter Oakley (son of John Henry Hoffecker) (Del.) Sept. 20, 1854–Jan. 23, 1934; House Nov. 6, 1900–01.

HOFFMAN, Carl Henry (Pa.) Aug. 12, 1896–Nov. 30, 1980; House May 21, 1946–47.

HOFFMAN, Clare Eugene (Mich.) Sept. 10, 1875–Nov. 3, 1967; House 1935–63; Chrmn. House Expenditures in the Executive Departments 1947–49; Chrmn. House Govern–ment Operations 1953–55.

HOFFMAN, Elmer Joseph (Ill.) July 7, 1899–June 25, 1976; House 1959–65.

HOFFMAN, Harold Giles (N.J.) Feb. 7, 1896–June 4, 1954; House 1927–31; Gov. Jan. 15, 1935–Jan. 18, 1938.

HOFFMAN, Richard William (Ill.) Dec. 23, 1893–July 6, 1975; House 1949–57.

HOGAN, Lawrence Joseph (Md.) Sept. 30, 1928–; House 1969–75.

HOGAN, Michael Joseph (N.Y.) April 22, 1871–May 7, 1940; House 1921–23.

HOGE, John (brother of William Hoge) (Pa.) Sept. 10, 1760–Aug. 4, 1824; House Nov. 2, 1804–05.

HOGE, Solomon Lafayette (S.C.) July 11, 1836–Feb. 23, 1909; House April 8, 1869–71, 1875–77.

HOGE, William (brother of John Hoge) (Pa.) 1762–Sept. 25, 1814; House 1801–Oct. 15, 1804, 1807–09.

HOGG, David (Ind.) Aug. 21, 1886–Oct. 23, 1973; House 1925–33.

HOGG, Herschel Millard (Colo.) Nov. 21, 1853–Aug. 27, 1934; House 1903–07.

HOGG, Robert Lynn (son of Charles Edgar Hogg) (W.Va.) Dec. 30, 1893–July 21, 1973; House Nov. 4, 1930–33.

HOGG, Samuel (Tenn.) April 18, 1783–May 28, 1842; House 1817–19.

HOKE, Martin Rossiter (Ohio) May 18, 1952–; House 1993–.

HOLADAY, William Perry (Ill.) Dec. 14, 1882–Jan. 29, 1946; House 1923–33.

HOLLAND, James (N.C.) 1754–May 19, 1823; House 1795–97, 1801–11.

HOLLENBECK, Harold Capistran (N.J.) Dec. 29, 1938–; House 1977–83.

HOLLIDAY, Elias Selah (Ind.) March 5, 1842–March 13, 1936; House 1901–09.

HOLLINGSWORTH, David Adams (Ohio) Nov. 21, 1844–Dec. 3, 1929; House 1909–11, 1915–19.

HOLLISTER, John Baker (Ohio) Nov. 7, 1890–Jan. 4, 1979; House Nov. 3, 1931–37.

HOLLOWAY, Clyde Cecil (La.) Nov. 28, 1943–; House 1987–93.

HOLLOWAY, David Pierson (Ind.) Dec. 7, 1809–Sept. 9, 1883; House 1855–57.

HOLMAN, Rufus Cecil (Oreg.) Oct. 14, 1877–Nov. 27, 1959; Senate 1939–45.

HOLMES, Adoniram Judson (Iowa) March 2, 1842–Jan. 21, 1902; House 1883–89.

HOLMES, Charles Horace (N.Y.) Oct. 24, 1827–Oct. 2, 1874; House Dec. 6, 1870–71.

HOLMES, David (Miss.) March 10, 1770–Aug. 20, 1832; House 1797–1809 (no party Va.); Senate Aug. 30, 1820–Sept. 25, 1825; Gov. 1809–17 (Miss. Terr.), Dec. 10, 1817–Jan. 5, 1820, Jan. 7–July 25, 1826 (Democratic Republican).

HOLMES, Otis Halbert (grandson of Dudley Chase Haskell) (Wash.) Feb. 22, 1902–July 27, 1977; House 1943–59.

HOLMES, Pehr Gustaf (Mass.) April 9, 1881–Dec. 19, 1952; House 1931–47.

HOLMES, Sidney Tracy (N.Y.) Aug. 14, 1815–Jan. 16, 1890; House 1865–67.

HOLT, Joseph Franklin III (Calif.) July 6, 1924–; House 1953–61.

HOLT, Marjorie Sewell (Md.) Sept. 17, 1920–; House 1973–87.

HOLTON, Hart Benton (Md.) Oct. 13, 1835–Jan. 4, 1907; House 1883–85.

HOOKER, Warren Brewster (N.Y.) Nov. 24, 1856–March 5, 1920; House 1891–Nov. 10, 1898.

HOOKS, Charles (great-grandfather of William Julius Harris) (N.C.) Feb. 20, 1768–Oct. 18, 1843; House Dec. 2, 1816–17, 1819–25.

HOOPER, Joseph Lawrence (Mich.) Dec. 22, 1877–Feb. 22, 1934; House Aug. 18, 1925–Feb. 22, 1934.

HOOPER, Samuel (Mass.) Feb. 3, 1808–Feb. 14, 1875; House Dec. 2, 1861–Feb. 14, 1875.

HOPE, Clifford Ragsdale (Kans.) June 9, 1893–May 16, 1970; House 1927–57; Chrmn. House Agriculture 1947–49, 1953–55.

HOPKINS, Albert Cole (Pa.) Sept. 15, 1837–June 9, 1911; House 1891–95.

HOPKINS, Albert Jarvis (Ill.) Aug. 15, 1846–Aug. 23, 1922; House Dec. 7, 1885–1903; Senate 1903–09.

HOPKINS, Benjamin Franklin (Wis.) April 22, 1829–Jan. 1, 1870; House 1867–Jan. 1, 1870.

HOPKINS, David William (Mo.) Oct. 31, 1897–Oct. 14, 1968; House Feb. 5, 1929–33.

HOPKINS, Larry Jones (Ky.) Oct. 25, 1933–; House 1979–93.

HOPKINS, Nathan Thomas (Ky.) Oct. 27, 1852–Feb. 11, 1927; House Feb. 18–March 3, 1897.

HOPKINS, Samuel (Ky.) April 9, 1753–Sept. 16, 1819; House 1813–15.

HOPKINS, Stephen Tyng (N.Y.) March 25, 1849–March 3, 1892; House 1887–89.

HOPWOOD, Robert Freeman (Pa.) July 24, 1856–March 1, 1940; House 1915–17.

HORAN, Walter Franklin (Wash.) Oct. 15, 1898–Dec. 19, 1966; House 1943–65.

HORN, John Stephen "Steve" (Calif.) May 31, 1931–; House 1933–.

HORR, Ralph Asley (Wash.) Aug. 12, 1884–Jan. 26, 1960; House 1931–33.

HORR, Roswell Gilbert (Mich.) Nov. 26, 1830–Dec. 19, 1896; House 1879–85.

HORTON, Frank Jefferson (N.Y.) Dec. 12, 1919–; House 1963–93.

HORTON, Frank Oglivie (Wyo.) Oct. 18, 1882–Aug. 17, 1948; House 1939–41.

HORTON, Valentine Baxter (Ohio) Jan. 29, 1802–Jan. 14, 1888; House 1855–59, 1861–63.

HOSKINS, George Gilbert (N.Y.) Dec. 24, 1824–June 12, 1893; House 1873–77.

HOSMER, Craig (Calif.) May 6, 1915–Oct. 11, 1982; House 1953–Dec. 31, 1974.

HOSTETTLER, John (Ind.) House, 1995–.

HOTCHKISS, Giles Waldo (N.Y.) Oct. 25, 1815–July 5, 1878; House 1863–67, 1869–71.

HOUGHTON, Alanson Bigelow (grandfather of Amory Houghton Jr.) (N.Y.) Oct. 10, 1863–Sept. 15, 1941; House 1919–Feb. 28, 1922.

HOUGHTON, Amory Jr. (grandson of Alanson Bigelow Houghton) (N.Y.) Aug. 7, 1926–; House 1987–.

HOUGHTON, Sherman Otis (Calif.) April 10, 1828–Aug. 31, 1914; House 1871–75.

HOUK, John Chiles (son of Leonidas Campbell Houk) (Tenn.) Feb. 26, 1860–June 3, 1923; House Dec. 7, 1891–95.

HOUK, Leonidas Campbell (father of John Chiles Houk) (Tenn.) June 8, 1836–May 25, 1891; House 1879–May 25, 1891.

HOUSTON, Robert Griffith (nephew of John Wallace Houston) (Del.) Oct. 13, 1867–Jan. 29, 1946; House 1925–33.

HOUSTON, Victor Stewart Kaleoaloha (Hawaii) July 22, 1876–July 31, 1959; House (Terr. Del.) 1927–33.

HOVEY, Alvin Peterson (Ind.) Sept. 6, 1821–Nov. 23, 1891; House 1887–Jan. 17, 1889; Gov. Jan. 1889–Nov. 21, 1891.

HOWARD, Benjamin (Ky.) 1760–Sept. 18, 1814; House 1807–April 10, 1810; Gov. (La. Terr.) 1810–12.

HOWARD, Guy Victor (Minn.) Nov. 28, 1879–Aug. 20, 1954; Senate Nov. 4, 1936–37.

HOWARD, Jacob Merritt (Mich.) July 10, 1805–April 2, 1871; House 1841–43 (Whig); Senate Jan. 17, 1862–71.

HOWARD, William Alanson (Mich.) April 8, 1813–April 10, 1880; House 1855–59, May 15, 1860–61; Gov. (Dakota Terr.) 1878–80.

HOWE, Albert Richards (Miss.) Jan. 1, 1840–June 1, 1884; House 1873–75.

HOWE, James Robinson (N.Y.) Jan. 27, 1839–Sept. 21, 1914; House 1895–99.

HOWE, Timothy Otis (Wis.) Feb. 24, 1816–March 25, 1883; Senate 1861–79; Postmaster Gen. Jan. 5, 1882–March 25, 1883.

HOWELL, Benjamin Franklin (N.J.) Jan. 27, 1844–Feb. 1, 1933; House 1895–1911.

HOWELL, George Evan (Ill.) Sept. 21, 1905–Jan. 18, 1980; House 1941–Oct. 5, 1947.

HOWELL, James Bruen (son of Elias Howell) (Iowa) July 4, 1816–June 17, 1880; Senate Jan. 18, 1870–71.

HOWELL, Jeremiah Brown (R.I.) Aug. 28, 1771–Feb. 5, 1822; Senate 1811–17.

HOWELL, Joseph (Utah) Feb. 17, 1857–July 18, 1918; House 1903–17.

HOWELL, Robert Beecher (Nebr.) Jan. 21, 1864–March 11, 1933; Senate 1923–March 11, 1933.

HOWEY, Benjamin Franklin (nephew of Charles Creighton Stratton) (N.J.) March 17, 1828–Feb. 6, 1895; House 1883–85.

HOWLAND, Benjamin (R.I.) July 27, 1755–May 1, 1821; Senate Oct. 29, 1804–09.

HOWLAND, Leonard Paul (Ohio) Dec. 5, 1865–Dec. 23, 1942; House 1907–13.

HRUSKA, Roman Lee (Nebr.) Aug. 16, 1904–; House 1953–Nov. 8, 1954; Senate Nov. 8, 1954–Dec. 27, 1976.

HUBBARD, Asahel Wheeler (father of Elbert Hamilton Hubbard) (Iowa) Jan. 19, 1819–Sept. 22, 1879; House 1863–69.

HUBBARD, Chester Dorman (father of William Pallister Hubbard) (W.Va.) Nov. 25, 1814–Aug. 23, 1891; House 1865–69 (1865–67 Unconditional Unionist).

HUBBARD, Demas Jr. (N.Y.) Jan. 17, 1806–Sept. 2, 1873; House 1865–67.

HUBBARD, Elbert Hamilton (son of Asahel Wheeler Hubbard) (Iowa) Aug. 19, 1849–June 4, 1912; House 1905–June 4, 1912.

HUBBARD, Joel Douglas (Mo.) Nov. 6, 1860–May 26, 1919; House 1895–97.

HUBBARD, John Henry (Conn.) March 24, 1804–July 30, 1872; House 1863–67.

HUBBARD, Levi (Mass.) Dec. 19, 1762–Feb. 18, 1836; House 1813–15.

HUBBARD, Thomas Hill (N.Y.) Dec. 5, 1781–May 21, 1857; House 1817–19, 1821–23.

HUBBARD, William Pallister (son of Chester Dorman Hubbard) (W.Va.) Dec. 24, 1843–Dec. 5, 1921; House 1907–11.

HUBBELL, James Randolph (Ohio) July 13, 1824–Nov. 26, 1890; House 1865–67.

HUBBELL, Jay Abel (Mich.) Sept. 15, 1829–Oct. 13, 1900; House 1873–83.

HUBBS, Orlando (N.C.) Feb. 18, 1840–Dec. 5, 1930; House 1881–83.

HUBER, Robert James (Mich.) Aug. 29, 1922–; House 1973–75.

HUCK, Winnifred Sprague Mason (daughter of William Ernest Mason) (Ill.) Sept. 14, 1882–Aug. 24, 1936; House Nov. 7, 1922–23.

HUDNUT, William Herbert III (Ind.) Oct. 17, 1932–; House 1973–75.

HUDSON, Grant Martin (Mich.) July 23, 1868–Oct. 26, 1955; House 1923–31.

HUFF, George Franklin (Pa.) July 16, 1842–April 18, 1912; House 1891–93, 1895–97, 1903–11.

HUFFINGTON, Michael (Calif.) Sept. 4, 1947–; House 1993–.

HUGHES, James Anthony (W.Va.) Feb. 27, 1861–March 2, 1930; House 1901–15, 1927–March 2, 1930.

HUKRIEDE, Theodore Waldemar (Mo.) Nov. 9, 1878–April 14, 1945; House 1921–23.

HULBURD, Calvin Tilden (N.Y.) June 5, 1809–Oct. 25, 1897; House 1863–69.

HULICK, George Washington (Ohio) June 29, 1833–Aug. 13, 1907; House 1893–97.

HULING, James Hall (W.Va.) March 24, 1844–April 23, 1918; House 1895–97.

HULINGS, Willis James (Pa.) July 1, 1850–Aug. 8, 1924; House 1913–15 (Progressive), 1919–21.

HULL, Harry Edward (Iowa) March 12, 1964–Jan. 16, 1938; House 1915–25.

HULL, John Albert Tiffin (Iowa) May 1, 1841–Sept. 26, 1928; House 1891–1911.

HULL, Merlin (Wis.) Dec. 18, 1870–May 17, 1953; House 1929–31 (Republican), 1935–May 17, 1953 (1935–47 Progressive).

HULL, Morton Denison (Ill.) Jan. 13, 1867–Aug. 20, 1937; House April 3, 1923–33.

HULL, William Edgar (Ill.) Jan. 13, 1866–May 30, 1942; House 1923–33.

HUMPHREY, Augustin Reed (Nebr.) Feb. 18, 1859–Dec. 10, 1937; House Nov. 7, 1922–23.

HUMPHREY, Gordon John (N.J.) Oct. 9, 1940–; Senate 1979–Dec. 4, 1990.

HUMPHREY, Herman Leon (Wis.) March 14, 1830–June 10, 1902; House 1877–83.

HUMPHREY, James (N.Y.) Oct. 9, 1811–June 16, 1866; House 1859–61, 1865–June 16, 1866.

HUMPHREY, Reuben (N.Y.) Sept. 2, 1757–Aug. 12, 1831; House 1807–09.

HUMPHREY, William Ewart (Wash.) March 31, 1862–Feb. 14, 1934; House 1903–17.

HUMPHREYS, Parry Wayne (Tenn.) 1778–Feb. 12, 1839; House 1813–15.

HUNGERFORD, John Newton (N.Y.) Dec. 31, 1825–April 2, 1883; House 1877–79.

HUNGERFORD, John Pratt (Va.) Jan. 2, 1761–Dec. 21, 1833; House March 4–Nov. 29, 1811, 1813–17.

HUNT, John Edmund (N.J.) Nov. 25, 1908–Sept. 22, 1989; House 1967–75.

HUNTER, Allan Oakley (Calif.) June 15, 1916–; House 1951–55.

HUNTER, Duncan Lee (Calif.) May 31, 1948–; House 1981–.

HUNTER, John (S.C.) 1732–1802; House 1793–95 (no party); Senate Dec. 8, 1796–Nov. 26, 1798.

HUNTER, Morton Craig (Ind.) Feb. 5, 1825–Oct. 25, 1896; House 1867–69, 1873–79.

HUNTER, Whiteside Godfrey (Ky.) Dec. 25, 1841–Nov. 2, 1917; House 1887–89, 1895–97, Nov. 10, 1903–05.

HUNTER, William (Vt.) Jan. 3, 1754–Nov. 30, 1827; House 1817–19.

HURLBUT, Stephen Augustus (Ill.) Nov. 29, 1815–March 27, 1882; House 1783–77.

HURLEY, Denis Michael (N.Y.) March 14, 1843–Feb. 26, 1899; House 1895–Feb. 26, 1899.

HUSTED, James William (N.Y.) March 16, 1870–Jan. 2, 1925; House 1915–23.

HUTCHINS, John (cousin of Wells Andrews Hutchins) (Ohio) July 25, 1812–Nov. 20, 1891; House 1859–63.

HUTCHINSON, Elijah Cubberley (N.J.) Aug. 7, 1855–June 25, 1932; House 1915–23.

HUTCHINSON, J. Edward (Mich.) Oct. 13, 1914–July 22, 1985; House 1963–77.

HUTCHINSON, Kathryn Ann "Kay" Bailey (Tex.) July 22, 1943–; Senate June 14, 1993–.

HUTCHINSON, Young Tim (Ark.) Aug. 11, 1949–; House 1993–.

HYDE, DeWitt Stephen (Md.) March 21, 1909–April 25, 1966; House 1953–69.

HYDE, Henry John (Ill.) April 18, 1924–; House 1975–; Chrmn. House Judiciary Committee 1995–.

HYDE, Ira Barnes (Mo.) Jan. 18, 1838–Dec. 6, 1926; House 1873–75.

HYDE, Samuel Clarence (Wash.) April 22, 1842–March 7, 1922; House 1895–97.

HYMAN, John Adams (N.C.) July 23, 1840–Sept. 14, 1891; House 1875–77.

HYNEMAN, John M. (Pa.) April 25, 1771–April 16, 1816; House 1811–Aug. 2, 1813.

ILSLEY, Daniel (Mass.) May 30, 1740–May 10, 1813; House 1807–09.

INGALLS, John James (Kans.) Dec. 29, 1833–Aug. 16, 1900; Senate 1873–91; elected Pres. pro tempore Feb. 25, 1887; March 7, 1889, April 2, 1889, Feb. 28, 1890, April 3, 1890.

INGERSOLL, Ebon Clark (Ill.) Dec. 12, 1831–May 31, 1879; House May 20, 1864–71.

INGHAM, Samuel Delucenna (Pa.) Sept. 16, 1779–June 5, 1860; House 1813–July 6, 1818, Oct. 8, 1822–29; Secy. of the Treasury March 6, 1829–June 20, 1831.

INGLIS, Robert Durden (S.C.) Oct. 11, 1959–; House 1993–.

INHOFE, James Mountain (Okla.) Nov. 17, 1934–; House 1987–1994, Senate 1995–.

IRELAND, Andrew Poysell "Andy" (Fla.) Aug. 23, 1930–; House 1977–93 (1977–July 5, 1984, Democrat).

IRELAND, Clifford Cady (Ill.) Feb. 14, 1878–May 24, 1930; House 1917–23.

IRVINE, William (N.Y.) Feb. 14, 1820–Nov. 12, 1882; House 1859–61.

IRVING, William (N.Y.) Aug. 15, 1766–Nov. 9, 1821; House Jan. 22, 1814–19.

IRWIN, Edward Michael (Ill.) April 14, 1869–Jan. 30, 1933; House 1925–31.

IRWIN, Harvey Samuel (Ky.) Dec. 10, 1844–Sept. 3, 1916; House 1901–03.

IRWIN, Jared (Pa.) Jan. 19, 1768–Sept. 20, 1818; House 1813–17.

ISTOOK, Ernest Jim (Okla.) Feb. 11, 1950–; House 1993–.

ITTNER, Anthony Friday (Mo.) Oct. 8, 1837–Feb. 22, 1931; House 1877–79.

IVES, Irving McNeil (N.Y.) Jan. 24, 1896–Feb. 24, 1962; Senate 1947–59.

JACK, Summers Melville (Pa.) July 18, 1852–Sept. 16, 1945; House 1899–1903.

JACKSON, Amos Henry (Ohio) May 10, 1846–Aug. 30, 1924; House 1903–05.

JACKSON, Donald Lester (Calif.) Jan. 23, 1910–May 27, 1981; House 1947–61.

JACKSON, Fred Schyler (Kans.) April 19, 1868–Nov. 21, 1931; House 1911–13.

JACKSON, George (father of John George Jackson and Edward Brake Jackson) (Va.) Jan. 9, 1757–May 17, 1831; House 1795–97, 1799–1803.

JACKSON, James (father of Jabez Young Jackson, grandfather of James Jackson, below) (Ga.) Sept. 21, 1757–March 19, 1806; House 1789–91 (no party); Senate 1793–95 (no party), 1801–March 19, 1806; Gov. Jan. 12, 1798–March 3, 1801 (Democratic Republican).

JACKSON, John George (son of George Jackson, brother of Edward Brake Jackson, grandfather of William Thomas Bland) (Va.) Sept. 22, 1777–March 28, 1825; House 1803–Sept. 28, 1810, 1813–17.

JACKSON, Oscar Lawrence (Pa.) Sept. 2, 1840–Feb. 16, 1920; House 1885–89.

JACKSON, William Humphreys (father of William Purnell Jackson) (Md.) Oct. 15, 1839–April 3, 1915; House 1901–05, 1907–09.

JACKSON, William Purnell (son of William Humphreys Jackson) (Md.) Jan. 11, 1868–March 7, 1939; Senate Nov. 29, 1912–Jan. 28, 1914.

JACOBS, Ferris Jr. (N.Y.) March 20, 1836–Aug. 30, 1886; House 1791–93.

JACOBS, Orange (Wash.) May 2, 1827–May 21, 1914; House (Terr. Del.) 1875–79.

JADWIN, Cornelius Comegys (Pa.) March 27, 1835–Aug. 17, 1913; House 1881–83.

JAMES, Addison Davis (grandfather of John Albert Whitaker) (Ky.) Feb. 27, 1850–June 10, 1947; House 1907–09.

JAMES, Amaziah Bailey (N.Y.) July 1, 1812–July 6, 1883; House 1877–81.

JAMES, Benjamin Franklin (Pa.) Aug. 1, 1885–Jan. 26, 1961; House 1949–59.

JAMES, Craig T. (Fla.) May 5, 1941–; House 1989–93.

JAMES, Darwin Rush (N.Y.) May 14, 1834–Nov. 19, 1906; House 1883–87.

JAMES, William Francis (Mich.) May 23, 1873–Nov. 17, 1945; House 1915–35.

JARMAN, John (Okla.) July 17, 1915–Jan. 15, 1982; House 1951–77 (1951–Jan. 24, 1975, Democrat).

JARRETT, Benjamin (Pa.) July 18, 1881–July 20, 1944; House 1937–43.

JAVITS, Jacob Koppel (N.Y.) May 18, 1904–March 7, 1986; House 1947–Dec. 31, 1954; Senate Jan. 9, 1957–81.

JEFFERIS, Albert Webb (Nebr.) Dec. 7, 1868–Sept. 14, 1942; House 1919–23.

JEFFORDS, Elza (Miss.) May 23, 1826–March 19, 1885; House 1883–85.

JEFFORDS, James Merrill (Vt.) May 11, 1934–; House 1975–89; Senate 1989–.

JEFFREY, Harry Palmer (Ohio) Dec. 26, 1901–; House 1943–45.

JEFFRIES, James Edmund (Kans.) June 1, 1925–; House 1979–83.

JEFFRIES, Walter Sooy (N.J.) Oct. 16, 1893–Oct. 11, 1954; House 1939–41.

JENCKES, Thomas Allen (R.I.) Nov. 2, 1818–Nov. 4, 1875; House 1863–71.

JENISON, Edward Halsey (Ill.) July 27, 1907–; House 1947–53.

JENKINS, John James (Wis.) Aug. 24, 1843–June 8, 1911; House 1895–1909.

JENKINS, Mitchell (Pa.) Jan. 24, 1896–Sept. 15, 1977; House 1947–49.

JENKINS, Robert (Pa.) July 10, 1769–April 18, 1848; House 1807–11.

JENKINS, Thomas Albert (Ohio) Oct. 28, 1880–Dec. 21, 1959; House 1925–59.

JENKS, Arthur Byron (N.H.) Oct. 15, 1866–Dec. 14, 1947; House 1937–June 9, 1938, 1939–43.

JENNER, William Ezra (Ind.) July 21, 1908–March 9, 1985; Senate Nov. 14, 1944–45, 1947–59; Chrmn. Senate Rules and Administration 1953–55.

JENNINGS, John Jr. (Tenn.) June 6, 1880–Feb. 27, 1956; House Dec. 30, 1939–51.

JENSEN, Benton Franklin (Iowa) Dec. 16, 1892–Feb. 5, 1970; House 1939–65.

JEPSEN, Roger William (Iowa) Dec. 23, 1928–; Senate 1979–85.

JEWETT, Daniel Tarbox (Mo.) Sept. 14, 1807–Oct. 7, 1906; Senate Dec. 19, 1870–Jan. 20, 1871.

JOHANSEN, August Edgar (Mich.) July 21, 1905–; House 1955–65.

JOHNS, Joshua Leroy (Wis.) Feb. 27, 1881–March 16, 1947; House 1939–43.

JOHNSON, Adna Romulus (Ohio) Dec. 14, 1860–June 11, 1938; House 1909–11.

JOHNSON, Albert (Wash.) March 5, 1869–Jan. 17, 1957; House 1913–33.

JOHNSON, Albert Walter (Pa.) April 17, 1906–; House Nov. 5, 1963–77.

JOHNSON, Andrew (father-in-law of David Trotter Patterson) (Tenn.) Dec. 29, 1808–July 31,1875; House 1843–53 (Democrat); Senate Oct. 8, 1857–March 4, 1862 (Democrat), March 4-July 31, 1875; Gov. Oct. 17, 1853–Nov. 3, 1857 (Democrat), March 12, 1862–March 4, 1865 (Military); Vice President March 4–April 15,1865; President April 15, 1865–69.

JOHNSON, Anton Joseph (Ill.) Oct. 20, 1878–April 16, 1958; House 1939–49.

JOHNSON, Calvin Dean (Ill.) Nov. 22, 1898–Oct. 13, 1985; House 1943–45.

JOHNSON, Fred Gustus (Nebr.) Oct.16, 1876–April 30, 1951; House 1929–31.

JOHNSON, Grove Lawrence (father of Hiram Warren Johnson) (Calif.) March 27, 1841–Feb. 1, 1926; House 1895–97.

JOHNSON, Henry Underwood (Ind.) Oct. 28, 1850– June 4, 1939; House 1891–99.

JOHNSON, Hiram Warren (son of Grove Lawrence Johnson) (Calif.) Sept. 2, 1866–Aug. 6, 1945; Senate March 16, 1917–Aug. 6, 1945; Gov. Jan. 3, 1911–March 15, 1917.

JOHNSON, Jacob (Utah) Nov. 1, 1847–Aug. 15, 1925; House 1913–15.

JOHNSON, James (Va.) ?–Dec. 7, 1825; House 1813–Feb. 1, 1820.

JOHNSON, James Paul (Colo.) June 2, 1930–; House 1973–81.

JOHNSON, Justin Leroy (Calif.) April 8, 1888–March 26, 1961; House 1943–57.

JOHNSON, Martin Nelson (N.Dak.) March 3, 1850–Oct. 21, 1909; House 1891–99; Senate March 4–Oct. 21, 1909.

JOHNSON, Nancy Lee (Conn.) Jan. 5, 1935–; House 1983–; Chrmn. House Standards of Official Conduct Committee 1995–.

JOHNSON, Noble Jacob (Ind.) Aug. 23, 1887–March 17, 1968; House 1925–31, 1939–July 1, 1948.

JOHNSON, Richard Mentor (brother of James Johnson born in 1774 and John Telemachus Johnson, uncle of Robert Ward Johnson) (Ky.) Oct. 17, 1780–Nov. 19, 1850; House 1807–19, 1829–37; Senate Dec. 10, 1819–29; Vice President 1837–41.

JOHNSON, Royal Cleaves (S.Dak.) Oct. 3, 1882–Aug. 2, 1939; House 1915–33.

JOHNSON, Samuel Robert (Tex.) Oct. 11, 1930–; House May 22, 1991–.

JOHNSON, William Richard (Ill.) May 15, 1875–Jan. 2, 1938; House 1925–33.

JOHNSON, William Ward (Calif.) March 9, 1892–June 8, 1963; House 1941–45.

JOHNSTON, James Thomas (Ind.) Jan. 19, 1839–July 19, 1904; House 1885–89.

JOHNSTON, Rowland Louis (Mo.) April 23, 1872–Sept. 22, 1939; House 1929–31.

JOHNSTON, Walter Eugene III (N.C.) March 3, 1936–; House 1981–83.

JOLLEY, John Lawlor (S.Dak.) July 14, 1840–Dec. 14, 1926; House Dec. 7, 1891–93.

JONAS, Charles Andrew (father of Charles Raper Jonas) (N.C.) Aug. 14, 1876–May 25, 1955; House 1929–31.

JONAS, Charles Raper (son of Charles Andrew Jonas) (N.C.) Dec. 9, 1904–Sept. 28, 1988; House 1953–73.

JONAS, Edgar Allan (Ill.) Oct. 14, 1885–Nov. 14, 1965; House 1949–55.

JONES, Alexander Hamilton (N.C.) July 21, 1822–Jan. 29, 1901; House July 6, 1868–71.

JONES, Evan John (Pa.) Oct. 23, 1872–Jan. 9, 1952; House 1919–23.

JONES, Francis (Tenn.) ?–?; House 1817–23.

JONES, Homer Raymond (Wash.) Sept. 3, 1893–Nov. 26, 1970; House 1947–49.

JONES, John Percival (Nev.) Jan. 27, 1829–Nov. 27, 1912; Senate 1873–1903.

JONES, John Sills (Ohio) Feb. 12, 1836–April 11, 1903; House 1877–79.

JONES, Phineas (N.J.) April 18, 1819–April 19, 1884; House 1881–83.

JONES, Robert Franklin (Ohio) June 25, 1907–June 22, 1968; House 1939–Sept. 2, 1947.

JONES, Walter (Va.) Dec. 18, 1745–Dec. 31, 1815; House 1797–99, 1803–11.

JONES, Walter B. Jr. (N.C.) House, 1995–.

JONES, Wesley Livsey (Wash.) Oct. 9, 1863–Nov. 19, 1932; House 1899–1909; Senate 1909–Nov. 19, 1932.

JONES, William (Pa.) 1760–Sept. 6, 1831; House 1801–03; Secy. of the Navy Jan. 19, 1813–Dec. 1, 1814.

JONES, William Theophilus (Wyo.) Feb. 20, 1842–Oct. 9, 1882; House (Terr. Del.) 1871–73.

JONKMAN, Bartel John (Mich.) April 28, 1884–June 13, 1955; House Feb. 19, 1940–49.

JORDAN, Leonard Beck (Idaho) May 15, 1899–June 30, 1983; Senate Aug. 6, 1962–Jan. 2, 1973; Gov. Jan. 1, 1951–Jan. 3, 1955.

JORDEN, Edwin James (Pa.) Aug. 30, 1863–Sept. 7, 1903; House Feb. 23–March 4, 1895.

JORGENSEN, Joseph (Va.) Feb. 11, 1844–Jan. 21, 1888; House 1877–83.

JOY, Charles Frederick (Mo.) Dec. 11, 1849–April 13, 1921; House 1893–April 3, 1894, 1895–1903.

JOYCE, Charles Herbert (Vt.) Jan. 30, 1830–Nov. 22, 1916; House 1875–83.

JOYCE, James (Ohio) July 2, 1870–March 25, 1931; House 1909–11.

JUDD, Norman Buel (grandfather of Norman Judd Gould) (Ill.) Jan. 10, 1815–Nov. 11, 1878; House 1867–71.

JUDD, Walter Henry (Minn.) Sept. 25, 1898–Feb. 13, 1994; House 1943–63.

JULIAN, George Washington (Ind.) May 5, 1817–July 7, 1899; House 1849–51 (Free-Soiler), 1861–71.

JUNKIN, Benjamin Franklin (Pa.) Nov. 12, 1822–Oct. 9, 1908; House 1859–61.

JUUL, Niels (Ill.) April 27, 1859–Dec. 4, 1929; House 1917–21.

KADING, Charles August (Wis.) Jan. 14, 1874–June 19, 1956; House 1927–33.

KAHN, Florence Prag (widow of Julius Kahn) (Calif.) Nov. 9, 1866–Nov. 16, 1948; House 1925–37.

KAHN, Julius (husband of Florence Prag Kahn) (Calif.) Feb. 28, 1861–Dec. 18, 1924; House 1899–1903, 1905–Dec. 18, 1924.

KALANIANAOLE, Jonah Kuhio (Hawaii) March 26, 1871–Jan. 7, 1922; House (Terr. Del.) 1903–Jan. 7, 1922.

KARNES, David Kemp (Nebr.) Dec. 12, 1948–; Senate March 13, 1987–89.

KASICH, John Richard (Ohio) May 13, 1952–; House 1983; Chrmn. House Budget Committee 1995–.

KASSEBAUM, Nancy Landon (Kans.) July 29, 1932–; Senate Dec. 23, 1978–1996; Chrmn. Senate Labor and Human Resources Committee 1995–.

KASSON, John Adam (Iowa) Jan. 11, 1822–May 19, 1910; House 1863–67, 1873–77, 1881–July 13, 1884.

KASTEN, Robert Walter Jr. (Wis.) June 19, 1942–; House 1975–79; Senate 1981–93.

KAYNOR, William Kirk (Mass.) Nov. 29, 1884–Dec. 20, 1929; House March 4–Dec. 20, 1929.

KEAN, Hamilton Fish (father of Robert Winthrop Kean, brother of John Kean) (N.J.) Feb. 27, 1862–Dec. 27, 1941; Senate 1929–35.

KEAN, John (brother of Hamilton Fish Kean, uncle of Robert Winthrop Kean) (N.J.) Dec. 4, 1852–Nov. 4, 1914; House 1883–85, 1887–89; Senate 1899–1911.

KEAN, Robert Winthrop (son of Hamilton Fish Kean, nephew of John Kean) (N.J.) Sept. 28, 1893–Sept. 21, 1980; House 1939–59.

KEARNEY, Bernard William (N.Y.) May 23, 1889–June 3, 1976; House 1943–59.

KEARNS, Carroll Dudley (Pa.) May 7, 1900–June 11, 1976; House 1947–63.

KEARNS, Charles Cyrus (Ohio) Feb. 11, 1869–Dec. 17, 1931; House 1915–31.

KEATING, Kenneth Barnard (N.Y.) May 18, 1900–May 5, 1975; House 1947–59; Senate 1959–65.

KEATING, William John (Ohio) March 30, 1927–; House 1971–Jan. 3, 1974.

KEEFE, Frank Bateman (Wis.) Sept. 23, 1887–Feb. 5, 1951; House 1939–51.

KEENEY, Russell Watson (Ill.) Dec. 29, 1897–Jan. 11, 1958; House 1957–Jan. 11, 1958.

KEIFER, Joseph Warren (Ohio) Jan. 30, 1836–April 22, 1932; House 1877–85, 1905–11; Speaker Dec. 5, 1881–83.

KEIGHTLEY, Edwin William (Mich.) Aug. 7, 1843–May 4, 1926; House 1877–79.

KEIM, William High (Pa.) June 13, 1813–May 18, 1862; House Dec. 7, 1858–59.

KEISTER, Abraham Lincoln (Pa.) Sept. 10, 1852–May 26, 1917; House 1913–17.

KEITH, Hastings (Mass.) Nov. 22, 1915–; House 1959–73.

KELLEY, Harrison (Kans.) May 12, 1836–July 24, 1897; House Dec. 2, 1889–91.

KELLEY, Patrick Henry (Mich.) Oct. 7, 1867–Sept. 11, 1925; House 1913–23.

KELLEY, William Darrah (Pa.) April 12, 1814–Jan. 9, 1890; House 1861–Jan. 9, 1890.

KELLOGG, Francis William (Ala.) May 30, 1810–Jan. 13, 1879; House 1859–65 (Mich.) July 22, 1868–69.

KELLOGG, Frank Billings (Minn.) Dec. 22, 1856–Dec. 21, 1937; Senate 1917–23; Secy. of State March 5, 1925–March 28, 1929.

KELLOGG, Stephen Wright (Conn.) April 5, 1822–Jan. 27, 1904; House 1869–73.

KELLOGG, William (Ill.) July 8, 1814–Dec. 20, 1872; House 1867–63.

KELLOGG, William Pitt (La.) Dec. 8, 1830–Aug. 10, 1918; Senate July 9, 1868–Nov. 1, 1872, 1877–83; House 1883–85; Gov. Jan. 13, 1873–Jan. 8, 1877.

KELLY, Melville Clyde (Pa.) Aug. 4, 1883–April 29, 1935; House 1913–15, 1917–35.

KELLY, Richard (Fla.) July 31, 1924–; House 1975–81.

KELLY, Sue W. (N.Y.) House, 1995–.

KELSEY, William Henry (N.Y.) Oct. 2, 1812–April 20, 1879; House 1855–59 (1855–57 Whig), 1867–71.

KEM, James Preston (Mo.) April 2, 1890–Feb. 24, 1965; Senate 1947–53.

KEMP, Jack French (N.Y.) July 13, 1935–; House 1971–89; Secy. of Housing and Urban Development Feb. 13, 1989–Jan. 20, 1993.

KEMPTHORNE, Dirk (Idaho) Oct. 29, 1951–; Senate 1993–.

KENAN, Thomas (N.C.) Feb. 26, 1771–Oct. 22, 1843; House 1805–11.

KENDALL, Elva Roscoe (Ky.) Feb. 14, 1893–Jan. 29, 1968; House 1929–31.

KENDALL, Nathan Edward (Iowa) March 17, 1868–Nov. 5, 1936; House 1909–13; Gov. Jan. 13, 1921–Jan. 15, 1925.

KENDALL, Samuel Austin (Pa.) Nov. 1, 1859–Jan. 8, 1933; House 1919–Jan. 8, 1933.

KENNEDY, Ambrose (R.I.) Dec. 1, 1875–March 10, 1967; House 1913–23.

KENNEDY, Charles Augustus (Iowa) March 24, 1869–Jan. 10, 1951; House 1907–21.

KENNEDY, James (Ohio) Sept. 3, 1853–Nov. 9, 1928; House 1903–11.

KENNEDY, John Lauderdale (Nebr.) Oct. 27, 1854–Aug. 30, 1946; House 1905–07.

KENNEDY, Robert Patterson (Ohio) Jan. 23, 1840–May 6, 1918; House 1887–91.

KENNEDY, William (N.C.) July 31, 1768–Oct. 11, 1834; House 1803–05, 1809–11, Jan. 30, 1813–15.

KENT, Joseph (Md.) Jan. 14, 1779–Nov. 24, 1837; House 1811–15, 1819–Jan. 6, 1826; Senate 1833–Nov. 24, 1837; Gov. Jan. 9, 1826–Jan. 15, 1829 (Democratic Republican).

KENYON, William Scheuneman (N.Y.) Dec. 13, 1820–Feb. 10, 1896; House 1859–61.

KENYON, William Squire (Iowa) June 10, 1869–Sept. 9, 1933; Senate April 12, 1911–Feb. 24, 1922.

KERR, Daniel (Iowa) June 18, 1836–Oct. 8, 1916; House 1887–91.

KERR, John (father of John Kerr Jr., cousin of Bartlett Yancey, great–uncle of John Hosea Kerr) (Va.) Aug. 4, 1782–Sept. 29, 1842; House 1813–15, Oct. 30, 1815–17.

KERR, Josiah Leeds (Md.) Jan. 10, 1861–Sept. 27, 1920; House Nov. 6, 1900–01.

KERR, Winfield Scott (Ohio) June 23, 1852–Sept. 11, 1917; House 1895–1901.

KERSHAW, John (S.C.) Sept. 12, 1765–Aug. 4, 1829; House 1813–15.

KERSTEN, Charles Joseph (Wis.) May 26, 1902–Oct. 31, 1972; House 1947–49, 1951–55.

KETCHAM, John Clark (Mich.) Jan. 1, 1873–Dec. 4, 1941; House 1921–33.

KETCHAM, John Henry (N.Y.) Dec. 21, 1832–Nov. 4, 1906; House 1865–73, 1877–93, 1897–Nov. 4, 1906.

KETCHUM, William Matthew (Calif.) Sept. 2, 1921–June 24, 1978; House 1973–June 24, 1978.

KETCHUM, Winthrop Welles (Pa.) June 29, 1820–Dec. 6, 1879; House 1875–July 19, 1876.

KEYES, Henry Wilder (N.H.) May 23, 1863–June 19, 1938; Senate 1919–37; Gov. Jan. 3, 1917–Jan. 2, 1919.

KIDDER, Jefferson Parish (Dakota) June 4, 1815–Oct. 2, 1883; House (Terr. Del.) 1875–79.

KIEFER, Andrew Robert (Minn.) May 25, 1832–May 1, 1904; House 1893–97.

KIEFNER, Charles Edward (Mo.) Nov. 25, 1869–Dec. 13, 1942; House 1925–27, 1929–31.

KIESS, Edgar Raymond (Pa.) Aug. 26, 1875–July 20, 1930; House 1913–July 20, 1930.

KILBOURNE, James (Ohio) Oct. 19, 1770–April 9, 1850; House 1813–17.

KILBURN, Clarence Evans (N.Y.) April 13, 1893–May 20, 1975; House Feb. 13, 1940–65.

KILGORE, David (Ind.) April 3, 1804–Jan. 22, 1879; House 1857–61.

KILLINGER, John Weinland (Pa.) Sept. 18, 1824–June 30, 1896; House 1859–63, 1871–75, 1877–81.

KIM, Jay C. (Calif.) March 27, 1939–; House 1993–.

KIMBALL, Alanson Mellen (Wis.) March 12, 1827–May 26, 1913; House 1875–77.

KIMBALL, Henry Mahlon (Mich.) Aug. 27, 1878–Oct. 19, 1935; House Jan. 3–Oct. 19, 1935.

KINDNESS, Thomas Norman (Ohio) Aug. 26, 1929–; House 1975–87.

KING, Carleton James (N.Y.) June 16, 1904–Nov. 19, 1977; House 1961–Dec. 31, 1974.

KING, Edward John (Ill.) July 1, 1867–Feb. 17, 1929; House 1915–Feb. 17, 1929.

KING, Peter Thomas (N.Y.) April 5, 1944–; House 1993–.

KING, Preston (N.Y.) Oct. 14, 1806–Nov. 12, 1865; House 1843–47 (Democrat), 1849–53 (Free-Soiler); Senate 1857–63.

KING, Samuel Wilder (Hawaii) Dec. 17, 1886–March 24, 1959; House (Terr. Del.) 1935–43; Gov. (Hawaii Terr.) Feb. 28, 1953–July 31, 1957.

KING, William Smith (Minn.) Dec. 16, 1828–Feb. 24, 1900; House 1875–77.

KINGSTON, John Heddens "Jack" (Ga.) April 24, 1955–; House 1993–.

KINKAID, Moses Pierce (Nebr.) Jan. 24, 1856–July 6, 1922; House 1903–July 6, 1922.

KINSEY, Charles (N.J.) 1773–June 25, 1849; House 1817–19, Feb. 2, 1820–21.

KINSEY, William Medcalf (Mo.) Oct. 28, 1846–June 20, 1931; House 1889–91.

KINZER, John Roland (Pa.) March 28, 1874–July 25, 1955; House Jan. 28, 1930–47.

KIRK, Andrew Jackson (Ky.) March 19, 1866–May 25, 1933; House Feb. 13, 1926–27.

KIRKPATRICK, Snyder Solomon (Kans.) Feb. 21, 1848–April 5, 1909; House 1895–97.

KIRKPATRICK, William (N.Y.) Nov. 7, 1769–Sept. 2, 1832; House 1807–09.

KIRKPATRICK, William Huntington (son of William Sebring Kirkpatrick) (Pa.) Oct. 2, 1885–Nov. 28, 1970; House 1921–23.

KIRKPATRICK, William Sebring (father of William Huntington Kirkpatrick) (Pa.) April 21, 1844–Nov. 3, 1932; House 1897–99.

KIRKWOOD, Samuel Jordan (Iowa) Dec. 20, 1813–Sept. 1, 1894; Senate Jan. 13, 1866–67, 1877–March 7, 1881; Gov. Jan. 11, 1860–Jan. 14, 1864, Jan. 13, 1876–Feb. 1, 1877; Secy. of the Interior March 8, 1881–April 17, 1882.

KIRTLAND, Dorrance (N.Y.) July 28, 1770–May 23, 1840; House 1817–19.

KISSEL, John (N.Y.) July 31, 1864–Oct. 3, 1938; House 1921–23.

KITCHELL, Aaron (N.J.) July 10, 1744–June 25, 1820; House 1791–93, Jan. 29, 1795–97, 1799–1801; Senate 1805–March 12, 1809.

KITCHEN, Bethuel Middleton (W.Va.) March 21, 1812–Dec. 15, 1895; House 1867–69.

KITTREDGE, Alfred Beard (S.Dak.) March 28, 1861–May 4, 1911; Senate July 11, 1901–09.

KLECZKA, John Casimir (Wis.) May 6, 1885–April 21, 1959; House 1919–23.

KLEPPE, Thomas Savig (N.Dak.) July 1, 1919–; House 1967–71; Secy. of the Interior Oct. 17, 1975–Jan. 20, 1977.

KLEPPER, Frank B. (Mo.) June 22, 1864–Aug. 4, 1933; House 1905–07.

KLINE, Ardolph Loges (N.Y.) Feb. 21, 1858–Oct. 13, 1930; House 1921–23.

KLINE, Isaac Clinton (Pa.) Aug. 18, 1858–Dec. 2, 1947; House 1921–23.

KLUG, Scott L. (Wis.) Jan. 16, 1953–; House 1991–.

KNAPP, Charles (father of Charles Junius Knapp) (N.Y.) Oct. 8, 1797–May 14, 1880; House 1869–71.

KNAPP, Charles Junius (son of Charles Knapp) (N.Y.) Oct. 8, 1797–May 14, 1880; House 1869–71.

KNAPP, Charles Luman (N.Y.) July 4, 1847–Jan. 3, 1929; House Nov. 5, 1901–11.

KNAPP, Chauncey Langdon (Mass.) Feb. 26, 1809–May 31, 1898; House 1855–59 (1855–57 American Party).

KNIGHT, Charles Landon (Ohio) June 18, 1867–Sept. 26, 1933; House 1921–23.

KNIGHT, Nehemiah (father of Nehemiah Rice Knight) (R.I.) March 23, 1746–June 13, 1808; House 1803–June 13, 1808.

KNOLLENBERG, Joseph Castl (Mich.) Nov. 28, 1933–; House 1993–.

KNOPF, Philip (Ill.) Nov. 18, 1847–Aug. 14, 1920; House 1903–09.

KNOWLAND, Joseph Russell (father of William Fife Knowland) (Calif.) Aug. 5, 1873–Feb. 1, 1966; House Nov. 8, 1904–15.

KNOWLAND, William Fife (son of Joseph Russell Knowland) (Calif.) June 26, 1908–Feb. 23, 1974; Senate

Aug. 26, 1945–59; Senate majority leader Aug. 4, 1953–55; Senate minority leader 1955–59.

KNOWLTON, Ebenezer (Maine) Dec. 6, 1815–Sept. 10, 1874; House 1855–57.

KNOX, James (Ill.) July 4, 1807–Oct. 8, 1876; House 1853–57 (1853–55 Whig).

KNOX, Philander Chase (Pa.) May 6, 1853–Oct. 12, 1921; Senate June 10, 1904–March 4, 1909, 1917–Oct. 12, 1921; Atty. Gen. April 5, 1901–June 30, 1904; Secy. of State March 6, 1909–March 5, 1913.

KNOX, Victor Alfred (Mich.) Jan. 13, 1899–Dec. 13, 1976; House 1953–65.

KNOX, William Shadrach (Mass.) Sept. 10, 1843–Sept. 21, 1914; House 1895–1903.

KNUTSON, Harold (Minn.) Oct. 20, 1880–Aug. 21, 1953; House 1917–49; Chrmn. House Ways and Means 1947–49.

KOLBE, James Thomas (Ariz.) June 28, 1942–; House 1985–.

KONNYU, Ernest Leslie (Calif.) May 17, 1937–; House 1987–89.

KOONTZ, William Henry (Pa.) July 15, 1830–July 4, 1911; House July 18, 1866–69.

KOPP, Arthur William (Wis.) Feb. 28, 1874–June 2, 1967; House 1909–13.

KORELL, Franklin Frederick (Oreg.) July 23, 1889–June 7, 1965; House Oct. 18, 1927–31.

KRAMER, Kenneth Bentley (Colo.) Feb. 19, 1942–; House 1979–87.

KRAUS, Milton (Ind.) June 26, 1866–Nov. 18, 1942; House 1917–23.

KREIDER, Aaron Shenk (Pa.) June 26, 1853–May 19, 1929; House 1913–23.

KRONMILLER, John (Md.) Dec. 6, 1858–June 19, 1928; House 1909–11.

KRUEGER, Otto (N.Dak.) Sept. 7, 1890–June 6, 1963; House 1953–59.

KUCHEL, Thomas Henry (Calif.) Aug. 15, 1910–; Senate Jan. 2, 1953–69.

KULP, Monroe Henry (Pa.) Oct. 23, 1858–Oct. 19, 1911; House 1895–99.

KUNKEL, John Christian (grandfather of John Crain Kunkel) (Pa.) Sept. 18, 1816–Oct. 14, 1870; House 1855–59 (1855–57 Whig).

KUNKEL, John Crain (grandson of John Christian Kunkel, great-grandson of John Sergeant, great-great-grandson of Robert Whitehill) (Pa.) July 21, 1898–July 27, 1970; House 1939–51, May 16, 1961–67.

KUPFERMAN, Theodore Roosevelt (N.Y.) May 12, 1920–; House Feb. 8, 1966–69.

KURTZ, Jacob Banks (Pa.) Oct. 31, 1867–Sept. 18, 1960; House 1923–35.

KUSTERMANN, Gustav (Wis.) May 24, 1850–Dec. 25, 1919; House 1907–11.

KUYKENDALL, Andrew Jackson (Ill.) March 3, 1815–May 11, 1891; House 1865–67.

KUYKENDALL, Dan Heflin (Tenn.) July 9, 1924–; House 1967–75.

KYL, John (Ariz.) House, 1995–.

KYL, John Henry (father of John Henry Kyl) (Ariz.) May 9, 1919–; House Dec. 15, 1959–65, 1967–73.

KYL, Jon Llewellyn (son of John Henry Kyl) (Ariz.) April 25, 1942–; House 1987–1995; Senate 1995–.

KYLE, Thomas Barton (Ohio) March 10, 1856–Aug. 13, 1915; House 1901–05.

LACEY, Edward Samuel (Mich.) Nov. 26, 1835–Oct. 2, 1916; House 1881–85.

LACEY, John Fletcher (Iowa) May 30, 1841–Sept. 29, 1913; House 1889–91, 1893–1907.

LACOCK, Abner (Pa.) July 9, 1770–April 12, 1837; House 1811–13; Senate 1813–19.

LADD, Edwin Freemont (N.Dak.) Dec. 13, 1859–June 22, 1925; Senate 1921–June 22, 1925.

LAFEAN, Daniel Franklin (Pa.) Feb. 7, 1861–April 18, 1922; House 1903–13, 1915–17.

LAFFERTY, Abraham Walter (Oreg.) June 10, 1875–Jan. 15, 1964; House 1911–15.

LAFLIN, Addison Henry (N.Y.) Oct. 24, 1823–Sept. 24, 1878; House 1865–71.

LA FOLLETTE, Charles Marion (great-grandson of William Heilman) (Ind.) Feb. 27, 1898–June 27, 1974; House 1943–47.

LA FOLLETTE, Robert Marion (father of Robert Marion La Follette Jr.) (Wis.) June 14, 1855–June 18, 1925; House 1885–91; Senate Jan. 2, 1906–June 18, 1925; Gov. Jan. 7, 1901–Jan. 1, 1906.

LA FOLLETTE, William Leroy (Wash.) Nov. 30, 1860–Dec. 20, 1934; House 1911–19.

LAFORE, John Armand Jr. (Pa.) May 25, 1905–; House Nov. 5, 1957–61.

LAGOMARSINO, Robert John (Calif.) Sept. 4, 1926–; House March 5, 1974–93.

LA GUARDIA, Fiorello Henry (N.Y.) Dec. 11, 1882–Sept. 20, 1947; House 1917–Dec. 31, 1919 (Republican) 1923–33 (1923–25 Republican, 1925–27 American Laborite).

LaHOOD, Ray (Ill.) House 1995–.

LAIDLAW, William Grant (N.Y.) Jan. 1, 1840–Aug. 19, 1908; House 1887–91.

LAIRD, James (Nebr.) June 20, 1849–Aug. 17, 1889; House 1883–Aug. 17, 1889.

LAIRD, Melvin Robert (Wis.) Sept. 1, 1922–; House 1953–Jan. 21, 1969; Secy. of Defense Jan. 22, 1969–Jan. 29, 1973.

LAMBERT, John (N.J.) Feb. 24, 1746–Feb. 4, 1823; House 1805–09; Senate 1809–15; Gov. Nov. 15, 1802–Oct. 29, 1803 (Democratic Republican).

LAMBERTSON, William Purnell (Kans.) March 23, 1880–Oct. 26, 1957; House 1929–45.

LAMPERT, Florian (Wis.) July 8, 1863–July 18, 1930; House Nov. 5, 1918–July 18, 1930.

LAMPORT, William Henry (N.Y.) May 27, 1811–July 21, 1891; House 1871–75.

LANDGREBE, Earl Frederick (Ind.) Jan. 21, 1916–June 29, 1986; House 1969–75.

LANDIS, Charles Beary (brother of Frederick Landis) (Ind.) July 9, 1858–April 24, 1922; House 1897–1909.

LANDIS, Frederick (brother of Charles Beary Landis) (Ind.) Aug. 18, 1872–Nov. 15, 1934; House 1903–07.

LANDIS, Gerald Wayne (Ind.) Feb. 23, 1895–Sept. 6, 1971; House 1939–49.

LANE, Henry Smith (Ind.) Feb. 24, 1811–June 18, 1881; House Aug. 3, 1840–43 (Whig); Senate 1861–67; Gov. Jan. 14–16, 1861.

LANE, James Henry (son of Amos Lane) (Kans.) June 22, 1814–July 11, 1866; House 1853–55 (Democrat Ind.); Senate April 4, 1861–July 11, 1866.

LANE, Joseph Reed (Iowa) May 6, 1858–May 1, 1931; House 1899–1901.

LANGEN, Odin Elsford Stanley (Minn.) Jan. 5, 1913–July 6, 1976; House 1959–71.

LANGER, William (N.Dak.) Sept. 30, 1886–Nov. 8, 1959; Senate 1941–Nov. 8, 1959; Chrmn. Senate Post Office and Civil Service 1947–49; Chrmn. Senate Judiciary 1953–55; Gov. Dec. 31, 1932–July 17, 1934 (Independent), Jan. 6, 1937–Jan. 5, 1939 (Independent).

LANGHAM, Jonathan Nicholas (Pa.) Aug. 4, 1861–May 21, 1945; House 1909–15.

LANGLEY, John Wesley (husband of Katherine Gudger Langley, son-in-law of James Madison Gudger Jr.) (Ky.) Jan. 14, 1868–Jan. 17, 1932; House 1907–Jan. 11, 1926.

LANGLEY, Katherine Gudger (wife of John Wesley Langley, daughter of James Madison Gudger Jr.) (Ky.) Feb. 14, 1888–Aug. 15, 1948; House 1927–31.

LANGSTON, John Mercer (Va.) Dec. 14, 1829–Nov. 15, 1897; House Sept. 23, 1890–91.

LANING, Jay Ford (Ohio) May 15, 1853–Sept. 1, 1941; House 1907–09.

LANKFORD, Menalcus (Va.) March 14, 1883–Dec. 27, 1937; House 1929–33.

LANMAN, James (Conn.) June 14, 1767–Aug. 7, 1841; Senate 1819–25.

LANNING, William Mershon (N.J.) Jan. 1, 1849–Feb. 16, 1912; House 1903–June 6, 1904.

LANSING, Frederick (N.Y.) Feb. 16, 1838–Jan. 31, 1894; House 1889–91.

LANSING, William Esselstyne (N.Y.) Dec. 29, 1821–July 29, 1883; House 1861–63, 1871–75.

LAPHAM, Elbridge Gerry (N.Y.) Oct. 18, 1814–Jan. 8, 1890; House 1875–July 29, 1881; Senate Aug. 2, 1881–85.

LARGENT, Steve (Okla.) House, 1995–.

LARNED, Simon (Mass.) Aug. 3, 1753–Nov. 16, 1817; House Nov. 5, 1804–05.

LARRAZOLO, Octaviano Ambrosio (N.Mex.) Dec. 7, 1859–April 7, 1930; Senate Dec. 7, 1928–29; Gov. Jan. 1, 1919–Jan. 1, 1921.

LARSON, Oscar John (Minn.) May 20, 1871–Aug. 1, 1957; House 1921–25.

LASH, Israel George (N.C.) Aug. 18, 1810–April 1, 1878; House July 20, 1868–71.

LATHAM, Henry Jepson (N.Y.) Dec. 10, 1908–; House 1945–Dec. 31, 1958.

LATHAM, Tom (Iowa) House, 1995–.

LATHROP, William (Ill.) April 17, 1825–Nov. 19, 1907; House 1877–79.

LaTOURETTE, Steven C. (Ohio) House, 1995–.

LATTA, Delbert Leroy (Ohio) March 5, 1920–; House 1959–89.

LAUGHLIN, Greg H. (Tex.) Jan. 21, 1942–; House 1989– (Democrat until 1995).

LAW, Charles Blakeslee (N.Y.) Feb. 5, 1872–Sept. 15, 1929; House 1905–11.

LAWRENCE, George Pelton (Mass.) May 19, 1859–Nov. 21, 1917; House Nov. 2, 1879–1913.

LAWRENCE, George Van Eman (son of Joseph Lawrence) (Pa.) Nov. 13, 1818–Oct. 2, 1904; House 1865–69, 1883–85.

LAWRENCE, Henry Franklin (Mo.). Jan. 31, 1868–Jan. 12, 1950; House 1921–23.

LAWRENCE, William (Ohio) June 26, 1819–May 8, 1899; House 1865–71, 1873–77.

LAWS, Gilbert Lafayette (Nebr.) March 11, 1838–April 25, 1907; House Dec. 2, 1889–91.

LAWSON, John Daniel (N.Y.) Feb. 18, 1816–Jan. 24, 1896; House 1873–75.

LAWYER, Thomas (N.Y.) Oct. 14, 1785–May 21, 1868; House 1817–19.

LAXALT, Paul Dominique (Nev.) Aug. 2, 1922–; Senate Dec. 18, 1974–87; Gov. Jan. 2, 1967–Jan. 4, 1971.

LAYTON, Caleb Rodney (Del.) Sept. 8, 1851–Nov. 11, 1930; House 1919–23.

LAZIO, Enrico A. "Rick" (N.Y.) March 13, 1958–; House 1993–.

LEACH, DeWitt Clinton (Mich.) Nov. 23, 1822–Dec. 21, 1909; House 1857–61.

LEACH, James Albert Smith (Iowa) Oct. 15, 1942–; House 1977–; Chrmn. House Banking and Financial Services Committee 1995–.

LEACH, Robert Milton (Mass.) April 2, 1879–Feb. 18, 1952; House Nov. 4, 1924–25.

LEAKE, Walter (Miss.) May 25, 1762–Nov. 17, 1825; Senate Dec. 10, 1817–May 15, 1820; Gov. Jan. 7, 1822–Nov. 17, 1825.

LEATHERWOOD, Elmer O. (Utah) Sept. 4, 1872–Dec. 24, 1929; House 1921–Dec. 24, 1929.

LEAVENWORTH, Elias Warner (N.Y.) Dec. 20, 1803–Nov. 25, 1887; House 1875–77.

LEAVITT, Scott (Mont.) June 16, 1879–Oct. 19, 1966; House 1923–33.

LeBOUTILLIER, John (N.Y.) May 26, 1953–; House 1981–83.

LE COMPTE, Karl Miles (Iowa) May 25, 1887–Sept. 30, 1972; House 1939–59; Chrmn. House Administration 1947–49, 1953–55.

LEE, Gary Alcide (N.Y.) Aug. 18, 1933–; House 1979–83.

LEE, Moses Lindley (N.Y.) May 29, 1805–May 19, 1876; House 1859–61.

LEE, Warren Isbell (N.Y.) Feb. 6, 1876–Dec. 25, 1955; House 1921–23.

LEECH, James Russell (Pa.) Nov. 19, 1888–Feb. 5, 1952; House 1927–Jan. 29, 1932.

LE FEVER, Jacob (father of Frank Jacob Le Fevre) (N.Y.) April 20, 1830–Feb. 4, 1905; House 1893–97.

LE FEVER, Joseph (Pa.) April 3, 1760–Oct. 17, 1826; House 1811–13.

LE FEVRE, Frank Jacob (son of Jacob Le Fever) (N.Y.) Nov. 30, 1874–April 29, 1941; House 1905–07.

LE FEVRE, Jay (N.Y.) Sept. 6, 1893–April 26, 1970; House 1943–51.

LEFFERTS, John (N.Y.) Dec. 17, 1785–Sept. 18, 1829; House 1813–15.

LEHLBACH, Frederick Reimold (nephew of Herman Lehlbach) (N.J.) Jan. 31, 1876–Aug. 4, 1937; House 1915–37.

LEHLBACH, Herman (uncle of Frederick Reimold Lehlbach) (N.J.) Jan. 31, 1876–Aug. 4, 1937; House 1915–37.

LEIB, Michael (Pa.) Jan. 8, 1760–Dec. 8, 1822; House 1799–Feb. 14, 1806 (no party); Senate Jan. 9, 1809–Feb. 14, 1814.

LEIGHTY, Jacob D. (Ind.) Nov. 15, 1839–Oct. 1912; House 1895–97.

LEISENRING, John (Pa.) June 3, 1853–Jan. 19, 1901; House 1895–97.

LEITER, Benjamin Franklin (Ohio) Oct. 13, 1813–June 17, 1866; House 1855–59.

LEMKE, William (N.Dak.) Aug. 13, 1878–May 30, 1950; House 1933–41 (Nonpartisan Republican), 1943–May 30, 1950.

LENROOT, Irvine Luther (Wis.) Jan. 31, 1869–Jan. 26, 1949; House 1909–April 17, 1918; Senate April 18, 1918–27.

LENT, Norman Frederick (N.Y.) March 23, 1931–; House 1971–93.

LEONARD, Fred Churchill (Pa.) Feb. 16, 1866–Dec. 5, 1921; House 1895–97.

LEONARD, John Edwards (great-nephew of John Edwards of Pa.) (La.) Sept. 22, 1845–March 15, 1878; House 1877–March 15, 1878.

LESSLER, Montague (N.Y.) Jan. 1, 1869–Feb. 17, 1938; House Jan. 7, 1902–03.

LETTS, Fred Dickinson (cousin of Lester Jesse Dickinson) (Iowa) April 26, 1876–Jan. 19, 1965; House 1925–31.

LEVY, David A. (N.Y.) Dec. 18, 1953–; House 1993–.

LEWIS, Barbour (Tenn.) Jan. 5, 1818–July 15, 1893; House 1873–75.

LEWIS, Charles Jeremy "Jerry" (Calif.) Oct. 21, 1934–; House 1979–.

LEWIS, Earl Ramage (Ohio) Feb. 22, 1887–Feb. 1, 1956; House 1939–41, 1943–49.

LEWIS, Fred Ewing (Pa.) Feb. 8, 1865–June 27, 1949; House 1913–15.

LEWIS, John Francis (Va.) March 1, 1818–Sept. 2, 1895; Senate Jan. 26, 1870–75.

LEWIS, John Henry (Ill.) July 21, 1830–Jan. 6, 1929; House 1881–83.

LEWIS, John William (Ky.) Oct. 14, 1841–Dec. 20, 1913; House 1895–97.

LEWIS, Robert Jacob (Pa.) Dec. 30, 1864–July 24, 1933; House 1901–03.

LEWIS, Ron E. (Ky.) Sept. 14, 1946–; House May 26, 1994–.

LEWIS, Thomas Francis Jr. (Fla.) Oct. 26, 1924–; House 1983–.

LEWIS, William (Ky.) Sept. 22, 1868–Aug. 8, 1959; House April 24, 1948–49.

LIBBEY, Harry (Va.) Nov. 22, 1843–Sept. 30, 1913; House 1883–87 (1883–85 Readjuster).

LICHTENWALTER, Franklin Herbert (Pa.) March 28, 1910–March 4, 1973; House Sept. 9, 1947–51.

LIGHTFOOT, James Ross (Iowa) Sept. 27, 1938–; House 1985–.

LILLEY, George Leavens (Conn.) Aug. 3, 1859–April 21, 1909; House 1903–Jan. 5, 1909; Gov. Jan. 6–April 21, 1909.

LILLEY, Mial Eben (Pa.) May 30, 1850–Feb. 28, 1915; House 1905–07.

LILLY, William (Pa.) June 3, 1821–Dec. 1, 1893; House March 4–Dec. 1, 1893.

LINCOLN, Abraham (Ill.) Feb. 12, 1809–April 15, 1865; House 1847–49 (Whig); President 1861–April 15, 1865.

LINCOLN, Enoch (son of Levi Lincoln, brother of Levi Lincoln Jr.) (Maine) Dec. 28, 1788–Oct. 8, 1829; House Nov. 4, 1818–21 (Mass.), 1821–26; Gov. Jan. 3, 1827–Oct. 8, 1829.

LINCOLN, Levi (father of Enoch Lincoln and Levi Lincoln, Jr.) (Mass.) May 15, 1749–April 14, 1820; House Dec. 15, 1800–March 5, 1801; Cont. Cong. (elected but did not attend) 1781; Atty. Gen. March 5, 1801–March 3, 1806; Gov. Dec. 10, 1808–May 1, 1809 (Democratic Republican).

LINCOLN, William Slosson (N.Y.) Aug. 13, 1813–April 21, 1893; House 1867–69.

LINDBERGH, Charles Augustus (Minn.) Jan. 20, 1859–May 24, 1924; House 1907–17.

LINDER, John Elmer (Ga.) Sept. 9, 1942–; House 1993–.

LINDQUIST, Francis Oscar (Mich.) Sept. 27, 1869–Sept. 25, 1924; House 1912–15.

LINDSAY, John Vliet (N.Y.) Nov. 24, 1921–; House 1959–Dec. 31, 1965.

LINDSEY, Stephen Decatur (Maine) March 3, 1828–April 26, 1884; House 1877–83.

LINDSLEY, James Girard (N.Y.) March 19, 1819–Dec. 4, 1898; House 1885–87.

LINEBERGER, Walter Franklin (Calif.) July 20, 1883–Oct. 9, 1943; House 1921–27.

LINN, James (N.J.) 1749–Jan. 5, 1821; House 1799–1801.

LINN, John (N.J.) Dec. 3, 1763–Jan. 5, 1821; House 1817–Jan. 5, 1821.

LINNEY, Romulus Zechariah (N.C.) Dec. 26, 1841–April 15, 1910; House 1895–1901.

LINTON, William Seelye (Mich.) Feb. 4, 1856–Nov. 22, 1927; House 1893–97.

LIPPITT, Henry Frederick (R.I.) Oct. 12, 1856–Dec. 28, 1933; Senate 1911–17.

LIPSCOMB, Glenard Paul (Calif.) Aug. 19, 1915–Feb. 1, 1970; House Nov. 10, 1953–Feb. 1, 1970.

LITTAUER, Lucius Nathan (N.Y.) Jan. 20, 1859–March 2, 1944; House 1897–1907.

LITTLE, Edward Campbell (Kans.) Dec. 14, 1858–June 27, 1924; House 1917–June 27, 1924.

LITTLE, John (Ohio) April 25, 1837–Oct. 18, 1900; House 1885–87.

LITTLE, Peter (Md.) Dec. 11, 1775–Feb. 5, 1830; House 1811–13, Sept. 2, 1816–29.

LITTLEFIELD, Charles Edgar (Maine) June 21, 1851–May 2, 1915; House June 19, 1899–Sept. 30, 1908.

LITTLEJOHN, De Witt Clinton (N.Y.) Feb. 7, 1818–Oct. 27, 1892; House 1863–65.

LIVERMORE, Arthur (son of Samuel Livermore, brother of Edward St. Loe Livermore) (N.H.) July 29, 1766–July 1, 1853; House 1817–21, 1823–25.

LIVINGSTON, Robert Linlithgow Jr. (La.) April 30, 1943–; House Sept. 7, 1977–; Chrmn. House Appropriations Committee 1995–.

LLOYD, Edward (Md.) July 22, 1779–June 2, 1834; House Dec. 3, 1806–09 (no party); Senate 1819–Jan. 14, 1826; Gov. June 9, 1809–Nov. 16, 1811 (Democratic Republican).

LLOYD, Sherman Parkinson (Utah) Jan. 11, 1914–Dec. 15, 1979; House 1963–65, 1967–73.

LOAN, Benjamin Franklin (Mo.) Oct. 4, 1819–March 30, 1881; House 1863–65 (1863–65 Unconditional Unionist).

LoBIONDO, Frank A. (N.J.) House, 1995–.

LOCKE, Matthew (uncle of Francis Locke, great-great-great-grandfather of Effiegene Locke Wingo) (N.C.) 1730–Sept. 7, 1801; House 1793–99 (1793–95 no party).

LODGE, Henry Cabot (grandfather of Henry Cabot Lodge Jr. and John Davis Lodge, great-grandson of George Cabot) (Mass.) May l2, 1850–Nov. 9, 1924; House 1887–93; Senate 1893–Nov. 9, 1924; Senate minority leader Aug. 24, 1918–19; Senate majority leader 1919–Nov. 9, 1924; elected Pres. pro tempore March 25, 1912 (to serve March 25–March 26, 1912).

LODGE, Henry Cabot Jr. (grandson of Henry Cabot Lodge, brother of John Davis Lodge, nephew of Augustus Peabody Gardner, great-great-great-grandson of George Cabot) (Mass.) July 5, 1902–Feb. 27, 1985; Senate 1937–Feb. 3, 1944, 1947–53.

LODGE, John Davis (grandson of Henry Cabot Lodge, brother of Henry Cabot Lodge Jr., nephew of Augustus Peabody Gardner, great-great-great-grandson of George Cabot) (Conn.) Oct. 20, 1903–Oct. 29, 1985; House 1947–51; Gov. Jan. 3, 1951–Jan. 5, 1956.

LOEFFLER, Thomas Gilbert (Tex.) Aug. 1, 1946–; House 1979–87.

LOFLAND, James Rush (Del.) Nov. 2, 1823–Feb. 10, 1894; House 1873–75.

LOGAN, George (Pa.) Sept. 9, 1753–April 9, 1821; Senate July 13, 1801–07.

LOGAN, John Alexander (Ill.) Feb. 9, 1826–Dec. 26, 1886; House 1859–April 2, 1862 (Democrat), 1867–71; Senate 1871–77, 1879–Dec. 26, 1886.

LOGAN, William (Ky.) Dec. 8, 1776–Aug. 8, 1822; Senate 1819–May 28, 1820.

LONG, Chester Isaiah (Kans.) Oct. 12, 1860–July 1, 1934; House 1895–97, 1899–March 4, 1903; Senate 1903–09.

LONG, Jefferson Franklin (Ga.) March 3, 1836–Feb. 4, 1901; House Dec. 22, 1870–71.

LONG, John Davis (Mass.) Oct. 27, 1838–Aug. 28, 1915; House 1883–89; Gov. Jan. 8, 1880–Jan. 4, 1883; Secy. of the Navy March 6, 1897–April 30, 1902.

LONGLEY, James B. Jr. (Maine) House, 1995–.

LONGNECKER, Henry Clay (Pa.) April 17, 1820–Sept. 16, 1871; House 1859–61.

LONGWORTH, Nicholas (nephew of Bellamy Storer) (Ohio) Nov. 5, 1869–April 9, 1931; House 1903–13, 1915–April 9, 1931; House majority leader 1923–25; Speaker Dec. 7, 1925–27, Dec. 5, 1927–29, April 15, 1929–31.

LONGYEAR, John Wesley (Mich.) Oct. 22, 1820–March 11, 1875; House 1863–67.

LOOFBOUROW, Frederick Charles (Utah) Feb. 8, 1874–July 8, 1949; House Nov. 4, 1930–33.

LOOMIS, Dwight (Conn.) July 27, 1821–Sept. 17, 1903; House 1859–63.

LORD, Bert (N.Y.) Dec. 4, 1869–May 24, 1939; House 1935–May 24, 1939.

LORD, Henry William (Mich.) March 8, 1821–Jan. 25, 1891; House 1881–83.

LORIMER, William (Ill.) April 27, 1861–Sept. 13, 1934; House 1895–1901, 1903–June 17, 1909; Senate June 18, 1909–July 13, 1912.

LORING, George Bailey (Mass.) Nov. 8, 1817–Sept. 14, 1891; House 1877–81.

LOTT, Chester Trent (Miss.) Oct. 9, 1941–; House 1973–89; Senate 1989–; Senate majority leader 1996–.

LOUD, Eugene Francis (Calif.) March 12, 1847–Dec. 19, 1908; House 1891–1903.

LOUD, George Alvin (Mich.) June 18, 1852–Nov. 13, 1925; House 1903–11, 1915–17.

LOUDENSLAGER, Henry Clay (N.J.) May 22, 1852–Aug. 12, 1911; House 1893–Aug. 12, 1911.

LOUGHRIDGE, William (Iowa) July 11, 1827–Sept. 26, 1889; House 1867–71, 1873–75.

LOUTTIT, James Alexander (Calif.) Oct. 16, 1848–July 26, 1906; House 1885–87.

LOVE, Francis Johnson (W.Va.) Jan. 23, 1901–House 1947–49.

LOVE, John (Va.) ?–Aug. 17, 1822; House 1807–11.

LOVE, William Carter (N.C.) 1784–1835; House 1815–17.

LOVEJOY, Owen (cousin of Nathan Allen Farwell) (Ill.) Jan. 6, 1811–March 25, 1864; House 1857–March 25, 1864.

LOVERING, William Croad (Mass.) Feb. 25, 1835–Feb. 4, 1910; House 1897–Feb. 4, 1910.

LOVETTE, Oscar Byrd (Tenn.) Dec. 20, 1871–July 6, 1934; House 1931–33.

LOVRE, Harold Orrin (S.Dak.) Jan. 30, 1904–Jan. 17, 1972; House 1949–57.

LOW, Frederick Ferdinand (Calif.) June 30, 1828–July 21, 1894; House June 3, 1862–63; Gov. Dec. 10, 1863–Dec. 5, 1867 (Union Republican).

LOW, Philip Burrill (N.Y.) May 6, 1836–Aug. 23, 1912; House 1895–99.

LOWDEN, Frank Orren (Ill.) Jan. 26, 1861–March 20, 1943; House Nov. 6, 1906–11; Gov. Jan. 8, 1917–Jan. 10, 1921.

LOWE, David Perley (Kans.) Aug. 22, 1823–April 10, 1882; House 1871–75.

LOWER, Christian (Pa.) Jan. 7, 1740–Dec. 19, 1806; House 1806–Dec. 19, 1806.

LOWERY, William David (Calif.) May 2, 1947–; House 1981–93.

LOWNDES, Lloyd Jr. (great-nephew of Edward Lloyd) (Md.) Feb. 21, 1845–Jan. 8, 1905; House 1873–75; Gov. Jan. 8, 1896–Jan. 10, 1900.

LOWNDES, William (brother of Thomas Lowndes) (S.C.) Feb. 11, 1782–Oct. 27, 1822; House 1811–May 8, 1822.

LUCAS, Frank Dean (Okla.) Jan. 6, 1960–; House May 17, 1995–.

LUCAS, John Baptiste Charles (Pa.) Aug. 14, 1758–Aug. 17, 1842; House 1803–05.

LUCAS, William Vincent (S.Dak.) July 3, 1835–Nov. 10, 1921; House 1893–95.

LUCE, Clare Boothe (stepdaughter of Albert Elmer Austin) (Conn.) April 10, 1903–Oct. 9, 1987; House 1943–47.

LUCE, Robert (Mass.) Dec. 2, 1862–April 17, 1946; House 1919–35, 1937–41.

LUFKIN, Willfred Weymouth (Mass.) March 10, 1879–March 28, 1934; House Nov. 6, 1917–June 30, 1921.

LUGAR, Richard Green (Ind.) April 4, 1932–; Senate 1977–; Chrmn. Senate Foreign Relations 1985–87; Chrmn. Senate Agriculture, Nutrition and Forestry Committee 1995–.

LUHRING, Oscar Raymond (Ind.) Feb. 11, 1879–Aug. 20, 1944; House 1919–23.

LUJAN, Manuel Jr. (N.Mex.) May 12, 1928–; House 1969–89; Secy. of the Interior Feb. 8, 1989–Jan. 20, 1993.

LUKENS, Donald Edgar "Buz" (Ohio) Feb. 11, 1931–; House 1967–71, 1987–Oct. 24, 1990.

LUNA, Tranquilino (N.Mex.) Feb. 25, 1849–Nov. 20, 1892; House (Terr.Del.) 1881–March 5, 1884.

LUNDIN, Frederick (Ill.) May 18, 1868–Aug. 20,1947; House 1909–11.

LUNGREN, Daniel Edward (Calif.) Sept. 22, 1946–; House 1979–89.

LUTHER, William P. Bell (Minn.) House, 1995–.

LYBRAND, Archibald (Ohio) May 23, 1840–Feb 7, 1910; House 1897–1901.

LYLE, Aaron (Pa.) Nov. 17, 1759–Sept. 24, 1825; House 1809–17.

LYMAN, Joseph (Iowa) Sept. 13, 1840–July 9, 1890; House 1885–89.

LYMAN, William (Mass.) Dec. 7, 1755–Sept. 2, 1811; House 1793–97 (1793–95 no party).

LYNCH, John (Maine) Feb. 18, 1825–July 21, 1892; House 1865–73.

LYNCH, John Roy (Miss.) Sept. 10, 1847–Nov. 2, 1939; House 1873–77, April 29, 1882–83.

LYON, Matthew (father of Chittenden Lyon, great-grandfather of William Peters Hepburn) (Ky.) July 14, 1746–Aug. 1, 1822; House 1797–1801 (Vt.), 1803–11.

MAAS, Melvin Joseph (Minn.) May 14, 1898–April 13, 1964; House 1927–33, 1935–45.

MacCRATE, John (N.Y.) March 29, 1885–June 9, 1976; House 1919–Dec. 30, 1920.

MacDOUGALL, Clinton Dugald (N.Y.) June 14, 1839–May 24, 1914; House 1873–77.

MACE, Daniel (Ind.) Sept. 5, 1811–July 26, 1867; House 1851–57 (1851–55 Democrat).

MacGREGOR, Clarence (N.Y.) Sept. 16, 1872–Feb. 18, 1952; House 1919–Dec. 31, 1928.

MacGREGOR, Clark (Minn.) July 12, 1922–; House 1961–71.

MACHTLEY, Ronald K. (R.I.) July 13, 1948–; House 1989–.

MACK, Connie III (step-grandson of Tom Connally, grandson of Morris Sheppard, great-grandson of John Levi Sheppard) (Fla.) Oct. 29, 1940–; House 1983–89; Senate 1989–.

MACK, Russell Vernon (Wash.) June 13, 1891–March 28, 1960; House June 7, 1947–March 28, 1960.

MACKEY, Edmund William McGregor (S.C.) March 8, 1846–Jan. 27, 1884; House 1875–July 19, 1876 (Independent Republican), May 31, 1882–Jan. 27, 1884.

MacKINNON, George Edward (Minn.) April 22, 1906–; House 1947–49.

MacLAFFERTY, James Henry (Calif.) Feb. 27, 1871–June 9, 1937; House Nov. 7, 1922–25.

MACLAY, Samuel (brother of William Maclay, father of William Plunkett Maclay) (Pa.) June 17, 1741–Oct. 5, 1811; House 1795–97 (no party); Senate 1803–Jan. 4, 1809.

MACLAY, William (Pa.) March 22, 1765–Jan. 4, 1825; House 1815–19.

MACLAY, William Plunkett (son of Samuel Maclay, nephew of William Maclay) (Pa.) Aug. 23, 1774–Sept. 2, 1842; House Oct. 8, 1816–21.

MACON, Nathaniel (uncle of Willis Alston and Micajah Thomas Hawkins, great-grandfather of Charles Henry Martin of North Carolina) (N.C.) Dec. 17, 1757–June 29, 1837; House 1791–Dec. 13, 1815 (no party); Senate Dec. 13, 1815–Nov. 14, 1828; Speaker Dec. 7, 1801–03, Oct. 17, 1803–05, Dec. 2, 1805–07; elected Pres. pro tempore May 20, 1826, Jan. 2, 1827, March 2, 1827; Cont. Cong. (elected but did not attend) 1785.

MACY, William Kingsland (N.Y.) Nov. 21, 1889–July 15, 1961; House 1947–51.

MADDEN, Martin Barnaby (Ill.) March 21, 1855–April 27, 1928; House 1905–April 27, 1928.

MADIGAN, Edward Rell (Ill.) Jan. 13, 1936–; House 1973–March 8, 1991; Secy. of Agriculture March 12, 1991–Jan. 20, 1993.

MADISON, Edmond Haggard (Kans.) Dec. 18, 1865–Sept. 18, 1911; House 1907–Sept. 18, 1911.

MAFFETT, James Thompson (Pa.) Feb. 2, 1837–Dec. 19, 1912; House 1887–89.

MAGEE, James McDevitt (Pa.) April 5, 1877–April 16, 1949; House 1923–27.

MAGEE, Walter Warren (N.Y.) May 23, 1861–May 25, 1927; House 1915–May 25, 1927.

MAGOON, Henry Sterling (Wis.) Jan. 31, 1832–March 3, 1889; House 1875–77.

MAGRADY, Frederick William (Pa.) Nov. 24, 1863–Aug. 27, 1954; House 1925–33.

MAGRUDER, Patrick (Md.) 1768–Dec. 24, 1819; House 1805–07.

MAHANY, Rowland Blennerhassett (N.Y.) Sept. 28, 1864–May 2, 1937; House 1895–99.

MAHON, Thaddeus Maclay (Pa.) May 21, 1840–May 31, 1916; House 1893–1907.

MAILLIARD, William Somers (Calif.) June 10, 1917–June 10, 1992; House 1953–March 5, 1974.

MAIN, Verner Wright (Mich.) Dec. 16, 1885–July 6, 1965; House Dec. 17, 1935–37.

MAJORS, Thomas Jefferson (Nebr.) June 25, 1841–July 11, 1932; House Nov. 5, 1878–79.

MALBY, George Roland (N.Y.) Sept. 16, 1857–July 5, 1912; House 1907–July 5, 1912.

MALLARY, Richard Walker (Vt.) Feb. 21, 1929–; House Jan. 7, 1972–75.

MALLORY, Rufus (Oreg.) Jan. 10, 1831–April 30, 1914; House 1867–69.

MALONE, George Wilson (Nev.) Aug. 7, 1890–May 19, 1961; Senate 1947–59.

MALONEY, Franklin John (Pa.) March 29, 1899–Sept. 15, 1958; House 1947–49.

MALONEY, Robert Sarsfield (Mass.) Feb. 3, 1881–Nov. 8, 1934; House 1921–23.

MANAHAN, James (Minn.) March 12, 1866–Jan. 8, 1932; House 1913–15.

MANDERSON, Charles Frederick (Nebr.) Feb. 9, 1837–Sept. 28, 1911; Senate 1883–95; elected Pres. pro tempore March 2, 1891.

MANLOVE, Joe Jonathan (Mo.) Oct. 1, 1876–Jan. 31, 1956; House 1923–33.

MANN, James Robert (Ill.) Oct. 20, 1856–Nov. 30, 1922; House 1897–Nov. 30, 1922; House minority leader 1911–19.

MANTLE, Lee (Mont.) Dec. 13, 1851–Nov. 18, 1934; Senate Jan. 16, 1895–99.

MANZULLO, Ronald (Ill.) March 24, 1944–; House 1993–.

MAPES, Carl Edgar (Mich.) Dec. 26, 1874–Dec. 12, 1939; House 1913–Dec. 12, 1939.

MARAZITI, Joseph James (N.J.) June 15, 1912–May 20, 1991; House 1973–75.

MARCHAND, David (father of Albert Gallatin Marchand) (Pa.) Dec. 10, 1776–March 11, 1832; House 1817–21.

MARION, Robert (S.C.) 1766–March 22, 1811; House 1805–Dec. 4, 1810.

MARKHAM, Henry Harrison (Calif.) Nov. 16, 1840–Oct. 9, 1923; House 1885–87; Gov. Jan. 8, 1891–Jan. 11, 1895.

MARKS, Marc Lincoln (Pa.) Feb. 12, 1927–; House 1977–83.

MARLENEE, Ronald Charles (Mont.) Aug. 8, 1935–; House 1977–93.

MARR, George Washington Lent (Tenn.) May 25, 1779–Sept. 5, 1856; House 1817–19.

MARRIOTT, David Daniel (Utah) Nov. 2, 1939–; House 1977–85.

MARSH, Benjamin Franklin (Ill.) 1839–June 2, 1905; House 1877–83, 1893–1901, 1903–June 2, 1905.

MARSHALL, Leroy Tate (Ohio) Nov. 8, 1883–Nov. 22, 1950; House 1933–37.

MARSHALL, Lycurgus Luther (Ohio) July 9, 1888–Jan. 12, 1958; House 1939–41.

MARSHALL, Thomas Frank (N.Dak.) March 7, 1854–Aug. 20, 1921; House 1901–09.

MARSTON, Gilman (N.H.) Aug. 20, 1811–July 3, 1890; House 1859–63, 1865–67; Senate March 4–June 18, 1889.

MARTIN, David O'Brien (N.Y.) April 26, 1944–; House 1981–93.

MARTIN, David Thomas (Nebr.) July 9, 1907–; House 1961–Dec. 31, 1974.

MARTIN, Eben Wever (S.Dak.) April 12, 1855–May 22, 1932; House 1901–07, Nov. 3, 1908–15.

MARTIN, Edward (Pa.) Sept. 18, 1879–March 19, 1967; Senate 1947–59; Chrmn. Senate Public Works 1953–55; Gov. Jan. 19, 1943–Jan. 2, 1947.

MARTIN, James Douglas (Ala.) Sept. 1, 1918–; House 1965–67.

MARTIN, James Grubbs (N.C.) Dec. 11, 1935–; House 1973–85; Gov. Jan. 5, 1985–.

MARTIN, James Stewart (Ill.) Aug. 19, 1826–Nov. 20, 1907; House 1873–75.

MARTIN, Joseph John (N.C.) Nov. 21, 1833–Dec. 18, 1900; House 1879–Jan. 29, 1881.

MARTIN, Joseph William Jr. (Mass.) Nov. 3, 1884–March 6, 1968; House 1925–67; House minority leader 1939–47, 1949–53, 1955–59; Speaker 1947–49, 1953–55; Chrmn. Rep. Nat. Comm. 1940–42.

MARTIN, Lynn Morley (Ill.) Dec. 26, 1939–; House 1981–91; Secy. of Labor Feb. 22, 1991–Jan. 20, 1993.

MARTIN, Patrick Minor (Calif.) Nov. 25, 1924–July 18, 1968; House 1963–65.

MARTIN, Thomas Ellsworth (Iowa) Jan. 18, 1893–June 27, 1971; House 1939–55; Senate 1955–61.

MARTINI, Bill (N.J.) House, 1995–.

MARVIN, Francis (N.Y.) March 8, 1828–Aug. 14, 1905; House 1893–95.

MARVIN, James Madison (N.Y.) Feb. 27, 1809–April 25, 1901; House 1863–69.

MASON, Armistead Thomson (son of Stevens Thomson Mason) (Va.) Aug. 4, 1787–Feb. 6, 1819; Senate Jan. 3, 1816–17.

MASON, Joseph (N.Y.) March 30, 1828–May 31, 1914; House 1879–83.

MASON, Noah Morgan (Ill.) July 19, 1882–March 29, 1965; House 1937–63.

MASON, Stevens Thomson (father of Armistead Thomson Mason) (Va.) Dec. 29, 1760–May 10, 1803; Senate Nov. 18, 1794–May 10, 1803 (Nov. 18, 1794–1803 no party).

MASON, William Ernest (father of Winnifred Sprague Mason Huck) (Ill.) July 7, 1850–June 16, 1921; House 1887–91, 1917–June 16, 1921; Senate 1897–1903.

MASSEY, William Alexander (Nev.) Oct. 7, 1856–March 5, 1914; Senate July 1, 1912–Jan. 29, 1913.

MASSEY, Zachary David (Tenn.) Nov. 14, 1864–July 13, 1923; House Nov. 8, 1910–11.

MASTERS, Josiah (N.Y.) Nov. 22, 1763–June 30, 1822; House 1805–09.

MATHEWS, Frank Asbury Jr. (N.J.) Aug. 3, 1890–Feb. 5, 1964; House Nov. 6, 1945–49.

MATHEWS, George Arthur (Dakota) June 4, 1852–April 19, 1941; House (Terr. Del.) March 4–Nov. 2, 1889.

MATHEWSON, Elisha (R.I.) April 18, 1767–Oct. 14, 1853; Senate Oct. 26, 1807–11.

MATHIAS, Charles McCurdy Jr. (Md.) July 24, 1922–; House 1961–69; Senate 1969–87; Chrmn. Senate Rules and Administration 1981–87.

MATHIAS, Robert Bruce (Calif.) Nov. 17, 1930–; House 1967–75.

MATTESON, Orsamus Benajah (N.Y.) Aug. 28, 1805–Dec. 22, 1889; House 1849–51 (Whig), 1853–Feb. 27, 1857 (Whig), March 4, 1857–59.

MATTHEWS, Charles (Pa.) Oct. 15, 1856–Dec. 12, 1932; House 1911–13.

MATTHEWS, Nelson Edwin (Ohio) April 14, 1852–Oct. 13, 1917; House 1915–17.

MATTHEWS, Stanley (uncle of Henry Watterson) (Ohio) July 21, 1824–March 22, 1889; Senate March 21, 1877–79; Assoc. Justice Supreme Court May 17, 1881–March 22, 1889.

MATTINGLY, Mack Francis (Ga.) Jan. 7, 1931–; Senate 1981–87.

MAXWELL, George Clifford (father of John Patterson Bryan Maxwell, uncle of George Maxwell Robeson) (N.J.) May 31, 1771–March 16, 1816; House 1811–13.

MAY, Catherine Dean Barnes (Wash.) May 18, 1914–; House 1959–71.

MAY, Edwin Hyland Jr. (Conn.) May 28, 1924–; House 1957–59.

MAYNARD, Horace (Tenn.) Aug. 30, 1814–May 3, 1882; House 1857–63 (1857–59 American Party, 1959–61 Opposition Party, 1861–63 Unionist), July 24, 1866–75 (1866–67 Unconditional Unionist); Postmaster Gen. Aug. 25, 1880–March 7, 1881.

MAYNE, Wiley (Iowa) Jan. 19, 1917–; House 1967–75.

MAYRANT, William (S.C.) ?–?; House 1815–Oct. 21, 1816.

McARTHUR, Clifton Nesmith (grandson of James Willis Nesmith) (Oreg.) June 10, 1879–Dec. 9, 1923; House 1915–23.

McBRIDE, George Wycliffe (brother of John Rogers McBride) (Oreg.) March 13, 1854–June 18, 1911; Senate 1895–1901.

McBRIDE, John Rogers (brother of George Wycliffe McBride) (Oreg.) Aug. 22, 1832–July 20, 1904; House 1863–65.

McCAIN, John Sidney III (Ariz.) Aug. 29, 1936–; House 1983–87; Senate 1987–; Chrmn. Senate Indian Affairs Committee 1995–.

McCALL, John Ethridge (Tenn.) Aug. 14, 1859–Aug. 8, 1920; House 1895–97.

McCALL, Samuel Walker (Mass.) Feb. 28, 1851–Nov. 4, 1923; House 1893–1913; Gov. Jan. 6, 1916–Jan. 2, 1919.

McCANDLESS, Alfred A. (Calif.) July 23, 1927–; House 1983–.

McCARTHY, Dennis (N.Y.) March 19, 1814–Feb. 14, 1886; House 1867–71.

McCARTHY, John Jay (Nebr.) July 19, 1857–March 30, 1943; House 1903–07.

McCARTHY, Joseph Raymond (Wis.) Nov. 14, 1908–May 2, 1957; Senate 1947–May 2, 1957; Chrmn. Senate Government Operations 1953–55.

McCLEARY, James Thompson (Minn.) Feb. 5, 1853–Dec. 17, 1924; House 1893–1907.

McCLEERY, James (La.) Dec. 2, 1837–Nov. 5, 1871; House March 4–Nov. 5, 1871.

McCLENACHAN, Blair (Pa.) ?–May 8, 1812; House 1797–99.

McCLINTOCK, Charles Blaine (Ohio) May 25, 1886–Feb. 1, 1965; House 1929–33.

McCLORY, Robert (Ill.) Jan. 31, 1908–July 24, 1988; House 1963–83.

McCLOSKEY, Paul Norton "Pete" Jr. (Calif.) Sept. 29, 1927–; House Dec. 12, 1967–83.

McCLURE, Addison S. (Ohio) Oct. 10, 1839–April 17, 1903; House 1881–83, 1895–97.

McCLURE, James Albertus (Idaho) Dec. 27, 1924–; House 1967–73; Senate 1973–; Chrmn. Senate Energy and Natural Resources 1981–87.

McCLURG, Joseph Washington (Mo.) Feb. 22, 1818–Dec. 2, 1900; House 1863–68 (1863–65 Unconditional Unionist); Gov. Jan. 12, 1869–Jan. 9, 1871.

McCOID, Moses Ayres (Iowa) Nov. 5, 1840–May 19, 1904; House 1879–85.

McCOLLISTER, John Yetter (Nebr.) June 10, 1921–; House 1971–77.

McCOLLUM, Ira William "Bill" Jr. (Fla.) July 12, 1944–; House 1981–.

McCOMAS, Louis Emory (grandfather of Katherine Edgar Byron, great-grandfather of Goodloe Edgar Byron) (Md.) Oct. 28, 1846–Nov. 10, 1907; House 1883–91; Senate 1899–1905.

McCONNELL, Addison Mitchell "Mitch" Jr. (Ky.) Feb. 20, 1942–; Senate 1985–; Chrmn. Senate Select Ethics Committee 1995–.

McCONNELL, Samuel Kerns Jr. (Pa.) April 6, 1901–April 11, 1985; House Jan. 18, 1944–Sept. 1, 1957; Chrmn. House Education and Labor 1953–55.

McCONNELL, William John (Idaho) Sept. 18, 1839–March 30, 1925; Senate Dec. 18, 1890–91; Gov. Jan. 2, 1893–Jan. 4, 1897.

McCOOK, Anson George (N.Y.) Oct. 10, 1835–Dec. 30, 1917; House 1877–83.

McCORD, Andrew (N.Y.) about 1754–1808; House 1803–05.

McCORD, Myron Hawley (Wis.) Nov. 26, 1840–April 27, 1908; House 1889–91; Gov. (Ariz. Terr.) 1897–98.

McCORMICK, Henry Clay (Pa.) June 30, 1844–May 26, 1902; House 1887–91.

McCORMICK, John Watts (Ohio) Dec. 20, 1831–June 25, 1917; House 1883–85.

McCORMICK, Joseph Medill (husband of Ruth Hanna McCormick) (Ill.) May 16, 1877–Feb. 25, 1925; House 1917–19; Senate 1919–Feb. 25, 1925.

McCORMICK, Richard Cunningham (N.Y.) May 23, 1832–June 2, 1901; House (Unionist Terr. Del. Ariz.) 1869–75, (Rep.) 1895–97; Gov. (Unionist Ariz. Terr.) 1866.

McCORMICK, Ruth Hanna (daughter of Marcus Alonzo Hanna, wife of Joseph Medill McCormick and of Albert

Gallatin Simms) (Ill.) March 27, 1880–Dec. 31, 1944; House 1929–31.

McCORMICK, Washington Jay (Mont.) Jan. 4, 1884–March 7, 1949; House 1921–23.

McCOWEN, Edward Oscar (Ohio) June 29, 1877–Nov. 4, 1953; House 1943–49.

McCRACKEN, Robert McDowell (Idaho) March 15 1874–May 16, 1934; House 1915–17.

McCRARY, George Washington (Iowa) Aug. 29, 1835–June 23, 1890; House 1869–77; Secy. of War March 12, 1877–Dec. 10, 1879.

McCREARY, George Deardorff (Pa.) Sept. 28, 1846–July 26, 1915; House 1903–13.

McCREDIE, William Wallace (Wash.) April 27, 1862–May 10, 1935; House Nov. 2, 1909–11.

McCREERY, William (Md.) 1750–March 8, 1814; House 1803–09.

McCRERY, James O. III (La.) Sept. 18, 1949–; House April 26, 1988–.

McCULLOCH, Roscoe Conkling (Ohio) Nov. 27, 1880–March 17, 1958; House 1915–21; Senate Nov. 5, 1929–Nov. 30, 1930.

McCULLOCH, William Moore (Ohio) Nov. 24, 1901–Feb. 22, 1980; House Nov. 4, 1947–73.

McCULLOGH, Welty (Pa.) Oct. 10, 1847–Aug. 31, 1889; House 1887–89.

McCUMBER, Porter James (N.Dak.) Feb. 3, 1858–May 18, 1933; Senate 1899–1923.

McDADE, Joseph Michael (Pa.) Sept. 29, 1931–; House 1963–.

McDILL, Alexander Stuart (Wis.) March 18, 1822–Nov. 12, 1875; House 1873–75.

McDILL, James Wilson (Iowa) March 4, 1834–Feb. 28, 1894; House 1873–77; Senate March 8, 1881–83.

McDONALD, Alexander (Ark.) April 10, 1832–Dec. 13, 1903; Senate June 22, 1868–71.

McDONALD, Jack H. (Mich.) June 28, 1932–; House 1967–73.

McDONALD, John (Md.) May 24, 1837–Jan. 30, 1917; House 1897–99.

McDONOUGH, Gordon Leo (Calif.) Jan. 2, 1895–June 25, 1968; House 1945–63.

McDOWELL, Alexander (Pa.) March 4, 1845–Sept. 30, 1913; House 1893–95.

McDOWELL, John Ralph (Pa.) Nov. 6, 1902–Dec. 11, 1957; House 1939–41, 1947–49.

McDOWELL, Joseph (N.C.) Feb. 15, 1756–Feb. 5, 1801; House 1797–99; Cont. Cong. (elected but did not attend) 1787.

McDUFFIE, John Van (Ala.) May 16, 1841–Nov. 18, 1896; House June 4, 1890–91.

McEWAN, Thomas Jr. (N.J.) Feb. 26, 1854–Sept. 11, 1926; House 1895–99.

McEWEN, Robert Cameron (N.Y.) Jan. 5, 1920–; House 1965–81.

McEWEN, Robert D. (Ohio) Jan. 12, 1950–; House 1981–93.

McFADDEN, Louis Thomas (Pa.) July 25, 1876–Oct. 1, 1936; House 1915–35.

McFARLAN, Duncan (N.C.) ?–Sept. 7, 1816; House 1805–07.

McGARVEY, Robert Neill (Pa.) Aug. 14, 1888–June 28, 1952; House 1947–49.

McGAVIN, Charles (Ill.) Jan. 10, 1874–Dec. 17, 1940; House 1905–09.

McGOWAN, Jonas Hartzell (Mich.) April 2, 1837–July 5, 1909; House 1877–81.

McGRATH, Raymond Joseph (N.Y.) March 27, 1942–; House 1981–93.

McGREGOR, J. Harry (Ohio) Sept. 30, 1896–Oct. 7, 1958; House Feb. 27, 1940–Oct. 7, 1958.

McGREW, James Clark (W.Va.) Sept. 14, 1813–Sept. 18, 1910; House 1869–73.

McGUGIN, Harold Clement (Kans.) Nov. 22, 1893–March 7, 1946; House 1931–35.

McGUIRE, Bird Segle (cousin of William Neville) (Okla.) Oct. 13, 1865–Nov. 9, 1930; House (Terr. Del.) 1903–07, (Rep.) Nov. 15, 1907–15.

McHUGH, John Michael (N.Y.) Sept. 29, 1948–; House 1993–.

McINDOE, Walter Duncan (Wis.) March 30, 1819–Aug. 22, 1872; House Jan. 26, 1863–67.

McINNIS, Scott (Colo.) May 9, 1953–; House 1993–.

McINTIRE, Clifford Guy (Maine) May 4, 1908–Oct. 1, 1974; House Oct. 22, 1951–65.

McINTIRE, William Watson (Md.) June 30, 1850–March 30, 1912; House 1897–99.

McINTOSH, David M. (Ind.) House, 1995–.

McINTOSH, Robert John (Mich.) Sept. 16, 1922–; House 1957–59.

McJUNKIN, Ebenezer (Pa.) March 28, 1819–Nov. 10, 1907; House 1871–Jan. 1, 1875.

McKEAN, James Bedell (nephew of Samuel McKean) (N.Y.) Aug. 5, 1821–Jan. 5, 1879; House 1859–63.

McKEE, George Colin (Miss.) Oct. 2, 1837–Nov. 17, 1890; House 1869–75.

McKEE, Samuel (Ky.) Oct. 13, 1774–Oct. 16, 1826; House 1809–17.

McKEE, Samuel (Ky.) Nov. 5, 1833–Dec. 11, 1898; House 1865–67 (Unconditional Unionist), June 22, 1868–69.

McKENNA, Joseph (Calif.) Aug. 10, 1843–Nov. 21, 1926; House 1885–March 28, 1892; Atty. Gen. March 5, 1897–Jan. 25, 1898; Assoc. Justice Supreme Court Jan. 26, 1898–Jan. 5, 1925.

McKENZIE, John Charles (Ill.) Feb. 18, 1860–Sept. 17, 1941; House 1911–25.

McKEON, Howard Philip "Buck" (Calif.) Sept. 9, 1939–; House 1993–.

McKERNAN, John Rettie Jr. (husband of Olympia Jean Bouchles Snowe) (Maine) May 20, 1948–; House 1983–87; Gov. 1987–.

McKEVITT, James Douglas "Mike" (Colo.) Oct. 26, 1928–; House 1971–73.

McKIM, Alexander (uncle of Isaac McKim) (Md.) Jan. 10, 1748–Jan. 18, 1832; House 1809–15.

McKINLAY, Duncan E. (Calif.) Oct. 6, 1862–Dec. 30, 1914; House 1905–11.

McKINLEY, William (Va.) ?–?; House Dec. 21, 1810–11.

McKINLEY, William Brown (Ill.) Sept. 5, 1856–Dec. 7, 1926; House 1905–13, 1915–21; Senate 1921–26.

McKINLEY, William Jr. (Ohio) Jan. 29, 1843–Sept. 14, 1901; House 1877–May 27, 1884, 1885–91; Gov. Jan. 11, 1892–Jan. 13, 1896; President 1897–Sept. 14, 1901.

McKINNEY, James (Ill.) April 14, 1852–Sept. 29, 1934; House Nov. 7, 1905–13.

McKINNEY, Stewart Brett (Conn.) Jan. 30, 1931–May 7, 1987; House 1971–May 7, 1987.

McKNEALLY, Martin Boswell (N.Y.) Dec. 31, 1914–June 14, 1992; House 1969–71.

McKNIGHT, Robert (Pa.) Jan. 20, 1820–Oct. 25, 1885; House 1859–63.

McLACHLAN, James (Calif.) Aug. 1, 1852–Nov. 21, 1940; House 1895–97, 1901–11.

McLAUGHLIN, James Campbell (Mich.) Jan. 26, 1858–Nov. 29, 1932; House 1907–Nov. 29, 1932.

McLAUGHLIN, Joseph (Pa.) June 9, 1867–Nov. 21, 1926; House 1917–19, 1921–23.

McLAUGHLIN, Melvin Orlando (Nebr.) Aug. 8, 1876–June 18, 1928; House 1919–27.

McLEAN, Alney (Ky.) June 10, 1779–Dec. 30, 1841; House 1815–17, 1819–21.

McLEAN, Donald Holman (N.J.) March 18, 1884–Aug. 19, 1975; House 1933–45.

McLEAN, George Payne (Conn.) Oct. 7, 1857–June 6, 1932; Senate 1911–29; Gov. Jan. 9, 1901–Jan. 7, 1903.

McLEAN, James Henry (Mo.) Aug. 13, 1829–Aug. 12, 1886; House Dec. 15, 1882–83.

McLEAN, John (brother of William McLean) (Ohio) March 11, 1785–April 4, 1861; House 1813–16; Postmaster Gen. July 1, 1823–March 9, 1829; Assoc. Justice Supreme Court Jan. 11, 1830–April 4, 1861.

McLEOD, Clarence John (Mich.) July 3, 1895–May 15, 1959; House Nov. 2, 1920–21, 1923–37, 1939–41.

McLOSKEY, Robert Thaddeus (Ill.) June 26, 1907–; House 1963–65.

McMAHON, Gregory (N.Y.) March 19, 1915–June 27, 1989; House 1947–49.

McMASTER, William Henry (S.Dak.) May 10, 1877–Sept. 14, 1968; Senate 1925–31; Gov. Jan. 4, 1921–Jan. 6, 1925.

McMILLAN, James (Mich.) May 12, 1838–Aug. 10, 1902; Senate 1889–Aug. 10, 1902.

McMILLAN, John Alex III (N.C.) May 9, 1932–; House 1985–.

McMILLAN, Samuel (N.Y.) Aug. 6, 1850–May 6, 1924; House 1907–09.

McMILLAN, Samuel James Renwick (Minn.) Feb. 22, 1826–Oct. 3, 1897; Senate 1875–87.

McMILLEN, Rolla Coral (Ill.) Oct. 5, 1880–May 6, 1961; House June 13, 1944–51.

McMORRAN, Henry Gordon (Mich.) June 11, 1844–July 19, 1929; House 1903–13.

McNARY, Charles Linza (Oreg.) June 12, 1874–Feb. 25, 1944; Senate May 29, 1917–Nov. 5, 1918, Dec. 18, 1918–Feb. 25, 1944; Senate minority leader 1933–44.

McNULTA, John (Ill.) Nov. 9, 1837–Feb. 22, 1900; House 1873–75.

McNULTY, Michael R. (N.Y.) Sept. 16, 1947–; House 1989–.

McPHERSON, Edward (Pa.) July 31, 1830–Dec. 14, 1895; House 1859–63.

McPHERSON, Isaac Vanbert (Mo.) March 8, 1868–Oct. 31, 1931; House 1919–23.

McPHERSON, Smith (Iowa) Feb. 14, 1848–Jan. 17, 1915; House 1899–June 6, 1900.

McRUER, Donald Campbell (Calif.) March 10, 1826–Jan. 29, 1898; House 1865–67.

McVEY, Walter Lewis Jr. (Kans.) Feb. 19, 1922–; House 1961–63.

McVEY, William Estus (Ill.) Dec. 13, 1885–Aug. 10, 1958; House 1951–Aug. 10, 1958.

McWILLIAMS, John Dacher (Conn.) July 23, 1891–March 30, 1975; House 1943–45.

MEADE, Wendell Howes (Ky.) Jan. 18, 1912–June 2, 1986; House 1947–49.

MEADER, George (Mich.) Sept. 13, 1907–; House 1951–65.

MEANS, Rice William (Colo.) Nov. 16, 1877–Jan. 30, 1949; Senate Dec. 1, 1924–27.

MECHEM, Edwin Leard (N.Mex.) July 2, 1912–; Senate Nov. 30, 1962–Nov. 3, 1964; Gov. Jan. 1, 1951–Jan. 1, 1955, Jan. 1, 1957–Jan. 1, 1959, Jan. 1, 1961–Nov. 30, 1962.

MEEKER, Jacob Edwin (Mo.) Oct. 7, 1878–Oct. 16, 1918; House 1915–Oct. 16, 1918.

MEIGS, Return Jonathan Jr. (Ohio) Nov. 17, 1764–March 29, 1825; Senate Dec. 12, 1808–May 1, 1810; Gov. Dec. 8, 1810–March 24, 1814 (Democratic Republican); Postmaster Gen. April 11, 1814–June 30, 1823.

MEIKLEJOHN, George de Rue (Nebr.) Aug. 26, 1857–April 19, 1929; House 1893–97.

MELLISH, David Batcheller (N.Y.) Jan. 2, 1831–May 23, 1875; House 1873–May 23, 1874.

MENGES, Franklin (Pa.) Oct. 26, 1858–May 12, 1956; House 1925–31.

MERCER, David Henry (Nebr.) July 9, 1857–Jan. 10, 1919; House 1893–1903.

MERCUR, Ulysses (Pa.) Aug. 12, 1818–June 6, 1887; House 1865–Dec. 2, 1872.

MERIWETHER, David (father of James Meriwether, grandfather of James A. Meriwether) (Ga.) April 10, 1755–Nov. 16, 1822; House Dec. 6, 1802–07.

MERRIAM, Clinton Levi (N.Y.) March 25, 1824–Feb. 18, 1900; House 1871–75.

MERRILL, D. Bailey (Ind.) Nov. 22, 1912–; House 1953–55.

MERRILL, Orsamus Cook (Vt.) June 18, 1775–April 12, 1865; House 1817–Jan. 12, 1820.

MERRITT, Edwin Albert (N.Y.) July 25, 1860–Dec. 4, 1914; House Nov. 5, 1912–Dec. 4, 1914.

MERRITT, Schyler (Conn.) Dec. 16, 1853–April 1, 1953; House Nov. 6, 1917–31, 1933–37.

MERROW, Chester Earl (N.H.) Nov. 15, 1906–Feb. 10, 1974; House 1943–63.

MESICK, William Smith (Mich.) Aug. 26, 1856–Dec. 1, 1942; House 1897–1901.

MESKILL, Thomas Joseph (Conn.) Jan. 30, 1928–; House 1967–71; Gov. Jan. 6, 1971–Jan. 8, 1975.

METCALF, Jack (Wash.) House, 1995–.

METCALF, Jesse Houghton (R.I.) Nov. 16, 1860–Oct. 9, 1942; Senate Nov. 5, 1924–37.

METCALF, Victor Howard (Calif.) Oct. 10, 1853–Feb. 20, 1936; House 1899–July 1, 1904; Secy. of Commerce and Labor July 1, 1904–Dec. 16, 1906; Secy of the Navy Dec. 17, 1906–Nov. 30, 1908.

METCALFE, Lyne Shackelford (Mo.) April 21, 1822–Jan. 31, 1906; House 1877–79.

MEYER, Herbert Alton (Kans.) Aug. 30, 1886–Oct. 2, 1950; House 1947–Oct. 2, 1950.

MEYERS, Jan (Kans.) July 20, 1918–; House 1985–; Chrmn. House Small Business Committee 1995–.

MICA, John L. (brother of Daniel Andrew Mica) (Fla.) Jan. 27, 1943–; House 1993–.

MICHAELSON, Magne Alfred (Ill.) Sept. 7, 1878–Oct. 26, 1949; House 1921–31.

MICHALEK, Anthony (Ill.) Jan. 16, 1878–Dec. 21, 1916; House 1905–07.

MICHEL, Robert Henry (Ill.) March 2, 1923–; House 1957–; House minority leader 1981–95.

MICHENER, Earl Cory (Mich.) Nov. 30, 1876–July 4, 1957; House 1919–33, 1935–51; Chrmn. House Judiciary 1947–49.

MIDDLETON, Henry (S.C.) Sept. 28, 1770–June 14, 1846; House 1815–19; Gov. Dec. 10, 1810–Dec. 10, 1812.

MILES, Frederick (Conn.) Dec. 19, 1815–Nov. 20, 1896; House 1879–83, 1889–91.

MILLARD, Charles Dunsmore (N.Y.) Dec. 1, 1873–Dec. 11, 1944; House 1931–Sept. 29, 1937.

MILLARD, Joseph Hopkins (Nebr.) April 20, 1836–Jan. 13, 1922; Senate March 28, 1901–07.

MILLARD, Stephen Columbus (N.Y.) Jan. 14, 1841–June 21, 1914; House 1883–87.

MILLER, Arthur Lewis (Nebr.) May 24, 1892–March 16, 1967; House 1943–59; Chrmn. House Interior and Insular Affairs 1953–55.

MILLER, Clarence Benjamin (Minn.) March 13, 1872–Jan. 10, 1922; House 1909–19.

MILLER, Clarence E. (Ohio) Nov. 1, 1917–; House 1967–93.

MILLER, Edward Edwin (Ill.) July 22, 1880–Aug. 1, 1946; House 1923–25.

MILLER, Edward Tylor (Md.) Feb. 1, 1895–Jan. 20 1968; House 1947–59.

MILLER, Frederick Daniel "Dan" (Fla.) May 30, 1942–; House 1993–.

MILLER, George Funston (Pa.) Sept. 5, 1809–Oct. 21, 1885; House 1865–69.

MILLER, Jack Richard (Iowa) June 6, 1916–Aug. 29, 1994; Senate 1961–73.

MILLER, James Monroe (Kans.) May 6, 1852–Jan. 20, 1926; House 1899–1911.

MILLER, John Franklin (uncle of John Franklin Miller, below) (Calif.) Nov. 21, 1831–March 8, 1886; Senate 1881–March 8, 1886.

MILLER, John Franklin (nephew of John Franklin Miller, above) (Wash.) June 9, 1862–May 28, 1936; House 1917–31.

MILLER, John Ripin (Wash.) May 23, 1938–; House 1985–93.

MILLER, Louis Ebenezer (Mo.) April 30, 1899–Nov. 1, 1952; House 1943–45.

MILLER, Orrin Larrabee (Kans.) Jan. 11, 1856–Sept. 11, 1926; House 1895–97.

MILLER, Pleasant Moorman (Tenn.) ?–1849; House 1809–11.

MILLER, Samuel Franklin (N.Y.) May 27, 1827–March 16, 1892; House 1863–65, 1875–77.

MILLER, Samuel Henry (Pa.) April 19, 1840–Sept. 4, 1918; House 1881–85, 1915–17.

MILLER, Thomas Byron (Pa.) Aug. 11, 1896–March 20, 1976; House May 9, 1942–45.

MILLER, Thomas Ezekiel (S.C.) June 17, 1849–April 8, 1938; House Sept. 24, 1890–91.

MILLER, Thomas Woodnutt (uncle of Clement Woodnutt Miller) (Del.) June 26, 1886–May 5, 1973; House 1915–17.

MILLER, Ward MacLaughlin (Ohio) Nov. 29, 1902–March 11, 1984; House Nov. 8, 1960–61.

MILLER, Warner (N.Y.) Aug. 12, 1838–March 21, 1918; House 1879–July 26, 1881; Senate July 27, 1881–87.

MILLER, Warren (W.Va.) April 2, 1847–Dec. 29, 1920; House 1895–99.

MILLER, William Edward (N.Y.) March 22, 1914–June 24, 1983; House 1951–65; Chrmn. Rep. Nat. Comm. June 1961–July 1964.

MILLER, William Jennings (Conn.) March 12, 1899–Nov. 22, 1950; House 1939–41, 1943–45, 1947–49.

MILLIKEN, Seth Llewellyn (Maine) Dec. 12, 1831–April 18, 1897; House 1883–April 18, 1897.

MILLIKEN, William H. Jr. (Pa.) Aug. 19, 1897–July 4, 1969; House 1959–65.

MILLIKIN, Eugene Donald (Colo.) Feb. 12, 1891–July 26, 1958; Senate Dec. 20, 1941–57; Chrmn. Senate Finance 1947–49, 1953–55.

MILLINGTON, Charles Stephen (N.Y.) March 13, 1855–Oct. 25, 1913; House 1909–11.

MILLS, Daniel Webster (Ill.) Feb. 25, 1838–Dec. 16, 1904; House 1897–99.

MILLS, Ogden Livingston (N.Y.) Aug. 23, 1884–Oct. 11, 1937; House 1921–27; Secy. of the Treasury Feb. 13, 1932–March 4, 1933.

MILLS, William Oswald (Md.) Aug. 12, 1924–May 24, 1973; House May 27, 1971–May 24, 1973.

MILLSPAUGH, Frank Crenshaw (Mo.) Jan. 14, 1872–July 8, 1947; House 1921–Dec. 5, 1922.

MILLWARD, William (Pa.) June 30, 1822–Nov. 28, 1871; House 1855–57 (Whig), 1859–61.

MILNES, Alfred (Mich.) May 28,1844–Jan. 15, 1916; House Dec. 2, 1895–97.

MINOR, Edward Sloman (Wis.) Dec. 13, 1840–July 26, 1924; House 1895–1907.

MINSHALL, William Edwin Jr. (Ohio) Oct. 24, 1911–Oct. 15, 1990; House 1955–Dec. 31, 1974.

MITCHELL, Alexander Clark (Kans.) Oct. 11, 1860–July 7, 1911; House March 4–July 7, 1911.

MITCHELL, Donald Jerome (N.Y.) May 8, 1923–; House 1973–83.

MITCHELL, Edward Archibald (Ind.) Dec. 2, 1910–Dec. 11, 1979; House 1947–49.

MITCHELL, John Hipple (Oreg.) June 22, 1835–Dec. 8, 1905; Senate 1873–79, Nov. 18, 1885–97, 1901–Dec. 8, 1905.

MITCHELL, John Inscho (Pa.) July 28, 1838–Aug. 20, 1907; House 1877–81; Senate 1881–87.

MITCHELL, John Murry (N.Y.) March 18, 1858–May 31, 1905; House June 2, 1896–99.

MITCHELL, William (Ind.) Jan. 19, 1807–Sept. 11, 1865; House 1861–63.

MITCHILL, Samuel Latham (N.Y.) Aug. 20, 1764–Sept. 7, 1831; House 1801–Nov. 22, 1804, Dec. 4, 1810–13; Senate Nov. 23, 1804–09.

MIZE, Chester Louis (Kans.) Dec. 25, 1917–Jan. 11, 1994; House 1965–71.

MIZELL, Wilmer David (N.C.) Aug. 13, 1930–; House 1969–75.

MOFFATT, Seth Crittenden (Mich.) Aug. 10, 1841–Dec. 22, 1887; House 1885–Dec. 22, 1887.

MOFFITT, John Henry (N.Y.) Jan. 8, 1843–Aug. 14, 1926; House 1887–91.

MOLINARI, Guy Victor (father of Susan Molinari) (N.Y.) Nov. 23, 1928–; House 1981–Jan. 1, 1990.

MOLINARI, Susan (daughter of Guy Victor Molinari, wife of L. William Paxon) (N.Y.) March 27, 1958–; House March 27, 1990–.

MONAHAN, James Gideon (Wis.) Jan. 12, 1855–Dec. 5, 1923; House 1919–21.

MONAST, Louis (R.I.) July 1, 1863–April 16, 1936; House 1927–29.

MONDELL, Franklin Wheeler (Wyo.) Nov. 6, 1860–Aug. 6, 1939; House 1895–97, 1899–1923; House majority leader 1919–23.

MONKIEWICZ, Boleslaus Joseph (Conn.) Aug. 8, 1898–July 2, 1971; House 1939–41, 1943–45.

MONROE, James (Ohio) July 18, 1821–July 6, 1898; House 1871–81.

MONSON, David Smith (Utah) June 20, 1945–; House 1985–87.

MONTGOMERY, Daniel Jr. (Pa.) Oct. 30, 1765–Dec. 30, 1831; House 1807–09.

MONTGOMERY, John (Md.) 1764–July 17, 1828; House 1807–April 29, 1811.

MONTGOMERY, Samuel James (Okla.) Dec. 1, 1896–June 4, 1957; House 1925–27.

MONTGOMERY, Thomas (Ky.) 1779–April 2, 1828; House 1813–15, Aug. 1, 1820–23.

MONTOYA, Nestor (N.Mex.) April 14, 1862–Jan. 13, 1923; House 1921–Jan. 13, 1923.

MOODY, Gideon Curtis (S.Dak.) Oct. 16, 1832–March 17, 1904; Senate Nov. 2, 1889–91.

MOODY, James Montraville (N.C.) Feb. 12, 1858–Feb. 5, 1903; House 1901–Feb. 5, 1903.

MOODY, Malcolm Adelbert (Oreg.) Nov. 30, 1854–March 19, 1925; House 1899–1903.

MOODY, William Henry (Mass.) Dec. 23, 1853–July 2, 1917; House Nov. 5, 1895–May 1, 1902; Secy. of the Navy May 1, 1902–June 30, 1904; Atty. Gen. July 1, 1904–Dec. 17, 1906; Assoc. Justice Supreme Court Dec. 17, 1906–Nov. 20, 1910.

MOON, John Wesley (Mich.) Jan. 18, 1836–April 5, 1898; House 1893–95.

MOON, Reuben Osborne (Pa.) July 22, 1847–Oct. 25, 1919; House Nov. 2, 1903–13.

MOONEY, William Crittenden (Ohio) June 16, 1855–July 24, 1918; House 1915–17.

MOORE, Allen Francis (Ill.) Sept. 30, 1869–Aug. 18, 1945; House 1921–25.

MOORE, Arch Alfred Jr. (W.Va.) April 16, 1923–; House 1957–69; Gov. Jan. 13, 1969–Jan. 17, 1977, Jan. 14, 1985–Jan. 16, 1989.

MOORE, Charles Ellis (Ohio) Jan. 3, 1884–April 2, 1941; House 1919–33.

MOORE, Edward Hall (Okla.) Nov. 19, 1871–Sept. 2, 1950; Senate 1943–49.

MOORE, Eliakim Hastings (Ohio) June 19, 1812–April 4, 1900; House 1869–71.

MOORE, Jesse Hale (Ill.) April 22, 1817–July 11, 1883; House 1869–73.

MOORE, Joseph Hampton (Pa.) March 8, 1864–May 2, 1950; House Nov. 6, 1906–Jan. 4, 1920.

MOORE, Nicholas Ruxton (Md.) July 21, 1756–Oct. 7. 1816; House 1803–11, 1813–15.

MOORE, Orren Cheney (N.H.) Aug. 10, 1839–May 12, 1893; House 1889–91.

MOORE, Oscar Fitzatien (Ohio) Jan. 27, 1817–June 24, 1885; House 1855–57.

MOORE, Robert (grandfather of Michael Daniel Harter) (Pa.) March 30, 1778–Jan. 14, 1831; House 1817–21.

MOORE, Samuel (Pa.) Feb. 8, 1774–Feb. 18, 1861; House Oct. 13, 1818–May 20, 1822.

MOORE, Thomas (S.C.) 1759–July 11, 1822; House 1801–13, 1815–17.

MOORE, William (N.J.) Dec. 25, 1810–April 26, 1878; House 1867–71.

MOORE, William Henson III (La.) Oct. 4, 1939–; House Jan. 7, 1975–87.

MOORE, William Robert (Tenn.) March 28, 1830–June 12, 1909; House 1881–83.

MOORE, William Sutton (Pa.) Nov. 18, 1822–Dec. 30, 1877; House 1873–75.

MOOREHEAD, Tom Van Horn (Ohio) April 12, 1898–Oct. 21, 1979; House 1961–63.

MOORES, Merrill (Ind.) April 21, 1856–Oct. 21, 1929; House 1916–25.

MOORHEAD, Carlos John (Calif.) May 6, 1922–; House 1973–.

MOORHEAD, James Kennedy (Pa.) Sept. 7, 1806–March 6, 1884; House 1859–69.

MORANO, Albert Paul (Conn.) Jan. 18, 1908–Dec. 16, 1987; House 1951–59.

MOREHEAD, John Motley (N.C.) July 20, 1866–Dec. 13, 1923; House 1909–11.

MORELLA, Constance Albanese (Md.) Feb. 12, 1931–; House 1987–.

MOREY, Frank (La.) July 11, 1840–Sept. 22, 1889; House 1869–June 8, 1876.

MOREY, Henry Lee (Ohio) April 8, 1841–Dec. 29, 1902; House 1881–June 20, 1884, 1889–91.

MORGAN, Charles Henry (Mo.) July 5, 1842–Jan. 4, 1912; House 1875–79 (Democrat), 1883–85 (Democrat), 1893–95 (Democrat), 1909–11.

MORGAN, Dick Thompson (Okla.) Dec. 6, 1853–July 4, 1920; House 1909–July 4, 1920.

MORGAN, Edwin Barber (brother of Christopher Morgan, nephew of Noyes Barber) (N.Y.) May 2, 1806–Oct. 13, 1881; House 1853–59 (1853–57 Whig).

MORGAN, Edwin Dennison (cousin of Morgan Gardner Bulkeley) (N.Y.) Feb. 8, 1811–Feb. 14, 1883; Senate 1863–69; Chrmn. Rep. Nat. Comm. 1856–64, 1872–76; Gov. Jan. 1, 1859–Jan. 1, 1863.

MORGAN, James (N.J.) Dec. 29, 1756–Nov. 11, 1822; House 1811–13.

MORGAN, Stephen (Ohio) Jan. 25, 1854–Feb. 9, 1928; House 1899–1905.

MORGAN, William Mitchell (Ohio) Aug. 1, 1870–Sept. 17, 1935; House 1921–31.

MORIN, John Mary (Pa.) April 18, 1868–March 3, 1942; House 1913–29.

MORPHIS, Joseph Lewis (Miss.) April 17, 1831 –July 29, 1913; House Feb. 23, 1870–73.

MORRELL, Daniel Johnson (Pa.) Aug. 8, 1821–Aug. 20, 1885; House 1867–71.

MORRELL, Edward de Veaux (Pa.) Aug. 7, 1863 Sept. 1, 1917; House Nov. 6, 1900–07.

MORRIL David Lawrence (N.H.) June 10, 1772–Jan. 28, 1849; Senate 1817–23; Gov. June 3, 1824–June 7, 1827.

MORRILL, Anson Peaslee (brother of Lot Myrick Morrill)

(Maine) June 10, 1803–July 4, 1887; House 1861–63; Gov. Jan. 3, 1855–Jan. 2, 1856.

MORRILL, Edmund Needham (Kans.) Feb. 12, 1834–March 14, 1909; House 1883–91; Gov. Jan. 14, 1895–Jan. 11, 1897.

MORRILL, Justin Smith (Vt.) April 14, 1810–Dec. 28, 1898; House 1855–67 (1855–57 Whig, 1857–67 Republican); Senate 1867–Dec. 28, 1898 (1867–73 Union Republican).

MORRILL, Lot Myrick (brother of Anson Peaslee Morrill) (Maine) May 3, 1813–Jan. 10, 1883; Senate Jan. 17, 1861–69, Oct. 30, 1869–July 7, 1876; Gov. Jan. 8, 1858–Jan. 2, 1861; Secy. of the Treasury July 7, 1876–March 9, 1877.

MORRILL, Samuel Plummer (Maine) Feb. 11, 1816–Aug. 4, 1892; House 1869–71.

MORRIS, Daniel (N.Y.) Jan. 4, 1812–April 22, 1889; House 1863–67.

MORRIS, Edward Joy (Pa.) July 16, 1815–Dec. 31, 1881; House 1843–46 (Whig), 1857–June 8, 1861.

MORRIS, Robert Page Walter (Minn.) June 30, 1853–Dec. 16, 1924; House 1897–1903.

MORRISON, Sidney Wallace (Wash.) May 13, 1933–House 1981–93.

MORROW, Dwight Whitney (N.J.) Jan. 11, 1873–Oct. 5, 1931; Senate Dec. 3, 1930–Oct. 5, 1931.

MORROW, John (Va.) ?–?; House 1805–09.

MORROW, William W. (Calif.) July 15, 1843–July 24, 1929; House 1885–91.

MORSE, Elijah Adams (Mass.) May 25, 1841–June 5, 1898; House 1889–97.

MORSE, Elmer Addison (Wis.) May 11, 1870–Oct. 4, 1945; House 1907–13.

MORSE, Frank Bradford (Mass.) Aug. 7, 1921–; House 1961–May 1, 1972.

MORSE, Freeman Harlow (Maine) Feb. 19, 1807–Feb. 5, 1891; House 1843–45 (Whig), 1857–61.

MORSE, Oliver Andrew (N.Y.) March 26, 1815–April 20, 1870; House 1857–59.

MORTON, Levi Parsons (N.Y.) May 16, 1824–May 16, 1920; House 1879–March 21, 1881; Vice President 1889–93; Gov. Jan. 1, 1895–Jan. 1, 1897.

MORTON, Marcus (Mass.) Dec. 19, 1784–Feb. 6, 1864; House 1817–21; Gov. Feb. 6–May 26, 1825, Jan. 18, 1840–Jan. 7, 1841, Jan. 17, 1843–Jan. 3, 1844.

MORTON, Oliver Hazard Perry Throck (Ind.) Aug. 4, 1823–Nov. 1, 1877; Senate 1867–Nov. l, 1877; Gov. Jan. 16, 1861–Jan. 23, 1867.

MORTON, Rogers Clark Ballard (brother of Thruston Ballard Morton) (Md.) Sept. 19, 1914–April 19, 1979; House 1963–Jan. 29, 1971; Chrmn. Rep. Nat. Comm. April 1969–Jan. 1971; Secy. of the Interior Jan. 29, 1971–April 30, 1975; Secy. of Commerce May 1, 1975–Feb. 2, 1976.

MORTON, Thruston Ballard (brother of Rogers Clark Ballard Morton) (Ky.) Aug. 9, 1907–Aug. 14, 1982; House 1947–53; Senate 1957–69; Chrmn. Rep. Nat. Comm. April 1959–June 1961.

MOSES, George Higgins (N.H.) Feb. 9, 1869–Dec. 20, 1944; Senate Nov. 6, 1918–33; elected Pres. pro tempore March 6, 1925, Dec. 15, 1927.

MOSHER, Charles Adams (Ohio) May 7, 1906–Nov. 16, 1984; House 1961–77.

MOSS, Hunter Holmes, Jr. (W.Va.) May 26, 1874–July 15, 1916; House 1913–July 15, 1916.

MOSS, John McKenzie (nephew of James Andrew McKenzie) (Ky.) Jan. 3, 1868–June 11, 1929; House March 25, 1902–03.

MOTT, Gordon Newell (Nev.) Oct. 21, 1812–April 27, 1887; House (Terr. Del.) 1863–Oct. 31, 1864.

MOTT, James (N.J.) Jan. 18, 1739–Oct. 18, 1823; House 1801–05.

MOTT, James Wheaton (Oreg.) Nov. 12, 1883–Nov. 12, 1945; House 1933–Nov. 12, 1945.

MOTT, Luther Wright (N.Y.) Nov. 30, 1874–July 10, 1923; House 1911–July 10, 1923.

MOTT, Richard (Ohio) July 21, 1804–Jan. 22, 1888; House 1855–59.

MOUSER, Grant Earl (father of Grant Earl Mouser, Jr.) (Ohio) Sept. 11, 1868–May 6, 1949; House 1905–09.

MOUSER, Grant Earl Jr. (son of Grant Earl Mouser) (Ohio) Feb. 20, 1895–Dec. 21, 1943; House 1929–33.

MOXLEY, William James (Ill.) May 22, 1851–Aug. 4, 1938; House Nov. 23, 1909–11.

MOYNIHAN, Patrick Henry (Ill.) Sept. 25, 1869–May 20, 1946; House 1933–35.

MOZLEY, Norman Adolphus (Mo.) Dec. 11, 1865–May 9, 1922; House 1895–97.

MRUK, Joseph (N.Y.) Nov. 6, 1903–; House 1943–45.

MUDD, Sydney Emanuel (father of Sydney Emanuel Mudd, below) (Md.) Feb. 12, 1858–Oct. 21, 1911; House March 20, 1890–91, 1897–1911.

MUDD, Sydney Emanuel (son of Sydney Emanuel Mudd, above) (Md.) June 20, 1885–Oct. 11, 1924; House 1915–Oct. 11, 1924.

MUHLENBERG, Frederick Augustus (great-great-grandson of Frederick Augustus Conrad Muhlenberg, great-great-great-nephew of John Peter Gabriel Muhlenberg) (Pa.) Sept. 25, 1887–Jan. 19, 1980; House 1947–49.

MULDOWNEY, Michael Joseph (Pa.) Aug. 10, 1889–March 30, 1947; House 1933–35.

MULKEY, Frederick William (nephew of Joseph Norton Dolph) (Oreg.) Jan. 6, 1874–May 5, 1924; Senate Jan. 23–March 3, 1907, Nov. 6–Dec. 17, 1918.

MULLINS, James (Tenn.) Sept, 15, 1807–June 26, 1873; House 1867–69.

MUMFORD, George (N.C.) ?–Dec. 31, 1818; House 1817–Dec. 31, 1818.

MUMFORD, Gurdon Saltonstall (N.Y.) Jan. 29, 1764–April 30, 1831; House 1805–11.

MUMMA, Walter Mann (Pa.) Nov. 20, 1890–Feb. 25, 1961; House 1951–Feb. 25, 1961.

MUNDT, Karl Earl (S.Dak.) June 3, 1900–Aug. 16, 1974; House 1939–Dec. 30, 1948; Senate Dec. 31, 1948–73.

MURDOCK, Victor (Kans.) March 18, 1871–July 8, 1945; House May 26, 1903–15.

MURFREE, William Hardy (uncle of David W. Dickinson) (N.C.) Oct. 2, 1781–Jan. 19, 1827; House 1813–17.

MURKOWSKI, Frank Hughes (Alaska) March 28, 1933–; Senate 1981–; Chrmn. Senate Veterans' Affairs 1985–87; Chrmn. Senate Energy and Natural Resources Committee 1995–.

MURPHY, Arthur Phillips (Mo.) Dec. 10, 1870–Feb. 1, 1914; House 1905–07, 1909–11.

MURPHY, Benjamin Franklin (Ohio) Dec. 24, 1867–March 6, 1938; House 1919–33.

MURPHY, Everett Jerome (Ill.) July 24, 1852–April 10, 1922; House 1895–97.

MURPHY, George Lloyd (Calif.) July 4, 1902–May 3, 1992; Senate Jan. 1, 1965–Jan. 2, 1971.

MURPHY, Maurice J. Jr. (N.H.) Oct. 3, 1927–; Senate Dec. 7, 1961–Nov. 6, 1962.

MURPHY, Nathan Oakes (Ariz.) Oct. 14, 1849–Aug. 22, 1908; House (Terr. Del.) 1895–97; Gov. (Ariz. Terr.) 1892–94, 1898–1902.

MURRAY, Ambrose Spencer (brother of William Murray) (N.Y.) Nov. 27, 1807–Nov. 8, 1885; House 1855–59 (1855–57 Whig).

MURRAY, George Washington (S.C.) Sept. 22, 1853–April 21, 1926; House 1893–95, June 4, 1896–97.

MURRAY, John (Pa.) 1768–March 7, 1834; House Oct. 14, 1817–21.

MURRAY, Reid Fred (Wis.) Oct. 16, 1887–April 29, 1952; House 1939–April 29, 1952.

MYERS, Amos (Pa.) April 23, 1824–Oct. 18, 1893; House 1863–65.

MYERS, Gary Arthur (Pa.) Aug. 16, 1937–; House 1975–79.

MYERS, John Thomas (Ind.) Feb. 8, 1927–; House 1967–.

MYERS, Leonard (Pa.) Nov. 13, 1827–Feb. 11, 1905; House 1863–69, April 9, 1869–75.

MYRICK, Sue (N.C.) House, 1995–.

NAPIER, John Light (S.C.) May 16, 1947–; House 1981–83.

NAREY, Harry Elsworth (Iowa) May 15, 1885–Aug. 18, 1962; House Nov. 3, 1942–43.

NASH, Charles Edmund (La.) May 23, 1844–June 21, 1913; House 1875–77.

NEAL, Henry Safford (Ohio) Aug. 25, 1828–July 13, 1906; House 1877–83.

NEAL, William Elmer (W.Va.) Oct. 14, 1875–Nov. 12, 1959; House 1953–55, 1957–59.

NEEDHAM, James Carson (Calif.) Sept. 17, 1864–July 11, 1942; House 1899–1913.

NEGLEY, James Scott (Pa.) Dec. 22, 1826–Aug. 7, 1901; House 1869–75, 1885–87.

NELLIGAN, James Leo (Pa.) Feb. 14, 1929–; House 1981–83.

NELSEN, Ancher (Minn.) Oct. 11, 1904–Nov. 30, 1992; House 1959–Dec. 31, 1974.

NELSON, Adolphus Peter (Wis.) March 28, 1872–Aug. 21, 1927; House Nov. 5, 1918–23.

NELSON, Arthur Emanuel (Minn.) May 10, 1892–April 11, 1955; Senate Nov. 18, 1942–43.

NELSON, Charles Pembroke (son of John Edward Nelson) (Maine) July 2, 1907–June 8, 1962; House 1949–57.

NELSON, Hugh (Va.) Sept. 30, 1768–March 18, 1836; House 1811–Jan. 14, 1823.

NELSON, John Edward (father of Charles Pembroke Nelson) (Maine) July 12, 1874–April 11, 1955; House March 27, 1922–33.

NELSON, John Mandt (Wis.) Oct. 10, 1870–Jan. 29, 1955; House Sept. 4, 1906–19, 1921–33.

NELSON, Knute (Minn.) Feb. 2, 1843–April 28, 1923; House 1883–89; Senate 1895–April 28, 1923; Gov. Jan. 4, 1893–Jan. 31, 1895.

NELSON, Roger (father of John Nelson) (Md.) 1759–June 7, 1815; House Nov. 6, 1804–May 14, 1810.

NELSON, Thomas Maduit (Va.) Sept. 27, 1782–Nov. 10, 1853; House Dec. 4, 1816–19.

NESBITT, Wilson (S.C.) ?–May 13, 1861; House 1817–19.

NETHERCUTT, George (Wash.) House, 1995–.

NEUMANN, Mark W. (Wis.) House, 1995–.

NEVIN, Robert Murphy (Ohio) May 5, 1850–Dec. 17, 1912; House 1901–07.

NEW, Anthony (Ky.) 1747–March 2, 1833; House 1793–1805 (1793–95 no party Va.), 1811–13, 1817–19, 1821–23.

NEW, Harry Stewart (Ind.) Dec. 31, 1858–May 9, 1937; Senate 1917–23; Chrmn. Rep. Nat. Comm. 1907–08; Postmaster Gen. March 4, 1923–March 5, 1929.

NEWBERRY, John Stoughton (father of Truman Handy Newberry) (Mich.) Nov. 18, 1826–Jan. 2, 1887; House 1879–81.

NEWBERRY, Truman Handy (son of John Stoughton Newberry) (Mich.) Nov. 5, 1864–Oct. 3, 1945; Senate 1919–Nov. 18, 1922; Secy. of the Navy Dec. 1, 1908–March 5, 1909.

NEWBOLD, Thomas (N.J.) Aug. 2, 1760–Dec. 18, 1823; House 1807–13.

NEWCOMB, Carman Adam (Mo.) July 1, 1830–April 6, 1902; House 1867–69.

NEWELL, William Augustus (N.J.) Sept. 5, 1817–Aug. 8, 1901; House 1847–51 (Whig), 1865–67; Gov. Jan. 20, 1857–Jan. 17, 1860, (Wash. Terr.) 1880–84.

NEWHALL, Judson Lincoln (Ky.) March 26, 1870–July 23, 1952; House 1929–31.

NEWSHAM, Joseph Parkinson (La.) May 24, 1837–Oct. 22, 1919; House July 18, l868–69, May 23, 1870–71.

NEWTON, Cleveland Alexander (Mo.) Sept. 3, 1873–Sept. 17, 1945; House 1919–27.

NEWTON, Thomas Jr. (Va.) Nov. 21, 1768–Aug. 5, 1847; House 1801–29, March 4, 1829–March 9, 1830, 1831–33.

NEWTON, Walter Hughes (Minn.) Oct. 10, 1880–Aug. 10, 1941; House 1919–June 30, 1929.

NEY, Bob (Ohio) House, 1995–.

NICHOLAS, John (brother of Wilson Cary Nicholas, uncle of Robert Carter Nicholas) (Va.) about 1757–Dec. 31, 1819; House 1793–1801 (1793–95 no party).

NICHOLAS, Wilson Cary (brother of John Nicholas, uncle of Robert Carter Nicholas) (Va.) Jan. 31, 1761–Oct. 10, 1820; Senate Dec. 5, 1799–May 22, 1804; House 1807–Nov. 27, 1809; Gov. Dec. 1, 1814–Dec. 1, 1816.

NICHOLS, Charles Archibald (Mich.) Aug. 25, 1876–April 25, 1920; House 1915–April 25, 1920.

NICHOLS, Matthias H. (Ohio) Oct. 3, 1824–Sept. 15, 1862; House 1853–59 (1853–55 Democrat).

NICHOLS, Richard (Kans.) April 29, 1926–; House 1991–93.

NICHOLSON, Donald William (Mass.) Aug. 11, 1888–Feb. 16, 1968; House Nov. 18, 1947–59.

NICHOLSON, John (N.Y.) 1765–Jan. 20, 1820; House 1809–11.

NICHOLSON, Joseph Hopper (Md.) May 15, 1770–March 4, 1817; House 1799–March 1, 1806.

NICHOLSON, Samuel Danford (Colo.) Feb. 22, 1859–March 24, 1923; Senate 1921–March 24, 1923.

NICKLES, Donald Lee (Okla.) Dec. 6, 1948–; Senate 1981–.

NIEDRINGHAUS, Frederick Gottlieb (uncle of Henry Frederick Niedringhaus) (Mo.) Oct. 21, 1837–Nov. 25, 1922; House 1889–91.

NIEDRINGHAUS, Henry Frederick (nephew of Frederick Gottlieb Niedringhaus) (Mo.) Dec. 15, 1864–Aug. 3, 1941; House 1927–33.

NIELSON, Howard Curtis (Utah) Sept. 12, 1924–House 1983–91.

NILES, Jason (Miss.) Dec. 19, 1814–July 7, 1894; House 1873–75.

NIMTZ, F. Jay (Ind.) Dec. 1, 1915–; House 1967–59.

NIXON, George Stuart (Nev.) April 2, 1860–June 6, 1912; Senate 1905–June 5, 1912.

NIXON, John Thompson (N.J.) Aug. 31, 1820–Sept. 28, 1889; House 1859–67.

NIXON, Richard Milhous (Calif.) Jan. 9, 1913–April 22, 1994; House 1947–Nov. 30, 1950; Senate Dec. 1, 1950–Jan. 1, 1953; Vice President 1953–61; President 1969–Aug. 9, 1974.

NOBLE, James (Ind.) Dec. 16, 1785–Feb. 26, 1831; Senate Dec. 11, 1816–Feb. 26, 1831.

NODAR, Robert Joseph Jr. (N.Y.) March 23, 1916–Sept. 11, 1974; House 1947–49.

NOLAN, John Ignatius (husband of Mae Ella Nolan) (Calif.) Jan. 14, 1874–Nov. 18, 1922; House 1913–Nov. 18, 1922.

NOLAN, Mae Ella (widow of John Ignatius Nolan) (Calif.) Sept. 20, 1886–July 9, 1973; House Jan. 23, 1923–25.

NOLAN, William Ignatius (Minn.) May 14, 1874–Aug. 3, 1943; House June 17–1929–33.

NOONAN, George Henry (Tex.) Aug. 20, 1828–Aug. 17, 1907; House 1895–91.

NORBECK, Peter (S.Dak.) Aug. 27, 1870–Dec. 20, 1936; Senate 1921–Dec. 20, 1936; Gov. Jan. 2, 1917–Jan. 4, 1921.

NORBLAD, Albin Walter Jr. (Oreg.) Sept. 12, 1908–Sept. 20, 1964; House Jan. 11, 1946–Sept. 20, 1964.

NORCROSS, Amas (Mass.) Jan. 26, 1824–April 2, 1898; House 1877–83.

NORMAN, Fred Barthold (Wash.) March 21, 1882–April 18, 1947; House 1943–45, Jan. 3–April 18, 1947.

NORRIS, Benjamin White (Ala.) Jan. 22, 1819–Jan. 26, 1873; House July 21, 1868–69.

NORTH, Solomon Taylor (Pa.) May 24, 1853–Oct. 19, 1917; House 1915–17.

NORTHWAY, Stephen Asa (Ohio) June 19, 1833–Sept. 8, 1898; House 1893–Sept. 8, 1898.

NORTON, Jesse Olds (Ill.) Dec. 25, 1812–Aug. 3, 1875; House 1853–57 (1853–55 Whig), 1863–65.

NORTON, Miner Gibbs (Ohio) May 11, 1857–Sept. 7, 1926; House 1921–23.

NORTON, Nelson Ira (N.Y.) March 30, l820–Oct.28, 1887; House Dec. 6, 1875–77.

NORTON, Patrick Daniel (N.Dak.) May 17, 1876–Oct. 14, 1953; House 1913–19.

NORWOOD, Charlie (Ga.) House, 1995–.

NUNN, David Alexander (Tenn.) July 26, 1833–Sept. 11, 1918; House 1867–69, 1873–75.

NUSSLE, James (Iowa) June 27, 1960–; House 1991–.

NUTE, Alonzo (N.H.) Feb. 12, 1826–Dec. 24, 1892; House 1889–91.

NUTTING, Newton Wright (N.Y.) Oct. 22, 1840–Oct. 15, 1889; House 1883–85, 1887–Oct. 15, 1889.

NYE, Frank Mellen (Minn.) March 7, 1852–Nov. 29, 1935; House 1907–13.

NYE, Gerald Prentice (N.Dak.) Dec. 19, 1892–July 17, 1971; Senate Nov. 14, 1925–45.

NYE, James Warren (Nev.) June 10, 1815–Dec. 25, 1876; Senate Dec. 16, 1864–73; Gov. (Nev. Terr.) 1861–64.

NYGAARD, Hjaimar Carl (N.Dak.) March 24, 1906–July 18, 1963; House 1961–July 18, 1963.

OAKEY, Peter Davis (Conn.) Feb. 25, 1861–Nov. 18, 1920; House 1915–17.

OAKMAN, Charles Gibb (Mich.) Sept. 4, 1903–Oct. 28, 1973; House 1953–55.

O'BRIEN, George Miller (Ill.) June 17, 1917–July 17, 1986; House 1973–July 17, 1986.

O'BRIEN, Joseph John (N.Y.) Oct. 9, 1897–Jan. 23, 1953; House 1939–45.

O'CONNOR, Charles (Okla.) Oct. 26, 1878–Nov. 15, 1940; House 1929–31.

ODDIE, Tasker Lowndes (Nev.) Oct. 20, 1870–Feb. 17, 1950; Senate 1921–33; Gov. Jan. 2, 1911–Jan. 4, 1915.

ODELL, Benjamin Baker Jr. (N.Y.) Jan. 14, 1854–May 9, 1926; House 1895–99; Gov. Jan. 1, 1901–Jan. 1, 1905.

O'DONNELL, James (Mich.) March 25, 1840–March 17, 1915; House 1885–93.

OGDEN, Charles Franklin (Ky.) ?–April 10, 1933; House 1919–23.

OGLE, Alexander (father of Charles Ogle, grandfather of Andrew Jackson Ogle) (Pa.) Aug. 10, 1766–Oct. 14, 1832; House 1817–19.

OGLESBY, Richard James (cousin of Woodson Ratcliffe Oglesby) (Ill.) July 25, 1824–April 24, 1899; Senate 1873–79; Gov. Jan. 16, 1865–Jan. 11, 1869, Jan. 13–Jan. 23, 1873, Jan. 30, 1885–Jan. 14, 1889.

O'GRADY, James Mary Early (N.Y.) March 31, 1863–Nov. 3, 1928; House 1899–1901.

O'HARA, James Edward (N.C.) Feb. 26, 1844–Sept. 15, 1905; House 1883–87.

O'HARA, Joseph Patrick (Minn.) Jan. 23, 1895–March 4,1975; House 1941–59.

O'KONSKI, Alvin Edward (Wis.) May 26, 1904–July 8, 1987; House 1943–73.

OLCOTT, Jacob Van Vechten (N.Y.) May 17, 1856–June 1, 1940; House 1905–11.

OLIN, Abram Baldwin (son of Gideon Olin, cousin of Henry Olin) (N.Y.) Sept. 21, 1808–Juiy 7, 1879; House 1857–63.

OLIN, Gideon (father of Abram Baldwin Olin, uncle of Henry Olin) (Vt.) Nov. 2, 1743–Jan. 21, 1823; House 1803–07.

OLIVER, George Tener (Pa.) Jan. 26, 1848–Jan. 22, 1919; Senate March 17, 1909–17.

OLIVER, Samuel Addison (Iowa) July 21, 1833–July 7, 1912; House 1875–79.

OLMSTED, Marlin Edgar (Pa.) May 21, 1847–July 19, 1913; House 1897–1913.

OLPP, Archibald Ernest (N.J.) May 12, 1882–July 26, 1949; House 1921–23.

O'NEILL, Charles (Pa.) March 21, 1821–Nov. 25, 1893; House 1863–71, 1873–Nov. 25, 1893.

ORMSBY, Stephen (Ky.) 1759–1844; House 1811–13, April 20, 1813–17.

ORR, Alexander Dalrymple (nephew of William Grayson, cousin of William John Grayson) (Ky.) Nov. 6, 1761–June 21, 1835; House Nov. 8, 1792–97 (Nov. 8, 1792–95 no party).

ORR, Jackson (Iowa) Sept. 21, 1832–March 15, 1926; House 1871–75.

ORTH, Godlove Stein (Ind.) April 22, 1817–Dec. 16, 1882; House 1863–71, 1873–75, 1879–Dec. 16, 1882.

OSBORN, Thomas Ward (Fla.) March 9, 1836–Dec. 18, 1898; Senate June 25, 1868–73.

OSBORNE, Edwin Sylvanus (Pa.) Aug. 7, 1839–Jan. 1, 1900; House 1885–91.

OSBORNE, Henry Zenas (Calif.) Oct. 4, 1848–Feb. 8, 1923; House 1917–Feb. 8, 1923.

OSMER, James H. (Pa.) Jan. 23, 1832–Oct. 3, 1912; House 1879–81.

OSMERS, Frank Charles Jr. (N.J.) Dec. 30, 1907–May 21, 1977; House 1939–43, Nov. 6, 1951–65.

OSTERTAG, Harold Charles (N.Y.) June 22, 1896–May 2, 1985; House 1951–65.

OTERO, Mariano Sabino (nephew of Miguel Antonio Otero) (N.Mex.) Aug. 29, 1844–Feb. 1, 1904; House (Terr. Del.) 1879–81.

OTIS, Norton Prentiss (N.Y.) March 18, 1840–Feb. 20, 1905; House 1903–Feb. 20, 1905.

OTJEN, Theobald (Wis.) Oct. 27, 1851–April 11, 1924; House 1895–1907.

OVERSTREET, Jesse (Ind.) Dec. 14, 1859–May 27, 1910; House 1895–1909.

OVERTON, Edward Jr. (Pa.) Feb. 4, 1836–Sept. 18, 1903; House 1877–81.

OWEN, James (N.C.) Dec. 7, 1784–Sept. 4, 1866; House 1817–19.

OWEN, William Dale (Ind.) Sept. 6, 1846–1906; House 1885–91.

OWENS, Thomas Leonard (Ill.) Dec. 21, 1897–June 7, 1948; House 1947–June 7, 1948.

OXLEY, Michael Garver (Ohio) Feb. 11, 1944–; House June 25, 1981–.

PACHECO, Romualdo (Calif.) Oct. 31, 1831–Jan. 23, 1899; House 1877–Feb. 7, 1878, 1879–83; Gov. Feb. 27–Dec. 9, 1875.

PACKARD, Jasper (Ind.) Feb. 1, 1832–Dec. 13, 1899; House 1869–75.

PACKARD, Ronald C. (Calif.) Jan. 19, 1931–; House 1983–.

PACKER, Horace Billings (Pa.) Oct. 11, 1861–April 13, 1940; House 1897–1901.

PACKER, John Black (Pa.) March 21, 1824–July 7, 1891; House 1869–77.

PACKWOOD, Robert William (Oreg.) Sept. 11, 1932–; Senate 1969–1995; Chrmn. Senate Commerce, Science and Transportation 1981–85; Chrmn. Senate Finance 1985–87, 1993–95.

PADDOCK, Algernon Sidney (Nebr.) Nov. 9, 1830–Oct. 17, 1897; Senate 1875–81, 1887–93.

PADDOCK, George Arthur (Ill.) March 24, 1885–Dec. 29, 1964; House 1941–43.

PAGE, Carroll Smalley (Vt.) Jan. 10, 1843–Dec. 3, 1925; Senate Oct. 21, 1908–23; Gov. Oct. 2, 1890–Oct. 6, 1892.

PAGE, Horace Francis (Calif.) Oct. 20, 1833–Aug. 23, 1890; House 1873–83.

PAGE, John (Va.) April 17, 1743–Oct. 11, 1808; House 1789–97 (1789–95 no party); Gov. Dec. 1, 1802–Dec. 1, 1805 (Democratic Republican).

PAIGE, Calvin DeWitt (Mass.) May 20, 1848–April 24, 1930; House Nov. 26, 1913–25.

PAINE, Halbert Eleazer (Wis.) Feb. 4, 1826–April 14, 1905; House 1865–71.

PALMER, Beriah (N.Y.) 1740–May 20, 1812; House 1803–05.

PALMER, Cyrus Maffet (Pa.) Feb. 12, 1887–Aug. 16, 1959; House 1927–29.

PALMER, Francis Wayland "Frank" (Iowa) Oct. 11, 1827–Dec. 3, 1907; House 1869–73.

PALMER, George William (nephew of John Palmer, cousin of William Elisha Haynes) (N.Y.) Jan. 13, 1818–March 2, 1916; House 1857–61.

PALMER, Henry Wilber (Pa.) July 10, 1839–Feb. 15, 1913; House 1901–07, 1909–11.

PALMER, John William (Mo.) Aug. 20, 1866–Nov. 3, 1958; House 1929–31.

PALMER, Thomas Witherell (Mich.) Jan. 25, 1830–June 1, 1913; Senate 1883–89.

PALMER, William Adams (Vt.) Sept. 12, 1781–Dec. 3, 1860; Senate Oct. 20, 1818–25; Gov. Oct. 18, 1831–Nov. 2, 1835 (Anti–Mason Democrat).

PARKER, Abraham X. (N.Y.) Nov. 14, 1831–Aug. 9, 1909; House 1881–89.

PARKER, Isaac Charles (Mo.) Oct. 15, 1838–Nov. 17, 1896; House 1871–75.

PARKER, James (Mass.) 1768–Nov. 9, 1837; House 1813–15, 1819–21.

PARKER, James (grandfather of Richard Wayne Parker) (N.J.) March 3, 1776–April 1, 1868; House 1833–37.

PARKER, James Southworth (N.Y.) June 3, 1867–Dec. 19, 1933; House 1913–Dec. 19, 1933.

PARKER, John Mason (N.Y.) June 14, 1805–Dec. 16, 1873; House 1855–59 (1855–57 Whig).

PARKER, Mel Michael "Mike" (Miss.) Oct. 31, 1949–; House May 17, 1980– (Democrat until 1995).

PARKER, Nahum (N.H.) March 4, 1760–Nov. 12, 1839; Senate 1807–June 1, 1810.

PARKER, Paul Michael "Mike" (Miss.) Oct. 31, 1949–; House 1989–.

PARKER, Richard Wayne (grandson of James Parker) (N.J.) Aug. 6, 1848–Nov. 28, 1923; House 1896–1911, Dec. 1, 1914–19, 1921–23.

PARRAN, Thomas (Md.) Feb. 12, 1860–March 29, 1955; House 1911–13.

PARRIS, Albion Keith (cousin of Virgil Delphini Parris) (Maine) Jan. 19, 1788–Feb. 11, 1857; House 1815–Feb. 3, 1818 (Mass.); Senate 1827–Aug. 26, 1828; Gov. Jan. 5, 1822–Jan. 3, 1827 (Democratic Republican).

PARRIS, Stanford E. (Va.) Sept. 9, 1929–; House 1973–75, 1981–91.

PARROTT, Marcus Junius (Kans.) Oct. 27, 1828–Oct. 4, 1879; House (Terr. Del.) 1857–Jan. 29, 1861.

PARSONS, Herbert (N.Y.) Oct. 28, 1869–Sept. 16, 1925; House 1905–11.

PARSONS, Richard Chappel (Ohio) Oct. 10, 1826–Jan. 9, 1899; House 1873–75.

PARTRIDGE, Donald Barrows (Maine) June 7, 1891–June 5, 1946; House 1931–33.

PARTRIDGE, Frank Charles (Vt.) May 7, 1861–March 2, 1943; Senate Dec. 23, 1930–March 31, 1931.

PASHAYAN, Charles "Chip" Jr. (Calif.) March 27, 1941–; House 1979–91.

PATERSON, John (N.Y.) 1744–July 19, 1808; House 1803–05.

PATTEN, John (Del.) April 26, 1746–Dec. 26, 1800; House 1793–Feb. 14, 1794 (no party), 1795–97; Cont. Cong. 1786.

PATTERSON, Francis Ford Jr. (N.J.) July 30, 1867–Nov. 30, 1935; House Nov. 2, 1920–27.

PATTERSON, George Robert (Pa.) Nov. 9, 1863–March 21, 1906; House 1901–March 21, 1906.

PATTERSON, George Washington (brother of William Patterson, uncle of Augustus Frank) (N.Y.) Nov. 11, 1799–Oct. 15, 1879; House 1877–79.

PATTERSON, James Thomas (Conn.) Oct. 20, 1908–Feb. 7, 1989; House 1947–59.

PATTERSON, James Willis (N.H.) July 2, 1823–May 4, 1893; House 1863–67; Senate 1867–73.

PATTERSON, John James (S.C.) Aug. 8, 1830–Sept. 28, 1912; Senate 1873–79.

PATTERSON, Roscoe Conkling (Mo.) Sept. 15, 1876–Oct. 22, 1954; House 1921–23; Senate 1929–35.

PATTERSON, Thomas (half-brother of John Patterson) (Pa.) Oct. 1, 1764–Nov. 16, 1841; House 1817–25.

PATTON, John (father of Charles Emory Patton and John Patton Jr., uncle of William Irvin Swoope) (Pa.) Jan. 6, 1823–Dec. 23, 1897; House 1861–63, 1887–89.

PATTON, John Jr. (son of John Patton, brother of Charles Emory Patton, cousin of William Irvin Swoope) (Mich.) Oct. 30, 1850–May 24, 1907; Senate May 5, 1894–Jan. 14, 1895.

PAUL, John (Va.) Dec. 9, 1883–Feb. 13, 1964; House Dec. 15, 1922–23.

PAUL, Ronald Ernest (Tex.) Aug. 20, 1935–; House April 3, 1976–77, 1979–85.

PAULDING, William Jr. (N.Y.) March 7, 1770–Feb. 11, 1854; House 1811–13.

PAXON, L. William (husband of Susan Molinari) (N.Y.) April 29, 1954–; House 1989–.

PAYNE, Frederick George (Maine) July 24, 1904–June 15, 1978; Senate 1953–59; Gov. Jan. 5, 1949–Dec. 25, 1952.

PAYNE, Sereno Blisha (N.Y.) June 26, 1843–Dec. 10, 1914; House 1883–87, 1889–Dec. 10, 1914; House majority leader 1899–1911.

PAYSON, Lewis Edwin (Ill.) Sept. 17, 1840–Oct. 4, 1909; House 1881–91.

PEARCE, Charles Edward (Mo.) May 29, 1842–Jan. 30, 1902; House 1897–1901.

PEARCE, John Jamison (Pa.) Feb. 28, 1826–May 26, 1912; House 1855–57.

PEARRE, George Alexander (Md.) July 16, 1860–Sept. 19, 1923; House 1899–1911.

PEARSON, James Blackwood (Kans.) May 7, 1920–; Senate Jan. 31, 1962–Dec. 23, 1978.

PEARSON, Richmond (N.C.) Jan. 26, 1852–Sept. 12, 1923; House 1895–99, May 10, 1900–01.

PEASE, Henry Roberts (Miss.) Feb. 19, 1835–Jan. 2, 1907; Senate Feb. 3, 1874–75.

PEAVEY, Hubert Haskell (Wis.) Jan. 12, 1881–Nov. 21, 1937; House 1923–35.

PECK, Erasmus Darwin (Ohio) Sept. 16, 1808–Dec. 25, 1876; House April 23, 1870–73.

PEDDIE, Thomas Baldwin (N.J.) Feb. 11, 1808–Feb. 16, 1889; House 1877–79.

PEELLE, Stanton Judkins (Ind.) Feb. 11, 1843–Sept. 4, 1928; House 1881–May 22, 1884.

PEGRAM, John (Va.) Nov. 16, 1773–April 8, 1831; House April 21, 1818–19.

PEIRCE, Robert Bruce Fraser (Ind.) Feb. 17, 1843–Dec. 5, 1898; House 1881–83.

PELHAM, Charles (Ala.) March 12, 1835–Jan. 18, 1908; House 1873–75.

PELLY, Thomas Minor (Wash.) Aug. 22, 1902–Nov. 21, 1973; House 1953–73.

PENDLETON, James Monroe (R.I.) Jan. 10, 1822–Feb. 16, 1889; House 1871–75.

PENNINGTON, William (cousin of Alexander Cumming McWhorter Pennington) (N.J.) May 4, 1796–Feb. 16, 1862; House 1859–61; Speaker Feb. 1, 1860–61; Gov. Oct. 27, 1837–Oct. 27, 1843 (Democratic Republican).

PENROSE, Boies (Pa.) Nov. 1, 1860–Dec. 31, 1921; Senate 1897–Dec. 31, 1921.

PEPPER, George Wharton (Pa.) March 16, 1867–May 24, 1961; Senate Jan. 9, 1922–27.

PERCE, Legrand Winfield (Miss.) June 19, 1836–March 16, 1911; House Feb. 23, 1870–73.

PERCY, Charles Harting (father-in-law of John Davison "Jay" Rockefeller IV) (Ill.) Sept. 27, 1919–; Senate 1967–85; Chrmn. Senate Foreign Relations 1981–85.

PEREA, Francisco (cousin of Pedro Perea) (N.Mex.) Jan. 9, 1830–May 21, 1913; House (Terr. Del.) 1863–65.

PEREA, Pedro (cousin of Francisco Perea) (N.Mex.) April 22, 1842–Jan. 11, 1906; House (Terr. Del.) 1899–1901.

PERHAM, Sidney (Maine) March 27, 1819–April 10, 1907; House 1863–69; Gov. Jan. 4, 1871–Jan. 7, 1874.

PERKINS, Bishop Walden (Kans.) Oct. 18, 1841–June 20, 1894; House 1883–91; Senate Jan. 1, 1892–93.

PERKINS, George Clement (Calif.) Aug. 23, 1839–Feb. 26, 1923; Senate July 26, 1893–1915; Gov. Jan. 8, 1880–Jan. 10, 1883.

PERKINS, George Douglas (Iowa) Feb. 29, 1840–Feb. 3, 1914; House 1891–99.

PERKINS, James Breck (N.Y.) Nov. 4, 1847–March 11, 1910; House 1901–March 11, 1910.

PERKINS, Randolph (N.J.) Nov. 30, 1871–May 25, 1936; House 1921–May 25, 1936.

PERLMAN, Nathan David (N.Y.) Aug. 2, 1887–June 29, 1952; House Nov. 2, 1920–27.

PERRY, Aaron Fyfe (Ohio) Jan. 1, 1815–March 11, 1893; House 1871–72.

PERRY, John Jasiel (Maine) Aug. 21, 1811–May 2, 1897; House 1855–57, 1859–61.

PERSON, Seymour Howe (Mich.) Feb. 2, 1879–April 7, 1957; House 1931–33.

PETERS, John Andrew (uncle of John Andrew Peters, below) (Maine) Oct. 9, 1822–April 2, 1904; House 1867–73.

PETERS, John Andrew (nephew of John Andrew Peters, above) (Maine) Aug. 13, 1864–Aug. 22, 1953; House Sept. 8, 1913–Jan. 2, 1922.

PETERS, Samuel Ritter (Kans.) Aug. 16, 1842–April 21, 1910; House 1883–91.

PETERSEN, Andrew Nicholas (N.Y.) March 10, 1870–Sept. 28, 1952; House 1921–23.

PETRI, Thomas Evert (Wis.) May 28, 1940–; House April 3, 1979–.

PETTIBONE, Augustus Herman (Tenn.) Jan. 21, 1835–Nov. 26, 1918; House 1881–87.

PETTIGREW, Richard Franklin (S.Dak.) July 23, 1848–Oct. 5, 1926; House (Terr. Del.) 1881–83; Senate Nov. 2, 1889–1901.

PETTIS, Jerry Lyle (husband of Shirley Neal Pettis) (Calif.) July 18, 1916–Feb. 14, 1975; House 1967–Feb. 14, 1975.

PETTIS, Shirley Neal (widow of Jerry Lyle Pettis) (Calif.) July 12, 1924–; House April 29, 1975–79.

PETTIS, Solomon Newton (Pa.) Oct. 10, 1827–Sept. 18, 1900; House Dec. 7, 1868–69.

PETTIT, John Upfold (Ind.) Sept. 11, 1820–March 21, 1881; House 1855–61.

PFEIFFER, William Louis (N.Y.) May 29, 1907–; House 1949–51.

PHEIFFER, William Townsend (N.Y.) July 15, 1898–Aug. 16, 1986; House 1941–43.

PHELPS, Darwin (Pa.) April 17, 1807–Dec. 14, 1879; House 1869–71.

PHELPS, Oliver (N.Y.) Oct. 21, 1749–Feb. 21, 1809; House 1803–05.

PHELPS, Timothy Guy (Calif.) Dec. 20, 1824–June 11, 1899; House 1861–63.

PHELPS, William Walter (N.J.) Aug. 24, 1839–June 17, 1894; House 1873–75 (no party), 1883–89.

PHILLIPS, Dayton Edward (Tenn.) March 29, 1910–Oct. 23, 1980; House 1947–51.

PHILLIPS, Fremont Orestes (Ohio) March 16, 1856–Feb. 21, 1936; House 1899–1901.

PHILLIPS, John (Calif.) Sept. 11, 1887–Dec. 18, 1983; House 1943–57.

PHILLIPS, Thomas Wharton (father of Thomas Wharton Phillips Jr.) (Pa.) Feb. 23, 1835–July 21, 1912; House 1893–97.

PHILLIPS, Thomas Wharton Jr. (son of Thomas Wharton Phillips) (Pa.) Nov. 21, 1874–Jan. 2, 1956; House 1923–27.

PHILLIPS, William Addison (Kans.) Jan. 14, 1824–Nov. 30, 1893; House 1873–79.

PHIPPS, Lawrence Cowle (Colo.) Aug. 30, 1862–March 1, 1958; Senate 1919–31.

PICKENS, Israel (Ala.) Jan. 30, 1780–April 24, 1827; House 1811–17 (N.C.); Senate Feb. 17–Nov. 27, 1826; Gov. Nov. 9, 1821–Nov. 25, 1825 (Democratic Republican).

PICKETT, Charles Edgar (Iowa) Jan. 14, 1866–July 20, 1930; House 1909–13.

PICKLER, John Alfred (S.Dak.) Jan. 24, 1844–June 13, 1910; House Nov. 2, 1889–97.

PIERCE, Charles Wilson (Ala.) Oct. 7, 1823–Feb. 18, 1907; House July 21, 1868–69.

PIERCE, Gilbert Ashville (N.Dak.) Jan. 11, 1839–Feb. 15, 1901; Senate Nov. 21, 1889–91; Gov. (Dakota Terr.) 1884–86.

PIERCE, Henry Lillie (Mass.) Aug. 23, 1825–Dec. 17, 1896; House Dec. 1, 1873–77.

PIERCE, Ray Vaughn (N.Y.) Aug. 6, 1840–Feb. 4, 1914; House 1879–Sept. 18, 1880.

PIERCE, Wallace Edgar (N.Y.) Dec. 9, 1881–Jan. 3, 1940; House 1939–Jan. 3, 1940.

PIKE, Austin Franklin (N.H.) Oct. 16, 1819–Oct. 8, 1886; House 1873–75; Senate 1883–Oct. 8, 1886.

PIKE, Frederick Augustus (Maine) Dec. 9, 1816–Dec. 2, 1886; House 1861–69.

PIKE, James (N.H.) Nov. 10, 1818–July 26, 1895; House 1855–59 (1855–57 American Party).

PILE, William Anderson (Mo.) Feb. 11, 1829–July 7, 1889; House 1867–69; Gov. (N.Mex. Terr.) 1869, 1870.

PILES, Samuel Henry (Wash.) Dec. 28, 1858–March 11, 1940; Senate 1905–11.

PILLION, John Raymond (N.Y.) Aug. 10, 1904–Dec. 31, 1978; House 1953–65.

PINCKNEY, Charles (father of Henry Laurens Pinckney, father-in-law of Robert Young Hayne) (S.C.) Oct. 26, 1757–Oct. 29, 1824; Senate Dec. 6, 1798–1801; House 1819–21; Cont. Cong. 1785–87; Gov. Jan. 26, 1789–Dec. 5, 1792, Dec. 8, 1796–Dec. 6, 1798, Dec. 9, 1806–Dec. 10, 1808.

PINE, William Bliss (Okla.) Dec. 30, 1877–Aug. 25, 1942; Senate 1925–31.

PINKNEY, William (Md.) March 17, 1764–Feb. 25, 1822; House March 4–Nov. 1791 (no party), 1815–April 18, 1816 (no party); Senate Dec. 21, 1819–Feb. 25, 1822; Atty. Gen. Dec. 11, 1811–Feb. 10, 1814.

PIPER, William (Pa.) Jan. 1, 1774–1852; House 1811–17.

PIRCE, William Almy (R.I.) Feb. 29, 1824–March 5, 1891; House 1885–Jan. 25, 1887.

PIRNIE, Alexander (N.Y.) April 16, 1903–June 12, 1982; House 1959–73.

PITNEY, Mahlon (N.J.) Feb. 5, 1858–Dec. 9, 1924; House 1895–Jan. 10, 1899; Assoc. Justice Supreme Court March 18, 1912–Dec. 31, 1922.

PITTENGER, William Alvin (Minn.) Dec. 29, 1885–Nov. 26, 1951; House 1929–33, 1935–37, 1939–47.

PLAISTED, Harris Merrill (Maine) Nov. 2, 1828–Jan. 31, 1898; House Sept. 13, 1875–77; Gov. Jan. 13, 1881–Jan. 3, 1883 (Democrat).

PLANTS, Tobias Avery (Ohio) March 17, 1811–June 19, 1887; House 1865–69.

PLATT, Edmund (N.Y.) Feb. 2, 1865–Aug. 7, 1939; House 1913–June 7, 1920.

PLATT, James Henry Jr. (Va.) July 13, 1837–Aug. 13, 1894; House Jan. 26, 1870–75.

PLATT, Orville Hitchcock (Conn.) July 19, 1827–April 21, 1905; Senate 1879–April 21, 1905.

PLATT, Thomas Collier (N.Y.) July 15, 1833–March 6, 1910; House 1873–77; Senate March 4–May 16, 1881, 1897–1909.

PLEASANTS, James (Va.) Oct. 24, 1769–Nov. 9, 1836; House 1811–Dec. 14, 1819; Senate Dec. 14, 1819–Dec. 15, 1822; Gov. Dec. 1, 1822–Dec. 10, 1825.

PLOESER, Walter Christian (Mo.) Jan. 7, 1907–; House 1941–49; Chrmn. House Select Committee on Small Business 1947–49.

PLUMB, Preston B. (Kans.) Oct. 12, 1837–Dec. 20, 1891; Senate 1877–Dec. 20, 1891.

PLUMB, Ralph (Ill.) March 29, 1816–April 8, 1903; House 1885–89.

PLUMLEY, Charles Albert (son of Frank Plumley) (Vt.) April 14, 1875–Oct. 31, 1964; House Jan. 16, 1934–51.

PLUMLEY, Frank (father of Charles Albert Plumley) (Vt.) Dec. 17, 1844–April 30, 1924; House 1909–16.

POFF, Richard Harding (Va.) Oct. 19, 1923–; House 1953–Aug. 29, 1972.

POINDEXTER, Miles (Wash.) April 22, 1868–Sept. 21, 1946; House 1909–11; Senate 1911–23.

POLAND, Luke Potter (Vt.) Nov. 1, 1815–July 2, 1887; Senate Nov. 21, 1865–67; House 1867–75, 1883–85.

POLLARD, Ernest Mark (Nebr.) April 15, 1869–Sept. 24, 1939; House July 18, 1905–09.

POLLARD, Henry Moses (Mo.) June 14, 1836–Feb. 24, 1904; House 1877–79.

POLLOCK, Howard Wallace (Alaska) April 11, 1920–; House 1967–71.

POLSLEY, Daniel Haymond (W.Va.) Nov. 28, 1803–Oct. 14, 1877; House 1867–69.

POMBO, Richard William (Calif.) Jan. 8, 1961–; House 1993–.

POMEROY, Charles (Iowa) Sept. 3, 1825–Feb. 11, 1891; House 1869–71.

POMEROY, Samuel Clarke (Kans.) Jan. 3, 1816–Aug. 27, 1891; Senate April 4, 1861–73.

POMEROY, Theodore Medad (N.Y.) Dec. 31, 1824–March 23, 1905; House 1861–69; Speaker March 3, 1869.

POND, Benjamin (N.Y.) 1768–Oct. 6, 1814; House 1811–13.

POOL, John (uncle of Walter Freshwater Pool) (N.C.) June 16, 1826–Aug. 16, 1884; Senate July 4, 1868–73.

POOL, Walter Freshwater (nephew of John Pool) (N.C.) Oct. 10, 1850–Aug. 25, 1883; House March 4–Aug. 25, 1883.

POOLE, Theodore Lewis (N.Y.) April 10, 1840–Dec. 23, 1900; House 1895–97.

PORTER, Albert Gallatin (Ind.) April 20, 1824–May 3, 1897; House 1859–63; Gov. Jan. 10, 1881–Jan. 12, 1885.

PORTER, Charles Howell (Va.) June 21, 1833–July 9, 1897; House Jan. 26, 1870–73.

PORTER, James (N.Y.) April 18, 1787–Feb. 7, 1839; House 1817–19.

PORTER, John Edward (Ill.) June 1, 1935–; House Jan. 22, 1980–.

PORTER, Peter Buell (grandfather of Peter Augustus Porter, uncle of Augustus Seymour Porter) (N.Y.) Aug. 14, 1773–March 20, 1844; House 1809–13, 1815–Jan. 23, 1816; Secy. of War May 26, 1828–March 9, 1829.

PORTER, Stephen Geyer (Pa.) May 18, 1869–June 27, House 1911–June 27, 1930.

PORTMAN, Robert Jones (Ohio) Dec. 19, 1955–; House May 5, 1993–.

POSEY, Francis Blackburn (Ind.) April 28, 1848–Oct. 31, 1915; House Jan. 29–March 3, 1889.

POST, Philip Sidney (Ill.) March 19, 1833–Jan. 6, 1895; House 1887–Jan. 6, 1895.

POSTON, Charles Debrille (Ariz.) April 20, 1825–June 24, 1902; House (Terr. Del.) Dec. 5, 1864–65.

POTTER, Charles Edward (Mich.) Oct. 30, 1916–Nov. 23, 1979; House Aug. 26, 1947–Nov. 4, 1952; Senate Nov. 5, 1952–59.

POTTER, John Fox (Wis.) May 11, 1817–May 18, 1899; House 1857–63.

POTTER, Samuel John (R.I.) June 29, 1753–Oct. 14, 1804; Senate 1803–Oct. 14, 1804.

POTTLE, Emory Bemsley (N.Y.) July 4, 1815–April 18, 1891; House 1857–61.

POTTS, David Matthew (N.Y.) March 12, 1906–Sept. 11, 1976; House 1947–49.

POULSON, C. Norris (Calif.) July 23, 1895–Sept. 25, 1982; House 1943–46, 1947–June 11, 1953.

POUND, Thaddeus Coleman (Wis.) Dec. 6, 1833–Nov. 21, 1914; House 1877–83.

POWELL, Samuel (Tenn.) July 10, 1776–Aug. 2, 1841; House 1815–17.

POWELL, Walter Eugene (Ohio) April 25, 1931–; House 1971–75.

POWER, Thomas Charles (Mont.) May 22, 1839–Feb. 16, 1923; Senate Jan. 2, 1890–95.

POWERS, Caleb (Ky.) Feb. 1, 1869–July 25, 1932; House 1911–19.

POWERS, David Lane (N.J.) July 29, 1896–March 28, 1968; House 1933–Aug. 30, 1945.

POWERS, Horace Henry (Vt.) May 29, 1835–Dec. 8, 1913; House 1891–1901.

POWERS, Llewellyn (Maine) Oct. 14, 1836–July 28, 1908; House 1877–79, April 8, 1901–July 28, 1908; Gov. Jan. 6, 1897–Jan. 2, 1901.

POWERS, Samuel Leland (Mass.) Oct. 26, 1848–Nov. 30, 1929; House 1901–05.

PRACHT, Charles Frederick (Pa.) Oct. 20, 1880–Dec. 22, 1950; House 1943–45.

PRATT, Charles Clarence (Pa.) April 23, 1854–Jan. 27, 1916; House 1909–11.

PRATT, Daniel Darwin (Ind.) Oct. 26, 1813–June 17, 1877; Senate 1869–75.

PRATT, Harcourt Joseph (N.Y.) Oct. 23, 1866–May 21, 1934; House 1925–33.

PRATT, Harry Hayt (N.Y.) Nov. 11, 1864–Nov. 13, 1932; House 1915–19.

PRATT, Henry Otis (Iowa) Feb. 11, 1838–May 22, 1931; House 1873–77.

PRATT, Joseph Marmaduke (Pa.) Sept. 4, 1981–July 19, 1946; House Jan. 18, 1944–45.

PRATT, Ruth Sears Baker (N.Y.) Aug. 24, 1877–Aug. 23, 1965; House 1929–33.

PRAY, Charles Nelson (Mont.) April 6, 1868–Sept. 12, 1963; House 1907–13.

PRESCOTT, Cyrus Dan (N.Y.) Aug. 15, 1836–Oct. 23, 1902; House 1879–83.

PRESSLER, Larry Lee (S.Dak.) March 29, 1942–; House 1975–79; Senate 1979–; Chrmn. Senate Commerce, Science and Transportation Committee 1995–.

PRESTON, Francis (father of William Campbell Preston, uncle of William Ballard Preston and William Preston, cousin of James Breckinridge, John Breckinridge, James Brown, and John Brown of Virginia and Kentucky) (Va.) Aug. 2, 1765–May 26, 1836; House 1793–97 (1793–95 no party).

PRICE, Hiram (Iowa) Jan. 10, 1814–May 30, 1901; House 1863–69, 1877–81.

PRICE, Hugh Hiram (son of William Thompson Price) (Wis.) Dec. 2, 1859–Dec. 25, 1904; House Jan. 18–March 3, 1887.

PRICE, Robert Dale (Tex.) Sept. 7, 1927–; House 1967–75.

PRICE, William Thompson (father of Hugh Hiram Price) (Wis.) June 17, 1824–Dec. 6, 1886; House 1883–Dec. 6, 1886.

PRINCE, Charles Henry (Ga.) May 9, 1837–April 3, 1912; House July 25, 1868–69.

PRINCE, George Washington (Ill.) March 4, 1854–Sept. 26, 1939; House Dec. 2, 1895–1913.

PRINDLE, Elizur H. (N.Y.) May 6, 1829–Oct. 7, 1890; House 1871–73.

PRINGEY, Joseph Colburn (Okla.) May 22, 1858–Feb. 11, 1935; House 1921–23.

PRITCHARD, George Moore (son of Jeter Connelly Pritchard) (N.C.) Jan. 4, 1886–April 24, 1955; House 1929–31.

PRITCHARD, Jeter Connelly (father of George Moore Pritchard) (N.C.) July 12, 1857–April 10, 1921; Senate Jan. 23, 1895–1903.

PRITCHARD, Joel McFee (Wash.) May 5, 1925–; House 1973–85.

PROCTOR, Redfield (Vt.) June 1, 1831–March 4, 1908; Senate Nov. 2, 1891–March 4, 1908; Gov. Oct. 3, 1878–Oct. 7, 1880; Secy. of War March 5, 1889–Nov. 5, 1891.

PROSSER, William Farrand (Tenn.) March 16, 1834–Sept. 23, 1911; House 1869–71.

PROUTY, Solomon Francis (Iowa) Jan. 17, 1854–July 16, 1927; House 1911–15.

PROUTY, Winston Lewis (Vt.) Sept. 1, 1906–Sept. 10, 1971; House 1951–59; Senate 1959–Sept. 10, 1971.

PRYCE, Deborah (Ohio) July 29, 1951–; House 1993–.

PUGH, John (Pa.) June 2, 1761–July 13, 1842; House 1805–09.

PUGH, John Howard (N.J.) June 23, 1827–April 30, 1905; House 1877–79.

PUGH, Samuel Johnson (Ky.) Jan. 28, 1850–April 17, 1895–1901.

PUGSLEY, Jacob Joseph (Ohio) Jan, 25, 1838–Feb. 5, 1920; House 1887–91.

PURMAN, William James (Fla.) April 11, 1840–Aug. 14, 1928; House 1873–Jan. 25, 1875, 1875–77.

PURNELL Fred Sampson (Ind.) Oct. 25, 1882–Oct. 21, 1939; House 1917–33.

PURSELL, Carl Duane (Mich.) Dec. 19, 1932–; House 1977–93.

PURTELL William Arthur (Conn.) May 6, 1897–May 31, 1978; Senate Aug. 29–Nov. 4, 1952, 1953–59.

PURVIANCE, Samuel Anderson (Pa.) Jan. 10, 1809–Feb. 14, 1882; House 1855–59 (1855–57 Whig).

PYLE, Gladys (S.Dak.) Oct. 4, 1890–; Senate Nov. 9 1938–39 (Congress was not in session between election and expiration of term).

QUACKENBUSH, John Adam (N.Y.) Oct. 15, 1828–May 11, 1908; House 1889–93.

QUARLES, Joseph Very (Wis.) Dec. 16, 1843–Oct. 7, 1911; Senate 1899–1905.

QUARLES, Tunstall (Ky.) about 1770–Jan. 7, 1855; House 1817–June 15, 1820.

QUAY, Matthew Stanley (Pa.) Sept. 30, 1833–May 28, 1904; Senate 1887–99, Jan. 16, 1901–May 28, 1904; Chrmn. Rep. Nat. Comm. 1888–91.

QUAYLE, James Danforth "Dan" (Ind.) Feb. 4, 1947–; House 1977–81; Senate 1981–Jan. 3, 1989; Vice President 1989–93.

QUIE, Albert Harold (Minn.) Sept. 18, 1923–; House Feb. 18, 1958–79; Gov. Jan. 1, 1979–Jan. 3, 1983.

QUIGG, Lemuel Ely (N.Y.) Feb. 12, 1863–July 1, 1919; House Jan. 30, 1894–99.

QUILLEN, James Henry (Tenn.) Jan. 11, 1916–; House 1963–.

QUINN, John Francis "Jack" (N.Y.) April 13, 1951–; House 1993–.

RADANOVICH, George P. (Calif.) House, 1995–.

RADCLIFFE, Amos Henry (N.J.) Jan. 16, 1870–Dec. 29, 1950; House 1919–23.

RADWAN, Edmund Patrick (N.Y.) Sept. 22, 1911–Sept. 7, 1959; House 1951–59.

RAILSBACK, Thomas Fisher (Ill.) Jan. 22, 1932–; House 1967–83.

RAINES, John (N.Y.) May 6, 1840–Dec. 16, 1909; House 1889–93.

RAINEY, Joseph Hayne (S.C.) June 21, 1832–Aug. 2, 1887; House Dec. 12, 1870–79.

RAMEY, Frank Marion (Ill.) Sept. 23, 1881–March 27, 1942; House 1929–31.

RAMEY, Homer Alonzo (Ohio) March 2, 1891–April 13, 1960; House 1943–49.

RAMSEY, Alexander (Minn.) Sept. 8, 1815–April 22, 1903; House 1843–47 (Whig Pa.); Senate 1863–75; Gov. April 2, 1849–53 (Minn. Terr.), Jan. 2, 1860–July 10, 1863; Secy. of War Dec. 10, 1879–March 5, 1881.

RAMSEY, John Rathbone (N.J.) April 25, 1862–April 10, 1933; House 1917–21.

RAMSEYER, Christian William (Iowa) March 13, 1875–Nov. 1, 1943; House 1915–33.

RAMSTAD, James (Minn.) May 6, 1946–; House 1991–.

RANDALL, Charles Sturtevant (Mass.) Feb. 20, 1824–Aug. 17, 1904; House 1889–95.

RANDALL, Clifford Ellsworth (Wis.) Dec. 25, 1876–Oct. 16, 1934; House 1919–21.

RANDOLPH, James Henry (Tenn.) Oct. 18, 1825–Aug. 22, 1900; House 1877–79.

RANDOLPH, Thomas Mann (son-in-law of Pres. Thomas Jefferson) (Va.) Oct. 1, 1768–June 20, 1828; House 1803–07; Gov. Dec. 1, 1819–Dec. 1, 1822.

RANEY, John Henry (Mo.) Sept. 28, 1849–Jan. 23, 1928; House 1895–97.

RANKIN, Jeannette (Mont.) June 11, 1880–May 18, 1973; House 1917–19, 1941–43.

RANNEY, Ambrose Arnold (Mass.) April 17, 1821–March 5, 1899; House 1881–87.

RANSDELL, Joseph Eugene (La.) Oct. 7, 1858–July 27, 1954; House Aug. 29, 1899–1913; Senate 1913–31.

RANSIER, Alonzo Jacob (S.C.) Jan. 3, 1834–Aug. 17, 1882; House 1873–75.

RANSLEY, Harry Clay (Pa.) Feb. 5, 1863–Nov. 7, 1941; House Nov. 2, 1920–37.

RAPIER, James Thomas (Ala.) Nov. 13, 1837–May 31, 1883; House 1873–75.

RATHBONE, Henry Riggs (grandson of Ira Harris) (Ill.) Feb. 12, 1870–July 15, 1928; House 1923–July 15, 1928.

RAUM, Green Berry (Ill.) Dec. 3, 1829–Dec. 18, 1909; House 1867–69.

RAVENEL, Arthur Jr. (S.C.) March 29, 1927–; House 1987–.

RAWSON, Charles Augustus (Iowa) May 29, 1867–Sept. 2, 1936; Senate Feb. 24–Dec. 1, 1922.

RAY, George Washington (N.Y.) Feb. 3, 1844–Jan. 10, 1925; House 1883–85, 1891–Sept. 11, 1902.

RAY, John Henry (N.Y.) Sept. 27, 1886–May 21, 1975; House 1953–63.

RAY, Joseph Warren (Pa.) May 25, 1849–Sept. 15, 1928; House 1889–91.

RAY, Ossian (N.H.) Dec. 13, 1835–Jan. 28, 1892; House Jan. 8, 1881–85.

RAY, William Henry (Ill.) Dec. 14, 1812–Jan. 25, 1881; House 1873–75.

RAYMOND, Henry Jarvis (N.Y.) Jan. 24, 1820–June 18, 1869; House 1865–67; Chrmn. Rep. Nat. Comm. 1864–66.

RAYMOND, John Baldwin (Dakota) Dec. 5, 1844–Jan. 3, 1886; House (Terr. Del.) 1883–85.

REA, John (Pa.) Jan. 27, 1756–Feb. 26, 1829; House 1803–11, May 11, 1813–15.

REAVIS, Charles Frank (Nebr.) Sept. 5, 1870–May 26, 1932; House 1915–June 3, 1922.

REBER, John (Pa.) Feb. 1, 1858–Sept. 26, 1931; House 1919–23.

REECE, Brazilla Carroll (husband of Louise Goff Reece, son-in-law of Guy Despard Goff) (Tenn.) Dec. 22, 1889–March 19, 1961; House 1921–31, 1933–47, 1951–March 19, 1961; Chrmn. Rep. Nat. Comm. 1946–48.

REECE, Louise Goff (widow of Brazilla Carroll Reece, daughter of Guy Despard Goff, granddaughter of Nathan Goff) (Tenn.) Nov. 6, 1898–May 14, 1970; House May 16, 1961–63.

REED, Chauncey William (Ill.) June 2, 1890–Feb. 9, 1956; House 1935–Feb. 9, 1956; Chrmn. House Judiciary 1953–55.

REED, Clyde Martin (Kans.) Oct. 19, 1871–Nov. 8, 1949; Senate 1939–Nov. 8, 1949; Gov. Jan. 14, 1929–Jan. 12, 1931.

REED, Daniel Alden (N.Y.) Sept. 15, 1875–Feb. 19, 1959; House 1919–Feb. 19, 1959; Chrmn. House Ways and Means 1953–55.

REED, David Aiken (Pa.) Dec. 21, 1880–Feb. 10, 1953; Senate Aug. 8, 1922–35.

REED, Joseph Rea (Iowa) March 12, 1835–April 2, 1925; House 1889–91.

REED, Philip (Md.) 1760–Nov. 2, 1829; Senate Nov. 25, 1806–13; House 1817–19, March 19, 1822–23.

REED, Stuart Felix (W.Va.) Jan. 8, 1866–July 4, 1935; House 1917–25.

REED, Thomas Brackett (Maine) Oct. 18, 1839–Dec. 7, 1902; House 1877–Sept. 4, 1899; Speaker Dec. 2, 1889–91, Dec. 2, 1895–97, March 15, 1897–99.

REEDER, William Augustus (Kans.) Aug. 28, 1849–Nov. 7, 1929; House 1899–1911.

REES, Edward Herbert (Kans.) June 3, 1866–Oct. 25, 1969; House 1937–61; Chrmn. House Post Office and Civil Service 1947–49, 1953–55.

REES, Rollin Raymond (Kans.) Jan. 10, 1865–May 30, 1935; House 1911–13.

REEVES, Albert Lee Jr. (Mo.) May 31, 1906–April 15, 1987; House 1947–49.

REEVES, Walter (Ill.) Sept. 25, 1848–April 9, 1909; House 1895–1903.

REGULA, Ralph Straus (Ohio) Dec. 3, 1924–; House 1973–.

REID, Charlotte Thompson (Ill.) Sept. 27, 1913–; House 1963–Oct. 7, 1971.

REID, Frank (Ill.) April 18, 1879–Jan. 25, 1945; House 1923–35.

REID, Robert Raymond (Ga.) Sept. 8, 1789–July 1, 1841; House Feb. 18, 1819–23; Gov. (Fla. Terr.) 1839–41.

REIFEL, Benjamin (S.Dak.) Sept. 19, 1906–Jan. 2, 1990; House 1961–71.

REINECKE, Edwin (Calif.) Jan. 7, 1924–; House 1965–Jan. 21, 1969.

REMANN, Frederick (Ill.) May 10, 1847–July 14, 1895; House March 4–July 14, 1895.

REVELS, Hiram Rhodes (Miss.) Sept. 27, 1827–Jan. 16, 1901; Senate Feb. 23, 1870–71.

REVERCOMB, William Chapman (W.Va.) July 20, 1895–Oct. 6, 1979; Senate 1943–49, Nov. 7, 1956–59; Chrmn. Senate Public Works 1947–49.

REYBURN, John Edgar (father of William Stuart Reyburn) (Pa.) Feb. 7, 1845–Jan. 4, 1914; House Feb. 18, 1890–97, Nov. 6, 1906–March 31, 1907.

REYBURN, William Stuart (son of John Edgar Reyburn) (Pa.) Dec. 17, 1882–July 25, 1946; House May 23, 1911–13.

REYNOLDS, Edwin Ruthvin (N.Y.) Feb. 16, 1816–July 4, 1908; House Dec. 5, 1860–61.

REYNOLDS, James B. (Tenn.) 1779–June 10, 1851; House 1815–17, 1823–25.

REYNOLDS, John Merriman (Pa.) March 5, 1848–Sept. 14, 1933; House 1905–Jan. 17, 1911.

REYNOLDS, Samuel Williams (Nebr.) Aug. 11, 1890–March 20, 1988; Senate July 3–Nov. 7, 1954.

RHEA, John (Tenn.) 1753–May 27, 1832; House 1803–15, 1817–23.

RHODES, John Jacob (father of John Jacob Rhodes III) (Ariz.) Sept. 18, 1916–; House 1953–83; House minority leader Dec. 7, 1974–81.

RHODES, John Jacob III (son of John Jacob Rhodes) (Ariz.) Sept. 8, 1943–; House 1987–93.

RHODES, Marion Edwards (Mo.) Jan. 4, 1868–Dec. 25, 1928; House 1905–07, 1919–23.

RICE, Alexander Hamilton (Mass.) Aug. 30, 1818–July 22, 1895; House 1859–67; Gov. Jan. 5, 1876–Jan. 1, 1879.

RICE, Benjamin Franklin (Ark.) May 26, 1828–Jan. 19, 1905; Senate June 23, 1868–73.

RICE, John Birchard (Ohio) June 23, 1832–Jan. 14, 1893; House 1881–83.

RICE, John Blake (Ill.) May 28, 1809–Dec. 17, 1874; House 1873–Dec. 17, 1874.

RICE, John Hovey (Maine) Feb. 5, 1816–March 14, 1911; House 1861–67.

RICE, William Whitney (Mass.) March 7, 1826–March 1, 1896; House 1877–87.

RICH, Carl West (Ohio) Sept. 12, 1898–June 26, 1972; House 1963–65.

RICH, Charles (Vt.) Sept. 13, 1771–Oct. 15, 1824; House 1813–15.

RICH, John Tyler (Mich.) April 23, 1841–March 28, 1926; House April 5, 1881–83; Gov. Jan. 1, 1893–Jan. 1, 1897.

RICH, Robert Fleming (Pa.) June 23, 1883–April 28, 1968; House Nov. 4, 1930–43, 1945–51.

RICHARDS, Jacob (Pa.) 1773–July 20, 1816; House 1803–09.

RICHARDS, John (brother of Matthias Richards) (Pa.) April 18, 1753–Nov. 13, 1822; House 1795–97.

RICHARDS, Mark (Vt.) July 16, 1760–Aug. 10, 1844; House 1817–21.

RICHARDS, Matthias (brother of John Richards) (Pa.) Feb. 26, 1758–Aug. 4, 1830; House 1807–11.

RICHARDSON, David Plunket (N.Y.) May 28, 1833–June 21, 1904; House 1879–83.

RICHARDSON, Harry Alden (Del.) Jan. 1, 1853–June 16, 1928; Senate 1907–13.

RICHARDSON, William Merchant (Mass.) Jan. 4, 1774–March 15, 1838; House Nov. 4, 1811–April 18, 1814.

RICHMOND, Hiram Lawton (Pa.) May 17, 1810–Feb. 19, 1885; House 1873–75.

RICKETTS, Edwin Darlington (Ohio) Aug. 3, 1867–July 3, 1937; House 1915–17, 1919–23.

RIDDICK, Carl Wood (Mont.) Feb. 25, 1872–July 9, 1960; House 1919–23.

RIDDLE, Albert Gallatin (Ohio) May 28, 1816–May 16, 1902; House 1861–63.

RIDGE, Thomas Joseph (Pa.) Aug. 26, 1945–; House 1983–.

RIEHLMAN, Roy Walter (N.Y.) Aug. 26, 1899–July 16, 1978; House 1947–65.

RIFE, John Winebrenner (Pa.) Aug. 14, 1846–April 17, 1908; House 1889–93.

RIGGS, Frank (Calif.) Sept. 5, 1950–; House 1991–93; 1995–.

RIKER, Samuel (N.Y.) April 8, 1743–May 19, 1823; House Nov. 5, 1804–05, 1807–09.

RINAKER, John Irving (Ill.) Nov. 1, 1830–Jan. 15, 1915; House June 5, 1896–97.

RINALDO, Matthew John (N.J.) Sept. 1, 1931–; House 1973–93.

RINGGOLD, Samuel (Md.) Jan. 15, 1770–Oct. 18, 1829; House Oct. 15, 1810–15, 1817–21.

RISK, Charles Francis (R.I.) Aug. 19, 1897–Dec. 26, 1943; House Aug. 6, 1935–37, 1939–41.

RITCHIE, David (Pa.) Aug. 19, 1812–Jan. 24, 1867; House 1853–59 (1853–57 Whig).

RITCHIE, James Monroe (father of Byron Foster Ritchie) (Ohio) July 28, 1829–Aug. 17, 1918; House 1881–83.

RITTER, Donald Lawrence (Pa.) Oct. 21, 1940–; House 1979–93.

RIVES, Zeno John (Ill.) Feb. 22, 1874–Sept. 2, 1939; House 1905–07.

RIZLEY, Ross (Okla.) July 5, 1892–March 4, 1969; House 1941–49.

ROACH, Sidney Crain (Mo.) July 25, 1876–June 29, 1934; House 1921–25.

ROARK, Charles Wickliffe (Ky.) Jan. 22, 1887–April 5, 1929; House March 4–April 5, 1929.

ROBBINS, Edward Everett (Pa.) Sept. 27 1860–Jan. 25, 1919; House 1897–99, 1917–Jan. 25, 1919.

ROBBINS, George Robbins (N.J.) Sept. 24, 1808–Feb. 22, 1875; House 1855–59 (1855–57 Whig).

ROBERTS, Anthony Ellmaker (grandfather of Robert Grey Bushong) (Pa.) Oct. 29, 1803–Jan. 25, 1885; House 1855–59 (1855–57 Independent Whig).

ROBERTS, Charles Patrick "Pat" (Kans.) April 20, 1936–; House 1981–; Chrmn. House Agriculture Committee, 1995–.

ROBERTS, Clint Ronald (S.Dak.) Jan. 30, 1935–; House 1981–83.

ROBERTS, Edwin Ewing (Nev.) Dec. 12, 1870–Dec. 11, 1933; House 1911–19.

ROBERTS, Ellis Henry (N.Y.) Sept. 30, 1827–Jan. 8, 1918; House 1871–75.

ROBERTS, Ernest William (Mass.) Nov. 22, 1858–Feb. 27, 1924; House 1899–1917.

ROBERTS, Jonathan (Pa.) Aug. 16, 1771–July 24, 1854; House 1811–Feb. 24, 1814; Senate Feb. 24, 1814–21.

ROBERTSON, Alice Mary (Okla.) Jan. 2, 1854–July 1, 1931; House 1921–23.

ROBERTSON, Charles Raymond (N.Dak.) Sept. 5, 1889–Feb. 18, 1951; House 1941–43, 1945–49.

ROBERTSON, Edward Vivian (Wyo.) May 27, 1881–April 15, 1963; Senate 1943–49.

ROBERTSON, George (Ky.) Nov. 18, 1790–May 16, 1874; House 1817–21.

ROBERTSON, Thomas Bolling (brother of John Robertson) (La.) Feb. 27, 1779–Oct. 5, 1828; House April 30, 1812–April 20, 1818; Gov. Dec. 18, 1820–Nov. 15, 1822 (Democratic Republican).

ROBERTSON, Thomas James (S.C.) Aug. 3, 1823–Oct. 13, 1897; Senate July 15, 1868–77.

ROBERTSON, William Henry (N.Y.) Oct. 10, 1823–Dec. 6, 1898; House 1867–69.

ROBESON, George Maxwell (nephew of George Clifford Maxwell) (N.J.) March 16, 1829–Sept. 27, 1897–; House 1879–83; Secy. of the Navy June 26, 1869–March 12, 1877.

ROBINSON, Arthur Raymond (Ind.) March 12, 1881–March 17, 1961; Senate Oct. 20, 1925–35.

ROBINSON, Christopher (R.I.) May 15, 1806–Oct. 3, 1889; House 1859–61.

ROBINSON, George Dexter (Mass.) Jan. 20, 1834–Feb. 22, 1896; House 1877–Jan. 7, 1884; Gov. Jan. 1884–Jan. 6, 1887.

ROBINSON, James Kenneth (Va.) May 14, 1916–April 8, 1990; House 1971–81

ROBINSON, James Sidney (Ohio) Oct. 14, 1827–Jan. 14, 1892; House 1881–Jan. 12, 1885.

ROBINSON, James Wallace (Ohio) Nov. 26, 1826–June 28, 1898; House 1873–75.

ROBINSON, John Buchanan (Pa.) May 23, 1846–Jan. 28, 1933; House 1891–97.

ROBINSON, Jonathan (brother of Moses Robinson) (Vt.) Aug. 11, 1756–Nov. 3, 1819; Senate Oct. 10, 1807–15.

ROBINSON, Milton Stapp (Ind.) April 20, 1832–July 28, 1892; House 1875–79.

ROBINSON, Thomas Jr. (Del.) 1800–Oct. 28, 1843; House 1839–41.

ROBINSON, Thomas John Bright (Iowa) Aug. 12, 1868–Jan. 27, 1958; House 1923–33.

ROBINSON, Tommy Franklin (Ark.) March 7, 1942–; House 1985–91 (1985–July 28, 1989 Democrat).

ROBISON, Howard Winfield (N.Y.) Oct. 30, 1915–Sept. 26, 1987; House Jan. 14, 1958–75.

ROBSION, John Marshall (father of John Marshall Robsion Jr.) (Ky.) Jan. 2, 1873–Feb. 17, 1948; House 1919–Jan. 10, 1930, 1935–Feb. 17, 1948; Senate Jan. 11–Nov. 30, 1930.

ROBSION, John Marshall Jr. (son of John Marshall Robsion Jr.) (Ky.) Aug. 28, 1904–; House 1953–59.

ROCKEFELLER, Lewis Kirby (N.Y.) Nov. 25, 1875–Sept. 18, 1948; House Nov. 2, 1937–43.

ROCKWELL Francis Williams (son of Julius Rockwell) (Mass.) May 26, 1844–June 26, 1929; House Jan. 17, 1884–91.

ROCKWELL, Robert Fay (Colo.) Feb. 11, 1886–Sept. 29, 1950; House Dec. 9, 1941–49.

RODENBERG, William August (Ill.) Oct. 30, 1865–Sept. 10, 1937; House 1899–1901, 1903–13, 1915–23.

RODEY, Bernard Shandon (N.Mex.) March 1, 1856–March 10, 1927; House (Terr. Del.) 1901–05.

RODGERS, Robert Lewis (Pa.) June 2, 1875–May 9, 1960; House 1939–47.

RODMAN, William (Pa.) Oct. 7, 1757–July 27, 1824; House 1811–13.

RODNEY, Caesar Augustus (cousin of George Brydges Rodney) (Del.) Jan. 4, 1772–June 10, 1824; House 1803–05, 1821–Jan. 24, 1822; Senate Jan. 24, 1822–Jan. 29, 1823; Atty. Gen. Jan. 20, 1807–Dec. 11, 1811.

ROGERS, Edith Nourse (widow of John Jacob Rogers) (Mass.) 1881–Sept. 10, 1960; House June 30, 1925–Sept. 10, 1960; Chrmn. House Veterans' Affairs 1947–49, 1953–55.

ROGERS, Harold Dallas (Ky.) Dec. 31, 1937–; House 1981–.

ROGERS, John Jacob (husband of Edith Nourse Rogers) (Mass.) Aug. 18, 1881–March 28, 1925; House 1913–March 28, 1925.

ROGERS, Thomas Jones (father of William Findlay Rogers) (Pa.) 1781–Dec. 7, 1832; House March 3, 1818–April 20, 1824.

ROHRABACHER, Dana (Calif.) June 21, 1947–; House 1989–.

ROHRBOUGH, Edward Gay (W.Va.) 1874–Dec. 12, 1956; House 1943–45, 1947–49.

ROLLINS, Edward Henry (N.H.) Oct. 3, 1824–July 31, 1889; House 1861–67; Senate 1877–83.

ROLPH, Thomas (Calif.) Jan. 17, 1885–May 10, 1956; House 1941–45.

ROMEIS, Jacob (Ohio) Dec. 1, 1835–March 8, 1904; House 1885–89.

ROMERO, Trinidad (N.Mex.) June 15, 1835–Aug. 28, 1918; House (Terr. Del.) 1877–79.

RONCALLO, Angelo Dominick (N.Y.) May 28, 1927–; House 1973–75.

ROOT, Elihu (N.Y.) Feb. 15, 1845–Feb. 7, 1937; Senate 1909–15; Secy. of War Aug. 1, 1899–Jan. 31, 1904; Secy. of State July 19, 1905–Jan. 27, 1909.

ROOTS, Logan Holt (Ark.) March 26, 1841–May 30, 1893; House June 22, 1868–71.

ROSE, John Marshall (Pa.) May 18, 1856–April 22, 1923; House 1917–23.

ROSENBLOOM, Benjamin Louis (W.Va.) June 3, 1880–March 22, 1965; House 1921–25.

ROS-LEHTINEN, Ileana (Fla.) July 15, 1952–; House Sept. 6, 1989–.

ROSS, Edmund Gibson (Kans.) Dec. 7, 1826–May 8, 1907; Senate July 19, 1866–71; Gov. (N.Mex. Terr.) 1885–89 (Democrat).

ROSS, John (father of Thomas Ross) (Pa.) Feb. 24, 1770–Jan. 31, 1834; House 1809–11, 1815–Feb. 24, 1818.

ROSS, Jonathan (Vt.) April 30, 1826–Feb. 23, 1905; Senate Jan. 11, 1899–Oct. 18, 1900.

ROSS, Robert Tripp (N.Y.) June 4, 1903–October 1, 1981; House 1947–49, Feb. 19, 1952–63.

ROSS, Sobieski (Pa.) May 16, 1828–Oct. 24, 1877; House 1873–77.

ROSSDALE, Albert Berger (N.Y.) Oct. 23, 1878–April 17, 1968; House 1921–23.

ROTH, Tobias Anton "Toby" (Wis.) Oct. 10, 1938–; House 1979–.

ROTH, William Victor Jr. (Del.) July 22, 1921–; House 1967–Dec. 31, 1970; Senate Jan. 1, 1971–; Chrmn. Senate Governmental Affairs 1981–87; Chrmn. Senate Governmental Affairs Committee 1995–.

ROUDEBUSH, Richard Lowell (Ind.) Jan. 18, 1918–; House 1961–71.

ROUKEMA, Margaret Scafati "Marge" (N.J.) Sept. 19, 1929–; House 1981–.

ROUSSELOT, John Harbin (Calif.) Nov. 1, 1927–House 1961–63, June 30, 1970–83.

ROUTZOHN, Harry Nelson (Ohio) Nov. 4, 1881–April 14, 1953; House 1939–41.

ROWAN, John (uncle of Robert Todd Lytle) (Ky.) July 12, 1773–July 13, 1843; House 1807–09; Senate 1825–31.

ROWBOTTOM, Harry Emerson (Ind.) Nov. 3, 1884–March 22, 1934; House 1925–31.

ROWE, Edmund (Ohio) Dec. 21, 1892–1972; House 1943–45.

ROWE, Frederick William (N.Y.) March 19, 1863–June 20, 1946; House 1915–21.

ROWELL, Jonathan Harvey (Ill.) Feb. 10, 1833–May 15, 1908; House 1883–91.

ROWLAND, Charles Hedding (Pa.) Dec. 20, 1860–Nov. 24, 1921; House 1915–19.

ROWLAND, John G. (Conn.) May 24, 1957–; House 1985–91.

ROYCE, Edward Randall (Calif.) Oct. 12, 1951–; House 1993–.

ROYCE, Homer Elihu (Vt.) June 14, 1819–April 24, 1891; House 1857–61.

ROYER, William Howard (Calif.) April 11, 1920–; House April 3, 1979–81.

ROYSE, Lemuel Willard (Ind.) Jan. 19, 1847–Dec. 18, 1946; House 1895–99.

RUDD, Eldon Dean (Ariz.) July 15, 1920–; House 1977–87.

RUDMAN, Warren Bruce (N.H.) May 13, 1930–; Senate Dec. 29, 1980–93; Chrmn. Senate Select Committee on Ethics 1985–87.

RUGGLES, Benjamin (Ohio) Feb. 21, 1783–Sept. 2, 1857; Senate 1815–33.

RUMPLE, John Nicholas William (Iowa) March 4, 1841–Jan. 31, 1903; House 1901–Jan. 31, 1903.

RUMSFELD, Donald Henry (Ill.) July 9, 1932–; House 1963–May 25, 1969; Secy. of Defense Nov. 20, 1975–Jan. 20, 1977.

RUPLEY, Arthur Ringwalt (Pa.) Nov. 13, 1868–Nov. 11, 1920; House 1913–15.

RUPPE, Philip Edward (Mich.) Sept. 29, 1926–; House 1967–79.

RUSK, Jeremiah McLain (Wis.) June 17, 1830–Nov. 21, 1893; House 1871–77; Gov. Jan. 2, 1882–Jan. 7, 1889; Secy. of Agriculture March 6, 1889–March 6, 1893.

RUSSELL, Charles Addison (Conn.) March 2, 1852–Oct. 23, 1902; House 1887–Oct. 23, 1902.

RUSSELL, Charles Hinton (Nev.) Dec. 27, 1903–Sept. 13, 1989; House 1947–49; Gov. Jan. 1, 1951–Jan. 5, 1959.

RUSSELL, John (N.Y.) Sept. 7, 1772–Aug. 2, 1842; House 1805–09.

RUSSELL, Joshua Edward (Ohio) Aug. 9, 1867–June 21, 1953; House 1915–17.

RUSSELL, William Augustus (Mass.) April 22, 1831–Jan. 10, 1899; House 1879–85.

RUTH, Earl Baker (N.C.) Feb. 7, 1916–; House 1969–75.

RUTHERFORD, Albert Greig (Pa.) Jan. 3, 1879–Aug. 10, 1941; House 1937–Aug. 10, 1941.

RUTHERFORD, Robert (Va.) Oct. 20, 1728–Oct. 1803; House 1793–97 (1793–95 no party).

RYAN, Thomas (Kans.) Nov. 25, 1837–April 5, 1914; House 1877–April 4, 1889.

RYAN, Thomas Jefferson (N.Y.) June 17, 1890–Nov. 10, 1968; House 1921–23.

SABIN, Dwight May (Minn.) April 25, 1843–Dec. 22, 1902; Senate 1883–89; Chrmn. Rep. Nat. Comm. 1883–84.

SACKETT, Frederick Mosley (Ky.) Dec. 17, 1868–May 18, 1941; Senate 1925–Jan. 9, 1930.

SADLAK, Antoni Nicholas (Conn.) June 13, 1908–Oct. 18, 1969; House 1947–59.

SAGE, Ebenezer (N.Y.) Aug. 16, 1755–Jan. 20, 1834; House 1809–15.

SAIKI, Patricia Fukuda (Hawaii) May 28, 1930–; House 1987–91.

SAILLY, Peter (N.Y.) April 20, 1754–March 16, 1826; House 1805–07.

ST. GEORGE, Katharine Price Collier (N.Y.) July 12, 1896–May 2, 1983; House 1947–65.

ST. JOHN, Charles (N.Y.) Oct. 8, 1818–July 6, 1891; House 1871–75.

SALMON, Matt (Ariz.) House, 1995–.

SALTONSTALL, Leverett (Mass.) Sept. 1, 1892–June 17, 1979; Senate Jan. 4, 1945–67; Chrmn. Senate Armed Services 1953–55; Gov. Jan. 5, 1939–Jan. 3, 1945.

SAMMONS, Thomas (grandfather of John Henry Starin) (N.Y.) Oct. 1, 1762–Nov. 20, 1838; House 1803–07, 1809–13.

SAMPSON, Ezekiel Silas (Iowa) Dec. 6, 1831–Oct. 7, 1892; House 1875–79.

SAMPSON, Zabdiel (Mass.) Aug. 22, 1781–July 19, 1828; House 1817–July 26, 1820.

SAMUEL, Edmund William (Pa.) Nov. 27, 1857–March 7, 1930; House 1905–07.

SANBORN, John Carfield (Idaho) Sept. 28, 1885–May 16, 1968; House 1947–51.

SANDERS, Archie Dovell (N.Y.) June 17, 1857–July 15, 1941; House 1917–33.

SANDERS, Everett (Ind.) March 8, 1882–May 12, 1950; House 1917–25; Chrmn. Rep. Nat. Comm. 1932–34.

SANDERS, Newell (Tenn.) July 12, 1850–Jan. 26, 1939; Senate April 11, 1912–Jan. 24, 1913.

SANDERS, Wilbur Fiske (Mont.) May 2, 1834–July 7, 1905; Senate Jan. 1, 1890–93.

SANDFORD, Thomas (Ky.) 1762–Dec. 10, 1808; House 1803–07.

SANDMAN, Charles William Jr. (N.J.) Oct. 23, 1921–Aug. 26, 1985; House 1967–75.

SANFORD, John (N.Y.) Jan. 18, 1851–Sept. 26, 1939; House 1889–93.

SANFORD, Mark (S.C.) House, 1995–.

SANFORD, Rollin Brewster (great-grandson of Jonah Sanford) (N.Y.) May 18, 1874–May 16, 1957; House 1915–21.

SANFORD, Stephen (son of John Sanford born in 1803, father of John Sanford born in 1851) (N.Y.) May 26, 1826–Feb. 13, 1913; House 1869–71.

SANTORUM, Rick (Pa.) May 10, 1958–; House 1991–1994; Senate 1995–.

SAPP, William Fletcher (nephew of William Robinson Sapp) (Iowa) Nov. 20, 1824–Nov. 22, 1890; House 1877–81.

SAPP, William Robinson (uncle of William Fletcher Sapp) (Ohio) March 4, 1804–Jan. 3, 1875; House 1853–57 (1853–55 Whig.).

SARASIN, Ronald Arthur (Conn.) Dec. 31, 1934–; House 1973–79.

SARBACHER, George William Jr. (Pa.) Sept. 30, 1919–March 4, 1973; House 1947–49.

SARGENT, Aaron Augustus (Calif.) Sept. 28, 1827–Aug. 14, 1887; House 1861–63, 1869–73; Senate 1873–79.

SAUERHERING, Edward (Wis.) June 24, 1864–March 1, 1924; House 1895–99.

SAUNDERS, Alvin (grandfather of William Henry Harrison of Wyoming) (Nebr.) July 12, 1817–Nov. 1, 1899; Senate March 5, 1877–83; Gov. (Nebr. Terr.) 1861–67.

SAVAGE, John (N.Y.) Feb. 22, 1779–Oct. 19, 1863; House 1815–19.

SAWYER, Frederick Adolphus (S.C.) Dec. 12, 1822–July 31, 1891; Senate July 16, 1868–73.

SAWYER, Harold Samuel (Mich.) March 21, 1920–; House 1977–85.

SAWYER, John Gilbert (N.Y.) June 5, 1825–Sept. 5, 1898; House 1885–91.

SAWYER, Lemuel (N.C.) 1777–Jan. 9, 1852; House 1807–13, 1817–23, 1825–29.

SAWYER, Philetus (Wis.) Sept. 22, 1816–March 29, 1900; House 1865–75; Senate 1881–93.

SAXBE, William Bart (Ohio) June 24, 1916–; Senate 1969–Jan. 3, 1974; Atty. Gen. Jan. 4, 1974–Feb. 3, 1975.

SAXTON, Hugh James (N.J.) Jan. 22, 1943–; House 1985– (elected Nov. 6, 1984, to fill a vacancy in the 98th Congress and to the 99th Congress but was not sworn in until Jan. 3, 1985).

SAY, Benjamin (Pa.) Aug. 28, 1755–April 23, 1813; House Nov. 16, 1808–June 1809.

SAYLER, Henry Benton (cousin of Milton Sayler) (Ind.) March 31, 1836–June 18, 1900; House 1873–75.

SAYLOR, John Phillips (Pa.) July 23, 1908–Oct. 28, 1973; House Sept. 13, 1949–Oct. 28, 1973.

SCARBOROUGH, Joe (Fla.) House 1995–.

SCHADEBERG, Henry Carl (Wis.) Oct. 12, 1913–Dec. 11, 1985; House 1961–65, 1967–71.

SCHAEFER, Daniel (Colo.) Jan. 25, 1936–; House March 29, 1983–.

SCHAFER, John Charles (Wis.) May 7, 1893–June 9, 1962; House 1923–33, 1939–41.

SCHALL, Thomas David (Minn.) June 4, 1878–Dec. 22, 1935; House 1915–25; Senate 1925–Dec. 22, 1935.

SCHENCK, Abraham Henry (uncle of Isaac Teller) (N.Y.) Jan. 22, 1775–June 1, 1831; House 1815–17.

SCHENCK, Paul Fornshell (Ohio) April 19, 1899–Nov. 30, 1968; House Nov. 6, 1951–65.

SCHENCK, Robert Cumming (Ohio) Oct. 4, 1809–March 23, 1890; House 1843–51 (Whig), 1863–Jan. 5, 1871.

SCHERER, Gordon Harry (Ohio) Dec. 26, 1906–Aug. 13, 1988; House 1953–63.

SCHERLE, William Joseph (Iowa) March 14, 1923–; House 1967–75.

SCHIFF, Steven Harvey (N.Mex.) March 18, 1947–; House 1989–.

SCHIFFLER, Andrew Charles (W.Va.) Aug. 10, 1889–March 27, 1970; House 1939–41, 1943–45.

SCHIRM, Charles Reginald (Md.) Aug. 12, 1864–Nov. 2, 1918; House 1901–03.

SCHMITT, Harrison Hagan (N.Mex.) July 3, 1935–; Senate 1977–83.

SCHMITZ, John George (Calif.) Aug. 12, 1930–; House June 30, 1970–73.

SCHNEEBELI, Gustav Adolphus (Pa.) May 23, 1853–Feb. 6, 1923; House 1905–07.

SCHNEEBELI, Herman Theodore (Pa.) July 7, 1907–May 6, 1982; House April 26, 1960–77.

SCHNEIDER, Claudine (R.I.) March 25, 1947–; House 1981–91.

SCHOEPPEL, Andrew Frank (Kans.) Nov. 23, 1894–Jan. 21, 1962; Senate 1949–Jan. 21, 1962; Gov. Jan. 11, 1943–Jan. 13, 1947.

SCHUETTE, William Duncan (Mich.) Oct. 13, 1953–; House 1985–91.

SCHULZE, Richard Taylor (Pa.) Aug. 7, 1929–; House 1975–93.

SCHUNEMAN, Martin Gerretsen (N.Y.) Feb. 10, 1764–Feb. 21, 1827; House 1805–07.

SCHURZ, Carl (Mo.) March 2, 1829–May 14, 1906; Senate 1869–75; Secy. of the Interior March 12, 1877–March 7, 1881.

SCHUYLER, Karl Cortlandt (Colo.) April 3, 1877–July 31, 1933; Senate Dec. 7, 1932–33.

SCHWABE, George Blaine (brother of Max Schwabe) (Okla.) July 26, 1886–April 2, 1952; House 1945–49, 1951–April 2, 1952.

SCHWABE, Max (brother of George Blaine Schwabe) (Mo.) Dec. 6, 1905–; House 1943–49.

SCHWEIKER, Richard Schultz (Pa.) June 1, 1926–; House 1961–69; Senate 1969–81; Secy. of Health and Services Jan. 22, 1981–Feb. 3, 1983.

SCHWENGEL, Frederick Delbert (Iowa) May 28, 1906–April 1, 1993; House 1955–65, 1967–73.

SCOBLICK, James Paul (Pa.) May 10, 1909–Dec. 4, 1981; House Nov. 5, 1946–49.

SCOFIELD, Glenni William (Pa.) March 11, 1817–Aug. 30, 1891; House 1863–75.

SCOTT, Charles Frederick (Kans.) Sept. 7, 1860–Sept. 18, 1938; House 1901–11.

SCOTT, Frank Douglas (Mich.) Aug. 25, 1878–Feb. 12, 1951; House 1915–27.

SCOTT, George Cromwell (Iowa) Aug. 8, 1864–Oct. 6, 1948; House Nov. 5, 1912–15, 1917–19.

SCOTT, Hardie (son of John Roger Kirkpatrick Scott) (Pa.) June 7, 1907–; House 1947–53.

SCOTT, Harvey David (Ind.) Oct. 18, 1818–July 11, 1891; House 1855–57.

SCOTT, Hugh Doggett Jr. (Pa.) Nov. 11, 1900–July 21, 1994; House 1941–45, 1947–59; Senate 1959–77; Senate minority leader Sept. 24, 1969–77; Chrmn. Rep. Nat. Comm. 1948–49.

SCOTT, John (Pa.) July 24, 1824–Nov. 29, 1896; Senate 1869–75.

SCOTT, John Roger Kirkpatrick (father of Hardie Scott) (Pa.) July 6, 1873–Dec. 9, 1946; House 1915–Jan. 5, 1919.

SCOTT, Lon Allen (Tenn.) Sept. 25, 1888–Feb. 11, 1931; House 1921–23.

SCOTT, Nathan Bay (W.Va.) Dec. 18, 1842–Jan. 2, 1924; Senate 1899–1911.

SCOTT, William Lloyd (Va.) July 1, 1915–; House 1967–73; Senate 1973–Jan. 1, 1979.

SCRANTON, George Whitfield (second cousin of Joseph Augustine Scranton) (Pa.) May 11, 1811–March 24, 1861; House 1859–March 24, 1861.

SCRANTON, Joseph Augustine (great-grandfather of William Warren Scranton, second cousin of George Whitfield Scranton) (Pa.) July 26, 1838–Oct. 12, 1908; House 1881–83, 1885–87, 1889–91, 1893–97.

SCRANTON, William Warren (great-grandson of Joseph Augustine Scranton) (Pa.) July 19, 1917–; House 1961–63; Gov. Jan. 15, 1963–Jan. 17, 1967.

SCRIVNER, Errett Power (Kans.) March 20, 1898–May 5, 1978; House Sept. 14, 1943–59.

SCROGGY, Thomas Edmund (Ohio) March 18, 1843–March 6, 1915; House 1905–07.

SCUDDER, Henry Joel (uncle of Townsend Scudder) (N.Y.) Sept. 18, 1825–Feb. 10, 1886; House 1873–75.

SCUDDER, Hubert Baxter (Calif.) Nov. 5, 1888–July 4, 1968; House 1949–59.

SCUDDER, Isaac Williamson (N.J.) 1816–Sept. 10, 1881; House 1873–75.

SCUDDER, John Anderson (N.J.) March 22, 1759–Nov. 6, 1836; House Oct. 31, 1810–11.

SCULL, Edward (Pa.) Feb. 5, 1818–July 10, 1900; House 1887–93.

SEARS, Willis Gratz (Nebr.) Aug. 16, 1860–June 1, 1949; House 1923–31.

SEASTRAND, Andrea (Calif.) House, 1995–.

SEATON, Frederick Andrew (Nebr.) Dec. 11, 1909–Jan. 16, 1974; Senate Dec. 10, 1951–Nov. 4, 1952; Secy. of the Interior June 8, 1956–Jan. 20, 1961.

SEAVER, Ebenezer (Mass.) July 5, 1763–March 1, 1844; House 1803–13.

SEBELIUS, Keith George (Kans.) Sept. 10, 1916–Aug. 5, 1982; House 1969–81.

SECCOMBE, James (Ohio) Feb. 12, 1893–Aug. 23, 1970; House 1939–41.

SEDGWICK, Charles Baldwin (N.Y.) March 15, 1815–Feb. 3, 1883; House 1859–67.

SEELEY, John Edward (N.Y.) Aug. 1, 1810–March 30, 1875; House 1871–73.

SEELY-BROWN, Horace Jr. (Conn.) May 12, 1908–April 9, 1982; House 1947–49, 1951–59, 1961–63.

SEGER, George Nicholas (N.J.) Jan. 4, 1866–Aug. 26, 1940; House 1923–Aug. 26, 1940.

SEIBERLING, Francis (cousin of John Frederick Seibering) (Ohio) Sept. 20, 1870–Feb. 1, 1945; House 1929–33.

SELLS, Sam Riley (Tenn.) Aug. 2, 1871–Nov. 2, 1935; House 1911–21.

SELVIG, Conrad George (Minn.) Oct. 11, 1877–Aug. 2, 1953; House 1927–33.

SENER, James Beverley (Va.) May 18, 1837–Nov. 18, 1903; House 1873–75.

SENSENBRENNER, Frank James Jr. (Wis.) June 14, 1943–; House 1979–.

SESSINGHAUS, Gustavus (Mo.) Nov. 8, 1838–Nov. 16, 1887; House March 2–3, 1883.

SESSIONS, Walter Loomis (N.Y.) Oct. 4, 1820–May 27, 1896; House 1871–75, 1885–87.

SETTLE, Thomas (uncle of David Settle Reid, grandfather of Thomas Settle, below) (N.C.) March 9, 1789–Aug. 5, 1857; House 1817–21.

SETTLE, Thomas (grandson of Thomas Settle, above) (N.C.) March 10, 1865–Jan. 20, 1919; House 1893–97.

SEVIER, John (Tenn.) Sept. 23, 1745–Sept. 24, 1815; House June 16, 1790–91 (no party N.C.), 1811–Sept. 24, 1815; Gov. March 30, 1796–Sept. 23, 1801 (Democratic Republican), Sept. 23, 1803–Sept. 19, 1809 (Democratic Republican).

SEWARD, William Henry (N.Y.) May 16, 1801–Oct. 10, 1872; Senate 1849–61 (1849–55 Whig); Secy. of State March 6, 1861–March 4, 1869; Gov. Jan. 1, 1839–Jan. 1, 1843 (Whig.).

SEWELL, William Joyce (N.J.) Dec. 6, 1835–Dec. 27, 1901; Senate 1881–87, 1895–Dec. 27, 1901.

SEXTON, Leonidas (Ind.) May 19, 1827–July 4, 1880; House 1877–79.

SEYBERT, Adam (Pa.) May 16, 1773–May 2, 1825; House Oct. 10, 1809–15, 1817–19.

SEYMOUR, Henry William (Mich.) July 21, 1834–April 7, 1906; House Feb. 14, 1888–89.

SEYMOUR, John (Calif.) Dec. 3, 1937–; Senate Jan. 10, 1991–Nov. 3, 1992.

SHADEGG, John (Ariz.) House, 1995–.

SHAFER, Paul Werntz (Mich.) April 27, 1893–Aug. 17, 1954; House 1937–Aug. 17, 1954.

SHAFFER, Joseph Crockett (Va.) Jan. 19, 1880–Oct. 19, 1958; House 1929–31.

SHALLENBERGER, William Shadrack (Pa.) Nov. 24, 1839–April 15, 1914; House 1877–83.

SHANKS, John Peter Cleaver (Ind.) June 17, 1826–Jan. 23, 1901; House 1861–63, 1867–75.

SHANNON, Richard Cutts (N.Y.) Feb. 12, 1839–Oct. 5, 1920; House 1895–99.

SHANNON, Thomas Bowles (Calif.) Sept. 21, 1827–Feb. 21, 1897; House 1863–65.

SHARON, William (Nev.) Jan. 9, 1821–Nov. 13, 1885; Senate 1875–81.

SHARP, Edgar Allan (N.Y.) June 3, 1876–Nov. 27, 1948; House 1945–47.

SHARP, Solomon P. (Ky.) 1780–Nov. 7, 1825; House 1813–17.

SHARTEL, Cassius McLean (Mo.) April 27, 1860–Sept. 27, 1943; House 1905–07.

SHATTUC, William Bunn (Ohio) June 11, 1841–July 13, 1911; House 1897–1903.

SHAW, Albert Duane (N.Y.) Dec. 21, 1841–Feb. 10, 1901; House Nov. 6, 1900–Feb. 10, 1901.

SHAW, Eugene Clay Jr. (Fla.) April 19, 1939–; House 1981–.

SHAW, George Bullen (Wis.) March 12, 1854–Aug. 27, 1894; House 1893–Aug. 27, 1894.

SHAW, Guy Loren (Ill.) May 16, 1881–May 19, 1950; House 1921–23.

SHAW, Henry (son of Samuel Shaw) (Mass.) 1788–Oct. 17, 1857; House 1817–21.

SHAW, Samuel (father of Henry Shaw) (Vt.) Dec. 1768–Oct. 23, 1827; House Sept. 6, 1808–13.

SHAYS, Christopher (Conn.) Oct. 18, 1945–; House Sept. 9, 1987–.

SHEATS, Charles Christopher (Ala.) April 10, 1839–May 27, 1904; House 1873–75.

SHEEHAN, Timothy Patrick (Ill.) Feb. 21, 1909–; House 1951–59.

SHEFFIELD, William Paine (father of William Paine Sheffield, below) (R.I.) Aug. 30, 1820–June 2, 1907; House 1861–63; Senate Nov. 19, 1884–Jan. 20, 1885.

SHEFFIELD, William Paine (son of William Paine Sheffield, above) (R.I.) June 1, 1857–Oct. 19, 1919; House 1909–11.

SHELBY, Richard Craig (Ala.) May 6, 1934–; House 1979–87; (Democrat); Senate 1987– (Republican from 1994).

SHELDEN, Carlos Douglas (Mich.) June 10, 1840–June 24, 1904; House 1897–1903.

SHELDON, Lionel Allen (La.) Aug. 30, 1828–Jan. 17, 1917; House 1869–75; Gov. (N.Mex. Terr.) 1881–85.

SHELDON, Porter (N.Y.) Sept. 29, 1831–Aug. 15, 1908; House 1869–71.

SHELDON, Socrates Norton (N.Y.) July 22, 1801–Feb. 1, 1873; House 1861–63.

SHELLABARGER, Samuel (Ohio) Dec. 10, 1817–Aug. 7, 1896; House 1861–63, 1865–69, 1871–73.

SHELTON, Samuel Azariah (Mo.) Sept. 3, 1858–Sept. 13, 1948; House 1921–23.

SHERBURNE, John Samuel (N.H.) 1757–Aug. 2, 1830; House 1793–97.

SHERMAN, James Schoolcraft (N.Y.) Oct. 24, 1856–Oct. 30, 1912; House 1887–91, 1893–1909; Vice President 1909–Oct. 30, 1912.

SHERMAN, John (Ohio) May 10, 1823–Oct. 22, 1900; House 1855–March 21, 1861; Senate March 21, 1861–March 8, 1877, 1881 –March 4, 1897; elected Pres. pro tempore Dec. 7, 1885; Secy. of the Treasury March 10, 1877–March 3, 1881; Secy. of State March 6, 1897–April 27, 1898.

SHERMAN, Judson W. (N.Y.) 1808–Nov. 12, 1881; House 1857–59.

SHERMAN, Lawrence Yates (Ill.) Nov. 8, 1858–Sept. 15, 1939; Senate March 26, 1913–21.

SHERWIN, John Crocker (Ill.) Feb. 8, 1838–Jan. 1, 1904; House 1879–83.

SHIPSTEAD, Henrik (Minn.) Jan. 8, 1881–June 26, 1960; Senate 1923–47 (1923–41 Farmer Laborite).

SHOEMAKER, Lazarus Denison (Pa.) Nov. 5, 1819–Sept. 9, 1893; House 1871–75.

SHONK, George Washington (Pa.) April 26, 1850–Aug. 14, 1900; House 1891–93.

SHORT, Dewey Jackson (Mo.) April 7, 1898–Nov. 19, 1979; House 1929–31, 1935–57; Chrmn. House Armed Services 1953–55.

SHORT, Don Levingston (N.Dak.) June 22, 1903–May 10, 1982; House 1969–65.

SHORTRIDGE, Samuel Morgan (Calif.) Aug. 3, 1861–Jan. 15, 1952; Senate 1921–33.

SHOTT, Hugh Ike (W.Va.) Sept. 3, 1866–Oct. 12, 1953; House 1929–33; Senate Nov. 18, 1942–43.

SHOUP, George Laird (great-grandfather of Richard Gardner Shoup) (Idaho) June 15, 1836–Dec. 21, 1904; Senate Dec. 18, 1890–1901; Gov. April 1889–90 (Idaho Terr.), Oct. 1–Dec. 1890.

SHOUP, Richard Gardner (great-grandson of George Laird Shoup) (Mont.) Nov. 29, 1923–; House 1971–75.

SHOWALTER, Joseph Baltzell (Pa.) Feb. 11, 1851–Dec. 3, 1932; House April 20, 1897–1903.

SHREVE, Milton William (Pa.) May 3, 1858–Dec. 23, 1939; House 1913–15, 1919–33.

SHRIVER, Garner E. (Kans.) July 6, 1912–; House 1961–77.

SHULTZ, Emanuel (Ohio) July 25, 1819–Nov. 5, 1912; House 1881–83.

SHUMWAY, Norman David (Calif.) July 28, 1934–; House 1979–91.

SHUSTER, E.G. "Bud" (Pa.) Jan. 23, 1932–; House 1973–; Chrmn. House Transportation and Infrastructure Committee 1995–.

SIBAL, Abner Woodruff (Conn.) April 11, 1921–; House 1961–65.

SIBLEY, Joseph Crocker (Pa.) Feb. 18, 1850–May 19, 1926; House 1893–95 (Democrat), 1899–1907 (1899–1901 Democrat).

SIEGEL, Isaac (N.Y.) April 12, 1880–June 29, 1947; House 1915–23.

SILER, Eugene (Ky.) June 26, 1900–; House 1955–65.

SILJANDER, Mark Deli (Mich.) June 11, 1951–; House April 21, 1981–87.

SIMKINS, Eldred (S.C.) Aug. 30, 1779–Nov. 17, 1831; House Jan. 24, 1818–21.

SIMMONS, James Samuel (nephew of Milton George Urner) (N.Y.) Nov. 25, 1861–Nov. 28, 1935; House 1909–13.

SIMMONS, Robert Glenmore (Nebr.) Dec. 25, 1891–Dec. 27, 1969; House 1923–33.

SIMMS, Albert Gallatin (husband of Ruth Hanna McCormick) (N.Mex.) Oct. 8, 1882–Dec. 29, 1964; House 1929–31.

SIMON, Joseph (Oreg.) Feb. 7, 1851–Feb. 14, 1935; Senate Oct. 8, 1898–1903.

SIMONDS, William Edgar (Conn.) Nov. 24, 1842–March 14, 1903; House 1889–91.

SIMPKINS, John (Mass.) June 27, 1862–March 27, 1898; House 1895–March 27, 1898.

SIMPSON, Alan Kooi (son of Milward Lee Simpson) (Wyo.) Sept. 2, 1931–; Senate Jan. 1, 1979–; Chrmn. Senate Veteran's Affairs 1981–85; Chrmn. Senate Veteran's Affairs Committee 1995–.

SIMPSON, Edna Oakes (widow of Sidney Elmer "Sid" Simpson) (Ill.) Oct. 28, 1891–May 15, 1984; House 1959–61.

SIMPSON, James Jr. (Ill.) Jan. 7, 1905–Feb. 29, 1960; House 1933–35.

SIMPSON, Kenneth Farrand (N.Y.) May 4, 1895–Jan. 25, 1941; House Jan. 3–Jan. 25, 1941.

SIMPSON, Milward Lee (father of Alan Kooi Simpson) (Wyo.) Nov. 12, 1897–June 10, 1993; Senate Nov. 6, 1962–67; Gov. Jan. 3, 1955–Jan. 5, 1959.

SIMPSON, Richard Murray (Pa.) Aug. 30, 1900–Jan. 7, 1960; House May 11, 1937–Jan. 7, 1960.

SIMPSON, Sidney Elmer "Sid" (husband of Edna Oakes Simpson) (Ill.) Sept. 20, 1894–Oct. 26, 1958; House 1943–Oct. 26, 1958; Chrmn. House District of Columbia 1963–55.

SINCLAIR, James Herbert (N.Dak.) Oct. 9, 1871–Sept. 5, 1943; House 1919–35.

SINGISER, Theodore Frelinghuysen (Idaho) March 15, 1845–Jan. 23, 1907; House (Terr. Del.) 1883–85.

SINNICKSON, Clement Hall (great-nephew of Thomas Sinnickson) (N.J.) Sept. 16, 1834–July 24, 1919; House 1875–79.

SINNOTT, Nicholas John (Oreg.) Dec. 6, 1870–July 20, 1929; House 1913–May 31, 1928.

SITTLER, Edward Lewis Jr. (Pa.) April 21, 1908–Dec. 26, 1978; House 1951–53.

SKEEN, Joseph Richard (N.Mex.) June 30, 1927–; House 1981–.

SKILES, William Woodburn (Ohio) Dec. 11, 1849–Jan. 9, 1904; House 1901–Jan. 9, 1904.

SKINNER, Charles Rufus (N.Y.) Aug. 4, 1844–June 30, 1928; House Nov. 8, 1881–85.

SKINNER, Richard (Vt.) May 30, 1778–May 23, 1833; House 1813–15; Gov. Oct. 13, 1820–Oct. 10, 1823 (Democratic Republican).

SKINNER, Thomson Joseph (Mass.) May 24, 1752–Jan. 20, 1809; House–Jan. 27, 1797–99, 1803–Aug. 10, 1804.

SKUBITZ, Joe (Kans.) May 6, 1906–; House 1963–Dec. 31, 1978.

SLAUGHTER, Daniel French Jr. (Va.) May 20, 1925–; House 1985–Nov. 5, 1991.

SLEMP, Campbell (father of Campbell Bascom Slemp) (Va.) Dec. 2, 1839–Oct. 13, 1907; House 1903–Oct. 13, 1907.

SLEMP, Campbell Bascom (son of Campbell Slemp) (Va.) Sept. 4, 1870–Aug. 7, 1943; House Dec. 17, 1907–23.

SLOAN, Andrew (Ga.) June 10, 1845–Sept. 22, 1883; House March 24, 1874–75.

SLOAN, Andrew Scott (brother of Ithamar Conkey Sloan) (Wis.) June 12, 1820–April 8, 1895; House 1861–63.

SLOAN, Charles Henry (Nebr.) May 2, 1863–June 2, 1946; House 1911–19, 1929–31.

SLOAN, Ithamar Conkey (brother of Andrew Scott Sloan) (Wis.) May 9, 1822–Dec. 24, 1898; House 1863–67.

SLOAN, James (N.J.) ?–Nov. 1811; House 1803–09.

SMALL, Frank Jr. (Md.) July 15, 1896–Oct. 24, 1973; House 1953–65.

SMALL, William Bradbury (N.H.) May 17, 1817–April 7, 1878; House 1873–75.

SMALLS, Robert (S.C.) April 5, 1839–Feb. 22, 1915; House 1875–79, July 19, 1882–83, March 18, 1884–87.

SMART, James Stevenson (N.Y.) June 14, 1842–Sept. 17, 1903; House 1873–75.

SMELT, Dennis (Ga.) about 1750–?; House Sept. 1, 1806–11.

SMILIE, John (Pa.) 1741–Dec. 30, 1812; House 1793–95 (no party), 1799–Dec. 30, 1812.

SMITH, Abraham Herr (Pa.) March 7, 1815–Feb. 16, 1894; House 1873–85.

SMITH, Addison Taylor (Idaho) Sept. 5, 1862–July 5, 1956; House 1913–33.

SMITH, Albert Lee Jr. (Ala.) Aug. 31, 1931–; House 1981–83.

SMITH, Ballard (Va.) ?–?; House 1815–21.

SMITH, Charles Brooks (W.Va.) Feb. 24, 1844–Dec. 7, 1899; House Feb. 3, 1890–91.

SMITH, Christopher Henry (N.J.) March 4, 1953–; House 1981–.

SMITH, Clyde Harold (husband of Margaret Chase Smith) (Maine) June 9, 1876–April 8, 1940; House 1937–April 8, 1940.

SMITH, Daniel (Tenn.) Oct. 28, 1748–June 6, 1818; Senate Oct. 6, 1798–99, 1805–March 31, 1809.

SMITH, Dennis Alan "Denny" (cousin of Steven Douglas Symms) (Oreg.) Jan. 19, 1938–; House 1981–91.

SMITH, Dietrich Conrad (Ill.) April 4, 1840–April 18, 1914; House 1881–83.

SMITH, Frank Leslie (Ill.) Nov. 24, 1867–Aug. 30, 1950; House 1919–21; elected to the Senate for the term beginning 1927 but was not permitted to qualify and resigned Feb. 9, 1928.

SMITH, Frederick Cleveland (Ohio) July 29, 1884–July 16, 1956; House 1939–51.

SMITH, George (Pa.) ?–?; House 1809–13.

SMITH, George Joseph (N.Y.) Nov. 7, 1859–Dec. 24, 1913; House 1903–05.

SMITH, George Luke (La.) Dec. 11, 1837–July 9, 1884; House Nov. 24, 1813–75.

SMITH, George Ross (Minn.) May 28, 1864–Nov. 7, 1952; House 1913–11

SMITH, George Washington (Ill.) Aug. 18, 1846–Nov. 30, 1907; House 1889–Nov. 30, 1907.

SMITH, H. Allen (Calif.) Oct. 8, 1909–; House 1957–73.

SMITH, Henry Cassorte (Mich.) June 2, 1856–Dec. 7, 1911; House 1899–1903.

SMITH, Henry P. III (N.Y.) Sept. 29, 1911–; House 1965–75.

SMITH, Hiram Ypsilanti (Iowa) March 22, 1843–Nov. 4, 1894; House Dec. 2, 1884–85.

SMITH, Horace Boardman (N.Y.) Aug. 18, 1826–Dec. 26, 1888; House 1871–75.

SMITH, Howard Alexander (uncle of Peter H. Dominick) (N.J.) Jan. 30, 1880–Oct. 27, 1966; Senate Dec. 7, 1944–59; Chrmn. Senate Labor and Public Welfare 1953–55.

SMITH, Isaac (Pa.) Jan. 4, 1761–April 4, 1834; House 1813–15.

SMITH, Israel (Vt.) April 4, 1759–Dec. 2, 1810; House Oct. 17, 1791–97 (no party), 1801–03 (no party); Senate 1803–Oct. 1, 1807; Gov. Oct. 9, 1807–Oct. 14, 1808 (Democratic Republican).

SMITH, James Strudwick (N.C.) Oct. 15, 1790–Aug. 1859; House 1817–21.

SMITH, James Vernon (Okla.) July 23, 1926–June 23, 1973; House 1967–69.

SMITH, Jedediah Kilburn (N.H.) Nov. 7, 1770–Dec. 17, 1828; House 1807–09.

SMITH, John (Ohio) about 1735–July 30, 1824; Senate April 1, 1803–April 25, 1808.

SMITH, John (Va.) May 7, 1750–March 5, 1836; House 1801–15.

SMITH, John (N.Y.) Feb. 12, 1752–Aug. 12, 1816; House Feb. 6, 1800–Feb. 23, 1804 (no party); Senate Feb. 23, 1804–13.

SMITH, John Ambler (Va.) Sept. 23, 1847–Jan. 6, 1892; House 1873–75.

SMITH, John Armstrong (Ohio) Sept. 23, 1814–March 7, 1892; House 1869–73.

SMITH, John M.C. (Mich.) Feb. 6, 1853–March 30, 1923; House 1911–21, June 28, 1921–March 30, 1923.

SMITH, John Quincy (Ohio) Nov. 5, 1824–Dec. 30, 1901; House 1873–75.

SMITH, Josiah (Mass.) Feb. 26, 1738–April 4, 1803; House 1801–03.

SMITH, Lamar Seeligson (Tex.) Nov. 19, 1947–; House 1987–.

SMITH, Larkin I. (Miss.) June 26, 1944–Aug. 13, 1989; House Jan. 3–Aug. 13, 1989.

SMITH, Lawrence Henry (Wis.) Sept. 15, 1892–Jan. 22, 1958; House Aug. 29, 1941–Jan. 22, 1958.

SMITH, Linda (Wash.) House, 1995–.

SMITH, Margaret Chase (widow of Clyde Harold Smith) (Maine) Dec. 14, 1897–; House June 3, 1940–49; Senate 1949–73.

SMITH, Nicholas Hart (Mich.) Nov. 5, 1934–; House 1993–.

SMITH, O'Brien (S.C.) about 1756–April 27, 1811; House 1805–07.

SMITH, Peter (Vt.) Oct. 31, 1945–; House 1989–91.

SMITH, Ralph Tyler (Ill.) Oct. 6, 1915–Aug. 13, 1972; Senate Sept. 17, 1969–Nov. 3, 1970.

SMITH, Robert Clinton (N.H.) March 30, 1941–; House 1985–Dec. 7, 1990; Senate Dec. 7, 1990–.

SMITH, Robert Freeman (Oreg.) June 16, 1931–; House 1983–.

SMITH, Samuel (Md.) July 27, 1752–April 22, 1839; House 1793–1803 (no party), Jan. 31, 1816–Dec. 17, 1822; Senate 1803–15, Dec. 17, 1822–33; elected Pres. pro tempore Dec. 2, 1805, March 18, 1806, March 2, 1807, April 16, 1808, May 15, 1828, March 13, 1829, May 29, 1830, March 1, 1831.

SMITH, Samuel (Pa.) ?–?; House Nov. 7, 1805–11.

SMITH, Samuel William (Mich.) Aug. 23, 1852–June 19, 1931; House 1897–1915.

SMITH, Sylvester Clark (Calif.) Aug. 26, 1858–Jan. 26, 1913; House 1905–Jan. 26, 1913.

SMITH, Virginia Dodd (Nebr.) June 30, 1911–; House 1975–91.

SMITH, Walter Inglewood (Iowa) July 10, 1862–Jan. 27, 1922; House Dec. 3, 1900–March 15, 1911.

SMITH, William (S.C.) about 1762–June 26, 1840; Senate Dec. 4, 1816–23, Nov. 29, 1826–31.

SMITH, William (S.C.) Sept. 20, 1751–June 22, 1837; House 1797–99.

SMITH, William Alden (Mich.) May 12, 1859–Oct. 11, 1932; House 1895–Feb. 9, 1907; Senate Feb. 9, 1907–19.

SMITH, William Alexander (N.C.) Jan. 9, 1828–May 16, 1888; House 1873–75.

SMITH, William Jay (Tenn.) Sept. 24, 1823–Nov. 29, 1913; House 1869–71.

SMITH, William Orlando (Pa.) June 13, 1859–May 12, 1932; House 1903–07.

SMITH, Wint (Kans.) Oct. 7, 1892–April 27, 1976; House 1947–61.

SMITH, Worthington Curtis (son of John Smith of Vt.) (Vt.) April 23, 1823–Jan. 2, 1894; House 1867–73.

SMOOT, Reed (Utah) Jan. 10, 1862–Feb. 9, 1941; Senate 1903–33.

SMYSER, Martin Luther (Ohio) April 3, 1851–May 6, 1908; House 1889–91, 1905–07.

SMYTH, Alexander (Va.) 1765–April 17, 1830; House 1817–25, 1827–April 17, 1830.

SMYTH, William (Iowa) Jan. 3, 1824–Sept. 30, 1870; House 1869–Sept. 30, 1870.

SNAPP, Henry (father of Howard Malcolm Snapp) (Ill.) June 30, 1822–Nov. 26, 1895; House Dec. 4, 1871–73.

SNAPP, Howard Malcolm (son of Henry Snapp) (Ill.) Sept. 27, 1855–Aug. 14, 1938; House 1903–11.

SNELL, Bertrand Hollis (N.Y.) Dec. 9, 1870–Feb. 2, 1958; House Nov. 2, 1915–39; House minority leader 1931–39.

SNIDER, Samuel Prather (Minn.) Oct. 9, 1845–Sept. 24, 1928; House 1889–91.

SNOVER, Horace Greeley (Mich.) Sept. 21, 1847–July 21, 1924; House 1895–99.

SNOW, Donald Francis (Maine) Sept. 6, 1877–Feb. 12, 1958; House 1929–33.

SNOWE, Olympia Jean Bouchles (wife of John Rhettie McKernan Jr.) (Maine) Feb. 21, 1947–; House 1979–1994; Senate 1995–.

SNYDER, Homer Peter (N.Y.) Dec. 6, 1863–Dec. 30, 1937; House 1915–25.

SNYDER, Marion Gene (Ky.) Jan. 26, 1928–; House 1963–65, 1967–87.

SNYDER, Melvin Claude (W.Va.) Oct. 29, 1898–; House 1947–49.

SNYDER, Oliver P. (Ark.) Nov. 13, 1833–Nov. 22, 1882; House 1871–75.

SOLOMON, Gerald Brooks Hunt (N.Y.) Aug. 14, 1930–; House 1979–; Chrmn. House Rules Committee 1995–.

SOMES, Daniel Eton (Maine) May 20, 1815–Feb. 13, 1888; House 1859–61.

SOSNOWSKI, John Bartholomew (Mich.) Dec. 8, 1883–July 16, 1968; House 1925–27.

SOUDER, Mark E. (Ind.) House, 1995–.

SOUTHARD, Henry (father of Isaac Southard and Samuel Lewis Southard) (N.J.) Oct. 7, 1747–May 22, 1842; House 1801–11, 1815–21.

SOUTHARD, James Harding (Ohio) Jan. 20, 1851–Feb. 20, 1919; House 1895–1907.

SOUTHWICK, George Newell (N.Y.) March 7, 1863–Oct. 17, 1912; House 1895–99, 1901–11.

SPRAIGHT, Richard Dobbs (grandfather of Richard Spraight Donnell, father of Richard Dobbs Spraight Jr.) (N.C.) March 25, 1758–Sept. 6, 1802; House Dec. 10, 1798–1801; Cont. Cong. 1783–85; Gov. Dec. 14, 1792–Nov. 19, 1795 (Anti-Federalist).

SPALDING, Burleigh Folsom (N.Dak.) Dec. 3, 1853–March 17, 1934; House 1899–1901, 1903–05.

SPALDING, George (Mich.) Nov. 12, 1836–Sept. 13, 1915; House 1895–99.

SPALDING, Rufus Paine (Ohio) May 3, 1798–Aug. 29, 1886; House 1863–69.

SPALDING, Thomas (Ga.) March 26, 1774–Jan. 5, 1851; House Dec. 24, 1805–06.

SPANGLER, Jacob (Pa.) Nov. 28, 1767–June 17, 1843; House 1817–April 20, 1818.

SPARKS, Charles Isaac (Kans.) Dec. 20, 1872–April 30, 1937; House 1929–33.

SPAULDING, Elbridge Gerry (N.Y.) Feb. 24, 1809–May 5, 1897; House 1949–51 (Whig), 1859–63.

SPAULDING, Oliver Lyman (Mich.) Aug. 2, 1833–July 30, 1922; House 1881–83.

SPEAKS, John Charles (Ohio) Feb. 11, 1859–Nov. 6, 1945; House 1921–31.

SPECTER, Arlen (Pa.) Feb. 12, 1930–; Senate 1981–; Chrmn. Senate Select Intelligence Committee 1995–.

SPEED, Thomas (Ky.) Oct. 25, 1768–Feb. 20, 1842; House 1817–19.

SPEER, Peter Moore (Pa.) Dec. 29, 1862–Aug. 3, 1933; House 1911–13.

SPEER, Thomas Jefferson (Ga.) Aug. 31, 1837–Aug. 18, 1872; House 1871–Aug. 18, 1872.

SPENCE, Floyd Davidson (S.C.) April 9, 1928–; House 1971–; Chrmn. House National Security Committee 1995–.

SPENCER, George Eliphaz (Ala.) Nov. 1, 1836–Feb. 19, 1893; Senate July 13, 1868–79.

SPENCER, John Canfield (son of Ambrose Spencer) (N.Y.) Jan. 8, 1788–May 18, 1855; House 1817–19; Secy. of War Oct. 12, 1841–March 3, 1843; Secy. of the Treasury March 8, 1843–May 2, 1844.

SPENCER, Selden Palmer (Mo.) Sept. 16, 1862–May 16, 1925; Senate Nov. 6, 1918–May 16, 1925.

SPERRY, Nehemiah Day (Conn.) July 10, 1827–Nov. 13, 1911; House 1895–1911.

SPINK, Cyrus (Ohio) March 24, 1793–May 31, 1859; House March 4–May 31, 1859.

SPINK, Solomon Lewis (Dakota) March 20, 1831–Sept. 22, 1881; House (Terr. Del.) 1869–71.

SPINNER, Francis Elias (N.Y.) Jan. 21, 1802–Dec. 31, 1890; House 1855–61 (1855–57 Democrat).

SPOONER, Henry Joshua (R.I.) Aug. 6, 1839–Feb. 9, 1918; House Dec. 5, 1881–91.

SPOONER, John Coit (Wis.) Jan. 6, 1843–June 11, 1919; Senate 1885–91, 1897–April 30, 1907.

SPRAGUE, Charles Franklin (grandson of Peleg Sprague of Maine) (Mass.) June 10, 1857–Jan. 30, 1902; House 1897–1901.

SPRAGUE, William (nephew of William Sprague, above) (R.I.) Sept. 12, 1830–Sept. 11, 1915; Senate 1863–75; Gov. May 29, 1860–March 3, 1863 (Unionist).

SPRAGUE, William Peter (Ohio) May 21, 1827–March 3, 1899; House 1871–75.

SPRIGG, Thomas (uncle of Richard Sprigg Jr.) (Md.) 1747–Dec. 13, 1809; House 1793–97.

SPRINGER, Raymond Smiley (Ind.) April 26, 1882–Aug. 28, 1947; House 1939–Aug. 28, 1947.

SPRINGER, William Lee (Ill.) April 12, 1909–Sept. 20, 1992; House 1951–73.

SPROUL, Elliott Wilford (Ill.) Dec. 28, 1856–June 22, 1935; House 1921–31.

SPROUL, William Henry (Kans.) Oct. 14, 1867–Dec. 27, 1932; House 1923–31.

SQUIRE, Watson Carvosso (Wash.) May 18, 1838–June 7, 1926; Senate Nov. 20, 1889–97; Gov. (Wash. Terr.) 1884–87.

STAFFORD, Robert Theodore (Vt.) Aug. 8, 1913–; House 1961–Sept. 16, 1971; Senate Sept. 16, 1971–89; Chrmn. Senate Environment and Public Works 1981–87; Gov. Jan. 8, 1959–Jan. 5, 1961.

STAFFORD, William Henry (Wis.) Oct. 12, 1869–April 22, 1957; House 1903–11, 1913–19, 1921–23, 1929–33.

STAHLE, James Alonzo (Pa.) Jan. 11, 1829–Dec. 21, 1912; House 1895–97.

STALKER, Gale Hamilton (N.Y.) Nov. 7, 1889–Nov. 4, 1985; House 1923–35.

STANARD, Edwin Obed (Mo.) Jan. 5, 1832–March 12, 1914; House 1873–75.

STANFIELD, Robert Nelson (Oreg.) July 9, 1877–April 13 1945; Senate 1921–27.

STANFILL, William Abner (Ky.) Jan. 16, 1892–June 12, 1971; Senate Nov. 19, 1945–Nov. 5, 1946.

STANFORD, Leland (Calif.) March 9, 1824–June 21, 1893; Senate 1885–June 21, 1893; Gov. Jan. 10, 1862–Dec. 10, 1863.

STANFORD, Richard (grandfather of William Robert Webb) (N.C.) March 2, 1767–April 9, 1816; House 1797–April 9, 1816.

STANGELAND, Arlan Ingehart (Minn.) Feb. 8, 1930–; House March 1, 1977–91.

STANLEY, Winifred Claire (N.Y.) Aug. 14, 1909–; House 1943–45.

STANTON, Benjamin (Ohio) June 4, 1809–June 2, 1872; House 1851–53 (Whig), 1855–61.

STANTON, John William (Ohio) Feb. 20, 1924–; House 1965–83.

STANTON, Joseph Jr. (R.I.) July 19, 1739–1807; Senate June 7, 1790–93 (no party); House 1801–07.

STARIN, John Henry (grandson of Thomas Sammons) (N.Y.) Aug. 27, 1825–March 21, 1909; House 1877–81.

STARKWEATHER, Henry Howard (Conn.) April 29, 1826–Jan. 28, 1876; House 1867–Jan. 28, 1876.

STARR, John Farson (N.J.) March 25, 1818–Aug. 9, 1904; House 1863–67.

STATON, David Michael (W.Va.) Feb. 11, 1940–; House 1981–83.

STAUFFER, Simon Walter (Pa.) Aug. 13, 1888–Sept. 26, 1975; House 1953–55, 1957–59.

STEARNS, Clifford Bundy (Fla.) April 16, 1941–; House 1989–.

STEARNS, Foster Waterman (N.H.) July 29, 1881–June 4, 1956; House 1939–45.

STEARNS, Ozora Pierson (Minn.) Jan, 15, 1831–June 2, 1896; Senate Jan. 23–March 3, 1871.

STEELE, George Washington (Ind.) Dec. 13, 1839–July 12, 1922; House 1881–89, 1895–1903; Gov. (Okla. Terr.) 1890–91.

STEELE, Robert Hampton (Conn.) Nov. 3, 1938–; House Nov. 3, 1970–75.

STEELMAN, Alan Watson (Tex.) March 15, 1942–; House 1973–77.

STEENERSON, Halvor (Minn.) June 30, 1852–Nov. 22, 1926; House 1903–23.

STEERS, Newton Ivan Jr. (Md.) Jan. 13, 1917–Feb. 11, 1993; House 1977–79.

STEFAN, Karl (Nebr.) March 1, 1884–Oct. 2, 1951; House 1935–Oct. 2, 1951.

STEIGER, Sam (Ariz.) March 10, 1929–; House 1967–77.

STEIGER, William Albert (Wis.) May 15, 1938–Dec. 4, 1978; House 1967–Dec. 4, 1978.

STEIWER, Frederick (Oreg.) Oct. 13, 1883–Feb. 3, 1939; Senate 1927–Jan. 31, 1938.

STEPHENS, Ambrose Everett Burnside (Ohio) June 3, 1862–Feb. 12, 1927; House 1919–Feb. 12, 1927.

STEPHENSON, Isaac (brother of Samuel Merritt Stephenson) (Wis.) June 18, 1829–March 15, 1918; House 1883–89; Senate May 17, 1907–15.

STEPHENSON, Samuel Merritt (brother of Isaac Stephenson) (Mich.) Dec. 23, 1831–July 31, 1907; House 1889–97.

STERLING, John Allen (brother of Thomas Sterling) (Ill.) Feb. 1, 1857–Oct. 17, 1918; House 1903–13, 1915–Oct. 17, 1918.

STERLING, Thomas (brother of John Allen Sterling) (S.Dak.) Feb. 21, 1851–Aug. 26, 1930; Senate 1913–25.

STEVENS, Aaron Fletcher (N.H.) Aug. 9, 1819–May 10, 1887; House 1867–71.

STEVENS, Charles Abbot (brother of Moses Tyler Stevens, cousin of Isaac Ingalls Stevens) (Mass.) Aug. 9, 1816–April 7, 1892; House Jan. 27–March 3, 1875.

STEVENS, Frederick Clement (Minn.) Jan. 1, 1861–July 1, 1923; House 1897–1915.

STEVENS, Thaddeus (Pa.) April 4, 1792–Aug. 11, 1868; House 1849–53 (Whig), 1859–Aug. 11, 1868.

STEVENS, Theodore Fulton "Ted" (Alaska) Nov. 18, 1923–; Senate Dec. 24, 1968–; Chrmn. Senate Select Committee on Ethics 1983–85; Chrmn. Senate Rules and Administration Committee 1995–.

STEVENSON, Job Evans (Ohio) Feb. 10, 1832–July 24, 1922; House 1869–73.

STEVENSON, William Henry (Wis.) Sept. 23, 1891–March 19, 1978; House 1941–49.

STEWART, Alexander (Wis.) Sept. 12, 1829–May 24, 1912; House 1895–1901.

STEWART, Andrew (Pa.) April 6, 1836–Nov. 9, 1903; House 1891–Feb. 26, 1892.

STEWART, David Wallace (Iowa) Jan. 22, 1887–Feb. 10, 1974; Senate Aug. 7, 1926–27.

STEWART, Jacob Henry (Minn.) Jan. 15, 1829–Aug. 25, 1884; House 1877–79.

STEWART, James Fleming (N.J.) June 15, 1851–Jan. 21, 1904; House 1895–1903.

STEWART, John (Pa.) ?–1820; House Jan. 15, 1801–05.

STEWART, John George (Del.) June 2, 1890–May 24, 1970; House 1935–37.

STEWART, John Knox (N.Y.) Oct. 20, 1853–June 27, 1919; House 1899–1903.

STEWART, John Wolcott (Vt.) Nov. 24, 1825–Oct. 29, 1915; House 1883–91; Senate March 24–Oct. 21, 1908; Gov. Oct. 6, 1870–Oct. 3, 1872.

STEWART, William (Pa.) Sept. 10, 1810–Oct. 17, 1876; House 1857–61.

STILLWELL, Thomas Neel (Ind.) Aug. 29, 1830–Jan. 14, 1874; House 1865–67.

STINESS, Walter Russell (R.I.) March 13, 1854–March 17, 1924; House 1915–23.

STINSON, K. William (Wash.) April 20, 1930–; House 1963–65.

STIVERS, Moses Dunning (N.Y.) Dec. 30, 1828–Feb. 2, 1895; House 1889–91.

STOBBS, George Russell (Mass.) Feb. 7, 1877–Dec. 23, 1966; House 1925–31.

STOCKBRIDGE, Francis Brown (Mich.) April 9, 1826–April 30, 1894; Senate 1887–April 30, 1894.

STOCKBRIDGE, Henry Jr. (Md.) Sept. 18, 1856–March 22, 1924; House 1891.

STOCKMAN, David Alan (Mich.) Nov. 10, 1946–; House 1977–Jan. 27, 1981.

STOCKMAN, Lowell (Oreg.) April 12, 1901–Aug. 9, 1962; House 1943–53.

STOCKMAN, Steve (Tex.) House, 1995–.

STOKES, Edward Lowber (Pa.) Sept. 29, 1880–Nov. 8, 1964; House Nov. 3, 1931–35.

STOKES, William Brickly (Tenn.) Sept. 9, 1814–March 14, 1897; House 1859–61 (Opposition Party), July 24, 1866–71 (July 24, 1866–67 Unconditional Unionist).

STONE, Charles Warren (Pa.) June 29, 1843–Aug. 15, 1912; House Nov. 4, 1890–99.

STONE, David (N.C.) Feb. 17, 1770–Oct. 7, 1818; House 1799–1801 (no party); Senate 1801–Feb. 17, 1807, 1813–Dec. 24, 1814; Gov. Dec. 12, 1808–Dec. 5, 1810 (Democratic Republican).

STONE, Eben Francis (Mass.) Aug. 3, 1822–Jan. 22, 1895; House 1881–87.

STONE, John Wesley (Mich.) July 18, 1838–March 24, 1922; House 1877–81.

STONE, Joseph Champlin (Iowa) July 30, 1829–Dec. 3, 1902; House 1877–79.

STONE, Ulysses Stevens (Okla.) Dec. 17, 1878–Dec. 8, 1962; House 1929–31.

STONE, William Alexis (Pa.) April 18, 1846–March 1, 1920; House 1891–Nov. 9, 1898; Gov. Jan. 17, 1899–Jan. 20, 1903.

STORER, Bellamy (uncle of Nicholas Longworth) (Ohio) Aug. 28, 1847–Nov. 12, 1922; House 1891–95.

STORER, Clement (N.H.) Sept. 20, 1760–Nov. 21, 1830; House 1807–09; Senate June 27, 1817–19.

STORM, Frederic (N.Y.) July 2, 1844–June 9, 1935; House 1901–03.

STORY, Joseph (Mass.) Sept. 18, 1779–Sept. 10, 1845; House May 23, 1808–09; Assoc. Justice Supreme Court Feb. 3, 1812–Sept. 10, 1845.

STOUGHTON, William Lewis (Mich.) March 20, 1827–June 6, 1888; House 1869–73.

STOVER, John Hubler (Mo.) April 24, 1833–Oct. 27, 1889; House Dec. 7, 1868–69.

STOW, Silas (N.Y.) Dec. 21, 1773–Jan. 19, 1827; House 1811–13.

STOWELL, William Henry Harrison (Va.) July 26, 1840–April 27, 1922; House 1871–77.

STRAIT, Horace Burton (Minn.) Jan. 26, 1835–Feb. 25, 1894; House 1873–79, 1881–87.

STRANG, Michael Lathrop (Colo.) June 17, 1929–; House 1985–87.

STRATTON, John Leake Newbold (N.J.) Nov. 27, 1817–May 17, 1899; House 1859–63.

STRATTON, William Grant (Ill.) Feb. 26, 1914–; House 1941–43, 1947–49; Gov. Jan. 12, 1953–Jan. 9, 1961.

STRAWBRIDGE, James Dale (Pa.) April 7, 1824–July 19, 1890; House 1873–75.

STRICKLAND, Randolph (Mich.) Feb. 4, 1823–May 5, 1880; House 1869–71.

STRINGFELLOW, Douglas R. (Utah) Sept. 24, 1922–Oct. 19, 1966; House 1953–55.

STRODE, Jesse Burr (Nebr.) Feb. 18, 1845–Nov. 10, 1924; House 1895–99.

STRONG, James George (Kans.) April 23, 1870–Jan. 11, 1938; House 1919–33.

STRONG, Julius Levi (Conn.) Nov. 8, 1828–Sept. 7, 1872; House 1869–Sept. 7, 1872.

STRONG, Luther Martin (Ohio) June 23, 1838–April 26, 1903; House 1893–97.

STRONG, Nathan Leroy (Pa.) Nov. 12, 1859–Dec. 14, 1939; House 1917–35.

STRONG, William (Vt.) 1763–Jan. 28, 1840; House 1811–15, 1819–21.

STROTHER, George French (Va.) 1783–Nov. 28, 1840; House 1817–Feb. 10, 1820.

STROTHER, James French (W.Va.) June 29, 1868–April 10, 1930; House 1925–29.

STRUBLE, Isaac S. (Iowa) Nov. 3, 1843–Feb. 17, 1913; House 1883–91.

STULL, Howard William (Pa.) April 11, 1876–April 22, 1949; House April 26, 1932–33.

STUMP, Robert Lee "Bob" (Ariz.) April 4, 1927–; House 1977– (1977–83 Democrat); Chrmn. House Veterans' Affairs Com-mittee 1995.

STURGISS, George Cookman (W.Va.) Aug. 16, 1842–Feb. 26, 1925; House 1907–11.

STURTEVANT, John Cirby (Pa.) Feb. 20, 1835–Dec. 20, 1912; House 1897–99.

SULLIVAN, Patrick Joseph (Wyo.) March 17, 1865–April 8, 1935; Senate Dec. 5, 1929–Nov. 20, 1930.

SULLIVAN, Patrick Joseph (Pa.) Oct. 12, 1877–Dec. 31, 1946; House 1929–33.

SULLOWAY, Cyrus Adams (N.H.) June 8, 1839–March 11, 1917; House 1897–1913, 1915–March 11, 1917.

SUMMERS, John William (Wash.) April 29, 1870–Sept. 25, 1937; House 1919–33.

SUMNER, Charles (Mass.) Jan. 6, 1811–March 11, 1874; Senate April 24, 1851–March 11, 1874 (1851–57 Free–Soiler).

SUMNER, Jessie (Ill.) July 17, 1898–Aug. 10, 1994; House 1939–47.

SUMTER, Thomas (grandfather of Thomas De Lage Sumter) (S.C.) Aug. 14, 1734–June 1, 1832; House 1789–93 (no party), 1797–Dec. 15, 1801; Senate Dec. 15, 1801–Dec. 16, 1810; Cont. Cong. (elected but did not attend) 1783.

SUNDQUIST, Donald Kenneth (Tenn.) March 16, 1936–; House 1983–.

SUNDSTROM, Frank Leander (N.J.) Jan. 5, 1901–May 23, 1980; House 1943–49.

SUTHERLAND, Daniel Alexander (Alaska) April 17, 1869–March 24, 1955; House (Terr. Del.) 1921–31.

SUTHERLAND, George (Utah) March 25, 1862–July 18, 1942; House 1901–03, Senate 1905–17; Assoc. Justice Supreme Court Oct. 2, 1922–Jan. 17, 1938.

SUTHERLAND, Howard (W.Va.) Sept. 8, 1865–March 12, 1950; House 1913–17; Senate 1917–23.

SWANSON, Charles Edward (Iowa) Jan. 3, 1879–Aug. 22, 1970; House 1929–33.

SWANWICK, John (Pa.) 1740–Aug. 1, 1798; House 1795–Aug. 1, 1798.

SWART, Peter (N.Y.) July 6, 1752–Nov. 3, 1829; House 1807–09.

SWARTZ, Joshua William (Pa.) June 9, 1867–May 27, 1959; House 1925–27.

SWASEY, John Philip (Maine) Sept. 4, 1839–May 27, 1928; House Nov. 3, 1908–11.

SWEENEY, David McCann "Mac" (Tex.) Sept. 15, 1955–; House 1985–89.

SWEET, Burton Erwin (Iowa) Dec. 10, 1867–Jan. 3, 1957; House 1915–23.

SWEET, John Hyde (Nebr.) Sept. 1, 1880–April 4, 1964; House April 9, 1940–41.

SWEET, Thaddeus C. (N.Y.) Nov. 16, 1872–May 1, 1928; House Nov. 6, 1923–May 1, 1928.

SWEET, Willis (Idaho) Jan. 1, 1856–July 9, 1925; House Oct. 1, 1890–95.

SWENEY, Joseph Henry (Iowa) Oct. 2, 1845–Nov. 11, 1918; House 1889–91.

SWICK, Jesse Howard (Pa.) Aug. 6, 1879–Nov. 17, 1952; House 1927–35.

SWIFT, Oscar William (N.Y.) April 11, 1869–June 30, 1940; House 1915–19.

SWIGERT, John Leonard (Colo.) Aug. 30, 1931–Dec. 27, 1982; elected to the House for the term beginning 1983 but did not serve.

SWINBURNE, John (N.Y.) May 30, 1820–March 28, 1889; House 1885–87.

SWINDALL, Charles (Okla.) Feb. 13, 1876–June 19, 1939; House Nov. 2, 1920–21.

SWINDALL, Patrick Lynn (Ga.) Oct. 18, 1950–House 1985–89.

SWING, Philip David (Calif.) Nov. 30, 1884–Aug. 8, 1963; House 1921–33.

SWITZER, Robert Mauck (Ohio) March 6, 1863–Oct. 28, 1952; House 1911–19.

SWOOPE, William Irvin (nephew of John Patton) (Pa.) Oct. 3, 1862–Oct. 9, 1930; House 1923–27.

SWOPE, King (Ky.) Aug. 10, 1893–April 23, 1961; House Aug. 2, 1919–21.

SYMES, George Gifford (Colo.) April 28, 1840–Nov. 3, 1893; House 1885–89.

SYMMS, Steven Douglas (Idaho) April 23, 1938–; House 1973–81; Senate 1981–93.

SYPHER, Jacob Hale (La.) June 22, 1837–May 9, 1905; House July 18, 1868–69, Nov. 7, 1870–75.

TABER, John (N.Y.) May 5, 1880–Nov. 22, 1965; House 1923–63; Chrmn. House Appropriations 1947–49, 1953–55.

TABOR, Horace Austin Warner (Colo.) Nov. 26, 1830–April 10, 1899; Senate Jan. 27–March 3, 1883.

TAFFE, John (Nebr.) Jan. 30, 1827–March 14, 1884; House 1867–73.

TAFT, Charles Phelps (brother of Pres. William Howard Taft, uncle of Robert Alphonso Taft, great-uncle of Robert Taft Jr.) (Ohio) Dec. 21, 1843–Dec. 31, 1929; House 1895–97.

TAFT, Kingsley Arter (Ohio) July 19, 1903–March 28, 1970; Senate Nov. 5, 1946–47.

TAFT, Robert Alphonso (son of Pres. William Howard Taft, father of Robert Taft Jr., nephew of Charles Phelps Taft) (Ohio) Sept. 8, 1889–July 31, 1953; Senate 1939–July 31, 1953; Chrmn. Senate Labor and Public Welfare 1947–49; Senate majority leader Jan. 3–July 31, 1953.

TAFT, Robert Alphonso Jr. (son of Robert Alphonso Taft, grandson of Pres. William Howard Taft, greatnephew of Charles Phelps Taft) (Ohio) Feb. 26, 1917–Dec. 7, 1993; House 1963–65, 1967–71; Senate 1971–Dec. 28, 1976.

TAIT, Charles (Ga.) Feb. 1, 1768–Oct. 7, 1835; Senate Nov. 27, 1809–19.

TALBOT, Isham (Ky.) 1773–Sept. 25, 1837; Senate Jan. 3, 1815–19, Oct. 19, 1820–26.

TALBOT, Joseph Edward (Conn.) March 18, 1901–April 30, 1966; House Jan. 20, 1942–47.

TALCOTT, Burt Lacklen (Calif.) Feb. 22, 1920–; House 1963–77.

TALENT, James Michael (Mo.) Oct. 18, 1956–; House 1993–.

TALLE, Henry Oscar (Iowa) Jan. 12, 1892–March 14, 1969; House 1939–59.

TALLMADGE, James Jr. (N.Y.) Jan. 20, 1778–Sept. 29, 1853; House June 6, 1817–19.

TALLMAN, Peleg (Mass.) July 24, 1764–March 12, 1840; House 1811–13.

TANNEHILL Adamson (Pa.) May 23, 1750–Dec. 23, 1820; House 1813–15.

TANNER, Adolphus Hitchcock (N.Y.) May 23, 1833–Jan. 14, 1882; House 1869–71.

TAPPAN, Mason Weare (N.H.) Oct. 20, 1817–Oct. 25, 1886; House 1855–61 (1855–57 American Party).

TARR, Christian (Pa.) May 25, 1765–Feb. 24, 1833; House 1817–21.

TATE, Randy (Wash.) House 1995–.

TATGENHORST, Charles Jr. (Ohio) Aug. 19, 1883–61; House Nov. 8, 1927–29.

TATOM, Absalom (N.C.) 1742–Dec. 20, 1802; House 1795–June 1, 1796.

TATTNALL, Josiah (Ga.) 1762–June 6, 1803; Senate Feb. 20, 1796–99; Gov. Nov. 7, 1801–Nov. 4, 1802 (Democratic Republican).

TAUKE, Thomas Joseph (Iowa) Oct. 11, 1950–; House 1979–91.

TAUL, Micah (grandfather of Tani Bradford) (Ky.) May 14, 1785–May 27, 1850; House 1815–17.

TAUZIN, Wilbert Joseph "Billy" (La.) June 14, 1943–; House May 17, 1980– (Democrat until 1995).

TAWNEY, James Albertus (Minn.) Jan. 3, 1855–June 12, 1919; House 1893–1911.

TAYLER, Robert Walker (Ohio) Nov. 26, 1852–Nov. 25, 1910; House 1895–1903.

TAYLOR, Abner (Ill.) 1829–April 13, 1903; House 1889–93.

TAYLOR, Alexander Wilson (Pa.) March 22, 1815–May 7, 1893; House 1873–76.

TAYLOR, Alfred Alexander (son of Nathaniel Green Taylor, brother of Robert Love Taylor) (Tenn.) Aug. 6, 1848–Nov. 25, 1931; House 1889–95; Gov. Jan. 15, 1921–Jan. 16, 1923.

TAYLOR, Caleb Newbold (Pa.) July 27, 1813–Nov. 15, 1887; House 1867–69, April 13, 1870–71.

TAYLOR, Charles Hart (N.C.) Jan. 23, 1941–; House 1991–.

TAYLOR, Dean Park (N.Y.) Jan. 1, 1902–Oct. 16, 1977; House 1943–61.

TAYLOR, Edward Livingston Jr. (Ohio) Aug. 10, 1869–March 10, 1938; House 1905–13.

TAYLOR, Ezra Booth (Ohio) July 9, 1823–Jan. 29, 1912; House Dec. 13, 1880–93.

TAYLOR, Gene (Mo.) Feb. 10, 1928–; House 1973–89.

TAYLOR, Herbert Worthington (N.J.) Feb. 19, 1869–Oct. 15, 1931; House 1921–23, 1925–27.

TAYLOR, Isaac Hamilton (Ohio) April 18, 1840–Dec. 18, 1936; House 1885–87.

TAYLOR, James Willis (Tenn.) Aug. 28, 1880–Nov. 14, 1939; House 1919–Nov. 14, 1939.

TAYLOR, John (Va.) Dec. 19, 1793–Aug. 20, 1824; Senate Oct. 18, 1792–May 11, 1794 (no party), June 4–Dec. 7, 1803, Dec. 18, 1822–Aug. 20, 1824.

TAYLOR, John (S.C.) May 4, 1770–April 16, 1832; House 1807–Dec. 30, 1810; Senate Dec. 31, 1810–Nov. 1816; Gov. Dec. 9, 1826–Dec. 10, 1828 (Democratic Republican).

TAYLOR, John (S.C.) ?–?; House 1815–17.

TAYLOR, John W. (N.Y.) March 26, 1784–Sept. 18, 1854; House 1813–33; Speaker Nov. 15, 1820–21, Dec. 5, 1825–27.

TAYLOR, Joseph Danner (Ohio) Nov. 7, 1830–Sept. 19, 1899; House Jan. 2, 1883–85, 1887–93.

TAYLOR, Vincent Albert (Ohio) Dec. 6, 1845–Dec. 2, 1922; House 1891–93.

TAYLOR, Waller (Ind.) before 1786–Aug. 26, 1826; Senate Dec. 11, 1816–25.

TAYLOR, Zachary (Tenn.) May 9, 1849–Feb. 19, 1921; House 1885–87.

TEAGUE, Charles McKevett (Calif.) Sept. 18, 1909–Jan. 1, 1974; House 1955–Jan. 1, 1974.

TELFAIR, Thomas (Ga.) March 2, 1780–Feb. 18, 1818; House 1813–17.

TEMPLE, Henry Wilson (Pa.) March 31, 1864–Jan. 11, 1955; House 1913–15 (Progressive), Nov. 2, 1915–33.

TEMPLETON, Thomas Weir (Pa.) Nov. 8, 1867–Sept. 5, 1935; House 1917–19.

TENER, John Kinley (Pa.) July 25, 1863–May 19, 1946; House 1909–Jan. 16, 1911; Gov. Jan. 17, 1911–Jan. 19, 1915.

TEN EYCK, John Conover (N.J.) March 12, 1814–Aug. 24, 1879; Senate 1859–65.

TERREL, William (Ga.) 1778–July 4, 1855; House 1817–21.

TERRY, John Hart (N.Y.) Nov. 14, 1924–; House 1971–73.

TEWES, Donald Edgar (Wis.) Aug. 4, 1916–; House 1957–59.

THATCHER, Maurice Hudson (Ky.) Aug. 15, 1870–Jan. 6, 1973; House 1923–33.

THAYER, Eli (father of John Alden Thayer) (Mass.) June 11, 1819–April 15, 1899; House 1857–61.

THAYER, Harry Irving (Mass.) Sept. 10, 1869–March 10, 1926; House 1925–March 10, 1926.

THAYER, John Milton (uncle of Arthur Laban Bates) (Nebr.) Jan. 24, 1820–March 19, 1906; Senate March 1, 1867–71; Gov. 1875–79 (Wyo. Terr.), Jan. 6, 1887–Jan. 15, 1891, May 5, 1891–Feb. 8, 1892.

THAYER, Martin Russell (Pa.) Jan. 27, 1819–Oct. 14, 1906; House 1863–67.

THEAKER, Thomas Clarke (Ohio) Feb. 1, 1812–July 16, 1883; House 1859–61.

THILL, Lewis Dominic (Wis.) Oct. 18, 1903–May 6, 1975; House 1939–43.

THISTLEWOOD, Napoleon Bonaparte (Ill.) March 30, 1837–Sept. 15, 1915; House Feb. 15, 1908–13.

THOMAS, Charles Randolph (N.C.) Feb. 7, 1827–Feb. 18, 1891; House 1871–75.

THOMAS, Christopher Yancy (Va.) March 24, 1818–Feb. 11, 1879; House March 5, 1874–75.

THOMAS, Craig (Wyo.) Feb. 17, 1933–; House May 2, 1989–1994; Senate 1995.

THOMAS, David (N.Y.) June 11, 1762–Nov. 27, 1831; House 1801–May 1, 1808.

THOMAS, Francis (Md.) Feb. 3, 1799–Jan. 22, 1876; House 1831–41 (1831–37 Jacksonian), 1861–69 (1861–63 Unionist, 1863–67 Unconditional Unionist); Gov. Jan. 3, 1841–Jan. 6, 1845 (Democrat).

THOMAS, George Morgan (Ky.) Nov. 23, 1828–Jan. 7, 1914; House 1887–89.

THOMAS, Henry Franklin (Mich.) Dec. 17, 1843–April 16, 1912; House 1893–97.

THOMAS, Isaac (Tenn.) Nov. 4, 1784–Feb. 2, 1859; House 1815–17.

THOMAS, Jesse Burgess (Ill.) 1777–May 3, 1853; House (Terr. Del.) Oct. 22, 1808–09 (no party Ind.); Senate Dec. 3, 1818–29.

THOMAS, John (Idaho) Jan. 4, 1874–Nov. 10, 1945 Senate June 30, 1928–33, Jan. 27, 1940–Nov. 10, 1945.

THOMAS, John Parnell (N.J.) Jan. 16, 1895–Nov. 19, 1970; House 1937–Jan. 2, 1950; Chrmn. House Un–American Activities 1947–49.

THOMAS, John Robert (Ill.) Oct. 11, 1846–Jan. 19, 1914; House 1879–89.

THOMAS, Lot (Iowa) Oct. 17, 1843–March 17, 1905; House 1899–1905.

THOMAS, Ormsby Brunson (Wis.) Aug. 21, 1832–Oct. 24, 1904; House 1885–91.

THOMAS, William Aubrey (Ohio) June 7, 1866–Sept. 8, 1951; House Nov. 8, 1904–11.

THOMAS, William David (N.Y.) March 22, 1880–May 17, 1936; House Jan. 30, 1934–May 17, 1936.

THOMAS, William Marshall (Calif.) Dec. 6, 1941–; House 1979–; Chrmn. House Oversight Committee 1995–.

THOMPSON, Albert Clifton (Ohio) Jan. 23, 1842–Jan. 26, 1910; House 1885–91.

THOMPSON, Charles James (Ohio) Jan. 24, 1862–March 27, 1932; House 1919–31.

THOMPSON, Fred (Tenn.) Senate, 1995–.

THOMPSON, John (N.Y.) March 20, 1749–1823; House 1799–1801, 1807–11.

THOMPSON, John (N.Y.) July 4, 1809–June 1, 1890; House 1857–59.

THOMPSON, John McCandless (brother of William George Thompson) (Pa.) Jan. 4, 1829–Sept. 3, 1903; House Dec. 22, 1874–75, 1877–79.

THOMPSON, Philip Rootes (Va.) March 26, 1766–July 27, 1837; House 1801–07.

THOMPSON, Ruth (Mich.) Sept. 15, 1887–April 5, 1970; House 1951–57.

THOMPSON, Standish Fletcher (Ga.) Feb. 5, 1925–; House 1967–73.

THOMPSON, William George (brother of John McCandless Thompson) (Iowa) Jan. 17, 1830–April 2, 1911; House Oct. 14, 1879–83.

THOMSON, Edwin Keith (Wyo) Feb. 8, 1919–Dec. 9, 1960; House 1955–Dec. 9, 1960; did not seek nomination but was elected to the Senate for the term beginning 1961, did not serve.

THOMSON, Vernon Wallace (Wis.) Nov. 5, 1905–April 12, 1988; House 1961–Dec. 31, 1974; Gov. Jan. 7, 1957–Jan. 5, 1959.

THONE, Charles (Nebr.) Jan. 4, 1924–; House 1971–79; Gov. Jan. 4, 1979–Jan. 6. 1983.

THORKELSON, Jacob (Mont.) Sept. 24, 1876–Nov. 20, 1945; House 1939–41.

THORNBERRY, William M. "Mac" (Tex.) House, 1995–.

THORNBURGH, Jacob Montgomery (Tenn.) July 3, 1837–Sept. 19, 1890; House 1873–79.

THORP, Robert Taylor (Va.) March 12, 1850–Nov. 26, 1938; House May 2, 1896–97, March 23, 1898–99.

THORPE, Roy Henry (Nebr.) Dec. 13, 1874–Sept. 19, 1951; House Nov. 7, 1922–23.

THROOP, Enos Thompson (N.Y.) Aug. 21, 1784–Nov. 1, 1874; House 1815–June 4, 1816; Gov. March 12, 1829–Jan. 1, 1833 (Jacksonian).

THROPP, Joseph Earlston (Pa.) Oct. 4, 1847–July 27, 1927; House 1899–1901.

THRUSTON, Buckner (Ky.) Feb. 9, 1763–Aug. 30, 1845; Senate 1805–Dec. 18, 1809.

THURMOND, James Strom (S.C.) Dec. 5, 1902–; Senate Dec. 24, 1954–April 4, 1956 (Democrat), Nov. 7, 1956– (Nov. 7, 1956–Sept. 16, 1964 Democrat); elected Pres. pro tempore Jan. 5, 1981; Chrmn. Senate Judiciary 1981–87; Gov. Jan. 21, 1947–Jan. 16, 1951 (Democrat); Chrmn. Senate Armed Services Committee 1995–.

THURSTON, John Mellen (Nebr.) Aug. 21, 1847–Aug. 9, 1916; Senate 1895–1901.

THURSTON, Lloyd (Iowa) March 27, 1880–May 7, 1970; House 1926–39.

THYE, Edward John (Minn.) April 26, 1896–Aug. 28, 1969; Senate 1947–59; Chrmn. Senate Select Committee on Small Business 1953–55; Gov. April 27, 1943–Jan. 8, 1947.

TIAHRT, Todd (Kans.) House 1995–.

TIBBOTT, Harve (Pa.) May 27, 1885–Dec. 31, 1969; House 1939–49.

TIFFIN, Edward (Ohio) June 19, 1766–Aug. 9, 1829; Senate 1807–09; Gov. March 3, 1803–March 4, 1807 (Democratic Republican).

TILLINGHAST, Thomas (cousin of Joseph Leonard Tillinghast) (R.I.) Aug. 21, 1742–Aug. 26, 1821; House Nov. 13, 1797–99 (Federalist), 1801–03.

TILLMAN, Lewis (nephew of Barclay Martin) (Tenn.) Aug. 18, 1816–May 3, 1886; House 1869–71.

TILSON, John Quillin (Conn.) April 5, 1866–Aug. 14, 1958; House 1909–13, 1915–Dec. 3, 1932; House majority leader 1925–31.

TIMBERLAKE, Charles Bateman (Colo.) Sept. 25, 1854–May 31, 1941; House 1915–35.

TINCHER, Jasper Napoleon (Kans.) Nov. 2, 1878–Nov. 6, 1951; House 1919–27.

TINKHAM, George Holden (Mass.) Oct. 29, 1870–Aug. 28, 1956; House 1915–43.

TIPTON, Thomas Foster (Ill.) Aug. 29, 1833–Feb. 7, 1904; House 1877–79.

TIPTON, Thomas Weston (Nebr.) Aug. 5, 1817–Nov. 26, 1899; Senate March 1, 1867–75.

TIRRELL, Charles Quincy (Mass.) Dec. 10, 1844–July 31, 1910; House 1901–July 31, 1910.

TOBEY, Charles William (N.H.) July 22, 1880–July 24, 1953; House 1933–39; Senate 1939–July 24, 1953; Chrmn. Senate Banking and Currency 1947–49; Chrmn. Senate Interstate and Foreign Commerce 1953; Gov. Jan. 3, 1929–Jan. 1, 1931.

TODD, Lemuel (Pa.) July 29, 1817–May 12, 1891; House 1855–57, 1873–75.

TOLLEFSON, Thor Carl (Wash.) May 2, 1901–Dec. 30, 1982; House 1947–65.

TOLLEY, Harold Sumner (N.Y.) Jan. 16, 1894–May 20, 1956; House 1925–27.

TOMPKINS, Arthur Sidney (N.Y.) Aug. 26, 1865–Jan. 20, 1938; House 1899–1903.

TOMPKINS, Caleb (brother of Daniel D. Tompkins) (N.Y.) Dec. 22, 1759–Jan. 1, 1846; House 1817–21.

TOMPKINS, Cydnor Bailey (father of Emmett Tompkins) (Ohio) Nov. 8, 1810–July 23, 1862; House 1857–61.

TOMPKINS, Emmett (son of Cydnor Bailey Tompkins) (Ohio) Sept. 1, 1853–Dec. 18, 1917; House 1901–03.

TONGUE, Thomas H. (Oreg.) June 23, 1844–Jan. 11, 1903; House 1897–Jan. 11, 1903.

TORKILDSEN, Peter Gerard (Mass.) Jan. 28, 1958–; House 1993–.

TOWE, Harry Lancaster (N.J.) Nov. 3, 1898–Feb. 8, 1991; House 1943–Sept. 7, 1951.

TOWELL, David Gilmer (Nev.) June 9, 1937–; House 1973–75.

TOWER, John Goodwin (Tex.) Sept. 29, 1925–April 5, 1991; Senate June 15, 1961–85; Chrmn. Senate Armed Services 1981–85.

TOWNER, Horace Mann (Iowa) Oct. 23, 1855–Nov. 23, 1937; House 1911–April 1, 1923; Gov. (P.R.) 1923–29.

TOWNSEND, Amos (Ohio) 1821–March 17, 1895; House 1877–83.

TOWNSEND, Charles Champlain (Pa.) Nov. 24, 1841–July 10, 1910; House 1889–91.

TOWNSEND, Charles Elroy (Mich.) Aug. 15, 1856–Aug. 3, 1924; House 1903–11; Senate 1911–23.

TOWNSEND, George (N.Y.) 1769–Aug. 17, 1844; House 1815–19.

TOWNSEND, Hosea (Colo.) June 16, 1840–March 4, 1909; House 1889–93.

TOWNSEND, John Gillis Jr. (Del.) May 31, 1871–April 10, 1964; Senate 1929–41; Gov. Jan. 17, 1917–Jan. 18, 1921.

TOWNSEND, Martin Ingham (N.Y.) Feb. 6, 1810–March 8, 1903; House 1875–79.

TOWNSEND, Washington (Pa.) Jan. 20, 1813–March 18, 1894; House 1869–77.

TRACEWELL, Robert John (Ind.) May 7, 1852–July 28, 1922; House 1895–97.

TRACEY, John Plank (Mo.) Sept. 18, 1836–July 24, 1910; House 1895–97.

TRACY, Uri (N.Y.) Feb. 8, 1764–July 21, 1838; House 1805–07, 1809–13.

TRAEGER, William Isham (Calif.) Feb. 26, 1880–Jan. 20, 1935; House 1933–35.

TRAIN, Charles Russell (Mass.) Oct. 18, 1817–July 28, 1889; House 1859–63.

TREADWAY, Allen Towner (Mass.) Sept. 16, 1867–Feb. 16, 1947; House 1913–45.

TREEN, David Conner (La.) July 16, 1928–; House 1973–March 10, 1980; Gov. March 10, 1980–March 12, 1984.

TRELOAR, William Mitchellson (Mo.) Sept. 21, 1850–July 3, 1935; House 1895–97.

TREMAIN, Lyman (N.Y.) June 14, 1819–Nov. 30, 1878; House 1873–75.

TRIBLE, Paul Seward Jr. (Va.) Dec. 29, 1946–; House 1977–83; Senate 1983–89.

TRIGG, Abram (brother of John Johns Trigg) (Va.) 1750–?; House 1797–1809.

TRIGG, John Johns (brother of Abram Trigg) (Va.) 1748–May 17, 1804; House 1797–May 17, 1804.

TRIMBLE, Carey Allen (Ohio) Sept. 13, 1813–May 4, 1887; House 1859–63.

TRIMBLE, David (Ky.) June 1782–Oct. 20, 1842; House 1817–27.

TRIMBLE, John (Tenn.) Feb. 7, 1812–Feb. 23, 1884; House 1867–69.

TROUP, George Michael (Ga.) Sept. 8, 1780–April 26, 1856; House 1807–15; Senate Nov. 13, 1816–Sept. 23, 1818, 1829–Nov. 8, 1833; Gov. Nov. 7, 1823–Nov. 7, 1827 (Democratic Republican).

TROUTMAN, William Irvin (Pa.) Jan. 13, 1905–Jan. 27, 1971; House 1943–Jan. 2, 1945.

TROWBRIDGE, Rowland Ebenezer (Mich.) June 18, 1821–April 20, 1881; House 1861–63, 1865–69.

TUCKER, Henry St. George (Va.) Dec. 29, 1780–Aug. 28, 1848; House 1815–19.

TUFTS, John Quincy (Iowa) July 12, 1840–Aug. 10, 1908; House 1875–77.

TUPPER, Stanley Roger (Maine) Jan. 25, 1921–; House 1961–67.

TURNER, Benjamin Sterling (Ala.) March 17, 1825–March 21, 1894; House 1871–73.

TURNER, Charles Jr. (Mass.) June 20, 1760–May 16, 1839; House June 28, 1809–13.

TURNER, Erastus Johnson (Kans.) Dec. 26, 1846–Feb. 10, 1933; House 1887–91.

TURNER, James (father of Daniel Turner) (N.C.) Dec. 20, 1766–Jan. 15, 1824; Senate 1805–Nov. 21, 1816; Gov. Dec. 6, 1802–05.

TURPIN, Charles Murray (Pa.) March 4, 1878–June 4, 1946; House June 4, 1929–37.

TWICHELL Ginery (Mass.) Aug. 26, 1811–July 23, 1883; House 1867–73.

TWYMAN, Robert Joseph (Ill.) June 18, 1897–June 28, 1976; House 1947–49.

TYLER, James Manning (Vt.) April 27, 1835–Oct. 13, 1926; House 1879–83.

TYLER, John (father of David Gardiner Tyler, son of Gov. John Tyler of Va.) (Va.) March 29, 1790–Jan. 18, 1862; House Dec. 16, 1817–21; Senate 1827–Feb. 29, 1836; elected Pres. pro tempore March 3, 1835; Gov. Dec. 10, 1825–March 4, 1827 (Democratic Republican); Vice President March 4–April 6, 1841 (Whig); President April 6, 1841–45 (Whig).

TYNDALL, William Thomas (Mo.) Jan. 16, 1862–Nov. 26, 1928; House 1905–07.

TYNER, James Noble (Ind.) Jan. 17, 1826–Dec. 5, 1904; House 1869–75; Postmaster Gen. July 13, 1876–March 12, 1877.

UDREE, Daniel (Pa.) Aug. 5, 1751–July 15, 1828; House Oct. 12, 1813–15, Dec. 26, 1820–21, Dec. 10, 1822–25.

UNDERHILL, Charles Lee (Mass.) July 20, 1867–Jan. 28, 1946; House 1921–33.

UPDEGRAFF, Jonathan Taylor (Ohio) May 13, 1822–Nov. 30, 1882; House 1879–Nov. 30, 1882.

UPDEGRAFF, Thomas (Iowa) April 3, 1834–Oct. 4, 1910; House 1879–83, 1893–99.

UPDIKE, Ralph Eugene (Ind.) May 27, 1894–Sept. 16, 1953; House 1925–29.

UPHAM, Nathaniel (N.H.) June 9, 1774–July 10, 1829; House 1817–23.

UPSON, Charles (Mich.) March 19, 1821–Sept. 5, 1885; House 1863–69.

UPSON, William Hanford (Ohio) Jan. 11, 1823–April 13, 1910; House 1869–73.

UPTON, Frederick Stephen (Mich.) April 23, 1953–; House 1987–.

UPTON, Robert William (N.H.) Feb. 3, 1884–April 28, 1972; Senate Aug. 14, 1953–Nov. 7, 1954.

URNER, Milton George (uncle of James Samuel Simmons) (Md.) July 29, 1839–Feb. 9, 1926; House 1879–83.

UTT, James Boyd (Calif.) March 11, 1899–March 1, 1970; House 1953–March 1, 1970.

UTTER, George Herbert (R.I.) July 24, 1854–Nov. 3, 1912; House 1911–Nov. 3, 1912; Gov. Jan. 3, 1905–Jan. 1, 1907.

VAIL, Richard Bernard (Ill.) Aug. 31, 1895–July 29, 1955; House 1947–49, 1951–53.

VAILE, William Newell (Colo.) June 22, 1876–July 2, 1927; House 1919–July 2, 1927.

VALENTINE, Edward Kimble (Nebr.) June 1, 1843–April 11, 1916; House 1879–85.

VAN AERNAM, Henry (N.Y.) March 11, 1819–June 1, 1894; House 1865–69, 1879–83.

VAN ALEN, James Isaac (half–brother of Martin Van Buren) (N.Y.) 1776–Dec. 23, 1870; House 1807–09.

VAN CORTLANDT, Philip (brother of Pierre Van Cortlandt Jr.) (N.Y.) Aug. 21, 1749–Nov. 1, 1831; House 1793–1809 (1793–95 no party).

VAN CORTLANDT, Pierre Jr. (brother of Philip Van Cortlandt) (N.Y.) Aug. 29, 1762–July 13, 1848; House 1811–13.

VANDENBERG, Arthur Hendrick (Mich.) March 22, 1884–April 18, 1951; Senate March 31, 1928–April 18, 1951; elected Pres. pro tempore Jan. 4, 1947; Chrmn. Senate Foreign Relations 1947–49.

VANDER JAGT, Guy Adrian (Mich.) Aug. 26, 1931–; House Nov. 8, 1966–93.

VANDEVER, William (Calif.) March 31, 1817–July 23, 1893; House 1859–Sept. 24, 1861 (Iowa) 1887–91.

VAN HORN, Burt (N.Y.) Oct. 28, 1823–April 1, 1896; House 1861–63, 1865–69.

VAN HORN, Robert Thompson (Mo.) May 19, 1824–Jan. 3, 1916; House 1865–71, 1881–83, Feb. 27, 1896–97.

VAN HORNE, Archibald (Md.) ?–1817; House 1807–11.

VAN HORNE, Isaac (Pa.) Jan. 13, 1754–Feb. 2, 1834; House 1801–05.

VAN NESS, John Peter (N.Y.) 1770–March 7, 1846; House Oct. 6, 1801–Jan. 17, 1803.

VAN PELT, William Kaiser (Wis.) March 10, 1905–; House 1951–65.

VAN SCHAICK, Isaac Whitbeck (uncle of Aaron Van Schaick Cochrane) (Wis.) Dec. 7, 1817–Aug. 22, 1901; House 1885–87, 1889–91.

VAN VALKENBURGH, Robert Bruce (N.Y.) Sept. 4, 1821–Aug. 1, 1888; House 1861–65.

VAN VOORHIS, Henry Clay (Ohio) May 11, 1852–Dec. 12, 1927; House 1893–1905.

VAN VOORHIS, John (N.Y.) Oct. 22, 1826–Oct. 20, 1905; House 1879–83, 1893–95.

VAN VORHES, Nelson Holmes (Ohio) Jan. 23, 1822–Dec. 4, 1882; House 1875–79.

VAN WINKLE, Marshall (great-nephew of Peter Godwin Van Winkle) (N.J.) Sept. 28, 1869–May 10, 1957; House 1905–07.

VAN WYCK, Charles Henry (Nebr.) May 10, 1824–Oct. 24, 1895; House 1859–63, 1867–69, Feb. 17, 1870–71 (N.Y.); Senate 1881–87.

VAN ZANDT, James Edward (Pa.) Dec. 18, 1898–Jan. 6, 1986; House 1939–Sept. 24, 1943, 1947–63.

VARE, William Scott (Pa.) Dec. 24, 1867–Aug. 7, 1934; House April 24, 1912–Jan. 2, 1923, 1923–27; elected to the Senate for the term beginning 1927 but was not permitted to qualify.

VARNUM, Joseph Bradley (Mass.) Jan. 29, 1750 or 1751–Sept. 21, 1821; House 1795–June 29, 1811 (no party); Speaker Oct. 26, 1807–09, May 22, 1809–11; Senate June 29, 1811–17; elected Pres. pro tempore Dec. 6, 1813.

VAUGHN, Albert Clinton Sr. (Pa.) Oct. 9, 1894–Sept. 1, 1951; House Jan. 3–Sept. 1, 1951.

VELDE, Harold Himmel (Ill.) April 1, 1910–Sept. 1, 1985; House 1949–57; Chrmn. House Un-American Activities 1953–55.

VERPLANCK, Daniel Crommelin (father of Gulian Crommelin Verplanck) (N.Y.) March 19, 1762–March 29, 1834; House Oct. 17, 1803–09.

VERREE, John Paul (Pa.) March 9, 1817–June 27, 1889; House 1859–63.

VESTAL, Albert Henry (Ind.) Jan. 18, 1875–April 1, 1932; House 1917–April 1, 1932.

VEYSEY, Victor Vincent (Calif.) April 14, 1916–; House 1971–75.

VIDAL, Michel (La.) Oct. 1, 1824–?; House July 18, 1868–69.

VINCENT, Bird J. (Mich.) March 6, 1880–July 18, 1931; House 1923–July 18, 1931.

VINCENT, Earl W. (Iowa) March 27, 1886–May 22, 1953; House June 4, 1928–29.

VOIGT, Edward (Wis.) Dec. 1, 1873–Aug. 26, 1934; House 1917–27.

VOLK, Lester David (N.Y.) Sept. 17, 1884–April 30, 1962; House Nov. 2, 1920–23.

VOLSTEAD, Andrew John (Minn.) Oct. 31, 1860–Jan. 20, 1947; House 1903–23.

VOORHIS, Charles Henry (N.J.) March 13, 1833–April 15, 1896; House 1879–81.

VORYS, John Martin (Ohio) June 16, 1896–Aug. 25, 1968; House 1939–59.

VREELAND, Albert Lincoln (N.J.) July 2, 1901–May 3, 1975; House 1939–43.

VREELAND, Edward Butterfield (N.Y.) Dec. 7, 1856–May 8, 1936; House Nov. 7, 1899–1913.

VUCANOVICH, Barbara Farrell (Nev.) June 22, 1921–; House 1983–.

VURSELL, Charles Wesley (cousin of Carl Bert Albert) (Ill.) Feb. 8, 1881–Sept. 21, 1974; House 1943–59.

WACHTER, Frank Charles (Md.) Sept. 16, 1861–July 1, 1910; House 1899–1907.

WADDILL, Edmund Jr, (Va.) May 22, 1855–April 9, 1931; House April 12, 1890–91.

WADE, Benjamin Franklin (brother of Edward Wade) (Ohio) Oct. 27, 1800–March 2, 1878; Senate March 15, 1851–69 (1851–57 Whig); elected Pres. pro tempore March 2, 1867.

WADE, Edward (brother of Benjamin Franklin Wade) (Ohio) Nov. 22, 1802–Aug. 13, 1866; House 1853–61 (1853–55 Free-Soiler).

WADE, William Henry (Mo.) Nov. 3, 1835–Jan. 13, 1911; House 1885–91.

WADLEIGH, Bainbridge (N.H.) Jan. 4, 1831–Jan. 24, 1891; Senate 1873–79.

WADSWORTH, James Wolcott (father of James Wolcott Wadsworth Jr., great-grandfather of James Wadsworth Symington) (N.Y.) Oct. 12, 1846–Dec. 24, 1926; House Nov. 8, 1881–85, 1891–1907.

WADSWORTH, James Wolcott Jr. (son of James Wolcott Wadsworth, grandfather of James Wadsworth Symington, father-in-law of Stuart Symington) (N.Y.) Aug. 12, 1877–June 21, 1952; Senate 1916–27; House 1933–51.

WADSWORTH, William Henry (Ky.) July 4, 1821–April 2, 1893; House 1861–65 (Unionist), 1885–87.

WAGONER, George Chester Robinson (Mo.) Sept. 3, 1863–April 27, 1946; House Feb. 26, 1901–03.

WAINWRIGHT, Jonathan Mayhew (N.Y.) Dec. 10, 1864–June 3, 1945; House 1923–31.

WAINWRIGHT, Stuyvesant II (N.Y.) March 16, 1921–; House 1953–61.

WAIT, John Turner (Conn.) Aug. 27, 1811–April 21, 1899; House April 12, 1876–87.

WAKEFIELD, James Beach (Minn.) March 21, 1825–Aug. 25, 1910; House 1883–87.

WAKEMAN, Seth (N.Y.) Jan. 15, 1811–Jan. 4, 1880; House 1871–73.

WALBRIDGE, David Safford (Mich.) July 30, 1802–June 15, 1868; House 1855–59.

WALCOTT, Frederic Collin (Conn.) Feb. 19, 1869–April 27, 1949; Senate 1929–35.

WALDEN, Madison Miner (Iowa) Oct. 6, 1836–July 24, 1891; House 1871–73.

WALDHOLTZ, Enid Greene (Utah) House, 1995–.

WALDO, George Ernest (N.Y.) Jan. 11, 1851–June 16, 1942; House 1905–09.

WALDOW, William Frederick (N.Y.) Aug. 26, 1882–April 16, 1930; House 1917–19.

WALDRON, Alfred Marpole (Pa.) Sept. 21, 1865–June 28, 1952; House 1933–35.

WALDRON, Henry (Mich.) Oct. 11, 1819–Sept. 13, 1880; House 1855–61, 1871–77.

WALKER, Amasa (Mass.) May 4, 1799–Oct. 29, 1875; House Dec. 1, 1862–63.

WALKER, David (brother of George Walker, grandfather of James David Walker) (Ky.) ?–March 1, 1820; House 1817–March 1, 1820.

WALKER, Felix (N.C.) July 19, 1753–1828; House 1817–23.

WALKER, James Alexander (Va.) Aug. 27, 1832–Oct. 21, 1901; House 1895–99.

WALKER, Joseph Henry (Mass.) Dec. 21, 1829–April 3, 1907; House 1889–99.

WALKER, Lewis Leavell (Ky.) Feb. 15, 1873–June 30, 1944; House 1929–31.

WALKER, Prentiss Lafayette (Miss.) Aug. 23, 1917-; House 1965–67.

WALKER, Robert Jarvis Cochran (Pa.) Oct. 20, 1838–Dec. 19, 1903; House 1881–83.

WALKER, Robert Smith (Pa.) Dec. 23, 1942–; House 1977–; Chrmn. House Science Committee 1995–.

WALL, William (N.Y.) March 20, 1800–April 20, 1872; House 1861–63.

WALLACE, Alexander Stuart (S.C.) Dec. 30, 1810–June 27, 1893; House May 27, 1870–77.

WALLACE, James M. (Pa.) 1750–Dec. 17, 1823; House Oct. 10, 1815–21.

WALLACE, John Winfield (Pa.) Dec. 20, 1818–June 24, 1889; House 1861–63, 1875–77.

WALLACE, Rodney (Mass.) Dec. 21, 1823–Feb. 27, 1903; House 1889–91.

WALLACE, William Copeland (N.Y.) May 21, 1856–Sept. 4, 1901; House 1889–91.

WALLACE, William Henson (Idaho) July 19, 1811–Feb. 7, 1879; House (Terr. Del. Wash.) 1861–63, (Terr. Del. Idaho) Feb. 1, 1864–65; Gov. (Idaho Terr.) 1863.

WALLHAUSER, George Marvin (N.J.) Feb. 10, 1900–Aug. 4, 1993; House 1959–65.

WALLIN, Samuel (N.Y.) July 31, 1856–Dec. 1, 1917; House 1913–15.

WALLOP, Malcolm (Wyo.) Feb. 27, 1933–; Senate 1977–; Chrmn. Senate Select Committee on Ethics 1981–83.

WALLS, Josiah Thomas (Fla.) Dec. 30, 1842–May 5, 1905; House 1871–Jan. 29, 1873 (no party), 1873–April 19, 1876.

WALSH, James Thomas (N.Y.) June 19, 1947–; House 1989–.

WALSH, Joseph (Mass.) Dec. 16, 1875–Jan. 13, 1946; House 1915–Aug. 2, 1922.

WALSH, William Francis (N.Y.) July 11, 1912–; House 1973–79.

WALTERS, Anderson Howell (Pa.) May 18, 1862–Dec. 7, 1927; House 1913–15, 1919–23, 1925–27.

WALTON, Charles Wesley (Maine) Dec. 9, 1819–Jan. 24, 1900; House 1861–May 26, 1862.

WALTON, Eliakim Persons (Vt.) Feb. 17, 1812–Dec. 19, 1890; House 1857–63.

WALTON, Matthew (cousin of George Walton) (Ky.) ?–Jan. 18, 1819; House 1803–07.

WAMP, Zach (Tenn.) House, 1995–.

WAMPLER, William Creed (Va.) April 21, 1926–; House 1953–55, 1967–83.

WANGER, Irving Price (Pa.) March 5, 1852–Jan. 14, 1940; House 1893–1911.

WARBURTON, Herbert Birchby (Del.) Sept. 21, 1916–July 30, 1983; House 1953–55.

WARBURTON, Stanton (Wash.) April 13, 1865–Dec. 24, 1926; House 1911–13.

WARD, Charles Bonnell (N.Y.) April 27, 1879–May House 1915–25.

WARD, Hamilton (N.Y.) July 3, 1829–Dec. 28, 1898; House 1865–71.

WARD, Jasper Delos (Ill.) Feb. 1, 1829–Aug. 6, 1902; House 1873–75.

WARD, Jonathan (N.Y.) Sept. 21, 1768–Sept. 28, 1842; House 1815–17.

WARD, Marcus Lawrence (N.J.) Nov. 9, 1812–April 25, 1884; House 1873–75; Gov. Jan. 16, 1866–Jan. 19, 1869; Chrmn. Rep. Nat. Comm. 1866–68.

WARD, Mike (Ky.) House, 1995–.

WARD, Thomas (N.J.) about 1759–March 4, 1842; House 1813–17.

WARD, William (Pa.) Jan. 1, 1837–Feb. 27, 1895; House 1877–83.

WARD, William Lukens (N.Y.) Sept. 2, 1856–July 16, 1933; House 1897–99.

WARE, John Haines III (Pa.) Aug. 29, 1908–; House Nov. 3, 1970–1975.

WARE, Nicholas (Ga.) 1769–Sept. 7, 1824; Senate Nov. 10, 1821–Sept. 7, 1824.

WARNER, John William (Va.) Feb. 18, 1927–; Senate Jan. 2, 1979–.

WARNER, Samuel Larkin (Conn.) June 14, 1828–Feb. 6, 1893; House 1865–67.

WARNER, Vespasian (Ill.) April 23, 1842–March 31, 1925; House 1895–1905.

WARNER, Willard (Ala.) Sept. 4, 1826–Nov. 23, 1906; Senate July 13, 1868–71.

WARNER, William (Mo.) June 11, 1840–Oct. 4, 1916; House 1885–89; Senate March 18, 1905–11.

WARNOCK, William Robert (Ohio) Aug. 29, 1838–July 30, 1918; House 1901–05.

WARREN, Francis Emroy (Wyo.) June 20, 1844–Nov. 24, 1929; Senate Nov. 18, 1890–93, 1895–Nov. 24, 1929; Gov. Feb. 1885–86 (Wyo. Terr.), March 1889–Sept. 1890 (Wyo. Terr.), Sept. 11–Nov. 24, 1890.

WASHBURN, Cadwallader Colden (brother of Israel Washburn Jr., Elihu Benjamin Washburne and William Drew Washburn) (Wis.) April 22, 1818–May 15, 1882; House 1855–61, 1867–71; Gov. Jan. 1, 1872–Jan. 5, 1874.

WASHBURN, Charles Grenfill (Mass.) Jan. 28, 1857–May 25, 1928; House Dec. 18, 1906–11.

WASHBURN, Henry Dana (Ind.) March 28, 1832–Jan. 26, 1871; House Feb. 23, 1866–69.

WASHBURN, Israel Jr. (brother of Elihu Benjamin Washburne, Cadwallader Colden Washburn and William Drew Washburn) (Maine) June 6, 1813–May 12, 1883; House 1851–Jan. 1, 1861 (1851–55 Whig); Gov. Jan. 2, 1861–Jan. 7, 1863.

WASHBURN, William Barrett (Mass.) Jan. 31, 1820–Oct. 5, 1887; House 1863–Dec. 5, 1871; Senate April 29, 1874–75; Gov. Jan. 3, 1872–April 17, 1874.

WASHBURN, William Drew (brother of Israel Washburn Jr., Elihu Benjamin Washburne and Cadwallader Colden Washburn) (Minn.) Jan. 14, 1831–July 29, 1912; House 1879–85; Senate 1889–95.

WASHBURNE, Elihu Benjamin (brother of Israel Washburn Jr., Cadwallader Colden Washburn and William Drew Washburn) (Ill.) Sept. 23, 1816–Oct. 23, 1887; House 1853–March 6, 1869 (1853–55 Whig); Secy. of State March 6–March 16, 1869.

WASON, Edward Hills (N.H.) Sept. 2, 1865–Feb. 6, 1941; House 1915–33.

WATERMAN, Charles Winfield (Colo.) Nov. 2, 1861–Aug. 27, 1932; Senate 1927–Aug. 27, 1932.

WATERS, Russell Judson (Calif.) June 6, 1843–Sept. 25, 1911; House 1899–1901.

WATKINS, Arthur Vivian (Utah) Dec. 18, 1886–Sept. 1, 1973; Senate 1947–59.

WATKINS, George Robert (Pa.) May 21, 1902–Aug. 7, 1970; House 1965–Aug. 7, 1970.

WATRES, Laurence Hawley (Pa.) July 18, 1882–Feb. 6, 1964; House 1923–31.

WATSON, Albert William (S.C.) Aug. 30, 1922–; House 1963–Feb. 1, 1965 (Democrat), June 15, 1965–71.

WATSON, Cooper Kinderdine (Ohio) June 18, 1810–May 20, 1880; House 1855–57.

WATSON, David Kemper (Ohio) June 8, 1849–Sept. 28, 1918; House 1895–97.

WATSON, Henry Winfield (Pa.) June 24, 1856–Aug. 27, 1933; House 1915–Aug. 27, 1933.

WATSON, James Eli (Ind.) Nov. 2, 1864–July 29, 1948; House 1895–97, 1899–1909; Senate Nov. 8, 1916–33; Senate majority leader 1929–33.

WATSON, Lewis Findlay (Pa.) April 14, 1819–Aug. 25, 1890; House 1877–79, 1881–83, 1889–Aug. 25, 1890.

WATTS, J.C. (Okla.) House, 1995–.

WATTS, John Sebrie (N.Mex.) Jan. 19, 1816–June 11, 1876; House (Terr. Del.) 1861–63.

WAUGH, Daniel Webster (Ind.) March 7, 1842–March 14, 1921; House 1891–95.

WEAKLEY, Robert (Tenn.) July 20, 1764–Feb. 4, 1845; House 1809–11.

WEAVER, Archibald Jerard (grandfather of Phillip Hart Weaver) (Nebr.) April 15, 1843–April 18, 1887; House 1883–87.

WEAVER, James Dorman (Pa.) Sept. 27, 1920–; House 1963–65.

WEAVER, Phillip Hart (grandson of Archibald Jerard Weaver) (Nebr.) April 9, 1919–April 16, 1989; House 1955–63.

WEAVER, Walter Lowrie (Ohio) April 1, 1851–May 26, 1909; House 1897–1901.

WEBBER, Amos Richard (Ohio) Jan. 21, 1852–Feb. 25, 1948; House Nov. 8, 1904–07.

WEBBER, George Washington (Mich.) Nov. 25, 1825–Jan. 15, 1900; House 1881–83.

WEBER, Edward Ford (Ohio) July 26, 1931–; House 1981–83.

WEBER, John Baptiste (N.Y.) Sept. 21, 1842–Dec. 18, 1926; House 1885–89.

WEBER, John–Vincent (Minn.) July 24, 1952–; House 1981–93.

WEBSTER, John Stanley (Wash.) Feb. 22, 1877–Dec. 24, 1962; House 1919–May 8, 1923.

WEDEMEYER, William Walter (Mich.) March 22, 1873–Jan. 2, 1913; House 1911–Jan. 2, 1913.

WEEKS, Charles Sinclair (son of John Wingate Weeks of Mass.) (Mass.) June 15, 1893–Feb. 7, 1972; Senate Feb. 8–Dec. 19, 1944; Secy. of Commerce Jan. 21, 1953–Nov. 10, 1958.

WEEKS, Edgar (cousin of John Wingate Weeks of Mass.) (Mich.) Aug. 3, 1839–Dec. 17, 1904; House 1899–1903.

WEEKS, John Eliakim (Vt.) June 14, 1853–Sept. 10, 1949; House 1931–33; Gov. Jan. 6, 1927–Jan. 8, 1931.

WEEKS, John Wingate (Mass.) April 11, 1860–July 12, 1926; House 1905–March 4, 1913; Senate 1913–19; Secy. of War March 5, 1921–Oct. 13, 1925.

WEEMS, Capell Lane (Ohio) July 7, 1860–Jan. 5, 1913; House Nov. 3, 1903–09.

WEICHEL, Alvin F. (Ohio) Sept. 11, 1891–Nov. 27, 1956; House 1943–55; Chrmn. House Merchant Marine and Fisheries 1947–49, 1953–55.

WEICKER, Lowell Palmer Jr. (Conn.) May 16, 1931–; House 1969–71; Senate 1971–89; Chrmn. Senate Small Business 1981–87; Gov. Jan. 9, 1991–.

WEIS, Jessica McCullough (N.Y.) July 8, 1901–May 1, 1963; House 1959–63.

WELBORN, John (Mo.) Nov. 20, 1857–Oct. 27, 1907; House 1905–07.

WELCH, Adonijah Strong (Fla.) April 12, 1821–March 14, 1889; Senate June 25, 1868–69.

WELCH, Frank (Nebr.) Feb. 10, 1835–Sept. 4, 1878; House 1877–Sept. 4, 1878.

WELCH, Richard Joseph (Calif.) Feb. 13, 1869–Sept. 10, 1949; House Aug. 31, 1926–Sept. 10, 1949; Chrmn. House Public Lands 1947–49.

WELDON, Dave (Fla.) House, 1995–.

WELDON, Wayne Curtis (Pa.) July 22, 1947–; House 1987–.

WELKER, Herman (Idaho) Dec. 11, 1906–Oct. 30, 1957; Senate 1951–57.

WELKER, Martin (Ohio) April 25, 1819–March 15, 1902; House 1865–71.

WELLER, Jerry (Ill.) House, 1995–.

WELLER, Ovington Eugene (Md.) Jan. 23, 1862–Jan. 5, 1947; Senate 1921–27.

WELLINGTON, George Louis (Md.) Jan. 28, 1852–March 20, 1927; House 1895–97; Senate 1897–1903.

WELLS, Alfred (N.Y.) May 27, 1814–July 18, 1867; House 1859–61.

WELSH, George Austin (Pa.) Aug. 9, 1878–Oct. 22, 1970; House 1923–May 31, 1932.

WENDOVER, Peter Hercules (N.Y.) Aug. 1, 1768–Sept. 24, 1834; House 1825–21.

WENTWORTH, John (Ill.) March 5, 1815–Oct. 16, 1988; House 1843–51 (Democrat), 1853–55 (Democrat), 1865–67.

WERDEL, Thomas Harold (Calif.) Sept. 13, 1905–Sept. 30, 1966; House 1949–53.

WERTZ, George M. (Pa.) July 19, 1856–Nov. 19, 1928; House 1923–25.

WEST, George (N.Y.) Feb. 17, 1823–Sept. 20, 1901; House 1881–83, 1885–89.

WEST, Joseph Rodman (La.) Sept. 19, 1822–Oct. 31, 1898; Senate 1871–77.

WESTLAND, Aldred John (Wash.) Dec. 14, 1904–Nov. 3, 1982; House 1953–65.

WETMORE, George Peabody (R.I.) Aug. 2, 1846–Sept. 11, 1921; Senate 1895–1907, Jan. 22, 1908–13; Gov. May 26, 1885–May 31, 1887.

WEVER, John Madison (N.Y.) Feb. 24, 1847–Sept. 27, 1914; House 1891–95.

WEYMOUTH, George Warren (Mass.) Aug. 25, 1850–Sept. 7, 1910; House 1897–1901.

WHALEN, Charles William Jr. (Ohio) July 31, 1920–; House 1967–79.

WHALLEY, John Irving (Pa.) Sept. 14, 1902–March 8, 1980; House Nov. 8, 1960–73.

WHARTON, Charles Stuart (Ill.) April 22, 1875–Sept. 4, 1939; House 1905–07.

WHARTON, James Ernest (N.Y.) Oct. 4, 1899–Jan. 12, 1990; House 1951–65.

WHARTON, Jesse (grandfather of Wharton Jackson Green) (Tenn.) July 29, 1782–July 22, 1833; House 1807–09; Senate March 17, 1814–Oct. 10, 1815.

WHEAT, William Howard (Ill.) Feb. 19, 1879–Jan. 16, 1944; House 1939–Jan. 16, 1944.

WHEELER, Frank Willis (Mich.) March 2, 1853–Aug. 9, 1921; House 1889–91.

WHEELER, Hamilton Kinkaid (Ill.) Aug. 5, 1848–July 19, 1918; House 1893–95.

WHEELER, Loren Edgar (Ill.) Oct. 7, 1862–Jan. 8, 1932; House 1915–23, 1925–27.

WHEELER, Nelson Platt (Pa.) Nov. 4, 1841–March 3, 1920; House 1907–11.

WHEELER, William Almon (N.Y.) June 30, 1819–June 4, 1887; House 1861–63, 1869–77; Vice President 1877–81.

WHERRY, Kenneth Spicer (Nebr.) Feb. 28, 1892–Nov. 29, 1951; Senate 1943–Nov. 29, 1951; Senate minority leader 1949–Nov. 29, 1951.

WHITE, Albert Smith (Ind.) Oct. 24, 1803–Sept. 24, 1864; House 1837–39 (Whig), 1861–63; Senate 1839–45 (Whig).

WHITE, Alexander (Ala.) Oct. 16, 1816–Dec. 13, 1893; House 1851–53 (Whig), 1873–75.

WHITE, Alexander Colwell (Pa.) Dec. 12, 1833–June 11, 1906; House 1885–87.

WHITE, Dudley Allen (Ohio) Jan. 3, 1901–Oct. 14, 1957; House 1937–41.

WHITE, George Elon (Ill.) March 7, 1848–May 17, 1935; House 1895–99.

WHITE, George Henry (N.C.) Dec. 18, 1852–Dec. 28, 1918; House 1897–1901.

WHITE, Harry (Pa.) Jan. 12, 1834–June 23, 1920; House 1877–81.

WHITE, Hays Baxter (Kans.) Sept. 21, 1855–Sept. 29, 1930; House 1919–29.

WHITE, James Bain (Ind.) June 26, 1835–Oct. 9, 1897; House 1887–89.

WHITE, John Daugherty (nephew of John White) (Ky.) Jan. 16, 1849–Jan. 5, 1920; House 1875–77, 1881–85.

WHITE, Michael Doherty (Ind.) Sept. 8, 1827–Feb. 6, 1917; House 1877–79.

WHITE, Milo (Minn.) Aug. 17, 1830–May 18, 1913; House 1883–87.

WHITE, Rick (Wash.) House, 1995–.

WHITE, Stephen Van Culen (N.Y.) Aug. 1, 1831–Jan. 18, 1913; House 1887–89.

WHITE, Wallace Humphrey Jr. (grandson of William Pierce Frye) (Maine) Aug. 6, 1877–March 31, 1952; House 1917–31; Senate 1931–49; Senate minority leader 1945–47; Senate majority leader 1947–49.

WHITE, Wilbur McKee (Ohio) Feb. 22, 1890–Dec. 31, 1973; House 1931–33.

WHITE, William John (Ohio) Oct. 7, 1850–Feb. 16, 1923; House 1893–95.

WHITEHILL, James (son of John Whitehill, nephew of Robert Whitehill) (Pa.) Jan. 31, 1762–Feb. 26, 1822; House 1813–Sept. 1, 1814.

WHITEHILL, John (father of James Whitehill, brother of Robert Whitehill) (Pa.) Dec. 11, 1729–Sept. 16, 1815; House 1803–07.

WHITEHILL, Robert (brother of John Whitehill, uncle of James Whitehill, great-great-grandfather of John Crain Kunkel) (Pa.) July 21, 1738–April 8, 1813; House Nov. 7, 1805–April 8, 1813.

WHITEHURST, George William (Va.) March 12, 1925–; House 1969–87.

WHITELEY, Richard Henry (Ga.) Dec. 22, 1830–Sept. 26, 1890; House Dec. 22, 1870–75.

WHITESIDE, Jenkin (Tenn.) 1772–Sept. 25, 1822; Senate April 11, 1809–Oct. 8, 1811.

WHITESIDE, John (Pa.) 1773–July 28, 1830; House 1815–19.

WHITFIELD, Edward (Ky.) House 1995–.

WHITING, Richard Henry (uncle of Ira Clifton Copley (Ill.) Jan. 17, 1826–May 24, 1888; House 1875–77.

WHITING, William (Mass.) March 3, 1813–June 29, 1873; House March 4–June 29, 1873.

WHITING, William (Mass.) May 24, 1841–Jan. 9, 1911; House 1883–89.

WHITLEY, James Lucius (N.Y.) May 17, 1959; House 1929–35.

WHITMORE, George Washington (Tex.) Aug. 26, 1824–Oct. 14, 1876; House March 30, 1870–71.

WHITTAKER, Robert Russell (Kans.) Sept. 18, 1939–; House 1979–91.

WHITTEMORE, Benjamin Franklin (S.C.) May 18, 1824–Jan. 25, 1894; House July 18, 1868–Feb. 24, 1870.

WICKER, Roger (Miss.) House, 1995–.

WICKERSHAM, James (Alaska) Aug. 24, 1857–Oct. 24, 1939; House (Terr. Del.) 1909–17, Jan. 7–March 3, 1919, March 1–3, 1921, 1931–33.

WICKES, Eliphalet (N.Y.) April 1, 1769–June 7, 1850; House 1805–07.

WICKHAM, Charles Preston (Ohio) Sept. 15, 1836–March 18, 1925; House 1887–91.

WIDGERY, William (Mass.) about 1753–July 31, 1822; House 1811–13.

WIDNALL, William Beck (N.J.) March 17, 1906–Dec. 28, 1983; House Feb. 6, 1950–Dec. 31, 1974.

WIGGINS, Charles Edward (Calif.) Dec. 3, 1927–; House 1967–79.

WIGGLESWORTH, Richard Bowditch (Mass.) April 25, 1891–Oct. 22, 1960; House Nov. 6, 1928–Nov. 13, 1958.

WILBER, David (father of David Forrest Wilber) (N.Y.) Oct. 5, 1820–April 1, 1890; House 1873–75, 1879–81, 1887–April 1, 1890.

WILBOUR, Isaac (R.I.) April 25, 1763–Oct. 4, 1837; House 1807–09; Gov. May 7, 1806–May 6, 1807 (Democratic Republican).

WILDE, Richard Henry (Ga.) Sept. 24, 1789–Sept. 10, 1847; House 1815–17, Feb. 7–March 3, 1825, Nov. 17, 1827–35.

WILDER, Abel Carter (Kans.) March 18, 1828–Dec. 22, 1875; House 1863–65.

WILDER, William Henry (Mass.) May 14, 1855–Sept. 11, 1913; House 1911–Sept. 11, 1913.

WILEY, Alexander (Wis.) May 26, 1884–May 26, 1967; Senate 1939–63; Chrmn. Senate Judiciary 1947–49; Chrmn. Senate Foreign Relations 1953–55.

WILEY, William Halsted (N.J.) July 10, 1842–May 2, 1925; House 1903–07, 1909–11.

WILKIN, James Whitney (father of Samuel Jones Wilkin) (N.Y.) 1762–Feb. 23, 1845; House June 7, 1815–19.

WILKINSON, Morton Smith (Minn.) Jan. 22, 1819–Feb. 4, 1894; Senate 1859–65; House 1869–71.

WILLARD, Charles Wesley (Vt.) June 18, 1827–June 8, 1880; House 1869–75.

WILLARD, George (Mich.) March 20, 1824–March 26, 1901; House 1873–77.

WILLEY, Earle Dukes (Del.) July 21, 1889–March 17, 1950; House 1943–45.

WILLEY, Waitman Thomas (W.Va.) Oct. 18, 1811–May 2, 1900; Senate July 9, 1861–63 (Va.), Aug. 4, 1863–71 (Aug. 4, 1863–65 Unionist).

WILLIAMS, Abram Pease (Calif.) Feb. 3, 1832–Oct. 17, 1911; Senate Aug. 4, 1886–87.

WILLIAMS, Andrew (N.Y.) Aug. 27, 1828–Oct. 6, 1907; House 1875–79.

WILLIAMS, Arthur Bruce (Mich.) Jan. 27, 1872–May 1, 1925; House June 19, 1923–May 1, 1925.

WILLIAMS, Charles Grandison (Wis.) Oct. 18, 1829–March 30, 1892; House 1873–83.

WILLIAMS, David Rogerson (S.C.) March 8, 1776–Nov. 17, 1830; House 1805–09, 1811–13; Gov. Dec. 10, 1814–Dec. 5, 1816 (Democrat Republican).

WILLIAMS, Elihu Stephen (Ohio) Jan. 24, 1835–Dec. 1, 1903; House 1887–91.

WILLIAMS, George Henry (Oreg.) March 26, 1823–April 4, 1910; Senate 1865–71; Atty. Gen. Jan. 10, 1872–May 15, 1875.

WILLIAMS, George Howard (Mo.) Dec. 1, 1871–Nov. 25, 1963; Senate May 25, 1925–Dec. 5, 1926.

WILLIAMS, George Short (Del.) Oct. 21, 1877–Nov. 22, 1961; House 1939–41.

WILLIAMS, Isaac Jr. (N.Y.) April 5, 1777–Nov. 9, 1860; House Dec. 20, 1813–15, 1817–19, 1823–25.

WILLIAMS, John (brother of Lewis Williams and Robert Williams, father of Joseph Lanier Williams, cousin of Marmaduke Williams) (Tenn.) Jan. 29, 1778–Aug. 10, 1837; Senate Oct. 10, 1815–23.

WILLIAMS, John James (Del.) May 17, 1904–Jan. 11, 1988; Senate 1947–Dec. 31, 1970.

WILLIAMS, John McKeown Snow (Mass.) Aug. 13, 1818–March 19, 1886; House 1873–75.

WILLIAMS, Lawrence Gordon (Pa.) Sept. 15, 1913–July 13, 1975; House 1967–75.

WILLIAMS, Lyle (Ohio) Aug. 23, 1942–; House 1979–85.

WILLIAMS, Marmaduke (cousin of John Williams of Tenn., Lewis Williams and Robert Williams) (N.C.) April 6, 1774–Oct. 29, 1850; House 1803–09.

WILLIAMS, Morgan B. (Pa.) Sept. 17, 1831–Oct. 13, 1903; House 1897–99.

WILLIAMS, Nathan (N.Y.) Dec. 19, 1773–Sept. 25, 1835; House 1805–07.

WILLIAMS, Richard (Oreg.) Nov. 15, 1836–June 19, 1914; House 1877–79.

WILLIAMS, Robert (brother of John Williams of Tenn. and Lewis Williams, cousin of Marmaduke Williams, uncle of Joseph Lanier Williams) (N.C.) July 12, 1773–Jan. 25, 1836; House 1797–1803; Gov. (Miss. Terr.) 1805–09.

WILLIAMS, Seward Henry (Ohio) Nov. 7, 1870–Sept. 2, 1922; House 1915–17.

WILLIAMS, Thomas (Pa.) Aug. 28, 1806–June 16, 1872; House 1863–69.

WILLIAMS, Thomas Hill (Miss.) 1780–1840; Senate Dec. 10, 1817–29.

WILLIAMS, Thomas Sutler (Ill.) Feb. 14, 1872–April 5, 1940; House 1915–Nov. 11, 1929.

WILLIAMS, William (Ind.) May 11, 1821–April 22, 1896; House 1867–75.

WILLIAMS, William Brewster (Mich.) July 28, 1826–March 4, 1905; House Dec. 1, 1873–77.

WILLIAMS, William Robert (N.Y.) Aug. 11, 1884–May 9, 1972; House 1951–59.

WILLIAMSON, John Newton (Oreg.) Nov. 8, 1855–Aug. 29, 1943; House 1903–07.

WILLIAMSON, William (S.Dak.) Oct. 7, 1875–July 15, 1972; House 1921–33.

WILLIS, Frank Bartlett (Ohio) Dec. 28, 1871–March 30, 1928; House 1911–Jan. 9, 1915; Senate Jan. 14, 1921–March 30, 1928; Gov. Jan. 11, 1915–Jan. 8, 1917.

WILLIS, Jonathan Spencer (Del.) April 5, 1830–Nov. 24, 1903; House 1895–97.

WILLIS, Raymond Eugene (Ind.) Aug. 11, 1875–March 21, 1956; Senate 1941–47.

WILLITS, Edwin (Mich.) April 25, 1830–Oct. 22, 1896; House 1877–83.

WILLOUGHBY, Westel Jr. (N.Y.) Nov. 20, 1769–Oct. 3, 1844; House Dec. 13, 1815–17.

WILMOT, David (Pa.) Jan. 20, 1814–March 16, 1868; House 1845–51 (Democrat); Senate March 14, 1861–63.

WILSON, Alexander (Va.) ?–?; House Dec. 4, 1804–09.

WILSON, Earl (Ind.) April 18, 1906–April 27, 1990; House 1941–59, 1961–65.

WILSON, Francis Henry (N.Y.) Feb. 11, 1844–Sept. 25, 1910; House 1895–Sept. 30, 1897.

WILSON, George Allison (Iowa) April 1, 1884–Sept. 8, 1953; Senate Jan. 14, 1943–49; Gov. Jan. 12, 1939–Jan. 14, 1943.

WILSON, George Washington (Ohio) Feb. 22, 1840–Nov. 27, 1909; House 1893–97.

WILSON, Henry (Mass.) Feb. 16, 1812–Nov. 22, 1875; Senate Jan. 31, 1855–73 (1855–59 Free Soiler/ American Party/ Democrat); Vice President 1873–Nov. 22, 1875.

WILSON, James (father of John Lockwood Wilson) (Ind.) April 9, 1825–Aug. 8, 1867; House 1857–61.

WILSON, James (Iowa) Aug. 16, 1835–Aug. 26, 1920; House 1873–77, 1883–85; Secy. of Agriculture March 6, 1897–March 6, 1913.

WILSON, James Falconer (Iowa) Oct. 19, 1828–April 22, 1895; House Oct. 8, 1861–69; Senate 1883–95.

WILSON, James Jefferson (N.J.) 1775–July 28, 1834; Senate 1815–Jan. 8, 1821.

WILSON, Jeremiah Morrow (Ind.) Nov. 25, 1828–Sept. 24, 1901; House 1871–75.

WILSON, John Henry (Ky.) Jan. 30, 1846–Jan. 14, 1923; House 1889–93.

WILSON, John Lockwood (son of James Wilson of Ind.) (Wash.) Aug. 7, 1850–Nov. 6, 1912; House Nov. 20, 1889–Feb. 18, 1895; Senate Feb. 19, 1895–99.

WILSON, John Thomas (Ohio) April 18, 1811–Oct. 6, 1891; House 1867–73.

WILSON, Joseph Gardner (cousin of James Willis Nesmith) (Oreg.) Dec. 13, 1826–July 2, 1873; House March 4–July 2, 1873.

WILSON, Nathan (N.Y.) Dec. 23, 1758–July 25, 1834; House June 3, 1808–09.

WILSON, Pete (Calif.) Aug. 23, 1933–; Senate 1983–Jan. 7, 1991; Gov. Jan. 7, 1991–.

WILSON, Robert Carlton (Calif.) April 5, 1916–; House 1953–81.

WILSON, Stephen Fowler (Pa.) Sept. 4, 1821–March 30, 1897; House 1865–69.

WILSON, Thomas (Pa.) 1772–Oct. 4, 1824; House May 4, 1813–17.

WILSON, William (Pa.) ?–?; House 1815–19.

WILSON, William Henry (Pa.) Dec. 6, 1877–Aug. 11, 1937; House 1935–37.

WILSON, William Warfield (Ill.) March 2, 1868–July 22, 1942; House 1903–13, 1915–21.

WINANS, James January (Ohio) June 7, 1818–April 28, 1879; House 1869–71.

WINDOM, William (Minn.) May 10, 1827–Jan. 29, 1891; House 1859–69; Senate July 15, 1870–Jan. 22, 1871, March 4, 1871–March 7, 1881, Nov. 15, 1881–83; Secy. of the Treasury March 8–Nov. 13, 1881, March 7, 1889–Jan. 29, 1891.

WINN, Edward Lawrence "Larry" Jr. (Kans.) Aug. 22, 1919– ; House 1967–85.

WINN, Richard (S.C.) 1750–Dec. 19, 1818; House 1793–97 (1793–95 no party), Jan. 24, 1803–13.

WINSLOW, Samuel Ellsworth (Mass.) April 11, 1862–July 11, 1940; House 1913–25.

WINSTON, Joseph (N.C.) June 17, 1746–April 21, 1815; House 1793–95 (no party), 1803–07.

WINTER, Charles Edwin (Wyo.) Sept. 13, 1870–April 22, 1948; House 1923–29.

WINTER, Thomas Daniel (Kans.) July 7, 1896–Nov. 7, 1951; House 1939–47.

WISE, Richard Alsop (son of Henry Alexander Wise, grandson of John Sergeant, brother of John Sergeant Wise, cousin of George Douglas Wise) (Va.) Sept. 2, 1843–Dec. 21, 1900; House April 26, 1898–99, March 12–Dec. 21, 1900.

WITCHER, John Seashoal (W.Va.) July 15, 1839–July 8, 1906; House 1869–71.

WITHERELL, James (Vt.) June 16, 1759–Jan. 9, 1838; House 1807–May 1, 1808.

WITHERSPOON, Robert (great-great-grandfather of Robert Witherspoon Hemphill) (S.C.) Jan. 29, 1767–Oct. 11, 1837; House 1809–11.

WITHROW, Gardner Robert (Wis.) Oct. 5, 1892–Sept. 23, 1964; House 1931–39 (1931–35 Republican, 1935–39 Progressive), 1949–61.

WOLCOTT, Edward Oliver (Colo.) March 26, 1848–March 1, 1905; Senate 1889–1901.

WOLCOTT, Jesse Paine (Mich.) March 3, 1893–Jan. 28, 1969; House 1931–57; Chrmn. House Banking and Currency 1947–49, 1953–55.

WOLD, John Schiller (Wyo.) Aug. 31, 1916– ; House 1969–71.

WOLF, Frank Rudolph (Va.) Jan. 30, 1939– ; House 1981– .

WOLF, William Penn (Iowa) Dec. 1, 1833–Sept. 19, 1896; House Dec. 6, 1870–71.

WOLFENDEN, James (Pa.) July 25, 1889–April 8, 1949; House Nov. 6, 1928–47.

WOLVERTON, Charles Anderson (N.J.) Oct. 24, 1880–May 16, 1969; House 1927–59; Chrmn. House Interstate and Foreign Commerce 1947–49, 1953–55.

WOLVERTON, John Marshall (W.Va.) Jan. 31, 1872–Aug. 19, 1944; House 1925–27, 1929–31.

WOOD, Abiel (Mass.) July 22, 1772–Oct. 26, 1834; House 1813–15.

WOOD, Alan Jr. (nephew of John Wood) (Pa.) July 6, 1834–Oct. 31, 1902; House 1875–77.

WOOD, Benson (Ill.) March 31, 1839–Aug. 27, 1915; House 1895–97.

WOOD, Ira Wells (N.J.) June 19, 1856–Oct. 5, 1931; House Nov. 8, 1904–13.

WOOD, John (uncle of Alan Wood Jr.) (Pa.) Sept. 6, 1816–May 28, 1898; House 1859–61.

WOOD, John M. (Maine) Nov. 17, 1813–Dec. 24, 1864; House 1855–59.

WOOD, John Travers (Idaho) Nov. 25, 1878–Nov. 2, 1954; House 1951–53.

WOOD, Walter Abbott (N.Y.) Oct. 23, 1815–Jan. 15, 1892; House 1879–83.

WOOD, William Robert (Ind.) Jan. 5, 1861–March 7, 1933; House 1915–33.

WOODBRIDGE, Frederick Enoch (Vt.) Aug. 29, 1818–April 25, 1888; House 1863–69.

WOODBURN, William (Nev.) April 14, 1838–Jan. 15, 1915; House 1875–77, 1885–89.

WOODFORD, Stewart Lyndon (N.Y.) Sept. 3, 1835–Feb. 14, 1913; House 1873–July 1, 1874.

WOODMAN, Charles Walhart (Ill.) March 11, 1844–March 18, 1898; House 1895–97.

WOODRUFF, John (Conn.) Feb. 12, 1826–May 20, 1868; House 1855–57 (American Party), 1859–61.

WODRUFF, Roy Orchard (Mich.) March 14, 1876–Feb. 12, 1953; House 1913–15 (Progressive), 1921–53.

WOODS, Frank Plowman (Iowa) Dec. 11, 1868–April 25, 1944; House 1909–19.

WOODS, Samuel Davis (Calif.) Sept. 19, 1845–Dec. 24, 1915; House Dec. 3, 1900–03.

WOODWARD, William (father of Joseph Addison Woodward) (S.C.) ?–?; House 1815–17.

WOODWORTH, James Hutchinson (Ill.) Dec. 4, 1804–March 26, 1869; House 1855–57.

WOODWORTH, Laurin Dewey (Ohio) Sept. 10, 1837–March 13, 1897; House 1873–77.

WOODYARD, Harry Chapman (W.Va.) Nov. 13, 1867–June 21, 1929; House 1903–11, Nov. 7, 1916–23, 1925–27.

WOOMER, Ephraim Milton (Pa.) Jan. 14, 1844–Nov. 29, 1897; House 1893–97.

WORCESTER, Samuel Thomas (Ohio) Aug. 30, 1804–Dec. 6, 1882; House July 4, 1861–63.

WORKS, John Downey (Calif.) March 29, 1847–June 6, 1928; Senate 1911–17.

WORTHINGTON, Henry Gaither (Nev.) Feb. 9, 1828–July 29, 1909; House Oct. 31, 1864–65.

WORTHINGTON, Thomas (Ohio) July 16, 1773–June 20, 1827; Senate April 1, 1803–07, Dec. 15, 1810–Dec. 1, 1814; Gov. Dec. 8, 1814–Dec. 14, 1818 (Democratic Republican).

WORTLEY, George Cornelius (N.Y.) Dec. 8, 1926–; House 1981–89.

WREN, Thomas (Nev.) Jan. 2, 1826–Feb. 5, 1904; House 1877–79.

WRIGHT, Ashley Bascom (Mass.) May 25, 1841–Aug. 14, 1897; House 1893–Aug. 14, 1897.

WRIGHT, Charles Frederick (brother of Myron Benjamin Wright) (Pa.) May 3, 1856–Nov. 10, 1925; House 1899–1905.

WRIGHT, George Grover (brother of Joseph Albert Wright) (Iowa) March 24, 1820–Jan. 11, 1896; Senate 1871–77.

WRIGHT, Myron Benjamin (brother of Charles Frederick Wright) (Pa.) June 12, 1847–Nov. 13, 1894; House 1889–Nov. 13, 1894.

WRIGHT, Robert (Md.) Nov. 20, 1752–Sept. 7, 1826; Senate Nov. 19, 1801–Nov. 12, 1806; House Nov. 29, 1810–17, 1821–23; Gov. Nov. 12, 1806–May 6, 1809 (Democratic Republican).

WURZBACH, Harry McLeary (uncle of Robert Christian Eckhardt) (Tex.) May 19, 1874–Nov. 6, 1931; House 1921–29, Feb. 10, 1930–Nov. 6, 1931.

WYANT, Adam Martin (Pa.) Sept. 15, 1869–Jan. 5, 1935; House 1921–33.

WYATT, Wendell (Oreg.) June 15, 1917–; House Nov. 3, 1964–75.

WYDLER, John Waldemar (N.Y.) June 9, 1924–Aug. 4, 1987; House 1963–81.

WYLIE, Chalmers Pangburn (Ohio) Nov. 23, 1920–; House 1967–93.

WYMAN, Louis Crosby (N.H.) March 16, 1917–; House 1963–65, 1967–Dec. 31, 1974; Senate Dec. 31, 1974–75.

WYNNS, Thomas (N.C.) 1764–June 3, 1825; House Dec. 7, 1802–07.

YANCEY, Bartlett (cousin of John Kerr) (N.C.) Feb. 19, 1785–Aug. 30, 1828; House 1813–17.

YARDLEY, Robert Morris (Pa.) Oct. 9, 1850–Dec. 8, 1902; House 1887–91.

YATES, John Barentse (N.Y.) Feb. 1, 1784–July 10, 1836; House 1815–17.

YATES, Richard (father of Richard Yates) (Ill.) Jan. 18, 1818–Nov. 27, 1873; House 1851–55 (Whig); Senate 1865–71; Gov. Jan. 14, 1861–Jan. 16, 1865.

YATES, Richard (son of Richard Yates) (Ill.) Dec. 12, 1860–April 11, 1936; House 1919–33; Gov. Jan. 14, 1901–Jan. 9, 1905.

YOST, Jacob (Va.) April 1, 1853–Jan. 25, 1933; House 1887–89, 1897–99.

YOUNG, Charles William "Bill" (Fla.) Dec. 16, 1930–; House 1971–.

YOUNG, Clarence Clifton (Nev.) Nov. 7, 1922–; House 1953–57.

YOUNG, Donald Edwin (Alaska) June 9, 1933–; House March 6, 1973–; Chrmn. House Resources Committee 1995–.

YOUNG, Edward Lunn (S.C.) Sept. 7, 1920–; House 1973–75.

YOUNG, George Morley (N.Dak.) Dec. 11, 1870–May 27, 1932; House 1913–Sept. 2, 1924.

YOUNG, Horace Olin (Mich.) Aug. 4, 1850–Aug. 5, 1917; House 1903–May 16, 1913.

YOUNG, Isaac Daniel (Kans.) March 29, 1849–Dec. 10, 1927; House 1911–13.

YOUNG, James Rankin (Pa.) March 10, 1847–Dec. 18, 1924; House 1897–1903.

YOUNG, Lafayette (Iowa) May 10, 1848–Nov. 15, 1926; Senate Nov. 12, 1910–April 11, 1911.

YOUNG, Milton Ruben (N.Dak.) Dec. 6, 1897–May 31, 1983; Senate March 12, 1945–81; elected Pres. pro tempore Dec. 4, 1980 (to serve Dec. 5, 1980).

YOUNG, Richard (N.Y.) Aug. 6, 1846–June 9, 1935; House 1909–11.

YOUNG, Samuel Hollingsworth (Ill.) Dec. 26, 1922–; House 1973–75.

YOUNG, Thomas Lowry (Ohio) Dec. 14, 1832–July 20, 1888; House 1879–83; Gov. March 2, 1877–Jan. 14, 1878.

YOUNGBLOOD, Harold Francis (Mich.) Aug. 7, 1907–May 10, 1983; House 1947–49.

YOUNGDAHL, Oscar Ferdinand (Minn.) Oct. 13, 1893–Feb. 3, 1946; House 1939–43.

YOUNGER, Jesse Arthur (Calif.) April 11, 1893–June 20, 1967; House 1953–June 20, 1967.

ZELIFF, William (N.H.) June 12, 1936–; House 1991–.

ZIHLMAN, Frederick Nicholas (Md.) Oct. 2, 1879–April 22, 1935; House 1917–31.

ZIMMER, Richard (N.J.) Aug. 16, 1944–; House 1991–.

ZION, Roger Herschel (Ind.) Sept. 17, 1921–; House 1967–75.

ZSCHAU, Edwin Van Wyck (Calif.) Jan. 6, 1940–; House 1983–87.

ZWACH, John Matthew (Minn.) Feb. 8, 1907–Nov. 11, 1990; House 1967–75.

Governors

ALABAMA

(became a state December 14, 1819)

LEWIS, David Peter. 1820–July 3, 1884; Nov. 25, 1872–Nov. 25, 1874.

HUNT, Harold Guy. June 17, 1933–; Jan. 19, 1987–April 22, 1993.

JAMES, Fob. Sept. 15, 1934–; 1995–.

ALASKA

(became a state January 3, 1959)

MILLER, Keith Harvey. March 1, 1925–; Jan. 29, 1969–Dec. 5, 1970.

HAMMOND, Jay Sterner. July 21, 1922–; Dec. 2, 1974–Dec. 6, 1982.

ARIZONA

(became a state February 14, 1912)

CAMPBELL, Thomas Edward. Jan. 18, 1878–March 1, 1944; Jan. 1, 1917–Dec. 25, 1917, Jan. 6, 1919–Jan, 1, 1923.

CAMPBELL, Thomas Edward. Jan. 6, 1919–Jan. 1, 1923 (for previous term see above).

PHILLIPS, John C. Nov. 13, 1870–June 25, 1943; Jan. 7, 1929–Jan. 5, 1931.

PYLE, John Howard. March 25, 1906–; Jan. 1951–Jan. 3, 1955.

FANNIN, Paul Jones. Jan. 29, 1907–; Jan. 5, 1959–Jan. 4, 1965; Senate 1965–77.

WILLIAMS, John Richard. Oct. 29, 1909–; Jan. 2, 1967–Jan. 6, 1975.

MECHAM, Evan. May 12, 1924–; Jan. 5, 1987–April 4, 1988.

SYMINGTON, Fife. Aug. 12, 1945–; March 6, 1991–.

ARKANSAS

(became a state June 15, 1836)

CLAYTON, Powell. Aug. 7, 1833–Aug. 25, 1914; July 2, 1868–March 17, 1871; Senate 1871–77.

Governors are listed in chronological order by state. Listed first are their birth and, if applicable, death dates, if available. Term or terms as governor are listed next, followed by any other government service.

HADLEY, Ozra A. June 30, 1826–July 18, 1915; March 17, 1871–Jan. 6, 1873.

BAXTER, Elisha. Sept. 1, 1827–May 31, 1899; Jan. 6, 1873–Nov. 12, 1874.

ROCKEFELLER, Winthrop (brother of Vice President Nelson Aldrich Rockefeller, uncle of John Davison "Jay" Rockefeller IV of W.Va., grandson of Sen. Nelson Wilmarth Aldrich of R.I., nephew of Rep. Richard Steere Aldrich of R.I.). May 1, 1912–Feb. 22, 1973; Jan. 10, 1967–Jan. 12, 1971.

CALIFORNIA

(became a state September 9, 1850)

STANFORD, Leland. March 9, 1824–June 21, 1893; Jan. 10, 1862–Dec. 10, 1863; Senate 1885–June 21, 1893.

BOOTH, Newton. Dec. 30, 1825–July 14, 1892; Dec. 8, 1871–Feb. 27, 1875; Senate 1875–81 (Anti-Monopolist).

PACHECO, Romualdo. Oct. 31, 1831–Jan. 23, 1899; Feb. 27–Dec. 9, 1875–; House 1877–Feb. 7, 1878, 1879–83.

PERKINS, George Clement. Aug. 23, 1839–Feb. 26, 1923; Jan. 8, 1880–Jan. 10, 1883; Senate July 26, 1893–1915.

WATERMAN, Robert Whitney. Dec. 15, 1826–April 12, 1891; Sept. 13, 1887–Jan. 8, 1891.

MARKHAM, Henry Harrison. Nov. 16, 1840–Oct. 9, 1923; Jan. 8, 1891–Jan. 11, 1895; House 1885–87.

GAGE, Henry Tifft. Dec. 25, 1852–Aug. 28, 1924; Jan. 3, 1899–Jan. 6, 1903.

PARDEE, George Cooper. July 25, 1857–Sept. 1, 1941; Jan. 6, 1903–Jan. 8, 1907.

GILLETT, James Norris. Sept. 20, 1860–April 20, 1937; Jan. 8, 1907–Jan. 3, 1911; House 1903–Nov. 4, 1906.

JOHNSON, Hiram Warren. Sept. 2, 1866–Aug. 6, 1945; Jan. 3, 1911–March 15, 1917; Senate March 16, 1917–Aug. 6, 1945.

STEPHENS, William Dennison. Dec. 26, 1859–April 25, 1944; March 15, 1917–Jan. 9, 1923; House 1911–July 22, 1916 (1911–15 Republican, 1915–July 22, 1916 Progressive).

RICHARDSON, Friend William. Dec. 1865–Sept. 6, 1943; Jan. 9, 1923–Jan. 4, 1927.

YOUNG, Clement Calhoun. April 28, 1869–Dec. 24, 1947; Jan. 4, 1927–Jan. 6, 1931.

ROLPH, James Jr. Aug. 23, 1869–June 2, 1934; Jan. 6, 1931–June 2, 1934.

MERRIAM, Frank Finley. Dec. 22, 1865–April 25, 1955; June 2, 1934–Jan. 2, 1939.

WARREN, Earl. March 19, 1891–July 9, 1974; Jan. 4,

1943–Oct. 5, 1953; Chief Justice United States Oct. 5, 1953–June 23, 1969.

KNIGHT, Goodwin Jess. Dec. 9, 1896–May 22, 1970; Oct. 5, 1953–Jan. 5, 1959.

REAGAN, Ronald Wilson. Feb. 6, 1911–; Jan. 5, 1967–Jan. 6, 1975; President 1981–89.

DEUKMEJIAN, George. June 6, 1928–; Jan. 3, 1983–Jan. 7, 1991.

WILSON, Peter Barton "Pete." Aug. 23, 1933–; Jan. 7, 1991–; Senate 1983–Jan. 7, 1991.

COLORADO

(became a state August 1, 1876)

ROUTT, John Long. April 25, 1826–Aug. 13, 1907; Nov. 3, 1876–Jan. 14, 1879, Jan. 13, 1891–Jan. 10, 1893.

PITKIN, Frederick Walker. Aug. 31, 1837–Dec. 18, 1886; Jan. 14, 1879–Jan. 9, 1883.

EATON, Benjamin Harrison. Dec. 15, 1833–Oct. 29, 1904; Jan. 13, 1885–Jan. 11, 1887.

COOPER, Job Adams. Nov. 6, 1843–Jan. 20, 1899; Jan. 10, 1889–Jan. 13, 1891.

ROUTT, John Long. Jan. 13, 1891–Jan. 10, 1893 (for previous term see above).

McINTIRE, Albert Wills. Jan. 15, 1853–Jan. 30, 1935; Jan. 8, 1895–Jan. 12, 1897.

PEABODY, James Hamilton. Aug. 21, 1852–Nov. 23, 1917; Jan. 13, 1903–Jan. 10, 1905, March 17, 1905.

McDONALD, Jesse Fuller. June 30, 1858–Feb. 25, 1942; March 17, 1905–Jan. 8, 1907.

BUCHTEL, Henry Augustus. Sept. 30, 1847–Oct. 22, 1924; Jan. 8, 1907–Jan. 12, 1909.

CARLSON, George Alfred. Oct. 23, 1876–Dec. 6, 1926; Jan. 12, 1915–Jan. 9, 1917.

SHOUP, Oliver Henry Nelson. Dec. 13, 1869–Sept. 30, 1940; Jan. 14, 1919–Jan. 9, 1923.

MORLEY, Clarence J. Feb. 9, 1869–Nov. 15, 1948; Jan. 13, 1925–Jan. 11, 1927.

CARR, Ralph L. Dec. 11, 1887–Sept. 22, 1950; Jan. 10, 1939–Jan. 12, 1943.

VIVIAN, John Charles. June 30, 1887–Feb. 10, 1964; Jan. 12, 1943–Jan. 14, 1947.

THORNTON, Daniel Isaac J. Jan. 31, 1911–Jan. 18, 1976; Jan. 9, 1951–Jan. 11, 1955.

LOVE, John A. Nov. 29, 1916–; Jan. 8, 1963–July 16, 1973.

VANDERHOOF, John David. May 27, 1922–; July 16, 1973–Jan. 14, 1975.

CONNECTICUT

(ratified the Constitution January 9, 1788)

HOLLEY, Alexander Hamilton. Aug. 12, 1804–Oct. 2, 1887; May 6, 1857–May 5, 1858.

BUCKINGHAM, William Alfred. May 28, 1804–Feb. 5, 1875; May 5, 1858–May 2, 1866; Senate 1869–Feb. 5, 1875.

HAWLEY, Joseph Roswell. Oct. 31, 1826–March 17, 1905; May 2, 1866–May 1, 1867; House Dec. 2, 1872–75, 1879–81; Senate 1881–1905.

JEWELL, Marshall. Oct. 20, 1825–Feb. 10, 1883; May 5, 1869–May 4, 1870, May 16, 1871–May 7, 1873; Postmaster Gen. Sept. 1, 1874–July 12, 1876; Chrmn. Rep. Nat. Comm. 1880–83.

ANDREWS, Charles Bartlett. Nov. 4, 1836–Sept. 12, 1902; Jan. 9, 1879–Jan. 5, 1881.

BIGELOW, Hobart B. May 16, 1834–Oct. 12, 1891; Jan. 5, 1881–Jan. 3, 1883.

HARRISON, Henry Baldwin. Sept. 11, 1821–Oct. 29, 1901; Jan. 8, 1885–Jan. 7, 1887.

LOUNSBURY, Phineas Chapman (brother of George Edward Lounsbury, below). Jan. 10, 1841–June 22, 1925; Jan. 7, 1887–Jan. 10, 1889.

BULKELEY, Morgan Gardner (cousin of Edwin Denison Morgan of N.Y.). Dec. 26, 1837–Nov. 6, 1922; Jan. 10, 1889–Jan. 4, 1893; Senate 1905–11.

COFFIN, Owen Vincent. June 20, 1836–Jan. 3, 1921; Jan. 9, 1895–Jan. 6, 1897.

COOKE, Lorrin Alamson. April 6, 1831–Aug. 12, 1902; Jan. 6, 1897–Jan. 4, 1899.

LOUNSBURY, George Edward (brother of Phineas Chapman Lounsbury, above). May 7, 1838–Aug. 16, 1904; Jan. 4, 1899–Jan. 9, 1901.

McLEAN, George Payne. Oct. 7, 1857–June 6, 1932; Jan. 9, 1901–Jan. 7, 1903; Senate 1911–29.

CHAMBERLAIN, Abiram. Dec. 7, 1837–May 15, 1911; Jan. 7, 1903–Jan. 4, 1905.

ROBERTS, Henry. Jan. 22, 1853–May 1, 1929; Jan. 4, 1905–Jan. 9, 1907.

WOODRUFF, Rollin Simmons. July 14, 1854–June 30, 1925; Jan. 9, 1907–Jan. 6, 1909.

LILLEY, George Leavens. Aug. 3, 1859–April 21, 1909; Jan. 6–April 21, 1909; House 1903–Jan. 5, 1909.

WEEKS, Frank Bentley. Jan. 20, 1854–Oct. 2, 1935; April 21, 1909–Jan. 4, 1911.

HOLCOMB, Marcus Hensey. Nov. 28, 1884–March 5, 1932; Jan. 6, 1915–Jan. 5, 1921.

LAKE, Everett John. Feb. 8, 1871–Sept. 16, 1948; Jan. 5, 1921–Jan. 3, 1923.

TEMPLETON, Charles Augustus. March 3, 1871–Aug. 15, 1955; Jan. 3, 1923–Jan. 7, 1925.

BINGHAM, Hiram. Nov. 19, 1875–June 6, 1956; Jan. 7–Jan. 8, 1925; Senate Dec. 17, 1924–33.

TRUMBULL, John Harper. March 4, 1873–May 21, 1961; Jan. 8, 1925–Jan. 7, 1931.

BALDWIN, Raymond Earl. Aug. 31, 1893–Oct. 4, 1986; Jan. 4, 1939–Jan. 8, 1941, Jan. 6, 1943–Dec. 27, 1946; Senate Dec. 27, 1946–Dec. 16, 1949.

BALDWIN, Raymond Earl. Jan. 6, 1943–Dec. 27, 1946 (for previous term see above).

McCONAUGHY, James Lukens. Oct. 21, 1887–March 7, 1948; Jan. 8, 1947–March 7, 1948.

SHANNON, James Coughlin. July 21, 1896–; March 7, 1948–Jan. 5, 1949.

LODGE, John Davis. Oct. 20, 1903–Oct. 29, 1985; Jan. 3, 1951–Jan. 5, 1955; House 1947–51.

MESKILL, Thomas Joseph. Jan. 30, 1928–; Jan. 6, 1971–Jan. 8, 1975; House 1967–71.

ROWLAND, John G. May 24, 1957–; 1995–.

DELAWARE

(ratified the Constitution December 7, 1787)

MARVIEL, Joshua Hopkins. Sept. 3, 1825–April 8, 1895; Jan. 15–April 8, 1895.

HUNN, John. June 23, 1849–Sept. 1, 1926; Jan. 15, 1901–Jan. 17, 1905.

LEA, Preston. Nov. 12, 1841–Dec. 4, 1916; Jan. 17, 1905–Jan. 19, 1909.

PENNEWILL, Simeon Selby. July 23, 1867–Sept. 9, 1935; Jan. 19, 1909–Jan. 21, 1913.

MILLER, Charles R. Sept. 30, 1857–Sept. 18, 1927; Jan. 21, 1913–Jan. 17, 1917.

TOWNSEND, John Gillis Jr. May 31, 1871–April 10, 1964; Jan. 17, 1917–Jan. 18, 1921; Senate 1929–41.

DENNEY, William Du Hamel. March 31, 1873–Nov. 22, 1953; Jan. 18, 1921–Jan. 20, 1925.

ROBINSON, Robert P. March 28, 1869–March 4, 1939; Jan. 20, 1925–Jan. 15, 1929.

BUCK, Clayton Douglass. March 21, 1890–Jan. 27, 1965; Jan. 15, 1929–Jan. 19, 1937; Senate 1943–49.

BACON, Walter W. Jan. 20, 1879–March 18, 1962; Jan. 21, 1941–Jan. 18, 1949.

BOGGS, James Caleb. May 15, 1909–; Jan. 20, 1953–Dec. 30, 1960; House 1947–53; Senate 1961–73.

BUCKSON, David Penrose. July 25, 1920–; Dec. 30, 1960–Jan. 17, 1961.

PETERSON, Russell Wilbur. Oct. 3, 1916–; Jan. 21, 1969–Jan. 16, 1973.

duPONT, Pierre Samuel "Pete" IV. Jan. 22, 1935–; Jan. 18, 1977–Jan. 15, 1985; House 1971–77.

CASTLE, Michael Newbold. July 2, 1939–; Jan. 15, 1985–Dec. 31, 1992; House 1993–.

WOLF, Dale Edward. Sept. 6, 1924–; Jan. 1–Jan. 19, 1993.

FLORIDA

(became a state March 3, 1845)

REED, Harrison. Aug. 26, 1813–March 25, 1899; July 9, 1868–Jan. 7, 1873.

HART, Ossian Bingley. Jan. 17, 1821–March 18, 1874; Jan. 7, 1873–March 18, 1874.

STEARNS, Marcellus Lovejoy. April 29, 1839–Dec. 8, 1891; March 18, 1874–Jan. 2, 1877.

KIRK, Claude Roy Jr. Jan. 7, 1926–; Jan. 3, 1967–Jan. 5, 1971.

MARTINEZ, Robert. Dec. 25, 1934–; Jan. 6, 1987–Jan. 8, 1991.

GEORGIA

(ratified the Constitution January 2, 1788)

BULLOCK, Rufus Brown. March 28, 1834–April 27, 1907; July 4, 1868–Oct. 23, 1871.

CONLEY, Benjamin. March 1, 1815–Jan. 10, 1886; Oct. 30, 1871–Jan. 12, 1872.

HAWAII

(became a state August 21, 1959)

QUINN, William Francis. July 31, 1919–; Aug. 21, 1959–Dec. 3, 1962.

IDAHO

(became a state July 3, 1890)

SHOUP, George Laird. June 15, 1836–Dec. 21, 1904; April 1889–90 (Idaho Terr.), Oct. 1–Dec. 1890; Senate Dec. 18, 1890–1901.

WILLEY, Norman Bushnell. March 25, 1838–Oct. 20, 1921; Dec. 19, 1890–Jan. 1, 1893.

McCONNELL, William John. Sept. 18, 1839–March 30, 1925; Jan. 2, 1893–Jan. 4, 1897; Senate Dec. 18, 1890–91.

MORRISON, John Tracy. Dec. 25, 1860–Dec. 20, 1915; Jan. 5, 1903–Jan. 2, 1905.

GOODING, Frank Robert. Sept. 16, 1859–June 24, 1928; Jan. 2, 1905–Jan. 4, 1909; Senate Jan. 15, 1921June 24, 1928.

BRADY, James Henry. June 12, 1862–Jan. 13, 1918; Jan. 4, 1909–Jan. 2, 1911; Senate Feb. 6, 1913–Jan. 13, 1918.

HAINES, John Michiner. Jan. 1, 1863–June 4, 1917; Jan. 6, 1913–Jan. 4, 1915.

DAVIS, David William. April 23, 1873–Aug. 5, 1959; Jan. 6, 1919–Jan. 1, 1923.

MOORE, Charles Calvin. Feb. 26, 1866–March 19, 1958; Jan. 1, 1923–Jan. 3, 1927.

BALDRIGE, H. Clarence. Nov. 24, 1868–June 8, 1947; Jan. 3, 1927–Jan. 5, 1931.

BOTTOLFSEN, Clarence Alfred. Oct. 10, 1891–July 19, 1964; Jan. 2, 1939–Jan. 6, 1941, Jan. 4, 1943–Jan. 1, 1945.

BOTTOLFSEN, Clarence Alfred. Jan. 4, 1943–Jan. 1, 1945 (for previous term see above).

ROBINS, Charles Armington. Dec. 8, 1884–Sept. 20, 1970; Jan. 6, 1947–Jan. 1, 1951.

JORDAN, Leonard Beck. May 16, 1899–June 30, 1983; Jan. 1, 1951–Jan. 3, 1955; Senate Aug. 6, 1962–Jan. 2, 1973.

SMYLIE, Robert Eben. Oct. 31, 1914–; Jan. 3, 1955–Jan. 2, 1967.

SAMUELSON, Don William. July 27, 1913–; Jan. 2, 1967–Jan. 4, 1971.

BATT, Phil. March 4, 1927–; 1995–.

ILLINOIS

(became a state December 3, 1818)

EDWARDS, Ninian. March 17, 1775–July 20, 1833; 1809–18 (Ill. Terr.), Dec. 6, 1826–Dec. 6, 1830; Senate Dec. 3, 1818–24.

BISSELL, William Harrison. April 25, 1811–March 18, 1860; Jan. 12, 1857–March 18, 1860; House 1849–55 (1849–53 Democrat, 1853–55 Independent Democrat).

WOOD, John. Dec. 20, 1798–June 11, 1880; March 21, 1860–Jan. 14, 1861.

YATES, Richard (father of Richard Yates, below). Jan. 18, 1818–Nov. 27, 1873; Jan. 14, 1861–Jan. 16, 1865; House 1851–55 (Whig); Senate 1865–71 (Republican).

OGLESBY, Richard James. July 25, 1824–April 24, 1899; Jan. 16, 1865–Jan. 11, 1869, Jan. 13–Jan. 23, 1873, Jan. 30, 1885–Jan. 14, 1889; Senate 1873–79.

PALMER, John Mc Auley. Sept. 13, 1817–Sept. 25, 1900; Jan. 11, 1869–Jan. 13, 1873; Senate 1891–97 (Democrat).

OGLESBY, Richard James. Jan. 13–Jan. 23, 1873 (for previous term see above).

BEVERIDGE, John Lourie. July 6, 1824–May 3, 1910; Jan. 23, 1873–Jan. 8, 1877; House Nov. 7, 1871–Jan. 4, 1873.

CULLOM, Shelby Moore. Nov. 22, 1829–Jan. 28, 1914; Jan. 8, 1877–Feb. 8, 1883; House 1865–71; Senate 1883–1913; Senate majority leader 1911–13.

HAMILTON, John Marshall. May 28, 1847–Sept. 22, 1905; Feb. 16, 1883–Jan. 30, 1885.

OGLESBY, Richard James. Jan. 30, 1885–Jan. 14, 1889 (for previous terms see above).

FIFER, Joseph Wilson. Oct. 28, 1840–Aug. 6, 1938; Jan. 14, 1889–Jan. 10, 1893.

TANNER, John Riley. April 4, 1844–May 23, 1901; Jan. 11, 1897–Jan. 14, 1901.

YATES, Richard (son of Richard Yates, above). Dec. 12, 1860–April 11, 1936; Jan. 14, 1901–Jan. 9, 1905; House 1919–33.

DENEEN, Charles Samuel. May 4, 1863–Feb. 5, 1940; Jan. 9, 1905–Feb. 3, 1913; Senate Feb. 26, 1925–31.

LOWDEN, Frank Orren. Jan. 26, 1861–March 20, 1943; Jan. 8, 1917–Jan. 10, 1921; House Nov. 6, 1906–11.

SMALL, Lennington. June 16, 1862–May 17, 1936; Jan. 10, 1921–Jan. 14, 1929.

EMMERSON, Louis Lincoln. Dec. 27, 1883–Feb. 4, 1941; Jan. 14, 1929–Jan. 9, 1933.

GREEN, Dwight Herbert. Jan. 9, 1897–Feb. 20, 1958; Jan. 13, 1941–Jan. 10, 1949.

STRATTON, William Grant. Feb. 26, 1914–; Jan. 12, 1953–Jan. 9, 1961; House 1941–43, 1947–49.

OGILVIE, Richard Buell. Feb. 2, 1923–May 10, 1988; Jan. 13, 1969–Jan. 8, 1973.

THOMPSON, James Robert. May 8, 1936–; Jan. 10, 1977–Jan. 14, 1991.

EDGAR, James. Jan. 22, 1946–; Jan. 14, 1991–.

INDIANA

(became a state December 11, 1816)

LANE, Henry Smith. Feb. 24, 1811–June 18, 1881; Jan. 14–Jan. 16, 1861; House Aug. 3, 1840–43 (Whig); Senate 1861–67.

MORTON, Oliver Hazard Perry Throck. Aug. 4, 1823–Nov. 1, 1877; Jan. 16, 1861–Jan. 23, 1867; Senate 1867–Jan. 13, 1873.

BAKER, Conrad. Feb. 12, 1817–April 28, 1885; Jan. 24, 1867–Jan. 13, 1873.

PORTER, Albert Gallatin. April 20, 1824–May 3, 1897; Jan. 10, 1881–Jan. 12, 1885; House 1859–63.

HOVEY, Alvin Peterson. Sept. 6, 1821–Nov. 23, 1891; Jan. 1889–Nov. 21, 1891; House 1887–Jan. 17, 1889.

CHASE, Ira Joy. Dec. 7, 1834–May 11, 1895; Nov. 21, 1891–Jan. 9, 1893.

MOUNT, James Atwell. March 24, 1843–Jan. 16, 1901; Jan. 11, 1897–Jan. 14, 1901.

DURBIN, Winfield Taylor. May 4, 1847–Dec. 18, 1928; Jan. 14, 1901–Jan. 9, 1905.

HANLY, James Franklin. April 4, 1863–Aug. 1, 1920; Jan. 9, 1905–Jan. 11, 1909; House 1895–97.

GOODRICH, James Putnam. Feb. 18, 1864–Aug. 15, 1940; Jan. 8, 1917–Jan. 10, 1921.

McCRAY, Warren Terry. Feb. 4, 1865–Dec. 19, 1938; Jan. 10, 1921–April 30, 1924.

BRANCH, Emmett Forest. May 16, 1874–Feb. 23, 1932; April 30, 1924–Jan. 12, 1925.

JACKSON, Edward L. Dec. 27, 1873–Nov. 18, 1954; Jan. 12, 1925–Jan. 14, 1929.

LESLIE, Harry Guyer. Aug. 6, 1878–Dec. 10, 1937; Jan. 14, 1929–Jan. 9, 1933.

GATES, Ralph Fesler. Feb. 24, 1893–July 28, 1978; Jan. 8, 1945–Jan. 10, 1949.

CRAIG, George North. Aug. 6, 1909–Dec. 17, 1992; Jan. 12, 1953–Jan. 14, 1957.

HANDLEY, Harold Willis. Nov. 27, 1909–Aug. 30, 1972; Jan. 14, 1957–Jan. 9, 1961.

WHITCOMB, Edgar Doud. Nov. 6, 1917–; Jan. 13, 1969–Jan. 8, 1973.

BOWEN, Otis Ray. Feb. 26, 1918–; Jan. 8, 1973–Jan. 12, 1981; Secy. of Health and Human Services Dec. 13, 1985–Jan. 20, 1989.

ORR, Robert Dunkerson. Nov. 17, 1917–; Jan. 12, 1981–Jan. 9, 1989.

IOWA

(became a state December 28, 1846)

LOWE, Ralph Phillips. Nov. 27, 1805–Dec. 22, 1883; Jan. 13, 1858–Jan. 11, 1860.

KIRKWOOD, Samuel Jordan. Dec. 20, 1813–Sept. 1, 1894; Jan. 11, 1860–Jan. 14, 1864, Jan. 13, 1876–Feb. 1, 1877; Senate Jan. 13, 1866–67, 1877–March 7, 1881; Secy. of the Interior March 8, 1881–April 17, 1882.

STONE, William Milo. Oct. 14, 1827–July 8, 1893, Jan. 14, 1864–Jan. 16, 1868.

MERRILL, Samuel. Aug. 7, 1822–Aug. 31, 1899; Jan. 16, 1868–Jan. 11, 1872.

CARPENTER, Cyrus Clay. Nov. 24, 1829–May 29, 1898; Jan. 11, 1872–Jan. 13, 1876; House 1879–83.

KIRKWOOD, Samuel Jordan. Jan. 13, 1876–Feb. 1, 1877 (for previous term see above).

NEWBOLD, Joshua G. May 12, 1830–June 10, 1903; Feb. 1, 1877–Jan. 17, 1878.

GEAR, John Henry. April 7, 1825–July 14, 1900; Jan. 17, 1878–Jan. 12, 1882; House 1887–91, 1893–95; Senate 1895–July 14, 1900.

SHERMAN, Buren Robinson. May 28, 1836–Nov. 4, 1904; Jan. 12, 1882–Jan. 14, 1886.

LARRABEE, William. Jan. 20, 1832–Nov. 16, 1912; Jan. 14, 1886–Feb. 26, 1890.

JACKSON, Frank Darr. Jan. 26, 1854–Nov. 16, 1938; Jan. 11, 1894–Jan. 16, 1896.

DRAKE, Francis Marion. Dec. 30, 1830–Nov. 20, 1903; Jan. 16, 1896–Jan. 13, 1898.

SHAW, Leslie Mortier. Nov. 2, 1848–March 28, 1932; Jan. 13, 1898–Jan. 16, 1902; Secy. of the Treasury Feb. 1, 1902–March 3, 1907.

CUMMINS, Albert Baird. Feb. 15, 1850–July 30, 1926; Jan. 16, 1902–Nov. 24, 1908; Senate Nov. 24, 1908–July 30, 1926; elected Pres. pro tempore May 19, 1919, March 7, 1921.

GARST, Warren. Dec. 4, 1850–Oct. 5, 1924; Nov. 24, 1908–Jan. 14, 1909.

CARROLL, Beryl Franklin. March 15, 1860–Dec. 16, 1939; Jan. 14, 1909–Jan. 16, 1913.

CLARKE, George W. Oct. 24, 1852–Nov. 28, 1936; Jan. 16, 1913–Jan. 11, 1917.

HARDING, William Lloyd. Oct. 3, 1877–Dec. 17, 1934; Jan. 11, 1917–Jan. 13, 1921.

KENDALL, Nathan Edward. March 17, 1868–Nov. 5, 1936; Jan. 13, 1921–Jan. 15, 1925; House 1909–13.

HAMMILL, John. Oct. 14, 1875–April 6, 1936; Jan. 15, 1925–Jan. 15, 1931.

TURNER, Daniel Webster. March 17, 1877–April 15, 1969; Jan. 15, 1931–Jan. 12, 1933.

WILSON, George Allison. April 1, 1884–Sept. 8, 1953; Jan. 12, 1939–Jan. 14, 1943; Senate Jan. 14, 1943–49.

HICKENLOOPER, Bourke Blakemore. July 21, 1896–Sept. 4, 1971; Jan. 14, 1943–Jan. 11, 1945; Senate 1945–69.

BLUE, Robert Donald. Sept. 24, 1898–Dec. 14, 1989; Jan. 11, 1945–Jan. 13, 1949.

BEARDSLEY, William S. May 17, 1901–Nov. 21, 1954; Jan. 13, 1949–Nov. 21, 1954.

ELTHON, Leo. June 9, 1898–April 16, 1967; Nov. 22, 1954–Jan. 13, 1955.

HOEGH, Leo Arthur. March 30, 1908–; Jan. 13, 1955–Jan. 17, 1967.

ERBE, Norman Arthur. Oct. 25, 1919–; Jan. 12, 1961–Jan. 17, 1963.

RAY, Robert D. Sept. 26, 1928–; Jan. 16, 1969–Jan. 14, 1983.

BRANSTAD, Terry Edward. Nov. 17, 1946–; Jan. 14, 1983–.

KANSAS

(became a state January 29, 1861)

ROBINSON, Charles Lawrence. July 21, 1818–Aug. 17, 1894; Feb. 9, 1861–Jan. 12, 1863.

CARNEY, Thomas. Aug. 20, 1824–July 28, 1888; Jan. 12, 1863–Jan. 9 , 1865.

CRAWFORD, Samuel Johnson (father-in-law of Arthur Capper, below). April 10, 1835–Oct. 21, 1913; Jan. 9, 1865–Nov. 4, 1868.

GREEN, Nehemiah. March 8, 1837–Jan. 12, 1890; Nov. 4, 1868–Jan. 11, 1869.

HARVEY, James Madison. Sept. 21, 1833–April 15, 1894; Jan. 11, 1869–Jan. 13, 1873; Senate Feb. 2, 1874–77.

OSBORN, Thomas Andrew. Oct. 26, 1836–Feb. 4, 1898; Jan. 13, 1873–Jan. 18, 1877.

ANTHONY, George Tobey. June 9, 1824–Aug. 5, 1896; Jan. 18, 1877–Jan. 13, 1879.

ST. JOHN, John Pierce. Feb. 26, 1833–Aug. 31, 1916; Jan. 13, 1879–Jan. 8, 1883.

MARTIN, John Alexander. March 10, 1839–Oct. 2, 1889; Jan. 13, 1885–Jan. 14, 1889.

HUMPHREY, Lyman Underwood. July 25, 1844–Sept. 12, 1915; Jan. 14, 1889–Jan. 9, 1893.

MORRILL, Edmund Needham. Feb. 12, 1834–March 14, 1909; Jan. 14, 1895–Jan. 11, 1897; House 1883–91.

STANLEY, William Eugene. Dec. 28, 1844–Oct. 13, 1910; Jan. 9, 1899–Jan. 12, 1903.

BAILEY, Willis Joshua. Oct. 12, 1854–May 19, 1932; Jan. 12, 1903–Jan. 9, 1906; House 1899–1901.

HOCH, Edward Wallis. March 17, 1849–June 1, 1925; Jan. 9, 1905–Jan. 11, 1909.

STUBBS, Walter Roscoe. Nov. 7, 1858–March 25, 1929; Jan. 11, 1909–Jan. 13, 1913.

CAPPER, Arthur (son-in-law of Samuel Johnson Crawford, above). July 14, 1865–Dec. 19, 1951; Jan. 11, 1915–Jan. 13, 1919; Senate 1919–49.

ALLEN, Henry Justin. Sept. 11, 1868–Jan. 17, 1950; Jan. 13, 1919–Jan. 8, 1923; Senate April 1, 1929–Nov. 30, 1930.

PAULEN, Benjamin Sanford. July 14, 1869–July 11, 1961; Jan. 12, 1925–Jan. 14, 1929.

REED, Clyde Martin. Oct. 19, 1871–Nov. 8, 1949; Jan. 14, 1929–Jan. 12, 1931; Senate 1939–Nov. 8, 1949.

LANDON, Alfred Mossman. Sept. 9, 1887–Oct. 12, 1987; Jan. 9, 1933–Jan. 11, 1937.

RATNER, Payne Harry. Oct. 3, 1896–Dec. 27, 1974; Jan. 9, 1939–Jan. 11, 1943.

SCHOEPPEL, Andrew Frank. Nov. 23, 1894–Jan. 21, 1962; Jan. 11, 1943–Jan. 13, 1947; Senate 1949–Jan. 21, 1962.

CARLSON, Frank. Jan. 23, 1893–May 30, 1987; Jan. 13, 1947–Nov. 28, 1950; House 1935–47; Senate Nov. 29, 1950–69.

HAGAMAN, Frank Leslie. June 1, 1894–June 23, 1966; Nov. 28, 1950–Jan. 8, 1951.

ARN, Edward Ferdinand. May 19, 1906–; Jan. 8, 1951–Jan. 10, 1955.

HALL, Frederick Lee. July 24, 1916–March 18, 1970; Jan. 10, 1955–Jan. 3, 1957.

McCUISH, John Berridge. June 22, 1906–March 12, 1962; Jan. 3–Jan. 14, 1957.

ANDERSON, John Jr. May 8, 1917–; Jan. 9, 1961–Jan. 11, 1965.

AVERY, William Henry. Aug. 11, 1911–; Jan. 11, 1965–Jan. 9, 1967; House 1955–65.

BENNETT, Robert Frederick. May 23, 1927–; Jan. 13, 1975–Jan. 8, 1979.

HAYDEN, John Michael "Mike." March 16, 1944–; Jan. 12, 1987–Jan. 14, 1991.

GRAVES, Bill. January 9, 1953–; 1995–.

KENTUCKY

(became a state June 1, 1792)

GREENUP, Christopher. 1750–April 27, 1818; June 1, 1804–June 1, 1808; House Nov. 9, 1792–97 (Nov. 9, 1792–95 no party).

BRADLEY, William O'Connell (uncle of Edwin Porch Morrow, below). March 18, 1847–May 23, 1914; Dec. 10, 1895–Dec. 12, 1899; Senate 1909–May 23, 1814.

TAYLOR, William Sylvester. Oct. 10, 1853–Aug. 2, 1928; Dec. 12, 1899–Jan. 31, 1900.

WILLSON, Augustus Everett. Oct. 13, 1846–Aug. 24, 1931; Dec. 10, 1907–Dec. 12, 1911.

MORROW, Edwin Porch (nephew of William O'Connell Bradley, above). Nov. 28, 1877–June 15, 1935; Dec. 9, 1919–Dec. 11, 1923.

SAMPSON, Flemon Davis. Jan. 25, 1875–May 25, 1967; Dec. 13, 1927–Dec. 8, 1931.

WILLIS, Simeon Slavens. Dec. 1, 1879–April 2, 1965; Dec. 7, 1943–Dec. 9, 1947.

NUNN, Louis Broady. March 8, 1924–; Dec. 12, 1967–Dec. 7, 1971.

LOUISIANA

(became a state April 30, 1812)

WARMOTH, Henry Clay. May 9, 1842–Sept. 30, 1931; June 29, 1868–Dec. 9, 1872.

PINCHBACK, Pinckney Benton Stewart. May 10, 1837–Dec. 21, 1921; Dec. 9, 1872–Jan. 13, 1873.

KELLOGG, William Pitt. Dec. 8, 1830–Aug. 10, 1918; Jan. 13, 1873–Jan. 8, 1877; Senate July 9, 1868–Nov. 1, 1872, 1877–83; House 1883–85.

TREEN, David Conner. July 16, 1928–; March 10, 1980–March 12, 1984; House 1973–March 10, 1980.

ROEMER, Charles Elson "Buddy" III. Oct. 4, 1943–; March 14, 1988–Jan. 8, 1992 (March 14, 1988–March 11, 1991 Democrat); House 1981–March 14, 1988 (Democrat).

MAINE

(became a state March 15, 1820)

LINCOLN, Enoch (son of Levi Lincoln of Mass., brother of Levi Lincoln Jr. of Mass., great-uncle of Frederick Robie). Dec. 28, 1788–Oct. 8, 1829; Jan. 3, 1827–Oct. 8, 1829; House Nov. 4, 1818–21 (Mass.), 1821–26.

MORRILL, Anson Peaslee (brother of Lot Myrick Morrill, below). June 10, 1803–July 4, 1887; Jan. 3, 1855–Jan. 2, 1856; House 1861–63.

HAMLIN, Hannibal. Aug. 27, 1809–July 4, 1891; Jan. 8–Feb. 25, 1857; House 1843–47 (Democrat); Senate June 8, 1848–Jan. 7, 1857 (Democrat), 1857–Jan. 17, 1861, 1869–81; Vice President 1861–65.

WILLIAMS, Joseph Hartwell. June 2, 1814–July 19, 1896; Feb. 26, 1857–Jan. 8, 1858.

MORRILL, Lot Myrick (brother of Anson Peaslee Morrill, above). May 3, 1813–Jan. 10, 1883; Jan. 8, 1858–Jan. 2, 1861; Senate Jan. 17, 1861–69, Oct. 30, 1869–July 7, 1876; Secy. of the Treasury July 7, 1876–March 9, 1877.

WASHBURN, Israel Jr. (brother of Cadwallader Colden Washburn of Wis.). June 6, 1813–May 12, 1883; Jan. 2, 1861–Jan. 7, 1863; House 1851–Jan. 1, 1861 (1851–55 Whig).

COBURN, Abner. March 22, 1803–Jan. 4, 1885; Jan. 7, 1863–Jan. 6, 1864.

CONY, Samuel. Feb. 27, 1811–Oct. 5, 1870; Jan. 6, 1864–Jan. 2, 1867.

CHAMBERLAIN, Joshua Lawrence. Sept. 8, 1828–March 2, 1908; Jan. 2, 1867–Jan. 4, 1871.

PERHAM, Sidney. March 27, 1819–April 10, 1907; Jan. 4, 1871–Jan. 7, 1874; House 1863–69 (Republican).

DINGLEY, Nelson Jr. Feb. 15, 1832–Jan. 13, 1899; Jan. 7, 1874–Jan. 5, 1876; House Sept. 12, 1881–Jan. 13, 1899.

CONNOR, Seldon. Jan. 25, 1839–July 9, 1917; Jan. 5, 1876–Jan. 8, 1879.

DAVIS, Daniel Franklin. Sept. 12, 1843–Jan. 9, 1897; Jan. 17, 1880–Jan. 13, 1881.

ROBIE, Frederick (great-great-nephew of Levi Lincoln of Mass., great-nephew of Levi Lincoln Jr. of Mass. and Enoch Lincoln). Aug. 12, 1822–Feb. 3, 1912; Jan. 3, 1883–Jan. 5, 1887.

BODWELL, Joseph Robinson. June 18, 1818–Dec. 15, 1887; Jan. 5–Dec. 15, 1887.

MARBLE, Sebastian Streeter. March 1, 1817–May 10, 1902; Dec. 16, 1887–Jan. 2, 1889.

BURLEIGH, Edwin Chick. Nov. 27, 1843–June 16, 1916; Jan. 2, 1889–Jan. 4, 1893; House June 21, 1897–1911; Senate 1913–June 16, 1916.

CLEAVES, Henry B. Feb. 6, 1840–June 22, 1912; Jan. 4, 1893–Jan. 6, 1897.

POWERS, Llewellyn. Oct. 14, 1836–July 28, 1908; Jan. 6, 1897–Jan. 2, 1901; House 1877–79, April 8, 1901–July 28, 1908.

HILL, John Fremont. Oct. 29, 1855–March 16, 1912; Jan. 2, 1901–Jan. 4, 1905; Chrmn. Rep. Nat. Comm. 1910–12.

COBB, William Titcomb. July 23, 1857–July 24, 1937; Jan. 4, 1905–Jan. 6, 1909.

FERNALD, Bert Manfred. April 3, 1858–Aug. 23, 1926; Jan. 6, 1909–Jan. 4, 1911; Senate Sept. 12, 1916–Aug. 23, 1926.

HAINES, William Thomas. Aug. 7, 1854–June 4, 1919; Jan. 1, 1913–Jan. 6, 1915.

MILLIKEN, Carl Elias. July 13, 1877–May 1, 1961; Jan. 3, 1917–Jan. 5, 1921.

PARKHURST, Frederick Hale. Nov. 5, 1864–Jan. 31, 1921; Jan. 5–Jan. 31, 1921.

BAXTER, Percival Proctor. Nov. 22, 1876–June 12, 1969; Jan. 31, 1921–Jan. 8, 1925.

BREWSTER, Ralph Owen. Feb. 22, 1888–Dec. 25, 1961; Jan. 8, 1925–Jan. 2, 1929; House 1935–41; Senate 1941–Dec. 31, 1952.

GARDINER, William Tudor. June 12, 1892–Aug. 3, 1953; Jan. 2, 1929–Jan. 4, 1933.

BARROWS, Lewis Orin. June 7, 1893–Jan. 30, 1967; Jan. 6, 1937–Jan. 1, 1941.

SEWALL, Sumner. June 17, 1897–Jan. 25, 1965; Jan. 1, 1941–Jan. 3, 1945.

HILDRETH, Horace Augustus. Dec. 2, 1901–; Jan. 3, 1945–Jan. 5, 1949.

PAYNE, Frederick George. July 24, 1904–June 15, 1978; Jan. 5, 1949–Dec. 25, 1952; Senate 1953–59.

CROSS, Burton Melvin. Nov. 15, 1902–; Dec. 26, 1952–Jan. 5, 1955.

HASKELL, Robert Nelson. Aug. 24, 1903–; Jan. 3–Jan. 8, 1959.

REED, John Hathaway. Jan. 5, 1921–; Dec. 30, 1959–Jan. 5, 1967.

McKERNAN, John Rettie Jr. (husband of Rep. Olympia Jean Bouchless Snowe). May 20, 1948–; Jan. 7, 1987–; House 1983–87.

MARYLAND

(ratified the Constitution April 28, 1788)

LOWNDES, Lloyd Jr. Feb. 21, 1845–Jan. 8, 1905; Jan. 8, 1896–Jan. 10, 1900; House 1873–75.

GOLDSBOROUGH, Phillips Lee. Aug. 6, 1865–Oct. 22, 1946; Jan. 10, 1912–Jan. 12, 1916; Senate 1929–35.

NICE, Harry Whinna. Dec. 5, 1877–Feb. 25, 1941; Jan. 9, 1935–Jan. 11, 1939.

McKELDIN, Theodore Roosevelt. Nov. 20, 1900–Aug. 10, 1974; Jan. 10, 1951–Jan. 14, 1959.

AGNEW, Spiro Theodore. Nov. 9, 1918–; Jan. 25, 1967–Jan. 7, 1969; Vice President 1969–Oct. 10, 1973.

MASSACHUSETTS

(ratified the Constitution February 6, 1788)

EUSTIS, William. June 10, 1753–Feb. 6, 1825; May 31, 1823–Feb. 6, 1825; House 1801–05, Aug. 21, 1820–23; Secy. of War March 7, 1809–Jan. 13, 1813.

MORTON, Marcus. Dec. 19, 1784–Feb. 6, 1864; Feb. 6–May 26, 1825, Jan. 18, 1840–Jan. 7, 1841, Jan. 17, 1843–Jan. 3, 1844; House 1817–21 (Republican).

BANKS, Nathaniel Prentice. Jan. 30, 1816–Sept. 1, 1894; Jan. 6, 1858–Jan. 2, 1861; House 1853–Dec. 24, 1857, Dec. 4, 1865–73, 1875–79, 1889–91 (1853–55 Democrat, 1855–57 American Party, March 4–Dec. 24, 1857 Republican, Dec. 4, 1865–67 Union Republican, 1867–73 Republican, 1875–77 Independent); Speaker Feb. 2, 1856–57.

ANDREW, John Albion. May 31, 1818–Oct. 30, 1867; Jan. 2, 1861–Jan. 4, 1866.

BULLOCK, Alexander Hamilton. March 2, 1816–Jan. 17, 1882; Jan. 4, 1866–Jan. 7, 1869.

CLAFLIN, William. March 6, 1818–Jan. 5, 1905; Jan. 7, 1869–Jan. 4, 1872; House 1877–81; Chrmn. Rep. Nat. Comm. 1868–72.

WASHBURN, William Barrett. Jan. 31, 1820–Oct. 5, 1887; Jan. 3, 1872–April 17, 1874; House 1863–Dec. 5, 1871; Senate April 29, 1874–75.

TALBOT, Thomas. Sept. 7, 1818–Oct. 6, 1886; April 29, 1874–Jan. 6, 1875, Jan. 1, 1879–Jan. 7, 1880.

RICE, Alexander Hamilton. Aug. 30, 1818–July 22, 1895; Jan. 5, 1876–Jan. 1, 1879; House 1859–67.

TALBOT, Thomas. Jan. 1, 1879–Jan. 7, 1880 (for previous term see above).

LONG, John Davis. Oct. 27, 1838–Aug. 28, 1915; Jan. 8, 1880–Jan. 4, 1883; House 1883–89; Secy. of the Navy March 6, 1897–April 30, 1902.

ROBINSON, George Dexter. Jan. 20, 1834–Feb. 22, 1896; Jan. 1884–Jan. 5, 1887; House 1877–Jan. 7, 1884.

AMES, Oliver. Feb. 4, 1831–Oct. 22, 1895; Jan. 5, 1887–Jan. 1, 1890.

BRACKETT, John Quincy Adams. June 8, 1842–April 6, 1918; Jan. 1, 1890–Jan. 7, 1891.

GREENHALGE, Frederic Thomas. July 19, 1842–March 5, 1896; Jan. 3, 1894–March 5, 1896; House 1889–91.

WOLCOTT, Roger. July 13, 1847–Dec. 21, 1900; March 5, 1896–Jan. 4, 1900.

CRANE, Winthrop Murray. April 23, 1853–Oct. 2, 1920; Jan. 4, 1900–Jan. 8, 1903; Senate Oct. 12, 1904–13.

BATES, John Lewis. Sept. 18, 1859–June 8, 1946; Jan. 8, 1903–Jan. 5, 1905.

GUILD, Curtis Jr. Feb. 2, 1860–April 6, 1915; Jan. 4, 1906–Jan. 7, 1909.

DRAPER, Eben Sumner. June 17, 1858–April 9, 1914; Jan. 7, 1909–Jan. 5, 1911.

McCALL, Samuel Walker. Feb. 28, 1851–Nov. 4, 1923; Jan. 6, 1916–Jan. 2, 1919; House 1893–1913.

COOLIDGE, John Calvin (cousin of William Wallace Stickney of Vt.). July 4, 1872–Jan. 5, 1933; Jan. 2, 1919–Jan. 6, 1921; Vice President 1921–Aug. 3, 1923; President Aug. 3, 1923–29.

COX, Charming Harris. Oct. 28, 1879–Aug. 20, 1968; Jan. 6, 1921–Jan. 8, 1925.

FULLER, Alvan Tufts. Feb. 27, 1878–April 30, 1958–Jan. 8, 1925–Jan. 3, 1929; House 1917–Jan. 5, 1921 (1917–19 Independent Republican).

ALLEN, Frank G. Oct. 6, 1874–Oct. 9, 1950; Jan. 3, 1929–Jan. 8, 1931.

SALTONSTALL, Leverett. Sept. 1, 1892–June 17, 1979; Jan. 5, 1939–Jan. 3, 1945; Senate Jan. 4, 1945–67.

BRADFORD, Robert Fiske. Dec. 15, 1902–March 18, 1983; Jan. 2, 1947–Jan. 6, 1949.

HERTER, Christian Archibald. March 28, 1895–Dec. 30, 1966; Jan. 8, 1953–Jan. 3, 1957; House 1943–53; Secy. of State April 22, 1959–Jan. 20, 1961.

VOLPE, John Anthony. Dec. 8, 1908–; Jan. 5, 1961–Jan. 3, 1963, Jan. 7, 1965–Jan. 22, 1969; Secy. of Transportation Jan. 22, 1969–Feb. 1, 1973.

VOLPE, John Anthony. Jan. 7, 1965–Jan. 22, 1969 (for previous term see above).

SARGENT, Francis Williams. July 29, 1915–; Jan. 22, 1969–Jan. 2, 1975.

WELD, William Floyd. July 31, 1945–; Jan. 3, 1991–.

MICHIGAN

(became a state January 26, 1837)

BINGHAM, Kinsley Scott. Dec. 16, 1808–Oct. 5, 1861; Jan. 3, 1855–Jan. 5, 1859; House 1847–51 (Democrat); Senate 1859–Oct. 5, 1861.

WISNER, Moses. June 3, 1815–Jan. 5, 1863; Jan. 5, 1859–Jan. 2, 1861.

BLAIR, Austin. Feb. 8, 1818–Aug. 6, 1894; Jan. 2, 1861–Jan. 4, 1865; House 1867–73.

CRAPO, Henry Howland. May 22, 1804–July 22, 1869; Jan. 4, 1865–Jan. 6, 1869.

BALDWIN, Henry Porter. Feb. 22, 1814–Dec. 31, 1892; Jan. 6, 1869–Jan. 1, 1873; Senate Nov. 17, 1879–81.

BAGLEY, John Judson. July 24, 1832–Dec. 27, 1881; Jan. 1, 1873–Jan. 3, 1877.

CROSWELL, Charles Miller. Oct. 31, 1825–Dec. 13, 1886; Jan. 3, 1877–Jan. 1, 1881.

JEROME, David Howell. Nov. 17, 1869–April 23, 1896; Jan. 1, 1881–Jan. 1, 1883.

ALGER, Russell Alexander. Feb. 27, 1836–Jan. 24, 1907; Jan. 1, 1885–Jan. 1, 1887; Senate Sept. 27, 1902–Jan. 24, 1907; Secy. of War March 5, 1897–Aug. 1, 1899.

LUCE, Cyrus Gray. July 2, 1824–March 18, 1905; Jan. 1, 1887–Jan. 1, 1891.

RICH, John Tyler. April 23, 1841–March 28, 1926; Jan. 1, 1893–Jan. 1, 1897; House April 5, 1881–83.

PINGREE, Hazen Stuart. Aug. 30, 1840–June 18, 1901; Jan. 1, 1897–Jan. 1, 1901.

BLISS, Aaron Thomas. May 22, 1837–Sept. 16, 1906; Jan. 1, 1901–Jan. 1, 1905; House 1889–91.

WARNER, Fred Maltby. July 21, 1865–April 17, 1923; Jan. 1, 1905–Jan. 1, 1911.

OSBORN, Chase Salmon. June 22, 1860–April 11, 1949; Jan. 1, 1911–Jan. 1, 1913.

SLEEPER, Albert Edson. Dec. 31, 1862–May 13, 1934; Jan. 1, 1917–Jan. 1, 1921.

GROESBECK, Alexander Joseph. Nov. 7, 1873–March 10, 1953; Jan. 1, 1921–Jan. 1, 1927.

GREEN, Fred Warren. Oct. 20, 1871–Nov. 30, 1936; Jan. 1, 1927–Jan. 1, 1931.

BRUCKER, Wilber Marion. June 23, 1894–Oct. 28, 1968; Jan. 1, 1931–Jan. 1, 1933.

FITZGERALD, Frank Dwight. Jan. 27, 1885–March 16, 1939; Jan. 1, 1935–Jan. 1, 1937, Jan. 2–March 16, 1939.

FITZGERALD, Frank Dwight. Jan. 2–March 16, 1939 (for previous term see above).

DICKENSON, Luren Dudley. April 15, 1859–April 22, 1943; March 16, 1939–Jan. 1, 1941.

KELLY, Harry Francis. April 19, 1895–Feb. 8, 1971; Jan. 1, 1943–Jan. 1, 1947.

SIGLER, Kim. May 2, 1894–Nov. 30, 1953; Jan. 1, 1947–Jan. 1, 1949.

ROMNEY, George Wilcken. July 8, 1907–; Jan. 1, 1963–Jan. 22, 1969; Secy. of Housing and Urban Development Jan. 20, 1969–Feb. 2, 1973.

MILLIKEN, William Grawn. March 26, 1922–; Jan. 22, 1969–Jan. 1, 1983.

ENGLER, John. Oct. 12, 1948–; Jan. 1, 1991–.

MINNESOTA

(became a state May 11, 1858)

RAMSEY, Alexander. Sept. 8, 1815–April 22, 1903; April 2, 1849–53 (Minn. Terr.), Jan. 2, 1860–July 10, 1863; House 1843–47 (Whig Pa.); Senate 1863–75; Secy. of War Dec. 10, 1879–March 5, 1881.

SWIFT, Henry Adoniram. March 23, 1823–Feb. 25, 1869; July 10, 1863–Jan. 11, 1864.

MILLER, Stephen. Jan. 17, 1816–Aug. 18, 1881; Jan. 11, 1864–Jan. 8, 1866.

MARSHALL, William Rogerson. Oct. 17, 1825–Jan. 8, 1896; Jan. 8, 1866–Jan. 9, 1870.

AUSTIN, Horace. Oct. 15, 1831–Nov. 2, 1905; Jan. 9, 1870–Jan. 7, 1874.

DAVIS, Cushman Kellogg. June 16, 1838–Nov. 27, 1900; Jan. 7, 1874–Jan. 7, 1876; Senate 1887–Nov. 27, 1900.

PILLSBURY, John Sargent. July 29, 1828–Oct. 10, 1901; Jan. 7, 1876–Jan. 10, 1882.

HUBBARD, Lucius Frederick. Jan. 26, 1836–Feb. 5, 1913; Jan. 10, 1882–Jan. 5, 1887.

McGILL, Andrew Ryan. Feb. 19, 1840–Oct. 31, 1905; Jan. 5, 1887–Jan. 9, 1889.

MERRIAM, William Rush. July 26, 1849–Feb. 18, 1931; Jan. 9, 1889–Jan. 4, 1893.

NELSON, Knute. Feb. 2, 1843–April 28, 1923; Jan. 4, 1893–Jan. 31, 1895; House 1883–89; Senate 1895April 28, 1923.

CLOUGH, David Marston (father-in-law of Roland Hill Hartley of Wash.) Dec. 27, 1846–Aug. 28, 1924; Jan. 31, 1895–Jan. 2, 1899.

VAN SANT, Samuel Rinnah. May 11, 1844–Oct. 3, 1936; Jan. 7, 1901–Jan. 4, 1905.

EBERHART, Adolph Olson. June 23, 1870–Dec. 6, 1944; Sept. 21, 1909–Jan. 5, 1915.

BURNQUIST, Joseph Alfred Arner. July 21, 1879–Jan. 12, 1961; Dec. 30, 1915–Jan. 5, 1921.

PREUS, Jacob Aall Ottesen. Aug. 28, 1883–May 24, 1961; Jan. 5, 1921–Jan. 6, 1925.

CHRISTIANSON, Theodore. Sept. 12, 1883–Dec. 9, 1948; Jan. 6, 1925–Jan. 6, 1931; House 1933–37.

STASSEN, Harold Edward. April 13, 1907–; Jan. 2, 1939–April 27, 1943.

THYE, Edward John. April 26, 1896–Aug. 28, 1969; April 27, 1943–Jan. 8, 1947; Senate 1947–59.

YOUNGDAHL, Luther Wallace. May 29, 1896–June 21, 1978; Jan. 8, 1947–Sept. 27, 1951.

ANDERSON, Clyde Elmer. March 16, 1912–; Sept. 27, 1951–Jan. 5, 1955.

ANDERSEN, Elmer Lee. June 17, 1909–; Jan. 2, 1961–March 25, 1963.

LEVANDER, Harold. Oct. 10, 1910–; Jan. 2, 1967–Jan. 4, 1971.

CARLSON, Arne. Sept. 24, 1934–; Jan. 7, 1991–.

MISSISSIPPI

(became a state December 10, 1817)

LEAKE, Walter. May 25, 1762–Nov. 17, 1826; Jan. 7 1822–Nov. 17, 1825; Senate Dec. 10, 1817–May 15, 1820.

ALCORN, James Lusk. Nov. 4, 1816–Dec. 19, 1894; March 10, 1870–Nov. 30, 1871; Senate Dec. 1, 1871–77.

POWERS, Ridgely Ceylon. Dec. 24, 1836–Nov. 11, 1912; Nov. 30, 1871–Jan. 4, 1874.

AMES, Adelbert. Oct. 31, 1835–April 12, 1933; Jan. 4, 1874–March 20, 1876; Senate Feb. 23, 1870–Jan. 10, 1874.

FORDICE, Kirk. Feb. 10, 1934–; Jan. 14, 1992–.

MISSOURI

(became a state August 10, 1821)

McCLURG, Joseph Washington. Feb. 22, 1818–Dec. 2, 1900; Jan. 12, 1869–Jan. 9, 1871; House 1863–68 (1863–65 Unconditional Unionist, 1865–68 Republican).

HADLEY, Herbert Spencer. Feb. 20, 1872–Dec. 1, 1927; Jan. 11, 1909–Jan. 13, 1913.

HYDE, Arthur Mastick. July 12, 1877–Oct. 17, 1947; Jan. 10, 1921–Jan. 12, 1925; Secy. of Agriculture March 6, 1929–March 4, 1933.

BAKER, Samuel Aaron. Nov. 7, 1874–Sept. 16, 1933; Jan. 12, 1925–Jan. 14, 1929.

CAULFIELD, Henry Stewart. Dec. 9, 1873–May 11, 1966; Jan. 14, 1929–Jan. 9, 1933; House 1907–09.

DONNELL, Forrest C. Aug. 20, 1884–March 3, 1980; Jan. 13, 1941–Jan. 8, 1945; Senate 1945–51.

BOND, Christopher S. "Kit." March 6, 1939–; Jan. 8, 1973–Jan. 10, 1977, Jan. 12, 1981–Jan. 14, 1985; Senate 1987–.

BOND, Christopher S. "Kit." Jan. 12, 1981–Jan. 14, 1985 (for previous term see above).

ASHCROFT, John May. 9, 1942–; Jan. 14, 1985–Jan. 11, 1993.

MONTANA

(became a state November 8, 1889)

RICKARDS, John Ezra. July 23, 1848–Dec. 26, 1927; Jan. 2, 1893–Jan. 4, 1897.

DIXON, Joseph Moore. July 31, 1867–May 22, 1934; Jan. 3, 1921–Jan. 4, 1925; House 1903–07; Senate 1907–13.

FORD, Samuel Clarence. Nov. 7, 1882–Nov. 25, 1961; Jan. 6, 1941–Jan. 3, 1949.

ARONSON, John Hugo. Sept. 1, 1891–Feb. 25, 1978; Jan. 5, 1953–Jan. 4, 1961.

NUTTER, Donald Grant. Nov. 28, 1915–Jan. 25, 1962; Jan. 4, 1961–Jan. 25, 1962.

BABCOCK, Tim M. Oct. 27, 1919–; Jan. 26, 1962–Jan. 6, 1969.

STEPHENS, Stan. Sept. 16, 1929–; Jan. 2, 1989–Jan. 4, 1993.

RACICOT, Marc Francis. July 24, 1948–; Jan. 4, 1993–.

NEBRASKA

(became a state March 1, 1867)

BUTLER, David C. Dec. 15, 1829–May 25, 1891; March 27, 1867–June 2, 1871.

JAMES, William Hartford. Oct. 16, 1831–Feb. 1, 1920; June 2, 1871–Jan. 13, 1873.

FURNAS, Robert Wilkinson. May 5, 1824–June 1, 1905; Jan. 13, 1873–Jan. 12, 1875.

GARBER, Silas. Sept. 21, 1833–Jan. 12, 1905; Jan. 12, 1875–Jan. 1879.

NANCE, Albinus. March 30, 1848–Dec. 7, 1911; Jan. 9, 1879–Jan. 4, 1883.

DAWES, James William. Jan. 8, 1844–Oct. 8, 1918; Jan. 4, 1883–Jan. 6, 1887.

THAYER, John Milton. Jan. 24, 1820–March 19, 1906; 1875–79 (Wyo. Terr.), Jan. 6, 1887–Jan. 15, 1891, May 5, 1891–Feb. 8, 1892; Senate March 1, 1867–71.

THAYER, John Milton. May 5, 1891–Feb. 8, 1892 (for previous term see above).

CROUNSE, Lorenzo. Jan. 27, 1834–May 13, 1909; Jan. 13, 1893–Jan. 3, 1895; House 1873–77.

DIETRICH, Charles Henry. Nov. 26, 1853–April 10, 1924; Jan. 3–May 1, 1901; Senate March 28, 1901–05.

SAVAGE, Ezra Perin. April 3, 1842–Jan. 8, 1920; May 1, 1901–Jan. 8, 1903.

MICKEY, John Hopwood. Sept. 30, 1845–June 2, 1910; Jan. 8, 1903–Jan. 3, 1907.

SHELDON, George Lawson. May 31, 1870–April 4, 1960; Jan. 3, 1907–Jan. 7, 1909.

SHALLENBERGER, Ashton Cockayne. Dec. 23, 1862–Feb. 22, 1938; Jan. 7, 1909–Jan. 5, 1911; House 1901–03, 1915–19, 1923–29, 1931–35.

ALDRICH, Chester Hardy. Nov. 10, 1862–March 10, 1924; Jan. 5, 1911–Jan. 9, 1913.

McKELVIE, Samuel Roy. April 15, 1881–Jan. 6, 1956; Jan. 9, 1919–Jan. 3, 1923.

McMULLEN, Adam. June 12, 1872–March 2, 1959; Jan. 8, 1925–Jan. 3, 1929.

WEAVER, Arthur J. Nov. 18, 1873–Oct. 17, 1945; Jan. 3, 1929–Jan. 8, 1931.

GRISWOLD, Dwight Palmer. Nov. 27, 1893–April 12, 1954; Jan. 9, 1941–Jan. 9, 1947; Senate Nov. 5, 1952–April 12, 1954.

PETERSON, Val Frederick Demar Erastus. July 18, 1903–Oct. 17, 1983; Jan. 9, 1947–Jan. 8, 1953.

CROSBY, Robert Berkey. March 26, 1911–; Jan. 8, 1953–Jan. 6, 1955.

ANDERSON, Victor Emanuel. March 30, 1902–Aug. 15, 1962; Jan. 6, 1955–Jan. 8, 1959.

BURNEY, Dwight Willard. Jan. 7, 1892–; Sept. 9, 1960–Jan. 6, 1961.

TIEMANN, Norbert Theodore. July 18, 1924–; Jan. 5, 1967–Jan. 7, 1971.

THONE, Charles. Jan. 4, 1924–; Jan. 4, 1979–Jan. 6, 1983; House 1971–79.

ORR, Kay A. Jan. 2, 1939–; Jan. 9, 1987–Jan. 9, 1991.

NEVADA

(became a state October 31, 1864)

BLASDEL, Henry Goode. Jan. 20, 1825–July 26, 1900; Dec. 5, 1864–Jan. 2, 1871.

KINKEAD, John Henry. Dec. 10, 1826–Aug. 15, 1924; Jan. 7, 1879–Jan. 1, 1883.

STEVENSON, Charles Clark. Feb. 20, 1826–Sept. 21, 1890; Jan. 4, 1887–Sept. 2, 1890.

BELL, Francis Jardine. Jan. 28, 1840–Feb. 13, 1927; Sept. 21, 1890–Jan. 5, 1891.

COLCORD, Roswell Keyes. April 25, 1839–Oct. 30, 1939; Jan. 6, 1891–Jan. 7, 1895.

ODDIE, Tasker Lowndes. Oct. 20, 1870–Feb. 17, 1950; Jan. 2, 1911–Jan. 4, 1915; Senate 1921–33.

BALZAR, Frederick Bennett. June 15, 1880–March 21, 1934; Jan. 3, 1927–March 21, 1934.

GRISWOLD, Morley Isaac. Oct. 10, 1890–Oct. 3, 1951; March 21, 1934–Jan. 7, 1935.

RUSSELL, Charles Hinton. Dec. 27, 1903–Sept. 13, 1989; Jan. 1, 1951–Jan. 5, 1959; House 1947–49.

LAXALT, Paul Dominique. Aug. 2, 1922–; Jan. 2, 1967–Jan. 4, 1971; Senate Dec. 18, 1974–87.

LIST, Robert Frank. Sept, 1, 1936–; Jan. 1, 1979–Jan. 3, 1983.

NEW HAMPSHIRE

(ratified the Constitution June 21, 1788)

MORRILL, David Lawrence. June 10, 1772–Jan. 28, 1849; June 3, 1824–June 7, 1827.

HAILE, William May 1807–July 22, 1876; June 4, 1857–June 2, 1859.

GOODWIN, Ichabod. Oct. 10, 1796–July 4, 1882; June 2, 1859–June 6, 1861.

BERRY, Nathaniel Springer. Sept. 1, 1796–April 27, 1894; June 6, 1861–June 3, 1863.

GILMORE, Joseph Albree. June 10, 1811–April 7, 1867; June 3, 1863–June 8, 1865.

HARRIMAN, Walter. April 8, 1817–July 25, 1884; June 6, 1867–June 2, 1869.

STEARNS, Onslow. Aug. 30, 1810–Dec. 29, 1878; June 3, 1869–June 8, 1871.

STRAW, Ezekiel Albert. Dec. 30, 1819–Oct. 23, 1882; June 6, 1872–June 3, 1874.

CHENEY, Person Colby. Feb. 25, 1828–June 19, 1901; June 10, 1875–June 6, 1877; Senate Nov. 24, 1886–June 14, 1887.

PRESCOTT, Benjamin Franklin. Feb. 26, 1833–Feb. 21, 1895; June 7, 1877–June 5, 1879.

HEAD, Nathaniel. May 20, 1828–Nov. 12, 1883; June 5, 1879–June 2, 1881.

BELL, Charles Henry (son of John Bell, nephew of Samuel Bell). Nov. 18, 1823–Nov. 11, 1893; June 2, 1881–June 7, 1883; Senate March 13–June 18, 1879.

HALE, Samuel Whitney. April 2, 1823–Oct. 16, 1891; June 7, 1883–June 4, 1885.

CURRIER, Moody. April 22, 1806–Aug. 23, 1898; June 4, 1885–June 2, 1887.

SAWYER, Charles Henry. March 30, 1840–Jan. 18, 1908; June 2, 1887–June 6, 1889.

GOODELL, David Harvey. May 6, 1834–Jan. 22, 1915; June 6, 1889–Jan. 8, 1891.

TUTTLE, Hiram Americus. Oct. 16, 1837–Feb. 10, 1911; Jan. 8, 1891–Jan. 5, 1893.

SMITH, John Butler. April 12, 1838–Aug. 10, 1914; Jan. 5, 189–Jan. 3, 1895.

BUSIEL, Charles Albert. Nov. 24, 1842–Aug. 29, 1901; Jan. 3, 1895–Jan. 7, 1897.

RAMSDELL, George Allen. March 11, 1834–Nov. 16, 1900; Jan. 7, 1897–Jan. 5, 1899.

ROLLINS, Frank West. Feb. 24, 1860–Oct. 27, 1915; Jan. 5, 1899–Jan. 3, 1901.

JORDAN, Chester Bradley. Oct. 15, 1839–Aug. 24, 1914; Jan. 3, 1901–Jan. 1, 1903.

BATCHELDER, Nahum Josiah. Sept. 3, 1859–April 22, 1934; Jan. 1, 1903–Jan. 5, 1905.

McLANE, John. Feb. 27, 1852–April 13, 1911; Jan. 5, 1905–Jan. 3, 1907.

FLOYD, Charles Miller. June 5, 1861–Feb. 3, 1923; Jan. 3, 1907–Jan. 7, 1909.

QUINBY, Henry Brewer. June 10, 1846–Feb. 8, 1924; Jan. 7, 1909–Jan. 5, 1911.

BASS, Robert Perkins. Sept. 11, 1873–July 29, 1960; Jan. 5, 1911–Jan. 2, 1913.

SPAULDING, Rolland Harty (brother of Huntley Nowel Spaulding, below). March 15, 1873–March 14, 1942; Jan. 7, 1915–Jan. 3, 1917.

KEYES, Henry Wilder. May 23, 1863–June 19, 1938; Jan. 3, 1917–Jan. 2, 1919; Senate 1919–37.

BARTLETT, John Henry. March 15, 1869–March 19, 1952; Jan. 2, 1919–Jan. 6, 1921.

BROWN, Albert Oscar. July 18, 1853–March 28, 1937; Jan. 6, 1921–Jan. 4, 1923.

BROWN, Fred Herbert. April 12, 1879–Feb. 3, 1955; Jan. 4, 1923–Jan. 1, 1925; Senate 1933–39.

WINANT, John Gilbert. Feb. 23, 1889–Nov. 3, 1947; Jan. 1, 1925–Jan. 6, 1927, Jan. 1, 1931–Jan. 3, 1935.

SPAULDING, Huntley Nowel (brother of Rolland Harty Spaulding, above). Oct. 20, 1869–Nov. 14, 1955; Jan. 6, 1927–Jan. 3, 1929.

TOBEY, Charles William. July 22, 1880–July 24, 1953; Jan. 3, 1929–Jan. 1, 1931; House 1933–39; Senate 1939–July 24, 1953.

WINANT, John Gilbert. Jan. 1, 1931–Jan. 3, 1935 (for previous term see above).

BRIDGES, Henry Styles. Sept. 9, 1898–Nov. 26, 1961; Jan. 3, 1935–Jan. 1937; Senate 1937–Nov. 26, 1861; Senate minority leader Jan. 8, 1952–53; elected Pres. pro tempore Jan. 3, 1953.

MURPHY, Francis Parnell. Aug. 16, 1877–Dec. 19, 1958; Jan. 7, 1937–Jan. 2, 1941.

BLOOD, Robert Oscar. Nov. 10, 1887–Aug. 3, 1975; Jan. 2, 1941–Jan. 4, 1945.

DALE, Charles Milby. March 8, 1893–Sept. 28, 1978; Jan. 4, 1945–Jan. 6, 1949.

ADAMS, Sherman. Jan. 8, 1899–Oct. 27, 1986; Jan. 6, 1949–Jan. 1, 1953; House 1945–47.

GREGG, Hugh. Nov. 22, 1917–; Jan. 1, 1953–Jan. 6, 1955.

DWINELL, Lane. Nov. 14, 1906–; Jan. 6, 1955–Jan. 1, 1959.

POWELL, Wesley. Oct.13, 1915–Jan. 6, 1981; Jan. 1, 1959–Jan. 3, 1963.

PETERSON, Walter Rutherford. Sept. 19, 1922–; Jan. 2, 1969–Jan. 4, 1973.

THOMSON, Meldrim Jr. March 8, 1912–; Jan. 4, 1973–Jan. 4, 1979.

ROY, Vesta M. March 26, 1925–; Dec. 1, 1982–Jan. 6, 1983.

SUNUNU, John Henry. July 2, 1939–; Jan. 6, 1983–Jan. 4, 1989.

GREGG, Judd Alan. Feb. 14, 1947–; Jan. 4, 1989–Jan. 7, 1993; House 1981–89.

MERRILL, Stephen "Steve." June 21, 1946– Jan. 7, 1993–.

NEW JERSEY

(ratified the Constitution December 18, 1787)

BLOOMFIELD, Joseph. Oct. 18, 1753–Oct. 3, 1823; Oct. 31, 1801–Oct. 28, 1802, Oct. 29, 1803–Oct. 29, 1812; House 1817–21.

SOUTHARD, Samuel Lewis. June 9, 1787–June 26, 1842; Oct. 26, 1832–Feb. 27, 1833; Senate Jan. 26, 1821–23 (Republican), 1833–June 26, 1842 (Whig); elected Pres. pro tempore March 11, 1841; Secy. of the Navy Sept. 16, 1823–March 3, 1829.

NEWELL, William Augustus. Sept. 5, 1817–Aug. 8, 1901; Jan. 20, 1857–Jan. 17, 1860, (Wash. Terr.) 1880–84; House 1847–51 (Whig), 1865–67 (Republican).

OLDEN, Charles Smith. Nov. 19, 1799–April 7, 1876; Jan. 17, 1860–Jan. 20, 1863.

WARD, Marcus Lawrence. Nov. 9, 1812–April, 25, 1884; Jan. 16, 1866–Jan. 19, 1869; House 1873–75; Chrmn. Rep. Nat. Comm. 1866–68.

GRIGGS, John William. July 10, 1849–Nov. 28, 1927; Jan. 21, 1896–Jan. 31, 1898; Atty. Gen. June 25, 1898–March 29, 1901.

VOORHEES, Foster MacGowan. Nov. 5, 1856–June 14, 1927; Feb. 1–Oct. 18, 1898, Jan. 17, 1899–Jan. 21, 1902.

WATKINS, David Ogden. June 8, 1862–June 20, 1938; Oct. 18, 1898–Jan. 16, 1899.

VOORHEES, Foster MacGowan. Jan. 17, 1899–Jan. 21, 1902 (for previous term see above).

MURPHY, Franklin. Jan. 3, 1846–Feb. 24, 1920; Jan. 21, 1902–Jan. 17, 1905.

STOKES, Edward Casper. Dec. 22, 1860–Nov. 4, 1942; Jan. 17, 1905–Jan. 21, 1908.

FORT, John Franklin. March 20, 1852–Nov. 17, 1920; Jan. 21, 1908–Jan. 17, 1911.

EDGE, Walter Evans. Nov. 20, 1873–Oct. 29, 1956; Jan. 15, 1917–May 16, 1919, Jan. 18, 1944–Jan. 21, 1947; Senate 1919–Nov. 21, 1929.

RUNYON, William Nelson. March 5, 1871–Nov. 9, 1931; May 16, 1919–Jan. 13, 1920.

CASE, Clarence Edwards. Sept. 24, 1877–Sept. 3, 1961; Jan. 13–Jan. 20, 1920.

LARSON, Morgan Foster. June 15, 1882–March 21, 1961; Jan. 15, 1929–Jan. 19, 1932.

POWELL, Clifford R. July 26, 1893–March 28, 1973; Jan. 3–Jan. 8, 1935.

PRALL, Horace Griggs. March 6, 1881–April 23, 1951; Jan. 8–Jan. 15, 1935.

HOFFMAN, Harold Giles. Feb. 7, 1896–June 4, 1954; Jan. 15, 1935–Jan. 18, 1938; House 1927–31.

EDGE, Walter Evans. Jan. 18, 1944–Jan. 21, 1947 (for previous term see above).

DRISCOLL, Alfred Eastlack. Oct. 25, 1902–March 9, 1975; Jan. 21, 1947–Jan. 19, 1954.

CAHILL, William Thomas. June 25, 1912–; Jan. 20, 1970–Jan. 15, 1974; House 1959–Jan. 19, 1970.

KEAN, Thomas H. April 21, 1935–; Jan. 19, 1982–Jan. 16, 1990.

WHITMAN, Christine Todd. Sept. 26, 1946–; Jan. 18, 1994–.

NEW MEXICO

(became a state January 6, 1912)

LINDSEY, Washington Ellsworth. Dec. 20, 1862–April 5, 1926; Feb. 19, 1917–Jan. 1, 1919.

LARRAZOLO, Octaviano Amrosio. Dec. 7, 1859–April 7, 1930; Jan. 1, 1919–Jan. 1, 1921; Senate Dec. 7, 1928–29.

MECHEM, Merrit Cramer (uncle of Edwin Leard Mechem, below). Oct. 10, 1870–May 24, 1946; Jan. 1, 1921–Jan. 1, 1923.

DILLON, Richard Charles. June 24, 1877–Jan. 4, 1966; Jan. 1, 1927–Jan. 1, 1931.

MECHEM, Edwin Leard (nephew of Merrit Cramer Mechem, above). July 2, 1912–; Jan. 1, 1951–Jan. 1, 1955, Jan. 1, 1957–Jan. 1, 1959, Jan. 1, 1961–Nov. 30, 1962; Senate Nov. 30, 1962–Nov. 3, 1964.

MECHEM, Edwin Leard. Jan. 1, 1957–Jan. 1, 1959 (for previous term see above).

MECHEM, Edwin Leard. Jan. 1, 1961–Nov. 30, 1962 (for previous terms see above).

BOLACK, Thomas Felix. May 18, 1918–; Nov. 30, 1962–Jan. 1, 1963.

CARGO, David Francis. Jan. 13, 1929–; Jan. 1, 1967–Jan. 1, 1971.

CARRUTHERS, Garrey Edward. Aug. 29, 1939–; Jan. 1, 1987–Jan. 1, 1991.

JOHNSON, Gary E. January 1, 1953–; 1995–.

NEW YORK

(ratified the Constitution July 26, 1788)

KING, John Alsop. Jan. 3, 1788–July 7, 1867; Jan. 1, 1857–Jan. 1, 1859; House 1849–51 (Whig).

MORGAN, Edwin Dennison (cousin of Morgan Gardner Bulkeley of Conn.). Feb. 8, 1811–Feb. 14, 1883; Jan. 1, 1859–Jan. 1, 1863; Senate 1863–69; Chrmn. Rep. Nat. Comm. 1856–64, 1872–76.

DIX, John Adams. July 24, 1798–April 21, 1879; Jan. 1, 1873–Jan. 1, 1875; Senate Jan. 27, 1845–49 (Democrat); Secy. of the Treasury Jan. 15–March 6, 1861.

CORNELL, Alonzo B. Jan. 22, 1832–Oct. 15, 1904; Jan. 1, 1880–Jan. 1, 1883.

MORTON, Levi Parsons. May 16, 1824–May 16, 1920; Jan. 1, 1895–Jan. 1, 1897; House 1879–March 21, 1881; Vice President 1889–93.

BLACK, Frank Swett. March 8, 1853–March 22, 1913; Jan. 1, 1897–Jan. 1, 1899; House 1895–Jan. 7, 1897.

ROOSEVELT, Theodore. Oct. 27, 1858–Jan. 6, 1919; Jan. 1, 1899–Jan. 1, 1901; Vice President March 4–Sept. 14, 1901; President Sept. 14, 1901–09.

ODELL, Benjamin Baker Jr. Jan. 14, 1854–May 9 1826; Jan. 1, 1901–Jan. 1, 1905; House 1895–99.

HIGGINS, Frank Wayland. Aug. 18, 1856–Feb. 12, 1907; Jan. 1, 1905–Jan. 1, 1907.

HUGHES, Charles Evans. April 11, 1862–Aug. 27, 1948; Jan. 1, 1907–Oct. 6, 1910; Assoc. Justice Supreme Court Oct. 10, 1910–June 10, 1916; Secy. of State March 5, 1921–March 4, 1925; Chief Justice United States Feb. 24, 1930–July 1, 1941.

WHITE, Horace. Oct. 7, 1865–Nov. 26, 1943; Oct. 6, 1910–Jan. 1, 1911.

WHITMAN, Charles Seymour. Aug. 28, 1868–March 29, 1947; Jan. 1, 1915–Jan. 1, 1919.

MILLER, Nathan Lewis. Oct. 10, 1868–June 26, 1953; Jan. 1, 1921–Jan. 1, 1923.

DEWEY, Thomas Edmund. March 24, 1902–March 16, 1971; Jan. 1, 1943–Jan. 1, 1955.

ROCKEFELLER, Nelson. Aldrich (brother of Winthrop Rockefeller of Ark., uncle of Sen. John Davison "Jay" Rockefeller IV, nephew of Rep. Richard Steere Aldrich, grandson of Sen. Nelson Wilmarth Aldrich). July 8, 1908–Jan. 26, 1979; Jan. 1, 1959–Dec. 18, 1973; Vice President Dec. 19, 1974–77.

WILSON, Malcolm. Feb. 26, 1914–; Dec. 18, 1973–Jan. 1, 1975.

PATAKI, George. June 24, 1945–; 1995–.

NORTH CAROLINA

(ratified the Constitution November 21, 1789)

TURNER, James. Dec. 20, 1766–Jan. 15, 1824; Dec. 6, 1802–05; Senate 1805–Nov. 21, 1816.

HOLDEN, William Woods. Nov. 24, 1818–March 1, 1892; May 29–Dec. 15, 1865, July 1, 1868–Dec. 15, 1870.

HOLDEN, William Woods. July 1, 1868–Dec. 15, 1870 (for previous term see above).

CALDWELL, Tod Robinson. Feb. 19, 1818–July 11, 1874; Dec. 15, 1870–July 11, 1874.

BROGDEN, Curtis Hooks. Nov. 6, 1816–Jan. 5, 1901; July 11, 1874–Jan. 1, 1877; House 1877–79.

HOLSHOUSER, James Eubert Jr. Oct. 8, 1934–Jan. 5, 1973–Jan. 8, 1977.

MARTIN, James Grubbs. Dec. 11, 1935–; Jan. 5, 1985–Jan. 9, 1993; House 1973–85.

NORTH DAKOTA

(became a state November 2, 1889)

MILLER, John. Oct. 6, 1843–Oct. 26, 1908; Nov. 4, 1889–Jan. 6, 1891.

BURKE, Andrew Horace. May 15, 1850–Nov. 17, 1918; Jan. 7, 1891–Jan. 3, 1893.

ALLIN, Roger. Dec. 18, 1848–Jan. 1, 1936; Jan. 7, 1895–Jan. 5, 1897.

BRIGGS, Frank Arlington. Sept. 16, 1858–Aug. 9, 1898; Jan. 5, 1897–Aug. 9, 1898.

DEVINE, Joseph McMurray. March 15, 1861–Aug. 31, 1938; Aug. 9, 1898–Jan. 3, 1899.

FANCHER, Frederick Bartlett. April 2, 1852–Jan. 10, 1944; Jan. 3, 1899–Jan. 10, 1901.

WHITE, Frank. Dec. 12, 1856–March 23, 1940; Jan. 10, 1901–Jan. 4, 1905.

SARLES, Elmore Yocum. Jan. 15, 1859–Feb. 14, 1929; Jan. 5, 1905–Jan. 9, 1907.

HANNA, Louis Benjamin. Aug. 9, 1861–April 23, 1948; Jan. 8, 1913–Jan. 3, 1917; House 1909–Jan. 7, 1913.

FRAZIER, Lynn Joseph. Dec. 21, 1874–Jan. 11, 1947; Jan. 3, 1917–Nov. 23, 1921; Senate 1923–41.

NESTOS, Ragnvald Anderson. April 12, 1877–July 15, 1942; Nov. 23, 1921–Jan. 7, 1925.

SORLIE, Arthur Gustav. April 26, 1874–Aug. 28, 1928; Jan. 7, 1925–Aug. 28, 1928.

MADDOCK, Walter Jeremiah. Sept. 13, 1880–Jan. 25, 1951; Aug. 28, 1928–Jan. 9, 1929.

SHAFER, George F. Nov. 23, 1888–Aug. 13, 1948; Jan. 9, 1929–Dec. 31, 1932.

OLSON, Ole H. Sept. 19, 1872–Jan. 29, 1954; July 17, 1934–Jan. 7, 1935.

WELFORD, Walter. May 21, 1868–June 28, 1952; Feb. 2, 1935–Jan. 6, 1937.

AANDAHL, Fred George. April 9, 1897–April 7, 1966; Jan. 4, 1945–Jan. 3, 1951; House 1951–53.

BRUNSDALE, Clarence Norman. July 9, 1891–Jan. 27, 1978; Jan. 3, 1951–Jan. 9, 1957; Senate Nov. 19, 1969–Aug. 7, 1960.

DAVIS, John Edward. April 18, 1913–; Jan. 9, 1957–Jan. 4, 1961.

OLSON, Allen Ingvar. Nov. 5, 1938–; Jan. 7, 1981–Jan. 8, 1985.

SCHAFER, Edward Thomas. Aug. 8, 1946– Jan. 5, 1993–.

OHIO

(became a state March 1, 1803)

CHASE, Salmon Portland (father-in-law of William Sprague of R.I.). Jan. 13, 1808–May 7, 1873; Jan. 14, 1856–Jan. 9, 1860; Senate 1849–55 (Free-Soiler), March 4–March 6, 1861 (Republican); Secy. of the Treasury March 7, 1861–June 30, 1864; Chief Justice United States Dec. 15, 1864–May 7, 1873.

DENNISON, William Jr. Nov. 23, 1815–June 15, 1882; Jan. 9, 1860–Jan. 13, 1862; Postmaster Gen. Oct. 1, 1864–July 16, 1866.

COX, Jacob Dotson. Oct. 27, 1828–Aug. 4, 1900; Jan. 8, 1866–Jan. 13, 1868; Secy. of the Interior March 5, 1869–Oct. 31, 1870; House 1877–79.

HAYES, Rutherford Birchard. Oct. 4, 1822–Jan. 17, 1893; Jan. 13, 1868–Jan. 8, 1872, Jan. 10, 1876–March 2, 1877; House 1865–July 20, 1867; President 1877–81.

NOYES, Edward Follansbee. Oct. 3, 1832–Sept. 4, 1890; Jan. 8, 1872–Jan. 12, 1874.

HAYES, Rutherford Birchard. Jan. 10, 1876–March 2, 1877 (for previous term see above).

YOUNG, Thomas Lowry. Dec. 14, 1832–July 20, 1888; March 2, 1877–Jan. 14, 1878; House 1879–83.

FOSTER, Charles. April 12, 1828–Jan. 9, 1904; Jan. 12, 1880–Jan. 14, 1884; House 1871–79; Secy. of the Treasury Feb. 25, 1891–March 6, 1893.

FORAKER, Joseph Benson. July 5, 1846–May 10, 1917; Jan. 11, 1886–Jan. 13, 1890; Senate 1897–1909.

McKINLEY, William Jr. Jan. 29, 1843–Sept. 14, 1901; Jan. 11, 1892–Jan. 13, 1896; House 1877–May 27, 1884, 1885–91; President 1897–Sept. 14, 1901.

BUSHNELL, Asa Smith. Sept. 16, 1834–Jan. 15, 1904; Jan. 13, 1896–Jan. 8, 1900.

NASH, George Kilborn. Aug. 14, 1842–Oct. 28, 1904; Jan. 8, 1900–Jan. 11, 1904,

HERRICK, Myron Timothy. Oct. 9, 1854–March 31, 1929; Jan. 11, 1904–Jan. 8, 1906.

HARRIS, Andrew Lintner. Nov. 17, 1835–Sept. 13, 1915; June 18, 1906–Jan. 11, 1909.

WILLIS, Frank Bartlett. Dec. 28, 1871–March 30, 1928; Jan. 11, 1915–Jan. 8, 1917; House 1911–Jan. 9, 1915; Senate Jan. 14, 1921–March 30, 1928.

DAVIS, Harry Lyman. Jan. 25, 1878–May 21, 1950; Jan. 10, 1921–Jan. 8, 1923.

COOPER, Myers Young. Nov. 25, 1873–Dec. 7, 1958; Jan. 14, 1929–Jan. 12, 1931.

BRICKER, John William. Sept. 6, 1893–March 22, 1986; Jan. 9, 1939–Jan. 8, 1945; Senate 1947–59.

HERBERT, Thomas James. Oct. 28, 1894–Oct. 26, 1974; Jan. 13, 1947–Jan. 10, 1949.

BROWN, John William. Dec. 28, 1913–; Jan. 3–Jan. 14, 1957.

O'NEILL, C. William. Feb. 14, 1916–Aug. 20, 1978; Jan. 14, 1957–Jan. 12, 1959.

RHODES, James Allen. Sept. 13, 1909–; Jan. 14, 1963–Jan. 11, 1971, Jan. 13, 1975–Jan. 10, 1983.

RHODES, James Allen. Jan. 13, 1975–Jan. 10, 1983 (for previous term see above).

VOINOVICH, George Victor. July 15, 1936–; Jan. 14, 1991–.

OKLAHOMA

(became a state November 16, 1907)

BELLMON, Henry Louis. Sept. 3, 1921–; Jan. 14, 1963–Jan. 9, 1967, Jan. 12, 1987–Jan. 14, 1991; Senate 1969–81.

BARTLETT, Dewey Follett. March 28, 1919–March 1, 1979; Jan. 9, 1967–Jan. 11, 1971; Senate 1973–79.

BELLMON, Henry Louis. Jan. 12, 1987–Jan. 14, 1991 (for previous term see above).

KEATING, Frank. February 10, 1944–; 1995–.

OREGON

(became a state February 14, 1859)

WOODS, George Lemuel. July 30, 1832–Jan. 7, 1890; Sept. 12, 1866–Sept. 14, 1870.

MOODY, Zenas Perry. May 27, 1832–March 14, 1917; Sept. 13, 1882–Jan. 12, 1887.

LORD, William Paine. July 1, 1839–Feb. 17, 1911; Jan. 14, 1895–Jan. 9, 1899.

GEER, Theodore Thurston. March 12, 1851–Feb. 21, 1924; Jan. 9, 1899–Jan. 14, 1903.

BENSON, Frank Williamson. March 20, 1858–April 14, 1911; March 1, 1909–June 17, 1910.

BOWERMAN, Jay. Aug. 15, 1876–Oct. 25, 1957; June 17, 1910–Jan. 8, 1911.

WITHYCOMBE, James. March 21, 1854–March 3, 1919; Jan. 12, 1915–March 3, 1919.

OLCOTT, Ben Wilson. Oct. 15, 1872–July 21, 1952; March 3, 1919–Jan. 8, 1923.

PATTERSON, Isaac Lee. Sept. 17, 1859–Dec. 21, 1929; Jan. 10, 1927–Dec. 21, 1929.

NORBLAD, Albin Walter. March 19, 1881–April 17, 1960; Dec. 22, 1929–Jan. 12, 1931.

SPRAGUE, Charles Arthur. Nov. 12, 1887–March 13, 1969; Jan. 9, 1939–Jan. 11, 1943.

SNELL, Earl Wilcox. July 11, 1895–Oct. 28, 1947; Jan. 11, 1943–Oct. 28, 1947.

HALL, John Hubert. Feb. 7, 1899–Nov. 14, 1970; Oct. 30, 1947–Jan. 10, 1949.

McKAY, Douglas James. June 24, 1893–July 22, 1959; Jan. 10, 1949–Dec. 27, 1952; Secy. of the Interior Jan. 21, 1953–April 15, 1956.

PATTERSON, Paul Linton. July 18, 1900–Jan. 31, 1956; Dec. 27, 1952–Jan. 31, 1956.

SMITH, Elmo Everett. Nov. 19, 1909–July 15, 1968; Feb. 1, 1956–Jan. 14, 1957.

HATFIELD, Mark Odom. July 12, 1922–; Jan. 12, 1959–Jan. 9, 1967; Senate Jan. 10, 1967–.

McCALL, Thomas Lawson. March 22, 1913–Jan. 8, 1983; Jan. 9, 1967–Jan. 11, 1975.

ATIYEH, Victor George. Feb. 20, 1923–; Jan. 8, 1979–Jan. 12, 1987.

PENNSYLVANIA

(ratified the Constitution December 12, 1787)

CURTIN, Andrew Gregg. April 22, 1815–Oct. 7, 1894; Jan. 15, 1861–Jan. 15, 1867; House 1881–87 (Democrat).

GEARY, John White. Dec. 30, 1819–Feb. 8, 1873; Jan. 15, 1867–Jan. 21, 1873.

HARTRANFT, John Frederick. Dec. 16, 1830–Oct. 17, 1889; Jan. 21, 1873–Jan. 18, 1879.

HOYT, Henry Martyn. June 8, 1830–Dec. 1, 1892; Jan. 21, 1879–Jan. 16, 1883.

BEAVER, James Addams. Oct. 21, 1837–Jan. 31, 1914; Jan. 18, 1887–Jan. 20, 1891.

HASTINGS, Daniel Hartman. Feb. 26, 1849–Jan. 9, 1903; Jan. 15, 1895–Jan. 17, 1899.

STONE, William Alexis. April 18, 1846–March 1, 1920; Jan. 17, 1899–Jan. 20, 1903; House 1891–Nov. 9, 1898.

PENNYPACKER, Samuel Whitaker. April 9, 1843–Sept. 2, 1916; Jan. 20, 1903–Jan. 15, 1907.

STUART, Edwin Sydney. Dec. 28, 1853–March 21, 1937; Jan. 15, 1907–Jan. 17, 1911.

TENER, John Kinley. July 25, 1863–May 19, 1946; Jan. 17, 1911–Jan. 19, 1915; House 1909–Jan. 16, 1911.

BRUMBAUGH, Martin Grove. April 14, 1862–March 14, 1930; Jan. 19, 1915–Jan. 21, 1919.

SPROUL, William Cameron. Sept. 16, 1870–March 21, 1928; Jan. 21, 1919–Jan. 16, 1923.

PINCHOT, Gifford. Aug. 11, 1865–Oct. 4, 1946; Jan. 16, 1923–Jan. 18, 1927, Jan. 20, 1931–Jan. 15, 1935.

FISHER, John Stuchell. May 25, 1867–June 25, 1940; Jan. 18, 1927–Jan. 20, 1931.

PINCHOT, Gifford. Jan. 20, 1931–Jan. 15, 1935 (for previous term see above).

JAMES, Arthur Horace. July 14, 1883–April 27, 1973; Jan. 17, 1939–Jan. 19, 1943.

MARTIN, Edward. Sept. 18, 1879–March 19, 1967; Jan. 19, 1943–Jan. 2, 1947; Senate 1947–59.

BELL, John Cromwell Jr. Oct. 25, 1892–March 18, 1974; Jan. 2–Jan. 21, 1947.

DUFF, James Henderson. Jan. 21, 1883–Dec. 20, 1969; Jan. 21, 1947–Jan. 16, 1951; Senate Jan. 18, 1951–57.

FINE, John Sydney. April 10, 1893–May 21, 1978; Jan. 16, 1961–Jan. 18, 1955.

SCRANTON, William Warren. July 19, 1917–; Jan. 15, 1963–Jan. 17, 1967; House 1961–63.

SHAFER, Raymond Philip. March 5, 1917–; Jan. 17, 1967–Jan. 19, 1971.

THORNBURGH, Richard Lewis. July 16, 1932–; Jan. 16, 1979–Jan. 20, 1987; Atty. Gen. Aug. 12, 1988–Aug. 9, 1991.

RIDGE, Tom. August 26, 1945–; 1995–.

RHODE ISLAND

(ratified the Constitution May 29, 1790)

DYER, Elisha II (father of Elisha Dyer III, below). July 20, 1811–May 17, 1890; May 26, 1857–May 31, 1859.

TURNER, Thomas Goodwin. Oct. 24, 1810–Jan. 3, 1875; May 31, 1859–May 1860.

BURNSIDE, Ambrose Evertt. May 23, 1824–Sept. 13, 1881; May 29, 1866–May 25, 1869; Senate 1875–Sept. 13, 1881.

PADELFORD, Seth. Oct. 3, 1807–Aug. 26, 1878; May 25, 1869–May 27, 1873.

HOWARD, Henry. April 2, 1826–Sept. 22, 1905; May 27, 1873–May 25, 1875.

LIPPITT, Henry (father of Charles Warren Lippitt, below). Oct. 9, 1818–June 5, 1891; May 25, 1875–May 29, 1877.

LITTLEFIELD, Alfred Henry. April 2, 1829–Dec. 21, 1893; May 25, 1880–May 29, 1883.

BOURN, Augustus Osborn. Oct. 1, 1834–Jan. 28, 1925; May 29, 1883–May 26, 1885.

WETMORE, George Peabody. Aug. 2, 1846–Sept. 11, 1921; May 26, 1885–May 31, 1887; Senate 1895–1907, Jan. 22, 1908–13.

TAFT, Royal Chapin. Feb. 14, 1823–June 4, 1912; May 29, 1888–May 28, 1889.

LADD, Herbert Warren. Oct. 15, 1843–Nov. 29, 1913; May 28, 1889–May 27, 1890, May 26, 1891–May 31, 1892.

LADD, Herbert Warren. May 26, 1891–May 31, 1892 (for previous term see above).

BROWN, Daniel Russell. March 28, 1848–Feb. 28, 1919; May 31, 1892–May 29, 1895.

LIPPITT, Charles Warren (son of Henry Lippitt, above). Oct. 8, 1846–April 4, 1924; May 29, 1895–May 26, 1897.

DYER, Elisha III (son of Elisha Dyer II, above). Nov. 29, 1839–Nov. 29, 1906; May 25, 1897–May 29, 1900.

GREGORY, William. Aug. 3, 1849–Dec. 16, 1901; May 29, 1900–Dec. 16, 1901.

KIMBALL, Charles Dean. Sept. 13, 1859–Dec. 8, 1930; Dec. 16, 1901–Jan. 6, 1903.

UTTER, George Herbert. July 24, 1854–Nov. 3, 1912; Jan. 3, 1905–Jan. 1, 1907; House 1911–Nov. 3, 1912.

POTHIER, Aram J. July 26, 1854–Feb. 3, 1928; Jan. 5, 1909–Jan. 5, 1915, Jan. 6, 1925–Feb. 3, 1928.

BEECKMAN, Robert Livingston. April 15, 1866–Jan. 21, 1935; Jan. 5, 1915–Jan. 4, 1921.

SAN SOUCI, Emery John. July 24, 1857–Aug. 10, 1936; Jan. 4, 1921–Jan. 2, 1923.

POTHIER, Aram J. Jan. 6, 1925–Feb. 3, 1928 (for previous term see above).

CASE, Norman Stanley. Oct. 11, 1888–Oct. 9, 1967; Feb. 4, 1928–Jan. 3, 1933.

VANDERBILT, William Henry. Nov. 24, 1901–April 14, 1981; Jan. 3, 1939–Jan. 7, 1941.

DEL SESTO, Christopher. March 10, 1907–Dec. 23, 1973; Jan. 6, 1959–Jan. 3, 1961.

CHAFEE, John Hubbard. Oct. 22, 1922–; Jan. 1, 1963–Jan. 7, 1969; Senate Dec. 29, 1976–.

DiPRETE, Edward Daniel. July 8, 1934–; Jan. 1, 1985–; Jan. 1, 1991–.

ALMOND, Lincoln C. June 16, 1936–; 1995–.

SOUTH CAROLINA

(ratified the Constitution May 23, 1788)

PINCKNEY, Charles (father-in-law of Robert Young Hayne, below). Oct. 26, 1757–Oct. 29, 1824; Jan. 26, 1789–Dec. 5, 1792, Dec. 8, 1796–Dec. 6, 1798, Dec. 9, 1806–Dec. 10, 1808; Cont. Cong. 1785–87; Senate Dec. 6, 1798–1801; House 1819–21.

MIDDLETON, Henry. Sept. 28, 1770–June 14, 1846; Dec. 10, 1810–Dec. 10, 1812; House 1815–19.

ORR, James Lawrence. May 12, 1822–May 5, 1873; Nov. 29, 1865–July 6, 1868; House 1849–69 (Democrat); Speaker Dec. 7, 1857–59.

SCOTT, Robert Kingston. July 3, 1826–Aug. 13, 1900; July 9, 1868–Dec. 7, 1872.

MOSES, Franklin J. Jr. 1838–Dec. 11, 1906; Dec. 7, 1872–Dec. 1, 1874.

CHAMBERLAIN, Daniel Henry. June 23, 1835–April 14, 1907; Dec. 1, 1874–April 10, 1877.

EDWARDS, James Burrows. June 24, 1927–; Jan. 21, 1975–Jan. 10, 1979.

CAMPBELL, Carroll Ashmore Jr. July 24, 1940–Jan. 14, 1987–1995; House 1979–87.

BEASLEY, David. Feb. 26, 1957; 1995–.

SOUTH DAKOTA

(became a state November 2, 1889)

MELETTE, Arthur Calvin. June 23, 1842–May 25, 1896; Nov. 2, 1889–Jan. 3, 1893.

SHELDON, Charles Henry. Sept. 12, 1840–Oct. 20, 1898; Jan. 3, 1893–Jan. 5, 1897.

HERREID, Charles Nelson. Oct. 20, 1857–July 6, 1928; Jan. 8, 1901–Jan. 3, 1905.

ELROD, Samuel Harrison. May 1, 1856–July 13, 1935; Jan. 3, 1906–Jan. 8, 1907.

CRAWFORD, Coe Isaac. Jan. 14, 1858–April 25, 1944; Jan. 8, 1907–Jan. 5, 1909; Senate 1909–15.

VESSEY, Robert Scadden. May 16, 1858–Oct. 18, 1929; Jan. 5, 1909–Jan. 7, 1913.

BYRNE, Frank Michael. Oct. 23, 1858–Dec. 24, 1927; Jan. 7, 1913–Jan. 2, 1917.

NORBECK, Peter. Aug. 27, 1870–Dec. 20, 1936; Jan. 2, 1917–Jan. 4, 1921; Senate 1921–Dec. 20, 1936.

McMASTER, William Henry. May 10, 1877–Sept. 14, 1968; Jan. 4, 1921–Jan. 6, 1925; Senate 1925–31.

GUNDERSON, Carl. June 20, 1864–Feb. 26, 1933; Jan. 6, 1925–Jan. 4, 1927.

GREEN, Warren Everett. March 10, 1870–April 27, 1945; Jan. 6, 1931–Jan. 3, 1933.

JENSEN, Leslie. Sept. 15, 1892–Dec. 14, 1964; Jan. 5, 1937–Jan. 3, 1939.

BUSHFIELD, Harlan John. Aug. 6, 1882–Sept. 27, 1948; Jan. 3, 1939–Jan. 5, 1943; Senate 1943–Sept. 27, 1948.

SHARPE, Merrell Quentin. Jan. 11, 1888–Jan. 22, 1962; Jan. 5, 1943–Jan. 7, 1947.

MICKELSON, George Theodore (father of George Speaker Mickelson, below). July 23, 1903–Feb. 28, 1965; Jan. 7, 1947–Jan. 2, 1951.

ANDERSON, Sigurd. Jan. 22, 1904–Dec. 21, 1990; Jan. 2, 1951–Jan. 4, 1955.

FOSS, Joseph Jacob. April 17, 1915–; Jan. 4, 1955–Jan. 6, 1959.

GUBBRUD, Archie M. Dec. 31, 1910–; Jan. 3, 1961–Jan. 5, 1965.

BOE, Nils Andreas. Sept. 10, 1913–; Jan. 5, 1965–Jan. 7, 1969.

FARRAR, Frank Leroy. April 2, 1929–; Jan. 7, 1969–Jan. 5, 1971.

JANKLOW, William John. Sept. 13, 1939–; Jan. 1, 1979–Jan. 6, 1987.

MICKELSON, George Speaker (son of George Theodore Mickelson, above). Jan. 31, 1941–April 19, 1993; Jan. 6, 1987–April 19, 1993.

MILLER, Walter Dale. Oct. 5, 1925–; April 20, 1993–1995.

JANKLOW, William J. Sept. 13, 1936–; 1995–.

TENNESSEE

(became a state June 1, 1796)

JOHNSON, Andrew. Dec. 29, 1808–July 31, 1875; March 12, 1862–March 4, 1865 (military).

BROWNLOW, William Gannaway. Aug. 29, 1805–April 29, 1877; April 5, 1865–Feb. 25, 1869; Senate 1869–75.

HAWKINS, Alvin. Dec. 2, 1821–April 27, 1905; Jan. 17, 1881–Jan. 15, 1883.

HOOPER, Ben Walker. Oct. 13, 1870–April 18, 1957; Jan. 26, 1911–Jan. 17, 1915.

TAYLOR, Alfred Alexander. Aug. 6, 1848–Nov. 25, 1931; Jan. 15, 1921–Jan. 16, 1923; House 1889–95.

DUNN, Bryant Winfield Culberson. July 1, 1927–; Jan. 16, 1971–Jan. 18, 1975.

ALEXANDER, Lamar. July 3, 1940–; Jan. 17, 1979–Jan. 17, 1987; Secy. of Education March 22, 1991–Jan. 20, 1993.

SUNDQUIST, Don. March 15, 1936–; 1995–.

TEXAS

(became a state December 29, 1845)

DAVIS, Edmund Jackson. Oct. 2, 1827–Feb. 7, 1883; Jan. 8, 1870–Jan. 15, 1874.

CLEMENTS, William Perry Jr. April 13, 1917–; Jan. 16, 1979–Jan. 18, 1983, Jan. 20, 1987–Jan. 15, 1991.

BUSH, George W. July 6, 1946; 1995–.

UTAH

(became a state January 4, 1896)

WELLS, Heber Manning. Aug. 11, 1859–March 12, 1938; Jan. 6, 1896–Jan. 1905.

CUTLER, John Christopher. Feb. 5, 1846–July 30, 1928; Jan. 2, 1905–Jan. 4, 1909.

SPRY, William. Jan. 11, 1864–April 21, 1929; Jan. 4, 1909–Jan. 1, 1917.

MABEY, Charles Rendell. Oct. 4, 1877–April 26, 1959; Jan. 3, 1921–Jan. 5, 1925.

LEE, Joseph Bracken. Jan. 7, 1899–; Jan. 3, 1949–Jan. 7, 1957.

CLYDE, George Dewey. July 21, 1898–April 2, 1972; Jan. 7, 1957–Jan. 4, 1965.

BANGERTER, Norman Howard. Jan. 4, 1933–; Jan. 7, 1985–Jan. 3, 1993.

LEAVITT, Michael Okerlund. Feb. 11, 1951–; Jan. 3, 1993–.

VERMONT

(became a state March 4, 1791)

FLETCHER, Ryland. Feb. 18, 1799–Dec. 19, 1885; Oct. 10, 1856–Oct. 10, 1858.

HALL, Hiland. July 20, 1795–Dec. 18, 1885; Oct. 10, 1858–Oct. 12, 1860; House Jan. 1, 1833–43 (Jan. 1–Jan. 3, 1833 no party, 1833–35 Anti-Jacksonian, 1835–43 Whig).

FAIRBANKS, Erastus. Oct. 28, 1792–Nov. 20, 1864; Oct. 12, 1860–Oct. 11, 1861.

HOLBROOK, Frederick. Feb. 15, 1813–April 28, 1909; Oct. 11, 1861–Oct. 9, 1863.

SMITH, John Gregory (father of Edward Curtis Smith, below). July 22, 1818–Nov. 6, 1891; Oct. 9, 1863–Oct. 13, 1865.

DILLINGHAM, Paul Jr. (father of William Paul Dillingham, below). Aug. 10, 1799–July 16, 1891; Oct. 13, 1865–Oct. 13, 1867; House 1843–47 (Democrat).

PAGE, John Boardman. Feb. 25, 1826–Oct. 24, 1885; Oct. 13, 1867–Oct. 15, 1869.

WASHBURN, Peter Thacher. Sept. 7, 1814–Feb. 7, 1870; Oct. 15, 1869–Feb. 7, 1870.

HENDEE, George Whitman. Nov. 30, 1832–Dec. 6, 1906; Feb. 7–Oct. 6, 1870; House 1873–79.

STEWART, John Wolcott. Nov. 24, 1825–Oct. 29, 1915; Oct. 6, 1870–Oct. 3, 1872; House 1883–91; Senate March 24–Oct. 21, 1908.

CONVERSE, Julius. Dec. 17, 1798–Aug. 16, 1885; Oct. 3, 1872–Oct. 8, 1874.

PECK, Asahel. Feb. 6, 1803–May 18, 1879; Oct. 8, 1874–Oct. 6, 1876.

FAIRBANKS, Horace (son of Erastus Fairbanks, above). March 21, 1820–March 17, 1888; Oct. 5, 1876–Oct. 3, 1878.

PROCTOR, Redfield Sr. (father of Fletcher Dutton Proctor and Redfield Proctor Jr., grandfather of Mortimer Robinson Proctor). June 1, 1831–March 4, 1908; Oct. 3, 1878–Oct. 7, 1880; Senate Nov. 2, 1891–March 4, 1908; Secy. of War March 5, 1889–Nov. 5, 1891.

FARNHAM, Roswell. July 23, 1827–Jan. 5, 1903; Oct. 7, 1880–Oct. 5, 1882.

BARSTOW, John Lester. Feb. 21, 1832–June 28, 1913; Oct. 5, 1882–Oct. 2, 1884.

PINGREE, Samuel Everett. Aug. 2, 1832–June 1, 1922; Oct. 2, 1884–Oct. 7, 1886.

ORMSBEE, Ebenezer Jolls. June 8, 1834–April 3, 1924; Oct. 7, 1886–Oct. 4, 1888.

DILLINGHAM, William Paul (son of Paul Dillingham Jr., above). Dec. 12, 1843–July 12, 1923; Oct. 4, 1888–Oct. 2, 1890; Senate Oct. 18, 1900–July 12, 1923.

PAGE, Carroll Smalley. Jan. 10, 1843–Dec. 3, 1925; Oct. 2, 1890–Oct. 6, 1892; Senate Oct. 21, 1908–23.

FULLER, Levi Knight. Feb. 24, 1841–Oct. 10, 1896; Oct. 6, 1892–Oct. 4, 1894.

WOODBURY, Urban Andrain. July 11, 1838–April 15, 1915; Oct. 4, 1894–Oct. 8, 1896.

GROUT, Josiah. May 28, 1841–July 19, 1925; Oct. 8, 1896–Oct. 6 1898.

SMITH, Edward Curtis (son of John Gregory Smith, above). Jan. 5, 1854–April 6, 1925; Oct. 6, 1898–Oct. 4, 1900.

STICKNEY, William Wallace (cousin of President John Calvin Coolidge). March 21, 1853–Dec. 15, 1932; Oct. 4, 1900–Oct. 3, 1902.

McCULLOUGH, John Griffith. Sept. 16, 1835–May 29, 1915; Oct. 3, 1902–Oct. 6, 1904.

BELL, Charles James. March 10, 1845–Sept. 25, 1909; Oct. 6, 1904–Oct. 4, 1906.

PROCTOR, Fletcher Dutton (father of Mortimer Robinson Proctor, son of Redfield Proctor Sr., brother of Redfield Proctor Jr.). Nov. 7, 1860–Sept. 27, 1911; Oct. 4, 1906–Oct. 8, 1908.

PROUTY, George Herbert. March 4, 1862–Aug. 19, 1918; Oct. 8, 1908–Oct. 5, 1910.

MEAD, John Abner. April 20, 1841–Jan. 12, 1920; Oct. 5, 1910–Oct. 3, 1912.

FLETCHER, Allen Miller. Sept. 25, 1853–May 11, 1922; Oct. 3, 1912–Jan. 7, 1915.

GATES, Charles Winslow. Jan. 12, 1856–July 1, 1927; Jan. 7, 1915–Jan. 4, 1917.

GRAHAM, Horace French. Feb. 7, 1862–Nov. 23, 1941; Jan. 4, 1917–Jan. 9, 1919.

CLEMENT, Percival Wood. July 7, 1846–Jan. 9, 1927; Jan. 9, 1919–Jan. 6, 1921.

HARTNESS, James. Sept. 3, 1861–Feb. 2, 1934; Jan. 6, 1921–Jan. 4, 1973.

PROCTOR, Redfield Jr. (son of Redfield Proctor Sr., brother of Fletcher Dutton Proctor, uncle of Mortimer Robinson Proctor). April 13, 1879–Feb. 5, 1957; Jan. 4, 1923–Jan. 8, 1925.

BILLINGS, Franklin Swift. May 11, 1862–Jan. 16, 1935; Jan. 8, 1925–Jan. 6, 1927.

WEEKS, John Eliakim. June 14, 1853– Sept. 10, 1949; Jan. 6, 1927–Jan. 8, 1931; House 1931–33.

WILSON, Stanley Calef. Sept. 10, 1879–Oct. 5, 1967; Jan. 8, 1931–Jan. 10, 1935.

SMITH, Charles Manley. Aug. 3, 1868–Aug. 12, 1937; Jan. 10, 1935–Jan. 7, 1937.

AIKEN, George David. Aug. 20, 1892–Nov. 19, 1984; Jan. 7, 1937–Jan. 9, 1941; Senate Jan. 10, 1941–75.

WILLS, William Henry. Oct. 26, 1882–March 6, 1946; Jan. 9, 1941–Jan. 4, 1945.

PROCTOR, Mortimer Robinson (son of Fletcher Dutton Proctor, grandson of Redfield Proctor Sr., nephew of Redfield Proctor Jr.). May 30, 1889–April 28, 1968; Jan. 4, 1945–Jan. 9, 1947.

GIBSON, Ernest William Jr. March 6, 1901–Nov. 4, 1969; Jan. 9, 1947–Jan. 14, 1950; Senate June 24, 1940–41.

ARTHUR, Harold John. Feb. 9, 1904–July 19, 1971; Jan. 16, 1950–Jan. 4, 1951.

EMERSON, Lee Earl. Dec. 19, 1898–May 21, 1976; Jan. 4, 1951–Jan. 6, 1955.

JOHNSON, Joseph Blaine. Aug. 29, 1893–Oct. 25, 1986; Jan. 6, 1955–Jan. 8, 1959.

STAFFORD, Robert Theodore. Aug. 8, 1913–; Jan. 8, 1959–Jan. 5, 1961; House 1961–Sept. 16, 1971; Senate Sept. 16, 1971–89.

KEYSER, Frank Ray Jr. Aug. 17, 1927–; Jan. 5, 1961–Jan. 10, 1963.

DAVIS, Deane Chandler. Nov. 7, 1900–Dec. 8, 1990; Jan. 9, 1969–Jan. 4, 1973.

SNELLING, Richard Arkwright. Feb. 18, 1927–Aug. 14, 1991; Jan. 3, 1977–Jan. 10, 1985, Jan. 10–Aug. 14, 1991.

SNELLING, Richard Arkwright. Jan. 10–Aug. 14, 1991 (for previous term see above).

VIRGINIA

(ratified the Constitution June 25, 1788)

NICHOLAS, Wilson Cary. Jan. 31, 1761–Oct. 10, 1820; Dec. 1, 1814–Dec. 1, 1816; Senate Dec. 5, 1799–May 22, 1804; House 1807–Nov. 27, 1809.

RANDOLPH, Thomas Mann (son-in-law of President Thomas Jefferson). Oct. 1, 1768–June 20, 1828; Dec. 1, 1819–Dec. 1, 1822; House 1803–07.

PLEASANTS, James. Oct. 24, 1769–Nov. 9, 1836; Dec. 1, 1822–Dec. 10, 1825; House 1811–Dec. 14, 1819; Senate Dec. 14, 1819–Dec. 15, 1822.

GILES, William Branch. Aug. 12, 1762–Dec. 4, 1830; March 4, 1827–March 4, 1830; House Dec. 7, 1790–Oct. 2, 1798 (no party), 1801–03 (Republican); Senate Aug. 11, 1804–15 (Republican).

GODWIN, Mills Edwin Jr. Nov. 19, 1914–; Jan. 16, 1966–Jan. 17, 1970 (Democrat), Jan. 12, 1974–Jan. 14, 1978.

HOLTON, Abner Linwood Jr. Sept. 21, 1923–; Jan. 17, 1970–Jan. 12, 1974.

GODWIN, Mills Edwin Jr. Jan. 12, 1974–Jan. 14, 1978 (for previous term see above).

DALTON, John Nichols. July 11, 1931–July 30, 1986; Jan. 14, 1978–Jan. 16, 1982.

ALLEN, George Felix. March 8, 1952–; Jan. 15, 1994–; House Nov. 12, 1991–93.

WASHINGTON

(became a state November 11, 1889)

PERRY, Elisha Peyre. Aug. 9, 1825–Oct. 14, 1895; Nov. 11, 1889–Jan. 9, 1893.

McGRAW, John Harte. Oct. 4, 1850–June 23, 1910; Jan. 9, 1893–Jan. 11, 1897.

McBRIDE, Henry. Feb. 7, 1856–Oct. 6, 1937; Dec. 26, 1901–Jan. 9, 1905.

MEAD, Albert Edward. Dec. 14, 1861–March 19, 1913; Jan. 9, 1905–Jan. 27, 1909.

COSGROVE, Samuel Goodlove. April 10, 1847–March 28, 1909; Jan. 27–March 28, 1909.

HAY, Marion E. Dec. 9, 1866–Nov. 21, 1933; March 29, 1909–Jan. 11, 1913.

HART, Louis Folwell. Jan. 4, 1862–Dec. 5, 1929; June 14, 1919–Jan. 12, 1925.

HARTLEY, Roland Hill (son-in-law of David Martson Clough of Minn.). June 26, 1864–Sept. 21, 1952; Jan. 12, 1925–Jan. 9, 1933.

LANGLIE, Arthur Bernard. July 25, 1900–July 24, 1966; Jan. 13, 1941–Jan. 8, 1945, Jan. 10, 1949–Jan. 14, 1957.

LANGLIE, Arthur Bernard. Jan. 10, 1949–Jan. 14, 1957 (for previous term see above).

EVANS, Daniel Jackson. Oct. 16, 1925–; Jan. 11, 1965–Jan. 12, 1977; Senate Sept. 12, 1983–89.

SPELLMAN, John D. Dec. 29, 1926–; Jan. 14, 1981–Jan. 16, 1985.

WEST VIRGINIA

(became a state June 19, 1863)

BOREMAN, Arthur Inghram. July 24, 1823–April 19, 1896; June 20, 1863–Feb. 26, 1869; Senate 1869–75.

FARNSWORTH, Daniel Duane Tompkins. Dec. 28, 1819–Dec. 5, 1892; Feb. 27–March 4, 1869.

STEVENSON, William Erskine. March 18, 1820–Nov. 29, 1883; March 4, 1869–March 4, 1871.

ATKINSON, George Wesley. June 29, 1845–April 4, 1925; March 4, 1897–March 4, 1901; House Feb. 26, 1890–91.

WHITE, Albert Blakeslee. Sept. 22, 1856–July 3, 1941; March 4, 1901–March 4, 1905.

DAWSON, William Mercer Owens. May 21, 1853–March 12, 1916; March 4, 1905–March 4, 1909.

GLASSOCK, William Ellsworth. Dec. 13, 1862–April 12, 1925; March 4, 1909–March 4, 1913.

HATFIELD, Henry Drury. Sept. 15, 1875–Oct. 23, 1962; March 4, 1913–March 4, 1917; Senate 1929–35.

MORGAN, Ephraim Franklin. Jan. 16, 1869–Jan. 15. 1950; March 4, 1921–March 4, 1925.

GORE, Howard Mason. Oct. 12, 1877–June 20, 1947; March 4, 1925–March 4, 1929; Secy. of Agriculture Nov. 22, 1924–March 4, 1925.

CONLEY, William Gustavus. Jan. 8, 1866–Oct. 21, 1940; March 4, 1929–March 4, 1933.

UNDERWOOD, Cecil Harland. Nov. 5, 1922–; Jan. 13, 1957–Jan. 16, 1961.

MOORE, Arch Alfred Jr. April 16, 1923–; Jan. 13, 1969–Jan. 17, 1977, Jan. 14, 1985–Jan. 16, 1989; House 1957–69.

MOORE, Arch Alfred Jr. Jan. 14, 1985–Jan. 16, 1989 (for previous term see above).

WISCONSIN

(became a state May 29, 1848)

BASHFORD, Coles. Jan. 24, 1816–April 25, 1878; March 25, 1856–Jan. 4, 1858; House (Terr. Del.) 1867–69 (Independent Ariz.).

RANDALL, Alexander Williams. Oct. 31, 1819–July 26, 1872; Jan. 4, 1858–Jan. 6, 1862; Postmaster Gen. July 25, 1866–March 4, 1869.

HARVEY, Louis Powell. July 22, 1820–April 19, 1862; Jan. 6–April 19, 1962.

SALOMON, Edward P. Aug. 11, 1828–April 21, 1909; April 19, 1862–Jan. 4, 1864.

LEWIS, James Taylor. Oct. 30, 1819–Aug. 4, 1904; Jan. 4, 1864–Jan. 1, 1866.

FAIRCHILD, Lucius. Dec. 27, 1831–May 23, 1896; Jan. 1, 1866–Jan. 1, 1872.

WASHBURN, Cadwallader Colden (brother of Israel Washburn Jr. of Maine). April 22, 1818–May 15, 1882; Jan. 1, 1872–Jan. 6, 1874; House 1855–61, 1867–71.

LUDINGTON, Harrison. July 30, 1812–June 17, 1891; Jan. 3, 1876–Jan. 7, 1878.

SMITH, William E. June 18, 1824–Feb. 13, 1883; Jan. 7, 1878–Jan. 2, 1882.

RUSK, Jeremiah McLain. June 17, 1830–Nov. 21, 1893; Jan. 2, 1882–Jan. 7, 1889; House 1871–77; Secy. of Agriculture March 6, 1889–March 6, 1893.

HOARD, William Dempster. Oct. 10, 1836–Nov. 22, 1918; Jan. 7, 1889–Jan. 5, 1891.

UPHAM, William Henry. May 3, 1841–July 2, 1924; Jan. 7, 1895–Jan. 4, 1897.

SCOFIELD, Edward. March 28, 1842–Feb. 3, 1925; Jan. 4, 1897–Jan. 7, 1901.

LA FOLLETTE, Robert Marion. June 14, 1855–June 18, 1925; Jan. 7, 1901–Jan. 1, 1906; House 1885–91; Senate Jan. 2, 1906–June 18, 1925.

DAVIDSON, James Ole. Feb. 10, 1854–Dec. 16, 1922; Jan. 1, 1906–Jan. 2, 1911.

McGOVERN, Francis Edward. Jan. 21, 1866–May 16, 1946; Jan. 2, 1911–Jan. 4, 1915.

PHILIPP, Emanuel Lorenz. March 25, 1861–June 15, 1925; Jan. 4, 1915–Jan. 3, 1921.

BLAINE, John James. May 4, 1875–April 16, 1934; Jan. 3, 1921–Jan. 3, 1927; Senate 1927–33.

ZIMMERMAN, Fred R. Nov. 20, 1880–Dec. 14, 1954; Jan. 3, 1927–Jan. 7, 1929.

KOHLER, Walter Jodok Sr. (father of Walter Jodok Kohler Jr., below). March 3, 1875–April 21, 1940; Jan. 7, 1929–Jan. 5, 1931.

HEIL, Julius Peter. July 24, 1876–Nov. 30, 1949; Jan. 2, 1939–Jan. 4, 1943.

GOODLAND, Walter Samuel. Dec. 22, 1862–March 12, 1947; Jan. 4, 1943–March 12, 1947.

RENNEBOHM, Oscar. May 25, 1889–Oct. 15, 1968; March 12, 1947–Jan. 1, 1951.

KOHLER, Walter Jodok, Jr. (son of Walter Jodok Kohler Sr., above). April 4, 1904–March 21, 1976; Jan. 1, 1951–Jan. 7, 1957.

THOMSON, Vernon Wallace. Nov. 5, 1905–April 2, 1988; Jan. 7, 1957–Jan. 5, 1959; House 1961–Dec. 31, 1974.

KNOWLES, Warren Perley. Aug. 19, 1908–May 11, 1993; Jan. 4, 1965–Jan. 4, 1971.

DREYFUS, Lee Sherman. June 20, 1926–; Jan. 1, 1979–Jan. 3, 1983.

EARL, Anthony Scully. April 12, 1936–; Jan. 3, 1983–Jan. 5, 1987.

THOMPSON, Tommy George. Nov. 19, 1941–; Jan. 5, 1987–.

WYOMING

(became a state July 10, 1890)

WARREN, Francis Emroy. June 20, 1884–Nov. 24, 1929; Feb. 1885–Nov. 1886 (Wyo. Terr.), March 1889–Sept. 1890 (Wyo. Terr.), Sept. 11–Nov. 24, 1890; Senate Nov. 18, 1890–93, 1895–Nov. 24, 1929.

BARBER, Amos Walker. July 25, 1861–May 18, 1915; Nov. 24, 1890–Jan. 2, 1893.

RICHARDS, William Alford. March 9, 1849–July 25, 1912; Jan. 7, 1895–Jan. 2, 1899.

RICHARDS, DeForest. Aug. 6, 1846–April 28, 1903; Jan. 2, 1899–April 28, 1903.

CHATTERTON, Fenimore. July 21, 1860–May 9, 1958; April 28, 1903–Jan. 2, 1905.

BROOKS, Bryant Butler. Feb. 5, 1861–Dec. 7, 1944; Jan. 2, 1905–Jan. 2, 1911.

CAREY, Joseph Maull (father of Robert Davis Carey, below). Jan. 19, 1845–Feb. 5, 1924; Jan. 2, 1911–Jan. 4, 1915; House (Terr. Del.) 1885–July 10, 1890; Senate Nov. 15, 1890–95.

CAREY, Robert Davis (son of Joseph Maull Carey, above). Aug. 12, 1878–Jan. 17, 1937; Jan. 6, 1919–Jan. 1, 1923; Senate Dec. 1, 1930–37.

LUCAS Franklin Earl. Aug. 4, 1876–Nov. 26, 1948; Oct. 2, 1924–Jan. 5, 1925.

EMERSON, Frank Collins. May 26, 1882–Feb. 18, 1931; Jan. 3, 1927–Feb. 19, 1931.

CLARK, Alonzo Monroe. Aug. 13, 1868–Oct. 12, 1952; Feb. 18, 1931–Jan. 2, 1933.

SMITH, Nels Hanson. Aug. 27, 1884–July 5, 1976; Jan. 2, 1939–Jan. 4, 1943.

CRANE, Arthur Griswold. Sept. 1, 1877–Aug. 12, 1955; Jan. 3, 1949–Jan. 1, 1951.

BARRETT, Frank Aloysius. Nov. 10, 1892–May 30, 1962; Jan. 1, 1951–Jan. 3, 1953; House 1943–Dec. 31, 1950; Senate 1953–59.

ROGERS, Clifford Joy "Doc." Dec. 20, 1897–May 18, 1962; Jan. 3, 1953–Jan. 3, 1955.

SIMPSON, Milward Lee. Nov. 12, 1897–June 10, 1993; Jan. 3, 1955–Jan. 5, 1959; Senate Nov. 6, 1962–67.

HANSEN, Clifford Peter. Oct. 16, 1912–; Jan. 6, 1963–Jan. 2, 1967; Senate 1967–Dec. 31, 1978.

HATHAWAY, Stanley Knapp. July 19, 1924–; Jan. 2, 1967–Jan. 6, 1975; Secy. of the Interior June 12–Oct. 9, 1975.

GERINGER, Jim. April 24, 1944–; 1995–.